ECONOMICS OF REGULATION AND ANTITRUST

ECONOMICS OF REGULATION AND ANTITRUST

Second Edition

W. Kip Viscusi
John M. Vernon
Joseph E. Harrington, Jr.

The MIT Press
Cambridge, Massachusetts
London, England

First MIT Press edition 1995
Second edition © 1995 Massachusetts Institute of Technology
First edition © 1992 D.C. Heath and Company

This book was set in Times Roman by Asco Trade Typesetting Ltd., Hong Kong, and was printed and bound in the United States of America.

Library of Congress Cataloging-in-Publication Data

Viscusi, W. Kip.
    Economics of regulation and antitrust / W. Kip Viscusi, John M.
Vernon, Joseph E. Harrington, Jr.—2nd ed.
        p. cm.
    Includes bibliographical references and index.
    ISBN 0-262-22049-0
    1. Industrial policy—United States. 2. Trade regulation—United States.
3. Antitrust law—United States. I. Vernon, John Mitcham, 1937– .
II. Harrington, Joseph Emmett, 1957– . III. Title.
HD3616.U47V57   1995
338.973—dc20   95-37648
                                                               CIP

This book is dedicated to:

Kira and Michael
Michelle, Julie, John, and Chris
Joe and Kathryn

Contents

Preface to the Second Edition

One of the most exciting areas of economic policy is government regulation and antitrust. These efforts affect virtually all aspects of our lives, ranging from the food we eat to the prices we pay. This policy area has undergone dramatic changes in the past two decades. The traditional topics in this area would have included issues such as setting appropriate trucking rates as well as conventional antitrust issues. However, in many areas of economic regulation there has been substantial deregulation as market forces in a larger and more competitive economy have been given more rein. New areas of economic regulation have developed, such as those pertaining to the regulation of cable television rates. In addition, there has been an entirely new wave of government regulation, chiefly relating to the environment and safety, which involves a substantial commitment of economic resources.

The emerging character of regulation has been accompanied by an intellectually vibrant economic literature. Economists have developed new theories to characterize firm behavior and to assess which market contexts warrant government intervention. Our view of which situations of apparently excessive market power warrant government interference has changed dramatically.

Economists have also developed new methodologies to deal with emerging health, safety, and environmental regulations. These regulatory efforts were largely nonexistent two decades ago, and the economic literature addressing these issues was similarly undeveloped. In this book we will attempt to convey the general character of the principles guiding economic regulation in this and other areas as well as the most salient aspects of these policies.

The traditional emphasis of economics textbooks on business and government is on the character of regulations and antitrust policies. This treatment is built around the question: what are these policy mechanisms, and how do they operate?

The orientation of *Economics of Regulation and Antitrust* is quite different. Rather than start with the institutional aspect of regulatory and antitrust policies, we begin with the economic issues at stake. What particular market failures provide a rationale for government intervention? How can economic theory illuminate the character of market operation, the role for government action, and the appropriate form of government action? What do formal empirical analyses of economic behavior and the effects of government intervention indicate about the direction that this intervention should take? To provide the most up-to-date answers to these important questions, we base our analysis on new developments in economic theory and empirical analysis that have been specifically devised to further understanding of regulations and antitrust policies.

Because this has been a fertile area of economic research for several decades, a large body of economic reasoning can be brought to bear in analyzing these issues. *Economics of Regulation and Antitrust* is the only economics textbook whose focus derives from the insights that economic reasoning can provide in analyzing regulatory and antitrust issues. This approach contrasts with previous treatments, which concentrate on the character of these policies and relegate the economic issues to a minor role.

This approach, which we established in the first edition, has been carried forward in this edition as well. New topics, such as the regulation of environmental tobacco smoke, have been added. Other topics, such as pharmaceutical regulation and the new price competition in electric power, have been given entirely new treatments to reflect the changing emphasis of government policy.

The chapters covering the airline, cable television, and telecommunications industries have been updated in light of more recent analyses and the evolving nature of technology and regulation. The most up-to-date studies assessing the impact of airline deregulation on market concentration, air fares, and airline safety have been covered. Important regulatory changes with regard to cable television rates have taken place in recent years. These developments are extensively reviewed, as are analyses that estimate the effect of regulatory policies on those rates. One of the major regulatory issues of the day relates to telecommunications and the digital convergence of communications, computers, and entertainment. Additional sections have been added to cover these regulatory issues as they pertain to both traditional and wireless local telephone, long-distance telephone, and cable television.

Our emphasis on economic principles in no way implies a neglect of the pertinent institutional features. This text includes extensive case studies of major areas of regulation and antitrust policy, including entire chapters devoted to such issues as government merger policies, cable television regulation, and transportation regulation. Indeed, this text is unique in its extensive coverage of several of these topics, as well as issues such as the role of the White House regulatory oversight process. Although this book discusses essential aspects of these regulations and their performance, our intent is not to provide students with a list of case names, government rules, and other institutional details. Rather, we hope to provide students not only with pertinent insights today but also with the economic tools to analyze the implications of regulations and antitrust policies a decade from now. Future policies may have a quite different structure from those presently in place, and it is the economic framework we use to approach these issues that will be of lasting value.

The minimum economics background needed for this book is an introductory price theory course. This background will enable students to grasp all of the empirical material as well as most of the theoretical developments. In some cases, the text advances to a level at which some background in intermediate microeconomic theory is desirable, but these more difficult sections can be omitted. A unique feature of this book is that it brings to bear on these issues new developments in industrial organization and game theory. Presentation of this more advanced material is self-contained, does not involve the use of calculus, and is incorporated in chapters in such a way that it can easily be omitted by an instructor with a different course emphasis.

We have used drafts of this book in our teaching at the undergraduate level and in business school curricula. Others have used this book in law schools and public policy schools. In no case did we use all of these chapters in any one course. Although the book's coverage is nearly encyclopedic, it is still not all-inclusive. It is doubtful whether any single course can successfully cover all the material included in this book, except perhaps in an intensive two-semester sequence. Because instructors have a variety of different interests and instructional needs, we have structured the book in a manner that will facilitate its use in a variety of contexts.

Organization of the Book

Economics of Regulation and Antitrust consists of two introductory chapters, followed by three parts. The beginning of the book sets the stage and introduces some of the overriding issues, such as ascertaining what the objective is that government regulators maximize and considering the appropriate division of labor between the states and the federal government.

The following three parts of the book present the core of the analytical material. Part I focuses on antitrust policy, Part II deals with economic regulation, and Part III focuses on social regulation and patent policy. Each of these parts is structured in a similar manner. The first chapter of each part provides an overview of the key economic issues as well as the pertinent methodology that will be employed. We discuss the principal market failures in this context, and how economic analysis is used to address them. In every case, the first chapter of each part can be viewed as essential reading. The instructor can then select which of the subsequent case studies to use. Chapters that require the student to have read another chapter within that part, other than the introductory chapter, are noted below. Otherwise, chapters within a part can be assigned in whatever order the instructor wishes. Any chapters that the instructor wishes to omit may be excluded.

Part I, which focuses on antitrust policy, includes a healthy dose of the analytical tools of modern industrial organization. Chapter 3 is an introductory overview of antitrust policy and of the other chapters in Part I. Efficiency and technical progress are explained in Chapter 4 as tools for evaluating policies. At least the first half of this chapter is probably necessary reading for understanding Chapters 5–9.

Oligopoly and collusive pricing (Chapter 5) is novel in introducing oligopoly through a game-theoretic approach and then relating the theoretical models to antitrust cases. Market structure and entry deterrence (Chapter 6) is mostly analytical; it can be skipped by instructors under time pressure in courses with a primary focus on antitrust cases. The remaining three chapters—horizontal and conglomerate mergers (Chapter 7), vertical mergers and restrictions (Chapter 8), and monopolization and price discrimination (Chapter 9)—are "stand-alone" chapters that can be assigned or not, depending on the instructor's preference.

Part II addresses the role of economic regulation. As evidenced by the dozen or so case studies in this part, economic regulation has been an integral part of the U.S. economy. Although there has been substantial deregulation of airlines, trucking, and long distance telephone, the debate over appropriate regulatory policies and re-regulation is still very active.

An overview of economic regulation, including its historical development and a summary of regulatory practices, is provided in Chapter 10. This chapter also provides the most in-depth textbook discussion of the efforts of social scientists to understand the extent of government regulation. The remainder of Part III is comprised of two pieces. Chapters 11–15 cover the regulation of natural monopolies. The recent theory of natural monopoly is presented in Chapter 11, while Chapter 12 reviews actual regulatory practices with respect to electric utilities and local telephone companies. Although regulation is the standard U.S. government response to natural monopolies, alternatives are available; these are discussed in Chapters 13 and 14. Chapter 13 addresses a new and promising approach, franchise bidding, and provides a detailed case study of cable television. A more traditional alternative is that of government enterprise. It is reviewed in Chapter 14, along with a comparative analysis of government ownership and regulation with respect to electric utilities. Then, in Chapter 15, some dynamic issues related to monopoly regulation are explored in the context of the rapidly changing long distance telecommunications market.

The regulation of markets that are potentially competitive receives in-depth treatment in the remaining three chapters of Part II. A theoretical investigation of the effects of regulation is provided in Chapter 16. These ideas are then applied to regulation in the transportation and energy industries. Chapter 17 closely examines airlines and surface freight transportation (in particular, trucking and railroads), while Chapter 18 covers the crude oil and natural gas industries.

Part III focuses on the new forms of risk and environmental regulation that emerged primarily after the 1970s. Chapter 19 introduces the principal methodological issues, including market failures such as externalities and inadequate risk information, the primary economic test of benefit-cost analysis that applies in this area, and the rather daunting task that economists face in assigning dollar values to outcomes such as a five-degree temperature change in the early part of the next century.

The task of assigning market prices to outcomes that, by their very nature, are not traded in efficient markets is the focus of Chapter 20. The primary case study concentrates on how economists attempt to assign a dollar value to risks to human life, which illustrates how economists have attempted to assess the pertinent tradeoff rates that should be used in evaluating government policies. The next four chapters deal with various types of social regulation policies, including environmental protection regulation (Chapter 21), product safety regulation (Chapter 22), occupational safety regulation (Chapter 23), and pharmaceutical regulation (Chapter 24). Chapter 22 presents the greatest variety of social regulation issues that have been of long-term interest to researchers in industrial organization and in law and economics. A major strength of all these chapters is that they confront the current policy issues now under debate, including topics such as global warming, the role of product liability law, and the social consequences of smoking.

Chapter 24, on patents and pharmaceuticals, is new to the second edition. It combines the theory of patents with a case study of their application to one of the most technologically progressive U.S. industries. It is a particularly timely addition to the book, given the current interest in health care reform.

Suggested Course Outlines

An intensive one-year course could cover this entire book. However, in most cases, instructors will be using the book in a context in which it is not feasible to cover all the material.

In Table A we have identified six different course approaches and the pertinent chapters that can be assigned for each one. The first type of

Table A
Suggested Course Outlines

Course Focus	Introduction		Part I							Part II									Part III					
	1	2	3	4	5	6	7	8	9	10	11	12	13	14	15	16	17	18	19	20	21	22	23	24
Balanced one-quarter course	√	√	√	√	√		√		√	√		√							√	√		√		
Antitrust			√	√	√	√	√	√	√															
Economic regulation	√	√		√						√	√	√	√	√	√	√	√	√					√	√
Social regulation	√	√		√															√	√	√	√	√	√
Industrial organization			√	√	√	√			√	√			√			√	√	√				√		√
Institutional	√	√	√		√		√		√	√		√							√	√	√	√	√	√

course is the balanced one-quarter course. Such a course would include the introductory material in Chapters 1 and 2 as general background; Chapters 3–5, 7, and 9 from Part I; Chapters 10 and 12 from Part II; and Chapters 19, 20, and 22 from Part III.

The second course approach is a conventional antitrust course. It would place the greatest reliance on Part I of the book, which includes Chapters 3–9. Instructors who wish to provide a broader perspective on some of the other topics in regulation might augment these chapters with the indicated chapters for the one-quarter course.

A course focusing on economic regulation would include primarily the introductory section and Part II of the book, or Chapters 1–2, 4, 10–18, 22, and 24. Similarly, a course focusing on social regulation would include the introductory section and Part III of the book, or Chapters 1–2, 4, and 19–24. In situations in which we have taught such narrowly defined courses, we have often found it useful to include the material from the balanced one-quarter course as well, to give the student a broader perspective on the most salient economic issues in other areas of government intervention.

Given the frontier treatment of industrial organization in Part I, this book could also be used in a policy-oriented course on industrial organization. With Chapters 3–6 providing the theoretical foundation in industrial organization, an instructor could select from the remaining chapters to cover a variety of policy issues. A suggestion is to use Chapter 9 (its coverage of monopolization practices follows up on the theory of strategic entry deterrence in Chapter 6), Chapters 10, 13, and 16–18 (to examine how different types of economic regulatory structures can affect competition), and Chapters 22 and 24 (to assess efforts such as product quality regulation).

The final course outline pertains to courses, particularly those in business schools, that wish to have a more institutional focus. For these courses, the objective is to focus on the empirical aspects of government regulation and antitrust policies, as well as the character of these policies. Moreover, these courses would require no advanced undergraduate economic methods. The chapters in the book that meet these tests and can be readily grasped with an introductory economics background are also indicated in Table A.

Acknowledgments

We would like to thank Terry Vaughn at MIT Press for his enthusiastic support, advice, and motivational comments.

Each of the authors has profited from the word processing and editorial input at his institution. At Duke University, we would like to thank Tracy Kuczak and Kris McGee. At Johns Hopkins, we would like to thank Donna Althoff and Joanna Wescott (for trying to get a ^ above a p).

A number of individuals have provided comments on parts of the manuscript or advice along the way. These include the following:

Gilbert Becker, St. Anselm College
Klaus G. Becker, Texas Tech University
Phillip A. Beutel, National Economic Research Associates, Inc.
Myong-Hun Chang, Cleveland State University
R. Morris Coats, Nicholls State University
Christopher B. Colburn, Old Dominion University
Andrew R. Dick, University of California–Los Angeles
Henry Grabowski, Duke University
Mark Kennet, Tulane University
Luther D. Lawson, University of North Carolina–Wilmington
Stanford L. Levin, Southern Illinois University at Edwardsville
Wesley A. Magat, Duke University
Matthew Marlin, Duquesne University
John Martin, Adelphi University
Sam Peltzman, University of Chicago
Robin A. Prager, Vanderbilt University
Michael A. Salinger, Boston University
Daniel F. Spulber, Northwestern University

1 Introduction

The government acts in many ways. The most familiar role of the government is the subject of public finance courses. The government raises money in taxes and then spends this money through various expenditure efforts. In addition, the government also regulates the behavior of firms and individuals. Our legal system is perhaps the most comprehensive example of the mechanism by which this regulation takes place.

This book will be concerned with government regulation of the behavior of both firms and individuals within the context of issues classified as regulation and antitrust. Regulation of firms involves much more than attempting to deal with monopoly power in the traditional textbook sense. The setting of prices for public utilities, the control of pollution emitted in the firm's production process, and the allocation of radio broadcast bands are all among the contexts in which government regulation plays a prominent role in influencing firm behavior.

The behavior of individuals has also come under increasing regulatory scrutiny. In some cases decisions are regulated directly, such as the requirement to wear seatbelts. In addition, individuals are affected by regulations that influence either market prices or the mix of products that are available. Product-safety standards, for example, serve to eliminate the high-risk end of the product-quality spectrum. The menu of products available to consumers and jobs available to workers is the subject of substantial regulatory influence.

To assess the pervasiveness of these efforts, consider a day in the life of the typical American worker. That worker awakes in the morning to the sound of his clock radio, where the stations he listens to and the wavelength they broadcast on are regulated by the Federal Communications Commission. Settling down to breakfast, the worker is greeted by the label on the cereal box whose content is strictly regulated by the Federal Trade Commission and the Food and Drug Administration to avoid misleading consumers about the health benefits of breakfast cereals. The orange juice from concentrate can also no longer be labeled "fresh" courtesy of a 1991 Federal Trade Commission action. The milk poured on the cereal is also regulated in a variety of ways, with perhaps the most important being the role of U.S. Department of Agriculture price supports (milk marketing orders). More recently, there has been substantial concern with the health-risk characteristics of milk in terms of the presence of hormones (bovine somatotrophin), which has been the object of substantial regulatory debate. If one chooses to add fruit to the cereal, it is reassuring to know that the Environmental Protection Agency (EPA) stringently regulates the pesticides that can be used on domestic produce. Unfortunately, imported produce that has been drenched in pesticides is not inspected with great frequency.

Heading to work, our regulated individual climbs into a Japanese car that was successful in not violating any import quotas. The worker will be safer en route to work than in earlier years, thanks to extensive safety regulations by the National Highway Traffic Safety Administration. The fuel used by the car is also less environmentally damaging than would have been the case in the absence of U.S Department of Transportation Fuel Economy standards and in the absence of EPA gasoline lead standards.

Once on the job, the worker is protected against many of the hazards of work by occupational safety and health regulations and is also assured a decent wage by minimum-wage regulation. A host of U.S. Department of Labor regulations, as well as Equal Employment Opportunity Commission stipulations, ensure that the worker will not be unduly discriminated against during the course of his employment.

Our worker's phone calls are billed at telephone rates set by regulation, although increasingly these rates have been influenced by market forces. Visiting business associates travel on planes whose availability and fares have been greatly influenced by regulatory changes. The safe arrival of these associates is due in part to the continued vigilance of the Federal Aviation Administration and the safety incentives created by tort liability lawsuits following airplane crashes.

Even when our individual escapes from work for an evening of relaxation and recreation, government regulations remain present. If the worker eats dinner at a restaurant, there is a good chance that he or she will be forbidden to smoke cigarettes or relegated to a smoking area. The U.S. Consumer Product Safety Commission, for example, has regulatory responsibility for a wide range of sports equipment, ranging from all-terrain vehicles to baseball helmets.

Although some deregulation has taken place in the past decade, the scope of government regulation remains quite broad. The role of regulation in our society remains ubiquitous. Various forms of government regulation touch almost every aspect of our activities and consumption patterns. The widespread impact of regulation is not unexpected, inasmuch as this represents a very potent mechanism by which the government can influence market outcomes.

The Rationale for Regulation and Antitrust Policies

If we existed in a world that functioned in accordance with the perfect competition paradigm, there would be little need for antitrust policies and other regulatory efforts. All markets would consist of a large number of sellers of a product, and consumers would be fully informed of the product's implications. Moreover, there would be no externalities present in this idealized economy, as all effects would be internalized by the buyers and sellers of a particular product.

Unfortunately, economic reality seldom adheres very closely to the textbook model of perfect competition. Many industries are dominated by a small number of large firms. In some instances, principally the public utilities, there may even be a monopoly. Consumers who use hazardous products and workers who accept risky employment may not fully understand the consequences of their actions. There are also widespread externalities that affect the air we breathe, the water we drink, and the future viability of the planet.

The government has two types of mechanisms at its disposal to address these departures from the perfectly competitive model. The first mechanism is price incentives. We can impose a tax on various kinds of activities in order to decrease their attractiveness. There is some attempt to have taxes that are product specific, as in the case of alcohol taxes and cigarette taxes, but there the notion has largely been that we should be taxing products perceived as luxuries. There certainly has not been any deliberate attempt to link these taxes to an assessment of market failures. The tax on cars that fail to meet fuel-economy standards, known as the gas-guzzler tax, perhaps best meets the notion of utilizing the price mechanism to influence economic behavior. Gasoline taxes, which remain well below their optimal level, serve a similar function.

An alternative to taxes is to try to control behavior directly. We do this in the field of antitrust by the government taking explicit action to block mergers that might threaten the competitive character of a market. In the area of utility regulation, a complex web of regulations prevents public utilities from charging excessive rates for their electricity, which is a commodity for which the electric companies have a captive market. Much health, safety, and environmental regulation similarly specifies the technological requirements that must be met or the pollution standards that cannot be exceeded. This book will consequently be concerned primarily with various forms of government action that limit behavior related to the kinds of market failures discussed above.

Not all market failures stem from actions by firms. In some cases, individuals also may be contributing to the market failures. If we fail to use seat belts as often as we should or dispose of our hazardous waste products in a reckless manner, then there will be a need for government regulation to influence our activities. Although the preponderance of regulatory policies is directed at business, the scope of regulation is sufficiently comprehensive to include all economic actors.

Antitrust Regulation

The first of the three parts of the book deals with antitrust policy. Beginning with the post–Civil War era, there has been substantial concern with antitrust issues. This attention was stimulated by a belief that consumers were vulnerable to the market power of monopolies. Because of the potential economic losses that result from monopolies, a number of states enacted antitrust laws at the end of the nineteenth century. The U.S. Congress also was particularly active in this area in the early part of the twentieth century, and many of the most important pieces of legislation governing the current antitrust policy date back to that time. The major federal statute continues to be the 1890 Sherman Act.

The Changing Character of Antitrust Issues

The scope of antitrust issues is quite broad. It encompasses the traditional concerns with a monopoly, but these issues are less prominent now than they once were. Several decades ago, major topics of debate concerned whether IBM, AT&T, General Motors, and other major firms had become too powerful and too dominant in their markets. Debates such as these would seem quaint today—perhaps useful as an exercise in an economic history course. Today these once-dominant companies are now humbled giants, weakened by the effects of foreign competition. In many respects we have a global market rather than a U.S. market for many products, so some of the earlier concerns about monopolies have been muted.

Indeed, in the 1980s we even witnessed a merger that would have been totally unthinkable three decades earlier. The merger of General Electric with RCA created a powerful electronics corporation of unprecedented size. The rationale for the merger was that a large scale was necessary to support the innovation needed to meet the threat of foreign competition. The competitive threat was certainly real. Whereas several decades ago these companies produced the great majority of all electronics items used in the United States, by the 1990s it was difficult to find a TV or VCR not made in Japan.

The current structure of antitrust policies is diverse in character and impact. The overall intent of these policies has not changed markedly over the past century. Their intent is to limit the role of market power that might result from substantial concentration in a particular industry. What has changed is that the concerns have shifted from the rise of single monopolies to mergers, leveraged buyouts, and other financial transactions that combine and restructure corporations in a manner that might fundamentally influence market behavior.

Reasoning behind Antitrust Regulations

The major concerns with monopoly and similar kinds of concentration are not that being big is necessarily undesirable. However, because of the control over the price exerted by a monopoly there are economic efficiency losses to society. Product quality and diversity may also be affected. Society could potentially be better off if limitations were imposed on the operation of a monopoly or a similar kind of concentrated industry.

Recent research has greatly changed how we think about monopolies. For example, one major consideration is not simply how big a firm currently is and what its current market influence is, but rather the extent to which there is a possible entry from a competitor. If firms fear the prospect of such entry, which has been characterized through the theory of contestable markets, then the behavior of a monopolist will be influenced in a manner that will promote more responsible behavior.

One of the reasons concentrated industries emerge is that some firms may have exclusive rights to some invention or may have been responsible for a technological change that has transformed the industry. Coca-Cola and Pepsi Cola are much more successful soft drink products than their generic counterparts because of their perceived superior taste. If their formulas were public and could be generally replicated, then their market influence would wane considerably.

Once a firm has achieved a monopolistic position, perhaps in part due to past innovation, we want it to continue to be dynamic in terms of its innovative efforts. A substantial controversy has long been waged by economists as to whether monopoly promotes or deters innovation. Will a monopolist, in effect, rest on its laurels and not have any incentive to innovate because of the lack of market pressure, or will monopolists be spurred on by the prospect of capturing all of the gains from innovation that a monopoly can obtain, whereas a firm in a perfectly competitive market would lose some of the benefits of innovation as its innovation is copied by the competitors? We will explore the relative merits of these arguments and the dynamics of monopolies but will not draw any general conclusions indicating the desirability of monopolies. The relative merits of monopolistic power tend to vary across market contexts.

Economic Regulation

In many contexts where natural monopolies have emerged, for reasons of economic efficiency it is desirable to have a monopolistic market structure. Nevertheless, these economic giants must be tamed so that they will not charge excessive prices. We do not wish to incur all of the efficiency and equity problems that arise as a result of a monopoly. Prominent examples include public utilities. It does not make sense to have a large number of small firms providing households with electricity, providing public transportation systems, or laying phone lines and cable TV lines. However, we also do not wish to give single firms free reign in these markets because the interests of a monopoly will not best advance the interests of society as a whole. What's good for General Motors is not necessarily good for America.

Other kinds of regulation affect energy prices and minimum wage levels. In some instances the focus of economic regulation is to control product price. This may be indirectly through profit regulation by, for example, limiting public utilities to a particular rate of return. In other cases, there are complex rules governing prices, as in the case of U.S. energy regulations and long distance telephone rate regulation.

Development of Economic Regulation

The genesis of these various kinds of economic regulation can be traced back to the late 1800s, as in the case of antitrust. Before the turn of the century, the U.S. Congress had created the Interstate Commerce Commission to regulate railroad rates, and the early twentieth century saw a surge in the number of regulatory agencies in the transportation, communication, and securities fields. It was during that period, for example, that the U.S. Congress established the Federal Communications Commission and the Securities and Exchange Commission. In the case of antitrust policy, the main thrust of these efforts has been to prevent the development of the kinds of market concentration that threaten the competitive functioning of markets. In contrast, economic regulation generally recognizes that market concentration not only is inevitable, but in many cases is a superior structure for the particular market. The intent is then to place limits on the performance of the firms in this market so as to limit the losses that might be inflicted.

Factors in Setting Rate Regulations

Establishing a rate structure that will provide efficient incentives for all parties is not a trivial undertaking. Consider the case of an electric power company. The objective is not to minimize the rate to consumers, inasmuch as very low rates may affect the desirability of staying in business for the electric company. In addition, it may affect the quality of the product being provided in terms of whether power is provided at off-peak times or whether power outages are remedied quickly. A series of complex issues affects the role of the dynamics of the investment process in technological improvements. We want the electric power company to innovate so that they will be able to provide cheaper power in the future. However, if we capture all the gains from innovation and give them to the consumers through lower prices, then the firm has no incentive to undertake the innovation. We cannot rely on market competition to force them to take such action, for there is little competition within this market structure. Thus we must strike a delicate balance between providing sufficient incentives for firms to undertake cost-reducing actions while at the same time ensuring that the prices for consumers are not excessive.

Key concerns that have arisen with respect to economic regulation pertain to the differing role of marginal costs and fixed costs. When the electric company provides service to your house or apartment, there are specific identifiable costs that can be attributed to the product that is delivered to you—the marginal costs. However, the electric company also incurs substantial fixed costs in terms of its plant and equipment that also must be covered. How should the electric company allocate these fixed costs? Should it simply divide them equally among the total number of customers? Should it allocate the costs proportionally to the total bills that the customers have? Should it distinguish among different groups depending on how sensitive they are to price? If businesses are less price-sensitive than are consumers, should the major share of these costs be borne by firms or by individual consumers?

Over the past several decades, economists have developed a very sophisticated series of frameworks for addressing these issues. The overall object of these analyses is to determine how we can best structure the price and incentive schemes for these firms so that we protect the interests of electricity customers while at the same time providing incentives and a reasonable return to the firms involved.

In the case of both antitrust and economic regulation, it is seldom possible to replicate an efficient market perfectly. There is generally some departure from the perfect competition situation that cannot be glossed over or rectified, even through the most imaginative and complex pricing scheme. However, by applying economic tools to these issues, we can obtain a much more sensible market situation than would emerge if there were no regulation whatsoever.

It is also noteworthy that economic analysis often plays a critical role in such policy discussions. Economic analyses based on the models discussed in this book frequently provide the basis for ratemaking decisions for public utilities. A prominent regulatory economist, Alfred E. Kahn, was responsible for the deregulation of the airlines, in large part because of his belief that competition would benefit consumers and create a more viable market structure than the previous system, in which airline market entry was dictated by a government bureaucracy. In contrast, economic analysis often does not play such a central role in the operation of a perfectly competitive market. The paradigmatic firm in a competitive market is a small enterprise operating in a sea of other small enterprises. Firms in this market do not routinely draw demand curves, marginal revenue curves, and marginal cost curves. Yet few economists are disturbed by this failure to apply economic tools explicitly, as economists since the time of Milton Friedman have argued that they implicitly apply the laws of economics, much as the billiard player applies the laws of geometry even though he may not have had any formal training in the subject. In the case of economic regulation, the application of economic reasoning is quite explicit. Economists play a prominent role in these regulatory agencies. Much of the policy debate turns on economic analyses and consideration of the merits of the kinds of economic issues that we will address in the course of this book.

Health, Safety, and Environmental Regulation

The newest form of regulation is the focus of Part 3 of the book. In the 1970s the U.S. Congress created a host of agencies concerned with regulating health, safety, and environmental quality. These new regulatory agencies included the U.S. Consumer Product Safety Commission, the Occupational Safety and Health Administration, the Environmental Protection Agency, the Nuclear Regulatory Commission, and the National Highway Traffic Safety Administration. Although these forms of regulation are often referred to as being social-regulation policies, the exact dividing line between what regulations are economic regulations and what regulations are social regulations is unclear. As a result, we will use the more specific designation of health, safety, and environmental regulation to encompass these forms of regulation.

The chief impetus for the health, safety, and environmental regulations is twofold. First, substantial externalities often result from economic behavior. The operation of businesses often generates air pollution, water pollution, and toxic waste. Individual consumption decisions are also the source of externalities, as the fuel we burn in our cars gives rise to air pollution. Informational issues also play a salient role. Because of the peculiar nature of information as an economic commodity, it is more efficient for the government to be the producer of much information and to disseminate the information broadly. Individual firms, for example, will not have the same kind of incentives to do scientific research unless they can reap the benefits of the information. As a result, it is largely through the efforts of government agencies that society has funded research into the implications of various kinds of hazards so that we can form an assessment of their consequences and determine the degree to which they should be regulated.

Many government policies in the safety and environmental area deal with aspects of market behavior that by their very nature do not involve voluntary bargains. We all suffer the effects of air pollution from local power plants, but we did not agree to consume this air pollution. No transaction ever took place, and we are not explicitly compensated for these losses. In the absence of such a market transaction, we do not have explicit estimates of the price. No specific price has been set for the loss in visibility, or for that matter the various kinds of health effects and materials damages that will result from air pollution. Thus the first task that must be undertaken is to assess the worth of these various kinds of policies, inasmuch as the benefit values do not necessarily emerge from market behavior. A case study that will be explored in Part 3 is how we attach a value to risks of life and death, which is perhaps the most difficult and most sensitive of these fundamental tradeoffs that we face.

The three dimensions of health, safety, and environmental regulation arise with respect to risks in our environment, risks in the workplace, and risks from the products we consume. Most of our regulatory influence over these risks is through direct government regulation. Several federal agencies promulgate detailed requirements on workplace technologies as well as overall performance requirements.

Role of the Courts

An increasingly prominent player in this regulatory area has been the courts. Whereas in the case of antitrust regulations the courts have been enforcing laws passed by Congress, in the case of these social regulation areas, the obligations that courts have been assessing pertain to the common-law requirements that have developed through decades of judicial decisions and precedents regarding how various kinds of accidents and other externalities are handled.

The incentives generated by the courts in many instances dwarf those created by regulatory agencies. The court awards for asbestos have been so substantial that the asbestos industry in the United States has been all but eliminated by the financial burdens. Liability costs have led the pharmaceutical industry largely to abandon research on contraceptive devices, and many vaccines have also been withdrawn from the market because of high liability burdens. Visitors at motels will notice that diving boards have disappeared—a consequence of the added liability-insurance costs associated with this form of recreational equipment. To understand the role of the government within the context of this type of regulation, one must assess not only how the regulatory agencies function but what doctrines govern the behavior of the courts. These matters will also be addressed in Part 3.

Criteria for Assessment

Ideally, the purpose of antitrust and regulation policies is to foster improvements judged in efficiency terms. We should move closer to the perfectly competitive ideal than we would have in the absence of this type of intervention. The object is to increase the efficiency with which the economy operates, recognizing that we may fall short of the goal of replicating a perfectly competitive market, but nevertheless we can achieve substantial improvements over what would prevail in the absence of such government intervention.

Put somewhat differently, our task is to maximize the net benefits of these regulations to society. Such a concern requires that we assess both the benefits and the costs of these regulatory policies and attempt to maximize their difference. If all groups in society are treated symmetrically, then this benefit-cost calculus represents a straightforward maximization of economic efficiency. Alternatively, we might choose to weight the benefits to the disadvantaged differently or make other kinds of distinctions, in which case we can incorporate a broader range of concerns than efficiency alone.

Although maximizing economic efficiency or some other laudable social objective may be touted by economists as our goal, in practice it is not what the regulators choose to maximize. Regulators respond to a variety of political constituencies. Indeed, in many instances the same kinds of market failures that led to the regulation also may influence the regulations that are undertaken. As a society, for example, we overreact to low-probability risks that have been called to our attention. We fear the latest highly publicized carcinogen, and we cancel our European vacation plans after a highly publicized terrorist attack. These same kinds of overreactions to risk also create pressures for regulatory agencies to take action against these hazards.

Moreover, even in instances in which government agencies do not suffer from irrationality or from irrational pressures, they will not necessarily maximize social welfare. The actions taken by government agencies will influence the fortunes of firms and particular groups in society in substantial ways. The granting of a cable TV franchise may make one a millionaire, and restrictions on foreign competition will greatly boost the fortune of firms in highly competitive international markets. There is a strong private interest in regulatory outcomes, and we will explore the economic foundations and mechanisms by which this private interest becomes manifest.

The net result of these private interests is that regulatory policies frequently do not perform in the manner that economists would intend in an ideal world. As Nobel laureate George Stigler demonstrated, economic regulation often advances private interests, such as increasing the profits of the industry being regulated. The apparent object is not always to maximize social welfare but rather to provide transfers in particular groups in society. Moreover, these transfers may be provided in an inefficient way, so that regulatory policies may fall far short of our ideal.

The successive disappointments with regulatory policy have given rise to the terminology "government failure" to represent the governmental counterpart of market failure. In much the same way as markets may fail because some of the idealized assumptions fail to hold, the government too may fail. Our task is not always to replace a situation of market failure with government action, for governmental intervention may not yield a superior outcome. We should always assess whether the particular kinds of intervention that have been chosen will actually enhance market performance and improve our welfare to as great an extent as possible. As we examine the various forms of regulation, we will consider the merits of the regulation as well as the test that we should use in assessing their adequacy.

Questions and Problems

1. Why should the government intervene in situations of market failure? Should the government intervene if a market is fully efficient in the sense of being perfectly competitive? What additional rationales are present if there is an inadequacy in the market?

2. Discuss some of the kinds of instances in which the government has an advantage in terms of informational capabilities as well as superior expertise to make decisions that consumers would not have.

3. Economists frequently use the yardstick of economic efficiency in judging the merits of alternative policies. What value judgments are implicit in the economic efficiency doctrine?

Recommended Reading

Two classics in regulatory economics are Alfred E. Kahn, *The Economics of Regulation: Principles and Institutions* (Cambridge, Mass.: MIT Press, 1988), and George J. Stigler, *The Citizen and the State* (Chicago: University of Chicago Press, 1975). An excellent analysis of the legal and policy issues appears in Stephen Breyer, *Regulation and Its Reform* (Cambridge, Mass.: Harvard University Press, 1982). Useful advanced texts are Daniel F. Spulber, *Regulation and*

Markets (Cambridge, Mass.: MIT Press, 1989); and Sanford V. Berg and John Tschirhart, *Natural Monopoly Regulation: Principles and Practice* (Cambridge: Cambridge University Press, 1988).

Appendix

Key Regulatory Agencies

BLS	Bureau of Labor Statistics
CAB	Civil Aeronautics Board
CEA	Council of Economic Advisors
CFTC	Commodity Futures Trading Commission
CPSC	Consumer Product Safety Commission
DOD	Department of Defense
DOT	Department of Transportation
EEOC	Equal Employment Opportunity Commission
EPA	Environmental Protection Agency
FAA	Federal Aviation Administration
FAO	Food and Agricultural Organization
FCC	Federal Communication Commission
FDA	Food and Drug Administration
FDIC	Federal Deposit Insurance Corporation
FEC	Federal Election Commission
FERC	Federal Energy Regulatory Commission
FHA	Federal Housing Administration
FMC	Federal Maritime Commission
FSLIC	Federal Savings and Loan Insurance Corporation
FTC	Federal Trade Commission
ICC	Interstate Commerce Commission
ITC	International Trade Commission
NHTSA	National Highway Traffic Safety Administration
NIH	National Institutes of Health
NIOSH	National Institute of Occupational Safety and Health
NLRB	National Labor Relations Board
NRC	National Regulatory Commission
OIRA	Office of Information and Regulatory Affairs
OMB	Office of Management and Budget
OSHA	Occupational Safety and Health Administration
SEC	Securities and Exchange Commission
USDA	United States Department of Agriculture

2 The Making of a Regulation

A stylized account of the evolution of regulation and antitrust policies is this: A single national regulatory agency establishes the government policy in an effort to maximize the national interest, where the legislative mandate of the agency defines its specific responsibilities in fostering these interests. The reality of regulatory policymaking differs quite starkly from this stylized view. The process is imperfect in that some observers claim that "government failure" may be of the same order of importance as market failure.[1]

One important difference is that not all regulation is national in scope. Much regulation occurs at the state and local levels. Recent political concern with the importance of reflecting the preferences and economic conditions at the local level has spurred an increased interest in regulatory activity other than at the federal level. It is noteworthy that from a historical standpoint most regulation, such as the rate regulations for railroads, began at the state level. These regulations were subsequently extended to the national level.

Even in situations in which it is a national regulatory body that is acting, this group may not be fostering the national interest. Special interest groups and their diverse array of lobbyists also have an influence on regulatory policy. Moreover, the legislative mandates of the regulatory agencies are typically specified much more narrowly than simply urging the agency to promote the national interest.

Another difference from the stylized model is that typically the regulatory agency is not the only governmental player. Congress and the judiciary provide one check, and more importantly the regulatory oversight process within the White House has substantial input as well. Each of these groups has its own agenda. Few observers would claim that any of these agendas coincides exactly with the national interest.

The final possible misconception is that it is a simple matter for the government to issue a regulatory policy or to make a decision regarding antitrust policy. There are explicit steps that government agencies must take before instituting regulations. At each of these stages, several governmental and private players have an input into the process and can influence the outcome. The nature of this process and the way it affects the regulatory outcomes is the subject of this chapter.

The underlying principles governing antitrust and regulation policies must be consistent with the legislative mandates written by Congress. Actions taken with these legislative stipulations in turn are subject to review by the courts. These two sets of influences are pertinent to all policy actions discussed in this book.

Other aspects of the character of these policies differ considerably. The U.S. Department of Justice's vigilance in pursuing antitrust actions varies with political administrations, in part because of differences in interpretation of the law. Although the U.S. Department of Justice occasionally issues formal regulations to guide industry behavior, such as procedures for implementing civil penalties, for the most part the main policy mechanism of influence is litigation against firms believed to be violating the antitrust statutes. This threat of litigation also produces many out-of-court settlements of antitrust cases.

Many of the economic-regulation agencies are independent regulatory commissions, such as the Interstate Commerce Commission, the Federal Trade Commission, and the Federal Communications Commission. In addition to initiating legal action, these agencies place extensive reliance on issuance of regulations to guide business behavior. The steps that must be taken in issuing these regulations follow the procedures discussed later in this chapter, except that there is no review by executive authority over regulatory commissions.

The final group of agencies consists of regulatory agencies within the Executive Branch. These agencies rely primarily on issuing formal regulations pursuant to their legislative mandates. For example, EPA has issued lead-emission standards in implementing the Clean Air Act. This regulatory activity is subject to review by the Office of Management and Budget and the full rulemaking process detailed later in this chapter.

Because the regulatory procedures for executive branch agencies are most complex, this chapter will focus on them as the most general case. The issues are of greatest pertinence to the policies to be considered in Part 3 of the book. However, the economic lessons involved are quite general. Government policies should not be regarded as a fixed object to be treated reverentially within courses on business and government. Rather, they are generated by a complex set of political and economic forces, not all of which produce desirable outcomes. Part of the task of the subsequent chapters is to ascertain which policies are beneficial and which are not.

State versus Federal Regulation: The Federalism Debate

Although regulation is frequently viewed as being synonymous with federal regulation, not all regulation is at the federal level. Restrictions on cigarette smoking in restaurants are determined at the local level, as are drinking ages. State regulatory commissions set utility rates and often are involved in complex legal battles over appropriate jurisdiction. Almost all insurance regulation occurs at the state level as well. Some states regulate insurance rates quite stringently, whereas in other states these insurance rates have been deregulated. The terms under which there are payouts under insurance schemes also vary with locale, as some states have adopted no-fault rules in accident contexts. States also differ in terms of the factors that they will permit insurance companies to take into account when setting rates. In some instances, the states prohibit the insurance company from factoring in the driver's age, sex, or race when setting automobile insurance rates. Finally, states differ in terms of whether they make automobile insurance mandatory and, if it is mandatory, the extent of the subsidy that is provided to high-risk drivers by the lower-risk drivers.

Advantages of Federalism

The existence of state regulations of various kinds is not simply the result of an oversight on the part of federal regulators. There are often sound economic reasons why we want regulation to take place at the state level. Indeed, particularly in the Reagan and Bush administrations there was an emphasis on transferring some of the control over the regulatory structure and regulatory enforcement to the states—an emphasis that comes under the general heading of "federalism." The extent of the impact of federalism principles has, however, been less than advocates of this approach intended. In recognition of this emphasis, the Office of Management and Budget issued the following regulatory policy guideline:

Federal regulations should not preempt State laws or regulations, except to guarantee rights of national citizenship or to avoid significant burdens on interstate commerce.[2]

A number of sound economic rationales underlie this principle of federalism. First, local conditions may affect both the costs and benefits associated with the regulation. Preferences vary locally, as do regional economic conditions. Areas where mass transit is well established can impose greater restrictions on automobiles than can states where there are not such transportation alternatives.

The second potential advantage to decentralized regulation is that citizens wishing a different mix of public goods can choose to relocate. Those who like to gamble can, for example, reside in states where gambling is permitted, such as Nevada or New Jersey. The entire theory of local public goods is built around similar notions whereby individuals relocate in an effort to establish the best match between the local public policies and their preferences. The diversity of options made possible through the use of state regulation permits such choices to be made, whereas if all regulatory policies and public decisions were nationally uniform, there would be no such discretion.

A third advantage of local regulation is that it can reflect the heterogeneity of costs and benefits in a particular locale. Ideally, we would like to set national standards that fully reflect benefits and cost differences across areas. We want to recognize, for example, the need to regulate pollution sources more stringently when there are large exposed populations at risk. Federal regulations seldom reflect this diversity. In contrast, state regulations are seldom structured in a way to meet the needs in other states rather than their own.

A related advantage stemming from the potential for heterogeneity with state regulation is also the potential for innovation. Many states have embarked on innovative regulatory policies. California has been a leader in this regard, as it has instituted labeling requirements for hazardous chemicals as well as efforts to drastically roll back automobile insurance rates. Being innovative does not necessarily imply that these innovations are beneficial, but there is a benefit that other states derive from these experiments since they can see which regulatory experiments work and which ones do not. Experimentation at the local level will generally be less costly than at the national level, should the regulatory experiments prove to be a mistake. Moreover, if the experiment proves to be successful, then other states can and typically will follow suit.

Advantages of National Regulations

Although the benefits of local regulation are considerable, one should also take into account the potential advantages of national regulatory approaches as well. First, the national regulatory agencies often have an informational advantage over the local agencies. The U.S. Food and Drug Administration, for example, administers a regulatory structure for pharmaceuticals that entails substantial product testing. Duplicating this effort at the local level would be extremely costly and inefficient. Moreover, most local regulatory agencies have not developed the same degree of expertise as is present at the national level in this or in many other scientific areas.

A second rationale for national regulations is that uniform national regulations are generally more efficient for nationally marketed consumer products. If firms had to comply with fifty different sets of safety and environmental pollution standards for automobiles, production costs would soar. Labeling efforts as well as other policies that affect products involved in interstate commerce likewise will impose less cost on firms if they are undertaken on a uniform national basis.

The efficiency rationale for federal regulation is often more general, as in the case of antitrust policies. If the product market is national in scope, then one would want to recognize impediments to competition in the market through federal antitrust policies rather than relying on each of the fifty states to pursue individual antitrust actions.

A third rationale for federal regulation is that many problems occur locally but have national ramifications. Air pollution from power plants in the Midwest is largely responsible for the problems with acid rain in the eastern United States and Canada. Indeed, many of the environmental problems we are now confronting are global in scope, particularly those associated with climate change. Policies to address global warming will affect all energy sources. There is a need not only for national regulation but also for recognition of the international dimensions of the regulatory policy problem.

A final rationale for national regulations is that we view certain policy outcomes as being sufficiently important that all citizens should be guaranteed them. A prominent example is civil-rights regulations. We do not, for example, permit some states to discriminate based on race and sex even if they would want to if not constrained by federal affirmative-action requirements.

The Overlap of State and Federal Regulations

Because national regulations tend to have a preemptive effect, even if there is no specific legal provision providing for preemption, the prevention of substantial encroachment on the legitimate role of the states requires some restraint on the part of federal regulators. In recent years there have been several attempts to recognize the legitimate state differences that may exist.

Many of the examples of policies providing for an increased role of the states pertain to the administration of federal regulation. Beginning in 1987, the Department of Health and Human Services gave the states more leeway in their purchases of computers and computer-related equipment for the Aid to Families with Dependent Children program. Previously, the states had to undertake substantial paperwork to get approval for their computer needs. Similarly, the Department of Transportation has eased the paperwork and reporting procedures associated with subcontract work undertaken by the states, as in their highway construction projects.

On a more substantive level, the U.S. Environmental Protection Agency (EPA) has delegated substantial authority to the states for the National Pollutant Discharge Elimination System. This program establishes the water-pollution permits that will serve as the firm's regulatory standard for its water pollution discharges. Many states have assumed authority for the enforcement of these environmental regulations, and EPA has begun granting the states greater freedom in setting the permitted pollution amount for the firms. The Occupational Safety and Health Administration (OSHA) has undertaken similar efforts, and many states are responsible for the enforcement of job-safety regulations that are set at the national level but are monitored and enforced using personnel under a state enforcement program.

Although the states continue to play a subsidiary role in the development and administration of antitrust and regulatory policies, there has been increased recognition of the important role that the states have to play. This increased emphasis on the role of the states stems from several factors. Part of the enthusiasm for state regulation arises from the natural evolution of the development of federal regulation. If we assume that the federal government will first adopt the most promising regulatory alternatives and then will proceed to expand regulation by adopting the less beneficial alternatives, eventually we will reach a point where there will be some policies that will not be desirable nationally but will be beneficial in some local areas. The states will play some role in terms of filling in the gaps left by federal regulation.

Another force that has driven the expanding role of state regulation has been the recognition that there are legitimate differences among states. In many instances, the states have taken the initiative to recognize these differences by taking bold regulatory action, particularly with respect to insurance rate regulation.

Finally, much of the impetus for state regulation stems from a disappointment with the performance of federal regulation. Indeed, it is not entirely coincidental that the resurgence of interest in federalism principles occurred during the Reagan administration, which was committed to deregulation. There has consequently been an increased emphasis on the economic rationales for giving the states a larger role in the regulatory process and in ascertaining that federal intervention is truly needed. The main institutional player in promoting this recognition of federalism principles has been the U.S. Office of Management and Budget (OMB) within the context of the regulatory oversight process, which we will consider in later sections.

The Character of the Rulemaking Process

Although federal regulatory agencies do have substantial discretion, they do not have complete leeway to set the regulations that they want to enforce. One constraint is provided by legislation. Regulations promulgated by these agencies must be consistent with their legislative mandate, or they run the risk of being overturned by the courts. In addition, regulatory agencies must go through a specified set of administrative procedures as part of issuing a regulation. These procedures do not provide for the same degree of accountability as occurs in situations where Congress votes on particular pieces of legislation. However, there are substantial checks in this process that have evolved substantially over time to provide increased control of the actions of regulatory agencies.

The Chronology of New Regulations

Figure 2.1 illustrates the current structure of the rulemaking process. The two major players in this process are the regulatory agency and the OMB. The first stage of the development of a regulation occurs at the time when the agency decides to regulate a particular area of economic activity. Once a regulatory topic is on the agency's regulatory agenda, it must be listed as part of its regulatory program if it is a significant regulatory action that is likely to have a substantial cost impact. OMB has the authority to review this regulatory program, where the intent of this review is to identify potential overlaps among agencies, to become aware of particularly controversial regulatory policies that are being developed, and to screen out regulations that appear to be particularly undesirable. For the most part, these reviews have very little effect on the regulations that the agency pursues, but they do serve an informational role in terms of alerting OMB to potential interagency conflicts.

The next stage in the development of a regulation is to prepare a Regulatory Impact Analysis (RIA). The requirements for such RIAs have become more detailed over time, and at present they require the agency to calculate benefits and costs and to determine whether the benefits of the regulation are in excess of the costs. The agency is also required to consider potentially more desirable policy alternatives.

After completing the RIA, which is generally a very extensive study of the benefits and costs of regulatory policies, the agency must send the analysis to OMB for its review, which must take place 60 days before the agency issues a Notice of Proposed Rulemaking (NPRM) in the *Federal Register*. During this period of up to sixty days, OMB reviews the proposed regulation and the analysis supporting it. In the great majority of the cases, OMB simply approves the regulation in its current form. In many instances, OMB negotiates with the agency to obtain improvements in the regulation, and in a few rare instances OMB rejects the regulation as being undesirable. At that point, the agency has the choice either to revise the regulation or to withdraw it.

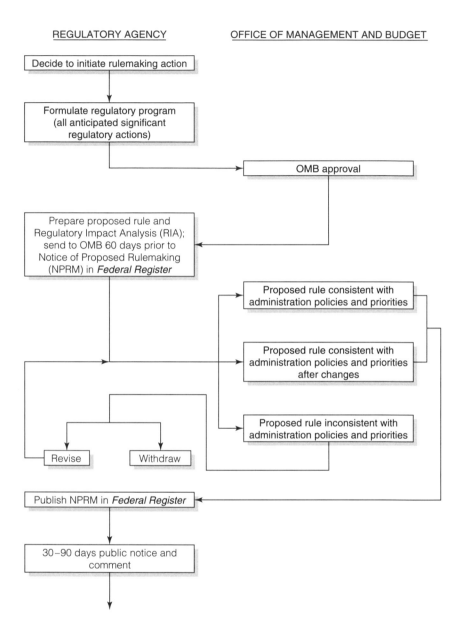

Figure 2.1
The Regulatory Management Process

Source: National Academy of Public Administration, *Presidential Management of Rule-making in Regulatory Agencies* (Washington D.C.: National Academy of Public Administration, 1987), p. 12. Reprinted by permission of the National Academy of Public Administration.

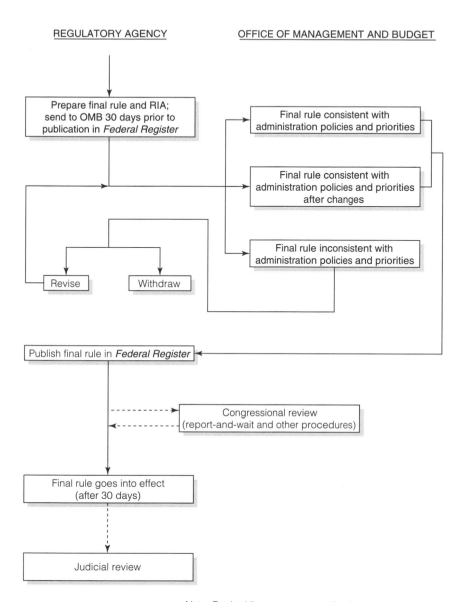

Figure 2.1 (cont.)

This OMB review is generally a secret process. Later in this chapter we will present overall statistics regarding the character of the regulatory decisions in terms of the numbers of regulations approved and disapproved. However, what is lacking is a detailed public description of the character of the debate between OMB and the regulatory agency. The secretive nature of this process is intended to enable the regulatory agency to alter its position without having to admit publicly that it has made an error in terms of the regulation it has proposed. It can consequently back down in a face-saving manner. Keeping the debate out of the public forum prevents the parties from becoming locked into positions for the purpose of maintaining a public image. The disadvantage of the secrecy is that it has bred some suspicion and distrust of the objectives of OMB's oversight process, and it excludes Congress and the public from the regulatory-policy debate. Moreover, because of this secrecy, some critics of OMB may have overstated the actual impact the review process has had in altering or blocking proposed regulations. Under the Clinton administration, OMB made a major effort to open up more aspects of this review to public scrutiny.

If the regulation is withdrawn, there is also one additional step that the agency can pursue. In particular, it can attempt to circumvent the OMB review by making an appeal to the president or to the vice president if he has been delegated authority for this class of regulatory issues.

After receiving OMB approval, the agency can publish the NPRM in the *Federal Register*. This publication is the official outlet for providing the text of all proposed and actual regulatory policies, as well as other official government actions. As a consequence, it serves as a mechanism for disseminating to the public the nature of the regulatory proposal and the rationale for it. Included in the material presented in the *Federal Register* is typically a detailed justification for the regulation, which often includes an assessment of the benefits and costs of the regulatory policy.

Once the regulatory proposal has been published in the *Federal Register*, it is now open to public debate. There is then a thirty to ninety day period for public notice and comment. Although occasionally the agency receives comments from disinterested parties, for the most part these comments are provided by professional lobbying groups for business, consumer, environmental, and other affected interests.

After receiving and processing these public comments, the regulatory agency must then put the regulation in its final form. In doing so, it finalizes its regulatory impact analysis, and it submits both the regulation and the accompanying analysis to OMB thirty days before publishing the final regulation in the *Federal Register*.

OMB then has roughly one month to review the regulation and decide whether to approve it. In many cases, this process is constrained even further by judicial deadlines or deadlines specified in legislation, which require the agency to issue a regulation by a particular date. In recent years regulatory agencies have begun to use these deadlines strategically, submitting the regulatory proposal and the accompanying analysis shortly before the deadline so that OMB will have little time to review the regulation before some action must be taken. Rejected regulations are returned to the agency for revision, and some of the most unattractive regulations may be eliminated altogether.

The overwhelming majority of regulations are, however, approved and published as final rules in the *Federal Register*. Congressional review is a very infrequent process, and the typical regulation goes into effect after thirty days. The regulation is still, of course, subject to judicial review in subsequent years.

Despite the multiplicity of boxes and arrows in Figure 2.1, there are very few binding external controls on the development of regulations. OMB has an initial chance at examining whether regulation should be on an agency's regulatory agenda, but at that stage so little is known that this approval is almost always automatic. Moreover, the OMB review process became less stringent in the Clinton administration than in the Reagan and Bush administrations. The only two reviews of consequence are those of proposed rules and final rules. OMB's approval is required for these stages, but this approval process is primarily influential at the margin. OMB review activities alter regulations in minor ways, such as introducing alternative methods of compliance that agencies might have that will be less costly but equally effective. Moreover, as we will see in Chapter 20, OMB is also successful in screening out some of the most inefficient regulations, such as those with costs per life well in excess of $100 million.

Although many of the other steps, particularly those involving public participation, are not binding in any way, the agency still must maintain its legitimacy. In the absence of public support, the agency runs the risk of losing its congressional funding and the support of the president, who appoints regulatory officials and, even in the case of commissioners to organizations such as the Interstate Commerce Commission, is responsible for periodic reappointments. Thus the public-comment process often has a substantive impact as well.

Nature of the Regulatory Oversight Process

The steps involved in issuing a regulation did not take the form outlined in Figure 2.1 until the 1980s. In the early 1970s, for example, there was no executive branch oversight. After the emergence of the health, safety, and environmental regulatory agencies in the 1970s, it became apparent that some oversight mechanism was needed to ensure that these regulations were in society's best interests. For the most part, these agencies have been on automatic pilot, constrained by little other than their legislative mandate and potential judicial review as to whether they were adhering to the mandate. Congress can, of course, intervene and pass legislation requiring that the agency take a particular kind of action, as it did with respect to the lawnmower standard for the Consumer Product Safety Commission. However, the routine regulatory actions seldom receive congressional scrutiny. Most important, there is no need for congressional approval for a regulatory agency to take action provided that it can survive judicial review. Proponents of the various types of "capture theories" of regulation would clearly see the need for such a balancing review.[3] If a regulatory agency has, in effect, been captured by some special interest group, then it will serve the interests of that group as opposed to the national interest. There are those who have speculated, for example, that labor unions exert a pivotal influence on the operation of OSHA and that the transportation industry wields considerable influence over the Interstate Commerce Commission.

The Nixon and Ford Administrations

The first of the White House review efforts was an informal "quality of life" review process instituted by President Nixon. The focus of this effort was to obtain some sense of the costs and overall economic implications of major new regulations.

This review process was formalized under the Ford administration through Executive Order No. 11821. Under this order, regulatory agencies were required to prepare inflationary impact statements for all major rules. These statements required that agencies assess the cost and price effects that their new regulations would have. Moreover, President Ford established a new agency within the White House, the Council on Wage and Price Stability, to administer this effort.

Although no formal economic tests were imposed, the requirement that agencies calculate the overall costs of their new regulations was a first step toward requiring that they achieve some balancing in terms of the competing effects that their regulations had. Before the institution of this inflationary-impact-statement requirement, regulatory agencies routinely undertook actions for which there was no quantitative assessment of the costs that would be imposed on society at large. Clearly, the costs imposed by regulation are a critical factor in determining its overall desirability. Knowledge of these cost effects ideally should promote sounder regulatory decisions.

The review process itself was not binding in any way. The Council on Wage and Price Stability examined the inflationary-impact analyses prepared by the regulatory agencies to ensure that the requirements of the Executive Order had been met. However, even in the case of an ill-conceived regulation, no binding requirements could be imposed provided that the agency had fulfilled its obligations to assess the costs of the regulation, however large they may have been.

The mechanism for influence on the regulatory process was twofold. First, the Council on Wage and Price Stability filed its comments on the regulatory proposal in the public record as part of the rulemaking process. Second, these comments in turn provided the basis for lobbying with the regulatory agency by various members of the Executive Office of the President. Chief among these participants were members of the President's Council of Economic Advisors and the president's domestic policy staff.

The Carter Administration

Under President Carter this process continued with two major additions. First, President Carter issued his Executive Order No. 12044, which added a cost-effectiveness test to the inflationary-impact requirement. The regulatory-impact analyses that were prepared by regulatory agencies now had also to demonstrate that the "least burdensome of the acceptable alternatives have been chosen." In practical terms, such a test rules out clearly dominated policy alternatives. If the government can achieve the same objective at less cost, it should do so. Reliance on this principle has often led economists, for example, to advocate performance-oriented alternatives to the kinds of command and control regulations that regulators have long favored.

In practice, however, the cost-effectiveness test only affects the most ill-conceived regulatory policies. For the most part, this test does not succeed in enabling one to rank policies in terms of their relative desirability. Suppose, for example, that we had one policy option that could save ten lives at a cost of $1 million per life, and we had a second policy option that could save twenty lives at a cost of $2 million per life. Also assume that these policy options are mutually exclusive: if we adopt one policy, we therefore cannot pursue the other. The first policy has a higher cost effectiveness in that there is a lower cost per life saved. However, this policy may not necessarily be superior. It may well be in society's best interest to save an additional ten lives even though the cost per life saved is higher because overall the total net benefits to society of the latter option may be greater. Comparison of total benefits and costs of regulatory impacts was a common focus of Carter's regulatory oversight program, but no formal requirements had to be met.

The other major change under President Carter was the establishment of the Regulatory Analysis Review Group. The primary staff support for this effort came from the Council on Wage and Price Stability and the President's Council of Economic Advisors. However, the impact that reviews by this group had was enhanced by the fact that it also included representatives from the President's Domestic Policy Staff, the Office of Management and Budget, and various cabinet agencies. The establishment of this group was a recognition that the executive oversight process had to be strengthened in some way, and the mechanism that was used for this strengthening was to bring to bear the political pressure of a consensus body on the particular regulatory agency. Moreover, the collegial nature of this group served an educational function as well in that there was a constant effort to educate regulatory officials regarding the proper economic approach to be taken within the context of regulatory analyses. For example, EPA officials present during a discussion of a proposed regulation by the National Highway Traffic Safety Administration could participate in a debate over the merits of the regulation and the appropriate means for assessing these merits, where the same kinds of generic issues were pertinent to their own agency as well. The reports by this group were not binding, but because they reflected the consensus view of the major branches of the Executive Office of the President as well as the affected regulatory agencies, they had an enhanced political import.

Even with these additional steps there was no binding test other than a cost-effectiveness requirement that had to be met. Moreover, the effectiveness of the informal political leverage in promoting sound regulatory policies was somewhat mixed. One famous case involved the OSHA cotton dust standard. OSHA proposed a standard for the regulation of cotton dust exposures for textile mill workers. The difficulty with this regulation in view of the regulatory oversight officials was that the cost of the health benefits achieved would be inordinately high—on the order of several hundred thousand dollars per temporary disability prevented. The head of the Council of Economic Advisors, Charles Schultze, went to President Carter with an assessment of the undue burdens caused by the regulation. These concerns had been voiced by the textile industry as well. President Carter first sided with the Council of Economic Advisors in this debate. However, after an appeal by Secretary of Labor Donovan, which was augmented by an expression of the affected labor unions' strong interests, Carter reversed his decision and issued the regulation. What this incident made clear is that even when the leading economic officials present a relatively cogent case concerning the lack of merit of a particular regulation, there are political factors and economic consequences other than simply calculations of benefits and costs that will drive a policy decision.

As a postscript, it is noteworthy that the Reagan administration undertook a review of this cotton dust standard shortly after taking office. Although Reagan administration economists were willing to pursue the possibility of overturning the regulation, at this juncture the same industry leaders who had originally opposed the regulation now embraced it, having already complied with the regulation, and they hoped to force the other, less technologically advanced firms in the industry to incur these compliance costs as well. The shifting stance by the textile industry reflects the fact that the overall economic costs imposed by the regulation, not the net benefit to society, are often the driving force behind the lobbying efforts involved in the rulemaking process.

The Reagan Administration

Under the Reagan administration there were several pivotal changes in the regulatory oversight mechanism. First, President Reagan moved the oversight function from the Council on Wage and Price Stability to OMB. Because OMB is responsible for setting the budgets of all regulatory agencies and has substantial authority over them, this change increases the institutional clout of the oversight mechanism. The second major shift was to increase the stringency of the tests being imposed. Instead of simply imposing a cost-effectiveness requirement, Reagan moved to a full-blown benefit-cost test in his Executive Order No. 12291:

Sec. 2. General Requirements. In promulgating new regulations, reviewing existing regulations, and developing legislative proposals concerning regulation, all agencies, to the extent permitted by law, shall adhere to the following requirements:

a. Administrative decisions shall be based on adequate information concerning the need for and consequences of proposed government action;

b. Regulatory action shall not be undertaken unless the potential benefits to society for the regulation outweigh the potential costs to society;

c. Regulatory objectives shall be chosen to maximize the benefits to society;

d. Among alternative approaches to any given regulatory objective, the alternative involving the least net costs to society shall be chosen; and

e. Agencies shall set regulatory priorities with the aim of maximizing the aggregate net benefits to society, taking into account the condition of the particular industries affected by regulations, the condition of the national economy, and other regulatory actions contemplated for the future.

If, however, the benefit-cost test conflicts with the agency's legislative mandate—as it does for all risk and environmental regulations—the test is not binding.

The third major change in the Executive Branch oversight process was the development of a formal regulatory planning process whereby the regulatory agencies would have to clear a regulatory agenda with the Office of Management and Budget. This procedure, which was accomplished through Executive Order No. 12498, was an extension of a concept begun under the Carter administration known as the Regulatory Calendar, which required the agency to list its forthcoming regulatory initiatives. This exercise has served to alert administration officials and the public at large as to the future of regulatory policy, but on a practical basis it has not had as much impact on policy outcomes as has the formal review process, coupled with a benefit-cost test.

The Bush Administration

Under President Bush, the regulatory oversight process remained virtually unchanged. The thrust of the effort was almost identical in character to the oversight procedures that were in place during the second term of the Reagan administration. For example, the same two key Executive Orders issued by Reagan remained in place under President Bush.

The Clinton Administration

President Clinton continued the regulatory oversight process in a manner that was not starkly changed from the two previous administrations. In his Executive Order No. 12866, President Clinton established principles for regulatory oversight similar to the emphasis on benefits, costs, and benefit-cost analysis of previous administrations. However, the tone of the Clinton Executive Order was quite different in that it was less adversarial with respect to the relationship with regulatory agencies. Moreover, this Executive Order correctly emphasized that many consequences of policies are difficult to quantify and that these qualitative concerns should be taken into account as well. The Clinton administration also raised the threshold for reviewing proposed regulations, restricting the focus to the truly major government regulations.

In 1995, both the House and the Senate passed regulatory reform legislation. Once the differences between the two bills are reconciled, the net effect will be to strengthen the test that must be applied to new regulations. The key congressional concerns were that regulations be based on an accurate assessment of the risks involved, not worst case scenarios, and that regulatory agencies proceed with regulations only if the benefits exceed the costs. The extent to which the benefit-cost provision will be influential hinges on whether the compromise legislation that is ultimately approved by the President includes a provision that overrides agencies' legislative mandates that in some cases may prohibit benefit-cost tests.

The Criteria Applied in the Oversight Process

Certainly the most dominant criteria that have been used in the oversight process over the last decade have been those pertaining to ensuring the cost effectiveness of the regulation and, more specifically, ascertaining that the benefits of the regulation exceed the costs. Although OMB has frequently been unable to enforce the benefit-cost requirements because of conflicts with the agency's legislative mandate, there have been several notable success stories that illustrate how effective regulation can be if approached in a sound economic manner.

Regulatory Success Stories

One of these success stories is visible every time we ride in an automobile. A prominent regulatory innovation has been the requirement that all cars have center-high mounted stop lamps. When the driver puts on his brakes, the brake lights go on as always, but so does a red light in the bottom center of the rear window. This 1983 regulation was the subject of an extensive analysis whereby the Department of Transportation demonstrated that the benefits of the regulation exceeded the costs. Equally important is that the Department of Transportation also conducted a series of tests with various fleets of automobiles to determine which of several stop-lamp designs would be the most effective in reducing rear-end collisions. Thus there was an explicit attempt to evaluate regulatory policy alternatives and to select the most attractive from among these alternatives.

Perhaps the greatest regulatory success story of the 1980s involving OMB is the phase-down of lead in gasoline. (Telephone deregulation did not involve OMB but was probably of greater consequence.) Through a series of regulations, EPA requirements have all but eliminated the use of lead in gasoline. This regulation was accompanied by a comprehensive regulatory analysis that clearly established that the benefits of the regulation exceeded the costs.[4] It is noteworthy that this regulation, one of the few where EPA clearly established the economic attractiveness of the policy in terms of benefit-cost ratio, is also one which had the greatest demonstrable impact of any pollution regulation instituted in the 1980s. Lead emissions declined dramatically in the 1980s, and the reduction in lead pollution represents the greatest environmental success story of that decade.

Promotion of Cost-Effective Regulation

One general way in which the government promotes the most cost-effective regulation is through the encouragement of performance-oriented regulation. Our objective is to promote outcomes that are in the interests of the individuals affected by regulations rather than simply to mandate technological improvements irrespective of their impact. This concern with ends rather than means leads to the promotion of the use of performance-oriented regulations whenever possible.

Rather than mandate nationally uniform standards, it is frequently desirable to give firms some discretion in terms of their means of compliance. The FDA's tamper-resistant packaging requirements impose effectiveness requirements on the packaging, but do not dictate particular types of packaging that must be used. Similarly, the child-resistant-cap requirements of the Consumer Product Safety Commission specify safety thresholds that the caps must meet in terms of preventing children from opening the bottles, but they do not prevent firms from adopting particular cap designs that they might believe are most appropriate for the product.

The adoption of performance-oriented alternatives has generally lagged behind economists' enthusiasm for these policies. Two principal reasons account for this discrepancy. First, the enforcement of some performance-oriented alternatives can be more expensive. If firms were simply given general guidelines to make their workplace safer but were not given any explicit instructions for doing so, then government inspectors would have a more difficult task in determining whether the firm had met the minimal safety requirements.[5]

Another major barrier to performance-oriented regulation has been political. In the case of air-pollution requirements, congressmen from soft-coal-producing states lobbied for legislation that required firms to develop technological solutions to air pollution (that is, use of scrubbers) as opposed to changing the type of fuel they used to a less polluting form of coal. This emphasis was dictated by regional economic self-interests, not by national efficiency concerns.

Distortion of Benefit and Cost Estimates

Another principle that has been promoted through the oversight process is the utilization of unbiased estimates of the benefits and costs. The need for lack of bias may appear to be both obvious and uncontroversial, but in fact it represents an ongoing problem with respect to risk regulations.

The scientific analyses underlying risk regulations typically include a variety of assumptions for the purpose of "conservatism," but which in effect distort the assessment of the merits of the regulation. For example, projections of the cancer-causing implications of some chemical may be made by relying upon the most sensitive animal species, as opposed to the animal species most relevant to extrapolation to humans. In addition, scientific analysts frequently focus on the upper end of the 95-percent-confidence interval, thus placing great emphasis on how high the risk potentially could be as opposed to their best estimate of how high the risk actually is.

Focusing on the upper limit of the potential risk distorts the policy mix in a number of ways. Most important is that it shifts our attention to those hazards about which the least is known, as opposed to those hazards that pose the greatest threat and will endanger the greatest number of lives. Because we often know the least about the very-low-probability events because we have little experience to guide us, the effect has often been to tilt policies in the direction of the inconsequential low-probability events that we dimly understand, whereas the major sources of accidents and illness that are precisely understood receive less attention.

In some cases, there are additional conservatism factors incorporated arbitrarily within the risk analysis process. For example, risk analysts assessing the reproductive toxicity of different chemicals may simply multiply these risk levels by a factor of 1000 for the purposes of "conservatism," but there is no justification for multiplying by any factor.

The problem that these conservatism adjustments pose from the standpoint of government policy is that when we address different regulations and are comparing their efficacy, we do not know the extent to which the benefits have been distorted. Various conservatism factors are used by different agencies in different contexts. These adjustments are seldom detailed in the regulatory analysis and are often compounded in the successive stages of analysis. Conservatism multipliers are often added in each round of the calculations. Such distortions prevent the regulatory policymakers from having the accurate information they need to choose among policies. The overall judgment as to how conservative society wishes to be in bearing risk or in incurring other outcomes is a social policy decision that should be made at the policy-making level of the regulatory agencies and the Executive Branch. Arbitrary conservatism factors incorporated in the risk analysis in effect involve little more than stealth policymaking that is masquerading as a scientific exercise.

The Regulatory Role of Price and Quality

A general principle that has guided the development of regulation and in particular the deregulation effort is that "regulation of prices and production in competitive markets should be avoided."[6] The price system has a legitimate role to play, as is evidenced in the discussion of markets in all elementary economics textbooks. Recognition of the role of the price mechanism has provided the impetus for the deregulation of the rate entry regulations that were formerly present in industries like airlines, trucking, and communications. Some regulations, such as minimum-wage requirements, explicitly interfere with these prices. The purported benefits of these regulations is that they will raise workers' income level to a fairer wage amount needed for subsistence, although most labor economists believe that the long-run effect of minimum wage regulations is to displace workers from jobs. It appears in this regard that teenagers, particularly minority teenagers, have been most hard-hit by the adverse employment effects of higher minimum wage levels.

Just as we do not want to standardize product prices, we also do not wish to standardize quality except when there are legitimate reasons for doing so, as in the case of provision of minimal safety levels for cars. Antilock brakes and passenger side airbags are beneficial safety features, but they are also quite expensive. We would like to give consumers the option to purchase such equipment; the more expensive cars typically offer these features. However, we do not require that all cars have them, for those features would comprise a substantial part of the product price for the low end of the market. Instead of mandating all available safety devices for all cars, we have required that certain minimal safety features be universal, and we permit other safety features to be optional. Consumers who place substantial value on safety can purchase the cars offering these additional features, and we can continually revise the nationally mandated safety standards to reflect the safety floor that is most sensible from the standpoint of being imposed on a universal basis.

The Impact of the Oversight Process

The objective of regulatory oversight is to foster better regulations, not necessarily less regulation. However, one consequence of improving regulation is that we will eliminate those regulations that are unattractive from the standpoint of advancing the national interest. Moreover, much of the impetus for regulatory oversight has been a concern with the excessive costs imposed by unattractive regulations, so that there has been considerable attention devoted to these costs.

The Cost of Regulation

The stakes involved are enormous. President Bush noted the staggering levels of costs involved:

Federal regulations impose estimated direct costs on the economy as high as $175 billion—more than $1,700 for every taxpayer in the United States. These costs are in effect indirect "taxes" on the American public—taxes that should only be levied when the benefits clearly exceed the costs.[7]

Roughly half of these costs are attributable to EPA regulations, as earlier estimates of the costs imposed by EPA policies indicated that these regulatory costs alone were in the range of $70–$80 billion per year.[8]

In the absence of regulatory reform efforts, these costs would be substantially higher. The Council of Economic Advisors estimates that airline deregulation led to $15 billion worth of gains to airline travelers and airline companies.[9] Similarly, estimates suggest that savings resulting from trucking deregulation have been in excess of $30 billion annually.[10] The annual benefits from railroad deregulation have also been substantial—on the order of $15 billion annually.[11] The total savings from these deregulation efforts in the transportation field are on the order of $60 billion per year—a substantial payoff indeed for a return to greater reliance on market forces.

Other Measures of the Size of Regulation

The most pertinent estimate of regulatory activity is the level of the costs that are generated by the regulation. Thomas Hopkins, once a prominent regulatory-oversight official, has compiled a comprehensive assessment of the costs of different Federal regulatory programs. This tally appears in Table 2.1, where the primary inputs to these calculations are the regulatory analysis prepared by government regulations on a prospective basis for new regulations.[12] Actual costs of regulations may of course differ from those that are estimated at the time of the regulation's promulgation. However, these cost measures are likely to be much more indicative of the scale of regulatory activity than are *Federal Register* counts.

As the information in Table 2.1 indicates, the cost of these regulations is substantial. The total cost level in 1991 was $413 billion, which excludes regulations that were simply transfers, such as the minimum wage. The minimum wage leads to higher wage payments for low income

Table 2.1
Annual Cost of Federal Regulation (Billions of 1991 Dollars)

	1977	1988	1991	2000
Environmental regulation	42	87	115	178
Other social regulation	29	30	36	61
Economics regulations—efficiency	120	73	73	73
Process regulation	122	153	189	221
Subtotal of costs	313	343	413	533
Economic regulations—transfers	228	130	130	130
Total costs	540	473	542	662

Source: Thomas D. Hopkins, "Costs of Regulation: Filling the Gaps." Report prepared for Regulatory Information Service Center, August 1992.

workers. From an economic standpoint this is not an efficiency loss, but simply an effort that passes money around in society. The gains to workers offset the losses to firms. However, from the standpoint of the potential costs to the rest of society, the appropriate amount to be recognized is the total regulatory cost of $542 billion in 1991 since it is this regulatory cost amount that firms (or consumers and workers) must pay. In practice, however, the shifting of this and other costs among consumers, shareholders, workers, and other parties is a very complex matter.

In 1991 the total gross domestic product was $5.7 trillion, so the regulatory cost share of the gross domestic product was 9.6 percent. Another useful measure of regulatory costs is the regulatory cost per household. In 1994 these costs are estimated to be $5,935 per household.[13] Regulatory costs consequently are not a trivial component of the gross domestic product, but it should also be taken into account that benefits are derived from these efforts as well. It is quite striking that for the 1991 federal regulatory costs, the largest component was for process regulation, or $189 billion in annual expenditures related to government paperwork requirements. Environmental regulation, such as that administered by the U.S. Environmental Protection Agency, was next greatest in importance at $115 billion, followed by economic regulation at $73 billion. The role of deregulation in the economic regulation context is apparent as economic regulations decreased in cost from 1977 to 1991. Moreover, there has been a substantial change in the mix of regulations, as environmental regulation has assumed increasing importance during the same period in which economic regulation has diminished in terms of the efficiency costs.

One of the most striking aspects of the regulatory cost mix is the substantial process regulation component of $189 million in 1991 federal paperwork costs. A concern with paperwork required by federal activities has long been widespread. Moreover, unlike the regulatory efforts themselves, paperwork often lacks the clearcut link to perceived societal benefits, such as improved environmental quality. Although politicians frequently voice commitments to reduce paperwork, this burden continues to grow. One difficulty is that gathering information generally appears to be attractive, inasmuch as more knowledge is better than less, but the benefits derived from the information are not always valued to determine whether the associated paperwork burden is justified. One frequently proposed policy that might address this issue is to establish a federal paperwork budget to limit the annual dollar value of paperwork costs.

A less precise tally of trends in regulatory burdens is provided by the index of the number of pages published in the *Federal Register*. One would expect there to be a correlation between the number of pages devoted to government rules and regulations and the cost these regulations impose. This need not be the case if, for example, agencies become adept at editing their regulatory documents to make them shorter but no less burdensome. Moreover, some *Federal Register* entries modify regulations and decrease costs rather than increase them. However, it is generally believed that there is a positive, albeit highly imperfect, correlation between the amount of federal regulation published in the *Federal Register* and the regulatory costs imposed.

Figure 2.2 indicates the trends in these costs for the past half-century. In 1936 the number of pages in the *Federal Register* was relatively modest—2,599. The pace of regulation increased steadily but slowly until 1970. It is apparent from Figure 2.2 that there was a rapid escalation in regulation beginning in that decade. The 1970s marked the establishment of the new wave of health, safety, and environmental regulation, which greatly expanded the role of the government and its regulatory activities. By 1980 the number of pages in the *Federal Register* reached 87,012. The first half of the 1980s marked a decrease in the dissemination of new regulation, which was consistent with the Reagan administration's efforts to deregulate and roll back regulations. However, by the second term of the Reagan administration there was renewed regulatory activity, which is also reflected in the recent increase in the number of pages of regulations published in the *Federal Register*.

Other measures of regulatory activity have similar implications. The *Code of Federal Regulations* summarizes the stock of existing regulations, whereas the *Federal Register* page count provides a measure of the flow of annual regulations. The total number of pages of regulation in the *Code of Federal Regulations* was under 10,000 in 1950, but had grown to in excess of 100,000 by 1980. By the end of that decade, the

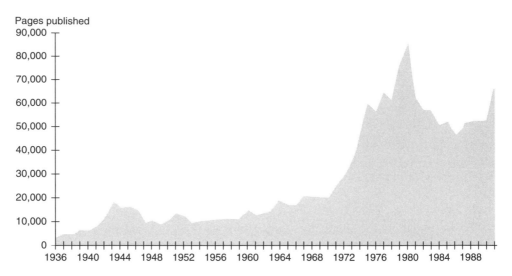

Pages published

Figure 2.2
Trends in Federal Register Analysis Pages, 1936–1991
Source: Office of the Federal Register.

number of pages in the *Code of Federal Regulations* was just over 50,000, which has been consistent with the effort to scale back the role of regulation, particularly in the transportation area. Regulatory budget and staffing trends, which appear in the appendix to Chapter 2, tell a similar story.

The Character of Regulatory Oversight Actions

It is also instructive to consider the mix of actions undertaken through the regulatory oversight to obtain an assessment of the nature of the oversight activity that has led to many of these changes. Table 2.2 summarizes the oversight actions undertaken in the 1980s. When the oversight process began, OMB approved almost 90 percent of regulations without change. At the present time, the overall approval rate is just under 75 percent as most regulations proposed by regulatory agencies are consistent with OMB's guideline without any modification.

The second largest category consists of regulations that are consistent with the guidelines after specific changes in the regulation have been made. Some of these changes have been quite consequential. For example, at OMB's insistence the Occupational Safety and Health Administration offered firms a variety of alternative means of compliance to reduce the explosion hazards arising from the dust levels in grain mills. This expanded flexibility did not impede the safety effects of the regu-

Table 2.2
Types of Actions Taken by the OMB Regulatory Oversight Process on Agency Rules 1981–1991

Action taken	Percentage in										
	1981	1982	1983	1984	1985	1986	1987	1988	1989	1990	1991
Consistent without change	87.3	84.1	82.3	78.0	70.7	68.3	70.5	70.9	73.8	71.8	63.2
Consistent with change	4.9	10.3	12.7	15.1	23.1	22.9	23.7	21.9	19.4	19.3	27.2
Withdrawn by agency	1.8	1.2	1.6	2.4	3.1	2.8	2.5	2.4	2.7	2.5	2.8
Returned for reconsideration	1.6	2.1	1.3	2.7	1.5	1.4	0.4	1.2	1.3	1.0	1.1
Suspended	NA	NA	NA	NA	NA	NA	NA	NA	0.7	2.7	2.7
Sent improperly or exempt	3.1	0.9	0.0	0.0	0.3	0.2	0.2	0.1	0.4	0.2	0.1
Emergency, statutory, or judicial deadline	1.4	1.4	2.0	1.7	1.2	4.3	2.5	3.5	1.6	2.5	3.0
Total	100.1	100.0	99.9	99.9	99.9	99.9	99.8	100.0	99.9	100.0	100.1

Source: U.S. Office of Management and Budget, *Regulatory Program of the United States Government, April 1, 1992–March 31, 1993* (Washington, D.C.: U.S. Government Printing Office).

lation, but it did lower the regulatory costs. Almost one-fifth of the regulations are those that are consistent with OMB principles after such changes are made. This high percentage, coupled with the extremely high approval rate of many regulations without any changes whatsoever, indicates that the dominant emphasis of the OMB process is to promote negotiated solutions to enhance regulatory policy as opposed to simply serving in an obstructionist role. The OMB oversight process has limited political resources so that it cannot afford to do battle in every regulatory arena, even though few would claim that 90 percent of the regulations proposed will in fact maximize the net benefits to society.

The percentage of instances in which OMB blocks regulations is quite small. In 1989, for example, 2.7 percent of all regulations were withdrawn by the regulatory agency and 1.3 percent were returned for consideration. Many of these regulations are among the most burdensome.

Perhaps the most interesting trend exhibited in Table 2.2 pertains to the first two rows of the table. The percentage of regulations that are consistent with OMB guidelines without any change dropped by 14 percent from 1981 to 1989, and the percentage of regulations that are consistent with change rose by a comparable amount over that period. The dominant emphasis of OMB actions has been either to approve regulations or to promote moderate modifications of them, and over time there has been an increased attempt to alter regulations in an incremental fashion rather than simply to approve them without any change whatsoever.

Such incremental modifications in regulation are where we would expect the regulatory oversight process to have its greatest influence because major conflicts, such as those over the entire thrust of a regulatory
policy, would be escalated to higher political levels. If all regulatory
policy decisions were escalated in this manner, the president would have
little opportunity to devote time to other national problems. In any
year, there are hundreds of major regulations and an even greater number of minor regulations that agencies will issue. In 1989, for example,
OMB reviewed 179 major regulations from the U.S. Department of Labor and 104 major regulations from the U.S. Environmental Protection
Agency.[14] Given the substantial volume of regulatory activity, the only
feasible way to address these issues is to remain within the interagency
negotiations between the regulatory agency and OMB, saving appeals
to a higher level for the small percentage of regulatory issues that
involve controversial issues of national policy. In the Reagan administration, one such policy meriting presidential involvement was the decision with respect to acid rain policies, and in the Bush administration
global-warming policies received the greatest presidential scrutiny. In
the Clinton administration there has been substantial high-level involvement in the rewriting of the Superfund law, which governs the
treatment of hazardous wastes. More routine regulations, such as standards for the combustion of municipal waste, are handled without a
national debate.

What Do Regulators Maximize?

In theory, regulatory agencies serve to maximize the national interest
subject to their legislative mandates. Similarly, OMB is presumably motivated to maximize the net benefits minus costs to society. Such a characterization of regulatory objectives is, unfortunately, excessively naive.
There are a number of diverse factors that influence policy decisions, many
of which have very little to do with these formal statements of purpose.

What is clear at this stage is that there are certainly influences at
work other than those that are formally specified. However, economists
have yet to reach a consensus regarding the specific formulation that
best captures the political mechanisms at work. A brief review of some
of these theories can, however, highlight the range and the types of
approaches that have been taken.

The Capture Theory

Under the capture theory of regulation, such as that espoused by
George Stigler, the regulatory agency is captured by the economic inter-

ests that it serves.[15] Stigler has been most successful in testing this model with respect to the economic regulation agencies, such as the Interstate Commerce Commission. Examples of how government regulation can foster industry interests abound. Regulation of airline fares can, for example, provide a floor on airline rates that enables firms to make greater profits than if there were price competition. Similarly, minimum quality standards for products can promote the interests of the more established and advanced firms in the industry, which will use these mandated quality standards to squeeze the producers with less advanced technological capabilities.

Most models based on the capture theory recognize the competing demands on regulatory agencies. Private interests as well as public interests may affect the political survival of the regulatory officials as well as the agency's budget. Although the most direct descendant of Stigler's work is that of Peltzman,[16] a number of authors have developed similar models reflecting the diversity of political influences at work. Roger Noll has developed an external signaling theory of regulation whereby regulatory agencies attempt to minimize the conflicting criticism that appears through signals from the economic and social environment in which the regulatory agency operates.[17] Noll proposes that agencies construct an administrative apparatus for the development and enforcement of their regulations to promote the ability of groups that approve their actions and to limit the ability of political forces that disapprove their actions.

Other Theories of Influence Patterns

Other researchers have also formulated models reflecting diverse patterns of influence, but have concluded that there are particular sets of influences that are most influential. For example, Wilson and Stewart suggest that regulatory agencies have substantial discretion with respect to the regulatory actions they take, so that it is the regulatory agency that plays the dominant role.[18] Other authors have advocated a quite different view in which Congress has the dominant role, not the regulatory agency.[19] The leverage of Congress stems from the fact that the congressional committees are responsible for setting the budgets of the regulatory agencies and for confirming the leading administrators in these agencies.

Comprehensive Models of Regulatory Objectives

In all likelihood, the actual outcomes are influenced by a multiplicity of factors that cannot be characterized by any simple, single model. The regulatory agency does not have sole control, nor does OMB. Moreover,

Congress and the judiciary play a restraining role, and lobbyists for and against the regulation can affect the political payoffs to the regulatory agency as well. The actual strength of the influences undoubtedly varies depending on the particular context.

An interesting case study of the extent to which there are multiple influences at work is provided through detailed analysis of the rulemaking process for the EPA regulations that implemented the industrial effluent standards that are used to control water pollution. The study by Magat, Krupnick, and Harrington highlights the types of outcomes that will ultimately be explained through an analysis of the competing interests affecting regulatory outcomes:

The factors determining the outcomes of EPA's effluent standard-setting process are by no means self-evident. For instance, on December 7, 1973, EPA proposed effluent discharge standards for water pollution from the leather tanning industry. These standards required that by 1977 discharges of biological oxygen demand (BOD) not exceed 40 milligrams per liter (mg/l) of waste water. Four months and two days later, EPA promulgated the final BOD standard for the industry of 102 mg/l. Why was the stringency of the standard weakened by 155 percent between its initial proposal and final promulgation? Why did EPA issue a tighter final standard for the meat packing industry, which produces wastes with similar characteristics to leather tanning, of only 24 mg/l BOD? And why did smaller firms receive weaker regulations?[20]

The heterogeneity of the regulation in different industries and for firms of different sizes clearly suggests that there is no simple or naive regulatory objective guiding behavior. Through detailed statistical analysis of a series of decisions made by EPA as part of this rulemaking process, Magat et al. have identified a variety of factors that were influential in the setting of these water pollution standards.

One such influence was efficiency concerns. EPA did adjust the stringency of regulations in different industries to reflect the differences in compliance costs across firms. This is the kind of heterogeneity one would want to promote, in that standards should not be as stringent for industries that must bear greater burdens to reduce pollution. In those contexts, the costs of compliance will be greater, so that to maximize the net benefits of the standard one would want to reflect these cost differences in the standard level.

Second, the quality of the economic analysis supporting the standard also was influential. Standards supported by high-quality economic analyses were more likely to lead to more stringent effluent guidelines than those lacking substantive support. This result as well suggests that there is a sense of economic rationality to the process whereby the strength of the analysis does affect the policy outcome. It should be noted, however, that the particular price and cost effects of the regulation did not appear to be as influential as the overall quality of the economic analysis.

Other players have an impact as well. The economic resources of the trade association for the particular industry affect the stringency of the standards in the expected manner. In particular, industries with large budgets for their trade association are able to obtain weaker standards, after taking into account other factors that should determine the stringency of the regulation. The total financial resources appear to be much more influential than the volume of industry comments provided, in that these resources presumably reflect the political clout of the agency more so than does the number of pages of comments submitted.

Conclusion

In later chapters we will develop a series of models of the regulatory process. All such models should be viewed as a simplification of the actual objectives guiding the regulatory agencies. Economists have made substantial progress in recent decades in developing approaches to indicate how regulators make decisions, which is often quite different than one would predict based on their legislative mandates or their stated agency objectives. A variety of political factors also are at work and will affect the policy outcomes that result.

Despite the multiplicity of these influences, one should not understate the pivotal role that legislative mandates have. These mandates, which are written by Congress, in many circumstances define the terms of the regulatory debate and impose stringent limits on the scope of discretion of the regulatory officials. It is through these mandates that Congress has a long-run influence on regulatory policy, even though most short-run regulatory decisions appear to be governed by actions of the regulatory agency, the influence of the regulatory oversight process, and recognition of the political factors at stake in the regulatory policy decision.

Questions and Problems

1. A frequent proposal has been to replace the oversight process through a system known as a "regulatory budget." Each agency would be assigned a total cost that it could impose on the American economy, and its task would be to select the regulations that best foster the national interest

subject to this cost. Can you identify any problems with the regulatory budget approach? How feasible do you believe it would be to calculate the costs of all the regulations of a particular agency? What, for example, are the costs associated with affirmative action? Are they positive or negative?

2. Inadequacies in government action are frequently called "government failure." In some cases, government failures reinforce market failures. In particular, the government may promote inefficient outcomes in a way that exacerbates the shortcomings of the market rather than alleviates these shortcomings. Can you think of any examples where such mutually reinforcing failures might occur and the reasons why they might occur?

3. One justification often given for the utilization of a variety of conservatism factors in risk analyses is that society is risk-averse, so that we should be conservative. Can you identify any flaws in this reasoning?

4. Regulatory agencies are not permitted to publicly release the details of their regulatory proposals until after the appropriate review by OMB, as outlined in Figure 2.2. How do you believe the process would change if the agency first issued the proposal publicly and then began its discussions with OMB? Do you believe this change would improve the regulatory decisionmaking process? What new factors would be brought to bear?

5. What are the problems in using measures such as *Federal Register* page counts to assess the costs imposed by regulation? In the chapter as well as in the appendix, the measures of regulatory trends include *Federal Register* page counts, page counts from the *Code of Federal Regulations*, agency budget trends, and agency staffing trends. Which of these sets of information do you believe is most informative with respect to the regulatory costs imposed on society? What other measures do you believe would be useful in assessing the changing regulatory burden?

Notes

1. Charles Wolf, "A Theory of Non-Market Failure," *Journal of Law and Economics*, April 1978.

2. U.S. Office of Management and Budget, *Regulatory Program of the United States Government. April 1, 1988–March 31, 1989* (Washington, D.C.: U.S. Government Printing Office, 1988), p. 20.

3. Most of the economic models along the lines of a capture theory are based at least in part on the work of George J. Stigler, *The Citizen and the Stage* (Chicago: University of Chicago Press, 1975).

4. U.S. Office of Management and Budget, *Regulatory Program*, pp. 16–17.

5. The government could utilize an outcomes-based performance measure, such as total worker deaths and injuries. However, such a measure would be more effective for large firms than for smaller firms, which have a sufficiently small sample of workers that precise inferences cannot be drawn regarding the firms' safety performance.

6. U.S. Office of Management and Budget, *Regulatory Program*, p. 18.

7. Statement by George Bush in U.S. Office of Management and Budget, *Regulatory Program of the United States Government, April 1, 1990-March 31, 1991* (Washington, D.C.: U.S. Government Printing Office, 1990), p. vii.

8. U.S. Office of Management and Budget, *Regulatory Program of the United States Government, April 1, 1988-March 31, 1989* (Washington, D.C.: U.S. Government Printing Office, 1988).

9. Council of Economic Advisors, *Economic Report of the President* (Washington, D.C.: U.S. Government Printing Office, 1988), p. 206.

10. Diane S. Owen, *Deregulation in the Trucking Industry* (Washington, D.C.: Federal Trade Commission, 1988).

11. Christopher C. Barnekov and Andrew N. Kleit, "The Efficiency Effects of Railroad Deregulation in the United States," *International Journal of Transport Economics* 17 (1990).

12. See Thomas D. Hopkins, "Costs of Regulation: Filling the Gaps," report prepared for Regulatory Information Service Center, August 1992.

13. See Thomas D. Hopkins, "Costs of Regulation: Filling the Gaps," report prepared for Regulatory Information Service Center, August 1992.

14. U.S. Office of Management and Budget, *Regulatory Program of the United States Government, April 1, 1990-March 31, 1991* (Washington, D.C.: U.S. Government Printing Office, 1990), p. 647.

15. George J. Stigler, "The Theory of Economic Regulation," *Bell Journal of Economics* 2 (1971): 3–21.

16. Sam Peltzman, "Toward a More General Theory of Regulation," *Journal of Law and Economics* 19 (1976): 211–40.

17. Roger Noll, *Reforming Regulation: Studies in the Regulation of Economic Activity* (Washington, D.C.: Brookings Institution, 1971), and Roger Noll, "Government Administrative Behavior and Private Sector Response: A Multi-Disciplinary Survey," Social Science Working Paper Number 62 (Pasadena: California Institute of Technology, 1976).

18. See James Q. Wilson, "The Politics of Regulation," in James W. McKie (ed.), *Social Responsibility and the Business Predicament* (Washington, D.C.: The Brookings Institution, 1974); and Richard B. Stewart, "The Reformation of American Administrative Law," *Harvard Law Review* 88 (1975): 1669–813.

19. See Barry R. Weingast and Mark J. Moran, "Bureaucratic Discretion or Congressional Control: Regulatory Policymaking by the Federal Trade Commission," *Journal of Political Economy* 91 (1983): 765–800.

20. Wesley A. Magat, Alan J. Krupnick, and Winston Harrington, *Rules in the Making: A Statistical Analysis of Regulatory Agency Behavior* (Washington, D.C.: Resources for the Future, 1986), pp. xi–xii.

Appendix.   Trends in Regulatory Agency Budgets and Staff

An instructive measure of the changing role of government regulation is provided by the magnitude of government expenditures in this area. Although the principal costs of regulations are those borne by business and the public at large, the levels of the budgets of the regulatory agencies do provide some index of the degree of regulatory activity.

The Center for the Study of American Business at Washington University, which is directed by Murray Weidenbaum (Chairman of President Reagan's Council of Economic Advisors), regularly compiles a series of tables summarizing these budgetary and staffing trends. Tables A.1 and A.2 summarize the key data. These patterns are generally consistent with those displayed by the *Federal Register* page counts. Regulation accelerated dramatically in the 1970s, as there was a substantial growth in the health, safety, and environmental regulation agencies. The deregulation in the transportation fields in the 1980s, coupled with the moderation in the health, safety, and environmental regulation area, led to some reduction in the regulatory effort in the early 1980s. However, there is some evidence of a resurgence in regulation in the latter 1980s and early 1990s.

Table A.1
Costs of Federal Regulatory Agencies (*Fiscal Years, Millions of Dollars in "Obligations"*)

Agency	1970	1975	1980	1985	1990	1991	1992	1993	(Estimated) 1994	(Estimated) 1995	% Change 1994–95
					Social Regulation						
Consumer Safety and Health											
Consumer Product Safety Commission	—	$37	$43	$36	$35	$37	$41	$47	$44	$41	–7.2%
Department of Agriculture:											
Agricultural Marketing Service	$190	$99	$67	$157	$160	$191	$196	$200	$216	$221	2.3%
Animal and Plant Health Inspection Service	101	373	259	342	423	448	494	476	498	481	–3.5%
Federal Grain Inspection Service	—	—	55	38	42	40	43	42	54	54	0.0%
Food Safety and Inspection Service	—	—	381	405	475	505	533	559	586	605	3.1%
Packers and Stockyards Admin.	3	5	8	8	10	11	12	12	12	12	0.0%
Subtotal	$294	$477	$770	$950	$1,110	$1,195	$1,278	$1,289	$1,366	$1,373	0.5%
Department of Health and Human Services:											
Food and Drug Administration	$80	$207	$334	$437	$603	$707	$778	$815	$964	$1,001	3.7%
Department of Housing and Urban Development:											
Consumer Protection Programs	*	$2	$4	$7	$6	$7	$7	$9	$8	$9	11.1%
Department of Justice:											
Drug Enforcement Admin.	$2	$12	$13	$18	$28	$35	$36	$38	$37	$36	–2.8%
Department of Transportation:											
Coast Guard	$94	$284	$498	$558	$910	$881	$1,026	$1,233	$1,316	$1,398	5.9%
Federal Aviation Administration	126	196	281	294	495	531	581	600	615	611	–0.7%
Federal Highway Administration	6	15	20	33	98	109	120	133	136	163	16.6%
Federal Railroad Administration	21	52	85	44	56	57	60	68	94	75	–25.3%
National Highway Traffic Safety Administration	32	104	136	114	142	156	177	188	192	180	–6.7%
Subtotal	$279	$651	$1,020	$1,043	$1,701	$1,734	$1,964	$2,222	$2,353	$2,427	3.0%

(*continued*)

Table A.1 (cont.)

Agency	1970	1975	1980	1985	1990	1991	1992	1993	(Estimated) 1994	(Estimated) 1995	% Change 1994–95
Department of the Treasury:											
Bureau of Alcohol, Tobacco and Firearms	$50	$95	$144	$173	$282	$323	$353	$394	$390	$396	1.5%
Chemical Safety and Hazard Investigation Board	—	—	—	—	—	—	—	—	$3	$4	25.0%
Federal Mine Safety and Health Review Commission	—	—	$4	$3	$4	$4	$5	$6	$6	$6	0.0%
National Transportation Safety Board	$5	$10	$17	$22	$27	$31	$35	$36	$37	$37	0.0%
Total—Consumer Safety and Health	$710	$1,491	$2,349	$2,689	$3,796	$4,073	$4,497	$4,856	$5,208	$5,330	2.3%
Job Safety and Other Working Conditions											
Department of Labor:											
Employment Standards Admin.	$37	$45	$124	$127	$155	$151	$155	$157	$162	$170	4.7%
Office of the American Workplace	12	29	55	57	79	31	31	27	27	34	20.6%
Pension and Welfare Benefits Administration	—	—	—	—	—	56	62	64	65	73	11.0%
Mine Safety and Health Admin.	27	67	144	150	167	173	181	191	195	203	3.9%
Occupational Safety and Health Admin.	—	96	191	220	267	284	300	290	300	323	7.1%
Subtotal	$76	$237	$514	$554	$668	$695	$729	$729	$749	$803	6.7%
Architectural and Transportation Barriers Compliance Board	—	—	—	$2	$2	$3	$3	$3	$3	$3	0.0%
Equal Employment Opportunity Comm.	$13	$55	$124	$163	$185	$198	$212	$223	$230	$246	6.5%
National Labor Relations Board	$39	$62	$108	$137	$141	$148	$162	$170	$171	$175	2.3%
Occupational Safety and Health Review Commission	—	$5	$7	$6	$6	$6	$7	$7	$7	$8	12.5%
Total—Job Safety and Other Working Conditions	$128	$359	$753	$862	$1,002	$1,050	$1,113	$1,132	$1,160	$1,235	6.1%

Environment

Council on Environmental Quality	*	$3	$8	$1	$1	$2	$3	$1	$1	*	—
Department of Defense:											
Army Corps of Engineers	$2	$20	$41	$54	$64	$75	$86	$87	$92	$110	16.4%
Department of Interior:											
Fish and Wildlife Service	$7	$24	$68	$90	$159	$206	$225	$266	$309	$369	16.3%
Office of Surface Mining Reclamation and Enforcement	—	—	174	422	346	354	334	358	379	279	−35.8%
Subtotal	$7	$24	$242	$512	$505	$560	$559	$624	$688	$648	−6.2%
Environmental Protection Agency	$205	$794	$1,360	$1,928	$3,594	$3,979	$4,411	$4,288	$4,324	$4,666	7.3%
Total—Environment	$214	$841	$1,651	$2,495	$4,164	$4,616	$5,059	$5,000	$5,105	$5,424	5.9%
Energy											
Department of Energy:											
Economic Regulatory Admin.	—	$127	$146	$24	$17	$14	$14	$12	$15	$13	−15.4%
Petroleum Regulation	—	—	—	12	11	12	13	14	15	15	0.0%
Federal Inspector for the Alaska Natural Gas Pipeline	—	—	8	*	*	*	*	—	*	—	—
Subtotal	—	$127	$154	$36	$28	$26	$27	$26	$30	$28	−7.1%
Nuclear Regulatory Commission	$64	$148	$396	$445	$434	$466	$514	$529	$609	$554	−9.9%
Total—Energy	$64	$275	$550	$481	$462	$492	$541	$555	$639	$582	−9.8%
Total Social Regulation	$1,116	$2,966	$5,303	$6,527	$9,424	$10,231	$11,210	$11,543	$12,112	$12,571	3.7%

(continued)

Table A.1 (cont.)

Agency	1970	1975	1980	1985	1990	1991	1992	1993	(Estimated) 1994	1995	% Change 1994–95
					Economic Regulation						
Finance and Banking											
Department of the Treasury:											
Comptroller of the Currency	$32	$65	$113	$170	$261	$382	$305	$345	$379	$391	3.1%
Farm Credit Administration	$4	$6	$12	$20	$36	$36	$39	$37	$41	$42	2.4%
Federal Deposit Insurance Corporation	$38	$63	$113	$232	$495	$259	$344	$577	$495	$425	−16.5%
Federal Reserve System:											
Federal Reserve Banks	n/a	n/a	$86	$152	$212	$237	$276	$329	$357	$357	0.0%
Federal Reserve System Board of Governors	5	7	20	28	30	38	43	51	54	54	0.0%
Subtotal	$5	$7	$106	$180	$242	$275	$319	$380	$411	$411	0.0%
National Credit Union Administration	$7	$10	$18	$22	$46	$53	$58	$61	$66	$68	2.9%
Total—Finance and Banking	$86	$151	$362	$624	$1,080	$1,005	$1,065	$1,400	$1,392	$1,337	−4.1%
Industry-Specific Regulation											
Civil Aeronautics Board	$11	$18	$29	$5	—	—	—	—	—	—	—
Commodity Futures Trading Comm.	2	3	17	28	39	44	47	47	48	52	7.7%
Federal Communications Commission	25	47	76	96	108	119	127	134	167	168	0.6%
Federal Energy Regulatory Comm.	18	33	68	98	114	121	140	140	183	176	−4.0%
Federal Maritime Commission	4	7	11	12	15	16	18	18	19	19	0.0%
Interstate Commerce Commission	27	47	78	50	44	44	47	51	53	53	0.0%
Renegotiation Board	4	5	—	—	—	—	—	—	—	—	—
Total—Industry-Specific Regulation	$91	$160	$279	$289	$320	$344	$379	$390	$470	$468	−0.4%

General Business

											%
Cost Accounting Standards Board	—	$1	$1	—	—	—	—	—	—	—	—
Council on Wage and Price Stability	—	$1	$9	—	—	—	—	—	—	—	—
Department of Commerce:											
International Trade Administration	$6	$9	$16	$38	$20	$24	$23	$28	$36	$33	−9.1%
Export Administration	—	—	—	—	$43	$44	$43	37	42	44	4.5%
Patent and Trademark Office	49	78	105	200	327	358	422	471	536	572	6.3%
Subtotal	$55	$87	$121	$238	$390	$426	$488	$536	$614	$649	5.4%
Department of Justice:											
Antitrust Division	$10	$18	$49	$43	$48	$54	$59	$62	$72	$75	4.0%
Federal Election Commission	—	—	$9	$13	$15	$17	$19	$21	$24	$27	11.1%
Federal Trade Commission	$21	$39	$66	$66	$70	$77	$83	$88	$94	$96	2.1%
International Trade Commission	$4	$9	$14	$25	$38	$39	$42	$43	$45	$45	0.0%
Library of Congress:											
Copyright Office	$3	$6	$14	$17	$20	$23	$26	$26	$26	$28	7.1%
Securities and Exchange Commission	$22	$45	$72	$105	$162	$188	$224	$252	$272	$310	12.3%
Total—General Business	$115	$206	$355	$507	$743	$824	$941	$1,028	$1,147	$1,230	6.7%
Total Economic Regulation	$292	$517	$996	$1,420	$2,143	$2,173	$2,385	$2,818	$3,009	$3,035	0.9%
GRAND TOTAL	$1,408	$3,483	$6,299	$7,947	$11,567	$12,404	$13,595	$14,361	$15,121	$15,606	3.1%

Notes: ∗ = less than $500,000
— = agency not operational
n/a = not available

Source: Melinda Warren, "Reforming the Federal Regulatory Process: Rhetoric of Reality?" Center for the Study of American Business, OP #138, 1994, pp. 17–19.

Table A.2
Costs of Federal Regulatory Agencies (Fiscal Years, Millions of Constant Dollars in "Obligations," 1987 = 100)

Agency	1970	1975	1980	1985	1990	1991	1992	1993	(Estimated) 1994	(Estimated) 1995	% Change 1994–95
						Social Regulation					
Consumer Safety and Health											
Consumer Product Safety Commission	—	$75	$60	$38	$31	$31	$34	$38	$35	$31	−9.3%
Department of Agriculture:											
Agricultural Marketing Service	$540	$201	$93	$166	$141	$162	$162	$161	$169	$169	−0.4%
Animal and Plant Health Inspection Service	$287	$758	$361	$362	$374	$380	$408	$383	$391	$367	−6.0%
Federal Grain Inspection Service	—	—	77	40	37	34	36	34	42	41	−2.7%
Food Safety and Inspection Service	—	—	531	429	420	429	440	450	460	462	0.5%
Packers and Stockyards Admin.	9	10	11	8	9	9	10	10	9	9	−2.7%
Subtotal	$835	$970	$1,074	$1,006	$981	$1,014	$1,055	$1,037	$1,071	$1,048	−2.2%
Department of Health and Human Services:											
Food and Drug Administration	$227	$421	$466	$463	$533	$600	$642	$656	$756	$764	1.1%
Department of Housing and Urban Development:											
Consumer Protection Programs	*	$4	$6	$7	$5	$6	$6	$7	$6	$7	9.5%
Department of Justice:											
Drug Enforcement Admin.	$6	$24	$18	$19	$25	$30	$30	$31	$29	$27	−5.3%
Department of Transportation:											
Coast Guard	$267	$577	$695	$591	$804	$748	$847	$992	$1,032	$1,067	3.4%
Federal Aviation Administration	358	398	392	311	437	451	480	483	482	466	−3.3%
Federal Highway Administration	17	30	28	35	87	93	99	107	107	124	16.7%
Federal Railroad Administration	60	106	119	47	49	48	50	55	74	57	−22.3%
National Highway Traffic Safety Administration	91	211	190	121	125	132	146	151	151	137	−8.8%
Subtotal	$793	$1,323	$1,423	$1,105	$1,503	$1,472	$1,622	$1,788	$1,845	$1,853	0.4%

Department of the Treasury:

Bureau of Alcohol, Tobacco and Firearms	$142	$193	$201	$183	$249	$274	$291	$317	$306	$302	−1.2%
Chemical Safety and Hazard Investigation Board	—	—	—	—	—	—	—	—	$2	$3	29.8%
Federal Mine Safety and Health Review Commission	—	$6	$3	$4	$3	$4	$5	$5	$5	$5	−2.7%
National Transportation Safety Board	$14	$20	$24	$23	$24	$26	$29	$29	$29	$28	−2.7%
Total—Consumer Safety and Health	$2,017	$3,030	$3,276	$2,849	$3,353	$3,458	$3,713	$3,907	$4,085	$4,069	−0.4%

Job Safety and Other Working Conditions

Department of Labor:

Employment Standards Admin.	$105	$91	$173	$135	$137	$128	$128	$126	$127	$130	2.1%
Office of the American Workplace	34	59	77	60	70	26	26	22	21	26	22.6%
Pension and Welfare Benefits Administration	—	—	—	—	—	48	51	51	51	56	9.3%
Mine Safety and Health Admin.	77	136	201	159	148	147	149	154	153	155	1.3%
Occupational Safety and Health Admin.	—	195	266	233	236	241	248	233	235	247	4.8%
Subtotal	$216	$482	$717	$587	$590	$590	$602	$586	$587	$613	4.3%
Architectural and Transportation Barriers Compliance Board	—	—	$2	$2	$2	$3	$2	$2	$2	$2	−2.7%
Equal Employment Opportunity Comm.	$37	$112	$173	$173	$163	$168	$175	$179	$180	$188	4.1%
National Labor Relations Board	$111	$126	$151	$145	$125	$126	$134	$137	$134	$134	−0.4%
Occupational Safety and Health Review Commission	—	$10	$10	$6	$5	$5	$6	$6	$5	$6	11.2%
Total—Job Safety and Other Working Conditions	$364	$730	$1,050	$913	$885	$891	$919	$911	$910	$943	3.6%

(continued)

Table A.2 (cont.)

Agency	1970	1975	1980	1985	1990	1991	1992	1993	(Estimated) 1994	(Estimated) 1995	% Change 1994-95
Environment											
Council on Environmental Quality	*	$6	$11	$1	$1	$2	$2	$1	$1	*	*
Department of Defense:											
Army Corps of Engineers	$6	$41	$57	$57	$57	$64	$71	$70	$72	$84	16.4%
Department of Interior:											
Fish and Wildlife Service	$20	$49	$95	$95	$140	$175	$186	$214	$242	$282	16.2%
Office of Surface Mining Reclamation and Enforcement	—	—	243	447	306	301	276	288	297	213	−28.4%
Subtotal	$20	$49	$338	$542	$446	$475	$462	$502	$540	$495	−8.3%
Environmental Protection Agency	$582	$1,614	$1,897	$2,042	$3,175	$3,378	$3,642	$3,450	$3,391	$3,562	5.0%
Total—Environment	$608	$1,709	$2,303	$2,643	$3,678	$3,919	$4,178	$4,023	$4,004	$4,140	3.4%
Energy											
Department of Energy:											
Economic Regulatory Admin.	—	$258	$204	$25	$15	$12	$12	$10	$12	$10	−15.6%
Petroleum Regulation	—	—	—	13	10	10	11	11	12	11	−2.7%
Federal Inspector for the Alaska Natural Gas Pipeline	—	—	11	*	*	*	*	—	*	—	*
Subtotal	—	$258	$215	$38	$25	$22	$22	$21	$24	$21	−9.2%
Nuclear Regulatory Commission	$182	$301	$552	$471	$383	$396	$424	$426	$478	$423	−11.5%
Total—Energy	$182	$559	$767	$510	$408	$418	$447	$447	$501	$444	−11.4%
Total Social Regulation	$3,170	$6,028	$7,396	$6,914	$8,325	$8,685	$9,257	$9,286	$9,500	$9,596	1.0%

Economic Regulation

Finance and Banking										
Department of the Treasury:										
Comptroller of the Currency	$91	$132	$158	$180	$231	$324	$252	$278	$297	$298	0.4%
Farm Credit Administration	$11	$12	$17	$21	$32	$31	$32	$30	$32	$32	−0.3%
Federal Deposit Insurance Corporation	$108	$128	$158	$246	$437	$220	$284	$464	$388	$324	−16.4%
Federal Reserve System:										
Federal Reserve Banks	n/a	n/a	$120	$161	$187	$201	$228	$222	$280	$273	−2.7%
Federal Reserve System Board of Govs.	$14	$14	$28	$30	$27	$32	$36	$41	$42	$41	−2.7%
Subtotal	$14	$14	$148	$191	$214	$233	$263	$306	$322	$314	−2.7%
National Credit Union Administration	$20	$20	$25	$23	$41	$45	$48	$49	$52	$52	0.3%
Total—Finance and Banking	$244	$307	$505	$661	$954	$853	$879	$1,126	$1,092	$1,021	−6.5%
Industry-Specific Regulation										
Civil Aeronautics Board	$31	$37	$40	$5	—	—	—	—	—	—	—
Commodity Futures Trading Comm.	$6	$6	$24	$30	$34	$37	$39	$38	$38	$40	5.4%
Federal Communications Commission	$71	$96	$106	$102	$95	$101	$105	$108	$131	$128	−2.1%
Federal Energy Regulatory Comm.	$51	$67	$95	$104	$101	$103	$116	$113	$144	$134	−6.4%
Federal Maritime Commission	$11	$14	$15	$13	$13	$14	$15	$14	$15	$15	−2.7%
Interstate Commerce Commission	$77	$96	$109	$53	$39	$37	$39	$41	$42	$40	−2.7%
Renegotiation Board	$11	$10	—	—	—	—	—	—	—	—	—
Total—Industry-Specific Regulation	$259	$325	$389	$306	$283	$292	$313	$314	$369	$357	−3.1%

(continued)

Table A.2 (cont.)

Agency	1970	1975	1980	1985	1990	1991	1992	1993	(Estimated) 1994	(Estimated) 1995	% Change 1994–95
General Business											
Cost Accounting Standards Board	—	$2	$1	—	—	—	—	—	—	—	—
Council on Wage and Price Stability	—	$2	$13	—	—	—	—	—	—	—	—
Department of Commerce:											
International Trade Administration	$17	$18	$22	$40	$18	$20	$19	$23	$28	$25	-10.8%
Export Administration	—	—	—	—	38	37	36	30	33	34	2.0%
Patent and Trademark Office	139	159	146	212	289	304	348	379	420	437	3.9%
Subtotal	$156	$177	$169	$252	$345	$362	$403	$431	$482	$495	2.9%
Department of Justice:											
Antitrust Division	$28	$37	$68	$46	$42	$46	$49	$50	$56	$57	1.4%
Federal Election Commission	—	—	$13	$14	$13	$14	$16	$17	$19	$21	9.5%
Federal Trade Commission	$60	$79	$92	$70	$62	$65	$69	$71	$74	$73	-0.6%
International Trade Commission	$11	$18	$20	$26	$34	$33	$35	$35	$35	$34	-2.7%
Library of Congress:											
Copyright Office	$9	$12	$20	$18	$18	$20	$21	$21	$20	$21	4.8%
Securities and Exchange Commission	$63	$91	$100	$111	$143	$160	$185	$203	$213	$237	10.9%
Total—General Business	$327	$419	$495	$537	$656	$699	$777	$827	$900	$939	4.4%
Total Economic Regulation	$830	$1,051	$1,389	$1,504	$1,893	$1,845	$1,969	$2,267	$2,360	$2,317	-1.8%
GRAND TOTAL	$4,000	$7,079	$8,785	$8,418	$10,218	$10,530	$11,226	$11,553	$11,860	$11,913	0.5%

Notes: * = less than $500,000
— = agency not operational
n/a = not available
Numbers may not add to totals due to rounding.

Source: Melinda Warren, "Reforming the Federal Regulatory Process: Rhetoric of Reality?" Center for the Study of American Business, OP #138, 1994, pp. 20–22.

I ANTITRUST

In this section we will be concerned with the unregulated sector of the economy. That is, we will consider industries that are not subject to governmental controls on product standards, prices, profits, or entry and exit. These are the industries in which competition is the primary mechanism that society relies on to produce good economic results.

It is generally believed that antitrust policy should seek to create and maintain market environments that enhance competitive processes. For example, antitrust law forbids firms from colluding on price, large firms from merging to create monopolies, and dominant firms from using predatory tactics against smaller rivals. Several chapters in this section of the book will examine these and similar antitrust rules.

The field in economics known as industrial organization is concerned with the types of issues raised above. According to Nobel laureate George J. Stigler of the University of Chicago, courses in industrial organization

have for their purpose the understanding of the structure and behavior of the industries (goods and services producers) of an economy. These courses deal with the size structure of firms (one or many, "concentrated" or not), the causes (above all the economies of scale) of this size structure, the effects of concentration on competition, the effects of competition upon prices, investment, innovation, and so on.[1]

The objective of this chapter is to provide a brief overview of some of the important concepts that have been developed by industrial organization specialists. We will also provide background information on the antitrust laws and their enforcement.

Industrial Organization Analysis

The theory of market structures, as presented in most microeconomics textbooks, consists of models of perfect competition, monopoly, oligopoly, and monopolistic competition. Because these theoretical models are so abstract, they have proved to be of limited value to economists interested in understanding real-world markets.

Industrial organization economists have extended the theory of market structures in several directions in order to make it a more useful tool for analyzing actual industrial markets. Important methods of extension have included the development of concepts more amenable to empirical measurement and the incorporation of a richer set of variables. Recently, game theory has been used extensively in the analysis of oligopolistic markets.[2]

Economists at Harvard University in the 1930s and 1940s are usually credited with starting the field of industrial organization. They often used a general methodological approach to the economic analysis of markets that is based on three key concepts: (1) structure, (2) conduct (or behavior), and (3) performance. The hypothesized linkage among these three concepts is that the structure (number of sellers, ease of entry, etc.) of a market explains or determines to a large degree the conduct (pricing policy, advertising, etc.) of the participants in the market, and the performance (efficiency, technical progress) of the market is simply an evaluation of the results of the conduct.

We should hasten to add that there is controversy at the present time among specialists in industrial organization concerning this structure-conduct-performance relationship. Some argue that there is neither good theoretical nor empirical evidence that supports the hypothesis that structure determines performance; others contend just the opposite. An increasingly influential viewpoint seems to be that differences among industries are so complex that simple generalizations (for example, fewer sellers lead to high profit rates) are invalid. What is advocated is to study industries on a case-by-case basis, applying and adapting economic models as appropriate to the industry in question. Given this rather unsettled state of knowledge, we shall simply refer the reader to a number of representative sources on this debate.[3]

While the structure-conduct-performance relationship is subject to debate, it nevertheless provides a useful framework for organizing and discussing a number of important concepts. Figure 3.1 presents a schematic representation of the structure-conduct-performance model. The dashed arrow between the conduct and structure blocks indicates that conduct can sometimes "feedback" to change structure. There are a

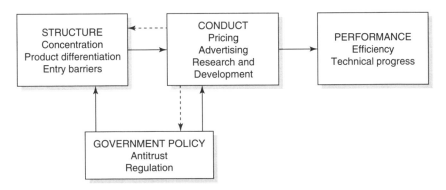

Figure 3.1
The Structure-Conduct-Performance Model of Industrial Organization

number of ways in which behavior of existing firms in a market can affect future market structure. Through investing in research and development a firm can lower its cost to a point where it can profitably price its competitors out of the market. Alternatively, firms can influence market structure by affecting the decisions of potential entrants to enter. As will be reviewed in Chapter 6, the profitability of entry can be influenced by existing firms' strategically manipulating price or capital. Perhaps the most blunt way in which conduct affects structure is through merger. The combination of existing firms directly impacts market structure.

For clarity, Figure 3.1 is limited to key elements of structure, conduct, and performance. Many additional elements could be added in a more comprehensive diagram. Although the elements of structure will be examined in detail in later chapters, it is useful to provide a short discussion of each here.

Concentration

Theories of competition, oligopoly, and monopoly typically assume sellers of equal size, and thereby specify only the number of sellers (many, few, one). Actual industries contain sellers of unequal size, and concentration is an attempt to capture the size distribution of the selling firms (one might also consider the concentration of buyers, but we ignore that here). A simple index that is commonly used is to rank firms by their market shares and to add the market shares of, say, the top four sellers. This is the four-firm concentration ratio.

An example is that the four-firm concentration ratio for the airline industry in the United States was 61 in 1990. That is, the market shares of the top four firms were:

American	18 percent
United	17 percent
Delta	14 percent
Northwest	12 percent
Total	61 percent

In sum, concentration is a better measure of the size distribution of sellers because it gives weight to the inequality of sizes. Otherwise, a simple count of sellers would weight American equally with, say, Southwest, which had only 2 percent of the market in 1990. (Although this is not the time to engage in a detailed discussion of the "definition of the market," it is important to qualify the points made above by noting the importance of the basis for market share calculation. If one were to calculate the concentration ratio for a "market" of carriers serving the New York-Los Angeles route, the answer would be quite different. In fact, this problem of market definition is often the most important issue in antitrust cases.)

Entry Barriers

For the present discussion, an entry barrier can be thought of as something that makes entry more costly or more difficult. The significance of entry barriers is that they may permit existing firms to charge prices above the competitive level without attracting entry. A clear example is a patent on a product that has no close substitutes. That is, the patent holder on a drug for which there are no available substitutes can charge a monopoly price for the legal life of the patent without fear of attracting entry.

As we will explain in detail in Chapter 6, the definition of entry barriers is a controversial issue. However, it should be helpful to indicate several other examples that have been given. If potential entrants into an industry have absolutely higher costs for all output levels than established firms, this would be an entry barrier. Some argue that economies of scale that are large relative to the total market demand constitute an entry barrier. The idea is that there may only be "room" in the market for a small number of firms of efficient size. Strong brand loyalties created through intensive advertising have been cited as an entry barrier to new firms. For example, new firms wanting to enter the photographic film market may have to offer very large price cuts in conjunction with heavy promotion to induce consumers to try a new, unknown product.

Product Differentiation

If consumers perceive that there are real differences among the products in a market, the competitive tactics of sellers may focus more on advertising and product design than if there are no differences. In markets where the product is homogeneous, such as wheat, steel, shares of common stock, oil, and so on, price may be the primary basis for competition. Differentiated products, such as breakfast cereals, autos, soft drinks, beer, and medicines are less likely to be sold primarily on a price basis. Hence this element of structure is important in its influence on the character of competitive tactics. And, as mentioned before, product differentiation can be important in the creation of barriers to entry.

The elements in the conduct block of Figure 3.1 are self-explanatory. The performance block contains two elements: efficiency and technical progress. Of course, one could list other desirable attributes of economic performance. For example, most would agree that industrial performance should facilitate full employment of labor and other resources. It can also be argued that the operations of industries should produce an equitable distribution of income.

While these additional elements of performance are important, they are heavily influenced by various macroeconomic policies, such as tax policy, and only marginally by antitrust. Hence in this book we shall focus on efficiency and technical progress.

Although the next chapter will be concerned with a detailed examination of these two elements of performance, we might note that, in a real sense, both deal with economic efficiency. That is, technical progress is the term used in the economics literature for what might be better called "dynamic efficiency." It is the efficiency with which an industry accomplishes technical change—developing new and better production methods and products. The term efficiency in Figure 3.1 refers to the efficiency of resource allocation with a given state of technology. For example, the monopolist that sets price above marginal cost causes a "deadweight loss" in economic surplus.

Figure 3.1 also shows a government policy block that contains the two major categories of policy to be examined in this book: antitrust and regulation. The arrows show that antitrust and regulation can be viewed as influencing the structure and conduct of an industry in order to improve the industry's economic performance.

An antitrust decision might lead to the dissolution of a monopoly into a number of independent sellers. This would directly affect the concentration, or industry structure. A 1911 antitrust case resulted in the creation of thirty-three companies by splitting up John D. Rockefeller's famous monopoly (or trust) of the oil-refining industry. Alternatively, antitrust laws against price fixing influence the conduct block (rather than the structure block).

The dashed arrow indicates a "feedback" relationship from the conduct block to government policy. Business firms often maintain public affairs departments and/or lobbyists whose purpose is to try to change government policy to favor themselves. The Robinson-Patman Act of 1936 is generally viewed as an economically harmful law enacted by Congress under strong political pressure from hundreds of small businessmen. The act was designed to protect these small businesses from the operations of large discount chains that emerged during the 1930s. Among other things, it made it illegal for large food chains to pay lower prices than smaller independent food stores for their produce (even though the large chains performed their own brokerage function). How economic agents influence the type of regulation in place will be examined in Chapter 10.

In summary, this schematic structure-conduct-performance model provides an overview of the book. We need to understand both the economics of how industries behave and the impact of government policies. And it is important to be able to evaluate economic performance under alternative policy variations. We now examine the antitrust laws and their enforcement in more detail.

Antitrust

The major federal antitrust statute in the United States, the Sherman Act of 1890, was the political reaction to the widespread growth of large-scale business combinations, or trusts, formed in the 1880s. Severe business depression had brought about pricing practices that were disastrous to firms in certain industries. To avoid this cutthroat competition, trusts were formed in many industries, including petroleum, meat packing, sugar, lead, coal, tobacco, and gunpowder. Farmers' organizations, labor unions, and small businessmen united in urging passage of a law to protect themselves from the economic power of these new trusts.

There are two main sections of the Sherman Act. Section 1 prohibits contracts, combinations, and conspiracies in restraint of trade. Penalties for violators can be imprisonment and/or a fine. Section 2 prohibits monopolization, attempts to monopolize, and combinations or conspiracies to monopolize "any part of the trade or commerce among the several states, or with foreign nations." Penalties are similar to those for Section 1. The classic target under Section 1 is price-fixing arrangements, while Section 2 is applied to market dominance. We shall examine price fixing in Chapter 5 and monopolization in Chapter 9.

As a result of dissatisfaction with the Sherman Act during the first few decades, two additional statutes were enacted in 1914. The Clayton Act was designed to define anticompetitive acts more clearly. It outlawed price discrimination, tying clauses and exclusive dealing agreements, interlocking directorates, and mergers between competitors. However, these practices were illegal only where they would "substantially lessen competition or tend to create a monopoly." Section 7, which dealt with mergers, was largely ineffective because of a legal loophole. This problem was remedied by the Celler-Kefauver Act of 1950, which amended Section 7. The law concerning mergers and vertical restrictions will be discussed in detail in Chapters 7 and 8. Also, Section 2, having to do with price discrimination, was heavily amended in 1936 by the Robinson-Patman Act. This will be discussed briefly in Chapter 9.

The second statute passed in 1914 was the Federal Trade Commission (FTC) Act. The objective of this legislation was to create a special agency that could perform both investigatory and adjudicative functions. Prior to this time, the Antitrust Division of the Justice Department was the sole enforcement agency in antitrust matters. The FTC Act also contained a section that outlawed "unfair methods of competition."

These three laws—the Sherman Act of 1890 and the Clayton and FTC acts of 1914—comprise the substantive framework for U.S. antitrust policy. (Key sections of these three statutes are reproduced in the appendix at the end of this chapter.) As indicated in our brief description above, the language is general and the interpretation has been left to the courts. Hence, to really understand what is legal and what is illegal in specific situations, one must be familiar with the important court decisions and the specific rules of law that have been developed in these decisions. In many situations there remains considerable uncertainty about what a future court might hold to be legal or illegal. This is true, for example, with regard to the term monopolization. If IBM has 70 percent of the general-purpose computer market, has it been guilty of monopolization? As we will see, the answer depends on the nature of the tactics IBM followed in winning its large market share.

Economists generally view antitrust as a set of laws designed to promote competition and, therefore, economic efficiency. The basic idea is, of course, that certain types of business behavior can lead to an inefficient allocation of resources. At first glance, this view seems to be consistent with the language of the Sherman and Clayton Acts. However, it should be observed that while economic analysis can and has influenced the development of antitrust doctrine, there are other important influences as well. One such influence is the political factor of protecting the small businessman. For example, because competition might lead to the bankruptcy of small, high-cost firms, in certain areas of antitrust the law has been interpreted to protect the small businesses even if higher costs result. To illustrate, one important Supreme Court decision contained the following statement:

It is competition, not competitors, that the Act protects. But we cannot fail to recognize Congress' desire to promote competition through the protection of viable, small, locally owned businesses. Congress appreciated that occasional higher costs and prices might result from the maintenance of fragmented industries and markets. It resolved these competing considerations in favor of decentralization. We must give effect to that decision.[4]

The viewpoint taken in this book is that economic efficiency should be the only objective in antitrust decisions. This position is consistent with the conclusion of the antitrust scholar Robert Bork:

Whether one looks at the texts of the antitrust statutes, the legislative intent behind them, or the requirements of proper judicial behavior, therefore, the case is overwhelming for judicial adherence to the single goal of consumer welfare in the interpretation of the antitrust laws. Only that goal is consistent with congressional intent, and equally important, only that goal permits courts to behave responsibly and to achieve the virtues appropriate to law.[5]

Enforcement and Remedies

As noted above, federal government enforcement is shared by the Antitrust Division of the Justice Department and the Federal Trade Commission (FTC). The states also have their own antitrust laws, enforced by the attorneys general of the individual states. In this book, we focus on the federal antitrust laws because they are far more important.

Antitrust laws are also enforced by private actions. For example, consumers or business firms that believe they have been harmed by price fixing or some other possible antitrust violations can bring a private antitrust suit. In fact, private suits have been the predominant form of antitrust enforcement for over fifty years. Table 3.1 shows the number of antitrust cases filed by the Antitrust Division, the FTC, and private parties in U.S. District Courts from 1970 to 1989. As the table shows, private cases account for around 93 percent of the total.

Table 3.1 also indicates that the number of private cases reached a peak of 1611 cases in 1977 and has been declining throughout the 1980s. This decline might be due to new antitrust interpretations of the late 1970s that have increased the burden on plaintiffs to prove their cases. This is especially the case in areas such as vertical restraints and predatory pricing (to be discussed in Chapters 8 and 9).

The types of cases brought by the federal government also differ from those brought by private parties. The government cases tend to be of larger import. The most lengthy and costly monopolization cases are government cases. Through the early 1980s about two-thirds of the Justice Department's cases involved horizontal price fixing, with the next most frequent cases involving monopolization. Next were merger cases. The FTC concentrated on price fixing and mergers. Price fixing is also the most common private case. In contrast to government cases, private parties bring relatively fewer monopolization and merger cases. Private cases more often involve practices such as tying, exclusive dealing, dealer termination, and price discrimination.

The outcomes of antitrust cases are varied. By far the most common outcome is some form of settlement—rather than a full-blown trial. Almost 90 percent of private cases are either settled or voluntarily dropped by the plaintiff.[6] Settlements often take the form of agreements by the

Table 3.1
Antitrust Cases Filed in U.S. District Courts, 1970–1989

Year	U.S. Cases	Private	Private as % of Total
1970	56	877	94.0
1971	70	1445	95.4
1972	94	1299	93.3
1973	72	1125	94.0
1974	64	1230	95.1
1975	92	1375	93.7
1976	70	1504	95.6
1977	78	1611	95.4
1978	72	1435	95.2
1979	78	1234	94.1
1980	78	1457	94.9
1981	142	1292	90.1
1982	111	1037	90.3
1983	95	1192	92.6
1984	101	1100	91.6
1985	90	1052	92.1
1986	84	838	90.9
1987	100	758	88.3
1988	98	654	87.0
1989	99	638	86.6
Total	1744	23153	93.0

defendants to pay damages in order to avoid a trial. The damages are usually less than those claimed by the plaintiff, but the uncertainty of the outcome of a trial can make it in both parties' interests to agree on some settlement amount and avoid a trial.

Government cases most frequently end by consent decrees, or orders.[7] These are agreements between the government and the defendant that specify certain actions that the defendant will take. For example, in 1982 AT&T agreed to divest its telephone operating companies (among other items) in return for the Justice Department's agreement to terminate its monopolization case.

In cases that proceed through the trial phase, the defendant may, of course, be found innocent or guilty. Various studies indicate that the plaintiff probably prevails less than one-third of the time. There are various penalties possible in cases where the defendant is found guilty.

In monopolization or mergers, a guilty defendant may be forced to divest certain assets. For example, in a merger case the defendant would likely be forced to sell the acquired firm.

Another remedy is an injunction. An injunction is a court order to prohibit an antitrust violator from some specified future conduct. For example, a firm may be prohibited from only leasing (and not also selling) its copying machines, or only selling film and development services as a package.

Fines or prison sentences may be used in criminal cases brought under the Sherman Act. These are usually reserved for price-fixing cases, such as occurred in the famous electrical equipment industry in the early 1960s. In that case, the judge sent seven defendants to jail for thirty days and fined the firms several million dollars.[8] Historically, however, fines have been a very weak deterrent. In the 1960s the average fine per price-fixing conviction was $131,000. This represented about two-tenths of 1 percent of the sales involved in the conspiracy.[9]

In private cases the successful plaintiffs can win treble damages, which can be a particularly strong remedy. For example, if firms are found guilty of fixing prices, damages can be measured as the excess payments made by customers over what the prices would have been in the absence of the conspiracy. While such damages are seldom easy to measure and are subject to further court litigation, the final amount is multiplied by three to determine the actual award. This trebling of actual damages can lead to very high awards. In the electrical equipment case referred to above, the total treble damages awarded to damaged customers in subsequent civil cases was approximately $400 million!

The trebling of damages is itself a controversial issue. On one hand, it clearly stimulates the initiation of private antitrust enforcement (as compared to awards equal to the actual damages only). This should not be viewed as an unqualified virtue, however, in that it can lead to perverse results. Some argue that a customer might knowingly encourage antitrust violations with the intention of bringing a suit to recover three times the damages.[10]

Another criticism of treble damages is the stimulation of so-called nuisance or extortion suits that have little merit in attacking likely antitrust violations. Rather, they are brought because they appear to be good investments. For example, assume that A can make up a story of plausible damage by B resulting from some possible antitrust violation. After trebling, the estimated award could be, say, $10 million. Given that the uncertainty of how the judge or jury might decide is often high in antitrust cases, it might pay B to offer A a settlement of, say, $500,000 even if B expects the chances of winning are relatively good. (Even if B thinks its probability of winning is 0.9, its expected damage payment is still $1 million with a trial. That is, in a statistical sense, the probability of losing, 0.1, times the $10 million is $1 million.)

Exemptions from Antitrust

Congress has granted certain industries and business activities exemptions from antitrust. These include labor unions, export cartels, agricultural cooperatives, regulated industries, and some joint research and development ventures.

Labor unions were exempted from antitrust in the Clayton Act itself. The reasoning for the exemption was to permit labor to match the bargaining power of employers. There are some limits to the exemption, however.

The Webb-Pomerene Act of 1918 exempted export associations. Hence, firms can combine in an association to fix prices on their foreign sales and to allocate markets. These practices would clearly violate the Sherman Act if done domestically.

The Capper-Volstead Act of 1922 authorized agricultural cooperatives of farmers, ranchers, and dairymen to market their commodities collectively. The rationale was to permit the cooperatives to offset the bargaining power on the demand side of the market.

The exemptions for regulated industries vary depending upon the industry. The rationale is that regulation itself—such as regulation by public utility commissions of electricity prices—will serve to protect the public from antitrust practices. The insurance industry, for another example, is currently being investigated by Congress with regard to removing its exemption because of perceived ineffective regulation by the states.

Professional sports teams are treated somewhat more leniently under antitrust. Baseball was actually granted immunity by the Supreme Court in a 1922 decision. One reason for the lenient treatment is the view that a sports league is not simply a collection of independent firms, such as, say, the steel industry. A sports league must cooperate in various ways in order to produce its product—competitive sports contests. An illustration of the leniency allowed is the practice of drafting new players. The league does not permit its teams to bid against each other for new players graduating from college or high school. Rather, the players are allocated by the league rules to particular teams. The (controversial) rationale is that this is necessary to promote "competitive balance."

Finally, some joint research and development ventures are exempt from antitrust. The rationale is that such ventures are needed to maintain the competitiveness of U.S. industry against foreign competition.

Summary and Overview of Part 1

This chapter has introduced some important concepts of antitrust economics. Also, the primary antitrust laws, their enforcement, and exceptions from antitrust were described.

For an economist interested in the evaluation of antitrust policy, the performance block of Figure 3.1 is especially important. Hence the entire next chapter is devoted to explaining the two performance dimensions: economic efficiency and technical progress.

Chapter 5 begins the study of antitrust policy with analysis of oligopoly theory and collusive pricing. As is true with other antitrust chapters, the relevant antitrust decisions will be described. The following chapter focuses on the structure block of Figure 3.1: concentration and entry barriers. It provides a useful background for examining antitrust policy toward mergers in Chapter 7.

Chapter 8 on vertical relationships and Chapter 9 on monopolization conclude the antitrust section of the book. These two final chapters can be differentiated from earlier chapters inasmuch as they focus on possible anticompetitive practices by firms acting alone. Previous chapters, such as those on collusion and mergers, deal with two or more firms acting together in possible anticompetitive acts.

Notes

1. George J. Stigler, *The Organization of Industry* (Homewood, Ill.: Irwin, 1968), p. 1.

2. A stimulating exchange between F. M. Fisher and C. Shapiro on the value of game theory in the analysis of oligopoly is contained in *The Rand Journal of Economics*, Spring 1989.

3. See Harold Demsctz, "Two Systems of Belief about Monopoly," and Leonard Weiss, "The Concentration-Profits Relationship and Antitrust," in Harvey J. Goldschmid et al. (eds.), *Industrial Concentration: The New Learning* (Boston: Little, Brown, 1974). Also, Richard Schmalensee, "Antitrust and the New Industrial Economics," *American Economic Review*, May 1982. A more recent overview is given in Jean Tirole, *The Theory of Industrial Organization* (Cambridge, Mass.: MIT Press, 1988), pp. 1–4.

4. Brown Shoe Company vs. United States, 370 U.S. 294, 344 (1962).

5. Robert H. Bork, *The Antitrust Paradox* (New York: Basic Books, 1978), p. 89.

6. Steven C. Salop and Lawrence J. White, "Private Antitrust Litigation: An Introduction and Framework," in Lawrence J. White (ed.), *Private Antitrust Litigation: New Evidence, New Learning* (Cambridge, Mass.: MIT Press, 1989).

7. Another possibility is a plea of nolo contendere in criminal proceedings. This means, "I do not wish to contend," and is not quite as strong as pleading guilty. It is advantageous to defendants because it cannot be used as proof of guilt in subsequent cases that might be brought by parties seeking damages.

8. A good book on the electrical equipment conspiracies is John G. Fuller, *The Gentlemen Conspirators: The Story of Price-Fixers in the Electrical Industry* (New York: Grove Press, 1962). A more technical analysis is Ralph G. M. Sultan, *Pricing in the Electrical Oligopoly* (Boston: Harvard Business School, 1974).

9. In the 1950s the average fine was only $40,000, which represented less than

one-tenth of the involved sales. These figures are from Richard A. Posner, *Antitrust Law* (Chicago: University of Chicago Press, 1976).

10. On this and the issue of optimal penalties for antitrust, see William Breit and Kenneth G. Elzinga, *Antitrust Penalty Reforms: An Economic Analysis* (Washington, D.C.: American Enterprise Institute, 1986).

Appendix.   Antitrust Statutes

Sherman Act

1. Every contract, combination in the form of trust or otherwise, or conspiracy, in restraint of trade or commerce among the several States, or with foreign nations, is declared to be illegal. Every person who shall make any contract or engage in any combination or conspiracy hereby declared to be illegal shall be deemed guilty of a felony, and, on conviction thereof, shall be punished by fine not exceeding one million dollars if a corporation, or, if any other person, one hundred thousand dollars or by imprisonment not exceeding three years, or by both said punishments, in the discretion of the court.

2. Every person who shall monopolize, or attempt to monopolize, or combine or conspire with any other person or persons, to monopolize any part of the trade or commerce among the several States, or with foreign nations, shall be deemed guilty of a felony, and, on conviction thereof, shall be punished by fine not exceeding one million dollars if a corporation, or, if any other person, one hundred thousand dollars or by imprisonment not exceeding three years, or by both said punishments, in the discretion of the court.

Clayton Act

2. a. It shall be unlawful for any person engaged in commerce, in the course of such commerce, either directly or indirectly, to discriminate in price between different purchasers of commodities of like grade and quality, where either or any of the purchases involved in such discrimination are in commerce, where such commodities are sold for use, consumption, or resale within the United States or any Territory thereof or the District of Columbia or any insular possession or other place under the jurisdiction of the United States, and where the effect of such discrimination may be substantially to lessen competition or tend to create a monopoly in any line of commerce, or to injure, destroy, or prevent competition with any person who either grants or knowingly receives the benefit of such discrimination, or with customers of either of them: Provided, That nothing herein contained shall prevent differentials which make only due allowance for differences in the cost of manufacture, sale, or delivery resulting from the differing methods or quantities in which such commodities are to such purchasers sold or delivered.

b. Upon proof being made, at any hearing on a complaint under this section, that there has been discrimination in price or services or facilities furnished, the burden of rebutting the prima facie case thus made by showing justification shall be upon the person charged with a violation of this section, and unless justification shall be affirmatively shown, the Commission is authorized to issue an order terminating the discrimination: Provided, however, That nothing herein contained shall prevent a seller rebutting the prima facie case thus made by showing that his lower price or the furnishing of services or facilities to any purchaser or purchasers was made in good faith to meet an equally low price of a competitor, or the services or facilities furnished by a competitor.

c. It shall be unlawful for any person engaged in commerce, in the course of such commerce, to pay or grant, or to receive or accept, anything of value as a commission, brokerage, or other compensation, or any allowance or discount in lieu thereof, except for services rendered in connection with the sale or purchase of goods, wares, or merchandise, either to the other party to such transaction or to an agent, representative, or other intermediary therein where such intermediary is acting in fact for or in behalf, or is subject to the direct or indirect control, of any party to such transaction other than the person by whom such compensation is so granted or paid.

d. It shall be unlawful for any person engaged in commerce to pay or contract for the payment of anything of value to or for the benefit of a customer of such person in the course of such commerce as compensation or in consideration for any services or facilities furnished by or through such customer in connection with the processing, handling, sale, or offering for sale of any products or commodities manufactured, sold, or offered for sale by such person, unless such payment or consideration is available on proportionally equal terms to all customers competing in the distribution of such products or commodities.

e. It shall be unlawful for any person to discriminate in favor of one purchaser against another purchaser or purchasers of a commodity bought for resale, with or without processing, by contracting to furnish or furnishing, or by contributing to the furnishing of, any services or facilities connected with the processing, handling, sale, or offering for sale of such commodity so purchased upon terms not accorded to all purchasers on proportionally equal terms.

f. It shall be unlawful for any person engaged in commerce, in the course of such commerce, knowingly to induce or receive a discrimination in price which is prohibited by this section.

3. It shall be unlawful for any person engaged in commerce, in the course of such commerce, to lease or make a sale or contract for sale of goods, wares, merchandise, machinery, supplies, or other commodities, whether patented or unpatented, for use, consumption, or resale within the United States or any Territory thereof or the District of Columbia or any insular possession or other place under the jurisdiction of the United States, or fix a price charged therefor, or discount from, or rebate upon, such price, on the condition, agreement, or understanding that the lessee or purchaser thereof shall not use or deal in the goods, wares, merchandise, machinery, supplies, or other commodities of a competitor or competitors of the lessor or seller, where the effect of such lease, sale, or contract for sale or such condition, agreement, or understanding may be to substantially lessen competition or tend to create a monopoly in any line of commerce.

4. No corporation engaged in commerce shall acquire, directly or indirectly, the whole or any part of the stock or other share capital and no corporation subject to the jurisdiction of the Federal Trade Commission shall acquire the whole or any part of the assets of another corporation engaged also in commerce, where in any line of commerce in any section of the country, the effect of such acquisition may be substantially to lessen competition, or to tend to create a monopoly. This section shall not apply to corporations purchasing such stock solely for investment and not using the same by voting or otherwise to bring about, or in attempting to bring about, the substantial lessening of competition. Nor shall anything contained in this section prevent a corporation engaged in commerce from causing the formation of subsidiary corporations for the actual carrying on of their immediate lawful business, or the natural and legitimate branches or extensions thereof, or from owning and holding all or a part of the stock of such

subsidiary corporations, when the effect of such formation is not to substantially lessen competition.

Federal Trade Commission Act

5. a. (1) Unfair methods of competition in or affecting commerce, and unfair or deceptive acts or practices in or affecting commerce, are declared unlawful.

(2) The Commission is empowered and directed to prevent persons, partnerships, or corporations, except banks, common carriers subject to the Acts to regulate commerce, air carriers and foreign air carriers subject to the Federal Aviation Act of 1958, and persons, partnerships, or corporations insofar as they are subject to the Packers and Stockyards Act, 1921, as amended, except as provided in section 406 (b) of said Act, from using unfair methods of competition in or affecting commerce and unfair or deceptive acts or practices in or affecting commerce.

4   Efficiency and Technical Progress

As indicated in the preceding chapter, *economic performance* is the term used to measure how well industries accomplish their economic tasks in society's interests. Clearly, to evaluate antitrust laws it is essential to have some well-defined objective. In order to evaluate a law that prohibits mergers between two rivals, it is important to have a conceptual tool that identifies the costs and benefits to society of that law.

The two dimensions of economic performance to be discussed here were referred to in the last chapter as *efficiency* and *technical progress*. In a sense, more descriptive terms would be static and dynamic efficiency—but we use the traditional terms in order to be consistent with the economics literature. The main distinction is that in discussing *efficiency* it will be assumed that the technology is given, and in discussing *technical progress* the assumption is that resources are being allocated to developing new technologies (for producing old products more cheaply and for producing completely new products).

Economic Efficiency

We begin by considering the theoretical world of perfect competition. Every microeconomics text devotes much attention to the perfectly competitive model. The key assumptions are:

1. Consumers are perfectly informed about all goods, all of which are private goods.

2. Producers have production functions that rule out increasing returns to scale and technological change.

3. Consumers maximize their preferences given budget constraints; producers maximize profits given their production functions.

4. All agents are price takers, and externalities among agents are ruled out.

5. A competitive equilibrium, that is, a set of prices such that all markets clear, is then determined.

An important welfare theorem that follows from the above assumptions is that the competitive equilibrium is *Pareto optimal*. In short, the equilibrium cannot be replaced by another one that would increase the welfare of some consumers without harming others. An important property of the equilibrium is that *price equals marginal cost* in all markets.

Note that the ideal competitive world described above would have no need for government intervention in the marketplace, except for policies affecting income distribution. This book ignores problems of income distribution—leaving those problems to the field of public finance (which studies taxation and transfer payments).

Many of the assumptions above will be relaxed and discussed in detail throughout this book. Of course, the key assumption to be discussed in this part of the book is the *price-taking* assumption. That is, antitrust economics is concerned with the causes and consequences of firms' abilities to set price above marginal cost.

Once we begin to relax the assumptions above, it becomes clear that we need to develop partial equilibrium tools. That is to say, it becomes incredibly complex to deal with a general equilibrium model in which some markets are monopolies, externalities exist, imperfect information about product quality obtains, and so on.[1] Hence we now turn to welfare economics concepts in the context of a single market, effectively ignoring the interactions with all other markets.

Partial Equilibrium Welfare Tools

The competitive model above was said to satisfy the condition of *Pareto optimality*. This is also referred to as *Pareto efficiency* or simply *economic efficiency*. One tool for evaluating the effect of a policy change (say, breaking up a monopoly) is the Pareto criterion. That is, if everyone is made better off by the change (or no one is made worse off, and at least one person is made better off), then the Pareto criterion would say that the change is "good." It is hard to argue with this criterion for evaluating public policies. The problem is that one is unlikely to find many "good" real-world policies. In most cases in the real world, at least some people will be harmed.

A generally accepted alternative standard in applied microeconomics is the *compensation principle*, which is equivalent to choosing policies that yield the highest total *economic surplus*. The basic idea is that if the "winners" from any policy change can, in principle, compensate the "losers" so that everyone is better off, then it is a "good" change. Note that actual compensation of the losers is not required. If it were required, of course, it would satisfy the Pareto criterion.

To illustrate, consider Figure 4.1. The figure shows the market demand and supply curves for video cassette recorders (VCRs). Recall first a few facts about these two curves. The competitive industry's supply curve is found by horizontal aggregation of the supply curves of individual firms. The individual firms' supply curves are their marginal cost curves; hence we can think of the supply curve in Figure 4.1 as the industry's marginal cost curve.

Another useful point is to recognize that the area under the marginal cost curve represents the sum of the incremental costs for all units of

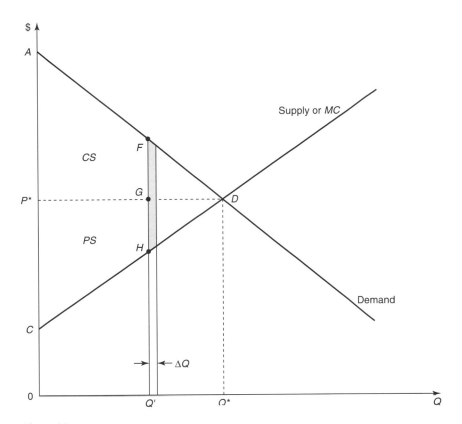

Figure 4.1
Demand and Supply Curves in Determination of Economic Surplus

output and, as a result, equals the total cost. Hence the total cost of producing Q^* VCRs is the area $0Q^*DC$ (this is exclusive of any fixed costs).

Under certain assumptions, the demand curve can be viewed as a schedule of the marginal *willingness-to-pay* by VCR customers.[2] For example, at the competitive equilibrium (price P^*, output Q^*) the marginal willingness-to-pay P^* exactly equals marginal cost at the output Q^*. Because the area under this schedule of marginal willingness-to-pay is total willingness-to-pay, consumers are willing to pay $0Q^*DA$ for output Q^*. The difference between total willingness-to-pay and total cost is therefore the area ACD and is referred to as the *total surplus* generated in the VCR market. Finally, it is common to divide *total surplus* into *consumer surplus* of AP^*D and *producer surplus* of P^*CD.

Consumer surplus is defined as the total willingness-to-pay $0Q^*DA$ less what the consumers must actually pay. Because consumers must pay the rectangle defined by price P^* and the output Q^* (that is, area

$0Q^*DP^*$), the area AP^*D in Figure 4.1 is the consumer surplus. Producer surplus, defined in an analogous manner, is equal to the profit of the firms in the industry. Because firms receive revenues of price P^* times output Q^* (that is, area $0Q^*DP^*$) and they incur costs equal to the area under the marginal cost curve, $0Q^*DC$, they earn a producer surplus of the difference, P^*CD.

Notice that maximizing total surplus is equivalent to maximizing the sum of consumer and producer surplus. We next show that maximizing total surplus is equivalent to selecting the output level at which price equals marginal cost. In Figure 4.1, assume that output Q' is being produced and sold at price $Q'F$. Clearly, at the output Q', the marginal willingness-to-pay $Q'F$ exceeds the marginal cost $Q'H$. Hence a small increase in output of ΔQ would increase surplus by the area of the slender shaded region (approximately FH height by ΔQ width). Output increases would continue to increase surplus up to output Q^*. Hence, maximizing surplus implies that output should be increased from Q' to Q^*, adding an increment to total surplus of area FHD. Of course, by an analogous argument, we can show that output increases beyond Q^* would reduce surplus since marginal cost exceeds marginal willingness-to-pay. In short, equating price and marginal cost at output Q^* maximizes total surplus.

It is useful to provide another interpretation for the area FHD in Figure 4.1. Recall that this area represents potential increases in total surplus if for some reason output is held at Q'. For illustrative purposes, assume that a cartel has agreed to restrict output to Q', charging price $Q'F$. This results in a so-called *deadweight loss* of surplus equal to area FHD. This is often referred to as the *social cost of monopoly*, or simply an *efficiency loss*. In other words, without the cartel, competition would cause price to equal marginal cost, yielding the higher total surplus of ACD as compared to the surplus under the cartel case of $ACHF$. As before, it is sometimes said that there is a deadweight loss in consumer surplus of the triangle FGD and a deadweight loss of producer surplus of the triangle GHD.

Now, consider the point made earlier about the compensation principle and the argument that if the winners can compensate the losers the policy change is a good one. Using a simple monopoly versus competition example, we will show that additional insights can be obtained by considering consumers and producers separately.

Monopoly versus Competition Example

In Figure 4.2 we show a monopoly equilibrium with price P_m and quantity Q_m. For simplicity, we assume that average cost AC is constant and

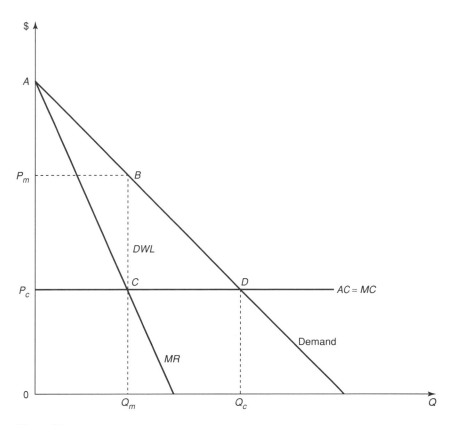

Figure 4.2
Monopoly versus Competition

therefore equal to marginal cost MC. Hence the monopolist chooses output Q_m where marginal revenue MR equals marginal cost. Profit, or producer surplus, equals price minus average cost multiplied by quantity, or area P_mP_cCB. Consumer surplus equals the triangle AP_mB.

Next, consider a policy to break up the monopoly and replace it with a competitive industry. Let us assume no change in costs, so that the competitive industry supply is the horizontal line at the level of MC. (This assumption may not be satisfied in practice, inasmuch as one reason for the existence of a monopoly may be some technological superiority that achieves lower costs of production.) Hence the new equilibrium is price P_c and output Q_c. Consumer surplus increases to the triangular area AP_cD, and producer surplus disappears.

In effect, the elimination of monopoly has led to a net gain in total surplus of triangle BCD. This triangle, the deadweight loss caused by the monopoly, is labeled as DWL in Figure 4.2.

To reinforce the points made above, we can use specific numerical demand and cost functions. In particular, assume

$Q = 100 - P$ demand

$MC = AC = 20$ marginal and average cost

The monopoly price is therefore $P_m = \$60$, $Q_m = 40$, and the competitive equilibrium is $P_c = \$20$, $Q_c = 80$.[3]

Monopoly

Total Surplus $= AP_cCB = \$2400$

    Consumer Surplus $= AP_mB = \$800$

    Producer Surplus $= P_mP_cCB = \$1600$

Competition

Total Surplus $= AP_cD = \$3200$

    Consumer Surplus $= AP_cD = \$3200$

    Producer Surplus $=$ zero

The procompetition policy leads to an increase in total surplus from $2400 to $3200. On this basis, it should be carried out. Notice, however, at the disaggregated level, producer surplus falls from $1600 to zero. The owners of the monopoly are therefore harmed. Consumers gain enough to compensate the monopoly owners and still be better off. That is, consumers gain by $3200 − $800 = $2400. In principle, consumers could compensate the monopoly owners with $1600 to offset their loss, and still have a net gain of $2400 − $1600 = $800. Of course, as discussed earlier, under the compensation principle the compensation need not be carried out. One can justify this by noting that if the government is worried about the income level of the monopoly owners, it can handle this directly through the tax system.

Oil Industry Application

An interesting application of this type of analysis of the oil industry was performed by Arrow and Kalt[4] in 1979. They evaluated the benefits and costs of removing oil price controls in the United States. While the controls will be examined in detail in Chapter 18, it is instructive to present their main findings here to illustrate efficiency losses and gains as compared with simple transfers of surplus from one group to another.

In the 1970s the federal government, concerned with inflation, held oil prices in the United States below what prices would have been in the absence of the controls. This resulted in efficiency losses, according to Arrow and Kalt, of approximately $2.5 billion per year. (A detailed analysis of these losses is provided in Chapter 18.)

Our analysis above, and that shared by most economists, is that this is as far as economists can legitimately go in evaluating public policies. It then becomes a political decision as to whether the transfers among groups are viewed as supporting or offsetting the efficiency analysis. For example, in the hypothetical monopoly example above, the transfer of surplus is from the monopoly owners to consumers, and this is presumably in the politically "correct" direction. That is, if one believes that consumers generally have lower incomes than monopoly owners, and that a more equal income distribution is good, breaking up the monopoly both eliminates efficiency losses and has politically correct distribution effects.

Arrow and Kalt took a further step by trying to evaluate the distribution effect of decontrolling oil prices. Roughly, the decontrol of oil prices would mean higher prices for consumers and higher profits for producers—a politically bad transfer. They were concerned with trying to compare the gain in efficiency with the loss in equity.

The transfer from consumers to producers was estimated to be about $2.8 billion. Arrow and Kalt then proposed, with numerous qualifications, that a dollar transfer from consumers to producers would lose about half its value. The resulting "equity cost" as they termed it would then be half of the $2.8 billion transfer, or $1.4 billion. Hence the efficiency gain of $2.5 billion[5] exceeded the equity cost of $1.4 billion, and they therefore recommended that oil price decontrol was in the public interest.

The key to Arrow and Kalt's analysis is their willingness to assign an "equity cost" of 50 cents per dollar transferred from consumers to producers. As noted earlier, the standard view of economists is that assigning an equity cost of this sort is arbitrary. Economic analysts currently have no empirical basis for assigning any specific value to these equity costs. Nevertheless, it is certainly true that the political process gives great weight to equity issues, and it is helpful for economists to at least set out the magnitude involved.

Some Complications

Economies of scale were implicitly assumed to be relatively small in the monopoly versus competition example. That is, we ignored the problem that arises when the representative firm's long-run average cost curve reaches its minimum at an output level that is large relative to the market demand. In other words, in our monopoly example, we assumed that

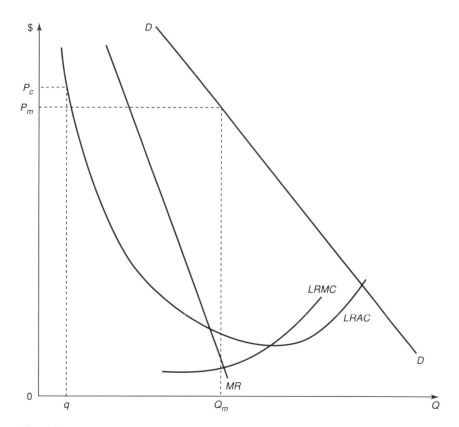

Figure 4.3
Economies of Scale and Natural Monopoly

the single firm could be replaced with a large number of firms with no effect on costs.

To take an extreme case, consider Figure 4.3. Economies of scale are such that the long-run average cost curve *LRAC* reaches its minimum at an output level that is very large relative to market demand. Situations of this kind are referred to as *natural monopolies,* to reflect that production can be most cheaply carried out by a single firm. The profit-maximizing monopolist would set price equal to P_m and output Q_m.

Suppose that it were known that in order to have a sufficient number of firms in the industry for competition to obtain, each firm would be able to produce an output of only q. As Figure 4.3 shows, the average cost of output q would be quite high and would result in a competitive price of P_c, *which exceeds the monopoly price.*

Clearly, economies of scale can make monopoly the preferred market organization. Public utilities to provide electric power or sewage treatment are notable examples. In extreme cases of the type depicted in

Figure 4.3, the policy problem becomes one of regulating the natural monopolist. The approach usually followed in public utility regulation is to force the monopolist to price so as to earn a "fair" rate of return on its investment. An alternative, although not often followed in the United States, is to create a public enterprise, owned and operated by the government. These topics will be discussed in detail in Part 2 of this book.

More relevant to antitrust policy is the intermediate case, where economies of scale are more moderate relative to market demand. For example, it may be imagined that the size of the automobile market is only large enough to support three or four firms, each producing at the minimum point on its long-run average cost curve. This situation would give rise to an industry of three or four firms, or an oligopoly. The key factor differentiating oligopoly from perfect competition and monopoly is that the small number of firms creates a high degree of interdependence. Each firm must consider how its rivals will respond to its own decisions.

Oligopoly theory does not yield any definite predictions analogous to the *price = marginal cost* prediction of perfect competition, or the *price greater than marginal cost* prediction of monopoly. Most theories of oligopoly imply that price will exceed marginal cost, but by less than under monopoly.

Yet oligopoly is quantitatively very significant in most industrial economies, and it is therefore an important topic for study. It should be stressed, in addition, that the prevalence of oligopoly does not necessarily imply that large-scale economies are the cause. In fact, whether or not economies of scale explain the existence of particular oligopolies is a key public policy concern. We will return to oligopoly theory in Chapter 5.

A second complication is the existence of *product differentiation.* Product differentiation refers to the situation in which some differences in the products of rival sellers are perceived by the buyers. The differences may be real differences, such as the differences in size, styling, horsepower, reliability, and so on, between Fords and Chevrolets—or they may be primarily the result of image differences conveyed through advertising. The main requirement is that consumers regard the differentiation sufficiently important that they willingly pay a somewhat higher price for their preferred brand.

E. H. Chamberlin[6] constructed the theory of monopolistic competition in which many competitors produce differentiated products. All firms that produce products that are reasonably close substitutes are members of the *product group.* Given these assumptions and the assumption of

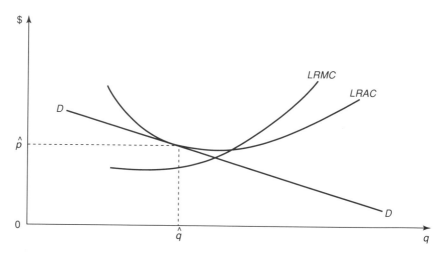

Figure 4.4
Equilibrium of Monopolist Competitor

free entry, the long-run equilibrium of a monopolistic competitor is given by the tangency of the firm's demand curve with its average cost curve. This is shown in Figure 4.4.

The monopolistic competitor earns zero profits in long-run equilibrium. This is a consequence of the assumption of free entry; the existence of a positive profit will attract entry until a firm's own demand is reduced sufficiently to make profits zero. The product differentiation assumption gives the firm's demand curve its slightly negative slope; that is, the firm can increase its price without losing all its sales to a competitor.

The relevant point here is that price exceeds marginal cost—the signal that there is a misallocation of resources. But consider Chamberlin's argument:

> The fact that equilibrium of the firm when products are heterogeneous normally takes place under conditions of falling average costs of production has generally been regarded as a departure from ideal conditions.... However, if heterogeneity is part of the welfare ideal, there is no prima facie case for doing anything at all. It is true that the same total resources may be made to yield more units of product by being concentrated on fewer firms.... But unless it can be shown that the loss of satisfaction from a more standardized product is less than the gain through producing more units, there is no "waste" at all, even though every firm is producing to the left of its minimum point.[7]

The key issue is the optimal amount of product variety, and this is a difficult theoretical problem. A large literature on this subject has developed in recent years.[8] In Chapter 6 we present a simple model that illustrates the tradeoffs involved.

X-Inefficiency

Other types of inefficiency may be important in monopoly. First, we consider X-inefficiency, so named by Leibenstein in his well-known 1956 article on the subject.[9] Thus far, we have assumed that both monopolists and perfect competitors combine their factors of production efficiently, thereby minimizing cost for each level of output. However, it can be argued that the pressures of competition force perfect competitors to be cost minimizers, whereas the freedom from competition makes it possible for the monopolist to be inefficient, or X-inefficient. That is, the monopolist may operate at a point *above* its theoretical cost curve.

Of course, X-inefficiency is inconsistent with the assumption that monopolists maximize profits. However, some economists have argued that the separation of ownership from control in large firms with market power permits the managers to substitute their own objectives for the profit objectives of the owners. Therefore, in such cases, X-inefficiency may arise.

Monopoly-Induced Waste

A third and final source of inefficiency created by monopoly is competition among agents to become a monopolist. Consider the example of a government-mandated monopoly in the form of a franchise. If Figure 4.2 depicts the relevant demand and cost curves, then the franchise owner will earn profits equal to $P_m P_c CB$. Knowing that the firm that receives this franchise will earn rents of $P_m P_c CB$, firms will invest resources in lobbying the legislature or the regulatory agency in order to become the recipient of this franchise. This competition to earn monopoly profits uses up real resources in the form of labor by lobbyists and lawyers. These wasted resources represent a cost to society, just as do the traditional deadweight loss and any X-inefficiencies. Competition among firms for rents is appropriately referred to as *rent-seeking* behavior.[10]

How large is the welfare loss from rent-seeking behavior? We know that it cannot exceed the amount of monopoly profits ($P_m P_c CB$ in Figure 4.2). No firm would find it optimal to spend in excess of that amount in order to become a monopolist. In some simple models it has been shown that if rent-seeking is perfectly competitive (that is, there are many identical firms), then all rents will be competed away.[11] In that case, the total welfare loss from monopoly is $P_m P_c DB$. More generally, $P_m P_c DB$ represents an upper bound on the welfare loss from monopoly (excluding any X-inefficiencies) while BCD is a lower bound.

There are a number of ways in which rent-seeking behavior may arise. As just mentioned, competition for rents could take the form of firms lobbying legislators in order to get favorable legislation passed, for example, entry regulation and import quotas. When these lobbying activities use up real resources, they represent a welfare loss associated with monopoly. Alternatively, if favorable government actions are achieved by bribing legislators or regulators, then this is not a welfare loss but rather simply a transfer from the briber to the bribee. However, one could take the rent-seeking argument one step further and argue that agents will compete to become legislators or regulators in order to receive the rents from bribes. If real resources are used at that stage, then they represent a welfare loss.

Rent-seeking behavior can also arise in the form of excessive nonprice competition. Suppose firms are able to collude so that price exceeds cost. The lure of this high price-cost margin could generate intensive advertising competition as firms compete for market share. Depending on the particular setting, this advertising may have little social value and simply be the byproduct of competition for rents. Historically, socially wasteful advertising has been thought to be a feature of the cigarette industry. As we will see in later chapters, nonprice rivalry among firms in a cartel or in a regulated industry can lead to excessive spending on product quality, product variety, and capacity as well as advertising.

Finally, unions have been found to be quite effective in extracting some of a firm's profits in the form of higher wages. This higher wage results in the private marginal cost of labor exceeding its social marginal cost, so that a firm tends to use too little labor in the production process. This inefficient input mix represents yet another source of welfare loss associated with monopoly. One study found that unions extract in excess of 70 percent of monopoly rents.[12]

Estimates of the Welfare Loss from Monopoly

Having identified various sources of welfare losses due to price exceeding marginal cost, it is natural to wonder about the quantitative size of these losses in the U.S. economy. One method for estimating the traditional deadweight welfare loss (which we will denote DWL) is as follows. From Figure 4.2, we know that DWL equals BCD when the monopoly price is charged. BCD can be approximated by $\frac{1}{2}(P_m - P_c)(Q_c - Q_m)$ where this approximation is exact if the demand function happens to be linear. More generally, if P^* is the price that firms charge and Q^* is the resulting level of demand, then DWL is approximated by $\frac{1}{2}(P^* - P_c)(Q_c - Q^*)$. Because P^* and Q^* are the actual price and quantity, one can collect data on P^* and Q^* for various firms or industries.

However, we typically do not know the competitive price without estimating marginal cost. It is difficult to get a reliable estimate of marginal cost for just a single industry. To do so for a significant portion of the U.S. economy would be a gargantuan task. We then need to find some alternative way of estimating DWL that does not require having data on P_c and Q_c.

In his pioneering study, Arnold Harberger used the following approach.[13] To begin, one can perform a few algebraic manipulations and show that:

$$\tfrac{1}{2}(P^* - P_c)(Q_c - Q^*) = \tfrac{1}{2}\eta d^2 P^* Q^* \tag{4.1}$$

where η is the absolute value of the market demand elasticity and d is the price-cost margin. More formally, $d = (P^* - P_c)/P^*$ and $\eta = |(\Delta Q/Q)/(\Delta P/P)|$ where $\Delta Q = Q_c - Q^*$ and $\Delta P = P^* - P_c$. Although data on industry revenue, P^*Q^*, are available, one needs to come up with estimates of d and η. In order to derive a ballpark figure of DWL, Harberger used the difference between an industry's rate of return and the average for the sample to estimate the price-cost margin d, and simply assumed that $\eta = 1$. With this back-of-the-envelope technique, Harberger found that DWL was on the order of $\tfrac{1}{10}$ of 1 percent of GNP. Though the assumption of unit elasticity is arbitrary, what is important is that the conclusion one draws from this estimate is robust to the value of η. Even increasing it five-fold will mean that DWL is only $\tfrac{1}{2}$ of 1 percent of GNP. Harberger concluded that the welfare losses from monopoly are very small indeed.

We thought it worthwhile to review Harberger's work in order to show how one might go about estimating welfare losses from monopoly. However, there are several reasons to question the relevance and accuracy of his low estimate of DWL. First, it is an estimate based on data from the 1920s. Whether such an estimate is relevant to today's economy is questionable. Second, we know that there are sources of welfare loss from monopoly other than DWL. Harberger estimated that the size of above-normal profits was around 3–4 percent of GNP. This leaves open the question of how much resources were used in competing for these rents. Depending on the extent of such competition, we know that the true welfare loss could be as high as 3–4 percent of GNP. The third and perhaps most important reason for questioning the validity of Harberger's estimate is that later researchers have performed more careful analyses and found higher values of DWL.

One such study was performed by Keith Cowling and Dennis Mueller.[14] They took a quite different approach to estimating DWL. Their approach avoided having to make an arbitrary assumption on the demand elasticity by assuming that firms maximize profit. The first step in their analysis is to note that a firm's profit-maximizing price P^* satisfies the following relationship:

$$\frac{P^*}{P^* - MC} = \eta \tag{4.2}$$

where MC is marginal cost. In words, a firm sets price so that the inverse of the price-cost margin equals the firm demand elasticity. Note that in a competitive industry η is infinity so that (4.2) tells us that $P^* = MC$. Recall that Harberger showed that DWL could be estimated by $\frac{1}{2}\eta d^2 P^* Q^*$ where $d = (P^* - MC)/P^*$ (and we have replaced P_c with MC). Because $1/d = P^*/(P^* - MC)$ and given (4.2), it follows that $\eta = 1/d$. Now substitute $1/d$ for η in the expression that estimates DWL [see equation (4.1)]:

$$DWL \cong \frac{1}{2}\eta d^2 P^* Q^* = \frac{1}{2}\left(\frac{1}{d}\right)d^2 P^* Q^* = \frac{1}{2}dP^* Q^* \tag{4.3}$$

Substituting $(P^* - MC)/P^*$ for d in Equation (4.3), it follows that

$$DWL \cong \frac{1}{2}\left(\frac{P^* - MC}{P^*}\right)P^* Q^* = \frac{1}{2}(P^* - MC)Q^* = \frac{1}{2}\Pi^* \tag{4.4}$$

where Π^* is firm profits. Because $\Pi^* = (P^* - AC)Q^*$, where AC is average cost, the last equality in (4.4) uses the assumption that marginal cost is constant so that $MC = AC$. Cowling and Mueller showed that the deadweight welfare loss created by a firm is approximately equal to half of its profits.

With this methodology, Cowling and Mueller collected data on Π^* for 734 U.S. firms for 1963–1966. Remember that Π^* represents *economic* profits, not *accounting* profits. Hence they used 12 percent as the normal return on capital in the economy and subtracted normal profits from accounting profits to estimate Π^*. Their estimate of DWL was around 4 percent of GNP, considerably higher than that found by Harberger. If one includes advertising expenditures as wasted resources associated with rent-seeking behavior, their measure jumps to 13 percent of GNP. Of course, inclusion of all advertising expenditures assumes that all advertising lacks any social value. This is clearly false, because some advertising reduces search costs for consumers. Thus one would expect Cowling and Mueller's best measure of the welfare loss from monopoly to lie somewhere between 4 and 13 percent of GNP. Nevertheless, it is interesting that under their most comprehensive measure, General Motors by itself created a welfare loss of $\frac{1}{4}$ of 1 percent of GNP!

It is clearly important to understand the quantitative size of the welfare loss from price exceeding marginal cost, whether it is due to monopoly, collusion, or regulation. Unfortunately, estimating welfare losses is an inherently precarious task because of data limitations. One must then interpret these estimates with considerable caution. A final point is that even if we knew for certain that monopoly welfare losses were, say, only 1 percent of GNP, this would not be grounds for abolishing antitrust. The reason is that the 1 percent figure would apply to an economy with antitrust in place. Perhaps if antitrust did not exist, the monopoly losses would be much larger.

Technical Progress

Efficiency in producing the desired bundle of known goods and services with a given technology is obviously important. Some argue, however, that economists place too much emphasis on this type of efficiency. They believe it is at least as important for industry to be efficient in generating new knowledge that saves resources in producing known products, as well as in creating new or higher-quality products. In short, industry should be technically progressive.

Importance of Technological Change

In a path-breaking 1957 study,[15] Nobel laureate Robert M. Solow of MIT estimated that about 80 percent of the increase in gross output per worker-hour from 1909 to 1949 in the United States could be attributed to technological change. Subsequent studies[16] have led to somewhat lower estimates, but Solow's general conclusion as to the relative importance of technological advance is unchanged. It should be useful to illustrate his analysis graphically in order to clarify the meaning of technological change.

In Figure 4.5, two production functions are shown. The functions apply to the economy as a whole and show that output per worker-hour Q, rises (at a decreasing rate) with the amount of capital per worker-hour, K. The lower production function represents the best technology known at time $t = 1$. New knowledge at time $t = 2$ leads to a shift upward in the function, enabling society to obtain higher Q for any given K. Thus the shift represents technological change between $t = 1$ and $t = 2$.

We can now indicate Solow's method of analysis. Suppose that at $t = 1$ the amount of capital per worker-hour is K_1 and at $t = 2$ it is K_2. Furthermore, suppose that Q_1 and Q_2 are the observed outputs per worker-hour on these two dates. The total increase in Q can be

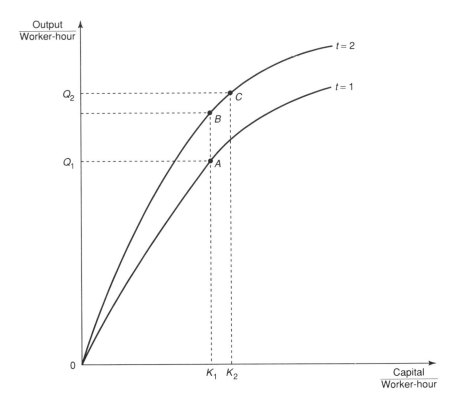

Figure 4.5
Technical Change Shifts the Production Function

conceived as consisting of two parts: the movement from A to B (the effect of technological change) and the movement along the production function from B to C (the effect of increased capital per worker-hour). As stated earlier, Solow found that the amount of the total increase in Q due to technological change (the movement from A to B) was greater than that due to increased capital per worker-hour (the movement from B to C).

The importance of new products is also clear. One has only to think of some examples: jet aircraft, VCRs, antibiotics, personal computers, nuclear power, and so forth. This dimension of technological change was not incorporated fully in Solow's estimates.

Granted that technological change is important, we must now consider what determines it. At the industry level, it is reasonable to expect a number of factors to be influential in determining the rate of technical advance. Undoubtedly, the amount of resources devoted to research and development (R & D) is important. But the amount of private resources allocated will depend upon profitability considerations, which, in turn, will depend on such things as the expected demand for the product and the technical feasibility of the project. And, what is particularly relevant in this book, the structure of the market should affect these profitability calculations.

Some quite persuasive economists have argued that some monopoly power is necessary to provide incentives for firms to undertake research and development programs. The rationale for existing patent policy rests to some extent upon this argument. Others, however, have taken the opposite position, namely, that it is competitive pressures that produce the higher rates of progressiveness.

The famous economist Joseph Schumpeter is usually credited with the view that some monopoly must be tolerated to obtain progressiveness. According to Schumpeter:

But in capitalist reality as distinguished from its textbook picture, it is not [perfect] competition which counts, but the competition from the new commodity, the new technology, the new source of supply, the new type of organization ... —competition which strikes not at the margins of the profits and the outputs of the existing firms but at their very foundations and their very lives.[17]

Before turning to a rivalry model that provides some insight into these issues, it may be helpful to explain several terms that will be used in our discussions. At the beginning there is *basic research*, which seeks knowledge for its own sake. Most industrial firms engage in *applied research*, which is directed toward a particular product or process. If successful, *invention* takes place, which is the discovery of new knowledge. After invention, *development* must take place, leading to the commercial application of the invention, or *innovation*. The last phase of technical change is the *diffusion* of the product or process throughout the industry, or economy.

An R & D Rivalry Model

F. M. Scherer and D. Ross have presented an instructive model of R & D rivalry in their book *Industrial Market Structure and Economic Performance*. Their model is useful in illuminating the conflicting incentives that market structure provides for innovation: (1) more rivals tend to stimulate more rapid innovation in order to be first with a new product and benefit from the disproportionate rewards of being first, and (2) more rivals split the potential benefits into more parts, making each firm's share less. Here we shall draw heavily on their expositional approach, which, in turn, is an attempt to simplify more mathematically complex models published elsewhere.

The model collapses innovative activity into a determination of the speed of new product development. That is, the model seeks to show what factors lead to the firm's choice of the number of years from beginning R & D to the market introduction of the product. We should note that it is incorrect to equate a shorter time necessarily with "socially preferred." While we often seem to identify higher rates of innovation as necessarily "good," it is of course possible for innovation to take place too rapidly.[18]

The situation is one of oligopoly with each firm competing through improved products. To improve one's product requires carrying out R & D for a certain time period prior to marketing. The time period can be compressed by expending more resources. Hence there is a cost-time tradeoff that is shown in Figure 4.6 as the curve CC'.

It is easy to explain the curve CC' by example. Let one plan be to spend $400,000 per year for 10 years. The present discounted value of this stream at 10 percent is $2.5 million. Hence this is one point on CC'.

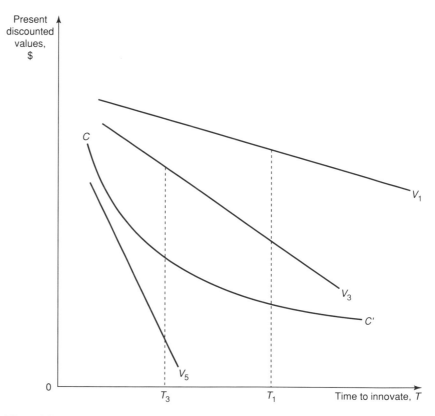

Figure 4.6
R & D Rivalry

Another plan is to spend $1 million per year for 5 years—with a present value of $3.8 million. This is a second point on CC'. Clearly the implication is that it costs more to shorten the time to innovation. There are several reasons for this: Costly errors can be made when development steps are taken concurrently instead of waiting for the information early experiments supply. Second, parallel experimental approaches may be necessary to hedge against uncertainty. Third, there are diminishing returns in the application of additional scientific and engineering manpower to a given technical project.[19]

It is assumed that firms choose the time to innovation T in order to maximize the present discounted value of their profits. Hence the next step is to introduce the function V, which represents how the present value of net revenues varies with T. The net revenues are equal to revenues from the sale of the product minus the production and marketing costs incurred. As shown in Figure 4.6 the V functions (each V function corresponds to a different number of rivals) slope down to the right. It is easy to explain the slope of V_1, which refers to a monopoly situation with no rivals.

Assume for simplicity that the net revenues from the product will be constant over time. Now, if somehow T happened to be zero, the vertical intercept of V_1 would equal the present value of this constant stream of net revenues from $T = 0$ forever. If the flow is $1 million per year, then the present value at 10 percent would be $10 million. Now as T increases, the early years of potential net revenues are lost, thereby reducing the present value and causing the V_1 function to slope down to the right. For example, if net revenues do not begin until year 3, the present value falls to $8.3 million.

In this monopoly case, the profit maximizing T is easily found graphically. It is simply that value of T that is associated with the largest vertical difference between the present value of net revenues and the present value of R & D costs. This is also found by locating the value of T where the slope of V_1 equals the slope of CC'. The optimal T is shown as T_1 in the figure.

Now consider a second situation in which there are, say, three rivals. This is represented with the function V_3. Two points should be noted about V_3 relative to V_1. It is lower, reflecting lower net revenues for each T, and it is steeper. Thus, V_3 is lower than V_1 simply because the total market potential net revenues must now be split three ways. That is, it is reasonable for a firm with two rivals to expect to share the market with the other two, to some degree. Notice that this shift downward reduces overall expected profits, but it does not eliminate them because V_3 still lies above CC'. This reduced expected appropriability of net revenues by the firm can lead to a situation in which the innovation is simply unprofitable—with a zero rate of innovation. Such a case is shown by the function V_5, which corresponds to five rivals. Presumably five rivals is "too many" and would result in too much imitation for R & D to be undertaken at all.

Return to the V_3 case and consider the second point made above. We see that V_3 is steeper than V_1. First note what this steeper slope implies about the optimal T. As the slope gets steeper, the optimal T falls until the V_3 function's slope equals that of CC', at T_3. This steepness, in other words, leads to a faster speed of development as compared to the monopoly case. This effect of increasing the number of rivals is therefore a stimulating effect on the rate of innovation—as long as the number of rivals does not increase too much and cause a situation where innovation is completely unprofitable.

What causes the slope of V_3 to be steeper than V_1 can be explained as follows. The idea is that the proportionate payoff to being first, and enjoying the whole market until imitation, grows with the number of rivals. In monopoly, there is little loss as one innovates later and later— the monopoly still has the whole market in later years. This means the slope of V_1 is relatively flat. Now in a three-firm market, the first firm enjoys the whole market until imitation occurs. Let us say that when imitation occurs, the leader's share falls to one-third—equal to each of the two imitators. The relative size of the leader's payoff to one of the two imitators' payoffs is what determines the slope of V_3. Clearly the relative payoff for a low T (and being first) is greater than the case of monopoly. Furthermore, in some cases the pioneer firm is even relatively better off because of brand loyalty developed during the early years. This makes it possible to keep a proportionately greater share of the market than its imitators. For example, brand loyalty may make it possible for the pioneer to keep half the market, with each imitator getting one-fourth.

Hence the model described above points clearly to the influence of market structure on innovation. While the complexity of the innovative process makes it difficult to obtain nice, neat results, one can infer that neither pole of perfect competition nor pure monopoly seems to be ideal. As Scherer and Ross put it in summarizing an extensive review of empirical work:

What is needed for rapid technical progress is a subtle blend of competition and monopoly, with more emphasis in general on the former than the latter, and with the role of monopolistic elements diminishing when rich technological opportunities exist.[20]

A more fundamental issue is that it may be naive to conceive of the public policy issue as one of choosing the optimal market structure to optimize the tradeoff between static allocative efficiency and progressiveness. The reason is that structure itself should perhaps be viewed as evolving endogenously as technological change occurs through time. Thus, firms that are successful in the innovation game will grow while others decline or drop out. And, over time, the industry's concentration will change as a result.

In Chapter 24 we consider a special policy toward technological change—the granting of patents to provide incentives for inventive activity. Although the model of R & D rivalry implicitly assumed patents to be unimportant, Chapter 24 goes to the other extreme and assumes that patents are essential. Most empirical studies conclude that the importance of patents varies greatly across industries, being especially important in pharmaceuticals and chemicals.

Summary

This chapter has examined two dimensions of economic performance: efficiency and technical progress. The major difference is that the efficiency section assumed a known technology while the technical progress discussion focused on the allocation of resources to develop new knowledge (for producing new products, and for producing existing products more cheaply).

An important lesson that this chapter tries to teach is the usefulness of total economic surplus in assessing public policies. That is, if total economic surplus rises as a result of a policy change, then under certain plausible assumptions, one can argue that the change is in the public interest. An example of such a change that was described was the decontrol of oil prices in the United States.

A hypothetical monopoly-versus-competition example was used to explain the concept of the deadweight loss caused by monopoly pricing. A short section discussed several empirical studies that have sought to estimate the social cost of monopoly in the United States.

In the technical progress section, a simple model of R & D rivalry was presented. The model illustrated how increasing the number of rivals can have two opposing effects on the speed of innovation. The key point of the model is that no simple relationship between the number of rivals and the rates of innovation exists—a larger number of rivals does not always produce better results for society.

Questions and Problems

1. Explain the difference between the Pareto criterion and the compensation principle as rules for deciding whether a particular policy change is in the public interest.

2. Assume, in the monopoly-versus-competition example in the text where demand is $Q = 100 - P$ and marginal cost MC = average cost AC = \$20, that MC under competition remains at \$20. However, assume that the reason the monopoly can continue to be a monopoly is that it pays \$10 per unit of output to reimburse lobbyists for their efforts in persuading legislators to keep the monopoly insulated from competition. For example, the lobbyists may be generating (false) studies that demonstrate that competition results in higher costs.

   a. Calculate the prices and quantities under monopoly and competition.

   b. Calculate total economic surplus under monopoly and competition. The difference is the social cost of monopoly.

   c. The social cost of monopoly can be disaggregated into two distinct types of cost. What are these two types of costs, and what are their respective magnitudes?

3. Discuss the concept of "equity cost" used in the oil industry study by Arrow and Kalt. Do you think it is generally true that "consumers" have lower incomes than "producers"? Does it matter to your answer that labor unions and senior citizens have large ownership interests in corporations through pension funds?

4. A (mini-) refrigerator monopolist, because of strong scale economies, would charge a price of \$120 and sell forty-five refrigerators in Iceland. Its average cost would be \$60. On the other hand, the Iceland Planning Commission has determined that five refrigerator suppliers would be sufficiently competitive to bring price into equality with average cost. The five-firm equilibrium would yield a price of \$100 and a total output of fifty refrigerators.

   a. Consumer surplus under the five-firm industry organization would be larger than under monopoly. If the demand curve is linear, by how much is consumer surplus larger?

   b. Producer surplus under monopoly is larger—by how much?

   c. If the Planning Commission thinks that total economic surplus is the correct criterion, which organization of the refrigerator industry will they choose?

5. What is the best market structure for promoting technical progress?

6. A study in 1975 estimated the effect of monopoly on equity as opposed to efficiency (W. Comanor and R. Smiley, "Monopoly and the Distribution of Wealth," *Quarterly Journal of Economics*, May 1975). For 1962, the wealthiest 0.27 percent of the population accounted for 18.5 percent of wealth. If all industries were competitive, this study estimated that the wealthiest 0.27 percent would have only 13 percent of wealth in 1962. Can you explain this finding? Hint: The wealthiest 0.27 percent held 30 percent of business ownership claims.

Notes

1. See R. G. Lipsey and K. Lancaster, "The General Theory of Second Best," *Review of Economic Studies*, 1956, for an analysis.

2. This interpretation is most easily understood if the demand curve is assumed to be made up of many heterogeneous consumers with demands for at most one VCR. Hence the individual with the highest valuation (or willingness-to-pay) for a VCR is represented by the vertical intercept of the demand curve, $0A$. The next highest valuation (for the second VCR) is slightly less than $0A$, and so forth. The person who actually has the marginal willingness-to-pay P^* is the person who obtains a zero (individual) consumer surplus—all others have positive surpluses. For example, the person with marginal willingness-to-pay of $Q'F$ has to pay P^* and has a surplus of FG. The key assumption necessary to make this interpretation generally valid is that the income effect for the good is "small." See R. Willig, "Consumer's Surplus without Apology," *American Economic Review*, September 1976, for support for this interpretation.

3. The monopolist sets marginal revenue MR equal to MC. MR is $100 - 2Q$ and MC is 20. Equating and solving for Q gives $Q = 40$. The competitive equilibrium is found by setting $P = MC$. So $100 - Q = 20$ gives $Q = 80$. In each case substitute the equilibrium value of Q into the demand function to obtain the value of P.

4. K. J. Arrow and J. P. Kalt, "Decontrolling Oil Prices," *Regulation*, September/October 1979.

5. Actually, Arrow and Kalt noted that the $2.5 billion efficiency gain from decontrol should be reduced to $1.9 billion to reflect the fact that the efficiency gains would accrue primarily to producers. Thus the final comparison was a $1.9 billion gain and a $1.4 billion loss in favor of decontrol.

6. E. H. Chamberlin, *The Theory of Monopolistic Competition* (Cambridge, Mass.: Harvard University Press, 1933).

7. E. H. Chamberlin, "Product Heterogeneity and Public Policy," *American Economic Review*, Vol. 40, May 1950.

8. See Richard Schmalensee, "Industrial Economics: An Overview," *Economic Journal*, September 1988, for a survey of this issue.

9. H. Leibenstein, "Allocative Efficiency vs. X-Inefficiency," *American Economic Review*, June 1966.

10. The pioneering work on rent-seeking behavior is Gordon Tullock, "The Welfare Costs of Tariffs, Monopolies and Theft," *Western Economic Journal* 5 (1967): 224–32. A more relevant piece for our analysis is Richard A. Posner, "The Social Costs of Monopoly and Regulation," *Journal of Political Economy* 83 (August 1975): 807–27.

11. William P. Rogerson, "The Social Costs of Monopoly and Regulation: A Game-Theoretic Analysis," *Bell Journal of Economics* 13 (Autumn 1982): 391–401.

12. Michael A. Salinger, "Tobin's *q*, Unionization, and the Concentration-Profits Relationship," *Rand Journal of Economics* 15 (Summer 1984): 159–70.

13. Arnold C. Harberger, "Monopoly and Resource Allocation," *American Economic Review* 44 (1954): 77–87.

14. Keith Cowling and Dennis C. Mueller, "The Social Costs of Monopoly Power," *Economic Journal* 88 (December 1978): 727–48. For a summary of many of these studies, see Paul Ferguson, *Industrial Economics: Issues and Perspectives* (London: Macmillan, 1988).

15. R. M. Solow, "Technical Change and the Aggregate Production Function," *Review of Economics and Statistics*, August 1957.

16. E. F. Denison, *Trends in American Economic Growth, 1929–1982* (Washington, D.C.: Brookings Institution, 1985).

17. Joseph A. Schumpeter, *Capitalism, Socialism, and Democracy* (New York: Harper & Row, 1975), p. 84.

18. See, for example, Yoram Barzel, "Optimal Timing of Innovation," *Review of Economics and Statistics*, August 1968.

19. F. M. Scherer and D. Ross, *Industrial Market Structure and Economic Performance*, 3rd ed. (Boston: Houghton Mifflin, 1990), p. 632.

20. Ibid., p. 660.

Oligopoly, Collusion, and Antitrust

Section 1 of the Sherman Act prohibits contracts, combinations, and conspiracies that restrain trade. Although this is rather general language, it usually refers to conspiracies to fix prices or share markets. In this chapter, we will trace major judicial decisions from the passage of the Sherman Act in 1890 to the present to show the evolution of the current legal rules toward price fixing.

Before beginning this task, however, we shall discuss the theories of collusive and oligopoly pricing. Oligopoly, of course, refers to a market structure with a small number of sellers—small enough to require each seller to take into account its rivals' current actions and likely future responses to its actions. Price-fixing conspiracies, or cartels, are not limited to a small number of sellers, although it is generally believed that the effectiveness of a cartel is greater when the number of participants is small.

Our coverage will proceed in the following manner. In order to explore the theory of oligopoly and collusion, we will need to be properly tooled. Toward this end, an introductory discussion of game theory is provided. With that under our belts, the plan is to review the Cournot model and a model of collusive behavior. The last section of this chapter discusses antitrust law and landmark price-fixing cases.

A very important assumption that underlies the analysis in this chapter is that potential entry is not a problem. We shall always assume that the number of active firms is fixed. Our focus is then upon the internal industry problems of firms reaching an equilibrium when the only competition comes from existing firms. Allowing for competition from new or potential entrants is delayed until the next chapter.

Game Theory

Example 1: Advertising Competition

Consider a duopoly in which firms do not compete in price because of collusion or regulation. Let the price be $15 and the quantity demanded be 100 units. If unit cost is $5, then profit per unit equals $10. That is, a firm receives revenue of $15 for each unit and it costs the firm $5 to produce that unit. Though it is assumed that firms have somehow been able to avoid competing in price, it is also assumed that firms do compete via advertising. To simplify matters, a firm can advertise at a low rate (which costs $100) or at a high rate (which costs $200). Also for simplicity, assume that advertising does not affect market demand but rather just a firm's market share. Specifically, a firm's market share depends on how much it advertises relative to its competitor. If both firms

Table 5.1
The Advertising Game

| | | FIRM 2 | |
		Low Advertising	High Advertising
FIRM 1	Low Advertising	400,400	150,550
	High Advertising	550,150	300,300

advertise an equal amount (whether low or high), then firms equally share market demand which means that each has demand of 50 units. However, if one firm advertises low and the other advertises high, then the high advertising firm dominates the market with a market share of 75 percent.

Given these data, we can calculate each firm's profits net of advertising expenditure for all of the possible advertising rates that firms can set. The result of these calculations is Table 5.1, which is called a profit matrix. This matrix comprises four cells. In each cell there are two entries, the first of which is firm 1's profit (net of advertising expenditure) and the second of which is firm 2's profit (also net of advertising expenditure). If both firms advertise at a low rate, then each firm's profit is 400. Each firm receives half of market demand, which is 50 units, and earns profit of $10 on each unit. This generates gross profit of $500. After subtracting the cost of advertising at a low rate, which is $100, we derive profit of $400. If instead firm 1 advertises at a low rate and firm 2 advertises at a high rate, then firm 1's profit is 150 $[= (10)(100)(0.25) - 100]$ and firm 2's profit is 550 $[= (10)(100)(0.75) - 200]$. Finally, if both firms advertise at a high rate, then each receives profits of 300 $[= (10)(100)(0.5) - 200]$.

Suppose that the two firms simultaneously choose how much to advertise. That is, each firm decides whether to spend $100 or $200 on advertising at the same time that its competitor decides. How much should each firm advertise if it wants to maximize its profits? Let's look at this decision from the perspective of firm 1. First notice that how much profit it earns depends on how intensively firm 2 advertises. If firm 2 advertises at a low rate, then firm 1 earns $400 from choosing a low rate of advertising and $550 from choosing a high rate. The higher profit from advertising at a high rate comes from the higher market share that firm 1 would receive, which is more than sufficient to offset the higher cost of advertising. Thus, if firm 1 believes that firm 2 will not advertise very much, then it should advertise intensively. If instead firm 1 believes that firm 2 will advertise at a high rate, then it earns $150 from low advertising but $300 from high advertising. Therefore, profit-maximizing behavior by firm 1 is to advertise intensively regardless of how much it believes firm 2 will advertise. By the symmetry of this setting, firm 2's decision process is identical. Our prediction as to how profit-maximizing firms would behave in this setting is that both firms would invest heavily in advertising. This is a stable outcome as each firm is maximizing its profits. Note, however, that joint profits are not maximized. Joint profits are $600 when both advertise intensively but are $800 if both pursue minimal advertising. The problem is that each firm has an incentive to advertise heavily but when they both do so then each firm's advertising is negated by the advertising of their rival.[1]

Example 2: Compatibility of Standards

Let us now consider a quite different setting. Suppose that firm 1 is a supplier of video cassette recorders and firm 2 is a supplier of video cassettes. Each firm's product can have either the Beta format or the VHS format. Further suppose that firm 1's cost of producing a VHS VCR is slightly less than its cost of producing a Beta VCR, while firm 2's cost of producing Beta cassettes is slightly less than producing a VHS cassette. These two firms are the sole exporters of these products to a country that currently has no VCRs or video cassettes. Each firm must decide whether to manufacture its product with the Beta format or the VHS format. (Assume that it is too costly to manufacture both formats.) The consumers in this country are indifferent between the two technologies. All they care about is that the format of the video cassettes sold is the same as the format of the VCRs sold.

Assume that the profit matrix for these two firms is Table 5.2. If both use VHS, then firm 1 earns $500 and firm 2 earns $200. If both use Beta, then firm 1 earns $400 and firm 2 earns $250. If they each supply a different format, then each earns zero profits as demand is zero.

What should firms do in this setting? If firm 1 believes that firm 2 is going to supply Beta cassettes, then firm 1 earns higher profits by also supplying Beta cassettes (compare $400 and 0). If firm 2 believes that firm 1 will supply Beta VCRs, then firm 2 is better off supplying Beta cassettes (compare $250 and 0). Both firms using the Beta format is then a stable outcome, as each firm is choosing the format that maximizes its profits given the format chosen by the other firm. No firm has an incentive to change its decision.

There is another stable outcome, however, in which both firms choose the VHS format. Firm 1 prefers this stable outcome to the one in which the Beta format is chosen, while firm 2 prefers the outcome with the

Table 5.2
The Compatibility Game

		FIRM 2	
		Beta	VHS
FIRM 1	Beta	400, 250	0, 0
	VHS	0, 0	500, 200

Beta format. We would predict that both firms would offer the same format, but which format that might be is unclear.

In contrast to Example 1, a firm's decision in this setting depends on the decision made by the other firm. A firm's profit-maximizing format is the one that matches the format that it believes the other firm is going to choose. This interdependence in firms' decisions is an essential feature of oligopolies.[2]

The Strategic Form of a Game

The above two examples are known as games. We are all familiar with the term game, but in fact there is a branch of applied mathematics known as *game theory*. In game theory, a "game" is a well-defined object. In this section, we describe what a game is and how one analyzes a game. The reason for spending time on game theory is that it is a tool designed for investigating the behavior of rational agents in settings for which each agent's best action depends upon what other agents are expected to do. As a result, game theory will prove to be very useful in investigating firm behavior in oligopolies and, more generally, in providing insight concerning the strategic behavior of firms.

Our goal is to understand the behavior of agents in a particular economic setting; for example, the decision by firms as to how much to advertise, how much to produce, or what technology to use. The first step in applying game theory is to define what the relevant game is (where "relevant" is defined by the researcher and the scientific community at large).

The *strategic form* (or normal form) of a game describes an economic setting by three elements: (1) a list of the agents who are making decisions, (2) a list of the possible decisions that each agent can make, and (3) a description of the way in which each agent evaluates different possible outcomes. Those agents who are making decisions are called *players*. The decision rule of a player is called a *strategy*. A strategy tells a player how to behave in the setting being modeled. A player's *strategy set* includes all the possible strategies that a player could choose. Finally, a player's *payoff function* describes how he evaluates different strategies.

That is, given the strategies chosen by all players, a player's payoff function tells him his state of well-being (or welfare or utility) from players having played those strategies.

In Example 2 the players are firms 1 and 2, a player's strategy is a format, and the strategy set of a player contains the two available formats: {Beta, VHS}. When a player is a firm, we typically assume that a player's payoff is just its profit. In Example 2 the payoff functions of the two players are represented by Table 5.2.[3]

Nash Equilibrium

Having modeled a particular economic setting as a game, one can use it to recommend to players how they should play or to make predictions as to how they will play. While game theory is perhaps better at the former, it is more commonly used for the latter and it is for the latter purpose that we will use it.

A strategy is a decision rule that instructs a player how to behave over the course of the game. A strategy may be very simple, like a rate of advertising, or very complicated, like what price to set at the beginning of each month in response to last month's sales. On a conceptual basis, it is useful to think of players as choosing their strategies simultaneously at the beginning of the game. Once their strategies are chosen, the game commences and players act according to their strategies.

Assuming that players are rational, a player chooses the strategy that gives him his highest payoff (if the player is a firm, this just means the firm is profit-maximizing). As shown in Tables 5.1 and 5.2, a player's payoff depends not only on his strategy but also on the strategy of the other player. This is an essential feature of games. Thus, in deciding which strategy is best, a player must take into account the strategies that he expects the other players to choose. To capture this interdependence, the concept of *Nash equilibrium* was developed. A list of strategies, one for each player, is a Nash equilibrium if each player's strategy maximizes his payoff given the strategies chosen by the other players and if this condition holds simultaneously for all players.

In Example 1 the only Nash equilibrium is the strategy pair (High, High). It is a Nash equilibrium because given firm 2 chooses High, firm 1 maximizes its profits (that is, its payoff) by also choosing High. In addition, given firm 1 chooses High, High is optimal for firm 2. In other words, each firm is choosing a profit-maximizing strategy given the (profit-maximizing) strategy chosen by the other firm. At each of the other three strategy pairs, (Low, Low), (Low, High), and (High, Low), at least one firm can increase its profit by choosing a different strategy. For example, at (Low, High), firm 1 prefers to use High rather than Low as it increases profit by 150. In Example 2, both (Beta, Beta) and (VHS, VHS) are Nash equilibria but (Beta, VHS) and (VHS, Beta) are not Nash equilibria. Note that the outcomes referred to as being stable in Examples 1 and 2 are Nash equilibria.

Oligopoly Theory

An oligopoly is an industry with a small number of sellers. How small is small cannot be decided in theory but only in practice. Nevertheless, in principle, the criterion is whether firms take into account their rivals' actions in deciding upon their own actions. In other words, the essence of oligopoly is *recognized interdependence* among firms. General Motors certainly considers the actions and likely future responses of Ford and Chrysler when it makes its decisions (whether concerning product design, price, advertising, or other factors). On the other hand, a Kansas wheat farmer would be silly to worry about any effect of his planned output on the planned output of the farmer next door.

Since the pioneering work of Augustin Cournot in 1838, many theories of oligopoly have been developed.[4] As it has turned out, the first model of oligopoly is still the most widely used one. In this section we will review Cournot's modeling of the oligopoly problem. Afterward, a brief discussion of some of the other models of oligopoly is provided.

The Cournot Solution

To simplify the analysis, we will work with a numerical example. Let marginal cost be constant at $40 and assume that the inverse market demand function is

$$P = 100 - Q \tag{5.1}$$

If industry supply is Q, then the price that equates supply and demand is $100 - Q$.

Prior to considering the oligopoly setting, let us review the monopoly case, as it will be a useful benchmark. Given (5.1), the marginal revenue curve of a monopolist is

$$MR = 100 - 2Q \tag{5.2}$$

Demand, marginal revenue, and marginal cost are depicted in Figure 5.1. A monopolist maximizes its profit by setting Q to equate marginal revenue and marginal cost. This results in a quantity of 30 and a price of $70. Monopoly profit equals $900.[5]

Now suppose that there are instead two firms, denoted firm 1 and firm 2. Both firms have constant marginal cost of $40 and produce iden-

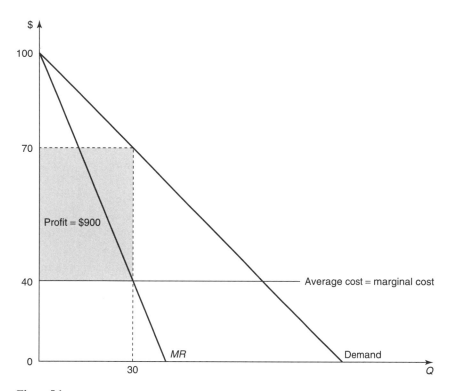

Figure 5.1
Monpoly Solution

tical products. The distinguishing features of the Cournot model are that firms choose quantity (rather than price) and do so simultaneously. The price of the good is set in the market so as to equate industry supply (which equals the sum of the firms' outputs) and demand. Thus, if q_1 and q_2 are the outputs of firms 1 and 2, respectively, then the resulting market price is

$$P = 100 - q_1 - q_2 \tag{5.3}$$

Though the Cournot model was developed more than a century before game theory, one can interpret the Cournot model as a game. In the Cournot game, the set of players is comprised of firms 1 and 2. The strategy of a firm is its quantity. Finally, a firm's payoff is simply its profits. For our numerical example, the profits of firms 1 and 2 are, respectively,

$$\pi_1 = (100 - q_1 - q_2)q_1 - 40q_1 \tag{5.4}$$

$$\pi_2 = (100 - q_1 - q_2)q_2 - 40q_2 \tag{5.5}$$

These profits clearly demonstrate the interdependence that character-izes oligopoly. The profit of firm 1 depends not only on its own output but also on the output of firm 2 (and, similarly, π_2 depends on q_1 and q_2). In particular, the higher q_2 is, the lower is π_1 (holding q_1 fixed). This is because the more that your competitor produces, the lower is the market price for the good, which means your revenue (and profit) is lower.

Having formulated the Cournot model, we next proceed to determine the behavior of firms implied by profit maximization. However, it is not sufficient to determine the quantity that maximizes firm 1's profit with-out also considering what quantity maximizes firm 2's profit, as the former depends on the latter. We need to find a quantity for each firm that results in each maximizing profits given the quantity of its com-petitor. This means finding a Nash equilibrium.

As an initial step in deriving a Nash equilibrium, consider the prob-lem faced by firm 1. It wants to select a quantity that maximizes π_1, taking into account the anticipated quantity of firm 2. Suppose firm 1 believes that firm 2 plans to produce 10 units. Using (5.3), the market price when firm 1 produces q_1 is then

$$P = 100 - q_1 - 10 = 90 - q_1 \qquad (5.6)$$

When $q_2 = 10$, it follows that firm 1's revenue is $(90 - q_1)q_1$. Its mar-ginal revenue is then $90 - 2q_1$. Firm 1 wants to choose q_1 to maximize its profits, which means equating firm marginal revenue with marginal cost. As shown in Figure 5.2, the profit-maximizing quantity is 25..

One can go through the same exercise to find the profit-maximizing output for firm 1 for each possible value of q_2. For example, if $q_2 = 30$, then firm 1's revenue is $(70 - q_1)q_1$ and its marginal revenue is $70 - 2q_1$. As shown in Figure 5.2, the profit-maximizing output is now 15. Doing this for all possible values of q_2, one finds that the value of q_1 that max-imizes firm 1's profit is

$$q_1 = 30 - 0.5q_2 \qquad (5.7)$$

Equation (5.7) is known as firm 1's best reply function because it gives the value of q_1 that is firm 1's best (in the sense of maximizing profits) reply to firm 2's output.[6] In the same manner, one can derive the best reply function of firm 2 to be

$$q_2 = 30 - 0.5q_1 \qquad (5.8)$$

In Figure 5.3, firm 1's best reply function is plotted. Note that it is downward sloping; the higher is firm 2's quantity, the lower is the profit-maximizing quantity of firm 1. The intuition lies in Figure 5.2. Note that

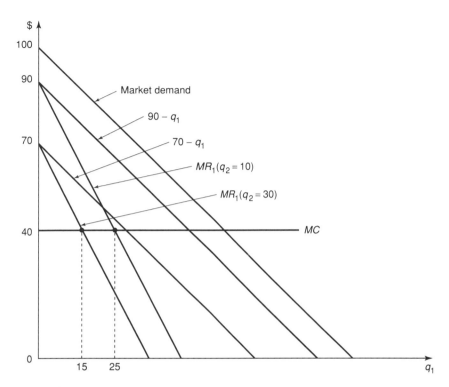

Figure 5.2
Profit Maximation by Firm 1

when q_2 is raised from 10 to 30, firm 1's demand and marginal revenue curves shift in. This reflects the fact that for any value of q_1, a higher value of q_2 results in firm 1 receiving a lower price for its product. Because its demand is weaker, firm 1 produces less in response to firm 2's producing more. Hence, firm 1's best reply function is downward sloping; that is, firm 1 produces less, the more firm 2 is anticipated to supply.

A Nash equilibrium is defined by a pair of quantities such that each firm's quantity maximizes its profit given the other firm's quantity. The appeal of such a solution is that no firm has an incentive to change its output given what its competitor is doing. We have already shown that a firm maximizes its profits only when it produces according to its best reply function. A Nash equilibrium is then defined by a pair of quantities such that both firms are simultaneously on their best reply functions, which is shown in Figure 5.4.

A Nash equilibrium is defined by each firm producing 20 units. That is, given that one's rival produces 20, an output of 20 maximizes a firm's profit. You should convince yourself that any other output pair is not a Nash equilibrium, as at least one firm is not maximizing its profit. For

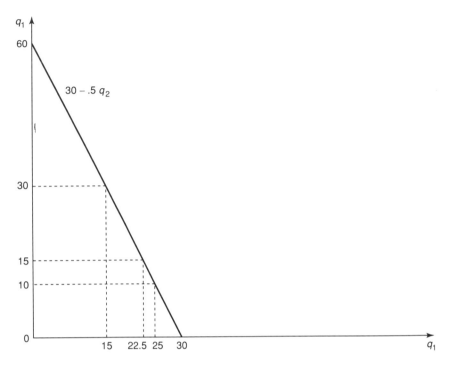

Figure 5.3
Firm 1's Best Reply Function

example, at $q_1 = 30$ and $q_2 = 15$, firm 2 is maximizing its profits (it is on its best reply function) but firm 1 is not. Given $q_2 = 15$, firm 1's profit-maximizing output is 22.5 (see Figure 5.3).

To summarize, the Nash equilibrium of the Cournot game (which we also refer to as the Cournot solution) is

$q_1 = 20 \qquad q_2 = 20$

$\pi_1 = 400 \qquad \pi_2 = 400$

$P = 60$

Note that the price at the Cournot solution exceeds the competitive price of 40 (which equals unit cost) but is less than the monopoly price of 70. This is a standard feature of the Cournot solution and is not particular to our numerical example. The Cournot price exceeds marginal cost because firms do not act as price takers. Firms are not small in the sense that their output decisions affect price and they realize this. They know that the more they produce, the lower is the market price. As a result, each firm supplies less than they would if they were price takers, which results in the Cournot price exceeding the competitive price.

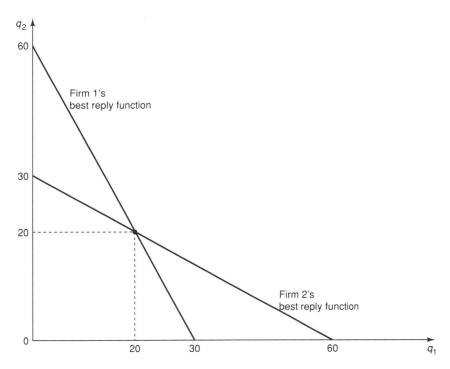

Figure 5.4
The Cournot Solution

The Cournot price is less than the monopoly price because each firm cares only about its own profits and not industry profits. When firm 1 considers increasing its output, it takes into account how this output increase affects π_1 but ignores how it affects π_2. As a result, in maximizing one's own profit, each firm produces too much from the perspective of maximizing industry profit. Hence the monopoly price (which is also the joint-profit-maximizing price under constant marginal cost) exceeds the Cournot price.

Though each firm is maximizing its own profit at the Cournot solution, both firms could simultaneously raise their profits by jointly reducing their output from 20 toward the joint-profit-maximizing output of 15. The problem is that neither firm has an incentive to do so. Suppose that firms were to communicate prior to choosing their output and agreed to each produce 15. If firm 1 actually believed that firm 2 would go along with the agreement and produce 15, firm 1 would do better by reneging and producing 22.5 (reading from its best reply function). Given $q_2 = 15, q_1 = 22.5$ yields profits of 506.25 for 1 firm 1 versus profits of 450 from $q_1 = 15$. Of course, firm 2 is no fool and thus would never produce 15 anyway. Note the similarity with the problem faced by firms in the advertising game of Example 1. In both games, the Nash equilibrium is Pareto inefficient in that firms could raise both of their profits by jointly acting differently.

In concluding this section, let us note that the Cournot solution predicts that the price-cost margin is inversely related to the number of firms, denoted n, and the elasticity of market demand, denoted η:

$$\frac{P - MC}{P} = \frac{1}{n\eta} \tag{5.9}$$

Recall that the elasticity of demand measures how responsive demand is to a change in price. According to this formula, as the number of firms increases, the right-hand side expression in (5.9) becomes smaller which implies that the price-cost margin shrinks. The reader is referred to Table 16.1 for a numerical example that establishes that the market price associated with the Cournot solution is decreasing in the number of firms. Equation (5.9) also tells us that as the industry becomes perfectly competitive (the number of firms approaches infinity), the price-cost margin converges to zero which means that price converges to the competitive price of marginal cost.[7]

Other Models of Oligopoly

In the more than 150 years since Cournot developed his pioneering analysis of oligopoly, many alternative models of oligopoly have been put forth. In 1934, Heinrich von Stackelberg proposed a modification of the Cournot model based on the observation that some industries are characterized by one firm being a leader in the sense that it commits to its output prior to its competitors doing so.[8] The *Stackelberg model* is a game with sequential moves in which the "leader" (say, firm 1) chooses output and then, after observing firm 1's output, the "follower" (firm 2) chooses its output.

Equilibrium behavior in the Stackelberg model entails the follower, firm 2, acting the same way as in the Cournot model (though not choosing the same quantity). In place of firm 2's conjecture as to what firm 1 will produce, firm 2 actually observes firm 1's output. Given the observed output of firm 1, firm 2 chooses its output to maximize its profit, which is just given by its best reply function. In contrast, firm 1, being the leader, acts quite differently. Rather than take firm 2's output as fixed (as it does in the Cournot model), firm 1 recognizes that firm 2 will respond to the output choice of firm 1. Taking into account the response of the follower, the leader chooses its output to maximize its profit.

Using the example from the preceding section, the Stackelberg leader chooses its quantity to maximize:

$$[100 - q_1 - (30 - 0.5q_1)]q_1 - 40q_1 \qquad\qquad (5.10)$$

This expression is firm 1's profit where we have substituted firm 2's best reply function, $30 - 0.5q_1$, for its quantity, q_2. This substitution reflects the fact that firm 1 influences firm 2's quantity choice. Solving for the value of q_1 that maximizes (5.10), one finds that the leader produces 30 units and the follower responds with a quantity of 15 ($= 30 - 0.5 \cdot 30$). Compared to the Cournot solution, firm 1 produces more and firm 2 produces less and thus the leader ends up with a higher market share. Firm 1 produces above the Cournot quantity because it knows that firm 2 will respond by producing less (recall that firm 2's best reply function is downward sloping). In other words, firm 1 takes advantage of moving first by committing itself to a higher quantity knowing that it will induce its rival to produce less.

A second class of oligopoly models assumes that firms choose price rather than output. The first piece of work in this line is that of Joseph Bertrand.[9] In a critique of Cournot's book, Bertrand briefly sketched a model in which firms make simultaneous price decisions. When firms offer identical goods and have constant marginal cost, there is a unique Nash equilibrium when firms choose price and it entails both firms pricing at marginal cost. The *Bertrand model* yields the surprising result that oligopolistic behavior generates the competitive solution! As it turns out, this result is very special. If firms' products are differentiated, price competition results in findings similar to those of the Cournot solution: each firm's price lies between the competitive price and the monopoly price.

In concluding this brief sketch, let us note that our basic findings for the Cournot model with homogeneous goods are robust to allowing firms' products to be differentiated as long as they are not too dissimilar.[10]

Product Differentiation

No discussion of oligopoly theory would be complete without at least a brief consideration of product differentiation. One of the most significant ways in which firms compete is by trying to make their product unique relative to the other products in the market. The reason is that the more differentiated is one's product, the more one is able to act like a monopolist. That is, you can set a higher price without inducing large numbers of consumers to switch to buying your competitors' products.

To consider the role of product differentiation, let us follow the suggestion of Bertrand and assume that firms make simultaneous price decisions with constant marginal cost—though, of course, we will assume that firms' products are differentiated. This means that consumers perceive these products as being imperfect substitutes. That is, there are consumers who are willing to buy one firm's product even though it is priced higher than its competitors'. It also typically means that a small change in a firm's price causes a small change in its demand. For a market with two firms, let $D_i(p_1, p_2)$ denote the number of units demanded of firm i's product when the prices are p_1 and p_2 ($i = 1, 2$). An example of a firm demand curve when products are differentiated is

$$D_1(p_1, p_2) = 100 - p_1 + 0.5p_2 \tag{5.11}$$

$$D_2(p_1, p_2) = 100 - p_2 + 0.5p_1 \tag{5.12}$$

Note that a firm's demand is decreasing in its own price but increasing in the price of its rival. The latter property reflects products being substitutes so when firm 2 raises its price, some consumers who previously purchased firm 2's product decide to switch to buying firm 1's product. Another notable property is that even if $p_1 > p_2$, firm 1 still has positive demand (as long as the difference between prices is not too great). Due to firm 1's product being distinct from that of firm 2, some consumers are willing to pay a premium for firm 1's product. Finally, note that a firm's demand is affected more by a change in its own price than a change in the price of its rival. If we assume each firm has constant marginal cost of 20 then firms' profit functions are

$$\pi_1(p_1, p_2) = (p_1 - 20)D_1(p_1, p_2) = (p_1 - 20)(100 - p_1 + 0.5p_2) \tag{5.13}$$

$$\pi_2(p_1, p_2) = (p_2 - 20)D_2(p_1, p_2) = (p_2 - 20)(100 - p_2 + 0.5p_1) \tag{5.14}$$

where firm i earns $p_i - 20$ on each unit sold.

To derive a Nash equilibrium for the differentiated products price game, one can use the same method that we used for the homogeneous goods quantity game (that is, the Cournot model). The first step is to derive each firm's profit-maximizing price given the price of its competitor, that is, the best reply function. For the profit functions above, one can show that the best reply functions are

$$p_1 = 60 + 0.25p_2 \tag{5.15}$$

$$p_2 = 60 + 0.25p_1 \tag{5.16}$$

In contrast to the Cournot game, a firm's best reply function is upward sloping (see Figure 5.5). The reason is as follows. Firm 1's demand rises

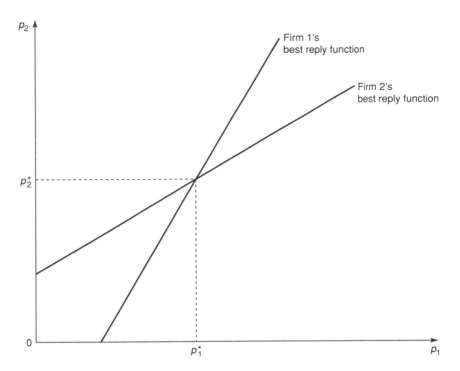

Figure 5.5
Differentiated Products Price Game

in response to firm 2 charging a higher price as some of firm 2's consumers decide to buy from firm 1. Generally, the stronger is a firm's demand, the higher is its profit-maximizing price. It follows that the higher
firm 2's price becomes, the higher is the price that maximizes firm 1's
profit so that its best reply function is upward sloping.

As with the Cournot game, Nash equilibrium occurs where the best
reply functions intersect so that each firm is choosing a price that maximizes its profit, given the other firm's price. Equilibrium then has firm 1
pricing at p_1^* and firm 2 pricing at p_2^*. For our example, the Nash equilibrium entails each firm pricing at 80. To convince yourself that this is
true, if you plug 80 for p_2 in (5.15), one finds that the resulting price for
firm 1 is 80 and if you plug 80 for p_1 in (5.16), one finds that the resulting
price for firm 2 is 80. Given one's rival prices at 80, it maximizes a firm's
profit to also price at 80. Since this argument applies to both firms, both
firms pricing at 80 is a (symmetric) Nash equilibrium.

An important result is that the more differentiated firms' products are,
the higher are equilibrium prices. To understand the intuition underlying this result, let us begin by considering the extreme case of homogeneous products. If firm 1 prices at the same level as firm 2, firms

equally share market demand, inasmuch as consumers are indifferent about buying from the two firms. Because consumers buy from the firm with the lower price, firm 1 can induce all of firm 2's consumers to buy from it by slightly undercutting firm 2's price. Thus a small drop in firm 1's price results in a doubling of its demand. This strong incentive to undercut your competitor's price results, in equilibrium, in prices being driven down to marginal cost.

As products become differentiated, the rise in demand from undercutting your competitor's price is reduced. Some consumers are willing to buy your competitor's product even at a higher price (this is what it means for products to be differentiated). Because a firm does not get as much of its competitor's demand from lowering its price, there is a reduced incentive for firms to set low prices. This results in prices being higher, in equilibrium, when firms' products are more differentiated. When firms' products are so differentiated that consumers do not even perceive them as being substitutes, each firm is effectively a "local" monopolist and charges the monopoly price for its market.

Collusion

Using the Cournot solution, we found that oligopolistic competition results in firms jointly producing too much. Although each firm is individually maximizing its profits, both firms are aware that industry profits are not maximized. Going back to the example in the preceding section, the Nash equilibrium entails each firm producing 20 units and receiving profits of 400. If they instead each produced half of the monopoly output of 30 then each would receive profit of 450. Of course, no individual firm has an incentive to do this because producing 20 units is optimal given one's rival is anticipated to supply 20 units. However, if they could find a way in which to coordinate and jointly reduce their production, they could increase profits for everyone. The lure of higher profits through coordination of their behavior is what collusion is all about.

Historically, there are many incidents of firms successfully coordinating their quantity and price decisions. Examples include the tobacco industry (including Reynolds or what is now RJR-Nabisco), the electrical equipment industry (including General Electric), and the folding-box industry, as well as many international cartels like OPEC. Since the Cournot solution predicts that firms do not maximize joint profits, how are we to explain the fact that, in some industries, firms are able to collude? What keeps each firm from deviating from the collusive agreement by producing at a higher rate and thereby earning higher profits?

A Theory of Collusion

The inadequacy of the Cournot solution lies in the limitations of the Cournot model. A critical specification is that firms make output decisions only once. In reality, firms live for many periods and are continually making output decisions. To correct for this weakness in the Cournot model, consider an infinitely repeated version of that model.[11] In each period, firms make simultaneous quantity decisions and expect to make quantity decisions for the indefinite future. For simplicity, assume that the demand curve and cost functions do not change over time.

There are several important differences between the standard (one-period) Cournot game and the infinitely repeated Cournot game. Because a firm chooses output more than once, a strategy is going to be a much more complicated object than simply some number of units. Rather than generally define a strategy, we will consider some examples below. Second, and this is very important, each firm will receive information over time in the form of past prices and quantities. Though firms choose output simultaneously in a given period, each firm can observe the other firm's past outputs as well as the resulting market price. Finally, each firm acts to maximize the sum of its discounted profits rather than just today's profit. We shall let r denote the interest (or discount) rate for each firm.

Let q_1^t and q_2^t denote the period t quantity of firm 1 and firm 2, respectively, where $t = 1, 2, 3, \ldots$. We first want to show that one Nash equilibrium for this game has each firm produce the Cournot output in every period: $q_1^t = 20$ and $q_2^t = 20, t = 1, 2, 3, \ldots$. Recall that this has each firm's per period profit as 400. A firm's payoff, which is just the sum of its discounted profits, is then[12]

$$\frac{400}{1+r} + \frac{400}{(1+r)^2} + \frac{400}{(1+r)^3} + \cdots = \frac{400}{r} \tag{5.17}$$

For example, if the interest rate is 10 percent, then a firm's payoff (and its market value) is $4,000.

Now consider firm 1 choosing a strategy in which its quantity differs from 20 for one or more periods. In all those periods for which $q_1^t \neq 20$, profits will be lower in those periods (as 20 units maximizes current profit) while profits in periods in which the firm continues to produce 20 remain the same. Hence the sum of discounted profits must be lower. It is then optimal for a firm to produce 20 in each period when it expects its competitor always to do so. One Nash equilibrium for the infinitely repeated Cournot game is then just a repetition of the Cournot solution.

Alternatively stated, repetition of a Nash equilibrium for the single-period game is a Nash equilibrium for the infinitely repeated game.

While a Nash equilibrium has been found for the infinitely repeated Cournot game, it does not put us any closer to understanding how firms can sustain a collusive outcome like the joint-profit maximum. Thus, let's consider a very different strategy from the one specified above. In particular, consider a strategy that allows a firm's output to depend on how much its competitor produced in the past. An example of such a strategy (for firm 1) is specified below:

$$q_1^1 = 15$$

$$q_1^t = \begin{cases} 15 & \text{if } q_1^\tau = 15 \text{ and } q_2^\tau = 15 \quad \text{for all } \tau = 1, \ldots, t-1 \\ 20 & \text{otherwise} \end{cases} \tag{5.18}$$

$$t = 2, 3, \ldots$$

This strategy says that firm 1 should produce 15 in period 1. Recall that 30 is the monopoly quantity so that each firm producing 15 maximizes joint profit. In any future period, it should produce 15 if and only if both firms produced 15 in all periods prior to the current one. Alternatively, if one or more firms deviated from producing 15 in some past period, then firm 1 should produce 20 (the Cournot output) in all remaining periods. This strategy is called a "trigger strategy" because a slight deviation from the collusive output of 15 triggers a breakdown in collusion. The strategy for firm 2 is similarly defined:

$$q_2^1 = 15$$

$$q_2^t = \begin{cases} 15 & \text{if } q_1^\tau = 15 \text{ and } q_2^\tau = 15 \quad \text{for all } \tau = 1, \ldots, t-1 \\ 20 & \text{otherwise} \end{cases} \tag{5.19}$$

$$t = 2, 3, \ldots$$

If both firms use these strategies, then each will produce 15 in period 1. Because each produced 15 in period 1 then, as prescribed by these strategies, each firm will produce 15 in period 2. By the same argument, the two firms will produce 15 in every period if they use these strategies. Hence the monopoly price is observed in all periods. If we can show that these strategies from a Nash equilibrium (that is, no firm has an incentive to act differently from its strategy), we will have derived a theory which can explain how profit-maximizing firms can sustain collusion.

Given that firm 2 uses the strategy in (5.19), firm 1 receives profit of 450 in each period from using (5.18) so that its payoff is $450/r$. Now consider firm 1 choosing a different strategy. Any meaningfully different strategy must entail producing a quantity different from 15 in some period. There is no loss of generality from supposing that this occurs in the first period. If $q_1^1 \neq 15$, then firm 2 learns after period 1 that firm 1 deviated from the collusive output. According to firm 2's strategy, it will respond by producing 20 in all future periods. Because firm 1 is aware of how firm 2 will respond, firm 1 will plan to produce 20 in all future periods after deviating from 15 in the current period, as doing anything else would lower firm 1's payoff from period 2 onward. It follows that if $q_1^1 \neq 15$, then firm 1's payoff is

$$[(100 - q_1^1 - 15)q_1^1 - 40q_1^1]\frac{1}{1+r} + \frac{400}{r(1+r)} \qquad (5.20)$$

The first term is period 1 discounted profits, while the second term is the sum of discounted future profits. Given that firm 1 deviates output from the collusive level of 15 in the first period, (5.20) shows that the amount by which q_1^1 differs from 15 affects current profits but not future profits. This is because the punishment for cheating is independent of how much a firm cheats. Therefore, (5.20) is maximized by setting $q_1^1 = 22.5$, as that output maximizes current profits (reading off of firm 1's best reply function in Figure 5.3 when $q_2 = 15$). Substituting 22.5 for q_1^1 in (5.20), one then derives the highest payoff that firm 1 can earn from choosing a strategy different from (5.18):

$$\frac{506.25}{1+r} + \frac{400}{r(1+r)} \qquad (5.21)$$

Figure 5.6 shows the time path of profit from going along with the collusive agreement—earn 450 every period—and cheating on the cartel—earn 506.25 in period 1 and 400 every period afterward. Thus, cheating gives higher profits up front but lower profits in the future as it intensifies competition.

Given that firm 2 uses the strategy in (5.19), firm 1 earns $450/r$ from using the strategy in (5.18), while the highest payoff it can get from choosing a different strategy is that in (5.21). Therefore the strategy in (5.18) maximizes firm 1's payoff if and only if

$$\frac{450}{r} \geq \frac{506.25}{1+r} + \frac{400}{r(1+r)} \qquad (5.22)$$

Working through the algebra, (5.22) holds if and only if $r \leq 0.89$. In other words, if firm 1 sufficiently values future profits (in other words, r is sufficiently small), it prefers to produce 15 each period rather than cheat and produce above 15. By the same argument one can show that firm 2's strategy in (5.19) maximizes the sum of its discounted profits if

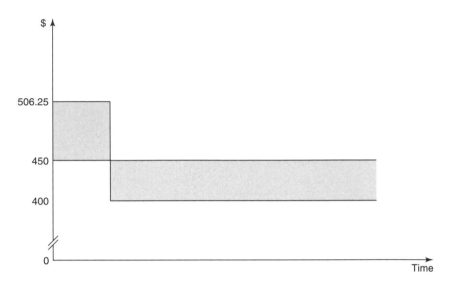

Figure 5.6
Profits from Colluding versus Cheating

and only if $r \le 0.89$. We conclude that (5.18) and (5.19) are a Nash equilibrium when the discount rate is sufficiently low.[13]

In contrast to the one-period game, we have shown that firms are able to produce at the joint-profit maximum without either firm having an incentive to cheat. What is critical for this result is that a firm's output decision depends on the past behavior of its competitor. Note that if firm 1 ever cheats on the collusive agreement by producing different from 15 units, firm 2 will respond by giving up collusion forever and producing the Cournot output of 20. This response to a deviation lowers firms 1's future profits (and also firm 2's future profits). A firm that cheats raises its current profits, but the punishment of future collusion breaking down lowers future profits. As long as a firm sufficiently values future profits, it will prefer not to cheat.

Of course, if $r > 0.89$, then these trigger strategies do not form a Nash equilibrium, which means that they cannot sustain the joint-profit maximum. In that event, each firm prefers to cheat and receive higher profit today. However, trigger strategies with a higher collusive output should form a Nash equilibrium. For example, if $0.89 < r \le 1.33$, one can show that firms can use trigger strategies to support an output of 16 though not an output of 15. Although price is below the monopoly level, it is still above the Cournot price.

Finally, let us note that it can be shown that collusion becomes more difficult as the number of firms grows. Specifically, as the number of firms increases, each firm must have a lower discount rate in order for cheating to be unprofitable at the joint-profit maximum. Intuitively, as the number of firms increases, two things happen. First, each firm has a smaller share of the market at the joint-profit maximum. This provides a firm with a bigger increase in current profit from cheating on the collusive agreement. On the other hand, the punishment from cheating—the Cournot solution—is more competitive as there are more firms. Because price falls more after cheating, the loss from cheating is greater when the number of firms is higher. This works in the opposite direction to make collusion easier. It has been shown that the first effect dominates, so that the net gain to cheating goes up as the number of firms increases. Hence, collusion is more difficult the greater the number of firms. Consistent with the static setting, we conclude that having more firms results in a lower price.

Cartel Problems

In developing a concise and instructive theory of collusion, many important issues related to collusion were ignored. This section will discuss some of the real-world complications associated with collusion that were not taken account of in our previous discussion.

One of the most difficult problems that a cartel faces is in reaching agreement on what price to set and how demand should be allocated among cartel members. Though our analysis focused upon firms colluding at the joint-profit-maximizing price, there are actually many possible collusive prices. Any price between the noncollusive equilibrium price (like the Cournot price) and the joint-profit-maximizing price yields higher profit than not colluding. The question then arises, How do firms coordinate on a particular collusive price? If firms' managers got together and discussed this matter, they should be able to solve this coordination problem. As we discuss in the next section, such overt conspiracies to raise price are illegal. Firms would prefer to solve the coordination problem without overt communication.

In practice, there have been several devices that firms have used to solve the coordination problem. One common institution is *price leadership*. The price leader might be the largest or lowest-cost firm, though this is not always so. The identity of the leader may even change over time. The essential idea is that the leader openly announces its intention to change its price, and the other firms normally follow with similar price changes. Of course, the leader must accurately assess what price is likely to be acceptable to its rivals. If the leader is too far off the mark, some rivals may elect not to follow. Price leadership through public announcements of fare changes (for example, in the *Wall Street Journal*) has been commonly practiced in the airline industry.

In 1994, the Justice Department settled a case involving airlines' pricing practices. A particular concern was that the airlines were using a commonly owned computer network to signal each other for the purpose of sustaining non-competitive prices. The computer system provides instantaneous transmission of more than 100,000 domestic fare changes daily. The network makes it easier for the airlines to enter the data in their computer reservation systems for travel agents.

It was conjectured that one of the pricing rules that airlines sought to establish and sustain was the rule that each airline gets to set the fares in its own hub. A 1989 encounter between America West and Northwest is evidence in support of this conjecture. America West set a low fare of $258 roundtrip for the Minneapolis-Los Angeles route. This low fare would largely attract passengers from Northwest as it has a hub in Minneapolis. Rather than lowering its $308 fare to match America West, Northwest set a new fare that struck directly at America West's hub in Phoenix. Northwest cut its $208 fare between Phoenix and New York to $168 and, most interestingly, initially made the fare available for only two days. Apparently, America West got the message. Five days after setting its low Minneapolis-Los Angeles fares, America West rescinded them. It has been reported that some airline executives have gone so far as to communicate their personal feelings with respect to being undercut by prefixing new fares with the letters "FU."

There are other practices and customs in particular industries that aid in reducing the uncertainties of collusive pricing. One example is the use of conventional *mark-up pricing* rules. If all firms in an industry become accustomed to calculating prices with the same formula, then pricing changes that reflect industry-wide cost changes are more likely to be understood and accepted.

Another practice is the use of a *basing point system* of pricing. This system is used in some industries where freight costs are relatively large and consumers are located at various distances from producers. An example is the Pittsburgh-plus system used in the steel industry until it was abandoned in 1924 because of an antitrust order. Under that system every steel producer could easily quote the same price to a customer in, say, Durham, North Carolina. The price would equal the price at the Pittsburgh mill plus the freight charge from Pittsburgh to Durham—even if the actual producer's mill was in Birmingham. Hence, basing point systems reduce what would otherwise be a very complicated price quotation problem to a relatively simple formula. Firms wishing to collude need only agree on a single price at the Pittsburgh mill.

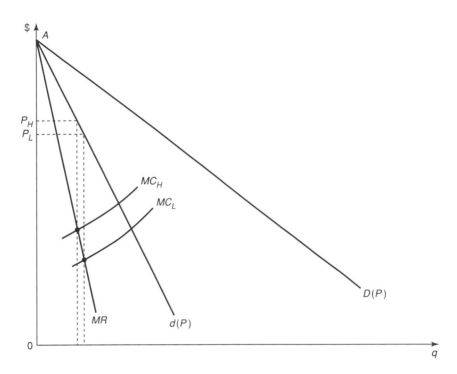

Figure 5.7
Preferred Prices of Duopolists Sharing the Market Equally

The difficulty in agreeing on a particular collusive outcome becomes even more acute when firms are noticeably different. To illustrate how cost differences can create difficulties in agreeing on a particular price, consider the following duopoly setting. Suppose that firms sell identical products but firm 1 has higher cost than firm 2. Assume that they agree to split the market equally. As shown in Figure 5.7, each firm faces the same demand curve $d(P)$, which is just half the market demand curve $D(P)$.

The profit-maximizing price for the low-cost firm, P_L, is determined by the intersection of marginal revenue and its marginal cost MC_L. In contrast, the high-cost firm prefers the higher price of P_H. Because both firms must set the same price (otherwise one of the firms would have zero demand), there is an obvious conflict. Firms must negotiate in order to resolve this difference. Thus, if firms have different cost functions or products, there is a bargaining problem that the cartel must solve. This compounds the usual coordination problem described above.

Clearly, the coordination problem becomes more difficult the larger the number of firms involved. While this problem is not to be underestimated, it is noteworthy that there have been a number of successful cartels involving a large number of firms. When collusion took place in the folding-box industry, no company had more than 10 percent of the market. In 1976 the courts found almost 50 executives in 22 companies guilty of price fixing. One of the convicted executives said,

Price agreements between competitors was a way of life. Our ethics were not out of line with what was being done in this company and, in fact, in this industry for a long time. I've been in this industry for 32 years, and this situation was not just a passing incident. That's just the way I was brought up in the business, right or wrong.[14]

A simplification in our model of collusion is that firms could perfectly observe the past output decisions of their competitors. In fact, one of the serious problems faced by some cartels is in determining whether or not someone cheated. Consider the following modification to the infinitely repeated Cournot game. Assume that each firm knows only its own past output decisions and past market prices. Thus a firm does not directly observe the past output decisions of its competitors. Also suppose that the market price depends on firms' outputs and on random forces that shift the market demand curve.

The monitoring problem faced by a cartel is as follows. If a firm cheats by producing above the collusive output, price will tend to be lower. However, if price is low, firms cannot infer for certain that someone cheated. A low price is consistent with no one cheating and random forces having shifted in the market demand curve (for example, recessionary forces). Because monitoring is imperfect, there is a stronger incentive to cheat because you may be able to get away with it. Although collusion is still supportable in such a setting, it is more difficult to sustain.[15]

The famous electrical equipment price-fixing cases of the early 1960s provide an example in which imperfect monitoring resulted in cheating and ultimately the breakdown of collusion. The four companies involved were General Electric, Westinghouse, Allis-Chalmers, and Federal Pacific. Their arrangement was to rotate the business on a fixed-percentage basis among the four firms. Sealed bids were made so that each firm would submit the low bid a sufficient number of times to obtain the agreed-on market share.

Richard Smith has described the breakup of this cartel in 1957 as follows.[16] The chairman of Florida Power & Light Company, Mac Smith, was buying about a million dollars' worth of circuit breakers that year and was pressuring G.E. and Westinghouse for price breaks: "Westinghouse had proposed to Florida Power that it add all its circuit-breaker orders to its order for Westinghouse transformers. In return, Westinghouse would take 4 percent off circuit-breaker book and hide the discount in the transformer order."[17] The problem arose when Smith decided to split the circuit-breaker order between G.E. and Westinghouse. G.E. had somehow discovered the attempt by Westinghouse to cheat, and had matched the discount. This quickly led to a series of deeper and deeper price cuts. Westinghouse offered Baltimore Gas & Electric 5 percent off. A week later Allis-Chalmers reduced its price to Potomac Electric by 12 percent. The process escalated until discounts of 60 percent were reached in the winter of 1957–1958!

In concluding, let us briefly mention two other complications that a cartel faces. We assumed that the demand curve and cost functions do not change over time. In fact, this is far from the truth for some industries. For example, many industries' demand curve shifts over time with the business cycle. When demand and cost conditions are changing, in principle, the collusive price should adjust. If it doesn't, then the incentive to cheat could change to the point that a firm may find it optimal to cheat. Historically, it has been observed that collusion is more likely to break down during recessions.[18]

Finally, the role of entry in destabilizing cartels has been ignored. Our focus has been only on internal stability (does any firm have an incentive to cheat?) to the exclusion of external stability (does a potential entrant have an incentive to enter?). It is very important to consider the role of entry when examining collusion. Unless there is some factor that prevents entry, one would expect collusion to attract entrants. Rather than discuss this important issue here, we will postpone it until the next chapter.

Collusion: Railroads in the 1880s

Because cartels were legal in the United States prior to 1890, the railroads entered a cartel agreement in 1879 in order to stabilize price. This agreement created the Joint Executive Committee (JEC). The role of the JEC was to set the rail rate of eastbound freight shipments from Chicago to the Atlantic seaboard.

In an empirical analysis, Robert Porter sought to determine whether the JEC maintained collusion through a mechanism similar to the trigger strategy described above.[19] The collusive device considered by Porter was distinct in two ways. First, the punishment for cheating is reversion to the Cournot solution (that is, a breakdown of collusion) for some finite number of periods rather than forever. Second, it was assumed that the JEC could only imperfectly monitor the firms' actions. Because of imperfect monitoring, this theory of collusion predicts that there will be episodes of what looks like cheating. As a result, there will be periodic reversions to the Cournot solution. One would then expect

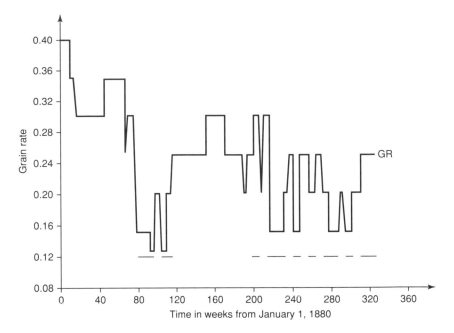

Figure 5.8
Cartel Pricing of Rail Rates: 1880–1886

to find periods in which firms are colluding, so that price is high, and periods in which collusion breaks down and firms revert to the Cournot solution.

Porter examined rail rates for grain during 1880–1886 and assessed whether there were periodic switches between collusion and competition. Figure 5.8 shows the movement in the grain rate from 1880 to 1886. The evidence shows that price was relatively high in weeks 0–80 and 120–220. There appeared to have been breakdowns in collusion (often referred to as "price wars") in weeks 80–120 and periodically over 220–360. The dark line below the grain rate indicates periods in which Porter concluded that collusion broke down. The railroad industry appears to have been colluding but not perfectly. Collusion was intermixed with periodic breakdowns, resulting in intense competition and lower prices.

Antitrust Law toward Price Fixing

Section 1 of the Sherman Act outlaws "every contract, combination ... or conspiracy in restraint of trade." If interpreted literally, this language would make nearly every type of business agreement or contract illegal.

Two lawyers, for example, who decide to form a partnership would be illegally in restraint of trade since they eliminate competition between themselves. In an early 1911 case, however, the Supreme Court stated that "the words 'restraint of trade' ... only embraced acts or contracts or agreements or combinations ... which, either because of their inherent nature or effect or because of the evident purpose of the acts, etc., injuriously restrained trade."[20]

These tests, as refined in subsequent opinions, have become known as the *per se rule* and the *rule of reason*. That is, when a practice can have no beneficial effects but only harmful effects, the "inherent nature" of the practice is injuriously restraining trade. Price fixing by a cartel seems to fit this description and is now illegal per se. This means that the behavior need only be proved to have existed and that there is no allowable defense.

If a certain practice does not qualify as a per se offense, the rule of reason applies. This term refers to the tests of "inherent effect" and "evident purpose." For example, a merger between two firms in the same market is not necessarily harmful or beneficial. Hence the court must then look to the "inherent effect" of the merger and its "evident purpose" or intent. The usual test of inherent effect has come to be the market share of the parties involved. In short, a merger would be judged as legal or illegal depending on an evaluation of the evidence concerning the actual intent of the firms to monopolize the market and the quantitative significance of the market shares involved.

Per se rule antitrust cases tend to be much shorter than the lengthy deliberations often found in rule of reason cases. The IBM monopolization case, an extreme example of a rule of reason antitrust case, lasted thirteen years and involved 950 witnesses, 726 trial days, 17,000 exhibits, and 104,400 trial transcript pages. Justice Thurgood Marshall has described the rationale for the per se category:

Per se rules always contain a degree of arbitrariness. They are justified on the assumption that the gains from imposition of the rule will far outweigh the losses and that significant administrative advantages will result. In other words, the potential competitive harm plus the administrative costs of determining in what particular situations the practice may be harmful must far outweigh the benefits that may result. If the potential benefits in the aggregate are outweighed to this degree, then they are simply not worth identifying in individual cases.[21]

Economic Analysis of Legal Categories

These categories are also generally consistent with economic analysis. A simple example should make this point clear. Consider the model

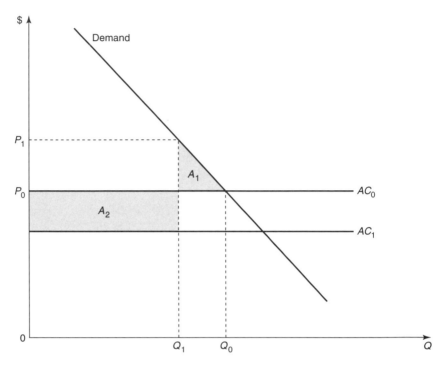

Figure 5.9
Benefits (A_2) and Costs (A_1) to Society of Merger

developed by Oliver Williamson to illustrate the possible tradeoffs created when two firms in the same market seek to merge.[22]

In Figure 5.9 the initial price is P_0 and output is Q_0. The degree of competition is assumed to be sufficient to force price down to AC_0. Now assume that a merger takes place that creates both cost savings and market power. Hence the postmerger equilibrium results in a price increase to P_1 and a cost reduction to AC_1. Output falls from Q_0 to Q_1.

The merger results in a deadweight loss in consumers' surplus equal to triangle A_1 in Figure 5.9. (Recall the discussion of deadweight loss in Chapter 4 at Figure 4.3.) On the other hand, there is a gain to society as a result of the cost savings, which is shown by the rectangle A_2 in Figure 5.9. That is, A_2 represents the cost savings in producing output Q_1 at an average cost of AC_1 rather than AC_0.

The analysis here follows that of Robert Bork.[23] He makes the point that the diagram can be used to illustrate all antitrust problems, because it shows the relationship between efficiency gains and losses. Bork also stresses that efficiency gains through cost savings are but one form of increased efficiency—and that area A_2 should be taken to symbolize any efficiency gain and not merely cost reductions. An example might be an improvement in competitive effectiveness achieved through combining a firm with marketing expertise with one possessing research and development skills.

Of course, not all mergers produce both gains and losses. Some may result in only one or the other, or neither. It is, however, appropriate for the courts to investigate this issue rather than simply declaring mergers to be illegal per se. Ideally, then, a rule of reason decision would find mergers with no gains but actual losses to be illegal. Similarly, mergers with positive gains and no losses would be legal.

The cases where both gains and losses occur are more difficult. The argument could be made that the antitrust authority should compare the loss of A_1 with the gain of A_2. If A_2 exceeds A_1, the merger should be permitted, and not otherwise. As we shall see, courts do not follow this benefit-cost approach. Rather, the rule of reason focuses on the question of the suppression of competition (that is, the existence of area A_1). If such losses are found, then the merger will be found to be illegal regardless of any cost savings. (We will return to this problem in detail in Chapter 7 where merger policy is discussed. There we will examine several important qualifications.)

A cartel, in contrast to a merger that integrates the productive activities of the firms, can lead only to the area A_1 losses. Cost savings are quite unlikely without actual integration. Hence it is quite sensible to place cartels that attempt to fix prices or allocate markets in the per se category. The "inherent nature" of price fixing is to suppress competition and there are no beneficial effects.[24]

Per Se Rule Cases

As we have noted, the courts have taken a clear position with regard to overt conspiracies by competitors to fix prices or share markets. A number of early railroad cases[25] struggled with the issue, as did an interesting case involving cast-iron pipe manufacturers. This latter case, Addyston Pipe, was decided on appeal by the Supreme Court in 1899.[26]

The opinion of the Circuit Court of Appeals, written by Judge (later President), William Howard Taft, is regarded by some as one of the greatest antitrust opinions in the history of the law. According to antitrust expert Robert Bork, Taft made "a remarkable attempt to settle the issue of goals and to provide the Sherman Act with a workable formula for judging restraints. The opinion is one of almost unparalleled suggestiveness, and yet its potentialities, after more than seventy years, remain almost entirely unexploited."[27] The case is also intriguing for the insight it provides into the economics of cartels. For these reasons we have included an appendix at the end of this chapter that contains details of the case and excerpts from the Addyston Pipe opinion.

The per se rule toward price fixing was firmly established in the Supreme Court's Trenton Potteries decision in 1927. Some twenty-three manufacturers of sanitary pottery belonged to an association that attempted to fix the prices of their products. The defendants had roughly 82 percent of the market. In its decision, the Court concluded:

The aim and result of every price-fixing agreement, if effective, is the elimination of one form of competition. The power to fix prices, whether reasonably exercised or not, involves power to control the market and to fix arbitrary and unreasonable prices. The reasonable price fixed today may through economic and business changes become the unreasonable price of tomorrow.... Agreements which create such potential power may well be held to be in themselves unreasonable or unlawful restraints, without the necessity of minute inquiry whether a particular price is reasonable or unreasonable as fixed and without placing on the Government in enforcing the Sherman Law the burden of ascertaining from day to day whether it has become unreasonable through the mere variation of economic conditions.[28]

Notwithstanding its rather strong statement in Trenton Potteries, the Supreme Court six years later seemed to refute its earlier opinion. The Appalachian Coals case concerned some 137 companies that joined together to form Appalachian Coals, Inc. The new company was to act as exclusive selling agent for the companies. These 137 firms accounted for 12 percent of all bituminous coal produced east of the Mississippi River and 54 percent of the production in the Appalachian region. A key fact was that the country was in the midst of the Great Depression and coal mining was especially depressed. Prices of coal fell by 25 percent from 1929 to 1933 and the majority of coal mining firms suffered losses.

The government brought suit and the district court in 1932 found Appalachian Coals in violation of the Sherman Act. However, upon appeal, the Supreme Court reversed the decision. The opinion observed that "a close and objective scrutiny of particular conditions and purposes is necessary in each case.... The mere fact that the parties to an agreement eliminate competition among themselves is not enough to condemn it."[29] This is clearly in opposition to the per se rule enunciated in Trenton Potteries. It can be explained perhaps by the "deplorable" conditions of the industry and the desire by the Court to assist in bringing about a "more orderly" marketing system. And, as Richard Posner has observed, "Faith in the policy of competition was deeply shaken by the depression of the 1930s; this more than anything may explain the outcome in the Appalachian Coals case."[30]

This apparent inconsistency was remedied by the Court in a 1940 decision when it once again issued a strong per se rule toward price fixing. We should note that the composition of the Court had changed significantly from the 1933 version. Also, by 1940 there was little remaining public support for cartelization as a remedy for depressions. (The National Industry Recovery Act, which promoted this idea, was ruled unconstitutional in 1935.)

The 1940 decision, Socony-Vacuum, involved the gasoline industry. Independent refiners were dumping gasoline at very low prices. During 1935 and 1936 more than a dozen major oil refiners, including Socony-Vacuum (now known as Mobil), agreed to a coordinated purchasing program to keep prices up. Each major refiner selected "dancing partners" (that is, independent refiners) and was responsible for buying the surplus gasoline placed on the market by its partners.

The Supreme Court, on appeal, sustained the verdict of guilty. The Court stated flatly that "price-fixing agreements are unlawful per se under the Sherman Act and that no showing of so-called competitive abuses or evils which those agreements were designed to eliminate may be interpreted as a defense."[31]

Since the 1940 decision, the per se rule toward price fixing has been perhaps the most unambiguous antitrust rule of law. Even so, there are difficult, gray areas of collective activity that pose problems. Trade association activities are an example.

Trade associations collect and disseminate information on a wide variety of topics to their members. While normally information helps make markets work better, price information can lead to diminished price competition, especially in oligopolistic markets. A detailed examination of trade association cases is beyond the scope of this book. Suffice it to say that the courts have adopted a rule of reason approach, and that no clear principles of what is legal or illegal have emerged.

A brief discussion of the applicability of the per se rule to the professions should be appropriate at this point. Until the 1970s doctors, lawyers, engineers, and other professions were apparently viewed as outside the jurisdiction of the Sherman Act. In the 1975 Goldfarb case, however, the Supreme Court found a bar association in violation of Section 1.[32]

The Virginia Bar Association, as was common practice at the time, had circulated a list of suggested minimum attorney's fees for various services. For example, the fee for title search in connection with the sale of real estate was 1 percent of the value of the property. The Bar Association issued an opinion that "evidence that an attorney habitually charges less than the suggested minimum fee schedule adopted by his local Bar Association, raises a presumption that such lawyer is guilty of misconduct." (Generally, professional associations argued that price competition would lead to reduced quality of services and that consumers— unable to judge quality—would be harmed.)

The Goldfarbs, planning to buy a house in Fairfax County, Virginia, believed the 1 percent fee for title search to be too high. Hence they consulted some thirty-six lawyers and none would give them a lower price. As a result, the Goldfarbs brought a price-fixing suit against the Bar Association. The Supreme Court ultimately decided in the Goldfarbs' favor. Subsequent cases have reinforced the interpretation that professional organizations cannot restrict price competition.

Interestingly, the United States stands alone in its per se rule against price fixing. Other industrial nations have adopted a rule of reason approach. For example, the United Kingdom has set forth eight "gateways" that can enable a price-fixing agreement to escape illegality. For example, one gateway is that the agreement can be legal if the court considers the agreement necessary to avoid serious and persistent unemployment effects.

We conclude this section on per se rule cases with a recent case involving college football.[33] The Supreme Court argued that because of the special characteristics of sports, the rule of reason should apply even though the alleged offense was horizontal price fixing.

The National Collegiate Athletic Association (NCAA) consists of some 850 voting members—colleges and universities with athletic programs. It serves as a regulatory body that sets playing rules, standards of amateurism, rules about recruitment of athletes, the size of athletic squads and coaching staffs, and so forth. The issue in the case here relates to the NCAA's restraint on its members' rights to negotiate their own television contracts for football games. In 1981 the NCAA negotiated contracts with two television networks, ABC and CBS, which limited the total number of games that could be televised and the number by each institution. It also effectively set the price that each institution could receive per telecast. A number of major college football programs decided to negotiate their own telecasts with NBC. In response to a publicly announced threat of disciplinary action by the NCAA, the major football programs filed an antitrust suit against the NCAA.

While a lower court held that the NCAA television plan constituted illegal per se price fixing, the Supreme Court held that the rule of reason should apply. The Court reasoned that college football is "an industry in which horizontal restraints on competition are essential if the product is to be available at all." Hence, unlike many industries like the steel industry, in which firms need not coordinate their activities, sports leagues need to do so to schedule games, set standards, and so on. In such cases, horizontal restraints are not, on balance, always harmful.

Despite opting for the rule of reason approach, the Court decided against the NCAA. The main justification put forth by the NCAA was that its television plan would protect live attendance at games. Fans who could watch Notre Dame on television might not go to a Podunk College game in their own city. The Court decided that protecting an inferior product from competition was inconsistent with the basic policy of the Sherman Act. "The rule of reason does not support a defense based on the assumption that competition itself is unreasonable."

Conscious Parallelism

A much more difficult antitrust problem is what is termed conscious parallelism. Suppose that there is no evidence that firms got together and made overt agreements to fix prices; however, the firms did behave in parallel fashion by charging identical prices. The key question is whether the conspiracy can be inferred from such conscious parallelism. The importance of this issue is that oligopoly pricing often has characteristics of conscious parallelism.

In particular, the model of tacit collusion requires no overt communication among the firms to reach a monopoly equilibrium. From the viewpoint of economic performance, this outcome is just as harmful as if the firms operated a cartel. Therefore, why should not both types of collusion be treated equally under the antitrust laws? One obvious problem is that the remedies would probably need to differ. A cartel could stop communicating, but tacit understandings might require a structural dissolution of the industry to be made ineffective.[34]

As we will see by reviewing the leading cases, the courts have taken what Richard Posner calls a "cops and robbers" approach to price fixing. By this he means that the weapons that the law had developed to deal with conspiracies in other areas were focused on price fixing. Hence the inquiry became limited to the question of whether the defendants had met or communicated with one another. "Once the conspiracy approach to explicit collusion became firmly ensconced in the minds of bench and bar, it was perhaps inevitable that tacit collusion would be considered beyond the reach of the antitrust laws because, by definition, it did not involve explicit, detectable acts of agreement or communication."[35]

Several early cases indicated that the courts would infer conspiracy from parallel behavior if some additional evidence existed. A 1939 case, Interstate Circuit, involved the manager of a motion picture exhibition chain in Texas and eight motion picture distributors. The exhibitor sent identical letters to the distributors (Paramount, RKO, and so on), naming all eight as addressees, and demanding certain restrictions. For example, the manager demanded that the distributors not release their first-run films to theaters charging less than 25 cents admission. After the letters were mailed, the distributors did exactly what the exhibitor had demanded. However, there was no evidence of meetings or other communications among the distributors. The parallel behavior of the distributors, plus the letter, was sufficient for the Supreme Court to find illegal conspiracy. According to the Court:

It taxes credulity to believe that the several distributors would, in the circumstances, have accepted and put into operation with substantial unanimity such far-reaching changes in their business methods without some understanding that all were to join, and we reject as beyond the range of probability that it was the result of mere chance.[36]

In the 1946 American Tobacco decision, the Court seemed to state that the cigarette industry was guilty of conspiracy based solely on its parallel pricing behavior. It observed that "no formal agreement is necessary to constitute an unlawful conspiracy. Often crimes are a matter of inference deduced from the acts of the person accused."[37]

Professor William Nicholls interpreted this decision as "a legal milestone in the social control of oligopoly" because it permitted "the inference of illegal conspiracy from detailed similarity of behavior."[38]

Briefly, the facts in the case that were viewed as particularly significant were as follows:

1. On June 30, 1931, Reynolds announced an increase in its wholesale cigarette price from \$6.40 to \$6.85. The other two major firms, American and Liggett & Myers, followed upward to the same price within twenty-four hours. This increase occurred in the midst of the Great Depression, when leaf prices and labor costs were falling.

2. In November 1932, after a loss of 23 percent of the market to smaller firms selling "economy brands," the Big Three dropped their prices, almost in unison, to \$5.50. This rapidly forced many of the economy brand suppliers out of business.

3. The Big Three bought large amounts of low-grade tobacco, thereby bidding up its price, even though they did not use it for their own cigarettes. It was the type of tobacco used for economy brands.

4. The Big Three declined to participate in leaf tobacco auctions unless buyers from all three companies were present, and they refrained from buying tobacco grades in which the others had a special interest.

These facts were sufficient for the courts to infer the existence of a conspiracy. However, more recent cases do not seem to support the view that parallel oligopoly pricing alone will be found to be illegal.

In the 1954 Theatre Enterprises decision the Supreme Court concluded:

The crucial question is whether respondents' conduct toward petitioner stemmed from independent decision or from an agreement, tacit or express. To be sure, business behavior is admissible circumstantial evidence from which the fact finder may infer agreement.... But this court has never held that proof of parallel business behavior conclusively establishes agreement or, phrased differently, that such behavior itself constitutes a Sherman Act offense. Circumstantial evidence of consciously parallel behavior may have made heavy inroads into the traditional judicial attitude toward conspiracy; but "conscious parallelism" has not yet read conspiracy out of the Sherman Act entirely.[39]

And, in a widely publicized case involving parallel pricing of tetracycline by five pharmaceutical manufacturers, a district court found the firms to be innocent. A key fact in this case was that Pfizer, Cyanamid, Bristol, Upjohn, and Squibb each charged the same price of $30.60 for its brand of tetracycline continuously from November 1953 until July 1960. Much attention was given to the low manufacturing cost of around $3.00, and therefore the extremely high profit margins.

In their defense the companies argued that it would make no sense for any one of them to cut its price. The market demand for tetracycline was price inelastic, so that a general price reduction would not expand the total market. Also, a price cut by one would be matched immediately by the others, making such a tactic self-defeating. Furthermore, entry was barred by virtue of Pfizer's patent; hence, there was no need to lower price to limit entry.[40] Therefore the maintenance of a common price of $30.60 by the five firms did not imply a conspiracy. The Court apparently agreed with this line of argument, concluding that "the parallel pricing among the tetracycline producers, standing alone, does not indicate price fixing."[41]

How can we reconcile these more recent decisions[42] with the earlier Tobacco case? Or, more to the point, how are the courts likely to draw the line in determining what circumstantial evidence warrants an inference of conspiracy? The accumulated precedents have been summarized as "parallelism plus." In the Tobacco case it can be argued that the "plus" could be inferred from the fact that the firms had advance knowledge of impending rival actions that could hardly have been gained without covert communications.

The current rule of law toward oligopoly pricing, without explicit collusion, is that it is perfectly legal. While some economists view oligopolistic markets (autos, steel, aluminum, and others) with concern and urge new legislation to deconcentrate such industries, a majority of economists do not. One reason for this lack of concern is the belief that tacit collusion is unlikely to be effective except in very unusual situations. Oliver Williamson's argument on this issue is perhaps a representative one:

More generally, the argument comes down to this: it is naive to regard oligopolists as shared monopolists in any comprehensive sense—especially if they have differentiated products, have different cost experiences, are differently situated with respect to the market in terms of size, and plainly lack a machinery by which oligopolistic coordination, except of the most primitive sort, is accomplished and enforced. Except, therefore, in highly concentrated industries producing homogeneous products, with nontrivial barriers to entry, and at a mature stage of development, oligopolistic interdependence is unlikely to pose antitrust issues for which dissolution is an appropriate remedy. In the usual oligopoly situation, efforts to achieve collusion are unlikely to be successful or, if they are, will require sufficient explicit communication that normal remedies against price fixing, including injunctions not to collude, will suffice.[43]

The beneficial effect of entry on oligopolistic performance was ignored intentionally in this chapter in order to achieve a more orderly presentation. Clearly, in the absence of entry barriers, any attempt by oligopolists to price noncompetitively would be frustrated by entry. In fact, it can be argued that the threat of entry is sufficient to bring about competitive pricing in the absence of barriers to entry. Given the obvious importance of entry barriers, we will devote a large part of the next chapter to this topic.

Chapter 7 will discuss another set of cooperative practices among firms that can eliminate competition: horizontal and conglomerate mergers. In the following two chapters we examine business behavior that harms competition by inflicting injury on rivals, such as monopolization through predatory techniques.

Summary

This chapter examined a variety of issues related to the behavior of firms in oligopolistic industries. An oligopoly is characterized by having a relatively small number of firms. The low number results in it being appropriate for each firm to take into account the actions and future responses of its competitors in deciding how much to produce or what price to set.

Though there are many models of oligopoly, this chapter focused upon the Cournot model, which specifies that firms make simultaneous output decisions. We chose the Cournot model for several reasons. First, it is widely used by industrial organization economists. Second, many of the qualitative results of the Cournot solution are intuitively plausible and are consistent with some empirical evidence. Finally, a number of the most important results generated by the Cournot model are representative of results from many other oligopoly models. Though the Cournot model is idiosyncratic in specifying that firms choose output and not price, its results are quite general.

It was shown that the Cournot solution entails a price that exceeds the competitive price but falls short of the monopoly price. Firms jointly produce too much relative to the joint-profit maximum. While each firm is individually maximizing its profit at the Cournot solution, firms could raise all of their profits by jointly reducing output and moving price toward the monopoly level.

It is the lure of higher profits that provides firms with the desire to collude in their output decisions. The problem that firms face in colluding is that each can increase its current profit by deviating from the agreed-on output or price. To explain and understand collusive behavior in practice, an infinite horizon extension of the Cournot model was developed. It was found that collusion is consistent with each firm acting to maximize its sum of discounted profits. A firm is deterred from deviating from the collusive outcome by the threat that cheating will induce a breakdown in collusion. While cheating raises current profits, it lowers future profits by inducing greater competition in the future.

With an understanding of how firms can collude, the chapter then turned to exploring antitrust law with respect to collusion or, as it is often called, price fixing. Although price fixing was made illegal with the Sherman Act (1890), the interpretation of this law took place only with key early cases like Addyston Pipe and Steel (1899) and Trenton Potteries (1927). These cases established the per se rule with respect to price fixing. This rule says that price fixing is illegal regardless of the circumstances. There is no allowable defense.

Current law is such that to prove that firms are guilty of price fixing one needs a "smoking gun," for example, a memo from a CEO to his competitor stating what the collusive price is to be. It is insufficient to show that the price decisions of firms are consistent with firms acting collusively. Although firms that collude without overtly communicating result in the same welfare losses as does a cartel that does overtly communicate, only the latter can be prosecuted under Section 1 of the Sherman Act.

Questions and Problems

1. In 1971 the federal government prohibited the advertising of cigarettes on television and radio. Can you explain why this ban on advertising might have raised the profits of cigarette manufacturers? Hint: Use the Advertising Game.

2. The inverse market demand for mineral water is $P = 200 - 10Q$, where Q is total market output and P is the market price. Two firms, A and B, have complete control of the supply of mineral water and both have zero costs.

   a. Find the Cournot solution.

   b. Find an identical output for each firm that maximizes joint profits.

3. Continuing with problem 2, assume that each firm can choose only two outputs—the ones from parts (a) and (b) in Question 2. Denote these outputs q_a and q_b.

   a. Compute the payoff/profit matrix showing the four possible outcomes.

   b. Show that this game has the same basic properties as the Advertising Game. In particular, each firm's optimal output is independent of what the other firm produces.

   Now consider firms playing an infinitely repeated version of this game and consider the following strategy for each firm: (i) produce q_b in period 1, (ii) produce q_b in period t if both firms produced q_b in all preceding periods, and (iii) produce q_a in period t if one or more firms did not produce q_b in some past period. Assume each firm acts to maximize its sum of discounted profits where the discount rate is r.

   c. Find the values for r such that this strategy pair is a Nash equilibrium.

4. Consider a duopoly with firms that offer homogeneous products where each has constant marginal cost of c. Let $D(P)$ denote market demand. Firms make simultaneous price decisions. Letting p_1 and p_2 be the prices of firms 1 and 2, respectively, the demand function of firm 1 is specified to be

$$D_1(p_1, p_2) = \begin{cases} D(p_1) & \text{if } p_1 < p_2 \\ [D(p_1/2] & \text{if } p_1 = p_2 \\ 0 & \text{if } p_1 > p_2 \end{cases}$$

   If firm 1's price is lower than firm 2's price, then all consumers buy from it so that its demand equals market demand. If both firms charge the same price, then they equally split market demand. If firm 1's price is higher than firm 2's price, then all consumers go to firm 2. Firm 2's demand function is similarly defined. Each firm chooses prices to maximize its profit.

   a. Show that both firms pricing at marginal cost is a Nash equilibrium.

   b. Show that any other pair of prices is not a Nash equilibrium.

   Suppose that we limit firms to choosing price equal to c, $2c$, or $3c$.

   c. Compute the payoff/profit matrix.

   d. Derive all of the Nash equilibrium price pairs.

5. In its rivalry with Westinghouse, General Electric instituted a "price protection" plan. This plan stated that if G.E. lowered its price, it would rebate the price difference to its past customers. Show that this plan makes collusion between G.E. and Westinghouse easier. Hint: G.E.'s gain from deviating is lower with the price protection plan in effect.

6. Assume an industry with two firms facing an inverse market demand of $P = 100 - Q$. The product is homogeneous and each firm has a cost function of $600 + 10q + .25q^2$. Assume firms agree to equally share the market.

    a. Derive each firm's demand curve.

    b. Find each firm's preferred price when it faces the demand curve in (a).

    Now assume that firm 1's cost function is instead $25q + q^2$ while firm 2's is as before.

    c. Find each firm's preferred price when it faces the demand curve in (a).

    d. Compute each firm's profit when firm 1's preferred price is chosen. Do the same for firm 2's preferred price. Which price do you think firms would be more likely to agree upon? Why?

    e. Show that neither price maximizes joint profits.

    f. Find the price that maximizes joint profits. Hint: It is where marginal revenue equals both firms' marginal cost.

    g. Would firm 1 find the solution in (f) attractive? If not, would a side payment from firm 2 to firm 1 of $500 make it attractive?

7. In the NCAA case, the Supreme Court held that the rule of reason was applicable even though horizontal price fixing was involved. Explain the rationale.

8. The Addyston Pipe case involved an internal bidding process by the cartel prior to one member's submission of the actual bid. Explain how this worked and whether it is an effective cartel procedure.

9. What are the benefits and costs of the per se rule?

10. What is the law toward parallel business behavior? Assume, for example, that three firms charge identical prices for a product and it is agreed by all observers that the price is unusually high compared to cost. Would this alone constitute a Sherman Act offense? Cite a relevant case to support your answer.

Notes

1. This game is more commonly known as the Prisoners' Dilemma. It is the most widely examined game in game theory. There are literally hundreds of papers that investigate this game theoretically or test it experimentally in the laboratory using human subjects, typically college students. For a discussion of the Prisoners' Dilemma, see Robert Gibbons, *Game Theory for Applied Economists* (Princeton: Princeton University Press, 1992).

2. This game is more commonly known as the Battle of the Sexes; see Gibbons, 1992.

3. In Example 1 the set of players is firms 1 and 2, a strategy is a rate of advertising, a strategy set is {Low, High}, and the payoff functions of the players are

represented by Table 5.1. For an introduction to game theory, see Gibbons, 1992.

4. Augustin Cournot, *Research into the Mathematical Principles of the Theory of Wealth*, English edition of Cournot, 1838, translated by Nathaniel T. Bacon (New York: Kelley, 1960).

5. Because revenue is $R = (100 - Q)Q$, marginal revenue equals the first derivative of $(100 - Q)Q$ with respect to $Q: dR/dQ = 100 - 2Q$. Equating MR and MC, $100 - 2Q = 40$, and solving for Q yields the profit-maximizing output of 30.

6. To derive firm 1's best reply function, find the value of q_1 that maximizes π_1. This is achieved where marginal profit is zero: $\partial \pi_1 / \partial q_1 = 100 - 2q_1 - q_2 - 40 = 0$. Solving this expression for q_1 yields $q_1 = 30 - 0.5q_2$. An analogous method yields firm 2's best reply function. What we are calling a firm's best reply function, Cournot called a firm's "reaction function." In his original treatment, Cournot provided a dynamic story to his static model that entails each firm's reacting to the other's output. However, the use of the term reaction function is a misnomer, as firms make simultaneous output decisions in the Cournot model so that there is no reaction.

7. The profit of firm i is

$$\pi_i = P(q_1 + \cdots + q_n)q_i - C(q_i)$$

The first-order condition is

$$\partial \pi_i / \partial q_i = P'(q_1 + \cdots + q_n)q_i + P(q_1 + \cdots + q_n) - C'(q_i) = 0$$

Adding the first-order condition over n firms gives $nP + qP' - nMC = 0$. Dividing through by n and using $\eta = -(1/P)(P/q)$, one gets $n - 1/\eta - nMC/P = 0$. Rearranging, one gets the expression in (5.9).

8. Heinrich von Stackelberg, *Marktform und Gleichgewicht* (Vienna: Julius Springer, 1934).

9. Joseph Bertrand, "Review of Theorie mathematique de la richesse sociale and Recherches sur les principes mathematiques de la theorie des richesses," *Journal des Savants*, 1883.

10. For a more complete discussion of oligopoly theory, see James W. Friedman, *Oligopoly Theory* (Cambridge: Cambridge University Press, 1983); Jean Tirole, *The Theory of Industrial Organization* (Cambridge, Mass.: MIT Press, 1988); and Carl Shapiro, "Theories of Oligopoly Behavior," in *Handbook of Industrial Organization*, Richard Schmalensee and Robert D. Willig (eds.) (Amsterdam: North-Holland, 1989).

11. It is not necessary that a firm literally live forever but rather that it can potentially live forever. In other words, there cannot be any known date in the future for which firms are certain that they will no longer be around. In fact, firms can be around for quite a long time. Currently, the oldest recorded firm still in existence is the Swedish firm Stora Kopparberg (it means Great Copper Mountain). Documents show that it was in existence in 1288!

12. The present value of receiving $V every period equals V/r, where r is the interest rate and V is received at the end of the period. To show this result, let S denote the present value of this infinite stream:

$$S = \frac{V}{1 + r} + \frac{V}{(1 + r)^2} + \frac{V}{(1 + r)^3} + \cdots$$

Multiply S by $[1/(1+r)]$:

$$\frac{S}{1+r} = \frac{V}{(1+r)^2} + \frac{V}{(1+r)^3} + \frac{V}{(1+r)^4} + \cdots$$

Subtract $S/(1+r)$ from S and one gets

$$\frac{S}{S-1+r} = \frac{V}{1+r}$$

Solving this equation for S, one finds that $S = V/r$.

13. This theory of collusion is due to James W. Friedman, "A Non-cooperative Equilibrium for Supergames," *Review of Economics Studies* 38 (1971): 1–12. Also see James W. Friedman, *Oligopoly and the Theory of Games* (Amsterdam: North-Holland, 1977). The earliest argument that firms would be able to collude successfully is due to Edward H. Chamberlin, *The Theory of Monopolistic Competition* (Cambridge, Mass.: Harvard University Press, 1933).

14. Jeffrey Sonnenfeld and Paul R. Lawrence, "Why Do Companies Succumb to Price Fixing?" *Harvard Business Review* 56 (July–August 1978): 145–57.

15. This discussion is based upon the theory of Edward J. Green and Robert H. Porter, "Noncooperative Collusion under Imperfect Price Information," *Econometrica* 52 (January 1984): 87–100. Also see George J. Stigler, "A Theory of Oligopoly," *Journal of Political Economy* 72 (1964): 44–61.

16. Richard A. Smith, *Corporations in Crisis* (Garden City, N.Y.: Doubleday, 1966).

17. Ibid., p. 132.

18. Valerie Suslow, "Stability in International Cartels: An Empirical Survey," Hoover Institution, Working Papers in Economics E–88–7, February 1988.

19. Robert H. Porter, "A Study of Cartel Stability: The Joint Executive Committee, 1880–1886," *Bell Journal of Economics* 14 (Autumn 1983): 301 14. A related analysis is performed for the steel industry in Jonathan A. Baker, "Identifying Cartel Policing under Uncertainty: The U.S. Steel Industry, 1933–1939," *Journal of Law and Economics* 32 (October 1989): S47–S76.

20. United States v. American Tobacco Co., 221 U.S. 106, 1979 (1911).

21. United States v. Container Corp. of America, 393 U.S. 333, 341 (1969).

22. Oliver E. Williamson, "Economies as an Antitrust Defense: The Welfare Tradeoffs," *American Economic Review*, 58 (1968): 18–36.

23. Robert H. Bork, *The Antitrust Paradox* (New York: Basic Books, 1978), Chapter 5.

24. This is not to say that there are never any circumstances in which agreements to fix reasonable prices produce better economic performance than competition. Possible circumstances might include the avoidance of cutthroat competition in industries with high fixed costs and cyclical demand patterns, and industries that need price cooperation to undertake research and development. However, it appears to be almost a consensus among economists that such cases are rare.

25. United States v. Trans-Missouri Freight Association, 166 U.S. 190 (1897) and United States v. Joint-Traffic Association, 171 U.S. 505 (1898).

26. United States v. Addyston Pipe & Steel Co., 175 U.S. 211 (1899).

27. Bork, The Antitrust Paradox, p. 26.

28. United States v. Trenton Potteries Company et al., 273 U.S. 392, 396–398 (1927).

29. Appalachian Coals, Inc. v. United States, 288 U.S. 344, 360 (1933).

30. Richard A. Posner, *Antitrust: Cases, Economic Notes, and Other Materials* (St. Paul, Minn.: West Publishing Co., 1974), p. 75.

31. United States v. Socony-Vacuum Oil Co. et al., 310 U.S. 150, 218 (1940).

32. Goldfarb v. Virginia State Bar, 421 U.S. 773 (1975).

33. NCAA v. University of Oklahoma et al., 468 U.S. (1984).

34. However, one possible direction that remedies, short of dissolution, might take is illustrated by the U.S. turbogenerator industry. The two rivals, G.E. and Westinghouse, were able to maintain stable prices for many years through the use of a pricing book and a "price protection" plan. Under the "price protection" plan, the sellers guaranteed that any discount on new orders would apply retroactively on all orders taken in the past six months. The effect of the plan was to make the incentive to "cheat" through secret price cuts much less. In 1977 the Justice Department got the companies to agree to drop the price protection plan; the hope is, of course, that price competition will be stimulated.

35. Richard A. Posner, *Antitrust Law: An Economic Perspective* (Chicago: University of Chicago Press, 1976), p. 40.

36. Interstate Circuit, Inc., et al., v. United States, 306 U.S. 208, 223 (1939).

37. American Tobacco Company et al. v. United States, 328 U.S. 781, 809 (1946).

38. William H. Nicholls, "The Tobacco Case of 1946," *American Economic Review*, May 1949.

39. Theatre Enterprises, Inc. v. Paramount Film Distributing Corp. et al., 346 U.S. 537 (1954).

40. Pfizer had licensed the other four firms to sell tetracycline. How this came about is a complicated story itself, but it is a separate issue and need not be described here.

41. Charles Pfizer & Company, Inc. et al. v. United States, 367. Supp. 91 (1973).

42. A case decided in 1984 by the U.S. Court of Appeals is consistent with the recent decisions in finding for the firms. Unlike the cases discussed above in which the legal issue was one of inferring conspiracy from parallel behavior, the FTC charged the firms with competing unfairly under the FTC Act. The charge was that the firms engaged in "facilitating practices" that made tacit collusion easier to achieve. The facilitating practices included quoting prices on a uniform delivered price basis, announcing price changes to customers well in advance of the effective date, and including a "price protection plan" similar to the one described in note 33. For a study of this case, see George A. Hay, "Practices that Facilitate Cooperation: The Ethyl Case," in John E. Kwoka, Jr., and Lawrence J. White (eds.), *The Antitrust Revolution* (Glenview, Ill.: Scott, Foresman, 1989).

43. Oliver E. Williamson, *Markets and Hierarchies: Analysis and Antitrust Implications* (New York: The Free Press, 1975), p. 246.

Appendix A

Game Theory: Formal Definitions

The strategic (or normal) form of a game is defined by three elements: (1) the set of players, (2) the strategy sets of the players, and (3) the payoff functions of the players. The set of players comprises those individuals making decisions. Let n

denote the number of players. The strategy of a player is a decision rule that prescribes how he should play over the course of the game. All of the strategizing by a player takes place with regards to his selection of a strategy. The strategy set of player i, which we denote S_i, comprises all feasible strategies. A player is constrained to choosing a strategy from his strategy set. The payoff function of player i gives player i's utility (or payoff) as a function of all players' strategies. An n-tuple of strategies, one for each player, is referred to as a strategy profile. Player i's payoff function is denoted $V_i(\cdot)$, where $V_i(s_1, \ldots, s_n)$ is the payoff to player i when player 1's strategy is s_1, player 2's is $s_2, \ldots$, player n's strategy is s_n.

A strategy profile $(s_1^*, \ldots s_n^*)$ is a Nash equilibrium if and only if each player's strategy maximizes his payoff given the other players' strategies. Formally,

$$V_i(s_1^*, \ldots s_n^*) \geq V_i(s_1^*, \ldots s_{i-1}^*, s_i, s_{i+1}^*, \ldots, s_n^*)$$

for all s_i in S_i and for all $i = 1, \ldots, n$.

Appendix B

The Addyston Pipe Case*

This case resulted from a price-fixing suit brought in 1896 against six cast iron pipe manufacturers located in Alabama, Kentucky, Tennessee, and Ohio. The industry was characterized by high fixed costs, fluctuating demand, high transportation costs, and product homogeneity. The main source of demand for cast iron pipe was from municipalities and utility companies for the distribution of water and gas.

The Addyston group, as the six firms were known, was in a geographical location that gave it a substantial transportation advantage over manufacturers in New Jersey, Pennsylvania, and New York (the production center of the United States at that time).

The six firms and their capacities in tons per year were:

	Capacity
Addyston Pipe and Steel, Cincinnati, Ohio	45,000
Dennis Long and Co., Louisville, Ky.	45,000
Howard-Harrison Iron Co., Bessemer, Ala.	45,000
Anniston Pipe and Foundary, Anniston, Ala.	30,000
South Pittsburg Pipe Works, South Pittsburg, Tenn.	15,000
Chattanooga Foundary, Chattanooga, Tenn.	40,000
Total	220,000

During the early 1890s a recession severely lowered the demand for pipe and stimulated firms to seek ways to restrict price competition. For example, in 1896 the Addyston group operated at only 45 percent capacity even though recovery had begun.

The first agreement among all six firms was made in 1894 and the following plan was adopted. Two types of territory were defined: "reserved" and "pay." Reserved territory consisted of cities whose business was assigned to certain

---

* This appendix draws heavily on Almarin Phillips, *Market Structure, Organization and Performance* (Cambridge, Mass.: Harvard University Press, 1962), Chapter 5.

member firms. Each firm generally reserved the cities to which it was closer than the others. Each firm was required to pay a "bonus" of $2 per ton to the cartel for all shipments to the reserved cities.

Pay territory was defined as all other cities west of New York and Pennsylvania and south of Virginia. The members of the Southern Associated Pipe Works (the official name of the cartel) could bid for jobs in pay territory in competition with other members, but had to pay a preestablished bonus of $1 to $4 per ton to the association. The bonus set for a particular city depended upon the cartel's locational advantage over outsiders.

Bonuses at the end of the year were to be distributed by the association to its members on the basis of a complicated formula, closely related to capacity. The following description of the formula is taken from the minutes of the association, which were placed in evidence at the trial:

> First. The bonuses on the first 90,000 tons of pipe secured in any territory, 16 and smaller, shall be divided equally among six shops. Second. The bonuses on the next 75,000 tons, 30 and smaller sizes, to be divided among five shops, South Pittsburg not participating. Third. The bonuses on the next 40,000 tons, 36 and smaller sizes, to be divided among four shops, Anniston and South Pittsburg not participating. Fourth. The bonuses on the next 15,000 tons, consisting of all sizes of pipe, shall be divided among three shops, Chattanooga, South Pittsburg, and Anniston not participating. The above division is based on the following tonnage of capacity: South Pittsburg, 15,000 tons; Anniston, 30,000 tons; Chattanooga, 40,000 tons; Bessemer, 45,000 tons; Louisville, 45,000 tons; Cincinnati, 45,000 tons. When the 220,000 tons have been made and shipped, and the bonuses divided as hereinafter provided, the auditor shall set aside into a reserve fund all bonuses arising from the excess of shipments over 220,000 tons, and shall divide the same at the end of the year among the respective companies according to the percentage of the excess of tonnage they may have shipped (of the sizes made by them) either in pay or free territory. It is also the intention of this proposition that the bonuses on all pipe larger than 36 inches in diameter shall be divided equally between the Addyston Pipe & Steel Company, Dennis Long & Co., and the Howard-Harrison Company.

Unfortunately for the cartel, the plan employing preestablished bonuses in pay territory did not work very well. As a result, the association decided to revise its agreement in an ingenious manner. The following is taken from a resolution passed May 27, 1895:

> Whereas, the system now in operation in this association of having a fixed bonus on the several states has not, in its operation, resulted in the advancement in the prices of pipe, as was anticipated, except in reserved cities, and some further action is imperatively necessary in order to accomplish the ends for which this association was formed: Therefore, be it resolved, that from and after the first day of June, that all competition on the pipe lettings shall take place among the various pipe shops prior to the said letting. To accomplish this purpose it is proposed that the six competitive shops have a representative board located at some central city, to whom all inquiries for pipe shall be referred, and said board shall fix the price at which said pipe shall be sold, and bids taken from the respective shops for the privilege of handling the order, and the party securing the order shall have the protection of all the other shops.

In short, the cartel would decide as a group what price would probably win a particular job. For example, Omaha requested bids for 519 pieces of 20-inch pipe and the cartel estimated that $23.40 per ton was just below what an outsider could bid. Then Bessemer bid the highest bonus of $8 per ton in the internal auction and won the right to bid $23.40 to Omaha. Other members then submitted bids to Omaha at prices greater than $23.40 to give the appearance of competition. This plan certainly moved the cartel closer to joint profit maximization.

The degree of success under the new plan is hard to judge since the cartel was discovered the following year. A Philadelphia pipe manufacturer underbid the cartel on an Atlanta job. The city rejected all bids because they were too high. Following this, a secretary of the cartel association agreed to make public the cartel's operations in return for a share of the damages. A suit was brought by the government in district court. The government lost and appealed the decision. The Court of Appeals found for the government, and the opinion was written by Judge William Howard Taft.

We turn now to Judge Taft's opinion, parts of which are reproduced below. Note the distinction Taft makes between "naked" and "ancillary" restraints. Naked restraints are those whose only effect is to eliminate competition; ancillary restraints are those where the elimination of competition is subordinate to other ends that may be socially beneficial. These concepts correspond to the economic analysis of the per se rule and the rule of reason discussed in the chapter. That is, naked restraints should fall in the per se category; ancillary restraints should be subject to the rule of reason.

The Opinion of the Court

"Two questions are presented in this case for our decision: First. Was the association of the defendants a contract, combination, or conspiracy in restraint of trade, as the terms are to be understood in the act? Second. Was the trade thus restrained trade between the states?

The argument for defendants is that their contract of association was not, and could not be, a monopoly, because their aggregate tonnage capacity did not exceed 30 percent of the total tonnage capacity of the country; that the restraints upon the members of the association, if restraints they could be called, did not embrace all the states, and were not unlimited in space; that such partial restraints were justified and upheld at common law if reasonable, and only proportioned to the necessary protection of the parties; that in this case the partial restraints were reasonable, because without them each member would be subjected to ruinous competition by the other, and did not exceed in degree of stringency or scope what was necessary to protect the parties in securing prices for their product that were fair and reasonable to themselves and the public; that competition was not stifled by the association because the prices fixed by it had to be fixed with reference to the very active competition of pipe companies which were not members of the association, and which had more than double the defendants' capacity; that in this way the association only modified and restrained the evils of ruinous competition, while the public had all the benefit from competition which public policy demanded.

For the reasons given, then, covenants in partial restraint of trade are generally upheld as valid when they are agreements (1) by the seller of property or business not to compete with the buyer in such a way as to derogate from the value of the property or business sold; (2) by a retiring partner not to compete with the firm; (3) by a partner pending the partnerships not to do anything to interfere, by competition or otherwise, with the business of the firm; (4) by the buyer of property not to use the same in competition with the business retained by the seller; and (5) by an assistant, servant, or agent not to compete with his master or employer after the expiration of his time of service. Before such agreements are upheld, however, the court must find that the restraints attempted thereby are reasonably necessary (1, 2, and 3) to the enjoyment by the buyer of the property, good will, or interest in the partnership bought; or (4) to the legitimate ends of the existing partnership; or (5) to the prevention of possible injury to the business of the seller from use by the buyer of the thing sold; or (6) to protection from the danger of loss to the employer's business caused by the unjust use on the part of the employee of the confidential knowledge acquired in such business.

This very statement of the rule implies that the contract must be one in which there is a main purpose, to which the covenant in restraint of trade is merely ancillary. The covenant is inserted only to protect one of the parties from the injury which, in the execution of the contract or enjoyment of its fruits, he may suffer from the unrestrained competition of the other. The main purpose of the contract suggests the measure of protection needed, and furnishes a sufficiently uniform standard by which the validity of such restraints may be judicially determined. In such a case, if the restraint exceeds the necessity presented by the main purpose of the contract, it is void for two reasons: First, because it oppresses the covenantor, without any corresponding benefit to the covenantee; and, second, because it tends toward a monopoly. But where the sole object of both parties in making the contract as expressed therein is merely to restrain competition, and enhance or maintain prices, it would seem that there was nothing to justify or excuse the restraint, that it would necessarily have a tendency to monopoly, and therefore would be void. In such a case there is no measure of what is necessary to the protection of either party, except the vague and varying opinion of judges as to how much, on principles of political economy, men ought to be allowed to restrain competition. There is in such contracts no main lawful purpose, to subserve which partial restraint is permitted, and by which its reasonableness is measured, but the sole object is to restrain trade in order to avoid the competition which it has always been the policy of the common law to foster.

Upon this review of the law and the authorities, we can have no doubt that the association of the defendants, however reasonable the prices they fixed, however great the competition they had to encounter, and however great the necessity for curbing themselves by joint agreement from committing financial suicide by ill-advised competition, was void at common law, because in restraint of trade, and tending to a monopoly. But the facts of the case do not require us to go so far as this, for they show that the attempted justification of this association on the grounds stated is without foundation.

The defendants, being manufacturers and vendors of cast-iron pipe, entered into a combination to raise the prices for pipe for all the states west and south of New York, Pennsylvania, and Virginia, constituting considerably more than three-quarters of the territory of the United States and significantly called by the associates 'pay territory.'

The freight upon cast-iron pipe amounts to a considerable percentage of the price at which manufacturers can deliver it at any great distance from the place of manufacture. Within the margin of the freight per ton which Eastern manufacturers would have to pay to deliver pipe in pay territory, the defendants, by controlling two-thirds of the output in pay territory, were practically able to fix prices. The competition of the Ohio and Michigan mills, of course, somewhat affected their power in this respect in the northern part of the pay territory; but, the further south the place of delivery was to be, the more complete the monopoly over the trade which the defendants were able to exercise, within the limit already described. Much evidence is adduced upon affidavit to prove that defendants had no power arbitrarily to fix prices, and that they were always obliged to meet competition. To the extent that they could not impose prices on the public in excess of the cost price of pipe with freight from the Atlantic seaboard added, this is true; but, within that limit, they could fix prices as they chose. The most cogent evidence that they had this power is the fact, everywhere apparent in the record, that they exercised it. The details of the way in which it was maintained are somewhat obscured by the manner in which the proof was adduced in the court below, upon affidavits solely, and without the clarifying effect of cross-examination, but quite enough appears to leave no doubt of the ultimate fact. The defendants were, by their combination, therefore able to deprive the public in a large territory of the advantages otherwise accruing to them from the proximity of defendants' pipe factories, and, by keeping prices just low enough to prevent competition by Eastern manufacturers, to compel the public to pay an increase over what the price would have been, if fixed by competition between defendants, nearly equal to the advantage in freight rates enjoyed by defendants over Eastern competitors. The defendants acquired this power by voluntarily agreeing to sell only at prices fixed by the committee, and by allowing the highest bidder at the secret "auction pool" to become the lowest bidder of them at the public letting. Now, the restraint thus imposed on themselves was only partial. It did not cover the United States. There was not a complete monopoly. It was tempered by the fear of competition, and it affected only a part of the price. But this certainly does not take the contract of association out of the annulling effect of the rule against monopolies.

It has been earnestly pressed upon us that the prices at which the cast-iron pipe was sold in pay territory were reasonable. A great many affidavits or purchasers of pipe in pay territory, all drawn by the same hand or from the same model, are produced, in which the affiants say that, in their opinion, the prices at which pipe has been sold by defendants have been reasonable. We do not think the issue an important one, because, as already stated, we do not think that at common law there is any question of reasonableness open to the courts with reference to such a contract. Its tendency was certainly to give defendants the power to charge unreasonable prices, had they chosen to do so. But, if it were important, we should unhesitatingly find that the prices charged in the instances which were in evidence were unreasonable.

Another aspect of this contract of association brings it within the terms used in the statute, "a conspiracy in restraint of trade." A conspiracy is a combination of two or more persons to accomplish an unlawful end by lawful means or a lawful end by unlawful means. In the answer of the defendants, it is averred that the chief way in which cast-iron pipe is sold is by contracts let after competitive bidding invited by the intending purchaser. It would have much interfered with the smooth working of defendants' association had its existence and purposes become known to the public. A part of the plan was a deliberate attempt to create in the minds of the members of the public inviting bids the belief that competition existed between the defendants. Several of the defendants were required to bid at every letting and to make their bids at such prices that the one already selected to obtain the contract should have the lowest bid. It is well settled that an agreement between intending bidders at a public auction or a public letting not to bid against each other, and thus to prevent competition, is a fraud upon the intending vendor or contractor, and the ensuing sale or contract will be set aside.

The largest purchasers of pipe are municipal corporations, and they are by law required to solicit bids for the sale of pipe in order that the public may get the benefit of competition. One of the means adopted by the defendants in this plan of combination was this illegal and fraudulent effort to evade such laws and to deceive intending purchasers. No matter what the excuse for the combination by defendants in restraint of trade, the illegality of the means stamps it as a conspiracy and so brings it within the term of the federal statute."

As an interesting footnote to this case, in May 1898, after Taft's decision in February, four of the cartel members merged to form the American Pipe and Foundry Company. The following year, American Pipe combined with the remaining two cartel members (along with other companies) and became known as the United States Cast Iron Pipe and Foundry Company. The new company had a total capacity of 450,000 tons per year, which was about 75 percent of the national market. (We might note that today such a "merger-to-monopoly" would not be allowed under antitrust law, although it was at that time.)

6 Market Structure and Strategic Competition

There are two key sources of competition in markets—existing firms and potential entrants. Chapter 5 focused on the behavior of existing firms while taking their number as being exogenously determined. This chapter extends this analysis in two important ways. First, we consider the determinants of the number of sellers. The factors analyzed are scale economies and entry conditions. Second, we consider the role of potential competition—specifically, the effect that the threat of entry has on the price-cost margin.

In the section on market structure, our discussion begins with the problem of measuring the concentration of an industry. The analysis then turns to investigating how scale economies and entry conditions affect actual and potential competition. In the discussion of dominant firm theory, we begin an exploration of how established firms can influence the future competitiveness of the industry. Although entry conditions are treated as being exogenous to firms in the section on market structure, the "Strategic Competition" section explores how established firms can affect entry conditions and thereby deter entry.

Market Structure

This section investigates two key elements of market structure—concentration and entry conditions. Our discussion of concentration is a continuation of our coverage of oligopoly theory and collusion in that its focus is the role of actual competition. We then investigate the determinants of concentration by considering scale economies and entry conditions. Our discussion of entry conditions is concerned with understanding their role in determining the extent of actual competition (that is, the number of firms) and the extent of potential competition. The discussion of entry conditions in this section presumes that they are exogenously determined. Later in this chapter, we will investigate ways in which existing firms can influence entry decisions.

Concentration

In our analysis of oligopoly theory in the preceding chapter, we assumed that firms were identical—having the same products and same cost functions. As long as the industry is symmetric, a single number—the number of sellers—accurately measures market concentration. While the abstract world is often specified to be symmetric in order to reduce the complexity of the analysis, in the real world there is typically great heterogeneity among firms. The implication of firms having different products and cost functions is that firms have very different market shares. As a result, a simple count of the number of firms can be a very misleading measure of the degree of concentration.

One of the traditional tasks in industrial organization has been to develop a statistic that allows a single number to measure reasonably the concentration of an industry. In constructing a useful index of concentration, one first needs to understand the purpose that a concentration index is to serve. From a welfare and antitrust perspective, a concentration index should measure the ability of firms to raise price above the competitive level. A higher value for a concentration index should indicate a higher price-cost margin or a higher likelihood of firms being able to collude successfully. Note that a concentration index is exclusively concerned with actual competition and ignores potential competition. For this reason, a concentration index cannot fully assess the competitiveness of a particular industry. Some other information will have to be provided so as to take account of the degree of potential competition.

Definition of the Market

To measure concentration, one must first define the limits of the market. Computation of firm market shares requires knowledge of the total sales of the market which itself requires defining which products sold to which consumers constitutes a well-defined market.

The issue of how markets should be defined from the viewpoint of economic theory has never been answered definitively. Economic theorists generally take the market as a given. However, when one engages in empirical work, it becomes necessary to make difficult judgments about what products and sellers constitute the market. For example, the outcome of one famous antitrust case hinged upon whether the relevant market was cellophane, or whether the correct market was "flexible wrapping materials" (that is, Saran, aluminum foil, brown paper, cellophane, and the like).[1]

Most economists agree that the ideal market definition must take into account substitution possibilities in both consumption and production. George Stigler has expressed this as follows:

An industry should embrace the maximum geographical area and the maximum variety of productive activities in which there is a strong long-run substitution. If buyers can shift on a large scale from product or area B to A, then the two should be combined. If producers can shift on a large scale from B to A, again they should be combined.

Economists usually state this in an alternative form: All products or enterprises with large long-run cross-elasticities of either supply or demand should be combined into a single industry.[2]

A further difficulty on the supply side is the distinction between "substitution" and "new entry." That is, where does the market stop and potential entry begin? Consider the airline industry. Should the market be, say, the "New York-Los Angeles market" or the entire United States? If the market is the New York-Los Angeles route, concentration would be relatively high, given this tight market definition. Entry would be "easy," though, as airlines serving Miami-San Francisco, for example, could easily switch. Alternatively, if the market is defined as the entire United States, concentration would be low but might include some airlines not well suited for the New York-Los Angeles route, for instance with aircraft designed for short hops and a small volume of traffic.

Of course, some definition must be followed. No harm is done if it is recognized that what is important is the competitive constraint on potential monopoly pricing. That is, one would get the same answer in analyzing pricing on the New York-Los Angeles route by viewing it either as a highly concentrated market with easy entry, or as part of the unconcentrated United States market.

F. M. Scherer has offered the following proposal: "At the risk of being somewhat arbitrary, we should probably draw the line to include as substitutes on the production side only existing capacity that can be shifted in the short run, i.e., without significant new investment in plant, equipment, and worker training."[3] A similar, though more specific, definition has been put forth by the Justice Department. It will be discussed in Chapter 7, where we examine merger cases.

Concentration Ratio

Although economists have devised many indices to measure concentration, the most widely used measure is the concentration ratio. The m-firm concentration ratio is simply the share of total industry sales accounted for by the m largest firms.

A fundamental problem with concentration ratios is that they describe only one point on the entire size distribution of sellers. Consider the size distributions of two hypothetical industries, as shown in Table 6.1. Clearly, industries X and Y have the same four-firm concentration ratio, namely, 80 percent. However, noting the other information in Table 6.1, most economists would regard the two industries as likely to exhibit quite different patterns of competitive behavior. Suppose, now, that we calculate the three-firm ratios: Industry Y is now seen to be "more concentrated" (75 percent versus only 60 percent for Industry X). The basic problem is simply that this type of measure wastes relevant data. On the other hand, the concentration ratio is superior to a simple count of sellers.

Table 6.1
Percentage of Sales Accounted for by the Five Leading Firms in Industries X and Y

Firm	Industry X	Industry Y
1	20	60
2	20	10
3	20	5
4	20	5
5	20	5
Total	100	85

To pursue this point, consider the size distributions of the two industries shown as concentration curves in Figure 6.1. The height of a concentration curve above any integer n on the horizontal axis measures the percentage of the industry's total sales accounted for by the largest firms. In general, the curves will rise from left to right, and at a continuously diminishing rate. In the limiting case of identical shares, such as in Industry X, the curve becomes a straight line. The curves reach their maximum height of 100 percent where n equals the total number of firms in the industry. If the curve of Industry Y is everywhere above the curve of X, then Y is more concentrated than X. However, when the curves intersect, as they do in Figure 6.1, it is impossible to state which is the "more concentrated" industry, unless we devise a new definition.

The most widely available concentration ratios are those compiled by the U.S. Bureau of the Census. Ideally, these ratios should refer to industries that are defined meaningfully from the viewpoint of economic theory. However, the census classifications of industries were developed over a period of years "to serve the general purposes of the census and other government statistics" and were "not designed to establish categories necessarily denoting coherent or relevant markets in the true competitive sense, or to provide a basis for measuring market power."[4] The census frequently includes products that are not close substitutes, and it sometimes excludes products that are close substitutes. An example of the latter is the existence of two separate "industries" for beet sugar and cane sugar. The census ignores both regional markets (for example, all bakeries are combined into a single national market) and foreign competition (steel imports are excluded from the steel industry).

Because we will refer occasionally to studies that have used census concentration ratios, it should be helpful to provide a brief description of their procedure for classifying industries. Their classification system (known as the Standard Industrial Classification, or SIC) makes use of a series of numbers in which each succeeding digit represents a finer degree of classification. Thus, in the manufacturing sector of the economy,

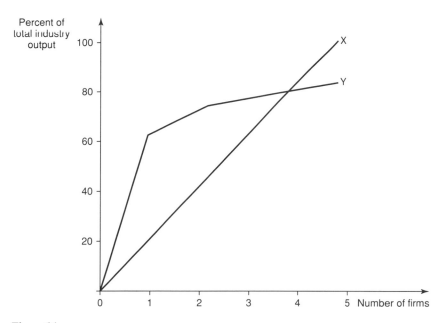

Figure 6.1
Concentration Curves for Industries X and Y

there are only 20 "two-digit" industries. An example is industry 20, the "food and kindred products" industry. Within this two-digit industry there are nine three-digit industries, such as industry 201, the "meat products" industry. Within this three-digit industry there are three four-digit industries, such as industry 2015, "poultry dressing plants." The Census Bureau has computed concentration ratios for the top four, eight, and twenty firms for some 450 four-digit industries; these are the ratios most often used in statistical studies of industrial organization.

In Table 6.2 we show four-firm concentration ratios for selected four-digit industries in 1987. The industries were chosen to cover a wide range of concentration ratios. It is immediately apparent that the theoretical market structures of perfect competition and monopoly do not provide useful categories for our real-world industries. Nor is it clear which industries should be classified as oligopolistic or competitive. Of course, most would agree that the industries at the top of Table 6.2 are oligopolies, but how far down the list should we descend?

HHI

In 1992, the Antitrust Division of the Justice Department and the Federal Trade Commission issued new guidelines concerning their policy toward mergers.[5] These guidelines are expressed in terms of the

Table 6.2
Concentration of Selected Industries, 1987

Industry	CR4	HHI
Chewing Gum	96	NA
Cigarettes	92	NA
Motor Vehicles and Car Bodies	90	NA
Cereal Breakfast Foods	87	2207
Greeting Cards	85	2830
Household Refrigerators and Freezers	85	2256
Turbines and Turbine Generators	80	2162
Glass Containers	78	2126
Photographic Equipment and Supplies	77	2241
Tires and Inner Tubes	69	1897
Distilled and Blended Liquors	53	883
Farm Machinery and Equipment	45	802
Blast Furnaces and Steel Mills	44	607
Paper Mills	33	432
Petroleum Refining	32	435
Meat Packing Plant Products	32	403
Pharmaceutical Preparations	22	273
Wood Kitchen Cabinets	16	91
Women's Dresses	6	24

CR4 = four-firm concentration ratio
HHI = Herfindahl-Hirschman Index for the fifty largest companies
Source: Census of Manufactures: Concentration Ratios in Manufacturing: 1987 (February 1992).

HHI (named for its inventors, O. C. Herfindahl and A. O. Hirschman). It is then important to define and discuss the HHI.

The HHI has the advantage of incorporating more information about the size distribution of sellers than the simple concentration ratio does. If we let s_i denote firm i's percentage of total industry sales (that is, its market share), then the HHI is defined as

$$HHI = (100s_1)^2 + (100s_2)^2 + \cdots + (100s_n)^2$$

where n equals the number of firms. The HHI is the weighted average slope of the concentration curve (recall from Figure 6.1 that industries with steeper sloped curves are more concentrated). The weight for the slope of each segment of the curve is the corresponding s_i for that segment.

If an industry consists of a single seller, then HHI attains its maximum value of 10,000. The index declines with increases in the number of firms and increases with rising inequality among a given number of firms. Hence, referring to our example in Table 6.1, while assuming firms 6, 7, and 8 in Industry Y each have 5 percent of the market, we can calculate their HHIs:

Industry X: $HHI = 20^2 + 20^2 + 20^2 + 20^2 + 20^2 = 2000$

Industry Y: $HHI = 60^2 + 10^2 + 5^2 + 5^2 + 5^2 + 5^2 + 5^2 + 5^2 = 3850$

Thus the HHI would indicate that Industry X would be more likely to exhibit competitive behavior.

The Justice Department regards an HHI of 1000 as critical. That is, if a merger leaves the HHI for the industry at 1000 or less, the merger is unlikely to be challenged as violating antitrust laws. Note the HHIs in Table 6.2.

One of the attractive features of the HHI is that it has foundations in oligopoly theory. Suppose that firms have homogeneous products and engage in Cournot competition. Let us allow firms to have different cost functions. Thus, c_i will denote the (constant) marginal cost of firm i, where $i = 1, \ldots, n$. One can show that the Cournot solution has a firm's market share being negatively related to its marginal cost. The lower firm i's marginal cost, the higher is its profit-maximizing output and thus the higher is firm i's share of the market. The important result is that the HHI is directly related to a weighted average of firms' price-cost margins from the Cournot solution:

$$s_1 \left(\frac{P^c - c_1}{P^c} \right) + s_2 \left(\frac{P^c - c_2}{P^c} \right) + \cdots + s_n \left(\frac{P^c - c_n}{P^c} \right) = \frac{HHI}{\eta}$$

where P^c is the Cournot price, s_i is firm i's market share, and η is the market demand elasticity. The higher is the HHI, the higher is the industry price-cost margin.[6]

Using Concentration Indices in Antitrust Policy

Empirical evidence has shown that a high concentration index for an industry is signal of a high price-cost margin.[7] Thus the relationship is true not only in theory but also in practice.

An important question is, What policy implications are one to draw? In answering this question, one must have a theory for why concentration and price-cost margins (or profits) are positively related. Traditionally, there have been two main hypotheses. The *collusion hypothesis* states that the more concentrated an industry is, the less competitive are firms and thus the higher is the price-cost margin. This finding we established in the preceding chapter. For the Cournot solution, the smaller the number of firms (and thus the greater the concentration), the higher is the price-cost margin. In addition, collusion was found to be easier as the number of firms decreases. A reasonable policy implication from this theory is that one should break up highly concentrated industries.

In contrast to the collusion hypothesis, Harold Demsetz's *differential efficiency hypothesis* (or superior efficiency hypothesis) argues that high concentration does not cause a high price-cost margin. Instead, high concentration tends to be observed with high price-cost margins. The argument is as follows. In some industries there are apt to be a few firms that have a differential advantage over their competitors. This advantage could be due to lower cost or a better product. In those industries these superior firms will tend to dominate the market—so that concentration is high—and be able to price considerably above cost—so that the price-cost margin and industry profit are high. This argument underlies the relationship between the HHI and the industry price-cost margin for the Cournot solution. When firms have different costs, the result is skewed market shares and a high HHI. While the differential efficiency hypothesis is really a statement about firms—those firms with high market share will tend to have a high price-cost margin—it also implies that at the industry level, after aggregating individual firm data, one will tend to observe high industry concentration with high industry price-cost margins. According to the differential efficiency hypothesis, one does not want to go around breaking up highly concentrated industries. To do so would be to penalize firms for being superior and thereby deter them from doing what we want them to do—provide better products at a lower cost.

Note that the prediction of the differential efficiency hypothesis is that firms with high market shares will tend to have high price-cost margins and profits. An implication of this relationship is that industry profit will tend to be positively related to industry concentration. In contrast, the collusion hypothesis predicts that higher concentration causes higher price-cost margins and profits. A number of empirical tests of these two competing hypotheses have been performed. The empirical evidence strongly supports the differential efficiency hypothesis.[8] The evidence shows that a firm's profit is strongly positively associated with its market share. There is typically a weak positive association between industry profit and concentration.

Scale Economies

Perhaps the most important explanation of why some industries are more concentrated than others is the magnitude of economies of scale relative to total market demand. In other words, what fraction of the market's output is needed by a firm to achieve minimum long-run average cost? For example, the automobile industry depends on large-scale production to achieve low unit costs, and there is "room" for only a small number of such large-scale firms in the market. On the other hand, gasoline service stations do not gain cost advantages significantly beyond a certain volume, and comprise a relatively unconcentrated industry.

The specialization of labor and equipment that can be achieved as a result of larger size is an important source of economies of scale. The classic example is again automobile assembly. As the rate of output increases, workers can specialize more narrowly and become highly efficient in a number of tasks. Rather than install a complete engine, a worker might be responsible for attaching one small part. Similarly, specialized automatic screw machines might be used in producing ball bearings rather than general-purpose lathes, if the output is sufficiently large.

Turning to the sources of diseconomies of scale, we find only one major explanation in the economics literature. This explanation is that as a firm increases in size, it becomes more and more difficult for the top management to exercise control over the entire organization. Thus this "control loss," as the number of layers of management increases, is a possible source of diseconomies of scale.

However, according to some experts, this problem can be partially mitigated by a decentralized multidivisional form of corporate organization. That is, by delegating authority and responsibility to operating divisions (such as General Motors did in creating Chevrolet, Buick, Oldsmobile, Pontiac, and so on), control loss can be largely offset.

While scale economies have been measured in various ways, many economists consider that the best way is to use engineering cost estimates. This is because engineers' cost estimates usually embody assumptions quite similar to those underlying the long-run average cost curve of economic theory. An engineering study can hold fixed relative factor prices, product homogeneity, location, technology, volume, and so forth, thereby isolating the effect of increases in the rate of output on cost.

The results of one such study—which estimated both efficient plant and efficient firm sizes—are given in Table 6.3. This 1975 study, conducted by Scherer, Beckenstein, Kaufer, and Murphy, obtained its estimates by interviews with technically qualified personnel working in the industries studied.[9] To obtain the estimates for their twelve industries, they interviewed personnel in 125 companies in six countries.

If we take the figures in Table 6.3 at face value, the second column (which gives "efficient firm" size as a percentage of the total market) indicates that scale economies are not particularly severe in most of the

Table 6.3
Minimum Efficient Scale of Plants and Firms as Percentage of U.S. National Market, 1967

Industry	Minimum Efficient Scale Plant as Percentage of Total Market	Minimum Efficient Scale Firm as Percentage of Total Market	Four-Firm Concentration Ratio
Beer Brewing	3.4	10–14	40
Cigarettes	6.6	6–12	81
Cotton Synthetic Fabrics	0.2	1	36
Paints, Varnishes, and Lacquers	1.4	1.4	22
Petroleum Refining	1.9	4–6	33
Shoes, Except Rubber	0.2	1	26
Glass Containers	1.5	4–6	60
Cement	1.7	2	29
Steel Works	2.6	3	48
Ball and Roller Bearings	1.4	4–7	54
Refrigerators and Freezers	14.1	14–20	73
Storage Batteries	1.9	2	61

Source: F. M. Scherer, A. Beckenstein, E. Kaufer, and R. D. Murphy, *The Economies of Multi-Plant Operation: An International Comparison Study* (Cambridge, Mass.: Harvard University Press, 1975).

twelve industries. Only in the refrigerator and freezer industry is as much as 20 percent of the market necessary for efficiency. The third column indicates that actual market shares of the leading firms are generally considerably greater than necessary to attain efficient size. For example, the average market share of the four leading firms in the storage battery industry is about 15 percent; yet the "efficient firm" market share is only 2 percent.

Two other studies using the engineering approach, one by Bain[10] and the other by Pratten,[11] found similar results for different samples of industries. That is to say, in only a few industries in each study did the estimated efficient shares approximate the actual shares of the leading firms.

Needless to say, the validity of such studies of economies of scale is not universally accepted. John McGee, for example, argues that there are some serious problems:

Such estimates cannot be forward-looking and are stale when done. They must implicitly embody some unspecified but homogeneous quality of production management, organization, and control, and must assume that some unspecified but given quality of overall management is imagined both to choose and to use the hypothetical physical plant that someone constructed on paper. Also, business problems are not solely engineering problems—which partly explains why not all successful businesses are run by practicing engineers.[12]

An extensive discussion of the various techniques used to estimate economies of scale—such as engineering cost estimates or econometric analysis of accounting data—is contained in a book by Scherer.[13] Unfortunately, space limitations prevent further discussion of this important topic here.

Entry Conditions

Thus far in our analysis, we have measured the competitiveness of an industry by the number of firms or some other measure of concentration. An equally important factor, however, is the ease with which entry can take place. Entry conditions are important for two reasons. First, the number of active firms is partially determined by the cost of entry as well as other factors like economies of scale. Thus, entry conditions play an important role in determining concentration. Second, entry conditions determine the extent of potential competition. It is generally believed that a credible threat of entry will induce active firms to compete vigorously. If they do not, so that the industry has a high price-cost margin, entry will take place and drive price down. According to this argument, entry conditions are then important because the cost or difficulty of entry affects the effectiveness of potential competition. Later in this chapter, we will examine the proposition that when entry is relatively costless, active firms must compete vigorously.

Defining the relevant set of entry conditions has proven to be a difficult and controversial subject in industrial organization. Nevertheless, here are some questions one needs to ask in order to assess entry conditions. How many prospective firms have the ability to enter in a reasonable length of time? How long does it take to enter this industry? How costly is entry? Will a new firm be at a disadvantage vis-à-vis established firms? Does a new firm have access to the same technology, the same products, the same information? Is it costly to exit the industry? You might wonder why the last question relates to entry conditions. Since an entrant is uncertain as to whether it will succeed, the cost of exit can be an important factor in the original decision to enter.

Equilibrium under Free Entry

Entry into an industry means acquiring the ability to produce and sell a product. In almost every industry, there is some cost to entry. This cost may represent investment in a production facility. If entry requires a license (as it does in many professional occupations), then the cost of this license contributes to the cost of entry. Entry into a consumer market often entails extensive advertising of one's product in order to introduce it to the market. Or it might mean the issuance of free samples. As an initial step in considering entry conditions, we begin by investigating the relationship between the cost of entry and the number of competing firms.

Consider an industry in which all active and prospective firms have access to the same production technology and input prices so that each firm has the same cost function. Further assume that all firms produce the same product. Let $\pi(n)$ denote each firm's profit per period when there are n active firms in the industry. For example, if we model active firms as simultaneously choosing output, then the Cournot solution applies so that $\pi(n) = P^c q^c - C(q^c)$, where q^c is the Cournot firm output (where a higher n implies a lower q^c), P^c is the Cournot price, and $C(q^c)$ is each firm's cost of producing q^c (not including the cost of entry). We will assume that firm profit, $\pi(n)$, is decreasing in the number of firms, n. This makes sense because more firms generally means a more competitive environment.

Assume that active firms operate in this industry forever and r is each firm's discount rate. If the industry has reached an equilibrium and it entails n active firms, then each active firm's sum of discounted future profits is $\pi(n)/r$. Using the condition that firm profit is decreasing in the number of firms, Figure 6.2 plots the present value of a firm (before netting out any cost of entry).

Suppose that this is a new industry and prospective firms simultaneously decide whether or not to enter. A *free-entry equilibrium* is defined by a number of entrants, denoted n^e, such that entry is profitable for each of the n^e entrants and entry would be unprofitable for each of the potential entrants who chose not to enter. If K denotes the cost of entry, the free-entry-equilibrium number of firms is defined by

$$\frac{\pi(n^e)}{r} - K > 0 > \frac{\pi(n^e + 1)}{r} - K \tag{6.1}$$

For the case in Figure 6.2, n^e equals five.

Suppose condition (6.1) does not hold; in particular, consider the first inequality not holding. In Figure 6.2 this means that six or more firms decide to enter. Because $[\pi(n)/r] - K < 0$ when $n > 5$, this could not be a free-entry equilibrium. Each of the prospective firms expects to have a negative present value from entering the industry. One or more of these entrants would prefer not to enter. Thus, six or more active firms is too many. Alternatively, suppose that the second inequality in (6.1) does not hold; that is, n firms plan to enter and $[\pi(n + 1)/r] - K > 0$ (for Figure 6.2, this means $n < 5$). In that case, entry of an additional firm is profitable, so that we would expect additional entry. Hence this is not a free-entry equilibrium either. Only when both inequalities in (6.1) are

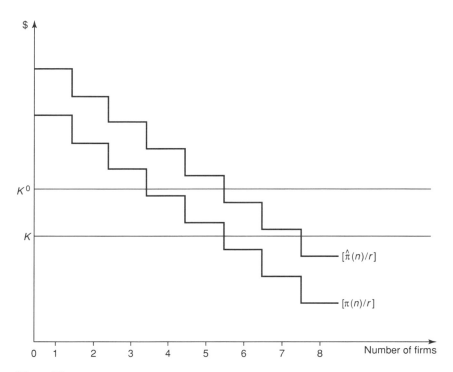

Figure 6.2
The Effect of the Cost of Entry on the Free-Entry Equilibrium Number of Firms

satisfied is an equilibrium achieved. In that case, entrants have a positive present value and nonentrants would have a negative present value if they entered.[14]

The relationship between the cost of entry and the number of active firms at a free-entry equilibrium is quite straightforward. If the cost of entry rises, fewer entrants find entry profitable. As shown in Figure 6.2, if the cost of entry is higher, say, at K^0, there would initially be less entry. Only three firms would enter.

This model of entry is useful in revealing how entry conditions influence the number of competing firms. However, it is unsatisfactory in that it ignores several important factors relevant to the role of entry. This model does not allow for asymmetries between firms, and it is these asymmetries that explain the observed inequality in market shares. In particular, asymmetries between existing firms and potential entrants are ignored in that this model only examines initial entry into an industry. In fact, the concern of antitrust analysis is largely with the entry conditions faced by potential entrants for a currently active industry. Of key importance is the effectiveness of the threat of entry in keeping price close to cost. The remainder of this chapter will focus on disadvantages that potential entrants might face compared to existing firms and, in particular, the ability of existing firms to create such disadvantages.

Prior to moving on in our analysis, we can at least touch upon this issue with the use of Figure 6.2. Suppose that, as shown in Figure 6.2, the cost of entry is K, so that five firms enter. Further suppose that, after some number of periods, an unanticipated and permanent shift outward of the market demand curve occurs. This rise in demand causes each firm's profit to rise so that the present value schedule shifts up (see Figure 6.2). As a result, each active firm is earning profit of $\hat{\pi}(5)$ rather than $\pi(5)$. If the cost of entry is still K, this rise in demand will induce two additional firms to enter. However, for reasons that will be considered shortly, the entry cost of a new firm may be higher than that for earlier entrants. If instead it costs K^0 for a firm to enter the industry today, additional entry will not occur in response to the rise in demand. As a result, the price-cost margin is higher but entry does not occur to stay its rise.

Barriers to Entry

The traditional wisdom in industrial organization is that serious and persistent monopolistic deviations of price from cost are likely only when two conditions coexist: sufficiently high seller concentration to permit (collusive) pricing, and high barriers to entry of new competition.[15]

We have reviewed collusive pricing, but what are *barriers to entry*? There is perhaps no subject that has created more controversy among industrial organization economists than that of barriers to entry. At one extreme, some economists argue that the only real barriers are government related. Examples include a franchise given by government to a local cable television company and the requirement that to operate a New York City taxicab one must own a government-issued medallion. A patent is another example in that it gives a firm a seventeen-year monopoly. At the other end of the spectrum, some economists argue that almost any large expenditure necessary to start up a business is a barrier to entry. Given this state of affairs, we cannot hope to provide a definitive answer. Our objective will be to discuss the various views and definitions and try to evaluate each of them.

A pioneer in this area (and a source of much of the controversy), Joe Bain defined a barrier to entry as "the extent to which, in the long run, established firms can elevate their selling prices above minimal average costs of production and distribution ... without inducing potential entrants to enter the industry."[16] One immediate problem with this definition is that it is a tautology: a barrier to entry is said to exist if existing firms earn above-normal profit without inducing entry. In other words, Bain defines a barrier to entry in terms of its outcome.

One gets a better idea of what Bain has in mind when he states what he considers to be barriers to entry. These include scale economies, the capital cost requirements of entry, government restrictions like tariffs and patents, and absolute cost advantages of existing firms. Sources of the latter include a better technology (protected through patents or trade secrets), control of low-cost raw material supplies, and the learning curve. The learning curve refers to the idea that a firm with greater experience (typically measured by total past output) has discovered more ways of improving its production process.

These barriers are quite diverse and certainly entail very different welfare implications. A government restriction like a tariff is typically welfare-reducing. It is then a "bad" barrier to entry. In contrast, superior efficiency of existing firms due to a better technology is a "good" barrier to entry. No reasonable economist believes that society is better off if existing firms are made less efficient. However, at least in the short run, welfare would be higher if existing firms were forced to share their know-how with new entrants. The important point to make here is that a barrier to entry, as defined by Bain, need not imply that its removal would raise welfare.[17]

A very different definition was put forth by Nobel laureate George Stigler: "a barrier to entry may be defined as a cost of producing (at some or every rate of output) which must be borne by firms which seek to enter an industry but is not borne by firms already in the industry."[18] The emphasis of this definition is on differential costs between existing firms and entrants. For example, suppose that later entrants have to advertise their product to consumers while existing firms do not. This cost of advertising is a barrier to entry according to Stigler's definition (and also Bain's). We believe it is correct to say that Stigler's definition is narrower than Bain's. That is, some things are barriers according to Bain but not according to Stigler (for example, scale economies), although the reverse is not true.[19]

A third definition comes from Christian von Weizsäcker: "Barriers to entry into a market ... can be defined to be socially undesirable limitations to entry of resources which are due to protection of resource owners already in the market."[20] This definition certainly is the best motivated. However, like Bain, it defines a barrier to entry by a particular outcome. Ideally, we would like a definition to point out those specific factors in industries that are reducing social welfare. Whether one can construct a welfare-based operational definition that antitrust economists and lawyers could then use is an open question.

In the remainder of this section, we want to focus upon the controversy related to the definition of entry barriers. The discussion has largely revolved around what Bain has labeled barriers to entry. For example, large amounts of capital necessary for entry are often cited as a source of cost disadvantage faced by new entrants. Richard Posner strongly disagrees with this position:

Suppose that it costs $10,000,000 to build the smallest efficient plant to serve some market; then, it was argued, there is a $10,000,000 "barrier to entry," a hurdle a new entrant would have to overcome to serve the market at no disadvantage vis-à-vis existing firms. But is there really a hurdle? If the $10,000,000 plant has a useful life of, for example, ten years, the annual cost to the new entrant is only $1,000,000. Existing firms bear the same annual cost, assuming that they plan to replace their plants. The new entrant, therefore, is not at any cost disadvantage at all.[21]

Posner does agree with a somewhat more subtle view of the capital requirements barrier. This is the view that the uncertainty of a new entrant's prospects may force the entrant to pay a higher risk premium to borrow funds than existing firms must pay. Others have observed that when truly huge amounts of capital are required, the number of possible entrants who can qualify is greatly reduced. And, although this may not bar entry, it could delay it.

Perhaps the most controversial entry barrier is that of scale economies. To get a feel for this controversy, we have constructed a fictitious conversation between Joe Bain and George Stigler.[22] The conversation concerns a market for which the firm average cost function is as shown in Figure 6.3. Average cost is declining until an output of $\hat{q}$ is reached, after which average cost is constant. Here $\hat{q}$ is the minimum efficient (or optimal) scale. Suppose that there is a single firm in the industry and it is producing q^0 and pricing at P^0. Note that its price exceeds average cost.

Joe: As is apparent from Figure 6.3, scale economies are a barrier to entry. The existing firm is pricing above cost, yet entry does not occur, as it would be unprofitable.

George: But Joe, why do you say that entry is unprofitable?

Joe: The reason is quite obvious. If a new firm comes in and produces at minimum efficient scale, the total industry supply would be $\hat{q} + q^0$. Because price falls below average cost, entry is unprofitable. Of course, a new firm could instead produce at a low rate and thereby reduce the extent by which price is depressed. However, because average cost is declining, the new firm would be at a considerable cost disadvantage and once again incurs losses. In either case, entry is unprofitable.

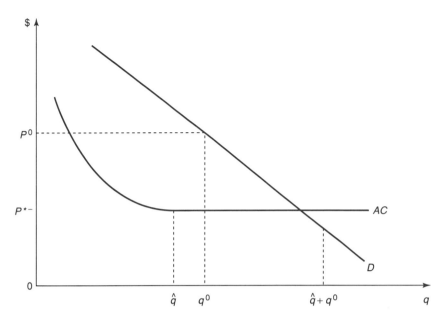

Figure 6.3
Scale Economies as a Barrier to Entry?

George: Why do you assume that the new firm expects the existing firm to maintain its output? Why can't the new firm enter and slightly undercut the existing firm's price of P^0? It would then get all of market demand and earn profit approximately equal to $[P^0 - AC(q^0)]q^0$. Entry is profitable!

Joe: Don't be silly, George. Do you really believe that a new firm could induce all consumers to switch to buying its product by setting a slightly lower price?

George: Why not?

Joe: There are lots of reasons. For example, it has been found empirically that consumers are hesitant to switch brands. Such brand loyalty makes sense as consumers have a lot less information about a new brand's quality since they lack personal experience. In order to offset brand loyalty, a new firm would have to offer a considerable price discount in order to lure consumers away.

George: Joe, we finally agree on something. What you've done is pointed out the real barrier to entry—that consumers have a preference for the existing firm's product. In order to overcome brand loyalty, a new firm must initially sell at a discount or perhaps even give away the product in the form of free samples. The cost of getting consumers familiar with its product is a measure of the true barrier to entry and it meets my definition. Scale economies are just a red herring.

Well, someone had to have the last word, and we let it be the economist with the Nobel Prize. In any event, we hope this dialogue gave you a taste of the controversy and difference of opinions related to scale economies as a barrier to entry.

Having mentioned brand loyalty as a barrier to entry, let us point out its relevance in the ReaLemon case. The ReaLemon brand of reconstituted lemon juice commanded a premium price over its rivals. The apparent reason was that consumers had greater experience with ReaLemon and were unwilling to experiment with unknown brands (without large price discounts). Several policies for eliminating this barrier are conceivable, but consider the one proposed by a Federal Trade Commission official: "For competition to enter the processed lemon juice industry, the barriers to entry which inhere in the ReaLemon trademark must be eliminated. As a consequence ... the only effective relief under the facts shown by the record in this case requires the licensing of the ReaLemon brand name to others wishing to enter the production, marketing and sale of processed reconstituted lemon juice."[23] The important question here is whether consumers will truly gain as a result of trademark licensing. Who will ensure that all licensees selling ReaLemon will maintain a high-quality product? In brief, the ReaLemon trademark has served to convey information to consumers, and licensing to remove the barrier to entry probably would raise information costs.

If you were paying attention, you should be quite confused about entry barriers. Join the crowd! The concept of barriers to entry lacks clarity, and one is never sure what to do with it. It is certainly not clear what are the welfare implications of any particular thing called a barrier to entry. The most unfortunate part is that some economists and antitrust lawyers throw the term entry barrier around like there is one accepted and meaningful definition when there is not. The best advice we can offer is to perform a two-stage inquiry. In the first stage, carefully examine the assumptions underlying the particular argument that something is a barrier. Determine whether it is indeed true that existing firms can maintain price above cost while deterring entry. In the second stage, consider whether there is a policy that could "remove" the barrier and improve social welfare.

Contestability and Sunk Costs

A different perspective on entry conditions is provided by the theory of *contestable markets* due to William Baumol, John Panzar, and Robert

Willig.[24] A market is *perfectly contestable* if three conditions are satisfied. First, new firms face no disadvantage vis-à-vis existing firms. This means that new firms have access to the same production technology, input prices, products, and information about demand. Second, there are zero *sunk costs*; that is, all costs associated with entry are fully recoverable. A new firm can then costlessly exit the industry. If entry requires construction of a production facility at cost K, then sunk costs are zero if, on exiting the industry, a firm can sell it for K (less any amount due to physical depreciation). If there is no market for such a facility and it must be sold for scrap at price R, then sunk costs equal $K - R$. The third condition is that the entry lag (which equals the time between when a firm's entry into the industry is known by existing firms and when the new firm is able to supply the market) is less than the price adjustment lag for existing firms (the time between when it desires to change price and when it can change price).

The central result is that if a market is perfectly contestable, then an equilibrium must entail a socially efficient outcome. For example, suppose that there are scale economies as in Figure 6.3 and a firm prices at P^0, which exceeds P^*, the price associated with average cost pricing.[25] If the market is perfectly contestable, then a new firm could enter, undercut the price of P^0 by a small amount, and earn profit of approximately $[P^0 - AC(q^0)]q^0$. Implicit in it earning that profit is that its product and cost function are the same as the incumbent firm and the incumbent firm is unable to adjust price prior to the new firm selling. Furthermore, when the incumbent firm eventually does respond by adjusting its price, the new firm is assured of being able to costlessly exit the industry with its above-normal returns intact because there are zero sunk costs. This type of hit-and-run entry will occur unless the incumbent firm prices at P^*. Contestability is a theory for which potential competition plays the dominant role in generating competitive behavior.

If there are positive sunk costs, then a new firm cannot costlessly exit. If the exit cost is sufficiently large, then it may swamp the above-normal profit earned before the incumbent firm responds. However, if sunk costs are close to zero, the price that the incumbent firm charges must be close to P^*. Baumol, Panzar, and Willig then interpret sunk cost as a barrier to entry.

This definition has close ties to Stigler's. It is also related to Posner's view about risk premiums being higher for potential entrants. The more expenditures that are sunk, the higher you would expect a new firm's cost of capital (due to the risk premium). Because there is a chance that this new firm will fail, higher sunk costs mean more costs that cannot be recovered on exit. For example, the cost of advertising one's product: Who would pay much of anything for the trademark of a failed product?

In concluding, we should note that the theory of contestable markets is quite controversial. One reason is that the theory is not robust to small changes in some of the assumptions. In particular, if the entry lag exceeds the price adjustment lag (which seems very plausible), then price could be considerably above P^*.[26] Although the theory is robust to the amount of sunk costs, it appears that most industries have considerable sunk costs. The relevance of the theory is then put into question. However, if nothing else, contestability has been instrumental in causing antitrust analyses to reduce their emphasis on concentration and take proper account of potential competition.

Dominant Firm Theory

Though the theory of monopoly is given a prominent place in textbooks, in fact there have been very few monopolies. There have been, however, many industries in which one firm was dominant. At the turn of the century, U.S. Steel (now USX) commanded 65 percent of the market and was more than ten times the size of its largest competitor. More recent examples include IBM and AT&T. IBM has long been the dominant firm in the mainframe computer market, where its market share exceeded 60 percent in the 1980s. Years after entry was allowed into the long-distance communications market, AT&T remains the dominant player with a market share exceeding 60 percent (see Chapter 15 for details).

Static Analysis

The standard dominant firm model assumes that there is one big firm and a large number of small price-taking firms, typically referred to as the "competitive fringe." Because of its position, the dominant firm is modeled as selecting a price that the fringe firms take as given in deciding how much to supply. Given that the fringe comprises price takers, their profit-maximizing output can be represented by a supply function, $S(P)$.[27]

Being strategic, the dominant firm knows that when it prices at P, the fringe will supply $S(P)$ to the market. The dominant firm's demand is specified to be what is left over of market demand after fringe supply is sold. Denoted $D_d(P)$, the dominant firm's demand function is then defined by

$$D_d(P) = D(P) - S(P)$$

where $D(P)$ is the market demand function. Figure 6.4 depicts the dominant firm's demand function along with the resulting marginal revenue

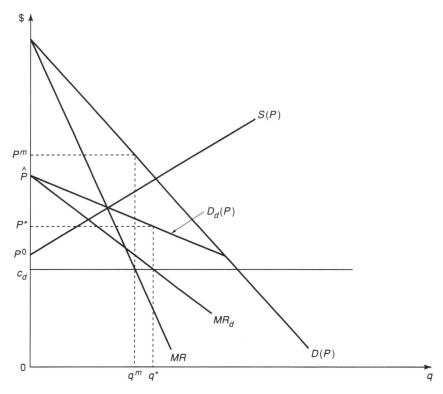

Figure 6.4
A Dominant Firm with a Competitive Fringe

curve MR_d. Because the fringe supply curve lies above the market demand curve when price exceeds $\hat{P}$, the fringe supplies all of demand when the dominant firm prices above $\hat{P}$. Therefore, $D_d(P) = 0$ when $P > \hat{P}$; the dominant firm prices itself out of the market. On the other hand, the dominant firm prices the fringe out of the market when its price is less than P^0, as $S(P) = 0$ for all $P < P^0$. In that case, the market demand curve and the dominant firm demand curve coincide. For prices between P^0 and $\hat{P}$, the market is supplied by both the dominant firm and fringe firms.

If the dominant firm's (constant) unit cost is c_d, then its profit is

$$\pi_d = (P - c_d)D_d(P) = (P - c_d)[D(P) - S(P)]$$

The dominant firm maximizes its profit by equating its marginal revenue MR_d with its marginal cost c_d. The intersection, shown in Figure 6.4, occurs at a dominant firm output of q^*. The price that the dominant firm charges is P^*, where it is read off of its demand curve: $q_d^* = D_d(P^*)$. The dominant firm solution entails a price of P^* with the fringe supplying

$S(P^*)$ and the dominant firm supplying the residual of $[D(P^*) - S(P^*)]$ or q^*.

The important insight provided by the dominant firm model is in showing how the existence of a competitive fringe restrains the dominant firm's pricing behavior. Suppose the fringe was absent so that the dominant firm was instead a monopolist. In that case its demand would equal market demand. As shown in Figure 6.4, its marginal revenue curve is MR, so that its profit-maximizing output would be q^m. Price would be P^m, which exceeds P^*. The existence of a competitive fringe results in the dominant firm charging a lower price.

The dominant firm sets a lower price because its demand is weaker as a result of the fringe. Furthermore, it takes into account how the fringe will respond to its price. Knowing that fringe supply is increasing in its price, the dominant firm sets a lower price in order to reduce fringe supply. By the same logic, one can show that if the fringe were to become larger (that is, if its supply curve shifted out), the dominant firm would set a price even lower than P^*.

Dynamic Analysis: Limit Pricing

One of the more interesting features of dominant firm industries is the manner in which they evolve. In the case of U.S. Steel, its dominance deteriorated over time. It had 65 percent of the market in 1901, but its market share was down to 42 percent by 1925 and just 24 percent by 1967. In contrast, Alcoa maintained a clearly dominant position in the aluminum industry from 1893 to 1940. Similarly, IBM has been able to maintain its dominance in mainframe computers as has AT&T in long-distance telecommunications. Why is it that some firms remained dominant and others did not?

To explore this and related issues, dynamic versions of the dominant firm model have been developed. The pioneering work in this area was by Darius Gaskins, though we will follow the more recent contribution of Kenneth Judd and Bruce Petersen.[28] The new factor that the dynamic model brings in is the way the size of the fringe changes over time. Of central importance is how the growth of the fringe depends on the pricing behavior of the dominant firm.

Rather than start with a supply function for the fringe, let us begin by specifying the cost function for a fringe firm and derive its supply that is consistent with the maximization of a fringe firm's profits. Assume that to produce one unit of output, a fringe firm must spend c_f on variable inputs and use one unit of capacity. If we denote $x(t)$ as the total capacity of the fringe at time t, the maximum amount of output that the fringe can produce at t is then $x(t)$. We will assume that the fringe's initial capacity is relatively low and that $c_f \geq c_d$, so that the dominant firm is at least as efficient as the fringe firms.

Given the dominant firm prices at $P(t)$ at time t, fringe profit at t from producing q units is $[P(t) - c_f]q$. When $P(t) > c_f$, fringe profit is higher the more it produces. In that case, each fringe firm maximizes its profits by producing at capacity. Thus, fringe supply is $x(t)$ when $P(t) > c_f$. When $P(t) < c_f$ then a fringe firm prefers to produce zero. It follows that the fringe supply function is

$$S(P(t)) = \begin{cases} x(t) & \text{if } P(t) \geq c_f \\ 0 & \text{if } P(t) < c_f \end{cases}$$

In order to be able to expand future production above existing capacity, fringe firms must invest in new capacity. Capacity is assumed to live forever and cost Z per unit. The key assumption in this analysis is how fringe firms finance investment in capacity. It is assumed that investment is financed solely from retained earnings. *Retained earnings* are that part of profit that is not given out as dividends. Suppose $P(t) \geq c_f$. Using the fringe supply function, fringe profit at t is then $[P(t) - c_f]x(t)$. Let $u(t)$ denote a fringe firm's *retention ratio*. It is the proportion of current profit retained by the firm. Assume that all retained earnings are invested in capacity. The growth in the fringe's capacity at t, denoted $\Delta x(t)$, is then

$$\Delta x(t) = [P(t) - c_f]x(t)u(t)\frac{1}{Z} \qquad \text{if } P(t) \geq c_f \tag{6.2}$$

In words, the fringe has profit of $[P(t) - c_f]x(t)$ at t, so that its retained earnings are $[P(t) - c_f]x(t)u(t)$. If a unit of capacity costs \$Z, then \$1 buys $(1/Z)$ units of capacity. Because it is spending $[P(t) - c_f]x(t)u(t)$ on capacity and \$1 buys $(1/Z)$ units of capacity then the fringe adds capacity equal to $[P(t) - c_f]x(t)u(t)(1/Z)$, as stated in (6.2). In addition to choosing how much to produce, each fringe firm decides on what retention ratio to set at each point in time. It acts so as to maximize the value of the firm, that is, the sum of future discounted dividends.

There are several important properties to note about the fringe capacity expansion Equation (6.2). If the dominant firm sets a higher price, fringe profit expands, which means that the fringe has more earnings for investment. If the retention ratio remains the same, the fringe will expand at a higher rate. Furthermore, the bigger is the fringe (as measured by its current capacity), the larger is its growth, as there is more profit that can be used for investment.

Before moving on, we should briefly discuss the assumption that investment must be done out of retained earnings. Although there are many reasons why capital market imperfections might make external finance either unavailable or too expensive, suffice it to say that, empirically, internal finance is important for small firms. In 1970–1979, corporations with less than $5 million in assets retained, on average, over 80 percent of their earnings. Even for corporations with assets between $5 million and $25 million, the average retention ratio was 75 percent.[29] It is common for new firms to retain all of their earnings and give out no dividends.

The dominant firm is going to choose a price for each t so as to maximize its sum of discounted profits. As shown in the static analysis, the optimal price depends on how much the fringe can supply today. In addition, however, it depends on the growth of the fringe as specified in (6.2). The higher today's price, the higher is fringe profit and, holding the retention ratio fixed, the more the fringe invests in capacity expansion. Because the dominant firm's demand is lower the greater fringe capacity becomes, higher growth of the fringe means that the dominant firm's future demand curve will be weaker. Hence the dominant firm's future demand will shift in more, the higher it prices today. The effect of the dominant firm's current price on its future demand will play a central role.

En route to describing the optimal price path for the dominant firm, let us consider two extreme strategies. One pricing strategy is for the dominant firm always to set price so as to maximize current profit. Let us call this *myopic pricing*. Typically, setting such a high price will cause the fringe to invest in capacity and expand. Because $x(t)$ is increasing over time, the dominant firm's demand curve will be shifting in. Weaker demand results in the myopic price falling over time along with the dominant firm's profit. Figure 6.5 shows the time path of price and fringe capacity; Figure 6.6 shows the time path of the dominant firm's profit. Depending on the relative unit cost of the dominant firm and the fringe, the dominant firm's market share could go to zero.

A firm whose behavior was consistent with a myopic pricing strategy was the Reynolds International Pen Corporation.[30] Reynolds was one of the inventors of the ballpoint pen. Starting in 1945, it sold its ballpoint pen for between $12 and $20 while unit cost was only 80 cents. In response to this high price, a hundred competitors rushed into the market. By 1948, Reynolds's market share was zero! However, it made off with considerable profits over that three-year period.

The polar opposite case is for the dominant firm to set price so as to prevent all fringe expansion. The price at which fringe expansion is zero is called the *limit price*. We will denote it by $\overline{P}$. Clearly, pricing at c_f will achieve the goal of zero fringe expansion, as fringe firms have no earn-

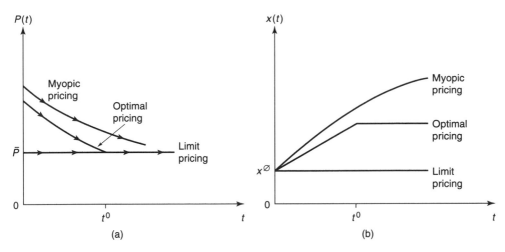

Figure 6.5
(a) Price Paths for a Dominant Firm. (b) Time Path of the Size of the Fringe

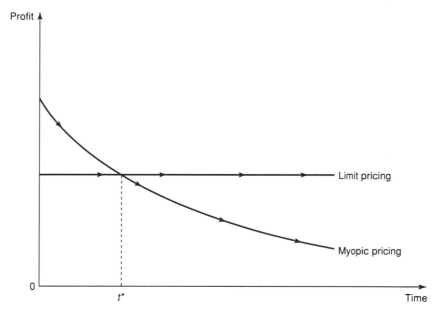

Figure 6.6
Profit Paths for a Dominant Firm

ings to finance investment. However, the limit price is actually higher than c_f. Though a price exceeding c_f does allow positive fringe profit, fringe firms find it optimal not to invest in capacity if they expect a price close to c_f into the future. The reason is as follows. To produce one more unit forever requires an initial investment of Z (the cost of the additional unit of capacity) and a per period cost of c_f. The present value of an initial cost of Z and c_f forever is $Z + (c_f/r)$, where r is the discount rate. If the fringe expects to get a price of P forever, its discounted revenue is P/r. It will choose to invest in another unit of capacity if and only if

$$\frac{P}{r} > Z + \frac{c_f}{r} \rightarrow P > rZ + c_f$$

Thus the limit price is $rZ + c_f$, which exceeds c_f.

In comparing myopic pricing and limit pricing in Figure 6.6, note that myopic pricing gives higher profits upfront (that is, before t^*) while limit pricing gives higher profits in the future (that is, after t^*). A dominant firm then prefers myopic pricing to limit pricing when its discount rate is high, as it values future profit much less than current profit. In contrast, if the dominant firm is very patient (that is, its discount rate is low), it would prefer limit pricing to myopic pricing, as the former yields a higher level of profit in the long run.

In fact, the price path that maximizes the dominant firm's sum of discounted profits entails neither myopic pricing nor limit pricing but rather something in between. The optimal price path is shown in Figure 6.5(a). Note that it starts out above the limit price but below that which maximizes current profit. Price falls over time until it reaches the limit price at time t^0 and then remains there forever. It follows that the fringe expands up to t^0, inasmuch as price exceeds the limit price, and stops growing after time t^0.[31]

The dominant firm's price path is determined by a crucial dynamic tradeoff. Setting a price closer to that which maximizes current profit raises current profit but reduces future profit, as it causes the fringe to expand at a faster rate. This causes the dominant firm's future demand curve to shift in at a faster rate. In order to slow down fringe expansion, the dominant firm prefers to charge a price below that which maximizes current profit.

An important property of the dominant firm's pricing path is that price falls over time. This occurs because the dominant firm's demand curve is shifting in because of the expansion of the fringe. Weaker demand results in a lower price. However, a second factor is also at play. From (6.2), note that the rate of fringe expansion is higher the bigger the fringe becomes, because its earnings are bigger. As a result, initially fringe expansion is relatively small because of its small size. Hence a high price early on is less costly because the fringe will expand slower than it would if that same price were set later when it is bigger.

Strategic Competition

When a firm acts to improve its future position in the market, it is said to engage in strategic competition. Among its many forms, this behavior can take the form of raising the cost of entry so as to reduce the number of future entrants or investing in cost-reducing capital so as to achieve a cost advantage vis-à-vis one's competitors. In the remainder of this chapter, we will review a variety of forms of strategic competition.

The analysis that we are about to pursue is quite distinct from what we have done thus far. In Chapter 5 and in the section on market structure in this chapter, we examined how market structure affects firm behavior. In contrast, strategic competition is concerned with the reverse causality—firm behavior affecting market structure. More specifically, an incumbent firm influencing its share of the market and the number and relative capabilities of its competitors. This issue was analyzed in the preceding section for the case where a dominant firm faces a competitive fringe. We showed that a dominant firm reduces price over time in order to reduce the growth of fringe firms. Although the dominant-firm model does consider how firm conduct affects future market structure, the analysis of this section differs in an important way. We assumed that the dominant firm's competitors were small price-taking firms. We now want to allow for all firms to be large in the sense that their output decisions affect the market price. All firms are assumed to be strategic.

The most extreme form of strategic competition involves reducing the number of one's competitors. This can entail driving some existing competitors out of the industry or deterring prospective firms from entering. *Predatory pricing* is a pricing strategy designed to promote the exit of other firms. It will be reviewed in Chapter 9. The branch of strategic competition concerned with preventing entry is referred to as *strategic entry deterrence*. It will be the central focus of our ensuing analysis. Because strategic entry deterrence is a form of monopolization practice, the theories that we will review here are relevant to the antitrust analysis performed in Chapter 9.[32]

Limit Pricing

There are two central questions underlying the literature on strategic entry deterrence. First, how can incumbent firms affect a potential entrant's decision to enter? Second, if they can influence that decision, how does this affect the behavior of incumbent firms? We can also ask: Even if entry does not occur, does the threat of entry force induce incumbent firms to act more competitively?

The earliest work exploring strategic entry deterrence was that of limit pricing. *Limit pricing* is the use of price by established firms to deter entry. A form of limit pricing was analyzed when we showed how a dominant firm could use price to prevent expansion by competitive fringe firms. Here we will assume that a new firm is not small and could be as large as established firms.

Bain-Sylos Model

The earliest model of limit pricing is due to Paolo Sylos-Labini and that industrial-organization legend Joe Bain.[33] (For a picture of Joe Bain, see the June 1983 issue of the *American Economic Review*.) A central assumption in this model is what is known as the *Bain-Sylos Postulate*:

The entrant believes that, in response to entry, each incumbent firm will continue to produce at its preentry output rate.

This can be illustrated using Figure 6.7. Assume that there is a single incumbent firm (or, alternatively, a perfectly colluding cartel) and that it is

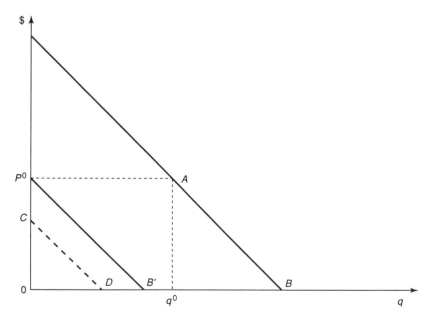

Figure 6.7
Residual Demand Curve under the Bain-Sylos Postulate

producing q^0 and selling it at P^0 prior to entry. Given the Bain-Sylos Postulate, this means that the output of the entrant will simply add to q^0, causing price to fall. In short, the line segment AB is the residual demand facing the potential entrant (where the entrant's origin is at q^0). For convenience, we can shift the residual demand curve AB leftward to P^0B', thereby making the origin for the entrant along the vertical axis.

Notice that the incumbent firm can manipulate the residual demand curve by its choice of its preentry output. For example, in Figure 6.7 higher output than q^0 would imply a lower residual demand curve (that is, the dashed curve CD). This means that the incumbent firm could choose its output so that the residual demand curve facing the potential entrant would make entry just unprofitable.

This is shown in Figure 6.8. The long-run average cost curve for a typical firm in this industry is $AC(q)$. This average cost function holds for both incumbent firms and new firms, so that there is no barrier to entry in terms of an absolute cost advantage. As shown, average cost declines until $\hat{q}$, minimum efficient scale, is reached and then becomes constant.

The key question is: Can the incumbent firm create residual demand curve for the entrant such that entry is unprofitable? The answer is yes. The residual demand curve $\overline{P}B'$ that is just tangent to $AC(q)$ is one for

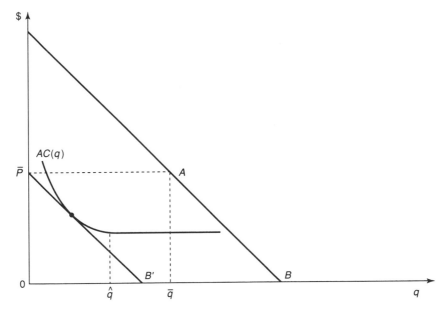

Figure 6.8
Determination of the Limit Price: Bain-Sylos Model

which there is no output for a new firm that gives it positive profit. Working backward from the residual demand curve, an incumbent firm output of $\bar{q}$ is necessary to generate the residual demand curve. The price associated with $\bar{q}$, denoted $\bar{P}$, is the *limit price*. It is the maximum price that deters entry. We then find that if the incumbent firm prices at $\bar{P}$, it deters entry and earns above-normal profit of $[\bar{P} - AC(\bar{q})]\bar{q}$.

Critique of the Bain-Sylos Postulate

The key assumption in this analysis is that a potential entrant expects the incumbent firm to respond to entry by maintaining its output at its preentry rate. Industrial organization economists generally consider the Bain-Sylos Postulate to be a "bad" assumption. First, it is generally thought to be undesirable to assume something about how an agent behaves other than that he acts to maximize his own well-being. In this light, the Bain-Sylos Postulate has been criticized in that it assumes how the incumbent will respond to entry (or how the potential entrant believes the incumbent will respond to entry, which is just as bad). Rather than make such an assumption, we want to *derive* how profit-maximizing incumbent firm will respond to entry.

This more methodological criticism aside, the Bain-Sylos Postulate is a bad assumption because an incumbent firm will typically choose not to behave in the manner that is assumed. In response to entry, an incumbent firm will typically want to reduce its output below its preentry level. Recall from the Cournot model that a firm's optimal output rate is lower the more its competitors produce. Because entry entails more output being provided by one's competitors, the profit-maximizing output of the incumbent firm should be *lower* after entry, not the same. In the Bain-Sylos model, entry is deterred only because the potential entrant believes the incumbent firm's threat to maintain its output. Yet the threat is not credible!

There is an even more basic point here. In fact, the entry decision is wholly independent of the incumbent firms' preentry output. To see this crucial point, consider a three-stage model in which the incumbent firms choose their outputs in stage 1, the potential entrant decides whether or not to enter in stage 2, and the active firms (which include the potential entrant if it entered) simultaneously choose output in stage 3 (that is, engage in Cournot competition). The profitability of entry depends on a new firm's profit at the Cournot solution in stage 3 as well as the cost of entry. The key question to ask is, How does the incumbent firm's output in stage 1 affect the Cournot solution achieved in stage 3? If the incumbent firm's preentry output is to affect the entry decision, it must affect the cost of entry and/or the postentry equilibrium. If the postentry demand and cost functions are independent of past output decisions, then the postentry equilibrium will be independent of the incumbent firms' preentry output. Hence the entry decision is independent of preentry output.[34]

Strategic Theories of Limit Pricing

For an incumbent firm to affect entry decisions, its preentry behavior must affect the profitability of entry. What might cause this to occur? The presumption is that if entry occurs, all active firms will achieve some oligopoly solution. As we found in Chapter 5, the determinants of an oligopoly solution include the market demand curve, firms' cost functions, and the number of firms (as well as, perhaps, firms' discount rates). It follows that for incumbent firms to influence the profitability of entry, they must affect the postentry demand function or their cost functions or a new firm's cost function. A central goal in the literature on strategic competition is to identify and explore the intertemporal linkage between incumbent firms' preentry behavior and the postentry structure in terms of cost and demand functions.

The way we will proceed in our discussion is as follows. In this section, we will describe some of the ways in which incumbent firms' preentry output or price decisions can affect the postentry demand or cost functions and thereby affect the profitability of entry. Having established a linkage between preentry decisions and the postentry outcome, the next step would be to examine how an incumbent firm might exploit this linkage. This will be postponed until the following section where we investigate the use of capacity to deter entry. Though capacity is the entry-deterring instrument, the method of analysis and general insight applies as well to when preentry price or output is the instrument used by incumbent firms.

In our discussion, let us assume there is just one incumbent firm and one potential entrant. In trying to find ways in which the incumbent firm's preentry output can affect the postentry equilibrium, one needs to think of reasons why past output would affect current demand or cost functions. One source of this intertemporal linkage is *adjustment costs*. In many manufacturing processes, costs are incurred in changing the rate of production. To increase output, a firm may need to bring new equipment on line. Installation of this equipment can require shutting down the production process, which is costly in terms of lost output. To reduce output, a firm may need to lay off workers, which is also costly. Adjustment costs are those costs incurred from changing the firm's rate of production.[35]

An example of a cost function with adjustment costs is

$$C(q^t) = 100 + 20q^t + \tfrac{1}{2}(q^t - q^{t-1})^2$$

where q^t is the period t output and q^{t-1} is output from the previous period. The cost to adjusting output is measured by $\tfrac{1}{2}(q^t - q^{t-1})^2$. Notice that it is minimized when $q^t = q^{t-1}$, so that there is no change in output. It is greater the bigger the change in output.

When the incumbent firm incurs a cost to adjusting its production rate, we want to argue that its preentry output will affect the profitability of entry. The more a firm produces today, the higher is its profit-maximizing output in the future. Because of the cost to adjusting its output, a firm will tend to produce an output close to its past output. Thus, if the postentry equilibrium is the Cournot solution, then the incumbent firm will produce at a higher rate after entry, the more it produced in the preentry period. As shown in Figure 6.9, increasing its preentry output shifts out the incumbent firm's postentry best reply function. A rise in its preentry output then shifts the postentry equilibrium from point A to B. Because the incumbent firm produces more at

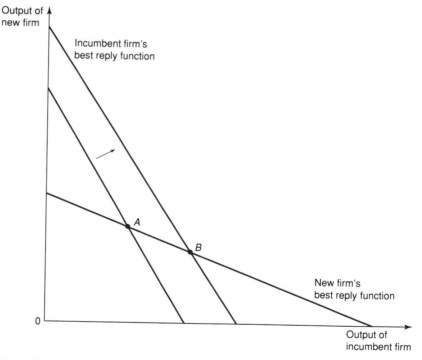

Figure 6.9
The Effect of the Preentry Output on the Postentry Equilibrium with Adjustment Costs

B, postentry profit for the new firm is less. An incumbent firm may then be able to deter entry by producing at a sufficiently high rate prior to the entry decision.

By the preceding analysis, one can motivate the Bain-Sylos Postulate by the assumption that the incumbent firm faces infinitely large adjustment costs, so that it would be too costly to change its output in response to entry. This is obviously a very extreme assumption, though it does make the Bain-Sylos Postulate an assumption on the structure of the model rather than an assumption on behavior.

What this analysis has shown is how the existence of adjustment costs can create the linkage between an incumbent firm's preentry output and the postentry equilibrium. Given that there is a way in which an incumbent firm can affect the profitability of entry, the next question is whether it is optimal to use it so as to deter entry. It is possible that it could take a very high preentry output in order to make entry unprofitable. In that case, an incumbent firm might prefer to produce a lower output and let entry occur. A detailed treatment of the decision to deter entry is provided in the next section, in which we explore capacity as the entry-deterring instrument.

Let us briefly mention several other ways in which the incumbent firm's preentry output or price can affect the profitability of entry. Some production processes have a learning curve; that is, the more experience a firm has with the process, the more ways it finds to lower cost. One reason is that intricate labor operations, such as in aircraft assembly and the manufacture of computer components, can become more efficient as workers gain experience. Using cumulative past output as a measure of experience, an example of a cost function with a learning curve effect is

$$C(q^t) = 100 + \left[20 + \frac{1}{1 + Y^t}\right] q^t$$

where Y^t is the sum of past outputs: $Y^t = q^{t-1} + q^{t-2} + \cdots$. Note that the more a firm produced in the past, the lower is its marginal cost today. Hence the higher an incumbent firm's preentry output becomes, the lower is its marginal cost after entry, which means the more it will produce in the postentry equilibrium. Hence, entry deterrence could occur by setting a high preentry output, which would lower the incumbent firm's marginal cost and give it a cost advantage vis-à-vis a new firm.[36]

Earlier in this chapter, we mentioned that consumers are hesitant to switch brands of a good because there are certain costs associated with doing so. To switch banks you must close out your account, which entails a certain amount of time and effort. If the quality of an untried brand is uncertain, then a consumer will have to incur costs associated with learning about the new brand. Such costs are avoided by sticking with the brand one is currently using, as personal experience has already relieved this uncertainty. Such costs are referred to as *switching costs*.

The demand for a new firm's product comes from consumers who currently buy from existing firms and consumers who are currently not in the market. If there are switching costs, a new firm is at a disadvantage when it comes to competing for the first type of consumer. It will have to offer such consumers a price discount to induce them to switch because of the costs associated with doing so. No such price discount has to be offered to consumers who are not currently buying. Incumbent firms can make entry less profitable by increasing the number of consumers who have attached themselves to an existing brand. This is most easily achieved by offering a low preentry price. A new firm would then have to offer a large price discount in order to get much of any demand for its product. The price discount required may be so low as to make entry unprofitable.[37]

In the preceding discussion we considered how the incumbent firm's preentry output can affect the postentry demand function or its postentry cost function. Given this linkage, the incumbent firm may be able to make the postentry equilibrium sufficiently unattractive so as to deter entry. Alternatively, if an entrant is uncertain about what demand and cost will be after entry, the incumbent firm may be able to deter entry by influencing a potential entrant's *beliefs* over postentry demand or cost functions rather than the actual demand or cost functions themselves.

To consider this possibility, suppose that the potential entrant is uncertain of the incumbent firm's marginal cost. Assume that entry is profitable when the incumbent firm's marginal cost is comparable to or higher than that of the potential entrant. If instead the incumbent firm has a considerable cost advantage, entry is assumed to be unprofitable. Because an incumbent firm's marginal cost affects its profit-maximizing output, one would expect its preentry output to provide information about its cost. A potential entrant would tend to infer from a high preentry output (or a low preentry price) that the incumbent firm has low marginal cost and, therefore, entry would be unprofitable. Of course, the incumbent firm might then produce a lot even if its marginal cost is high, in order to try and mislead the potential entrant into believing that it has low cost. Hence, the incentive to signal that you have low cost results in the incumbent firm producing at a higher rate than it would if there were no threat of entry. Whether the incumbent firm is successful in deterring entry depends on the particular model. Nevertheless, this signaling phenomenon does generate a role for potential competition in keeping an incumbent firm's price below the monopoly level even if entry never takes place.[38]

In summary, there are two important conclusions from the limit-pricing literature. First, there are a number of different ways in which pre-entry output or price can affect the postentry equilibrium and thereby influence the decision to enter. Second, even if entry is deterred, the threat of entry will generally induce incumbent firms to produce at a higher rate.

Investment in Cost-Reducing Capital

In a pioneering paper, Avinash Dixit provided some fundamental insight that has fueled much of the research into strategic entry deterrence.[39] Because his paper is representative of the type of analysis and insight in models of strategic competition, we will consider it in some depth.

Let us begin with a description of the technology available to firms. To operate at all in this industry, a firm must incur some fixed cost which we denote K. In order to produce one unit, a firm needs one unit of capacity, which costs r, and variable inputs that cost w. If a firm currently has a capacity stock of x, its cost function is then

$$C(q) = \begin{cases} K + rx + wq & \text{if } q \leq x \\ K + (w + r)q & \text{if } q > x \end{cases}$$

Given preexisting capacity stock of x, a firm has fixed (and sunk) cost of $K + rx$. To produce q when it does not exceed capacity requires only variable inputs that cost wq. However, if output is in excess of capacity, one must buy $(q - x)$ additional units of capacity. This costs $r(q - x)$, which means total cost is $K + wq + rx + r(q - x) = K + (w + r)q$.

There are three stages to the game and two firms—one incumbent firm and one potential entrant. Firms have homogeneous products. Initially, neither firm has any capacity.

Stage 1: The incumbent firm invests in capacity, denoted x.

Stage 2: The potential entrant observes the incumbent firm's capacity and decides whether or not to enter. Entry costs $K > 0$.

Stage 3: Active firms simultaneously choose how much to invest in capacity and how much to produce. The incumbent firm carries x from stage 1.

If there was entry, there would be two active firms in stage 3. Otherwise there is just one—the incumbent firm.

To derive an equilibrium for this game, let us begin with the thought experiment of what would happen in stage 3 if entry occurred and how

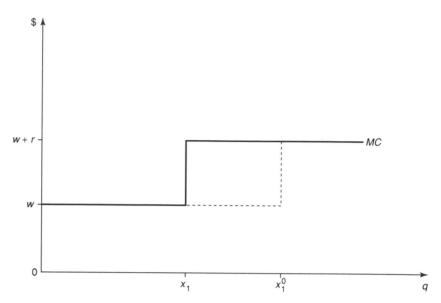

Figure 6.10
Incumbent Firm's Marginal Cost Curve

would this depend on the incumbent firm's initial investment in capacity. The presumption is that each firm chooses a quantity so as to maximize its profit which means a Nash equilibrium. The point we want to argue is that, generally, the higher is the initial capacity of the incumbent firm, the higher is the incumbent firm's postentry Nash equilibrium quantity and the lower is the new firm's postentry Nash equilibrium quantity. In Figure 6.10 is the marginal cost curve that the incumbent firm faces in stage 3 given an initial capacity of x_1. Marginal cost is w if the incumbent firm produces below its initial capacity and jumps to $w + r$ if it produces above x_1 as it must add capacity which costs r per unit. If the incumbent firm's initial capacity is instead x_1^0 then its marginal cost is lower for all quantities between x_1 and x_1^0. Generally, when a firm's marginal cost is lower, it desires to produce more. As a result, in the postentry game, the incumbent firm finds it optimal to produce at a higher rate when its initial capacity is x_1^0 than when it is x_1. Because this higher quantity means that the new firm can expect a lower market price for any quantity that it would produce, it chooses to produce a lower amount. In other words, higher initial capacity for the incumbent firm credibly commits it to producing more in stage 3 because its marginal cost is lower. This commitment induces a new firm to produce less. We can further conclude that a new firm's postentry profit is then lower, the greater is the initial capacity investment (in stage 1)

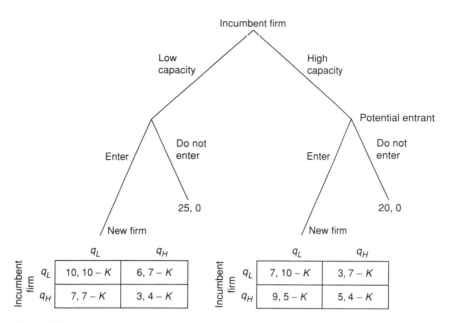

Figure 6.11
Modified Dixit Game

of the incumbent firm because any firm's profit is lower when its rival produces more.

What we have described is a linkage between the incumbent firm's preentry capacity investment and the postentry profit for a new firm. Through this linkage, the incumbent firm may have an instrument for deterring entry. By having sufficiently great capacity, the incumbent firm may be able to depress postentry profit for a new firm to the point that entry would be unprofitable.

To explore whether the incumbent firm will choose to deter entry, we will consider a simplified version of the Dixit game as shown in Figure 6.11. To read this diagram, start from the top and read downward. At the start, the incumbent firm has two choices: low capacity (Low) or high capacity (High). Thus, we are restricting x_1 to being one of two values. One can think of building a small plant or a large plant. After it makes its investment decision, the potential entrant decides whether to enter. If entry does not occur, the incumbent firm earns the profit associated with being a monopolist. This is specified to be 25 when the incumbent chooses Low in the capacity stage and 20 when it chooses High. Without the threat of entry, it would then choose to invest a low amount in capacity.

If entry does take place, then firms make simultaneous quantity decisions where each firm can decide to produce at a low rate (q_L) or at a high rate (q_H). A matrix lists the profits for the two firms from the four possible quantity pairs. The first number in a cell of a matrix is the profit for the incumbent firm, whereas the second number is the profit for the new firm (recall that K is the cost of entry). For example, if the incumbent firm chooses $x_1 =$ Low, entry occurs, and both firms produce q_H, then the profits of the incumbent firm and the new firm are 3 and $4 - K$, respectively. Implicit in these profit numbers is that the incumbent firm prefers to produce at a high rate when it invests heavily in capacity (as its marginal cost is low) and prefers to produce at a low rate when it does not invest heavily in capacity (as its marginal cost is high for a high rate of production).

If $x_1 =$ Low and entry occurs, the postentry (Nash) equilibrium has both firms producing q_L. Given that the new firm produces q_L, the incumbent firm earns 10 by producing q_L and 7 by producing q_H, so it prefers q_L. Given that the incumbent firm produces q_L, the new firm earns $10 - K$ by producing q_L and $7 - K$ by producing q_H, so it prefers q_L. You should prove to yourself that the other three possible outcomes, $(q_L, q_H), (q_H, q_L)$, and (q_H, q_H), are not Nash equilibria. If instead $x_1 =$ High, then the postentry equilibrium has the incumbent firm producing q_H and earning 9, and the new firm producing q_L and earning $5 - K$.

How will the potential entrant behave? Well, it depends on the cost of entry and on the incumbent firm's capacity. If $x_1 =$ Low, then the postentry equilibrium profit for a new firm is $10 - K$. Hence, if $x_1 =$ Low, entry is profitable (and will occur) if and only if $K < 10$ (note that the potential entrant always earns 0 from not entering). If $x_1 =$ High, then postentry profit is $5 - K$ so that it enters if and only if $K < 5$.

The final step in deriving equilibrium behavior for this three-stage game is to determine the optimal behavior of the incumbent firm at the capacity stage. There are three cases to consider. Case 1 is when the cost of entry is high: $K > 10$. Because entry is unprofitable regardless of the incumbent firm's capacity, the incumbent firm will choose the same capacity as if there were no threat of entry: $x_1 =$ Low. In Case 2, the cost of entry is intermediate: $5 < K < 10$. Under Case 2, the incumbent firm deters entry when $x_1 =$ High but entry occurs when $x_1 =$ Low. It then earns 10 from $x_1 =$ Low and 20 from $x_1 =$ High. Hence it optimally chooses to set $x_1 =$ High and deters entry. Note that it invests more in capacity than if there were no threat of entry. Finally, Case 3 is when entry is relatively inexpensive: $K < 5$. Entry occurs regardless of the incumbent's capacity. The incumbent then earns 10 from $x_1 =$ Low and 9 from $x_1 =$ High, so that it invests a low amount in capacity. Thus the incumbent firm chooses the same capacity as a monopolist would who had no threat of entry. In a more general model, the incumbent firm would strategically raise its capacity in anticipation of entry in order to reduce the new firm's output.

There are several important lessons to be learned from the preceding analysis. Since capacity is durable and lasts into the postentry period, an incumbent firm's capacity investment affects its future cost function and thereby affects the postentry equilibrium. Because of its durability, capital is a natural instrument for strategically deterring entry and, more generally, for improving one's position in the market. A second lesson is that even if there is a strategy that effectively deters entry, an incumbent firm may not choose to use it. In the game above, when $5 < K < 10$, entry was strategically deterred by the incumbent investing a lot in capacity. However, suppose that we made high capacity relatively more expensive so that the incumbent firm's profit when it chooses $x_1 = $ High is only a third of what it is in Figure 6.11. In that case, by having high capacity and deterring entry, its profit is 20/3, which is less than its profit by having low capacity and allowing entry, which is 10.

Raising Rivals' Costs

We have thus far discussed a number of ways in which an incumbent firm can improve its future position in the market by giving itself a cost advantage over its competitors. This could involve, for example, a learning curve or cost-reducing investment. In this section, we consider a strategy in which an incumbent firm gives itself a cost advantage by raising its rivals' costs rather than lowering its own cost.

We will consider one strategy, of which there are several, for raising the cost of a rival.[40] Suppose that firm 1 has a relatively capital-intensive production process while its competitor, firm 2, has a relatively labor-intensive production process. Further suppose that the industry is unionized and the union bargaining process works in the following manner. The union first bargains with firm 1 concerning its wage. On agreement with firm 1, the union demands that firm 2 pay the same wage. The (credible) threat of a strike by the union should be able to induce firm 2 to accept the wage that resulted from negotiations between the union and firm 1. Bargaining between the United Auto Workers and the domestic auto manufacturers takes place in this manner.

From a strategic perspective, it may actually be in firm 1's best interests to agree to a relatively high wage with the union. Though a higher wage raises its cost, it raises firm 2's cost even more as firm 2 uses more labor in producing its product. Agreeing to a high wage then gives firm 1 a cost advantage over firm 2, even though firm 1's cost has increased!

The rise in firm 2's marginal cost will cause it to reduce its output, which will raise firm 1's revenue. As long as this revenue increase is bigger than the increase in firm 1's cost, firm 1 will have raised its profits by agreeing to a higher wage.

Preemption and Brand Proliferation

Consider a market where there are two possible products: X and Y. Assume that these products are imperfect substitutes and that all firms have access to the technology to produce either one. Initially, the industry is characterized as follows. There is a lone incumbent firm that produces only X. Suppose that demand for Y is sufficiently weak so that it is unprofitable for the incumbent firm to offer Y, nor is it profitable for a new firm to come in and offer Y. Furthermore, it is assumed that a potential entrant would find it unprofitable to enter and produce X, as it would put it in direct competition with the incumbent firm.

Now suppose that there is an unanticipated permanent increase in the demand for Y. Under this new demand structure, let $\Pi(A, B)$ denote the profit to a firm if its product line is A and its competitor's product line is B. There are four possible product lines: product X, product Y, products X and Y (denoted XY), and no products (denoted N). For example, $\Pi(XY, Y)$ is the profit of a firm offering both X and Y when its competitor offers just Y. To produce product Y, a firm has to incur a fixed cost of F_Y.

Assume that if there was no threat of entry, the incumbent firm would choose not to offer Y:

$$\Pi(X, N) > \Pi(XY, N) - F_Y \tag{6.3}$$

The left-hand side is the profit from a monopolist offering only X and the right-hand side is the profit from it expanding to offering Y as well. Equation (6.3) will hold if the increase in demand for Y is sufficiently small relative to the fixed cost F_Y. We will further assume that entry by a new firm with product Y is profitable if the incumbent firm offers only X and is unprofitable if it offers both products:

$$\Pi(Y, X) - F_Y > 0 > \Pi(Y, XY) - F_Y \tag{6.4}$$

Here, $\Pi(Y, X) - F_Y$ is the profit to a new firm from exclusively offering Y and $\Pi(Y, XY) - F_Y$ is the profit to a new firm from offering Y if the incumbent firm offers both X and Y. Note that $0 > \Pi(Y, XY) - F$ is natural if competition is sufficiently intense when two firms offer the same product.

Note that (6.3) and (6.4) are quite consistent. Because products X and Y are substitutes, if product Y is offered, the demand for product X will fall. Although introduction of Y generates positive profit, it reduces profit from the sale of X. Of course, a new firm that offers only Y does not care about the reduced profits on X. In contrast, when the incumbent firm considers offering Y, it cares about total profits. Thus it values the introduction of Y by the profits earned from Y less the reduction in profits earned from X.

In considering how the incumbent firm will behave in response to the rise in demand for Y, let us assume that it could put Y on the market before a new firm could. This assumption is actually not important for the story we are telling though it is a natural one. For example, the incumbent firm is apt to learn about the rise in demand for Y before anyone else. We know that if the incumbent firm does not offer Y, then entry will occur. In that case, the incumbent firm's profit is $\Pi(X, Y)$. If instead it was to introduce Y, entry would be unprofitable [as $\Pi(Y, XY) - F_Y < 0$] and thus would not occur. The incumbent firm's profit from offering Y is then $\Pi(XY, N) - F_Y$. Thus the incumbent firm will find it optimal to preempt entry by introducing Y if and only if

$$\Pi(XY, N) - F_Y > \Pi(X, Y) \tag{6.5}$$

Rearranging (6.5), one derives:

$$\Pi(XY, N) - \Pi(X, Y) > F_Y \tag{6.6}$$

Recall from (6.4) that it was assumed that $\Pi(Y, X) > F_Y$. Thus, if the right-hand side of (6.6) is at least as great as $\Pi(Y, X)$ then, because $\Pi(Y, X) > F_Y$, it must exceed F_Y. It follows that (6.6) holds if the following is true:

$$\Pi(XY, N) - \Pi(X, Y) \geq \Pi(Y, X) \tag{6.7}$$

Rearranging the expression in (6.7) gives us

$$\Pi(XY, N) \geq \Pi(X, Y) + \Pi(Y, X) \tag{6.8}$$

Thus, if (6.8) holds, then the incumbent firm will introduce product Y and thereby deter a new firm from doing so.

The left-hand side of (6.8) is profit earned by a single firm offering both products X and Y. The right-hand side is industry profit from one firm offering product X and a second firm offering product Y. Because there are two competing firms in the market, generally competition will drive prices down below the level that a two-product monopolist would set (unless the two firms were to perfectly collude). Assuming that there is no cost disadvantage from offering both products, (6.8) must then be true. One two-product firm earns more than two single-product firms competing against one another.

The point here is simple and quite intuitive. If a new firm enters and offers Y, there will be two firms competing in the market—one with product X and one with product Y. This competition results in prices being driven below that which would be set by a single firm selling both products. In contrast, the incumbent firm can coordinate the pricing of products X and Y if it offers Y. Hence the value of introducing Y to the incumbent firm is greater than that to a new firm, so that the incumbent firm will introduce product Y before a new firm can.

Although we gave the incumbent firm first shot at offering product Y, this is not important to the story. Suppose that, instead of assuming that demand for Y suddenly increases, we assume it rises slowly over time in an anticipated manner. At some point in time, call it t^*, entry by a new firm with product Y yields a normal return (that is, the sum of discounted profits equals zero). Entry before t^* results in a below-normal return while entry after t^* results in an above-normal return (assuming no one else has introduced Y). By the reasoning given above, the incumbent firm earns positive profit from offering Y at t^* (more than a new firm would earn) because it can coordinate the pricing of X and Y. Hence the incumbent firm must earn positive profit by introducing product Y just before t^*. In contrast, a new firm would not offer it anytime before t^* as it would be unprofitable. We then find that the incumbent firm will preempt entry by introducing product Y before a new firm would find it profitable to do so.

The strategy outlined here is referred to as *brand proliferation*.[41] Incumbent firms offer new brands in order to fill niches in the market that would have provided room for profitable entry. Note that, in the absence of the threat of entry, product Y would not have been introduced (see [6.3]). Hence, its introduction is solely for the purpose of deterring entry. As is discussed in Chapter 9, the leading manufacturers of ready-to-eat breakfast cereal were accused by the Federal Trade Commission of using an entry-deterring strategy of brand proliferation, though the case was eventually dropped.

Generally, society is better off having a new firm supply product Y than having the incumbent firm do so. The reason is that entry results in lower prices and higher consumer surplus. It is important to emphasize, however, that it may or may not be socially optimal for product Y to be supplied at all. Although the introduction of Y increases product variety, the resulting rise in consumer welfare may be inadequate to compensate for the fixed cost F_Y. This could be true even if entry by a new firm with product Y is profitable.

The reasoning as to why competition may not result in the socially optimal product variety is as follows. A new firm will enter with product Y when it results in positive profits. Part of these profits come from taking part of the incumbent firm's demand. This part of a new firm's profits do not add to social welfare but are simply a transfer from the incumbent firm to the entrant. Recall that the change in social welfare from entry equals the sum of the change in industry profits (which equals the sum of new firm's profits and the change in profits of existing firms) and the change in consumer surplus. Although the change in consumer surplus is typically positive and a new firm's profits are positive (otherwise there would be no entry), industry profits are usually reduced.

It is possible for industry profits to fall more than consumer surplus rises so that entry actually reduces social welfare. As an example, consider the case when products X and Y are close substitutes so that the introduction of product Y would not greatly improve product variety. If firms anticipate colluding in price, then entry will not improve product variety very much nor will price be much lower. The cost of entry could overwhelm these gains so as to reduce industry profits and social welfare (even though consumer surplus is higher). Competition may not result in the socially optimal product variety.

A few final remarks. First, the strategy of preemption has also been shown to apply to the construction of new plants and to the patenting of new innovations. Second, an important assumption in the foregoing analysis is that it is very costly for the incumbent firm to take a product off the market. In particular, it is assumed that if the incumbent firm introduced Y, then, if a new firm came in and sold Y, it would not be optimal for the incumbent firm to take Y off the market. If, in fact, product exit costs are not high, it would actually be profitable for the incumbent firm to take Y off the market but it would not be profitable for a new firm to do so. Thus, if exit costs are low, the preemption strategy will not work.[42]

Summary

In Chapters 5 and 6 we have analyzed the feedback relationship between market structure and firm conduct. Initially, market structure was taken as exogenous and we examined how concentration and entry conditions influence the way firms behave. Our analysis then turned to exploring how firm behavior can affect structure. Under the title of strategic competition, we found there to be many ways in which firms can influence their future market share and the number of firms. Examples include creating a cost advantage over one's existing competitors by raising their costs or preempting future entry through one's product decisions. Although for many years industrial organization economists treated entry conditions as being exogenous to firms, in fact entry conditions are partially determined by the behavior of established firms.

Questions and Problems

1. The HHI can be argued to be a better measure of industrial concentration than the concentration ratio. Comment.

2. Suppose that an industry has ten firms with market shares of the following percentages: 25, 15, 12, 10, 10, 8, 7, 5, 5, and 3.

   a. Derive the four-firm concentration ratio.

   b. Derive the HHI.

   c. Derive the effect of a merger between the fifth and sixth largest firms on the HHI.

   d. Suppose the government decides that it wants this industry to have a four-firm concentration ratio of 40 percent or less. How might this be achieved?

3. In 1972 a U.S. senator proposed the Industrial Reorganization Act. Among other things, this act required that firms in an industry be broken up if (i) their after-tax return on stockholders' equity exceeded 15 percent for five consecutive years, or (ii) the four-firm concentration ratio exceeded 50 percent. Discuss whether or not you think this piece of legislation should have been enacted. (By the way, it was not.)

4. How would you define a barrier to entry?

5. Sunk cost has been said to be a barrier to entry. Explain the mechanism for this to be true. State which definition you are using.

6. Suppose that the demand for long-distance telephone service is $D(P) = 50 - 2P$, where P is price. Prior to recent deregulation, this market was monopolized by AT&T. Assume that AT&T's cost function is $C(q) = 100 + 5q$.

   a. If AT&T had been an unregulated monopolist, derive the price that it would have charged.

   b. Derive the price that a regulatory agency would set if it was interested in maximizing consumer welfare subject to AT&T earning at least normal profits.

   Since deregulation, AT&T has continued to be the dominant firm. Suppose AT&T's competitors are small price-taking firms that can be represented by the supply function $S(P) = 2P - 20$.

   c. Using the static dominant firm model, derive the price that AT&T would charge. Derive AT&T's market share.

   d. How much is AT&T willing to pay to be an unregulated monopolist?

   Suppose that we extend this model to a multiperiod setting and assume that the fringe finances growth through retaining earnings.

   e. Will AT&T's current price be higher or lower than that derived in (c)?

7.   Ace Washtub Company is currently the sole producer of washtubs. Its cost function is $C(q) = 49 + 2q$ and the market demand function is $D(P) = 100 - P$. There is a large pool of potential entrants, each of which has the same cost function as Ace. Assume the Bain-Sylos Postulate. Let the incumbent firm's output be denoted q^I.

a. Derive the residual demand function for a new firm.

b. Given that the incumbent firm is currently producing q^I, if a potential entrant was to enter, how much would it produce?

c. Find the limit price. Hint: Find the output for Ace such that the slope of a new firm's average cost curve equals the slope of a new firm's residual demand curve.

Suppose, instead of assuming the Bain-Sylos Postulate, that we assume active firms expect to achieve a Cournot solution.

d. Does entry depend on q^I? Explain.

e. Will there be entry?

8.   Consider the Dixit capacity investment model when the inverse market demand curve is $P(Q) = 100 - Q, w = 10, r = 30$, and $K = 156.25$.

a. Derive a new firm's postentry best reply function.

b. Given initial capacity of x, derive the incumbent firm's postentry best reply function.

c. Given x, derive the postentry equilibrium profit of a new firm.

d. Derive the minimum capacity that makes entry unprofitable.

e. Derive the optimal capacity choice of the incumbent firm.

9.   From 1979 to 1987, Kellogg introduced the following brands of cereal: Graham Crackos; Most; Honey & Nut Corn Flakes; Raisins, Rice & Rye; Banana Frosted Flakes; Apple Frosted Mini Wheats; Nutri-Grain; Fruity Marshmallow Krispies; Strawberry Krispies; Crispix; Cracklin' Oat Bran; C-3PO; Apple Raisin Crisp; Fruitful Bran; OJ's; Raisin Squares; Just Right/ Nugget & Flake; All Bran with Extra Fiber; Apple Cinammon Squares; All Bran Fruit & Almonds; Strawberry Squares; Pro Grain; Muselix; Nutri-Gran Nuggets; and Nutrific.

a. Should the Antitrust Division of the Justice Department be concerned?

b. Five other companies introduced a total of fifty-one new brands over that same period. Does this fact change your answer in (a)?

10.   The demand for product X is $P_x = 10 - 2X - Y$, where Y is the quantity of a substitute product that is currently not being produced. The marginal cost of X is a constant equal to $1. Entry is completely barred and a monopolist, "Incumbent," produces X.

a. Find Incumbent's price, quantity, and profit.

b. Incumbent wishes to investigate the possibility of introducing Y, which is also protected from entry by other firms. The demand for Y is $P_y = 10 - 2Y - X$ and it also has a constant marginal cost of $1. However, there is a fixed cost of introducing Y of $4. Find the values of X, Y, P_x, P_y, and profit for Incumbent. Will Incumbent introduce Y?

c. Would it be in society's interests to have Incumbent introduce Y?

d. Now assume that entry is no longer barred. For simplicity, assume that if a new firm, "Entrant," decides to introduce Y, then Entrant and Incumbent will collude perfectly and settle at the joint profit maximum. Of course, given the demands and costs as assumed above, the prices and quantities found in part (b) will apply. Will Entrant have an incentive to introduce Y?

e. Still assuming that entry is not barred, will Incumbent have an incentive to preempt the entry by Entrant and offer Y first? (It is assumed that if Incumbent offers Y, then a second seller of Y will have negative profits.)

f. If the fixed cost of introducing Y is now taken to be \$6, answer (d) and (e). Is it in society's interests to have Y introduced?

g. Society's calculation of benefits for comparison with the \$6 introduction cost consists of three parts: the increase in consumer surplus due to Y, the increase in producer surplus from Y, and the loss in producer surplus from X. On the other hand, Entrant compares only one of these parts with the \$6. Is it ever possible for these two "decision rules" to give the same answer? That is, is it possible for social and private decision rules to coincide such that private decisions are socially "correct"? Explain.

11.   Assume the same demand and cost curves as in problem 10, except now take the fixed introduction cost of Y to depend upon bidding by Incumbent and Entrant. That is, assume that a third party owns a patent on Y and has requested bids for the right to produce Y.

a. Referring to your answers in parts (d) and (e) in problem 10, what would be the maximum amounts each would be willing to pay for the patent?

b. Assume now that a Cournot solution holds if Incumbent sells X and Entrant sells Y. Find the equilibrium prices, quantities, and profits.

c. Under the Cournot solution scenario find the maximum amounts that Incumbent and Entrant would pay for the patent so as to become the sole producer of Y.

d. Explain the intuition underlying your answer to (c) and why it differs in a qualitative way from the answer to (a).

Notes

1. United States v. E. I. duPont de Nemours and Co., 351 U.S. 377 (1956).

2. George J. Stigler, "Introduction," in National Bureau of Economic Research, *Business Concentration and Price Policy* (Princeton, N.J.: Princeton University Press, 1955), p. 4.

3. F. M. Scherer, *Industrial Market Structure and Economic Performance*, 2nd ed. (Chicago: Rand-McNally, 1980), p. 61.

4. U.S. Bureau of the Census, *Concentration Ratios in Manufacturing Industry*, 1963, Part I (Washington, D.C., 1966), p. viii.

5. These guidelines are discussed in detail in Chapter 7.

6. Keith Cowling and Michael Waterson, "Price-Cost Margins and Market Structure," *Economica* 43 (1976): 267–74.

7. For example, Ian Domowitz, R. Glenn Hubbard, and Bruce C. Petersen, "Business Cycles and the Relationship between Concentration and Price-Cost Margins," *Rand Journal of Economics* 17 (Spring 1986): 1–17.

8. James Bothwell, Thomas Cooley, and Thomas Hall, "A New View of the Market Structure-Performance Debate," *Journal of Industrial Economics* 32 (June 1984): 397–417; and David Ravenscraft, "Structure-Profits Relationship at the Line of Business and Industry Level," *Review of Economics and Statistics* 65 (February 1983): 22–31. For a recent review article, see Michael A. Salinger, "The Concentration-Margins Relationship," *Brookings Papers on Economic Activity*, 1990, pp. 287–335.

9. F. M. Scherer et al., *The Economics of Multi-Plant Operation: An International Comparison Study* (Cambridge, Mass.: Harvard University Press, 1975).

10. Joe S. Bain, *Barriers to New Competition* (Cambridge, Mass.: Harvard University Press, 1956).

11. C. F. Pratten, *Economies of Scale in Manufacturing Industry* (London: Cambridge University Press, 1971).

12. John S. McGee, "Efficiency and Economies of Size," in H. J. Goldschmid et al. (eds.), *Industrial Concentration: The New Learning* (Boston: Little, Brown, 1974), p. 102.

13. Scherer, 1980.

14. This theory ignores the difficult coordination problem faced by firms simultaneously making entry decisions. If all potential entrants are identical, how do they decide which *n* should enter? In fact, there is another free-entry equilibrium for this model in which each potential entrant enters with some probability. In that case, there could be too little entry or too much entry.

15. F. M. Scherer, *Industrial Market Structure and Economic Performance* (Chicago: Rand-McNally, 1970), p. 233.

16. Joe S. Bain, *Industrial Organization*, 2nd ed. (New York: John Wiley & Sons, 1968), p. 252.

17. Although one can remove government restrictions, how can one remove scale economies? Scale economies are due to existing technological know-how, and knowledge cannot be removed (unless one lives in the world created by George Orwell in *Nineteen Eighty-Four*). However, one can talk about breaking up firms so that each firm takes less advantage of economies of scale.

18. George J. Stigler, *The Organization of Industry* (Homewood, Ill.: Richard D. Irwin, 1968), p. 67.

19. For a discussion of entry barriers, see Harold Demsetz, "Barriers to Entry," *American Economic Review* 72 (March 1982): 47–57. Demsetz criticizes the definitions of Bain and Stigler for focusing solely on the differential opportunities of existing firms and potential entrants. He argues that this ignores legal barriers to entry like the requirement that one must have a license in order to operate but where licenses are traded freely (so that the incumbent firm and the potential entrant have the same opportunity costs). It is a matter of interpretation whether Bain ignores such barriers.

20. Christian C. von Weizsäcker, *Barriers to Entry* (Berlin: Springer-Verlag, 1980), p. 13.

21. Richard A. Posner, "The Chicago School of Antitrust Analysis," *University of Pennsylvania Law Review*, April 1979, p. 929.

22. It is important to emphasize that this conversation is not based on any stated opinions of Bain and Stigler, but on the current authors' interpretation of their writings.

23. Quoted in Richard Schmalensee, "On the Use of Economic Models in Antitrust: The ReaLemon Case," *University of Pennsylvania Law Review*, April 1979.

24. William J. Baumol, John C. Panzar, and Robert D. Willig, *Contestable Markets and the Theory of Industry Structure* (San Diego: Harcourt Brace Jovanovich, 1982).

25. The socially efficient solution referred to here is defined as the social-welfare optimum, subject to the constraint that firms earn at least normal profits. This solution entails a single firm pricing at average cost and meeting all demand. This analysis, however, does ignore the use of nonlinear pricing schemes like two-part tariffs. For details see Chapter 11.

26. Marius Schwartz and Robert J. Reynolds, "Contestable Markets: An Uprising in the Theory of Industry Structure: Comment" *American Economic Review* 73 (June 1983): 488–90.

27. Because each fringe firm is small, its output decision does not affect price. Hence the additional revenue from one more unit is just price, so that marginal revenue equals the market price for a fringe firm. Hence, a fringe firm chooses its output q so as to equate its marginal cost $MC(q)$ to price. It follows that an individual fringe firm's supply function $s(P)$ is defined by $P = MC[s(P)]$. If there are n fringe firms (where n is large), the fringe supply function is then $S(P) = ns(P)$.

28. Darius W. Gaskins, "Dynamic Limit Pricing: Optimal Pricing under the Threat of Entry," *Journal of Economic Theory* 3 (September 1971): 306–22; and Kenneth L. Judd and Bruce C. Petersen, "Dynamic Limit Pricing and Internal Finance," *Journal of Economic Theory* 39 (August 1986): 368–99.

29. Judd and Petersen, 1986, p. 374.

30. Scherer, 1980, p. 240.

31. There are a number of assumptions made to derive this result, including that the market demand function be linear.

32. There have been a number of review articles concerning strategic competition. Recent reviews include Drew Fudenberg and Jean Tirole, *Dynamic Models of Oligopoly* (London: Harwood, 1986); Joseph E. Harrington, Jr., "Strategic Behaviour and Market Structure," in John Eatwell, Murray Milgate, and Peter Newman (eds.), *The New Palgrave: Dictionary of Economics* (London: Macmillan, 1987); Richard Gilbert, "Mobility Barriers and the Value of Incumbency," and Janusz A. Ordover and Garth Saloner, "Predation, Monopolization and Antitrust," in Richard Schmalensee and Robert D. Willig (eds.), *Handbook of Industrial Organization* (Amsterdam: North-Holland, 1989).

33. This model was developed independently by Bain, 1956, and Paolo Sylos-Labini, *Oligopoly and Technological Progress* (Cambridge, Mass.: Harvard University Press, 1962).

34. This point was originally made in James W. Friedman, "On Entry Preventing Behavior," in Steven J. Brams et al. (eds.), *Applied Game Theory* (Vienna: Physica-Verlag, 1979).

35. For an analysis of entry deterrence when there are adjustment costs, see M. Therese Flaherty, "Dynamic Limit Pricing, Barriers to Entry and Rational Firms," *Journal of Economic Theory* 23 (October 1980): 160–82. This was one of the earliest pieces in the recent line of work on entry deterrence.

36. For an analysis of strategic competition when there is a learning curve, see Drew Fudenberg and Jean Tirole, "Learning-by-Doing and Market Performance," *Bell Journal of Economics* 14 (Autumn 1983): 522–30.

37. See Richard Schmalensee, "Product Differentiation Advantages of Pioneering Brands," *American Economic Review* 72 (June 1982): 349–65; and Paul Klemperer,

"Entry Deterrence in Markets with Consumer Switching Costs," *Economic Journal* 97 (March 1987): 99–117.

38. See Paul Milgrom and D. John Roberts, "Limit Pricing and Entry under Incomplete Information," *Econometrica* 50 (March 1982): 443–59; and Joseph E. Harrington, Jr., "Limit Pricing When the Potential Entrant Is Uncertain of Its Cost Function," *Econometrica* 54 (March 1986): 429–37.

39. Avinash Dixit, "The Role of Investment in Entry Deterrence," *Economic Journal* 90 (1980): 95–106.

40. See Steven C. Salop and David T. Scheffman, "Raising Rivals' Costs," *American Economic Review* 73 (May 1983): 267–71.

41. The preceding analysis is based upon the work of Richard Schmalensee, "Entry Deterrence in the Ready-to-Eat Breakfast Cereals Industry," *Bell Journal of Economics* 9 (Spring 1978): 378–93. Also see B. Curtis Eaton and Richard G. Lipsey, "The Theory of Market Preemption: The Persistence of Excess Capacity and Monopoly in Growing Spatial Markets," *Economica* 46 (1979): 149–58.

42. See Kenneth L. Judd, "Credible Spatial Preemption," *Rand Journal of Economics* 16 (Summer 1985): 153–66.

7 Mergers

In Chapter 5 we examined price-fixing agreements among firms and the evolution of antitrust law toward such conspiracies. In this chapter we continue our study of how cooperation among rivals (in this chapter, by merging) can harm competition. As we have observed previously, the other way that competition can be harmed is through actions by competitors that inflict injury on their rivals. Monopolization and exclusionary practices of this type will be treated in Chapters 8 and 9.

Horizontal mergers are defined as those in which rivals in the same market merge. An example of a horizontal merger is the merger of two steel companies: LTV's Jones & Laughlin Steel and Republic Steel. Of course, all horizontal mergers do not harm competition. However, the potential to harm competition is clear since the result is to reduce the number of rivals. Mergers, unlike price-fixing cartels, involve the integration of the firm's facilities, which raises the possibility of socially beneficial economies of combined operations. This explains the fact that price fixing is a per se offense while mergers are considered under the rule of reason.

Vertical mergers are those between two firms with potential or actual buyer-seller relationships. An example is the acquisition of Detroit Steel Corporation by Cleveland-Cliffs Iron (a supplier of iron ore). All other mergers—which are neither horizontal nor vertical—are classified as conglomerates. Actually, the conglomerate merger category has been subdivided into three further classes by the Federal Trade Commission. A product extension merger occurs when firms merge who sell noncompeting products but use related marketing channels or production processes. The Pepsico acquisition of Pizza Hut is an example.

A market extension merger is the joining of two firms selling the same product but in separate geographic markets. An example would be the acquisition by a chain of supermarkets in Florida of a supermarket chain in California. Finally, there is the "pure" category of conglomerate mergers between firms with no obvious relationships of any kind. The merger between R. J. Reynolds (tobacco) and Burmah Oil and Gas is an example.

While the mechanism that permits horizontal mergers potentially to harm competition is clear, this is not so for conglomerate and vertical mergers. Perhaps the most obvious way for conglomerate mergers to harm competition is through agreements to remove potential competitors. This was the government's claim in the Procter & Gamble–Clorox merger. That is, Procter & Gamble (a giant detergent manufacturer) was alleged to have been eliminated as a potential entrant into the bleach market when it acquired Clorox. In this respect, horizontal and conglomerate mergers are quite similar in their potential threats to competition, that is, the elimination of rivals (actual or potential).

The threats to competition from vertical mergers are less obvious and can be viewed as unilateral actions that potentially inflict harm on rivals. Note, for example, that the merger of an iron-ore supplier and a steel manufacturer does not change the number of competitors in either market. One popular complaint by judges has been that such mergers "foreclose" markets to rivals. Simply put, rival iron ore suppliers are harmed by no longer having the acquired steel manufacturer as a possible buyer, and this is thought to harm competition. Because vertical mergers are perhaps best viewed as an exclusionary activity, we will postpone discussion of vertical mergers until the next chapter, where we will also consider other vertical relationships.

The next section briefly describes historical trends in merger activity and changes in the applicable antitrust laws. The remaining sections of this chapter will examine the reasons for mergers and provide detailed analyses of horizontal and conglomerate mergers.

Antitrust Laws and Merger Trends

There has been an interesting interdependence between antitrust law and the trend of mergers in the United States. Four major merger "waves" have taken place. The first wave—roughly 1890 to 1904—has been described as the "merger for monopoly" wave. According to Professor Jesse Markham, "The conversion of approximately 71 important oligopolistic or near-competitive industries into near-monopolies by merger between 1890 and 1904 left an imprint on the structure of the American economy that fifty years have not erased."[1]

Perhaps the most famous of these mergers occurred in the steel industry. During the 1880s, over two hundred iron and steel makers were merged into twenty larger firms. In 1901, J. P. Morgan engineered a merger among twelve of these larger firms to form United States Steel Corporation—with about 65 percent of the market. The result was a sharp rise in prices and a handsome $62.5 million share of these monopoly rewards for Mr. Morgan. Other well-known firms created in this period through mergers include General Electric, American Can, DuPont, Eastman Kodak, Pittsburgh Plate Glass, American Tobacco, and International Paper.

Although the Sherman Antitrust Act was passed in 1890, it was not enforced vigorously until the early 1900s. The first decision to have a chilling effect on the merger wave was the Northern Securities decision in 1904. Of course, the Sherman Act did not contain specific antimerger provisions; Section 1 concerns combinations in restraint of trade and Section 2 deals with monopolization. In Northern Securities, the government's attack was based on both sections, and the attempt to combine the two railroads (Northern Pacific and Great Northern) was found to be illegal. Also, in 1911, two famous monopolies, or trusts as they were called, were found guilty and were broken up (Standard Oil and American Tobacco).

Because the Sherman Act applied to mergers only when the merging firms were on the verge of attaining substantial monopoly power, the Clayton Act was passed (in part) in 1914 to remedy this. Section 7 read:

That no corporation engaged in commerce shall acquire, directly or indirectly, the whole or any part of the stock or other share capital of another corporation engaged also in commerce where the effect of such acquisition may be to substantially lessen competition between [the two firms] or to restrain such commerce in any section or community or tend to create a monopoly of any line of commerce.

Unfortunately, the reference to stock acquisitions left a large loophole. By purchasing a competitor's assets, mergers could escape the reach of the Clayton Act.

The second merger wave took place over the period 1916–1929. Mergers to monopoly were now discouraged by the antitrust laws. However, "mergers to oligopoly" became the rule. For example, Bethlehem Steel was formed as the number-two steel firm by combining several smaller companies. The Great Depression ended this second wave.

The third wave began after World War II, peaking in 1968. It, too, differed from its predecessors. The reason for this difference was the passage of the Celler-Kefauver Act of 1950 and the strict judicial interpretations of that legislation. As we will see later in this chapter, horizontal and vertical mergers involving relatively small market shares were found to be illegal.

The Celler-Kefauver Act was passed in response to a rising concern by Congress over the beginnings of the third merger wave. An influential Federal Trade Commission report suggested that unless something was done, "the giant corporations will ultimately take over the country."[2] While the report was criticized by many economists, it and a government defeat in a steel merger case led to the Celler-Kefauver Act. It amended Section 7 of the Clayton Act to read:

That no corporation engaged in commerce shall acquire, directly or indirectly, the whole or any part of the stock or other share capital and no corporation subject to the jurisdiction of the Federal Trade Commission shall acquire the

Table 7.1
Distribution of Large Manufacturing and Mining Company Assets Acquired by Type of Merger, 1948–1978

Type of Merger	Percentage of All Assets Acquired			
	1948–1953	1956–1963	1963–1972	1974–1978
Horizontal	36.8	19.2	12.4	18.7
Vertical	12.8	22.2	7.8	7.8
Conglomerate				
Product Extension	44.8	36.0	39.3	26.1
Market Extension	2.4	6.7	7.3	3.1
Pure	3.2	15.9	33.2	44.3
Total	100.0	100.0	100.0	100.0

Source: Federal Trade Commission, *Statistical Report on Mergers and Acquisitions*, various years.

whole or any part of the assets of another corporation engaged also in commerce, where in any line of commerce in any section of the country, the effect of such acquisition may be substantially to lessen competition, or to tend to create a monopoly.

The principal change, of course, was to plug the asset acquisition loophole of the original law.

The changes in merger activity resulting from the new antimerger law can best be seen by examining Table 7.1. That is, the composition of mergers has been directly affected by the tougher antitrust policy toward horizontal and vertical mergers. Horizontal mergers have declined from 37 percent to 19 percent, while vertical mergers have fallen to 8 percent from 13 percent. The result, of course, has been an increasing percentage of conglomerate mergers.

The 1980s witnessed a fourth merger wave that rose from a total value of acquisitions of $50 billion in 1983 to over $200 billion in 1988. Some of the larger acquisitions in 1988 included Philip Morris's purchase of Kraft for $13.44 billion, Eastman Kodak's purchase of Sterling Drug for $5.1 billion, and Campeau Corporation's acquisition of Federated Department Stores for $6.51 billion. And in 1989 the closing of the largest acquisition ever took place—the so-called leveraged buyout (LBO) of RJR-Nabisco by Kohlberg, Kravis, Roberts & Co. (KKR)—for $25 billion.

LBOs became very popular in the 1980s. An investor group headed by either the company's top managers or buyout specialists (like KKR) puts up about 10 percent of the bid price in cash. They then borrow against the company's assets and raise, say, 60 percent in secured bank loans and 30 percent or so from "junk bonds." (Junk bonds are very risky bonds that must promise a high return because of the risk.) The investor group then buys all the outstanding stock of the company, taking the company private.

Normally, the new owners begin selling off parts of the company to reduce its debt. The new owners also try to cut costs and lay off employees to increase profitability and to ensure that the huge new debt can be serviced. Eventually, the investor group hopes to reap large profits by taking the streamlined company public again.

The huge magnitudes of the LBOs and the increasing corporate debt that they create have led to substantial concern. Some economists worry that such high debt is unsafe, not just for a company but for the entire economy. Others see it as beneficial for new owners to cut costs and make the new, smaller companies more efficient.

Although these LBOs have attracted a lot of attention and do pose possible policy concerns, they do not appear to represent antitrust issues. Antitrust concerns might be raised when the various units of the acquired company are sold. For example, if KKR should try to sell its cigarette business to Philip Morris, this would surely raise market-power issues. Finally, by the early 1990s, these types of acquisitions had diminished greatly.

A final comment regarding the magnitudes of the four merger waves is appropriate. Despite the huge size of some of the recent mergers cited above, the fact remains that the first merger wave (1890–1904) was by far the most significant in terms of its size relative to GNP.

Reasons for Mergers

There are many diverse reasons for mergers. It is not possible to examine all of these here; however, it is important to realize that not all mergers take place for anticompetitive reasons or to gain economies. Of course, given the focus of this chapter on antitrust policy, it follows that these motives are our primary interest. We shall examine several representative explanations for mergers below.

Monopoly

As we discussed earlier, the first merger wave around the turn of the century consisted of numerous "mergers for monopoly." The classic example was J. P. Morgan's series of mergers leading to the formation of United States Steel (now USX). It is inconceivable that such overt attempts to monopolize a market would be attempted in today's tough antitrust environment. Nevertheless, mergers leading to lesser degrees of market power are possible.

Economies

There may be economies from combining two firms that can lead to greater profitability. These cost savings can take many forms. Two broad categories are pecuniary and real economies. Pecuniary economies are monetary savings from buying goods or services more cheaply. For example, the larger size resulting from the merger may give the combined firm bargaining strength relative to its suppliers. On the other hand, real economies represent true resource savings because of increased specialization or scale economies of some kind. Clearly, real economies are socially beneficial and should be encouraged; pecuniary economies merely reflect redistributions of income between buyers and sellers.

Scherer has described an example of real economies in a horizontal merger involving three English antifriction bearing manufacturers.[3] These three firms were able to revamp production assignments among their plants so as to eliminate duplication and lengthen runs. This led to a 40 percent increase in output per employee within three years. We might note that this is perhaps an exceptional case since scale economies are usually realized through the construction of larger plants—which was not the case here.

Of course, production economies are not the only possibilities in mergers. Marketing can be improved in certain cases through the pooling of sales forces, the use of common advertising campaigns, and so on. Economies in finance, research and development, and other areas are also possible.

Reducing Management Inefficiencies

Takeovers of one firm by another can lead to savings by replacing an inefficient management with a more efficient one. The idea here is based on the problem of separation of management and control in modern corporations. In brief, there is a conflict in the objectives of the owners (shareholders) and the management: shareholders seek maximum profits and management cares greatly about profits but also has other interests. Managers care about their salaries, job security, power in controlling corporate resources, size of office and staff, and so on. A simple graphic depiction of these interactions, which economists call the principal-agent relationship, is given in Figure 7.1.

The principal (or owners) hires an agent (management) to run the business and earn maximum profits for the principal. Owners are uncertain about the profit possibilities that result from managerial decisions. In Figure 7.1 this "profit possibility frontier" is shown as a relation be-

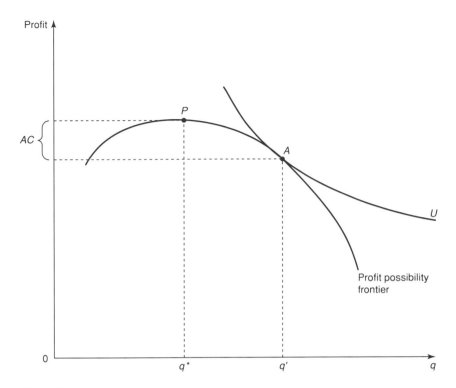

Figure 7.1
Principal-Agent Problem

tween profit and output q. For simplicity, think of q as a proxy variable that represents some of the variables that managers care about in addition to profit—for example, the size of the firm in and of itself (managers' salaries tend to be higher, the larger the firm). In contrast to management, the owners do not have good information on this frontier. They must try to induce the management to pick the point on it that the owners prefer. If owners could "see" the frontier, they would simply order the management to choose output q^* or be replaced. (Of course, q^* corresponds to maximum profit.)

Management has a utility function that represents its preferences for profit and q. The indifference curve U shows this tradeoff and indicates that management's choice is to give up some potential profit (AC for agency cost) for a higher output q'. Management picks point A at the tangency between the profit frontier and the indifference curve since this maximizes utility. The owners would prefer point P. In short, the agency cost AC is what the principal must give up because it has to contract with the agent to manage the firm, and the principal's lack of information about the profit frontier makes it impossible simply to require the agent to pick point P. The principal, of course, tries to use various profit-sharing plans, stock options, and the like, to induce the agent to operate closer to P, but the basic conflict in objectives means that AC will never be zero.

Jensen has argued that this conflict between managers and owners played an important role in explaining the large number of acquisitions in the 1980s.[4] He noted that it was particularly important in the oil industry. For various reasons, the industry was characterized by large cash flows in excess of the funds required for investment projects that promised positive net present values. According to Jensen, the industry needed to reduce investments in exploration and development because excess capacity meant that these investments would have negative returns. Management, though, would see reduced exploration and development investment, and paying out the excess cash flows as dividends, as undesirable. It would tend to reduce the size of the firm, leading to reductions in the company's exploration and development divisions. It could be seen as a symptom of a dying company. Hence, management would tend to resist the reduced investments that owners would prefer.

A simple numerical example may be helpful. Assume that Jones Oil has oil reserves and other assets that are worth $500 million and its management invests in exploration and development with a net present value of $-$100 million. Jones is then valued at $400 million by the stock market. Another oil company could acquire Jones via a takeover for $400 million (or, say, $450 million if needed to induce Jones's shareholders to sell), stop the wasteful investments, and wind up with a nice gain.

According to Jensen, "Total gains to shareholders in the Gulf/Chevron, Getty/Texaco and DuPont/Conoco mergers, for example, were over $17 billion." While these gains are extremely large, there is some dispute about whether true efficiency gains are that high.[5]

Other Motives

Owners of firms may wish to sell out for many reasons: financial distress, retirement, estate and income tax advantages, and so on. Also, firms may merge with quite different businesses in order to diversify and thereby stabilize their earnings. Finally, we might mention the desire by some business leaders who wish to acquire other firms for simple "empire-building" reasons. One such leader has been quoted as follows: "No mountain is high enough for us, nothing is impossible.... I came to this country without a penny, and built a company with 100,000 employees. This is what America is all about."[6]

We now turn to more detailed analyses of horizontal and conglomerate mergers. In each section we shall consider the particular benefits and costs from society's viewpoint, and then review the relevant antitrust cases.

Horizontal Mergers

As noted earlier, a horizontal merger provides the clearest example of possible anticompetitive effects. The reason, of course, is that any such merger reduces the number of competitors and therefore raises the possibility of creating market power. On the other hand, because mergers result in the integration of the firms' productive facilities, there is also the possibility of achieving socially beneficial cost savings.

In Chapter 5 we sketched a tradeoff model developed by Williamson that compares the social benefits and costs of horizontal mergers.[7] We shall reconsider that model here in more depth and examine various qualifications.

Benefits and Costs

In Figure 7.2 the horizontal line AC_0 represents the level of average costs of two firms before combining, and AC_1 shows the average costs after merger. Before merger the degree of competition is sufficient to force price down to AC_0. After merger, costs fall and market power is created—which leads to price increasing from P_0 to P_1.

The merger results in a deadweight loss in consumers' surplus equal to the shaded triangle A_1. However, there is a gain to society because of the cost savings, given by the shaded rectangle A_2. That is, A represents the cost savings in producing output q_1 at the lower average cost.

The main result of this analysis is that a relatively small percentage cost reduction will offset a relatively large price increase, thereby making society indifferent to the merger. For example, if a merger is expected to increase price by 20 percent, only a 2.4 percent cost reduction is required to equate areas A_1 and A_2 in Figure 7.2.[8] (These particular numbers also assume a unitary elasticity of demand.) Table 7.2 presents the cost reductions required for alternative assumptions about price increases and demand elasticities.

It is important to note that the model presented here assumes a merger that creates both market power and economies. This does not mean that such is typical of horizontal mergers. If the merger creates neither, or only one or the other, the benefits and costs should be particularly easy to evaluate. However, where both market power and cost savings are present, the economic analysis is most interesting—and this is why the model has been presented here.

Before turning to several qualifications, we should observe also that experts are divided on the issue of the usefulness of the analysis. That is, problems involved in quantifying areas A_1 and A_2 strike some scholars as being insuperable. Hard empirical evidence would be necessary on

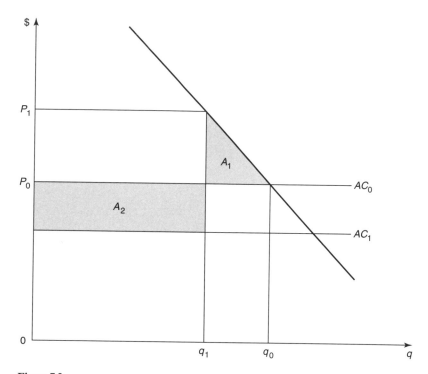

Figure 7.2
Benefits (A_2) and Costs (A_1) to Society of Horizontal Merger

Table 7.2
Percentage Cost Reduction Sufficient to Offset Percentage Price Increases for Selected Values of η (Elasticity of Demand)

$\frac{\Delta P}{P}$	η			
	3	2	1	$\frac{1}{2}$
5	0.44	0.27	0.13	0.06
10	2.00	1.21	0.55	0.26
20	10.38	5.76	2.40	0.95

Source: Computed by authors using formula in note 8.

the degree to which the merger would lower costs, raise prices, reduce output, and so on.

Cost savings would be especially difficult for antitrust authorities to authenticate because the firms involved would have to be relied upon for such information—and their incentives would be to overstate cost savings. Uncertainty about the effects of combining operations on costs is also great, even for the managements involved.

Judge Richard Posner has argued as follows:

> Not only is the measurement of efficiency ... an intractable subject for litigation; but an estimate of a challenged merger's cost savings could not be utilized in determining the total economic effect of the merger unless an estimate was also made of the monopoly costs of the merger—and we simply do not know enough about the effect of marginal increases in the concentration ratio ... to predict the price effects.[9]

Williamson, though recognizing the practical problems of implementation, has responded with several recommendations. One is that, at a minimum, the courts should explicitly recognize the merits of an economies defense in principle, even though they may disallow it as a practical defense in certain instances. He has also argued that "sensitivity to economies in antitrust policy formulation is enormously important. Such sensitivity is promoted by engaging in a dialogue concerning an economies defense, even though full-blown implementation of the specific tradeoff apparatus is never contemplated."

There are a number of qualifications of the model that we turn to now.

Preexisting Market Power

If price exceeds average cost in the premerger period, rather than equaling average cost as assumed above, the analysis must be modified. Such a modification by Williamson in later work led to the finding that somewhat greater economies are needed to offset the welfare losses of a postmerger price increase.

Timing

It may be the case that the economies can be realized through internal expansion if not by merger. Hence, preventing the merger may simply delay the achievement of the economies rather than eliminating them forever. This will occur most easily if the market in question is growing, thereby enabling the firms to grow to efficient sizes without necessarily increasing their market shares at the expense of rivals.

The basic idea is that the areas A_1 and A_2 in Figure 7.2 are no longer to be viewed as constants—rather, they will change over time. Consider Figure 7.3, which is similar to Figure 7.2 but also includes a new average

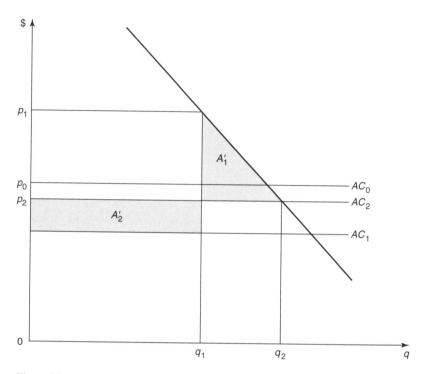

Figure 7.3
Benefits (A_2') and (A_1') to Society in Second Year after Proposed Merger

cost, AC_2. Figure 7.3 represents the market in question, say, two years after the date of the proposed merger; AC_2 is the level of average cost that would be realized by internal expansion, that is, if the merger were prohibited.

If the benefits and costs of the merger were to be calculated two years later, the shaded areas are these current values. Comparing A_1' with A_1 (in Figure 7.2) and A_2' with A_2 (also in Figure 7.2), it is apparent that the benefits are declining and the costs are increasing over time. A sophisticated analysis would then calculate the present discounted values of the streams of benefits and costs. Clearly, even with benefits greater than costs initially, it is possible for their present values to reverse this result.

The particular areas shown in Figure 7.3 depend on the assumption that competition without merger will be sufficiently vigorous to keep price equal to (falling) average cost. While other plausible assumptions can be made, the main point here is to show that the cost savings advantages of the merger will be lessened by rapid internal achievement of the potential economies. That internal growth is often a good alternative to horizontal merger is, in fact, a frequently made argument in support of tough antimerger policy.

Industry-Wide Effects

While the economies of the merger are limited to the two combining firms, the market power effects may lead to price increases by other firms as well. Hence the costs (deadweight losses) in Figures 7.2 and 7.3 may be understated.

An interested related issue here is how the other firms in the industry react to the merger between two rivals. Consider two possibilities—in case one the merger leads to efficiencies only, and in case two it leads to market power effects only. Rivals would likely oppose the merger in case one and welcome it in case two. Similarly, one might expect the stock prices of rivals to reflect these differences. In case one, assuming that lower costs lead to lower market prices, the rivals' stock prices might fall upon the announcement of the merger. Conversely, in case two, the rivals' stock prices might rise reflecting the expectation of higher industry-wide profits.[11]

Technological Progress

The analysis thus far has been concerned with cost savings of a static kind. To the extent that good predictions can be made about the effect of the merger on technological progress, this information should also be incorporated.

Income Distribution

Finally, we mention the effect of the merger on income distribution. The monopoly profit created is, of course, at the expense of consumers' surplus and is therefore a transfer from one group to another (although some individuals may belong to both groups). While such transfers do not entail efficiency effects, they are certainly important politically.

Cases

Before we describe the leading horizontal merger cases, it is useful to emphasize that the benefit-cost analysis above is the approach many economists advocate—it is not the way courts necessarily evaluate the legality of mergers. As we shall see, courts have not followed the Williamson methodology.

As discussed earlier, Section 7 of the Clayton Act was amended in 1950 to plug the "asset loophole." The Supreme Court's first ruling under the new Section 7 came in the Brown Shoe case of 1962.[12]

This case involved the merger of Brown, the fourth largest manufacturer of shoes in the United States, with about 4 percent of the market, and G. R. Kinney Co., the twelfth largest, with a 0.5 percent share. Both companies were also engaged in shoe retailing. Brown had 2.1 percent of the national retail market and Kinney had 1.6 percent. While the case involved both horizontal and vertical dimensions, we shall deal only with the horizontal aspects here.

The first step the Court took was to discuss the definition of the relevant retail shoe market.[13] That is, should total retail shoes sold in the United States be the market, or should men's shoes and women's shoes in large cities be separate relevant markets? It clearly matters since the two firms had a combined share of only about 4 percent of the national market, while they had 57 percent of the market for women's shoes in Dodge City, Kansas. According to the Court,

The "area of effective competition" must be determined by reference to a product market (the "line of commerce") and a geographic market (the "section of the country").

The outer boundaries of a product market are determined by the reasonable interchangeability of use or the cross-elasticity of demand between the product itself and substitutes for it. However, within this broad market, well-defined submarkets may exist which, in themselves, constitute product markets for antitrust purposes. The boundaries of such a submarket may be determined by examining such practical indicia as industry or public recognition of the submarket as a separate economic entity, the product's peculiar characteristics and uses, unique production facilities, distinct customers, distinct prices, sensitivity to price changes, and specialized vendors.

Applying these considerations to the present case, we conclude that the record supports the District Court's findings that the relevant lines of commerce are men's, women's, and children's shoes. These product lines are recognized by the public; each line is manufactured in separate plants; each has characteristics peculiar to itself rendering it generally noncompetitive with the others; and each is, of course, directed toward a distinct class of customers.

Next, the Court turned to the geographic dimensions of the market:

The criteria to be used in determining the appropriate geographic market are essentially similar to those used to determine the relevant product market. Congress prescribed a pragmatic, factual approach to the definition of the relevant market and not a formal, legalistic one. The geographic market selected must, therefore, both "correspond to the commercial realities" of the industry and be economically significant. Thus, although the geographic market in some instances may encompass the entire Nation, under other circumstances it may be as small as a single metropolitan area.

The Court then found that the relevant geographic markets were "every city with a population exceeding 10,000 and its immediate contiguous surrounding territory in which both Brown and Kinney sold shoes at retail through stores they either owned or controlled."

The Court found some high combined market shares. For example, the maximum was the 57 percent in Dodge City noted above. However, this was atypical. The most important statistic seemed to be that in 118 separate cities the combined share of one of the relevant product lines exceeded 5 percent. Hence

If a merger achieving 5 percent control were now approved, we might be required to approve future merger efforts by Brown's competitors.... The oligopoly Congress sought to avoid would then be furthered and it would be difficult to dissolve the combinations previously approved.

Thus the Court gave a lot of weight to its reading of the intent of Congress. "What Congress saw as the rising tide of economic concentration ... [and provided authority] for arresting mergers at a time when the trend to a lessening of competition ... was still in its incipiency."

It is useful to contrast the Court's opinion in Brown Shoe with the Williamson tradeoff analysis described earlier. The small market shares found hardly seem likely to give rise to monopolistic price increases. However, the Court's view was to stop a trend toward increased concentration in its incipiency. It noted, for example, that there was a 10 percent decrease in the number of shoe manufacturers between 1947 and 1954.

What about cost savings? In Brown Shoe the Court recognized that integrated operations could create efficiencies; however, such efficiencies were not regarded to be as important as maintaining a "decentralized" industry.

The retail outlets of integrated companies, by eliminating wholesalers and by increasing the volume of purchases from the manufacturing division of the enterprise, can market their own brands at prices below those of competing independent retailers. Of course, some of the results of large integrated or chain operations are beneficial to consumers. But we cannot fail to recognize Congress' desire to promote competition through the protection of viable, small, locally owned businesses. Congress appreciated that occasional higher costs and prices might result from the maintenance of fragmented industries and markets. It resolved these competing considerations in favor of decentralization. We must give effect to that decision.

In a 1967 decision in a conglomerate merger case, the Court made an even stronger statement concerning cost savings: "Possible economies cannot be used as a defense to illegality."[14]

Various interpretations are possible. One is that the measurement problem is so great that cost savings cannot be used practically as a defense in a judicial process. An alternate interpretation, which almost all economists find distasteful, is that cost savings are harmful because they lead to the failure of small, inefficient retailers. That this latter interpretation is not unreasonable was illustrated by the attempt by United Technologies in 1978 to take over Carrier Corporation. According to Scherer, Carrier tried to avert being taken over by claiming in antitrust suit "that the merger would make Carrier a more technologically progressive, potent competitor."[15]

A third interpretation of the Brown Shoe decision is that antitrust has multiple objectives, and economic efficiency is only one. Thus the objective of maintaining many small retailers must be balanced (somehow) against the higher costs to consumers. One antitrust expert, Robert Bork, has disputed the view that Congress intended multiple goals for antitrust:

In Brown Shoe, in fact, the Supreme Court went so far as to attribute to Congress a decision to prefer the interests of small, locally owned businesses to the interests of consumers. But to put the matter bluntly, there simply was no such congressional decision either in the legislative history or in the text of the statute.... The Warren Court was enforcing its own social preferences, not Congress'.[16]

Two merger cases were decided by the Supreme Court in 1964 that we shall briefly describe. One involved a merger between a tin-can manufacturer and a glass-bottle maker.[17] In this case the Court found the relevant market to be metal cans and glass bottles combined. The two companies, Continental Can and Hazel-Atlas Glass, had 22 percent and 3 percent shares, respectively, and the Court found these to be too high.

The second 1964 case was a merger between Alcoa, a producer of aluminum electrical conductor cable, and Rome Cable, a specialist in copper cable.[18] However, Rome did produce a small amount of aluminum cable. In this case, selecting from many possible choices for the relevant market, the Court elected a market which included only aluminum cable. And Alcoa's 27.8 percent and Rome's 1.3 percent were found to be illegal.

Hence, in the first case tin cans and glass bottles were considered substitutes, and in the second aluminum cable and copper cable were not considered substitutes. According to one expert these two decisions are logically inconsistent. Also,

the Alcoa-Rome and Continental-Hazel-Atlas decisions exhibit a different sort of consistency: the consistent willingness of the courts to accept market definitions that resolve inherent doubts on the side of preventing mergers with possible anticompetitive effects.[19]

The Von's decision in 1966 has been especially significant as a precedent.[20] Von's was the third largest grocery chain in the Los Angeles area in 1960 when it acquired the sixth ranked chain, Shopping Bag Food Stores. The combined firm had only 7.5 percent of the market and was second to Safeway Stores.

Despite the low share of 7.5 percent, the Court found the merger to be illegal. The emphasis in the decision was on the trend toward fewer owners in single grocery stores in Los Angeles. Thus the number declined from 5365 in 1950 to 3818 in 1961. Also, from 1953 to 1962 the number of chains with two or more grocery stores increased from 96 to 150. According to Justice Black, "The basic purpose of the 1950 Celler-Kefauver bill was to prevent economic concentration in the American economy by keeping a large number of small competitors in business."

In a 1974 case the Supreme Court handed the Justice Department its first defeat on a market definition issue.[21] The issue was whether coal production or uncommitted coal reserves was the appropriate variable for calculating market shares. With its composition changed by the addition of new conservative judges, the Court found that market shares based on coal reserves were not significant enough to find the merger unlawful.

In a 1993 book, Shenefield and Stelzer summarized the current attitude of the courts toward horizontal mergers. (Shenefield served as assistant attorney general in charge of the Antitrust Division of the Justice Department from 1977 to 1980.) Quoting their summary in part:

Under the current case law, market shares at the time of merger are only the beginning point. They are used to establish a presumption of illegality. The precise level at which that presumtion is triggered, however, has changed remarkably over the years. As recently as the late 1960s, aggregate market shares of under 10 percent in a relatively unconcentrated Los Angeles grocery store market were sufficient to support a finding of unlawfulness. Since that time, the triggering point for illegality has risen steadily. In the 1970s, acquisitions that resulted in aggregate shares of approximately 10–20 percent could be held unlawful. More recently, aggregate shares in excess of 25 percent may well be approved by the courts.[22]

We now turn to a description of merger guidelines issued jointly by the Antitrust Division of the Justice Department and the Federal Trade Commission (collectively, the "Agency") in 1992. The Guidelines serve the function of informing the business community about the types of mergers that are likely to be challenged by the Agency. Of course, as we have seen, the final word on the legality of a merger is that of the Supreme Court; however, the enforcement agencies play an important role in determining what cases the Court will consider. And there is an

important interaction effect, inasmuch as enforcement agencies are unlikely to bring lawsuits where their expectation of winning is low.

1992 Merger Guidelines

The 1992 Guidelines[23] are quite similar to guidelines issued in 1982 by
the Justice Department alone. The 1982 version made substantial
changes in earlier guidelines. Here we focus on the substance of the
present Guidelines and do not concern ourselves with slight differences
between the 1982 and 1992 versions.

A major contribution of the Guidelines is in defining the relevant
antitrust market. As we noted in the discussion of the cases above, the
delimitation of the relevant market is vital in determining the legality of
a merger.

The Agency defines the market conceptually as follows:

A market is defined as a product or group of products and a geographic area in
which it is sold such that a hypothetical profit-maximizing firm, not subject to
price regulation, that was the only present or future producer or seller of those
products in that area likely would impose at least a "small but significant and
nontransitory" increase in price, assuming the terms of sale of all other products
are held constant. A relevant market is a group of products and a geographic
area that is no bigger than necessary to satisfy this test.[24]

An example should be instructive. For simplicity, assume that the
product, gravel, has no close substitutes. Hence we can focus on the
geographical dimension of the market. Furthermore, assume that a
merger between two gravel suppliers located in Centerville is being examined by the Justice Department. At the present time the market in
Centerville is competitive and the price is $100. Furthermore, assume
that the cost per unit by suppliers everywhere is $100, and that it costs
25 cents per ton to haul a ton of gravel one mile. The issue is to determine the geographical limits of the market. Should it stop at the city
limits of Centerville? Given that it is costly to haul gravel from suppliers
outside the city limits, how many miles should the market extend beyond
the city limits?

In Figure 7.4 the horizontal axis shows Centerville located along a
"highway" that extends to the east and west, where the numbers indicate
the number of miles from Centerville's city limits. The height of the
vertical line at Centerville represents the $100 competitive price at that
location. The lines sloping upward to the east and west have vertical
heights equal to $100 plus the miles away from Centerville multiplied by
25 cents per mile. Hence, at a distance of 20 miles to the east, the height
of the sloping line is $100 + (0.25)(20) = $105. This can be interpreted

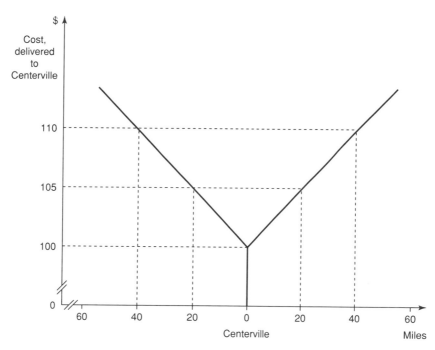

Figure 7.4
Geographical Market Definition

as the delivered price that a supplier 20 miles to the east could sell gravel for in Centerville.

The Guidelines provide the answer to the market definition problem. The market should include all suppliers who would need to be part of a hypothetical cartel such that the price in Centerville could be raised by, say, 5 percent, to $105 on a nontransitory basis. If it costs 25 cents per mile to transport a ton of gravel, then a supplier 20 miles away could sell in Centerville at $105. Hence, all suppliers within 20 miles of Centerville should be part of the market. Notice that if the price increase is taken to be 10 percent, then the market boundaries should extend out to 40 miles, implying a market with more suppliers.

The example makes the important point that one must decide on the percentage price increase before the market boundaries can be determined. In short, market power is a continuous variable—there is no magical way to determine a market without incorporating some standard. In fact, there were arguments at the Justice Department as to whether a 5 percent or 10 percent increase should be specified. Although 5 percent was specified, the Guidelines point out that it is not "an inflexible standard that will be used regardless of the circumstances of a given case." A higher price increase of course means a broader market and thereby permits more mergers to slip by unattacked than a lower price. (Two particular merging firms will have lower market shares in a 40-mile market than in a 20-mile market; and as we shall explain below, the Guidelines are more likely to endorse mergers that involve lower market shares.) A lower price increase means possibly prohibiting relatively harmless mergers or those that may promote efficiency.

In applying the Guidelines the Agency uses the HHI concentration index that was explained in Chapter 6. The HHI is used to determine which mergers qualify as being safe from challenge because they are unlikely to have adverse competitive effects. Those that do not fall into these "safe harbors" are then analyzed further with respect to entry conditions, efficiency considerations, and so on to determine if they will be challenged.

There are three categories of market concentration: Unconcentrated (HHI below 1000), Moderately Concentrated (HHI between 1000 and 1800), and Highly Concentrated (HHI above 1800). For example, if the Census Industries in Table 6.2 were relevant markets, "Household Refrigerators and Freezers" with an HHI of 2256 would be Highly Concentrated. Similarly, "Paper Mills" with an HHI of 432 would be Unconcentrated.

The safe harbors are shown as the shaded region in Figure 7.5. That is, the Agency will consider not only the post-merger market concentration, but also the increase in concentration resulting from the merger. Hence, all mergers with post-merger HHI values of 1000 or less are safe. Mergers that produce an increase in HHI of less than 100 points in Moderately Concentrated markets post-merger are also safe.

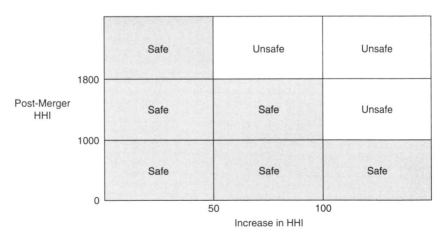

Figure 7.5
Safe Harbors for Mergers under 1992 Merger Guidelines

Example: A market shared equally by eight firms would have an HHI of 1250. If two firms merged, the HHI would increase by $25^2 - 12.5^2 - 12.5^2 = 312.5$. Hence, in this case the merger would be viewed as likely to have adverse competitive effects and the Agency would study other factors to determine if a challenge should be made.

Finally, mergers that produce an increase in HHI of 50 points or less in Highly Concentrated markets (1800 or above) are safe.

Example: A market shared equally by five firms would have an HHI of 2000. If two firms merged, the HHI would increase by 800, and this would fall outside of the safe harbors shown in Figure 7.5. Hence, the Agency would presume that the merger is likely to create or enhance market power or facilitate its exercise. Unless further analysis showing entry is easy or that important efficiencies are created, the Agency would challenge the merger.

An interesting application of the HHI was made by the FTC in 1986. The FTC challenged a proposed merger between Coca-Cola and Dr. Pepper. They argued that the proposed merger would increase the HHI for the carbonated soft drink industry by 341 points to a level of 2646. This clearly violated the Guidelines, and the FTC was successful in halting the merger.[25]

Finally, we should consider in more detail the Agency's viewpoint on the Williamson analysis. That is, will the cost savings be weighed against market power inefficiencies?

The Guidelines indicate that the [Agency] will consider various types of efficiencies including economies of scale, better integration of production facilities, plant specialization, and lower transportation costs. The [Agency] also will consider general selling, administrative and overhead expenses; however, as a practical matter, these types of efficiencies may be difficult to demonstrate. In addition, the [Agency] will reject claimed efficiencies if equivalent or comparable savings can reasonably be achieved by the parties by other means. Moreover, the greater the competitive concerns that the merger raises under the other standards of the Guidelines, the greater will be the level of expected efficiencies that the parties must establish.

Conglomerate Mergers

Conglomerate mergers involve firms that are not sellers in the same market nor do they stand in a buyer-seller relationship. Our earlier example of a "pure" conglomerate merger was the merger between the cigarette manufacturer R. J. Reynolds and Burmah Oil and Gas. Two other categories of conglomerate mergers discussed were product extension (Pepsico and Pizza Hut) and market extension (grocery chains in Florida and California). These latter two categories are more likely to be challenged by the antitrust authorities. The reason is a concern for reducing potential competition.

We will consider the potential competition theory shortly. First, however, we turn to some of the efficiency-enhancing characteristics of conglomerate mergers.

Potential Benefits

One well-known conglomerate is International Telephone and Telegraph (ITT). In 1960, ITT was a large manufacturer of telecommunication equipment and an operator of telephone systems. It embarked on a diversification program in that year largely through conglomerate mergers. Along the way, it acquired such diverse firms as Hartford Fire Insurance, Continental Baking, Sheraton Hotels, Avis Rent-a-Car, Canteen (vending machines), and over a hundred more. By 1980, ITT had become the thirteenth largest industrial firm in the United States. Although ITT is an extreme example of conglomerate merger growth, it certainly raises the issue of whether such firms are beneficial or harmful to the economy.

Of course, conglomerate firms vary widely in their internal organizational structure. In some, the central management staff may be quite knowledgeable about the operating problems of each division. In others, the top management may be concerned only with the profit and loss statements of its components. For this reason, it is hazardous to generalize about the efficiency properties of conglomerates.

Nevertheless, it can be argued that certain conglomerate organizations are superior to the capital market in allocating investment funds. The idea is that the top management of a conglomerate has access to information and possesses the controls to change the operations of its division. Banks and stockholders are much further removed from the internal operations of firms. Also, as Williamson has observed,

the general management and its support staff can perform a further capital market function—assigning cash flows to high yield uses. Thus, cash flows ... are exposed to an internal competition.... Moreover, because the costs of communicating and adapting internally are normally lower than would be incurred in making an investment proposal to the external capital market, it may be practicable to ... [employ] a sequential decision process (in which additional financing is conditional on prior stage results).... The transactions costs of effectuating such a process through the capital market, by contrast, are apt to be prohibitive.[26]

In short, such conglomerates serve effectively as "miniature capital markets."

A second benefit of conglomerate mergers, especially if other mergers are restricted by antitrust authorities, is the takeover threat. The idea is that managements are constantly being pressured to perform efficiently by the threat of a takeover by another firm. That is, suppose that firm A is run by a slack or incompetent management team making only 80 percent of its potential profits. Firm B will then have an incentive to buy A, fire its management, and boost A's profits by 20 percent. Recall that examples from the oil industry were discussed earlier in this chapter.

Of course, the stockholders of firm A also have an incentive to fire the inefficient management; however, the costs of organizing a sufficiently powerful group of stockholders to carry out this plan may be too high. Hence, conglomerate mergers can have beneficial results in providing incentives for managerial efficiency.

Anticompetitive Effects and Cases

Numerous anticompetitive claims have been made against conglomerate mergers. They have been charged with creating the opportunities for reciprocal dealing and predatory pricing, producing politically undesirable giant size, and eliminating potential competition.

Reciprocal dealing refers to the practice of buying from a supplier only on the condition that the supplier buys from you. For example, in one case, Consolidated Foods tried to get its suppliers to buy their onion and garlic needs from its newly acquired Gentry division. The competitive effects caused by this practice are controversial; for instance, some argue that reciprocity may inhibit competitive pricing and others that it can actually invigorate competition.[27]

Predatory pricing refers to deliberately pricing below cost to drive out rivals, and raising the price to the monopoly level after their exit. This tactic, as well as reciprocal dealing, is not confined to conglomerate firms; also, predatory pricing will be treated in depth in Chapter 9. Furthermore, the Merger Guidelines cite the elimination of potential competition as their only concern regarding conglomerate mergers. For these reasons, we will restrict further discussion here to potential competition.

First, we should clarify the meaning of a potential competitor. That is to say, how can one distinguish between an actual and a potential competitor? Clearly, if a firm could quickly shift from producing zero widgets to producing and selling positive quantities, arguably it could fit either category. To resolve this definitional problem, the Guidelines have offered the following arbitrary rule. An actual competitor is one that "has existing productive and distributive facilities that could easily and economically be used to produce and sell the relevant product within one year in response to a small but significant and nontransitory increase in price."[28] Hence, actual competitors are included as part of the relevant market. On the other hand potential competitors are those that "must construct significant new productive or distributive facilities in order to produce and sell the relevant product."

We shall use the Procter & Gamble case[29] of 1967 as an example of how the elimination of potential competition can be effected by conglomerate merger. Procter & Gamble, the dominant producer of soaps and detergents in the United States with 1957 sales of $1.1 billion, acquired Clorox with sales of only $40 million. Clorox, however, was the leading manufacturer of household liquid bleach, with 49 percent of the national market.

The Supreme Court held that the merger violated Section 7 of the Clayton Act for several reasons. Here, we confine the discussion to the Court's opinion regarding potential competition.

The Commission also found that the acquisition of Clorox by Procter eliminated Procter as a potential competitor.... The evidence clearly shows that Procter was the most likely entrant.... Procter was engaged in a vigorous program of diversifying into product lines closely related to its basic products. Liquid bleach was a natural avenue of diversification since it is complementary to Procter's products, is sold to the same customers through the same channels, and is advertised and merchandised in the same manner.... Procter had considered the possibility of independently entering but decided against it because the acquisition of Clorox would enable Procter to capture a more commanding share of the market.

It is clear that the existence of Procter at the edge of the industry exerted considerable influence on the market. First, the market behavior of the liquid bleach industry was influenced by each firm's predictions of the market behavior of its competitors, actual and potential. Second, the barriers to entry by a firm of Procter's size and with its advantages were not significant. There is no indication that the barriers were so high that the price Procter would have to charge would be above the price that would maximize the profits of the existing firms. Third, the number of potential entrants was not so large that the elimination of one would be insignificant. Few firms would have the temerity to challenge a firm as solidly entrenched as Clorox.

Thus, by acquiring Clorox, Procter removed itself as a potential competitor. Because Procter was the most likely entrant and perhaps unique in its capability to enter, the Court viewed this merger as removing an important constraint on pricing policies in the bleach market. It is also generally believed by antitrust authorities that other forms of entry by Procter would have been preferable to acquisition of the leading firm.

That is, more procompetitive alternatives would have been either new entry or entry by a so-called "toehold" acquisition of a small competitor.

In the Merger Guidelines, several criteria are given that must be met before a potential competition merger will be challenged:

1. The HHI must exceed 1800.

2. Entry must be difficult.

3. The eliminated potential competitor must have been one of only three or fewer firms having comparable advantages in entering the market.

4. The acquired firm's market share must be at least 5 percent.

Steiner has provided a useful graphical analysis of potential competition.[30] He introduces the concept of the "general condition of entry" (GCE) schedule. Potential competitors are assumed to have cost disadvantages, and the GCE ranks them in order of increasing disadvantage. Several possible GCE schedules are shown in Figure 7.6, where we assume that the average cost of existing firms in the widget industry is C^*.

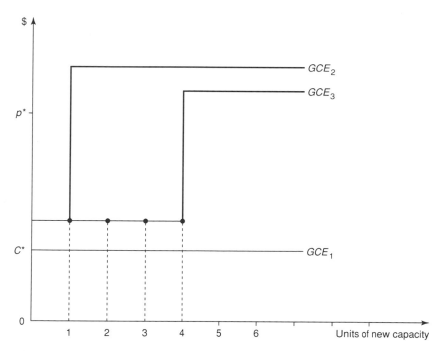

Figure 7.6
Alternative General Condition of Entry (GCE) Schedules

The vertical axis measures costs per unit of output and the horizontal axis measures the number of potential entrants. For simplicity, it is assumed that each entrant would construct one unit of capacity. Thus, GCE_1 shows a case in which wholly unimpeded entry would exist. In such cases, potential entry would force price to be set equal to C^*.

Now assume that p^* represents the monopoly price existing firms would like to charge if entry were blockaded. GCE_2 then represents a case in which a merger would be challenged if the single low-cost potential entrant acquired an existing firm. Clearly, the removal of that firm as a potential entrant means that entry would be effectively blocked, and price could rise to p^*.

The schedule GCE_3 shows a case in which the removal of a potential competitor would not be challenged. The reason, of course, is that three other potential competitors with comparable costs would remain as threats to entry.

Although the potential competition principle is certainly correct in theory, there are difficult problems involved in establishing empirically who the potential competitors are and what their respective costs are. Even more difficult to establish is whether a firm forbidden to enter by acquiring the leading firm might then enter by building new capacity or by acquiring a smaller firm. Some experts claim that potential competition cases are no longer even the subject of serious debate in the antitrust community.

Summary

In this chapter we have examined the economics of horizontal and conglomerate mergers. These mergers can be viewed as cooperative actions that can possibly harm competition. The other type of merger, vertical acquisitions of suppliers by customers (or vice versa), will be analyzed in the next chapter, where we will also examine vertical restraints.

A major part of this chapter dealt with the Justice Department and Federal Trade Commission Guidelines. These guidelines make use of the HHI index of concentration to spell out the conditions under which the government is likely to challenge a proposed merger. Another important contribution of the Guidelines is a new conceptual approach to market definition.

Questions and Problems

1. Assume the following facts concerning the horizontal merger model developed by Williamson and shown in Figure 7.2. Demand is $q = 100 - P$;

average cost premerger, $AC_0 = \$50$; average cost postmerger, $AC_1 = \$44$; and premerger price, $p_0 = \$50$. Assume that the postmerger price, $p_1 = \$70$, results from the market power created from the merger.

a. Calculate the value of the deadweight loss, area A_1.

b. Calculate the value of the cost savings created by the merger, area A_2.

c. Should the merger be allowed? What qualifications should be considered?

2. Assume all of the facts in problem 1 except that now take the premerger price, p_0, to be $52. How does this affect your answers to problem 1?

3. Assume a homogeneous good market for cellular phones. Two firms, 1 and 2, have a combined demand of $q = 40 - .4P$ and all manufacturers of cellular phones have constant marginal and average costs of $50. Initially, the price is $50.

(a) Firms 1 and 2 have decided to merge. They can lower their cost curve from $50 to $48 because of economies of combined operations. They expect that as the market leader they can lead the industry to a new price of $60. Ignore industry-wide effects—i.e., use the above demand curve—and compute social costs and benefits of the merger. On this basis should the merger be approved?

(b) Now recognize that the two firms above were intitally a part of a five-firm industry in which each firm acts as if it has a "share-of-the-market" demand curve of 20 percent of the market demand. The market demand is $Q = 100 - P$. (Note that the combined demand curve referred to above is in fact 40 percent of the market demand.) Would firm 3 favor or oppose the merger assuming that the phone price rises to $60 and it operates on its "share-of-the-market" demand curve, $q = 20 - .2P$?

(c) If social benefits and costs are now computed on an "industry-wide" basis, should the merger be approved?

(d) Now assume that greater cost savings are expected by firms 1 and 2. Their cost curve will shift down to $45 rather than to $48. It is now a real possibility that the new combined firm will decide to cut price to $50 (or just a bit below) and take over the entire market. Find the new firm's profits under the price increase strategy (of $60) and under the monopolization strategy. Given that the new firm will follow the most profitable strategy, will firm 3 favor or oppose the merger now?

(e) How might information about rival firms' attitudes toward a merger (or their stock prices) be useful to antitrust enforcement agencies?

4. A criticism of the model in problem 1 is that price is not related to cost through the standard monopoly theory. That is, if the merger creates monopoly power, then the postmerger price is precisely related to the postmerger cost (and the elasticity of demand). Is this a valid criticism?

5. In a merger between Owens Illinois and Brockway Glass in 1987 the premerger HHI was 1538. The two merging firms had market shares of 22.7 percent and 15 percent of the glass bottle market. Would this merger be safe under the Merger Guidelines?

6. Explain how the Agency would decide whether to include, say, plastic bottles, in the market referred to in problem 5.

7. According to some economists, horizontal mergers may not always be profitable even though they reduce the number of suppliers. For example, assume a three-firm industry in which the firms behave according to the

Cournot model. Let market demand be $Q = 20 - P$. Each firm has a constant average cost of \$4. Now assume that a merger reduces the number of firms to two. Calculate the combined profits of the two firms premerger, and then calculate the profit of the combined firm in the postmerger situation—a Cournot duopoly. Is this a reasonable way of modeling the profitability of horizontal mergers? For further background, see M. K. Perry and R. H. Porter, "Oligopoly and the Incentive for Horizontal Merger," *American Economic Review*, March 1985.

8. In what ways do conglomerate mergers merit the attention of antitrust authorities?

Notes

1. Jesse W. Markham, "Survey of the Evidence and Findings on Mergers," in National Bureau of Economic Research, *Business Concentration and Price Policy* (Princeton, N.J.: Princeton University Press, 1955), p. 180.

2. U.S. Federal Trade Commission, *The Merger Movement: A Summary Report* (Washington, D.C.: Federal Trade Commission, 1948), p. 68.

3. F. M. Scherer, *Industrial Market Structure and Economic Performance*, 2nd ed. (Chicago: Rand-McNally, 1980).

4. M. C. Jensen, "Takeovers: Their Causes and Consequences," *Journal of Economic Perspectives*, Winter 1988.

5. F. M. Scherer, "Corporate Takeovers: The Efficiency Arguments," *Journal of Economic Perspectives*, Winter 1988.

6. This quotation is from Charles G. Bludhorn of Gulf & Western. See *Business Week*, July 5, 1969, p. 34.

7. Oliver E. Williamson, "Economies as an Antitrust Defense: The Welfare Tradeoffs," *American Economic Review*, March 1968.

8. The calculations use $A_1 = \frac{1}{2}(\Delta p)(\Delta q)$ and $A_2 = (\Delta AC)q_1$. Substituting for Δq from the definition of price elasticity, η, we get

$$A_1 = \frac{1}{2}\frac{(\Delta p)(\eta q_0 \Delta p)}{p_0}.$$

Equating A_1 and A_2 yields

$$(\Delta AC)q_1 = \frac{1}{2}\frac{(\Delta p)(\eta q_0 \Delta p)}{p_0}.$$

Because $AC_0 = p_0$, divide the left side by $(AC_0)q_1$ and the right side by $p_0 q_1$. The result is

$$\frac{\Delta AC}{AC_0} = \frac{1}{2}\eta\left(\frac{q_0}{q_1}\right)\left(\frac{\Delta p}{p_0}\right)^2.$$

Finally, assuming a constant elasticity demand curve,

$$\frac{q_0}{q_1} = \left(\frac{1}{1 + \Delta p/p_0}\right)^\eta$$

So for $\eta - -1$, $\Delta p/p_0 = 0.2$, we get $q_0/q_1 = 1.2$, and therefore $\Delta AC/AC_0 = 0.024$.

9. Richard A. Posner, *Antitrust Law: An Economic Perspective* (Chicago: University of Chicago Press, 1976), p. 112.

10. Oliver E. Williamson, "Economies as an Antitrust Defense Revisited," *University of Pennsylvania Law Review*, 1977.

11. For an empirical test in the case of a merger of two airlines, see George W. Douglas, "The Importance of Entry Conditions: Texas Air's Acquisition of Eastern Airlines," in John E. Kwoka, Jr. and Lawrence J. White (eds.), *The Antitrust Revolution* (Glenview, Ill.: Scott, Foresman, 1989).

12. Brown Shoe Company v. United States, 370 U.S. 294 (1962).

13. The horizontal dimensions of the shoe-manufacturing market were not at issue before the Supreme Court. The district court found that the merger of Brown's and Kinney's manufacturing facilities was economically too insignificant to be illegal, and the government did not appeal the lower court's decision.

14. Federal Trade Commission v. Procter & Gamble Co. et al., 386 U.S. 368, 580 (1967).

15. Scherer, *Industrial Market Structure*, p. 554.

16. Robert H. Bork, *The Antitrust Paradox* (New York: Basic Books, 1978), p. 65.

17. United States v. Continental Can Co. et al., 378 U.S. 441 (1964).

18. United States v. Aluminum Co. of America et al., 377 U.S. 271 (1964).

19. Scherer, *Industrial Market Structure*, p. 554.

20. United States v. Von's Grocery Co. et al., 384 U.S. 270 (1966).

21. United States v. General Dynamics Corp. et al., 415 U.S. 486 (1974).

22. John H. Shenefield and Irwin M. Stelzer, *The Antitrust Laws: A Primer* (Washington, D.C.: The AEI Press, 1993), p.59.

23. The 1984 Guidelines are reprinted in *Trade Regulation Reports*, June 5, 1992.

24. Ibid.

25. See L. J. White, "Application of the Merger Guidelines: The Proposed Merger of Coca-Cola and Dr. Pepper," in Kwoka and White (eds.), *The Antitrust Revolution*.

26. Oliver E. Williamson, *Markets and Hierarchies: Analysis and Antitrust Implications* (New York: The Free Press, 1975), p. 147.

27. See Scherer, *Industrial Market Structure*, p. 344, for further discussion.

28. Justice Department Guidelines.

29. Federal Trade Commission v. Procter & Gamble Co. et al., 386 U.S. 568 (1967).

30. Peter O. Steiner, *Mergers* (Ann Arbor: University of Michigan Press, 1975).

8 Vertical Mergers and Restrictions

In previous chapters we have examined anticompetitive acts that result from cooperation among competitors. For example, rivals may cooperate to divide markets or fix prices. Rivals also may merge in order to achieve market power. In this chapter we begin the analysis of how firms can harm competition by inflicting injury on their rivals.

The focus in this chapter is on vertical relationships between buyers and sellers. For example, by buying or merging with some of its customer-firms a competitor can exclude its rivals from selling to those customer-firms. This is known as foreclosure in the antitrust literature. The possible harm to competition resulting from foreclosure will be a major topic.

Another type of vertical restriction is known as tying. Eastman Kodak, prior to 1954, required its customers of color film to buy its photofinishing service simultaneously. That is, Kodak sold every roll of film with an advance charge for processing included. Customers had no choice if they wanted the film except to purchase the right to have that film developed and printed also. This tying of one product to another is viewed harshly by the courts; it is seen as parlaying market power over, say, color film into a second monopoly over photofinishing. Tying will be considered in this chapter in some depth.

Other vertical restrictions that will be described and analyzed in this chapter include exclusive dealing, resale price maintenance, and territorial restraints.

Vertical Mergers

Vertical mergers link firms in buyer-seller relationships. Examples of vertical integration are numerous. The petroleum industry consists of many firms that are vertically integrated, from crude oil discovery and production to refineries to retail gasoline stations. The Federal Trade Commission undertook antitrust actions in the 1960s to block a series of vertical mergers between cement manufacturers and ready-mixed concrete firms. In this section we shall examine the possible benefits and costs of such combinations and review the evolution of antitrust law toward vertical mergers.

Benefits

The most common, yet subtle, benefit of vertical integration—either through internal growth or merger—is that it produces the efficient organizational form. Basically, all firms have to decide whether to "make or buy" an input. That is, should a particular input be manufactured by the firm itself or should the firm simply buy it on the market? One antitrust case was concerned with Ford Motor Company's decision to acquire the spark plug supplier Autolite so as to make spark plugs internally as opposed to continuing to buy plugs on the market.

Reducing Transactions Costs

Transactions costs are costs of using the market. In the Ford Motor Company example, these are costs that Ford would incur in searching among possible suppliers for the lowest price for spark plugs, and in negotiating the contracts to spell out exactly what the terms of sale are (product specifications, credit arrangements, delivery dates, and so on).

Another cost of buying rather than making has been termed the "cost of reduced flexibility." For example, Ford might be locked into long-term purchases of a certain type of spark plug. Many unforeseen events could occur to make these purchases no longer desirable. For example, innovations could create technically superior spark plugs, or Ford's car sales could fall, causing a decline in their demand for the particular type of spark plug. If Ford manufactured its own spark plugs, it would have the flexibility to respond to unexpected changes in a more efficient manner.

Of course, there are also reasons for firms to continue using the market rather than being completely integrated. A major reason is the increasing problem of coordination and management of the firm's activities as more and more functions are added. Also, there may be strong scale economies in a particular activity such that the firm's own needs are too small to achieve the efficient output rate.

As a further illustration of the nature of transactions costs, consider the pharmaceutical manufacturer Pfizer. Why is Pfizer integrated vertically into research and development of new ethical drugs? That is, in principle Pfizer could contract with independent laboratories for the discovery and development of new drugs, and perform internally only the manufacturing and marketing functions.

When one reflects on the uncertainty involved in drug discovery, and what the contracts with an independent lab would be like, it becomes clear why such integration exists. For example, would Pfizer seek a fixed supply price for a new antibiotic drug with certain specified therapeutic properties? Given the uncertainty, the lab would probably require a large risk premium to compensate it for the probability that it might be unable to deliver. There would also need to be contingencies negotiated for payments in the event of only partial success, or in the event of unexpected harmful side effects.

If Pfizer believed the risk premium to be too high, it might decide on a "cost-plus" contract, thereby bearing the risk itself. But cost-plus arrangements are well known to provide poor incentives for holding down costs. Hence a better solution for Pfizer than "using the market" may be vertical integration, that is, organizing research and development through direct managerial controls. The fundamental phenomenon here, of course, is that the market transaction costs of contract negotiation (price haggling, product specifications, incorporation of contingencies, and the like) are greater than performing the activity internally.

Another example is the connection between Western Electric and the Bell System operating companies that was severed in 1984 by an antitrust action. Western Electric manufactured most of the telephone switching equipment and trunks used by the operating companies. It was argued that since they were all part of one company (AT&T), Western could coordinate orders from the operating companies and plan its production scheduling so as to minimize cost. Some of these planning economies may be lost because of the greater uncertainty resulting from the divestiture. Of course, there were also believed to be benefits to society from the divestiture.[1]

Technological Economies

There are also benefits from vertical integration that arise from purely technological considerations. The classic example here is the integration of ironmaking and steelmaking, where physical proximity eliminates the need for reheating the iron before it is made into steel.

A further benefit of vertical integration, though one of a "second best" character, is the elimination of successive monopolies, or dissolving bilateral monopoly bargaining stalemates. The idea in both cases is that monopoly exists at both levels of a vertical chain. By merging, only a single integrated firm is created, and it can be shown to be socially preferable to the "double" monopolies. The term second best was used because society's "first best" would be competition at both levels.

Eliminating Successive Monopolies

The *successive monopolies* (or, sometimes termed, double marginalization) case can be illustrated with Figure 8.1. Assume that an "upstream" motor monopolist sells to a "downstream" boat monopolist.[2] The boat monopolist adds other inputs to the motor and produces the final product, a boat, at a constant conversion cost of C per unit, or $100 per unit. Hence, fixed proportions production is assumed to hold for boat production. Each boat requires exactly one motor and C dollars worth of

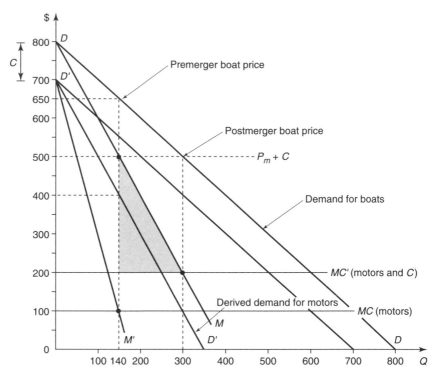

Figure 8.1
Successive Monopoly: Pre- and Postmerger

other inputs. We can therefore use the symbol Q to refer to both the quantity of motors and the quantity of boats.

The boat monopolist is assumed to have no monopsony power—that is, it accepts whatever price is set for the motor as fixed. (The opposite assumption—that the boat monopolist *does* have monopsony power—is the case of bilateral monopoly.)

Figure 8.1 shows the final demand curve for boats DD and the derived demand for motors $D'D'$. Finding the derived demand for motors is actually the heart of the analysis. The approach is to use the equilibrium condition for the downstream boat monopolist. That is, it maximizes profit by equating marginal revenue and marginal cost. Or,

$MR = P_m + C \dots$ marginal revenue equals marginal cost

so,

$P_m = MR - C \dots$ the derived demand for motors

Note that the boat monopolist's marginal cost is its conversion cost C plus the price of a motor, P_m. Hence, the derived demand for motors is just marginal revenue minus the conversion cost C. The curve $D'D'$ in Figure 8.1 is obtained by finding the marginal revenue curve corresponding to DD (the line DM) and shifting it downward by the constant C (that is, by $100).

Of course, the boat monopolist's input demand $D'D'$ is also the motor monopolist's product demand curve. The motor monopolist therefore maximizes profit by setting its marginal revenue curve, $D'M'$, equal to the marginal cost of motors MC (constant at $100). The profit-maximizing quantity is 140 motors, shown in Figure 8.1. The price can be found on the $D'D'$ curve as $P_m = \$400$.

The motor monopolist now equates its marginal revenue for boats DM to its marginal cost (the horizontal line at $500, labeled $P_m + C$). They intersect at $Q = 140$, yielding a boat price of $650.

If the two monopolists merged, the integrated firm would maximize profit by setting marginal revenue DM equal to marginal cost MC' (MC of motors $+ C$, or $200). The profit-maximizing quantity becomes 300 and the final price is $500. Hence, merger leads to a lower price ($500 versus $650) and a larger quantity (300 versus 140) as compared to successive monopoly. It is also true that total profit is larger (by the shaded triangular area in Figure 8.1). Hence, both the firms and consumers gain from the merger!

The shaded triangular area in Figure 8.1 represents incremental profit because profit equals the area beneath the marginal revenue curve less the area beneath the marginal cost curve. That is, the area under marginal revenue DM is total revenue and the area under marginal cost MC' is total cost. Expansion of output from 140 to 300 as a result of the vertical integration therefore adds the triangular area to profit.

Anticompetitive Effects

Perhaps the most common complaint raised in legal proceedings against vertical merger is foreclosure. As the Supreme Court stated in its famous Brown Shoe decision: "the diminution of the vigor of competition which may stem from a vertical arrangement results primarily from a foreclosure of a share of the market otherwise open to competitors."[3] As an example, the acquisition of ready-mixed concrete firms by cement suppliers was said to foreclose the market for cement to nonintegrated cement suppliers.

For foreclosure to create anticompetitive problems, one or both levels involved must possess some degree of market power. If both levels have large numbers of firms, vertical acquisitions can best be viewed as a method of nonprice competition. In the case where both levels are unconcentrated, suppliers could obtain secure markets by vertical acquisitions,

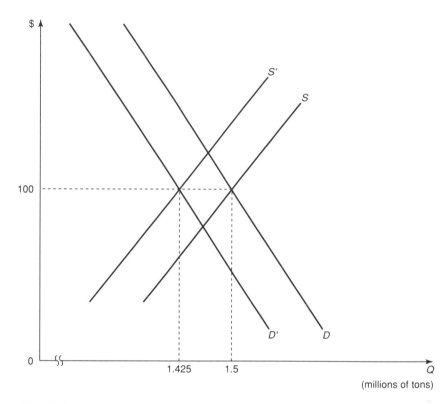

Figure 8.2
Cement Market Equilibrium before and after Vertical Merger between One buyer and One Seller

and this might cause harm to rivals who were slower to integrate. However, it can be argued that foreclosure used to increase market share will be costly to the firm attempting it, and therefore the rationality of foreclosure as a method of nonprice competition is suspect.

To see this argument, assume a situation in which twenty equal-sized cement suppliers sell to twenty equal-sized ready-mixed concrete firms. Now consider Ace Cement's strategy of acquiring a single buyer, say Jones Ready-Mix Concrete. At present, Ace sells 75,000 tons of cement at the market price of $100. Jones buys 75,000 tons of cement.

Before the merger, the demand and supply curves in the cement market are shown as *D* and *S* in Figure 8.2. The equilibrium price is $100 and the quantity traded in the market is 1.5 million tons.

After the merger Ace transfers all of its 75,000 tons internally to its Jones division, thereby removing its supply and Jones's demand from the market. The new demand and supply curves are now *D'* and *S'*. The equilibrium price is still $100, but the quantity traded in the market falls

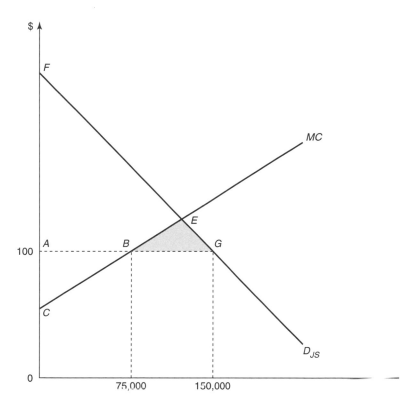

Figure 8.3
Cost of Foreclosing Cement Market to Rival Suppliers

by 75,000 tons to 1.425 million. Clearly, the foreclosure of Jones as a buyer has not disadvantaged the remaining cement suppliers. They may need to rearrange their actual sales patterns if they had been selling some cement to Jones, but in equilibrium the price is still $100.

Next, consider an alternate strategy by Ace.[4] Let Ace acquire two buyers, say, Jones and Smith, each of whom buys 75,000 tons of cement. Hence the thrust of Ace's strategy is now to increase its ready-mix market share at the expense of other cement suppliers.

In Figure 8.3 we show the horizontal summation of the demand curves for cement of Jones and Smith, D_{JS}, and Ace's marginal cost schedule for cement, MC. If the strategy of Ace is to withdraw all of the purchases of Jones and Smith from the market, the maximum profit can be obtained at point E where D_{JS} and MC intersect. Total revenue equals the area under the D_{JS} schedule and total cost equals the area below MC. Hence, profit equals the triangular area FEC.

Before the vertical acquisition, however, the sum of the profits of Ace, Jones, and Smith was larger by the shaded triangular area EGB. With the market price of $100, Ace made a profit of triangle *ABC* and the combined profits of Jones and Smith equaled triangle *FGA*. This means that foreclosure is costly, where the cost equals the foregone profit *EGB*.

A final point is that the vertical acquisition itself is not what is costly. The integrated firm could earn exactly the same profit as before the acquisition if it used the market price of $100 as its "transfer price." That is, the three "divisions" should be told to buy and sell at the $100 transfer price so as to maximize divisional profits. The result of this would be that each division would buy or sell exactly the same quantities as before the merger, with exactly the same profits.

One might imagine a situation in which Ace buys all of the ready-mixed concrete firms. This would surely constitute a serious "foreclosure." This would be true, of course, but the real problem in this case is horizontal monopoly, not vertical foreclosure. That is, it would not matter who bought all of the firms—it could have been a fast-food chain.

Now, in contrast to the discussion above, we relax the assumption that both levels are unconcentrated and reconsider the foreclosure arguments. Suppose, for example, that concentration is relatively high at the supplier level. For illustrative purposes, assume that there are four equal-sized suppliers, two of whom are vertically integrated. A vertical merger now means that the "open" sector is now reduced to only 25 percent of the total. The claim is that competition is harmed because of heightened entry barriers.

A potential entrant at the supply level has only half as big an open market as before the merger. Scale economies may now cause entry problems (as described in Chapter 6), given the reduced market. And if the entrant elects to enter at both levels simultaneously, capital requirements will be greater and may delay or forestall entry.

The Merger Guidelines (explained in Chapter 7) explain this point as follows:

More capital is necessary to enter two markets than to enter one. Standing alone, however, this additional capital requirement does not constitute a barrier to entry to the primary market. If the necessary funds were available at a cost commensurate with the level of risk in the secondary market, there would be no adverse effect. In some cases, however, lenders may doubt that would-be entrants to the primary market have the necessary skills and knowledge to succeed in the secondary market and, therefore, in the primary market. In order to compensate for this risk of failure, lenders might charge a higher rate for the necessary capital.

A recent theoretical model developed by Ordover, Saloner, and Salop shows that, under certain rather strong assumptions, a vertical merger can cause anticompetitive results through the general mechanism known

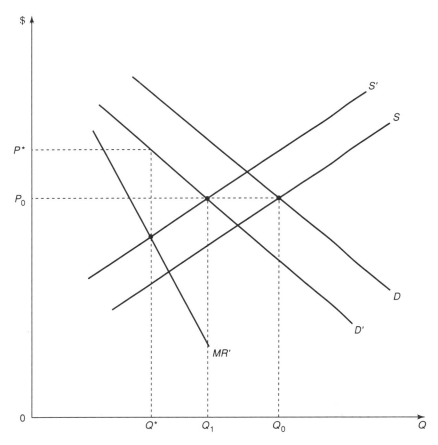

Figure 8.4
Raising Rivals' Costs Due to Vertical Merger

as raising rivals' costs.[5] The key idea of their model can be explained most simply with Figure 8.4.

The demand and supply curves for an input of the Hi-Tec Company, D and S, are shown in Figure 8.4. Initially, the competitive equilibrium price and quantity are P_0 and Q_0, as determined by the intersection of D and S. Hence, Hi-Tec and its rivals all pay equal input prices.

Now, assume that Hi-Tec merges with an input supplier and no longer deals in the open market. It simply transfers the input internally at P_0, which is the input's marginal cost. If the input market remains competitive after the merger, the new demand and supply curves, D' and S', continue to intersect at P_0. Of course, the open market output is lower (Q_1 compared to Q_0) because Hi-Tec's transactions are now internal to the merged firm. Notice that Hi-Tec's rivals continue to pay P_0 for the input, so they are in no way disadvantaged.

However, it is assumed by Ordover, Saloner, and Salop that the input supplier market structure is changed by the loss of Hi-Tec's merger partner. The reduced number of suppliers permits the remaining input suppliers to behave monopolistically. Hence they equate marginal revenue MR' to marginal cost S' at output Q^*, leading to a price increase to P^*.

Hi-Tec's vertical merger has led to a situation in which Hi-Tec pays only P_0 for its input compared to the higher P^* paid by its rivals. These lower input costs permit Hi-Tec to make higher profits in its competition with its higher-cost rivals. The monopoly pricing of inputs, which did not occur before the merger, is clearly anticompetitive. (Of course, in a real sense this is a horizontal problem of monopoly in the input supplier market—although it is a result of the vertical merger.)

In addition to foreclosure, it is also feared by some that vertical integration, combined with high concentration at one level, may permit an extension of that market power to the other level. A price squeeze is an example. Alcoa, with a monopoly over aluminum ingot and integrated downstream into fabrication, was alleged to have squeezed independent fabricators by charging a high price for ingot and low prices for fabricated products. Assume that Alcoa charged 15 cents per pound for ingot (which it sold to rivals) and 35 cents per sheet for aluminum (which it sold in competition with rivals). Clearly, by raising the ingot price to 20 cents and holding the sheet price fixed, Alcoa could squeeze its rival sheet suppliers.

M. J. Peck, a former member of the President's Council of Economic Advisers, has observed that the explanation for the Alcoa squeeze was more likely an attempt to protect its sheet market from competition from steel rather than an attempt to eliminate independent fabricators.[6] Still, the effect of the squeeze was to jeopardize the economic viability of the fabricators regardless of the intent of Alcoa's management.

It is also possible to have situations where vertical mergers may facilitate collusion in an already highly concentrated manufacturing industry. The Guidelines suggest two cases:

A high level of vertical integration by upstream firms into the associated retail market may facilitate collusion in the upstream market by making it easier to monitor price. Retail prices are generally more visible than prices in upstream markets, and vertical mergers may increase the level of vertical integration to the point at which the monitoring effect becomes significant.

The elimination by vertical merger of a particularly disruptive buyer in a downstream market may facilitate collusion in the upstream market. If upstream firms view sales to a particular buyer as sufficiently important, they may deviate from the terms of a collusive agreement in an effort to secure that business, thereby disrupting the operation of the agreement. The merger of such a buyer with an upstream firm may eliminate that rivalry, making it easier for the upstream firms to collude effectively.

In summary, we have suggested that harmful effects from vertical integration are unlikely to occur unless there is preexisting market power at one level or both. While this seems to indicate that the real problem is horizontal market power that should be attacked directly, perhaps this is not always possible. Hence we shall pursue the analysis from a somewhat different angle.

Suppose we recognize that market power at one level can be extended to another level. Does the creation of a "second" monopoly have any harmful consequences for economic efficiency? If it does not, then the merger may have been effected for other reasons—for example, socially beneficial transaction-cost savings. In this case, economic efficiency might be better served by favoring such mergers.

Extension of Monopoly: Fixed Proportions

Consider an admittedly extreme example. A monopolist supplier sells to a perfectly competitive industry. Assume that the monopolist extends its monopoly downstream, acquiring the competitive industry through a series of vertical mergers. Does this monopolization at a second level result in any additional efficiency losses? Also, from the monopolist's perspective, can monopoly profits be increased? As we will show, the answers to all these questions are negative as long as the competitive industry uses fixed-proportions production.

Fixed-proportions production simply means that each unit of output requires a fixed proportion of the various inputs. Some economists think that this assumption is applicable to situations where a manufacturer sells to retailers; that is, retailers combine the manufacturer's goods with other inputs in fixed proportions. Earlier, we made this assumption in our discussion of successive monopolies. There, each boat required exactly one motor plus C dollars' worth of all other inputs.

We can use that same example here by assuming that boat supply is perfectly competitive and motors are monopolized. Hence we want to examine the consequences of vertical monopolization of boats by the motor supplier.

Figure 8.5 illustrates the case. First, consider the premerger situation. The final demand for boats is DD. Subtracting the fixed conversion cost per unit, C, we obtain the derived demand for motors, $D'D'$[7]. The motor monopolist equates its marginal revenue, $D'M'$, with its marginal cost of motors, MC. It therefore charges a price of $400 and sells 300 motors. The competitive boat industry has a horizontal supply schedule of $400

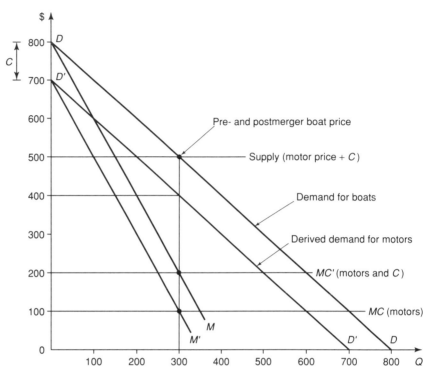

Figure 8.5
Vertical Monopolization with Fixed Proportions Production

plus the $100 conversion cost, or $500, and therefore sells 300 motor-boats for $500 each. The motor monopolist earns a profit of $400 less $100, multiplied by 300 units, or $90,000.

Now, assume the motor monopolist monopolizes downstream. The marginal revenue corresponding to the final demand for boats is DM. The marginal cost MC' of the combined operation is $200, or the sum of the marginal cost of motors ($100) and the conversion cost ($100). Equating DM and MC' gives an output of 300 boats and a price of $500. The integrated firm has a profit of $500 less $200, multiplied by 300 units, or $90,000.

The result is that the monopolist gains nothing by monopolizing downstream. Profit is the same pre- and postmerger. The motor mo-nopolist is able to extract all of the potential profit by choosing its price of motors. And from society's viewpoint there is absolutely no differ-ence. Price and output are unaffected also. Presumably, in cases where fixed-proportions production obtains, vertical monopolization must have some motivation other than increased monopoly profits.

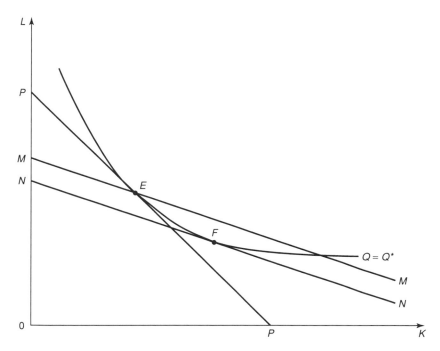

Figure 8.6
Potential Cost Savings, *MN*, from Vertical Integration with Variable Proportions Production

Extension of Monopoly: Variable Proportions

In this section we relax the assumption of fixed-proportions production. As an example, assume that shoe manufacturing is a competitive industry that is characterized by variable-proportions production. For simplicity, assume that only two inputs are required: shoe-making capital equipment, K, and labor, L. That is, a given number of shoes, Q, can be produced with alternative quantities of K and L Figure 8.6 shows these alternate production possibilities as the isoquant $Q = Q^*$. (An isoquant is the locus of the various combinations of K and L that can be used to produce a particular output level.)

Next, Sam's Shoe Machinery is assumed to have a monopoly over K. As before, we want to examine the incentives for, and efficiency consequences of, a vertical acquisition by Sam's of the shoe manufacturing industry. Can Sam's extract all of the profit by an appropriate choice of the price of K, as was true in the fixed proportions case? And will the price of shoes be affected by vertical acquisition?

In anticipation of the results of the analysis, a key difference between the two cases is the following: as p_k, the price of K, is increased by

Sam's, the shoe manufacturing industry will substitute away from K and use a more labor-intensive input mix. In the fixed-proportions case, this was not possible. No matter what price for motors was charged, more of the other inputs could not substitute for a motor. Every motorboat required one motor.

Let labor be priced at its true opportunity cost (that is, labor is supplied competitively) and take the marginal cost of K to be MC_k. The slope of isocost line NN in Figure 8.6 is the ratio of MC_k to the labor price. Hence, point F represents the least-cost input mix from society's viewpoint for producing Q^* shoes. Because $p_k > MC_k$ by assumption, the actual isocost line facing the shoe industry premerger has a steeper slope, such as PP. Hence the shoe industry picks input mix E, which minimizes its expenditures on inputs. Because the industry's payments to Sam's include a monopoly profit, the expenditures on inputs that it minimizes are not equivalent to true resource costs.

The true resource costs at E are higher than at F by the vertical distance MN (measured in units of L). In other words, setting a monopoly price on K causes inefficient production in shoe manufacturing—costs of production are too high because the input mix is incorrect (from society's viewpoint).

If Sam's monopolized forward into shoe manufacturing, the production of shoes would shift from E to F because the integrated monopoly would minimize costs using the true opportunity costs of K and L. The cost saving MN would then constitute a profit incentive for the vertical acquisition.

Thus far it would appear that such a merger should be permitted; costs of production would be lowered. However, there is a further step in our analysis. Namely, what price will the integrated monopolist charge for shoes, given the lower real cost of production? Unfortunately, mathematical analysis shows that the price can either rise or fall—although the most likely case is probably an increase.[8] And if price rises, we are back in a tradeoff situation where the benefits are cost savings and the costs are deadweight losses due to monopoly pricing.

In summary, we have shown that in the case of variable-proportions production, vertical monopolization will be profitable. The welfare effects can be either positive or negative depending upon the particular parameters (elasticity of demand, elasticity of substitution in production, and so on). However, we should not lose sight of the fact that the real problem is the horizontal monopoly that was assumed to exist in shoe machinery. Only if antitrust authorities could do nothing about this horizontal problem does the analysis here become relevant.

Cases

The Brown Shoe case in 1962, discussed earlier under horizontal merger cases, also had important vertical dimensions.[9] The Court held that the relevant market was the entire United States and noted with concern a trend toward increasing vertical integration.

> Since the diminution of the vigor of competition, which may stem from a vertical arrangement, results primarily from a foreclosure of a share of the market otherwise open to competitors, an important consideration in determining whether the effect of a vertical arrangement [is illegal] is the size of the share of the market foreclosed.

In Brown Shoe the size of the market foreclosed was on the order of 1 percent! That is, Brown (primarily a shoe manufacturer) could be expected to force Kinney (primarily a shoe retailer) to take only a small volume of Brown shoes, to the exclusion of other shoe manufacturers. However, as in the horizontal part of the case, the Court gave great weight to the trend and the concern to stop the process in its incipiency.

In the Ford Motor Company decision in 1972, the Supreme Court held that Ford's acquisition from Electric Autolite Co. of the name Autolite and associated spark-plug manufacturing assets was illegal. One basis for the decision was that the merger resulted in "the foreclosure of Ford as a purchaser of about ten percent of total industry output."[10]

Finally, we should mention the Merger Guidelines, discussed earlier in connection with possible anticompetitive effects of vertical mergers. While the 1968 Guidelines stated that vertical mergers between a supplier with a 10 percent share and a buyer with a 6 percent share might be challenged, the new Guidelines have no similar statements about foreclosure percentages. Rather, they merely caution that vertical mergers will be challenged only where they have anticompetitive horizontal effects. In particular, if a vertical merger creates barriers to entry, facilitates collusion, or enhances the ability to evade rate regulation, it may be challenged.

We turn now to a set of business practices that sometimes exists between suppliers and dealers or manufacturers and retailers that can be viewed as forms of vertical integration—but fall somewhat short of complete vertical integration. That is, these practices often accomplish some of the objectives of vertical integration, but through contractual means rather than a complete merging of firms.

The various practices that we shall examine are resale price maintenance (known as RPM), territorial restraints, exclusive dealing, and tying. They often come in combinations and in many differing forms. For this reason, we begin by providing concrete examples of each practice.

Vertical Restrictions

Resale price maintenance or RPM means that the supplier requires the dealer to resell its product at some set price. (It is sometimes referred to as vertical price fixing.) Usually, RPM is either a minimum resale price or a maximum resale price. An example of minimum RPM would be if Nintendo required its retailers to sell its video games at no less than $40. An example of a maximum resale price would be if the *New York Times* required its home delivery distributors to sell the newspaper for no more than $4 per week. Note that a vertically integrated firm would set its own resale price to final customers—so RPM is a partial substitute for vertical integration.

A territorial restraint is an agreement between the supplier and the dealer that the supplier will not allow any other dealer to locate within a certain area—thereby preserving an exclusive marketing territory to that dealer. Such agreements are widespread in the automobile industry. An example would be if Ford Motor Company agreed to allow only one Ford dealership in a city. Again, of course, if Ford Motor was completely integrated into retailing its cars, it would obviously choose where it would locate its retail outlets.

Exclusive dealing can be illustrated by a hypothetical agreement between Exxon and an independent service station that the service station would buy all its gasoline and motor oil supplies from Exxon. Exclusive dealing can be viewed as a way of accomplishing vertical integration by contract.

The last vertical restriction that we shall consider is known as tying. Tying refers to the practice of a supplier agreeing to sell its customer one product (the tying good) only if the customer agrees to purchase all of its requirements for another product (the tied good) from the supplier. A well-known example was IBM's former practice of leasing its tabulating machines only on the condition that the customer purchase all of its needs for tabulating cards from IBM.

The four practices are generally judged under either Section 1 of the Sherman Act or Section 3 of the Clayton Act. As we will see in reviewing the cases, RPM has been held to be illegal per se under the Sherman Act. It is viewed by the courts as simply a (vertical) form of price fixing. This view is not shared by many economists, however. The reason is that many economists view the economics of RPM as being similar to territorial restraints, and the courts apply a rule of reason to judging the legality of territorial restraints. The similarity follows from the fact that both practices can offer some market power to retailers—in one case the supplier can provide the dealer with a noncompetitive margin by fixing both the dealer's costs and its resale price, and in the other case the dealer has an exclusive market and can set its own noncompetitive price. (We will explain below why the supplier might want to provide a dealer with a "healthy" profit margin.)

Section 3 of the Clayton Act specifically mentions both exclusive dealing and tying, and holds them to be illegal "where the effect ... may be to substantially lessen competition or tend to create a monopoly." While exclusive dealing comes under the rule of reason, tying is judged under a "modified" per se rule.

Resale Price Maintenance

As we discussed above, RPM can be either a requirement by the supplier that the dealer not sell below a minimum price, or that the dealer not sell above a maximum price. It is possible to describe certain situations where the supplier would prefer the minimum resale price, and others where the supplier would prefer the maximum resale price.

The simplest explanation is perhaps that pertaining to the desire of a supplier to require maximum resale prices. To understand this case the reader should refer to the discussion earlier in this chapter on successive monopolies. There we discovered that vertical integration could lead to a lower final price and higher combined profits of the successive monopolists. If the supplier and dealer both have market power—thereby satisfying the assumptions of the successive monopolies model—it is clear that the ability of the supplier to limit the dealer's price will increase its own profitability. Incidentally, this will also improve society's welfare, given that the supplier's monopoly cannot be eliminated.

The explanation for the opposite type of RPM—setting minimum resale prices—is more complex. After all, it seems counterintuitive to think that a manufacturer might prefer higher distribution costs than competition among its retailers could bring about. However, minimum-price RPM might be wise in cases where the supplier wants to ensure the provision of certain presale informational services that are necessary for the marketing of technically complex products.

Consider a personal computer. Before buying an Apple computer, the consumer would like to learn as much about it as possible. A retail computer store that sells Apples is ideal—the consumer can consult with technically trained salesmen and operate the computer, getting advice on special programming problems. Then, however, the consumer might decide to purchase the Apple through a mail-order outlet that has lower prices for Apples because they need not provide floor space for demonstrations and technically trained salesmen. In other words, the

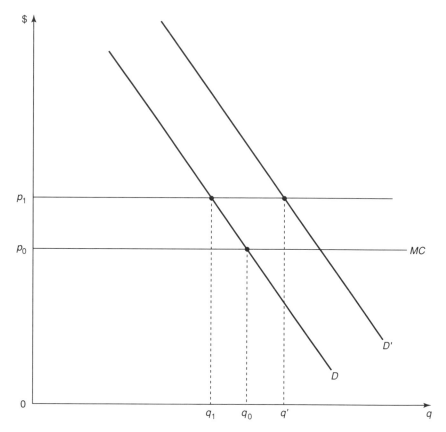

Figure 8.7
An Explanation for RPM: Shifting Out Demand

mail-order outlets are "free-riding" on the retail computer stores.[11] The concern of the supplier is that the mail-order outlets may make it unprofitable for the retail stores to continue to provide the informational services that are necessary for Apple to compete against IBM and other computer suppliers. This is a case where setting minimum resale prices may be sensible from the point of view of the supplier.

A graphical explanation may be helpful. In Figure 8.7 a retailer is shown whose marginal cost MC is equal to the price charged by the manufacturer (for simplicity, we assume the retailer's only cost is the manufacturer's product). Vigorous competition from other retailers brings price down to MC. Assume now that the manufacturer sets a minimum resale price at p_1, while continuing to sell to the retailer at MC. This might seem irrational because the demand D would imply that quantity sold would fall to q_1. Hence the manufacturer would necessarily lose money.

The key point, however, is that the retail margin $p_1 - MC$ enforced by the manufacturer is expected to lead to promotional activities by the retailer, which shifts the demand to D'. The net effect is shown in Figure 8.7 as an increase in quantity to q'.

While the particular case shown in Figure 8.7 is one possibility, other cases are also plausible, since the demand shift can be of various magnitudes. A detailed analysis of various cases by Scherer and Ross[12] suggests that RPM can be either efficiency increasing or decreasing, depending on the magnitude of the assumed demand shift.

There can be other anticompetitive effects of RPM as well. It is conceivable that either a cartel of dealers or a cartel of suppliers might be fostered through RPM. For example, the dealers might get together and insist that the supplier require minimum resale prices for all dealers. This would be very helpful in making the cartel work. Of course, it would not be in the supplier's best interest. It would also have to be a product that did not face substantial interbrand competition. For example, if Apple dealers could raise their prices, it might be quite profitable if they did not have to reckon with IBM, Compaq, Toshiba, NeXt, and so on.

The point about interbrand competition should be amplified. That is, many cases of minimum RPM have to do with intrabrand competition. If all dealers selling Apples eliminate intrabrand competition, it is not likely to be an effective cartel because consumers can shift to other brands of computers. And reduced intrabrand competition might make Apple a more effective interbrand competitor.

Since 1911, however, RPM has been illegal per se—despite the possible procompetitive arguments given above. The key case was Dr. Miles Medical Co. v. John D. Park & Sons.[13] Dr. Miles, a manufacturer of proprietary medicines, had established a set of minimum resale prices that applied throughout its distribution chain. John D. Park, a drug wholesaler, refused to enter into the restrictive agreements and instead was able to buy Dr. Miles products from other wholesalers at discounted prices. Dr. Miles brought a suit against John D. Park for interfering with the contracts between Dr. Miles and the other wholesalers. The Supreme Court held that the contracts were illegal, observing that "agreements or combinations between dealers, having for their sole purpose the destruction of competition and the fixing of prices, are injurious to the public interest and void."

It should be pointed out that there must be a conspiracy among the manufacturer and dealer to fix the prices. It is not illegal for a manufacturer unilaterally to set resale prices and refuse to deal with retailers who do not comply. Two recent cases,[14] have established the standards necessary to infer such a conspiracy. The first case, Monsanto v. Spray-Rite Service, involved a Monsanto herbicide dealer selling at discount prices. There was evidence that other dealers had complained to Monsanto, and Monsanto subsequently terminated the dealer. The Court said that evidence of complaints was not sufficient unless additional evidence tended to exclude the possibility of independent action by Monsanto.

The second case, a Supreme Court decision in 1988, also supports the view that the conditions for RPM to be found illegal per se are quite restrictive. In Business Electronics v. Sharp, two retailers of electronic calculators, Business Electronics and Hartwell, and the manufacturer, Sharp, were involved in a dispute in the Houston area. Hartwell complained to Sharp about Business Electronics low prices—below Sharp's suggested retail prices—and in June 1973 gave Sharp an ultimatum that Hartwell would terminate his dealership unless Sharp ended its relationship with Business Electronics. Sharp then terminated Business Electronics' dealership in July 1973; Business Electronics then brought suit alleging a conspiracy that was illegal per se. Business Electronics won at the District Court level, but the decision was reversed by the Court of Appeals. The Supreme Court then agreed with the Circuit Court's decision, which found that

to render illegal per se a vertical agreement between a manufacturer and a dealer to terminate a second dealer, the first dealer must expressly or impliedly agree to set its prices at some level, though not a specific one. The distributor cannot retain complete freedom to set whatever price it chooses.

Before turning to the next practice, territorial restraints, we should note that RPM has had an interesting history. During the Depression individual states enacted "fair trade" laws that allowed minimum price RPM. The reason was to "protect" small, independent retailers from the fierce price competition of the newly emerging chains. However, such laws generally affected goods in interstate commerce and as a result were in conflict with federal antitrust laws. In 1937 Congress passed the Miller-Tydings Act, which exempted state fair trade laws from the reach of the Sherman Act. By 1975 there was a strong lobby to repeal the fair trade laws, and the Consumer Goods Pricing Act was passed—making the per se illegality of RPM under the Sherman Act once again clear.

Territorial Restraints

Territorial restraints or, as it is also known, vertical market division, can be closely related to RPM. That is, we discussed above a hypothetical case of why Apple Computer might find minimum-price RPM a wise business decision—the reason being that the dealers would then be able to provide presale informational services to consumers without the "free-rider" problem. Allocating exclusive marketing territories to its dealers can operate in much the same way—each dealer would have some market power in its territory.

An important social benefit of territorial restraints is that distribution costs might be lowered by enabling each dealer to obtain scale economies. That is, by spreading fixed costs over a higher volume of sales, the costs of distribution can be reduced.

The potentially anticompetitive effects of territorial restraints are also similar to RPM—the fostering of cartel behavior among dealers or manufacturers. An interesting case of territorial restraints exists in the soft drink industry. The major soft drink syrup manufacturers—Coke, Pepsi, Dr. Pepper, and so on—allocate exclusive territories to their bottlers. A 1973 study by the Federal Trade Commission said that the reduced intrabrand competition had been costly to consumers because concentration at the syrup level was high.[15] That is, Coke buyers could not benefit from competition among Coke bottlers, but only from competition among Coke, Pepsi, Dr. Pepper, and so on. The FTC was prevented from pursuing the case, however, when Congress passed legislation that specifically exempted the soft-drink industry's territorial restrictions.

The cases on territorial restraints have led to a rule of reason approach as opposed to the per se illegality of RPM. Many economists believe this asymmetric treatment of economically similar practices to be wrong. Generally, the view of the critics is that both should be rule of reason offenses.

The key case is Continental T.V., Inc., et al., v. GTE Sylvania, Inc., which was decided by the Supreme Court in 1977.[16] GTE Sylvania was a manufacturer of television sets that in 1962 had only 1 or 2 percent of the national market. In 1962 Sylvania began a new marketing plan. It phased out its wholesale distributors and began to sell its television sets directly to a smaller and more select group of franchised retailers. The objective was to decrease the number of competing Sylvania retailers in the hope of attracting a smaller group of more aggressive and competent retailers who could increase Sylvania's market share. To accomplish this, Sylvania limited the number of franchises granted for any given region and required each dealer to sell only from the location at which the dealer was franchised. Interestingly, Sylvania retained the discretion to increase the number of retailers in a region depending upon the success of the retailers in developing the market.

In 1965 a Sylvania dealer in San Francisco, Continental T.V., wanted to open a store in Sacramento but was prohibited from doing so by Sylvania; Sylvania was doing exceptionally well in Sacramento and did not believe another dealer would be beneficial. As a result, Continental filed suit against Sylvania under the Sherman Act, Section 1.

The Supreme Court decided in favor of Sylvania and in so doing made it clear that the case should be decided on a rule of reason basis:

> Vertical restrictions promote interbrand competition by allowing the manufacturer to achieve certain efficiencies in the distribution of his products.... For example, new manufacturers and manufacturers entering new markets can use the restrictions in order to induce competent and aggressive retailers to make the kind of investment of capital and labor that is often required in the distribution of products unknown to the consumer. Established manufacturers can use them to induce retailers to engage in promotional activities or to provide service and repair facilities necessary to the efficient marketing of their products.... Certainly there has been no showing ... that vertical restrictions have or arc likely to have a "pernicious effect on competition" or that they "lack ... any redeeming virtue."

Exclusive Dealing

Exclusive dealing is a contract between a supplier and a dealer stating that the dealer will buy all of its supplies from that supplier. For example, a gasoline service station agrees to buy all of its gasoline and motor oil from, say, Exxon. In effect, exclusive dealing is an alternative way of accomplishing vertical integration—it is "contractual" integration rather than the more permanent ownership integration that we discussed earlier. And just as vertical mergers worry the courts because of possible foreclosure of rivals, exclusive dealing is believed to have the same anticompetitive effect.

Just as vertical integration is often the efficient organizational form because it reduces transactions costs, the same can be said in favor of exclusive dealing. Benefits may include lower selling expenses by the supplier and lower search costs by the dealer. Also, the supplier may find it worthwhile to invest in developing the skills of the dealers if he knows that the dealers will be devoting all their efforts to selling his products. Another factor is that the supplier may find it worthwhile to promote the products nationally if he knows that the dealers will not substitute a lower-priced nonadvertised brand when consumers flock to their stores.

The courts have treated exclusive dealing harshly. In a 1922 case, Standard Fashion Company v. Magrane-Houston Company, the Court found an exclusive dealing arrangement between a manufacturer of dress patterns and a dry-goods store to be illegal.[17] The reason was that it was believed that rival pattern manufacturers were foreclosed from the market. The Supreme Court approved an evaluation of the problem given by the Circuit Court of Appeals:

The restriction of each merchant to one pattern manufacturer must in hundreds, perhaps in thousands, of small communities amount to giving such single pattern manufacturer a monopoly of the business in such community.

The Circuit Court went on to observe that this could lead to ever higher concentration in the pattern business nationally "so that the plaintiff ... will shortly have almost, if not quite, all the pattern business." This is not sound analysis, however, since it ignores the issue of what a pattern manufacturer must give up to obtain an exclusive dealing arrangement in the first place. That is, the dry-goods stores can benefit by tough bargaining with potential pattern suppliers before signing up with a particular one. In short, this theory of monopolizing through foreclosure is no more persuasive than the foreclosure arguments that we have discussed earlier in this chapter.

In a more recent case decided in 1961 the Supreme Court refused to strike down an exclusive dealing arrangement between Tampa Electric Company and Nashville Coal Company.[18] The reason was that the arrangement involved only about 0.77 percent of total coal production and this was insufficient to qualify as a substantial lessening of competition in the relevant market. On the other hand, in a 1949 case involving an exclusive dealing arrangement between Standard Oil Company of California and about 6000 retail service stations, the Court held that 6.7 percent of the market was sufficient for illegality.[19] Hence, whether exclusive dealing is likely to be illegal seems to depend upon the market shares involved.

Tying

Tying is the practice of a seller conditioning the sale of one product on the sale of another. Earlier we used the example of IBM requiring its tabulating machine customers to buy its tabulating cards from IBM. Many similar examples have arisen in antitrust cases. Some examples include the tie-in of salt to salt dispensers, ink to duplicating machines, cans to can-closing machines, and staples to stapling machines.

Such examples generally have the characteristic that the customer buys or leases a "machine" and then must purchase the inputs that are used with the machine from the same supplier. The inputs used with the machine will vary with the intensity of use that various customers make of the machine. This variable-proportions case is only one type of tying arrangement. Another type, prevalent in the movie industry, involves fixed proportions. For example, a movie distributor may require a theater owner to take movie B if he wants movie A. This is generally referred to as block booking.

One's first reaction to this practice may be that it is irrational. For example, why would a film distributor try to force movie B on an owner who may have taken A alone but will refuse to take the package deal? He could have made money on A and now will make zero. Economists and the courts have puzzled over these practices and have presented numerous explanations. Perhaps the most widely accepted one among economists is that tying is a method of extracting higher profits through price discrimination. The courts, on the other hand, have viewed tying as a device for extending monopoly over one product, such as duplicating machines, to the tied product, ink. This is known as the "leverage theory" of tying.

Leveraging or Extension-of-Monopoly

In a 1912 case involving the tying of ink to patented duplicating machines, Chief Justice White offered the following observations on the danger of tying (the judge was distressed that the majority opinion declared the tie to be legal):

Take a patentee selling a patented engine. He will now have the right by contract to bring under the patent laws all contracts for coal or electrical energy used to afford power to work the machine or even the lubricants employed in its operation. Take a patented carpenter's plane. The power now exists in the patentee by contract to validly confine a carpenter purchasing one of the planes to the use of lumber sawed from trees grown on the land of a particular person.... My mind cannot shake off the dread of the vast extension of such practices which must come from the decision of the court now rendered. Who, I submit, can put a limit upon the extent of monopoly and wrongful restriction which will arise.[20]

Clearly, the judge was overstating the possibilities in fearing that a patent monopoly could be extended to most other products in the economy through tying. After all, the demand for the patented product is not infinite, and only so much consumer surplus can be extracted. Furthermore, Burstein has argued that "the simple and natural view, so favored by the courts, that ... tie-in sales are primarily for the purpose of extension of monopoly into new markets" must be discarded.[21] "Why do I discard the extension-of-monopoly hypothesis? ... [I]t simply does not fit the facts of many litigated cases and of numerous instances of business practice that have not necessarily been litigated."

Burstein then observes:

Can it sensibly be accepted that G.S. Suppiger Co. tied salt to its salt-dispensing machinery as part of a scheme to monopolize the American salt market? Did Morgan Envelope tie its toilet paper to its dispenser as part of a grand scheme to monopolize the American bathroom tissue market? Why do we see again and again ... cases involving the tying of rivets, staples, windshield wipers, repair parts, varnish, etc., when the tying monopolist's share of the market for the tied product remains minuscule?

Burstein next argues that price discrimination is the true explanation of many of these practices.

Hence, extension-of-monopoly (or leveraging) and price discrimination are two explanations for tying, although they are by no means the only explanations. Others include efficiency, quality control, evasion of price controls, and to prevent substitution away from a monopolized input.

We should make clear that extension-of-monopoly appears to be a very limited rationale for tying.[22] Consider an example where two products are used in fixed proportions: color film and photofinishing. A film monopolist could tie film to photofinishing (supplied by a competitive industry). But why would the monopolist bother? The same reasoning given earlier for the failure of fixed-proportions vertical monopolization to increase profits is applicable here. The monopolist of film could extract the maximum profit by its choice of the price of film—requiring the consumer to buy the combination of film and photofinishing for a single higher price would not increase profits.

We now turn to a consideration of the price discrimination hypothesis in more detail, followed by brief treatments of the other explanations mentioned.

Price Discrimination

A useful way to think about price discrimination can be shown by example. In Figure 8.8 we depict the usual profit-maximizing monopolist equilibrium where the monopolist is permitted to select a single price. The solution is determined by the usual marginal revenue (MR) equals marginal cost (MC) condition, and the price equals P^*. The monopolist's profit is the area $ABCP^*$. As we explained in Chapter 4, the area under the demand curve equals the total willingness-to-pay by consumers, and the area under the marginal cost curve equals total cost. This implies that total "potential profit" is larger than the actual profit by the amount of the two shaded triangles. (Total potential profit is equal to the area of triangle RSC; it would be the profit under perfect price discrimination.) In other words, it is in the monopolist's interest to try to extract a larger profit by price discrimination.

In many of the tying cases, the firm practicing tying has either a patent monopoly or some market power over the tying product. Hence it is useful to think in terms of tying as a pricing scheme designed to extract

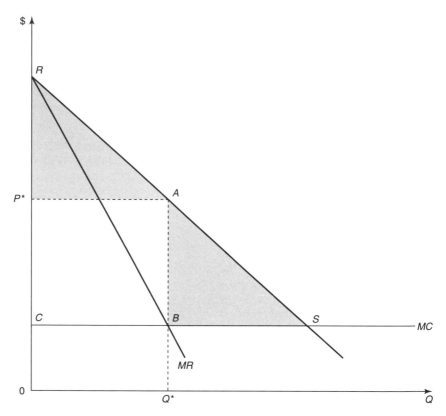

Figure 8.8
Potential Profit Not Captured through Single Monopoly Price

more of the consumers' surplus—or to appropriate some of the triangular shaded areas in Figure 8.8.

A simple block-booking example illustrates the point.[23] Assume that the maximum values to theater owners for two movies are as given below:

Maximum Value to Theater Owners

	Movie A	Movie B
Fox Theater	$100	$70
York Theater	$60	$80

To obtain the maximum revenue, the movie distributor has several possibilities, although some may be ruled out because of illegality or nonfeasibility. First, perfect price discrimination would entail charging separately the maximum value for each movie to each individual:

Perfect Price Discrimination: Revenue = $100 + $70 + $60 + $80 = $310

Thus the maximum potential revenue is $310. The ability to charge separate prices may not be possible, though. Assume then that the distributor can charge only one price for each movie. An examination of the values in the table indicates that the best he could do would be to charge $60 for movie A and $70 for movie B. This "normal" pricing outcome would yield:

Normal Pricing Case: Revenue = $60 + $60 + $70 + $70 = $260

There is one further possibility—block booking. Suppose that the distributor offers a bundle of movies A and B for a single price. The bundled price for movies A and B to the Fox Theater could be $170, but this would cause the York Theater to decline the bundle and generate a total revenue of only $170. Hence the best bundled price would be $140, inasmuch as this would keep both theaters as customers.

Block Booking Case: Revenue = $140 + $140 = $280

Of course, the point is that block booking yields higher revenue than normal pricing. This does not always work, however. In this case, Fox will pay more for A than York will, and York will pay more for B than Fox. If, for example, Fox will pay more for both movies, block booking gives results identical to normal pricing.

The courts take a harsh view of block booking. In the Loew's, Inc., case that was decided by the Supreme Court in 1962, six major film distributors of pre-1948 copyrighted films for television exhibition were found guilty of block booking.[24] As one example, Associated Artists Productions negotiated a contract with one television station for $118,800 in which the station had to take a bundle of 99 films. To get *Casablanca*, for example, the station had to take *Tugboat Annie Sails Again*.

According to Justice Goldberg:

This Court has recognized that "tying agreements serve hardly any purpose beyond the suppression of competition." They are an object of antitrust concern for two reasons—they may force buyers into giving up the purchase of substitutes for the tied product, and they destroy the free access of competing suppliers of the tied product.... The standard of illegality is that the seller must have "sufficient economic power with respect to the tying product to appreciably restrain free competition in the market for the tied product." ... The requisite economic power is presumed when the tying product is patented or copyrighted.

Hence the Court is concerned that tying can foreclose rivals from the tied market and this is harmful to competition. Again, our discussion earlier in this chapter on foreclosure applies here as well. The question remains of course as to the appropriate public policy if we accept the view that the fundamental explanation is price discrimination. Price discrimination is known to have ambiguous welfare effects—in some cases prices discrimination raises total economic surplus and in others it has a negative effect. In cases involving patents there is an additional consideration—it may increase the appropriability of the returns to innovation and therefore be socially beneficial. (Of course, one must hold the belief that generally innovators are able to appropriate an inadequate fraction of the social returns to innovation.) We will consider the welfare effects of price discrimination further in our next example.

We now turn to a highly simplified illustration of tying of the variable-proportions type.[25] The example is of a monopolist of copying machines who has two potential customers with different preferences for copying services. This difference in preferences is an essential part of the rationale for tying. The general idea is that tying gives the monopolist the ability to tailor his prices to "fit" his customers better than if he could charge only a single price to everyone.

The monopolist has constant costs of producing copying machines of $1000 per unit. The customers derive no utility from the machines but only from the copying services that they produce in combination with paper. The number of packages of paper can be assumed to measure the quantity of services consumed by the customers. Hence we assume that the two consumers have the demand curves for copying services (paper) as shown in Figure 8.9:

Demand by Customer 1: $q_1 = 100 - p_1$

Demand by Customer 2: $q_2 = 200 - 2p_2$

For convenience, we will assume that paper is supplied competitively and at a price of zero (the zero price makes the calculations easier). Hence, consider the monopolist's problem in confronting the two demand curves in Figure 8.9. Ignoring income effects, the areas under the demand curves and above the horizontal axes represent the consumer surpluses. That is, with the price of paper equal to zero, the areas give the surpluses of the consumers from copying services. These are shown as $5000 and $10,000. So the monopolist could charge $5000 per machine and sell to both customers, or charge $10,000 and sell to only customer 2. That is, customer 1 would not pay any more than $5000 for a copying machine since $5000 extracts his total surplus. (We assume implicitly that the monopolist cannot charge separate prices of $5000 to customer 1 and $10,000 to customer 2.) The two cases give profits of:

Profit at Machine Price of $5000 = 2($5000 − $1000) = $8000

Profit at Machine Price of $10,000 = $10,000 − $1000 = $9000

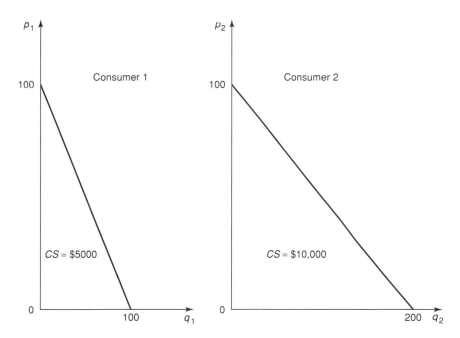

Figure 8.9
Demand for Copying Services with Consumer Surpluses for Zero Price Case

Hence the monopolist would do better by selling at a price of $10,000 and forcing the first customer out of the market.

Now, assume that the monopolist decides to practice tying. He can buy the paper on the market (at the zero price) and mark it up to sell to his copying machine customers. That is, the monopolist simply says that he will now charge a fixed price P for the machine and a price per unit for paper p. All paper must, of course, be purchased from the monopolist even though it is cheaper in the competitive market. This may present enforcement problems for the monopolist, but we will ignore that here. (It is also necessary to ensure that the two customers do not get together and share one machine.)

Figure 8.10 shows the profit-maximizing solution.[26] The monopolist should charge a machine price of $2812.50 and a paper price of $25. As shown in the figure, the first customer will buy 75 packages of paper at the $25 price. The consumer surplus is then $2812.50, which is extracted completely as the price of the machine. The second customer buys 150 packs and also pays the $2812.50 price for the machine. Hence, total profit under tying is

Profit under Tying: $2(\$2812.50 - \$1000) + \$25(75 + 150) = \$9250$

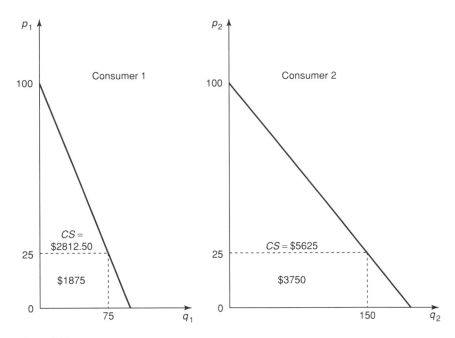

Figure 8.10
Tying Solution: Charge $2812.50 for Machine and $25 for Paper

The first term above is the profit from the machine sales and the second term is the profit on paper. The point, of course, is that tying permits the monopolist to extract a higher overall profit. Tying has permitted the monopolist more flexibility—he can lower the machine price, thereby attracting customer 1 into the market, and make up for lowering the machine price by making profits on paper sales.

Notice also that the monopolist is no longer limited to obtaining equal revenues from both customers. Under the solution in Figure 8.10, the monopolist gets $4687.50 from customer 1 and $6562.50 from customer 2. They pay equal machine prices, but customer 2 buys more paper because of its higher demand for copying services. Hence the paper plays the role of metering the demand for copying services, where the customer with the higher demand pays more. In principle, the tying of paper would be irrelevant if an actual meter could be used to record usage and a fee could be charged based upon usage. This means that tying here is a form of two-part pricing, where a fixed charge is made plus a price per unit. It is a type of pricing often used by public utilities.

Turning now to the public policy concern of whether tying is socially harmful, we can calculate total economic surplus with and without tying. First, assume the case of no-tying. The monopolist would choose to charge $10,000 for the machine, as explained above. Hence there is a consumer surplus of $10,000 (captured by the monopolist from customer 2—customer 1 stays out of the market) and the monopolist incurs costs of $1000. The welfare measure is

Total Surplus (No-Tying) = $10,000 − $1000 = $9000

Allowing tying, the total surplus can be seen easily by referring to Figure 8.10. It equals the two consumer surplus triangles ($2812.50 for customer 1 and $5,625 for customer 2) plus the two areas representing payments for paper ($1875 for customer 1 and $3750 for customer 2) less the costs for two machines ($2000). The welfare measure is therefore

Total Surplus (Tying) = $12,062.50

Hence, for this particular example, tying leads to a higher total surplus. However, this is not a general finding. As is often true, price discrimination can either increase welfare or decrease it—it depends on the particular situation. Schmalensee, who was responsible for regulatory and antitrust issues within President Bush's Council of Economic Advisers, has analyzed this issue in general and concluded that his work "provides little support for antitrust hostility toward tying contracts based on monopoly power over fixed inputs."[27]

For the interested student, an example that leads to the opposite result is simply to change customer 2's demand to $q_2 = 130 - p_2$. In this new situation, total surplus from no-tying is $11,450 and only $11,225 for tying. This is true despite the fact that tying is more profitable for the monopolist.[28] A key difference between the two situations is that in the latter case the consumers have more similar demand curves, and the no-tying solution keeps both customers in the market. Note that if no-tying keeps both consumers in the market, tying *must* cause total surplus to fall because consumers go from a paper price equal to marginal cost to a price above marginal cost.

Efficiency

It is obvious that many cases of tying are merely situations in which it is more efficient for the product to be sold as a tie-in. The classic case is an automobile. It is possible to imagine a car sold as a group of separate products: basic automobile, tires, radio, battery, etc. Because consumers are interested in the "package," transactions costs are reduced by the tie-in.

Quality Control

A defense often given in tying cases is that the tied good is necessary for the satisfactory performance of the tying good. IBM argued that it had to tie its cards to its tabulating machines because inferior cards would cause the machines to malfunction—causing a loss of good will from its customers. Of course, if this is correct, such tying is socially beneficial. The courts have generally not agreed with this argument, however, and have observed that the manufacturer of the tying good could simply state the specifications necessary for the tied goods. It would, of course, be in the interests of the customers to use only the "proper" tied goods.

In Siegel et al. v. Chicken Delight, Inc., a 1971 case decided by a Circuit Court of Appeals, Chicken Delight used such a quality control defense unsuccessfully.[29] Chicken Delight licensed several hundred franchisees to operate its stores. It did not charge its franchisees a franchise fee or royalties; rather, it allowed its franchisees to use its trademark and follow its business methods in exchange for purchasing their cooking equipment and certain supplies from Chicken Delight. It was also the case that the prices for these purchases were higher than the prices charged by other suppliers.

The court held that Chicken Delight could have achieved the necessary quality control by specification of the appropriate cooking equipment and supplies. It was therefore unnecessary in the court's view for Chicken Delight to require purchases of these items from itself.

There are several nagging questions about the view that simply stating the required specifications is a perfect substitute for the tie-in. One point is that it may be costly to convince buyers of the need for the specifications stated when cheaper alternatives exist. Another point is that Chicken Delight might have a "free rider" problem. The reputation of Chicken Delight could be damaged if a few franchisees decided to use cheap, low-quality equipment and supplies knowing that customers in general would identify with the regional reputation of Chicken Delight for good quality. That is, the few franchisees using inferior supplies would continue to have customers who relied on the overall quality of all Chicken Delight stores (even though their loyal repeat business might be small). Hence, these franchisees could free-ride off the high quality of the rest, and tying the supplies might be a way of combating this problem.

A successful defense using the quality-control argument was made in a 1960 case involving a cable television-system supplier, Jerrold Electronics.[30] Jerrold sold only on a complete systems basis—including installation, equipment, and maintenance. However, the legality of Jerrold's tying was restricted to the "early years" of the industry when the technology was in its infancy. After the technology had been in existence for a number of years, ensuring the availability of competent independent suppliers and service personnel, such tying was no longer legal.

Evasion of Price Controls

Tying can be used as a way of avoiding price controls. For example, when gasoline was under maximum price controls in the 1970s, the excess demand was great. Cars lined up for miles in certain cities to buy gasoline. Because the price could not be increased to clear the market, a gasoline station might tie its gasoline to other products or services to avoid the price ceiling. For example, one station was alleged to have offered gasoline at the controlled price to anyone who purchased a rabbit's foot for $5!

Prevent Substitution

The possibility also exists that tying could be used to prevent substitution away from a monopolized input. Here, the reader should refer to the discussion earlier in this chapter entitled "Extension of Monopoly: Variable Proportions." The analysis here is simply an alternative way of solving the problem that was solved there by vertical integration. That is, a monopolist of input K could not achieve all of its possible profits because the buyer of K would substitute L, the other input, for the monopoly priced K. The buyer of the two inputs (a competitive industry) uses them in variable proportions to produce the final product Q.

As an alternative to vertical integration, the monopolist of K could, in principle, tie the sale of L to the sale of K. The input L, priced competitively, would be bought by the monopolist and marked up for resale to the buyer. The markup would be set such that the ratio of prices confronting the buyer would be exactly equal to the ratio of marginal costs of K and L—thereby ensuring that the buyer would choose the efficient combination of the input to minimize true opportunity cost.[31] The final point is that the monopolist would choose the margins over marginal costs by the exact amount necessary to obtain the same profit that could be obtained under vertical integration.

Our discussion of the various reasons for tying does not include every possible reason that has appeared in the large literature on tying. However, our discussion should be sufficient to indicate that it is a complicated practice and that many of the reasons for tying are probably not anticompetitive. We will conclude the discussion with a few more remarks on the current law toward tying found in important opinions.

Current Law toward Tying

International Salt Co., Inc., v. United States, decided in 1947, is a landmark case and has usually been cited in subsequent tying cases.[32] The

International Salt Company had a patent over salt-dispensing machines used in food processing. The company required all users of the machines to buy their salt from the company as well. They argued that only their salt was of sufficient quality to function properly in their machines, and the tie-in was necessary to preserve goodwill. The Supreme Court, however, disagreed:

If others cannot produce salt equal to reasonable specifications for machine use, it is one thing; but it is admitted that, at times, at least, competitors do offer such a product. They are, however, shut out of the market by a provision that limits it, not in terms of quality, but in terms of a particular vendor. Rules for use of leased machinery must not be disguised restraints of free competition.

In a 1958 case, Northern Pacific Railway Company et al. v. United States, the Court spelled out its rule toward tying as what might be termed a "modified" per se rule.[33] The case concerned a railroad selling land along its right of way on the condition that the buyer ship over the railroad's line. A difference between this case and International Salt is that the market power in the salt dispenser case was due to a patent. Here, the tying product is land and the railroad was found to have sufficient market power to find the tie-in sale illegal:

Tying arrangements deny competitors free access to the market for the tied product.... At the same time buyers are forced to forego their free choice between competing products. For these reasons "tying agreements fare harshly under the laws forbidding restraints of trade." They are unreasonable in and of themselves whenever a party has sufficient economic power with respect to the tying product to appreciably restrain free competition in the market for the tied product and a "not insubstantial" amount of interstate commerce is affected.

An interesting and important case[34] decided in 1984 by the Supreme Court involved the tying of anesthesiological services to hospital services. The so-called Hyde case was a private lawsuit in which Dr. Edwin Hyde, an anesthesiologist, charged the East Jefferson Hospital in the New Orleans area with tying the services of a firm of anesthesiologists, Roux & Associates, to its hospital services. As a result of the tie-in, Dr. Hyde was denied permission to practice at the hospital.

The hospital had signed an exclusive contract with Roux & Associates for all of its anesthesiological services. An important institutional fact was that every patient who had surgery there paid Roux & Associates directly for their services. This is important because anticompetitive tying is supposed to involve the monopolist of the tying product (East Jefferson Hospital) increasing its profits through the tie of a second product (the services provided by Roux) over which it does not initially have a monopoly. As Lynk explains in his analysis of this case: "[anticompetitive tying] is not likely to involve the channeling of that profit into someone else's pocket."[35] In short, there is a real problem in the application of the standard leverage theory of tying to this case.

The Court unanimously found for the defendant, though there was a difference of opinion among the Justices as to the reason. The majority opinion of five Justices, written by Justice Stevens, held that there was no basis for a finding that the Hospital had market power. There was actually very little evidence in the record on this issue. Recall that the modified per se rule for tying requires that there be market power over the tying good. The four other Justices issued a concurring opinion, written by Justice O'Connor, but disagreed on the market power issue. They found that even though there was market power, there "is no sound economic reason for treating surgery and anesthesia as separate services" and therefore "the Hospital can acquire no *additional* market power by selling the two services together."

The four Justices also indicated their desire to drop the per se rule approach and move to a rule of reason for tying. Given the theoretically diverse welfare outcomes for tying, this would seem to be a good idea. Alternatively, an approach that was contained in the Justice Department's 1985 Guidelines regarding tying would seem sensible. That is, according to those Guidelines, the Department would use a two-step approach and drop any investigation in which the tying product's market share was less than 30 percent. If the share was over 30 percent, they generally would follow a rule of reason analysis. Because they were controversial, President Clinton's Assistant Attorney General for Antitrust, Anne Bingaman, dropped the 1985 Guidelines regarding tying and other vertical restraints in August of 1993.

A 1992 tying case, *Kodak*, was also a Supreme Court decision, and it left the per se approach intact.[36] It was a controversial decision because of the economic analysis used. The tie-in was a tie of repair services to parts for Kodak photocopiers. The tie-in excluded independent service companies from repairing Kodak photocopiers, and they brought the suit against Kodak. The market for photocopiers was agreed by all to be unconcentrated. However, the majority of Justices held that it was possible for Kodak to have a monopoly in parts[37]; the minority opinion was that it is not possible to have market power in a derivative market like repair parts if the original equipment copiers is competitive. That is, they argued that buyers would take into account both the equipment cost *and* the cost of maintaining the copier over time when they purchase a Kodak machine rather than a competitive machine. Justice Scalia, in his dissent, made the interesting observation that if Kodak had required consumers to purchase a lifetime parts and service contract with each machine, that tie-in would be immune from the law. The reason is that the tying product would then be photocopiers, and that market lacks the required market power.

Hence the rule is that tying is illegal when the seller possesses sufficient market power in the market of the tying product and the amount of commerce involved is substantial. Of course, it is possible for the tying to be "reasonable" in the sense that it was in the Jerrold case described earlier.

Summary

This chapter has discussed the possible benefits of vertical integration as well as possible anticompetitive consequences. A major reason for vertical integration is to reduce transactions costs, and these are often hard for policy analysts to identify. Hence it may be prudent to assume that such economies are present if no market power rationale for vertical integration is obvious.

Vertical restrictions such as resale price maintenance, territorial restraints, exclusive dealing, and tying were also examined. It was noted that these restrictions often have explanations that are in society's interests. Nevertheless, they are often treated harshly under the antitrust laws.

Questions and Problems

1. Consider a business firm that has an organization that you understand well. Try to explain why the firm buys certain inputs and makes the remainder (in the context of minimizing transactions costs).

2. Assume that firm M (the manufacturer) sells an input (a lawnmower) to firm R (the retailer). Now R sells the lawnmower to the public, incurring a constant cost of $5 per lawnmower for its services. Fixed-proportions production holds for R. Let X therefore represent the number of lawnmowers. If both M and R are monopolists, and P_L is the lawnmower price charged to the public with the demand $X = 100 - P_L$, answer the following questions.

    a. Find the derived demand for lawnmowers facing M. Hint: Find the marginal revenue equal marginal cost condition for R, where R's marginal cost is the sum of the $5 services cost and the price P_x that it must pay M per lawnmower. Solving for X gives the derived demand.

    b. If M's total cost function is $10 + 5X + X^2$, find the equilibrium prices and quantity, P_L, P_x, and X, and the profits of the two firms.

    c. Assume now that M and R form a single vertically integrated firm M-R. Find the equilibrium values of P_L and X and the profit of M-R.

d. Compare the unintegrated case (b) with the integrated case (c). Is it true that both the firms and the public would prefer (c)? Explain.

3.   Assume the same facts as in problem 2 except that monopolist R is now replaced with competitive industry R.

a. Find the derived demand for lawnmowers facing the manufacturing monopolist M. Hint: Make use of the fact that perfect competition equilibrium is defined by demand equals supply where supply is simply a horizontal line $P_L = 5 + P_x$. Solving for X gives the derived demand.

b. Find the equilibrium prices and quantity, P_L, P_x, and X, and the profit of M.

c. Assume that M vertically integrates forward into the competitive industry R, thereby extending its monopoly to cover both manufacturing and retailing. Find the equilibrium values of P_L and X and the profit of the combined firm M-R.

d. Compare the unintegrated case (b) with the integrated case (c). Is it profitable to monopolize forward? What is the intuitive explanation for your result?

4.   Assume a situation where a monopolist of input M sells to a competitive industry Z and the competitive industry Z has a production function characterized by variable proportions. A second competitive industry sells its output L to the competitive industry Z and Z combines M and L according to the production function $Z = L^{.5}M^{.5}$.

The price of L and its marginal cost are both \$1. The demand for the product of industry Z is $Z = 20 - P_Z$. It can be shown that the monopolist will charge \$26.90 for M to maximize its profit, given that its marginal cost of M is \$1. (This can be found by first obtaining the derived demand facing the monopolist using the price equal marginal cost condition in industry Z, and also using the condition for least cost production by industry Z.)

The competitive industry Z will have a constant marginal cost of \$10.37 and sell 9.63 units at a price of \$10.37.

a. Calculate the competitive industry Z's actual combination of L and M that it will use to produce the 9.63 units. Find the true economic cost to society of these inputs (not Z's actual payments to its suppliers, in that its payment to the monopolist includes a monopoly margin). Hint: The optimal input mix can be found by the simultaneous solution of two equations: the equality of the marginal product per dollar of the inputs and the production function equated to 9.63 units.

b. Assume that the monopolist decides to vertically integrate forward into the competitive industry Z—thereby extending its monopoly to cover industry Z. What will be the least-cost combination of L and M and its true economic cost in producing the 9.63 units? Hint: The vertically integrated firm will "charge" itself the marginal cost for M in determining its input mix.

c. What is the cost saving that the vertically integrated monopolist will obtain if it produces 9.63 units? That is, what is the saving compared to the cost found in (a)?

d. What makes this vertical integration profitable? Is it in society's interest if the monopolist holds its output fixed at 9.63 units after vertical integration?

e. In fact, after the vertical monopolization of Z the firm M-Z would have a constant marginal cost of \$2. Given this fact, what is the profit maximizing price P_Z and output Z? Draw a figure to illustrate the overall social benefits and costs of this vertical integration.

5. Assume that the maximum values to theater owners for movies A and B are as follows. The Fox Theater values A at \$100 and B at \$70. The York Theater values A at \$60 and B at \$50. Is block booking more profitable than charging a single price for each movie? Explain.

6. Consider a problem faced by Kamera Company. They have developed a patented new camera that can be produced at a constant unit cost of \$1. The film F is available competitively at a zero price. Consumers derive utility only from the combined services of the camera and film—which can be measured by packs of film consumed per period. Assuming two consumers with inverse demands:

$$p_1 = 8 - 4f_1/3 \quad \text{and} \quad p_2 = 12 - 3f_2/2$$

a. Consumers will purchase only one camera at most—hence, consumer surplus can be viewed as measuring what they would be willing to pay for a camera. If Kamera must charge both customers the same price for a camera, what is the price it will charge and what is its profit?

b. Assume now that Kamera decides to tie film to its camera. It requires customers to purchase film from Kamera if they wish to buy a camera. Kamera simply buys film on the market at the zero price and resells it. What are the prices of camera and film that Kamera will charge, and what is its profit? Is tying profitable?

c. Compare total economic surplus in case (a) with that in case (b).

d. If customer 2 has a different demand curve, say, $p_2 = 10 - 5f_2/4$, it reverses the result of (c). What is the intuitive reason for this reversal?

Notes

1. A major expected benefit was that regulation of the monopolistic operating companies would be improved. That is, the nonregulated Western Electric arm of AT&T had an incentive to charge artificially high prices to the regulated arm of AT&T—the operating companies. The reason was that the higher the prices, the higher the operating companies' "rate bases" and, therefore, the higher their allowed profits. The 1982 Department of Justice Guidelines cite this "evasion of rate regulation" problem as one basis for challenging vertical mergers.

2. The analogy to a stream is simply that the sales "flow" downstream from raw materials to final product.

3. Brown Shoe Company v. United States, 370 U.S. 294 (1962).

4. This example is based on Bruce T. Allen, "Vertical Integration and Market Foreclosure: The Case of Cement and Concrete," *Journal of Law and Economics*, April 1971.

5. J. A. Ordover, G. Saloner, and S. C. Salop, "Equilibrium Vertical Foreclosure," *American Economic Review*, March 1990. A clear discussion of "raising rivals' costs" more generally is given in the article by T. Krattenmaker and S. Salop in the December 1983 *Yale Law Journal*.

6. M. J. Peck, *Competition in the Aluminum Industry: 1945–1958* (Cambridge, Mass.: Harvard University Press, 1961).

7. The competitive industry is in equilibrium when $P_b = C + P_m$; that is, when the price of boats P equals marginal cost (which is just the sum of the fixed conversion cost C and the price of motors P_m). So, rewriting this condition as $P_b - C = P_m$, we have the derived demand curve, $P_b - C$.

8. For further results, see F. M. Westfield, "Vertical Integration: Does Product Price Rise or Fall?," *American Economic Review*, June 1981. The analysis here was originally published in J. M. Vernon and D. A. Graham, "Profitability of Monopolization by Vertical Integration," *Journal of Political Economy*, July/August 1971.

9. Brown Shoe Co. v. United States, 370 U.S. 294 (1962).

10. Ford Motor Co. v. United States, 405 U.S. 562 (1972).

11. The "free-riding" argument was originally made by L. G. Telser, "Why Should Manufacturers Want Fair Trade?," *Journal of Law and Economics*, October 1960. For an analysis of cases that do not seem to fit the free-rider theory of Telser, see H. P. Marvel and S. McCafferty, "Resale Price Maintenance and Quality Certification," *Rand Journal of Economics*, Autumn 1984.

In particular, they argue that in many cases dealers do not provide tangible presale services; rather their idea is that certain high-quality retailers—Macy's, Neiman Marcus, etc.—"serve as the consumer's agent in ascertaining the quality or stylishness of commodities." The retailers who invest in "certifying" the quality of the goods are then subject to free riding by other retailers.

12. F. M. Scherer and D. Ross, *Industrial Market Structure and Economic Performance*, 3rd ed. (Boston: Houghton Mifflin, 1990), Chapter 15.

13. Dr. Miles Medical Company v. John D. Park & Sons, 220 U.S. 373 (1911).

14. Monsanto Corporation v. Spray-Rite Service Corp., 465 U.S. 752 (1984) and Business Electronics Corp. v. Sharp Electronics Corp., 485 U.S. 717 (1988).

15. See Barbara Katz, "Competition in the Soft Drink Industry," *Antitrust Bulletin*, Summer 1979.

16. Continental T.V., Inc., et al. v. GTE Sylvania, Inc., 433 U.S. 36 (1977). See also Lee E. Preston, "Territorial Restraints: GTE Sylvania," in J. E. Kwoka, Jr., and L. J. White (eds.), *The Antitrust Revolution* (Glenview, Ill.: Scott, Foresman, 1989).

17. Standard Fashion Company v. Magrane-Houston Company, 258 U.S. 346 (1922).

18. Tampa Electric Company v. Nashville Coal Company, 365 U.S. 320 (1961).

19. Standard Oil Company of California v. United States, 337 U.S. 293 (1949).

20. Henry v. A.B. Dick Company, 224 U.S. 1 (1912).

21. M. L. Burstein, "A Theory of Full-Line Forcing," *Northwestern Law Review*, March–April 1960.

22. In a 1990 article, Whinston has developed some rather specialized models in which tying can serve as a mechanism for leveraging market power. His models assume that the tied good market is oligopolistic and that, in certain cases, the monopolist of the tying good can make it unprofitable for rivals in the tied good market to continue operations. M. D. Whinston, "Tying, Foreclosure, and Exclusion," *American Economic Review*, September 1990.

23. See George J. Stigler, *The Organization of Industry* (Homewood, Ill.: Richard D. Irwin, 1968), Chapter 15, for the original analysis of block booking.

24. United States v. Loew's, Inc., 371 U.S. 38 (1962).

25. The example here is based on the theoretical analysis contained in Walter Y. Oi, "A Disneyland Dilemma: Two-Part Tariffs for a Mickey Mouse Monopoly," *Quarterly Journal of Economics*, February 1971.

26. The solution is found as follows. To keep both customers in the market, the machine price should equal the consumer surplus (after the price of paper is increased) of customer 1. Hence, express the machine price as the area of the consumer surplus triangle: $\frac{1}{2}(100 - p)(100 - p)$. Then profit can be written as a function of the price of paper only:

$$(100 - p)(100 - p) + p(300 - 3p) - 2000$$

The first and second terms are revenues from machines and paper respectively, while the last term is the machine costs. The value of p that maximizes profit is $25. Note that the best profit with only one customer is $9000, and tying would not be employed.

27. Richard Schmalensee, "Monopolistic Two-Part Pricing Arrangements," *Bell Journal of Economics*, Autumn 1981.

28. In this case, the tying solution is to charge $3612.50 for the machine and $15 for paper. The profit is $8225 as compared with only $8000 under no-tying.

29. Siegel v. Chicken Delight, Inc., 448 F. 2d43 (9th Cir. 1971). For an interesting analysis of this case, see B. Klein and L. F. Saft, "The Law and Economics of Franchise Tying Contracts," *Journal of Law and Economics*, May 1985.

30. United States v. Jerrold Electronics Corporation, 187 F. Supp. 545 (1960).

31. In terms of Figure 8.6, the efficient input combination is point F. The slope of NN equals the ratio of prices that the tying monopolist should choose. See R. Blair and D. Kaserman, "Vertical Integration, Tying and Antitrust Policy," *American Economic Review*, June 1978, for a more formal analysis.

32. International Salt Co., Inc., v. United States, 332 U.S. 392 (1947).

33. Northern Pacific Railway Company et al. v. United States, 356 U.S. 1 (1958).

34. Jefferson Parish Hospital Dist. No. 2 v. Hyde, 466 U.S. 1 (1984).

35. W. J. Lynk, "Tying and Exclusive Dealing: Jefferson Parish Hospital v. Hyde," in J. E. Kwoka, Jr., and L. J. White (eds.), *The Antitrust Revolution*, 2nd ed. (New York: HarperCollins, 1994).

36. Eastman Kodak v. Image Technical Services, Inc., 112 S.Ct. 2072 (1992).

37. The monopoly could be due to information imperfections on the part of consumers, according to some economists. This line of reasoning is pursued in S. C. Salop, "Exclusionary Vertical Restraints Law: Has Economics Mattered?" *American Economic Review*, May 1993.

9 Monopolization and Price Discrimination

A major policy concern in the United States has long been the so-called dominant firm. Although few true monopolies exist in real-world markets, there are many industries inhabited by a single, dominant firm. Examples include IBM, Microsoft, Eastman Kodak, Boeing, Xerox, Campbell Soup, and Gillette. In years past, many such firms have been involved in monopolization antitrust cases—for instance, Standard Oil, United States Steel, Alcoa, and IBM. These cases and the evolution of the law toward dominant firms are the main topics to be discussed in this chapter.

A final section of this chapter discusses price discrimination and the Robinson-Patman Act. Price discrimination is not necessarily related to monopolization, although it can be. For example, as is well known, a monopolist can increase its profits by practicing price discrimination. On the other hand, secret, discriminatory price cutting through cheating on rivals is often the downfall of cartels. Predatory pricing—a strategy of pricing below cost to kill off one's rivals—can be viewed as price discrimination if the would-be monopolist charges higher prices elsewhere.

Turning to the problem of monopolization, recall first the wording of Section 2 of the Sherman Act:

> Every person who shall monopolize, or attempt to monopolize, or combine or conspire with any other person or persons, to monopolize any part of the trade or commerce among the several states, or with foreign nations, shall be deemed guilty of a felony.

Three types of acts are condemned—monopolization, the attempt to monopolize, and conspiring to monopolize. Here we shall focus on the first act—monopolization—because the most important cases are of this type.

It is important to note that the law forbids the act of monopolizing and not monopoly itself. Judge Irving Kaufman explained the reason for this in a 1979 case in which Eastman Kodak was charged with monopolization: "[O]ne must comprehend the fundamental tension—one might almost say the paradox—that is near the heart of Section 2."[1] Judge Kaufman then quoted a famous passage from an earlier decision involving Alcoa: "The successful competitor, having been urged to compete, must not be turned upon when he wins."[2]

The problem is, of course, to distinguish dominant firm situations built upon and maintained by superior efficiency from those achieved and maintained by, for example, predatory tactics. That is, if a firm is able to win the entire market through its lower cost performance (or superior product), this is what society should want. Hence, such performance should not be discouraged by antitrust penalties.

As we will see in discussing the important monopolization cases, bases for dominant firm status vary considerably. The earlier cases, for example, were concerned with monopolies achieved through mergers. Standard Oil was alleged to have become dominant by both mergers and predatory pricing tactics. Alcoa began its domination of aluminum through patents and economies of scale. These differences mean that monopolization cases are truly difficult "rule of reason" cases.

As we explained in Chapter 5, there are two parts to rule of reason cases: inherent effect and intent. The currently accepted Supreme Court statement on monopolization was given in the 1966 Grinnell case:

The offense of monopoly under Section 2 of the Sherman Act has two elements: (1) the possession of monopoly power in the relevant market, and (2) the willful acquisition or maintenance of that power as distinguished from growth or development as a consequence of a superior product, business acumen, or historic accident.[3]

Both parts raise difficulties in real-world situations. It will be useful to consider briefly some of these problems before turning to the cases in more detail.

The Possession of Monopoly Power

The usual graphic depiction of a monopoly is as shown in Figure 9.1. The monopolist is the sole supplier of the output Q, and therefore chooses the profit-maximizing output Q^* (where marginal revenue MR equals marginal cost MC). Economic profits are shown by the shaded area. This type of analysis contains two strong implicit assumptions: (1) the product is homogeneous and, therefore, the market is a "given," and (2) entry is ignored (or blockaded). Hence, this "monopolist" is easily identified.

A simple definition of monopoly power is the ability to set price above marginal cost. Hence, if we divide the price-marginal cost difference by price, we have one well-known index of the amount of monopoly power. It is known as the Lerner index.[4] This index, L, is defined as

$$L = \frac{P - MC}{P} = \frac{1}{e} \tag{9.1}$$

where

$P = $ price

$MC = $ marginal cost

$e = $ elasticity of demand

Note: All values are measured at the firm's profit-maximizing output.

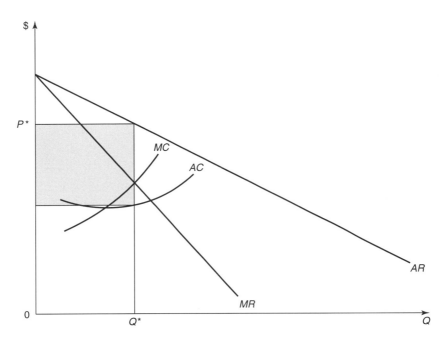

Figure 9.1
Monopoly Equilibrium

Notice that the Lerner index equals the reciprocal of the elasticity of demand.[5] For example, if the firm's price is double the marginal cost and $L = 0.5$, we also know that the elasticity of demand is 2. Furthermore, it follows that very large elasticities imply very little monopoly power. Recall that competitive firms face infinitely large elasticities and, therefore, have Lerner indexes of zero.

The short-run monopoly power measured by L should not be relevant in antitrust unless it is "large" and is expected to persist for a reasonably long period of time.[6] Hence, barriers, or obstacles, to easy entry should exist for there to be a serious antitrust concern.

An alternative index of monopoly power is the Bain index, B.[7] The index is essentially a profit index, and is

$$B = R - C - D - iV \tag{9.2}$$

where

R = total annual sales revenue

C = currently incurred costs for materials, wages, and salaries

D = depreciation of capital investment

i = interest rate for capital funds

V = owners' investment

Hence the Bain index measures economic profits, in that it subtracts all costs from revenues, including the opportunity cost of the owners' investment, iV. As Bain observed, "Although excess profits are not a sure indication of monopoly, they are, if persistent, a probable indication."[8]

Estimating the Bain index using accounting data has many well-known difficulties.[9] Accountants do not capitalize certain investments (advertising and research and development) that should be capitalized for economic analysis. Assets that have been sold may also include in their accounting value the present value of monopoly profits, and this makes it impossible to detect economic profits. Excess profits might be attributable to rapidly growing demand or superior efficiency, and not monopoly power. Many other problems could be cited.

One useful lesson from this short review of the economic definition of monopoly power is that it is not an "either-or" concept. It is a matter of degree. Schmalensee has expressed the difference between the economic and legal view as follows:

Both short-run and long-run monopoly power are logically continuous variables, in the sense that they can take on a whole range of values. The questions about monopoly power that usually interest economists involve its sources and importance, rather than its existence. Courts, on the other hand, often seem to treat the existence and importance of monopoly power as though they were equivalent.[10]

In the real world, we do not see monopolies (as in Figure 9.1) with homogeneous products and with blockaded entry. Rather, we see firms with large shares of "markets" that contain various products that are imperfect substitutes. In fact, disputes over where to draw the boundaries in defining the "markets" occupies much of the time and effort in monopolization cases.

In Chapter 7 the definition of the relevant market in merger cases was examined in depth. The concept explained there was that a market should include all firms and products that a hypothetical cartel would need to control in order to raise the existing price in a permanent way. Of course, the same general principle is applicable in monopoly situations. A good example is a famous market definition problem involving flexible wrapping materials, to which we now turn.

In the 1956 Cellophane case, the issue turned on whether the relevant market was cellophane only, or whether it was much broader (including other types of flexible wrapping materials: wax paper, greaseproof paper, glassine, foil, and others).[11] If cellophane alone were the market, duPont would have had a 75 percent market share, and the Court would have found monopoly power. Fortunately for duPont, the Court held that the relevant market was the broader flexible wrapping materials market (of which duPont's share was only 18 percent).

An important point can be illustrated by an economic error made by the Court in the Cellophane case. A high degree of substitution by consumers between two products must exist at competitive prices for the two products to be placed in the same market.

Cellophane was indeed a close substitute for other wrapping materials at the going price for cellophane. However, it has been argued by critics that cellophane's price contained a monopolistic margin over its marginal cost.[12] A rational monopolist would, in fact, raise price until its product became a substitute for alternatives. Hence, substitutes in consumption should be evaluated at prices that are reasonably close to marginal costs.

Summing up, one should begin with the product at issue—cellophane—and ask what other products, if any, duPont would need to control in order to charge a price, say, 5 percent, above its marginal cost. The evidence cited above is that no other products were necessary. Hence the market should be defined as cellophane only.

In addition to the demand-side substitution emphasized above, supply-side substitution is equally important in defining the relative market. Three types of substitution are possible: (1) competitors currently producing the product may have the ability to increase output from existing facilities; (2) producers of products not considered substitutes in consumption may be able to easily convert to production of relevant products (example: consumers cannot substitute between residential buildings and commercial buildings, but firms constructing commercial buildings could easily shift to home building); (3) entry of new competition.

Fisher has argued persuasively that the tendency of antitrust cases to be focused on determining the relevant market is often seriously misleading. In his view, "monopoly power is present when a firm is sufficiently insulated from competitive pressures to be able to raise prices ... without concern for its competitors' actions because its rivals cannot offer customers reasonable alternatives."[13] Thus, Fisher's view is that in trying to identify monopoly, the courts should focus on the constraints on the pricing power of the monopolist. He observes that

there is no positive harm in engaging in the market definition exercise. Indeed, viewed correctly, arguments concerning whether products are in or out of the market which are made in terms of demand and supply substitutability and hence in terms of constraints are exactly the arguments which one would have to decide in looking at the constraints directly. The trouble is that it is too easy to forget what the analysis is all about. By focusing on whether products are in or out of the market, one converts a necessarily continuous question into a question of yes or no. The temptation is to regard products which are in as all counting equally and products which are out as not counting at all.[14]

The attention paid to market share as the determinant of monopoly power is due in part to the famous opinion of Judge Hand in the 1945 Alcoa case.[15] He observed that a 90 percent market share "is enough to constitute a monopoly; it is doubtful whether sixty or sixty-four percent would be enough; and certainly thirty-three percent is not."

Intent to Monopolize

Given the existence of monopoly power, the second part of the rule of reason test is to determine whether the monopoly was acquired and/or maintained by practices that cannot qualify as superior efficiency or historic accident. That is, a monopoly over widgets because of superior efficiency in producing widgets is not in violation of the Sherman Act. A widget producer who used predatory pricing to bankrupt all of his rivals in acquiring the monopoly would be in violation.

Distinguishing predatory pricing from hard price competition can sometimes be difficult. For example, IBM developed a computer system in the 1960s that consisted of the central processing unit, input-output devices, memory devices, and so on. A number of companies found it profitable to begin selling memory devices that could be "plugged" into the IBM system. When IBM recognized that it was losing sales to these memory suppliers, it responded by vigorously cutting its own prices. These smaller companies suffered losses and some were forced out of the market. Was IBM maintaining monopoly power by predatory pricing, or was it simply being forced by competition to lower its prices (to the benefit of its customers)?

Distinguishing the two polar cases—superior efficiency and predatory pricing—in the earlier widget examples was clear. However, what about practices that are "in-between"? In the United Shoe Machinery case, Judge Wyzanski found that the use of certain leasing practices satisfied the second part of the test for illegal monopolization.[16] The judge viewed leasing provisions as constituting an "intermediate case where the cause of an enterprise's success ... [was not] the skill with which the business was conducted, but rather some practice which without being predatory, abusive, or coercive was in economic effect exclusionary."

Needless to say, Judge Wyzanski's opinion has been controversial. Some critics have argued that no such category of intermediate practices even exists. We shall return to these issues in the review of the leading monopolization cases, to which we now turn.

Cases

One antitrust expert has suggested that there have been three more or less distinct eras of Section 2 interpretation.[17] The first period, 1890–1940, was one in which the courts required, in addition to a large market share, evidence of abusive or predatory acts to show intent. In the second period, 1945–1970, the courts did not require evidence of abusive acts to infer intent; it was sufficient "to achieve a monopoly by maneuvers which, though 'honestly industrial,' were not economically inevitable."[18]

The third period, 1970 to the present, appears to be characterized by the willingness of the courts to allow more aggressive practices by dominant firms without inferring intent to monopolize. We will follow this breakdown of the monopolization cases in the discussion below.

1890–1940: Standard Oil and United States Steel

In 1911 the Supreme Court handed down two significant decisions. In the first, the Standard Oil Company, organized by the Rockefeller brothers, was found guilty of monopolization and dissolved into thirty-three geographically separated companies.[19] Two weeks later, James B. Duke's Tobacco Trust was also found guilty of monopolization.[20] It was divided into sixteen successor companies. Although both monopolies were accused of numerous predatory and abusive tactics, we will focus on Standard Oil because it has become a famous example of predatory pricing.

The Rockefellers built their trust by acquiring more than 120 rivals. They also were accused of engaging in predatory pricing to drive competitors out of business, of buying up pipelines in order to foreclose crude oil supplies to rivals, of securing discriminatory rail freight rates, and of conducting business espionage. As a result, Standard Oil obtained a 90 percent share of the refining and sale of petroleum products in the 1880s and 1890s.

The Supreme Court stated in its opinion that the crime of monopolization required two elements: First, the firm must have acquired a monopoly position. The 90 percent market share met this requirement. Second, there must be evidence of intent to acquire the monopoly position. The Court found that intent could be inferred from the predatory tactics described above.

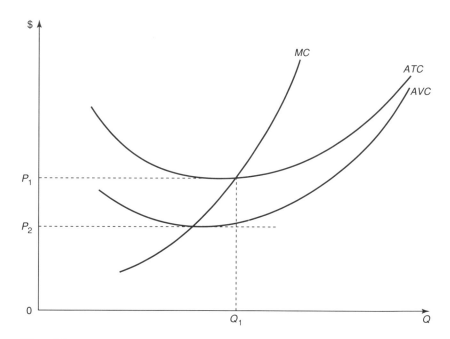

Figure 9.2
Short-Run Average Total Cost (ATC), Average Variable Cost (AVC), and Marginal Cost (MC) Curves

Because we have referred to predatory pricing several times, it is appropriate to consider this concept in more detail. Although there is no universally accepted definition of predatory pricing, one that will serve our purposes is:

pricing at a level calculated to exclude from the market an equally or more efficient competitor.

Pricing at a level to exclude from the market less efficient competitors is, of course, what competition is supposed to do. Pricing to exclude equally or more efficient competitors would be irrational because it would imply losses to the predator—unless the predator planned to drive the competitor out of business and then raise the price to the monopoly level. In short, the predator would be investing in losses for a period with the prospect of high returns upon becoming a monopolist.

Figure 9.2 should be instructive. Suppose both predator and victim are equally efficient and have short-run cost curves as shown.

Any price below P_1 would be sufficient to drive a firm from the market in the long run. That is, if a firm believed that price would never cover its average total costs (ATC), it should exit the industry. In order to drive a firm out of the market more quickly, the price should be be-

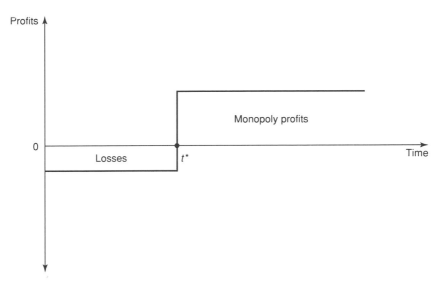

Figure 9.3
Pattern of Predatory Pricing Profits and Losses

low P_2. A price at this lower level would mean that the firm could not even cover its average variable costs (AVC), and it would be better off if it shut down production.

Of course, there is necessarily a large role here for strategic considerations. That is, the predator must make the victim believe that the predatory price is permanent and not just a bluff.

Figure 9.3 shows a simple time profile of an investment in predatory pricing. Losses will be incurred by the predator until time t^*, at which time the victim exits the industry. The predator then raises price to the monopoly level and begins to earn a return on its investment. Economists have long argued that such an investment is likely to be unwise in most circumstances, though perhaps not all. We consider the reasoning for this skepticism below.

First, the predator would need to have a "deep pocket," or substantial financial resources. At least, the predator must be able to finance losses over a longer period than its victim can. Second, these losses will increase if the victim fails to match the predatory price. The reason is that the predator must supply the whole market (its own customers plus the customers of the victim). These losses must continue until time t^*, which is that date beyond which the predator estimates the victim will not re-enter the market. Clearly, if the victim simply reopens its plant when the price is increased, the hoped-for profits will not materialize. As Professor McGee has observed:

If we look at predation as an investment to achieve or increase future monopoly profits, we should keep the arithmetic straight. Future monopoly profits must be discounted appropriately, and may be a long time coming, if they come at all. Near-term costs weigh more heavily and are more certain.

A one-dollar loss incurred today costs one dollar. At a 10 percent discount rate, an additional dollar profit three years hence is worth about 75 cents. A dollar profit deferred for five years is worth only 62 cents. If it cannot be realized in 10 years, it is worth only 38.5 cents. A dollar profit 25 years hence is worth less than a dime today. It may not pay to count the hereafter.[21]

A final point that may make predatory pricing appear to be unwise is the role of entry barriers. A monopoly price after t^* cannot be sustained without high barriers to entry. In short, there are many reasons to view predatory pricing as an activity that is probably rare.

Of course, claims of predatory pricing are often made by rivals who are damaged by tough price competition. A 1986 Supreme Court decision provides a good example of a baseless claim of predatory pricing. The case, Matsushita v. Zenith, began in 1970 with charges made by American television set manufacturers that seven large Japanese firms were conspiring to destroy the American television industry. By setting monopoly prices in Japan, the seven firms were argued to use those profits to subsidize "below-cost" U.S. prices. Ultimately, the Japanese were supposed to set monopoly prices in the United States too.

Using economic studies submitted in the case, Elzinga has produced some interesting figures that reveal the implausibility of the predatory pricing hypothesis.[22] That is, he shows that the investment, even with an eventual monopoly that lasts forever, would fail to break even. Specifically, the assumptions included a ten-year predation period with the price of television sets being 62 percent of the "but for predation" price. Also, using a demand elasticity of about 1.2, the postpredation price ranged from 119 to 138 percent of the "but for predation" price. Finally, a 12.2 percent opportunity cost of capital was assumed—equal to the average return on assets in Japan at that time.

In short, for these and other reasons that we will not discuss here, the hypothesis of predatory pricing was viewed by the Court as being one that simply made no economic sense. A judgment for the defendants was confirmed. The more likely explanation was that the Japanese firms were trying to win larger shares of the U.S. market through lower prices. (A final note to support this is that the Japanese firms never gained more than about 50 percent of the market.)

Of course, predatory pricing may make more sense if used in conjunction with a takeover strategy. Some economists argue that this is what happened in the Standard Oil case.[23] The key idea is that buying rivals rather than bankrupting them would have been the better tactic for the Rockefellers. If they bought up their rivals, there would be no period of losses—monopoly profits could have begun immediately. And with ownership of the production facilities of the rivals, there would be no danger of reentry by others using those facilities. Finally, an occasional predatory pricing episode could be used to persuade rivals to sell out cheaply.[24]

Of course, today it is no longer possible to create a monopoly through acquisition of rivals. The 1950 Celler-Kefauver Amendment to Section 7 of the Clayton Act has been enforced vigorously, as we discussed in Chapter 7. Horizontal mergers are challenged when significant market power is likely to be achieved. Given this situation, predatory pricing may be employed in certain cases where mergers would be preferred by the potential monopolizer. Hence, while predatory pricing may be rare, logically it cannot be ruled out as a method of monopolization. For this reason, we will return to some proposed legal definitions of predatory pricing at the end of the chapter.

The government brought suit in 1911 charging United States Steel with monopolization.[25] It was formed in 1901 through mergers that gave United States Steel control of over 65 percent of the domestic iron and steel business.

In 1907 the chairman of United States Steel, Judge E. H. Gary, began a series of dinner meetings with the heads of rival firms. These so-called Gary Dinners were designed to help stabilize pricing and create good will among the industry leaders. Apparently they accomplished this mission because in the trial no competitors had any harsh words for United States Steel's conduct. Unlike the predatory and abusive tactics that existed in the Standard Oil and American Tobacco cases, United States Steel was viewed as a "good citizen" by its rivals. One result of its price leadership was a gradual loss of market share that reached 52 percent by 1915. United States Steel seemed to hold a price "umbrella" up for its smaller rivals, allowing these rivals to offer lower prices, thereby increasing their share of the business.

The Supreme Court decided in its 1920 opinion that United States Steel was not guilty. The Court concluded that even if the company did have monopoly power, it had not exercised that power: "the law does not make mere size an offense or the existence of unexerted power an offense." Hence the law seemed to be clear in this period—dominant firms would violate the Sherman Act's Section 2 only if they engaged in predatory or aggressive acts toward rivals.

1940–1970: Alcoa and United Shoe Machinery

Twenty-five years after the United States Steel decision, another significant monopolization case was decided.[26] The Aluminum Company of

America (Alcoa) was the sole American producer of primary aluminum until 1940. In 1945 Circuit Judge Learned Hand set forth the opinion that Alcoa was guilty of illegal monopolization even though it had engaged in none of the aggressive and predatory tactics that characterized earlier convictions. Although the decision was not a Supreme Court ruling, it had the effect of one because the Circuit Court of Appeals was empowered by Congress to act as the court of last resort. A quorum of the Supreme Court was not available because several Justices disqualified themselves because of a previous connection with the litigation.

Alcoa was the holder of the patents of Charles Hall, who in 1886 invented a commercially feasible electrolytic process for converting alumina (concentrated aluminum oxide) into aluminum. Thanks to the Hall patent and other patents, Alcoa had protection from competition until 1909. After 1909 Alcoa was protected from foreign competition by high tariffs on imported aluminum. In addition, Alcoa protected its monopoly by buying up many of the low-cost bauxite (the ore containing aluminum) deposits and cheap electric power sites (aluminum production is electricity-intensive). Many economists also believe that Alcoa made entry less attractive by limit pricing—unlike United States Steel's strategy, discussed earlier.

Leonard Weiss has concluded that Alcoa's price and output performance in its years as a monopoly were very impressive. Aluminum prices generally declined over this period and output grew rapidly. Weiss quotes one Alcoa official as explaining that their profits "were consistently held down in order to broaden markets. Aluminum has no markets that have not been wrested from some other metal or material."[27]

The aluminum industry can be divided into the four vertical stages shown in Figure 9.4. Each stage involves a distinct technology and can be located in different regions. For example, bauxite is mined largely in the Caribbean area. Bauxite is processed into alumina near the Gulf Coast ports. Large-scale economies exist in the alumina plants (stage 2 in Figure 9.4)—in fact, until 1938 there was only one alumina plant in the United States. Because the reduction of alumina into aluminum ingots requires large amounts of electricity, these plants are located near cheap hydroelectric power sites (in the Northwest and Tennessee Valley). The first three stages in Figure 9.4 constitute the production of primary aluminum.

The fourth stage, fabrication, is technically similar to fabrication of other metals. Hence there are independent fabricators who buy aluminum ingot from primary producers and compete with the fabricated output of the primary producers. Again, until the 1940s Alcoa was the only primary producer in the United States.

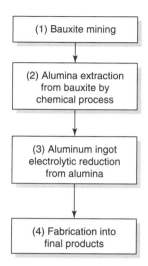

Figure 9.4
Vertically Related Stages of Aluminum Industry

It is important to understand the vertical structure of the industry in order to evaluate the market definition selected by Judge Hand. Also, one further technical fact is needed. As a durable good, scrap aluminum can be reprocessed and used by fabricators as a substitute for primary aluminum. This so-called secondary aluminum output was approximately one-quarter of the primary aluminum output in the 1940s.

Judge Hand considered three market share definitions for Alcoa:

1. $$\frac{\text{Alcoa's Sales}}{\text{Total Primary + Secondary + Imports}} = 33 \text{ percent}$$

2. $$\frac{\text{Alcoa's Sales + Internal Use}}{\text{Total Primary + Secondary + Imports}} = 64 \text{ percent}$$

3. $$\frac{\text{Alcoa's Sales + Internal Use}}{\text{Total Primary + Imports}} = 90 \text{ percent}$$

In the first definition, Alcoa's consumption of its own primary aluminum production for fabrication purposes is excluded. By adding it back, the second definition is attained—leading to an increase in market share from 33 percent to 64 percent. The third definition yields a share of 90 percent by excluding secondary aluminum from the denominator.

As we noted earlier in this chapter, Judge Hand stated that 90 percent "is enough to constitute a monopoly; it is doubtful whether sixty or sixty-four percent would be enough; and certainly thirty-three percent is not." He argued that 90 percent is the correct share for the following reasons.

First, "All ingot—with trifling exceptions—is used to fabricate intermediate, or end, products; and therefore all intermediate, or end, products which Alcoa fabricates and sells, pro tanto reduce the demand for ingot itself." Hence, "Internal Use" should appear in the numerator.

Second, Alcoa in the past had control of the primary aluminum that reappears as secondary aluminum in the present. Hence, Alcoa "always knew that the future supply of ingot would be made up in part of what it produced at the time, and if it was as far-sighted as it proclaims itself, that consideration must have had its share in determining how much to produce." For this reason, Judge Hand excluded secondary from the denominator and concluded Alcoa's share was 90 percent.

However, according to Judge Hand, "it does not follow that because Alcoa had such a monopoly, that it had 'monopolized' the ingot market: it may not have achieved monopoly; monopoly may have been thrust upon it." And, "a single producer may be the survivor out of a group of active competitors, merely by virtue of his superior skill, foresight and industry."

Judge Hand ruled out these possibilities in the Alcoa case. As he put it,

The only question is whether it falls within the exception established in favor of those who do not seek, but cannot avoid, the control of a market. It seems to us that that question scarcely survives its statement. It was not inevitable that it should always anticipate increases in the demand for ingot and be prepared to supply them. Nothing compelled it to keep doubling and redoubling its capacity before others entered the field.

Hence the Alcoa decision was a major change in the legal definition of monopolization. Predatory and aggressive acts were no longer necessary. Simply building capacity ahead of demand could be sufficient to indicate intent to monopolize by a dominant firm.

The remedy in the Alcoa case was to create two new competitors (Reynolds Metals and Kaiser Aluminum) by the sale of government-owned plants. The plants were built at government expense during World War II for military purposes. Divestiture of Alcoa was not a feasible alternative in any case since Alcoa had only two alumina plants, and one was almost obsolete.

The 1953 United Shoe Machinery case[28] was important in providing another example of a business practice that could indicate illegal monopolization by a dominant firm. The leasing practices of United Shoe were found to be exclusionary, and therefore evidence of illegal monopolization.

United Shoe supplied between 75 and 85 percent of the shoe machinery in the United States and there was no question of its dominance. United would not sell its machines to shoe manufacturers, but leased them for ten-year terms. There was a requirement that lessees had to use United machines if work was available. Also, the practice of United was to provide free repair services, and the Court viewed this as restricting entry since rivals of United would have to offer repair services as well. That is, independent repair firms would not exist given United's zero charges. Having to offer repair services in addition to shoe machinery would raise a capital requirement barrier.

The remedy in the United Shoe case was to purge the leases of their restrictive practices. Divestiture into three separate manufacturing plants was proposed by the government. However, the Court held this to be unrealistic because all of United's machine manufacture was conducted in a single plant in Massachusetts.

The leasing practices of United have been argued by some critics as not being effective exclusionary practices. That is, if rival shoe machinery suppliers were excluded from potential customers tied to ten-year leases, would they have been excluded less if potential customers bought the machinery?

Another issue that is puzzling is why shoe manufacturers would be willing to go along with restrictive leasing practices that are designed to provide United Shoe with monopoly power toward them. Consider Judge Richard Posner's example:

> Suppose that a competing shoe-machinery manufacturer offers to lease a machine for $10,000 a year under a lease terminable at will, while United offers to lease a similar machine for $9,000 a year but insists on a ten-year lease designed to destroy competing producers and enable United to raise its price to $20,000 at the end of the term. The $9,000 price is no bargain to the shoe manufacturers since the deal offered by United imposes an additional cost on the purchaser measured by the present value of the higher price in the future. If that value is, say $2,000 a year, United's offer is tantamount to charging the lessee $11,000.[29]

An alternative explanation is that United induced shoe manufacturers to lease its machinery by making the terms of the lease very attractive. According to Posner, the record of the United Shoe Machinery case indicated that United in fact offered extensive financial concessions to induce shoe manufacturers to lease its machinery. This explanation suggests that United was giving up part of its possible monopoly profits for market share. This is, of course, analytically similar to limit pricing by a dominant firm.

1970 to Present: Kodak, Cereals, IBM, and Others

During the current period, a number of "big cases" have been brought by antitrust agencies. IBM, Xerox, AT&T, and three breakfast cereal manufacturers were charged with monopolization. The latter case was unusual in that Kellogg, General Mills, and General Foods were charged by the Federal Trade Commission (FTC) with "shared monopoly." There were also a number of private suits that have received much attention, including a number of cases by smaller computer firms against IBM, and Berkey Photo against Eastman Kodak.

None of these cases reached the Supreme Court. Hence the final word on new judicial attitudes toward monopolization has yet to be heard. The IBM case was dismissed in 1982 by the Justice Department, thirteen years after the charges were first brought. Assistant Attorney General Baxter dropped the case after reviewing the evidence and concluding that the case was without merit. (We will discuss the IBM case in some detail later.) The Berkey-Kodak case was decided by the Second Circuit Court of Appeals in 1979—the Supreme Court declined to review the decision.

The Berkey-Kodak case involved a photofinisher (Berkey) charging monopolization against Eastman Kodak—with its 60 to 90 percent shares of most segments of the photography industry.[30] Berkey claimed that when in 1972 Kodak introduced its 110 Pocket Instamatic photographic system, which required a new Kodacolor II film, rival film and photofinishing suppliers were foreclosed from that market. According to Berkey, Kodak should have predisclosed its innovation to rivals so that they could compete immediately on introduction. Judge Kaufman concluded that Kodak "did not have a duty to predisclose information about the 110 system." He went on to explain his reasoning:

It is the possibility of success in the marketplace, attributable to superior performance, that provides the incentives on which the proper functioning of our competitive economy rests. If a firm that has engaged in the risks and expenses of research and development were required in all circumstances to share with its rivals the benefits of those endeavors, this incentive would very likely be vitiated.

The other "big cases" mentioned above were terminated by consent decrees (Xerox and AT&T) and by a decision by an FTC administrative law judge (breakfast cereals case). A consent decree is a negotiated settlement between the two parties subject to court approval. In the Xerox settlement in 1975 it was agreed that Xerox would license patents, supply "know-how" to competitors, sell as well as lease copy machines, and alter its pricing policies. In the AT&T settlement in 1982, AT&T divested its telephone-operating companies. Among other things, this separated the regulated telephone utilities from their main unregulated equipment supplier, Western Electric. (This important divestiture will be described in detail in Chapter 15 on telecommunications.)

The "shared monopoly" theory presented by the FTC against Kellogg, General Mills, and General Foods was a novel approach to a highly concentrated oligopoly.[31] The three firms had collectively 81 percent of the ready-to-eat cereals market, with Kellogg—the largest of the three—holding 45 percent. The FTC charged that the companies had engaged "in certain interdependent acts and practices in order to achieve a highly concentrated, noncompetitive market structure and shared monopoly power."

An example of one of these acts was termed "brand proliferation." By introducing some 150 brands between 1950 and 1970, the companies were alleged to have left "no room" for new entrants. The economic theory follows closely the Bain-Sylos limit-pricing model. The key idea is that brands are located in a "product characteristics space," and each competes only with brands located nearby exhibiting similar product characteristics. Fixed launching costs make it necessary to achieve a relatively large sales volume to be economically viable. So, if the "room" between brands is small (because of brand proliferation), new entrants will be deterred because they cannot expect to attain large enough sales. (This type of entry barrier was discussed in more detail in Chapter 6.)

The FTC judge, however, saw brand proliferation as "nothing more than the introduction of new brands, which is a legitimate means of competition.... There is no evidence of a conspiracy or intent to deter entry by means of new product introductions." After considering other acts, and rejecting them as being illegal, the judge dismissed the complaint. In 1982 the FTC commissioners decided to let the dismissal stand rather than appeal the decision to a higher court.[32]

The Justice Department filed its case against IBM in 1969, following a lengthy internal investigation of the leading computer firm. The case, dismissed in 1982, involved huge resource costs—over $200 million in legal costs, 950 witnesses, 726 trial days, 17,000 exhibits and 104,400 trial transcript pages.[33] One government witness earned a total of $465,000 in consulting fees.

The government argued that IBM had about 70 percent of the market for medium-size, business-oriented, "general purpose," electronic, digital computer systems. Not unexpectedly, IBM argued that the market was much broader, and should include companies selling "parts of systems" and computer systems for scientific and military purposes. IBM's share under the broader definition was less than 50 percent.

IBM's dominant position in the computer industry is usually attributed to its strong position before computers existed in the punched-card office equipment business. This gave IBM strong ties to the potential computer users. IBM delivered its first computer, the IBM 650, in 1954. Thus, while not being the technical leader in computers, IBM supplied both hardware and software that performed well.

According to the government, IBM engaged in numerous practices that enabled it to maintain its monopoly power. These practices were argued to be neither "inevitable nor honestly industrial." They were leasing, bundling, differentiation of software, fighting machines, tying of products, manipulation of purchase-to-lease price ratios, and education allowances. Unfortunately, we do not have the space to examine all of these practices in depth.

A particularly interesting set of practices by IBM was directed at peripherals companies. These were companies that supplied printers, tape drives, disk drives, and other pieces of equipment that can be "plugged" into the central computer system. For example, in 1970 peripherals manufacturers (such as Calcomp, Memorex, and Telex) were making combined net profits of $17.7 million through selling plug-compatible equipment to owners of IBM systems.

IBM responded by an integrated strategy of price cuts and "fighting machines." One such fighting machine was described by the government as follows:

IBM struck first at peripherals manufacturers by announcing the 2319A disk drive as a "new" disk drive. In fact it was essentially a physical rearrangement of its standard 2314-drive announced for attachment to the 370/145 computer. The 2319A represented a significant price reduction per spindle over IBM's standard 2314. Independent peripherals manufacturers had made significant inroads into the market. With the 2319A IBM attempted to foreclose the peripherals manufacturers from the 370/145 marketplace by integrating part of the control unit (a "competitive" product) for the disk drive into the computer unit (a "noncompetitive" product) of the 370/145. The rest of the control unit was placed into the box with the disk drive making it more difficult for [peripherals manufacturers] to interface with the IBM system in providing their products.[34]

This, plus a number of similar tactics, led to a $17.6 million loss for these peripherals manufacturers in 1971, and a $43 million loss in 1972.

Many of these peripherals manufacturers filed private antitrust cases against IBM. In every case, IBM has prevailed. For example, in the Calcomp v. IBM case the court concluded that IBM's conduct was not "unreasonably restrictive of competition."[35]

And, as stated earlier, the Justice Department dropped the IBM case in January 1982. According to the Assistant Attorney General, the government's chances of winning were "only one in ten thousand."

Finally, we note a private case that was decided by the Supreme Court in 1985.[36] The facts in the case, *Aspen Skiing Company v. Aspen Highlands Skiing*, are unusual and even though the Court found illegal monopolization, it does not appear to represent a significant change in the Court's treatment of monopolization. The Court found that Aspen Skiing Company had monopolized the market for skiing services in Aspen, Colorado. It owned three of the four major mountain ski facilities in that market, and used a marketing arrangement to harm its rival. That is, after many years in which the two rivals jointly offered six-day tickets to skiers that could be used at any facility, Aspen Skiing refused to do so any longer after a dispute over sharing the joint revenues. The Court found that there were no valid business reasons for Aspen Skiing's refusal, and that it represented a practice that tended to exclude competition.

Predatory Pricing: Proposed Legal Definitions

In 1975, two law professors, Areeda and Turner, published an important article in the *Harvard Law Review* in which they proposed a definition of predatory pricing to be used by the courts in identifying illegal predation.[37] Their proposed rule has been adopted by a number of judges, although some view it as too permissive. In this section we plan to review the Areeda-Turner rule and the justification for it. Then we will examine some of the criticisms and alternative tests for predation that have been put forth.

The legal definition of predatory pricing—if and when it becomes widely accepted—will be of great importance. In effect, it will be the rule by which firms must play the "competitive game." For example, suppose that price cutting is deemed predatory when a price is set below average total cost—as a number of courts have ruled in the past. This means that a dominant firm, faced with entry by an aggressive new rival, must be very careful not to price below its average total cost in responding to that new rival. The result may be that much healthy price competition will be stifled.

Of course, errors can be made in the other direction as well. That is, if the test for predatory pricing is made too permissive, then monopoly power might be fostered through predatory pricing. Hence it is useful to bear in mind that two types of errors are possible in searching for the optimal definition.

Viewpoints concerning the optimal definition are heavily influenced by one's expectation about the likelihood of the occurrence of predatory pricing. As we discussed earlier in this chapter, most economists consider predatory pricing to be a rare phenomenon. One antitrust expert, Robert Bork, has even argued that there should be no legal rules against it:

It seems unwise, therefore, to construct rules about a phenomenon that probably does not exist or which, should it exist in very rare cases, the courts would have grave difficulty distinguishing from competitive price behavior. It is almost certain that attempts to apply such rules do much more harm than good.[38]

Given the long history of predatory pricing as the subject of numerous antitrust cases, this position seems unlikely to prevail. Hence we will consider the Areeda-Turner rule, which is apparently becoming widely accepted by numerous lower courts. A particularly strong economic argument favoring the Areeda-Turner rule was given by Circuit Judge Breyer (now Supreme Court Justice) in a 1983 decision, Barry Wright v. ITT Grinnell.[39]

In considering the Areeda-Turner rule, it is helpful to refer to the typical short-run cost curves shown in Figure 9.5. Areeda and Turner argue that any price below marginal cost (MC) will cause the monopolist to lose money on some units of output—which is consistent with the pred-

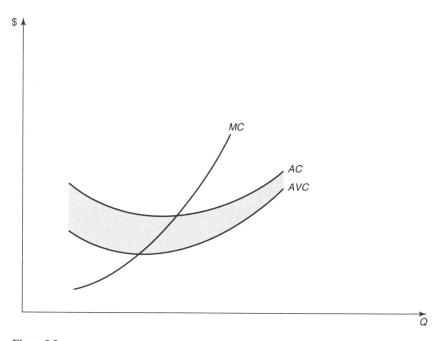

Figure 9.5
Region Showing Predatory Prices under ATC Rule That Are Not Predatory under Final Areeda-Turner Rule

atory pricing strategy. Also, pricing below short-run marginal cost is well known to be economically inefficient. For these reasons, they would classify such prices as predatory and therefore illegal. However, for outputs to the right of Q^*, average cost (AC) is less than marginal cost. Because prices above average cost (but below marginal cost) would not exclude equally efficient rivals, they would permit such prices (even though they would be economically inefficient).

Finally, because "marginal cost data are typically unavailable," Areeda and Turner propose to substitute average variable cost (AVC) for marginal cost. Their conclusion is:

a.   A price at or above reasonably anticipated average variable cost should be conclusively presumed lawful.

b.   A price below reasonably anticipated average variable cost should be conclusively presumed unlawful.

The Areeda-Turner proposal has stimulated a large number of criticisms and alternative proposals—too many for a comprehensive treatment here. For our purposes, it is appropriate to review three of the various alternatives that have been proposed. The three can be identified briefly as the *ATC* (average total cost) rule, the output restriction rule, and the Joskow-Klevorick two-stage rule.

The ATC Rule

A number of economists have independently proposed some version of what we term the ATC rule. A key reason given for preferring the ATC rule to the Areeda-Turner rule is that the latter rule is too permissive, allowing predators to escape too easily.

Because the final version of the Areeda-Turner rule is that only prices below average variable cost (AVC) are predatory, the shaded region in Figure 9.5 illustrates how it differs from the ATC rule.

Greer has argued that the ATC rule "produces a defendant's paradise, a monopolist's heaven." He goes on to observe that "a monopolist with abundant financial reserves could, under the [Areeda-Turner] rule, drive less financially secure but equally efficient rivals from the market without fear of prosecution merely by pricing below ATC and above AVC."[40]

Rather than make all pricing below ATC predatory, Greer's proposal is to have a two-part standard. Hence, illegal pricing would be shown by (1) pricing below ATC, plus (2) substantial evidence of predatory intent. Evidence of intent could include pricing below AVC as well as ATC, "documents revealing long-term business plans of injurious price-cutting activity," and "building immense new capacity in a market which is clearly not large enough to utilize fully that capacity at a profitable price."

The Output Restriction Rule

Williamson has proposed an alternative to the cost-based rules discussed above.[41] The focus of his analysis that we will review here is the case of an established dominant firm seeking to deter new entry.

Williamson stresses that predatory pricing should be evaluated as a long-run business strategy. The Areeda-Turner rationale that price below marginal cost is inefficient is correct but not of great significance to him. Rather, he argues that one must consider both the predatory pricing period (which may be short) and the postpredation period in efficiency terms. Moreover, the adaptation of the dominant firm to the legal standard is also important. For example, if the firm knows that the law forbids an increase in output in response to entry, this may induce the firm to build more capacity than otherwise in anticipation of entry. These "side effects" of rules against predatory pricing must be examined in designing the optimal rules.

Although we cannot review Williamson's complicated analysis in detail, a brief overview of his approach and results will be presented. Figures 9.6 and 9.7 show how the dominant firm will adjust to anticipated entry under an output restriction rule and a short-run marginal cost standard, respectively. That is, these two possible rules against predatory pricing are evaluated:

1. *The Output Restriction Rule, $Q \leq Q_0$.* Q_0 is the dominant firm's preentry level of output and Q is the postentry level of output. Hence this rule states that in the period after entry occurs the dominant firm cannot increase output above the preentry level.

2. *The Marginal Cost Rule, $P \geq$ SRMC.* This rule permits the dominant firm to increase output in the postentry period subject to the condition that price will not fall below short-run marginal cost.

Williamson's analysis uses the Bain-Sylos model of limit pricing that we described in Chapter 6. However, for analytical convenience, his long-run average cost curve (available to all firms) falls in steps rather than continuously. A key assumption is that

Dominant firms are assumed to be influenced by predatory pricing rules in the following way: whatever rule is in effect, dominant firms will invest in plant and equipment in an amount and kind such that the profits of any entrant, were one to appear, would be reduced to zero if the dominant firm responded to entry in

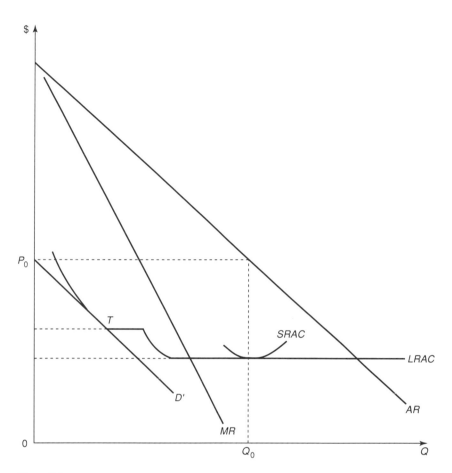

Figure 9.6
Output Restriction Rule Equilibrium

the most aggressive manner allowed by the prevailing rule. An aggressive (as opposed to a conciliatory) response involves producing the maximum output consistent with the prevailing rule. Given that investment is determined with this strategic objective in mind, the dominant firm behaves in all pre-entry periods by maximizing short-run profits.[42]

Under the output restriction rule, the dominant firm picks output Q_0 and charges a price of P_0. This is shown in Figure 9.6. The residual demand curve D' shows that the best the entrant could do would be to produce at point T and make zero profit.

In comparison, under the marginal cost rule, Figure 9.7 shows that preentry output is lower at Q_2 and price is higher at P_2. Under this rule, the dominant firm can increase output if entry occurs—from Q_2 to Q_0 along the SRMC curve. The residual demand curve D'' is flatter because of the assumed capability of the dominant firm to expand output in

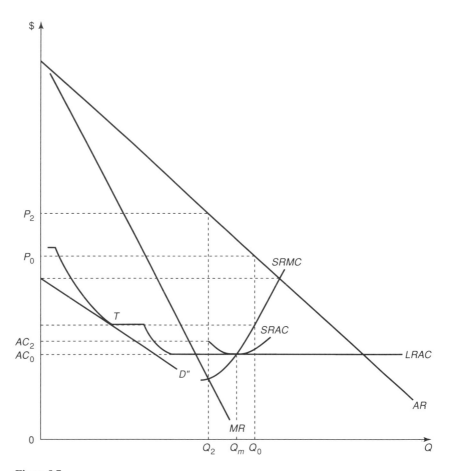

Figure 9.7
Marginal Cost Rule Equilibrium

response to entry.[43] Hence the marginal cost rule induces the dominant firm to build a smaller plant (minimum SRAC at Q_m as compared to Q_0) and charge a higher preentry price (P_2 compared to P_0) than for the output restriction rule case. The dominant firm also produces its preentry output at a higher average cost (AC_2 versus AC_0).

Based on these comparisons, Williamson concludes that the output restriction rule is superior on welfare grounds. He also concludes that it is superior to the average total cost (ATC) rule, although we will not describe that comparison here.

Finally, it can be argued that it may be easier to determine if a firm increases output than if it cuts price below cost. Estimating marginal and average costs is a very difficult business and can lead to endless arguments among accountants and other experts.

Joskow-Klevorick Two-Stage Rule

In a 1979 article[44] Joskow and Klevorick proposed a two-stage approach to predatory pricing. The first stage would require an examination of the market structure to determine if structure is likely to permit predation to be successful. For example, if entry barriers are low, the finding would be that predation is not likely to be a viable strategy, and the case would not be pursued. The second stage would use cost-based tests and pricing behavior tests. For example, price below average variable cost would be an indication of predation. Another indication would be if price were cut, but not below average total cost, and then raised significantly within two years without a corresponding increase in cost or demand. While the Supreme Court has yet to specify its view on what cost-based rule is correct, it can be argued that it supports a two-stage approach that focuses first on market structure and the alleged predator's ability to recoup its investment in foregone short-run profits. Circuit Judge Easterbrook argued in a 1989 case that in two 1986 Supreme Court cases the Supreme Court found that recoupment would be so unlikely that antitrust inquiry could not be justified.[45]

In one of those 1986 cases, the *Matsushita* case discussed earlier in this chapter, the Court said simply that predatory pricing means "pricing below some appropriate measure of cost." It then observed that "there is a good deal of debate, both in the cases and in the law reviews, about what cost is relevant in such cases. We need not resolve this debate here." The Court went on to observe that "it is not enough simply to achieve monopoly power, as monopoly pricing may breed quick entry by new competitors eager to share in the excess profits. The success of any predatory scheme depends on *maintaining* monopoly power for long enough both to recoup the predator's losses and to harvest some additional gain." Then, the Court noted that "if predatory pricing conspiracies are generally unlikely to occur, they are especially so where, as here, the prospects of attaining monopoly power seem slight."

The most recent Supreme Court decision was in the *Brooke* case,[46] decided in 1993. In this case, Liggett (a cigarette firm owned by Brooke) charged that Brown and Williamson introduced its generic cigarettes at predatory prices to try to harm Liggett's own generic business. The Court found that the market structure was such that Brown and Williamson could not recoup its predatory losses. A major factor was that Brown and Williamson had only a 12 percent share of the cigarette market, and the Court argued that recoupment would require coordinated pricing with other companies—an unlikely event in the Court's view.

Price Discrimination and the Robinson-Patman Act

The Clayton Act provision that price discrimination is illegal where it substantially lessens competition or tends to create a monopoly was amended in 1936 by the Robinson-Patman Act. The resulting, quite lengthy Section 2 of the Clayton Act is reproduced in the appendix of Chapter 3.

According to Judge Posner, "The Robinson-Patman Act ... is almost uniformly condemned by professional and academic opinion, legal and economic."[47] It was passed during the Great Depression largely to protect small, independent retailers from the newly emerging chains. For example, it outlaws brokerage fees unless an independent broker is involved. A&P was found to be in violation for buying directly from suppliers and performing its own wholesaling function. The "discrimination" was seen as A&P paying lower prices for supplies than independent stores pay who buy through brokers or wholesalers. The fact that A&P was lowering its distribution costs—an economic benefit for society—by performing its own wholesaling function was irrelevant.

The economic definition of price discrimination—charging different customers prices that are not in proportion to marginal costs—is almost completely turned on its head in the Robinson-Patman Act and its enforcement. For example, in cases where some injury to competition has been found, the Act has been interpreted as holding simple price differences to be illegal, regardless of cost differences. (Strictly, cost differences are a possible defense in the language of the law, but in practice it is virtually impossible to employ this defense. A second possible defense is that the discrimination was required to "meet competition.")

We begin by reviewing the economics of price discrimination. The traditional analysis considers a monopolist and examines equilibrium prices, profitability, and efficiency. This is referred to here as systematic (or persistent) discrimination to distinguish it from unsystematic (or temporary) discrimination. Unsystematic discrimination means situations of disequilibrium in which shifts of demand or cost lead to price changes that are not uniform to all buyers. In other words, normal competitive processes of adjustment to new equilibria can involve differences in prices that might be viewed (incorrectly) as price discrimination by antitrust authorities.

Systematic Discrimination

Price discrimination was discussed in Chapter 8, where tying and block booking were examined. There are three types of price discrimination:

first-degree or perfect discrimination (in which the monopolist obtains all of the consumer surplus), second-degree (such as tying), and third-degree (in which demanders are partitioned into groups and each group is charged a different price—such as discounts for children at the movie theater).

The distinction between second- and third-degree is that in second-degree discrimination all demanders confront the same price schedule, but they pay different average prices depending on their preferences[48]; in third-degree discrimination the seller separates demanders into different groups based upon some external characteristic (such as age) and confronts the groups with different prices. Clearly, in third-degree situations the seller must be able to keep resales from occurring. If children's tickets could be used by adults, no adults would pay the higher price of an adult ticket. It is also necessary for the seller to possess some degree of market power—otherwise there is no way prices can differ (in as much as price equals marginal cost in competitive markets).

The economics of third-degree discrimination can be explained by example. Consider duPont's patented superstrength synthetic fiber, Kevlar.[49] To simplify, assume that there are only two uses: in undersea cables and in tires. Because tire companies have the option of using low-cost substitutes in tires—steel and fiberglass—the demand for Kevlar by tire companies is more elastic (at a given price) than that by cable companies. That is, because of its technical characteristics, Kevlar is far superior to possible substitutes in undersea cables.

Assume hypothetically that the demand curves for Kevlar are

$q_c = 100 - p_c \ldots$ for use in undersea cables

$q_t = 60 - p_t \ldots$ for use in tires

For simplicity, let the marginal cost (MC) be constant at \$20. This situation is shown in Figure 9.8, where cable demand is shown on the right and tire demand on the left. That is, we have "flipped" tire demand to the left of the origin and so we measure its output as increasing left to right. This is done to make the diagram less cluttered.

First, consider the profit-maximizing solution assuming that duPont can charge different prices to tire and cable companies if it is profitable to do so. The logic is simple. Set the marginal revenue (MR_c) from cable companies equal to the marginal revenue (MR_t) from tire companies, and set both equal to MC. Clearly, if the marginal revenues differed, duPont would find it profitable to shift a unit from the lower marginal revenue market to the higher. The solution ($MR_c = MC$ at point N and

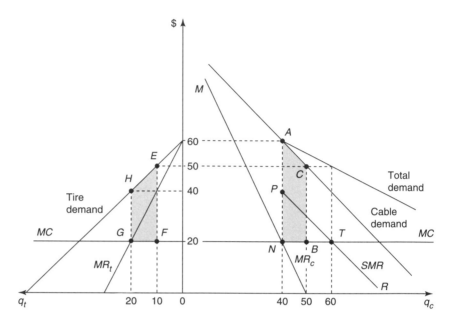

Figure 9.8
Price Discrimination That Decreases Total Surplus

$MR_t = MC$ at point G) is to sell 40 units to the cable market at a price of $60 and 20 units to the tire market at a price of $40. The profits in the two markets are found by computing revenues less costs, or $1600 from cable users and $400 from tire users, for a total of $2000.[50]

It is instructive to note that the higher price is charged in the market in which the elasticity of demand is lower. That is, at the equilibrium, the elasticity of demand is 1.5 in the cable market and 2 in the tire market.[51] If the elasticities were not different, the prices would be the same and discrimination would not be profitable.[52]

Next, consider the discrimination-disallowed, or single-price, equilibrium. Here it is necessary to aggregate the two demands by adding them horizontally to get the total demand curve. This is a kinked curve where the kink is at point A. Above point A, the total demand curve corresponds to cable demand only, because the tire users will pay no more than $60. The marginal revenue curve associated with the total demand curve, SMR,[53] intersects MC at a total output of 60 (at point T). Hence the single price is $50, and at this price cable users buy 50 units and tire users buy 10 units. Finally, the profit is again found by computing revenues minus costs, or $1800. As anticipated, profit is lower if discrimination is not permitted.

Summarizing,

Discrimination	Single Price
$p_c = \$60$	$p_c = p_t = \$50$
$q_c = 40$	$q_c = 50$
$p_t = \$40$	$q_t = 10$
$q_t = 20$	$q_c + q_t = 60$
$q_c + q_t = 60$	
total profit $= \$2000$	total profit $= \$1800$

The Kevlar example makes it clear that third-degree discrimination, the subject of the Robinson-Patman Act, is profitable. The next question is to examine the efficiency of price discrimination. For our Kevlar example, we can compare total economic surplus under the two scenarios—discrimination and single price. It turns out that in situations where there are linear demand curves, and where both demand groups buy positive amounts in the single price case, total surplus always falls when discrimination is allowed. This is the case in our example.

In Figure 9.8 it is easy to see this result graphically. In the cable market, the area of the shaded trapezoid $ANBC$ gives the loss in total surplus in moving from the single price of \$50 to the discriminatory price of \$60. Total value[54] of Kevlar to cable users is reduced by the area under the demand curve and between outputs of 40 and 50. Subtracting the cost saving from reducing output (the area under MC and between these two outputs) yields the trapezoid $ANBC$. This area equals \$350.

Similarly, the area of shaded trapezoid $HGFE$ in the tire market gives the gain in total surplus in moving from the single price of \$50 to the lower discriminatory price of \$40. This area equals \$250. Hence the net change in total surplus is a gain in the tire market of \$250 minus a loss in the cable market of \$350, or a net loss of \$100. For cases like this example (with linear demands), it is always true that the output changes in the two markets are exactly equal and opposite in direction—that is, total output is unchanged. Hence the two trapezoids are equal in width, but the loss trapezoid is taller.

It is important to provide an intuitive explanation for the net loss result in this example. Total output is unchanged and all that happens is a reallocation of output from high-value users (at the margin) to low-value users. In the single-price case, all users end up with the same marginal valuation. This "gap" is the inefficiency that produces the net loss.

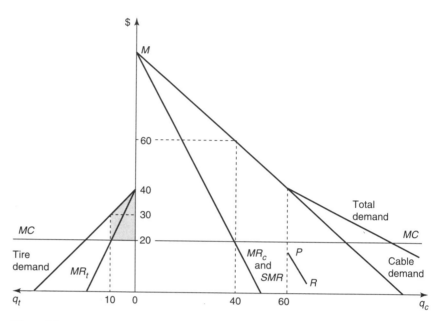

Figure 9.9
Price Discrimination That Increases Total Surplus

Trading between cable users and tire users, which is not allowed by du-Pont, would make both groups better off. (It is instructive to note that duPont's enforcement of different prices was attacked by a customer as an antitrust violation.)

As noted, we have been examining a rather special case. To show a different welfare result, we need change our example only slightly. Assume now that the demand for Kevlar by cable companies is unchanged, as is the marginal cost. However, now assume that the demand by tire users is smaller than before. In particular, let

$$q_t = 40 - p_t \dots \quad \text{for use in tires}$$

Carrying through the same analysis as before, we find that in Figure 9.9 the discrimination solution is where $MR_c = MC$ and $MR_t = MC$, so $p_c = \$60$ and $p_t = \$30$. Now, however, the single price equilibrium where $SMR = MC$ yields a price of $\$60$.[55] Given that the tire users will pay at most $40, the tire users will obviously buy zero units of Kevlar. They will simply use fiberglass and steel in their tires. This situation is therefore different from the case in Figure 9.8, where the tire users did buy positive amounts of Kevlar when a single price was used.

Summarizing,

Discrimination	Single Price
$p_c = \$60$	$p_c = p_t = \$60$
$q_c = 40$	$q_c = 40$
$p_t = \$30$	$q_t = 0$
$q_c = 10$	$q_c + q_t = 40$
$q_c + q_t = 50$	
total profit $= \$1700$	total profit $= \$1600$

Discrimination, as before, yields higher profits ($1700 versus $1600). Now, however, total output increases under discrimination. This increase is, of course, simply the output purchased by tire users who were not in the market when the single price was used. There has been no change whatsoever in the cable market, so the only change is that discrimination has permitted purchases of Kevlar by tire users. The interesting result is that welfare has been improved by discrimination. Not only is total surplus higher, by the shaded area in Figure 9.9, but this is an increase in welfare under the Pareto criterion as well. Notice that no one is harmed—the cable market is unchanged—and both duPont and tire users gain. The duPont company gains by a profit increase of $100 (the square area of the shaded region), and the tire users gain by $50 (the triangular portion of the shaded area).

Finally, we should note that in cases of nonlinear demand curves the welfare result can be either positive or negative. It is very difficult to provide any general conditions in this situation. It is true, however, that total output must increase if discrimination is to improve welfare.[56]

Unsystematic Discrimination

Unsystematic discrimination refers to various situations in which prices differ because of temporary changes taking place in the market. Movements toward equilibria are always taking place in competitive markets as shifts in demand or costs occur. That is, the long-run competitive equilibrium described in microeconomics texts is best viewed as a target that is constantly shifting, and competitive markets are always adjusting toward that equilibrium. For example, prices in one geographical region may rise temporarily because of a demand increase until new supplies can be made available (either through capacity additions or transport from distant regions). These temporary "discriminatory" situations clearly are necessary for markets to function efficiently and should not be forbidden by law.

A different situation that can be considered under this category is the cheating of a cartel member. A cartel member may decide that secretly shading the cartel price to a few large customers will be profitable. An across-the-board cut to all customers would be too dangerous because fellow cartel members would probably discover the cheating and match the cut. Nevertheless, such cheating has a tendency to spread and has often led to the deterioration of cartel price structures—a socially beneficial result. A good example is probably the nineteenth-century railroad cartels, which were known for frequent breakdowns of their agreed-on freight rates.

In summary, there are cases of unsystematic, or temporary, discrimination that are clearly socially beneficial. The difficulty is to distinguish in practice between this type of discrimination and systematic discrimination practiced by an entrenched monopolist that may be harmful. Hence, laws against price discrimination are difficult to write and enforce if they are to promote competition.

In recent years the Federal Trade Commission has brought few complaints under the Robinson-Patman Act, although there are still actions brought by private parties. Because of this trend, we will discuss only two of the best-known cases here.

Cases

Two main categories of Robinson-Patman cases are those involving primary-line discrimination and those involving secondary-line discrimination. Primary-line discrimination refers to situations in which the seller practicing discrimination injures its own rivals. Predatory pricing is an extreme example since it requires prices set below costs. Less severe discrimination that harms one's rivals without being predatory also qualifies as primary-line discrimination.

Secondary-line discrimination occurs when injury to competition takes place in the buyers' market. The idea is that buyers who get preferentially low prices will have an advantage over their rivals.

We consider two famous cases—one in each category. The primary-line case is a private case known as Utah Pie.[57] A small frozen dessert pie manufacturer in Salt Lake City, Utah Pie Company, brought the suit against three large rivals: Continental Baking, Carnation, and Pet Milk. The three large rivals had manufacturing facilities in California, but not in Utah. Hence, when Utah Pie opened its frozen pie plant in Utah, it obtained a significant cost advantage over its larger rivals. Utah Pie had market-share percentages of 66.5 in 1958, 34.3 in 1959, 45.5 in

1960, and 45.3 in 1961. Also, the market was expanding rapidly over this period, and Utah Pie's actual sales steadily rose as well.

The Supreme Court noted in its opinion that Continental, for example, set a price in Salt Lake City that was "less than its direct cost plus an allocation for overhead." Also, the rivals tended to charge less in Utah than they did in other locations. According to the Court,

At times Utah Pie was a leader in moving the general level of prices down, and at other times each of the respondents also bore responsibility for the downward pressure on the price structure. We believe that the Act reaches price discrimination that erodes competition as much as it does price discrimination that is intended to have immediate destructive impact.

Hence, Utah Pie won its case even though the decision has been regarded by most scholars as a mistake. Justice Stewart, in a dissenting opinion, put the argument clearly when he said that the market should be viewed as more competitive in 1961 than it was in 1958, not less competitive as the Court held. One reason is that the dominant firm, Utah Pie, had a 66.5 percent share of the market in 1958 but only 45.3 percent in 1961. According to Justice Stewart, "the Court has fallen into the error of reading the Robinson-Patman Act as protecting competitors, instead of competition."

The 1948 Morton Salt case is the landmark case involving secondary-line discrimination.[58] Morton Salt sold its Blue Label salt to wholesalers and to chain stores according to the following table of discounts:

	Price/Case
Less-than-carload purchases	$1.60
Carload purchases	1.50
5,000-case purchases in any consecutive 12 months	1.40
50,000-case purchases in any consecutive 12 months	1.35

Only five customers ever bought sufficient quantities of salt to obtain the $1.35 per case price. These were large chain stores, and the Court was concerned that small independent food stores could not compete with the chains because they had to pay, say, $1.60 per case. As the Court put it: "Congress was especially concerned with protecting small businesses which were unable to buy in quantities, such as the merchants here who purchased in less-than-carload lots."

Morton Salt tried to defend itself by claiming that the discounts were available to all customers. However, the Court rejected this claim saying that "theoretically, these discounts are available to all, but functionally they are not."

In conclusion, although economic analysis reveals that there are cases in which prohibiting price discrimination is socially beneficial, there are many cases in which it should not be prohibited. The Robinson-Patman Act appears to be a poor instrument for distinguishing the cases, and reforming the Act may be too difficult. This is similar to the criticism of predatory pricing law in that the attempt to prohibit certain harmful practices may be, on balance, more harmful than doing nothing. This is true because of the chilling effect on socially desirable price competition that such laws may cause.

Former judge Robert Bork has put the point colorfully: "One often hears of the baseball player who, although a weak hitter, was also a poor fielder. Robinson-Patman is a little like that. Although it does not prevent much price discrimination, at least it has stifled a great deal of competition."[59]

Summary

The law toward monopolization is one of the most difficult antitrust laws to understand. In part, this is because there are a number of ways (some good, some bad) of winning a large market share—for instance, through superior management, economies of scale, or predatory tactics. This was shown by examining a series of important decisions and how the interpretation of the law has changed since the Sherman Act was passed in 1890. Currently, there seems to be a greater leniency by the courts toward practices of dominant firms to protect their market shares than was true in the 1940–1970 period. The practice of predatory pricing was found to be a relatively unlikely event, and a number of alternative proposals for identifying predatory pricing were discussed. Finally, we discussed the Robinson-Patman Act—or the price discrimination law—and found that it is generally an anticompetitive law. Fortunately, enforcement by the Federal Trade Commission has declined in recent years.

Questions and Problems

1. If a large firm is found to possess monopoly power, what else is needed to find the firm guilty of monopolization? Why is possessing monopoly power insufficient for illegality?

2. In Chapter 7 the Merger Guidelines were described. In particular, the relevant market was defined as consisting of all products and firms such that a hypothetical cartel could raise its price by 5 percent and not have to re-

scind it because of unprofitability. In light of the duPont Cellophane case, how might this rule be modified to avoid the "error" of defining the market to be too broad?

3. Which of the three market definitions considered by Judge Hand in the Alcoa case do you think is most defensible?

4. IBM redesigned its disk drive 2319A to make it more difficult for rivals to interface with IBM computer systems. The Justice Department regarded this as anticompetitive. Comment.

5. A three-firm Cournot industry has a demand curve of $Q = 20 - P$. Each firm has an annual total cost of $4q_i + 12$. Find the equilibrium price, output of each firm, and profit per firm.

    a. The management of firm 1 is considering a strategy of predatory pricing since they believe monopoly profits would far exceed their current profits. What are the potential monopoly profits in this industry?

    b. Ignoring any antitrust concerns, the management wants at least to do an investment analysis of predatory pricing. They decide that to drive the other two firms out of the market a price of $2 per unit is needed and that it must be maintained for at least three years. Other assumptions were put forth, but the consensus was the $2 price, three-year assumption. Given that a six-year time horizon and a 14 percent cost of capital are standard assumptions for firm 1 in its investment decisions, is predatory pricing profitable? Present value formulas show that at 14 percent interest a stream of $1 receipts for three years has a present value of $2.322 and a stream of $1 receipts from year 4 to year 6 has a present value of $1.567.

    c. Assume that whatever the numbers above show, the management could choose numbers that make the investment profitable. If it did appear profitable, say, net present value is $10, should predation be pursued? What other considerations should the management want further information about?

6. A new chemical has been discovered that can be produced at a constant marginal cost of $10 by its patent holder, Johnson, Inc. Two industries A and B find the chemical, Cloreen, to be useful in their production processes. Industry A has a demand for Cloreen of $q_a = 100 - p_a$. Industry B's demand is $q_b = 60 - p_b$.

    a. If Johnson can prevent resales between industries A and B, what prices will it charge to A and B? It can be assumed that the patent gives Johnson monopoly power. What quantities will be sold to the two industries and what will be Johnson's profit?

    b. Assume now that it is illegal for Johnson to charge different prices to A and B. What price will Johnson now charge and what will its profit be? What is Johnson's quantity sold?

    c. Is total economic surplus higher in (a) or in (b)? What is the difference in total surplus in the two cases?

    d. Assume now that the demand for Cloreen by industry B is less than above, and is $q_b = 40 - p_b$. Aside from this change, the facts are as given above. Answer (a), (b), and (c) given the changed demand by industry B.

7. Assume a third-degree discrimination situation and you are to decide whether it is in society's interest. Assume that under the "no discrimination

allowed" case one group of users (group B) of a new product finds its price too high to buy any of the product. But under discrimination they would buy a positive amount at the lower price offered them. Further, assume that the price charged to the original group of buyers (group A) remains unchanged after discrimination is permitted.

a. The legal permission to price-discriminate would benefit the monopolist, but the original group of buyers (group A) would be harmed. Do you agree or disagree? Why?

b. The legal permission to discriminate would benefit group B buyers and the monopolist, and group A buyers would be unaffected, so the permission to discriminate is a Pareto superior move compared to the no-discrimination situation. Do you agree or disagree? Why?

c. A Pareto superior move will always pass the "increase in total economic surplus" test, but the reverse is not true. True or false? Why?

Notes

1. Berkey Photo v. Eastman Kodak Co., 603 F. 2d 263 (2d Cir. 1979).

2. United States v. Aluminum Co. of America, 148 F. 2d 416 (2d Cir. 1945).

3. United States v. Grinnell Corps., 384 U.S. 563 (1966).

4. See Abba Lerner, "The Concept of Monopoly and the Measurement of Monopoly Power," *Review of Economic Studies*, June 1934.

5. This result was developed in Chapter 5, Equation (5.9), for the case of n firms. By setting $n = 1$, the monopoly result here is obtained.

6. It is useful to observe that L might be large but might involve only very little economic activity. A better measure of monopoly power for purposes of deciding whether the government should bring antitrust charges is probably the deadweight loss that it causes. It can be shown, for example, that for a monopolist with constant marginal cost and linear demand, the deadweight loss, $DW = L$ (Monopolist's Revenue)/2. Hence it is clear that the deadweight loss would be small if the revenue involved is small, regardless of L. See R. Schmalensee, "Another Look at Market Power," *Harvard Law Review*, June 1982.

7. Joe S. Bain, "The Profit Rate as a Measure of Monopoly Power," *Quarterly Journal of Economics*, February 1941.

8. Ibid.

9. F. M. Scherer, *Industrial Market Structure and Economic Performance*, 2nd ed. (Chicago: Rand-McNally, 1980), p. 272. Also, F. M. Fisher and J. J. McGowan, "On the Misuse of Accounting Rates of Return to Infer Monopoly Profits," *American Economic Review*, March 1983.

10. R. Schmalensee, "On the Use of Economic Models in Antitrust: The Realemon Case," *University of Pennsylvania Law Review*, April 1979, p. 1009.

11. United States v. E. I. duPont de Nemours and Co., 351 U.S. 377 (1956).

12. For example, see G. W. Stocking and W. F. Muellar, "The Cellophane Case and the New Competition," *American Economic Review*, March 1955.

13. F. M. Fisher, J. J. McGowan, and J. E. Greenwood, *Folded, Spindled, and Mutilated: Economic Analysis and U.S. v. IBM* (Cambridge, Mass.: MIT Press, 1983), p. 99.

14. F. M. Fisher, "Diagnosing Monopoly," *Quarterly Review of Economics and Business*, Summer 1979, p. 16.

15. United States v. Aluminum Co. of America, 148 F. 2d 416 (2d Cir. 1945).

16. United States v. United Shoe Machinery Corporation, 110 F. Supp. 295 (D. Mass. 1953).

17. D. F. Greer, *Business, Government, and Society* (New York: Macmillan, 1983), p. 148.

18. United States v. United Shoe Machinery Corp., 110 U.S. 1 (1911).

19. Standard Oil Co. of New Jersey v. United States, 221 U.S. 1 (1911).

20. United States v. American Tobacco Co., 221 U.S. 106 (1911).

21. John S. McGee, "Predatory Pricing Revisited," *Journal of Law and Economics*, October 1980.

22. Kenneth G. Elzinga, "Collusive Predation: Matsushita v. Zenith (1986)," in John E. Kwoka, Jr., and Lawrence J. White (eds.), *The Antitrust Revolution* (Glenview, Ill.: Scott, Foresman, 1989).

23. The study by John McGee was the first to argue that predatory pricing probably did not occur in the Standard Oil case. John S. McGee, "Predatory Price Cutting: The Standard Oil (N.J.) Case," *Journal of Law and Economics*, October 1958.

24. An interesting econometric test that finds that American Tobacco used this strategy is Malcolm R. Burns, "Predatory Pricing and the Acquisition Cost of Competitors," *Journal of Political Economy*, April 1986.

25. United States v. United States Steel Corp., 251 U.S. 417 (1920).

26. United States v. Aluminum Co. of America, 148 F. 2d 416 (2d Cir. 1945).

27. L. W. Weiss, *Economics and American Industry* (New York: John Wiley & Sons, 1961), p. 203.

28. United States v. United Shoe Machinery Corp., 110 F. Supp. 295 (D. Mass. 1953).

29. Richard A. Posner, *Antitrust Law: An Economic Perspective* (Chicago: University of Chicago Press, 1976), p. 203.

30. Berkey Photo, Inc. v. Eastman Kodak Co., 603 F. 2d 263 (2d Cir. 1979).

31. In re Kellogg Company, Docket No. 8883, F.T.C., 1981.

32. *Wall Street Journal*, January 18, 1982, p. 6.

33. For details of this case, see Fisher et al., Folded, Spindled, and Mutilated. For an opposite view, see L. W. Weiss, "The Structure-Conduct-Performance Paradigm and Antitrust," *University of Pennsylvania Law Review*, April 1979.

34. U.S. Department of Justice, Antitrust Division, "An Economic Analysis of the Market for General Purpose Electronic Digital Computer Systems," December 19, 1974, mimeo.

35. California Computer Products, Inc., et al. v. International Business Machines, 613 F. 2d 727 (9th Cir. 1979). See also Gerald W. Brock, "Dominant Firm Response to Competitive Challenge: Peripheral Equipment Manufacturers' Suits against IBM (1979–1983)," in Kwoka and White, *The Antitrust Revolution*.

36. Aspen Ski Company v. Aspen Highland Skiing Corporation, 472 U.S. 585 (1985).

37. P. Areeda and D. F. Turner, "Predatory Pricing and Related Practices under Section 2 of the Sherman Act," *Harvard Law Review*, February 1975.

38. Robert H. Bork, *The Antitrust Paradox* (New York: Basic Books, 1978), p. 154.

39. Barry Wright Corporation v. ITT Grinnell Corporation et al., 724 F. 2d 227 (1st Cir. 1983).

40. Greer, *Business, Government, and Society*, p. 166.

41. Oliver E. Williamson, "Predatory Pricing: A Strategic and Welfare Analysis," *Yale Law Journal*, December 1977.

42. Ibid., p. 294.

43. The residual demand is the horizontal difference between the demand curve and the marginal cost curve.

44. P. L Joskow and A.K. Klevorick, "A Framework for Analyzing Predatory Pricing Policy," *Yale Law Journal*, December 1979.

45. Judge Easterbrook's argument is cited in A. K. Klevorick, "The Current State of the Law and Economics of Predatory Pricing," *American Economic Review*, May 1993.

46. Brooke Group v. Brown and Williamson Tobacco, 113 S.Ct. 2578 (1993). For an account of this case that disputes the Court's decision, see W. B. Burnett, "Predation by a Nondominant Firm: The Liggett Case," In Kwoka and White, *The Antitrust Revolution*.

47. Richard A. Posner, *The Robinson-Patman Act: Federal Regulation of Price Differences* (Washington, D.C.: American Enterprise Institute, 1976).

48. For example, in the tying illustration discussed in Chapter 8, the two customers faced the same price schedule (a copying machine price of $2812.50 and a price per package of copying paper of $25); however, one customer paid an average price per "unit of copying services" of $62.50 compared to only $43.75 for the other customer. This was because the two customers' demands for copying services differed.

49. This example is based on J. A. Hausman and J. K. Mackie-Mason, "Price Discrimination and Patent Policy," *Rand Journal of Economics*, Summer 1988.

50. Profit from cable users $= p_c q_c - (MC)q_c$
$$= (60)(40) - (20)(40) = \$1600$$

Profit from tire users $= p_t q_t - (MC)q_t$
$$= (40)(20) - (20)(20) = \$400$$

51. The elasticity of demand is $-(dq/dp)(p/q)$, so substituting $p_c = 60$, $q_c = 40$, and $dq/dp = 1$, we get 1.5. Similarly, in the tire market the elasticity is 2.

52. This can be understood by recalling the standard formula $MR = p(1 - 1/e)$, where e is the elasticity. Hence, if $MR_c = MR_t$, then $p_c(1 - 1/e_c) = p_t(1 - 1/e_t)$, and if $e_c = e_t$, then $p_c = p_t$.

53. The SMR is actually MNPTR, not just PTR. There is a discontinuous jump upward at point N where the kink in total demand occurs. We denote this SMR for "simple marginal revenue" following the exposition in Joan Robinson, *The Economics of Imperfect Competition* (London: Macmillan, 1933), Chapter 15. The SMR should not be confused with the aggregate MR schedule, which is the horizontal sum of MR_c and MR_t. We do not need that schedule here because of the assumption that MC is constant. The aggregate MR schedule is used in the discrimination case for determining total output when MC is not constant.

54. Because the demanders are firms rather than individuals, the demand curves are marginal revenue product schedules, and the area under these curves represents total revenue to the buying firms.

55. Similar to the point made in note 53, the SMR coincides with MR_c up to output 60; it then jumps vertically from a negative value to point P and includes segment PR.

56. See R. Schmalensee, "Output and Welfare Implications of Monopolistic Third-Degree Discrimination," *American Economic Review*, March 1981.

57. Utah Pie v. Continental Baking, 386 U.S. 685 (1967). An interesting analysis of this case is K. G. Elzinga and T. F. Hogarty, "Utah Pie and the Consequences of Robinson-Patman," *Journal of Law and Economics*, October 1978.

58. Federal Trade Commission v. Morton Salt Co., 334 U.S. 37 (1948).

59. Bork, *The Antitrust Paradox*, p. 382.

II ECONOMIC REGULATION

What is Economic Regulation?

The essence of free enterprise is that individual agents are allowed to make their own decisions. As consumers and laborers, each person decides how much to spend, how much to save, and how many hours to work. Firms decide which products to produce, how much to produce of each product, what price to charge, which inputs to use and from which suppliers to buy them, and how much to invest. In all modern economies, there is also an entity called government, which decides on such things as the income tax rate, the level of national defense expenditure, and the growth rate of the money supply. Government decisions like these affect both the welfare of agents and how they behave. For example, raising the income-tax rate induces some individuals to work fewer hours and some not to work at all. Although an income tax influences how a laborer behaves, the laborer is left to decide how many hours to work. In contrast, in its role as regulator, a government literally restricts the choices of agents. More formally, regulation has been defined as "a state imposed limitation on the discretion that may be exercised by individuals or organizations, which is supported by the threat of sanction."[1]

As has long been noted, the key resource of government is the power to coerce. Regulation is the use of this power for the purpose of restricting the decisions of economic agents. In contrast to the income tax, which does not restrict the choices of individuals (though it does affect their welfare), the minimum wage is a regulation in that it restricts the wages that firms can pay their laborers. Economic regulation typically refers to government-imposed restrictions on firm decisions over price, quantity, and entry and exit. Economic regulation is to be contrasted with social regulation which is discussed in Part III of this book.

When an industry is regulated, industry performance in terms of allocative and productive efficiency is codetermined by market forces and administrative processes. Even if it so desires, a government cannot regulate every decision as it is physically impossible for a government to perfectly monitor firms and consumers. As a result, market forces can be expected to play a significant role regardless of the degree of government intervention. For example, under airline regulation, the government controlled price but not the quality of service. This induced firms to shift competition from the price dimension to the quality dimension. Even in a government-controlled economy like the former Soviet Union, market forces were at work. Although production and price were set by the state, the (effective) market-clearing price was set in the market. If a good is in short supply, people will wait in line for it. The effective price to them is the price paid to the state plus the value of their time spent in line. In equilibrium, people stand in line until the effective price clears the market.

Instruments of Regulation

Although economic regulation can encompass restrictions on a wide array of firm decisions, the three key decision variables controlled by regulation are price, quantity, and the number of firms. Less frequently controlled variables include product quality and investment.

Control of Price

Price regulation may specify a particular price that firms must charge or may instead restrict firms to setting price within some range. If the concern of the government is with a regulated monopolist setting price too high, regulation is apt to specify a maximum price that can be charged. For example, in 1989 the Federal Communications Commission (FCC) instituted price caps to regulate AT&T's long-distance rates. If the regulated firm has some unregulated competitors, the regulatory agency may also be concerned with the regulated firm engaging in predatory pricing (that is, pricing so as to force its competitors to exit the market). In that situation, regulation is likely to entail a minimum price as well as a maximum price. In some cases, like the control of oil prices in the 1970s, regulation required that a specific price be set.

More often than not, regulation specifies more than a single price. It can put an entire price structure in place. The regulation of AT&T in the intercity telecommunications market requires the FCC to specify long-distance rates for different times of day and for different days of the week. The specification of a price structure as opposed to just a single price greatly increases the complexity of implementing economic regulation and can result in additional welfare losses, as we will observe.

In practice, price regulation may be the means by which a regulatory agency achieves an ultimate objective of limiting industry profit. A regulatory agency often sets price so that the regulated firm earns a normal rate-of-return. This is standard practice in the regulation of public utilities and has been used in other regulated industries such as the airline industry prior to its deregulation. Because firm profit is determined by a variety of factors (with price being just one of them), a regulatory agency may have a difficult time in achieving its goal of a normal rate-of-return. Regulatory lag in changing price in response to new cost and demand conditions can result in a regulated firm earning either too high or too low a rate of return. During the inflationary period of the 1970s, rising input prices resulted in public utilities' often earning a below normal rate-of-return because the regulatory agency was slow to adjust price. Alternatively, a regulated firm that experiences an innovation in its production technology will reap above-normal profits until the regulatory agency realizes the cost function has shifted down and responds by lowering price. A detailed discussion of rate-of-return regulation is provided in Chapter 12.

Control of Quantity

Restrictions on the quantity of a product or service that is sold may be used either with or without price regulation. From the 1930s up until around 1970, many oil-producing states, among them Texas and Oklahoma, placed maximum production limits on crude-oil producers. Although quantity was controlled by the state, price was determined nationally or globally (though obviously these quantity controls influenced the market price). Alternatively, a common form of quantity regulation that is often imposed upon a common carrier is that it "meet all demand at the regulated price." This requirement is used in regulating electric utilities. Finally, regulation may place restrictions upon the prices that firms set while leaving their quantity decision unregulated. For example, there were no quantity restrictions imposed when natural gas prices were regulated. Because these regulated prices were set below their market-clearing levels and firms were not required to meet all demand, the obvious implication was excess demand and shortages.

Control of Entry and Exit

As we will see in our studies of economic regulation, the two critical variables that regulators have controlled are price and the number of firms, the latter through restrictions on entry and exit. These variables are critical because price and the number of firms are key determinants of both allocative and productive efficiency.

Entry may be regulated on several levels. First, entry by new firms may be controlled, as is typically done in the regulation of public utilities. A key step toward deregulating the intercity telecommunications market was the FCC's allowing MCI to enter in 1969. MCI was the first entrant in the market since the industry's regulation at the turn of the twentieth century.

In addition to controlling entry by new firms, a regulatory agency may also control entry by existing regulated firms. These markets may already be served by other regulated firms or may be unregulated markets. As an example of the latter, the FCC placed restrictions on AT&T's entry into the computer market in the 1980s. The former case is exemplified by airline and trucking regulation. Their respective regulatory agencies made it very difficult for an existing firm to enter a geographic market already served by another regulated firm. As of the mid-1990s, these issues were at the center of the telecommunications industry. The regional Bell operating companies were interested in expanding their domain from local telephone to both long-distance and cable service, while cable companies like Time-Warner and long-distance telephone companies like MCI were proposing to provide local telephone service. The degree to which firms can freely enter these various markets is likely to have a major impact on the speed with which the "information superhighway" is completed.

A basis for exit regulation is that regulation strives to have services provided to a wider set of consumers than would be true in a free market. This may entail regulated firms serving unprofitable markets and, hence, the need for regulations that forbid a regulated firm from abandoning a market without regulatory approval. As we will see, restricting the decision to exit was an important issue in the regulation of the railroad industry.

Control of Other Variables

The essence of economic regulation is the limitation of firm behavior regarding price, quantity, and entry into and exit out of markets. Obviously, firms choose many other decision variables. One of these is the quality of the product or service that they produce. A regulatory agency may specify minimum standards for reliability of a service. If an electric utility has regular blackouts, the regulatory agency is likely to intervene and require an increase in capacity in order to improve service reliability. Although product quality may also be controlled for reasons like product safety, economic regulation does not typically place serious restrictions on it.

One reason for the minimal use of quality regulation is the cost of implementing it. To control any variable, the relevant economic agents have to be able to agree on what the variable is and what restrictions are placed on it. In the case of price and quantity, this is not difficult. The price is the amount paid by the consumer for the good, which is relatively easy to observe. Furthermore, restrictions take the simple form of numbers: a maximum price and a minimum price. Similarly, the measurability of quantity allows a regulatory agency to specify restrictions on it. However, quality is typically not so well defined nor so easily observable. For example, the quality of airline service encompasses an array of variables, including on-time performance, safety, on-board services, seat width, and luggage handling. In principle, a regulatory agency could attempt to control each of these variables and thus control quality, but it would be very costly to do so. In the case of airline regulation, these variables were not controlled except for minimal standards on safety. As a result, airlines competed vigorously in terms of quality. Generally, economic regulation has not placed severe restrictions on the quality of products or services that firms offer with the notable exception of product safety.

Another variable that is sometimes (though infrequently) regulated is firm investment. In contrast to the other decision variables we have considered, regulation of investment entails government intervention into the production process; that is, a firm's choice of technology and inputs. A regulatory agency may intervene in the capital decisions of a public utility like an electric utility or a local telephone company. One significant example is state regulation of investment decisions by hospitals. Certificate of Need programs require a hospital to obtain state approval before undertaking certain investment projects. The presumed objective is to avoid duplicate facilities.

Brief History of Economic Regulation

Formative Stages

What is typically meant by economic regulation in the United States began in the 1870s.[2] Two important events took place around that time. First, a key Supreme Court decision provided the basis for the regulation of monopolies. Second, forces were building in the railroad industry that would result in its being the first major industry subject to economic regulation at the federal level.

Munn v. Illinois (1877)

In 1877 the landmark case of *Munn v. Illinois* was decided. This case established that the state of Illinois could regulate rates set by grain elevators and warehouses. As stated in the opinion of the majority, the important principle promulgated by this decision was that

property does become clothed with public interest when used in a manner to make it of public consequence, and affect the community at large. When, therefore, one devotes his property to a use in which the public has an interest, he, in effect, grants to the public an interest in that use, and must submit to be controlled by the public for the common good.

Munn v. Illinois provided the foundation for regulation to be used to prevent monopolistic exploitation of consumers.

Interstate Commerce Act of 1887

Around the time of the *Munn v. Illinois* decision, the railroad industry was going through a turbulent period. Throughout the 1870s and 1880s the railroad industry was subject to spurts of aggressive price wars intermixed with periods of relatively stable prices (see Figure 5.7 in Chapter 5). At the same time, the railroads were practicing price discrimination across different consumers. Those consumers who were charged relatively high prices (due to relatively inelastic demand) were calling for government intervention. At the same time, the railroads were seeking government assistance to stabilize prices (perhaps near the monopoly level). The result of these forces was the *Interstate Commerce Act of 1887*, which created the Interstate Commerce Commission (ICC) for the purpose of regulating rail rates. Although only with later acts of Congress was the ICC given the necessary powers to regulate price, the Interstate Commerce Act represents an important landmark in Congressional regulatory legislation.

Nebbia v. New York (1934)

A common interpretation of *Munn v. Illinois* was that it was constitutional for government to regulate certain monopolistic industries. A stricter interpretation was that regulation could only be applied to public utilities. However, in its 1934 decision of *Nebbia v. New York*, the Supreme Court outlined a much wider realm for economic regulation. In that case, the state of New York was regulating the retail price of milk. The defense argued that the milk industry was competitive and could not be classified as a public utility so that there was no basis for state regulation. The majority opinion stated:

So far as the requirement of due process is concerned, and in the absence of other constitutional restriction, a state is free to adopt whatever economic policy may reasonably be deemed to promote public welfare, and to enforce that policy by legislation adapted to its purpose.

The Supreme Court tore down any constitutional barrier to economic regulation as long as, in the state's judgment, such regulation was in the public interest.

Trends in Regulation

Early regulation focused on the railroads and public utilities like electricity, telephone (which encompassed both local telephone and long

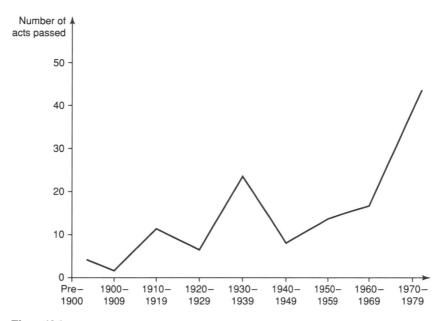

Figure 10.1
Number of Economic Regulatory Legislative Acts

Source: Center for the Study of American Business. This figure is from James F. Gatti, "An Overview of the Problem of Government Regulation," in James F. Gatti (ed.), *The Limits of Government Regulation* (New York: Academic Press, 1981).

distance communications), and city transit. The Massachusetts state commission began regulating such industries in 1885, but not until the period of 1907–1930 did most state legislatures create public-service commissions. In addition to federal regulation of railroads officially dating from 1887, regulation over interstate telephone service came with the Mann-Elkins Act of 1910.

Figure 10.1 depicts the growth of regulatory legislation. Three spurts of legislative activity have been identified.[3] The first two occurred during the periods of 1909–1916 and 1933–1940. During these years, federal regulatory powers were greatly expanded to encompass a large number of vital industries in the United States. The third burst of legislative activity took place over 1973–1980 and entailed the partial or full deregulation of many of the regulated industries.

The economic historian Richard Vietor has put forth the intriguing hypothesis that these regulatory and deregulatory booms are due to a fundamental change in people's perception of how an economy and its government interacts.[4] He attributes the regulatory wave of the 1930s to the downfall of faith in a laissez-faire economy emanating from the Great Depression. The deregulatory period of the 1970s occurred during

a period of serious stagflation—high inflation and high unemployment—which Vietor argues shook our faith in the ability of the government to provide a constructive influence on the economy. Though this
hypothesis is speculative and has not been tested (nor is it clear how one
could test it), it is both interesting and plausible.

1930s: Wave of Regulation

Due to several factors, including the *Nebbia v. New York* decision and
the dire economic conditions of the Great Depression, a wave of economic regulation took place over 1933–1940. At the state level, control
over the production of crude oil producers was being implemented
by oil-producing states. At the federal level, there were several pieces
of major legislation that greatly expanded the realm of economic
regulation.

A list of these legislative acts is provided in Table 10.1. With legislative acts in 1935 and 1940, the ICC's domain expanded from railroads
to the entire interstate surface-freight transportation industry, which
included trucks, water barges and oil pipelines (the last goes back to
1906). The one key exception was ocean shipping, which was regulated
by the Federal Maritime Commission beginning in 1936. Regulation of
long-distance passenger transportation was divided between the ICC
(railroads and buses) and the newly created Civil Aeronautics Board
(airlines).

Table 10.1
Major Economic Regulatory Legislation, 1887–1940

Year	Legislative Act	Agency Created
1887	Interstate Commerce Act	Interstate Commerce Commission
1910	Mann-Elkins Act	
1916	Shipping Act	
1920	Transportation Act	
1930	Oil prorationing (Oklahoma, Texas)	
1933	Banking Act Securities Act	
1934	Banking Act Communications Act	Federal Communications Commission
1935	Motor Carrier Act Public Utility Act Securities Exchange Act	Federal Power Commission Securities and Exchange Commission
1938	Civil Aeronautics Act Natural Gas Act	Civil Aeronautics Board
1940	Transportation Act	

To deal with the technologically progressive communications market, the Federal Communications Commission was established in 1934 to regulate broadcasting and to take over the duty of regulating the intercity telecommunications market from the ICC. Although electricity and natural gas had long been regulated at the state and local level, federal regulation of interstate commerce with respect to these two energy sources was only established in 1935 (for electricity) and in 1938 (for natural gas). Initially, natural gas regulation only covered its transportation. Regulation of natural gas prices did not take place until the mid-1950s.

The unsatisfactory performance of financial markets in the Great Depression was followed by a wave of federal legislation relating to the banking and securities industries. Among other restrictions, the Banking Acts of 1933 and 1935 created the Federal Deposit Insurance Corporation, forbade commercial banks from paying interest on ordinary checking accounts, and, in what has been referred to as the Glass-Steagall Act, prohibited both commercial banks from participating in investment banking and investment banks from accepting deposits. The Securities Act of 1933 mandated disclosure of information by issuers of securities, and the Securities Exchange Act of 1934 created the Securities and Exchange Commission, the main purpose of which was to monitor the activities of the securities industry.

1940–1970: Continued Growth of Regulation

Between the two legislative peaks of 1933–1940 and 1973–1980, legislative activity continued on a modest but steady path of expansion of federal regulatory powers. Two industries that were particularly affected were energy and communications. Although cable television was initially left unregulated at the federal level, it became subject to FCC regulation beginning in 1968. Until 1954, federal regulation of the oil and natural gas industries was only over pipelines and, at the state level, over production of crude oil. Due to a Supreme Court decision in 1954, the Federal Power Commission began controlling the wellhead price of natural gas. Then the price of oil was regulated beginning in 1971. Foreshadowing the deregulation that was to come, the FCC permitted MCI to enter the intercity telecommunications market in 1969. This represented a crucial first step in the partial deregulation of that market.

1971–1989: Wave of Deregulation

The decades of the 1970s and 1980s were characterized by extensive deregulation (see Table 10.2). In 1977, fully regulated industries produced 17 percent of the U.S. Gross National Product. By 1988, this had been

Table 10.2
Major Economic Deregulatory Initiatives: 1971–1989

Year	Initiative
1971	Specialized Common Carrier Decision (FCC)
1972	Domestic satellite open skies policy (FCC)
1975	Abolition of fixed brokerage fees (SEC)
1976	Railroad Revitalization and Reform Act
1977	Air Cargo Deregulation Act
1978	Airline Deregulation Act Natural Gas Policy Act
1979	Deregulation of satellite earth stations (FCC) Urgent-mail exemption (Postal Service)
1980	Motor Carrier Reform Act Household Goods Transportation Act Staggers Rail Act Depository Institutions Deregulation and Monetary Control Act International Air Transportation Competition Act Deregulation of cable television (FCC) Deregulation of customer premises equipment and enhanced services (FCC)
1981	Decontrol of crude oil and refined petroleum products (Executive Order) Deregulation of radio (FCC)
1982	Bus Regulatory Reform Act Garn–St. Germain Depository Institutions Act AT&T settlement
1984	Space commercialization Cable Television Deregulation Act Shipping Act
1986	Trading of airport landing rights
1987	Sale of Conrail Elimination of fairness doctrine (FCC)
1988	Proposed rules on natural gas and electricity (FERC) Proposed rules on price caps (FCC)
1989	Natural Gas Wellhead Decontrol Act of 1989

Source: Updated table from *Economic Report of the President*, January 1989.

reduced to 6.6 percent.[5] In the area of transportation, several pieces of legislation over 1978–1982 deregulated airlines (Airline Deregulation Act of 1978), railroads (Staggers Act of 1980), trucking (Motor Carrier Act of 1980), and passenger buses (Bus Regulatory Reform Act of 1982). In communications, entry regulation of the intercity telecommunications market was torn down over the course of several decisions that ranged from the FCC's Specialized Common Carrier Decision in 1971 to the breakup of AT&T in 1984 as a result of the U.S. Justice Department's antitrust case. Also during this period, cable television was deregulated at the federal level. Finally, oil price controls were lifted by President Ronald Reagan in January 1981; partial deregulation of natural gas prices had begun in 1978. Only in 1989 were natural-gas price controls removed.

Current Regulatory Policy

With most of the clear-cut cases of inappropriate regulation having been dismantled, the current trend is a mixture of re-regulation and further deregulation. For example, recent legislation not only now permits the regulation of cable rates but also requires it. Although deregulation of long-distance telephone service has stalled (it is still in a mode of partial deregulation in which AT&T's fares require FCC approval), current forces may result in the partial or full dismantling of the barriers between long distance companies, local telephone companies, and cable companies. There have been regular calls for the re-regulation of railroads and airlines coming from corners without much political influence nor much substantive evidence to support their claims. As far as the future, the primary architect of airline deregulation, Alfred Kahn, sees us at a point of no return:

> The evolution of regulatory policy will never come to an end. The path it takes—and we should make every effort to see that it takes—however, is the path not of a full circle or pendulum, which would take us back to where we started, but of a spiral, which has a direction. This is in a sense only an expression of a preference for seeking consistently to move in the direction of first-best functioning of a market economy, rather than the second- or third-best world of centralized command and control.[6]

The Regulatory Process

Overview of the Regulatory Process

Stage 1: Legislation

There are two key stages in the regulation of an industry. The first stage entails that the U.S. Congress, a state legislature, or a local government body like a city council enact a piece of legislation that establishes regulatory powers over a particular industry. Numerous agents are involved at this stage of the regulatory process. Because regulation restricts firm decisions, it is expected to influence firms' profits and consumers' welfare. Hence, one would anticipate that both firms and consumer advocates lobby the government to try to influence what the piece of legislation looks like as well as whether or not it passes. Obviously, legislators are key actors during this stage. Depending on their jurisdiction, legislators may represent producers, consumers, or just their electorate at large. Because industry workers are likely to be affected by legislation, one can also expect them to be involved in this process, particularly if workers are organized into a labor union.

Stage 2: Implementation

Having passed a piece of legislation, the second stage in the regulatory process is the implementation of this legislation. Although the legislature can influence its implementation, the immediate responsibility falls to the regulatory agency. Thus, regulators replace legislators as central actors at the implementation stage while producers and consumers continue to be relevant. Other important actors may include potential entrants who desire to enter this regulated industry.

Stage 3: Deregulation

There is sometimes a third stage in this process, which is the deregulation of the industry. Although one typically imagines deregulation being achieved via a legislative act, both the regulatory agency and the judiciary have proven to be instrumental forces in deregulating an industry. If the regulatory agency and the judiciary are in favor of deregulation, they may be able to achieve it even if the Congress is against it. Long before the Airline Deregulation Act, the airline industry was being deregulated by the Civil Aeronautics Board. In this light, the White House can play a significant role in their choice of regulatory commissioners; it was no mistake that President Jimmy Carter appointed the free-market advocate Alfred Kahn as CAB chairman. Due to its role in deregulating a number of industries, the Circuit Court of Appeals for the District of Columbia has been dubbed the "Supreme Court" for regulations.[7] In addition to the three branches of government, all agents significantly connected with the industry are typically involved in the deregulatory process including producers, consumers, labor, and prospective firms.

Regulatory Legislation

Selection of the Regulatory Agency

Legislation performs two key tasks in the regulatory process. First, it states which bureaucratic agency has jurisdiction over regulating certain dimensions of an industry. In many cases, like the Interstate Commerce Act of 1887 and the Federal Communications Act of 1934, legislation actually creates the bureaucratic agency. In other cases, legislation extends the realm of an existing agency as the Motor Carrier Act of 1935 did in bringing motor carriers within the realm of the ICC.

Powers of the Regulatory Agency

The second objective of legislation is in outlining the powers of the regulatory agency. The two key powers are control of price and entry into and exit from the industry. Although the Interstate Commerce Act of 1887 gave the ICC regulatory jurisdiction over the railroad industry, it took the Hepburn Act of 1906 and the Transportation Act of 1920 for the ICC to have the power to control rail rates. Sometimes it is unclear as to the powers given to the regulatory agency by a piece of legislation. Until a 1954 Supreme Court decision, the Federal Power Commission believed that the Natural Gas Act of 1938 did not give it the power to control the wellhead price of natural gas.

General Policy Objectives

Finally, regulatory legislation often specifies some general policy objectives for the regulatory agency to follow. In most cases, legislation instructs the regulatory agency to set "reasonable and just" prices and to see that service is made available to all consumers. Thus, the FCC and the CAB sought to expand long distance communications and airline service, respectively, to as wide a geographic area as was possible. Another common policy goal is to discourage regulated firms from practicing price discrimination.

Independent Regulatory Commissions

An independent regulatory commission at the federal level is typically comprised of five or more members. Table 10.3 provides a listing of some major regulatory agencies at the federal level. Federal regulatory commissioners are appointed, though in some states public utility commissioners are elected.[8] The appointment is for a fixed term, and the terms of the commissioners are staggered. There is an important degree of independence from the executive branch bestowed on regulatory commissioners. A commissioner can be removed for cause, but not at the discretion of the president.

In light of the lack of political accountability of regulatory commissioners, it has been argued that they are set up in the manner of judges.[9] In particular, Section 557 of the 1946 Administrative Procedure Act requires all administrative decisions by a regulatory commission to be substantiated by findings of fact and law.

Members of a Regulatory Agency

Political scientist James Q. Wilson has identified three different kinds of employees of a regulatory agency.[10] The *careerist* is an employee who anticipates a long-term relationship with the regulatory agency and whose major concern is that the regulatory agency continue to exist and grow. Not surprisingly, the careerist frowns on deregulation. The *politician* envisions eventually leaving the agency for an elective or appoin-

Table 10.3
Major Federal Economic Regulatory Commissions

Agency	Number of Members	Jurisdiction	Size of Staff (FTE)			
			1970	1980	1985	1990
Interstate Commerce Commission (1887)	7	Railroads (1887) Trucks (1935) Water Carriers (1940) Telephone (1910–1934) Oil Pipelines (1906–1977)	1912	1940	839	661
Federal Communications Commission (1934)	7	Telephone (1934) Broadcasting (1934) Cable Television (1968)	1645	2156	1828	1839
Securities and Exchange Commission (1934)	5	Securities (1934)	1436	2100	2046	2451
Federal Power Commission (1935) Federal Energy Regulatory Commission (1977)	5	Wholesale electricity (1935) Natural gas (1938) Oil pipelines (1977)	1164	1605	1533	1500
Civil Aeronautics Board (1938)	5	Airlines (1938)	686	753	0	0

Source: This is an adapted version of tables from Leonard W. Weiss, "The Regulatory Reform Movement" in Leonard W. Weiss and Michael W. Klass (eds.), *Regulatory Reform: What Actually Happened* (Boston: Little, Brown, 1986); and Melinda Warren and Kenneth Chilton, "Regulation's Rebound: Bush Budget Gives Regulation a Boost," Occasional Paper No. 81, Center for the Study of American Business, Washington University, May 1990.

tive position, with the regulatory agency a stepping stone for bigger and better things. Most commissioners are classified as politicians. Finally, the *professional* is more identified with certain skills than with the regulatory agency and strives to maintain professional esteem to allow career advancement.

The incentives of an employee of a regulatory agency depend very much on his type. Understanding how members of a regulatory agency are motivated is important in explaining the policies that are implemented. For example, consider the implementation of price regulation. The professional may desire to use this opportunity to show technical expertise. As a result, the professional might prefer a highly complex pricing structure. In contrast, the careerist might support a simple pricing structure so as to avoid any major problems which might result in legislative action. Finally, because the politician is concerned with not aggravating interest groups, he would be less inclined to allow price discrimination because it might alienate some consumers. Our ensuing analysis of regulation will not allow for such a rich set of motivations underlying the implementation of regulatory policy, but it is important that we at least recognize their presence.

Regulatory Procedures

Given the general and vague policy objectives provided by legislation, a regulatory agency is often left with considerable discretion as to how it regulates the industry. When a regulatory agency is told to set "reasonable and just" rates, there may be a wide array of rates that one could argue meet these criteria. Alternatively, some legislation is very specific about the duties of a regulatory agency. The Emergency Petroleum Allocation Act (1973–1975) and the Energy Policy and Conservation Act (1975–1981) provided a detailed formula as to the price structure for domestic crude oil. This resulted in the Federal Energy Administration having minimal discretion over the regulation of crude-oil prices.

Rulemaking Process

Two basic approaches have been pursued to rulemaking. First, a regulatory agency may act on a case-by-case approach by individually considering each proposal. The most important proposals concern rate changes and petitions for entry or exit. When the burden of a case-by-case approach becomes too great, a regulatory agency will often turn to substantive rulemaking. Hearings are conducted which lead to the formulation of a general rule which is applicable to a wide class of situations. The move to substantive rulemaking from a burdensome case-by-case approach was done by the FPC in regulating natural gas prices (the first case took five years for it to complete) and by the FCC in deciding on entry into a segment of the intercity telecommunications market (the first case took six years to complete).

If the participants do not agree with the decision of a regulatory decision, they have the right to appeal it in a U.S. Court of Appeals. This tactic has indeed been used. When the FCC told MCI that it was not allowed to operate in the long distance telephone service segment of the intercity telecommunications market, MCI went to the U.S. Court of Appeals where, in the Execunet I decision (1978), the courts reversed the FCC's decision. Two years after its 1992 ruling that local telephone companies must allow competitors direct access to the local phone network, the FCC found its decision overturned by a federal appeals court.

Delay and Strategic Manipulation of Regulatory Proceedings

An important property of regulatory procedures is that they are biased towards maintaining the status quo. By replacing market forces with administrative processes, regulation imposes due-process requirements on any changes. In some sense, producers and consumers have legal rights to the status quo and it can only be overthrown through due process. This is very much in contrast to the market where the status quo is regularly overthrown, and there is no legal recourse as long as no antitrust laws were violated.

Another property of regulation that favors the status quo is the extent of delay in regulatory proceedings. An agent who is interested in maintaining the status quo can pursue tactics such as litigation in order to lengthen the proceedings. Regardless of the reason for delay, its existence is hard to deny. For the CAB and the ICC, licensing proceedings averaged 170 days for the prehearing stage, 190 days for the hearing stage, and 220 days for the agency review stage. The total length of time was in excess of nineteen months. Ratemaking proceedings were even worse. On average, ratemaking cases by the CAB, FMC, FPC, and the ICC took over twenty-one months.[11] However, as mentioned earlier, a regulatory agency can reduce delay by replacing a case-by-case approach with substantive rulemaking.

In addition to generating delay in regulatory proceedings, agents can strategically manipulate the regulatory process in other ways. An important avenue for regulated firms is to control the flow of information to the regulators. For example, in considering a ratemaking case, a regulatory agency usually depends on the regulated firm for estimates of cost and demand conditions. Although outside expert witnesses can be used, their information is simply not as good as that which the firm has at its disposal. Another tactic is for regulated firms to coopt the experts, for example, by keeping the best law firms on retainer.[12]

The Theory of Regulation

Why is there regulation? In a free-market economy like that of the United States, why does the government choose to place restrictions on the decisions of agents? One of the objectives of a theory of regulation is to answer this question. Such a theory should make predictions concerning who benefits from regulation, which industries are most likely to be regulated, and what form regulation will take.[13] A proper addressing of these issues should allow us better to understand the effects of regulation. For example, if we know that there is a general tendency for price regulation to benefit producers, it is logical to expect price to be set significantly above cost in regulated industries.

In this section, we will outline the evolution of thought which addresses the question, Why is there regulation? There have been three stages in this evolution. The first hypothesis put forth was that regulation occurs in industries plagued with market failures. Originally called the *public interest theory*, more recently it has been referred to as *normative analysis as a positive theory* (NPT).[14] Largely due to empirical evidence that was inconsistent with NPT, economists and political scientists developed the capture theory (CT). Basically, the CT states that whether by design or not, the agency that is meant to regulate an industry is "captured" by that industry. The implication is that regulation promotes industry profit rather than social welfare. For reasons described later, NPT and the CT are actually not theories but rather hypotheses or statements about empirical regularities. This is to be contrasted to the third stage in this evolution of thought which is the economic theory of regulation (ET). This is indeed a theory in the proper sense in that it generates testable hypotheses as logical implications from a set of assumptions. Although the ET is an important advancement and explains some of the observed regulatory activity in the United States over the last hundred years, much evidence is still inconsistent with this theory.

Normative Analysis as a Positive Theory

Normative Rationale for Regulation

There is a basis for government intervention in that under certain conditions unrestrained competition does not work very well. Two common circumstances are that an industry is a natural monopoly or that it is plagued by externalities.

A market is a *natural monopoly* if, at the socially optimal quantity, industry cost is minimized by having only one firm produce. For the single-product case, if the average cost curve is declining for all quantities, then the cost of producing any industry quantity is minimized by having one firm produce it. In that case, the market is a natural monopoly regardless of market demand. Natural monopolies are likely to exist when there is a large fixed-cost component to cost. For example, most public utilities, like local distribution of electricity and local telephone, are natural monopolies. In those cases, fixed costs (in particular, the cost of connecting homes and businesses to the distribution system) are large relative to marginal costs. Hence, average cost is declining for a wide range of outputs. For the relevant region of market demand, these markets are natural monopolies.

The problem with a natural monopoly is that there is a fundamental conflict between allocative efficiency and productive efficiency. Productive efficiency requires that only one firm produce, because only then is the value of resources used to supply the market minimized. However, a lone producing firm will be inclined to set price above cost in its objective of maximizing profit. But then allocative efficiency is not achieved. To generate allocative efficiency, we need enough firms that competition drives price down to marginal cost. But then there is productive inefficiency because there are too many firms producing in the market. Thus we have an argument for government intervention when a market is a natural monopoly.

An *externality* exists when the actions of one agent, say agent A, affects the utility or production function of another agent, say agent B, *and* agent A does not care how his behavior affects agent B's welfare. When an externality is present, perfect competition does not result in an optimal allocation of resources. Suppose I am considering buying an Italian submarine sandwich for lunch. Let us suppose that the restaurant market is competitive so that the price of the sandwich equals marginal cost. If the input markets are also competitive, then the value of resources used by society in supplying that sandwich equals the price charged for it, which we will denote as P. Now suppose the maximum amount that I am willing to pay for that sandwich (taking into account my alternative opportunities for lunch) is V. If $V > P$, then I will buy the sandwich and receive a surplus of $V - P$. If there are no externalities from my consuming that sandwich, then the net welfare gain to society is $V - P$, which is positive. Thus, such a transaction should (and will) take place. Now let us assume that my consumption of the sandwich generates an externality. In particular, suppose the sandwich has onions on it (as any good Italian sub does) and I am planning to travel on a crowded subway after eating it. Unfortunately, the individual who sits next to me on the subway will have to smell my bad breath. Suppose that this individual would be willing to pay up to W dollars to get me to sit elsewhere (however, there are no seats left on the subway). The net welfare effect of my buying and consuming the Italian sub is not $V - P$ but instead $(V - P) - W$. If $W > V - P$, then welfare is actually reduced by my consuming the sub, even though I am personally better off. Hence, with the existence of an externality, competitive behavior can result in welfare-reducing transactions.

Externalities come in many forms. The example we have just considered is referred to as a negative externality. Other examples of negative externalities are noise and water pollution. In deciding whether to drive to work or take mass transit, the typical automobile driver does not consider the effect of his decision on the quality of the air that everyone must breathe. A common pool problem is a different type of negative externality. It occurs when there are several property owners to a resource: several firms may extract oil from a common reservoir, and several fishermen may fish from the same lake. In their pursuit of utility or profit maximization, these agents do not take into account how their activity reduces the resource and thus raises the cost of production to other agents.

Generally, when there are negative externalities, unregulated competition results in too much of an activity being pursued, whether it is too many Italian subs being consumed or too much oil being pumped out of a reservoir. There are also cases of positive externalities. For example, if I am immunized for a disease, I not only make myself better off but also reduce the spread of the disease, which makes others better off. Just as there is typically too much activity when there is a negative externality, there is typically too little activity when there is a positive externality.

When a market failure occurs—whether due to natural monopoly, externalities, or some other source—there is a potential rationale for government intervention. In the case of a natural monopoly, price and entry regulation may allow both allocative and productive efficiency. Entry regulation permits only one firm to produce (as required for productive efficiency) whereas price regulation restricts the firm to setting the socially optimal price (as required for allocative efficiency). In the case of externalities, imposition of a tax (subsidy) on an activity that generates a negative (positive) externality can result in a socially preferred allocation. When there is a market failure, in theory regulation may be able to raise social welfare. Whether it does so in practice is an altogether different issue and will be of central concern to us in the following chapters.

Description of Theory

Understanding when regulation *should* occur is normative analysis. This is to be contrasted to a positive theory which explains when regulation *does* occur. Normative analysis as a positive theory (NPT) uses normative analysis to generate a positive theory by saying that regulation is supplied in response to the public's demand for the correction of a market failure or for the correction of highly inequitable practices (for example, price discrimination, or firms' receiving windfall profits due to some change in industry conditions). According to this theory, if a market is a natural monopoly, then the public will demand the industry be regulated because a first-best solution is not achieved in the absence of regulation. Unfettered competition will result in either too many firms producing and/or price exceeding the socially optimal level. By regulating the industry, net welfare gains result and it is this potential for welfare gains that generates the public's demand for regulation. In this way, the public interest theory uses normative analysis (when should regulation occur?) to produce a positive theory (when does regulation occur?).

Critique of Normative Analysis as a Positive Theory

There are at least two major problems with NPT. First, it is at best a very incomplete theory. NPT puts forth the hypothesis that regulation occurs when it should occur because the potential for a net social welfare gain generates public demand for regulation. Lacking in this analysis is a description of the mechanism that allows the public to bring this about. Regulation occurs through legislative action and the behavior of the regulatory agency. NPT does not address the issue of how the potential for net social welfare gains induces legislators to pass regulatory legislation and regulators to pursue the proper actions. NPT does not generate the testable prediction that regulation occurs to correct a market failure, but rather assumes it.

The second major criticism of NPT, and the key reason for why it has lacked supporters for several decades, is the large amount of evidence that refutes it. Many industries have been regulated that are neither natural monopolies nor plagued by externalities; for example, price and entry regulation in the trucking, taxicab, and securities industries. In 1974, Richard Posner concluded, "Some fifteen years of theoretical and empirical research, conducted mainly by economists, have demonstrated that regulation is not positively correlated with the presence of external economies or diseconomies or with monopolistic market structure."[15]

Further evidence that is difficult to rectify with NPT is that, in many cases, firms supported or even lobbied for regulation. This was true with the regulation of the railroads in the late 1880s and of local and long-distance telephone where AT&T supported regulation (and thereby eliminated all other competitors from the market). Though firm support is not necessarily inconsistent with NPT, it does not sit comfortably. If a market is a natural monopoly but there are several active firms, competition could be driving price down below average cost so that firms are incurring losses. Regulation would allow at least one of them to earn normal profits. It is unlikely, however, that firms would be in support of regulation if all it could generate would be normal profits. A more plausible explanation is that regulation is anticipated to provide a stable level of above-normal profits to be earned, and this is why an industry may be in favor of its regulation.

A third but weaker line of evidence in conflict with NPT is that the regulation of even a natural monopoly does not always really constrain firm pricing behavior. In a well-known study, George Stigler and Claire Friedland examined the effect of regulation on the pricing of electric utilities over 1912–1937.[16] They found that regulation had an insignificant, though downward, effect on prices. In contrast, NPT would predict that regulation would have a strong downward effect on prices because it forces a monopolist to price at average cost rather than at the profit-maximizing level.

Reformulation of NPT

In light of the contradictory evidence, NPT was reformulated. This reformulation says that regulation is originally put in place to correct a market failure but then is mismanaged by the regulatory agency. However, even this reformulated hypothesis is unsatisfactory. First, it is subject to the same criticism of the original formulation in that it merely states a hypothesis rather than generating that hypothesis as a conclusion from a model. To be specific, it does not explain why the regulatory agency is mismanaged. Second, the reformulated hypothesis is still inconsistent with the evidence that industries are regulated that are not subject to significant market failures and that industries have often supported regulation. The reformulated hypothesis of NPT does not appear to be a substantive improvement on the original hypothesis.

Capture Theory

Genesis of the Capture Theory

A review of the history of regulation in the United States since the late nineteenth century reveals that regulation is not strongly correlated with the existence of market failures. At least up to the 1960s, one empirical regularity is that regulation is pro-producer in that it tends to raise industry profit. In potentially competitive industries like trucking and taxicabs, regulation supported prices above cost and prevented entry from dissipating rents. In naturally monopolistic industries like electric utilities, there was some evidence that showed that regulation had little effect on price, so that above-normal profit was allowed to be earned. The empirical evidence seemed to support the claim that regulation was inherently pro-producer.[17]

These empirical observations resulted in the development of the *capture theory* (CT). In stark contrast to NPT, the CT states that either regulation is supplied in response to the industry's demand for regulation (in other words, legislators are captured by the industry) or the regulatory agency comes to be controlled by the industry over time (in other words, regulators are captured by the industry).[18]

Critique of the Capture Theory

In that it is in greater agreement with regulatory history, the CT is more compelling than NPT. Nevertheless, the CT is subject to the same two criticisms leveled against NPT. Like NPT, the CT has no theoretical underpinnings because it does not explain how regulation comes to be controlled by the industry. In light of there being several interest groups affected by regulation, including consumer and labor groups as well as firms, why should regulation be controlled by the industry rather than these other interest groups? In its original form, the CT does not provide an explanation. Rather, it merely states the hypothesis that regulation is pro-producer.

Although there is much evidence supportive of the CT, there is also some empirical regularities that are inconsistent with it. Two common properties of regulation are cross-subsidization and a bias towards small producers. Although we will go into greater detail in later chapters, *cross-subsidization* is when a multiproduct firm prices some goods below average cost and makes up for the losses through revenue collected from the sale of other goods priced above average cost. Such pricing behavior is inconsistent with profit maximization and thus cannot be considered pro-producer. Cross-subsidization has been regularly observed in such regulated industries as railroads, airlines, and intercity telecommunications. It often takes the form of uniform prices' being charged to different consumers even though the marginal cost of supplying these consumers differs greatly. The other property is that regulation is often biased toward small producers. Small producers are allowed to earn greater profits relative to larger firms under regulation than they would have earned in an unregulated market. This was certainly true of small oil refiners under oil price controls.

Perhaps the strongest evidence against the CT is the long list of regulations that were not supported by the industry and have resulted in lower profits. The list includes oil and natural gas price regulation and social regulation over the environment, product safety, and worker safety. Finally, the CT has a difficult time explaining both why many industries were regulated *and* why they were later deregulated.

Economic Theory of Regulation

In summarizing the evidence, one finds that regulation is not strongly associated with the existence of market failure (in conflict with NPT) and is not exclusively pro-producer (in conflict with the CT). Depending on the regulated industry, the welfare of different interest groups is improved by regulation. One then needs a theory that can explain this phenomenon. In addition, a theory must also explain why we have observed both the regulation and (partial or full) deregulation of such industries as railroads (regulated in 1887, deregulated in 1980), intercity telecommunications (regulated in 1910, partially deregulated starting in 1971), trucking (regulated in 1935, deregulated in 1980), airlines (regulated in 1938, deregulated in 1978), natural gas (price regulated in 1954, deregulated in 1989), and oil (regulated in 1971, deregulated in 1981). It must also tackle the simultaneous decline of economic regulation and rise of social regulation in the past two decades.

The Stiglerian Approach

The major breakthrough in the theory of regulation occurred in a 1971 article by Nobel laureate George Stigler, "The Theory of Economic Regulation."[19] The value of this contribution was not so much in the predictions that it generated (it basically produced predictions along the lines of the CT), but in the way it approached the question, Why is there regulation? In contrast to NPT and the CT, Stigler put forth a set of assumptions and generated predictions about which industries would be regulated and what form regulation would take as logical implications of these assumptions.

The initial premise of Stigler's analysis is that the basic resource of the state is the power to coerce. An interest group that can convince the state to use its power of coercion to that interest group's benefit can improve its well-being. The next premise is that agents are rational in the sense of choosing actions that are utility maximizing. These two assumptions result in the hypothesis that regulation is supplied in response to the demands of interest groups acting to maximize their income. Regulation is one avenue by which an interest group can increase its income by having the state redistribute wealth from other parts of society to that interest group. As is typically the case, Stigler states it best:

We assume that political systems are rationally devised and rationally employed, which is to say that they are appropriate instruments for the fulfillment of desires of members of the society.[20]

With this fundamental insight, one can construct a theory that will make predictions as to which industries will be regulated and what form regulation will take. The remainder of the section on the *economic theory of regulation* (ET) describes some of the formal models under this rubric and describes their resulting predictions.

Stigler/Peltzman Model

Stigler's contribution did not stop with this analysis. He went on to discuss the different factors that determine which interest group(s) will control regulation. A later paper by Sam Peltzman formalized the analysis of Stigler, and both of these papers have built on the work of Mancur Olson.[21]

There are three crucial elements to the Stigler/Peltzman formulation. First, regulatory legislation redistributes wealth. It may do other things, but implicitly Stigler and Peltzman argue that the primary determinant of the form of regulation is the way in which it transfers wealth among members of society. Second, the behavior of legislators is driven by their desire to remain in office, which implies that legislation is designed to maximize political support. Third, interest groups compete by offering political support in exchange for favorable legislation.

The general result that follows is that regulation is likely to be biased toward benefiting interest groups that are better organized (so that they are more effective at delivering political support) and gain more from favorable legislation (so that they are willing to invest resources in acquiring political support). More specifically, regulation is likely to benefit small interest groups with strongly felt preferences at the cost of large interest groups with weakly felt preferences. The reasons lie in recognition and implementation. For an interest group to recognize the need for certain legislation, each member must have the potential of gaining a lot from it. Interest-group behavior is driven by the desires of its individual members. It is insufficient for some group potentially to realize a large gain from regulation. What is important is that each of its members stand to gain a lot, for only then does each member have the incentive to invest the resources to learn about the issues and about what needs to be done to achieve favorable legislation. This argues to the point that interest groups for which the per-capita benefit from regulation is relatively high are more likely to recognize how legislation can be designed to serve their interests. Of course, it is insufficient simply to recognize a desire for a particular piece of legislation. To benefit, that legislation must be implemented. This requires delivering political support—both in terms of votes and money—to legislators who can see that the appropriate bill is written, proposed, and passed. Here, big groups are at a disadvantage because of a free-rider effect. A person who makes a financial donation on behalf of his interest group benefits everyone in the group though the cost is specific to him. For example, a union worker who contributes dues of $50 incurs the full cost, but all union members share in the increased political power from the additional $50. This tendency to undercontribute is stronger the larger the group because the marginal impact of one person's contribution is smaller, though the cost to that person is independent of the group size. Of course, if everyone acts in that manner, contributions will be quite small. The smaller the size of the interest group, the weaker is this free-rider effect because each member's contribution has a proportionately bigger impact on the eventual impact of the group. Thus, in terms of both recognition of a need for regulation and implementation of that regulation, the advantage rests in small interest groups for which the per-capita benefits from regulation are high.

This argument provides some insight into why much of observed regulation favors producers. Producer groups are typically small in number, with each firm benefiting a large amount from regulation, whereas the primary opposition is consumers, of which there are typically millions, and the harm that regulation creates, while large in the aggregate, is small for each consumer.

U.S. Peanut Program

An example of a small group's benefiting from regulation at the cost of a large group is the peanut-quota system. Since 1949 the federal government has run a program that limits the number of farmers who can sell peanuts in the United States. Imports are also severely restricted. On top of these restrictions, price supports are used to guarantee that farmers with peanut quotas can cover their production costs for each year. This generally results in the minimum selling price being about 50 percent higher than the world price.

For 1982–1987, it was estimated that the average annual consumer-to-producer transfer was $255 million (in 1987 dollars) with an associated deadweight welfare loss of $34 million.[22] In 1982 there were 23,046 peanut farmers, which means that each received a net transfer of $11,100. In contrast, the cost to the average consumer of this program was only $1.23. Few consumers would be willing to spend their own time and money to dismantle the peanut program when they would only gain $1.23. However, the program is worth $11,100 to the average peanut farmer and that would certainly make it worth one's while to see that the program continues.

Predicting the Type of Industry to Be Regulated

The key assumption of the Stigler/Peltzman model is that the individuals who control regulatory policy (presumably the legislators) choose policy so as to maximize their political support. Although this is not the only assumption one could make, it is certainly a plausible one inasmuch as legislators desire to be reelected, and this is best achieved by maximizing political support. In deciding on government policies (which could include policies other than price and entry regulation), a legislator decides the size of the group to be benefited by regulation and how much wealth is to be transferred to them. For example, a legislator decides on the price structure and, in so doing, which consumers are benefited (their price is set below cost), which consumers are hurt (their price is set above cost), and how much firms are benefited (in terms of the level of profits).

Let us address in greater depth the issue of which industries are most likely to be regulated. For this purpose, Peltzman provides a model specifically designed for price and entry regulation. A legislator/regulator chooses price so as to maximize political support. Let the political support function be represented by $M(P, \pi)$ where P is price and π is industry profit. $M(P, \pi)$ is assumed to be decreasing in price because consumers increase their political opposition when price is higher while it is increasing in industry profit because firms respond with greater support. Profit depends on price where $\pi(P)$ will denote the profit function. In particular, $\pi(P)$ is increasing in P for all prices less than P^m (the monopoly price) and is decreasing in P for all prices above P^m. The profit function is shown in Figure 10.2. For $P < P^m$, note that if a legislator raises price, he raises consumer opposition—since $M(P, \pi)$ is decreasing in P—but also raises industry support—since $\pi(P)$ is increasing in P and $M(P, \pi)$ is increasing in π.

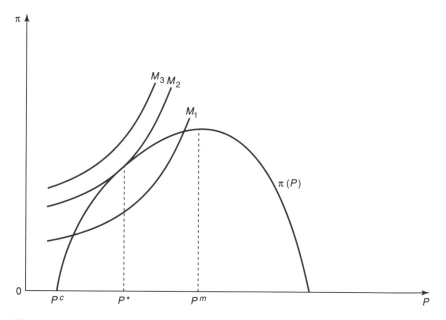

Figure 10.2
Optimal Regulatory Policy: Peltzman Model

Let us characterize the price that maximizes the political support function $M(P, \pi)$ subject to $\pi = \pi(P)$. To do so, we have put in Figure 10.2 indifference curves for a legislator. The curve M_1 represents all pairs of price and profit that generate the level M_1 of political support. Note that the slope of an indifference curve is positive. This reflects the fact that if price is higher (hence, consumer support is reduced) then profit must be higher (which raises industry support) if the same level of political support is to be achieved. Because $M(P, \pi)$ is decreasing in P and increasing in π, political support is increasing in a northwesterly direction, so that $M_3 > M_2 > M_1$. The optimal price for the legislator, denoted P^*, is that which achieves the highest level of political support subject to the constraint that profit equals $\pi(P)$. Note that P^* lies between the competitive price, P^c, where profit is zero and the monopoly price, P^m, where industry profit is maximized. Thus, we have formally derived the result that a legislator/regulator will not set a price so as to maximize industry profit.

The characterization of the optimal regulated price provides important insight into which industries are likely to gain the most from regulation. If the equilibrium price an industry would achieve in the absence of regulation is close to the price that would exist under regulation, P^*, then regulation is unlikely. The interest group that would benefit from regulation will not expect to gain a large amount because price would be relatively unaffected. Hence, it would not warrant the investment of resources to get the industry regulated. Because the regulated price lies in between P^c and P^m, this argument also suggests that the industries most likely to be regulated are those that are either relatively competitive (so that the unregulated equilibrium price is near P^c) or relatively monopolistic (so that the unregulated equilibrium price is near P^m). In both cases, some interest group will gain considerably from regulation. Firms will gain in the case of a competitive industry while consumers will gain in the case of a monopolistic industry.

Casual observation suggests that it is indeed these two extremes that tend to be subject to economic regulation. Monopolistic industries include local and long-distance telephone, electric and gas utilities, and railroads. Relatively competitive industries include agriculture (regulation takes the form of price supports), trucking, taxicabs, crude-oil and natural-gas production, and securities.

Becker Model

The Stigler/Peltzman modeling of the economic theory of regulation is based on a legislator or regulator choosing regulatory policy so as to maximize political support. In contrast, the formulation of Gary Becker

focuses instead on competition between interest groups.[23] He suppresses
the role of the legislator/regulator by assuming that "Politicians, political parties, and voters ... transmit the pressure of active groups."[24] True
to the economic theory of regulation, Becker assumes regulation is used
to increase the welfare of more influential interest groups.

For simplicity, suppose there are two interest groups denoted group 1
and group 2. An interest group can raise its welfare by influencing regulatory policy. The wealth transfer that group 1 gets depends on both the
pressure it exerts on legislators and regulators (denoted p_1) and the
pressure exerted by group 2 (denoted p_2). The amount of pressure is determined by the number of members in the group and the amount of resources used. Greater pressure by group 1 as well as less pressure by
group 2 implies that group 1 has more influence on the political process.
Greater influence translates into group 1 receiving a bigger wealth
transfer. In particular, if T is group 1's increase in wealth due to regulation, then $T = I(p_1, p_2)$, where $I(p_1, p_2)$ is called the influence function.
It is assumed that $I(p_1, p_2)$ is increasing in the pressure of group 1 and
decreasing in the pressure of group 2. In order to transfer wealth of
amount T to group 1, it is assumed that group 2's wealth must be reduced by $(1 + x)T$, where $x \geq 0$. When $x > 0$, more wealth is taken
from group 2 then is transferred to group 1. This "disappearing" wealth
is measured by xT and is the welfare loss from regulation.

A property of the Becker model is that aggregate influence is fixed.
The implication is that what is important for determining the amount of
regulatory activity (as measured by the wealth transfer) is the influence
of one group *relative* to the influence of another group. Each group
chooses a level of pressure so as to maximize its welfare given the pressure level chosen by the other group. Because greater pressure uses up
the group's resources, each group will not want to apply too much pressure. On the other hand, the less pressure a group applies, the greater
the influence of the other group. Hence, by reducing p_1, the relative
influence of group 1 declines so that the wealth transfer it gets will be
smaller. Taking into account the benefits and costs of pressure, one can
derive the optimal value of p_1, given any value for p_2. This optimal level
of pressure for group 1 is denoted $\psi_1(p_2)$ and is plotted in Figure 10.3.
$\psi_1(p_2)$ is referred to as groups 1's "best response function" because it tells
groups 1 what level of pressure is best (in terms of its own welfare) in response to group 2's level of pressure. For example, if group 2 is expected
to apply pressure of $\hat{p}_2$ then group 1's optimal level of pressure is $\psi_1(\hat{p}_2)$,
which is denoted $\hat{p}_1$ in Figure 10.3. Because the more pressure that
group 2 exerts the lower is the influence of group 1, group 1 finds it

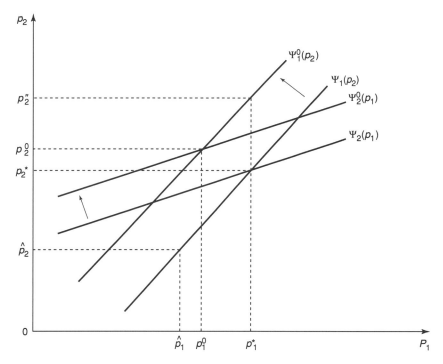

Figure 10.3
Political Equilibrium: Becker Model

optimal to apply more pressure to offset the greater pressure of group 2. This implies that $\psi_1(p_2)$ is increasing in p_2, as shown in Figure 10.3.

A political equilibrium is defined as a pair of pressure levels such that neither group has an incentive to change their decision. In other words, the pair of pressure levels (p_1^*, p_2^*) is a *political equilibrium* if, given group 2 applies pressures p_2^*, p_1^* is the pressure that maximizes group 1's welfare *and*, given group 1 applies pressure p_1^*, p_2^* is the pressure that maximizes group 2's welfare.[25] A political equilibrium is then defined by the intersection of the two best response functions $\psi_1(p_2)$ and $\psi_2(p_1)$ as at that intersection both interest groups are simultaneously exerting optimal levels of pressure. The political equilibrium in Figure 10.3 is then the pair (p_1^*, p_2^*).

The political equilibrium has both interest groups investing in pressure so as to influence the political process. The optimal pressure for each group is very much dependent on the level of pressure exerted by the other group because what determines regulatory policy is *relative* influence. As a result, the free-riding problem inherent in all groups is not as important as had been previously thought. Because all groups are subject to free-riding, what is important is the *relative* severity of free-riding. When the free-riding problem is less severe in group 1 than in group 2 (perhaps because group 1 has fewer members), group 1 will have a relative advantage over group 2. This is regardless of whether or not group 1 has a severe free-riding problem in some absolute sense.

Another important property to note about the equilibrium is that it is not Pareto optimal. Both groups could invest fewer resources and achieve the same level of relative influence. Because relative influence is all that matters, the political outcome would be the same but at a lower cost for both groups. As an example of this phenomenon, consider the case of competition among cable operators for the cable television franchise in the New York City boroughs of Brooklyn, Queens, Staten Island and the Bronx:

All the [franchise] applicants have hired influential lawyers and public-relations consultants, a roster of whom reads like a Who's Who of former city and state officials.... [A vice president for one of the applicants] contends that these friends at city hall (who typically command fees of about $5,000 per month) have tended to cancel one another out.[26]

Competition among groups for influence in the political process uses up economic resources to obtain the wealth transfer, resulting in a Pareto-inefficient outcome. The logic behind this result is exactly the same as that for the Pareto-inefficiency of the Cournot outcome in the oligopoly setting (see Chapter 5).

Given the theory of a political equilibrium, let us now use it to generate testable hypotheses concerning the properties of regulation. One important result is that if the marginal deadweight loss from regulation, x, increases then the amount of regulatory activity decreases (measured by the amount of wealth transfer T). An increase in the marginal deadweight loss means that group 2 incurs a bigger loss for any given transfer received by group 1. This greater potential loss spurs group 2 to apply more pressure for any given anticipated level of pressure by group 1. This effect of a rise in x on group 2's behavior is then represented by a shift in its best response function from $\psi_2(p_1)$ to $\psi_2^0(p_1)$ (see Figure 10.3). For example, if group 1 is expected to apply pressure p_1^* then group 2 now chooses to apply pressure p_2'' rather than p_2^* because now the welfare loss imposed on group 2 is higher for any given value of T (due to a higher value of x). This higher value of x also implies that group 1 will get a smaller wealth transfer for any given tax of group 2. Because group 1 has less of an incentive to invest resources to increase regulatory activity, it will apply less pressure. This is represented by its best response function shifting from $\psi_1(p_2)$ to $\psi_1^0(p_2)$ in response to an increase in the marginal deadweight loss from regulation. As a result, the new political equilibrium is (p_1^0, p_2^0), which entails more pressure by group 2, as $p_2^0 > p_2^*$, and less pressure by group 1, as $p_1^0 < p_1^*$. Because the amount of the transfer, T, equals $I(p_1, p_2)$ and $I(p_1, p_2)$ is increasing in p_1 and decreasing in p_2, it follows that $I(p_1^0, p_2^0) < I(p_1^*, p_2^*)$. As measured by the amount of wealth transfer, regulatory activity is reduced due to an increase in the marginal deadweight loss associated with it.

An important implication of this result is that regulatory policies that are welfare-improving are more likely to be implemented than ones that are not. Suppose that industry A is a natural monopoly and industry B is competitive. The deadweight welfare loss from regulating industry B is greater than that for industry A, ceteris paribus, because industry B is already achieving a welfare optimum while industry A is not. The implication of the above analysis is that the greater marginal deadweight loss associated with regulation of industry B means that more pressure will be applied for regulation in industry A than in industry B. The Becker model suggests that industries plagued by market failures (so that the marginal deadweight loss from regulation is relatively low or even negative) are more likely to be regulated. The beneficiary groups have greater potential for gains so that they will apply more pressure. Groups harmed by regulation will not be harmed as much because of the lower deadweight loss, so that they will apply less pressure against regulation.

In contrast to the Stigler/Peltzman model of regulation, the Becker model provides some justification for NPT. Where there are market failures, there are potential welfare gains from regulation. Some interest groups stand to gain a lot from regulation, whereas other groups stand to lose a little (relative to interest groups in industries not subject to market failure) because of the absence of relatively large deadweight welfare losses. As a result, there is relatively great pressure for regulation of industries subject to market failure. However, the Becker model, in contrast to NPT, does not state that regulation occurs only when there is a market failure. What determines regulatory activity is the relative influence of interest groups and this influence is determined not only by the welfare effects of regulation but also by the relative efficiency of interest groups in applying pressure to legislators and regulators.

Taxation by Regulation

One of the many perplexing aspects of economic regulation is the common use of cross-subsidization. Cross-subsidization is the use of revenue from the sale of one product to subsidize the sale of another product. More specifically, the price of one product is set to exceed its average cost while the price of a second product is set below its average cost.

Such pricing behavior is perplexing because it appears to be inconsistent with both profit maximization and welfare maximization.

An explanation for cross-subsidization is provided by Richard Posner.[27] He puts forth the thesis that one of the functions of regulation is to assist the government in its role of redistributing resources. In this light, cross-subsidization is interpreted as a means for redistributing wealth from one group of consumers to a second group of consumers. For example, price regulation entails charging a uniform price for providing local telephone service. Thus, a consumer who lives in a city, where the marginal cost of hooking him up to the system is low, pays the same fee as a consumer who lives in a rural area, where the marginal cost of hookup is considerably greater. Another example is airline pricing, where, under CAB regulation, the fare was often the same for routes of similar length even though average cost is much higher on low density routes than on high density routes. Posner's argument assumes that society desires to redistribute resources from one class of consumers to another class of consumers and concludes that this could be aided through cross-subsidization. In practice, it would appear that consumers in less densely populated areas tend to be subsidized at the cost of consumers in more densely populated areas.

The analysis of Posner fits in with the model of Becker. One can interpret the outcome of cross-subsidization as revealing that some consumers (those with price below cost) have relatively more influence on the political process than other consumers (those with price above cost). Although cross-subsidization cannot be explained by either NPT (as it is inconsistent with welfare maximization) or the CT (as it is inconsistent with profit maximization), it can be explained as the result of competition among interest groups to influence government policy for the purpose of raising their welfare.

Summary of Results

We have derived four major results using the Stiglerian approach to the theory of regulation. These results take the form of predicting the form of regulation and which industries will be regulated. First, there is a tendency for regulation to be designed to benefit relatively small groups with strong preferences over regulation at the cost of relatively large groups with weak preferences over regulation. In many cases, the implication of this result is that regulation will be pro-producer. Second, even if regulation is pro-producer, policy (in particular, price) will not be set so as to maximize industry profit. Because of the constraining influence of consumer groups, price will be set below the profit-maximizing level. A third result is that regulation is most likely in relatively competitive or relative monopolistic industries as it is in those industries that regulation will have the biggest impact on some group's well-being. Finally, the presence of a market failure makes regulation more likely because the gain to some interest groups is large relative to the loss to other interest groups. As a result, the former will have more influence on the legislative process, ceteris paribus.

Critique of ET: Modeling the Regulatory Process

An important assumption in the models of Stigler, Peltzman, and Becker is that interest groups directly influence regulatory policies. However, when one thinks about the process by which regulation is determined, one realizes there are numerous actors. Voters and special interest groups determine who the legislators are, legislators determine the piece of regulatory legislation (in conjunction with the chief executive), and regulators influence the actual policy that is implemented. In order for interest groups to have a significant impact on regulatory policy, it must be true that the process works the right way. First, interest groups must have a strong impact on the outcome of elections. Second, legislators must be sufficiently constrained by the threat of losing interest group support that they implement the policies supported by the interest groups that got them into office (and are presumably needed for reelection). Third, regulators must be sufficiently under the control of legislators if the policy that is implemented is not to deviate from that desired. An important critique of economic theories of regulation is that they ignore some important elements of the regulatory process by assuming interest groups adequately control legislators and legislators adequately control regulators.

Legislators obviously care about being reelected (and thus want to appease the interest groups that originally elected them), but they also care about other things. Like voters, legislators have preferences over issues even if they are not directly affected by them. Such preferences have been referred to as an ideology where "ideologies are more or less consistent sets of normative statements as to best or preferred states of the world."[28] Because interest groups cannot perfectly control or perfectly monitor the activities of legislators, legislators can be expected to periodically "shirk" their responsibilities to their interest groups and instead pursue their own ideology (which may or may not conflict with the desires of their interest groups).

In addition to legislators not being puppets of their interest groups, regulators need not be puppets of legislators. Regulators are difficult to control because they have access to information not available to legislators and because it is very costly for legislators to draft new legislation to redirect regulatory policy. As a result, regulators can have considerable discretion in implementing policy.[29] On the other hand, it has been argued that Congressional oversight committees can be quite effective in controlling regulators.[30] With its budgetary powers, the Congress can punish regulatory agencies that pursue the wrong policies. In spite of this threat, regulators clearly have a nontrivial amount of freedom from legislators.

Finally, the role of judiciary has been ignored in the ET. The courts have shown that they can be a key player in the regulatory process:

Judicial consent is necessary when a statute must be reinterpreted in order to implement a change. For instance, reinterpretation of the existing statutes was necessary for the deregulation of airline, trucking, telecommunications and several other industries, and the deregulation of various environmental, health and safety standards. Deregulation occurred *only* in those cases which were approved by the judiciary. Further, where it did occur, the opposition from committees of Congress was irrelevant.[31]

We are aware of ways in which interest groups can pressure the President and the Congress but how can they influence judiciary decisions? What motivates judges? These are important questions which the ET has not addressed.

Does the Empirical Evidence Support the Economic Theory of Regulation?

The central empirical challenge to the ET is to explain both the regulation and deregulation of such industries as railroads, trucking, intercity telecommunications, and crude oil. To address this issue, one should pose the question: What changes in the regulatory environment would induce deregulation?

According to NPT, deregulation would occur when there are changes in cost or demand conditions such that a market failure is either eliminated or sufficiently reduced so as to make deregulation socially optimal. Alternatively, the ET would predict deregulation when the relative influence of interest groups that are benefited by regulation is reduced. This could happen as a result of changes in cost or demand conditions (by affecting such things as the deadweight loss associated with regulation) or changes in the cost of organizing groups; for example, a new mechanism or technology may be discovered that reduces the free-rider problem. In the case of consumer groups, this new technology may be the arrival of a political entrepreneur like Ralph Nader who is proficient in organizing people and forming coalitions.

A casual survey of the the recent deregulatory movement suggests that the evidence is mixed.[32] The deregulation of the railroad industry in 1976–1980 would appear to be broadly consistent with the ET. The original regulation of the industry is explained by the industry being more influential in the political process. Although regulation originally allowed above-normal profits, it eventually reduced firm profitability due to a variety of reasons. In response, one would expect the industry to pressure for deregulation, which is what it did beginning in the mid 1950s. Unexplained, however, is why it took so long for significant deregulation to take place. On the other hand, the deregulation of trucking appears quite inconsistent with the ET. The trucking industry was earning large rents from regulation at the time of its deregulation. Further, one is hard pressed to find a reason why consumers of trucking services would have become more influential in the political process relative to trucking firms and the Teamsters Union. Finally, a case that can be argued to be supportive of either the ET or NPT is the deregulation of the intercity telecommunications market. As we will see in Chapter 15, deregulation can be explained as being a response to the industry no longer being a natural monopoly, as NPT would predict. A weakness in this argument is that, originally, the FCC allowed very limited entry and was steadfastly against allowing entry into certain segments of the market (in particular, long distance telephone service). This policy is difficult to rectify with NPT. It could be explained by the ET in that technological changes brought forth a new interest group in the form of prospective firms (initially, MCI). This interest group was influential enough to pressure the FCC to allow partial entry, but AT&T was too influential to allow full entry. It was only the U.S. Court of Appeals that eventually expanded entry.

More systematic and direct tests of the ET have been conducted and this work seeks to determine whether regulation tends to favor interest groups with a low cost of organizing and a high per-capita benefit from regulation. This empirical work investigates why states allow reciprocity for dentist licenses,[33] what determines the pricing of nuclear energy,[34] and why some states went from rate-of-return regulation to price caps in regulating the intrastate long distance rates of AT&T.[35]

A review of the record reveals that while the ET is an important advancement in understanding government intervention, there is still much empirical evidence that would seem to be inconsistent with it. It appears that we have a considerable journey ahead of us in understanding why regulation occurs when it does and why it takes the form that it does. A fuller analysis of the political side of regulation will be dealt with when we examine particular industries. Our studies will include an examination of the political economy of railroad and trucking regulation (Chapter 17), Congressional voting on strip-mining regulation (Chapter

19), and the 1984 Drug Price Competition and Patent Restoration Act (Chapter 24).

Taxicab Regulation

Regulatory History

Before the 1920s the taxicab industry was largely unregulated. As the automobile became an integral part of transportation, the demand and supply functions of taxicab services shifted out. The 1920s proved to be a growth phase for both taxicab services and taxicab regulations. Fare regulation became increasingly common, as did other legal restrictions such as the requirement that taxicabs be insured. Though regulation of the taxicab industry grew during the 1920s, local government left entry into the industry largely unregulated.

After the onset of the Great Depression, massive entry took place into the taxicab industry. Some of this entry was due to the sharp rise in the number of unemployed workers. With few other job opportunities available, some individuals took to driving taxicabs. With the increased number of competitors, fare competition heated up and taxicab drivers and owners faced falling profits. What ensued was local governments' placing restrictions on entry into the taxicab industry:

The regulation movement spread throughout the country. In Massachusetts, Frank Sawyer [owner of Checker Taxi Company] urged the state to regulate taxis, and in 1930 the legislature limited the number of cabs in Boston to 1,525 (the same as in 1980). New York City first limited the number of cabs in 1932 under the sponsorship of Mayor Jimmy Walker, but when Walker was forced to resign when it was discovered that he had been bribed by one of the taxi companies, the attempt at regulation failed. Five years later, however, the Haas Act in New York City froze the number of taxi medallions at 13,500.[36]

This appears to be a classic example of the Economic Theory of Regulation. Each taxicab company would gain a lot from regulation, while each consumer would only be harmed a little. Furthermore, there are many fewer taxicab companies than consumers, so that the cost of organizing political support is much lower for the former. As a result, the taxicab companies were more effective in getting regulation put in place than were consumers in preventing regulation.

The regulatory program that took place in the 1930s had a lasting impact on the industry. To an extent to be described below, regulation has prevented entry in most taxicab markets. A notable exception is Washington, D.C., which does allow entry. Since 1979 there has been a minor deregulatory movement in a few cities that has reduced restrictions on fares and the number of taxicabs. Nevertheless, the taxicab industry has largely escaped the program of deregulation that took place in the 1970s and 1980s.

Entry Restrictions

Taxicab regulation encompasses control over price, the number of competitors, and certain practices. Cities set either fares or ceilings for fares. Entry restrictions take different forms in different cities. A common way in which entry is restricted is to mandate that, in order to operate, a taxicab must own a medallion. Medallions are issued by the city and are limited in supply. The number of medallions provides an upper bound on the number of taxicabs (the number of taxicabs can be less than the number of medallions if a taxi company chooses not to use a medallion it owns). In most cities medallions can be sold and their ownership transferred. Cities that have pursued this type of entry regulation include Baltimore, Boston, Chicago, Detroit, New York City, and San Francisco. An alternative method of limiting the number of competitors is to limit the number of taxi companies, and possibly the number of taxicabs as well. This practice has been used in Cleveland, Dallas, Houston, Los Angeles, Philadelphia, Pittsburgh, and Seattle.[37]

In practice, cities have constrained the number of taxicabs. 13,566 medallions were issued in New York City in 1937. With nearly 2,000 returned to the city around World War II, the supply of medallions today is only 11,787 (as mandated by law in 1971). With a growing population, New York City residents have had to suffer with a declining number of taxicabs per capita. Similar experiences have occurred in most major cities. In Boston, the number of taxicabs has been fixed at 1,525 since 1930. In Detroit, the number has been 1,310 for over forty years. Although the number of taxicabs in Chicago has been a bit less stagnant, it is not much of an improvement. The city of Chicago allowed 4,108 taxicabs to operate in 1934, then reduced this number to 3,000 in 1937. Since 1963, 4,600 taxicabs have been allowed to operate.[38]

Evidence of the extent of entry restrictions is provided by the response to recent deregulation. In a survey of 103 cities, it was found that from 1979–1984, sixteen cities substantially relaxed entry restrictions, whereas seventeen cities relaxed fare regulations.[39] Three of the cities that allowed greater freedom of entry were Portland, Seattle, and San Diego. From 1979 to late 1983, Portland experienced a 12 percent rise in the number of taxi permits, Seattle a 30 percent rise, and San Diego a whopping 128 percent rise.[40] For the case of Seattle, the number of licensed taxicabs rose 21 percent from 1979 to mid 1981, and the number of taxicab companies increased nearly 50 percent.[41]

The Value of a Medallion

Perhaps the best method for assessing the value of entry restrictions is to determine how much a firm is willing to pay in order to operate in the industry. Although this is often a difficult piece of information to acquire, it is a simple task for the taxicab industry. Because in many cities a taxicab must have a medallion in order to operate and since the number of medallions is fixed, prospective taxicab operators must purchase a medallion in a secondary market. If the price in the market for medallions is positive then the number of competitors must be less than the number that would exist under free entry (where, effectively, the price of a medallion is zero).

The market value of a medallion is more than just a rough indicator of the effectiveness of entry restrictions. A medallion's price tells us exactly what the most informed agents believe to be the discounted stream of above-normal profits from economic regulation. To see this, consider an individual with a taxicab who is faced with two alternatives. He can freely enter and operate in Washington, D.C., or he can buy a New York City medallion and operate in New York City. The equilibrium price of a medallion is set by the market so that a prospective firm is indifferent between the two alternatives. If it were not, the market for medallions would not be in equilibrium; if firms could expect to earn more by buying a medallion and operating in New York City, then this would increase the demand for New York City medallions and drive the price up until the price made firms indifferent between the two alternatives. Because the Washington, D.C., market is subject to free entry, it is logical to presume that normal profits are being earned by firms there. Thus, the price of a medallion in New York City must equal the additional profits that can be earned by operating in a regulated market as opposed to an unregulated market. Specifically, it is equal to the discounted sum of future excess profits that are earned by a taxicab operating in New York City. For example, suppose operating a taxicab in a regulated market yields above-normal profits of $5,000 per year for the infinite future. If the interest rate is 5 percent, then the market value of a medallion is $5,000/.05 or $100,000. Competition for medallions should then drive the price up to $100,000.

Table 10.4 provides the market price of a taxicab medallion in a variety of U.S. cities. The values run as high as $210,000 for an independent taxicab in New York City. The total market value of taxicab medallions in New York City is then on the order of $2 billion. This represents above-normal profits achieved through fare and entry regulation. It is then not surprising that entry restrictions persist in most U.S. cities. A

Table 10.4
Prices of Taxicab Medallions

City	Date	Price Range
Boston	1983	$32,000–$33,000
Cambridge, MA	1983	$20,000–$25,000
Chicago	1970	$15,000 or more
Dallas	1976	$3,000
Houston	1983	$10,000–$12,000
Indianapolis	1980	$400–$500
Miami	1979	$18,000
Minneapolis	1983	$8,000–$12,000
Newark	1983	$9,000
New Orleans	1976	$3,000
New York City	1993	$210,000
Oakland, CA	1979	$2,000–$3,000
Portland, OR	1979	$3,000–$9,000
San Diego	1979	$8,000–$15,000
San Diego	1983	$1,000–$2,000
San Francisco	1983	$15,000–$20,000
Seattle	1967–1979	$1,000–$12,000
Somerville, MA	1983	$25,000

Source: Updated table from Mark W. Frankena and Paul A. Pautler, *An Economic Analysis of Taxicab Regulation*, Bureau of Economics Staff Report, Federal Trade Commission, May 1984.

current holder of a New York City medallion would stand to lose over $200,000 if free entry were allowed. In comparison, the value of deregulation to each consumer of taxicab services would be much much lower. Furthermore, the holding of medallions is typically concentrated in a few large taxicab companies, which makes this interest group more effective in providing political support in exchange for continued entry restrictions.

Summary and Overview of Part II

As with any sort of economic phenomenon, there are certain empirical regularities associated with economic regulation. It typically entails regulation over price, quantity, and/or the number of active firms. Regulatory activity also has certain time-series properties. We have witnessed periodic bursts of legislation. A large amount of economic regulation took place after the Great Depression, whereas deregulation was hot in the 1980s.

This chapter provided a brief review of the regulatory process, but it could hardly do justice to the complexity of this process. Many economic agents are involved at the time of regulation's inception, implementation, and, perhaps, its dismantling. To understand why the regulatory environment looks the way it does, one must understand the motives of consumers, firms, unions, legislators, regulatory commissioners, and government bureaucrats. Several theories of why regulation takes the form that it does were discussed. Different variants of the economic theory of regulation appear to be most consistent with the evidence. Nevertheless, there is still much regulation that this theory cannot explain. More research is required before we will have a complete theory of regulation.

In concluding this chapter, let us provide a brief overview of Part II. The chapters on economic regulation are divided into two segments: the regulation of natural monopoly and the regulation of potentially competitive markets. Because natural monopoly is perhaps the most important basis for economic regulation, considerable attention is given to understanding what is a natural monopoly, how best to regulate it, and what are the effects of regulation. Chapter 11 provides an introduction to natural monopoly. The standard form of natural monopoly regulation along with a discussion of its effects are provided in Chapter 12. In light of its importance, we also consider alternative methods for handling the problem of natural monopoly. Chapter 13 analyzes franchise bidding, using cable television as an application; Chapter 14 considers public enterprise, using municipally owned electric utilities as an application. The final chapter on natural monopoly focuses on dynamic issues related to regulation. This is performed in Chapter 15, where the intercity telecommunications market provides an interesting case study.

Chapters 16 through 18 assess the effects of regulation in industries that are potentially competitive. A theoretical discussion of these effects and how one might estimate their quantitative size is provided in Chapter 16. Analyses of the regulation of transportation is provided in Chapter 17 where we focus on the price and entry/exit regulation of the railroad, trucking, and airline industries. Concluding Part II, Chapter 18 considers price regulation in the crude oil and natural gas industries.

Questions and Problems

1. Do you agree with the *Nebbia v. New York* decision? If not, what do you think would have been a better judicial decision?

2. What are the roles of the legislature, the judiciary, and the regulatory agency in deregulation? How do interest groups affect deregulation? Should they be allowed to affect regulatory policy?

3. Sometimes, former regulatory commissioners are hired by the industry that they previously regulated. What effect do you think this has on the relationship between a regulatory agency and the industry? Should this be allowed? Discuss the advantages and disadvantages from prohibiting this practice.

4. Is there a theory that can explain why a competitive industry like taxicabs is regulated *and* why a monopolistic industry like local telephone is regulated? What about an oligopolistic industry like the airlines?

5. Can one explain why the railroad industry was regulated and then deregulated almost a century later? What about the regulation and deregulation of trucking?

6. What is the empirical evidence for and against the economic theory of regulation?

7. What would be the effect on regulatory practices if regulatory agencies were comprised of seven members where two members represent firms, two members represent workers, and three members represent consumers? More generally, how do you think regulatory commissioners should be chosen?

8. Use the economic theory of regulation to explain the existence of trade barriers like tariffs and quotas.

9. What do you think caused the wave of deregulation that took place during the 1970s and 1980s?

10. In 1993, a New York City taxicab medallion had a market value of $210,000. If the interest rate is 6 percent and entry restrictions are not expected to change in the future, what is the amount of above-normal profits earned annually?

11. If you bought a New York City taxicab medallion and operated a taxicab, would you be earning an above-normal rate of return on your investment?

12. Suppose a taxicab company is expected to earn annual above-normal profits of $10,000. Assume the interest rate is 5 percent.

    a. Derive the price of a medallion if entry regulation is expected to continue forever.

    b. Suppose it is announced by the city government that they will allow free entry into the taxicab industry in exactly two years. Derive the change in the price of a medallion in response to this announcement. Would this price differ from the price it would be selling for next year?

Notes

1. Alan Stone, *Regulation and Its Alternatives* (Washington, D.C.: Congressional Quarterly Press, 1982), p. 10.

2. For a discussion of early (municipal) regulation prior to the 1880s, see M. H. Hunter, "Early Regulation of Public Service Corporations," *American Economic Review* 7 (September 1917): 569–81.

3. Elizabeth Sanders, "The Regulatory Surge of the 1970s in Historical Perspective," in Elizabeth E. Bailey (ed.), *Public Regulation: New Perspectives on Institutions and Policies* (Cambridge, Mass.: MIT Press, 1987).

4. Richard H. K. Vietor, *Contrived Competition: Regulation and Deregulation in America* (Cambridge, Mass.: Harvard University Press, 1994).

5. Clifford Winston, "Economic Deregulation: Days of Reckoning for Micro-economists," *Journal of Economic Literature* 31 (September 1993): 1263–89. This paper also provides a comprehensive summary of the predicted and measured effects of economic deregulation.

6. Alfred E. Kahn, "Deregulation: Looking Backward and Looking Forward," *Yale Journal on Regulation* 7 (Summer 1990): 325–54.

7. For an analysis of the role of the judiciary in the deregulation process, see Krishna K. Ladha, "The Pivotal Role of the Judiciary in the Deregulation Battle between the Executive and Legislature," unpublished paper, Washington University, March 1990.

8. For a discussion and comparative analysis of appointed and elected state public utility commissioners, see Kenneth W. Costello, "Electing Regulators: The Case of Public Utility Commissioners," *Yale Journal on Regulation* 2 (1984): 83–105.

9. Stone, 1982.

10. James Q. Wilson, "The Politics of Regulation," in James Q. Wilson (ed.), *The Politics of Regulation* (New York: Basic Books, 1980).

11. "Delay in the Regulatory Process" in *Study on Federal Regulation*, Volume IV, U.S. Senate, Committee on Governmental Affairs, July 1977.

12. For an insightful discussion of the strategic manipulation of the regulatory process, see Bruce M. Owen and Ronald Braeutigam, *The Regulation Game* (Cambridge, Mass.: Ballinger Publishing Company, 1978).

13. These objectives for a theory of regulation are laid out in George J. Stigler, "The Theory of Economic Regulation," *Bell Journal of Economics and Management Science* 2 (Spring 1971): 3–21.

14. Paul L. Joskow and Roger G. Noll, "Regulation in Theory and Practice: An Overview," in Gary Fromm (ed.), *Studies in Public Regulation* (Cambridge: MIT Press, 1981).

15. Richard A. Posner, "Theories of Economic Regulation," in *Bell Journal of Economics and Management Science* 5 (Autumn 1974): 335–58.

16. George J. Stigler and Claire Friedland, "What Can Regulators Regulate? The Case of Electricity," *Journal of Law and Economics* 5 (October 1962): 1–16.

17. This position was articulated in William A. Jordan, "Producer Protection, Prior Market Structure and the Effects of Government Regulation," *Journal of Law and Economics* 15 (April 1972): 151–76.

18. The hypothesis of a life cycle for a regulatory agency is discussed in Marver H. Bernstein, *Regulating Business by Independent Commission* (Princeton, N.J.: Princeton University, 1955).

19. Stigler, 1971.

20. Ibid., page 4.

21. Sam Peltzman, "Toward a More General Theory of Regulation," *Journal of Law and Economics* 19 (August 1976): 211–40; Mancur Olson, *The Logic of Collective Action* (Cambridge, Mass.: Harvard University Press, 1965).

22. Randal R. Rucker and Walter N. Thurman, "The Economic Effects of Supply Controls: The Simple Analytics of the U.S. Peanut Program," *Journal of Law and Economics* 33 (October 1990): 483–515.

23. Gary S. Becker, "A Theory of Competition Among Pressure Groups for Political Influence," *Quarterly Journal of Economics* 98 (August 1983): 371–400.

24. Ibid., page 372.

25. For those who read the section on game theory in Chapter 5, a political equilibrium is just a Nash equilibrium for a game in which groups simultaneously choose how much pressure to apply.

26. Lauro Landro, "New York Today Picks Its Cable-TV Winners for Four Boroughs," *Wall Street Journal*, November 18, 1981, pp. 1, 22.

27. Richard A. Posner, "Taxation by Regulation," *Bell Journal of Economics and Management Science* 2 (Spring 1971): 22–50.

28. Joseph P. Kalt and Mark A. Zupan, "Capture and Ideology in the Economic Theory of Politics," *American Economic Review* 74 (June 1984): 279–300. This article provides a nice discussion of how ideology fits into the theory of regulation.

29. For analyses that explore the implications of regulators having better information than legislators, see Pablo T. Spiller, "Politicians, Interest Groups, and Regulators: A Multiple-Principals Agency Theory of Regulation, or 'Let Them Be Bribed,'" *Journal of Law and Economics* 22 (April 1990): 65–101, and Jean-Jacques Laffont and Jean Tirole, *A Theory of Incentives in Procurement and Regulation* (Cambridge, Mass.: The MIT Press, 1993).

30. Barry R. Weingast and Mark J. Moran, "Bureaucratic Discretion or Congressional Control? Regulatory Policymaking by the Federal Trade Commission," *Journal of Political Economy* 5 (October 1983): 765–800.

31. Ladha, 1990, p. 46.

32. For surveys see Theodore E. Keeler, "Theories of Regulation and the Deregulation Movement," *Public Choice*, 44 (1984): 103–45, and Sam Peltzman, "The Economic Theory of Regulation after a Decade of Deregulation," in Martin Neil Baily and Clifford Winston (eds.), *Brookings Papers on Economic Activity: Microeconomics 1989* (Washington, D.C.: Brookings Institution, 1989).

33. Gilbert Becker, "The Public Interest Hypothesis Revisited: A New Test of Peltzman's Theory of Regulation," *Public Choice* 49 (1986): 223–34.

34. Charles D. Delorme, Jr., David R. Kamerschen, and Herbert G. Thompson, Jr., "Pricing in the Nuclear Power Industry: Public or Private Interest?" *Public Choice* 73 (June 1994): 385–96.

35. David L. Kaserman, John W. Mayo, and Patricia L. Pacey, "The Political Economy of Deregulation: The Case of Intrastate Long Distance," *Journal of Regulatory Economics* 5 (March 1993): 49–63.

36. Gorman Gilbert and Robert E. Samuels, *The Taxicab* (Chapel Hill: University of North Carolina Press, 1982), pp. 70–71.

37. Mark W. Frankena and Paul A. Pautler, *An Economic Analysis of Taxicab Regulation*, Bureau of Economics Staff Report, Federal Trade Commission, May 1984.

38. Ibid.

39. Ibid.

40. Robert Cervero, "Revitalizing Urban Transit," *Regulation*, May/June 1984: 36–42.

41. Richard O. Zerbe, Jr., "Seattle Taxis: Deregulation Hits a Pothole," *Regulation*, November/December 1983: 43–48.

11 Theory of Natural Monopoly

As we discussed in Chapter 10, there are a number of market-failure arguments for economic regulation. Perhaps the most important and widely accepted is natural monopoly, and it provides the rationale for regulating electric-power and natural-gas distribution, local telephone service, water supply, and some common-carrier transportation services. We begin this chapter with a discussion of the theory of natural monopoly. Actual regulation of natural monopoly will be the subject of the next two chapters.

We will be taking an economic efficiency view of natural monopoly here. In previous chapters we have discussed various explanations for the existence of regulation, including market failure and capture theory hypotheses. In this chapter we focus exclusively on the natural-monopoly market-failure argument and various theoretical and actual solutions.

This chapter is primarily theoretical, but it also serves as an introduction to the next few chapters. Chapter 12 will be concerned with the practice of natural monopoly regulation and an evaluation of its benefits and costs. Chapters 13–15 will discuss several alternatives to regulation that are introduced only briefly here.

The Natural Monopoly Problem

An industry is a natural monopoly if the production of a particular good or service by a single firm minimizes cost. The typical example is production of a single commodity where long-run average cost (LRAC) declines for all outputs. Such a case is illustrated in Figure 11.1. Because LRAC is declining, long-run marginal cost (LRMC) necessarily lies everywhere below it.

The case shown in Figure 11.1 makes clear the public-policy dilemma. Simply stated, the problem is how society can benefit from least-cost production—which obviously requires single-firm production—without suffering from monopoly pricing. The idea, of course, is that a single firm would eventually win the entire market by continuing to expand output and lowering its costs. Having won the market, it could then set the monopoly price.[1]

Shortly, we will turn to an analysis of the variety of solutions to this problem that have been proposed. Before that, however, we will examine more carefully the definition and characteristics of natural monopoly.

Permanent and Temporary Natural Monopoly

An important distinction is that of permanent versus temporary natural monopoly.[2] Figure 11.1 illustrates the case of permanent natural mo-

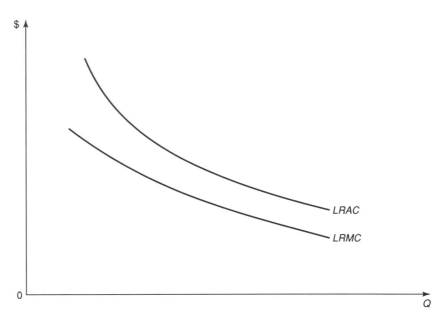

Figure 11.1
Cost Curves of Natural Monopolist

nopoly. The key is that LRAC falls continuously as output increases. No matter how large market demand is, a single firm can produce it at least cost.

A temporary natural monopoly is shown in Figure 11.2. Observe that LRAC declines up to output Q^* and then becomes constant thereafter. Hence, as demand grows over time, a natural monopoly when demand DD prevails can become a workably competitive market when demand D_1D_1 holds.

One can argue that such a cost curve can be used to describe intercity telephone service. There are several factors that give rise to sharp unit-cost savings at low volumes of telephone calls, but they play out as volume increases.

For example, a microwave telephone system consists of a number of stations—about twenty to forty miles apart—that transmit signals of specific frequencies. Each station requires land, a building, a tower and antennas, electronic equipment, and so on. These inputs do not all increase proportionately with the number of circuits, and therefore as volume increases the fixed costs can be spread over more calls. This spreading effect becomes less and less significant, however, as volume grows.

As an example, long-distance telephone service between New York and Philadelphia required only 800 circuits in the 1940s. At this ca-

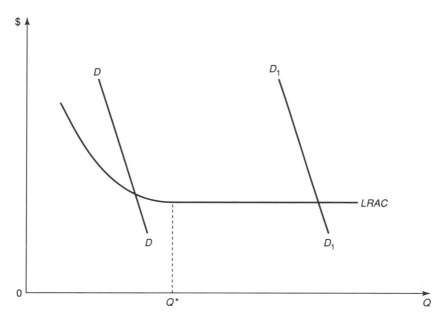

Figure 11.2
Temporary Natural Monopoly

pacity, unit costs were falling and constituted a natural monopoly situation. In the late 1960s the number of circuits had risen to 79,000
(largely because of the requirements of television), and this volume
was such that unit costs were essentially flat (beyond Q^* in Figure
11.2). Hence, by the late 1960s the temporary natural monopoly had
disappeared.

This phenomenon is not rare. Railroads possessed significant cost advantages in the late 1800s, and these advantages were eroded considerably with the introduction of trucking in the 1920s. This example
introduces a new element, namely, technological change.[3] That is, over
long periods of time it is likely that the cost function will shift as new
knowledge is incorporated into the production process. Hence, permanent natural monopoly is probably a rare category. Technical change
can shift cost functions so as to render competition workable. And as we
will see later, a serious deficiency of regulation seems to be that it often
fails to "disappear" when the natural monopoly does.

Subadditivity and Multiproduct Monopoly

In the real world a single-commodity producer is rare. Electric utilities
supply high and low voltage, peak and off-peak power; telephone companies provide local and long-distance service; and so on. It turns out

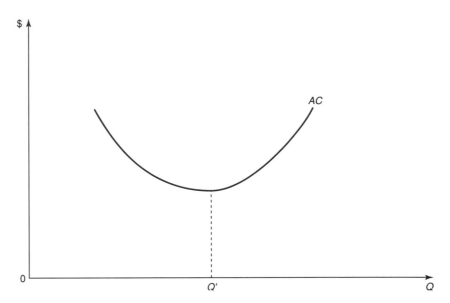

Figure 11.3
Economies of Scale up to Output Q'

that multiple-product natural monopoly is not only more realistic, but it also creates important theoretical issues that do not exist in the single-product case.

The definition of natural monopoly is that the cost function is subadditive.[4] We begin by explaining this concept in the single-product case because it can be illustrated graphically.

Consider the average cost curve shown in Figure 11.3. Average cost declines until the output Q' is reached, and then begins to increase. Economies of scale are said to exist at all outputs less than Q' and diseconomies at all outputs greater than Q'.

Subadditivity refers to whether it is cheaper to have one firm produce total industry output, or whether additional firms would yield lower total cost. For outputs less than Q', one firm is the least-cost solution, and therefore cost is subadditive for that range of outputs.

In order to examine the least-cost solution for outputs greater than Q', we introduce the minimum average cost function for two firms, AC_2. This curve and the single-firm AC curve from Figure 11.3 are both shown in Figure 11.4.

The curve AC_2 is obtained by construction from AC in the following manner. We know that for least-cost production, each firm must produce at the same output rate and thereby have the same marginal cost. Hence, for a given point on the AC curve, simply double the output rate

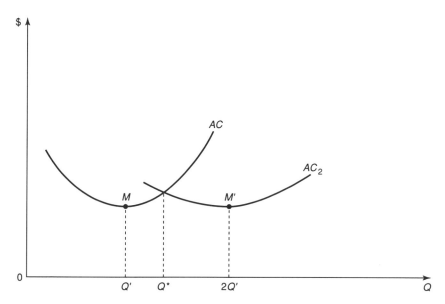

Figure 11.4
Minimum Average Cost Curve for Two Firms, AC_2

to obtain a point on the AC_2 curve. For example, at the minimum average cost point M on AC, double Q' to get $2Q'$, which corresponds to the minimum point M' on AC_2.

The intersection of AC and AC_2 at output Q^* defines the range of subadditivity. For all outputs less than Q^*, a single firm yields least-cost production. Hence the cost function is subadditive for outputs less than Q^*. Notice that subadditivity is the best way to define natural monopoly. Even though diseconomies of scale obtain between Q' and Q^*, it would be in society's interest to have a single firm produce in that range. An important point is that economies of scale (declining average cost) are not necessary for a single-product natural monopoly (although they are sufficient).

When we turn to multiple-product natural monopoly, the distinction between subadditivity and economies of scale becomes even greater. Again, the proper definition of natural monopoly is that the cost function is subadditive. That is, whatever the combination of outputs desired (say, 85 cars and 63 trucks, or 25 cars and 78 trucks), it is cheaper for a single firm to produce that combination if the cost function is subadditive.

In the multiple-output case, it can be shown that economies of scale are neither necessary nor sufficient for costs to be subadditive! Economies of scale would hold, for example, if the total cost of producing, say, a 10-percent greater quantity of each commodity increased by some amount less than 10 percent. The reason that economies of scale are neither necessary nor sufficient for subadditivity is that in the production of multiple outputs, the interdependence among outputs also becomes important.

Although various ways have been proposed for measuring these interdependencies, the concept of economies and diseconomies of scope is appealing intuitively.[5] Economies of scope mean that it is cheaper to produce, say, 85 cars and 63 trucks within a single firm than it is for specialty firms to produce the required outputs. If you think of peak-period electric power and off-peak power as different commodities, then economies of scope are clearly present—the two commodities can share the same power plant and distribution system.

Sharkey has given an example of a cost function that possesses economies of scale for all outputs, but which is nowhere subadditive.[6] His example is

$$C(Q_1, Q_2) = Q_1 + Q_2 + (Q_1 Q_2)^{1/3} \tag{11.1}$$

Notice that the total cost after increasing each output by 10 percent is

$$C(1.1Q_1, 1.1Q_2) = 1.1Q_1 + 1.1Q_2 + 1.1^{2/3}(Q_1 Q_2)^{1/3}$$

whereas the total cost increased by 10 percent is

$$1.1C(Q_1, Q_2) = 1.1Q_1 + 1.1Q_2 + 1.1(Q_1 Q_2)^{1/3}$$

Because the former is less than the latter, economies of scale exist. Nevertheless, the function has diseconomies of scope that sufficiently outweigh the economies of scale to make cost nowhere subadditive.

To see this, note that the third term in the cost function, equation (11.1), adds a positive amount to cost whenever both outputs are produced together. If, for example, all Q_1 was produced by firm A and all Q_2 was produced by firm B, then the sum of the total costs of the two firms would be less than if all production was carried out in a single firm, C. Specifically:

$$C_A = Q_1, \quad C_B = Q_2, \quad \text{so} \quad C_A + C_B = Q_1 + Q_2$$

$$C_C = Q_1 + Q_2 + (Q_1 Q_2)^{1/3}$$

Because $C_A + C_B < C_C$, production in the specialty firms, A and B, is cheaper than in a single firm, C. Thus, economies of scale are not sufficient for cost to be subadditive because of the diseconomies of scope.

In summary, the definition of natural monopoly in the multiple-output case is that the cost function must be subadditive. Subadditivity of the cost function simply means that the production of all combinations of outputs is accomplished at least cost by a single firm. It is a complex matter to specify the necessary and sufficient conditions for costs to be subadditive. We have shown through some simple examples, however, that it generally depends on both economies of scale and economies of scope. If both exist, then subadditivity will likely obtain.[7] Economies of scale alone, however, can be outweighed by diseconomies of scope. Thus, although economies of scale in the single-product case imply natural monopoly, this does not hold true for the multiple-product case.

Before turning to the various policy solutions to the natural monopoly problem, we shall briefly explain a related concept known as sustainability. It can be explained best by reference to Figure 11.5.

Figure 11.5 reproduces the cost function for the single-product case from Figure 11.4. Recall that the cost function is subadditive for outputs less than Q^*. Now consider a case in which market demand DD intersects average cost somewhere between Q' and Q^*, where AC is rising. If a single firm were to supply all output demanded at a price equal to average cost (at price P_0 and output Q_0 so that the firm would just cover all its costs), the natural monopoly would be termed unsustainable. That is, under certain assumptions, a potential entrant would have an in-

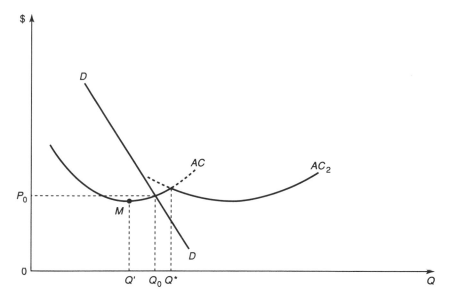

Figure 11.5
Sustainable Natural Monopoly up to Output Q'

centive to enter the market and produce a share of total output even though this would increase the cost of producing the total industry output.

The assumptions referred to above are that the entrant expects the incumbent firm to keep its price unchanged for some period of time after entry, and that the incumbent will supply the residual output.[8] Under these assumptions, the entrant would perceive that it could profit by offering to sell output Q' in Figure 11.4 at some price above its minimum average cost (point M) but slightly less than the price P_0 being charged by the incumbent.

By contrast, a sustainable natural monopoly would be one where market demand intersects AC in Figure 11.5 to the left of Q'. In this case an entrant cannot undercut the incumbent and therefore has no incentive to enter. The concept of sustainability is relevant where a regulatory agency must decide whether to allow entry in a particular market of a multiple-product natural monopolist.

Alternative Policy Solutions

In this section we examine various alternatives that have been proposed (and, in some cases, implemented) to correct the natural monopoly inefficiency. These alternatives include "doing nothing"; various "ideal" solutions; competition among bidders for the right to the monopoly franchise; and, finally, actual regulation, as practiced in the United States, and public enterprise, as exemplified by the Postal Service.

The first alternative mentioned above—doing nothing—might be appropriate if the potential monopoly power is not great. For example, a cable-television system might be viewed as a natural monopoly, but one with quite limited capacity for earning excess returns, for substitutes for cable television are rather close. Over-the-air broadcasting is one of them. Others are apparently becoming more important over time as new technologies are perfected. They include subscription television and satellite master antenna systems.

We consider first a collection of "ideal" pricing solutions. The adjective "ideal" is employed to indicate that we are assuming that the firm is to be operated in the public interest and that the only issue is what prices produce economic efficiency.

Ideal Pricing

The most obvious candidate for the efficient price is, of course, marginal cost.[9] A natural monopolist that charges marginal cost for each product is said to practice linear (or uniform) marginal cost pricing. In other words, a customer's expenditure for a product is a linear function of price and quantity sold, PQ. On the other hand, if the firm charges a fixed fee F, regardless of the amount bought, and also a per-unit charge P, nonlinear (or nonuniform) pricing would be in effect. Then the customer's expenditure would be a nonlinear function, $F + PQ$.

In our ideal pricing discussion, we begin with the linear marginal cost pricing solution. After considering nonlinear pricing we examine the so-called Ramsey pricing alternative, which applies to multiproduct cases. The section concludes with a discussion of a theoretical proposal by Loeb and Magat to induce profit-maximizing firms to price efficiently.

Linear Marginal Cost Pricing

Consider a single-product natural monopolist with decreasing average costs over the relevant output range. Figure 11.6 shows such a situation where market demand is DD.

The marginal cost price would be P_0 with output Q_0. The price does meet the well-known requirement for efficiency; however, on closer examination, several serious difficulties arise. An obvious difficulty is the loss, shown by the shaded rectangle RP_0ST.[10] Any enterprise would need a subsidy to continue to operate at this output level, because price

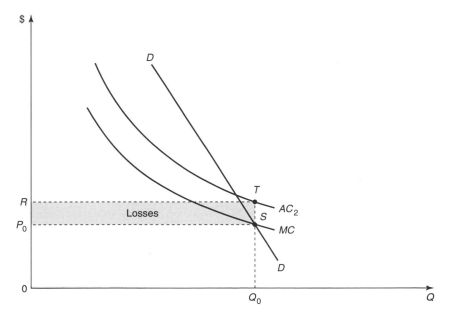

Figure 11.6
Marginal Cost Pricing Can Cause Losses

is less than average cost. The next question is to ask where the subsidy is to come from and what effect this will have on economic efficiency.

The only "correct" solution is for the government to raise the subsidy through a lump sum tax, that is, a tax that would not distort other decisions throughout the economy. Such taxes are rarely, if ever, used in practice. Income taxes and sales taxes are unacceptable because they create inefficiencies themselves by introducing wedges between prices and marginal costs. Even this "correct" solution (lump-sum tax to pay subsidy) is subject to some rather persuasive opposing arguments. Three frequently mentioned arguments are listed below.

1. If total costs are not covered by consumer expenditures, it is possible that total consumer benefits (given by the area under the demand curve)[11] are less than total costs—which means the good should not be produced at all. Figure 11.7 provides such a case. Total costs $AOQB$ (the area under the MC curve) exceed total benefits $DOQB$. Only if consumers are required to actually cover total costs can we be sure that the good is socially beneficial.

2. Because the enterprise's management knows losses will be subsidized, the incentive and capacity to control costs is weakened. Postal

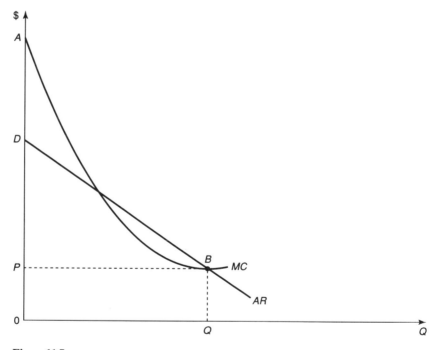

Figure 11.7
Natural Monopoly with Costs Exceeding Benefits

Service employees, for example, have an advantage in bargaining with management, inasmuch as both sides know that the enterprise will not fail if revenues are less than costs. The Treasury can always be counted on to subsidize the Postal Service in a pinch. Steel industry labor unions do not have this advantage.

3. On distributional grounds, it can be argued that nonbuyers of the natural monopoly good should not be required to subsidize the marginal cost buyers. That is, why should the taxes paid by individuals without telephone service be used to subsidize individuals who purchase such service at a loss-creating price?

A major point of the analysis above is that enterprises should price so that their revenues cover costs. Furthermore, in the United States, because most public utilities are privately owned firms, it is politically unrealistic to imagine government subsidizing the losses of private firms. Hence we conclude that there are compelling reasons to accept the constraint that natural monopolies should operate such that total revenues and total costs are equated.

In the single-product case, linear pricing implies that price must equal average cost if total revenues must equal total costs. This is shown in Figure 11.8 as price P_0 and output Q_0. This departure from marginal

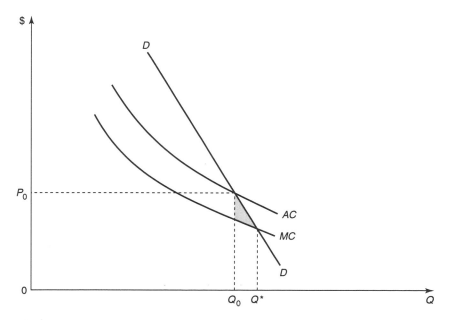

Figure 11.8
Welfare Loss with Average Cost Pricing

cost pricing leads, of course, to the welfare loss given by the shaded triangular area.[12]

The argument above refers to linear pricing; that is, the buyer pays a single price per unit and therefore the buyer's total expenditure is proportional to total consumption. An important alternative is nonlinear pricing.

Nonlinear Pricing

A two-part tariff is nonlinear and consists of a fixed amount or fee, regardless of consumption, plus a price per unit. If the price per unit equals marginal cost, then it is possible to have efficient pricing and have total revenues of the firm equal to its total costs.

For example, if the loss under linear marginal cost pricing is estimated to be K (the shaded rectangle in Figure 11.6), the fixed fee of the two-part tariff could be set so that the sum over all customers equals K. There are various ways for this to be true—the simplest is to set the fixed fee equal to K/N, where N equals the number of consumers.

There are possible problems with this nondiscriminatory two-part tariff. Because consumers usually vary considerably in terms of their demands for the good, it is possible for some consumers to be driven from the market if K/N exceeds their consumer surpluses at price equal to marginal cost. One might expect this to be more likely for, say, telephone service than for such "necessities" as electricity and water. Hence, efficiency losses will occur if these excluded consumers would have been willing to pay marginal cost. It is also true that in some markets it is not feasible to enforce a fixed fee for the "right-to-buy" at a price per unit. Consumers would have an incentive to have one person purchase for all, thereby paying only one fixed fee. This is not a problem for most public utilities.

The obvious thing to do to avoid excluding consumers is to charge different fixed fees to different consumers, or classes of consumers. In short, discriminatory two-part tariffs could tailor the fixed fees to the consumers' willingnesses-to-pay where the sum of the fixed fees should add up to K. Although this solution is best in terms of efficiency, it may be illegal to so discriminate.

If all consumers must be charged the same fixed fee, it will still be more efficient to use a two-part tariff than to use linear pricing (which in the case of a single product implies average cost pricing). The reason is simply that by using a fixed fee to make a contribution to revenues, the price per unit can be lowered toward marginal cost—thereby reducing deadweight losses. (In principle, one can pick some fixed fee, no matter how small, that will not drive anyone from the market and will permit a lowering of the price.)

The next logical question is, What is the optimal two-part tariff? Here, we explain only the economic principle involved.[13] Suppose initially that the fee is zero and price equals marginal cost. The result is, of course, a deficit that must be covered by increasing either the fee or the price per unit, or both. In essence, the derivation depends on a balancing of efficiency losses because of exclusion of additional consumers as the fixed fee rises against the increased consumption losses as price per unit increases above marginal cost. Hence the optimal two-part tariff generally will involve a price per unit that exceeds marginal cost and a fixed fee that excludes some consumers from the market.

Multipart tariffs are often used by public utilities. Consider the following example of the type of tariff sometimes used for local telephone service (such tariffs are often referred to as declining-block tariffs).

Fixed fee per month—$5

+10 cents per call for up to 100 calls

+5 cents per call for all calls between 100 and 200

+0 cents per call for all calls above 200

Notice that the marginal price falls as one moves to successively larger calling "blocks"—from 10 cents to 5 cents to 0 cents. This multipart tariff is plotted in Figure 11.9 as the bold segmented line *ABCD*. (The reason for the extensions of these segments in Figure 11.9 will become clear shortly.) Hence the figure shows "total consumer expenditure" vertically as a function of total "calls per month" horizontally.

A rationale often given for the declining blocks is that utilities are characterized by economies of scale, and falling marginal prices stimulate consumption—which, in turn, permit the construction of larger, lower-unit-cost plants. An alternative rationale is to view the declining-block tariff as a "self-selecting" set of two-part tariffs, and a set of such tariffs can increase economic efficiency along the lines discussed earlier.

Recall that discriminatory two-part tariffs permit the firm to tailor the tariffs to fit the differences in willingnesses-to-pay across consumers. The efficient solution can be achieved if no consumers are excluded from the market and all pay marginal cost per unit. As an approximation to this "ideal," one can use the multipart tariff in Figure 11.9 to cause consumers to self-select a two-part tariff that they prefer—wherein consumers with high willingnesses-to-pay pay high fixed fees in return for low prices per unit.

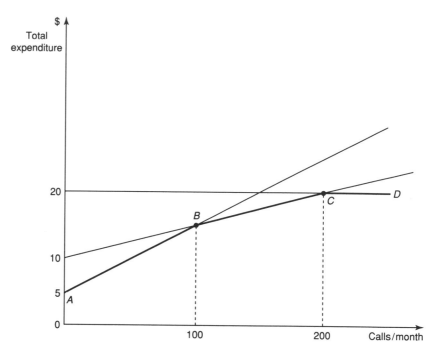

Figure 11.9
Multipart Tariff for Local Telephone Service

The three "self-selecting" two-part tariffs are

Fixed Fee	Price/Unit
$5	10 cents
$10	5 cents
$20	0 cents

One can represent a two-part tariff by a vertical intercept (for the fixed fee) and a straight line with slope equal to the price per unit. The three such lines in Figure 11.9 represent the three two-part tariffs referred to above. (Notice that no consumer would wish to consume on portions of the tariffs other than the lower boundary *ABCD*. Hence it does not matter that these "dominated" portions of the two-part tariffs are not actually part of the declining-block tariff.) The point is that the declining-block tariff has the same effect as confronting consumers with two-part tariffs that are tailored to their demands. And, of course, all consumers are free to choose the particular tariff that they prefer, so that there is no discrimination involved that is likely to be disallowed.

Up to this point our discussion of ideal pricing has been limited to a single-product natural monopolist. We now turn to the case of a multiple-product natural monopolist and describe what has become known as Ramsey pricing.

Ramsey Pricing

In a famous article published in 1927, Frank Ramsey suggested the following pricing (and taxing) method.[14] It is applicable to a multiple-product natural monopolist that would generate losses if linear marginal cost pricing were used. In essence, Ramsey prices are those linear prices that satisfy the total-revenues equal-total cost constraint and minimize the deadweight welfare losses. Note that Ramsey prices are linear prices—one for each product—so that we are implicitly ruling out multipart tariffs.

It is useful to illustrate Ramsey pricing with a numerical example. Let the natural monopoly be a two-product firm with total cost

$$C = 1800 + 20X + 20Y$$

The market demands for the two goods X and Y are given by

$$X = 100 - P_x$$

$$Y = 120 - 2P_y$$

An important assumption that we will make for our example is that the demands are independent—the demand for X does not depend on the price of Y, and vice versa. The more general case of interdependent demands involves much more complex mathematics and is beyond the scope of the discussion here.[15]

It should be obvious that the marginal costs of X and Y are each \$20, and that marginal cost prices would exactly cover the variable costs but not the fixed cost of \$1800. Because the firm must cover its total costs, it is clear that the prices will necessarily exceed their respective marginal costs. One possibility would be to raise the prices by the same proportion above marginal costs until total costs are covered. This is shown in Figure 11.10(a).

The figure shows that prices would need to be raised from \$20 to \$36.1 to generate sufficient revenues just to cover total costs.[16] In particular, the contribution that product Y makes toward fixed cost equals the rectangle $CEFD$. This is just price minus the constant unit variable cost of \$20, multiplied by the output of 47.7. Similarly, the contribution that product X makes equals rectangle $CEKJ$. The sum of these two rectangles is \$1800. (The fact that the demands intersect at the price equals marginal cost point for each is not necessary, and was chosen merely to make the graphical exposition simpler.)

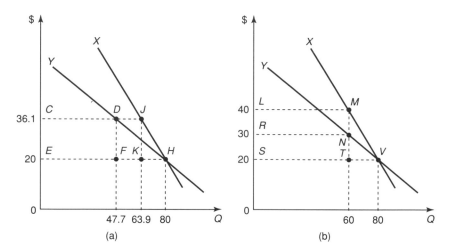

Figure 11.10
Proportionate Price Increase versus Ramsey Pricing

Now consider the deadweight losses that this proportionate price increase method causes. The deadweight loss triangle for product Y is triangle DFH, and is JKH for product X. The actual numerical values are $260 and $130, respectively, or a total of $390. Hence, one way of summing up this method is to observe that it "costs" $390 in deadweight welfare losses to generate the $1800 necessary for the firm to break even. The question becomes whether one can find another method for raising prices to generate the $1800 that entails a lower welfare cost.

A bit of reflection while examining Figure 11.10(a) might suggest differential price increases. That is, it is clear that the same price increase produces a smaller contribution to fixed cost from product Y at a higher cost in terms of deadweight loss. This is not surprising when one realizes that product X has a more inelastic demand (at point H) than does product Y. This suggests that it would be better to raise the price of X more than the price of Y.

The Ramsey pricing "rule" that gives the prices that minimize the deadweight losses is to raise prices in inverse proportion to demand elasticities. Mathematically, the rule[17] is

$$\frac{P_i - MC_i}{P_i} = \frac{\lambda}{e_i}$$

where

P_i = price of good i

MC_i = marginal cost of i

e_i = elasticity of demand of good i

λ = constant

Using this rule, one can derive the actual Ramsey prices.[18] They are shown in Figure 11.10(b). Hence the firm would minimize the welfare losses by charging $40 for good X and $30 for good Y. At these prices, the demand elasticities are 0.67 and 1.0, respectively. The deadweight loss triangles are $200 for good X (triangle MTV) and $100 for good Y (triangle NTV) for a total of $300. This is, of course, a lower "cost" in terms of welfare by $97 than the proportionate method of Figure 11.10(a).

Another interesting fact about Ramsey prices is apparent in Figure 11.10(b). The proportionate decrease in output from the price equals marginal cost output (outputs of 80 for both) is the same for the two goods. That is, both outputs are cut by $(80 - 60)/80$, or 25 percent. This is an alternative way of describing Ramsey pricing: cut output of all goods by the same proportion until total revenue just equals total cost. This way of stating the rule for Ramsey pricing is more general than the inverse elasticity rule, and holds true for the case of interdependent demands.

The Ramsey pricing rule can be viewed as providing theoretical justification for so-called "value of service" pricing that has been used for years in the railroad industry. It has been common for rail rates for shipping gravel, sand, potatoes, oranges, and grapefruits to be lower relative to shipping costs than for liquor, electronic equipment, cigarettes, and the like. The reason is that the elasticities of demand for shipping products that have low values per pound are higher than for products that have relatively high values per pound. (We are assuming that the actual costs of shipping are proportional to weight.)

In summary, all of the "ideal" pricing schemes discussed have problems (except for the two-part tariff with price equal to marginal cost and no exclusion of consumers by the fixed fee). It should be kept in mind that we have assumed away the very real difficulty of designing incentive systems that will induce enterprise managers to implement these pricing schemes. In short, managers of private firms are presumably interested in maximizing profits, not total economic surplus. Managers of public enterprises may also have objectives other than economic efficiency. Economists have recently begun to explore theoretical models of how regulatory agencies might provide incentives for natural monopolies to price efficiently. We will briefly describe the Loeb-Magat proposal below.

Loeb-Magat Proposal

Of course, if regulators had perfect information as to the monopolist's costs and demands, the ideal pricing schemes discussed above could be put into effect by command. However, such is not the case. Although the monopolist may not have perfect information itself, most people would probably agree that the monopolist has much better knowledge of its costs than the regulators do. Because the firm's profits will increase with higher prices, the firm has an incentive to overstate its costs (which is the usual basis that a regulator uses to set prices).

Loeb and Magat (L-M) assumed that the monopolist knows costs and demand information perfectly, but that the regulator knows demand only.[19] Hence, given this asymmetry of information and the assumption that the monopolist's objective is to maximize profit, what might the agency do to induce efficient pricing? The L-M scheme can be explained easily with the aid of Figure 11.11, which shows a single-product natural monopolist.

The monopolist has declining average cost (AC) and demand curve (AR). For simplicity, we assume the total cost function is $K + vX$; hence, marginal cost (MC) is constant and equal to v. The L-M proposal is to

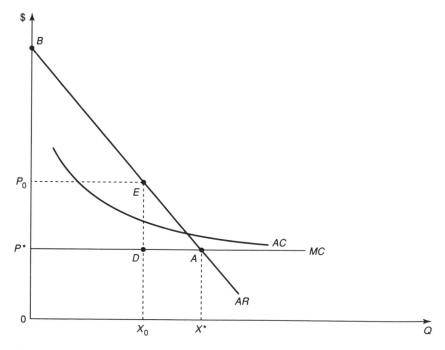

Figure 11.11
Loeb and Magat Incentive Scheme

allow the monopolist to choose its own price—this differs from the usual practice of the regulatory agency setting the price. However, they propose to have the agency subsidize the firm by an amount equal to consumer surplus at the selected price.

Suppose that the monopolist selects the price P_0. Its profits will be $P^*DEB - K$. The firm collects $0X_0EP_0$ from customers and P_0EB from the regulatory agency. Its variable cost is $0X_0DP^*$, leaving a variable profit of P^*DEB. Subtracting the fixed cost of K leaves the profit asserted above. Observe, however, that the firm can do better by lowering price. For example, if the monopolist selected P^*, it is easy to show that its profits will increase to $P^*AB - K$. That is, profits increase by the usual deadweight loss triangle DAE. This is, in fact, the profit-maximizing solution for the monopolist! Convince yourself that any other price will reduce profits. (Alternatively, note that the proposal causes the demand curve AR to become the monopolist's marginal revenue curve, and setting MC equal to marginal revenue is the profit-maximizing solution.)

The explanation for this price equal to marginal cost result is simply that the regulator has changed the firm's objective function by the subsidy. Now, in effect, the monopolist is maximizing total surplus—the total area under the demand curve minus costs.

The solution is economically efficient, but most people would find it objectionable on distributional grounds. The monopolist is appropriating the total economic surplus! To rectify this problem L-M suggest that a franchise bidding scheme (or a tax scheme) could recover some of the subsidy for the general treasury. In the case shown in Figure 11.11, the regulatory agency would auction off the right to operate the monopoly franchise. The key idea is that above-normal returns (of amount $P^*AB - K$) are available to the firm that operates the monopoly and that bidding for the franchise would continue until that amount is bid. Note that the subsidy is not completely recovered—there remains a net subsidy of an amount equal to fixed cost, K.[20]

Obviously, the L-M proposal is not the perfect solution to natural monopoly. Informational problems about the demand curve and the existence of a subsidy make it an unlikely substitute for the present regulatory process. It has, however, stimulated research by economists toward the goal of understanding how the regulatory process might be improved with respect to providing better incentive structures for natural monopolists.

In the next section we return to the discussion of alternative policy solutions to the natural monopoly problem. In contrast to the ideal pricing solutions that we have been examining heretofore, we now turn to actual solutions that have been used. The first is franchise bidding.

Franchise Bidding

Harold Demsetz has argued that the "theory of natural monopoly is deficient for it fails to reveal the logical steps that carry it from scale economies in production to monopoly price in the market place."[21] His point is that it may be possible to have bidding for the right to supply the entire demand (in effect, bidding for a franchise to serve a certain market). Even though only the single firm submitting the low bid would actually produce, there could be competition among potential suppliers. For example, given the situation shown in Figure 11.8, the low bid presumably would be a price of P_0 for Q_0 units.

Note that P_0 is not the efficient price. Nevertheless, P_0 would be an improvement over the natural monopoly price (a price above P_0). Then P_0 would be the lowest price bid for the right to supply the market inasmuch as any lower price would result in losses. At P_0 the winning bidder would just cover costs, including a normal return on investment.

This bidding for the franchise argument has stimulated a great deal of useful thinking about alternatives to natural monopoly regulation. However, the highly abstract example here oversimplifies many of the problems that such bidding would raise. A detailed discussion will be provided in Chapter 13.

Actual Solutions

In this section we briefly consider actual solutions that have been implemented in response to the natural monopoly problem. There are basically two distinct solutions: the regulatory agency and public enterprise. Extensive discussions of each will be presented in subsequent chapters; only a short treatment is given here.

Regulation

The typical natural monopoly in the United States is a private firm: Consolidated Edison, AT&T, El Paso Natural Gas, and so on. The firm is controlled by a regulatory agency that must approve the prices the monopolist can charge. A key goal is that the firm's revenues just cover its costs.

The measurement of costs is obviously a major task for the agency. Indeed, the attempt by the agency to estimate the proper return on capital investment is perhaps its most time-consuming activity. For example, a typical regulatory hearing involves testimony by numerous experts as to the "true" cost of capital for the firm.

In contrast, relatively little of the agency's resources are expended on the issue of the correct pricing structure. Recently, this has changed and agencies are becoming more interested in, for example, marginal cost pricing. In short, regulatory agencies try very hard to ensure that the monopolist's revenues equal its costs, and historically have been less concerned with the pricing structure used.

As a result, there is no simple way to describe the pricing structures used under regulation. Price discrimination is often employed both across customer groups (industrial, commercial, residential, and so on) and within groups (declining block rates, for instance, 5 cents per unit for the first 300 units, 4 cents per unit for the next 500 units, and so on).

Richard Schmalensee has observed,

> To the extent that utility regulators in the United States have been concerned with rate structures, they have tended to focus on prices paid by different classes of users. But this focus has typically been motivated and informed by considerations of equity or fairness rather than efficiency.[22]

Hence, regulatory agencies often try to prohibit undue discrimination across customer groups. They require the firm to allocate its total costs to customer groups and then adjust their prices if the revenues by groups do not correspond to the groups' "fully distributed costs."

There is a serious problem implicit in this procedure, however, because a large proportion of a firm's costs are usually common costs. For example, high-voltage power lines are used in common by all customer groups. And although arbitrary accounting rules can be made up to apportion these costs among groups (for instance, in proportion to their respective annual purchases of the product), none are meaningful in an economic sense as a basis for setting prices.

In summary, the predominant solution to natural monopoly in the United States is regulation. The regulatory solution is not an attempt to implement the ideal pricing schemes discussed earlier. Regulators do not see as their primary objective achieving economic efficiency. Rather, they appear to seek a set of prices that are not unduly discriminatory but that permit total revenues to cover total costs. Recently, however, regulatory agencies have become more interested in pricing schemes that promote economic efficiency. For example, peak pricing—charging more when demand presses on capacity, and, therefore, marginal cost is higher—is being implemented by electric utilities in various parts of the country.

Public Enterprise

The second actual solution to natural monopoly is public enterprise, or government ownership and operation of the monopoly. This is not as common in the United States as it is in other countries. The Postal Service is an example in the United States. Other examples include various government-owned electric utilities (for instance, the Tennessee Valley Authority) and Amtrak, the government-owned passenger service railroad.

In other countries, public enterprise is a frequent solution in the public utility sector. For example, electricity, telecommunications, gas, and railroads are primarily public enterprises in Europe. However, in recent years a number of countries such as Great Britain have been "privatizing" their public enterprises. That is, they are selling public enterprises to private investors and then instituting regulation.

In principle, public enterprise would appear to be a sensible alternative. Managers would be directed to maximize economic surplus—there would be no need for regulators to try to channel the decisions of profit-maximizing firms closer to the public interest. The efficacy of public enterprise as compared to regulation, however, is a complex issue and will be examined further in Chapter 14.

Summary

This chapter has been an introduction to natural monopoly. Theoretical issues have been introduced and discussed. First, the definition of natural monopoly was developed in both the single-product and the multiple-product cases. Second, alternative policy solutions and their difficulties were discussed. The solutions included "doing nothing," various efficient pricing solutions, competition among bidders for the right to the monopoly franchise, actual regulation, and public enterprise.

In the next chapter we will elaborate extensively on the regulation alternative. Chapter 15 will examine further issues in natural monopoly regulation, with an emphasis on telecommunications.

Questions and Problems

1. Consider a single-product natural monopoly situation with the usual U-shaped long run average cost curve. Is the range of output over which natural monopoly holds from zero to the output corresponding to minimum average cost? If not, explain how to determine the appropriate range.

2. Assume a natural monopoly with total costs $C = 500 + 20Q$. Market demand is $Q = 100 - P$.

    a. If price is set at marginal cost, what is the monopolist's profit?

    b. The answer to (a) implies that linear (or uniform) marginal cost pricing has a scrious problem in natural monopoly situations. Suppose that average cost pricing is employed. Find price, output, and the deadweight loss compared to (a).

c. Now consider two-part pricing—a type of nonlinear (or nonuniform) pricing. Each consumer must pay a fixed fee regardless of consumption level plus a price per unit. Assume that the market consists of ten consumers with identical demand curves for the product. If the price is set equal to marginal cost, what is the largest fixed fee that a consumer would pay for the right to buy at that price? What fixed fee would permit the monopolist to break even? What is the deadweight loss in this case?

3. Assume the same facts as in question 2 but that now there are six "rich" consumers with each having inverse demands: $p = 100 - 6.3q$; also, there are four "poor" consumers each with demands: $p = 100 - 80q$.

a. What is the largest fixed fee that a poor consumer would pay for the right to buy at marginal cost?

b. Because the poor consumers would not be willing to pay the uniform fixed fee of $50 necessary for the monopolist to break even, the rich consumers would have to pay a fixed fee of $83.33. What is the deadweight loss in this case?

c. Third-degree price discrimination could be a solution. That is, if it is legal, resales are not feasible, and consumers could be identified by the monopolist as being rich or poor, the monopolist could charge different fixed fees to the two consumer types. If the price per unit is still equal to marginal cost, what are two fixed fees that are feasible? In this case, what is the deadweight loss?

4. If third-degree price discrimination is not a feasible alternative in 3(c), consider the optimal two-part tariff. That is, what is desired is the two-part tariff that minimizes deadweight loss—or that maximizes total surplus. One way to think about it is to imagine the case of a zero fixed fee and price equal to marginal cost. This causes a loss of $500 that must be covered. Imagine raising both the fixed fee and the price simultaneously—both can cause losses: the fee by excluding poor consumers and the price by causing deadweight consumption losses. One possibility is to exclude poor consumers and go to solution 3(b). The other possibility is to keep all consumers in the market; this implies that the fixed fee should equal the consumer surplus of a poor consumer. It is optimal to take all of the poor consumers' surpluses as a fee. To see why, consider the opposite case where the poor have some excess of surplus over the fee. Then the price could be lowered, reducing deadweight losses and the surplus could be used to offset the reduction in revenues without excluding the poor from the market.

a. Find the sum of consumer and producer surplus minus the $500 fixed cost (that is, find total surplus) for case 3(b) where the poor are excluded.

b. Find total surplus for the case of all consumers retained in the market. Hint: An equation in P can be defined that equates to $500 the total contributions to fixed cost (10 times the fixed fee, equal to the consumer surplus of a poor consumer, plus the revenues net of variable cost generated by consumption). Hence, what is the optimal two-part tariff where all are retained in the market?

c. Compare the efficiency of the tariffs in (a) and (b).

5.   A multipart tariff can be superior to the optimal two-part tariff found in
     question 4. A multipart tariff involves a fixed fee plus multiple prices per
     unit, which depend upon predefined blocks of consumption.

     a. Show that by making an additional two-part tariff available to the
     consumers that they can use at their option, the "two" two-part tariffs are
     Pareto superior to the optimal tariff in question 4 (that is, $F = \$38.55$, $P =$
     $\$21.50$). Let the optional two-part tariff be $P = \$20.50$ and $F = \$51$. These
     two two-part tariffs are equivalent to a multipart tariff that has a fixed fee
     of $\$38.55$ and a price of $\$21.50$ for the first 12.4 units and a price of $\$20.50$
     for all units above 12.4. Show this by plotting the two tariffs on a graph
     that has total expenditure on the vertical axis and total units on the hori-
     zontal axis. The two straight lines representing the tariffs intersect at 12.4
     units. Because consumers will always operate on the lowest line that they
     can attain to minimize expenditure, the multipart tariff is just the lower
     boundary (that is, the kinked line defined by $F = \$38.55$ and the marginal
     prices of $\$21.50$ for the first 12.4 units and $\$20.50$ thereafter).

     b. Demonstrate that the two two-part tariffs are Pareto superior to the
     optimal two-part tariff in 4(b). Note that the optional tariff will not change
     the poor consumers' behavior at all. Why?

     c. As a result we can focus solely on the rich consumers and the mo-
     nopoly. If both are made better off by the optional tariff and the poor are
     kept the same, then the optional tariff results in a Pareto improvement—
     which is a stronger welfare statement than simply saying one tariff yields a
     higher total surplus. (That is, if we focus on total surplus comparisons, we
     ignore the fact that some people may be made worse off even though total
     surplus is higher.) Find the consumer surplus of a rich consumer under the
     two-part tariff of 4(b).

     d. Find the consumer surplus of a rich consumer under the multipart
     tariff.

     e. Find the change in profit of the monopolist. Hence a movement from
     two-part tariffs to multipart tariffs clearly has the potential for gains in
     efficiency. The intuition is that the more the "parts," the better the tariff
     can be tailored to the differences in willingness-to-pay across consumers.

6.   Assume that a water distribution monopoly serves two consumer types:
     industrial and residential. The demands by the two classes are as follows.
     Industrial: $Q_I = 30 - P_I$ and Residential: $Q_R = 24 - P_R$. The company has
     no costs other than the fixed cost of the pipeline, which is $\$328$. Find the
     Ramsey prices.

7.   Assume a natural monopoly with total cost $500 + 20Q$ facing a demand of
     $Q = 100 - P$.

     a. Find the price that enables the monopolist to break even. (This is the
     same problem as 2(b).) Call this price P^*.

     b. Loeb and Magat show that if the monopolist is allowed to choose its
     own price and to have the regulatory agency subsidize the firm by an
     amount equal to consumer surplus at the selected price, the monopoly will
     select price equal to marginal cost. What is the price and amount of gov-
     ernment subsidy?

     c. Loeb and Magat also note that a bidding process for the monopoly
     franchise would enable the government to recover some of the subsidy.
     What is the amount recovered and what is the net subsidy after bidding?

d. An alternate proposal would make use of two-part tariffs. For example, assume that the current regulated price is P^*. Now assume that the regulatory agency offers the firm the right to select any two-part tariff that it wishes as long as the consumer continues to have the option of buying at P^*. (For simplicity, assume a single consumer.) What is the two-part tariff that the monopolist will choose and what is its profit? What is the deadweight loss?

e. Assume that the government uses a bidding process to eliminate the monopoly profit in (d). The bid is in the form of a single price, like P^*, that the consumer will always have as an option to the two-part tariff. That is, the same rules are in effect as in (d) except that now the bidding is for the right to offer a two-part tariff optional to some P^* that the bidding will determine. What is the low bid?

f. Compare the Loeb and Magat proposal in (c) with the proposal in (e). Do both proposals give efficient prices? Are there any substantive differences?

Notes

1. Entry, induced by the monopoly price, is usually assumed to be unlikely in natural monopoly situations.

2. The term permanent is perhaps misleading inasmuch as one can never rule out dramatic technological changes that could convert a natural monopoly into a competitive structure industry.

3. Strictly speaking, technical change in lowering costs was also present in the telephone service example above.

4. An important article that defines natural monopoly this way is W. J. Baumol, "On the Proper Cost Tests for Natural Monopoly in a Multiproduct Industry," *American Economic Review*, December 1977.

5. See, for example, J. C. Panzar and R. D. Willig, "Economies of Scope," *American Economic Review*, May 1981.

6. William W. Sharkey, *The Theory of Natural Monopoly* (New York: Cambridge University Press, 1982).

7. For a rigorous analysis, see W. J. Baumol, J. C. Panzar, and R. D. Willig, *Contestable Markets and the Theory of Industry Structure* (New York: Harcourt Brace Jovanovich, 1982).

8. A further assumption is that the entrant perceives no entry barriers in the form of "sunk" costs. That is, the entrant believes that whatever investment is required can be recovered by transferring it elsewhere or by sale. All of these assumptions have been subject to controversy since the sustainability literature was introduced by Baumol, Panzar, and Willig.

9. See Chapter 4 for a detailed rationale. For a rigorous treatment of efficient pricing, see R. R. Braeutigam, "Optimal Policies for Natural Monopolies," in R. Schmalensee and R. D. Willig (eds.), *Handbook of Industrial Organization*, Vol. 2 (Amsterdam: North-Holland, 1989), and D. F. Spulber, *Regulation and Markets* (Cambridge, Mass.: MIT Press, 1989). For a more geometrical treatment, see K. E. Train, *Optimal Regulation* (Cambridge, Mass.: MIT Press, 1991).

10. The loss is equal to the difference between price and average cost, multiplied by output.

11. Throughout this chapter we make the common assumption that the area under the demand curve measures total willingness-to-pay by consumers. This requires one to assume that the income elasticity of demand is zero (or small enough to make the error unimportant). See R. D. Willig, "Consumer's Surplus without Apology," *American Economic Review*, September 1976.

12. For a discussion of welfare loss determination, see Chapter 4.

13. See Stephen J. Brown and David S. Sibley, *The Theory of Public Utility Pricing* (New York: Cambridge University Press, 1986), p. 93, for a formal analysis.

14. Frank Ramsey, "A Contribution to the Theory of Taxation," *Economic Journal*, March 1927.

15. The interested reader should consult Brown and Sibley, *The Theory of Public Utility Pricing*, p. 42.

16. Because P_x and P_y must be equal under the assumption that the marginal costs are both $20, the $36.1 value can be found by solving the equation that equates total revenues and total costs.

17. See Brown and Sibley, p. 39, for a formal derivation.

18. Computations are made simpler by using the alternative rule for Ramsey prices that will be given shortly involving proportionate quantity changes. That rule implies that the two products will have equal outputs. Hence this fact together with the total revenues equal total costs equation yields the Ramsey prices.

19. Martin Loeb and Wesley Magat, "A Decentralized Method for Utility Regulation," *Journal of Law and Economics*, 1969. Some additional research on this same issue can be found in Ingo Vogelsang and Jorg Finsinger, "A Regulatory Adjustment Process for Optimal Pricing by Multiproduct Monopoly Firms," *Bell Journal of Economics*, 1979; D. P. Baron and R. B. Myerson, "Regulating a Monopolist with Unknown Costs," *Econometrica*, 1982; D. Sappington, "Optimal Regulation of a Multiproduct Monopoly with Unknown Technological Capabilities," *Bell Journal of Economics*, 1983. A comprehensive though difficult recent survey is D. P. Baron, "Design of Regulatory Mechanisms and Institutions," in R. Schmalensee and R. D. Willig (eds.), *Handbook of Industrial Organization*.

20. For a variation on the Loeb and Magat proposal that eliminates the net subsidy and the need of the regulator to know demand, see D. A. Graham and J. M. Vernon, "A Note on Decentralized Natural Monopoly Regulation," *Southern Economic Journal*, July 1991.

21. Harold Demsetz, "Why Regulate Utilities?," *Journal of Law and Economics*, April 1968.

22. Richard Schmalensee, *The Control of Natural Monopolies* (Lexington, Mass.: Lexington Books, 1979).

The theory of natural monopoly and alternative policy solutions were the main topics of the last chapter. The most common policy solution in the United States—regulation—is the subject of this chapter. Electric power will be used as our primary example, although some references to other regulated natural monopolies will be made, such as telephone service, natural gas distribution, and water supply.

In examining regulation, it is useful to keep in mind the benefits and costs. The benefit is to reduce deadweight losses in efficiency that would exist under unregulated monopoly. The costs are less obvious, but include the direct costs of regulatory agencies as well as unintended side effects of regulation. An important side effect is higher costs because of changed incentive structures of regulated firms.

The technology for centralized production and distribution of electric power was first put into operation in September 1882 in New York City, where Thomas Edison began producing electricity in the famous Pearl Street plant of the Edison Electric Illuminating Company. In 1876, Alexander Graham Bell received a patent on the telephone. Hence these two important utilities have been in existence only for about a hundred years.

During the early years the common method of regulation was by the award of a franchise by the town or city. The city would normally grant a franchise for exclusive operation within the city in return for an agreement by the firm that it would provide a certain quality of service at certain rates. As the technology changed and firms began to serve larger regions and even entire states, community regulation became ineffective. It also became more efficient to have regulatory experts at the state level only, rather than having duplicate experts in every community. Finally, the franchise agreement was not very flexible in dealing with constantly changing economic conditions. All these factors led to the institution of the regulatory commission at the state level. The first such commissions began in 1907 in New York, Wisconsin, and Georgia. All states have regulatory commissions today.

Most of the discussion in this chapter will be concerned with state regulatory commissions, but we should observe that several federal regulatory agencies are also involved in natural monopoly regulation. For example, the Federal Energy Regulatory Commission (FERC) regulates interstate wholesale transactions of electricity and natural gas pipelines. The Federal Communications Commission (FCC) regulates interstate telephone service. Although this list is not complete, it does indicate a diverse group of regulators and regulated industries.

The regulatory commission is usually appointed by the governor or President, although in some states the commissioners are elected or appointed by the legislature. A typical commission consists of three to twelve commissioners who arc assisted by a staff of up to 2500 members. Many state commissions are smaller. The staff members are trained in accounting, engineering, economics, and the law.

Some data on the North Carolina Utilities Commission in a recent year are instructive. The North Carolina Utilities Commission, with seven commissioners and 147 staff members, regulated over 1000 utility companies. Many of these companies were small trucking companies and water and sewer companies. Three large electric utilities supplied power in the state, three large companies distributed natural gas, and two large telephone companies were operative.

The commissions typically focus on prices charged by the monopolist. Their mandate is usually somewhat vague, such as requiring that prices be "just and reasonable" and that there be no "undue discrimination." The procedure is that prices are set in rate cases and are generally fixed until the next case. Rate cases are similar to civil court cases. Expert witnesses on various topics are heard (for instance, economists testify on the cost of capital) with the final decision being made by the commissioners. In certain cases, appeal to higher courts is possible.

In the next section we will discuss the typical features of the rate case. The following sections focus on so-called rate level and rate structure issues. The rate level concerns the relation of overall revenues to costs, whereas the rate structure deals with how individual prices are set.

The Rate Case

The company being regulated usually initiates the rate case by applying for an increase in the prices (or rates) that it charges. A "test period" is selected—usually the last accounting period. Adjustments are made to reflect known changes that affect financial data. For example, it might be known that a natural gas distribution company will have to pay higher prices in the future for the gas it purchases from the pipeline. These changes are factored into the computation of the company's rate of return.

Accounting Equation

In essence, the following accounting equation describes the process:

$$\sum_{i=1}^{n} p_i q_i = \text{Expenses} + s(RB) \tag{12.1}$$

where

p_i = price of ith service

q_i = quantity of ith service

n = number of services

s = allowed or "fair" rate of return

RB = the rate base, a measure of the value of the regulated firm's investment

The underlying idea, of course, is that the company's revenues must just equal its costs, so that economic profit is zero. Notice that economically efficient prices are not required by the equation, only prices that cover total costs.

As observed above, it is common to discuss the regulation of natural monopoly in two parts: the rate-level problem and the rate-structure problem. The rate-level problem is concerned primarily with finding s so that the company will have the appropriate level of earnings on its investment (or rate base). The rate structure problem deals with issues of price discrimination among customer classes and products, that is, the p_i on the left-hand side of equation (12.1).

To begin a rate case, a company will submit detailed financial exhibits that show, for example, that at current prices its rate of return on its rate base for the test period is too low. It probably will argue that its true cost of capital is such that it needs a higher return in order "to continue to attract capital." Basically, what the company is arguing is that the prices it is now charging—as set in the last rate case—are too low. The commission staff will probably argue that the company's requested rate of return is too high, and that prices need not be raised as much as the company wants.

Eventually, after much testimony, the commissioners must make a determination of what they believe the rate of return should be, that is, the value of s. Assuming that they choose an s value that is higher than the company is now earning, the prices on the left-hand side in equation (12.1) will be adjusted to yield the new rate of return allowed by the commission. (Raising the prices will change the quantities bought, so correct regulatory decisionmaking requires information on demand elasticities.)

Regulatory Lag

Once the new prices are set, they remain unchanged until the next rate case. Hence the period during which prices remain fixed provides an incentive for the company to be cost efficient. The company is able to

Table 12.1
North Carolina Natural Gas Corporation Statement

	Year Ended Dec. 31, 19xx	Adjustments for Rate Increase	After Adjustments for Rate Increase
Revenues	$29,572,747	$2,832,332	$32,405,079
Expenses			
(1) Purchased gas	$19,411,430		$19,411,430
(2) Labor	2,968,387		2,968,387
(3) Depreciation	1,234,798		1,234,798
(4) Taxes	4,338,300	358,500	4,696,800
Total expenses	27,952,915	358,500	28,311,415
(5) *Net Operating Income*	1,619,832		4,093,664
Rate Base			
Plant less depreciation	41,871,387		41,871,387
Working capital	1,002,989		1,002,989
(6) Total	42,874,376		42,874,376
(7) Rate of return [(5)/(6)]	3.77%		9.54%

earn higher rates of return than allowed if it can reduce its costs and, of course, earn lower rates of return if its costs rise. This incentive for cost efficiency is often referred to as the result of regulatory lag. That is, if the commission were somehow able continuously to adjust prices to keep the company's rate of return always equal to s, there would be no lag and, importantly, no incentive for cost efficiency.

Before turning to more detailed discussion of the rate level and rate structure problems, it should be instructive to examine Table 12.1. This table presents an abbreviated exhibit used in a past rate case by North Carolina Natural Gas Corporation. It shows the effect of a proposed rate increase that the company requested.

The first of the three columns shows the financial data for the year ended December 31, 19xx. Hence the company had total revenues (the left-hand side of (12.1)) of over $29 million. After subtracting its expenses for purchasing gas, labor, depreciation, and taxes, it had a net operating income (row 5) of $1.6 million. The company's net investment or rate base is shown in row 6 as $42.9 million. This yields a rate of return of only 3.77 percent (that is, net operating income divided by the rate base).

The second column shows the adjustment for an increase in prices that is expected to raise an additional $2.8 million in revenues. These higher revenues require higher taxes, as is also shown in this column. Other adjustments could also be shown in this column—such as for higher costs for purchased gas—but we have suppressed additional adjustments for clarity.

The third column shows the way the company would like their financial results to look. That is, the company has estimated that the allowed rate of return s should be 9.54 percent, and so it has built-in price increases necessary to increase its rate of return to that figure. As we will see in the next section, the rate level problem is almost completely that of determining the appropriate value of s.

The Rate Level

The rate-level problem, as we observed earlier, is concerned with determining the values of the variables on the right-hand side of equation (12.1). That is, what are the legitimate expenses of the firm, including its required return on investment? The expenses (fuel costs, wages and salaries, taxes, and depreciation) usually account for about 80 to 85 percent of the total costs of the firm, with the remainder being the return on investment. Although these expenses are large, commissions typically do not spend much time monitoring them. They sometimes question advertising expenses (which might be viewed as trying to persuade the public that the company needs a rate increase). Sometimes they examine the salaries of top management. If the company purchases its inputs from a wholly owned subsidiary, it certainly needs to decide if the prices charged are reasonable.

Rate Base Valuation

In recent years, some commissions have taken a tough approach on whether to allow certain investments to become part of the rate base. This, and regulatory lag, appear to be the main forces that provide incentives for regulated firms to be cost efficient. Consider, for example, the following excerpt from a recent annual report of the California Public Utilities Commission:

In May 1987, the PUC Public Staff Division's Diablo Canyon Team recommended that of the $5.518 billion that PG&E spent before commercial operation of Diablo Canyon Nuclear Power Plant, the utility should only be allowed to collect $1.150 billion in rates.... The Public Staff Division alleges that unreasonable management was to blame for a large part of this cost overrun.[1]

Generally, the largest portion of a rate case is devoted to the issue of what the proper return to investment should be—or what should be the values of s and RB in equation (12.1). In terms of Table 12.1, the company proposed that s should be 9.54 percent and that the rate base should be $42.9 million.

One point that should be obvious is that what really matters is the product of the two variables, that is, 0.0954 times $42.9 million, or $4 million. In fact, much controversy used to surround the determination of both variables. At the present time it appears that many commissions have turned to an original cost method of valuing the rate base, and thus turned most of their attention to the appropriate value of s. That is, original cost valuation is simply the amount that the company originally paid for their plant and equipment, less depreciation. There can be little debate about the actual numbers in original cost valuation (aside, of course, from the issue of imprudent investment). Other valuation methods are much more subject to judgment calls. For example, valuing the rate base by reproduction cost means to estimate the current cost of reproducing the plant, even though some of the plant may be twenty years old.

One concern about using original cost is that in periods of inflation the reproduction cost rate base will exceed the original cost rate base. That is, an electric utility might have built much of its capacity at much lower plant prices twenty years ago. To reproduce the plants at current prices might cost five times original cost. And, because the economically correct prices should reflect current marginal costs, it might be thought that original cost leads to a setting of prices that are too low. This is certainly a possibility if the commission determines price by simply dividing the sum of "Expenses" and $s(RB)$ by quantity.

However, in principle the commission is not bound by this method. Ideally, the prices should depend on current marginal costs, and if these prices yield total revenues that are too high or too low in terms of the rate-level "solution," it is necessary only to adjust fixed fees in an appropriate manner. (Recall from Chapter 11 that economic efficiency generally requires only that prices per unit equal marginal costs—fixed fees, independent of output, can be adjusted to cover deficits or return additional revenues.)

There are other valuation methods that we should also mention. Replacement cost refers to what it would cost to replace the capacity with plants embodying the newest technology—as opposed to simply reconstructing the older-technology plants at today's prices. Another valuation method is simply to add up the value of all of the company's outstanding stocks and bonds, as given daily in the *Wall Street Journal*. This method has the defect that it is circular. The purpose of finding a rate base is so that the prices and returns can be determined; but the market-value method just described takes as the rate base a value that depends on prices and returns set by the commission in the past. (As we shall discuss shortly, the value of a share of common stock is a function of the firm's earnings per share.) In any case, we will proceed to discuss the determination of the allowed rate of return s under the assumption that the rate base is valued at original cost.

Actually, utilities are financed by investors in bonds, preferred stock, and common stock. For this reason, the allowed rate of return s that we seek is a weighted average of the costs of these three types of securities. For example, a 1993 rate case included the following estimate:

	Percent of Capitalization	Percent Cost
Bonds	48	9.34
Preferred stocks	14	8.22
Common stocks	38	12.5
	100	10.4 (weighted average)

The first two types of securities, bonds and preferred stocks, are not controversial because they have easily determined costs. The 9.34 percent figure for bonds is the so-called embedded cost; that is, it is the actual cost in interest payments that the company incurred when it issued all of its bonds in the past. Preferred stock also has a known yield. Hence the really controversial issue is what value should be used for the cost of common stock, which we shall denote by k. In the example above $k = 12.5$ percent, and therefore $s = 10.4$ percent. (That is, $s = (0.48)(9.34) + (0.14)(8.22) + (0.38)(12.5)$.)

Cost of Equity Capital

The estimation of the cost of equity capital, k, is the subject of an extensive literature in finance.[2] We can indicate only briefly here how it might be estimated. Although alternate conceptual methods exist, perhaps the most popular method is the discounted cash-flow method. Consider a share of common stock of Commonwealth Edison currently traded on the New York Stock Exchange at a price P. How is this price determined? One view is that it is equal to the present value of the stream of dividends expected by investors. In equation form,

$$P = \frac{D_1}{1+k} + \frac{D_2}{(1+k)^2} + \cdots + \frac{D_i}{(1+k)^i} + \cdots \tag{12.2}$$

where

P = price of stock

D_1 = expected dividend in year 1

D_2 = expected dividend in year 2

D_i = expected dividend in year i

k = cost of equity capital

Hence, k is simply the discount rate used by investors—it is the rate of return the investors can obtain on their next best opportunity at the same degree of riskiness. Now if we assume that investors expect dividends to grow at some constant rate g, where g is less than k, equation (12.2) can be solved for the unknown k:

$$k = D_1/P + g \qquad (12.3)$$

Assume that the current dividend yield D_1/P is 8 percent and investors expect that dividends will grow over time at 7 percent. Then equation (12.3) would yield 15 percent as the cost of equity capital.

A moment's thought reveals that this method of determining k is subject to great uncertainty. How should the dividend yield be measured? Should it be the yield security analysts expect? Or should it be the last year's dividend divided by the average stock price? Perhaps even more difficult is how to choose g. Should it be the average growth rate over the last three or five or ten years? In fact, past growth rates may be totally unrelated to what happens in the future. Also, should the estimates of k be based on the particular company under review, or should they be based on averages of a group of companies with about the same degree of risk for investors? Clearly, the possibilities for differences of opinion on the value of k are numerous.[3]

A somewhat subtle unintended cost of regulation can be noted here. The value of k depends upon the riskiness of the firm as perceived by investors. Simply put, a typical risk-averse investor in security A with a certain return of 8 percent would require, perhaps, 10 percent from security B if its return were subject to some uncertainty. That is, the investor would require a risk premium to compensate for the uncertainty. To the extent that the uncertainty is due to the behavior of the regulatory agency itself—for example, by setting rates in a very unpredictable manner—the cost of equity capital will be higher than necessary.

It is appropriate to step back at this point and consider the economic function of the rate of return. In competitive markets the function of the rate of return is to attract capital into the industry (that is, by paying for capital) and to provide an incentive for efficiency. Firms in competitive markets are rewarded by high profits if they are efficient, and punished by low profits or losses if not. Generally, commissions seem to regard the first function as the more important. This has a legal basis. A famous Supreme Court decision in 1944, *Federal Power Commission v. Hope Natural Gas Co.*, held that rates should be set to enable the company to operate successfully, to maintain its financial integrity, to attract capital, and to compensate its investors for the risks involved.

Recently, however, there have been some steps taken by commissions to reward efficient utilities and penalize the inefficient ones. Although these new steps do not necessarily operate by adjusting the allowed rate of return, it is instructive to consider the possibility of tying s to the firm's performance. There are undoubtedly serious problems in measuring a firm's performance, but one often-heard problem is not true— namely, that the firm must have a value of s that is not less than its cost of capital or it cannot attract capital.

Suppose for simplicity that a firm is known to have a cost of capital of 10 percent and the commission allows it a rate of return of $s = 10$ percent. The firm could raise capital by selling stock and using the proceeds to invest in new plant, earning the necessary 10 percent rate of return. Now suppose that the commission elects to cut its s value from 10 to 9 percent to penalize the firm for some inefficient behavior. Would the firm now be unable to raise capital to build needed new capacity? Clearly, the answer is that the firm *could* raise new capital—but its stock price would fall, inflicting losses on its existing owners. It is also true that the company would resist raising capital under the conditions cited, but it could do so. The point is that temporary adjustments in the allowed rate of return could be made without fear of the company being unable to attract capital.

The Sliding Scale Plan

Joskow and Schmalensee have analyzed a variety of proposals for incentive regulation of electric utilities.[4] One method, known as a "sliding scale" plan, is described below. It is interesting in that it has been used in practice (although rarely), and it also has some features that theoretical work has suggested as desirable. The essential property is that it permits the sharing of risks and rewards between the owners and consumers.

Let r^* be the target rate of return and let r_t be the actual rate of return at the prices that prevail initially in year t. The sliding scale would adjust prices so that the actual rate of return, r_a, at the new prices would be

$$r_a = r_t + h(r^* - r_t) \tag{12.4}$$

where h is a constant between zero and unity. Notice that if $h = 1$, regulation is essentially "cost-plus." That is, prices are always adjusted to give the firm a rate of return of r^*. The firm would neither benefit from being efficient nor be hurt by being inefficient.

Similarly, if $h = 0$, then regulation is basically "fixed-price." All gains from efficiency accrue to the firm, and all unexpected cost increases beyond management's control also affect the firm alone. An h value of 0.5, however, would share unexpected benefits and costs equally. The "optimal" value of h is unknown; however, one would think that neither extreme is likely to be best.

Price Caps and Performance Standards

In recent years, "price cap" regulation for telephone companies has been used by the FCC and some states in lieu of rate-of-return regulation. It is a form of regulation used in Britain for their recently "privatized" industries—such as telephones, gas, and water. ("Privatized" refers to the fact that government-owned industries were sold to private investors.)

The price cap used by the FCC is set so that AT&T is free to raise its prices at the rate of inflation minus some amount selected to reflect expected productivity. For example, the productivity might be 3 percent and if inflation is 5 percent, AT&T could raise its prices at $5 - 3 = 2$ percent per year. Of course, the company would be free to charge lower prices if this should appear to be more profitable. Price cap regulation is viewed as providing incentives for the firms so regulated to be cost efficient. In a sense, it builds regulatory lag into the process in a non-accidental way. And, of course, it is quite similar to the sliding scale plan described above inasmuch as consumers are permitted to share in productivity gains.

Although price cap regulation in long-distance telephone service is relatively new, a 1989 study by Mathios and Rogers has found evidence that favors price cap regulation in comparison with rate-of-return regulation.[5] They examined the thirty-nine states that have more than one Local Access and Transportation Area (LATA). The 161 LATAs in the United States were created as a result of the AT&T antitrust case that was settled in 1982. Basically, local telephone companies are allowed to provide long-distance service within LATAs, but not from one LATA to another. Hence, AT&T and other long-distance companies provide the inter-LATA, intrastate service. It is these intrastate, inter-LATA markets that the study investigated.

According to Mathios and Rogers, twenty-eight of the thirty-nine multi-LATA states moved to some form of price cap regulation of this long-distance service between 1984 and 1987. Kansas, for example, permits increases in rates by 4 percent and decreases by 7 percent without the need for a rate case. The authors found that "states that allowed pricing flexibility had lower 1987 prices than other states for all mileage bands."

In a 1993 article, Braeutigam and Panzar reported that some twenty-two states have recently moved to combined sliding-scale-price caps (SS-PC) incentive regulatory schemes for telephone companies. "A common form allows the telephone company to retain all earnings under PC rates as long as the rate of return is less than some specified amount, typically in the neighborhood of about 13 percent." Then, for example, the firm may be allowed to retain half of any additional earnings for a rate of return between 13 and 15 percent, and refund all additional earnings over 15 percent.

Braeutigam and Panzar conclude:

The limited U.S. evidence available supports the view that PC regulation is an effective means of controlling the *prices* of dominant firms when the control of their *profits* is left to the competitive marketplace. Thus, as has been observed many times, PC regulation is probably most effective as a transitory step on the path toward total deregulation and full competition.[6]

Finally, to round out our discussion of incentives to create efficiency, we note that the use of performance standards for electric power plants is becoming increasingly popular. For example, a specified norm for plant performance is defined. Penalties are imposed for performance below the norm and rewards are given for above-norm performance.

Joskow and Schmalensee have described a standard that the Arizona Public Service Company's nuclear plant, Palo Verde 1, had imposed on it. The target is the plant's capacity factor—the actual amount of electricity the plant generated divided by the amount it could generate running continuously throughout the year. Ideally, because of the low running costs of a nuclear plant, it should have a high capacity factor. The incentive provision is that if the capacity factor is between 60 and 75 percent, no penalty or reward is actuated. However, if the factor is between 75 and 85 percent, the company's reward equals 50 percent of the fuel-cost saving from running the plant more. Conversely, capacity factors between 50 and 60 percent result in a penalty equal to half of the additional fuel costs incurred by running more costly plants.

Averch-Johnson Effect

We turn now to an example of how rate-of-return regulation can create perverse incentives. The model we describe is an analysis of rate-of-return regulation published in 1962 by Averch and Johnson.[7] Their work led to a large outpouring of both theoretical and empirical research. Using what some today regard as very strong assumptions about how regulation constrains the firm, Averch and Johnson found that firms would choose too much capital relative to other inputs. As a result, the output would be produced at an inefficiently high cost. The key idea is that because allowed profit varies directly with the rate base (capital), the firm will tend to substitute too much capital for other inputs.

In mathematical terms, the problem is one of maximizing profit subject to a rate-of-return constraint. We will not develop the complete analysis, but it should be instructive to formulate the problem and provide the solution.

Hence the problem is to choose the quantities of labor and capital to maximize profit—that is, revenue minus the costs of the inputs, labor and capital. Maximize

$$\Pi = R(K, L) - wL - rK \tag{12.5}$$

subject to

$$\frac{R(K, L) - wL}{K} = s \tag{12.6}$$

where

Π = profit

R = revenue function

K = quantity of capital

L = quantity of labor

w = wage rate

r = cost of capital

s = allowed rate of return

The rate-of-return constraint, equation (12.6), implies that the firm is continuously restricted to a rate of return equal to s. The numerator equals total revenue minus the cost of labor, divided by capital—that is, the rate of return on capital. This, of course, is not strictly correct because the firm's prices are fixed from one rate case to the next, and therefore the firm's rate of return can be greater than or less than s during these periods of regulatory lag.

Another key assumption is that s is greater than r. In other words, it is assumed that the regulatory agency permits the firm to earn a higher rate of return on capital than the true cost of capital. Of course, the opposite case of s less than r would imply that the firm would prefer to shut down if this were to be a long-term situation. And if s and r were equal, the firm would be indifferent among the quantities of K and L inasmuch as its profit would be zero for all choices. Hence, Averch and Johnson argued that $s > r$ is the interesting one.

Using a standard mathematical solution technique (the Lagrangian multiplier method), Averch and Johnson found that

$$\frac{MP_k}{MP_l} = \frac{r - \alpha}{w} \tag{12.7}$$

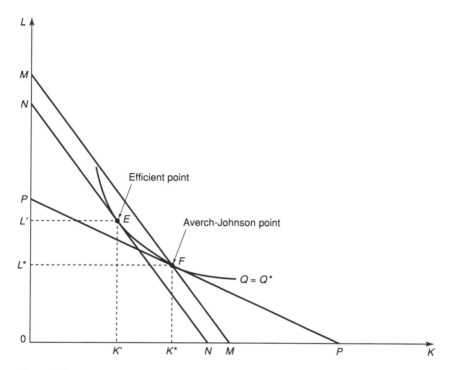

Figure 12.1
The Averch-Johnson Effect versus Least-Cost Production

where

$$\alpha = \frac{\lambda(s-r)}{1-\lambda} > 0$$

MP_k = marginal product of capital

MP_l = marginal product of labor

The α variable is positive because $s - r > 0$ and λ, the so-called Lagrangian multiplier, can be shown to be between 0 and 1. (The economic interpretation of λ is that it measures the increase in profit of a \$1 increase in allowed profit; hence its value between 0 and 1 is sensible.)

The result above can be explained by reference to Figure 12.1. The figure shows the isoquant for the level of output chosen by the regulated firm, Q^*. The axes show the quantities of the inputs, K and L, that can be used to produce output Q^*.

The economic theory of production requires that to minimize the cost of producing Q^*, it is necessary to equate the slope of the isoquant, that is, the ratio of marginal products, to the ratio of input prices. Equation

(12.7) implies that the Averch-Johnson regulated firm would meet this requirement if $\alpha = 0$. However, $\alpha > 0$, and the firm acts as if the cost of capital is cheaper than it actually is. That is, the firm acts as if its cost of capital is $r - \alpha$.

In Figure 12.1, let the slope of lines MM and NN equal r/w and the slope of line PP equal $(r - \alpha)/w$. Then, cost minimization requires operation at point E, where the slope of NN equals the slope of the isoquant. Note, however, that the regulated firm will choose to operate at point F, which equates the slope of PP (or $(r - \alpha)/w$) with the slope of the isoquant. The result shows that the regulated firm uses too much capital, K^*, and too little labor, L^*, as compared to the least-cost solution, K' and L'. The excess cost can be measured in units of labor by the distance MN on the vertical axis. That is, the actual cost of producing Q^* is OM units of labor inasmuch as MM passes through point F. However, the least-cost production of Q is ON units of labor.

A less rigorous explanation is as follows. The key point is that the regulated firm perceives that its cost of capital, $r - \alpha$, is less than the true cost r. For simplicity, take $s = 10$ percent, $r = 8$ percent, and $r - \alpha = 6$ percent. The regulated firm can earn a "bonus" of 2 percent on each dollar of new capital (costing 8 percent) because it is allowed to earn 10 percent. This "bonus" of 2 percent per dollar can be interpreted roughly as a 2 percent discount—making its perceived cost of capital only 6 percent.

It is very difficult to test for the existence of an Averch-Johnson (A-J) effect empirically. Some economists have argued that it is common knowledge that utilities often choose capital-intensive production, and this supports the A-J effect. One example is the resistance by electric utilities to highly integrated power pooling. The idea here is that utilities prefer to have their own capacity to meet peak demands rather than purchasing power from nearby companies. Although it might be least-cost to purchase power, these expenses are simply reimbursed under rate-of-return regulation. Investing in peak capacity, on the other hand, expands the rate base and thereby increases allowed profit.

A number of econometric tests for the A-J effect have also been performed. Using statistical analysis—usually in the electric power industry—the results have been mixed. Some have found support for the effect, and others have not.[8]

One reason for these mixed results might be that the regulatory environment in the United States was changing over the period of the statistical studies. Joskow, for example, has observed that until the early 1970s, electric power regulators did not really monitor rates of return carefully.[9] They were rather concerned with nominal electricity prices, because it is these prices that cause concern to consumers. Hence, if, as appears to be the case, nominal prices tended to stay constant or fall prior to the early 1970s, electric utilities could earn high rates of return without fear of having price decreases imposed. This clearly conflicts with the assumptions of the A-J model.

We should mention one possible beneficial effect of the A-J bias toward capital intensity. For most regulated industries, technological change takes place through the substitution of capital for other inputs. For example, direct long-distance dialing replaced many operators with automatic switching equipment. Hence one might argue that the A-J effect has possibly stimulated innovation. (Other characteristics of regulation, however, can be argued to retard innovation, so the net effect of regulation on innovation is unclear. For example, profits created through innovation can be expected to be reduced through price decreases at the next rate case.)

Finally, consider the two-product monopolist and the incentive to increase capital to increase profits. Noll and Owen have explained this problem for regulators succinctly:

Suppose that at all feasible prices, one market has elastic demand, while another has inelastic demand. If a regulated firm lowers the price in the former, it will increase sales by a relatively large amount, requiring that it commit substantially more capital to that market. But if it increases prices in the latter market, it will suffer a relatively small reduction in sales, and hence a small reduction in capital requirements. Thus, changing both prices simultaneously this way increases the total required capital.... This, in turn, increases the firm's allowed profits.[10]

Rate Structure

The rate structure has to do with how prices vary across customer classes and products. In the preceding chapter we described the prices that are economically efficient under various conditions. Of course, economically efficient prices (for instance, prices equal to marginal costs) are often not the prices set under regulation. Recently a movement toward peak load pricing (a type of marginal cost pricing) has become important in electric power. We will examine this topic in depth later in this section.

A common method of pricing used by regulatory commissions is to begin by allocating all of the utility's costs to various customer classes and services. Most utilities provide a variety of services to different customer groups. They also have many facilities that are used in common by these customers and services. For example, power plants and transmission lines, telephone switching centers, and pipelines all represent common costs that apply to most customer classes or services.

FDC Pricing

To illustrate concretely one such pricing method, fully distributed cost (FDC) pricing, consider a simple two-product natural monopolist that sells electricity to two classes of customers. We denote the electricity sold to residential buyers by X and to industrial customers by Y. (Electricity sold to residential customers is usually at a lower voltage than industrial customers require, and therefore there truly are two different products.)

Assume the cost functions below:

To produce X alone : $C_x = 700 + 20X$ $\qquad\qquad$ (12.8)

To produce Y alone : $C_y = 600 + 20Y$ $\qquad\qquad$ (12.9)

To produce both : $C_{xy} = 1050 + 20X + 20Y$ $\qquad$ (12.10)

Note that the joint production of X and Y is subadditive. That is, least-cost production requires that X and Y be produced together because fixed-cost is $1050, as compared to a total of $1300 if produced separately. The $1050 fixed-cost also represents common costs that must be allocated to each product in order to implement FDC pricing.

Kahn has observed that utilities' common costs "may be distributed on the basis of some common physical measure of utilization, such as minutes, circuit-miles, message-minute-miles, gross-ton-miles, cubic feet, or kilowatt-hours employed or consumed by each. Or they may be distributed in proportion to the costs that can be directly assigned to the various services."[11]

The particular method may appear quite reasonable, but the essential point is that it is necessarily arbitrary. And more importantly, such cost allocations lead to prices that have no necessary relationship to marginal costs. To take an example, assume that some "reasonable" method leads to an allocation of 75 percent of the common costs to product X and 25 percent to product Y. Hence, FDC average costs would be

$$AC_x = 787.5/X + 20 \qquad \text{and} \qquad AC_y = 262.5/Y + 20 \qquad (12.11)$$

That is, the average cost of X equals its 75 percent share of the $1050 common cost, divided by the units of X sold, plus the clearly attributable variable cost of X per unit of $20.

At this point, the demands for the two products must be specified. Assume that the demand functions are

$$P_x = 100 - X \qquad \text{and} \qquad P_y = 60 - 0.5Y \qquad (12.12)$$

With the demand information, the actual FDC prices can be found by equating equations (12.11) and (12.12). This simply sets $P_x = AC_x$ and $P_y = AC_y$, ensuring that total revenues are equal to total costs. The result is

$$P_x = AC_x = \$31.5 \qquad \text{and} \qquad P_y = AC_y = \$23.6$$
$$X = 68.5 \qquad\qquad\qquad Y = 72.8 \qquad\qquad (12.13)$$

Hence the FDC prices above clearly satisfy the requirement that total revenues equal total costs. Again, however, there is no basis for expecting these prices to be the economically efficient prices. In general, such prices lead to deadweight losses.

It is easy to show that the efficient prices in this case are the Ramsey prices (as explained in Chapter 11):

$$P_x = \$30 \qquad \text{and} \qquad P_y = \$25$$
$$X = 70 \qquad\qquad\qquad Y = 70 \qquad\qquad (12.14)$$

Figure 12.2 illustrates the Ramsey solution. By definition, the Ramsey prices have the smallest deadweight loss triangles (shaded in Figure 12.2) for all possible pairs that yield revenues equal to costs.

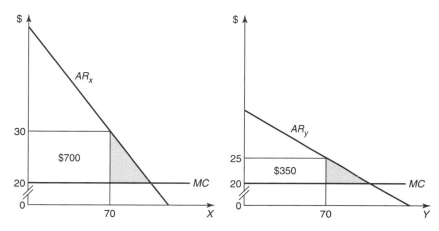

Figure 12.2
Ramsey Pricing

Although we have implicitly assumed that two-part pricing is not feasible in the example, notice that if it were feasible, the "first best" solution would be to charge marginal cost prices to each group; that is, each price would be $20. Then the fixed fees would be set to just cover the fixed cost of $1050. And in this case, in achieving economic efficiency it would make no difference how the $1050 was allocated between the two groups. (This point was also explained in Chapter 11.)

One problem that FDC pricing raises is that "reasonable" allocations of common costs lead to disputes among customer classes. It is natural to expect residential customers to argue that their share should be lower than 75 percent and for industrial customers to argue that their share should be lower than 25 percent. Commissions have long been concerned with "undue discrimination" across customer classes, and we turn to that subject next.

Undue Discrimination

Undue discrimination is really not an efficiency issue; rather, it has to do with the fairness of the existing set of prices in the sense of whether one group may be "subsidizing" another group. It is clearly a controversial issue for commissions inasmuch as a rate case may find intervenors representing residential customers and industrial customers in total opposition to each other. Both groups may argue that they are paying too large a share of the common costs! This is basically an equity issue—which we have avoided for the most part in this book—but there are some clarifications that economic analysis can offer to the debate.

Economists argue that if one must examine cross-subsidization issues (assuming Ramsey prices are not used), the most logical tests are the so-called stand-alone average cost and the average incremental cost tests—which are, in fact, equivalent.[12]

Consider the stand-alone average costs for product X for an output of X of 70 units. That is, returning to equation (12.8), the average cost of X is $30. The Ramsey price of $30 for the same output therefore does not give an incentive for customers of X to break away and produce X alone. This test therefore would classify the Ramsey price as subsidy-free. Similarly, the Ramsey price of Y is also subsidy-free. (Note that the FDC price of X for 68.5 units is $31.5, which exceeds the stand-alone average cost of $30.2. It therefore fails the subsidy-free test.)

Another test is the average incremental cost test. Here, we compute the average incremental cost, AIC, of producing X in joint production with Y. Thus, subtract the cost of producing Y alone from the cost of producing X and Y jointly to get the incremental cost of X. The AIC of

X is, therefore, $20 + 450/X$, or $26.4 for $X = 70$. Similarly, the AIC for Y at $Y = 70$ is $25. Here, the test for subsidy-free prices is that the prices equal or exceed their respective AICs. The logic is that if each product contributes to total revenue an amount that at least covers the extra costs it causes (when added to the production of the other products), then it should be viewed as a beneficial addition. To the extent that its incremental revenues exceed its incremental costs, the revenues required from the other products are reduced. The Ramsey prices of $30 and $25 also pass this test. In fact, these two tests always give the same answers. (Note that the FDC price of Y for 72.8 units is $23.6 while the AIC of Y is $24.8. Hence the FDC prices fail the subsidy-free test by this test too.)

It should be pointed out that FDC prices do not necessarily fail subsidy-free tests. They may pass the subsidy-free tests and still be economically inefficient.

Under certain conditions of subadditivity of cost (that is, when the natural monopoly is sustainable), it is true that Ramsey prices are subsidy-free in the sense that no outsider would find it profitable to enter. Hence the regulator need not be concerned about whether permitting entry would be socially beneficial. This assumes, of course, that the regulator permits the monopolist to charge Ramsey prices (rather than hold it to the FDC prices given above). On the other hand, there are cases in which the cost function is subadditive and yet subsidy-free prices do not exist. This is another way of viewing the case of a natural monopoly that is unsustainable—least-cost production requires a single firm, but there are no prices that can keep all of the monopolist's products invulnerable to entry.

Here is an example. Three towns are in need of a well for water supply. One deep well could supply all three towns at a cost of $660. This is the least-cost solution and would imply a price of $660/3 =$220 per town. Two towns could go together and dig a shallower well for $400, and each town alone could dig an even shallower well for $300. Clearly, $660 is lower than any of the alternatives. If each town had its own well, the total would be $900, and if two went in together for $400 and the third went alone at $300, the total would be $700.

The problem is that $220 per town would provide an incentive for two of the towns to join forces at $400, or a price of $200 each. One can think of it as (any) two towns, if they go along with the three-town project, subsidizing the third town in the amount of $20 each. Clearly, there is no way to avoid the subsidies if one is going to achieve least-cost production.

In anticipation of the next section on peak-load pricing, we provide a final example of "unfair" subsidization. Consider two groups of electricity customers: day customers and night customers. A plant costing K dollars is necessary to meet the day customers' demand, which is larger than the night demand. Because electricity cannot be easily stored, the plant must be large enough to supply power on demand.

The plant, of course, can be used to supply the smaller night demand as well. Under certain assumptions to be discussed in the next section, the economically efficient solution is to charge day customers for the total cost of the plant, K! Even though both groups use the plant, the day customers pay for the entire plant cost, plus fuel costs for their output. Night customers pay only for their fuel costs. It is certainly "unfair" in certain senses—however, it is the demand of day customers that necessitates such a large plant, and it would be inefficient if the price they paid did not signal the cost of the larger capacity.

In conclusion, the major point of this section is to make clear that the objective of economic efficiency may sometimes require pricing that conflicts with common notions of fairness. One justification for opting for efficiency, of course, is that the "size of the pie" is larger as a result, and authorities can in principle make everyone better off by appropriate taxes and/or subsidies.

Peak-Load Pricing

A major development in electric power in recent years has been the gradual movement toward the implementation of peak-load pricing. This term refers to the variation in prices by time of use—for example, in the middle of the day more electricity is demanded than in the middle of the night. The marginal cost of electricity is, as a result, much higher in the middle of the day than it is at night. Setting prices that vary over the day in proportion to the variation in marginal costs is a form of peak-load pricing. Until recently, in the United States most consumers paid electricity prices that did not vary over the day.

Costs of Power Production

It is useful to examine the cost structure of a typical electric power system before continuing with our discussion of peak-load pricing principles. A major point is that it is generally too costly (or impossible) to store electricity, and therefore sufficient capacity must be on hand to supply the demand at all times. This implies that capacity is determined by the amount of peak demand.

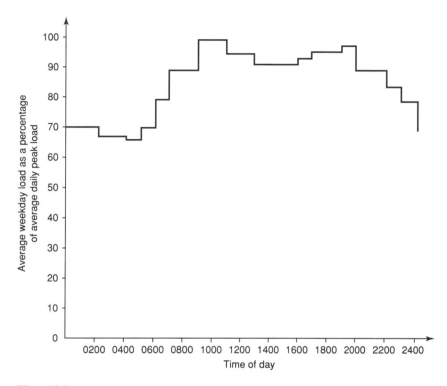

Figure 12.3
Average Daily Load Curve for Electricity

Demand for electric power typically varies in a reasonably predictable cyclical pattern—daily, weekly, monthly, and seasonally. The demand might follow the pattern in Figure 12.3 for a typical weekday. Hence, peak demand occurs at midmorning and is only 70 percent of that amount at midnight. Demand over the weekend might equal only 50 percent of the high during the week.

In a recent year, Duke Power Company produced some 55 billion kilowatt hours of electricity. If it had experienced a constant rate of demand over the year, Duke Power could have produced that amount of electricity with a capacity of 6300 megawatts (assuming, for simplicity, no downtime for maintenance or for other reasons). In fact, during one hour on January 11, Duke had its peak demand for the year, requiring a capacity of 11,145 megawatts! The company actually had some 13,234 megawatts of installed capacity. (Installed capacity is higher than expected peak demand to provide a reliability margin in view of the uncertainty in demand and to allow for unplanned outages of power plants.)

Duke Power's capacity consisted of

7,423 megawatts (MW) of coal-fired plants

3,760 MW of nuclear plants

1,452 MW of hydroelectric plants

  599 MW of combustion turbine plants

13,234 MW total

A typical electric-power system has a mixture of plant types because it leads to a lower overall cost of supplying the variable pattern of demand. Nuclear plants have relatively low variable or "running" costs, but have relatively high fixed (capital) costs. They are, therefore, suited for running as the "base load" plants—as many hours per year as possible. Combustion turbines, on the other hand, have relatively high running costs but low fixed costs. They are used to meet peak demands that last for only a small number of hours per year.

The result is that the short-run marginal cost curve of a power system is similar to the rising curve shown in Figure 12.4. The costs given by segment *AB* might represent the base load nuclear plants' running costs; *BC*, the costs of coal-fired plants of varying ages and efficiency; and *CD*, the costs of the peaking plants (such as combustion turbines). In this context, it is easy to realize that since demand varies continuously over

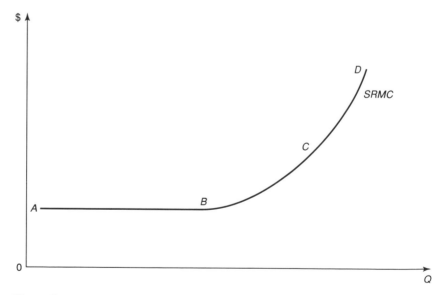

Figure 12.4
Short-Run Marginal Cost Curve for Electric Power System

timc, charging a pricc cqual to short-run marginal cost (SRMC) would require a continuously changing price.

In order to explain the principles of peak-load pricing most clearly, it will help to abstract greatly from the real-world complexity just described. Hence we turn now to a vastly simplified model.[13]

Peak-Load Pricing Model

In Figure 12.5 we make the assumption that demand is given by the peak demand curve for exactly half of the day, and by the off-peak demand curve for the other half of the day. For simplicity, it is assumed that the two demands are independent—the price in the peak period, for instance, does not affect the quantity demanded in the off-peak period.[14] Also, it is assumed that "running" costs—for example, fuel for electricity production—are constant at the level b until capacity is reached at K. At the output K, no further output is possible, as indicated by the vertical line that is labeled $SRMC$. Hence we have a so-called "rigid" plant with the $SRMC$ curve being equal to b for outputs less than K, and then becoming vertical at the plant capacity. One can think of this as an approximation to the smoothly increasing $SRMC$ curve in Figure 12.4.

The dashed horizontal line at the level $b + \beta$ is labeled long-run marginal cost ($LRMC$). The assumption here is that β represents the cost of an additional unit of capacity, and that it is possible to add capacity in

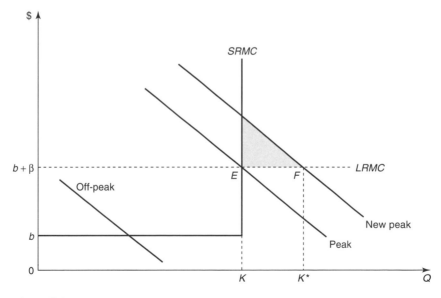

Figure 12.5
Peak-Load Pricing—Firm Peak

increments of single units if desired.[15] The economically efficient solution is to charge a price equal to $SRMC$ in order to use the existing plant optimally. The $LRMC$ comes into play in order to decide whether the existing plant capacity is optimal. Hence, in Figure 12.5 the off-peak price should be b and the peak price should be $b + \beta$. Notice that the peak price is equal to both $SRMC$ and $LRMC$. This indicates that the capacity is in fact optimal. The reason is that the price can be interpreted as the "marginal willingness-to-pay," and $b + \beta$ represents the marginal cost to supply one more unit.

If, for example, the peak price exceeded $b + \beta$, it would pay society to increase capacity. This is shown by the demand curve labeled new peak. This new peak demand intersects $SRMC$ at a price higher than $b + \beta$. This means that an increase in consumer surplus can be had by expanding capacity out to K^*. This increase in consumer surplus is equal to the area under the demand curve between K and K^*—which represents willingness-to-pay—minus the cost of supplying the additional output, rectangle $EFKK^*$. Subtracting the cost from willingness-to-pay gives the shaded triangle that represents the increase in consumer surplus attributable to the capacity increase. Hence, at the new capacity K^*, price is again equal to $SRMC$ and $LRMC$—indicating that K^* is the optimal capacity.

Now, assume that the electric utility follows the practice of charging a single price that does not vary over the day, say, a price of P^*. This situation is shown in Figure 12.6. As we mentioned earlier, this would represent the pricing policy generally followed in the United States before peak-load pricing began to be implemented. In order to satisfy demand at the peak at this price, capacity of K_0 is required. Because optimal capacity is K where price equals $LRMC$, the single-price policy leads to too much capacity. The deadweight loss associated with this is shown as the shaded triangle EFG. It equals the difference between the cost of the excess capacity, rectangle $EFKK_0$, and the willingness-to-pay for that incremental capacity, $EGKK_0$. Intuitively, the peak demanders are not charged enough for the actual costs that they cause.

There is a second deadweight loss triangle in Figure 12.6, and it is associated with the nonoptimal use of the plant in the off-peak period. That is, with the price P^* charged in the off-peak period, consumption in the off-peak period is too low—at Q_0 rather than at Q where price would equal $SRMC$.

We should observe that the economically efficient prices that we have been discussing are what society should prefer, not necessarily what a profit-maximizing regulated utility would desire. In fact, the utility would have total revenues equal to total costs in either case (peak-load

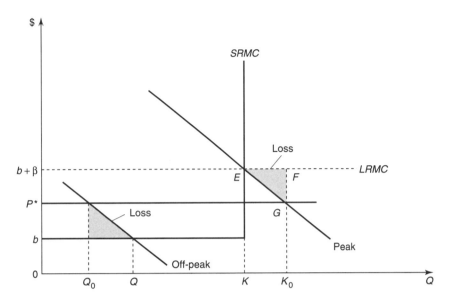

Figure 12.6
Dead Weight Losses Due to Nonpeak Pricing

prices or single price). What gave the impetus to regulated electric utilities moving toward peak-load pricing was probably a combination of
pressures—the energy crisis of the 1970s, high inflation, and other factors that made regulators seek alternatives to the traditional rate structures. In addition, Congress passed a law in 1978, the Public Utilities
Regulatory Policies Act, that among other things required state commissions to study peak-load pricing for possible implementation in their
state.

The cases of peak-load pricing described so far indicate that peak
demanders pay $b + \beta$ whereas off-peak demanders pay only b. That is,
peak demanders pay all capacity costs and off-peak pay none. This is
true, however, only for the particular case shown—known as the firm
peak case. An alternative case is the shifting peak case, which has the
property that the demands are "closer" together. Figure 12.7 illustrates
this case.

To see why this case is known as the shifting peak case, consider the
effect of charging the peak demanders all the capacity costs and the off-
peak demanders none. For simplicity, we assume that $b = 0$ in this
case—this makes the figure less cluttered and doesn't affect the key
points. The result is easily seen in Figure 12.7. Peak demanders would
demand R units of capacity (where price $= \beta$) and off-peak demanders
would want S units (where price $= 0$), or a greater capacity than peak

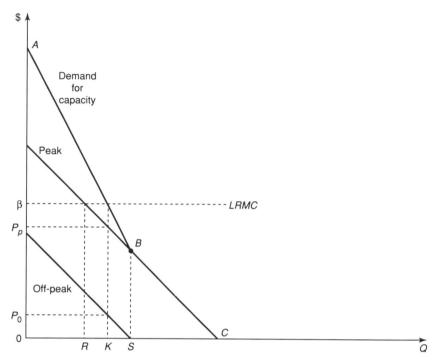

Figure 12.7
Demand for Capacity in Shifting Peak Case

demanders! Intuitively, this suggests that the prices are wrong. The correct set of prices can be found in conjunction with solving for the optimal capacity.

To obtain the optimal capacity, construct the "demand for capacity." Conceptually, think of the plant as a public good—it can be used by both peak and off-peak demanders (though at different times). This implies that the total willingness-to-pay for the plant is obtained by adding vertically the demand curves for the two groups of demanders. This total willingness-to-pay curve, the kinked curve ABC, is the demand for capacity. For example, at the output K the marginal willingness-to-pay is P_p by peakers and P_o by off-peakers, for a total of β. Because the capacity cost is β, K is the optimal capacity. The efficient prices for using this capacity are P_p and P_o, which, of course, add to β. Hence, in this case, the two groups share the capacity costs, unlike the firm peak case. (If we had a nonzero b, the prices in each period would also include b.)

In practice, each day is not divided into two distinct periods of peak and off-peak demands. Rather, demand changes continually over the day, and there are also changes from week to week and season to season. This implies that the implementation of peak-load pricing requires judgment as to the metering of demand and how to fix periods during which prices are held constant. That is, one needs to recognize that it is not practical to have prices changing every few minutes—consumers would not be willing to respond to such constantly changing prices—and the costs of metering consumption in such short periods would be too high.

For these reasons, the typical pattern of peak-load prices for a residential customer would be similar to those below:

Weekdays 6 P.M.–6 A.M.	4 cents/kwh
Weekdays 6 A.M.–2 P.M.	7 cents/kwh
5 P.M.–6 P.M.	
Weekdays 2 P.M.–5 P.M.	14 cents/kwh
Weekends	4 cents/kwh

In addition to the time varying rates, there would normally be a fixed charge per billing period. The rates above indicate that for this particular electric utility the peak period is on weekdays between 2 P.M. and 5 P.M., and the off-peak period is from 6 P.M. to 6 A.M. and all weekend. It might also be the case that the summer peak would exceed the winter peak. Hence the utility might have the rates above in effect for, say, May through October, and another schedule with somewhat lower rates for November through April. If the costs of metering small residential customers is viewed as too high to charge rates that vary over the day, the summer-winter scheme might be the only peak load pricing implemented. (The point here is that the cheaper metering equipment simply accumulates total electricity consumed by the month; more expensive equipment is needed to measure use by time of day.)

Regulation/Deregulation of Electric Power

In this section we consider two topics. The first topic is the question of whether regulation of electric power utilities has been effective. That is, what evidence is there on the basic question of whether electricity prices have been restrained relative to what they would have been in the absence of regulation? The second topic is that of deregulation of electric power, or the emergence of price competition in various parts of the electric power industry.

Effectiveness of Price Regulation

Has regulation of electric power made a difference? The best-known study is one published in 1962 by Stigler and Friedland (S-F).[16] Their idea was to compare the price of electricity in states with regulation to the price in states without regulation. Unfortunately, because state regulation now exists almost everywhere, S-F had to go back to the 1920s and 1930s to find states without regulation.[17] This data problem consequently makes their results of limited relevance to the present time.

To illustrate the nature of their study, S-F found that in 1922 the average price of electricity was 2.44 cents per kilowatt-hour in states with regulation and 3.87 cents in states without regulation. Of course, this simple comparison is invalid because prices vary for reasons other than the existence of regulation. However, once they controlled through multiple regression analysis for other variables (such as the percent of power generated in hydroelectric plants—which is less costly than power in coal plants), S-F claimed that no statistically significant difference in price remained.

Some critics have argued that S-F did find some beneficial effects of regulation at slightly lower standards of statistical significance. They have also observed that the study period covered a time when regulation was just getting started, and that regulators are more effective today. Finally, critics have argued that the threat of regulation (observed in an adjacent state) could cause unregulated firms to hold down their prices in the hope of avoiding regulation.

Other analysts have tried alternative methods to answer the fundamental question of regulation's effectiveness in electric power. Meyer and Leland used data for 1969 and 1974 in their study, which attempted to answer the following question.[18] To what extent do the prices charged by regulated firms differ from what unregulated profit-maximizing firms would charge? They made use of econometric estimates of demand and costs to find the hypothetical unregulated prices. They found that the regulated prices were significantly lower, but that even lower prices would have been preferred. Similar work by Greene and Smiley found that unregulated prices for electricity are 20–50 percent higher than actual regulated prices.[19] The appeal of this methodology is that it can be applied to current data. However, very strong assumptions are needed to calculate the profit-maximizing prices, and this makes their findings somewhat less persuasive.

Of course, given the problems with full regulation discussed earlier, if changing technologies can make it possible for competition to work at least in certain sectors of the industry, that is likely to be preferred to regulation. We now turn to this possibility in electric power.

Trend toward Competition

A major step toward price competition in electric power was taken by the passage of the Energy Policy Act of 1992. While the Act had many

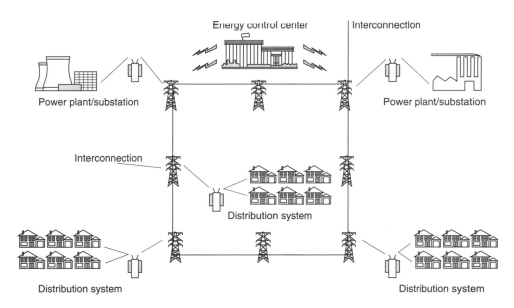

Figure 12.8
A Simple Electric System

provisions unrelated to electricity, the relevant provision for our purposes gave the Federal Energy Regulatory Commission (FERC) the right to order utilities to "wheel" power over their transmission lines. If Utility A wants to sell power to non-adjacent Utility B, and can only do so by using Utility C's transmission lines, then Utility C can assist in the transaction by wheeling the power from A to B.

To understand better the emerging competition in electric power, it is useful to consider a few basic facts about electric power systems. Figure 12.8 is a simplified power system. There were some 3,241 systems in the United States in 1990—most were small publicly owned systems. However, the 267 privately owned utilities accounted for 71 percent of the sales of electricity.[20]

Traditionally, most of the large privately owned electric utilities in the United States have been vertically integrated—owning power plants, substations, transmission lines, and distribution systems. The energy control center shown in Figure 12.8 coordinates the operation and dispatch of all power-system components within a geographic region. The control center is required because electricity must be generated as it is needed.

The interconnection shown in Figure 12.8 illustrates the fact that utilities are linked to others through a national grid. This linkage makes possible the sale of power from one utility to another—so-called wholesale transactions, or wholesale wheeling. Technological developments in high-voltage transmission have improved the feasibility of increasing numbers of these transactions. It should also be noted that wholesale power is also being sold by so-called independent power producers who are not subject to rate-of-return regulation.

One writer about the nature of the emerging electricity market has made a helpful analogy to a water system:

Hundreds of utilities and wholesale power producers buy and sell electricity over the superhighway every day, in an increasingly competitive wholesale market. The system can be envisioned as a complex of water pipes, in which pressure must be maintained within a certain range. In a typical transaction, an electricity seller increases its level of power production, raising the "pressure" and causing electricity to flow into the network, while the buyer decreases its power production proportionately, lowering its "pressure" and thereby drawing a roughly equivalent amount out of the system.[21]

FERC is charged with regulating the price of these wholesale transactions, and has been moving away from traditional rate-of-return price setting toward market based transactions. In 1994 a further important step was taken by some sixty utilities in an area covering approximately the western third of the United States plus British Columbia. They have agreed to remove barriers to wheeling among themselves and FERC has agreed to permit market-based pricing within upper and lower limits.[22]

In addition to traditional utilities selling wholesale power to each other, other independent power producers who only generate power are becoming more important. The 1978 Public Utility Regulatory Policy Act (PURPA) required utilities to purchase power from "qualifying facilities" (QFs). These QFs are companies that install cogeneration equipment (e.g., companies that produce steam for heating and use the excess steam to generate power) and certain small power-production facilities that make use of renewable energy sources and a variety of waste fuels.[23] The Energy Policy Act of 1992 created another category of independent power producers not subject to regulation. These producers are termed "exempt wholesale generators" (EWGs). A large fraction of the the first applicants for EWG status consisted of affiliates of existing utilities.

As one might expect, as wholesale wheeling has become increasingly important, large industrial buyers have begun to demand participation. They would like to have the right to buy power from any utility directly, not just from the utility that serves their geographic area. That is, "retail wheeling" would allow a retail customer to purchase power from Utility X and have it delivered through its local utility. The local utility would be paid for the cost of delivering the power.

The incentive for retail wheeling is great given the wide variation in power rates around the country. Some industrial customers pay only 4 cents per kilowatt-hour, whereas others pay up to 12.[24] Utilities with high costs would find themselves losing customers and, given their large fixed costs, would either have to raise rates to their remaining customers or take large losses. The 1992 Energy Policy Act restricted retail wheeling but left state authority in such matters untouched.[25] It will clearly be a controversial issue for the near future.[26]

Although some power companies dispute the technical feasibility of a fully competitive market including retail wheeling, it should be noted that such a market already exists in England and Wales. At least, any buyer who consumes more than one megawatt of power each year can purchase power from any producer in England and Wales.[27] In April 1994 the California Public Utilities Commission also proposed new regulations that would allow all electric power users, including homeowners, the right to choose their electricity supplier by 2002.[28]

Summary

This chapter has discussed numerous problems of rate-of-return regulation. Cost-minimizing behavior is not encouraged by such cost-plus regulation. Firms that cut costs do not receive full cost savings, inasmuch as prices will be reduced to the new level of costs. However, the "accidental" institution of regulatory lag and the practice of disallowing certain expenses or additions to the rate base are factors that tend to offset this problem. The new price cap regulation in telephones and performance standards in electric power are also likely to encourage economic efficiency.

The Averch-Johnson effect leads to a capital bias and higher costs than are necessary. However, the applicability of the A-J model is not accepted by all economists due to the strong assumptions of that model.

Peak-load pricing is clearly an important development of the 1980s that has improved efficiency significantly. Although price regulation in electric power has probably resulted in lower prices than would have existed otherwise, a major current change that should be socially beneficial is the emergence of price competition at the wholesale level. Competition at the retail level is much further in the future, although it already exists to some extent in England and Wales.

Questions and Problems

1. The rate base can be valued in various ways. What, if anything, is wrong with the utility commission valuing the rate base at its value according to the stock market and the bond market? That is, use the market value of the firm rather than, say, the original cost of assets less depreciation.

2.   Utility company executives are often quoted as saying that if their allowed
      rate of return is too low, they will be unable to attract capital to pay for
      capacity to meet increasing demands. Does this mean that regulators can-
      not use the allowed return as a device to provide incentives for utilities—
      raising the rate for good performance and lowering it for poor perfor-
      mance?

3.   Consider the Edison Electric Company with a production function $Q = K^{.5}L^{.5}$, where Q is output, K is capital, and L is labor. The market rental
      rate of capital is $0.50 and the wage rate is $0.50 also. The utility com-
      mission has set the allowed rental rate at $0.80. (Rental rates of capital are
      in dollars per unit of capital per year. With zero depreciation they are re-
      lated to percentage costs of capital in the following way. Suppose that the
      utility must invest in a generator at a cost of $5 per kilowatt of capacity,
      and 10 percent is its cost of capital; then the rental rate per year is 10 per-
      cent of the $5 per unit, or $0.50. Similarly, the percentage allowed rate of
      return would be 16 percent since 16 percent of $5 is $0.80. Rental rates are
      therefore comparable to wage rates and other factor costs in applying
      standard static production theory.)

      Edison faces a demand curve with the constant elasticity of demand
      2.857, or $Q = P^{-2.857}$. If Edison were unregulated, it would produce effi-
      ciently at a constant average and marginal cost of $1. However, because of
      Averch-Johnson effects, it uses too much capital under regulation and
      produces at an average cost of $1.01. Edison charges a price of $1.35 and
      sells $Q = 0.42$.

      a. Find the price and quantity if Edison were an unregulated monopoly.
      Hint: Marginal revenue is $P(1 - 1/2.857)$.

      b. Find the sum of consumer and producer surplus for the case where Ed-
      ison is regulated and where it is not. Hint: Using calculus, it can be shown
      that consumer surplus is $(0.54)Q^{0.65}$. Does regulation, even though im-
      perfect because of Averch-Johnson effects, nevertheless result in an im-
      provement over an unregulated monopoly case?

      c. Of course, the first-best case of price-equal marginal cost and efficient
      production is superior to regulation. Find the efficient solution. Draw a
      figure that shows the two types of losses that regulation causes as com-
      pared to the efficient solution.

      d. Assume now that the utility commission decides to lower the allowed
      rental rate from $0.80 closer to the market rate of $0.50. Assume that it
      picks $0.58. It can be shown that Edison will now choose to sell 0.67 units
      at a price of $1.15. Its average cost of production rises to $1.04. Compare
      this Averch-Johnson equilibrium with the earlier one in terms of total
      economic surplus. This, in fact, is the socially optimal allowed rental rate.
      Lower rates actually reduce total surplus. For further details, see A. Kle-
      vorick, "The Optimal Fair Rate of Return," *Bell Journal of Economics and
      Management Science*, Spring 1971.

4.   How does the Averch-Johnson characterization of the regulatory process
      differ from reality?

5.   Edison Electric Company's president has been arguing that residential
      electric rates need to be raised relative to industrial rates. His reason is
      that the rate of return that the company earns on its assets is higher from

its industrial customers than from its residential customers. Is this a good reason? Hint: How can Edison determine its assets dedicated to the two classes of customers?

6. In a certain city where all parking is controlled by the city, it is possible to provide parking facilities in the downtown area at a constant marginal capital investment of $10,000 per space. Costs of operation can be neglected. There are three equal periods during the day of eight hours each, and spaces are rented only for complete eight-hour periods. During the peak period of each of 250 days per year, the demand for parking is given by $P = a - bQ$, where P is the price per period for a parking space. During the other two off-peak periods of those 250 days, the spaces demanded are half that in the peak period, for each possible price. On other days demand is zero. Assume that the interest rate is 10 percent and the facilities do not depreciate.

a. If $a = \$16$, $b = 0.08$, and existing spaces are 120, what would be the socially optimal prices during the three periods?

b. What is the optimal number of spaces and what are the corresponding prices?

c. The above case is a so-called firm peak case, with peak demanders paying all capital costs. Now suppose that $a = \$5$ and $b = 0.08$. If peak demanders pay all capital costs, what quantity is demanded by peak demanders? If off-peak demanders pay zero, what is their quantity demanded? (Fractions of spaces are legitimate.) This is the shifting-peak case.

d. For the demand curves in (c), find the optimal number of spaces and the corresponding prices.

Notes

1. State of California, *Public Utilities Commission Annual Report 1986–1987*, p. 13.

2. The book by A. Lawrence Kolbe and James A. Read, Jr., with George R. Hall, *The Cost of Capital: Estimating the Rate of Return for Public Utilities* (Cambridge, Mass.: MIT Press, 1984), contains a good description of five methods of estimating the cost of capital.

3. A recent article reported that in rate cases over the 1980–1984 period, the average k requested by firms was 17.02 percent and the average k recommended by the Commissions' staffs was 15.11 percent. Interestingly, the average k allowed by the Commissions was 15.39 percent—a figure much closer to the staffs' recommendations than to the firms' requested values. S. B. Caudill, B. Im, and D. L. Kaserman, "Modeling Regulatory Behavior," *Journal of Regulatory Economics*, September 1993.

4. Paul L. Joskow and Richard Schmalensee, "Incentive Regulation for Electric Utilities," *Yale Journal of Regulation* 4, No. 1 (1986).

5. A. D. Mathios and R. P. Rogers, "The Impact of Alternative Forms of State Regulation of AT&T on Direct-Dial, Long-Distance Telephone Rates," *The Rand Journal of Economics*, Autumn 1989.

6. R. R. Braeutigam and J. C. Panzar, "Effects of the Change from Rate-of-Return to Price-Cap Regulation," *American Economic Review*, May 1993.

7. H. Averch and L. Johnson, "Behavior of the Firm Under Regulatory Constraint," *American Economic Review*, December 1962.

8. For example, H. C. Petersen, "An Empirical Test of Regulatory Effects," *Bell Journal of Economics*, Spring 1975, found support for the A-J effect. W. J. Boyes, "An Empirical Examination of the Averch-Johnson Effect," *Economic Inquiry*, March 1976, did not find support for it.

9. Paul L. Joskow, "Inflation and Environmental Concern: Structural Change in the Process of Public Utility Price Regulation," *Journal of Law and Economics*, October 1974.

10. Roger G. Noll and Bruce M. Owen, "The Anticompetitive Uses of Regulation: United States v. AT&T (1982)," in J. E. Kwoka, Jr. and L. J. White (eds.), *The Antitrust Revolution*, 2nd ed. (New York: HarperCollins, 1994), p. 338.

11. Alfred E. Kahn, *The Economics of Regulation: Principles and Institutions*, Vol. 1 (New York: John Wiley & Sons, 1971), p. 151.

12. For proof, see Stephen J. Brown and David S. Sibley, *The Theory of Public Utility Pricing* (New York: Cambridge University Press, 1986).

13. The exposition follows Peter O. Steiner, "Peak Loads and Efficient Pricing," *Quarterly Journal of Economics*, November 1957.

14. This assumption is probably too strong. A well-known counterexample occurred in 1964 when AT&T began lower rates for long-distance telephone calls after 5 P.M. They found themselves deluged with calls from people who formerly called during the day. The interdependence of demands can be handled with an increase in mathematical complexity. See I. Pressman, "A Mathematical Formulation of the Peak-Load Pricing Problem," *Bell Journal of Economics*, 1970.

15. The production function underlying this model is one of fixed coefficients. Much of the early literature employed this assumption. While the suitability of this assumption to describe, say, electric power production is an empirical question, the alternative variable-proportions technology is somewhat more difficult to exposit.

16. G. J. Stigler and C. Friedland, "What Can Regulators Regulate? The Case of Electricity," *Journal of Law and Economics*, October 1962.

17. And, as Joskow and Rose have observed, the states without regulation cannot be considered to be completely unregulated. Prior to state regulation most companies were regulated to some extent at the municipal level. P. L. Joskow and N. L. Rose, "The Effects of Economic Regulation," in R. Schmalensee and R. D. Willig (eds.), *Handbook of Industrial Organization*, Volume II, North-Holland, 1989.

18. R. A. Meyer and H. E. Leland, "The Effectiveness of Price Regulation," *Review of Economic and Statistics*, November 1980.

19. W. H. Greene and R. H. Smiley, "The Effectiveness of Utility Regulation in a Period of Changing Economic Conditions," in M. Marchand et al. (eds.), *The Performance of Public Enterprises: Concepts and Measurement* (Amsterdam: Elsevier, 1984).

20. Office of Technology Assessment, *Energy Efficiency: Challenges and Opportunities for Electric Utilities*, September 1993.

21. Matthew C. Hoffman, "Power Moves," *Reason*, June 1994, p. 52.

22. John Douglas, "Buying and Selling Power in the Age of Competition," *EPRI Journal*, June 1994.

23. P. L. Joskow, "Regulatory Failure, Regulatory Reform, and Structural Change in the Electrical Power Industry," *Brookings Papers: Microeconomics*, 1989, p. 163.

24. Hoffman, "Power Moves," p. 53.

25. OTA, *Energy Efficiency*, p. 44.

26. For an argument that opposes deregulation along these lines, see D. Gegax and K. Nowotny, "Competition and the Electric Utility Industry: An Evaluation," *Yale Journal on Regulation*, Winter 1993.

27. Hoffman, "Power Moves," p. 54.

28. Douglas, "Buying and Selling Power," p. 8.

13 Franchise Bidding and Cable Television

In spite of considerable deregulation in the 1980s, the government has continued to play a significant role in markets that are firmly believed to be natural monopolies. Most economists argue that there is a need for government intervention in some capacity when social optimality requires a single firm to produce some good or service. It is because we foresee a continued role for government intervention that we have dedicated several chapters to analyzing issues related to natural monopoly.

This and the following chapter investigate alternatives to regulation for the case of a natural monopoly. The approach explored in this chapter is the auctioning off of a franchise for the provision of a monopoly service. Referred to as *franchise bidding*, it entails issuing the franchise to the firm that proposes the lowest price for service while meeting certain criteria concerning quality of service. As will be made clear, it substitutes competition at the bidding stage for regulation. Our case study will concern cable television, where franchise bidding has been used extensively.

A second alternative, which is investigated in Chapter 14, is having the service provided by a public (or government) enterprise as opposed to regulating a privately owned firm. As an alternative to regulation, public ownership has been used rather widely in the distribution of electricity at the municipal level as well as for water utilities. Municipal electric utilities will be used as a case study in assessing the performance of publicly owned firms.

The main purpose of the two chapters is to explore these two policies—franchise bidding and public enterprise—and to assess whether they represent attractive alternatives to the traditional solution of regulation in solving the natural monopoly problem.

Theory of Franchise Bidding

If an industry is a natural monopoly, then cost efficiency requires a single firm to operate in the industry. Of course, in an unregulated environment with only one supplier, one would expect price to be set at the monopoly level. Because this entails price exceeding marginal cost, deadweight welfare losses would result, a situation that may not maintain itself. Potential entrants would observe one supplier in the industry earning above-normal profits and recognize that there is room for profitable entry by undercutting the monopolist's price. Entry drives price down, but it results in there being too many firms operating in the industry. Given scale economies, average cost is higher than if only one firm produced. In an unregulated environment with a natural monopoly, we would expect to observe a price that is too high and/or excessive entry into the industry.

This scenario provides the rationale for the regulation of a natural monopoly. To ensure the efficient number of firms in an industry, entry regulation is typically proposed to prevent more than one supplier from operating. Without the threat of entry, however, a monopolist is certain to set price at the monopoly level. To avoid welfare losses induced by an excessively high price, price regulation is used to keep price at the level that maximizes social welfare.

In an important article in 1968, Harold Demsetz questioned the accepted belief that a natural monopoly must be regulated in order to achieve the social welfare optimum.[1] In place of regulation, he proposed that there be franchise bidding. Specifically, the government would award a franchise to one firm for the provision of this service. The franchise would be awarded via competitive bidding, where a bid would take the form of the proposed price that would be charged for service. The prospective firm that offered the lowest bid would be awarded the franchise. If there is sufficient competition at the bidding stage, then price should be bid down to average cost ($\hat{P}$ in Figure 13.1) and the winner would earn normal profits. The role for government would be to act as an auctioneer rather than as a regulator.

Competition at the Bidding Stage

An Example of Franchise Bidding—A Modified English Auction

The motivating force of franchise bidding is that ex ante competition at the bidding stage keeps price and profit at the competitive level. Thus, ex ante competition serves the role usually played by active competition in the industry. To appreciate the effectiveness of ex ante competition, let us consider a particular auction form through which franchise bidding could take place.

The *English (or oral ascending) auction* is probably the most commonly used auction form.[2] When an item like a painting or an oil lease is to be sold, the English auction works as follows. The auctioneer announces a bid to which the bidders respond by signaling whether they are willing to buy at that price. If there are at least two active bidders (a bidder is active if he signals he is willing to buy at the going bid), the auctioneer raises the bid. He keeps raising it until there is only one active bidder. The last remaining bidder wins the item and pays a price equal to the final bid.

With franchise bidding, the franchise is instead awarded to the bidder who offers the lowest price for service, so that we need to slightly modify

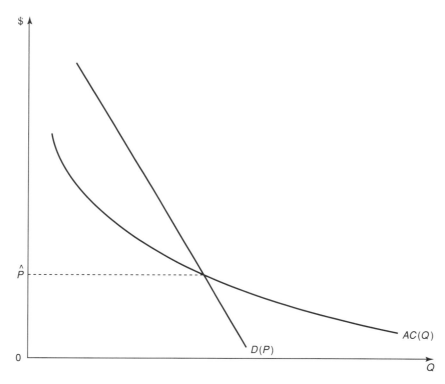

Figure 13.1
Average Cost Pricing

the English auction. Assume that the auctioneer starts at a high bid and lowers the bid as long as there are two or more active bidders. As soon as the bid is lowered to the point at which there is only one remaining bidder, the franchise is awarded to that bidder. In exchange for the franchise, the winning bidder is to charge a price for service equal to the final bid.

Suppose there are four firms bidding for the franchise. Let $AC_i(Q)$ represent the average cost function for firm i ($i = 1, 2, 3, 4$). As depicted in Figure 13.2, the firms have different cost functions. This could be due to firms having different production technologies as the result of patents or trade secrets. Alternatively, some firms might simply be more efficient than other firms. Constrained to linear pricing (that is, a constant per unit price), the social welfare optimum is to have firm 1 supply the good at a price of $\hat{P}_1$. This entails the most efficient firm pricing at average cost.

If the franchise is awarded via a modified English auction, the first question to ask is, What will be the optimal bidding strategy for a firm? Imagine that prior to the start of the auction, a firm decides on the bids

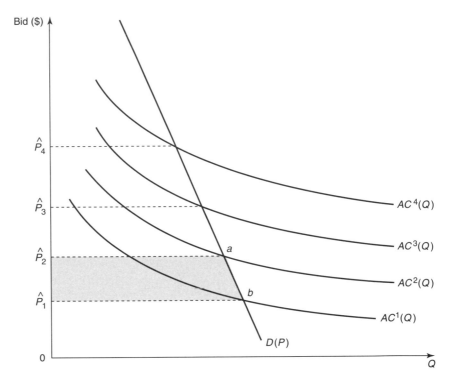

Figure 13.2
Franchise Bidding Using a Modified English Auction

for which it will remain active. It should be clear that firm i will choose to remain an active bidder when the bid B is greater than $\hat{P}_i$. If B exceeds $\hat{P}_i$ and firm i wins, it then earns above-normal profits as it ends up being able to charge a price which exceeds average cost. If B is less than $\hat{P}_i$, then firm i leaves the bidding because if it should win with a bid less than $\hat{P}_i$ it will have to charge a price less than average cost and thereby incur losses. Thus the optimal bidding strategy for firm i is to remain active as long as B is at least as great as $\hat{P}_i$. At a bid of $\hat{P}_i$, firm i would earn normal profits, as winning the franchise would result in average cost pricing.

Now let us determine what the outcome of franchise bidding will be if firms 1, 2, 3, and 4 compete via a modified English auction and use the bidding rule described above. Suppose that the auctioneer starts at a bid above $\hat{P}_4$. All four bidders will signal they are active. Because there is more than one bidder active, the auctioneer lowers the bid. Once B falls below $\hat{P}_4$, firm 4 will drop out of the bidding. However, the bid will continue to fall because there are still three active bidders. Firm 3 will drop out once B is less than $\hat{P}_3$, which leaves firms 1 and 2 competing.

As soon as B falls just below $\hat{P}_2$, firm 2 will leave the bidding. Because this leaves firm 1 as the only active bidder, the outcome of the auction is that firm 1 wins the franchise and charges a price slightly less than $\hat{P}_2$ (the final winning bid).

There is good and bad news resulting from the auctioning-off of the franchise. The good news is that the firm with the lowest average cost curve is the franchise owner. This will always be true because the firm that is most efficient can always outbid the other firms. The bad news is that price is approximately equal to $\hat{P}_2$, which exceeds the franchise owner's average cost. Consumer's surplus is lower by the shaded area $\hat{P}_2ab\hat{P}_1$ than when average cost pricing is used.

The reason price is set too high is that there is insufficient competition. Firm 1 does not face other firms that are as efficient as it is. Suppose instead that there are two firms with average cost functions $AC^1(Q)$ instead of just one firm. In the auction, when the bid falls below $\hat{P}_2$, there will still be two active bidders (the ones with average cost function $AC^1(Q)$). Thus the bid will fall until it reaches $\hat{P}_1$.[3] At that bid, the two firms are indifferent to winning the franchise. Once the bid falls below $\hat{P}_1$, both drop out. To decide on the winner, the auctioneer will have to choose randomly between the last two bidders. What is important is that the outcome of the auction entails a firm with the lowest cost structure producing and pricing at the socially optimal level of $\hat{P}_1$. Thus the ability of franchise bidding to result in a desirable social outcome is very much dependent on there being sufficient competition in the most efficient average cost range.

Analysis of Franchise Bidding

As long as there is sufficient competition at the bidding stage, franchise bidding results in average cost pricing and the most efficient firm operating. Although regulation could also achieve this outcome, the advantage to franchise bidding is that it imposes no informational requirements on a government agency. With regulation, the regulatory agency must have cost and demand information in order to achieve average cost pricing. Under franchise bidding, no such information is required, as competition, rather than a regulator's decision, results in average cost pricing. Thus, franchise bidding can achieve the same outcome as regulation but at lower cost since less information is required and a regulatory agency need not be established. A second advantage is that the inefficiency of rate-of-return regulation is avoided. With franchise bidding, there is no incentive to overcapitalize (the A-J effect; see Chapter 12). The franchise owner has every incentive to efficiently utilize resources because it retains all profits.

Thus far we have painted an excessively rosy picture of franchise bidding. It is best to think of our analysis up to this point as representing the potential of franchise bidding. In the next section we will be concerned with how franchise bidding performs in a more realistic setting. However, aside from any practical problems with franchise bidding, one criticism of it is that it does not result in marginal cost pricing.[4] Average cost pricing is certainly preferable to price being set at a monopoly level, but we know from Chapter 11 that a two-part tariff with per-unit price equal to marginal cost generally yields higher social welfare than average cost pricing.[5]

Although this criticism is valid, it should be noted that franchise bidding can be adapted so as to allow for two-part tariffs. However, we now need to assume that the government knows the market-demand function (though it still does not need cost information, in contrast to the case where regulation is used). Knowledge of the demand function gives the government a measure of how much consumers value a two-part tariff. Instead of awarding the franchise to the bidder who offers the lowest price, the government awards it to the one with the two-part tariff that maximizes social welfare (that is, the two-part tariff that consumers most prefer). Competition results in the franchise's being awarded to the firm that offers the two-part tariff that maximizes consumers' surplus, subject to profits being normal.

Consider the demand and cost function in Figure 13.3. Let us first show that there is a two-part tariff that beats out average cost pricing, so that a firm offering a price equal to average cost cannot win the franchise. A two-part tariff entails the payment of a fixed fee by a consumer, which gives that consumer the right to buy the good, plus a per-unit price for each unit purchased. For ease of analysis, let us assume the demand curve is perfectly income-inelastic.[6] If a firm bids a price equal to average cost and is awarded the franchise, then consumers' surplus is triangle abc. Now consider a second firm that offers a price equal to marginal cost and a fixed fee of F. Because marginal cost pricing increases consumers' surplus by the area $bcde$, consumers are better off with the two-part tariff as long as $bcde$ exceeds NF where N is the number of customers. That is, in order to have price lowered from average cost to marginal cost, consumers are willing to pay up to $bcde$. Thus, if it costs them less than $bcde$, they are better off with the two-part tariff. In order for a firm to earn at least normal profit, it must set F (given price equals marginal cost) such that NF exceeds $defg$ where rectangle $defg$ represents the losses from pricing below average cost. Because $bcde$ exceeds $defg$, there exists a two-part tariff that yields higher welfare for consumers than average cost pricing and allows the firm to earn above-

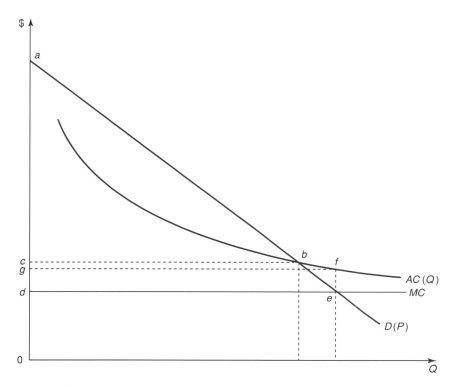

Figure 13.3
Franchise Bidding Using Two-Part Tariffs

normal profit; that is, $bcde > NF > defg$. As long as there is sufficient competition, the fixed fee will be bid down to $(defg/N)$ so that the franchise winner earns normal profit. We conclude that if the government has demand information, franchise bidding will result in a two-part tariff with marginal-cost pricing.[7]

As a final remark, it is important to stress that it is essential that the franchise be auctioned off to the firm that proposes the tariff with the highest social welfare. In contrast, suppose the franchise was awarded to the firm that was willing to pay the highest fee to the government and it was allowed to price freely. We know that the franchise owner would set price at the monopoly level P^m (see Figure 13.4). Because this yields profits of $\pi^m = [P^m - AC(Q^m)]Q^m$, firms are willing to pay up to π^m for the franchise. Hence, competition results in the franchise being awarded to the firm that offers π^m. The winner's effective average cost is then $([(\pi^m/Q) + AC(Q)])$. As shown in Figure 13.4, at the monopoly price P^m the franchise owner earns normal profit. Although normal profit was also earned when the franchise was auctioned off to the firm offering the lowest price for service, a major difference is the market price. With

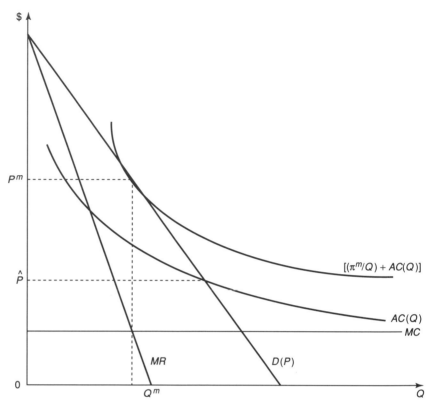

Figure 13.4
Bidding over the Franchise Fee

average-cost pricing, the latter franchise bidding scheme results in a price of $\hat{P}$ versus P^m. This lower price yields higher welfare. The conclusion one draws is that for franchise bidding to lead to a socially desirable solution, the franchise must be auctioned off to the firm offering the lowest price for service and not the highest franchise fee.

Quality of Service

If the service is homogeneous, then competition over pricing at the bidding stage leads to the social welfare optimum. Typically, however, a firm chooses the characteristics of the service it offers in terms of such variables as durability and reliability. For example, auto manufacturers do not just set the price of the automobiles they sell. Considerable time and expense is devoted to choosing the product characteristics in terms of design, motor size, and optional features like a rear window defroster and an intermittent wiper. Product performance is also a choice variable in terms of durability (is the body protected against rust?) and reliability (will the car start every winter morning?). Better paint jobs and stronger batteries result in higher quality.

Suppose that product quality is a choice variable and per-unit cost is increasing in the level of quality. If franchise bidding takes place over the price of service, competition will drive down not only price but also quality. The winning bidder will be the one that offers the lowest quality product at a price equal to average cost. The problem with franchise bidding in this situation is that society may not desire the low-quality, low-price alternative. Consumers may be willing to pay a higher price (at least as great as average cost) for higher-quality service. However, because competition takes place only over price, franchise bidding results in the lowest price, which implies the lowest level of quality.

There are several methods for adapting franchise bidding to when products can be differentiated. One is for the relevant government agency to specify the quality of service that is to be provided by the franchise owner. Franchise bidding can then take place over price without driving down quality. A second approach is to have multidimensional bidding in which firms not only propose a price for service but also the attributes of the service it will offer. These attributes determine the level of quality. The bidding procedure is now considerably more complex, as there is a tradeoff between higher quality and a lower price that has to be evaluated by the bidders and the franchising agency.

There are two difficulties inherent in both of these methods. First, they require the franchising agency to have information on consumers' valuation of quality. This will be needed in order to specify the required characteristics of a service or to analyze the tradeoff between quality and price in awarding the franchise. A second difficulty is in enforcing the agreement made with the franchise winner regarding quality. Quality is considerably more difficult to monitor than price. For example, assessing the performance of a long-distance telephone call in terms of static interference and connection time is no easy task. The same is true for determining the reliability of service, inasmuch as this requires monitoring service over a period of time. Thus the monitoring of a quality agreement is much more costly than the monitoring of a price agreement. Furthermore, there is generally going to be an incentive on the part of the franchise owner to reduce quality. Because price is fixed and higher quality increases cost, a firm has a tendency to reduce quality in order to reduce cost and increase profit. Of course, reducing quality will also reduce demand and this effect will tend to counteract the incentive to reduce quality. Nevertheless, we should expect lower quality than if there was perfect monitoring of quality by the relevant government agency.

Introducing the quality dimension into the franchise bidding process greatly complicates matters. It is important to note that to handle these complications a bigger role for government is required. This includes monitoring quality (as well as, of course, price) and specifying the attributes of the service to be provided by the franchise owner. Because the main attraction of franchise bidding is the minimal role for government, the advantage of franchise bidding over regulation is reduced as more realistic elements, like product quality, are introduced into the analysis.

Rent-Seeking Activity

When firms compete in terms of quality of service as well as price, the bids are multidimensional and highly complicated. In that situation, one should not use as simple a device as the English auction and award the franchise to the bidder with the lowest price. Some firms might bid a high price but, at the same time, promise a high-quality product. In selecting a franchise owner, the franchising agency will have to weigh both the price and quality dimensions.

In contrast to the case where competition takes place only in price and an auction mechanism is used, one cannot be assured that the winner of the franchise will be the one that maximizes welfare. One reason is that the franchising agency is likely to lack information about how consumers are willing to trade off price and quality. Thus, even if they wanted to act so as to maximize welfare, they are unable to do so. However, the franchising agency might not simply be interested in maximizing welfare. They might instead choose a proposal that serves their own purposes and not society's. For example, local politicians might choose the proposal that generates the most government revenue because it will allow them to reduce tax rates and thereby increase their chances of being reelected. Recognizing that the determination of the franchise owner depends on a variety of factors and not just social welfare, bidders will put forth proposals that cater to the desires of the franchising agency. Thus, firms will compete in ways that reduce welfare but raise their chance of winning. Such activity is referred to as *rent-seeking behavior* (see Chapter 4).

Rent is defined as the amount of payment to an agent that exceeds the minimum amount required to keep him in his current activity. Rent-seeking activity occurs when agents act to earn rent. In our context, rent is the amount of above-normal profit earned by the franchise owner. Firms pursue rent-seeking activities when they compete for this franchise by offering fees to the local government, performing public service

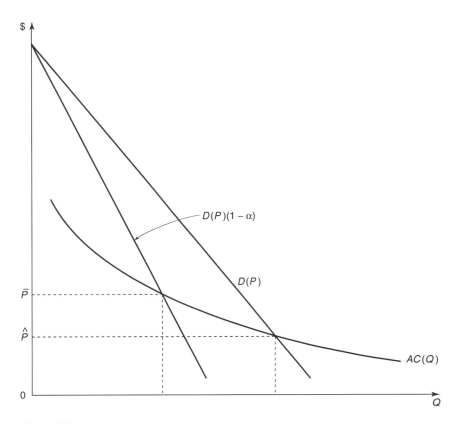

Figure 13.5
Franchise Bidding under a Proportional Franchise Fee

tasks, or even bribing elected local government officials with direct cash payments or contributions to their campaign funds.

If there is sufficient competition, rent-seeking activity will compete away any above-normal profit so that the franchise winner earns only normal profit. However, such activity may still reduce social welfare. For example, suppose that the franchise owner has to pay an annual fee that is some percentage of gross revenues. In that event, firms will not compete price down to $\hat{P}$ (see Figure 13.5). In order for them to earn normal profit, a higher price will have to be charged in order to cover cost and the franchise fee. For example, suppose that the franchise owner has to pay 100α percent of gross revenue to the local government. Firm revenue is then $PD(P)(1-\alpha)$ where $D(P)$ is the market demand function. The effective demand curve faced by the franchise winner is then $D(P)(1-\alpha)$. If competition drives price to average cost, the winning bid will be $\bar{P}$, which exceeds $\hat{P}$.

It is important to note that the welfare loss from the imposition of a franchise fee is due to the resulting higher price. The fee itself does not represent a reduction in welfare, as it is just a transfer from the franchise winner to politicians and/or taxpayers (via the local government). The other source of welfare loss from rent-seeking activity is the use of real resources, for example, attorney fees and the provision of public services. Although such expenditures have some value, the value of the resources used usually falls short of their resulting value. Rather, such expenditures are made in order to acquire rent.

We can conclude that if the franchising process allows room for rent-seeking behavior, social welfare is not as high as if the institution prevented it. When competition takes place over more than just price, we would expect firms to propose services that appeal to the franchising agency in spite of their negative impact on social welfare.

Contractual Arrangements for the Postbidding Stage

In our analysis thus far, we have assumed that bidding, whether over price or price and quality, is performed once and for all. Such a situation is suitable if the environment never changes. As we all know too well, the environment does change, and most often in ways that are quite unanticipated. Input prices and technology change over time, which causes the average cost curve to shift. The demand function changes as income and preferences change. In order to allow price to adjust in the future, franchise bidding will have to be supplemented with a contract that specifies how changes in cost and demand conditions are to be handled. In an important article in 1976, Oliver Williamson provided a detailed analysis of different types of contracts to handle future, unanticipated events.[8]

Recurrent, Short-Term Contracts

One approach is to use recurrent, short-term contracts. This approach avoids having to specify too much in the contract. Periodically, the franchise is to be put up for auction, at which time a new award is made and a new contract is issued. Thus, cost and demand changes are handled through recontracting. This procedure provides the current franchise owner with the incentive to honor its current contract, especially concerning quality. If it does not, it may be penalized in the next round of bidding through differentially disadvantageous treatment by the government agency.

The key element to the success of recurrent short-term contracts is that there be bidding parity at renewal time. If there is a lack of parity among bidders, in particular if the incumbent firm has an advantage, it may be able to renew the contract at noncompetitive terms. One ad-

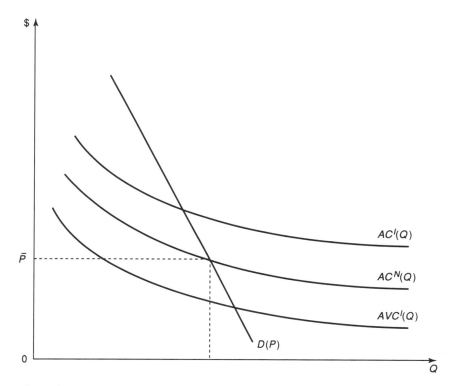

Figure 13.6
Franchise Bidding at Rcncwal Time

vantage the current franchise owner does have is that it has already invested in plant and equipment. In contrast, a new firm would have to
make this major investment. Thus, while the incumbent firm would be
willing to bid down to average variable cost, a new firm would not bid
below its average total cost. The result is that a new firm could be more
efficient than the current franchise owner but the latter would outbid it.
In Figure 13.6 the new firm has average cost curve $AC^N(Q)$, while the
incumbent has average cost curve $AC^I(Q)$ and average variable cost
curve $AVC^I(Q)$. Even though $AC^N(Q) < AC^I(Q)$, the franchise is renewed by the current owner because $AVC^I(Q) < AC^N(Q)$. The resulting
price would be $\bar{P}$.

This problem can be rectified by the transfer of capital from the previous franchise owner to the new one. The government could mandate a
compulsory transfer of assets in a fair and efficient manner. Thus a new
firm need not have to invest from scratch but could instead purchase the
existing plant and equipment from the previous franchise owner. In
response to this proposal, Williamson argued that this transfer is by
no means trivial. Requiring the incumbent to sell at original cost less

depreciation provides room for it to inflate the true value of its assets. In addition, what about human capital? Workers and management learn over time and build up knowledge as to how to best run the company. If a new firm comes in with new personnel, this capital cannot be transferred. Of course, a new firm is likely to hire these people, recognizing their marginal product is the greatest.

It is a valid point that the transfer of capital is indeed not a trivial problem. Nevertheless, if the franchise was won by a new firm, it would be in both firms' interest to transfer those assets. This is then just a bargaining problem, and one would expect it to be resolved since it is in the best interests of both firms to come to an agreement.

Another source of advantage to the existing franchise owner at renewal time may be imposed by the government agency monitoring the industry. It is often believed that bureaucrats try to maintain the status quo. Change brings additional work, for example, having to assist in the transfer of assets to the new franchise owner. Furthermore, if the change turns out for the worse, bureaucrats are likely to be blamed. In contrast, there is little lost from maintaining the status quo. Because of all this, the government agency is apt to favor the incumbent firm at renewal time as long as it has performed reasonably well. The degree of this advantage is unclear and it has not been adequately verified empirically. However, it is an effect that should be recognized when comparing franchise bidding to regulation.

Incomplete, Long-Term Contracts

The main alternative to recurrent short-term contracts is incomplete, long-term contracts, where long-term is on the order of fifteen to twenty years. The contracts are incomplete in the sense that all contingencies are not provided for but will instead be handled through negotiation and implicit understandings. An advantage to the long-term contract is that it gives the franchise owner the proper incentives to invest in long-lived assets, inasmuch as it is assured of being around to receive the returns from this investment. In contrast, with short-term contracts, a franchise owner may be less inclined to make long-term investments, given that its contract may not be renewed and there is uncertainty over the transfer of assets. This issue is particularly important for natural monopolies, as capital investment is typically a large portion of costs.

A disadvantage of the long-term contract is that it is difficult to write. It must allow for price to be changed in the future in response to changes in cost and/or demand conditions. Thus a price formula will need to be specified that relates the cost of inputs to the price of service. Monitoring of quality will be essential and the contract will have to provide for penalties if quality is not kept up to the specified level. With recurrent short-term contracts, penalties are less essential because the incumbent firm can be penalized at renewal time.

Ex-Post-Opportunistic Behavior

As we mentioned earlier, the current franchise owner will typically have certain advantages over prospective franchise owners. These advantages include having already made the necessary capital investment, better knowledge about the technology through learning-by-doing, better information on market demand, and greater familiarity with the franchising process. These advantages may provide the current franchise owner with the ability to hold up the local government opportunistically by forcing them to make favorable changes in their contract.

Recall that when an incomplete long-term contract is used, the local government and the franchise owner will have to negotiate prices and quality over time as new information arrives concerning the cost of providing the service as well as the demand for the service. If cost turns out to be higher than anticipated or demand turns out to be weaker than anticipated (weaker demand means higher average cost when there are economies of scale), price will have to be raised. One strategy for a prospective firm at the bidding stage is to offer a low price and then, if the franchise is won, to petition for a price increase on the basis that average cost was underestimated or demand was overestimated. As long as the franchise owner has already made some investment in capital and the proposed rate increase is not too great, the government agency is likely to concede to this request rather than have to incur the cost of performing another round of franchise bidding and having a new franchise owner commit resources.

Several devices are available for reducing the incentive of a franchise owner to engage in opportunistic holdup. Depending on the degree of renewal competition, the current franchise owner can be punished for opportunistic behavior by being relieved of his franchise at renewal time. However, punishment need not be limited to renewal time. A government agency has several devices for disciplining the franchise owner over the life of the contract. First, there are penalty clauses for reneging on one's proposal that are built into the franchise contract. Second, because the contract is incomplete, there are issues left open that need to be negotiated over the life of the contract. A government agency can punish for opportunistic holdup through the way they behave during these negotiations. Another mechanism may exist when a firm operates franchises in several markets. A reputation for opportunistic holdup can harm one's chances of winning a new franchise. Finally, a government agency can always threaten a franchise owner with public ownership of the franchise.

Finally, it should be mentioned that opportunistic holdup may also work in the other direction. Once a firm has sunk considerable resources, the government agency has power emanating from its monopsonistic position. By controlling the franchise owner's access to the market, the government agency is acting as an agent for buyers. If fixed costs are sunk, then the franchise owner will operate as long as price is at least as great as average variable cost. Thus a government agency may take advantage of its position by forcing the firm to price at average variable cost even though the firm would not have made the original investment if it anticipated a price below average cost. A government agency might implement such a policy by requiring that the franchise owner keep price fixed over time in an inflationary environment. If price were initially at average cost, price would fall below average cost over time as long as the inflation rate is positive.

Just as reputational effects are important for controlling the behavior of the franchise owner, they can be effective in deterring opportunistic behavior by the government. If prospective firms believe that price will not be adjusted over time for inflation, this will affect their initial bidding behavior. Specifically, they will not bid price down to average cost because they know a price equal to today's average cost may mean normal profit today but will mean losses in the future as the real price falls below real average cost. Though opportunistic behavior is potentially a problem when agents invest specific resources in their relationship with one another, it is at least partially mitigated by the disciplining influence of reputation.

Assessment of Franchise Bidding

Williamson makes a valid point when he says that uncertainty about the future creates a bigger role for government in the bidding process. In the case of incomplete, long-term contracts, franchise bidding differs from regulation as a matter of degree and not of kind. A government agency must specify quality and monitor the performance of the franchise owner. It must also negotiate price changes with the supplier. This point is made even more evident once one recognizes that regulation is itself an incomplete, long-term contract in which the firm is guaranteed a fair rate of return and there is an established procedure for making changes.

In an ideal environment, franchise bidding appears quite superior to regulation. It accomplishes the same outcome at lower cost. There is no need for a regulatory agency and no incentives for the monopolist to act inefficiently. However, as we introduce product quality and uncertainty, franchise bidding begins to look more and more like regulation. The apparent advantages to franchise bidding become less outstanding. Still, franchise bidding is an interesting alternative to regulation and it has considerable potential. The next section will analyze how franchise bidding has performed with regard to cable television. This application will provide us with some insight as to how franchise bidding has fared in practice in solving the natural monopoly problem.

Cable Television

The first cable systems were constructed in the late 1940s for the purpose of improving the reception of broadcast signals sent by local television stations. By expanding the market of a local television station, cable service was complementary to the service provided by local broadcasters. Then, beginning in the late 1950s and early 1960s, cable systems sought to expand the demand for their services by importing signals from other regions via microwave relay stations. In addition to providing better reception of local stations, cable service also offered a wider selection of broadcasts. The importation of signals then meant that cable services also represented an alternative to local television broadcasts. In this sense, cable service was a substitute for local broadcasting. This dual aspect of cable service—being both a substitute and a complement to local television broadcasting—will be most relevant when it comes to understanding regulatory policy with respect to cable television.[9]

With a few exceptions, each of the approximately 11,000 cable systems that exist today have a local monopoly over cable service. However, it is important to recognize that there are a number of substitutes for cable service. To begin, almost 40 percent of the households that could have cable service choose not to have it. Many of these households have chosen to rely on local television broadcasts. If they want the variety and reception of cable service, they have the option of purchasing a satellite dish, for which there are a number of available technologies. Although a cable company may have a monopoly over cable service, it is important to keep in mind that cable service must compete with other forms of video entertainment.

Historical/Regulatory Background

The Communications Act of 1934 created the Federal Communications Commission (FCC) and gave it the power to regulate wire and radio communication. Of particular relevance is that the FCC was given regulatory authority over television broadcasting. During the early period of cable television in the 1950s, cable television was allowed to grow with a minimum of regulatory interference. The FCC even went so far as to refuse to accept regulatory jurisdiction over cable television on the basis that it was neither a broadcasting facility nor a wire common carrier. Its general policy was to allow auxiliary services to television, like cable systems, to develop in an unfettered environment.

It is significant that at the time of the FCC's decision not to regulate cable television, cable services were very much complementary to television broadcasting in that they improved the reception of signals and thereby expanded a local television station's market. During the period 1959–1966, cable systems began to actively import signals via microwave relay stations. Importation was a relatively inexpensive way to increase the demand for cable services. Of course, imported channels are substitutes for local broadcasters so that the latter's advertising revenue would be expected to fall.

As the economic theory of regulation would predict, television broadcasters pressured the FCC to regulate cable television. The FCC responded in 1962 by forbidding the importation of a distant signal into a market for which the same broadcast was carried by a local television station. Then, in 1966, the FCC asserted full regulation over cable television. It required a cable system to carry all local television stations and prohibited the importation of any additional signals in the top 100 television markets. The FCC ended this freeze on importation in 1972 although, in its stead, it instituted a complex set of rules that still greatly limited the importation of signals. Even with these burdensome restrictions, the number of cable systems and the number of subscribers experienced healthy growth. From 1965 to 1975 the number of subscribers increased more than sevenfold from 1.2 million to 8.5 million viewers. The penetration ratio, which is the ratio of the number of subscribers to the number of households for which cable is available, had risen to 12.4 percent by 1975 from only 2.3 percent ten years earlier.[10]

The launch of the Satcom I satellite in 1975 provided cable systems with a relatively inexpensive technology for receiving distant programming. At the same time, the FCC was beginning to loosen its restrictions on the importation of signals. On top of these developments, the Home Box Office decision gave cable systems the right to compete freely with broadcast television. These events allowed a tremendous increase in the services provided by cable television. Prior to 1971, only 6 percent of all cable systems had more than twelve active channels. By 1980, almost 50 percent had more than twelve channels and 13 percent provided more

Table 13.1
Cable Television Industry Growth, 1976–1993

Year	Subscribers (millions)	Saturation	Penetration	Revenue ($billion)
1976	11.8	31.2%	51.1%	.932
1977	12.6	32.7	52.1	1.200
1978	14.2	35.3	53.0	1.476
1979	15.8	37.9	53.9	1.875
1980	19.2	43.2	55.0	2.549
1981	23.0	50.7	55.0	3.656
1982	27.5	59.3	55.6	4.984
1983	31.4	66.7	56.2	6.425
1984	34.2	70.9	56.5	7.774
1985	36.7	74.5	56.7	8.938
1986	39.7	78.4	57.2	10.144
1987	42.6	81.7	58.3	11.765
1988	45.7	84.7	59.2	13.595
1989	49.3	89.2	59.5	15.678
1990	51.7	92.2	60.1	17.855
1991	53.4	93.7	60.4	19.463
1992	55.2	94.7	60.9	21.044
1993	57.4	96.4	61.8	22.863

Saturation = number of U.S. households passed by cable systems/number of U.S. households

Penetration = number of U.S. households subscribing/number of U.S. households passed by cable systems

Source: Data are from Paul Kagan Associates and U.S. Department of Commerce, Bureau of Census. Table is from Thomas W. Hazlett, "Regulating Cable Television Rates: An Economic Analysis," University of California—Davis, Program on Telecommunications Policy, Working Paper No. 3, July 1994.

than thirty channels. As of 1992, 90 percent of cable subscribers receive more than twenty channels.

These developments were followed with tremendous growth in the cable television industry (see Table 13.1). In the 1970s less than a third of all households had access to cable. Now, cable service is nearly universal with it being available to more than 96 percent of households. Commensurate with this rise in availability has been a rise in subscribership. From 1976 to 1993, the number of subscribing households increased fivefold and stood at over 57 million. Growth in revenue has been equally spectacular as nominal revenue has increased more than twentyfold. A sign of the growing importance of cable service is the meteoric rise in advertising revenue. Since 1980 it has risen from almost nothing—less than $60 million—to close to $4 billion in 1993.[11]

During this phase in which cable service became ubiquitous, the regulatory issues were very different from those in the early part of cable's history. Since the early 1980s, the central regulatory issues have concerned cable rates and competition to cable operators. These issues will be discussed in a later section.[12]

Cable Television as a Natural Monopoly

In this section our objective is to analyze the rationale for government intervention in cable television. After reviewing the technology of cable systems and estimates of the degree of scale economies, we will conclude that current evidence is consistent with the hypothesis that cable television is a natural monopoly.

Technological Background

A cable system comprises three key components: (1) the headend, (2) the distribution plant, and (3) the subscriber interface. Figure 13.7 depicts

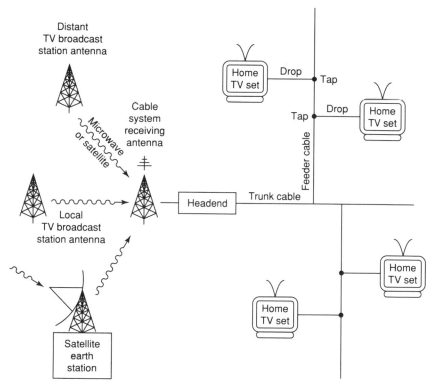

Figure 13.7
Physical Design of a Cable System

the physical design of a cable system. The purpose of the headend is to receive signals and process them for distribution. A major part of the headend is the antenna, which receives the signals. (It is for this reason that cable systems were originally referred to as community-antenna television, or CATV.) Once received, the signals are then distributed via the distribution plant, which has historically used coaxial cable—though now fiber optics is the preferred technology. As of 1993, TCI, the largest cable operator, planned to spend $2 billion to install fiber optics.[13] Its intention is to have the new system reach 90 percent of its customers. An important benefit from upgrading its system is that it will have the technology to offer phone service to its cable subscribers. (For more on this issue, see Chapter 15.) The final element of the cable system is the subscriber interface. It connects a subscriber to the distribution plant.

The capacity of the system, in terms of the number of channels, is determined by the distribution plant. Until the early 1980s most systems had a capacity of forty channels. At that time, the standard became a coaxial cable with fifty-four channels. The advent of fiber optics introduces the potential of near unlimited capacity. It is quite feasible to have hundreds of cable channels on a system.

A major portion of the cost of a cable system is in the purchase and construction of the distribution plant; in particular, the cost of laying the cable. This can be done aerially through the use of existing utility lines or underground though the latter is considerably more expensive. If a consumer is in the geographic region covered by the distribution plant, the marginal cost of a subscriber is relatively low, inasmuch as it just entails installing a subscriber interface. Given that marginal cost is relatively low and the cost of the distribution plant and the headend are fixed with respect to the number of subscribers, a cable system is generally considered to experience declining average cost per subscriber.

Estimates of Scale Economies

There are two important issues related to the optimal industry structure for cable television. First, for a given geographic market, is industry cost minimized by having cable systems not overlap? In other words, should each cable system have exclusive rights over the geographic area covered by its distribution plant? This is a particular type of scale economies which is referred to as *economies of density*.[14] If there are economies of density, then cost efficiency requires that there be no duplication of cable services; that is, each cable company's distribution plant should not overlap. However, even if there are economies of density, this does not necessarily imply that a metropolitan area should be served by a single cable company. A separate but related issue is whether cost efficiency requires a single firm to supply the entire geographic market or instead that the market be subdivided and have a different firm supply each submarket. We will deal with each of these issues in turn.

To examine the degree of economies of density, we need to estimate the average cost per subscriber for a fixed plant size. There are different measures of plant size though the most commonly used measures are the number of homes for which cable is available and the number of cable miles. Using a 1979 data set comprising seventeen cable systems in New Jersey, G. Kent Webb estimated an average cost curve for a system size of a thousand miles of cable and a density of one hundred households per mile of cable.[15] As shown in Figure 13.8, average cost per subscriber is clearly declining in the number of subscribers. This cost study provides empirical evidence supportive of the hypothesis that cable television experiences economies of density. For example, as market penetration is doubled from 40 percent to 80 percent, average cost declines by over 40 percent from approximately $14 to $8. A study by Eli Noam used cost data for nearly all 4200 cable systems for the year 1981.[16] He found that a 10 percent increase in the number of subscribers reduced unit cost by about 0.5 percent. Finally, Bruce Owen and Peter Greenhalgh used an alternative methodology by projecting cost figures. This study constructed a data set from 160 franchising proposals submitted over the period of 1979–1982.[17] Though this data set is inferior in that it comprises estimates of proposed cable systems rather than the actual cost of cable systems, the evidence is consistent with that of the other studies. It considers a hypothetical system with the characteristics of the average proposal which means 30,481 subscribers, 56.3 channels, and 428 miles of cable. For this system, the average monthly cost per subscriber was $39.33. If the number of subscribers is reduced by 50 percent, average cost per subscriber rises by 14 percent to $44.75. Thus, if two cable systems fully wired a geographic area and each served half of the market, the increase in cost relative to having a single supplier would be 14 percent. These studies support the hypothesis that cable systems exhibit economies of density. Cost efficiency then requires that the distribution plants of cable systems not overlap.

A second, and related, issue is whether it is more efficient to have one cable system for an entire geographical area or instead to subdivide the area with each cable system serving a submarket (and have no two cable systems overlapping). Cost studies have shown slight economies of scale of this variety. The New Jersey study by Webb estimated average cost per cable mile while holding market penetration constant (see

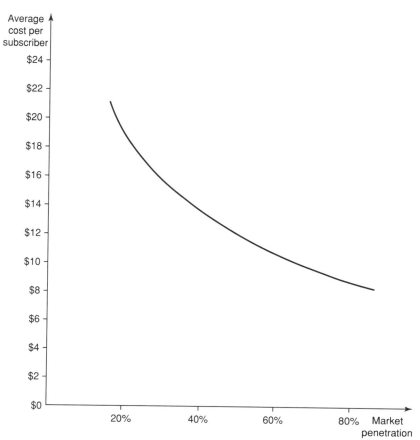

System size: 1,000 miles of cable.
Subscriber density: 100 households per mile of cable.

Figure 13.8
Average Total Cost for Cable Television Given Fixed Plant Size (1982 Dollars)

Source: Bruce M. Owen and Paul D. Gottlieb, "The Rise and Fall and Rise of Cable Television Regulation," in Leonard W. Weiss and Michael W. Klass, *Regulatory Reform: What Actually Happened* (Boston: Little Brown, 1986). Copyright 1986 by Leonard W. Weiss and Michael W. Klass. Reprinted by permission of HarperCollins Publishers.

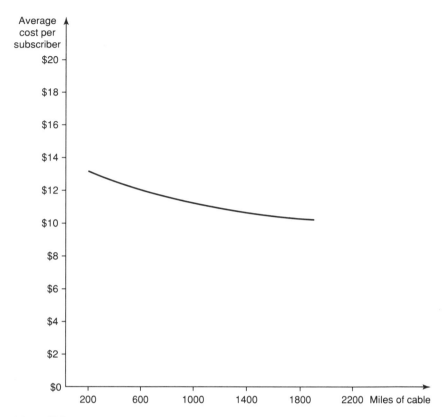

Figure 13.9
Average Total Cost for Cable Television Given Fixed Market Penetration (1982 Dollars)
Source: G. Kent Webb, *The Economics of Cable Television* (Lexington, Mass.: Lexington Books, 1983).

Figure 13.9). Economies of scale are present, but they are not particularly strong. The study by Noam estimated the elasticity of cost with respect to the number of homes passed. The elasticity was estimated to be 1.02, which means that a 10 percent increase in the size of the cable system (as measured by the number of homes passed by cable) results in a decrease in unit cost of only 0.2 percent.[18]

In summarizing this evidence, it appears that there are significant economies to having cable systems not overlap but that there are only slight cost savings from having a single cable system serve a geographic area, as opposed to subdividing it and having different cable systems serve these different submarkets. Taking into account both types of economies, it was estimated that the overall elasticity of scale was 1.096, so that a 10 percent increase in size (which includes both a 10 percent increase in homes passed and a 10 percent increase in subscribers) reduced unit cost by almost 1 percent.[19] Although the evidence is supportive of the hypothesis that cable television is a natural monopoly, it is not overwhelming.

Franchising Process

Given that the available evidence is supportive of cable systems exhibiting economies of density, there exists a rationale for a government providing exclusive rights to a cable company over a geographic area. The evidence we have considered also suggests that there may be little cost inefficiency from allowing several firms to serve a metropolitan area as long as their systems do not overlap. In this section we will briefly describe the process used by local governments in issuing a franchise; in the following section we will assess how franchise bidding has performed.

Procedural Steps in Franchise Bidding

The franchising process usually begins with the local government soliciting proposals from prospective cable operators. Often applicants are already cable operators in other markets in the United States. Once proposals are received, this initiates a negotiation process between the local government and the prospective cable operators. Typically, the local government will select a few applicants and ask them to submit bids. Eventually, a franchise is awarded or, if the local government is unsatisfied with the bids, the process is restarted.[20]

The length of time for this process to complete itself can be considerable. In the case of the franchising of the cable system in Oakland, California, the following timetable was observed:

June 19, 1969—The City of Oakland passed an ordinance allowing the issuing of a franchise for cable television.

April 30, 1970—The City of Oakland notified five applicants that their applications would be considered.

July 1, 1970—Bids were made by the five chosen applicants.

November 10, 1970—The franchise was awarded to Focus Cable.

December 23, 1970—Focus Cable accepted the franchise.[21]

The total length of time of the franchising process was in excess of eighteen months. While eighteen months may seem like a long time, the typical franchising process takes between two and ten years.[22] An extreme case is that of Philadelphia. Four rounds of franchise bidding took place starting in 1966; twenty years later Philadelphia had still not issued a franchise. The delay due to this process is certainly not trivial.

Description of Proposal and Contract

The proposal submitted by an applicant to the local government typically provides a technical account of the proposed system, the programming services, and prices. A description of the proposed system includes the number of channels, the pay channels that will be available, and any auxiliary services like two-way interactive channels. Price information includes the basic monthly price per subscriber and the price of pay channels.

Generally, much greater information than this is required. In the state of Massachusetts, the Cable Television Commission requires the franchise proposal to include:

(1) duration of the license (not to exceed 15 years); (2) area(s) to be served; (3) line extension policy; (4) construction schedule; (5) initial rates and charges; (6) amount and type of bond and insurance; (7) plan for local supervision; (8) criteria to be used in assessing applicant qualifications; (9) location of any free installations (e.g., public schools, police and fire stations, and other public buildings); and (10) equal employment opportunity practices. Suggested items are: (1) capability of the system; (2) plan for access channels and facilities; (3) plan for municipal coordination with the licensee; (4) types and patterns of ownership; (5) coordination with contiguous communities; and (6) subscriber rights of privacy.[23]

More generally, one would expect bidders to include any items in a proposal which are likely to give them an edge over competing bids. A discussion of such items will be provided later.

The most common contract used by the franchising authority is the long-term, nonexclusive contract. It is typically fifteen years in length. Nonexclusivity gives the local government the right to put the franchise up for auction if it finds the current franchise owner to be performing in an unsatisfactory manner.

Assessment of Franchise Bidding

In assessing the performance of franchise bidding, there are several issues that need to be addressed. To begin, a necessary condition for franchise bidding to work is that there be sufficient competition at the bidding stage. It is then important that we assess the degree of ex ante competition. However, recall from our discussion of rent-seeking behavior that it is vital that competition be of a certain type. Bidders must compete in terms of price and quality and not in terms of activities that benefit local governments but reduce social welfare. Activities of the latter variety are referred to as *nonprice concessions*.

The effectiveness of franchise bidding in generating a socially desirable solution depends not only on behavior at the bidding stage but also on how well the franchise owner performs over time. Related to this issue is the degree of opportunistic holdup. We will need to investigate whether franchise winners implement their proposals or renege on them by raising price and reducing quality. Finally, a key ingredient in the success of franchise bidding is that competition at the renewal stage be effective. If it is absent, the current franchise owner may be able to renew its franchise at terms that yield an abnormally high price without commensurate quality. In addition, renewal competition can be an important instrument for deterring opportunistic holdup.

Competition at the Bidding Stage

Generally, franchise bidding brings forth four or five applicants. A study of 92 franchise bidding cases in Massachusetts over 1973–1981 found that the number of applicants per case to range from 1 to 17 with an average of 5.2.[24] Furthermore, the average number of applicants was observed to rise from 2.6 in 1973–1978 (with 14 cases) to 5.7 over 1979–1981 (with 78 cases).[25] However, more recent evidence shows a declining number of applicants. In 27 of the largest franchises awarded after 1982, the average number of bidders was only 2.7.[26] The franchise bidding process in Baltimore brought forth only a single proposal.

Although the number of bidders for a franchise has not been large, it is nevertheless at a level that may generate an adequate level of competition. However, it is important to note that many of the same bidders compete for franchises in different communities. As of 1990, the five largest cable companies controlled nearly 50 percent of the U.S. cable market. The industry leader, TCI, had a market share of 22 percent.[27] Because many of the same firms are competing against one another for franchises, such an environment is conducive for collusion among bidders. However, there has been no test of this hypothesis.

There are four major areas in which competition for a franchise has taken place. One, obviously, is the price of cable service. Table 13.2 lists some of the major franchise awards over 1980–1982 including the range of bids for basic cable service. As one can see, the bids are often rather disparate. To examine the effect of the number of bidders on the winning bid price, Robin Prager surveyed sixty-six cable firms in 1984.[28] She found that for each additional bidder in the franchise auction, the price of basic cable service declined by $0.15 per month per subscriber, whereas the price of a pay channel declined by $0.16 per month per subscriber. As one would expect, an increase in the degree of ex ante competition reduced the winning bid.

A second dimension of competition is product quality. This includes channel capacity and programming as well as technical standards con-

Table 13.2
Major Franchise Awards, 1980–1982

Company/City	Cost of Basic Cable	Channel Capacity	Households in Franchise Area (thousands)	System Length (miles)	Capital Cost (millions of dollars)
ATC					
Indianapolis	$6.50	42	140	1,052	24.3
Cablevision					
Boston	$2.00–8.00	108	250	750	95
COX					
Tucson	$6.92–13.95	108	135	1,060	38.9
New Orleans	$7.95–11.95	108	220		
Omaha	$0.00–10.95	108 (80 in use)	125	1,095	33.7
Sammons					
Ft. Worth	$3.95–10.95	54	160	1,430	50.0
United					
Scottsdale	$5.95–11.95	54	50	400	19.0
Warner Amex					
Cincinnati	$3.95–10.95	138 (86 in use)	161	1,525	25.0
Dallas	$2.95–9.95	108	400	2,360	41.6
Pittsburgh	$5.35–9.45	80 (60 in use)	181	700	

Source: Adopted from Peter Falco, senior industry specialist, Merrill Lynch, *Cable Investment* (New York, 1983): 14. Table from G. Kent Webb, *The Economics of Cable Television* (Lexington, Mass.: Lexington Books, 1983).

cerning signal quality and reliability. Although firms compete in ways other than price and quality, these other dimensions of competition may tend to reduce social welfare. Such activities include franchise fees and nonprice concessions. The local government that is franchising cable service typically demands payment of a fixed fee and/or a percentage of gross revenues. However, competition in terms of financial payments to local governments is limited by federal regulation. The 1972 FCC rules set a maximum of 3 percent of gross revenues which was then raised to 5 percent in 1984.

Because of these restrictions on financial payments, bidders have actively competed in providing nonprice concessions. A common nonprice concession is the provision of channels for public service, educational use, and governmental use. Also included are free hookups, public parks, local origination studios, and excess capacity. Nonprice concessions are estimated to comprise about 26 percent of building costs and 11 percent of operating expenses.[29] Every dollar spent on nonprice concessions was found to raise the monthly rate per subscriber for basic cable service by $0.35.[30] On average, monthly basic rates are lower by

Table 13.3
Politically Imposed Costs of Franchise Monopoly (per month per subscriber)

	Uneconomic Investment	Delay	Lobbying	Franchise Fees	Total Costs
Low Estimate	$4.81	0.97	0.71	1.29	7.78
Mid-Point Estimate	$5.41	1.84	1.21	1.58	10.04
High Estimate	$6.00	2.72	1.71	1.88	12.31

Source: Assorted Sources. Table is from Thomas W. Hazlett, "Private Monopoly and the Public Interest: An Economic Analysis of the Cable Television Franchise," *University of Pennsylvania Law Review* 134 (July 1986): 1335–409.

$0.49 per subscriber if all nonprice concessions are eliminated.[31] As our analysis of rent-seeking behavior predicts, nonprice concessions tend to raise the price of cable service.

A study by Phillip Beutel estimated which aspects of a proposal are conducive to winning a franchise.[32] His study took account of the basic price per channel, the number of high-demand channels available, the total number of channels, and the number of public-access channels (with the last variable capturing nonprice concessions). It was found, rather interestingly, that a higher price actually raised one's chances of being awarded the franchise. A likely explanation is that the local government prefers to issue the franchise to a firm whose proposal will generate above-normal profit. The gain to the local government from doing so is that it provides a politically acceptable source of tax revenue. An alternative explanation is that franchising authorities are skeptical of proposals with absurdly low prices. Prospective cable operators have been known to offer free basic service, yet not be awarded the franchise. The franchising authority may have suspected that the proposal of free basic service meant either future rate increases or higher rates on other services.

In concluding, let us discuss a study that provides some rough estimates of some of the costs imposed by the franchising process. First, as discussed above, nonprice concessions result in uneconomic investment. As shown in Table 13.3, estimates of these costs are between $4.81 and $6.00 per subscriber per month. Second, the delay in the franchising process results in foregone consumer surplus, as consumers await cable service, and foregone profits, as firms await being able to supply cable service. The estimated cost is between $0.97 and $2.72. Third, the cost of lobbying by bidders (for example, in hiring consultants and attorneys) ranges from $0.71 to $1.71. Finally, franchise fees incur a cost of between $1.29 and $1.88. The total cost is between $7.78 and $12.31 per subscriber per month. This works out to about one-third of gross revenues. Even taking into account the roughness of these estimates, the politically imposed costs of franchising appear to be considerable.

Performance After the Initial Award

Clearly, there is anecdotal evidence of franchise owners reneging on their proposal once the franchise is issued. The winning proposal for the Milwaukee franchise called for a 108-channel system at a monthly basic service price of $4.95. Not long after the award was issued, the franchise winner renegotiated its contract and instead installed a 54-channel system at a monthly basic service price of $11.95.[33]

The systematic evidence is rather mixed. On the one hand, cable franchises were renegotiated in twenty-one of the thirty largest television markets, including eight before any homes were wired.[34] Of course, this evidence does not describe the degree of renegotiation. Other evidence suggests that opportunistic holdup is not a serious problem. A survey of the trade press over 1980–1986 revealed only sixty cases of cable operators' reneging on their contract from a pool of over three thousand cable operators.[35] Evidence from a survey of franchises in Massachusetts over 1973–1984 found that construction schedules and quality levels were generally consistent with the accepted proposals.[36] More important, the average time between the issuance of the franchise and the first rate increase was almost thirty-three months while the average time between the first rate increase and the second rate increase was over twenty-nine months.[37] On average, cable operators waited a considerable length of time before requesting a rate increase. Furthermore, of sixty-two franchises, forty-nine experienced a decrease in the real price of cable service from the time of the award until June 1984, while only thirteen had a real increase in the price of cable service.[38]

Another study tested the degree to which opportunistic holdup was prevented by reputational effects.[39] Recall that a cable operator who plans to compete for cable franchises in other markets may be penalized for opportunistic holdup because of the reputation it creates for not fulfilling its side of the contract. Communities may find the proposals of cable operators with such a reputation to be less credible and thus be less inclined to award them franchises. This study surveyed 221 communities served by franchised cable operators. Multiple-system operators were found to be less likely than single-system operators to have construction delays and more likely to provide voluntary improvements in the cable system. If we assume that a cable operator who currently serves several markets is more likely than a single system operator to compete for other cable franchises in the future then this empirical finding is supportive of reputational effects deterring opportunistic holdup.

Table 13.4
Deviation between Terms of Initial Contract and Renewal Contract

Term of Trade	Average for Initial Contract Sample	Estimated Deviation in Renewal Sample
Channel Capacity	46.4	9 fewer channels
Franchise Fee	2.9 percent	0.2 percent higher
Community Channels	2.8	0.8 fewer channels
Basic System Price (Monthly)	$9.35	$0.35 lower
Basic Price per Channel Offered	$0.52	$0.01 higher
Lead Pay Channel Price (Monthly)	$9.51	$1.13 higher*

*Indicates the difference is statistically significant at the 0.05 level in a one-tailed test.

Source: Mark A. Zupan, "Cable Franchise Renewals: Do Incumbent Firms Behave Opportunistically?" *RAND Journal of Economics* 20 (1989): 473–82.

In terms of competition at the renewal stage, the most significant statistic is that of 3516 refranchising decisions, only seven resulted in the local government's removing the current franchise owner.[40] The question, however, is whether this statistic is indicative of the satisfaction of the local government with the performance of the initial franchise owner or whether it is indicative of the lack of competition at the renewal stage. To investigate this issue, a study by Mark Zupan examined fifty-nine randomly chosen renewal agreements over 1980–1984 and compared the terms of the initial contract with the renewal contract. The results are shown in Table 13.4. From the perspective of the franchise owner, the renewal contract tends to be more favorable than the initial contract. Quality is lower at renewal time as, on average, channel capacity is reduced by nine channels, while the number of community channels is reduced by 0.8. The monthly basic price per channel is higher by $0.01 per subscriber and the monthly pay channel price is higher by $1.13. However, the monthly basic system price is reduced by $0.35 and the franchise fee is increased by 0.2 percent.

Rates and Rate Regulation

One of the main advantages of the long-term contract is that it avoids the costly process of frequent bidding and provides the franchise owner with the necessary long-term incentives for investment. On the downside, a long-term contract needs to make provisions for adjusting rates in response to changing cost and demand conditions. Ultimately, local governments chose to handle this problem through the regulation of rates. The typical procedure was for the cable operator to propose rate changes to a government authority as is done with regulated public utilities like local telephone. By 1979 at least ten states had some form of rate regulation.

This regulatory movement was cut short by federal legislation. Price controls over pay channels were discontinued in 1979 and, beginning in December 1986, the Cable Communications Policy Act of 1984 prohibited federal and state or local regulation of basic cable prices.[41] Continued regulation would be allowed only where effective competition was absent. The FCC considered a cable company to face effective competition if it competed with three or more over-the-air television stations. This meant that only 3 percent of the cable systems in the United States were subject to rate regulation.

In addition to prohibiting local authorities from controlling cable rates, the 1984 Act also constrained competition. First, it mandated that all cable systems be franchised by local governments. This eliminated the threat of entry from a second cable operator as a downward pressure on cable rates. Second, the 1984 Act made it more difficult for a local government to fail to renew a cable company's franchise. To do so, the cable company must have violated the franchise agreement and, even in that case, the company had to be given adequate opportunity to rectify the situation. The threat of not renewing a company's franchise because rates were too high was then considerably weakened. Finally, the act codified the FCC's 1970 ban on a local telephone company's providing cable service in its jurisdiction.

Cable rates became unregulated on December 29, 1986, and thereafter followed a steady rise exceeding the rate of inflation (see Figure 13.10). By mid-1991, basic cable rates had risen 36.5 percent in real terms. Before jumping to conclusions that cable companies have taken advantage of their market power, let us next note that the average basic package experienced an increase in channels of almost 30 percent, from twenty-nine to thirty-seven channels. Furthermore, cable operators have increased spending on basic programming from around $300 million to over $1 billion. Since deregulation of cable rates, we have then observed both a rise in price and in quality.[42]

A study by Robert Rubinovitz, an economist at the Antitrust Division of the Department of Justice, estimated the effect of the 1984 Act on quality-adjusted rates.[43] He compared the price and characteristics of basic cable packages in 1984 (the regulated benchmark) with that in 1990 (the unregulated benchmark). During that time, the real price of cable service rose 42 percent. After taking account of changes in the cost of a cable operator providing service and, most importantly, in the changes in the quality of service (for example, the number of channels),

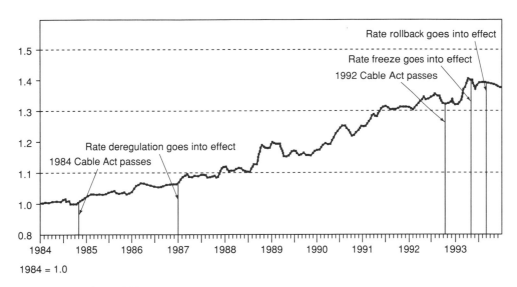

Figure 13.10
Real Cable Television Rates, 1984–1993
Source: Thomas W. Hazlett, "Regulating Cable Television Rates: An Economic Analysis,"
University of California–Davis, Program on Telecommunications Policy, Working Paper
No. 3, July 1994.

Rubinovitz concluded that real cable rates were higher by 18–23 percent. This price rise is attributed to the increase in market power associated with the deregulation of cable rates. Quality-adjusted cable rates have risen since deregulation.

Rising cable rates soon brought pressure on regulators and legislators to reinstitute some form of regulation. In June 1991, the FCC commissioners voted 5–0 to reinstate local rate regulation for many cable television operators. The following year the Congress passed the Cable Television Consumer Protection and Competition Act of 1992. It required that rates for basic cable service be regulated by the franchising authority or by the FCC. This reintroduced rate regulation to almost all cable markets. The FCC implemented this plan in April 1993 by requiring a roll back of basic rates of 10 percent per channel. Due to certain loopholes, some cable rates actually rose in response! The FCC then increased the required reduction to 17 percent less than a year later.

An economist specializing on the cable television, Thomas Hazlett described the progression from the 1984 Act to the 1992 Act:

While the profitability of the cable industry has never been higher, its political vulnerability has never been more evident—and the two events are connected. By fortuitously steering themselves through the regulatory maze to arrive at the bliss point of a legally protected but unregulated monopolist [as created by the

1984 Act], cable companies have traded friends for wealth in the political game.[44]

Is Government Intervention Welfare-Improving?

Natural monopoly is one of the few economic rationales for government intervention. Though the statistical evidence supports the hypothesis that cable television is a natural monopoly, some economists have argued that recent events put into question the social value of government intervention and, in particular, the use of franchise bidding.[45]

Price Regulation

Recent experience with rate regulation is not promising in that the government does not appear to have control over the instruments to achieve a socially preferred outcome. Cable program services are divided into basic, premium, and pay-per-view. Rate regulation only applies to basic service. Thus, in response to a government authority like the FCC requiring a reduction in basic cable rates, a cable company can respond by retiering—shifting better channels to unregulated tiers—or moving the better channels to à la carte status. Even if the regulation specifies a reduction in the average price per channel of basic service, the cable company can simply replace the shifted channels with cheaper, lower quality channels. Soon after the 1992 Act, jokes began circulating about "The Fireplace Channel" and the "The Fish Bowl Network." Though the Congress tried to take account of these strategic responses in their 1992 Act, loopholes remained. This is how some cable systems' basic rates rose after the 10 percent rate rollback mandated by the FCC.

Can the government effectively regulate cable rates? This is the question. The difficulty lies in that the cable companies have numerous unregulated instruments to get around or offset rate regulation. Of particular importance is adjusting the quality of the service. Lower rates do not imply that consumers are better off if cable companies reduce the quality of the service at the same time. Regulating quality is intrinsically difficult, and, in addition, cable regulators are legally prevented from controlling programming because cable operators have First Amendment rights as "electronic publishers." Even if cable operators are using their market power to set rates, it is not clear that regulating rates can lead to an improvement for consumers.

Entry Regulation

When an industry is a natural monopoly, we know that, in theory, price and entry regulation can improve social welfare. Whether it is true in

Table 13.5
Competitive Versus Monopolistic Cable Systems

	Sample Size (Subs)	Mean $Rev/Mo	Mean Basic Rate* ($)	Mean Basic Channels* (#)	Price/ Channel ($)
Monopoly (11,354 systems)	54.89 mm	32.12	19.08	35	.55
Competitive (103 systems)	1.13 mm	25.08	17.49	40	.44
Price/Quality Difference		−21.9%	−8.3%	+14.3%	−19.8%

* On most popular tier of basic programming.

Source: Data are from Paul Kagan Associates, General Accounting Office, and National Cable Television Assocation. Table is from Thomas W. Hazlett, "Regulating Cable Television Rates: An Economic Analysis," University of California–Davis, Program on Telecommunications Policy, Working Paper No. 3, July 1994.

practice depends on the particular industry and the constraints that regulators face. Recently, some economists have questioned the role of government intervention in the cable industry in spite of it being a natural monopoly. In light of the difficulty of regulating rates, it has been suggested that all regulation be removed, including the prohibition of entry.

Although the standard is for a cable operator to have a monopoly over the provision of cable service, there are a few communities for which there is competition among cable operators. That is, companies' distribution plants overlap so that consumers have two cable systems from which to choose. When two systems overlap, it is referred to as an *overbuild*. As of early 1992, overbuilds comprised just 1 percent of cable households. Though involving duplication of facilities, the evidence on those overbuilds is quite encouraging. As shown in Table 13.5, cable operators in competitive systems (those with two or more cable operators) had over fourteen more basic channels and the price of the basic service was 8 percent lower. Compared to the average monopoly system, the price per channel of basic service was 20 percent lower for the average competitive system. Furthermore, it appears that two cable operators can profitably coexist. For the average cable market with one cable operator, Thomas Hazlett estimated that a second cable operator who reduced rates by 20 percent and increased total penetration by 20 percent could expect to earn a rate-of-return of 16 percent.[46]

If the government should decide to pursue a policy of no price or entry regulation, an important element of this policy would be to repeal the current cross-ownership ban of local telephone and cable service. An area's local telephone company represents a significant potential entrant into cable. If a policy of no regulation is to be pursued, then it is crucial to make potential competition as intense as is feasible.

Summary

Theoretically, franchise bidding is a very attractive alternative to standard public utility regulation. Through the use of potential competition, as opposed to active competition, franchise bidding can, in principle, achieve the social welfare optimum without imposing the costs of a regulatory structure. Competition for the franchise can drive price down to average cost. Because price is fixed and the franchise owner retains all profit, it has every incentive to be efficient. In principle, franchise bidding is an ideal solution to the natural monopoly problem. It results in an efficient market structure, cost minimization, and socially optimal pricing.

In practice, franchise bidding is considerably more complicated and less effective in generating a socially desirable solution. As we observed in the case of cable television, bidding takes place over many more dimensions than just price. Because quality is a firm choice variable, the bid must encompass this information. This makes it a considerably more difficult task for a local government to award a franchise. Furthermore, the process creates nonwelfare-improving ways in which prospective franchise owners can compete. These rent-seeking activities may benefit the local government, but they are generally wasteful from society's perspective. As it currently stands, the franchising process generates considerable welfare losses in the case of cable television. These losses are largely due to the political nature of the process.

In the case of cable television, we have witnessed a topsy-turvy progression towards standard public utility regulation—entry is prohibited (with renewal competition being weak), and prices are set by the government. This raises the question of whether franchise bidding can really work in practice. Or perhaps the problem lies not with franchise bidding per se, but rather in the way in which it has been conducted. Perhaps the problems that arose in the case of cable television may be solved through a superior design of the franchising process. Only further applications of franchise bidding can answer these questions.

Questions and Problems

1. Assume a franchise is to be auctioned off where market demand is $100 - P$. Suppose there are just two firms competing for this franchise.

One firm's cost function is $C_1(q) = 100 + q$ while the other firm's cost function is $C_2(q) = 12q$. The franchise is auctioned off using a modified English auction where the firm offering the lowest price for service wins the franchise.

a) Who will win the franchise?

b) What will the winning bid be?

2.   Continuing with question #1, suppose the local government decides to issue the franchise to the firm that offers the biggest fee. An English auction is used where the firm offering the biggest payment to the local government wins the franchise. The franchise owner is free to charge any price that it likes. (Note: The marginal revenue curve is $100 - 2Q$.)

a) Who will win the franchise?

b) What will the winning franchise fee be?

c) What will price be?

(Hint: Calculate monopoly profit for each of the two bidders.)

3.   Which of the two methods described in questions 1 and 2 should a local government use if it wants to:

a) Maximize consumer welfare

b) Maximize government revenue

c) Maximize the number of consumers who buy this service.

d) For each of these objectives, can you think of a better method than the one described in question 1 or 2?

4.   Compare the following three methods of franchise bidding:

a) Recurrent short-term contracts

b) Long-term contracts

c) Recurrent short-term contracts in which the local government owns the capital.

5.   In practice, almost all cable television franchises are renewed.

a) Do you think this is evidence that franchise owners are performing in a satisfactory way or that competition at renewal time is weak?

b) How would you go about determining which hypothesis is correct?

6.   In 1984, Congress prohibited the regulation of the price of cable services. In response to the passage of this legislation, one study found that the market value of a cable system was (statistically speaking) unchanged in the top one hundred broadcast markets but went up in other markets. Explain.

7.   What are the technological sources of cable television being a natural monopoly?

8.   Should we allow free entry into cable television? In discussing this question, consider whether cable television is a contestable market.

9.   Should we use franchise bidding for local telephone? Can you think of any other markets for which franchise bidding would be a viable alternative to monopoly regulation?

10. Should local telephone companies be allowed to operate a cable system? If so, how should they be regulated?

Notes

1. Harold Demsetz, "Why Regulate Utilities?" *Journal of Law and Economics* 11 (April 1968): 55–65.

2. For some historical background on the use of auctions, see R. Cassady, Jr., *Auctions and Auctioneering* (Berkeley: University of California Press, 1967).

3. This assumes, of course, the two bidders do not collude and try to keep the bid above $\hat{P}_1$. For example, one firm could agree to drop out of the bidding at $\overline{P}$, where $\hat{P}_1 < \overline{P} < \hat{P}_2$, in exchange for a cash payment. This would allow both firms to earn higher profits in comparison to when the bid is driven down to $\hat{P}_1$. The inability to collude is then an essential condition if franchise bidding is to achieve a socially desirable outcome.

4. This criticism was originally made by Lester Telser in "On the Regulation of Industry: A Note," *Journal of Political Economy* 77 (November/December 1969): 937–52.

5. Recall that a two-part tariff has a customer pay a fixed fee for the right to purchase a good and a per unit price for each unit purchased.

6. The significance of this assumption is that the demand curve will not shift as we change the fixed fee. Increasing the fixed fee is equivalent to reducing consumer income. If the demand curve was not perfectly income-inelastic, it would shift in as we increase the fixed fee under the assumption that the good is normal. In order to simplify the analysis, we assume the demand curve is not responsive to changes in income.

7. One can show that there is always a two-part tariff that is Pareto-superior to average cost pricing. See Robert D. Willig, "Pareto-Superior Nonlinear Outlay Schedules," *Bell Journal of Economics* 9 (Spring 1978): 56–69. The idea of franchise bidding with two-part tariffs is analyzed in Daniel A. Graham and John M. Vernon, "A Note on Decentralized Utility Regulation," Duke University, mimeo, 1986.

8. Oliver E. Williamson, "Franchise Bidding for Natural Monopolies—In General and with Respect to CATV," *Bell Journal of Economics* 7 (Spring 1976): 73–104.

9. For a detailed analysis of cable television see G. Kent Webb, *The Economics of Cable Television* (Lexington, Mass.: Lexington Books, 1983).

10. Thomas W. Hazlett, "Cabling America: Economic Forces in a Political World," in Cento Veljanovski (ed.), *Freedom in Broadcasting* (Institute of Economic Affairs, 1989).

11. Thomas W. Hazlett, "Regulating Cable Television Rates: An Economic Analysis," University of California, Davis, Program on Telecommunications Policy Working Paper No. 3, July 1994.

12. For more background on the regulatory and judicial history of cable television, see Webb, 1983; Stanley M. Besen and Robert W. Crandall, "The Deregulation of Cable Television," *Law and Contemporary Problems*, Winter 1981; Bruce M. Owen and Paul D. Gottlieb, "The Rise and Fall and Rise of Cable Television," in Leonard W. Weiss and Michael W. Klass (eds.), *Regulatory Reform: What Actually Happened* (Boston: Little, Brown, 1983); and Thomas W.

Hazlett, "Private Monopoly and the Public Interest: An Economic Analysis of the Cable Television Franchise," *University of Pennsylvania Law Review* 134 (July 1986): 1335–1409.

13. "TCI Rushes to Install Fiber Optic Cable," *Baltimore Sun*, April 13, 1993.

14. This terminology is used in Hazlett, 1986.

15. Webb, 1983.

16. Eli M. Noam, "Economies of Scale and Regulation in CATV," in Michael A. Crew (ed.), *Analyzing the Impact of Regulatory Change in Public Utilities*, 1985.

17. Bruce M. Owen and Peter R. Greenhalgh, "Competitive Considerations in Cable Television Franchising," *Contemporary Policy Issues* 4 (April 1986): 69–79.

18. Noam, 1985.

19. Ibid.

20. For case studies of franchise bidding, see Webb, 1983, who analyzed Philadelphia; Williamson, 1976, who analyzed Oakland; and Robin A. Prager, "Franchise Bidding for Natural Monopoly: The Case of Cable Television in Massachusetts," *Journal of Regulatory Economics* 1 (1989): 115–31.

21. Williamson, 1976.

22. Hazlett, 1986.

23. Prager, 1989, p. 118.

24. Prager, 1989.

25. Ibid.

26. Mark A. Zupan, "The Efficacy of Franchise Bidding Schemes in the Case of Cable Television: Some Systematic Evidence," *Journal of Law and Economics* 22 (October 1989): 401–56.

27. FCC data; quoted in Leland L. Johnson, "Telephone Company Entry into Cable Television," RAND Report, 1992.

28. Prager, 1989.

29. Zupan, 1989.

30. Ibid.

31. Ibid.

32. Phillip A. Beutel, "City Objectives in Monopoly Franchising: The Case of Cable Television," Miami (Ohio) University, mimeo, May 1989.

33. Thomas D. Hazlett, "Wiring the Constitution for Cable," *Regulation*, 1988: 30–34. For additional anecdotal evidence, see Thomas W. Hazlett, "Franchise Bidding and Natural Monopoly: The Demsetz Solution on Cable," University of California–Davis, mimeo, June 1989.

34. Hazlett, 1988.

35. Zupan, 1988.

36. Prager, 1989.

37. Ibid.

38. Ibid.

39. Robin A. Prager, "Firm Behavior in Franchise Monopoly Markets," Owen Graduate School of Management, Vanderbilt University, Working Paper 88–05, October 1989.

40. Mark A. Zupan, "Cable Franchise Renewals: Do Incumbent Firms Behave Opportunistically?" *RAND Journal of Economics* 20 (Winter 1989): 473–82.

41. For estimates of the effect of deregulation on the value of cable franchises, see Adam B. Jaffee and David M. Kantner, "Market Power of Local Cable Television Franchises: Evidence from the Effects of Deregulation," *RAND Journal of Economics* 21 (Summer 1990): 226–34.

42. Thomas A. Hazlett, "Cable TV Reregulation: The Episodes You Didn't See on C-SPAN," *Regulation*, 1993, No. 2: 45–52.

43. Robert N. Rubinovitz, "Market Power and Price Increases for Basic Cable Service Since Deregulation," *RAND Journal of Economics* 24 (Spring 1993): 1–18.

44. Thomas W. Hazlett, "Should Telephone Companies Provide Cable TV?" *Regulation*, Winter 1990: 72–80.

45. For a discussion of these issues, see Thomas W. Hazlett, "Duopolistic Competition in CATV: Implications for Public Policy," *Yale Journal on Regulation* 7 (Winter 1990): 65–119.

46. Hazlett, 1994.

Public Enterprise

The ultimate objectives of any government policy that is designed to handle the natural monopoly problem are to have a single firm producing efficiently and pricing at the socially optimal level. The first objective can be achieved relatively easily by issuing a monopoly for the provision of the service to a privately owned firm. In acting to maximize its profit, the firm will produce efficiently. Unfortunately, the objective of profit maximization also leads to a price above the social optimum and thereby creates deadweight welfare losses.

To induce the firm to price in a socially efficient manner, we have thus far analyzed two alternative policies. One policy is to establish a regulatory agency that sets price and constrains the firm to earn a normal rate of return. Some of the problems with this approach are that the regulatory agency lacks the necessary information to make effective pricing decisions and that the profit constraint may lead the regulated firm to produce inefficiently. Two examples of the latter are a reduced incentive to adopt cost-reducing innovations, as additional profits earned cannot be fully retained by the firm, and overcapitalization due to the A-J effect. An alternative approach considered in the preceding chapter is to auction off a franchise to the firm that proposes the lowest price for service. Ideally, this scheme solves all problems because the franchise owner has every incentive to produce efficiently and competition at the bidding stage results in socially optimal pricing. Unfortunately, in practice, franchise bidding and regulation differ only by a matter of degree and not of kind.

A common element to both of these policies is to have the service provided by a privately owned firm and then to design an institution that forces the firm to price at the socially optimal level. Regulation achieves this objective through the enforcement powers of a regulatory agency, whereas franchise bidding uses ex ante competition to achieve it. The idea is to change the constraints faced by the profit-maximizing monopolist in order to induce it to set a lower price than it would otherwise.

In this chapter we consider a policy that is intrinsically different from both regulation and franchise bidding. Rather than constrain a privately owned firm, the approach is based on altering the objective of the firm from profit maximization to social welfare maximization. This rather quixotic objective is pursued by having the service provided by a *public enterprise*. In contrast to the privately owned firm, a public (or government) enterprise is owned and operated by the government. The potential of such an approach lies in that the objectives of a public enterprise may be more likely to be in line with the maximization of social welfare. In contrast to the manager of a private enterprise, who is accountable to shareholders, the manager of a public enterprise is ultimately accountable to voters.

This chapter is concerned with assessing public enterprise as an approach to handling the problem of natural monopoly. Of specific interest is comparing its performance to the regulation of a privately owned firm, which is the most common policy in the United States. In contrast, public enterprises are used quite extensively in Europe. Prior to beginning this task, we should first recognize that public enterprises are used for a variety of tasks, of which handling the natural monopoly problem is just one. Thus, let us first consider public enterprise from a more general perspective before embarking on our more narrow goal.

General Background

Public enterprises have a long and tainted history. In the ancient days of Athens, the government owned the mines. Prior to the second century B.C., the Ch'in dynasty in China had government monopolies over the provision of salt and iron. The Roman Empire had a large number of public enterprises that handled such diverse activities as recreation (specifically, games and circuses) and defense (for example, weaponry). A more modern example is the provision of postal service, which is performed by a public enterprise in almost all countries today. In the case of the United States, the postal system was created by the first Congress in 1789. While originally a department of the federal government, it became a semiautonomous, publicly owned firm in 1971 and was placed under the jurisdiction of the Postal Rate Commission.

Public enterprise is used in place of private enterprise for a variety of reasons. The purpose we are concerned with in this chapter is to handle the natural monopoly problem. Rather than attempt to cover all of the other reasons for their use, let us just discuss some examples so as to highlight the diversity of origins of public enterprise.

In the case of Communist-ruled countries like China and Cuba, the choice of public enterprise is largely based on ideological reasons. Privately owned firms that act to maximize owners' wealth are anathema to Marxist systems. It was also for political reasons that France expropriated Renault after World War II. At the time, Renault was one of the three largest automobile manufacturers in France. As punishment for cooperating with the Germans during the occupation of France, the French government took control of Renault. It has performed well under public ownership and is currently the largest auto maker in France.

Less by design and more by accident, the Italian government controls vast parts of the industrial sector including almost all of shipbuilding. This came about during the depression in the 1930s. At that time, the government created the Institute for Industrial Reconstruction to handle the assets of failed banks. The end result was considerable government control of assets in the industrial sector. For similar reasons but more by design, the U.S. Congress created the Consolidated Rail Corporation (Conrail) to help the ailing railroad industry.[1] Created by the Railroad Revitalization and Regulatory Reform Act of 1976, Conrail was formed by merging seven bankrupt railroads, including the Penn Central. Until its bankruptcy in 1970, the Penn Central handled about 20 percent of rail-freight movement in the United States.

Public enterprises may also be used in order to raise revenue. This is certainly one of the reasons for the use of state-owned and -operated lotteries and liquor retailing outlets. Besides often being quite profitable and a source of revenue, the fact that they are vices may also explain why they are state-controlled. It is thought by some that free enterprise and vices like gambling and liquor are not a suitable combination. The fear is that private enterprise will lead to abuses. Whatever the reasons, an increasing number of states are operating lotteries, and sixteen states have handled liquor retailing for many years.

There are widely differing opinions on the proper role of public enterprises. This diversity is evidenced by the variety of international experience. Beginning with the Industrial Revolution and especially since World War II, Europe has shown a much greater inclination than the United States to use public enterprise. For example, 75 percent of the railroad industry and all airlines are privately owned in the United States, whereas both industries are almost wholly government-owned in most European countries.

This difference in approach is not just observed across countries but also across time within the same country. A classic case is that of Great Britain. When in power, the Labour Party has been inclined to nationalize certain industries, such as steel. In contrast, when the Conservative Party is in control, they typically pursue a policy of privatization and restore these firms to the status of private ownership. This was the policy of the Conservative administration under Margaret Thatcher. Both British Airways and British Telcom (BT) were sold to private citizens. In the case of BT, a most interesting strategy was pursued:

All employees on privatisation will be given £70-worth of free shares—and will get two free shares for each one bought up to a limit of £100. Similarly, each telephone subscriber who buys shares of £250 (payable in three calls) will qualify for an £18 rebate on his quarterly telephone bill. The aim is no secret: the more people become shareholders, the more difficult it will be for a Labour government to renationalise BT.[2]

Positive Theory of Public Enterprise

Everywhere else in this book, we assume that firm behavior is motivated by the desire to maximize profit. Profit maximization seems to be the single most plausible objective of a privately owned firm, as it results in the maximization of shareholders' wealth. By specifying the objective of a firm (or, more generally, an economic agent), we can make predictions as to how it will respond to government policies. Such predictions are essential in determining the effects of those policies. For example, the A-J effect tells us that rate-of-return regulation results in a profit-maximizing firm overcapitalizing. By assuming that a firm maximizes profit subject to rate-of-return regulation, we are then able to identify an inefficiency resulting from government policy.

To compare a policy of regulation with one of public enterprise, we need to provide a theory as to how a public enterprise behaves. Because it is not privately owned, it is unlikely to maximize profit. It would be nice if a public enterprise were to maximize social welfare, but it would be hasty to jump to the conclusion that it does so. This is the difference between positive and normative economics. From a normative perspective, a public enterprise designed to handle the natural monopoly problem should pursue social welfare maximization. A positive theory tells us, in contrast, how a public enterprise actually does indeed behave. In order to derive such a theory, we will present a more general model of the firm than has been previously discussed.

Managerial Model of a Firm

An element common to almost all large organizations is a separation of ownership and managerial control. The modern private corporation is a classic example. Ownership is held by many shareholders, each with typically a small or negligible percentage of shares. As a result, day-to-day control of the firm rests with the appointed manager, though ultimate control lies with the shareholders. This is analogously true for most public enterprises, as ownership rests in the populace of the relevant political jurisdiction but control lies in the manager appointed by an elected official or a government bureaucrat, whichever it may be. In today's economy it is fair to say that the separation of ownership and control is indicative of almost all large organizations.

Let us construct a model of the firm based upon the recognition that managerial control does not rest with the owners but rather with a paid employee. If owners have as much information as managers and can perfectly monitor the actions of the manager, this separation issue is of no importance. In that case, if the manager does not do exactly what is in the owners' best interest, she will be fired. In spite of the separation of ownership and control, the results are the same as when the organization is owner-operated.

Of course, it is quite unreasonable to assume that owners can even come close to perfectly monitoring the manager. It is generally not in the best interests of any individual owner to spend the resources required to closely observe the manager's actions. Furthermore, through her day-to-day intimacy with the operations of the firm, the manager has much better information than the owners. Thus, even if the owners did observe the actions of the manager (for example, in choosing project A over project B), it is difficult for the owners to determine whether the manager is acting in their best interests.

These two conditions—the separation of ownership and control and the imperfect monitoring of managerial behavior—are characteristic of most major private and public enterprises. The managerial model of the firm has been developed to describe how such an organization behaves. A central assumption of this model is that the manager acts to maximize her own utility subject to the constraints and incentives instituted by the owners. Within this model, the goal of the owners is to construct a set of constraints and incentives so as to induce the manager to act in their best interests. Of course, the goal of the manager is to maximize her own utility. Our goal is to derive predictions as to how such a firm behaves.

In terms of her relationship with the firm, a manager's utility depends on income, nonpecuniary benefits, and effort. The manager's utility is greater, the greater is income and the greater are nonpecuniary benefits. The latter may include such items as the prestige of having a large staff or having a company jet at her disposal. In contrast, utility is less, the more effort the manager exerts. We can think of more effort as entailing less leisure, and less leisure generally reduces utility.

Not being perfectly monitored, the manager is likely to choose less effort and more nonpecuniary benefits than are in the owners' best interests. This is why the owners must design incentive schemes and create constraints in order to induce the manager to work hard and act efficiently (note that choosing to have a large staff for the purpose of prestige can be inefficient because it may not sufficiently increase productivity so as to warrant its cost).

Thus far we have not had to specify whether the firm is a private or a public enterprise, because the manager in both organizations will tend to act the same, ceteris paribus. Where the differences in the two organizations lie are in (1) the interests of the owners and (2) the mechanisms available to induce the manager to act properly.

Managerial Model of a Private Enterprise

In a private enterprise, owners want the manager to act so as to maximize profit. A key mechanism to induce such behavior is to make the manager's financial compensation depend on the profitability of the firm, that is, the use of an incentive scheme in which income increases with firm profit. This often takes the form of bonuses and/or issuing stock to the manager so as to make her a shareholder. Of course, this hardly solves the problem because the manager knows that if she works harder and increases profit, she will only get a small part of that profit increase. Making income depend on firm profit provides the right incentives, but it cannot entirely solve the problem of the separation of ownership and control.

An implicit incentive scheme also arises in the labor market. If a manager works hard and results in the firm earning a high rate of return, this will increase her reputation as a productive manager. Her value in the labor market will rise, which will result in higher future income. Thus, not only does superior performance increase current income, through bonuses and stock holdings, but future income is increased as well by enhancing the manager's reputation.

A final mechanism that induces the manager of a private enterprise to maximize profit is the threat of being fired if the firm performs poorly under her management. If owners observe poor performance, they can pursue actions to have the manager dismissed. Such a dismissal not only reduces current income but also future earnings as well, by deteriorating her reputation in the labor market. In reality, this is not a very effective constraint on managerial behavior because it is unlikely to be used. Given the wide dispersal of ownership in most privately owned firms, the owners are not usually in a position to credibly threaten such a response.

Nevertheless, the threat of being fired can arise quite effectively via the capital market. A firm that is being run inefficiently presents a profitable opportunity for investors. Because it is operating below its potential, the shares of the firm are selling at a relatively cheap price. Thus, investors (or, in today's parlance, a raider) can purchase shares at this low price, install new and efficient management, and return the firm to efficiency. The increase in profit earned by the firm is the financial return to the investors. In some cases, the investors immediately resell the firm at the higher share price. Thus, even if the ownership of a firm is widely dispersed, poor firm performance will induce investors to buy shares and concentrate ownership in order to replace ineffective management.

Even though the manager of a private enterprise has an incentive not to act in the owners' best interests, it is generally thought by most, but by no means all, economists that the constraints of the capital and labor markets as well as proper reward schedules induce the manager to act approximately like a profit maximizer.[3] Hence, for the modern private corporation, it is thought that profit maximization is a good approximation as to how it truly behaves.

Managerial Model of a Public Enterprise

Is there a similarly strong case to be made for the manager of a public enterprise to act in the owners' best interests and thus maximize social welfare? For two reasons, this is unlikely to be true. First, welfare, unlike profit, is difficult to measure. The use of imperfect indicators should provide opportunities for the manager to act in his own interests and not those of society. Second, the constraints posed on the manager of a private enterprise by the capital market are conspicuously absent. This will give the manager of a public enterprise greater discretion in his actions.

Although welfare is difficult to measure, there are substitutes that elected officials and voters can use to gauge the performance of a public enterprise. One obviously is price. A second set is attributes of output, for example, reliability of the service provided by the public enterprise. For the case of an electric utility, frequent blackouts would signal poor performance to the electorate.

Several theories of public enterprise behavior have been formulated on the premise that managers act to maximize political support and this is achieved by producing those attributes that signal good performance. By increasing political support, a manager raises his income and the likelihood of increased job tenure. In "A Theory of Government Enterprise," Cotton Lindsay notes,

[M]anagers are therefore influenced to divert resources from the production of attributes which will not be monitored to those which will. In so doing they will increase the perceived value of the [public enterprise's] output.[4]

For example, suppose that the quality of a service is easily observable but cost is not. The manager will then tend to choose too high a level of quality in order to increase political support. The important point is that the imperfections inherent in using attributes to measure managerial performance are likely to lead to strategic behavior by the manager. The manager will tend to produce those attributes to a degree that is excessive from society's perspective.

Sam Peltzman proposed a different theory, in which the manager of a public enterprise uses price to maximize political support.[5] This theory yields several interesting results. Let us suppose that political/voter support is greater, the smaller is the subsidy given to the public enterprise. This is reasonable because the higher the subsidy, the more tax revenue must be raised, and voters dislike tax increases. If we assume that the public enterprise must earn a normal rate of return if it is to raise new capital, then the subsidy will equal $-\pi(P)$ where $\pi(P)$ is profit for a given price, P. If $\pi(P) > 0$, then the subsidy is negative as the public enterprise adds to government revenues. Let us also assume that voter support is greater at lower prices, inasmuch as voters are also consumers.

One prediction of this model is that a public enterprise's manager will set a price below that which maximizes profit. To show why this is true, consider price being set at the profit-maximizing level, which we denote as P^m. Recall that marginal profit (that is, the change in profit from a small change in price) equals zero at a price of P^m. The reason is that if marginal profit was positive, then profit could be increased by raising price, which contradicts P^m being the profit-maximizing price. Similarly, if marginal profit was negative at P^m, then profit could be increased by lowering price. Hence, marginal profit must be zero at P^m.

Now consider the public enterprise charging a price slightly less than P^m. There is a direct and an indirect effect on political support. The direct effect is that voters care about price in their role as consumers. The indirect effect is that price affects firm profit, which affects the amount of the government subsidy. Voters care about the amount of the subsidy as they are also taxpayers. Because marginal profit at P^m is zero, a very slight reduction in price does not affect firm profit, so that it does not affect the amount of the subsidy. The indirect effect on political support from charging a price slightly less than P^m is then zero. On the other hand, the direct effect of charging a lower price raises political support, as voters always like lower prices, ceteris paribus. It follows that a public enterprise manager's political support is increased by setting a price below that which maximizes profit. We conclude that a public enterprise will charge a lower price than a private enterprise. For a closely related analysis, see the discussion surrounding Figure 10.2 in Chapter 10.

A second result is that price will be lower for voters than nonvoters. Consider a public enterprise located in political jurisdiction A but which serves residents of both A and jurisdiction B. The owners of the public firm are just the voters in A. By setting a higher price for consumers in B, the manager can increase profit and reduce taxes, thereby raising political support. This is achieved without having to increase the price charged to voters (that is, consumers in A). Of course, there is an upper bound to the price that can be charged to residents of B, as they can always decide to form their own public enterprise or have a private enterprise supply them.

A third prediction from the Peltzman model is that a public enterprise will pursue less price discrimination than a private enterprise in order to provide a more uniform treatment of consumers. Differential treatment can reduce political support because it alienates certain voters. Thus, relative to a private enterprise, one would expect less discrimination between industrial and residential users of the service as well as less discrimination over time-of-day usage.

Although managers certainly desire political support, it is an overly narrow perspective to think that they act simply so as to maximize political support. Managers also value nonpecuniary benefits and leisure, not just income. For the case of a private enterprise, we argued that the capital market is an important force in constraining the manager in her desire to divert resources to nonpecuniary benefits and to shirk in performing his duties. The threat of the firm's being acquired and current management's being replaced can be an effective deterrent against the manager of a private enterprise's acting too inefficiently.

Perhaps the most important difference between public and private enterprise is that there is no comparable disciplining force faced by the manager of a public enterprise. The reason is that there is no feasible mechanism by which the ownership of a public enterprise can be transferred. An owner of a public firm can forgo his share of ownership only by moving to another political jurisdiction. Hence, there is no comparable mechanism to concentrating ownership as occurs in the capital market. The fact that owners can shift their ownership to another jurisdiction in response to poor performance is unlikely anyway. The performance of public enterprise is just one factor among many that influence an individual's decision as to where to locate.

The significance of the nontransferability of ownership is that it gives the manager of a public enterprise considerably more discretion than his private-enterprise counterpart in pursuing his own personal interests. To make his work environment more pleasant, a manager may choose to minimize labor strife by providing higher wages. Similarly, he may choose to overinvest in capacity to prevent potential shortages and consumer strife. It has also been suggested that a manager will choose simpler pricing schedules and adjust them less frequently than a manager of a private enterprise. All these actions tend to increase nonpecuniary benefits from the job.

Comparison of Public and Private Enterprise

Relative to an unregulated private enterprise, our analysis suggests that a public enterprise will price lower, practice less price discrimination, and earn lower profits. There also seems to be a plausible case for public enterprise to be less efficient. A manager of a public enterprise has a tendency to use more capital and labor in order to reap nonpecuniary benefits like fewer consumer complaints and an absence of labor strife.

These differences in behavior are generated by two factors. First, income and job tenure are raised by increasing firm profit for the manager of a private enterprise but are raised by increasing political support for a public enterprise's manager. This results in lower prices for a public enterprise and greater inefficiency, for example, overinvesting in product reliability to gain consumer-voter support. The second factor is that the manager of a private enterprise is threatened by the disciplining force of the capital market. If she performs poorly, there is a mechanism by which to replace her even though ownership may be widely dispersed. Because of the nontransferability of ownership in the case of a public enterprise, there is no similar constraint on the manager of a public enterprise. He then has greater discretion to use resources to maximize his own utility rather than social welfare.

Of greater relevance to our objective, however, is the comparison between a public enterprise and a regulated private enterprise. How this comparison differs from the one above depends very much on the effectiveness of the regulatory constraint. If regulation is not very binding on the firm, then the above analysis applies. However, suppose that the regulatory constraint is binding. We know that regulation will cause price and profit to be lower, just as we found for a public enterprise. Whether price and profit differ much between the two institutions is then an empirical question. This issue will be addressed shortly.

In contrast, there is no reason to expect a regulated private enterprise not to practice price discrimination extensively. This is a potential source of difference from a public enterprise. We know by the A-J effect that a private enterprise that is subject to rate-of-return regulation also has a tendency to overcapitalize. However, it still does not have the discretion to act inefficiently, like a public enterprise.[6] Even for a regulated private enterprise, the capital market presents a constraining force on inefficient behavior. Furthermore, any increase in cost between rate hearings will reduce firm profit. Thus, one would expect a regulated private enterprise to be more efficient than a public enterprise.

According to this analysis, both a regulated private enterprise and a public enterprise will experience productive inefficiencies. Rate-of-return regulation results in the private firm overcapitalizing, whereas the public firm has less incentive to act efficiently inasmuch as its manager is interested more in political support than profit. From a productive efficiency standpoint, which approach to the natural monopoly problem is preferred is then an empirical question. In the next section we will examine how regulation and public enterprise have performed in the provision of electricity in municipalities.

Municipal Electric Utilities

In the United States there is significant governmental involvement in the generation and distribution of electricity at the federal, state, and local levels. In total, about 25 percent of supply comes from public power systems. Certainly the best-known federal project is the Tennessee Valley Authority (TVA). Created in 1933, its residential customers pay about one-half the average price for electricity in the United States. There are also large power systems at the state level in both New York and Nebraska.

The role of municipal electric utilities is quite different from the federal and state power projects. Municipal utilities tend to be small and often only distribute electricity. Rather than generate it themselves, they frequently purchase it in the wholesale market. For example, the TVA sells about one-half of their power to distributors, of which about a hundred are municipal utilities. Though small, municipal utilities are numerous and are responsible for about 20 percent of sales of electricity in the United States.[7]

Pricing Behavior

If the degree of regulatory constraint is not too severe, our analysis predicts that a public enterprise will set lower prices than would a regulated private enterprise. By setting a price below the profit-maximizing level, the manager of a public enterprise increases political support and, as a result, income and job tenure.

The evidence on the effect that regulation has on electricity prices is mixed. In a widely cited study using data from 1912–1937, George Stigler and Claire Friedland analyzed the pricing behavior of regulated and unregulated privately owned electric utilities.[8] Controlling for such factors as fuel cost and per-capita income, they found that although regulation did tend to reduce prices, the effect was rather small and insignificant. In light of the poor information that regulatory agencies typically have about demand and, especially, cost functions, such a finding is not surprising. Because the firm has a significant information advantage, a regulatory agency may often have little choice but to accept the proposed tariff. On the other hand, other studies have found electricity prices to be severely constrained by regulation. In some cases it was estimated that the monopoly price was 20 to 50 percent higher than actual regulated prices.[9]

If regulation does not have much of an effect on pricing behavior, we would expect a public enterprise to set lower prices than a privately owned utility. A study by Thomas Moore strongly supports this hypothesis.[10] Moore estimated the monopoly price for a firm sample that included privately owned regulated utilities and publicly owned utilities. Using data from 1962, he then compared these prices to the actual prices. Moore found the prices of regulated private utilities to be 5 to 6 percent below the monopoly price, indicating a small but negative effect of regulation on price. In contrast, the prices of the publicly owned utilities were 10 to 22 percent below the monopoly prices.

In a 1971 study, Peltzman derived similar empirical results. Table 14.1 shows the difference in pricing behavior. The publicly owned utilities consistently priced lower than the privately owned utilities. It is interesting to note, however, that Peltzman concluded that this difference in pricing can be explained by the tax-exempt status of public utilities. By not being taxed, they could charge lower rates. Nevertheless, the evidence available clearly supports the hypothesis that a publicly owned utility sets lower prices than a regulated privately owned utility.

A second hypothesis is that a public enterprise pursues less price discrimination. The reason is that more uniform pricing schedules reduce the alienation of consumer groups and this tends to increase political support. In addition, because they are easier to handle, a more uniform pricing schedule increases nonpecuniary benefits from the job. Peltzman did indeed find that publicly owned utilities used a smaller number of rate schedules on average than private utilities (see Table 14.2). Although both types of utilities did practice price discrimination (as is evident in Table 14.1), it was more extensive for privately owned utilities. Also consistent with the belief that public-enterprise managers have greater discretion to pursue an easier life, Peltzman found that public enterprises adjusted price less frequently.

Allocative Efficiency Comparison

Because publicly owned utilities set lower prices, it is tempting to conclude that they perform better than regulated privately owned utilities

Table 14.1
Mean Electricity Prices (cents per kwh) for Residential, Commerical, and Industrial Customers

Service Class and Consumption Level (kwh per month)	Private Utilities		Govt. Utilities		Absolute Difference		Government Price as Percentage of Private Price	
	Average Price	Marginal Price	Average Price	Marginal Price	Average Price	Marginal Price	Average Price	Marginal Price
Residential								
100	3.92¢	3.42¢	3.42¢	3.01¢	.50¢	.41¢	87.2%	88.0%
250	2.95	2.31	2.54	1.95	.41	.36	84.1	84.4
500	2.06	1.18	1.88	1.22	.18	−.04	91.3	103.4
750	1.90	1.58	1.68	1.30	.22	.28	88.4	82.3
1000	1.86	1.75	1.60	1.36	.26	.39	86.0	77.7
Commercial								
375	3.94	3.94	3.26	3.26	.68	.68	82.7	82.7
750	3.69	3.43	2.99	2.71	.70	.72	81.0	79.0
1500	3.50	3.31	2.76	2.53	.74	.78	78.9	76.4
6000	2.71	2.45	2.21	2.03	.50	.42	81.5	82.9
10000	2.40	1.92	2.01	1.71	.39	.21	83.7	89.1
Industrial								
15000	2.31	2.31	1.89	1.89	.42	.42	81.8	81.8
30000	2.10	1.85	1.74	1.56	.36	.29	82.9	84.3
60000	1.92	1.74	1.61	1.47	.31	.27	83.9	84.5
100000	1.84	1.70	1.55	1.45	.29	.25	84.2	85.3
200000	1.72	1.61	1.48	1.40	.24	.21	86.0	87.0

Source: Federal Power Commission Typical Electric Bills; Typical Net Monthly Bills for Residential, Commercial & Industrial Services (1966). The private utility sample consists of seventy-one cities for all customer classes; the government utility sample comprises sixty-four cities for residential rates and fifty-seven cities for commercial and industrial rates. Average price is the total bill for each indicated consumption level divided by the consumption level. Marginal price is the charge for one kwh at or below each indicated consumption level, but above the next lowest consumption level. (For 100 kwh and below, residential service, the marginal kwh price applies to consumption above the number of kwh included in the minimum monthly bill.) In S. Peltzman, "Pricing in Public and Private Enterprises: Electric Utilities in the United States," *Journal of Law and Economics*, April 1971.

Table 14.2
Degree of Price Discrimination in Private Versus Public Utilities

	Average Number of Rate Schedules per City Served by:		Difference (Standard Error)
	Private Utilities (69 Cities)	Public Utilities (69 Cities)	
Residential service	1.884	1.464	0.420 (0.147)
Non-residential service	6.507	3.826	2.681 (0.458)
Total	8.391	5.290	3.101 (0.520)

Source: Federal Power Commission, National Electric Book; 1968 from Sam Peltzman, "Pricing in Public and Private Enterprises: Electric Utilities in the United States," *Journal of Law and Economics*, April 1971.

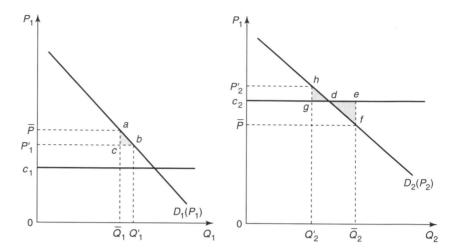

Figure 14.1
The Effects of Price Discrimination

on an allocative efficiency basis. By charging a price closer to that which maximizes profit, privately owned utilities cause greater deadweight welfare losses. However, even though average price may be higher, there can still be greater welfare associated with privately owned utilities because of more extensive price discrimination.

To understand this point, let us consider the two demand curves in Figure 14.1. The unit cost of supplying good 1 (2) is denoted c_1 (c_2). For the sake of simplicity, suppose that a firm discriminates between these two markets and sets price equal to P'_1 in market 1 and P'_2 in market 2. Now consider a nondiscriminating price $\overline{P}$ such that the following relationship holds:

$$\overline{P} < \frac{Q'_1}{Q'_1 + Q'_2} P'_1 + \frac{Q'_2}{Q'_1 + Q'_2} P'_2$$

so that average price is lower. Comparing prices P'_1 and $\overline{P}$ in market 1, welfare is higher with P'_1 as measured by the sum of triangle abc and $(P'_1 - c)(Q'_1 - \overline{Q})$. In addition, a price of $\overline{P}$ in market 2 yields lower welfare than P'_2 by triangle def less triangle dgh. The discriminatory pricing schedule yields higher welfare even though it results in a higher average price. For this example, setting a uniform price results in price being too high in market 1 (as marginal cost is low) and too low in market 2 (as marginal cost is high). Price discrimination allows consumers to get the right signals about which service is more costly.

Empirical evidence by Peltzman shows that greater price discrimination by privately owned utilities resulted in higher average sales of electricity per customer. In estimating the effects of the type of ownership on average sales per customer, he first controlled for other factors that could affect the difference in average sales. These factors included income, population size, regional differences, and average price. Once holding these factors constant, Peltzman found that average sales per customer were higher for privately owned utilities than for public utilities.

Given this evidence, it is difficult to determine which institution generates greater allocative efficiency. Although publicly owned utilities do seem to set lower average prices, privately owned utilities appear to practice greater price discrimination.

Productive Efficiency Comparison

Our previous analysis suggested that both regulated private utilities and publicly owned utilities tend to overcapitalize. The former will do so in order to increase profit through the expansion of their rate base under rate-of-return regulation. A public utility overinvests in capital in order to produce the attributes that garner political support, for example, increasing capacity in order to reduce the likelihood of blackouts and brownouts. We also expect a public enterprise to act more inefficiently than a private enterprise because of greater managerial discretion.

In his 1970 study, Moore estimated the ratio of peak demand to total capacity for twenty-seven publicly owned and thirty-six privately owned utilities. He found that ratio to be smaller for publicly owned firms, indicating that they had greater capacity relative to peak demand. Though there is certainly evidence supporting the A-J effect (see Chapter 12 for details), the Moore study suggests that the incentive to overcapitalize is greater for public enterprises.

To gauge productive efficiency, Thomas DiLorenzo and Ralph Robinson, in their 1982 study, measured average productivity of labor for both public and private utilities.[11] They found, on average, that one laborer generated 15.734 kilowatt hours of electricity in a publicly owned utility. In contrast, the comparable figure for a private utility was 16.566. A publicly owned utility was found to be less efficient, but this difference was not statistically significant.

Contradictory evidence is provided in a study by Donn Pescatrice and John Trapani.[12] They estimated cost and input demand functions with a data set made up of thirty-three private utilities and twenty-three public utilities. Their empirical results showed that a private utility's costs were 23.5 percent higher in 1965 and 32.9 percent higher in 1970 than the costs incurred by a public utility.

Assessment of Private versus Public Utilities

It is clear that the evidence concerning the relative efficiency of regulated privately owned utilities and publicly owned utilities is mixed. Nevertheless, a survey of comparative studies provides general support for the hypothesis that there is greater productive efficiency with private enterprise. Table 14.3 lists a number of such studies for industries ranging from electric utilities to refuse collection to weather forecasting. Most of these studies conclude that publicly owned firms are less efficient than privately owned firms.

Perhaps the major advantage of a privately owned firm is that it is subject to the disciplining force of the capital market. A study by Louis DeAlessi supports the hypothesis that the constraints placed on the manager of a public enterprise are not as great.[13] He assessed relative job tenure over 1962–1971 for a sample of a hundred private utilities and a hundred public utilities. Table 14.4 presents some of his results. As is quite apparent, job tenure was considerably greater for the manager of a public enterprise. Twice as many public firms as private firms did not change managers over the ten-year period. This evidence is consistent with the hypothesis that the manager of a public enterprise is subject to fewer constraints and devotes more resources to gain political support in order to raise job tenure.

Airlines

In the case of municipal electric utilities, the empirical evidence is inconclusive concerning the hypothesis that regulated privately owned firms are more efficient than publicly owned firms. In his 1977 study of the Australian airline industry, David Davies derives strong evidence to support the hypothesis that unregulated private firms are more efficient than public firms.[14]

Australia has two interstate airlines: Trans-Australian Airlines (TAA) and Ansett Australian National Airway. The former is a public enterprise while the latter is privately owned. Using data from 1958–1974, Davies compares the productive efficiency of these two types of ownership.

Davies chose a good pair of firms to test the relative efficiency hypothesis as, except in terms of ownership, TAA and Ansett are quite comparable. They serve similar routes and have comparable frequency of flights. Both charge identical passenger and freight rates and have a similar mix of services. Given these similarities, it is reasonable to believe that any differences in efficiency are probably due to the type of ownership.

Table 14.3
Comparisons of Private and Public Performance

Area, Author, and Year of Study	Findings
Utilities:	
Electricity	
Wallace and Junk (1970)	Public firms have 40–75% higher operating costs and 40% higher investment cost per kwh.
Meyer (1975)	Public firms have lower operating costs but higher transport and distribution costs.
Spann (1977)	Private firms are as efficient, and probably more efficient, with respect to operating costs.
Junker (1975)	No difference between public and private costs.
Neuberg (1977)	Public cost 23% less than private.
Pescatrice and Trapani (1980)	Public costs less than private.
Primeaux (1977, 1978)	Competition reduces costs of public provision.
DeAlessi (1974)	Private sector supply lower cost than public.
DiLorenzo and Robinson (1982)	Public firms are slightly less productive.
Atkinson and Halvorsen (1986)	Public and private firms are equally cost inefficient.
Water	
Mann and Mikesell (1976)	Public firms have 20% higher costs.
Morgan (1977)	Public firms have 15% higher costs.
Crain and Zardkoohi (1978)	Public firms are 40% less productive.
Health and Insurance Hospitals	
Clarkson (1972)	In nonprofit-making hospitals "red tape" is more prevalent.
Wilson and Jadlow (1980)	Proprietary hospitals deviate less than public hospitals from perfect efficiency index.
Insurance Claims	
Frech (1979)	Mutual insurance firms are 45–80% more costly than proprietary firms.
Refuse Collection	
Pier, Vernon, and Wicks (1974)	Municipal suppliers are more efficient.
Kitchen (1976)	Municipal suppliers are more costly than private ones.
Pommerehne and Frey (1976)	Operating costs are significantly lower for private than the for municipal firms.
Stevens and Savas (1977)	Municipal firms are 10–30% more costly than private firms.
Collins and Downes (1977)	Non significant cost differences.
Spann (1977)	Public firms are 45% more costly.
Savas (1974, 1977)	Private less costly than public.
Edwards and Stevens (1978)	Public service less costly than private.
Bennett and Johnson (1979)	Private less costly than public provision.
Transport:	
Railroads	
Oelert (1976)	Public firms have on average 160% higher costs compared with the contract price of private firms.

(continued)

Table 14.3 (cont.)

Area, Author, and Year of Study	Findings
Caves, Christensen, and Swanson (1980)	No significant differences in productivity; CN (Canadian National) was less efficient during the highly regulated period before 1965; its productivity has since increased more rapidly than that of CP (Canadian Pacific).
Airlines	
Davies (1977)	Private airline is clearly more efficient than the public one.
Services:	
Banks	
Nichols (1967)	Mutual firms have 13–30% higher operating costs.
Davies (1982)	In private banks productivity and profitability are higher than in public banks.
Cleaning	
Bundesrechnungshof (1972)	The cleaning of offices is 42–66% more expensive if undertaken by the public corporation itself than if it is contracted out.
Fischer-Mendershausen (1975)	Cleaning costs could be reduced by 30% if 80% of the space were contracted out.
Weather Forecasting	
Bennett and Johnson (1980)	Government service is 50% more costly.

Source: "Government Divestments and the Regulation of Natural Monopolies in the UK: The Case of British Gas," Mike Wright, *Energy Policy* 15, No. 3 (June 1987): 143–216.

Table 14.4
Frequency of Change in Top Executive of Firms in the Electric Power Industry, 1962–1971

Ownership Category	Frequency of Change Sample						Size
	0	1	2	3	4	5	
Public	36	42	17	3	1	1	100
Private	18	59	18	4	1	0	100

Source: Louis DeAlessi, "Managerial Tenure under Private and Government Ownership in the Electric Power Industry," *Journal of Political Economy*, May/June 1974.

Davies estimated three measures of productivity. They are presented in Table 14.5. For all three measures, the privately owned firm, Ansett, experienced greater efficiency than publicly owned TAA. Over the entire period of 1958–1974, an Ansett employee, on average, carried twice as much freight and mail as an employee of TAA. Similarly, passengers carried and revenue earned per employee were higher for the privately owned firm.

This is a good study with which to conclude our analysis of public enterprise because it presents clear and strong results. Although no single study is conclusive, the Australian airline industry does support the hypothesis that public enterprises are less efficient than privately owned firms.

Summary

In comparing the three approaches to the natural monopoly problem, we can draw some general conclusions. From a theoretical perspective, it seems that franchise bidding is preferred to regulation and regulation is preferred to public enterprise. This ordering is also the same in terms of the degree of competitive constraint forced on the firm. Competition is strongest in the case of franchise bidding, as firms compete for the franchise through quality and price. A regulated privately owned firm does not face such competition but is constrained by the threat of takeover and the replacement of existing management if the firm performs poorly. Finally, a public enterprise does not face either type of constraint, which thus allows it greater discretion to stray from efficiency.

In practice, it is more difficult to provide an ordering of the alternatives. As we have seen in the case of cable television, the role of government in franchise bidding is not as different from that of regulation as one might have believed from the theory. Similarly, although regulated private electric utilities appear to perform more efficiently than publicly owned utilities, the evidence is not strong. In addition, private utilities tend to set prices that are too high. Offsetting this is the fact that they practice greater price discrimination.

It is difficult to draw any definitive conclusions, especially because franchise bidding is a relatively new policy. If one alternative had to be chosen to offer the greatest potential, it would probably be franchise bidding. It provides the greatest role for competitive forces, and it is such forces that we count on for achieving social optimality. If franchise bidding is given greater experience, we are more likely to be able to determine whether it is the best method for handling natural monopolies.

Table 14.5
Productivity Measures for the Australian Airline Industry

Year	Tons of Freight and Mail Carried per Employee	Passengers Carried per Employee	Revenue Earned per Employee
Ansett Airline (Private Firm)			
1958–59	10.69	282	$ 7172
1959–60	10.77	309	7758
1960–61	10.96	337	8679
1961–62	10.84	331	8425
1962–63	11.09	316	8510
1963–64	11.06	324	9071
1964–65	12.14	352	9705
1965–66	11.08	354	10479
1966–67	10.34	348	10829
1967–68	9.57	363	12080
1968–69	9.54	392	13185
1969–70	9.35	414	14118
1970–71	8.75	417	15558
1971–72	8.82	437	17280
1972–73	9.07	468	17829
1973–74	10.02	532	21461
Average	10.25	373	12009
Trans Australian Airlines (Public Firm)			
1958–59	4.42	217	$ 6104
1959–60	4.57	259	7016
1960–61	4.52	228	7052
1961–62	4.64	246	7367
1962–63	4.69	255	7726
1963–64	4.83	274	8093
1964–65	5.02	287	8553
1965–66	4.88	294	9072
1966–67	5.11	316	9954
1967–68	5.41	337	11033
1968–69	5.34	356	11734
1969–70	5.80	390	13146
1970–71	5.70	399	14522
1971–72	5.63	414	15644
1972–73	5.62	449	16541
1973–74	6.06	496	19183
Average	5.14	326	10740

Source: Ansett Transport Industries Ltd. Annual Report, 1958–1974, and Trans Australian Airlines Annual Report, 1958–1974, from David Davies, "Property Rights and Economic Efficiency: The Australian Airline Revisited," *Journal of Law and Economics*, April 1977.

Thus, more definitive conclusions than the ones we have offered may present themselves in the near future.

Questions and Problems

1. Do you think that social welfare is higher with a regulated private enterprise or a public enterprise? Does your answer depend on the industry? What about for the distribution of electricity?

2. Why do public enterprises practice less price discrimination than regulated private enterprises? Does it have anything to do with the Robinson-Patman Act?

3. Privatization is a central economic issue for Eastern Europe. Should all public enterprises be privatized? Of those privatized, which should be regulated?

4. Why do public enterprises tend to have higher costs than private enterprises? Do you think this reason is sufficient to always prefer regulated private enterprises over public enterprises?

5. Compare regulation, franchise bidding, and public enterprise. Discuss the advantages and disadvantages of each. If you had to choose one method for all natural monopolies, which would it be?

6. Compare the change in price for an unregulated private enterprise, a regulated private enterprise, and a public enterprise in response to:

   a. The legislature becoming more pro-consumer.

   b. An increase in fixed costs.

   c. A fall in marginal cost.

7. Between a regulated private enterprise and a public enterprise, which do you think would be quicker to adopt a cost-reducing innovation? What about a product-improving innovation?

Notes

1. For a discussion of Conrail as well as some other rather interesting government enterprises, see Lloyd Musolf, *Uncle Sam's Private, Profit-Seeking Corporations* (Lexington, Mass.: Lexington Books, 1983).

2. *The Economist*, October 6, 1984, p. 89.

3. This is certainly the view ascribed to by the Chicago School. For example, see Eugene Fame, "Agency Problems and the Theory of the Firm," *Journal of Political Economy* 88 (April 1980): 288–307. For a particularly egregious case of a manager's not acting in the interests of the owners, see Bryan Burrough and John Helyar, *Barbarians at the Gate: The Fall of RJR Nabisco* (New York: Harper & Row, 1990).

4. Cotton M. Lindsay, "A Theory of Government Enterprise," *Journal of Political Economy* 84 (October 1976): 1065.

5. Sam Peltzman, "Pricing in Public and Private Enterprises: Electric Utilities in the United States," *Journal of Law and Economics* 14 (April 1971): 109–47.

6. Recall that when a regulated firm overcapitalizes, it does so in order to maximize profits by increasing its rate base. Although the capital-labor ratio is inefficient from a production perspective, the resulting ratio is the one that maximizes profits.

7. Important sources for this section include Louis DeAlessi, "An Economic Analysis of Government Ownership and Regulation: Theory and Evidence from the Electric Power Industry," *Public Choice* 19 (Fall 1974): 1–42; and Louis DeAlessi, "The Economics of Property Rights: A Review of the Evidence," *Research in Law and Economics* 2 (1980): 1–47.

8. George J. Stigler and Claire Friedland, "What Can Regulators Regulate? The Case of Electricity," *Journal of Law and Economics* 5 (October 1962): 1–16.

9. R. H. Smiley and W. H. Greene, "Determinants of the Effectiveness of Electric Utility Regulation," *Resources and Energy* 5 (1983): 65–81.

10. Thomas G. Moore, "The Effectiveness of Regulation of Electric Utility Prices," *Southern Economic Journal* 36 (April 1970): 365–75.

11. Thomas J. DiLorenzo and Ralph Robinson, "Managerial Objectives Subject to Political Market Constraints: Electric Utilities in the U.S.," *Quarterly Review of Economics and Business* 22 (Summer 1982): 113–25.

12. Donn R. Pescatrice and John M. Trapani III, "The Performance and Objectives of Public and Private Utilities Operating in the United States," *Journal of Public Economics* 13 (April 1980): 259–76.

13. Louis DeAlessi, "Managerial Tenure under Private and Government Ownership in the Electric Power Industry," *Journal of Political Economy* 82 (May/June 1974): 645–53.

14. David G. Davies, "The Efficiency of Public versus Private Firms: The Case of Australia's Two Airlines," *Journal of Law and Economics* 14 (April 1971): 149–65; and David G. Davies, "Property Rights and Economic Efficiency: The Australian Airline Revisited," *Journal of Law and Economics* 20 (April 1977): 223–26.

15 Dynamic Issues in Natural Monopoly Regulation: Telecommunications

Handling rate cases is perhaps the most commonly performed duty of a regulatory agency, but it is by no means its only duty. Because regulators are ultimately responsible for maintaining a healthy industry and maximizing social welfare, their tasks can be very far-ranging. This chapter is concerned with examining some of the more important tasks related to the evolution of a regulated industry.

The first task we will investigate is the decision to maintain regulation. At any time, changes in the market can result in an industry no longer being a natural monopoly. An important task for a regulatory agency is to identify when such a transformation has taken place and to then open the industry up to entry and eliminate price controls. The next few sections consider how an industry may be transformed from a natural monopoly into a potentially competitive market and provide an assessment of the welfare effects of different regulatory policies. These concepts will be applied to events that have taken place in the intercity telecommunications market over the last few decades. Their future relevance to the local telephone market is also discussed.

A second issue regulators may face is whether to allow a regulated monopolist to enter unregulated markets. Referred to as the separations issue, it has arisen in recent years in such industries as telecommunications, cable television, and electric power. After discussing the benefits and costs of different regulatory policies to handle this situation, we will use these concepts to understand the 1982 decision to break up AT&T.

We conclude the chapter with a discussion of the current and future status of the telecommunications industry. It is an industry that is currently undergoing fundamental changes brought on by technological advances and modifications in regulatory policy. Some of the central regulatory issues of the day concern the telecommunications industry.

Transformation of a Natural Monopoly

The formulation of regulatory policy would be a considerably simpler task if the environment within which it was made was static and never-changing. Having determined that a particular industry was a natural monopoly, regulators would then need to determine the socially optimal price and require the monopolist to meet all demand at that price. Once regulation was put in place, the only role for regulators would be to enforce regulatory policy.

Unfortunately, the environment in which economic agents act is anything but static. Demand shifts over time for such reasons as exogenous changes in consumer preferences or changes in income due to the business cycle or changes in productivity. Innovations are constantly taking place that alter the production technology or introduce unregulated substitute products. In response to these changes, regulators must adapt policy. With regard to monopoly regulation, we can identify two potential dilemmas resulting from changes in the environment. First, the shifting of cost and/or demand functions changes the socially optimal price. Regulators must adjust the regulated price in response to these events. A second and perhaps more troublesome problem arises when shifts in these functions are so severe as to call into question the need for monopoly regulation. In other words, cost and demand conditions may change to the point that the industry is no longer a natural monopoly.

This section will explore the sources of such a transformation and assess the effects of different regulatory policies when such a transformation has been thought to occur. We will then apply these concepts to events that have taken place in the intercity telecommunications market since World War II. Before undertaking this investigation, let us first briefly review the conditions under which monopoly regulation is socially desirable.

Basis for Natural Monopoly Regulation

A natural monopoly exists at an output rate Q^o if the total cost of producing Q^o is minimized by having a single firm produce. If this condition holds, then the cost function, $C(Q)$, is said to be subadditive at Q^o. For example, if a cost function is subadditive at Q^o, then it is cheaper for one firm to produce Q^o than to have two firms each produce half of Q^o. If social welfare is maximized by supplying an amount Q^o of this good, then the efficient market structure is to have a single firm, as it minimizes the resources used in producing Q^o.

In order to assess whether a particular industry is a candidate for regulation, we need to determine whether the firm cost function is subadditive at the socially optimal industry output. This requires both cost and demand information, where the latter is needed in order to calculate the socially optimal output. There is one exception, however, and this is when $C(Q)$ is subadditive at all quantities. In that case, cost efficiency requires single-firm production regardless of the level of demand. We know from Chapter 11 that for the single-product firm, scale economies imply that the cost function is subadditive. Referring back to Figure 11.1, a cost function is exhibited for which scale economies are never exhausted (that is, average cost is always declining). Even without knowledge of the market demand curve, this industry is a natural monopoly which makes it a prime candidate for regulation.

If the firm cost function exhausts economies of scale at some output, then demand information is required in order to determine the appro-

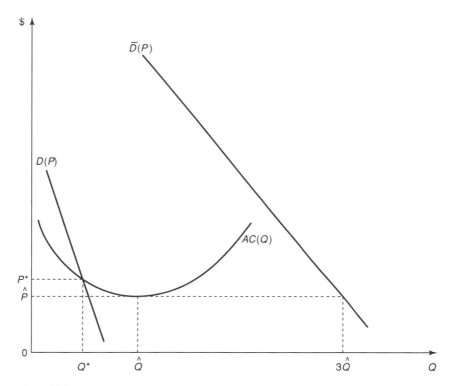

Figure 15.1
Natural Monopoly

priateness of regulation. Consider the U-shaped average cost curve in Figure 15.1. Scale economies are exhausted at an output of $\hat{Q}$. If the market demand curve is $D(P)$, this industry is a natural monopoly because $D(P)$ intersects $AC(Q)$ at Q^* and at that quantity average cost is falling which means that $C(Q^*)$ is subadditive. If the regulators were restricted to using linear pricing (see Chapter 11 for details), the optimal policy would be to allow only one firm to operate and to set a price equal to P^* (that is, average cost pricing). This regulatory policy is socially optimal for two reasons. First, P^* is the price that maximizes social welfare subject to the constraint that firm profit is nonnegative. Second, total cost is minimized at Q^*, as only one firm is operating in the industry.

To understand the importance of the role of market demand in determining the proper regulatory policy, consider the same average cost curve in Figure 15.1 but now assume the demand curve is $\overline{D}(P)$. The socially optimal price is then $\hat{P}$ (equal to minimum average cost of $AC(Q)$). At that price, market demand is $3\hat{Q}$, which is sufficient to support three firms at the efficient size of $\hat{Q}$. There would appear to be little basis for regulating such an industry.

The general rule of thumb is that monopoly regulation is appropriate when the minimum efficient size of the firm (that is, the lowest output at which average cost is minimized) is approximately equal to or larger than market demand at the socially optimal price. In Figure 15.1, when the demand curve is $D(P)$, the efficient firm size, $\hat{Q}$, is larger than market demand (at a price equal to average cost) of Q^*, so that a regulated monopoly is likely to be appropriate for this industry. In contrast, when $\overline{D}(P)$ is the demand curve, market demand at a price of $\hat{P}$ is three times the efficient firm size. In that situation, an unregulated environment is likely to be the appropriate policy.

A peculiar feature of the preceding example is that the socially optimal supply is an integer multiple of minimum efficient scale. Specifically, when demand is $\overline{D}(P)$, market demand at a price equal to minimum average cost is exactly equal to three times minimum efficient scale. Because one would not generally expect such a coincidence to occur, it is important that we show our analysis is robust to it.

Actually, engineering estimates suggest that a U-shaped average cost curve is not typical. Generally, average cost declines until minimum efficient scale is achieved and is then flat for some range of output. An example of such a cost function is depicted in Figure 15.2. Average cost is minimized as long as output lies between $\underline{Q}$ and $\overline{Q}$. Note that $\underline{Q}$ is then minimum efficient scale. For this average cost function, if the market demand function is $D(P)$, then a natural monopoly exists, while this is not true with $\overline{D}(P)$. If, for example, $\underline{Q} < Q^o/2 < \overline{Q}$, then industry cost is minimized by having two firms, each producing $Q^o/2$. We then find that our earlier result holds more generally if the average cost curve has a range of outputs that minimize average cost. Rather than use such an average cost function in future examples in this chapter, we will use the standard U-shaped average cost curve, though remembering that results are robust if we consider a more realistic average cost function of the type in Figure 15.2.

Sources of Natural Monopoly Transformation

Suppose the cost and demand conditions for a particular market call for monopoly regulation. In this subsection, we want to consider changes over time that would make continued regulation unjustified. Alternatively, this issue could be analyzed from the opposite perspective. That is, one could investigate how an industry can be transformed into (rather than out of) a natural monopoly. The sources of the transformation would be the same, only their direction would differ. The de-

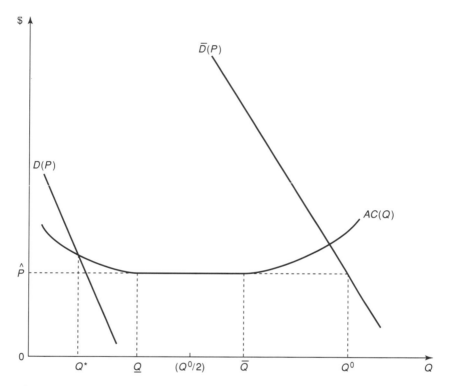

Figure 15.2
Efficient Market Structure with a Flat-Bottomed Average Cost Curve

cision to analyze the case when an industry is transformed into a potentially competitive market was determined by our later application to the intercity telecommunications market.

Demand Side

The sources of transformation are those events that make efficient firm size smaller relative to market demand at the socially optimal price. From the demand side, an industry can be transformed away from being a natural monopoly if the market demand curve shifts upward sufficiently, since it will raise the socially optimal output. For example, in Figure 15.1, if the demand curve shifted from $D(P)$ to $\overline{D}(P)$ over time, the optimal output would increase from Q^* to $3\hat{Q}$. Given an efficient firm size of $\hat{Q}$, the basis for monopoly regulation would no longer exist.

There are, of course, many sources of exogenous increase in demand. These include, for example, an exogenous change in consumer preferences toward the good, an increase in consumer income (if the product is a normal good), a reduction in the price of a complement, or even the

development of a complementary product that raises the value attached
to the good by consumers.

Cost Side

Recall that the firm cost function is determined by the best available
production technology and current input prices. It follows that the average and marginal cost curves will change when there is a technological
innovation that alters the best available technology or when there is a
change in input prices. A change in the cost structure can affect the conditions for the industry to be a natural monopoly in two ways. First, the
efficient firm size can change. Second, a change in the cost structure can
affect the socially optimal output. The qualitative nature of these two
effects is very much dependent on how exactly the cost function is
affected by the change in technology or input prices.

To analyze this issue, let us recall that total cost is composed of fixed
costs, denoted FC, and variable costs, denoted $VC(Q)$:

$$C(Q) = FC + VC(Q)$$

The average cost of a firm is then

$$AC(Q) = (FC/Q) + AVC(Q)$$

where $AVC(Q)$ is average variable cost. Let us assume that $AVC(Q)$ is
increasing in output. As Q increases, fixed costs are spread out over
more output so that FC/Q falls. On the other hand, average variable
cost is increasing in output. When Q is small, fixed costs loom large relative to variable costs, so that the reduction in average fixed cost from
increasing Q dominates the rise in average variable cost. Hence, when Q
is initially low, average cost declines as Q increases. As output is increased further, the reduction in average fixed cost from increasing output becomes less as output is already spread out over a lot of units. If
average variable cost rises sufficiently fast, then eventually average cost
will stop falling. Minimum efficient scale is achieved when the slope of
the average cost function is zero so that average cost is minimized. As
output rises above minimum efficient scale, average cost rises. This argument is what lies behind the standard U-shaped average cost curve
shown in Figure 15.3.

What happens when there is a reduction in fixed costs? Clearly, there
is a reduction in average cost. Since cost is lower, the socially optimal
output is higher. In addition, since fixed costs make up a smaller part of
total cost, minimum efficient scale falls. This is depicted in Figure 15.3.
A fall in fixed costs shifts the average cost curve from $AC(Q)$ to $\overline{AC}(Q)$.

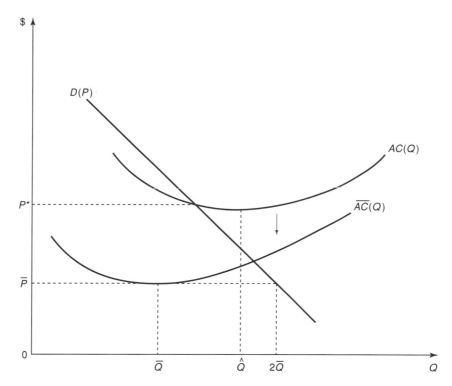

Figure 15.3
The Effect of a Change in Fixed Costs on the Efficient Market Structure

Minimum efficient scale falls from $\hat{Q}$ to $\overline{Q}$. Prior to the fall in fixed costs, the socially optimal price was defined where price equals average cost: P^*. With average cost at $\overline{AC}(Q)$, the socially optimal price equals minimum average cost, $\overline{P}$. Because demand is $2\overline{Q}$, the efficient market structure is to have two firms, not one. Thus an innovation that reduces fixed costs makes it less likely that an industry is a natural monopoly. For the case in Figure 15.3, the reduction in fixed costs moves the industry from being a natural monopoly to one in which two firms can profitably exist at the socially optimal price.

Although a fall in fixed costs makes it less likely that an industry is a natural monopoly, a change in variable costs has an ambiguous effect. For example, suppose that a rise in input prices caused average variable cost to rise. A likely effect on the average cost curve is depicted in Figure 15.4, where the rise in variable costs shifted the average cost curve to $\overline{AC}(Q)$. Obviously, average cost is higher. Because fixed costs now make up a smaller proportion of total cost, minimum efficient scale has fallen from $\hat{Q}$ to $\overline{Q}$. A smaller minimum efficient scale makes the industry less

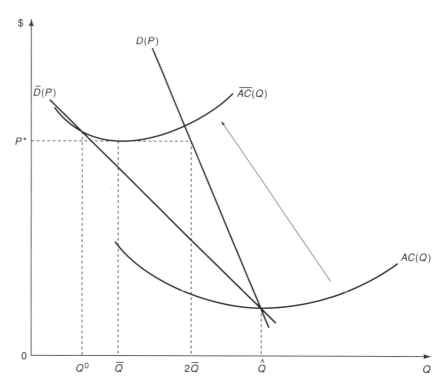

Figure 15.4
The Effect of a Change in Variable Costs on the Efficient Market Structure

likely to remain a natural monopoly. However, higher average cost reduces the socially optimal output, which works in the opposite direction.
The net effect depends on the elasticity of market demand. If the demand curve is highly inelastic, like $D(P)$, then the socially optimal output does not fall very much. In this case, it declines from $\hat{Q}$ to $2\overline{Q}$.
Because two efficient-sized firms can profitably exist at the socially optimal price, monopoly regulation is no longer appropriate. However, if
the demand curve is instead $\overline{D}(P)$, which is relatively elastic, the optimal
output falls a lot, from $\hat{Q}$ to Q^o. Hence a natural monopoly still exists
even though minimum efficient scale has fallen.

To summarize these results, we find that technological innovations
and changes in input prices affect the cost and demand conditions
underlying the rationale for monopoly regulation. Reductions in the
fixed-cost component of the cost function clearly make the industry less
suited for single-firm production by reducing efficient firm size and increasing the socially optimal industry output rate. Changes in the varia-
ble-cost function have less clear effects, as their impact depends on the
elasticity of market demand.

Regulatory Response

Suppose that a regulated monopoly has experienced the type of change just described. Perhaps an innovation occurred that reduced fixed costs or a complementary product was developed that shifted out the market demand curve. In either case, events have taken place that called into question the social desirability of monopoly regulation. The objective of this section is to consider and briefly analyze the policy alternatives available to regulators when faced with this type of situation.

Policy Alternatives

When faced with the situation just described, regulators have basically three alternative policies that they can pursue. The first alternative is to continue price and entry regulation. This is obviously the appropriate policy if they think it is very likely that the industry is still a natural monopoly. If a natural monopoly no longer exists, the pursuance of such a policy generates welfare losses from preventing competition which would lower price and produce a more efficient allocation of production among firms. A second policy is full deregulation: allowing free entry and removing price controls. A necessary condition for this policy to be appropriate is that the industry no longer be a natural monopoly or, if it is still a natural monopoly, that scale economies are relatively small so that any resulting productive inefficiencies from having more than one firm are likely to be offset by the general benefits of competition. However, the loss of natural monopoly status may not be sufficient to justify full deregulation. It may be preferable to pursue a gradual transition from a regulated environment to a deregulated one. Not only could such a policy be justified on grounds of efficiency and equity, but it also may be politically necessary as the severe transitional pains that could arise from full deregulation may induce intense lobbying effort to prevent it. Partial deregulation may be acceptable to all concerned groups. Ultimately, of course, full deregulation would be desirable if the industry is no longer a natural monopoly.

The third policy option is to pursue a course of partial deregulation. This would entail loosening entry restrictions by either allowing free entry or instituting relatively lenient standards for entry. The key feature of partial deregulation is that some substantive controls are kept on price. One possibility is for a regulatory agency to specify minimum and maximum limits on price and allow firms considerable flexibility within those bounds. Alternatively, an agency could continue to require regulatory approval for all rate changes but pursue a policy of rate freedom except when they believe the intentions of a firm are anticompetitive, whether to drive out competitors or achieve collusion. Price regulation could either be applied equally to all firms or differentiated between the established firm and entrants. One form of such an asymmetric regulatory policy is to allow considerable price freedom to new firms while continuing to subject the established firm to the rate approval process. In the absence of continued price regulation, it is possible that the dominant position of the established firm, along with possibly greater financial resources than new firms, might allow it to effectively engage in a predatory policy of pricing below cost so as to drive out new firms. Partial deregulation can be a useful intermediate policy when there is considerable uncertainty faced by regulators over cost and demand conditions. Alternatively, it could be used as a transitional policy to ease the adjustment to full deregulation.

Asymmetric Regulation and Creamskimming

One could imagine a number of distortions that could arise from a regulatory policy that treats the established firm and new firms differently. One such distortion is that it is possible for an industry to still be a natural monopoly and the established firm to be pricing so that it earns normal profit, yet a new firm could find entry profitable if it was allowed to freely set its price. The profitability of entry in that context is generated by distortions created by a regulatory policy that restricts the pricing of the established firm but not entrants.

This possibility is generated by a regulatory pricing practice known as *cross-subsidization*. Cross-subsidization occurs when the price of one product is set so as to generate additional revenues that are used to subsidize the sales of a second product offered by the regulated firm. This practice has been observed in many regulated industries including telephone, airlines, and railroads. It usually entails setting the price on a low-cost product too high and the price on a high-cost product too low. Revenue earned from the former is used to help cover the cost of supplying the latter.[1]

To examine the implications of cross-subsidization, suppose that the regulated monopolist offers two products, X and Y. Q_X is defined to be the number of units of product X produced, and Q_Y is defined analogously. The total cost of producing both products is represented by $C(Q_X, Q_Y)$. We want to suppose that a multiproduct natural monopoly exists. For this reason, it is assumed that the cost function has *economies of scope*. Economies of scope mean that it is cheaper for one two-product firm to produce Q_X and Q_Y than to have one firm produce Q_X and a second firm produce Q_Y. In other words:

$$C(Q_X, Q_Y) < C(Q_X, 0) + C(0, Q_Y)$$

The left-hand side is the cost of a two-product firm supplying both products X and Y. The right-hand side is the total cost of having Q_X produced by one firm and Q_Y produced by another firm.

In addition to assuming that there are economies of scope, we will assume that there are *product-specific economies of scale*. For the single-product case, economies of scale mean that average cost is declining. Product-specific economies of scale are a similar concept but defined instead for the multiproduct case. The incremental cost of producing Q_X is defined to be the added cost from producing Q_X, given that Q_Y of product Y is already being produced:

$$IC(Q_X) = C(Q_X, Q_Y) - C(0, Q_Y)$$

Average incremental cost of X is then

$$AIC(Q_X) = \frac{C(Q_X, Q_Y) - C(0, Q_Y)}{Q_X}$$

If product X has product-specific economies of scale, then the average incremental cost of producing X is declining. We assume that the regulated monopolist has product-specific economies of scale with respect to both products X and Y.

We now want to argue that if a multiproduct cost function has both economies of scope and product-specific economies of scale, then it is a multiproduct natural monopoly. That means the cost of producing Q_X and Q_Y is minimized by having a single firm in the industry. Suppose that there are m firms producing product X and m firms producing product Y. Because there are economies of scope, total industry cost is reduced by having these $2m$ firms combine into m two-product firms. That is, the average cost of a single firm producing X, $AC(Q_X)$, exceeds the average incremental cost of a two-product firm producing Q_X, $AIC(Q_X)$ [see Figure 15.5(a)]. Given product-specific economies of scale, average cost is lower, the more a firm produces. Thus, total cost is reduced by having the m two-product firms combine into a single firm. This means, of course, that the industry is a natural monopoly.

Let us return now to considering cross-subsidization. Suppose that the demand curves for X and Y are as shown in Figure 15.5. One cross-subsidization scheme entails pricing product X at P_X^o and product Y at P_Y^o where the regulated firm earns normal profits:

$$P_X^o Q_X^o + P_Y^o Q_Y^o - C(Q_X^o, Q_Y^o) = 0$$

so that the regulated firm earns normal profit. We have assumed that the price of product Y is less than its average incremental cost [Figure

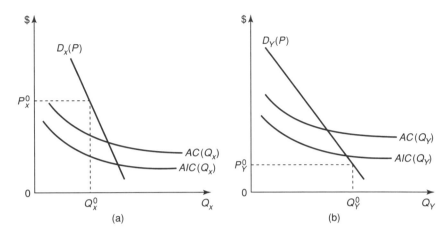

Figure 15.5
Cross-Subsidization and Creamskimming

15.5(b)]. In order for losses from the sale of Y to be covered, the price of product X must then be relatively high (Figure 15.5).

What we want to show now is that there is room for wasteful entry under partial deregulation even though the monopolist is earning normal profit and it is a natural monopoly. Recall that partial deregulation allows entry but continues price regulation for the regulated firm. Depicted in Figure 15.5(a) is the average cost curve of a single-product firm. A new firm can profitably enter by pricing slightly less than P_X^o. Note that entry will not take place into market Y because it is unprofitable. This practice of entering only the more profitable markets is known as *creamskimming*.[2] Entrants are taking the "cream" from the established firm and leaving the "milk," that is, the less profitable markets.

There are two important facts to note about creamskimming. First, it entails wasteful entry since single-firm production is cost-minimizing at every output pair. As shown in Figure 15.5(a), the average cost of a single-product firm exceeds the average (incremental) cost of the regulated two-product firm for product X. The second remark is that cross-subsidization is a socially inefficient way to price. By setting price too high for product X, the wrong signals are being sent out to potential entrants. If the regulators instead pursued Ramsey pricing (see Chapter 11), entry would not occur by less efficient firms, because Ramsey prices are sustainable.[3]

Intercity Telecommunications Market

Recent events in the intercity telecommunications market (ITM) provide a unique opportunity to apply the analysis presented in the preceding section.[4] The service provided in this market is the sending of a message to a particular place at a particular time. This transference occurs between geographical regions as opposed to a local or intracity basis. There are basically three different types of services offered in the ITM. They are message-toll service (MTS), which is what we usually think of as long-distance telephone service; wide-area telephone service (WATS); and private-line service (PLS). The last of these is a circuit that connects two or more points to meet the communication needs of specific users for full-time access to certain points. For example, a PLS may be used by a manufacturer to provide point-to-point communications between two factories. The users of PLS are typically medium- or large-sized firms or government organizations.

Regulatory Background

Federal regulation of the ITM finds its roots in the Mann-Elkins Act of 1910. This piece of legislation gave the Interstate Commerce Commission (ICC) the power to regulate interstate telephone service. Its ability to control entry resulted in American Telephone & Telegraph (AT&T) achieving a de jure monopoly in long-distance voice transmission. The ICC also had the power to set maximum and minimum rates for services. The Communications Act of 1934 transferred power over the ITM to the newly created Federal Communications Commission (FCC). The FCC had control over most aspects of competition through its control of price, entry, and interconnection. Interconnection is the linking of long-distance lines with local telephone lines. Until the late 1950s, the ITM was a classic case of a regulated monopolist. AT&T was the sole supplier of MTS, WATS, and PLS. The FCC controlled price and prevented any other firm from competing with AT&T.

The basis for regulation of the ITM was that it was considered to be a natural monopoly. For many years the best available production technology was the open-wire line system, which involves stringing wires between poles in order to send messages across geographical regions. Because of the very high fixed costs of such a system and the relatively low marginal cost of adding another customer, economies of scale were believed to exist at the relevant portion of the demand curve.

In the 1930s, AT&T developed coaxial cable, which replaced the open wire line system as the best available technology. Coaxial cable is able simultaneously to carry a much greater number of long-distance communications lines. However, while a technological improvement, coaxial cable also entails sufficiently large fixed costs so that a natural monopoly existed even for the largest intercity telecommunication routes.

Thus, cost efficiency demanded single-firm production, and that firm was AT&T.

Transformation of a Natural Monopoly

Though microwave transmission existed prior to World War II, it was not commercially viable until certain technological breakthroughs were achieved by the research and development program funded by the U.S. government as part of the war effort. The economic significance of microwave transmission rests in its ability to inexpensively transmit large amounts of information via radio beams. In contrast to open-wire line or coaxial cable, which require a physical connection between two points, microwave transmission is achieved through a series of microwave relay stations every twenty to thirty miles. Each station receives the microwave signal, amplifies it, and transmits it to the next station. The first microwave radio relay system in the United States for telephone service was installed between Boston and New York in 1947.[5]

By obviating the need for a physical connection between two points in a communications network, microwave radio technology greatly reduced the fixed cost of providing telecommunication services. As we know from our earlier analysis, a reduction of the fixed-cost component of the cost function results in a smaller efficient firm size. This fact was evidenced in the 1950s as many private firms and government organizations petitioned the FCC to allow them to build their own private line systems. On the cost side, we can conclude that the advent of microwave transmission reduced minimum efficient firm size and this made the ITM more amenable to having several suppliers.

At the same time, the demand for telecommunication services was shifting out for several reasons. First, income had been trending upward since the late 1940s. From 1949 to 1984, real per-capita disposable personal income rose at an annual rate of almost 2.2 percent.[6] In his review of the empirical literature, Lester Taylor finds that the estimates of long-run income elasticity of demand for long-distance telephone service range from 0.038 up to 2.76, which clearly indicates it is a normal good.[7] Given this sensitivity of the demand for long-distance telephone service to income, the upward trend in personal income caused the demand curve in the ITM to rise over time.

A second factor affecting market demand was that the advent of microwave technology altered some of the characteristics of the product itself. This new technology allows communications to be used for a wider range of purposes. Hence, market demand would be expected to shift up. An FCC report stated some of the duties that a microwave system could perform for a manufacturer:

Thus the central station in a microwave system can start, stop, slow or speed unattended equipment; open and close valves; record pressure, temperature, engine speed, rate of processing and other data; telemeter voltage, current and power; locate line faults, and perform other supervisory functions.[8]

In contrast, the open-wire line system was quite limited in its ability to perform tasks outside of standard telephone service.

Finally, the demand for intercity telecommunications exogenously increased with the development of computers in the 1950s and their later widespread use. Computers represent a product that is complementary to telecommunication service, inasmuch as the latter provides data processing and transmission service. All three of the factors described caused the demand curve in the ITM to shift out.

In analyzing both the cost and the demand side, it is clear that events since the late 1940s called into question the natural monopoly status of the ITM. The minimum efficient firm size had fallen and market demand had increased. At issue, however, is whether the size of these changes was sufficient for the industry to be transformed into one in which monopoly regulation is no longer desirable. As can be seen in Figure 15.6, there are two possible scenarios. Under one scenario, the

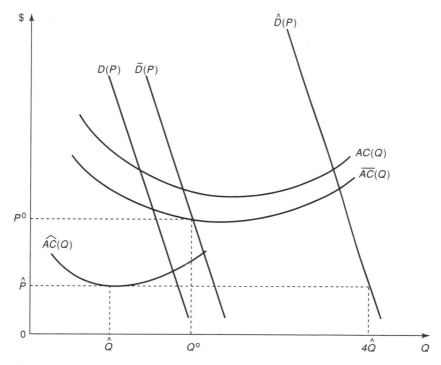

Figure 15.6
Potential Transformation of a Natural Monopoly

average-cost curve shifts from $AC(Q)$ to $\overline{AC}(Q)$ while market demand rises from $D(P)$ to $\overline{D}(P)$. In this case, a natural monopoly still exists, as the cost function is subadditive at Q^o. On the other hand, suppose that the quantitative effects are greater so that the average cost curve shifts from $AC(Q)$ to $\hat{A}C(Q)$ and demand from $D(P)$ to $\hat{D}(P)$. At the socially optimal price of $\hat{P}$, the market can support four firms at the efficient size. It is clear from the evidence that changes have occurred in the direction shown. The difficulty lies in determining which scenario better represents what has transpired in the ITM.

The empirical evidence on this issue is quite mixed. As a starting point, consider the cost studies done by AT&T and Motorola in July 1962 for an FCC hearing on the Telpak tariff proposed by AT&T.[9] The estimated average cost curves for a 200-mile microwave system are depicted in Figure 15.7. There are clearly economies of scale though the

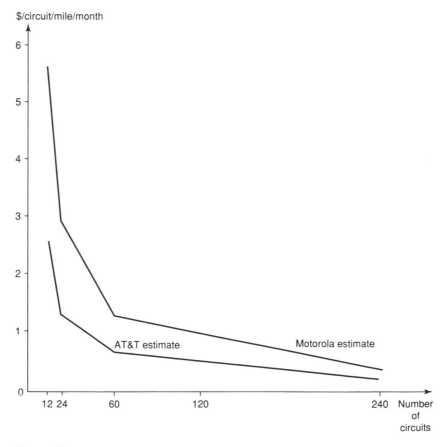

Figure 15.7
Economies of Scale for Intercity Telecommunication Services

average cost curve seems to be flattening out around 240 circuits. If economies of scale are exhausted around that size, then a natural monopoly would have existed for many telecommunication routes in the late 1940s. However, with the increase in demand since the 1950s, only the very low-density routes would still be a natural monopoly at 240 circuits. The larger intercity routes have demand of several thousand circuits, which suggests that many efficient-sized firms could have profitably existed. It should be noted that these conclusions are restricted by the fact that they are true only for 1962 and that our conjecture as to what the average cost curve looks like after 240 circuits is correct.

In his 1975 study, Leonard Waverman found for the mid-1960s that scale economies were exhausted at around 1000–1200 circuits.[10] In the late 1960s the New York–Philadelphia route had demand of around 79,000 circuits. In light of his estimate of minimum efficient scale of 1000–1200 circuits, he concluded that several suppliers could have existed on many intercity routes. Econometric work by David Evans and James Heckman in 1982 also supports this conclusion.[11] They estimated a multiproduct cost function for the Bell System based on data during the period 1958–1977. Their empirical estimates show that the cost function was not subadditive at any output configuration for AT&T over that period.

In contrast, other studies have found quite significant economies of scale for AT&T over the period 1947–1976.[12] The estimates of (Average Cost/Marginal Cost) ranged from 1.58 up to 2.12. If average cost is high relative to marginal cost, then average cost must be falling, which implies that there are economies of scale. It is important to note that these studies considered only product-specific economies of scale and not economies (or diseconomies) of scope. In contrast, the Evans and Heckman study allowed for both. It should be noted, however, that Evans and Heckman comment on the poor quality of data available for performing this type of analysis.

Regulatory Policy in the Microwave Era

With the advent of microwave technology, many private firms and government organizations began petitioning the FCC in the early 1950s to allow them to build and operate their own point-to-point communication networks. These demands led to the Above 890 Mc decision in 1959. In this decision, the FCC stated that frequencies above 890 megacycles would be shared by AT&T (the common carrier) with private users. What was significant in this decision is that a system built by a noncommon carrier could be used only for private demand. A firm could not sell telecommunication services. In response to the Above 890

Mc decision, AT&T entered the Telpak tariff, which called for volume discounts on PLS. Presumably, AT&T's objective was to make it profitable for businesses to buy AT&T's services rather than build their own system. Ultimately, the FCC disallowed the Telpak tariff because it was not justified by the cost estimates.

Microwave Communications Incorporated (MCI) petitioned the FCC in 1963 to allow them to enter the St. Louis–Chicago PLS market as a common carrier. That is, MCI desired to supply private line systems and act as a competitor to AT&T in this market. After six years of hearings and $10 million of expenses incurred by MCI, its application was approved in 1969. Once the MCI decision was made, the FCC found itself inundated with requests by other firms desiring to enter the PLS market. Furthermore, MCI, as well as the other new carriers, had to petition to enter each individual route. The MCI decision in 1969 only gave MCI permission to service the St. Louis–Chicago route. In response to this demand, the FCC made the Specialized Common Carrier (SCC) decision in 1971. It allowed free entry into the PLS market. A firm needed only to submit an application so that lengthy regulatory hearings were avoided.

Entry was extended to the message toll service (MTS) market with MCI's introduction of Execunet service in 1975. The MTS market represented considerably larger revenues than the PLS market. Later that year the FCC ruled in Execunet I that the SCC decision opened up entry only into the PLS market, so that MCI must discontinue their Execunet service. With the U.S. Court of Appeals for the District of Columbia overruling this decision in 1978, entry was extended from the PLS market to the entire ITM.

Starting in 1969 with the MCI decision, the FCC pursued a policy of partial deregulation. While allowing entry into the PLS market and then, by court order, into the MTS market, the FCC continued to regulate rates. In particular, they maintained the practice of cross-subsidization. This occurred at two levels. First, there was the use of long-distance rates to subsidize local service rates charged by AT&T. Within the ITM, AT&T was also forced to use rates on high-density, long-distance routes to subsidize rates on low-density routes. This specifically took the form of charging the same rate independent of the amount of traffic, even though average cost is lower, the greater the amount of traffic. A major reason for continuing price regulation was the fear that AT&T would set artificially low rates in order to drive competitors out of the ITM. Presumably, below-cost rates would be funded by AT&T pricing above cost in its monopoly markets in local telephone service.

Given these facts, it is not surprising that entry initially took place in the high-density markets. Because demand was largest there, these markets could best support several firms. Furthermore, because AT&T's prices were above cost, there was room for profitable entry. It is also not surprising that AT&T complained that entrants like MCI were less efficient and found entry profitable only because of creamskimming.[13] The allegation of being less efficient is very difficult to determine empirically. Nevertheless, because of cross-subsidization, the FCC certainly opened up the possibility that less efficient firms could find entry into the high-density markets profitable. Evidence against AT&T's claim, however, is the fact that MCI eventually entered all of the MTS markets.

As a result of a seven-year antitrust case against AT&T by the Department of Justice, AT&T agreed on January 8, 1982, to sever its connections with its twenty-two telephone operating companies. These twenty-two companies were made into seven holding companies, the regional Bell operating companies (RBOCs). Local Bell system operations were subdivided into 161 "local exchange and transport areas" (LATAs) with each LATA being assigned to one of the RBOCs. The key restriction on RBOCs is that they are not allowed to provide interLATA services. In exchange for spinning off its telephone operating companies, AT&T was permitted to retain Western Electric (its manufacturing division), Bell Labs (its research and development division), and Long Lines, which supplies intercity telecommunication services. In addition, the 1956 consent decree, which prevented AT&T from entering any unregulated markets, would be erased. The result of the breakup, which took place on January 1, 1984, is that AT&T is no longer involved in any monopoly markets. Because a major impetus for continued price regulation in the ITM is the fear that AT&T would fund predatory pricing from revenue generated by its monopolized markets, the breakup makes it feasible eventually to achieve full deregulation in the ITM.

Regulated Monopoly to Regulated Competition

Though the ITM has been in a deregulatory mode for over two decades, full deregulation has yet to be achieved. Stuck in a holding pattern, the FCC continues to regulate interstate interLATA rates while thirty-nine state regulatory agencies control intrastate interLATA rates. The form of this regulation is peculiar in that it applies to AT&T but, in practice, not to any of the other long-distance carriers. AT&T is required to serve all customers, file tariffs whenever it offers a new service, and average rates across broad customer segments.[14] Competing providers like MCI and Sprint are unconstrained by the regulatory authorities in their pricing, their provision of new services, and in their movements into and out of markets. To add to this unequal treatment, almost every new tariff by AT&T is challenged by its competitors, with the typical basis being that it is not cost-justified and thereby predatory in intent.[15]

The exact method of regulating AT&T has evolved since the 1984 breakup of the Bell system. In the mid 1980s, the FCC used rate-of-return regulation that allowed AT&T to set rates commensurate with a return of 12.2 percent.[16] With falling access charges to be paid to the local exchange system over the last decade, this rate-of-return constraint has forced AT&T to lower its rates. Then, in March 1989, the FCC approved the use of price caps. Rather than regulate AT&T's return, the FCC now directly regulates its rates. After adjusting for inflation, AT&T is required to reduce its rates each year by a productivity factor of 2.5 percent and a "consumer dividend" of 0.5 percent. This regulatory policy groups AT&T's services into three baskets: residential toll, 800 service, and all other business services; and specifies that AT&T cannot increase or decrease prices of any of the three baskets by more than 5 percent.[17] The replacement of rate-of-return regulation with price caps has also been popular at the state level where regulatory agencies control intrastate long-distance rates. Of the thirty-nine states with more than one LATA (so that there is such a thing as a long-distance phone call), twenty-eight of them went to price caps over 1984–1987.

The basis for this asymmetric regulatory policy is the dominant position of AT&T. A fear is that if AT&T was left unregulated, its market position and its financial and technological clout could allow it to drive out its competitors and thereby reestablish its monopoly position in the ITM. While the advent of competing long-distance suppliers has resulted in almost 40 percent of the market being served by carriers other than AT&T, the industry is still dominated by the presence of AT&T (see Table 15.1). The ITM is characterized by one very large firm, AT&T, two considerably smaller full-line competitors, MCI and Sprint, one specialized but growing competitor, LDDS Communications, and hundreds of tiny resellers of long distance service that lease their lines from the four above-mentioned firms. AT&T's only serious competitors in the residential market are MCI and Sprint and AT&T dwarfs both of them. The dominant position of AT&T is even more striking if one examines some significant submarkets. In 800 services, AT&T's market share was 74 percent while MCI stood at 17 percent and Sprint at 7 percent.[18] Though MCI's market share has been rising recently, AT&T commanded 75 percent of the Collect Call market in 1993 to only 11 percent for MCI and 9 percent for Sprint.[19]

Table 15.1
Market Shares in Long-Distance Telephone

Company	Market Share (%)		
	1984	1988	1993
AT&T	90.0	75.4	61.0
MCI	4.9	9.9	18.7
Sprint	3.1	6.2	9.6
Other	2.0	8.5	10.7

Source: Data for 1984 and 1988 are from Arsen J. Darnay and Marlita A. Reddy, *Market Share Reporter—1994* (Detroit: Gale Research Inc., 1994); data for 1993 are from *Fortune*, June 13, 1994.

Due to the dominant position of AT&T, there are two possible scenarios associated with full deregulation that are of concern.[20] The first scenario is one in which an unregulated AT&T substantially raises its rates. Whether AT&T would choose to do so and what impact that would have on the ITM depends on the ease with which customers would switch to other providers and the ability of competing providers to meet this increase in demand. If customers find other providers' service comparable to that of AT&T and those providers have excess capacity, then any significant price hike by AT&T is likely to prove to be unprofitable in that it would result in a significant drop in AT&T's demand. Recent experience suggests that this would indeed be the case. Customers have already shown their willingness to switch to competing providers, as evidenced by almost 40 percent of the market currently using an alternative provider. The use of fiber optics has resulted in considerable excess capacity so that competitors would be quite capable of meeting a sharp rise in their demand. An FCC study estimated that non-AT&T carriers could supply 146 percent of the market.[21] Though Sprint currently has around 10 percent of the market, it has enough fiber in place to carry all long-distance traffic.[22] The above analysis suggests that an unregulated AT&T would be quite unlikely to raise its rates and if it did that the impact on the market would be seriously mitigated by customers switching to other suppliers. A caveat is if AT&T was able to persuade its main competitors to also raise their rates. But that is an antitrust issue, not a regulatory one.

The second scenario, and perhaps the more relevant one, entails an unregulated AT&T pursuing a predatory policy of pricing very low, so as to force its competitors out of the market, and, once gone, raising its rates. This seems unlikely as well. Given its large market share, a policy of below-cost pricing would be very costly to AT&T and, given the size and financial strength of MCI and Sprint, it would take a long and in-

tense price war to drive them out of the industry. MCI earned net profits
of $732 million in 1993 and Sprint earned $687 million (Sprint also
owns some local telephone and cellular properties). Although these
numbers pale in comparison to AT&T's net profit of $4.262 billion,
it would take a lot to bankrupt MCI or Sprint.[23] Furthermore, the investment of MCI and Sprint in their long-distance networks, whether
microwave or fiber optics, is largely sunk so that the marginal cost of
operation is relatively low. The bottom line is that it would take a price
war of biblical proportions for AT&T to drive out either MCI or Sprint.
An alternative strategy is for AT&T to use a price war to induce one of
its largest competitors to be bought out, but it is unlikely that the antitrust authorities would allow AT&T to purchase or merge with any of
its main competitors.

Industry Trends and the Prognosis for Full Deregulation

Is the industry moving to a state of relatively balanced and aggressive
competition? Such a state would provide the basis for fully deregulating
the ITM. In examining the conduct of firms, the first striking piece of
evidence is that interstate rates, after controlling for inflation, have
fallen by 50 percent since 1984 (see Table 15.2). During that time, demand has approximately doubled. Is this indicative of an increasingly
competitive environment? To address this question properly, one must
first determine whether there have been cost reductions that could explain the fall in rates. Indeed, there have been large cost reductions and

Table 15.2
Long-Distance Rates, 1984 and 1991

Calling Distance (in airline miles)	January 1984	July 1991	Percent Change
1–10	$1.76	$1.70	−3.4%
11–22	2.38	1.80	−24.4
23–55	3.00	1.90	−36.7
56–124	3.90	2.09	−46.4
125–292	4.09	2.09	−48.9
293–430	4.37	2.30	−47.4
431–925	4.49	2.30	−48.8
926–1910	4.60	2.44	−47.0
1911–3000	5.15	2.45	−52.4
3001–4250	5.35	2.91	−45.6
4251–5750	5.56	3.20	−42.4

Source: Rates are for AT&T for a ten-minute direct-dialed daytime call within the U.S.
Data are from the FCC and the table is from "Special Report: Telecommunications," *Wall
Street Journal*, October 4, 1991.

some economists have argued that they are entirely responsible for the fall in rates. Since the breakup, there has been a shifting of the recovery of the fixed costs of local telephone systems from long-distance companies to final consumers. This has manifested itself as falling access charges for long-distance companies to connect to the local exchange system and higher monthly subscriber line charges for final consumers. A series of accounting changes has also reduced interstate costs and raised intrastate costs. Compared to 1984, one finds that AT&T's carrier access charges were $9.266 billion less in 1991, while its rate reductions translated into $8.22 billion less of revenue.[24] Although it is not clear that reduced access charges can explain all of the fall in rates, their magnitude puts into doubt the claim that falling rates reflect an increasingly competitive ITM.

As regards the competitiveness of the ITM, economists are divided in their opinions. Some characterize the ITM as having a price umbrella with AT&T setting the standard rates.[25] The idea is that AT&T sets artificially high rates and tolerates its competitors' setting slightly lower rates (though not too much lower). Other economists paint a different picture. They point to the steady eroding of AT&T's market share and the rate competition associated with discount programs like MCI's "Family and Friends."[26] That advertising by the top three long-distance suppliers accelerated from $524 million in 1992 to $800 million in 1993 may be evidence to be applied to either position.[27] It is consistent with increasing competitiveness, but there is also concern that heightened nonprice competition is reflective of reduced price competition.

With regard to market structure, two trends are at work, both of which are likely to be procompetitive. The steady decline of AT&T's market share has resulted in the industry becoming less concentrated over time. At the same time, there has been widespread consolidation through a series of mergers and acquisitions. Examples include Allnet and Lextel in 1985, GTE Sprint and US Telcom in 1986, and MCI and Telecom*USA in 1990 (when the latter was the fourth largest carrier). LDDS Communications has pursued an explicit strategy of growth through acquisition. Only the eleventh largest carrier in 1991, LDDS is now the fourth largest. Its activities include combining with the sixth and seventh largest carriers. Though consolidation means rising concentration, this trend may prove to be procompetitive in that it may generate a larger number of firms that have the size to compete head-to-head with AT&T in a variety of markets.

Another potentially important element in the competitiveness of the ITM is the degree of potential competition. If consolidation continues and the largest carriers were able to achieve an amicable arrangement, are there new firms to enter and restore more than a modicum of competition? In fact, a number of the Regional Bell Operating Companies (RBOCs) have expressed considerable interest in entering the ITM. Legally, this would require repeal of the 1982 consent decree that broke up the Bell System. Practically, the presence of four fiber-optic systems has resulted in excess capacity which would seem to make it unwise to construct another nationwide system. Of course, an entrant could lease lines like five hundred or so resellers are currently doing. However, because those lines would be leased from one of the top four long-distance carriers, there is a limit to the degree that a reseller can increase competition.

On net, it would seem that the ITM is moving towards a more balanced competitive environment. If this trend continues then the full deregulation of the ITM may ultimately become a reality.

Local-Exchange Telecommunications Market

Just as technological advances put into question the natural monopoly status of the ITM, a similar process may be in its inception in the local telephone market (LTM). The two key innovations are in the area of wireless communications and digital switches. Entry into the LTM has been occurring and further entry of much greater proportions is imminent.

The natural monopoly argument for the LTM is analogous to that for the ITM prior to the advent of microwave technology. Historically, local telephone service has been provided using a wire-based system that entails large fixed costs and low marginal costs of adding a subscriber or conducting a call. Because it entails wasteful duplication to have more than one wire running into a home, productive efficiency demands a single provider. In addition, switching services, which allow customers to place and receive calls, were characterized by such a degree of scale economies that it was highly economical to have an area served by a single switching facility.

Cellular Telephone Technology

Cellular radio systems replace wires with radio signals.[28] The system is comprised of radio relay stations or "cell sites." Each station includes a few short antennas and a receiver-transmitter and its task is to pick up signals from wireless telephones. The stations are then linked together by wires or microwave transmission. Adding a subscriber no longer entails a physical wire but rather allocating a part of the spectrum. Prior to the 1980s, the available spectrum could only support 140,000 subscribers nationwide. A solution to the problem of limited spectrum has been known since 1947, when scientists at Bell Labs came up with "cellular" radio networks. The idea is that radio telephones would be low-power, short-range devices. The same frequencies could then be reused in sufficiently distant areas in the manner that is done today with millions of cordless telephones. A geographic area would be divided into cells (hence the name cellular telephone) with each cell served by its own low-power transmitter. The capacity of a cellular system could then be increased by shrinking the size of cells and thus increasing their number. Although this theoretical solution has been known for decades, it was only with the advent of microelectronics in the 1970s that it became implementable. A cellular telephone system requires sophisticated transmitters and receivers and massive coordination among cells to "hand off" calls and coordinate frequencies as a phone moves between cells.

Regulatory Policy

The FCC has taken a procompetitive stance towards cellular telephony. It initially split the allocation of new radio-telephone frequencies between local telephone operating companies (telcos) and nonwire companies, or awarded licenses on an "open entry" basis to the best applicants. The FCC permitted two competitors for each area. Although cellular telephony is experiencing explosive growth (the number of subscribers having increased by 45 percent in 1993), in absolute terms there were only 16 million subscribers in 1993. This is a penetration ratio of only 8 percent.[29] Cellular telephone usage is a puny (though still valuable) portion of the LTM.

The FCC has been following a policy of auctioning off the spectrum rather than handing it out. Beginning in 1994, auctions are being conducted for what are called personal communications services (PCS). The FCC plans to auction off 160 megahertz in each metropolitan area. This is four times the size of the spectrum allocated for existing cellular, and this allocation could end up creating three to six wireless networks.

Is Local Telephone Still a Natural Monopoly?

The argument that the local telephone market is not a natural monopoly rests on two points.[30] First, the development of digital switching technology has greatly reduced the economies of scale associated with switching services. It is now economically feasible to have a local neighborhood connected to multiple switching facilities which is essential for competition as each carrier would have its own facility. Innovations like this one lie behind some preliminary estimates that the local telcos may no longer be a natural monopoly.[31]

The preceding argument deals with the switching technology. The second argument that the LTM is no longer a natural monopoly is based on advances in transmission. Specifically, it is that cellular telephony has greatly reduced fixed costs by replacing wire with radio. Still, a major issue is whether cellular telephones can effectively replace wire-based telephones. Cellular systems are currently handling 16 million subscribers, but, even with the PCS auctions, can they handle 100 million subscribers? What type of further innovations are required for that to be a reality? Currently, cellular systems need wire-based systems to function in that the local exchange completes 98 percent of all cellular calls. For the foreseeable future, it would then appear that local telcos hold an irreplaceable position in the LTM. In their analysis of this question, Bruce Greenwald and William Sharkey, economists at Bell Communications Research (the research arm of the RBOCs), conclude:

Taken as a whole, therefore, new transmission technologies have increased the number of potential competitors to the local exchange companies, but have not yet decisively eliminated economies of scale in low volume local transmission.[32]

The transformation of the LTM to a potentially competitive industry must await further technological progress.

Separation of Regulated Monopolies and Competitive Markets

For more than half a century, AT&T was a regulated monopolist in almost every respect. Its telephone-operating companies monopolized local service for a very large share of the U.S. population. Western Electric, the manufacturing arm of the Bell System, was the sole supplier of terminal equipment for those customers serviced by the Bell operating companies.[33] Its dominance was evidenced by the fact that the Bell System owned approximately 80 percent of the telephones in the United States in 1956. Finally, the Long Lines division had an undisputed monopoly of intercity telecommunications, which included long-distance telephone service. By the time of the breakup in 1984, however, it was clear that a regulated monopoly no longer properly characterized the Bell System. Instead, AT&T was operating in a mixture of regulated and competitive markets.

The change in the structure of AT&T's markets began taking place in the late 1960s. In its 1968 Carterphone decision, the FCC decided that the final users of telephone services could purchase their own terminal equipment. Before that time customers were restricted to connecting Western Electric equipment to Bell telephone lines. The Carterphone decision allowed them to buy equipment from alternative suppliers subject to quality standards set by AT&T. This action opened up the terminal equipment market to competition.[34] Then, in 1969, the FCC began a policy of free entry into the private line service market with the MCI decision and later with its Specialized Common Carrier decision in 1971. Competition was extended to the remainder of the intercity telecommunications market in 1975 with MCI's Execunet service. This market continues to be subject to price regulation, though it has not been a serious impediment to competition.

By the late 1970s AT&T was involved in markets that ranged from regulated monopoly (local telephone service) to regulated competition (long-distance telephone service) to unregulated competition (terminal equipment). The decision to break up AT&T was a statement that such a mixed situation was untenable. AT&T was forced to divest itself of its regulated monopolies, that is, the twenty-two Bell telephone-operating companies. This left AT&T with Long Lines, Western Electric, and Bell Labs, all of which were operating in markets that were unregulated or being deregulated. In line with AT&T being transformed into an unregulated firm, the Justice Department erased the 1956 consent decree, which prevented AT&T from entering unregulated markets. Thus the breakup of the Bell system had resulted in an AT&T that was stripped of its regulated monopolies in local telephone service and was prepared to compete freely in the remainder of the communications industry.

The objective of this section is to analyze the general issue underlying the decision to break up AT&T. This issue is concerned with whether regulated monopolies should be allowed to compete in unregulated markets or should instead be separated from them. Referred to as the separations issue, it has arisen not only in the telephone industry but also in the cable television and electric utility industries. The next few subsections consider the benefits and costs of separation and then applies this analysis to understanding the decision to break up the Bell System.

Benefits and Costs of Separation

The issue before us is whether a firm that is subject to monopoly regulation in one market should be allowed to enter and compete freely in markets that are unregulated and potentially competitive. We will observe that there are certain anticompetitive effects that can arise when a market consists of a regulated monopolist and unregulated firms. On the other hand, separation may result in certain cost inefficiencies.

Policy Options

One policy that is available to handle this type of situation is that of separation, which prohibits the regulated firm from participating in unregulated markets. There are actually two approaches to pursuing a policy of separation. Suppose that market X is the regulated market and market Y is the unregulated market. Separation can be achieved by restricting the regulated firm to participating only in market X. This was the approach implicit in the 1956 consent decree. A second method is to make both markets X and Y subject to monopoly regulation. When market Y is potentially competitive, such a policy would generally be undesirable.[35] Thus our attention will be directed to the first approach. An alternative policy option to that of separation is to allow the regulated monopolist to compete with other firms in market Y. Market Y could be left totally unregulated, or the regulatory agency could limit the degree of competition through price controls (setting maximum and minimum prices) or some other form of regulation.

Benefits of Separation

We want to consider the benefits of a policy that prohibits a regulated monopolist from competing in unregulated markets. The benefits of such a policy are defined in relation to what would occur if a policy of no separation was pursued. In particular, there are certain anticompetitive practices that might result from allowing a regulated monopolist to compete against unregulated firms. The benefits of separation rest in preventing such practices from taking place.

Suppose that the regulated monopolist was allowed to compete freely in an unregulated market. One possible undesirable effect is that the monopolist would use profits earned from its regulated markets to fund a policy of predatory pricing in the unregulated markets. By setting a very low price it can impose losses on its competitors and perhaps induce them to exit the industry. The advantage of the regulated firm is having regulated markets as a source of revenue to fund such activities.

A second, and perhaps more serious, anticompetitive practice may arise if the products in the regulated and unregulated markets are related—in particular, if product X (regulated) is an input in the production of product Y (unregulated). The regulated monopolist can then control the supply of competitors through its supply of product X. Alternatively, it may choose to give competitors a lower-quality product. Thus, consumers may find the regulated monopolist's product preferable to that of its competitors. The exact effects of this type of anticompetitive practice are very much dependent on the relationship between products X and Y. A more detailed analysis will be provided later when we look at applications.

Finally, the regulated monopolist may be able to charge a higher price in its regulated market under a policy of no separation. Because there is likely to be some capital that is shared by products X and Y, the regulated firm has some discretion in assigning costs. Because it is required to set price in market X so that revenue equals cost, it will find it optimal to assign all joint costs to product X. This will increase the price it can set in the regulated market and thus increase profit. This practice is not anticompetitive for market Y, but it does lead to a price in the regulated market that is above the socially optimal level.

The benefits of separation rest in preventing these types of practices. Under a policy of separation, we may observe both a lower price in the unregulated market and in the regulated market.

Costs of Separation

The primary cost of separation is the elimination of a potential competitor (the regulated monopolist) from the market. If there is free entry into the market and the regulated monopolist offers no advantages over other firms, then there is little lost from preventing it from competing. On the other hand, suppose that the regulated monopolist does possess an advantage. One plausible source of advantage is that it can produce the unregulated product at lower cost because of economies of scope between the regulated and unregulated products. By prohibiting the regulated monopolist from supplying the unregulated product, the most efficient firm is then eliminated from the market. The value of the increased resources used to supply the unregulated product represents a cost to society from separation.

If the two products are inputs in the production of the same good or service, there may be gains from vertical integration, specifically, lower transaction costs from coordinating activities.[36] A policy of separation would obviously prevent these gains from being realized and would be another cost to such a policy.

In summary, the main benefits from a policy of separation are the prevention of anticompetitive practices in the unregulated market and shifting of costs from the unregulated to the regulated market. This should result in a lower price than would be the case without separation. The potential cost to such a policy is the wasted resources due to preventing the most efficient firm from competing. This would tend to raise price. The social optimality of separation then depends on the ability of the regulated monopolist to pursue anticompetitive practices in an unregulated market and the degree of economies of scope that may exist between the regulated and unregulated products.

Breakup of AT&T

On November 20, 1974, the Department of Justice filed an antitrust suit against AT&T for violation of Section Two of the Sherman Act.

AT&T was accused of attempting to monopolize the telecommunications industry by using its dominant position in three segments of that industry: local exchange, long distance, and terminal equipment. The case went to court on January 15, 1981, and on January 7, 1982, two weeks before AT&T was scheduled to complete its case, AT&T and the Department of Justice reached a settlement. As described earlier, AT&T agreed to divest itself of its local telephone operating companies in exchange for repeal of the 1956 consent decree and retention of Western Electric, Bell Labs, and Long Lines. Judge Harold Greene, presiding over the trial, approved the settlement on August 11, 1982, and, on August 24, 1982, entered a modified final judgment. The divestiture was consummated on January 1, 1984.

The 1982 consent decree that broke up AT&T was a decision that a policy of separation was appropriate. At the time of the breakup, AT&T had a regulated monopoly in local telephone service but was competing with other firms in the partially deregulated ITM. By requiring AT&T to divest itself of its twenty-two telephone-operating companies, the Justice Department separated these two markets. In this subsection, we consider some of the effects of this policy.

As mentioned above, the major benefit of separation is to make the unregulated market better suited for equal and unconstrained competition among firms. Because price regulation was still in effect in the long-distance market, separation was not required to prevent predatory pricing. It is interesting to note, however, that on several occasions the FCC prevented AT&T from drastically reducing rates in the ITM. In the Telpak decision in 1964, the FCC disallowed a tariff offering by AT&T that reduced rates on private line services. The reason was that it was not cost-justified because the estimated rate of return would have been under 1 percent. It would appear that the FCC was concerned that the tariff was predatory. Similarly, the FCC disallowed the HiLo tariff proposed by AT&T, which sought lower rates on high-density routes being entered by MCI and other specialized common carriers. On the St. Louis–Chicago route, MCI was charging a full-time rate per channel of $481.65 at the time of the tariff in 1974. AT&T proposed to charge $341.85. However, in fairness to AT&T, it was probably not so much interested in pricing predatorily as in simply trying to eliminate cross-subsidization so to be able to compete.

The real problem arose in that the two products were interrelated. To provide long-distance service, a competitor like MCI had to interconnect with the local service lines provided by AT&T. The initial response of AT&T to entry in 1969 by MCI was simply to refuse to interconnect with them. In the SCC decision in 1971, the FCC said AT&T should interconnect with their competitors, but the terms were left open to AT&T. This did not improve the situation, because AT&T placed considerable restrictions on the specialized common carriers.[37] Only in 1974 did the FCC order interconnection in its Bell System Tariff Offering decision. When MCI expanded entry into message toll service, the same problem arose. Their entry was approved by the U.S. Court of Appeals in 1975, but not until 1978 was AT&T was forced to interconnect with MCI's Execunet service.[38]

Only in 1978 were firms like MCI allowed to interconnect with the local operating company as Long Lines. Even after achieving this right, the competitors to AT&T in the ITM were still not treated equally. It is generally believed that AT&T's competitors were given poorer-quality connections by the Bell operating companies. Customers had to dial twenty digits to make a long-distance call with MCI, but only eleven with AT&T. The result was that consumers saw AT&T as offering a higher-quality product, which forced its competitors to offer a discount to compete. It was this type of behavior that led to the original antitrust suit against AT&T.

Under the current separation policy, the local operating companies no longer have an incentive to offer discriminating service, as they have been divested from AT&T. Under current FCC policy, the ITM has moved to a position where AT&T, MCI, Sprint, and other common carriers will be on an equal basis from which to compete. This is clearly the major benefit from separation.

AT&T did point out that there are also costs from a policy of separation through foregone economies of scope. It was believed that there were cost savings ("network effects") from having one firm supply both local service and intercity service. Although there is certainly a need for coordination, it is unclear that it cannot be effectively achieved through the market rather than within the firm. Furthermore, the cost study by Evans and Heckman in 1983 did not find any such economies of scope. Thus there is little evidence to suggest that separation incurred much of a reduction in cost efficiency.

A particularly interesting endnote to this study is that the spun-off Bell regional operating companies are seeking permission from the FCC to enter the ITM. Not only does this reintroduce the separations issue, but if the FCC does permit them to enter, it calls into question the original purpose of breaking up the Bell System. This issue is discussed below in the section "The Future of the Telecommunications Industry: Digital Convergence."

Telecommunications and Computers[39]

During the time in which major technological advances were taking place in the ITM, there were also significant developments occurring in the computer industry.[40] The war effort in the 1940s not only led to the development of microwave technology but also to the first electronic computer. Completed in late 1945, it was referred to as the ENIAC (electronic numerical integrator and computer). An economic expert on the computer industry, Gerald Brock describes the ENIAC as

a monstrously large and unwieldy machine. It was two stories tall, weighed thirty tons, and covered 1,500 square feet of floor space. It contained 18,000 vacuum tubes, which required regular replacement, and consumed vast amounts of power. Its 700,000 resistors, 6,000 switches, and other components were held together with 500,000 soldered joints. It could only be reprogrammed by physically changing the complex wiring. However, it contained a unique computing capability, which allowed the numerical solution of complex differential equations that had previously daunted the most determined teams of mechanical calculator operators.[41]

Computers became commercially viable in the early 1950s with Remington Rand's Univac I and IBM's 701. The shifting of technology from vacuum tubes to transistors in 1958 led to major advances and resulted in both a lower price and a smaller size for a given set of capabilities.

Technological advances have continued to occur rapidly in the computer industry. Of particular interest are developments that have led to the intertwining of computers and communication networks. Telephone switchboards use computers to allocate calls to telephone lines. Computers use telecommunication services to transmit data. By the 1970s the computer and telecommunication industries were technologically interrelated to such a degree that it was only a matter of time before firms would begin offering bundled services.

In light of these events, it is not surprising that AT&T sought to enter the computer industry in the late 1970s. However, the FCC was wary of allowing AT&T to offer computer products because the market was unregulated. There was the possibility of predatory pricing (though such behavior seems quite unlikely in light of the dominant position of IBM). A more serious concern was the allocation of cost to the regulated markets that belonged to the computer division. This would result in higher local and long-distance telephone service rates (more likely the former, given competition in the ITM). Another possibly significant effect from permitting AT&T to enter the computer industry freely was that they might be

inclined to deny to AT&T's competitors the access to local networks that is essential to many new computer-based services and products. It was feared that, in the highly complex world of electronic interfaces, there might be temptingly subtle ways by which one of AT&T's local phone companies could make life easier for its parent and harder for its parent's rivals.[42]

For these reasons, the FCC pursued a policy of separation. However, rather than simply prohibit AT&T from competing in the computer industry, the FCC allowed it to enter through a wholly distinct subsidiary. In its Computer II decision in 1980, the FCC imposed the following requirements on the subsidiary: (1) accounts were to be totally separate from those of the remainder of AT&T, (2) no facilities could be shared between the subsidiary and the remainder of AT&T, (3) the subsidiary could sell no telecommunication transmission services, and (4) any software that AT&T makes available to the subsidiary must be made available on the same terms to all others. Meeting these requirements, AT&T formed a subsidiary by the name of American Bell, which became AT&T Information Systems in 1984.

This case gives us an opportunity to assess the costs of separation in greater detail. If two products share capital, then this implies the existence of economies of scope. Fixed costs are lower for a firm offering both products than for two single-product firms, as some capital need not be duplicated. By preventing the sharing of facilities, the Computer II decision led to the duplication of capital. Not being able to offer a package of computer and telecommunication services made it more costly to provide certain services, as they had to be purchased separately and coordinated ex post facto. William Baumol and Robert Willig also suggested in their 1985 study that there is less of an incentive for research and development under separation. Innovations achieved by the subsidiary could not be shared with the rest of AT&T without having to offer it to others on the same terms. This would reduce the incentive to invest in R & D. Though AT&T certainly preferred being allowed to enter the computer industry through a subsidiary over a policy of allowing no entry, it did not appear to alleviate any of the associated social costs from separation.

The Future of the Telecommunications Industry: Digital Convergence

Historically, cable television, local telephone, and long-distance telephone have been distinct markets with distinct providers. The future of the industry appears to involve these distinctions melting away as we witness the convergence of communications, computers, and entertainment. The source of this convergence is technological, but the speed at which it is achieved will be heavily influenced by regulatory policy. As we write, the U.S. Congress is constructing legislation that would redesign the regulatory environment. This is arguably the central regulatory issue of the day.

Table 15.3
The Status of the Telecommunications Industry

Market	Dominant Firm	Competitors	Future or Potential Competitors
Local Telephone	Local telco (RBOCs, GTE)	CAPs (MFS Comm.) Cellular (AT&T/McCaw)	Cable TV companies (Time Warner) Telcos from other regions Long-distance cos. (MCI) PCS
Long-Distance Telephone	AT&T	MCI, Sprint LDDS Comm. Resellers	Local telcos (Ameritech)
Cable Television	Local cable co.	Satellite TV Network TV	Local telcos (Bell Atlantic)

Examples are provided in parentheses.
RBOC—Regional Bell Operating Company
CAP—Competitive Access Provider
Telco—Telephone Company
PCS—Personal Communications Services

Industry Forces

Prior to reviewing the technological and regulatory developments underlying the convergence of cable, local telephone, and long distance, let us begin by describing the current status of this process. This assessment is summarized in Table 15.3.

Entry into the Local Telephone Market

There are currently two sources of competition to local telcos. Although the local telcos have a considerable presence in cellular telephony, every cellular telephone market has at least one provider that is not a local telco, like McCaw Cellular (which is scheduled to be acquired by AT&T). In the mid 1980s, the FCC began to allow entry by what are known as Competitive Access Providers (CAPs). These companies use fiber-optic systems to provide special access and private line service (not basic local service) to communications-intensive businesses and government entities. CAPs have experienced considerable growth in recent years, but they are still very small. The largest CAP is MFS Communications, and its 1992 revenue was only $108 million. As described below, a recent FCC decision could allow considerable expansion of the services provided by CAPs. This has spurred MFS to go public with its company so as to raise over $200 million for expansion.[43]

A large number of prospective competitors are on the horizon. First, there very likely will be several more wireless communication networks in place within a year or so. The FCC is scheduled to conduct PCS auctions that may increase severalfold the number of wireless providers. Second, cable companies have expressed interest in providing local telephone service and are on the verge of beginning to do so. Cable systems already have access to more than 90 percent of U.S. homes, but the provision of telephone service would require an upgrading of their systems from coaxial cable to fiber optic. Cable industry leader TCI has already announced plans to spend $2 billion on installing a fiber optic system for 90 percent of its 9.5 million customers by 1996.[44] In Great Britain, cable companies are currently providing local telephone, and it appears that customers in Rochester, New York, will be the first within the United States to have local telephone service provided by their cable company. In May 1994 the New York Public Service Commission chose to allow Time Warner's local cable unit to offer phone service starting in 1995.[45] In exchange for entry into its market, the Rochester Telephone Corporation will get a significant loosening of regulatory restrictions. This type of trade-off may be a common occurrence if one is to avoid lobbying efforts by local telcos designed to derail any intrusion on their markets.

Long-distance companies like MCI have also developed plans to offer local telephone service. In January 1994, MCI announced its intentions to spend $2 billion on the construction of its own local exchange system in the manner of a CAP. Using Western Union's old telegraph right-of-way, its plans are to do this in twenty cities over the next few years with a long-term plan of providing local service in two hundred cities.[46]

Entry into the Intercity Telecommunications Market

Because this was reviewed in the section "Intercity Telecommunications Market," we will provide only a brief description here. There are currently four providers with a physical network: AT&T, MCI, Sprint, and LDDS; and hundreds of resellers that lease unused capacity. The most likely entrants into the ITM are the local telcos. Given that the 1982 consent decree prohibits the Regional Bell Operating Companies (RBOCs) from offering interLATA service, four of the RBOCs filed a motion in July 1994 to have the decree repealed.[47] A more aggressive stance has been taken by Ameritech, one of the RBOCs, in proposing to open its phone network to local competition in exchange for entry into long distance and video.

Entry into Cable Television

For 99 percent of cable customers, cable service is provided by a company that has a local monopoly over cable service. The other 1 percent are in markets with more than one cable company. The provision of cable service by local telcos is currently in motion. In July 1994 Bell Atlantic was given approval by the FCC to offer video services in Toms River, New Jersey, that would compete with the local cable company.[48] Bell Atlantic would provide transmission, and a nonlocal cable company would provide programming.

Combinations

Coincident with this entry process has been a growing number of combinations between various firms. The apparent purpose is to have the appropriate corporate structure and talent to handle local telephone, long distance, and cable TV. In July 1993, AT&T announced its intention to acquire McCaw Cellular for $12.6 billion. This deal has received clearance from the antitrust authorities and appears very likely to be consummated. That same year, Sprint bought the ninth-largest cellular carrier, Centel, for $4.5 billion. RBOCs have been forming alliances with themselves and other cellular carriers in order to establish a bigger presence in cellular telephone markets.[49] RBOCs have also been acquiring cable companies outside of their territory. Southwestern Bell acquired Hauser Communications (which is located in the territory of Bell Atlantic) and U.S. West has a considerable stake in Time Warner. It is not clear that this form of combination will continue, however, in that Southwestern Bell has decided to sell Hauser Communications and a proposed merger between Bell Atlantic and TCI collapsed.

Technology and Regulation

Technological Developments

Fiber optics and digital electronics are the technological bases for the convergence that is taking place. Fiber optics provide tremendous capacity and reliability relative to coaxial cable and microwave relay systems. Joined with digital electronic technology, the resulting network has the ability to transmit vast amounts of data and video at high speeds. Augmenting these advances are innovations in signal compression that allow more information to be transported for a given system. There are even technologies being developed that may permit a local telco to provide video using their "antiquated" copper wire system. Finally, there are the development in cellular radio.

Regulatory Policy

The FCC has taken a procompetitive stance in handling the arrival of entrants spawned by new technology. It chose to allow CAPs to compete with local telcos and to allow competition in cellular telephone and has auctioned off spectrum to expand the number of wireless communication carriers. In 1992 it adopted rules allowing local telcos to offer "video dial tone" services for other companies that want to distribute TV programming. This means that cable companies are likely to face increasing competition. The FCC's 1992 Interconnection Decision greatly expanded the services that CAPs could provide by allowing them to connect to the local telco's network (though the Court of Appeals overturned this decision in 1994 and a further appeal is pending). FCC Chairman Reed Hundt expressed this procompetitive stance when he said, "the best way to get the maximum number of new communications services is by competition in all communications markets—voice, video, and data."[50]

There is a concern, however, that some of this entry may be profitable only because of current regulatory pricing policies. Just as we discussed the creamskimming argument with regard to MCI's entry into AT&T's more lucrative markets, local telcos have argued that the CAPs have only been serving the large business and government users, argued to be the more profitable customers. The issue is whether cross-subsidization in pricing, with prices above cost in some markets, is what is creating profitable opportunities for non-telco companies. Arguing against this position, one can point to the superior product that CAPs provide with fiber optics as opposed to the local telco's copper-wire system.

Another dimension to this issue is local access charges. Long-distance carriers are required to pay a fee for being connected to the local exchange. Although the payment of a fee is appropriate, the current level of that fee may be excessive. For MCI, local access fees consume 45 percent of revenue, and an internal study showed that MCI could cut their access costs to 20–30 percent of revenue by providing their own local fiber optic system. This would mean savings of as much as $300 million annually.[51] If access charges are too high, then companies like MCI might find it profitable to offer local service even if the natural monopoly argument for local telephone still applies. Such duplication may then be socially wasteful though privately profitable.

Policy Issues

How Far Should Entry Be Allowed to Go?

Any answer to this question implicitly defines the government's role. If one responds, "as far as it can go," then the implied government role is to stay out. Such an opinion was voiced by John Malone, chairman of cable industry leader TCI, when he proclaimed; "The government should be mainly a cheerleader."[52]

There are a number of legal obstacles to entry. The 1982 consent decree that broke up the Bell System expressly forbids RBOCs from providing interLATA service.[53] The 1984 Cable Act codified a longtime FCC rule that prevented local telcos from offering cable services in their territory. A recent Court of Appeals decision overturned the FCC's decision to allow CAPs to connect to the local telco network.

The Congress is seriously considering legislation that would open up a number of markets. The House of Representatives overwhelmingly passed a bill in 1994 that would have allowed RBOCs into interLATA markets, local telcos to offer cable service, and cable companies to offer local telephone service. A more restrictive bill was proposed in the Senate and ultimately no legislation was passed. As regards the 1982 consent decree, Judge Greene has stated his intentions to keep the restrictions on the RBOCs as long as they control access to local subscribers. The basis for the decree was that the local exchange is a bottleneck in that a caller must go through the local exchange system to complete a call. In spite of the explosive growth of cellular telephones, 98 percent of all cellular calls end up going through the local wire-based exchange. Currently, CAPs are much too small to have much of an effect on this bottleneck. It would appear that the original basis for the consent decree continues to this day though there is the hope that continued technological developments will eliminate this bottleneck.

How Far Would Entry Go?

Even if all entry restrictions are removed, will all of the companies that have expressed an interest in entering various segments of the telecommunications market actually do so? How serious are local telcos about providing cable service? It is estimated that it would cost about $1500 per subscriber to install fiber optics.[54] Will the additional service that is provided make such a large investment worthwhile? On a more promising note, Bell Atlantic is making some technological breakthroughs in signal compression that may allow the use of copper wire to transmit video. If successful, this could reduce the investment to $500 per subscriber.

Thus far there are a variety of competitors to the wire-based local telco but all are small. How big could they become if all entry restrictions were removed? How many subscribers can a radio-based system handle? Will CAPs continue to provide service only to non-residential customers and, if so, will residential customers be the only customers left with a single provider? If businesses are subsidizing residential rates and local telcos lose many of their business customers to CAPs, what will this mean in terms of residential rates? Will competition end up benefiting only some consumers at the cost of others and, if so, is deregulation politically feasible?

Summary

The moral of this chapter is that there is more to regulating a natural monopoly than simply setting price and preventing entry. The purpose of regulation is to raise social welfare relative to what it would have been in the absence of regulation. With the decision to regulate come many responsibilities, two of which we have examined in detail in this chapter. One task of a regulatory agency is to decide which markets a regulated firm can serve. When some of those markets are competitive, there may be anticompetitive effects from allowing a regulated firm to enter. On the other hand, a regulated firm might be able to provide the product or service at a lower cost than other firms because of economies of scope. A regulatory agency must consider these benefits and costs in deciding this issue.

Perhaps the most important responsibility that society subsumes when it regulates an industry is that it must know when such regulation is no longer necessary. In our technologically progressive world, there should be no presumption that an industry that is a natural monopoly today will be a natural monopoly tomorrow. Just as much as regulating a natural monopoly can be welfare-improving, regulating an industry that is no longer a natural monopoly can be welfare-reducing. Although it is ultimately the responsibility of legislators to decide when regulation is no longer appropriate, the first line of change in regulatory policy rests with the regulatory agency. It can choose to allow entry and to loosen controls on price. Ideally, the regulatory agency should be society's agent in representing our best interests with respect to the industry it regulates.

Unfortunately, there are obstacles inherent in the bureaucratic structure of a regulatory agency that can impede deregulation even when it is required. Historically, regulatory agencies appear to be resistant to major changes in the industries they control. Change requires bureaucratic resources and brings forth political risks if the change happens to result in higher prices or an unhealthy industry. Perhaps a more significant impediment is that deregulation means a curtailment of the duties of a regulatory agency and perhaps even its ultimate demise. This means reduced power, prestige, and income for the regulators. Though deregulation may be optimal from society's perspective, it may not be optimal from a regulator's perspective. Although the FCC, along with MCI, was an important force in opening the intercity telecommunications market to entry, it is also clear that the FCC delayed entry and sought to reduce the extent of entry.

There are two basic lessons to be learned from the past chapters on the regulation of natural monopoly. One lesson is that regulating an industry is a difficult task. Even in a static setting, a regulatory agency must attempt to set the socially optimal price in spite of having very imperfect information about cost and demand conditions. The problems become even more difficult when the environment changes in significant ways over time. A regulatory agency must make decisions about which markets a regulated firm should be allowed to serve and whether regulatory controls should be loosened in response to changes in cost and demand conditions. The second lesson is that although regulation has the potential to raise welfare, there are many side effects to regulation that are welfare-reducing. When considering a policy of regulation, even of a natural monopoly, one must evaluate these potential side effects. All this is not to say that regulation is a useless policy tool, but rather only to point out that we must be cautious in the use of such a blunt and powerful instrument as the economic regulation of an industry.

Questions and Problems

1. Suppose that the firm cost function is $C(Q) = 100 + 10Q + Q$. This cost function generates a U-shaped average cost curve with minimum efficient scale of 10. Determine whether this industry is a natural monopoly when the market demand function is

   a. $D(P) = 100 - 3P$

   b. $D(P) = 90 - 3P$

   c. $D(P) = 100 - 2P$

2. For the past twenty years the intercity telecommunications market has been open to entry while the FCC continues to regulate prices. Should the FCC fully deregulate this market? Should the FCC have fully deregulated it twenty years ago? What are the relevant issues in determining the appropriate regulatory policy?

3. When MCI originally entered the intercity telecommunications market, AT&T argued that MCI was creamskimming. What is creamskimming? How would one go about assessing the validity of AT&T's claim?

4. Why did the FCC allow entry into the private line service market but prevent entry into the message toll service market?

5. Is there a multiproduct natural monopoly with respect to products X and Y if the firm cost function is $C(Q_X, Q_Y) = 100 + 20Q_X + 10Q_Y - Q_X Q_Y$? Assume that $Q_X \leq 10$ and $Q_Y \leq 10$.

6. Do you think there are economies of scope between local telephone service and long-distance service? How about between local telephone service and cable television service? What difference does the existence of economies of scope make for the optimal regulatory policy?

7. Should the Regional Bell Operating Companies—which provide local telephone service—be allowed to provide long-distance service?

8. Should there be a general policy that regulated monopolies cannot provide products or services in unregulated markets? What are the benefits and costs of such a policy?

Notes

1. For a more complete analysis of cross-subsidization and some of its effects, see Gerald Faulhaber, "Cross-Subsidization: Pricing in Public Enterprise," *American Economic Review* 65 (December 1975): 966–77.

2. Optimal regulatory policy to prevent creamskimming by less efficient firms is analyzed in William Brock and David Evans, "Creamskimming," in David Evans (ed.), *Breaking Up Bell* (New York: North Holland, 1983).

3. This result is proven in William Baumol, Elizabeth Bailey, and Robert Willig, "Weak Invisible Hand Theorems on the Sustainability of Prices in a Multiproduct Monopoly," *American Economic Review* 67 (June 1977): 350–65.

4. The first study to analyze the issue of natural monopoly transformation with relation to the ITM is Leonard Waverman, "The Regulation of Intercity Telecommunications," in Almarin Phillips (ed.), *Promoting Competition in Regulated Markets* (Washington, D.C.: The Brookings Institution, 1975). The most complete study of this industry is Gerald Brock, *The Telecommunications Industry* (Cambridge, Mass.: Harvard University Press, 1981).

5. *FCC Annual Report*, June 30, 1957.

6. *Economic Report of the President*, February, 1986, Table B-26. In 1949, real per capita disposable personal income was $4,915 in 1982 dollars. By 1984, it had grown to $10,427.

7. Lester Taylor, *Telecommunications Demand: A Survey and Critique* (Cambridge, Mass.: Ballinger, 1980).

8. *FCC Annual Report*, June 30, 1956, p. 34.

9. *FCC Reports* 38 (January 22, 1965–July 9, 1965): 385–86.

10. Waverman, 1975.

11. David Evans and James Heckman, "Multiproduct Cost Function Estimates and Natural Monopoly Tests for the Bell System," in *Breaking Up Bell*.

12. M. Ishaq Nadiri and Mark Schankerman, "The Structure of Production, Technological Change, and the Rate of Growth of Total Factor Productivity in the U.S. Bell System," in Thomas Cowing and Rodney Stevenson (eds.), *Productivity Measurement in Regulated Industries* (New York: Academic Press, 1981). Also see Laurits Christensen, Diane Cummings, and Phillip Schoeh, "Econometric Estimation of Scale Economies in Telecommunications" in Leon Courville, Alain DeFontenay, and Rodney Dobell (eds.), *Economic Analysis of Telecommunications* (Amsterdam: North-Holland, 1983). For good reviews of these studies as well as studies performed on Bell Canada, see Melvin Fuss, "A Survey of Recent Results in the Analysis of Production Conditions in Tele-

communications," in Courville, DeFontenay, and Dobell, and Leonard Waver-man, "U.S. Interexchange Competition," in Robert W. Crandall and Kenneth Flamm (eds.), *Changing the Rules* (Washington, D.C.: The Brookings Institution, 1989). The studies of Bell Canada also found product-specific economies of scale, though the results were not as strong as those for AT&T.

13. As a matter of fact, in response to the SCC decision, AT&T tried to reduce cross-subsidization practices with their HiLo tariff in 1973. This tariff proposed lower rates on the high-density routes. The FCC did not approve it.

14. Richard H. K. Vietor, *Contrived Competition: Regulation and Deregulation in America* (Cambridge, Mass.: The Belknap Press of Harvard University Press, 1994).

15. Robert W. Crandall, "Halfway Home: U.S. Telecommunications (De)Regu-lation in the 1970s and 1980s," in Jack High (ed.), *Regulation: Economic Theory and Practice* (Ann Arbor: University of Michigan Press, 1991).

16. Vietor, 1994.

17. Ibid.

18. Arsen J. Darnay and Marlita A. Reddy, *Market Share Reporter—1994* (De-troit: Gale Research Inc., 1994).

19. Ibid.

20. This analysis is based upon Michael Katz and Robert Willig, "Deregulation of Long Distance Telephone Service: A Public Interest Assessment," Princeton University Discussion Paper No. 47, May 1983. Also see Roger Noll, "The Fu-ture of Telecommunications Regulation," California Institute of Technology Discussion Paper No. 432, July 1982.

21. Peter W. Huber, "Telephones, Competition, and the Candice-Coated Mo-nopoly, *Regulation*, 1993, Number 2: 34–43.

22. Peter W. Huber, Letter to the Editor, *Regulation*, 1993, Number 3: 4–6.

23. Data on net profit is from *Value Line*, July 15, 1994.

24. William E. Taylor and Lester D. Taylor, "Postdivestiture Long-Distance Competition in the United States," *American Economic Review* 83 (May 1993): 185–90.

25. Peter W. Huber, *Regulation*, 1993, Number 2.

26. Peter Pitsch, Letter to the Editor, *Regulation*, 1993, Number 3: 2–4.

27. *Advertising Age*, September 28, 1994.

28. This description is based upon Huber, *Regulation*, 1993, Number 2.

29. "Baby Bells Call Up Wireless Partners," *Advertising Age*, August 8, 1994.

30. This section is based upon Bruce C. Greenwald and William W. Sharkey, "The Economics of Deregulation of Local Exchange Telecommunications," *Journal of Regulatory Economics* 1 (1989): 319–39.

31. For estimates that put into question the subadditivity of the local telco's cost function, see Richard T. Shin and John S. Ying, "Unnatural Monopolies in Local Telephone," *RAND Journal of Economics* 23 (Summer 1992): 171–83; and John S. Ying and Richard T. Shin, "Viable Competition in Local Telephone: Superadditive Costs in the Post-divestiture Period," University of Delaware, photocopy, June 1994.

32. Ibid., p. 322.

33. Terminal equipment is that equipment used to terminate a telephone line at the final user's premises. It includes the ordinary telephone.

34. For a detailed analysis of competition in the terminal equipment market, see Gerald Brock, *The Telecommunications Industry*.

35. In the case of local telephone service (market X) and long-distance telephone service (market Y), some economists believed the optimal policy was to place both under monopoly regulation even if the ITM is no longer a natural monopoly. The reason is that Ramsey pricing requires that prices be regulated in both industries in order to maximize social welfare.

36. For more details on the cost savings from vertical integration, the reader is referred to Chapter 8.

37. For example, AT&T only provided interconnection with private line service in which one phone was connected only to just one other phone. Thus, more sophisticated private line services were not able to interconnect.

38. In Execunet II (1975), the FCC stated that AT&T did not have to interconnect with MCI's Execunet service. This decision was overturned, like Execunet I, by the U.S. Court of Appeals in 1978.

39. Much of the analysis of this section draws from William Baumol and Robert Willig, "Telephones and Computers—The Costs of Artificial Separation," *Regulation*, March/April 1985: 23–32.

40. For a discussion of the computer industry, see Gerald Brock, *The U.S. Computer Industry: A Study of Market Power* (Cambridge, Mass.: Ballinger, 1975).

41. Gerald Brock, "The Computer Industry," in Walter Adams (ed.), *The Structure of American Industry* (New York: Macmillan, 1986), p. 25.

42. Baumol and Willig, 1985, p. 25.

43. *Prospectus: MFS Communications Company, Inc.*, May 19, 1993.

44. "TCI Rushes to Install Fiber Optic Cable," *Baltimore Sun*, April 13, 1993.

45. "Battleground: Rochester," *Business Week*, May 30, 1994.

46. "MCI Is Planning Local Networks in Major Cities," *Wall Street Journal*, December 30, 1993.

47. "Four Baby Bells Begin Battle to End Consent Decree, Promising Lower Rates," *Wall Street Journal*, July 7, 1994.

48. "Bell Atlantic Becomes First Phone Firm Allowed to Compete with Cable TV," *Wall Street Journal*, July 7, 1994.

49. *Advertising Age*, August 8, 1994.

50. "Crossing Signals," *Barrons*, July 4, 1994.

51. "MCI Is Planning Local Networks in Major Cities," *Wall Street Journal*, December 30, 1993.

52. *Business Week*, January 24, 1994.

53. In fact, AT&T needed Judge Greene's approval to acquire McCaw Cellular; "AT&T Gains Waiver of 1982 Decree, Clearing Hurdle in Bid to Buy McCaw," *Wall Street Journal*, August 26, 1994.

54. Robert W. Crandall, "Relaxing the Regulatory Stranglehold on Communications," *Regulation*, Summer 1992: 26–35.

16 The Regulation of Potentially Competitive Markets: Theory and Estimation Methods

When a market is a natural monopoly, government intervention is warranted on the basis that competition may not work very well. Because a natural monopoly is characterized by declining average cost, production efficiency requires that there be a single firm producing in the industry. However, in order to achieve allocative efficiency, typically there must be several active firms competing so as to drive price down towards marginal cost.[1] Due to this tension between productive efficiency and allocative efficiency, a natural monopoly is unlikely to attain a socially desirable outcome in the absence of government intervention. While far from an ideal solution, government regulation can be a preferable alternative to that of unfettered competition.

Though natural monopoly is one of the few convincing arguments for the economic regulation of an industry, it is nevertheless true that economic history is full of episodes in which potentially competitive markets have been subject to vast forms of regulation.[2] This and the following chapters in Part 2 are concerned with analyzing the regulation of potentially competitive markets.

Our analysis will address two important issues. First, if there is no market failure, why then is there regulation? Because unregulated competition is thought to be the most effective way in which to achieve the social welfare optimum, the regulation of such markets suggests that it may be in place for private, and not social, gain. An issue with greater public policy relevance is to assess the effects of regulating potentially competitive markets. Our interest lies in understanding how and to what degree regulation impacts price, service, market structure, productivity, and other relevant economic variables. Of concern is the effect of regulation not only on static welfare but also on dynamic efficiency. While the latter is typically harder to predict and quantify, a plausible argument can be made that dynamic welfare losses from regulation greatly exceed their static counterpart.

This chapter provides an introductory theoretical analysis of the implications of price and entry/exit regulation for firm behavior and social welfare. Although this theory is relevant to most forms of economic regulation, it is of particular relevance to the regulation of the transportation industry. As an application of this theory, we analyze the regulation of the railroad, trucking, and airline industries in Chapter 17. In Chapter 18, the regulation of crude oil and natural gas is investigated. At that time, additional theoretical analysis is provided which is of particular relevance in understanding the welfare implications of energy regulation. In addition to providing an introduction into the theory of economic regulation, this chapter reviews and applies the different methods for estimating the quantitative effects of regulation.

Theory of Price and Entry/Exit Regulation

The major task before us is to understand how price regulation, along with entry/exit regulation, can directly and indirectly affect the decisions of firms and thereby influence social welfare. Because price regulation is common to most forms of economic regulation, this analysis should be applicable to most regulated industries. The particular form of price regulation which we consider is the specification of the price at which firms must sell their product or service. Modeling regulation in this manner is clearly an abstraction inasmuch as price regulation can take the form of a regulatory agency setting a maximum and/or minimum price which can be charged. Assuming that instead the agency sets a specific price considerably simplifies the analysis and is often an adequate approximation for actual regulatory practices. As is true of most regulated industries, it is assumed that firms are required to meet all demand at the prices set by the regulatory agency. When price exceeds marginal cost, it is clearly optimal for firms to do so.

Two rather general cases of price regulation will be considered. One case is when price is set above cost and entry is prohibited. The second case is when price is set below cost and exit is prohibited. In the transportation industry, the latter is characteristic of past regulatory policies with respect to railroads, whereas the former is characteristic of past regulatory policies with respect to the trucking and airline industries.

It is important to keep in mind that the objective of this section is to offer some initial insight into how price and entry/exit regulation affects firm behavior and to provide some theoretical foundation for when we investigate the regulation of the transportation industry. This section does not attempt to cover all of the effects of regulation. Price and entry/exit regulation are indeed common to most regulated industries, but each industry also has its own idiosyncratic set of rules. These rules often depend on the particular product being regulated, the history of the industry, the ideologies of the regulatory agency's commissioners and other industry-specific factors. It is important that these industry-specific rules be considered in assessing the welfare effects of regulation as they can have a significant influence on firm behavior. Although the analysis of this section will not be concerned with the effects of idiosyncratic rules of regulatory agencies, our case studies of the transportation and energy industries will be.

Direct Effects of Price and Entry/Exit Regulation: The Competitive Model

The welfare effects of regulation are derived by comparing the industry equilibrium under regulation with the equilibrium that would have occurred in an unregulated environment. Performing this task requires making conjectures as to the properties of the industry equilibrium in the absence of regulation. It is natural to suppose first that an unregulated industry would achieve a competitive equilibrium. In order to derive some clear and concise results, this is the assumption we initially make. Although this assumption may be appropriate for some markets, in others it is not. Industries in which the minimum efficient size of a firm is not small relative to market demand may entail an equilibrium market structure of only a few firms. In that situation, a competitive equilibrium is unlikely to be achieved unless there is intense pressure from potential entrants. Recognizing that the competitive solution is not always a good approximation for the equilibrium of an industry, we consider the effects of price regulation in an imperfectly competitive model in a later section.

First-Best Effects

In determining the welfare effects of regulation, the first point to note is that a competitive equilibrium achieves a social welfare optimum. Thus, if price regulation causes price to deviate from marginal cost in an economy that is currently at a competitive equilibrium, then regulation must result in a suboptimal allocation of resources. If price is set in excess of marginal cost, then there is too little of the regulated product produced and consumed. If instead price is set artificially low, then either too much of the product is consumed (if firms are required to meet demand) or too little is consumed and shortages prevail (if firms are left unregulated in their supply decisions). Generally, the farther is price set from the competitive level, the greater is the welfare loss to society.

To consider the effects of entry restrictions along with the regulation of price, suppose the market demand curve and the firm average cost curve are as depicted in Figure 16.1. The competitive equilibrium price, denoted P^*, is where price equals minimum average cost. According to Figure 16.1, the competitive equilibrium entails twenty firms, each producing at minimum efficient scale of $\hat{q}$. Recall from Chapter 6 that minimum efficient scale is the smallest output for a firm such that average cost is minimized. Social welfare is maximized at the competitive equilibrium because price equals marginal cost (so that allocative efficiency is achieved) and the total cost of producing $Q^*(= 20\hat{q})$ is minimized because the efficient market structure is in place (so productive efficiency is achieved).

Now put in place regulation that specifies that firms must set a price of $\overline{P}$, which exceeds P^*. The reduction in consumer surplus from the rise in price is measured by trapezoid $\overline{P}abP^*$. Of course, part of this loss in

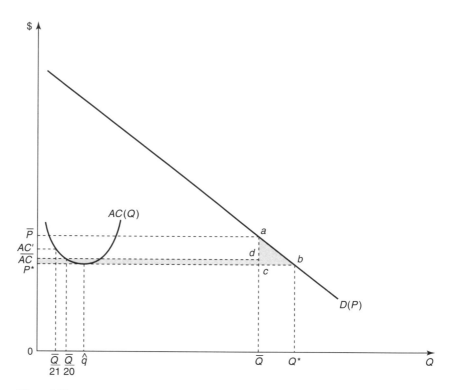

Figure 16.1
The Effects of Price and Entry Regulation: The Competitive Model

consumer surplus is transferred to firms in the form of additional profits. Suppose the regulatory agency prohibits any entry into the industry. In that case, each of the twenty firms will produce $\overline{Q}/20$, so that average cost is $\overline{AC}$, and firm profits will equal $(\overline{P} - AC)(\overline{Q}/20)$; that is, rectangle $\overline{P}ad\overline{AC}$. Substracting total industry profits from the loss in consumer surplus, the welfare loss from regulation is then the shaded area in Figure 16.1.

There are two distinct sources of welfare loss. First, there is the reduction in welfare resulting from the reduction of output from Q^* to $\overline{Q}$. This loss is measured by triangle abc. The second source of welfare loss is due to the inefficient market structure maintained under regulation. Each firm is producing at $\overline{Q}/20$. Because this falls below minimum efficient scale, each firm's average cost is higher under regulation. The rectangle $\overline{AC}dcP^*$ measures the value of additional resources used to produce $\overline{Q}$ relative to the preregulation equilibrium.

It is interesting to note that given price regulation, the imposition of entry regulation raises social welfare. Because the regulated price $\overline{P}$ exceeds average cost, there is an incentive for firms to enter the industry. For example, suppose one firm entered. The new equilibrium would still have a price of $\overline{P}$, as that is mandated by the regulatory agency, but each firm would now be producing slightly less; specifically, the amount $\overline{Q}/21$. Because profits for the new firm equal $(\overline{P} - AC')(\overline{Q}/21)$, which are positive, entry would occur. However, note that firm average cost has increased from $\overline{AC}$ to AC' in response to entry. Thus, the total cost of providing industry supply of $\overline{Q}$ has been increased by the amount $(AC' - \overline{AC})\overline{Q}$. To avoid this additional welfare loss, it is best that the regulatory agency prohibit entry *given* it is regulating price. Actually, it may even be best for the regulatory agency to go a step further and actually reduce the number of firms in order to achieve a more efficient market structure. Decreasing the number of firms from twenty to nineteen raises firm output from $\overline{Q}/20$ to $\overline{Q}/19$. If $\overline{Q}/19$ is still less than minimum efficient scale, then firm average cost is lower at a firm output rate of $\overline{Q}/19$ than at an output rate of $\overline{Q}/20$. In that case, the total cost of supplying $\overline{Q}$ is reduced by eliminating one of the firms. Of course, these conclusions concerning the optimality of restricting entry are conditional on price regulation already being in place. Regulation of entry may raise welfare given price regulation, but it is clear that price and entry regulation together reduce welfare.

Second-Best Effects

If all markets in an economy are at a competitive equilibrium, then the regulation of one market, so that price deviates from the competitive equilibrium price, must reduce social welfare. Now suppose the economy is not initially at a competitive equilibrium because of some preexisting distortion like imperfect competition or regulation or taxes. If a further distortion is imposed through regulation, does social welfare decline? The theorem of second best says, "not necessarily."[3] If there already exist distortions in the economy such that price is not equal to marginal cost in some markets, further distortions could either increase or decrease social welfare. This issue is of particular relevance for the case of economic regulation in the United States as one historical pattern that has emerged is for one product to be regulated and then for regulation to be extended to cover substitutes for that product. The theorem of second best tells us that the spread of regulation need not be welfare-reducing.

To see this point, let us examine the case of two products. In the market for product A, there are two types of suppliers. Type 1 firms specialize in product A and are able to produce it at a constant marginal cost, c_1. Type 2 firms concentrate on supplying a similar product, good B, to a

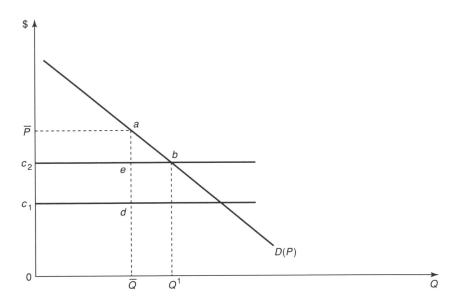

Figure 16.2
Second-Best Effects of Price Regulation on Productive Efficiency

different market but can also supply product A though at a higher unit
cost, c_2, than a type 1 firm's cost. Figure 16.2 depicts the marginal cost
curves for the two different types of firms and the market demand curve
for good A. In the absence of regulation, a competitive equilibrium is
achieved in which only type 1 firms supply product 1 and do so a price
of c_1. Suppose the initial situation is that type 1 firms are required by
government to set a price no lower than $\overline{P}$, where $\overline{P}$ exceeds not just the
unit cost of type 1 firms but also that of type 2 firms. In that case, the
equilibrium has (unregulated) type 2 firms supplying Q^1 units of product
A at a price of c_2.

Now suppose that further regulation is imposed in that *all* firms supplying product A are required to set price no lower than $\overline{P}$. Furthermore, assume consumers slightly prefer the product provided by
type 1 firms so that if both type 1 and type 2 firms sell at the same price,
all demand will go to type 1 firms. Under this assumption, the equilibrium under the new regulatory regime has all firms pricing at $\overline{P}$ but
only type 1 firms supplying the market. What is the welfare effect of expanding regulation? First, price goes up from c_2 to $\overline{P}$, which reduces
consumers surplus by $\overline{P}abc_2$. Second, more efficient firms are producing
so that industry profits rise by $\overline{P}adc_1$. If rectangle c_2edc_1 exceeds triangle
abe, then the expansion of regulation has actually raised social welfare.
The reason for this is that the initial regulatory regime had less efficient

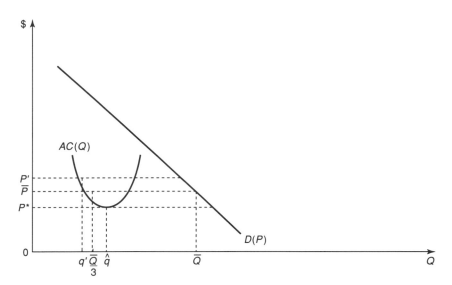

Figure 16.3
The Effects of Price and Entry Regulation: The Imperfectly Competitive Model

firms producing because price regulation discriminated against more efficient firms. By bringing all firms under price regulation, the more efficient firms ended up being the ones that supplied the market. These cost savings could be sufficiently large so as to compensate consumers for the rise in price from expanded regulation. This line of reasoning will be relevant when we examine the effects of simultaneous price regulation in the railroad and trucking industries.

Direct Effects of Price and Entry/Exit Regulation: The Imperfectly Competitive Model

Let us now consider a market in which minimum efficient scale is not small relative to market demand so that there are only a few active firms in the industry. In this situation, each firm supplies a significant share of the market and presumably recognizes that their output decisions have a noticeable impact on the market price. Firms are then expected to act competitively in the sense of being price-takers. Our objective is to assess the effects of price regulation in such a market.

To perform this analysis, we will use the Cournot model of oligopoly (which was presented in Chapter 5). In this model, each firm chooses its quantity so as to maximize its profit given the quantity decisions of the other firms in the industry. Of importance is that a firm takes into account how its quantity choice affects the market price. In Figure 16.3, we have supposed that the Cournot equilibrium involves three firms with each producing q', so that the resulting market price is P'. By the analysis in Chapter 5, we know that firms typically earn positive profits at a Cournot equilibrium because firms restrict supply in order to keep price above cost.

Let us consider the welfare effects of price regulation in this setting. Since price is already too high, as P' exceeds the competitive equilibrium price P^*, it follows that if regulation causes price to be raised above the Cournot equilibrium price, welfare will fall. On the other hand, if price is reduced, welfare will rise as price is pushed closer to the competitive level. As long as the reduction in price is not too great, regulation that reduces price below the equilibrium level may actually raise welfare when the industry is characterized by imperfect competition.

In evaluating the effects of entry regulation on social welfare, the most important point to realize is that free entry does not necessarily result in an efficient market structure when the market is imperfectly competitive. Recall that for a competitive market, firms are small so that their output decisions do not affect price. Thus, entry by a single firm does not affect existing firms' profits nor does it affect consumer surplus (because it does not affect the market price). The change in welfare from entry is then measured by the profits of the new firm. In a competitive industry, entry is profitable (and thereby occurs) if and only if it raises social welfare. The interests of society and the interests of individual firms perfectly coincide. Entry then occurs until the point at which social welfare is maximized.

This harmony of interests breaks down when there is imperfect competition. In that situation firms are not small, so that entry and the ensuing change in industry output do affect the market price. The change in welfare from entry is measured by the change in consumer surplus plus the change in industry profits, which comprises the new firm's profits and the change in existing firms' profits. The key point is that entry occurs if and only if a new firm's profits are positive, but entry is welfare-improving if and only if a new firm's profits plus the change in consumer surplus plus the change in existing firms' profits are positive. Clearly, the criterion for the private optimality of entry (that is, for entry to be profitable) differs from the criterion for the social optimality of entry. Just because the profits for a new firm are positive, so that it enters, it need not be true that entry is welfare-improving. Although consumer surplus is generally higher with entry, as price typically declines, industry profits are generally lower due to the fall in price. If the latter exceeds the former then entry can be welfare-reducing even though it is profitable. Similarly, entry could be welfare-increasing but unprofitable. For example, if a new firm expects to greatly intensify

Table 16.1
Profits and Social Welfare for the Cournot Solution

Number of Firms	Price	Firm Profits	Consumer Surplus	Social Welfare
1	55	1875	1013	2888
2	40	750	1800	3300
3	33	356	2278	3347
4	28	174	2592	3288
5	25	75	2813	3188
6	23	15	2976	3067
7	21	−23	3101	2937

competition so that its entry drastically reduces price, entry will probably be unprofitable. At the same time, it would have probably increased welfare because of the rise in consumer surplus emanating from the sharp fall in price. In this case, there would be too few firms in the industry at the free-entry equilibrium.

To be more concrete, consider the Cournot model with firms offering homogeneous products. Assume the market demand function is $D(P) = 100 - P$, the firm cost function is $C(q) = 10q$, and the cost of entry is 150. The entry cost might come from the construction of a production facility or advertising to introduce one's product. Given a fixed number of active firms, one can calculate the Cournot equilibrium. This is done when the number of firms lies between 1 and 7. The resulting levels of price, firm profits, consumer surplus, and social welfare are listed in Table 16.1. First note that the free-entry equilibrium is defined by six firms producing in the industry. If a seventh entered, the new firm's profits (as well as that of every other firm) would be negative, so that entry is unprofitable. Furthermore, all six active firms are earning positive profits, so that none has an incentive to exit the industry. Thus, this is a free-entry equilibrium. Note, however, that social welfare is not maximized when there are six firms. Rather, it is maximized when there are only three firms. Although price is higher with three as opposed to six firms (so that consumer surplus is lower), there are considerable cost savings from having only three firms (specifically, entry costs of 450 are saved by having three fewer firms enter). As a result, industry profits are sufficiently higher with three firms so as to compensate for lower consumer surplus. Free entry then results in too much entry. One can show that there are always too many firms relative to the social optimum under Cournot competition with homogeneous products. If instead firms offer differentiated products and consumers sufficiently value product diversity, it has been shown that free entry can entail too few active firms.[4] The key point is that the private interests of a firm generally do not coincide with the interests of society.

Because free entry need not result in an efficient industry structure under imperfect competition, it is unclear as to whether entry/exit regulation raises or lowers social welfare. No general conclusions can be made. Each particular case must be analyzed on its own merits. As an example of such an analysis, let us consider the case depicted in Figure 16.3. In the absence of regulation, the equilibrium price is P', with each firm producing below minimum efficient scale. Thus, price is excessively high, and there are too few firms in the industry. Suppose regulation sets price below P' at $\overline{P}$ and prohibits both entry and exit. Each firm now supplies $\overline{Q}/3$ instead of q'. Because $\overline{Q}/3$ is quite close to minimum efficient scale, it appears that the industry has the optimal number of firms for supplying $\overline{Q}$. Although there were too many firms when price was P', there are now the correct number of firms when price is lowered to $\overline{P}$. In this situation, the prohibition of any entry or exit is in society's best interests given the regulation of price. As a matter of fact, regulation is clearly welfare-improving in this case.

Although regulation can be welfare-improving in an imperfectly competitive market, it is perhaps unwise to support a regulatory policy that attempts to fine tune such markets. One major obstacle to implementing such a policy is that it is often extremely difficult to determine which markets are candidates for regulation as well as at what level price should be set. This latter problem is especially troublesome when cost and demand conditions change substantially over time. That a market has only a few firms is not a sufficient condition for regulation to be welfare-improving, inasmuch as competition may nevertheless be strong due to firms being innately competitive or due to potential competition forcing them to be so. Regulation in such markets is likely to reduce welfare. A policy of trying to fine tune imperfectly competitive markets through price regulation is a perilous task that has been shown historically to be self-defeating. A general policy of relying on unfettered competition seems advisable in markets that are not natural monopolies.

Some Indirect Effects of Price and Entry Regulation

A commonly observed regulatory policy is one in which price is set above cost, which allows firms to at least initially earn above-normal profits, and new firms are prohibited from entering the industry. Entry is usually not expressly forbidden. Rather, the regulatory agency says that a firm may apply to enter but that entry will be permitted if and only if certain (very stringent) standards are satisfied. A common procedure is for an applicant to be given a hearing at which the regulatory commissioners decide whether the standards for entry have been meant. Historically, it has been observed that this procedure can effectively be equivalent to a simple prohibition of entry. Finally, let us assume that although price and entry are regulated, product quality is subject to minimal or no regulation. For reasons described in Chapter 10, quality regulation is inherently difficult.

Excessive Nonprice Competition

By specifying the price at which firms must sell or a relatively small range within which price must be set, regulation effectively eliminates price as an instrument through which firms compete. To increase the demand for their product, one would expect firms to turn to nonprice methods. Because a firm cannot differentiate its product from other firms' products via price, it will use other means to do so. There exist many nonprice methods by which a firm can raise demand for its product. These include improving the quality of the product, changing its characteristics, providing or extending a warranty, and advertising to make the product appear more attractive.

The intensity of nonprice competition varies from industry to industry as it depends on the available technology for differentiating products as well as the degree of competition. Some products are naturally easy to differentiate, like automobiles, while others are inherently similar and thus resistant to differentiation, like natural gas. Even in the latter case, firms can compete by providing better service to go along with the product. A second factor that influences the degree of nonprice competition is the ability of firms to collude. A regulated industry is fertile ground for collusion as the same firms interact over time and without fear of entry disrupting a collusive arrangement. If firms can cooperate and prevent excessive nonprice competition (recall that regulation has taken care of the need to collude over price), firms may be able to retain above-normal profits. Otherwise, they may end up competing away above-normal profits through nonprice competition.

Let us consider the welfare effects of excessive nonprice competition. To simplify the analysis, suppose that a product can be produced at either high or low quality. All consumers prefer the high quality product (good h) to the low quality product (good l). The products are imperfect substitutes so that the demand curve of product h depends on the price of product l, P_l, as well as the price of product h, P_h. Similarly, the demand curve for product l depends on both P_l and P_h. Because product h is higher quality, consumers will purchase product l only if the price of product l is less than the price of product h and, further, more consumers will buy product l as the price of product l is lower than product h's

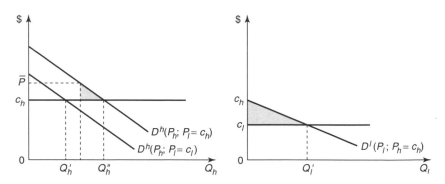

Figure 16.4
The Effects of Price Regulation on Nonprice Competition

price. It is also assumed that the unit cost of product h, denoted c_h, exceeds the unit cost of product l, denoted c_l. This seems reasonable because it says that a better product costs more to make.

Prior to regulation, it is assumed that the industry is at a competitive equilibrium. This is depicted in Figure 16.4. The competitive equilibrium has price equal to marginal cost so that $P_h = c_h$ and $P_l = c_l$. The associated quantities are Q'_h and Q'_l for products h and l, respectively. Q'_h is the demand for product h when its price is c_h and the demand curve is $D^h(P_h; P_l = c_l)$. Implicit in the demand curve for product h is that the price of the lower quality substitute is c_l. An analogous argument applies to the determination of Q'_l. Given that product h is priced at c_h, note that the demand for product l is zero when product l is also priced at c_h. This reflects the fact that if the prices are the same, then every consumer prefers the high quality product so that the demand for the low-quality product is zero.

Now consider a regulatory policy which specifies that firms must price their products at c_h regardless of quality. Nonprice competition is presumed to take the form of switching to producing the higher quality product. The demand and supply of product l is then zero. Because now, by law, product l must be priced at c_h, the demand curve for product h shifts out to $D^h(P_h; P_l = c_h)$ as the price of a substitute product has increased. The equilibrium under regulation entails Q''_h units of product h being produced and consumed while product l is no longer produced.

The welfare loss from regulation is measured by the shaded triangle under the demand curve $D^l(P_l; P_h = c_h)$ inasmuch as this is the consumer surplus foregone from no longer having the option to buy the low-quality, low-priced product. It is important to note that the increased area under the demand curve for good h, due to its shifting out to $D^h(P_h; P_l = c_h)$, does *not* represent a welfare gain. Rather, this area measures the increased willingness to pay for product h given that product l is no longer available. The increased area under the demand curve for product h tells us that there is a greater welfare loss from eliminating product h when product l is not available relative to when product l is available. A second point to make is that the increase in cost from supplying market demand, which equals $(Q_h'' c_h - Q_h' c_h - Q_l' c_l)$, is not a measure of the loss realized by consumers from regulation. It is true that consumers who previously purchased the low-quality product are now paying a higher price of c_h as opposed to c_l, but it is also true that they are receiving a higher quality product than before. Because this is certainly of value to them, it partially offsets the increase in production costs. Finally, in the event that regulation sets price above c_h, say at $\overline{P}$, the welfare loss is then the sum of the two shaded triangles. In addition to the loss from product l's being "regulated out of the market," there is the welfare loss from product h's being priced above cost.

The basic point to be made is that while regulation limits some avenues through which firms compete, it is difficult to restrict all avenues. In their efforts to maximize profits, firms will shift their activities to those avenues which are unimpeded by regulation. In the case of price regulation, firms will compete more intensively through nonprice methods like product quality and advertising. From a firm's perspective, such competition tends to reduce the above-normal profits generated by price and entry regulation. From society's perspective, such behavior is likely to result in excessive nonprice competition. Regulatory-induced nonprice competition played a central role in the airline industry.

Productive Inefficiency

If price regulation allows firms to earn above-normal profits and entry regulation prevents these profits from being competed away via the arrival of new firms, then workers, especially if they are unionized, are likely to try and extract part of the surplus. One obvious way is to demand higher wages. Although a straight transfer of rent from shareholders to workers is not necessarily welfare-reducing, higher wage rates result in the firm's substituting away from labor and toward other inputs like plant and equipment. Although the firm is still choosing the capital-labor ratio, which minimizes its cost, the ratio is not optimal from a social perspective because the cost of labor to the firm (that is, the wage rate) exceeds the opportunity cost of labor to society. Alternatively, workers may extract rent by increasing nonpecuniary benefits— for example, better working conditions. Such activities use up valuable resources and reduce productive efficiency though they are of value to workers.

A second source of productive inefficiency from price and entry regulation is the continued operation of inefficient firms that would have perished under free entry. In an unregulated environment, new firms replace those firms that are relatively inefficient. Entry regulation neutralizes the mechanism by which efficient firms are rewarded and inefficient firms perish. This analysis suggests that if a regulated industry is deregulated, one would expect entry and exit to occur simultaneously: exit taking place by the less efficient firms and entry occurring to replace those firms.

Some Indirect Effects of Price and Exit Regulation

Now consider a policy opposite to the one just considered. The regulated price is set below cost and firms are prevented from exiting the market. Given that price is below cost, there is certainly little incentive to enter the industry. Thus, if there is any need for regulation of market structure, it is through the prohibition of firms leaving the market. As before, firms are required to meet all demand at the set price, and there is minimal regulation of product quality.

Cross-Subsidization

A common regulatory policy is to set price below cost in some markets served by the regulated industry and then, in order to cover losses incurred in those markets, to set price above cost in some other markets. This policy is referred to as cross-subsidization and often takes the form of a product's being identically priced in different geographic markets even though the cost of supplying the product differs in these markets.[5]

To measure the welfare effects of a policy of cross-subsidization, consider a regulated industry that offers products 1 and 2. Assume that the demand curves for these two products are independent; that is, the price of one product does not affect the demand for the other product. For whatever reason, the regulatory agency desires to raise the supply of the high-cost product, which is presumed to be product 2. The regulated price for product 2 is set at $\overline{P}_2$ where $\overline{P}_2 < c_2$, and c_2 is the unit cost of producing good 2 (see Figure 16.5). The immediate welfare loss from such a policy is, of course, triangle abc. However, note that the industry is incurring losses equal to $(c_2 - \overline{P}_2)\overline{Q}_2$ or rectangle $c_2bc\overline{P}_2$. If the firm is to earn at least normal profits, which is necessary in order to raise new capital and avoid bankruptcy, the regulatory agency must increase the price of product 1 from the socially efficient level of c_1 to $\overline{P}_1$. Here $\overline{P}_1$ is set to allow a regulated firm to earn normal profits: $(\overline{P}_1 - c_1)\overline{Q}_1 + (\overline{P}_2 - c_2)\overline{Q}_2 = 0$. The welfare loss of a policy designed to subsidize the supply of product 2 is then the sum of triangles abc and def. In pursuing

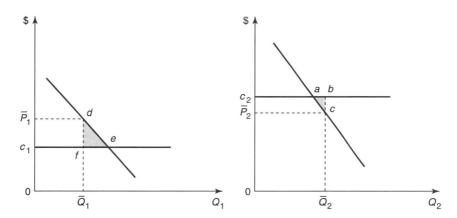

Figure 16.5
Cross-Subsidization

a policy of increasing the supply of one product, cross-subsidization is often used even though it entails the spread of deadweight welfare losses to other markets. A notable example is setting identical prices for local phone service for both urban and rural consumers even though it is more costly to provide it in the latter case. Subsidizing rural consumers was argued to be necessary to achieve universal phone service.

Reduced Capital Formation

As we just observed, if a firm is forced to serve unprofitable markets, it is likely to have a difficult time earning at least normal profits. This can result in long-run problems through its effect on investment. If some investment is financed internally, reduced profits decrease the amount of capital formation. In addition, the firm faces an increased chance of bankruptcy due to having to serve unprofitable markets. In order for investors to be willing to take the additional risk associated with a firm that has a relatively high probability of bankrupty, the firm has to offer a higher return to investors. This increases its cost of capital and therefore reduces the amount of investment. The end result is likely to be a short-run deterioration of the firm's capital stock, which reduces capacity, productivity, and product quality. Such a deterioration is likely to be myopic from society's long-run perspective. Reduced capital formation is a possible implication of price and exit regulation when it constrains a firm to serve markets at unprofitable prices.

Regulation and Innovation

Thus far we have considered the static welfare effects of price and entry/exit regulation. Another important impact of regulation is with respect to dynamic efficiency; specifically, its effect on the incentive to invest in research and development (R&D) as well as the incentive to adopt new innovations. The importance of technological innovation in the modern economy cannot be underestimated. In his famous 1957 study, Nobel laureate Robert Solow concluded that 90 percent of the doubling of per-capita nonfarm output in the United States over the period of 1909–1949 was due to technical advance.[6] Given the importance of technological innovation in the economy, it is essential to consider the ramifications of regulation on the pace of technological progress.

Before beginning our analysis, a proviso of sorts is in order. It is one thing to determine how regulation affects the incentive to invest in R&D and the rate of technological innovation but it is quite another thing to determine whether regulation results in a suboptimal rate of innovation. Dynamic efficiency does not necessarily imply that firms invest at the greatest rate possible, but rather that there is a particular rate of investment that is socially optimal. More innovation is not always better because resources must be used in order to discover and adopt innovations. Although a competitive equilibrium results in static efficiency, it is not at all clear as to whether it results in dynamic efficiency. Thus, if regulation results in less investment in R&D relative to a competitive equilibrium, it need not imply that there are dynamic welfare losses because there might be too much R&D expenditure at a competitive equilibrium.

Historically, it has been observed that new firms are an important source of innovation. For lack of a better word, new firms are thought to be vital entrepreneurs that play a crucial role in developing and adopting technological advances. Innovation provides a prospective firm with the opportunity to profitably enter an industry. Regulation that prevents entry or keeps price so low that entry is generally unprofitable closes the door to these entrepreneurs.

If regulation keeps price above cost and allows firms to earn above-normal profits, it is then possible for regulation to result in a greater rather than lower rate of innovation. Retained earnings can be an important source of funds for R&D expenditure, and so if regulation increases the level of industry profits, this could lead to more investment and more innovations. Alternatively, if price is kept below cost and firms incur losses, this should reduce the amount of investment in R&D.

A third effect of price regulation on innovation is through nonprice competition. Recall that with price set by the regulatory authorities, firms will attempt to differentiate their product in order to increase demand. Investing in R&D to achieve product innovations so as to offer a "new and improved" product can be an important avenue for nonprice competition. If this is important then regulation that keeps price excessively high may result in more product innovations taking place.

The Role of Regulatory Lags on Innovation

If a regulatory agency prevents a regulated firm from reaping the return from innovating by always making it price at average cost, then the regulated firm will have little or no incentive to innovate. In this regard, lags in the regulatory process are conducive to regulated firms' innovating. Any cost savings from adopting an innovation are retained by the firm until the regulatory agency is able to adjust price. Thus, the time between regulatory reviews allows the regulated firm to have price in excess of average (production) cost and thereby receive a return to innovating.

It has also been shown that regulatory lags not only influence whether a regulated firm adopts an innovation but also affect the speed at which adoption takes place.[7] To see why this is so, assume the regulatory agency always sets price equal to average cost and that the regulated firm's current production technology generates a constant average cost of c. As shown in Figure 16.6, the regulated price will be c. Now suppose

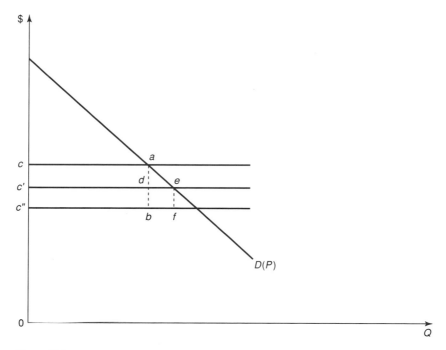

Figure 16.6
The Effects of Regulatory Lags on the Adoption of Innovations

an innovation becomes available to the regulated firm that would lower average cost to c''. The regulated firm can do one of three things. First, it can choose not to adopt the innovation. Second, it can adopt the innovation, reduce cost to c'', and receive profits measured by the rectangle $cabc''$. Of course, these above-normal profits are received only for one period, where a period is defined as the time between regulatory reviews. Once the regulatory agency meets, it will reduce price to c'' so that the regulated firm no longer earns a return from adopting the innovation. As long as the cost to adopting the innovation (for example, having to shut down production) is less than $cabc''$, the existence of a regulatory lag provides the regulated firm with the necessary incentive to adopt the innovation. However, a third alternative may be available, which is to gradually adopt the innovation over time. Suppose the regulated firm can partially adopt the innovation and reduce its cost to c'. After the next regulatory review (which will reduce price to c'), it can complete the adoption and reduce its cost to c''. From this strategy, the regulated firm earns profits of $cadc'$ in the first period and $c'efc''$ in the second period. Ignoring discounting and assuming the cost of full and gradual adoption are the same, the regulated firm earns higher profits (measured by $defb$) by gradually adopting the innovation. Thus, regulatory lag not only influences the incentives to adopt cost-savings innovations but also the speed at which adoption takes place.

Estimate of the Effect of Regulation on Productivity Growth

It is well known that the growth rate of productivity in the United States (as measured by, for example, output per person-hour) fell considerably in the 1960s and 1970s. It is also noteworthy that the extent of government intervention in the economy accelerated after the mid-1960s. It is natural to wonder to what extent the slowdown in productivity growth is due to a rise in the amount of regulation.

A recent study explored this question by estimating the determinants of labor productivity in U.S. manufacturing over 1958–1977.[8] Three different measures of aggregate regulation were used: (1) the cumulative number of major pieces of regulatory legislation in effect; (2) federal expenditures on regulatory activities; and (3) the number of full-time federal personnel engaged in regulatory activities. Depending on which measure of regulatory intensity was used, it was estimated that between 12 and 21 percent of the slowdown in the growth of labor productivity in U.S. manufacturing during 1973–1977, as compared to 1958–1965, was due to the growth in federal regulation.

Methods for Estimating the Effects of Regulation

There are two fundamental reasons for why we should be concerned with estimating the quantitative effects of regulation on price, product quality, productive efficiency, and other relevant variables. Having put forth a theory as to the effects of regulation, we now must determine its validity. Are the predictions of the theory consistent with actual regulatory experiences? For example, do we indeed find that price and entry regulation induces excessive nonprice competition? Does price and exit regulation that keeps price above cost result in reduced capital formation? A second motivation for estimating the effects of regulation is to determine, quantitatively, the welfare implications of alternative policies, in particular, of deregulation. Such estimates should be central to public-policy debates with respect to regulation. For both of these reasons, this section investigates different methods for quantitatively estimating the effects of economic regulation.[9]

Overview of Estimation Methods

The situation we are faced with is as follows. An industry is or has been subject to price and entry/exit regulation. Our objective is to estimate the impact that regulation has had on important economic variables. These variables include price, cost, product quality, product characteristics, capital investment, wages, and technological innovation. All these variables are relevant to assessing the welfare implications of regulation, as they affect allocative efficiency, productive efficiency, and dynamic efficiency.

To determine the effects of regulation, we must compare what values these variables would have taken in the absence of regulation with what values they actually did take under regulation. Because the industry is or has been regulated, in principle there is no difficulty in collecting data on these variables under regulation. Of course, in practice, some of these variables can be quite difficult to measure, for example, the quality of a product. This difficulty aside, one of the central tasks in estimating the effects of regulation is to derive a nonregulatory benchmark—that is, to determine what values these variables would have taken in the absence of regulation. There are three basic methods that have been used to estimate a nonregulatory benchmark, and we now turn to them.

Intertemporal Approach

The intertemporal (or time-series) approach compares the industry under study during years for which it was regulated with years for which it was not regulated. The nonregulatory benchmark is then the industry under study at a different time. This method requires that the sample period for which one has data includes years for which the industry was regulated and years for which it was not. We refer to this as the intertemporal approach because it compares variables across time.

In assessing the effects of regulation it can be quite misleading to compare values for the relevant economic variables in years with regulation with values for those same variables in years without deregulation. Given that many factors other than the regulatory environment change over time, the movement in economic variables may be only partly due to changes in regulation. For example, suppose one observes that profits are lower after an industry is deregulated. This could be due to regulation's having kept prices artificially high, but it could also be due to the business cycle. If the economy moved into a recession about the time of deregulation, lower profits might be due to the recession-induced shift of the market-demand curve, and not because deregulation reduced prices. Therefore, when utilizing the intertemporal approach, one must consider other relevant factors that might be changing across time. The demand curve might shift across time due to the business cycle, changes in preferences, or the degree of foreign competition. In estimating the effects of regulation on productive efficiency, one needs to control for exogenous changes across time in input prices and the production technology.

With the intertemporal approach, a valuable indicator of the effect of regulation on firm profits is the share price of a firm's common stock. Referred to as an event study, this method entails observing how a firm's share price changes in response to policy announcements concerning deregulation.[10] Because the share price is an index of the market value of the firm based on the information available to stock-market traders, a fall in it reveals that these traders expect deregulation to reduce the future stream of firm profits. This suggests that regulation was beneficial to firms, perhaps because prices were kept artifically high and entry was prohibited. On the other hand, if the share price was to rise in response to an announcement that the industry will be deregulated, then this reveals a belief among market participants that regulation depressed firm profits. This could be due to keeping price too low or stifling innovations. In using the event study approach, it is important to keep in mind that movements in a firm's share price reflect, at best, all of the information that is currently available. If an announcement of deregulation depresses the share price, it indicates that, based on current information, regulation was beneficial to firms. Because information is inherently incomplete, whether in fact regulation was beneficial is another matter.

Application: New York Stock Exchange

From its inception in 1792 until major deregulatory legislation in 1975, the New York Stock Exchange (NYSE) set minimum commission rates on transactions conducted by its members.[11] Given that its members always chose to set their rates equal to that minimum, in practice the NYSE set commission rates. The NYSE also required that commission rates be independent of the size of the order. Its members were not allowed to offer quantity discounts even though there are obvious scale economies in performing securities transactions. Finally, we should note that while the NYSE set standards for member behavior, these standards were enforced by the industry's regulatory arm: the Securities and Exchange Commission (SEC).

Regulation resulted in considerable discrepancies between commission rates and cost. In December 1968, the commission rate set by the NYSE was $.39 per share. Table 16.2 describes the relationship between the established rate and the estimated cost per share. Because of scale economies in transactions, the average cost per share was declining in the number of shares transacted. As the numbers reveal, cross-subsidization took place as consumers with relatively large orders subsidized consumers with relatively small orders.

The deregulation of rates began in the early 1970s. In 1971, the SEC ordered the NYSE to allow its members and their clients to freely negotiate commission rates on large orders, specifically, on the portion of an order in excess of $500,000. This deregulation largely applied to institu-

Table 16.2
Commission Rate, Cost, and Profit on $40 Stock by Order Size (1968)

Shares per Order	Commission[a] per Share	Estimated Cost[b] per Share	Profit per Share
100	$0.39	$0.55	$(0.16)
200	0.39	0.45	(0.06)
300	0.39	0.41	(0.02)
400	0.39	0.39	0.00
500	0.39	0.37	0.02
1,000	0.39	0.32	0.07
5,000	0.39	0.24	0.15
10,000	0.39	0.23	0.16
100,000	0.39	0.21	0.18

[a] Based on commission schedule in effect as of December 5, 1968.
[b] Cost estimate based on survey for 1969 by National Economic Research Associates.
Source: Gregg A. Jarrell, "Change at the Exchange: The Causes and Effects of Deregulation," *Journal of Law and Economics* 27 (October 1984): 273–312.

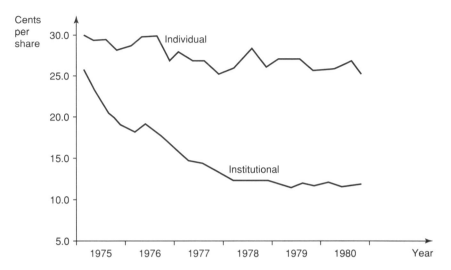

Figure 16.7
Average Commission Rates on the NYSE
Source: Data from the SEC. Figure from Gregg A. Jarrell, *Journal of Law and Economics*
27 (October 1984): 273–312. Reprinted by permission of The University of Chicago Press.

tional investors like managers of pension funds. The SEC continued to
deregulate throughout the early 1970s by reducing the minimum order
size at which negotiation was allowed. The legislative branch of the
government entered the deregulatory process by passing the Securities
Act Amendments of 1975. This legislation mandated that the SEC prohibit the NYSE from fixing commission rates.

Figure 16.7 provides a time-series of average commission rates for individual and institutional investors during the first five years of deregulation. Rates fell drastically. Almost immediately rates dropped about
25 percent in response to deregulation. Because of cross-subsidization,
deregulation resulted in commission rates rising for small orders (at
least for non-institutional transactions) and falling for large orders.
Rates fell in excess of 50 percent for orders in excess of 10,000 shares.

Intermarket Approach

If an industry is currently regulated and has been so for some time, the
intertemporal approach is not very useful. For one reason, data might
not exist that go back to the time when the industry was not regulated.
Even if data do exist, it still may not allow one to determine what the
effects of regulation would be today. If it has been a considerable length
of time since the market was unregulated, the industry is liable to have
changed so much that one could not reasonably determine what the effects of regulation are today or what would be the effect of deregulation.

The deregulation of many industries in the 1980s provided economists with the data which allowed the use of an intertemporal approach. However, before that time, when industries had been regulated for decades, economists looked to other markets for a nonregulatory benchmark. Referred to as the intermarket comparison approach (or the cross-sectional approach), it compares two markets that offer similar products and have similar demand and cost functions. However, they differ in an essential way—one market is regulated whereas the other is not. By comparing economic variables for these two markets, one can derive estimates of the effect of regulation.

Typically, the markets differ geographically in that firms provide similar products or services with similar technologies but provide this product or service in different geographic areas, for example, different states. In the case of the intertemporal approach, one has to be careful to control for changes over time in factors other than regulation if one is to isolate the effects of regulation. There is a related concern for the intermarket approach. Since one is comparing two markets at the same point in time, one does not have to be concerned with such things as the business cycle or changes in technologies. On the other hand, one is comparing two distinct markets and they are likely to differ more than just geographically. They could differ in terms of input prices like wages or the elasticity of demand. To use effectively the intermarket approach to estimate the effects of regulation, one needs to control for these differences in the two markets.

Application: Advertising of Eyeglasses

In studying regulation, one is often struck by its pervasiveness and its idiosyncrasies. It is not surprising that electric utilities and local telephone companies are regulated. But why should state regulatory agencies control the advertising of eyeglasses and eye examinations? Yet, in the 1960s, approximately three-quarters of states did just that. Some states outlawed the advertising of just price information; others prohibited the advertising of any information concerning eyeglasses and eye examinations.

A ban on advertising may either raise or lower price. By advertising, a firm may be able to differentiate its product and thereby increase the demand for its product. Generally, this would result in a higher price. Based on that effect, an advertising ban would tend to reduce price. On the other hand, advertising reduces search costs incurred by consumers, which leads to more comparison shopping and thus more intense price competition. Furthermore, when advertising takes place on price, a firm's demand curve is more elastic with respect to its own price. Given that advertising makes it less costly for consumers to learn which firm has the lowest price, a firm with a high price will experience lower demand, whereas a firm with a low price will experience higher demand compared to when advertising is prohibited. Because a firm's demand curve is more sensitive to price, a firm will tend to set a lower price in order to realize a sizable increase in its sales. The end result is more intense price competition among firms and lower prices. According to this analysis, it is unclear whether regulation that restricts advertising would raise or lower price.

To estimate the effect of advertising regulation on price, a study by Lee Benham compared the price of eyeglasses in states without regulation with that in states with regulation.[12] His data was a 1963 national survey of individuals who had purchased eyeglasses. Hence, the data set was not a time-series but rather a cross-section of individuals in different states at a particular point in time. It was found that the average price paid for eyeglasses in states without advertising restrictions was $26.34, while in states with advertising restrictions was $33.04. This evidence supports the hypothesis that advertising restrictions reduced the intensity of price competition by raising consumer search costs and thereby raised the price of eyeglasses.

In any empirical study, it is critical to play the devil's advocate by trying to think of other factors that could explain one's findings. With respect to the case at hand, could the observed price differential be due to factors other than state regulations? All eyeglasses are not the same. Suppose that consumers with higher income tend to buy higher quality eyeglasses. If states with advertising regulations also tend to have higher income (for whatever reason), it is then possible that the observed price differential is not due to advertising restrictions but rather differences in the purchased quality of eyeglasses. To attempt to control for this and other factors, Benham estimated the price paid for eyeglasses as a function of family income, sex, age, family size, and, of course, whether or not the state restricted advertising. He found that state regulations caused price to be higher by $7.48. This price differential is actually higher than the $6.40 estimated above. The evidence in this study clearly supports the hypothesis that advertising regulation raises prices.

Counterfactual Approach

If neither an intertemporal nor an intermarket approach can be used, then one can, so to speak, create a nonregulatory benchmark. This is achieved by using data for the regulated industry to simulate what the industry would look like if it had not been regulated. The counterfactual approach has been used, for example, to estimate regulatory-induced allocative inefficiencies from crude-oil price controls.

A typical application of the counterfactual approach is as follows. One first estimates the market-demand curve and the firm marginal-cost curve. The next step is to compare quantity under regulation with the quantity derived by evaluating the estimated market-demand curve at a price equal to marginal cost. If a competitive equilibrium would be achieved in the absence of regulation and the estimates of the market-demand curve and marginal cost are relatively precise, then one can derive an estimate of industry supply in an unregulated market. With regulated supply and the estimate of unregulated supply, one can then estimate the effect of regulation on consumer surplus.

The counterfactual approach is the least desirable of the three methods of estimation. One reason is that it requires making numerous assumptions about what the industry would have looked like in the absence of regulation. It is typically assumed that the cost curves would be the same with and without regulation and that a competitive equilibrium would be achieved. Because regulation often reduces productivity, assuming that cost is the same probably underestimates the benefits from deregulation. On the other hand, the postregulation market may be one of imperfect competition. Assuming a competitive equilibrium would then overestimate the gains from deregulation. A second drawback from the counterfactual approach is that it rarely can shed any light on productive inefficiences created by regulation. Who knows what innovations would have taken place in the absence of regulation? No one predicted that deregulation of the airline industry would cause the widespread adoption of the hub-and-spoke system.

When the data is available, the counterfactual approach has been used in conjunction with either the intertemporal or intermarket approach. In trying to estimate the effects of regulation, the intertemporal approach compares data in years with and without regulation. Alternatively, one might ask what the regulated years would have looked like if they had not been regulated. To address that question, one can use data from the unregulated years to estimate how exogenous variables like input prices, prices of substitutes, and the business cycle impact the industry equilibrium in terms of price, the number of firms, and other endogenous variables. With this estimated relationship, one then plugs in the values for these exogenous variables for the regulated years to come up with a simulated unregulated industry equilibrium. For the regulated years, one can then compare these simulated values with the actual observed values to derive a measure of the effects of regulation that is distinct from a pure intertemporal approach. If instead data are available for regulated and unregulated markets for only one year, one can perform an analogous experiment by using the intermarket approach in conjunction with the counterfactual approach.

Application: State Usury Laws

Aristotle considered money to be sterile, and thus the breeding of money to be unnatural. Attitudes such as this one have persisted throughout time and have periodically led to laws that either prevent interest from being paid on loans or, more generally, limit the rate of interest. Regulations which specify a maximum rate of interest that an institution can charge for lending money are known as usury laws.

Most states in the 1970s had some form of usury law. With regard to conventionally financed residential mortgages, only eight states had no usury ceiling, and fifteen states had usury ceilings of 10 percent or lower. A 10 percent usury ceiling means that a bank could not lend money at an interest rate exceeding 10 percent. Many of these laws had been in place for decades, but they had no real economic impact for much of that time because market-clearing interest rates generally fell below the legal maximum. However, the rampant inflation of the 1970s drove interest rates up so that suddenly these usury ceilings became a binding constraint faced by lending institutions.

To understand the implications of usury ceilings, one first needs to understand that borrowers and lendors care about the real rate of interest and only indirectly care about the interest rate at which they trade, which economists' refer to as the *nominal interest rate*. By subtracting the rate of inflation from the nominal interest rate, one derives the *real interest rate*. For example, if the nominal rate is 9 percent and the inflation rate is 5 percent, then the real interest rate is 4 percent. Consider someone borrowing $10,000 on January 1, 1994, under the agreement that it is to be paid back with interest on December 31, 1994. If the bank lends the money at a 5 percent (nominal) rate, then the borrower must pay back $10,500 at the end of the year. If the inflation rate was 5 percent in 1994, then the $10,500 the bank receives at the end of the year buys the same amount of goods that $10,000 purchased at the beginning of the year (as prices have risen by 5 percent). For having forgone the use of $10,000 for a year, the bank has nothing to show for it! If instead the inflation rate had been 0 percent, then that $10,500 received on December 31, 1994, means $500 more in goods that the bank could have bought at the beginning of the year. In this case the real interest rate is 5 percent, whereas in the former case it was 0 percent. What matters for lending and borrowing decisions is the real interest rate.

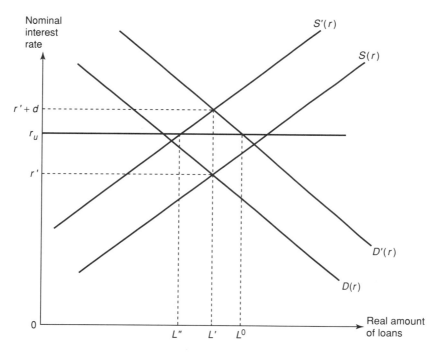

Figure 16.8
The Effects of a Usury Ceiling

To consider the effects of a usury ceiling, plotted in Figure 16.8 is the demand curve for real loans (that is, after controlling for the inflation rate), denoted $D(r)$, and the supply curve, $S(r)$, where r is the nominal interest rate (what is observed in the market). Let i denote the inflation rate associated with these demand and supply curves. In an unconstrained market, equating the supply and demand curves yields an equilibrium or market-clearing interest rate of r'. Note that the associated real interest rate is then $r' - i$. With a usury ceiling of r_u, regulation is not binding because the market-clearing rate of r' falls below r_u. Now suppose the rate of inflation jumps up to $i + d$. Holding the nominal rate fixed, the rise in inflation lowers the real interest rate. As a result, consumers demand more loans at a given nominal rate so that the market demand curve shifts out to $D'(r)$. Of course, a higher rate of inflation means that lending institutions are less willing to supply loans at a given nominal rate so that the market supply curve shifts in to $S'(r)$. In the absence of a usury ceiling, the new market-clearing rate would be $r' + d$, which is just the original nominal rate r' plus the change in the rate of inflation. Note that the real amount of loans remains at L'. As long as the nominal rate of interest can freely adjust with the rate of inflation, all that happens is that the nominal numbers change. Real economic activity remains the same. Now let us consider the implications of having a usury ceiling of r_u. When inflation rises to $i + d$, the nominal interest rate is prevented by law from fully adjusting to $r' + d$. It is only allowed to rise to r_u. Because the real interest rate has been reduced from $r' - d$ to $r_u - i - d$ (recall that the real interest rate remained the same if the nominal rate rose to $r' + d$), there is excess demand for loans. With an inflation rate of $i + d$ and a nominal interest rate of r_u, consumers demand L^o loans but only L'' are supplied. Excess demand is then $L^o - L''$.

This is the situation that arose in the market for residential loans in the mid-1970s. In those states with usury ceilings, the allowed nominal rates often fell below what was required to equate supply and demand. Because there are more loans demanded than are supplied by lending institutions, how were these scarce loans allocated among consumers? One argument is that the loans went to those consumers who were willing to accept the least attractive terms. Lending institutions have plenty of demand for loans and are thus in the position of being able to demand terms that make the loan less risky to them. In the case of residential loans, this could take the form of requiring a higher downpayment (which makes the loan less risky to lendors since the ratio of loan to property value is higher) or loans of shorter length.

The basic theoretical prediction is as follows. Let r_m^e denote the market-clearing nominal interest rate for residential mortgages. If $r_m^e > r_u$, then the usury ceiling is binding. In that case, the theory predicts that the greater is the distortion, as measured by $r_m^e - r_u$, the greater is excess demand and the more attractive are loan terms to lenders. This takes the form of a higher average ratio of loan to property value and a shorter average loan maturity. The difficulty in testing this theory is that the market-clearing rate r_m^e is not observed when the usury ceiling is binding. As is described below, some researchers solved this problem by jointly using the counterfactual and intertemporal approaches.

To estimate the effects of usury ceilings on loan terms, a study by Steven Crafton examined quarterly data during 1971–1975 for residential mortgages.[13] What is interesting about that time period is that usury ceilings were binding in some but not all quarters. The research strategy was to use data from those quarters for which the market-clearing interest rate for residential mortgages was observable (that is, the usury ceiling was not binding) to estimate the relationship between exogenous variables and that market-clearing rate. The estimated relationship was as follows:

$$r_m^e = 3.186 + .4526 r_{AAA} + 1.471 r_{adv} + .1195(r_m)_{-1}$$

where the variables on the right-hand side of the equality are the exogenous variables. r_{AAA} is the rate of AAA-rated bonds, r_{adv} is the interest rate paid by lending institutions to borrow funds from the Federal Home Loan Bank Board, and $(r_m)_{-1}$ is the mortgage rate from the previous quarter. What all this says is that when the usury ceiling is unbinding, the market-clearing rate for residential mortgages is approximately equal to 3.186 plus .4526 multiplied by the value for r_{AAA} plus 1.471 multiplied by the value for r_{adv} plus .1195 multiplied by the value for $(r_m)_{-1}$.

This relationship can be used to come up with an estimate of r_m^e when the usury ceiling was binding. For a quarter in which it was binding, one plugs in the values for r_{AAA}, r_{adv}, and $(r_m)_{-1}$ in the above equation. The resulting number is the simulated value for r_m^e, which we will denote $\hat{r}_m^e$. The estimated distortion in nominal interest rates due to the usury ceiling is then estimated to be $\hat{r}_m^e - r_u$. The final step in this approach is to determine, when the usury ceiling was binding, whether there was a relationship between the estimated distortion $\hat{r}_m^e - r_u$ and the terms of the average residential mortgage. Recall that the theory predicts that the greater is the discrepancy between the market-clearing rate and the usury ceiling, the more favorable are the terms of the loan to the lenders because of greater excess demand. Consistent with the theory, it was found that the greater was $\hat{r}_m^e - r_u$, the greater was the ratio of loan to property value (as lenders were demanding higher downpayments) and the smaller was the maturity of the loan.

Summary

This chapter had two objectives. First, we sought to provide an introductory analysis of the effects of price and entry/exit regulation on allocative and productive efficiency. We found that the static welfare effects of price regulation depend on whether entry is also regulated, on whether there exists unregulated substitutes for the regulated product, and whether the industry is imperfectly competitive. There were also some indirect effects of price and entry/exit regulation identified. Setting price above cost can result in excessive nonprice competition and productive inefficiencies while setting price below cost can spread welfare losses to other markets (through cross-subsidization) and result in reduced capital formation. Although dynamic welfare effects are more difficult to classify, we argued that they could be substantial. Price regulation reduces the incentive to innovate because it limits the returns to innovating. Fortunately, regulatory lags can offset this and thus provide greater incentive to adopt cost-saving innovations. Entry regulation cuts off a source of innovation in the form of entrepreneurs.

The second objective of this chapter was to briefly describe alternative methods for estimating the quantitative effects of regulation. We found that one can measure the impact of regulation by comparing regulated and unregulated markets at a point in time, by comparing a market before and after regulation, and by comparing a regulated market with projections of what it would look like if it was deregulated. The ensuing chapters focus on applying this theory and the methods for measuring the effects of regulation. In particular, the regulation of the transportation industry, reviewed in the following chapter, provides a most relevant application of the concepts provided in this chapter.

Questions and Problems

1. Assume the market demand function is $D(P) = 100 - P$ and the firm cost function is $C(q) = 20q$. The industry is populated by many small firms that offer identical products. In the absence of regulation, a competitive equilibrium would be achieved. However, regulation is in place and requires that a firm's price be at least as great as 30. Derive the effect of regulation on quantity, firm profits, and social welfare.

2. In following up Question 1, now suppose that a firm in the industry discovers and patents a technological innovation which reduces its unit cost to 10.

    a) Derive the welfare gain from deregulation.

    b) How does your answer to (a) change if the firm with the innovation can license other firms to use its technology?

3. For the case in Table 16.1, find the per firm subsidy or tax that results in the socially optimal number of firms.

4. Assume the market demand function is $D(P) = 1000 - 20P$, the firm cost function is $C(q) = 10q$, and there are twenty firms in the industry. Regulation requires that each firm set a price of 20. Suppose that an innovation becomes available to all firms that will reduce unit cost from 10 to 5. The cost of adopting this innovation is 50.

    a) Derive the value of this innovation under regulation.

    b) Derive the value of this innovation under deregulation.

5. Suppose the government considers regulating the price of automobiles. What difference does it make if it also regulates the quality of the automobile sold?

6. The number of seats on the New York Stock Exchange is a set number. Ownership of a seat is transferable and sold for about $850,000 in 1994. What does the market value of a seat on the NYSE measure?

7. In 1970, seats on the NYSE traded between a low price of $130,000 and a high price of $320,000. In 1974, they traded between $65,000 and $105,000.

What do you think caused this reduction in the market value of a NYSE seat? Was it deregulation or something else?

8. In 1979, New Jersey had a usury law that restricted the interest rate on conventionally financed residential mortgages to not exceed 9.5 percent. This usury ceiling was more restrictive than the one in the state of New York. Recognizing that people who work in New York City can choose to live in suburbs located either in New Jersey or New York, what effect does the more restrictive usury ceiling in New Jersey have on housing prices in the New Jersey suburbs relative to housing prices in the New York suburbs?

9. Until the 1977 Supreme Court decision *Bates v. State Bar of Arizona*, all states prohibited advertising by attorneys. That decision gave constitutional protection to an attorney's right to advertise the availability of their services and their fees to perform routine legal services. What effect do you think the 1977 decision has had on legal fees?

Notes

1. As we discussed in Chapter 13, active competition can sometimes be replaced with potential competition via franchise bidding.

2. It should be noted that there is also a role for regulation in responding to other types of market failures like externalities.

3. See Richard Lipsey and Kelvin Lancaster, "The General Theory of Second Best," *Review of Economic Studies* 24 (December 1956): 11–32.

4. See N. Gregory Mankiw and Michael D. Whinston, "Free Entry and Social Inefficiency," *Rand Journal of Economics* 17 (Spring 1986): 48–58; and Martin K. Perry, "Scale Economies, Imperfect Competition, and Public Policy," *Journal of Industrial Economics* 32 (1984): 313–33.

5. For a more detailed analysis of cross-subsidization, see the relevant section in Chapter 15.

6. Robert Solow, "Technical Change and the Aggregate Production Function," *Review of Economic Studies* 39 (August 1957): 312–20.

7. This analysis is from George Sweeney, "Adoption of Cost-Saving Innovations by a Regulated Firm," *American Economic Review* 71 (June 1981): 437–47.

8. Gregory B. Christainsen and Robert H. Haveman, "Public Regulations and the Slowdown in Productivity Growth," *American Economic Review* 71 (May 1981): 320–25.

9. Also see Paul L. Joskow and Nancy L. Rose, "The Effects of Economic Regulation," in Richard Schmalensee and Robert D. Willig (eds.), *Handbook of Industrial Organization*, Vol. 2 (Amsterdam: North-Holland, 1989); and Robert W. Hahn and John A. Hird, "The Costs and Benefits of Regulation: Review and Synthesis," *Yale Journal on Regulation* 8 (Winter 1991): 233–78.

10. See G. William Schwert, "Using Financial Data to Measure Effects of Regulation," *Journal of Law and Economics* 24 (April 1981): 121–58. The usefulness of this methodology has been put into question, however, in John J. Binder, "Measuring the Effects of Regulation with Stock Price Data," *Rand Journal of Economics* 16 (Summer 1985): 167–83.

11. This section is based upon Susan M. Phillips and J. Richard Zecher, *The SEC and the Public Interest* (Cambridge, Mass.: MIT Press, 1981); and Gregg A.

Jarrell, "Change at the Exchange: The Causes and Effects of Regulation," *Journal of Law and Economics* 27 (October 1984): 273–312.

12. Lee Benham, "The Effect of Advertising on the Price of Eyeglasses," *Journal of Law and Economics* 15 (October 1972): 337–52.

13. Steven M. Crafton, "An Empirical Test of the Effect of Usury Laws," *Journal of Law and Economics* 23 (April 1980): 135–45. See also James R. Ostas, "Effects of Usury Ceilings in the Mortgage Market," *Journal of Finance* 31 (June 1976): 821–34.

17 Economic Regulation of Transportation: Surface Freight and Airlines

From the mid-1970s to the early 1980s, the United States witnessed an unprecedented program of deregulation. Industries that had been long under government control found themselves "free at last." From the perspective of society, this period of deregulation is important because it generated considerable welfare gains. From the perspective of economic science, it is also a most significant period. Episodes of deregulation provide economists with natural experiments for testing theories concerning the effects of regulation. By investigating how prices, product quality, product variety, productive efficiency, and other important economic variables respond to deregulation, we can learn about the effects of regulatory policies. In other words, we can gain information as to what would have taken place in the absence of government regulation.

The objective of the current chapter is to put the theory of Chapter 16 into practice by exploring the impact of regulatory policies in several important markets of the U.S. transportation industry. We should note that our interest in the transportation industry is solely as a case study of the effects of economic regulation. It is not intended to be a comprehensive review of the transportation industry.[1]

Transportation Industry

Simply stated, the service provided by a transport firm is the physical movement of a good from one point in geographic space to a second point in geographic space. In attempting to define the transportation industry, it becomes immediately apparent that a wide array of markets is encompassed. Taxicabs transport travelers and small packages within metropolitan area. Airlines move travelers and small packages (as well as some larger ones) across metropolitan areas. Railroads transport large loads like boxcars of coal and grain across long distances. Although they are confined to transporting a small number of raw materials like natural gas and oil, pipelines also provide transportation services. Even intercity telecommunication companies provide transportation services of a sort in that they move information between local exchanges. All these firms provide some form of transportation service, but it should be obvious that all do not serve the same market. When it comes to the transportation of manufactured goods from the plant to the wholesaler, trucks and railroads can effectively compete though taxicabs cannot. Airlines, railroads, and buses compete to transport travelers long distance, but pipelines are hardly capable of providing such a service.[2] The transportation industry, broadly defined, comprises many varied markets.

We can define a market in the transportation industry as comprising those consumers who demand a particular type of product to be transported from one geographic location to a second geographic location and those firms that can effectively compete to provide that service. It is important to note that firms can offer services that are quite good substitutes for one another, yet use very dissimilar technologies in providing those services. In transporting travelers between geographic locations, airlines and railroads can, in some markets, be quite effective substitutes, for example, in the Washington-Philadelphia market. However, they use very different technologies. In light of this definition, a market would then be, for example, the transportation of travelers from Boston to Dallas or the transportation of steel from Pittsburgh to Chicago. How it is done is not important as long as consumers perceive firms as providing reasonable substitutes for one another's services.

For the purpose of exploring the effects of economic regulation, our interest is not so much in any particular market but rather in classes of markets. By class of markets we are referring to markets that have some essential properties in common, specifically, those properties that are essential in assessing the impact of regulation. One such property is the distance over which a good is transported. It is important to differentiate between local transportation (for example, within a metropolitan area) and long distance transportation (across metropolitan areas). A second property is the type of good being transported. At a minimum we need to differentiate between the transportation of passengers and of freight. Freight can be partitioned into bulk goods and nonbulk goods, where bulk goods include many raw materials like coal, grain, and oil, whereas nonbulk goods include many manufactured goods.

The transportation industries we will examine in this chapter include long-distance freight and long distance passenger. With regard to long-distance freight transportation, the main suppliers include railroads, trucks, water barges, pipelines, and airlines (see Table 17.1). Our concern will be with goods that are generally too large for airlines to be an effective competitor. We will also not be concerned with goods that can be moved by pipelines. As a result, the relevant competitors are railroads, trucks, and water barges. Because the impact of regulation has been most strongly felt in the railroad and trucking industries, we will concentrate on surface freight transportation and ignore water barges.

With respect to long-distance passenger travel, the most important mode of transportation is airlines. Railroads and passenger buses can be adequate substitutes in some markets, but there are many markets for which they are not effective competitors to airlines because of the distance being traveled and consumers' valuation of time. In those markets,

Table 17.1
Modal Shares of Intercity Freight Ton Miles, Selected Years, 1929–1988*

Year	Rail	Truck	Great Lakes	Rivers and Canals	Oil Pipelines	Air
1929	74.9	3.3	16.0	1.4	4.4	0.0
1939	62.4	9.7	14.0	3.7	10.2	0.0
1944	68.6	5.4	10.9	2.9	12.2	0.0
1950	56.2	16.3	10.5	4.9	12.1	0.0
1960	44.1	21.7	7.7	9.2	17.4	0.0
1970	39.8	21.3	5.9	10.5	22.3	0.2
1975	37.3	21.7	4.9	11.9	24.0	0.2
1980	37.5	22.3	3.9	12.5	23.6	0.2
1987	36.8	25.1	2.8	12.8	22.2	0.3
1988	37.0	25.2	2.8	12.7	21.9	0.3

*Includes both for-hire and private carriers

Source: Clifford Winston, Thomas M. Corsi, Curtis M. Grimm, and Carol A. Evans, *The Economic Effects of Surface Freight Deregulation* (Washington, D.C.: The Brookings Institution, 1990).

there is no adequate substitute for airline travel. Hence, it is not too severe a restriction to focus solely on airlines in the provision of long-distance passenger travel.

These two transportation subindustries—surface freight and airlines—are common in that they have a long history of economic regulation. In addition, both have been deregulated to at least some degree in recent years and, as a result, should provide informative case studies of the impact of economic regulation.

Surface Freight Transportation

In this section we will explore the regulation of the railroad and trucking industries in the United States. In assessing the effects of the regulation of surface freight transportation, it is important to consider the cross-effects between the regulation of one mode of transportation to a second mode. One would expect the regulation of rail rates to affect not only the supply and demand for rail services but also for trucking services since the two are competitors in some markets. In light of this fact, we will consider both modes simultaneously.[3]

Regulatory History

To understand the historical roots of regulation in the transportation industry, one has to start with the railroad industry in the second half of the nineteenth century. At that time railroads were the predominant form of long-distance transportation, whether passenger or freight. The most interesting feature of the railroad industry in the 1870s and 1880s was the volatile movements in rail rates, with many episodes of aggressive price wars. In response, the railroads attempted to coordinate their pricing decisions in order to stabilize prices at profitable levels. This led to the formation of the Joint Executive Committee (JEC) in 1879. As it turned out, the JEC was only mildly effective in keeping price above cost inasmuch as there were episodes of price wars in 1881, 1884, and 1885.[4]

Interstate Commerce Act of 1887

By the mid- to late 1880s the railroads came to the realization that for rates to be stabilized at profitable levels would require a more effective authority than the JEC. The JEC was replaced by the federal government with the Interstate Commerce Act of 1887. This act established the Interstate Commerce Commission (ICC) for the purpose of regulating the railroads. It was the job of the ICC to see that rail rates were "reasonable and just," that higher rates not be charged for short hauls than for long hauls, and that the railroads not discriminate among persons or shippers.

Only with additional legislation did the ICC actually acquire the requisite powers for controlling the railroad industry. The Hepburn Act of 1906 gave the ICC the power to set maximum rates, whereas the Transportation Act of 1920 allowed the ICC to set minimum rates and to control the entry and exit of firms from rail routes. The power to control the range over which firms could set rates as well as entry and exit decisions was extensively used by the ICC throughout the period of railroad regulation.

Until the 1920s the ICC had no difficulty in ensuring that the railroads earned at least a fair rate of return. However, in that decade, both trucks in the surface freight market and buses in the passenger market arose as vigorous competitors. Partly due to lobbying pressure from the railroads, the Motor Carrier Act of 1935 was passed, which brought motor carriers under ICC regulatory control. In addition, the Transportation Act of 1940 placed certain water barge transportation within the domain of the ICC. As in the case of railroads, the ICC controlled both rate-setting and entry into and exit out of markets served by regulated motor carriers and water barges.

Path to Deregulation

Rather interestingly, it was not long after this spurt of additional regulation that the railroads began lobbying for *less* ICC control, at least of railroads. When the Motor Carrier Act was passed, poor road conditions and the limited size of trucks prevented the diversion of much rail traffic. This situation changed drastically in the 1950s with the development of the interstate highway system and the presence of an unregulated trucking sector comprising owner-operators, who carried exempt commodities, and manufacturers and wholesalers providing their own freight transportation.[5] Railroads found that ICC regulations made it increasingly difficult to respond to this increased competition from alternative modes of transportation. All this led the industry to lobby for increased flexibility in setting rail rates. What ultimately came to pass was the Transportation Act of 1958. As a result of this legislation, the ICC approved some of the lower rates requested by the railroads and allowed railroads to discontinue passenger service in some markets that were considered unprofitable. However, the ICC turned down many other rate change requests, and the railroads still demanded increased rate flexibility. By the 1970s the railroads were demanding increases due to rising fuel costs as result of the oil price shocks. The bottom line is that by the mid-1970s, the railroad industry was lobbying hard for reduced regulatory control.

Spurred on by lobbying pressure from the railroads and the bankruptcy of Penn Central, the Railroad Revitalization and Regulatory Reform Act of 1976 (4R Act) was passed. The 4R Act set up a "zone of reasonableness" within which railroads could adjust rates with the exception that if railroads had "market dominance" over a certain route, the ICC could maintain its strict control. Using an encompassing definition of "market dominance," the ICC maintained considerable control over rail rates. A second important aspect of the 4R Act was to give railroads increased freedom in abandoning unprofitable routes. Although the 4R Act was the first step in deregulation, it did very little to relieve the pressures for reduced government control.

Quite in contrast to the case of railroads, the ICC took it on itself to deregulate the trucking industry. As early as 1975, the ICC made entry into trucking routes easier. Deregulation was moving at quite a strong pace by the late 1970s as the ICC had reduced restrictions over entry into routes and reduced the power of rate bureaus to establish rates, thus allowing more rate freedom for trucking firms.

Deregulation

The major pieces of legislation mandating deregulation came in 1980 with the Staggers Rail Act and the Motor Carrier Act of 1980. The Staggers Act overturned much of the Interstate Commerce Act of 1887 by giving railroads considerable freedom in setting rates, except where there is "market dominance" (which was not to be so often appealed to by the ICC), and in allowing freedom of entry and exit. The Motor Carrier Act of 1980 put into law much of the deregulation that the ICC had pursued in the late 1970s, though it did limit or rescind some ICC regulatory reforms. Nevertheless, after 1980 the surface freight transportation market was largely deregulated. Firms faced unprecedented freedom to compete and to move freely in and out of markets.

Why Was There Regulation?

It would appear that the formation of the ICC was a response to the inability of the railroad industry to maintain stable prices at profitable levels. One explanation for such price instability is that the railroads were attempting to keep rail rates artificially high so as to reap above-normal profits. If that is true, then price wars were not indicative of "destructive competition" but rather of collusive pricing, which created the incentive for a firm to undercut the agreed-on price for the purpose of raising short-run profits (though at the cost of future profits since it was likely to induce price war). Under this view, the ICC's role is as a cartel rate-setter, which is clearly not in society's best interests. On the other hand, a natural monopoly argument can be made for railroad regulation. An examination of the production technology suggests that average cost might have been declining in output. There are several components of cost that do not rise proportionately with traffic volume, including right-of-way, the cost of track, and certain equipment like locomotive power and train stations. If marginal cost lies significantly below average cost and competition leads to marginal cost pricing, then firms will earn below-normal profits when they are unable to coordinate their pricing decisions. In that case, there is an economic rationale for regulation.

Regardless of the rationale, empirical evidence reveals that financial markets expected the profitability of the railroads to improve with regulation.[6] Robin Prager examined movements in the stock prices of railroad firms in response to events surrounding the passage of the Interstate Commerce Act. Using monthly stock-price data from January 1883 to December 1887, the study revealed that the members of the Joint Executive Committee earned excess returns of 13.4 percent in the month in which the Senate passed the Cullom bill, which was the Senate's version of the Interstate Commerce Act. Non-JEC members earned even higher returns.

In contrast, there would appear to be no natural monopoly argument that one can make for the trucking industry. Economies of scale would appear to be exhausted at relatively low rates of production. The most plausible hypothesis for why trucking was regulated is that the presence of an unregulated trucking sector made it difficult for the ICC to effectively regulate the railroads. Given that the railroads and truckers compete in many markets, it would be difficult to achieve a particular outcome for the railroad industry as long as the ICC could only control what the railroad companies did.

The regulation of surface freight transportation appears to be consistent with the economic theory of regulation (see Chapter 10). The railroads formed a small and well-organized group that recognized the potential gains from price stability and how price and entry regulation would achieve that stability. Although the benefits of regulation were concentrated among a few firms, the cost of regulation was spread out across the many users of rail services. It is then not surprising that regulation should have passed that favored the railroads. It also appears that the ICC was "captured" by the railroads in that the regulation of the trucking industry was apparently a response to the competitive pressures felt by railroads. Of course, eventually all this was to change. Ultimately, regulation came to reduce the profitability of the railroad companies and increase the profitability of truckers as reflected in their respective lobbying practices.

Description of Regulatory Practices

Although regulation encompasses a wide array of restrictions, the most important restrictions are generally those placed on price and entry into and exit from markets. A reading of the relevant legislation suggests that railroads and trucking were subject to similar ICC control. In both industries, rate changes had to be requested and approved by the ICC and, in order to operate in a particular market, a certificate of convenience from the ICC was required. Exit from a market also required ICC approval. Despite the similarities in their respective pieces of legislation, in practice ICC control of price and entry and exit was quite different between railroads and trucking.

Price Regulation

In railroads, the ICC was very active in exercising its control over the setting of maximum and minimum rates. Its pricing practice was dictated by two basic principles: value-of-service pricing and equalizing discrimination. Value-of-service pricing entails charging higher rates for higher-valued commodities, regardless of whether there is a cost difference in transporting goods of different value. Because of value-of-service pricing, for many decades the railroads were forced to set higher rates for manufactured goods than for raw materials and agricultural products.

The principle of equalizing discrimination is that rates should not discriminate between shippers or between the size of the shipment, despite the fact that cost may vary across shippers (for example, some ocean ports are more costly to transport to) as well as the size of the shipment (typically, smaller shipments have a higher per-ton cost than larger shipments). The principle of equalizing discrimination meant that cost played a subordinate role in determining rail rates and typically resulted in rates for manufactured goods subsidizing rates for non-manufactured goods. This practice is referred to as cross-subsidization (see Chapter 16).

The setting of rates in the trucking industry was quite different from the practice observed in the railroad industry. To begin, the ICC allowed the trucking industry to establish rate-making bureaus that were exempt from antitrust prosecution by the Reed-Bulwinkle Act of 1948. Typically, the ICC automatically approved rate changes made by these bureaus unless they were protested by a shipper or a trucking firm. However, like the railroads, trucking rates were not allowed to be cut selectively. In particular, rates could not vary across routes of similar distances even though the density of the routes might vary and higher density results in lower unit cost, ceteris paribus. The density of the route refers to the volume of goods transported per mile. As a result, rates on high-density routes subsidized rates on low-density routes. In contrast to railroads, rates were allowed to vary across other dimensions that affect cost including the size of the shipment and the characteristics of the shipper.

The hypothesis that rail rates were set to equalize discrimination whereas truck rates were set in accordance with cartel pricing has been empirically tested. The methodology used was to determine how freight rates varied with demand elasticities and costs of service. To understand how freight rates vary with cost depending on whether rates are set to equalize discrimination or maximize industry profit, let us suppose marginal cost is related to shipment size according to the following formula: $MC = 12/(1 + S)$ where S is the shipment size. Thus, higher shipment size reduces marginal cost. For example, if the shipment size is 1 then marginal cost is 6 while if shipment size is doubled to 2 then marginal cost is reduced by a third, to 4. Equalizing discrimination would imply the same price being charged for all shipment sizes, say a per unit price of 8, so that a shipment of size S would cost $8 \cdot S$ to ship. To consider joint profit maximization, let $P^*(S)$ denote the profit-maximizing price (per unit being shipped) for a shipment of size S. Note that the total required payment for a shipment of size S is then $P^*(S) \cdot S$. Let η denote the absolute value of the elasticity of demand. Recall that demand elasticity measures how responsive demand is to a change in price. One can show that if price is set to maximize industry profit then $P^*(S)$ must equal $MC \cdot [\eta/(\eta - 1)]$. Substituting our formula for marginal cost, one derives $P^*(S) = [12/(1 + S)][\eta/(\eta - 1)]$, which implies that price is decreasing in S. Hence, if price was set so as to maximize industry profit, then the per unit price should be lower for larger shipments. Intuitively, because the profit-maximizing price must equate marginal revenue and marginal cost, if marginal cost is lower for larger shipments, then price must be set so that marginal revenue is lower, and this requires a lower price (assuming marginal revenue is declining in price). For example, if demand elasticity is constant at a value of 2, then the profit-maximizing price equals $24/(1 + S)$. In that case, if the shipment size is 1, then a profit-maximizing cartel would set a per unit price of 12, whereas if the shipment is of size 2, then a per unit price of 8 would be charged. A profit-maximizing cartel sets a lower per unit price for larger shipments, but this is not the case under equalizing discrimination, where, for our example, a per unit price of 8 is charged regardless of shipment size. Also note that industry profit maximization implies that the per unit price is higher for submarkets for which demand is less responsive to change in price (that is, demand is more inelastic, which is represented by a smaller value for η). No such relationship is observed under equalizing discrimination.

Using 1972 rail and truck rates (the rate being cents per hundredweight shipping charges), the dependence of these rates on cost and demand factors was estimated.[7] The proxy for cost of service was the size of the shipment because marginal cost is typically less the larger the shipment (as we assumed in our example). The empirical analysis revealed that rail rates were unaffected by shipment size, whereas truck rates were lower for larger shipments. It was also found that truck rates were higher the more inelastic the demand. These empirical findings are supportive of the hypothesis that rail rates were set so as to equalize discrimination whereas truck rates were set in line with maximizing industry profits. It is interesting to note that the railroad industry was in support of deregulation whereas the trucking industry was not. This would make sense if truck rates were set in a profit-maximizing manner and rail rates were not.

Entry and Exit Regulation

Although both the railroad and trucking industries required the approval of the ICC to enter and exit markets, the constraint varied between the two industries because of the rate-making practices described above. From the railroads' perspective, the effective constraint was with regards to exiting rather than entering markets. The policy of equalizing discrimination resulted in cross-subsidization, so that railroads were operating in some markets at a loss. The ICC was adamant that the railroads not abandon these markets. In contrast, the pricing policy for the trucking industry permitted considerable profits to be earned. This profit would normally be dissipated through entry (as market demand gets divided among more firms), but the ICC prevented any such entry. Specifically, a petition for entry into a particular route required the petitioner to establish that demand could not be effectively met by existing suppliers. This clearly placed the burden of proof on the firm seeking entry, and in fact most petitions for entry were turned down by the ICC. Generally, the only way to enter was to purchase the operating license of another trucking firm. Of course, this did not expand the number of competitors, but only changed the identities of the firms. It is important to note that the ICC limited entry into routes as well as into the industry so that even existing motor carriers found it difficult to enter routes that were currently being served.

Effects of Regulation

As described in Chapter 16, economic regulation can induce welfare losses through both allocative and productive inefficiencies. Allocative inefficiency is the misallocation of resources among different goods. It typically results from prices deviating from marginal cost. If the price of a good exceeds its marginal cost, we know that a suboptimal amount of that good is produced, ceteris paribus. It is also true that if two goods, say x and y, are substitutes and the price of x is above its marginal cost, it may be optimal to have the price of y above its marginal cost as well by the theory of second best. Therefore, in considering welfare losses from price regulation, one is concerned not only with the relation between rail rates and the cost of rail service but also the relation between rail rates and truck rates, inasmuch as they are substitutes in some markets. If rail rates are priced high relative to truck rates, then there is apt to be greater truck services supplied then is socially optimal. This is true even if truck rates are above cost, for the service is more efficiently supplied by railroads. Productive inefficiencies occur when inputs are not effectively used in production. Likely culprits are distorted input prices that result in a suboptimal input mix and wasted inputs due to the lack of competitive pressure. There are also dynamic sources of productive inefficiencies including the stifling of the discovery and adoption of innovations and distorted investment decisions. The ensuing analysis will consider allocative and productive inefficiencies created by regulation.

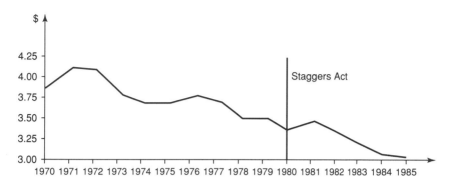

Figure 17.1
Average Real Revenue per Ton-Mile for Railroads

Source: Transportation Policy Associates, *Transportation in America*, 4th edition, March 1986, various tables. The 1985 figures are from the 1987 edition. These figures are taken from Kenneth D. Boyer, "The Costs of Price Regulation: Lessons from Railroad Deregulation, *Rand Journal of Economics* 18 (Autumn 1987): 408–16. Copyright 1987. Reprinted with permission of RAND.

Price and Quality of Service

To begin, let us assess the regulatory impact on surface freight rates. Our initial approach is to compare rates during the period of regulation with rates after deregulation. This approach is intertemporal (or time-series) in that it involves analyzing prices over time. Presented in Figure 17.1 is the time path of average real revenue per ton-mile of freight for rail services; Figure 17.2 shows the same variable for motor carrier services. (Except where noted, all dollar figures in this chapter are in 1985 dollars.) These rates are calculated by taking a weighted average of the actual rates charged. It is clear from Figure 17.1 that rail rates have declined since the Staggers Act. Real rail rates fell by over 12 percent between 1981 and 1985. Recall that the deregulation of motor carrier rates began prior to the Motor Carrier Act of 1980, as the ICC deregulated rates beginning in the late 1970s. During the period of the late 1970s, Figure 17.2 shows that motor-carrier rates did indeed decline. Interestingly, however, rates have actually risen since the Motor Carrier Act of 1980, having gone up over 5 percent between 1981 and 1985.

Prior to drawing any conclusions about the effect of regulation on rail and truck rates from Figures 17.1 and 17.2, we should carefully consider the data at hand. In using an intertemporal approach it is important to recognize that there are likely to be many important variables that can influence rates and that they may be changing over the sample period. Deregulation is not the only event that would be expected to affect average revenue per ton-mile. There are at least two other important changes over this period that would be expected to influence this variable. One

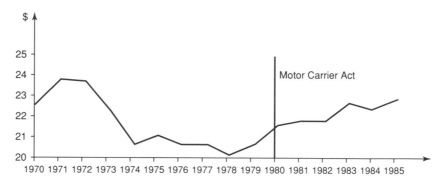

Figure 17.2
Average Real Revenue per Ton-Mile for Trucking
Source: Transportation Policy Associates, *Transportation in America*, 4th edition, March 1986, various tables. The 1985 figures are from the 1987 edition. These figures are taken from Kenneth D. Boyer, "The Costs of Price Regulation: Lessons from Railroad Deregulation," *Rand Journal of Economics* 18 (Autumn 1987): 408–16. Copyright 1987. Reprinted with permission of RAND.

is the recession that took place in 1981–1983. By shifting in the demand curve for transportation services, the recession would be expected to decrease average revenue per ton-mile in that firms would be chasing fewer consumers, which would intensify competition and lower rates. However, is the recession wholly responsible for the movement in surface freight rates? Most likely not. Observe that rail rates continued to fall through the recovery of 1984 and 1985. Trucking rates did indeed rise in 1983, but they declined in 1984, only to rise again in 1985.

A second factor confounding the effect of deregulation on surface freight rates is one that is endogenous to deregulation: the composition of traffic. Even if actual rates remained the same, average revenue per ton-mile could change if the types of commodities being transported were to change over the sample period. For example, if railroads switched to transporting more bulk goods, which have a lower rate than other goods, then average revenue would decline even if rates remained constant over time. An empirical analysis partially controlled for changes in the composition of traffic in order to assess the effect of deregulation on rail rates.[8] The proxy for the change in traffic composition used is the average weight of freight trains, as such a variable would be expected to rise if railroads transported more bulk commodities. Using the rail rates in Figure 17.1, it was found that 90 percent of the change in rates over the period 1971–1985 was due to the change in the average weight of freight trains. This suggests that deregulation is apt to have had a large impact on the mix of commodities being transported by railroads. After controlling for changes in the average weight of freight trains, it was found that rail rates were actually *higher* by 2 percent in the deregulated period 1980–1985.

It is presumed in that study that the effects of deregulation occurred immediately on enactment of the Staggers Act in 1980. Actually, deregulation was much more gradual. A study by economists at the Federal Trade Commission allowed for the gradual process of deregulation by observing the number of contracts between railroads and shippers.[9] One of the important implications of regulation was to prohibit such contracts. As deregulation progressed, an increasing number of contracts were made between railroads and shippers. This study measured the relationship between the number of rail contracts and average revenue per ton-mile, under the assumption that a greater number of rail contracts was associated with a greater degree of deregulation. The effect of changes in cost were taken account of by controlling for the percentage of rail shipments that were bulk goods, fuel prices, and average length of rail haul. Using data from 1970–1986, it was estimated that deregulation, as measured by the number of rail contracts, *reduced* rail rates by around 14 percent.

In light of the mixed empirical evidence, what is one to conclude about the effect of regulation on rail rates? Did regulation keep rates too high or too low? Examination of specific products shows that rates have gone up for some goods but gone down for other goods, perhaps explaining the mixed empirical evidence. For example, rail rates for the shipment of Kansas wheat to Gulf ports declined 34 percent between 1980 and 1985 and the average revenue per ton for farm products declined over 33 percent from $23.41 in 1980 to $15.57 in 1985.[10] On the other hand, rail rates for shipping coal rose 3 percent above the inflation rate over 1980–1984.[11]

With respect to motor carrier rates, Figure 17.2 fails to provide a clear picture of the impact of regulation. More disaggregated data show that regulation kept motor carrier rates too high. One piece of evidence dates from the mid-1950s, when the ICC exempted poultry and fruits and vegetables from the regulation of motor carrier rates. In response to this exemption, motor carrier rates fell 19 percent for fruits and vegetables and 33 percent for poultry.[12] More recent evidence comes from surveys of shippers (who are demanders of motor carrier service) taken after the Motor Carrier Act of 1980. A survey of some thirty-five shippers revealed that truckload rates fell by 25 percent from 1975 to 1982 and less-than-truckload rates fell by 11 percent over the same period. A larger survey of 2200 shippers of manufactured goods taken shortly after deregulation found that 65 percent of those polled said that truck rates were lower. In contrast, only 23 percent found rail rates to be lower.[13]

Finally, a recent study examined rates charged by sixty-one motor carriers of general freight from 1975 to 1985.[14] It found that deregulation had lowered rates by 15–20 percent by 1983 and by 25–35 percent by 1985. The growing effect of deregulation on motor carrier rates may be due to increased productivity growth. Such growth will be reviewed later.

Additional evidence comes from the state level. Around the same time as the Motor Carrier Act of 1980, a number of states also deregulated intrastate trucking. In fact, the first full deregulation in the U.S. transportation industry occurred when Florida deregulated trucking on July 1, 1980. State regulation was quite comparable to that on the federal level, both in terms of pricing and entry policy. One study examined the effect of deregulation in Florida and in Arizona, which was deregulated in July 1982.[15] Controlling for several factors that influence rates, including the commodity class, the shipment size, and the type of motor carrier, changes in motor carrier rates were examined for Arizona from January 1980 to October 1984 and for Florida from January 1979 to October 1984. It was found that deregulation caused average intrastate motor carrier rates to fall for half of the routes in Arizona and all of the routes in Florida. A second study focused upon motor-carrier rates for Florida for the more limited time period of June 1980 to September 1982.[16] It found that average rates fell by almost 15 percent.

Interpreting the evidence on the effect of regulation on surface freight rates is difficult because of there being so many different commodities and so many different routes. Nevertheless, the available evidence is supportive of the hypothesis that regulation kept rail rates too low, on average, though too high for some commodities, and kept motor carrier rates too high. To learn more about the effects of regulation, let us analyze what happened to traffic composition. The evidence here shows that the transportation of manufactured goods shifted away from railroads to trucks. In contrast, for bulk goods, in particular fruits and vegetables, railroads increased their share while trucking reduced theirs. A sample of shares of manufactured commodities in Table 17.2 reveals that deregulation reinforced the trend in which railroads were providing a smaller market share of these services. On the other hand, as shown in Table 17.3, the transportation of fruits and vegetables by railroads more than doubled from 1978 to 1982. It is also interesting to note that deregulation appears to have stopped the long-term trend whereby the percentage of freight (in ton-miles) carried by railroads has declined. In the 1920s railroads carried 75 percent of all freight (not just surface freight). By 1950 it had only 56.2 percent and by 1982 only 35.8 percent. However, this trend was reversed with deregulation and railroads had almost 37 percent of all traffic by 1985.[17]

Table 17.2
Shares of Average Commodity for Sampled Manufactured Goods

Year	Rail	For-Hire Motor Carrier	Private Motor Carrier
1963	32.8	46.6	16.5
1967	34.0	45.3	18.0
1972	30.8	45.1	20.6
1977	22.9	43.0	28.6
1983	16.0	47.4	26.0

Source: Census of Transportation, 1963–1983. Table is from Kenneth D. Boyer, "The Costs of Price Regulation: Lessons from Railroad Deregulation," *Rand Journal of Economics* 18 (Autumn 1987): 408–16. Reprinted by permission of RAND.

Table 17.3
Index of Rail Carloadings of Various Types of Traffic (1978 = 100)

Traffic	1969	1975	1978	1979	1980	1981	1982	1983
Fruit	632	274	100	104	136	196	232	260
Vegetables	538	284	100	92	140	203	232	192
Coal	116	106	100	119	129	130	127	118
Grain	96	100	100	107	117	101	94	103

Source: Freight Commodity Statistics, 1970–1982, American Railway Association. Taken from Thomas Gale Moore, "Rail and Trucking Reform," in Leonard W. Weiss and Michael W. Klass (eds.), *Regulatory Reform: What Actually Happened* (Boston: Little, Brown, 1986). Copyright © 1986 by Leonard W. Weiss and Michael W. Klass. Reprinted by permission of HarperCollins Publishers.

Associated with this switch in the commodities being carried, there has been a sharp decline in single-car shipments by railroads and a sharp increase in multicar shipments. The decline of single-car shipments may represent a transfer of the short-haul gathering function from railroads to trucking as the railroads have abandoned branch lines. Furthermore, railroads being able to set multicar rates has made them more competitive vis-à-vis trucking and perhaps has allowed them to reclaim medium-distance traffic. This movement by railroads from fewer short hauls to more medium hauls may also explain the decline in average revenue per ton-mile since the Staggers Act.[18]

Having recognized the change in traffic composition, the data in Figures 17.1 and 17.2 are now more understandable. Average rail revenue per ton-mile has declined even though some rates have actually risen because railroads have moved to transporting bulk commodities, which have lower rates. On the other hand, motor-carrier rates have fallen, in spite of average revenue per ton-mile rising over 1981–1985, because they have moved away from transporting goods with lower rates.

Table 17.4
Quality of Service after Motor Carrier Act of 1980

	Sample Size	Improved	Percentage Unchanged	Worse
Quality of trucks	71	24	68	8
Promptness of service	70	47	46	7
Availability of service	71	73	17	10
Reliability	71	37	52	11
Adjustment of claims	71	18	63	19
Need for supervision	70	14	69	17
Willingness to serve off-line points	71	34	42	24
Overall		35	51	14

Source: Thomas Gale Moore, "Rail and Trucking Deregulation," in Leonard W. Weiss and Michael W. Klass (eds.), *Regulatory Reform: What Actually Happened* (Boston: Little, Brown, 1986), p. 35. Copyright © 1986 by Leondard W. Weiss and Michael W. Klass. Reprinted by permission of HarperCollins Publishers.

Because the evidence shows that motor carrier rates were set considerably above cost, the theory of Chapter 16 suggests that one might expect excessive nonprice competition as truckers compete for economic rent. If this were so, then one would anticipate reduced service quality in response to deregulation. Rather surprisingly, the evidence shows *increased* service competition after deregulation. Table 17.4 provides the results of a survey of seventy shippers and reveals a clear rise in service quality. For motor carrier rates to be above normal and service quality not to be excessive, the trucking industry must have been quite effectively cartelized. Not only was price competition controlled but firms were also prevented from competing away above-normal profits through excessive nonprice competition. This assessment is partially confirmed, as we will observe later, by the large profits earned under regulation.

It is quite apparent that regulation distorted rail and motor carrier rates. Though calculating the amount of welfare loss from allocative inefficiency is an extremely difficult task, many economists have tackled this important problem. Although the estimates are so far-ranging as to question their usefulness, most studies from the 1980s fall in the range of $1 to $1.5 billion per year.[19] One of the most recent studies uses counterfactual analysis and estimates a much higher number.[20] Using shipper, carrier, and labor behavior during the deregulated year of 1985, it estimated what 1977 would have been like *if* the industry had been deregulated in that year. The simulated data for an "unregulated" 1977 was then compared with the actual (regulated) data for 1977. Looking at the effect on the welfare of shippers, who are the consumers of transportation services, it was estimated (in 1977 dollars) that the deregulation of motor carrier rates increased their welfare by almost $4 billion per year. Although the deregulation of rail rates was found to reduce grain rates, which raised shippers' welfare by about $280 million per year, it raised all other rates (on average) and this reduced welfare by $1.35 billion. Thus, shippers' welfare went up by $2.89 billion annually due to the change in surface freight rates from deregulation. Of course, this measure does not net out the transfer from shippers to carriers.[21]

Static Productive Inefficiency

One important source of productive inefficiency is restrictions on entry and exit. Entry restrictions prevent more efficient firms from replacing less efficient firms, whereas exit restrictions can keep firms producing in markets that are not socially efficient to serve. Let us initially consider the effect of entry and exit restrictions in the surface freight transportation industry.

As described in the description of regulatory practices, the ICC was influential in affecting the exit decisions of firms in the railroad industry. The evidence on rail rates shows that the ICC kept rates too low in some markets and, by prohibiting exit, forced railroads to serve unprofitable markets. In response to the Staggers Act giving firms the freedom to exit markets, railroads have abandoned unprofitable markets. A notable example is Conrail, which immediately abandoned 2600 route miles after the Staggers Act. While this comprised 15 percent of total track miles for Conrail, it generated only 1 percent of revenue.[22] It has been estimated that to provide rail services at 1969 levels at minimum cost would have required only 20–25 percent of existing capacity. The annual cost savings from reduced capacity was estimated to be on the order of $750 million to $1.5 billion.[23]

In contrast, the binding restriction on the motor-carrier industry was the limitation of entry. Because motor-carrier rates were above cost, and given the lack of excessive nonprice competition, trucking firms were earning above-normal profits. The prohibition on entry prevented these profits from being competed away. The response to the open door policy for prospective firms brought about by the Motor Carrier Act of 1980 was remarkable. From 1978 to 1985, the number of ICC certified motor carriers doubled from 16,874 to 33,823 and exceeded 40,000 by 1990. Nearly 17,000 companies entered between 1978 and 1985; over 6,000 failed.[24] As shown in Figure 17.3, bankruptcies rose dramatically in the early 1980s because of deregulation and the recession.

Since deregulation, new firms have entered because of the lure of above-normal profits. A continual flow of new firms forces the less effi-

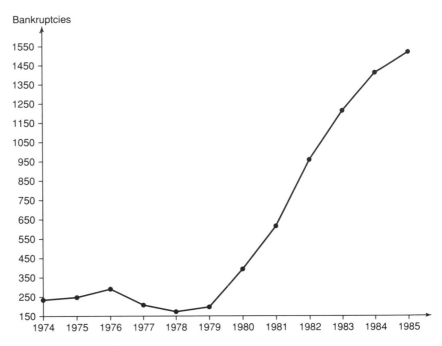

Figure 17.3
Bankruptcies among Trucking Firms
Source: Data from Dun and Bradstreet's *Business Failure Record.*

cient ones to exit; thus large entry and exit have been observed simultaneously. That firms are more efficient since deregulation is supported by
the estimated unit-cost data in Figure 17.4a and b. They show the distribution of average cost per ton-mile for "other specialized commodity"
carriers under regulation (1977) and under deregulation (1983). This
class of trucking firms typically carry just one type of good, so that we
need not worry about changes in traffic composition affecting cost estimates. As shown in Figure 17.4a, there was a wide distribution of unit
costs under regulation. Unit cost ranged from .0084 to 2.798, with an
average across firms of .3438. After deregulation, Figure 17.4b shows
that the range of unit costs was from .0032 to .6343 with an average of
only .1001. Not only is industry unit cost lower but there is a much
greater concentration of firms having the lowest unit cost. The most
plausible explanation is that deregulation resulted in the most inefficient
firms being forced out of the industry.

Besides maintaining inefficient firms, ICC regulation of the motor-
carrier industry resulted in productive inefficiency by raising wages. Because trucking firms earned above-normal profits, the Teamsters Union
was able to extract some of these rents through higher wages. Using

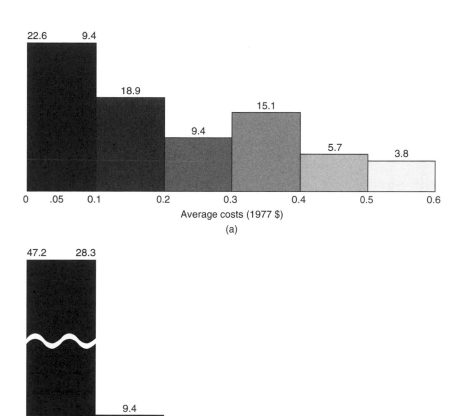

Figure 17.4
(a) Distribution of Estimated Unit Costs in 1977. (b) Distribution of Estimated Unit Costs in 1983

Source: B. Starr McMullen and Linda R. Stanley, "The Impact of Deregulation on the Production Structure of the Motor Carrier Industry," *Economic Inquiry* 26 (April 1988): 299–316. Reprinted by permission.

data from 1973–1978, it was estimated that a wage premium of 50 percent was paid to union workers in the trucking industry; that is, union workers earned a wage 50 percent higher than non-union workers performing comparable work with comparable skills. In contrast, from 1979 to 1985 (in the absence of regulation) the union premium was only 27 percent, which is very close to the national average of 28 percent.[25] By opening these markets to competition, laborers in trucking realized that they would have to settle for lower wages or watch workers being laid off as firms go bankrupt. Labor as an input was priced too high under regulation, which led to a reduced supply of transportation services and a socially inefficient input mix biased towards other inputs.

There are also many idiosyncratic sources of productive inefficiencies from the regulation of surface freight regulation. Let us briefly mention two examples. With respect to the motor-carrier industry, the ICC required truckers to charge the same rates on back hauls even though this resulted in many of them being empty. It would have been both welfare-improving and profit-improving to allow them to charge lower rates because the opportunity cost of providing the service is lower (as the trucks are traveling to their next haul anyway). It was estimated that the annual welfare loss due to empty back hauls was over $300 million.[26] Since deregulation, empty backhauls have fallen from 28 percent to 20 percent.[27]

Finally, did you know that the regulation of rail rates reduced the competitiveness of the flour market? The higher cost of transporting flour under regulation reduced the geographic size of flour markets. Because this meant that each market had fewer firms competing, railroad regulation reduced the intensity of price competition in flour markets.[28]

Dynamic Productive Inefficiency

By requiring railroads to serve unprofitable markets, regulation restricted the ability of railroads to finance investment. By the late 1970s, $15 billion of investment on track maintenance had been deferred or postponed. With deregulation and the ensuing ability to profitably adjust rates to market conditions, there was a tremendous increase in investment. During 1981–1985, $27 billion was spent on railroad structures, roadways, and maintenance of way while $30 billion was invested in rail cars, locomotives, and other equipment.[29]

A second source of dynamic inefficiency is the stifling of innovations. If regulation restricts railroads in their utilization of innovations (for example, through proper pricing), fewer innovations will be adopted. It is very difficult to directly measure how regulation affects the discovery and adoption of innovations. However, we can estimate what pro-

Table 17.5
Overall Productivity Growth for U.S. and Canadian Railroads (average annual percentages)

	1956–1963	1963–1974	1956–1974
Canada	1.7	4.0	3.3
United States	0.6	0.1	0.5
Canadian National	1.8	4.3	3.3
Canadian Pacific	1.7	3.3	2.7
Atchison, Topeka and Santa Fe	1.4	1.0	1.1
Southern Pacific	3.1	0.4	1.4

Source: Douglas W. Caves, Laurits R. Christensen, and Joseph A. Swanson, "The High Cost of Regulating U.S. Railroads," *Regulation*, January/February 1981: 41–46. Reprinted with the permission of The American Enterprise Institute for Public Policy Research, Washington, D.C.

ductivity growth would have been in the absence of regulation. Of course, this estimate will encompass all sources of reduced productivity growth, including reduced innovations and reduced investment.

For this purpose, cross-country analysis was performed that compared the growth in total productivity for U.S. railroads over 1956–1974 to the growth achieved for Canadian railroads during the same time period. Growth in total productivity of inputs is equivalent to a decline in cost per unit of output. Although both industries had access to the same innovations, the Canadian railroads were subject to much less regulation than U.S. railroads. As shown in Table 17.5, for 1956–1974 total productivity growth in the railroad industry was 3.3 percent in Canada, but only 0.5 percent in the United States. Because there is a large number of small and relatively weak railroads in the United States, the study sought to control for differences in U.S. and Canadian railroads by selecting a comparable subsample. Those chosen were Canadian National and Canadian Pacific for Canada and Atchison, Topeka and Santa Fe and Southern Pacific for the United States. At least for the period 1963–1974, this subsample supports the hypothesis that regulation reduced productivity growth. If U.S. railroads had experienced the growth in productivity that Canadian railroads had, it has been estimated that the cost of providing rail services in 1974 would have been $13.83 billion lower (in 1985 dollars). This is striking evidence of the productive inefficiencies brought about by the regulation of the railroad industry.

It was estimated that deregulation of the motor-carrier industry caused productivity to fall by .05 percent in the first year of deregulation but to grow every year thereafter (the data went up to 1984). By 1984, productivity was 16 percent higher. The initial fall is thought to be due to the adjustment that deregulation required. It is also important to note that the 16 percent rise is for those motor carriers that were still operating in 1984. Because deregulation presumably caused the least efficient firms to exit, the actual productivity gains were higher.[30]

Effect of Regulation on Profits

One of the more impressive accomplishments of deregulation is the resurrection of the profitability of the railroads. From 1980 to 1984, the average return on net depreciated investment for railroads was just over 4 percent. This is a modest return, but it is extraordinary from the perspective of the railroad industry in that it is double the return achieved over 1976–1980. As a matter of fact, when the railroads earned in excess of a 4 percent return in 1980–1981, it was the first time in over twenty-five years.[31] Where did this increased profitability come from? The most likely sources are: 1) freedom to exit unprofitable markets; 2) rate flexibility that allowed railroads to raise rates when demand is strong and reduce rates when demand is weak; 3) reduced labor costs; 4) increased investment to promote efficiency; and 5) the ability to enter into long-term contracts (something that was not allowed under regulation). Long-term contracts provide firms with a stable source of revenue, which allows them to make long-term investment.

In light of the evidence that regulation kept truck rates too high, it is not surprising that regulation benefited trucking firms. A recent study estimated the effect of ICC regulatory changes and Congressional legislation on the equity share price of thirty-two publicly traded trucking firms.[32] Nineteen separate events (an event being either a legislative or regulatory act) were identified from November 1978 to October 1981 that affected the regulatory environment. Because the share value of a firm reflects the market's beliefs on the future profit stream, by examining how the share value of trucking firms responded to these events one can measure how the stock market interpreted the effect of regulatory changes on future profitability. It was found that these regulatory reforms reduced the total value of motor carrier firms by 8–19 percent. This evidence is consistent with the hypothesis that motor-carrier rates were set in a cartel fashion. A second study performed along similar lines examined twenty-seven publicly traded trucking firms from 1974 to 1980.[33] The study also found that ICC actions had a significant negative effect on share values but that the Motor Carrier Act of 1980 had a much smaller negative effect that was not statistically different from zero. In contrast to the railroad industry, where the Staggers Act had a major effect, in the trucking industry it appears that the major effect was from the deregulatory actions of the ICC as opposed to Congressional legislation. However, one should not underestimate the long-term effects of the Motor Carrier Act of 1980, inasmuch as it put into law many of the changes made by the ICC.

Summarizing many of the studies that estimated the welfare loss from the regulation of surface freight transportation, Professors Robert D. Willig and William J. Baumol state:

> Various studies estimated, for example, that between 1950 and 1980 more than a billion dollars a year was wasted in transporting freight by truck rather than by rail. Another billion dollars a year was wasted in transporting freight on rail routes that were too long or were utilized with too little traffic density. Another $1.5 billion a year or more (in 1977 dollars) was wasted on unnecessary mileage traversed by empty cars, unnecessary demurage-time between car unloadings and loadings, and circuitous loaded routings.[34]

There are several lessons to be learned from the regulation of surface freight transportation. First, once put in motion, regulation can be imperialistic. Beginning with the railroad industry, ICC control soon spread to motor carriers and water barges. There was no economic basis for regulating truckers except that it made for more effective regulation of the railroad industry. A second lesson is the potentially large welfare losses from product substitution. Much of the allocative inefficiencies were due not so much to rail and truck rates being different from marginal cost, but rather to rail and truck rates being set nonoptimally with respect to one another. As a result, traffic for which it would have been more efficient to be carried by railroad—produce, for example—was instead carried by trucks because rail rates were set too high. Similarly, there are examples of intermodal substitution going the other way. A third lesson is that reduced price flexibility brought on by regulation can have disastrous consequences. It seriously threatened the long-term profitability of the railroad industry.

Current Status of Deregulation

In spite of the considerable welfare gains from deregulation, there has been periodic lobbying for reregulation of the railroad industry.[35] As we observed, rail rates have gone up for some commodities because regulation kept them too low. However, it has been argued that this rise is due to the market dominance of the railroads. In response to the rise in rail rates for transporting coal, utilities and coal shippers have lobbied for reregulation. The Staggers Act allowed for this in permitting the ICC to continue regulation in those markets for which the railroads have substantial market power.

In concluding, let us note that regulation of trucking remains at the state level. This is significant because two-thirds of all trucking of manufactured goods is intrastate. As of 1991, only six states had passed comprehensive legislation that deregulated intrastate trucking; another two never had regulation. Many of the regulated states have a regulatory structure comparable to that at the federal level prior to the Motor Carrier Act of 1980. Many of them have gone on to relax entry and rate regulation by way of bureaucratic initiative and limited legislation.[36]

The regulation of intrastate but not interstate rates has led to some notable distortions. For example, Cargill supplies flour to Lubbock, Texas, from its plant in Wichita, Kansas, even though it has a plant in Fort Worth, Texas, that is 162 miles closer. Because intrastate rates are regulated, supplying from the latter plant would cost about 28 percent more. Steel imported from out-of-state to Spokane through Seattle costs $14 per ton to transport it from Seattle. However, steel produced in Seattle costs 31 percent more to be transported to Spokane.[37]

Airlines

Regulation has been a feature of the airline industry from almost its inception. Then, quite suddenly, things began to change in the late 1970s. An intensive program of deregulation was begun which ultimately led to the complete absence of price and entry controls. There is perhaps no industry for which deregulation has caused such radical changes, and with these changes so much controversy. No one can deny that the airline industry has been drastically altered as a result of deregulation. The issue is what exactly has changed and has it been for the better.[38]

Regulatory History

The commercial airline industry began in the late 1920s with the hauling of mail for the U.S. Postal Service. Passenger service followed shortly thereafter in the early 1930s. Initially, the U.S. Postal Service had authority over mail rates, though this came under the realm of the Interstate Commerce Commission (ICC) with the Airmail Act of 1934. To allocate mail routes, the ICC set up a competitive bidding system whereby the airline that offered the lowest price per mile received a route franchise. In response to this system, the existing airlines pursued a strategy of submitting very low bids to assure the retention of their routes with the anticipation that they could raise rates afterwards. As it turned out, the ICC did not permit such rate increases so that many airlines found themselves on the verge of bankruptcy from having to provide mail service at a price considerably below cost. This episode is significant with regard to later airline regulation, as it was used as evidence by supporters of government regulation that an unregulated airline industry would be plagued by "destructive competition." Regulation was seen by some as a necessary condition for the airline industry to develop into a stable and healthy segment of the transportation sector of the U.S. economy.

Civil Aeronautics Act of 1938

With the Civil Aeronautics Act of 1938, the airline industry came under federal regulation. This act created the Civil Aeronautics Authority, which two years later became the Civil Aeronautics Board (CAB). The CAB was given control over the setting of maximum and minimum rates where the procedure for rate-making was taken from the Interstate Commerce Act of 1887. In addition, the number of competitors was placed under the domain of the CAB. This meant not only that entry into and exit out of the industry was subject to CAB approval but also that the CAB had the power to govern the route structures of firms. It could prevent an existing airline from entering a route or, alternatively, abandoning a route it was currently serving. In addition to control over price and market structure, the CAB was initially given responsibility for airline safety. This task was transferred to the Federal Aviation Administration (FAA) in 1958.

From its inception until the wheels of deregulation began to turn in the mid-1970s, the CAB was not shy about controlling air fares and the number of competitors. In a rather strong display of this power, the CAB implemented a route moratorium in the early 1970s. Because of excess capacity among airlines and declining industry profits, the CAB prohibited any firm from entering route markets. This kept new firms from entering the industry and existing firms from expanding the number of routes they served. The CAB feared that route expansion would intensify competition, which would negatively impact industry profit.

Path to Deregulation

By the mid-1970s pressure was building to reform airline regulation. Academics had long argued that regulation stifled competition and generated considerable welfare losses.[39] In 1975 Senate hearings held by Senator Edward Kennedy seriously explored the idea of regulatory reform. The Department of Transportation was also engaged in designing regulatory reform and even the CAB, under new chairman John Robson, strongly supported not just regulatory reform but full deregulation.

As CAB chairman, John Robson provided the initial step in deregulation by relaxing entry restrictions. He lifted the route moratorium and allowed entry into currently served markets for the first time since the 1960s. With Alfred Kahn's arrival as the new CAB chairman in June

1977, the pace of deregulation accelerated as he further reduced entry restrictions and controls over fares. Major fare-cutting followed.

Airline Deregulation Act of 1978

In response to these CAB reforms, fares were lower *and* industry profits were actually up in 1978. With such positive results from increased competition, Congress passed the Airline Deregulation Act (ADA) in 1978, which called for the phased deregulation of the airline industry. As prescribed by the ADA, the CAB's authority over routes was to terminate on December 31, 1981, its authority over fares to terminate on January 1, 1983, and, finally, its very existence to terminate on January 1, 1985. The actual pace of deregulation turned out to be considerably faster than outlined in the ADA. Within a year of its enactment, airlines were free to serve any route. By May 1980 the CAB allowed unlimited downward flexibility in fares and considerable upward flexibility. Independent pricing was being strongly encouraged by the CAB. Even prior to January 1, 1983, the date for which CAB control over entry and fares was to end, airlines were competing in an unregulated environment.

Description of Regulatory Practices

The main objectives underlying CAB policies during the regulatory period were to keep the airline industry financially sound and to promote air service. Toward this end, they extensively exercised control over price, the number of competitors, and route structures.

Price Regulation

The setting of fares by the CAB was characterized by four properties. First, fares were set with the intention of allowing airlines to earn a reasonable rate of return. Though this objective was an implicit feature of regulatory policy for a long time, it was not made explicit until 1960. In fact, before World War II air fares were typically set at the first-class rail fare, railroads being the main competitor to airlines. In 1960, the General Passenger Fare Investigation set fares so as to allow the industry to earn a rate of return of 10.5 percent while in 1970 the Domestic Passenger Fare Investigation (DPFI) was designed to generate an industry rate of return of 12 percent.

A second important feature of CAB pricing policy was that prices were generally set independent of cost. At least until 1970, the key criterion was profitability. Then the DPFI did introduce some role for cost in that it related fares to the length of the route, which is indeed related to cost of service. However, the CAB set fares above cost for routes exceeding four hundred miles and below cost for routes less than four hundred miles. This cross-subsidization from long-haul to short-haul markets was done primarily to promote air service to less dense routes.

A third property of CAB rate-setting was that fare changes were typically across-the-board rather than selective. This practice reduced fare flexibility and contributed to distortions in the fare structure. The fourth and final property was that the CAB strongly discouraged price competition. Requests for fare changes that were deemed as being a competitive response to other airlines' fares were not treated well by the CAB. Presumably, the CAB feared that fare competition would make it more difficult for the industry to maintain profitability. Related to an earlier point, fare competition might have been interpreted by the CAB as leading to destructive competition.

Entry and Exit Regulation

With the introduction of regulation in 1938, sixteen airlines, referred to as trunk carriers, were "grandfathered" and became certificated carriers. From 1938 to 1978, the CAB did not allow the entry of a single new trunk carrier. In preventing such entry, it denied seventy-nine applications during 1950–1974.[40] At the time of deregulation, only ten trunk carriers remained; six having disappeared through merger.

Whether a prospective firm wanted to enter the airline industry or an existing airline wanted to enter a currently served route, the CAB placed the burden of proof on the prospective entrant. The process by which a firm applied for entry into a route was long and expensive. Although the CAB did not allow entry that would directly compete in a major way with the trunk carriers, it did allow entry by local-service carriers. Local-service carriers did not serve major routes, though there was some still minor competition by trunk carriers. To a large extent the local-service carriers picked up short-haul business abandoned (with approval of the CAB) by the trunk carriers.

Entry into routes by existing airlines was permitted to a limited degree, though we know by the route moratorium of 1969–1974 that the CAB could prevent that as well. Only 10 percent of applications by existing airlines to enter an existing route were approved from 1965 to 1974.[41] In high-density markets, the CAB was more apt to allow entry, preferring an expansion in the number of competitors to a reduction in fares. As a general principle, the CAB chose not to have more than two or three carriers serving the same route.

Comparison to Motor-Carrier Regulation

In practice, airline regulation is quite comparable to the regulation of motor carriers. Prices were generally set to allow reasonable profits and entailed cross-subsidization from high-density to low-density markets. Similarly, entry was controlled into routes as well as into the industry. However, it is generally believed that the CAB was more lenient than the ICC in terms of allowing existing firms to enter currently served routes. Regardless of the similarities in regulatory practices, the effects of regulation differed considerably between trucking and airlines. As we will observe, this difference is largely due to technological differences in the service being provided, as well as to airlines' responding to regulation in a quite different manner from that of motor carriers.

Effects of Regulation

In comparing the effects of price and entry/exit regulation across industries, certain regularities arise. One common effect of regulation is that it reduces productivity growth. This was observed for the railroad industry, and we will find it also to be true for the airline industry. Another common effect of regulation is that the prevention of entry maintains inefficient firms in the industry. This was found to be true for the motor-carrier industry inasmuch as deregulation induced a large number of bankruptcies while simultaneously inducing considerable entry. Entry regulation will be seen to have had the same effect in the airline industry. But there are typically also effects of regulation that are unique to an industry or at least the extent to which these effects are significant is more extreme than in other industries. This is due to interindustry differences with respect to the product or service being offered and the type of production technology as well as the idiosyncratic features of any particular regulatory structure.

The regulation of the airline industry offers a case study of two classic effects of price and entry/exit regulation. First, if the government takes away price as a competitive instrument, then firms will turn to competing in other ways. In the case of airlines, firms aggressively competed through quality of service. Second, it is very difficult to predict the effects of regulation, because it is difficult to predict the new and innovative means of providing a better product at a lower cost that competition would have brought about. The development of the hub-and-spoke system since deregulation is such an innovation. The stifling of the adoption of the hub-and-spoke system was an unanticipated but yet substantial effect of regulation.

Price and Quality of Service

Our first task is to establish the effect of CAB regulation on air fares. One method for doing this is to compare air fares in regulated and unregulated markets over the same time period. In Chapter 16, this

Table 17.6
Differential between Intrastate Fares in California and Interstate Fares, 1972

	Intrastate Fare/Mile (in cents)	Interstate Fare/Mile (in cents)
Very short haul (65 miles)	16.923	23.585
Short haul (109 miles)	9.363	16.858
Short-medium haul (338–373 miles)	5.021	9.685

Source: Simat, Helliesen and Eichner, Inc., "The Intrastate Air Regulation Experience in Texas and California," in Paul W. MacAvoy and John W. Snow (eds.), *Regulation of Passenger Fares and Competition among the Airlines* (Washington, D.C.: American Enterprise Institute for Public Policy Research, 1977). Reprinted with permission of The American Enterprise Institute for Public Policy Research, Washington, D.C.

method was referred to as the intermarket approach. Although all interstate markets were subject to CAB regulation, intrastate markets were not. We can then assess the effect of regulation on air fares by comparing fares on intrastate and interstate routes that are of similar length and density. To be able to make such a comparison, one must consider intrastate routes in large states like California and Texas where routes are of sufficient length and density to allow a reasonable comparison to be made with some interstate routes.

Table 17.6 compares fares for intrastate routes in California and comparable interstate routes subject to CAB regulation. Fares in unregulated intrastate markets were considerably below fares for CAB-regulated markets. Also note that this differential was greater, the longer the length of the route. Fares for some specific routes in Texas for 1975 are provided in Table 17.7. Southwest Airlines was the primary intrastate carrier in Texas and consistently provided lower fares than were set by CAB-regulated carriers. Cross-sectional data on fares during the time of CAB regulation establishes that air fares were kept excessively high in some markets.

An alternative method for determining the effects of regulation on air fares is to observe how fares changed over time as the industry moved from a regulated to an unregulated status. Figure 17.5 shows the change in average real air fares between 1978 and 1993. Fares have fallen substantially for routes exceeding one thousand miles but have risen substantially for routes less than five hundred miles. From a different perspective, air fares between major large metropolitan areas declined by 8.7 percent for long-haul markets and by 14.5 percent for short-haul markets between 1976 and 1983, whereas fares rose on routes between small cities by 13.2 percent for short-haul markets and over 50 percent for medium-haul markets.[42] Consistent with the intermarket evidence in

Table 17.7
Comparison of Interstate and Intrastate Fare Levels in Selected Texas Markets, December 1, 1975

Fare Type	Dallas-Houston	Dallas-Harlingen	Dallas-San Antonio	Houston-Harlingen
Cab Interstate				
First Class	$48.00		$51.00	
Coach	35.00	$57.00	37.00	$42.00
Economy	32.00	51.00	33.00	38.00
Southwest Intrastate				
"Executive Class"	25.00	40.00	25.00	25.00
"Pleasure Class"	15.00	25.00	15.00	15.00

Source: Simat, Helliesen and Eichner, Inc., "The Intrastate Air Regulation Experience in Texas and California," in Paul W. MacAvoy and John W. Snow (eds.), *Regulation of Passenger Fares and Competition among the Airlines* (Washington, D.C.: American Enterprise Institute for Public Policy Research, 1977). Reprinted with the permission of The American Enterprise Institute for Public Policy Research, Washington, D.C.

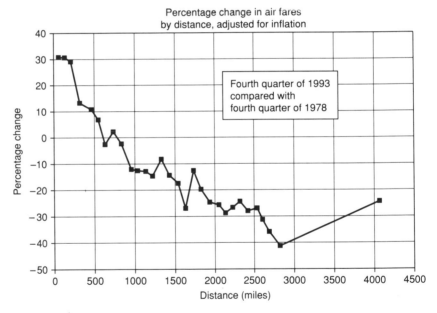

Figure 17.5
Percentage Change in Air Fares by Distance, Adjusted for Inflation

Source: Steven A. Morrison and Clifford Winston, "The Evolution of the Airline Industry," Northeastern University, manuscript, August 1994.

Tables 17.6 and 17.7, the intertemporal evidence confirms the hypothesis that CAB price regulation was characterized by cross-subsidization, with fares in high-density markets being set above cost and fares in low-density markets being set below cost. Another important change in the fare structure since deregulation is the sizable increase in discount fares and the ensuing increase in the number of passengers traveling on discount fares. In major markets only about a quarter of passengers traveled on discount fares in 1976 while almost three-quarters did so in 1983. In low-density markets, the rise in the use of discount fares was even greater.[43]

If fares were set above cost in some markets, an airline would be very interested in increasing its sales in those markets. Because fare reduction was discouraged by the CAB, airlines were forced to compete by making the service they provided more attractive to consumers. To understand the form of this competition, one must first examine a consumer's decision as to which airline to fly. To begin, the effective price of air travel to a consumer includes more than just the price of the airline ticket. Because consumers value their time, one measure of the cost of travel is the air fare plus the value of a consumer's time used during travel. The farther is the actual departure time of a flight from a consumer's ideal departure time, the greater the effective price of travel. The longer the travel time, the greater the effective price of travel. Thus, even if all airlines charge the same air fare, the effective price can differ across airlines as well as across consumers. The effective price depends on travel time, departure times, and a consumer's value of time.

In addition to affecting the time cost of travel through the frequency of flights and the availability of nonstop flights, airlines can influence the pleasure derived from air travel. An airline that is less crowded, has better on-board services, and a better safety record is more desired by consumers. Ceteris paribus, such an airline will have greater demand. Table 17.8 provides estimates of the average consumer's willingness to pay for improvements in some of these nonprice factors. It shows that, on average, a consumer is willing to pay $5.67 for a ten minute reduction in travel time. In other words, if two airlines offered identical services except that one airline's travel time was ten minutes less, the average consumer (flying the average route) would prefer the faster airline as long as its air fare was no more than $5.67 more expensive than the slower airline. If an airline raised the reliability of a flight being on time by ten percentage points, consumers would be willing to pay a higher air fare by the amount of $12.13. Of particular interest is the value attached to safety. For a consumer to be indifferent between an airline that had a fatal accident in the last six months and one that did

Table 17.8
Consumers' Willingness to Pay for Better Airline Service

Improvement in Service	Willingness-to-Pay (dollars/round trip)
Ten-minute reduction in travel time	$5.67
Ten-minute reduction in transfer time	6.67
Ten percentage points increase in flights on time	12.13
Carrier not to have a fatal accident in the preceding six months	77.80

Source: Steven A. Morrison and Clifford Winston, "Enhancing the Performance of the Deregulated Air Transportation System," in Martin Neil Baily and Clifford Winston (eds.), *Brookings Papers on Economic Activity: Microeconomics 1989* (Washington, D.C.: The Brookings Institution, 1989). Reprinted by permission.

not (holding all other characteristics the same), the airline with the recent accident must offer a fare which is $77.80 cheaper.

Because the decision of which airline to fly is influenced by factors other than price, airlines are able to compete through nonprice methods in order to raise the demand for their service. One important nonprice variable is flight frequency and, associated with that, load factor. Load factor is the number of passengers on a flight divided by the number of seats. Under fare regulation, airlines competed by offering a wide array of flights that resulted in low load factors. By doing so, an airline was more likely to have the departure time desired by a consumer and, in addition, low load factors resulted in less crowded and thus more pleasant flights.

By examining time-series evidence we can consider the effect of regulation on load factors. From a cost perspective, it is optimal for airlines to use larger aircrafts for longer distances. Because the cost of a seat rises with distance, the optimal load factor also rises with distance. One would then predict load factors to rise with distance in an unregulated environment. However, if regulation induced excessive nonprice competition, then one would expect load factors to *fall* with distance. Fares were more above cost on long-haul markets, so nonprice competition would be stronger in those markets, which means that load factors should have been lower. The estimated relationship between load factors and distance for the regulation year 1969 and for the deregulation years of 1976 and 1981 is shown in Figure 17.6. As expected, load factors did indeed fall with distance under regulation and rose with distance after deregulation. By keeping fares above cost, regulation induced heightened nonprice competition in terms of increased flight frequency and low load factors. Although consumers valued the lower load factors, regulation induced a nonoptimal mix of fares and load factors. Con-

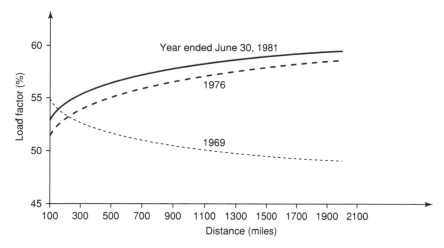

Figure 17.6
Load Factors and Distance
Source: David R. Graham, Daniel P. Kaplan, and David S. Sibley, "Efficiency and Competition in the Airline Industry," *Bell Journal of Economics* 14 (Spring 1983), 118–38. Copyright 1983. Reprinted with permission of RAND.

sumers would have been willing to accept lower fares and higher load factors relative to that achieved under CAB regulation.[44]

Excessive nonprice competition was also observed in terms of on-board services. From 1976 to 1982, the Consumer Price Index for food rose 62 percent, whereas the cost of food for airlines rose only 40 percent.[45] Because deregulation reduced the difference between fares and cost, it reduced the level of competition in terms of the quality of food. Over the same time period, the number of flight attendants per passenger fell 16 percent.[46] Both these changes show that firms achieved a higher level of nonprice competition under regulation.

Fares in some markets have fallen since deregulation, but the above evidence suggests that quality has also fallen (though further evidence presented below puts that into question). A rough indicator that, on net, consumers are better off is to look at what has happened to the volume of air travel. It has exploded since the industry was deregulated. From 1977 to 1990, domestic air travel rose by 120 percent.[47] A bit more refined measure shows that in 1988 air travel was 41 percent above the level projected by the trend established during the regulated period 1955–1978.[48]

Development of the Hub-and-Spoke System

From the evidence thus far, it would seem that regulation resulted in airlines offering a high-priced, high-quality product. The welfare loss to consumers was then in not having the option of choosing a low-priced low-quality product. In assessing the welfare implications of regulation, it would then seem that one must consider both the welfare loss from higher fares and the welfare gain from better quality of service. It is indeed true that regulation raised quality by having lower load factors and greater on-board services, but in terms of one important quality dimension regulation actually resulted in *lower* quality of air service. Flight frequency has risen since the airline industry was deregulated. Consumers now have a wider array of departure times from which to choose. That flight frequency could increase in spite of higher load factors is due to the adoption of the hub-and-spoke system.

To understand the hub-and-spoke system, consider an airline that serves three cities: A, B, and C; and thus three routes: A to B (and, of course, B to A), A to C, and B to C. There are two alternative route systems an airline could adopt. First, it could offer direct flights between the three cities. Alternatively, it could make one of these cities a hub (let it be B) and redirect traffic going from A to C and C to A through B. That is, a traveler going from A to C would get there by going from A to B and then from B to C. In this case, B is the hub and A and C are spokes, so that all traffic is routed into B. The concentration of traffic in B allows for larger aircraft, which are more economical, and a larger number of flights because of the higher volume of traffic at the hub.

One of the unanticipated developments since deregulation has been the wide-spread adoption of the hub-and-spoke system. To see how drastically route structures have changed, Figure 17.7 shows the route structure of Western Airlines before and after deregulation. As should be apparent, the two hubs are Salt Lake City and Los Angeles. By restricting the entry of existing carriers into currently served markets, CAB regulation prevented the massive route restructuring required to move to a hub-and-spoke system.

In spite of reduced nonprice competition, the development of the hub-and-spoke system puts into doubt the claim that the overall quality of service is lower under deregulation, because the hub-and-spoke system trades off longer travel time (as there are fewer direct flights so that more flights require a transfer) for a wider array of departure times. To address this question, a study analyzed 812 city pairs with and without regulation. It used actual data on fares and flight frequency for 1977 as the regulatory benchmark. To ascertain the effect of regulation, these data are compared with projected data for 1977 conditional on the route structure and fares being what they were under deregulation (specifically, 1983). Table 17.9 shows that real fares declined in medium hub–large hub and large hub–large hub routes but rose in all other markets.

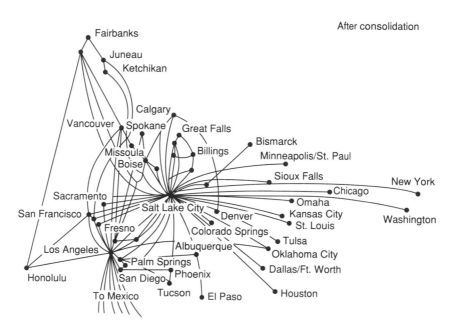

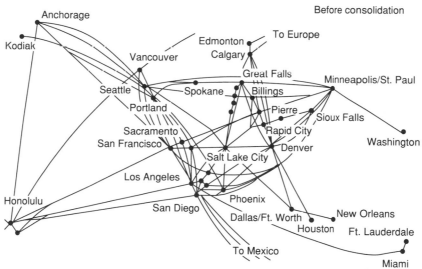

Figure 17.7
The Adoption of the Hub-and-Spoke System by Western Airlines

Source: Figure from Steven Morrison and Clifford Winston, *The Economic Effects of Airline Deregulation* (Washington, D.C.: The Brookings Institution, 1986). Copyright 1985 by The New York Times Company. Reprinted by permission.

Table 17.9
Weighted Average Percentage Change in Fares and Frequency from Deregulation (1977)

Category of Route	Number of City Pairs	Coach Fare	Discount Fare	Frequency
Nonhub–nonhub	51	21.2	22.1	33.9
Nonhub–small hub	52	22.5	12.3	1.4
Nonhub–medium hub	45	5.4	−0.4	24.3
Nonhub–large hub	53	16.3	9.1	28.7
Small hub–hub	60	15.3	11.3	33.9
Small hub–medium hub	69	18.7	10.4	20.8
Small hub–large hub	57	25.0	8.1	19.2
Medium hub–medium hub	69	15.6	2.0	−4.3
Medium hub–large hub	161	17.4	−6.8	14.4
Large hub–large hub	205	8.6	−17.6	−3.5

Source: Steven Morrison and Clifford Winston, *The Economic Effects of Airline Deregulation* (Washington, D.C.: The Brookings Institution, 1986). Reprinted by permission.

This is consistent with air fares being set above cost in dense markets and below cost in less dense markets. With the movement to hub-and-spoke systems, flight frequency increased for most markets. For example, there were a third more flights for nonhub–nonhub and small hub–small hub. Overall, the route-weighted average frequency increased by 9.2 percent as a result of the restructuring of the route system.

The development of the hub-and-spoke system points out an important lesson from economic regulation: it is difficult to predict what unfettered competition will generate. This was perhaps best said by Alfred E. Kahn, former chairman of the CAB:

The essence of the case for competition is the impossibility of predicting most of its consequences. The superiority of the competitive market is the positive stimuli it provides for constantly improving efficiency, innovating, and offering consumers diversity of choices.[49]

Before deregulation economists generally believed that regulation caused a nonoptimal product mix; fares were too high and quality of service was too high. What was not recognized was that regulation, through restrictions on entry, was holding back a restructuring of the route system that would result in lower costs and greater flight frequency. Deregulation reduced quality of service by raising load factors and travel time and reducing on-board services, but it raised quality by increasing the number of departures. The development of the hub-and-spoke system points out that it is only in retrospect that we can adequately understand the effects of regulation.

Welfare Estimates from Changes in Price and Quality

In considering the welfare effects of regulation, let us begin by focusing on the initial period of deregulatory activity by looking at movements in

Table 17.10
Annual Gains to Travelers from Airline Deregulation (billions of 1993 dollars)

Category	Gain
Fares	12.4
Travel Restrictions	−3.3
Frequency	10.3
Load Factor	−0.6
Number of Connections	−0.8
Mix of Connections (On-line/Interline)	0.8
Travel Time	−3.3
Total	15.6

Source: Steven A. Morrison and Clifford Winston, "The Evolution of the Airline Industry," Northeastern University, manuscript, August 1994.

fares and travel times and delays from the end of 1976 to the end of 1978.[50] This period captures the initial effect of price deregulation, but not the effect of the restructuring of the route system. The average real standard coach fare fell by almost 5 percent while first-class fares went from being 150 percent of the coach fare to 120 percent. Because lower fares brought forth greater volume of traffic, load factors rose from 55.6 percent to 61.0 percent. Once taking into account the effect of deregulation on travel time and delays, the estimated gain to consumers was about 10 percent of an average prederegulation round trip fare or about $25 to $35 per round trip (recall that all figures are in 1985 dollars). Any undesirable changes in travel time and delay were more than compensated for by the reduction in fares. It is important to note that this welfare measure does not take into account lower welfare due to reduced on-board services and higher load factors.

Table 17.10 provides the most up-to-date estimates of the welfare gains from deregulation. Consumers are gaining $12.4 billion annually from lower fares under deregulation and $10.3 billion from greater flight frequency. On the downside, increases in travel restrictions, travel time, load factors, and the number of connections have all reduced consumer welfare. On net, the gains are quite impressive, on the order of $15 billion annually.

Regulation not only reduced consumers' welfare but also negatively affected industry profits. If the industry had not been regulated in 1977, industry profits would have been higher by over $4 billion.[51] This is a surprising finding inasmuch as the airline industry has performed rather poorly since deregulation. Although it earned an annual rate of return of 1.30 percent over 1970–1977, it earned an even more feeble annual return of 0.10 percent over 1979–1986.[52] However, the airline industry

Table 17.11
Average Annual Percentage Decline in Unit Cost

	1970–1975		1975–1983	
Sources	U.S.	Non-U.S.	U.S.	Non-U.S.
Operating Characteristics	1.8	3.1	2.2	2.0
Technical Efficiency	1.2	1.4	1.1	0.8
Total Productive Efficiency	3.0	4.5	3.3	2.8

Source: Douglas W. Caves, Laurits R. Christensen, Michael W. Tretheway, and Robert J. Windle, "An Assessment of the Efficiency Effects of U.S. Airline Deregulation via an International Comparison," in Elizabeth E. Bailey (ed.), *Public Regulation: New Perspectives on Institutions and Policies* (Cambridge, Mass.: MIT Press, 1987).

has been hit by a number of negative profit shocks since deregulation, in particular, the recession of 1981–1983, a sharp rise in fuel prices, and several strikes by union employees. More recently, the industry has been plagued by excess capacity because airlines apparently overestimated the demand for air travel.

Dynamic Productive Inefficiency

To assess the effect of regulation on productivity growth, a cross-country study was performed that examined productivity growth for twenty-one U.S. airlines (including all trunk airlines) with that achieved by twenty-seven non-U.S. airlines for the period 1970–1983. This is a reasonable comparison inasmuch as countries' airline industries are similar in many respects except for the regulatory environment and labor costs. Aircraft and fuel are sold in world markets, while operation and maintenance of aircraft is governed by strict international standards.

Dating the beginning of deregulation at 1976, Table 17.11 compares the annual percentage decline in unit costs over periods of regulation and deregulation and across U.S. and non-U.S. airlines. Operating characteristics include changes due to traffic, route density, firm size, load factor, and capacity utilization. Technical efficiency is composed of all other sources of change in factor productivity. Under regulation, the annual decline in unit cost for U.S. airlines was only 3.0 percent compared to 4.5 percent for non-U.S. airlines. After deregulation, U.S. airlines outperformed non-U.S. airlines by experiencing a 3.3 percent annual decrease in unit cost. Consistent with the experience in the railroad industry, airline regulation reduced productivity growth.

Airline Safety

A constant fear expressed in public forums is that deregulation would cause airline safety to deteriorate. On the surface, this would seem to be an irrational fear, because airline safety is controlled by the Federal

Aviation Administration and safety regulations were unaffected by the Airline Deregulation Act. Further reflection, however, raises the potential for concern because nonprice competition may generate levels of safety exceeding that mandated by law. If deregulation reduced nonprice competition and intensified efforts to keep cost down, then perhaps it could have reduced safety. How might this take place? Perhaps a greater need to keep costs low resulted in airlines using less experienced and less well-rested pilots and skimping on aircraft maintenance. Furthermore, safety is also influenced by the amount of traffic and congestion, both of which have risen since deregulation. On the other hand, there are some factors that could cause safety to have risen since deregulation. Increased air travel requires more planes, which means that the average age of the fleet is lower. Increased competition could result in more efficient practices so that costs are lower and safety is higher. Finally, there is continual technological progress that increases airline safety.

There are numerous ways in which to measure airline safety including fatalities, accidents, and incidents (for example, the number of near mid-air collisions). These variables could be measured per departure or per passenger mile. Regardless of which measure is used, the conclusion is the same: the long-term rise in airline safety has continued during the years of deregulation.[53] Figure 17.8 shows the steady decline in the total accidents per million departures. If one looks at the number of fatalities per passenger mile (not showed in Figure 17.8), there is no clear trend as the measure is quite volatile. The crash of a single large aircraft typically dominates the annual number. Still, the fatality risk for a passenger on a U.S. domestic jet flight was 1 in every 2.5 million flights in 1971–1978 and 1 in every 7.4 million flights in 1979–1986.[54] As further evidence that safety has not deteriorated during the years of deregulation is that aviation insurance rates have not risen.[55] As perceived by insurance specialists, deregulation has not compromised airline safety.

That airline safety has not suffered with a 52 percent increase in passenger-miles over 1976 to 1986 is striking. As mentioned, this may simply reflect a long-term trend in improvements in safety due to better equipment and practices. There is also some evidence that deregulation has resulted in more efficient practices. One study examined the maintenance practices of seven airlines. It found that the length of time between maintenance shop visits for jet engines increased since deregulation but that there was no effect on the probability of an engine shutdown.[56]

Competition and Antitrust Policy after Deregulation

If an industry is subject to price and entry regulation, then there is a greatly reduced need for antitrust policy. With prices being set by the

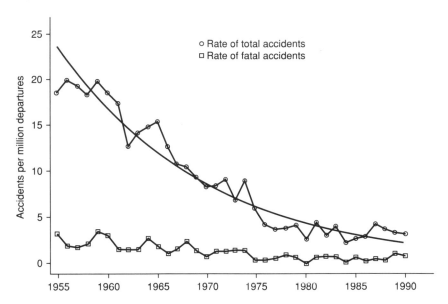

Figure 17.8
Actual and Predicted Accident Rates, 1955–1990

Source: Nancy L. Rose, "Fear of Flying? Economic Analyses of Airline Safety," *Journal of Economic Perspectives* 6 (Spring 1992): 75–94.

regulatory agency, collusion in price is irrelevant though one might still need to be concerned about firms colluding along unregulated dimensions like product quality. With entry restrictions, there is little need for concern about entry-deterring or predatory tactics designed to increase concentration. However, once an industry is deregulated, an active role for antitrust policy reemerges. Because the benefits from deregulation are predicated upon firms not conspiring to raise price, not acting to deter entry, and not predatorily driving new competitors out of the industry, antitrust policy can be critical in achieving those benefits. The Airline Deregulation Act of 1978 (ADA) took account of the important postderegulation role for antitrust policy in its mandating that the CAB put additional emphasis on the standards for mergers outlined by Section 7 of the Clayton Act. All mergers or acquisitions were to require prior approval.

Reconcentration of the Airline Industry

To measure industry concentration, we will use the number of "effective competitors," which is defined as the inverse of the sum of each firm's market share squared (or, the inverse of the HHI multiplied by 10,000). Thus, if s_i is the market share of firm i and there are n firms then the

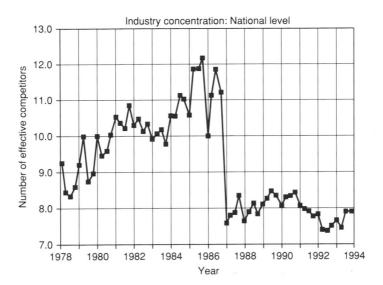

Figure 17.9
Industry Concentration: National Level

Source: Market share data used in calculating the number of effective competitors is a carrier's share of domestic passenger miles. Figure from Steven A. Morrison and Clifford Winston, "The Evolution of the Airline Industry," Northeastern University, manuscript, August 1994.

number of effective competitors equals $1/[s_1^2 + s_2^2 + \cdots + s_n^2]$. This measure takes account of how market share is distributed, and not simply the number of firms, in assessing how many competitive the industry is. In other words, the effective number of competitors for an industry is the number of equal-sized firms that would give the same level of HHI. For example, if there is but a single firm, so that its market share is one, then the number of effective competitors is one (which makes sense). If there are n firms with equal market share, then the number of effective competitors is $1/[(1/n)^2 + \cdots + (1/n)^2] = 1/[n(1/n^2)] = n$. However, if there are n firms and market share is skewed so that a few firms have a large part of the market then the number of effective competitors is less than n.

Using market share data at the national level, Figure 17.9 shows how the number of effective competitors has changed between the passage of the ADA in 1978 and 1993. During the early years after deregulation, entry by new airlines and the expansion of regional airlines resulted in a rise in the number of effective competitors (concentration went down). Then a consolidation process started to emerge, with its being particularly intense around 1986. Some airlines went bankrupt and some were acquired. By 1987, none of the original postderegulation entrants had

Table 17.12
Major Airline Mergers Since Deregulation

Year	Carriers	Status
1979	Pan American-National	Approved by CAB
	Texas International-National	Approved by CAB
		Not consummated
	Eastern-National	Anticompetitive finding by CAB
		Not consummated
	Continental-Western	Rejected by CAB
	North Central-Southern	Approved by CAB
1980	Republic-Hughes Air West	Approved by CAB
1981	Continental-Western	Approved by CAB
		Not consummated
	Texas International-Continental	Approved by CAB
1982	Air Florida-Western	Approved by CAB
		Not consummated
1985	United-Pan American (Pacific Division)	Opposed by DOJ
		Approved by DOT
1986	Delta-Western	Approved by DOT
	Texas Air-People Express	Not-anticompetitive finding by DOJ
		Approved by DOT
	Texas Air-Eastern	Approved by DOT after sale of slots to Pan Am Shuttle
	Trans World Airlines-Ozark	Opposed by DOJ
		Approved by DOT
	Northwest-Republic	Opposed by DOJ
		Approved by DOT
1987	USAir-Piedmont	Approved by DOT
	American-Air California	Approved by DOT
	USAir-Pacific Southwest	Approved by DOT

Source: Steven A. Morrison and Clifford Winston, "Enhancing the Performance of the Deregulated Air Transportation System," in Martin Neil Baily and Clifford Winston (eds.), *Brookings Papers on Economic Activity: Microeconomics 1989* (Washington, D.C.: The Brookings Institution, 1989). Reprinted by permission.

more than 1 percent of industry revenue.[57] Today, all of them have disappeared. Table 17.12 describes the intense merger activity that took place. At least at a national level, the number of effective competitors is lower than it was under deregulation.

Antitrust policy has been conspicuously absent during the years in which the airline industry has been deregulated. The CAB was quite lenient in their standards for airline mergers and the Department of Transportation (DOT) (which has handled airline mergers since 1984) has approved every airline merger, some against the recommendation of the Department of Justice (see Table 17.12). Under this laissez-faire policy, twenty airlines merged in 1985–1987. In response to these events, former CAB chairman Alfred E. Kahn stated,

[The] reconcentration of the industry reflects in part the deplorable failure of the Department of Transportation to disallow even one merger, or, in all but one case, even to set conditions to mitigate possible anticompetitive consequences. The DOT seems to have no appreciation whatever of the dangers our antitrust laws were set up almost a century ago to forestall.[58]

Deterrents to Entry

On top of an industry-wide trend of rising concentration, there are several factors that may limit entry. One factor is the threat of predatory retaliation from the industry leaders. Former Chairman Kahn speaks again:

I take perverse satisfaction in predicting the demise of price-cutting competitors like World and Capital Airways if we did nothing to limit the predictable geographically discriminatory response of the incumbent carriers to their entry.[59]

A more pervasive factor is travel agents' use of reservation systems supplied by carriers. The two dominant systems are American Airlines' Sabre and United Airlines' Apollo. By determining the order in which carriers' flights show up on a travel agent's computer screen, an airline reservation system can influence the distribution of demand among airlines. For example, in response to a request for a 3:00 P.M. flight, the Apollo system would show a 1:00 P.M. United flight prior to showing a 3:00 P.M. flight of its competitors. Although airline reservation systems aid travel agents in servicing customers, they can provide an anticompetitive advantage to the airlines providing systems. It has also been argued that this advantage is accentuated by merger.[60]

Another deterrent to entering certain route markets is difficulty in gaining airport access. Takeoff and landing slots are in short supply at O'Hare in Chicago, LaGuardia and Kennedy in New York, and National Airport in Washington, D.C. To improve efficiency at those four slot-constrained airports, the DOT allowed resale of slots beginning in April 1986. The need to purchase slots is an additional cost to entry and makes potential competition less effective in disciplining carriers. A second source of difficulty in airport access is the concentration of control over gates at hubs. Carriers may attempt to gain near monopoly control over gates in order to prevent entry. For example, after its acquisition of Ozark Airlines in 1986, TWA controlled over 75 percent of the gates at the St. Louis airport. Shortly thereafter, TWA raised fares by 13–18 percent for its flights out of St. Louis.[61] Finally, the existence of frequent-flyer programs makes successful entry by smaller carriers more difficult. The more routes it covers, the more valuable a carrier's frequent-flyer program to a customer, which gives an advantage to larger carriers.

Concentration and Air Fares

What has a smaller number of airlines and deterrents to entry meant in terms of air fares? This question must be examined at the level of the route for that is the relevant geographic market. Industry-wide concentration is still relevant, however, as the number of U.S. airlines provides a short-run upper bound on the number of competitors for a particular route. Fewer airlines may mean fewer active competitors and certainly means fewer potential competitors.

We know from Figure 17.9 that the number of potential competitors has fallen. What has happened to the number of actual competitors on various routes? Averaged across routes, the number of effective competitors at the route level has been persistently higher since deregulation. At the time of deregulation, there were, on average, 1.7 effective competitors per route This number has exceeded 2.0 since the early 1980s and, as of 1993, stood between 2.2 and 2.5 (depending on the exact measure used).[62] However, the picture is not so rosy when one looks at individual routes. The hub-and-spoke system has resulted in a number of routes being dominated by a single carrier. For example, Delta has 84 percent of enplanements at the Atlanta airport, USAir has 89 percent at Pittsburgh, and American has 77 percent at Nashville.[63] As of 1993 there were only three airports that were hubs for two carriers: Chicago's O'Hare with American and United, Dallas/Fort Worth with American and Delta, and Denver with Continental and United.[64]

The hub-and-spoke system has reduced the number of effective competitors at various airports. The significance of airport concentration is as follows. Suppose a passenger travels from Baltimore to Los Angeles through Pittsburgh. Despite USAir's large market share in Pittsburgh, it has no real market power over the Baltimore–Los Angeles route, for a traveler could easily go from Baltimore to Los Angeles by using, for example, American through Dallas/Fort Worth or United through Chicago. However, a passenger whose final destination is Pittsburgh has little choice but to travel on USAir. Passengers whose origin or destination is a hub with a single dominant firm may be forced to pay higher fares.

A study by Severin Borenstein found that the average fare per mile is higher for travelers whose origin or destination is the carrier's major hub. A dominant airline with 70 percent of the traffic might be able to charge a price 2–12 percent higher than a rival with only a 10 percent market share.[65] For the thirty largest airports, Table 17.13 provides the airport premium, which is the average ratio of fares on local routes from these airports compared to the national average fares on routes of the same distance. The airport premium measures the additional fare that must be paid for traveling on routes for which a hub carrier is likely to have a dominant position. For example, travelers using Chicago's O'Hare for local travel paid a premium of almost 15 percent. In Minne-

Table 17.13
Hubbing and Fares at the 30 Largest U.S. Airports

Airport	Percent Changing Planes	Airport Fare Premium	Rank by Size
Charlotte	75.7%	18.8%	20
Atlanta	69.0%	17.2%	3
Memphis	67.7%	27.4%	29
Dallas/Ft. Worth	65.8%	20.5%	2
Pittsburgh	62.1%	15.9%	16
Salt Lake City	61.3%	19.1%	28
St. Louis	56.2%	−4.0%	13
Chicago, O'Hare	55.7%	14.8%	1
Denver	54.1%	15.3%	7
Minneapolis	51.0%	31.5%	15
Houston, Intercontinental	49.5%	15.6%	19
New York, Kennedy	47.3%	2.9%	6
Detroit	43.6%	−0.7%	11
Baltimore	40.5%	9.1%	26
Phoenix	33.1%	−28.4%	9
Miami	31.0%	−14.3%	14
Seattle	27.3%	8.7%	24
San Francisco	25.3%	−1.5%	5
Los Angeles	25.2%	−5.3%	4
Philadelphia	24.9%	11.2%	22
Honolulu	22.4%	−20.8%	17
Newark	19.6%	11.5%	12
Las Vegas	18.9%	−27.8%	23
Houston, Hobby	17.5%	−23.4%	30
Orlando	16.8%	−15.6%	21
Boston	13.8%	9.0%	10
Washington D.C., National	11.1%	10.7%	18
Tampa	11.0%	−12.4%	27
San Diego	6.6%	−18.1%	25
New York—La Guardia	6.2%	9.5%	8

Source: Severin Borenstein, "The Evolution of U.S. Airline Competition," *Journal of Economic Perspectives* 6 (Spring 1992): 45–73.

apolis–St. Paul, where Northwest controls 82 percent of enplanements, the premium is 31.5 percent. The evidence is that market dominance does result in abnormally high fares for some consumers.

The above analysis used an intermarket approach in that it compared fares across routes that varied in the degree of concentration. One can also use an intertemporal approach by examining how fares along a particular route change as concentration changes. This approach was used by examining how airline mergers that increased concentration along some routes affected air fares. An analysis of twenty-seven mergers in 1985–1988 revealed that the merging airlines, on average, raised air fares by 9.4 percent more on those routes for which they both previously provided service. Furthermore, rival airlines on those routes responded by increasing their air fares by 12.2 percent.[66] The majority of the evidence supports the hypothesis that increasing concentration has translated into higher fares.

An important lesson to be learned from the deregulation of the airline industry is that if we are to realize the potential gains from deregulation, then regulatory policy and antitrust policy must work together. Dismantling regulation creates a void that needs to be filled by antitrust policy. It is important to understand that deregulation does not eliminate a role for government. Rather, it means a change in the role for government from one of controlling the industry to one of maintaining a competitive environment.

Although the trucking and airline industries were subject to similar regulatory practices, it is clear that the effects of regulation have been quite distinct. In the case of trucking, firms did not vigorously engage in nonprice competition, and this allowed them to earn substantial above-normal profits under regulation. In contrast, airlines competed away most of the potential profits that abnormally high fares created. They did this through the provision of frequent flights, low load factors, and high-quality on-board services. Why did regulation induce excessive nonprice competition in the airline industry but not in the trucking industry? One possible answer is that the demand for passenger air service is more responsive to nonprice factors than is the demand for surface freight service. If demand is very elastic with respect to these factors, a firm has a strong incentive to invest in them since a relatively small investment can result in a sharp rise in firm demand. Of course, if all firms do this, then there may be a lot of canceling out of these effects so that everyone's demand is only a little higher and considerable expenditure has been incurred.

There are at least two important lessons to be learned from CAB regulation of passenger air service. First, competition will follow the path of least regulatory resistance. Because no authority can fully control every dimension of competition, firms will compete via the least regulated dimensions. In the case of airline regulation, the CAB prevented fare competition but left uncontrolled competition over quality of service. As a result, regulation raised fares *and* raised the quality of service. A second lesson to be learned is that it is very difficult to predict the effects of regulation. Because competition entails coming up with new ways to provide a better product at a lower cost, it is typically beyond the creative abilities of a few economists to anticipate what innovations might have arisen in the absence of regulation. Although economists long predicted the welfare gains from deregulation, they were unable to anticipate the development of the hub-and-spoke system, a development stifled by the entry restrictions put in place by the CAB. As a result of the hub-and-spoke system deregulation has reduced fares in many markets, but it has not reduced quality of service as much as was anticipated.

Summary

The transportation industry is an informative case study for understanding the effects of regulation. There are several lessons to be stressed. The regulation of surface freight transportation highlights the imperialistic tendencies of regulation. It is difficult enough to regulate an industry. It is even more difficult to regulate only part of an industry. This is what the ICC discovered when it regulated the railroads but not the motor carriers. With rail rates being set above cost, truckers were free to set rates so as to undercut the railroads and take demand that would be more efficiently served by the railroads. Because of the difficulties inherent in such a situation, the Motor Carrier Act of 1935 extended ICC control from railroads to motor carriers.

A second lesson highlighted by the airline industry is that when regulation controls price, firms will find other ways to compete. The implication is that firms engage in nonprice competition. In the case of the airline industry, firms provided high-quality service at a high price. Consumers valued the higher quality resulting from regulation, but they were hurt by the absence of a low-priced, low-quality alternative.

A third lesson is that regulation has a tendency to maintain inefficient practices. This may entail railroads being prevented from abandoning unprofitable lines or allowing inefficient truckers to continue to operate. Restricting freedom of entry and exit destroys one of the most important features of competition: the efficient survive and the inefficient perish.

The final and perhaps most important lesson is that regulation can reduce welfare in ways that are difficult to anticipate. Regulation can stifle innovations that would have occurred in an unregulated market. It was found for both the railroad and airline industries that regulation reduced growth in factor productivity. A case in point is the development of the hub-and-spoke system since airline deregulation. Because of this unanticipated restructuring of the industry, deregulation allowed for lower fares *and* improved flight frequency.

Questions and Problems

1.   How would one measure the effect of regulation on the profitability of the trucking industry? Did regulation cause profits to go up or down?

2. Why were the railroads in favor of regulation in the 1880s but in favor of deregulation in the 1950s?

3. The Staggers Act gave railroads considerable freedom in setting rates except on routes where there was market dominance. From the perspective of a social planner, how would you choose to define market dominance?

4. During the years of CAB regulation, the unit cost for U.S. airlines declined 3 percent annually whereas the unit cost for non-U.S. airlines declined 4.5 percent. What are the ways in which regulation might have caused smaller productivity gains?

5. Was the deregulation of the railroad industry a Pareto improvement? How about the deregulation of the trucking industry? If these were not Pareto improvements, who gained and who lost from deregulation?

6. What was the role of antitrust policy after airline deregulation? What do you think should be the role of antitrust policy after an industry is deregulated?

7. In both the airline and trucking industries, rates were generally set too high on many routes. Why did nonprice competition tend to compete away most of the rents in the airline industry but not in the trucking industry? Was this nonprice competition welfare-improving?

8. Have all consumers been made better off by airline deregulation?

9. Why did the deregulation of prices cause wages in the airline and trucking industries to fall?

10. Using the economic theories of regulation from Chapter 10, can one explain the deregulation of the transportation industry?

11. What are the different ways in which to estimate the effect of regulation on air fares?

12. In response to truckers taking away an increasing amount of business from the railroads, the trucking industry was regulated in 1935. Would it have been better to have left the trucking industry deregulated? Would it have been better to have deregulated the railroad industry?

Notes

1. For the reader interested more generally in the economics of transportation as opposed to just the effects of regulation on the transportation industry, see Clifford Winston, "Conceptual Developments in the Economics of Transportation: An Interpretive Survey," *Journal of Economic Literature* 23 (March 1985): 57–94, and the references cited within.

2. A notable exception took place in the 1987 James Bond movie *The Living Daylights.* A Russian defector is transported across the Iron Curtain in a capsule propelled through a pipeline. This is fictional, but who knows whether some day pipelines might be able to compete with airlines in providing rapid long-distance transportation services.

3. General background references used for our discussion of the regulation of surface freight transportation are Stephen Breyer, *Regulation and Its Reform*

(Cambridge, Mass.: Harvard University Press, 1982); Theodore E. Keeler, *Railroads, Freight, and Public Policy*, (Washington, D.C.: The Brookings Institution, 1983); and Thomas Gale Moore, "Rail and Trucking Deregulation," in Leonard W. Weiss and Michael W. Klass (eds.), *Regulatory Reform: What Actually Happened* (Boston: Little, Brown, 1986).

4. For a discussion of the JEC's role in setting rail rates, see Robert H. Porter, "A Study of Cartel Stability: The Joint Executive Committee, 1880–1886," *Bell Journal of Economics* 14 (Autumn 1983): 301–14; and Chapter 5.

5. Clifford Winston, Thomas M. Corsi, Curtis M. Grimm, and Carol A. Evans, *The Economic Effects of Surface Freight Deregulation* (Washington, D.C.: The Brookings Institution, 1990).

6. Robin A. Prager, "Using Stock Price Data to Measure the Effects of Regulation: the Interstate Commerce Act and the Railroad Industry," *RAND Journal of Economics* 20 (Summer 1989): 280–90.

7. Kenneth D. Boyer, "Equalizing Discrimination and Cartel Pricing in Transport Rate Regulation," *Journal of Political Economy* 89 (April 1981): 270–86.

8. Kenneth D. Boyer, "The Costs of Price Regulation: Lessons from Railroad Deregulation," *RAND Journal of Economics* 18 (Autumn 1987): 408–16.

9. Christopher C. Barnekov and Andrew N. Kleit, "The Costs of Railroad Regulation: A Further Analysis," Bureau of Economics, Federal Trade Commission, Working Paper No. 164, May 1988.

10. Christopher C. Barnekov, "The Track Record," *Regulation* 1 (1987): 19–27.

11. "Why Won't the Coal and Utility People Negotiate?," *Railway Age*, December 1984.

12. John W. Snow, "The Problem of Motor Carrier Regulation and the Ford Administration's Proposal for Reform" in Paul W. MacAvoy and John W. Snow (eds.), *Regulation of Entry and Pricing in Truck Transportation* (Washington, D.C.: American Enterprise Institute, 1977).

13. Both survey data is from Moore, 1986.

14. John S. Ying and Theodore E. Keeler, "Pricing in a Deregulated Environment: The Motor Carrier Experience," *RAND Journal of Economics* 22 (Summer 1991): 264–73.

15. Richard Beilock and James Freeman, "Effect of Removing Entry and Rate Controls on Motor Carrier Levels and Structures," *Journal of Transport Economics and Policy* 21 (May 1985): 167–88.

16. Roger D. Blair, David L. Kaserman, and James T. McClave, "Motor Carrier Deregulation: The Florida Experiment," *Review of Economics and Statistics* 68 (February 1986): 159–84.

17. L. Adkins, "After Deregulation: Railroads Learn to Compete," *Dun's Business Monthly*, May 1985.

18. James M. MacDonald, "Railroad Deregulation, Innovation, and Competition: Effects of the Staggers Act on Grain Transportation," *Journal of Law and Economics* 32 (April 1989): 63–95.

19. Richard C. Levin, "Surface Freight Transportation: Does Rate Regulation Matter?" *Bell Journal of Economics* 9 (Spring 1978): 18–45; Anne F. Friedlaender and Richard Spady, *Freight Transport Regulation: Equity, Efficiency, and Competition in Rail and Trucking Industries* (Cambridge, Mass.: MIT Press, 1980); Clifford Winston, "The Welfare Effects of ICC Rate Regulation Revisited," *Bell Journal of Economics* 12 (Spring 1981): 232–44; and Ronald R.

Braeutigam and Roger G. Noll, "The Regulation of Surface Freight Transportation: The Welfare Effects Revisited," *Review of Economics and Statistics* 56 (February 1984): 80–87.

20. Winston et al., 1990.

21. Winston et al., 1990, also consider some indirect effects of rate deregulation on service, in particular, rail transit time, and find very large welfare gains even after netting out the loss in carriers' profits and labor's wages. Large estimates of the welfare gain from deregulation are also found by Barnekov and Kleit, 1988.

22. Thomas Gale Moore, "Rail and Truck Reform: The Record So Far," *Regulation*, November/December 1983: 33–41.

23. Keeler, 1983.

24. B. Starr McMullen and Linda R. Stanley, "The Impact of Deregulation on the Production Structure of the Motor Carrier Industry," *Economic Inquiry* 26 (April 1988): 299–316; and Thomas Gale Moore, "Unfinished Business in Motor Carrier Deregulation," *Regulation*, Summer 1991: 49–57.

25. Nancy L. Rose, "Labor Rent Sharing and Regulation: Evidence from the Trucking Industry," *Journal of Political Economy* 95 (December 1987): 1146–78.

26. John R. Felton, "The Impact of Rate Regulation Upon ICC-Regulated Truck Back Hauls," *Journal of Transport Economics and Policy* 15 (September 1981): 253–67.

27. Moore, 1991.

28. Noel D. Uri and Edward J. Rifkin, "Geographic Markets, Causality and Railroad Deregulation," *Review of Economics and Statistics* 67 (August 1985): 422–28.

29. All data in this paragraph is from Robert D. Willig and William J. Baumol, "Using Competition as a Guide," *Regulation* 1 (1987): 28–35.

30. John S. Ying, "The Inefficiency of Regulating Competitive Industry: Productivity Gains in Trucking Following Reform," *Review of Economics and Statistics* 72 (May 1990): 191–201.

31. Willig and Baumol, 1987.

32. Nancy L. Rose, "The Incidence of Regulatory Rents in the Motor Carrier Industry," *Rand Journal of Economics* 16 (Autumn 1985): 299–318.

33. Katherine Schipper, Rex Thompson, and Roman L. Weil, "Disentangling Interrelated Effects of Regulatory Changes on Shareholder Wealth: The Case of Motor Carrier Deregulation," *Journal of Law and Economics* 30 (April 1987): 67–100.

34. Willig and Baumol, 1987, p. 31.

35. Christopher Conte, "Push for Tighter U.S. Supervision of Railroads is a Threat to Success of Reagan Deregulators," *Wall Street Journal*, January 7, 1985.

36. Paul Teske, Samuel Best, and Michael Mintrom, "The Economic Theory of Regulation and Trucking Deregulation: Shifting to the State Level," *Public Choice* 79 (June 1994): 246–56.

37. Moore, 1991.

38. General background references used for our discussion of airline regulation are Theodore E. Keeler, "The Revolution in Airline Regulation," in Leonard W. Weiss and Michael W. Klass (eds.), *Case Studies in Regulation: Revolution and Reform* (Boston: Little, Brown, 1981); Stephen Breyer, *Regulation and Its Reform*

(Cambridge, Mass.: Harvard University Press, 1982); and Elizabeth E. Bailey, David R. Graham, and Daniel P. Kaplan, *Deregulating the Airlines*, (Cambridge, Mass.: MIT Press, 1985).

39. The first academic study to propose deregulation was Lucile S. Keyes, *Federal Control of Entry into Transportation* (Cambridge, Mass.: Harvard University Press, 1951).

40. Breyer, 1982.

41. Ibid.

42. Thomas Gale Moore, "U.S. Airline Deregulation: Its Effects on Passengers, Capital, and Labor," *Journal of Law and Economics* 29 (April 1986): 1–28.

43. Ibid.

44. This nonoptimal mix was shown for 1971 by George W. Douglas and James C. Miller, III, *Economic Regulation of Domestic Air Transport: Theory and Policy* (Washington, D.C.: The Brookings Institution, 1974).

45. Moore, 1986.

46. Ibid.

47. Severin Borenstein, "The Evolution of U.S. Airline Competition," *Journal of Economic Perspectives* 6 (Spring 1992): 45–73.

48. Richard B. McKenzie, "Making Sense of the Airline Safety Debate," *Regulation*, Summer 1991: 76–84.

49. Alfred E. Kahn, "Deregulation and Vested Interests: The Case of Airlines," in Roger G. Noll and Bruce M. Owen (eds.), *The Political Economy of Deregulation* (Washington, D.C.: American Enterprise Institute, 1983), p. 140.

50. Donald W. Koran, "The Welfare Effects of Airline Fare Deregulation in the United States," *Journal of Transport Economics and Policy* 18 (May 1983): 177–89.

51. Steven Morrison and Clifford Winston, *The Economic Effects of Airline Deregulation* (Washington, D.C.: The Brookings Institution, 1986).

52. Alfred E. Kahn, "Surprises of Airline Deregulation," *American Economic Review* 78 (May 1988): 316–22.

53. Nancy L. Rose, "Fear of Flying? Economic Analyses of Airline Safety," *Journal of Economic Perspectives* 6 (Spring 1992): 75–94.

54. Arnold Barnett and Mary Higgins, "Airline Safety: The Last Decade," *Management Science* 35 (January 1989): 1–21.

55. Steven A. Morrison and Clifford Winston, "Air Safety, Deregulation, and Public Policy," *The Brookings Review*, Winter 1988: 10–15.

56. D. Mark Kennet, "Did Deregulation Affect Aircraft Engine Maintenance? An Empirical Policy Analysis," *Rand Journal of Economics* 24 (Winter 1993): 542–58.

57. Michael E. Levine, "Airline Competition in Deregulated Markets: Theory, Firm Strategy, and Public Policy," *Yale Journal of Regulation* 4 (1987): 393–494.

58. Alfred E. Kahn, "I Would Do It Again," *Regulation*, 1988, Number 2: 22–28.

59. Alfred E. Kahn, "Surprises of Airline Deregulation," *American Economic Review* 78 (May 1988): 316–22.

60. Franklin M. Fisher, "Pan American to United: The Pacific Division Transfer Case," *Rand Journal of Economics* 18 (Winter 1987): 492–508.

61. "Happiness is a Cheap Seat," *The Economist*, February 4, 1989, pp. 68, 71.

62. Steven A. Morrison and Clifford Winston, "The Evolution of the Airline Industry," Northeastern University, photocopy, August 1994.

63. Data is for 1992; Morrison and Winston, 1994.

64. Alfred E. Kahn, "The Competitive Consequences of Hub Dominance: A Case Study," *Review of Industrial Organization* 8 (August 1993): 381–405.

65. Severin Borenstein, "Hubs and High Fares: Dominance and Market Power in the U.S. Airline Industry," *RAND Journal of Economics* 20 (Autumn 1989): 344–65.

66. E. Han Kim and Vijay Singal, "Mergers and Market Power: Evidence from the Airline Industry," *American Economic Review* 83 (June 1993): 544–69.

At least since the industrial revolution, the energy industry has been critical in the world economy. Energy is an essential input in almost all production processes, whether it is the use of gasoline by truckers to transport commodities, the use of electricity to run computers in an office, the use of natural gas to heat residential homes, or the use of coal to run a manufacturing plant. Because of its importance to economic activity, the price of energy and the availability of energy sources can have substantial ramifications on an economy. It is believed that energy prices play an important role in the business cycle. Figure 18.1 shows that of the six recessions in the United States between 1947 and 1975, all but one were preceded by a dramatic increase in the price of crude oil. The average lag between this upward price shock and the onset of a recession was around nine months. In addition to their impact on the supply and demand for energy, this evidence suggests that energy prices have significant macroeconomic implications as well.

There is considerable diversity in the sources of energy. The variety of energy sources as well as their relative importance have changed remarkably over time. Since 1850, the major sources of energy in the United States have been wood, coal, crude oil, natural gas, hydroelectric power, and nuclear power. Before 1900 wood and coal were the dominant sources of energy. During the period 1900–1950 wood became quite insignificant, while oil and gas joined coal as the central energy sources. Since 1950 oil and gas have increasingly replaced coal, while nuclear power has entered the market as a new energy source.[1] Because these products are very different in a physical sense, the standard unit of measurement for energy is the British thermal unit (BTU), where one BTU equals the amount of heat required to raise the temperature of one pound of water by one degree Fahrenheit.

In considering the energy market, it is important to recognize that it is inherently international in scope. Because coal and oil are relatively inexpensive to transport, there are significant international flows of these energy sources. Being more expensive to transport, there are considerably smaller flows of natural gas across countries. Figure 18.2 depicts the relative size of these flows. Because the international nature of the energy market creates a role for government policies, countries as well as producers and consumers are players in the world market for energy.

The objective of this chapter is to review and evaluate the economic regulation of the U.S. energy market. Our focus will be on government intervention in the crude-oil and natural-gas industries. State and federal regulation of the production of crude oil dates back to the early part of the twentieth century, whereas federal regulation of crude oil prices

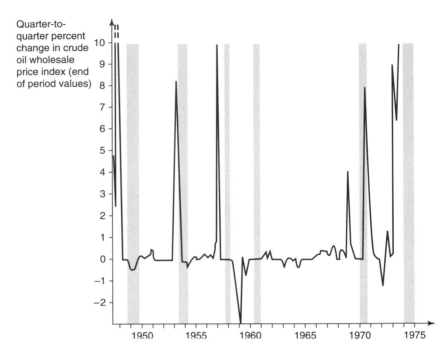

Figure 18.1
Changes in Crude Oil Prices and U.S. Recessions, 1947–1975
Source: James D. Hamilton, "Oil and the Macroeconomy since World War II," *Journal of Political Economy* 91 (April 1983): 228–48. Reprinted by permission of The University of Chicago Press.

took place during the 1970s. Although the natural-gas market has been subject to federal regulation since the 1930s, price regulation did not take place until the mid-1950s. In spite of considerable deregulation in 1985, the natural gas industry was only fully deregulated in 1989.

As we will observe, the regulatory regimes for the oil and gas industries were quite distinct, but they are common in that both regimes entailed the establishment of price ceilings that acted to constrain the price that oil and gas producers could charge for their products. Recall that a similar pricing constraint was placed upon the railroad industry during its time of regulation. However, a critical distinction exists between railroad price regulation and energy price regulation. The railroad was considered to be a common carrier, so that it was required by the Interstate Commerce Commission to meet all demand at the government established price. In contrast, oil and gas producers were under no such obligation. As a result, price ceilings generated shortages in the oil and gas markets as consumers demanded more units than firms were willing to supply.

World crude oil flow, 1986

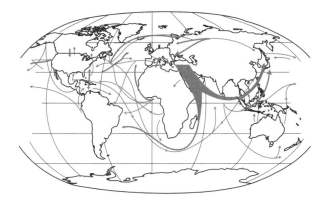

World natural gas flow, 1986

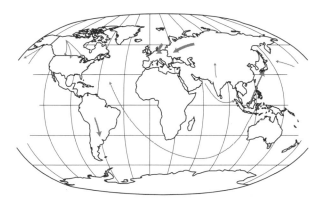

World coal flow, 1986

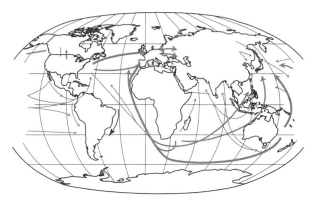

Figure 18.2
International Energy Flows
Source: International Energy Annual, Department of Energy, 1986.

In the next section, we briefly review the welfare implications of economic regulation that is characterized by price being set below the competitive equilibrium price and in which firms' supply decisions are left unregulated. With this foundation, we will examine the regulation of the domestic crude oil producing industry. In addition to reviewing the implications of federal price regulation, we will investigate the state regulation of production through what is called prorationing. Our analysis will then turn to assessing the implications of price regulation in the natural gas industry.

The Theory of Price Ceilings

The objective of this section is to provide a simple analysis of the welfare implications of price ceilings. Once we review the regulatory practices used in the oil and gas industries, it will become apparent that price regulation was considerably more complex than the regulatory structure analyzed in this section. In spite of this, our analysis should be relevant to more complex systems of price regulation as long as they involve some form of a price ceiling.

Consider the market for a product and let us suppose that in the absence of any government regulation that it is competitive. In Figure 18.3 the market supply function $S(P)$ is shown along with the market demand function $D(P)$. At a competitive equilibrium, the market clears at a price of P^* with Q^* units being sold. Now impose a price ceiling on this market; that is, the government restricts firms to setting price no higher than the ceiling. If the price ceiling is at least as great as P^*, then government regulation is nonbinding. Given current supply and demand conditions, firms and consumers have no desire to change their decisions so as to move price towards the price ceiling and away from P^*. Of course, if market demand shifted out or market supply shifted in, then the market-clearing price would rise, in which case the price ceiling might become binding.

To consider the case of a binding price ceiling, suppose it is set at $\overline{P}$ and $\overline{P}$ is less than the competitive equilibrium price P^* (see Figure 18.3). At a price of $\overline{P}$, market demand of $D(\overline{P})$ exceeds $S(\overline{P})(=\overline{Q})$, which is the amount that firms are willing to supply at a price of $\overline{P}$. The implications of this price ceiling is that output is reduced from Q^* to $\overline{Q}$. In contrast to the case of unfettered competition, consumers gain the rectangle $P^*df\overline{P}$ from paying $P^* - \overline{P}$ less per unit on $\overline{Q}$ units. On the other hand, consumers lose surplus measured by triangle bcd as $Q^* - \overline{Q}$ less units are supplied. Thus, the net gain to consumers is the difference be-

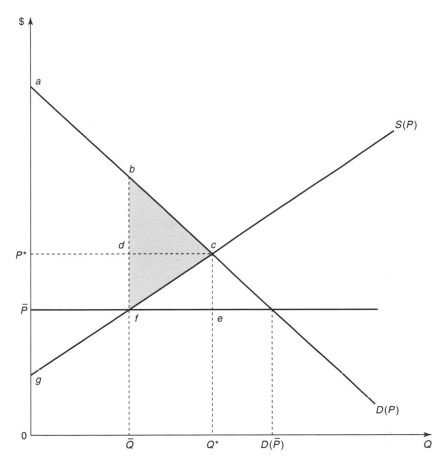

Figure 18.3
The Effects of a Price Ceiling

tween rectangle $P^*df\overline{P}$ and triangle bcd. On the other hand, firms clearly lose by the imposition of a price ceiling. In its absence, producer surplus is the triangle P^*cg. With the price ceiling, producers lose surplus of triangle dcf on the reduced supply of $Q^* - \overline{Q}$ and lose rectangle $P^*df\overline{P}$ to consumers through the lower price. Summing the change in consumer and producer surplus, the net effect of the price ceiling is a welfare loss measured by the shaded triangle bcf.

In confining the welfare loss to the triangle bcf, an implicit and important assumption is made. We have assumed that the $\overline{Q}$ units supplied by the market go to the consumers that value them the most; that is, the consumers whose demand is represented by the demand curve from 0 to $\overline{Q}$. Because there is excess demand of $D(\overline{P}) - \overline{Q}$, it is important from a welfare perspective as to how the $\overline{Q}$ units are allocated among consumers.

To analyze this issue in a simple manner, assume that each consumer wants to buy one unit or nothing. Consumers differ by their reservation price, the highest price that a consumer is willing to pay for the good. That is, at a price for the good equal to his reservation price, a consumer is indifferent between purchasing the good at that price and not purchasing the good. Obviously, if the market price is less than his reservation price, a consumer strictly prefers to buy the good. According to this formulation, we can then interpret the market-demand function as stating that there are a total of $D(P)$ consumers with a reservation price at least as great as P.

Now suppose that the $\overline{Q}$ units are randomly allocated to consumers, perhaps by government mandate. At a price $\overline{P}$, a total of $D(\overline{P})$ consumers want to buy the available $\overline{Q}$ units. Therefore, only a fraction $\overline{Q}/D(\overline{P})$ of consumers who want to buy the good at a price of $\overline{P}$ are able to do so. With random allocation of the $\overline{Q}$ units, this means that, for example, only $[\overline{Q}/D(\overline{P})]D(P')$ of the $D(P')$ consumers with a reservation price at least as high as P' will be able to purchase the good. The allocation rule is then depicted as the curve $[\overline{Q}/D(\overline{P})]D(P)$ in Figure 18.4. Let us now reexamine the welfare loss due to the imposition of a price ceiling reveals. In addition to the welfare loss of triangle bcf due to reduced supply, there is a welfare loss of triangle abf resulting from the limited supply not being allocated to those consumers who value the good the most. For the good to be properly allocated, the $\overline{Q}$ units should go to those consumers with reservation prices at least as high as P^o. Their surplus equals trapezoid $abf\overline{P}$. Alternatively, with random allocation of the $\overline{Q}$ units, only a fraction $\overline{Q}/D(\overline{P})$ of those consumers get to buy the good. The remaining units are allocated to consumers who value them less; specifically, those consumers with reservation prices ranging from $\overline{P}$ to P^o. Because now the consumers' surplus is only triangle $af\overline{P}$, random allocation results in an additional welfare loss of triangle abf and a total welfare loss of triangle acf.

An important implicit assumption in the above analysis is that consumers cannot resell the good (or, alternatively, cannot resell the right to buy the good). If they are allowed to do so, then the welfare loss abf may be avoided. Consumers fortunate enough to be allocated the good can resell it to the highest bidder through the secondary market. If the costs of engaging in this transaction are small, then the units should end up in the hands of those consumers who value them the most, regardless of to whom they were initially given. In that case, the only effect of random allocation is to distribute surplus to those consumers who are lucky enough to be given property rights over this valuable commodity.

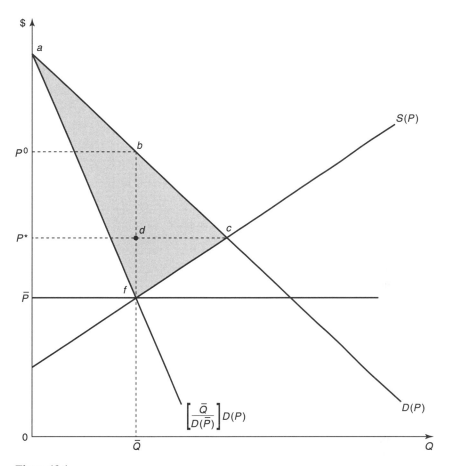

Figure 18.4
The Effects of a Price Ceiling with Random Allocation

Suppose instead that the allocation of the $\overline{Q}$ units is determined not by random allocation but rather by the suppliers. One would expect consumers to compete for the $\overline{Q}$ units and for those consumers with the highest reservation prices to spend the most in trying to get them. This might entail providing some form of bribe to a firm, or perhaps simply waiting in line. Competitive activity for the purpose of gaining access to products in short supply was regularly observed in the Soviet Union for standard household items and in the United States for such items as concert tickets. With competition being the mechanism for allocating the good, there is no longer the welfare loss that occurred from random allocation. However, there is instead a different type of welfare loss. If consumers use real resources to compete for these goods, then the value of those resources to society represents an additional welfare loss from price regulation. If instead consumers compete by using pecuniary resources, such as paying a financial bribe to a firm, then there is only a transfer and thus no associated welfare loss.

Two basic points are to be derived from this analysis. First, the imposition of a binding price ceiling reduces social welfare by decreasing the amount exchanged in the market. Second, in light of there being excess demand, how the good is allocated to consumers can create additional welfare losses. The good may not end up with those consumers who value it the most and/or consumers may use resources in competing with one another for the right to purchase the good at the government restricted price.

Price and Quantity Regulation of the Crude Oil Industry

Although the first oil well in the United States dates from 1859, oil did not become an important energy source until the early twentieth century. Even as late as 1920, oil made up only 11 percent of energy consumption in the United States.[2] The term *petroleum* is often equated with crude oil, but it actually refers to all natural hydrocarbons except for those in the coal family. In particular, petroleum includes natural gas as well as crude oil. In this section, we will focus upon the regulation of the production and pricing of domestic crude oil.

Technological Structure

The oil industry comprises three divisions: production, refining, and distribution. Because oil is normally found in underground reservoirs, the first step in production is exploration to discover an oil reservoir. The second step is development of the reservoir. This entails drilling a hole that creates a low-pressure point in the reservoir that then forces oil up to the surface. The third and final step in production is extraction of oil from the reservoir.[3] On its extraction, the next step in the process is the refining of crude oil into usable products. Finally, refined oil is distributed to retailers and consumers where distribution entails both the transportation and marketing of the product. Many firms in the oil industry are vertically integrated in that they perform production, refining, and distribution.

Economic Background

There are several notable features to the market for crude oil. Because of the relatively low cost of transportation and the geographic concentration of oil reserves, the market for oil is international in scope. (This is clear from Figure 18.2). As a result, major players include not only firms and consumers but also governments. Two particularly important players are, on the demand side, the United States and, on the supply side, the Organization of Petroleum Exporting Countries (OPEC).

A second important characteristic of the oil market is that it has a rather volatile history. There are several sources of this volatility. First, energy demand moves with the business cycle. When an economy moves into a recession, demand for manufactured goods fall so that inventories build up. In response to increased inventories, manufacturing production slows down. Because energy is an input in manufacturing, demand for energy then falls as an economy moves into a recession. By the same logic, an economic boom raises the demand for energy inputs. Thus, one source of volatility in the energy market is the sensitivity of energy demand to the business cycle. Of course, this is by no means sufficient to explain all volatility because many products are sensitive to the business cycle yet are not as volatile in terms of price and supply as is the market for energy.

On the supply side, an important source of volatility is that new discoveries of oil reserves can cause quite drastic increases in the size of known reserves. Typically, the result is an upward shock in supply and a downward shock in price. Finally, the geographic concentration of oil reserves creates the opportunity for short-run supply shocks due to disruptions in production and/or transportation. Table 18.1 lists the major events that have caused sharp increases in the price of crude oil since World War II.

Finally, one must note the importance of the United States in the world oil market. Originally, the United States was the dominant producer of oil, supplying 88 percent of world crude oil in 1880, 71 percent in 1925, and 52 percent in 1950. However, its importance has been declining throughout most of this century and particularly since World War II. By 1960, U.S. production was down to 27 percent of world production, and this had fallen to 16 percent by 1984.[4] On the consumption side, the United States has been and continues to be an important force. U.S. consumption of oil has grown tremendously since 1900, rising tenfold from 1900 to 1919 and another tenfold from 1919 to 1964. It peaked around 1978.[5]

OPEC

Even the briefest of descriptions of the oil industry must cover the the greatest cartel of our time—OPEC. Formed in September 1960, OPEC initially comprised the major oil exporting nations of Iran, Iraq, Kuwait, Saudi Arabia, and Venezuela. In addition to these five countries,

Table 18.1
Principal Causes of Crude Oil Price Increases, 1947–1981

Oil Price Episode	Principal Factors
1947–48	Previous investment in production and transportation capacity inadequate to meet postwar needs; decreased coal production resulting from shorter work week; European reconstruction.
1952–53	Iranian nationalization; strikes by oil, coal, and steel workers; import posture of Texas Railroad Commission.
1956–57	Suez crisis.
1969	Secular decline in U.S. reserves; strikes by oil workers.
1970	Rupture of trans-Arabian pipeline; Libyan production cutbacks; coal price increases (strikes by coal workers; increased coal exports; environmental legislation).
1973–74	Stagnating U.S. production; OPEC embargo.
1978–79	Iranian revolution.
1980–81	Iran-Iraq war; removal of U.S. price controls.

Source: James D. Hamilton, "A Brief Postwar History of Oil Prices and the U.S. Economy," University of Virginia, mimeo, 1982.

OPEC consists today of Algeria, Indonesia, Libya, Nigeria, and the United Arab Emirates.

Generally, the OPEC cartel has functioned by establishing a price for crude oil and then allocating output quotas among its members so as to maintain this price. The key member of the cartel is Saudi Arabia. As the member with the largest oil reserves, Saudi Arabia has been the "swing producer" whose responsibility was to adjust its production in order that the cartel price be achieved. Saudi Arabia has been regularly called upon to produce below its quota in order to compensate for overproduction by its fellow OPEC members. After persistent cheating by cartel members throughout the 1980s, Saudi Arabia eventually chose to forsake its role as the swing producer.

As a cartel, OPEC was not very successful until the early 1970s. At the beginning of October 1973 the posted price of Saudi Arabian light crude oil was $2.80 per barrel. However, by October 16 the price had jumped to $4.76 per barrel. This dramatic price increase was caused by an Arab embargo on oil shipments to the United States as a result of the fourth Arab-Israeli war. But the worse was yet to come for the oil-importing nations. An even greater price shock occurred in January 1974 as the price of crude oil rose to $10.84 per barrel. In the span of less than four months, the price of crude oil had increased almost fourfold.

Due to the events listed in Table 18.1, oil prices have continued to be subject to large price shocks. In response to the Iranian revolution and the ensuing Iran-Iraq war, the price of a barrel of crude oil increased from \$13.34 in January 1979 to \$34.00 by October 1981.[6] Throughout much of the 1980s, OPEC was subject to considerable overproduction by its members with the result being a falling price for crude oil. However, the price of oil can always shoot back up in response to new events; witness the 1990 Iraqi occupation of Kuwait.

Regulatory History

Beginning with the Standard Oil case in 1911, there is a long history of government involvement in the U.S. oil industry. Of course, that case concerned the oil-refining industry and the focus of this chapter is on the oil-producing industry. The consumers in our study are made up of domestic refining companies whereas the producers are domestic and foreign firms that extract oil from wells. To provide an overview, state and federal regulation from the early part of this century to about 1970 was designed to limit the supply of crude oil. This was achieved through restrictions on the production of domestic firms and on exports to the United States by foreign oil producers. From 1970 to 1981 federal regulation switched from this pro-producer stance to one less favorable to the oil industry as regulation constrained the price that domestic oil companies could charge for their product.

Prorationing

The goal of regulating domestic oil production dates to 1909, when Oklahoma authorized its Corporation Commission to limit the production of wells in the state. Similar powers were given to the Railroad Commission in Texas in 1919. However, not until 1928 were the first individual field proration orders issued. These orders limited production by allocating the total production allowed pro rata among wells. Such a mechanism is referred to as *prorationing*.

Events in 1926–1931 spurred a wave of state intervention in the production of oil. One critical event was the discovery of new reserves, in particular, the East Texas oil field in 1930. This was a 5.5 billion barrel reservoir that by 1933 had 1,000 firms with a total of 10,000 wells pumping oil from it.[7] Because of this massive increase in supply, along with the reduction in oil demand resulting from the Great Depression, oil prices fell sharply. Pursuing the lead of Oklahoma, Texas instituted prorationing in 1930 and Kansas followed in 1931. The federal government aided the oil-producing states by passing the Connally "Hot Oil" Act of 1935, which prohibited the interstate shipment of oil that was extracted in violation of state regulations.

In addition to prorationing, oil production was restricted through the requirement of minimum spacing between oil wells. States typically required at least twenty acres per well while the federal government, due to the need for conservation during World War II, required a minimum of forty acres. After World War II, an additional twenty-two states added conservation laws that gave state government the right to restrict oil production.

Mandatory Oil Import Program

Before 1957 the United States had no controls on the import of crude oil. In that year, motivated by rising imports, President Dwight Eisenhower called for a voluntary reduction by domestic oil refiners. Previously, the oil-producing states had responded to an increase in oil imports by reducing prorationing orders so as to maintain the domestic price. Needless to say, this policy of voluntary restraint did not work. The program then became involuntary in 1959 with the Mandatory Oil Import Program (MOIP).

Oil Price Controls

With rising inflation, President Richard Nixon instituted an economy-wide price freeze in August 1971. Two years after this freeze, Phase IV decontrolled all prices with the exception of crude oil. These controls were set to expire in April 1974, but oil price regulation continued unabated until President Ronald Reagan, in his first act, decontrolled oil prices. A synopsis of crude oil price controls from 1971 to 1989 is provided in Table 18.2.

By the early 1970s the other two forms of regulation had become extinct. States had stopped restricting domestic oil production while MOIP was ended in 1973. In November 1973, Phase IV was replaced with the Emergency Petroleum Allocation Act (EPAA). It instituted price ceilings on oil and an entitlements program for allocating this price-controlled oil to refiners. To be able to process one barrel of price-controlled domestic oil, a refiner needed one entitlement. Control over oil prices moved from the Cost of Living Council to the Federal Energy Administration (FEA) in May 1974.

Although President Gerald Ford favored decontrol of oil prices, the Energy Policy Conservation Act (EPCA) went into effect in December 1975. This program rolled back some oil prices, but it called only for gradual decontrol starting in early 1976. Interested in further decontrolling oil prices, President Jimmy Carter put forth a plan of gradual decontrol from June 1979 to September 1981, at which time EPCA was to expire. Concerned with the transfer of wealth from consumers to domestic oil producers under decontrol (as prices would presumably rise),

Table 18.2
Crude Oil Price Controls, 1971–1988

Program	Period	Price Regulations
Economic Stabilization		
Phase I	8/71 to 11/71	Economy-wide price freeze.
Phase II	11/71 to 1/73	Controlled price increases to reflect cost increase with profit limitations.
Phase III	1/73 to 8/73	Voluntary increases up to 1.5% annually for cost increases.
Special Rule No. 1	3/73 to 8/73	Mandatory controls for 23 largest oil companies.
Phase IV	8/73 to 11/73	Two-tier pricing; old oil at level of 5/15/73 plus $0.35, new oil, stripper oil, and "released" oil uncontrolled.
Reaction to Shortage		
Emergency Petroleum Allocation Act (EPAA)	11/73 to 12/75	Same as Phase IV plus entitlements program.
Energy Policy and Conservation Act (EPCA)	12/75 to 9/81	Lower tier (old) oil at $5.25, upper tier (new) oil at $11.28, stripper oil decontrolled (9/76), composite price at $7.66, provision for inflation increases.
Compromising Decontrol		
Administrative Decontrol	6/79 to 1/81	Under EPCA authority, phased decontrol of lower and upper tier oil.
Windfall Profits Tax	3/80 to 8/88	Tax on difference between controlled prices and market price.

Source: This is an adapted and updated version of Chart 10-1 in Richard H. K. Vietor, *Energy Policy in America Since 1945* (Cambridge: Cambridge University Press, 1984). Reprinted by permission of Cambridge University Press.

President Carter instituted the Crude Oil Windfall Profits Tax of 1980. In actuality, this was not a profits tax but rather an excise tax on oil. Ahead of the schedule outlined by President Carter, President Reagan lifted all remaining oil price controls in January 1981. Finally, in October 1988, President Reagan signed a bill repealing the Windfall Profits Tax.

Oil Prorationing

Regulatory Practices

Regulatory procedures varied across states. The following is representative of the process by which oil was prorationed.[8] To begin, each oil well in a state is assigned a maximum allowable rate of production. Let Q^a denote the sum of these maximum allowable rates across all wells. For each month, the prospective market demand is estimated at the current price for oil. Adjusting this demand projection for anticipated changes in inventories, the resulting number is the target rate of production. Let us denote it Q^t. If Q^t exceeds Q^a, then each well was restricted to producing no more than its maximum allowable rate. If instead Q^a exceeds Q^t then total oil production in the state is restricted to Q^t. In that case, Q^t is allocated in the following manner. First, production is allocated to those special wells that are exempt from prorationing. Let the total production of these wells be denoted Q^e. The remainder, $Q^t - Q^e$, is allocated to non-exempt wells in proportion to their respective maximum allowable rates. For example, a well with an allowable rate of Q^o would be allowed to produce $(Q^o/Q^a)(Q^t - Q^e)$. Table 18.3 shows the average percentage of the maximum allowable rates in several oil-producing states during 1948–1966. Prorationing clearly imposed severe restrictions on oil production.

Table 18.3
Annual Average of Monthly Market Demand Factors (Percentage)

Year	Texas	Louisiana	New Mexico[a]	Oklahoma
1948	100	[b]	63	[c]
1949	65	[b]	61	[c]
1950	63	[b]	69	[c]
1951	76	[b]	74	[c]
1952	71	[b]	68	[c]
1953	65	90	63	[c]
1954	53	61	57	[c]
1955	53	48	57	60
1956	52	42	56	53
1957	47	43	56	52
1958	33	33	49	45
1959	34	34	50	41
1960	28	34	49	35
1961	28	32	49	31
1962	27	32	50	35
1963	28	32	54	31
1964	28	32	54	28
1965	29	33	56	27
1966	34	35	65	38

[a] Southeast area only.
[b] No fixed allowable schedule.
[c] Comparable data not available.

Source: Respective state conservation committees. Table is from Stephen L. McDonald, *Petroleum Conservation in the United States: An Economic Analysis* (Baltimore: Johns Hopkins University Press, 1971). Reprinted by permission of Resources for the Future, Washington, D.C.

Rationale for Prorationing

State Government as a Cartel Manager

One interpretation of prorationing is that it is a scheme whereby the state acts as a cartel manager. By restricting production, the price of oil is kept above the competitive level; this allows above-normal profits to be earned by the oil companies. Because the loss in consumer surplus from output restrictions is distributed over the entire United States but the gain in firm profits is largely concentrated in the oil-producing states, one could imagine a policy of prorationing to be in the welfare interests of an individual state, though certainly not in the interests of the United States as a whole.

Common Pool Problem

An alternative rationale, and one with quite different welfare implications, is that prorationing solves a common pool problem. A common pool problem arises when two or more individuals share property rights over some resource. As explained below, these common property rights can result in the inefficient use of a resource.

To begin, let us consider the case of a resource which is owned by a single individual.[9] Consider a newly discovered oil reservoir and suppose it is entirely contained within the landholdings of a single individual. The landowner (or the company to which he has assigned mineral rights) has to decide how fast to extract the oil. For simplicity, suppose there are just two periods: period 1 (today) and period 2 (tomorrow). We will need to introduce a little notation. Let P_t and Q_t denote the price and extraction rate, respectively, in period t. $MC_t(Q)$ denotes the marginal cost of extracting at a rate Q in period t.

Suppose that the landowner is initially thinking about pumping Q_1 barrels of oil today and Q_2 tomorrow. If he considers pumping a little more oil today, the change in today's profit is $P_1 - MC_1(Q_1)$. The landowner sells that additional barrel for P_1 and it costs him $MC_1(Q_1)$ to extract it. In addition, extracting more oil today has an impact on tomorrow's profit. The technology of oil reservoirs is such that pumping at a faster rate reduces the amount of oil that can ultimately be recovered. If extraction is too fast, then there is a loss in subsurface pressure so that pockets of oil become trapped. Less oil can then be retrieved from the well. Let b denote the number of units of oil that cannot be extracted tomorrow due to an additional barrel being extracted today. The discounted loss in tomorrow's profit from extracting a little more today is then $b(1/(1+r))[P_2 - MC_2(Q_2)]$ where r is the interest rate. In other words, for each additional barrel pumped today, b fewer barrels can be pumped tomorrow and each of those barrels represents foregone profit of $P_2 - MC_2(Q_2)$. This loss is discounted since it is not incurred until tomorrow. We conclude that the discounted marginal return to pumping another barrel today is

$$[P_1 - MC_1(Q_1)] - b(1/(1+r))[P_2 - MC_2(Q_2)]$$

The landowner can go through the same thought exercise concerning tomorrow's rate of extraction. By pumping a little more oil tomorrow, he will receive additional revenue of P_2 at a cost of $MC_2(Q_2)$ so that his discounted marginal return is $(1/(1+r))[P_2 - MC_2(Q_2)]$.

Let Q_1^* and Q_2^* denote the rates of extraction for today and tomorrow, respectively, that maximize the present value of the landowner's profit stream. We will argue that these rates must be set so as to equate the marginal return from pumping another barrel today and pumping another barrel tomorrow:

$$P_1 - MC_1(Q_1^*) - b(1/(1+r))[P_2 - MC_2(Q_2^*)] = (1/(1+r))[P_2 - MC_2(Q_2^*)] \tag{18.1}$$

To see that profit maximization requires this to be true, suppose that the marginal return from pumping more today exceeded the marginal return from pumping more tomorrow:

$$P_1 - MC_1(Q_1) - b(1/(1+r))[P_2 - MC_2(Q_2)] > (1/(1+r))[P_2 - MC_2(Q_2)]$$

By shifting the pumping of one barrel from tomorrow to today, the landowner loses discounted profit of $(1/(1+r))[P_2 - MC_2(Q_2)]$ but gains discounted profit of

$$P_1 - MC_1(Q_1) - b(1/(1+r))[P_2 - MC_2(Q_2)]$$

Because the latter expression is bigger, the net change in the present value of the profit stream is positive. But if this is true, then the original extraction rates must not have been optimal. Therefore, if the marginal returns from pumping more today and more tomorrow are not equated, the landowner can shift extraction between the two periods so as to increase the present value of his profit stream. We conclude that profit maximization requires that those marginal returns be equated, as expressed in (18.1). Furthermore, because P_t is presumed to measure the marginal social benefit from a unit of oil in period t, profit maximization also achieves the rates of extraction that maximize social welfare.

Where the common pool problem arises is if the oil reservoir spans the property of two or more individuals. According to U.S. law, property rights over the oil reservoir are determined by the rule of capture. This rule states that any extracted oil belongs to the landowner who captures it through a well on his land. Thus, if an oil reservoir spans several properties, there are several individuals who have the right to extract oil from it. To capture the effect of other landowners extracting oil from a common reservoir, let x be the fraction of a barrel drained by neighbors by postponing pumping another unit today. That is, if a landowner considers pumping one less barrel today, he will not find that entire barrel in the reservoir tomorrow. Only a fraction $1 - x$ of that barrel would remain for his neighbors would have extracted the other fraction x of it. The condition for profit maximization is no longer (18.1) but instead the following expression:

$$P_1 - MC_1(\overline{Q}_1) - (1 - x)b(1/(1 + r))(P_2 - MC_2(\overline{Q}_2)) =$$
$$(1 - x)(1/(1 + r))[P_2 - MC_2(\overline{Q}_2)] \tag{18.2}$$

where $\overline{Q}_1$ and $\overline{Q}_2$ denote the new profit-maximizing rates of extraction. Note that if $x = 0$ (as is true if there is no common pool problem), (18.2) is the same as (18.1). The key implication of $x > 0$ is that a landowner has an incentive to extract at a faster rate today; that is, $\overline{Q}_1 > Q_1^*$. For every barrel of oil not pumped today, a landowner loses x of that barrel to his neighbors. Because the pool is shrinking over time because of one's neighbors also drawing from it, an individual landowner has an incentive to speed up extraction so as to acquire oil before it is acquired by the other landowners. Each landowner engages in this practice of fast extraction so that the overall rate of extraction is higher than when it is owned by one individual.

With a common pool problem such as this one, profit maximization by each landowner results in a rate of extraction that exceeds the socially optimal rate. Each owner is induced to pump more today, relative to the social optimum, because postponing extraction is costly because the other landowners will drain the field in the meantime. To see this result graphically, we can rewrite equation (18.1) as follows:

$$P_1 = MC_1(Q_1) + SUC$$

where

$$SUC = (1 + b)(1/(1 + r))[P_2 - MC_2(Q_2)]$$

and SUC stands for "social user cost." P_1 is the marginal revenue from pumping one more barrel today while $MC_1(Q_1) + SUC$ is the marginal cost to society from pumping that additional barrel. It comprises the marginal cost of pumping it, $MC_1(Q_1)$, and SUC, which is the future

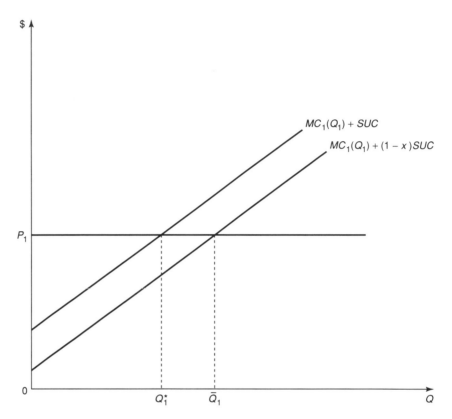

Figure 18.5
The Effect of Oil Prorationing on the Extraction Rate

cost to society of pumping another unit today. When there is just one landowner, private user cost is the same as social user cost. It follows that the profit-maximizing rate of extraction then satisfies

$$P_1 = MC_1(Q_1^*) + SUC$$

This is depicted in Figure 18.5. When instead there is a common pool problem, the cost to an individual landowner from extracting one more barrel is less than the cost to society. The reason is that the landowner is concerned about leaving a barrel in the ground because it may be extracted by one's neighbors. However, society does not care who extracts the oil (assuming that all landowners are equally efficient in extraction). When there is more than one landowner extracting oil from the same reservoir, an individual landowner's private user cost equals $(1 - x)SUC$, which falls short of social user cost. The profit-maximizing rate of extraction, $\overline{Q}_1$, then satisfies

$$P_1 = MC_1(\overline{Q}_1) + (1 - x)SUC$$

As shown in Figure 18.5, the common pool problem results in the rate of extraction exceeding the socially optimal rate.

Competition did indeed appear to cause excessive early extraction in the Texas oil fields during the 1920s and 1930s. It is estimated that the actual recovery of oil from a particular reservoir was around 20–25 percent of total oil reserves. In contrast, with controlled withdrawal, one could have extracted 80–95 percent.[10] Of course, this is not necessarily evidence that extraction was too fast because the social optimum might have called for quick extraction to the point of low ultimate recovery if the marginal social benefit from a barrel of oil in the early years was high relative to what it was expected to be in later years. However, the lack of variation in price over time and the substantial amount of oil lost through such fast rates of extraction would suggest that it is unlikely that such a fast rate of extraction rate was socially optimal.

Thus far we have shown competition results in excessive extraction for a given number of wells. In addition, owners might find it optimal to build more wells than is socially optimal in order to increase the rate of extraction. For example, the social optimum may require only one well for the reservoir, whereas profit maximization results in each landowner having at least one well. Because the construction of these additional wells uses up real resources, the value of those resources represent an additional welfare loss. If some of the additional oil that is pumped is not sent immediately to market but rather is stored, the cost of storage is another welfare loss for it is socially optimal to store oil in the ground. However, when a landowner is competing with other landowners for oil from the same reservoir, storage in the ground is costly as some of it will be extracted by other landowners in the future. It may be more profitable to pump it early and store it above ground.

There are several other implications from the common pool problem. The fact that other firms are extracting at a fast pace reduces a firm's profits from a well and thus reduces the potential gains from exploration, relative to an environment in which production is controlled in a socially optimal manner. Thus, the common pool problem can reduce the incentive to explore. One can also expect greater volatility in oil prices. When a new discovery is made, all landowners will rush to pump out oil before everyone else does. As a result, there is an upward shock in supply, which causes a downward shock in price. Once the extraction is completed, price then increases again.

Solutions to the Common Pool Problem

Although competition does not result in the social welfare optimum when there is a common pool problem, this need not imply a role for government intervention. As it turns out, there are several private mechanisms that may be able to solve the common pool problem. In some ways the simplest solution is to have a single individual own all the land over an oil reservoir (or at least the mineral rights). Of course, this is feasible only if a single landowner can earn greater profits than the sum of the profits that would be earned by the multiple landowners. Only then would an individual be able to buy up the land from the various landowners and turn a profit by doing so. When there is a common pool problem, this is indeed true because a single landowner can coordinate extraction on different lands and thereby earn a higher return. As a result, it is possible for an individual to pay each landowner an amount in excess of what they would otherwise earn and for the total payments made to the landowners to be less than the value of the combined land.

Alternatively, one could achieve the same objective through unitization. Unitization involves one of the owners being selected to develop the reservoir, but with the returns shared by all parties. Of course, parties must agree ex ante as to how to share these returns. A third solution is for the landowners to privately agree to prorationing and thereby limit their production.

In light of all these private solutions, why has there then been state intervention? These private solutions sound simple, but they can be rather difficult to implement. First, there are the transactions costs entailed in putting together any contract. If there are several hundred landowners, it will be quite costly for an individual to negotiate to buy several hundred properties. By similar reasoning, unitization and private prorationing will have large transactions costs when there are many landowners. A second problem is getting all of the landowners to agree. Each will probably have different information on and opinions about the value of the reservoir. In addition, some landowners are likely to try to hold out for a higher price for their land or a higher share of profits in the case of unitization or a higher share of production in the case of private prorationing. Such behavior can prevent an agreement from being reached. The costly and difficult nature of many agents coming to an agreement can often prevent these private mechanisms from solving the common pool problem. As a matter of fact, economists have studied attempts at private prorationing in Oklahoma and Texas during 1926–1935. They found that success in contracting was lower, the less concentrated was landownership. This suggests that the costs of reaching an agreement were indeed influential.[11]

In light of these difficulties, there can be a rationale for government intervention in the production of crude oil. When a common pool problem exists and private solutions are costly to implement, social welfare may be increased by the government imposition of production restrictions.

Effects of Prorationing

The evidence on the effects of instituting prorationing is both weak and relatively unsubstantive, but it still provides some insight into the potential welfare implications of this form of state regulation. First, anecdotal evidence has shown that prorationing increased the ultimate recovery of oil reservoirs. The productive lives of twenty fields in Arkansas, Louisiana, Oklahoma, and Texas were examined. Ten fields were developed before and ten after prorationing. For the pre-prorationing fields, the production rate in the fifteenth year was, on average, 8.6 percent of the peak production rate. In contrast, for the post-prorationing fields, the production rate was 73.9 percent of the peak rate in the fifteenth year.[12] This evidence is consistent with the predicted effect of prorationing, which is that it reduces early extraction rates and thereby increases ultimate recovery. However, conclusions drawn from this analysis are tentative in that it does not control for differences in the fields and does not compare these rates to the social optimum.

The predicted effect of prorationing on drilling costs is ambiguous. Because the maximum allowable production set by the state was directly dependent on the number of wells, there is an incentive to drill more wells. On the other hand, prorationing reduces production rates and thus reduces the need for more wells. The net effect on the number of wells is unclear. However, theory does predict that prorationing would increase the incentive to drill more costly wells because deeper wells were allocated a higher allowable rate of production and stripper wells, which produce at a low rate and high cost, were exempt from prorationing.

The evidence suggests that prorationing did increase the cost of production. It is believed that prorationing resulted in 23,000 additional wells in the East Texas oil field in the early 1930s.[13] As a result, the original maximum allowable production of 225 barrels per day set by the Railroad Commission in September 1931 had to be reduced to 37 barrels per day by December 1932 in order to maintain total production at a specified level.[14] A more systematic study estimated the additional exploration and drilling costs due to prorationing. It found for 1961 that these annual costs were higher by $2.15 billion (in 1961 dollars) as a result of prorationing.[15]

In evaluating prorationing, it appears to have raised drilling costs by increasing the incentive to drill wells. On the other hand, it is likely to have resulted in a more socially preferred rate of extraction as well as a higher degree of ultimate recovery. Unfortunately, the available evidence on the impact of prorationing is sufficiently sparse so as to make it difficult to draw any definitive conclusion concerning its net welfare effect.

Mandatory Oil Import Program

Regulatory Practices

The Mandatory Oil Import Program (MOIP) was put in place in 1959. While restrictions on oil imports were loosened in 1970, the MOIP was not suspended until April 1973. Officially, the rationale for limiting oil imports was that the United States was becoming too dependent on foreign oil and this created a national security risk. A more likely reason was to prop up domestic oil prices and increase the profits of domestic oil-producing firms. Whether or not this was intended, it was certainly an outcome of the program.

The MOIP initially restricted crude oil imports to 9 percent of projected domestic demand for oil. Due to the ambiguity of this criterion, the quota was changed to 12.2 percent of domestic oil production in 1962. Crude oil imports were subject to this quota, but residual fuel oil was not. It is notable that the MOIP applied only to oil refiners. Every oil refiner was given an import quota, regardless of their demand for oil imports prior to MOIP.

Effects of Regulation

In Figure 18.6, we have $D(P)$ denoting the domestic demand curve for oil and $S_d(P)$ denoting the supply curve of domestic oil producers. The world supply curve, denoted $S_w(P)$, is assumed to be horizontal at the world price P_w. To consider the effects of the MOIP, we first need to derive the market equilibrium in its absence. With no restrictions on oil imports, U.S. consumers would be supplied with $S_d(P)$ units of oil for prices less than or equal to P_w. At a price of P_w, there would be limitless supply, as represented by the world supply curve. Therefore, in the absence of the MOIP, the domestic equilibrium is defined by the intersection of $D(P)$ and $S_w(P)$. This results in a domestic price equal to the world price. Of the $D(P_w)$ units of demand, domestic oil producers would supply $S_d(P_w)$ whereas oil imports would be $D(P_w) - S_d(P_w)$.

Now consider the implementation of MOIP.[16] For simplicity, let us ignore the fact that residual fuel oil was exempt from the oil quota. In that case, oil imports were allowed to be 12.2 percent of domestic pro-

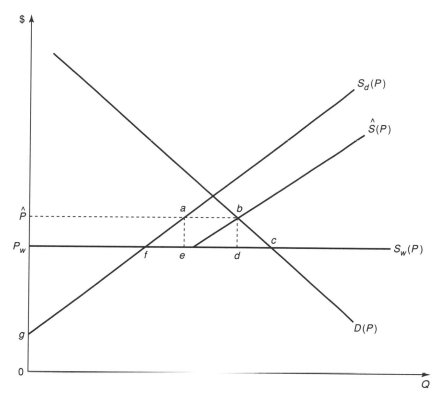

Figure 18.6
Equilibrium under the Mandatory Oil Import Program

duction. It follows that the supply curve faced by U.S. consumers, which we denote as $\hat{S}(P)$, is:

$$\hat{S}(P) = \begin{cases} S_d(P) & \text{if } 0 \le P < P_w \\ 1.122 S_d(P) & \text{if } P \ge P_w \end{cases}$$

If price is less than P_w, then it is below the world price so that total supply is that which is provided by domestic producers which is $S_d(P)$. If price is at least as high as P_w, then foreign producers are willing to supply as much as is demanded. However, the MOIP limits imports to 12.2 percent of domestic supply so that total supply is domestic supply of $S_d(P)$ plus oil imports of $(.122)S_d(P)$. This gives us the supply curve $\hat{S}(P)$.

According to Figure 18.6, the equilibrium price under MOIP is $\hat{P}$, which exceeds the world price. Notice that the MOIP has achieved its objective of reducing oil imports as they have fallen from $D(P_w) - S_d(P_w)$ (or distance cf) to $D(\hat{P}) - S_d(\hat{P})$ (or distance ba). In assessing the welfare effects of limiting oil imports, first note that consumers are worse off by the sum of rectangle $\hat{P}aeP_w$ and triangle bcd. Because demand decreases from $D(P_w)$ to $D(\hat{P})$, consumers lose surplus measured by triangle bcd. In addition, consumers have to pay a higher price of $\hat{P}$ on its remaining demand. However, this higher price is paid only for domestic oil so that its expenditure increases by $(\hat{P} - P_w)S_d(\hat{P})$ or rectangle $\hat{P}aeP_w$. Although consumers are made worse off, domestic oil producers receive higher profits because of the increase in demand for domestically produced oil. Oil import quotas increase domestic oil producers' profits from triangle P_wfg to triangle $\hat{P}ag$. Thus, domestic producer surplus rises by $\hat{P}afP_w$. Summing up the change in consumer surplus and domestic producer surplus, the welfare loss from MOIP is measured by the sum of triangles aef and bcd. Triangle bcd measures the foregone consumer surplus from the fall in demand from $D(P_w)$ to $D(\hat{P})$, whereas triangle aef measures the value of wasted resources from having domestic oil producers supply an additional amount of $S_d(\hat{P}) - S_d(P_w)$ rather than have it supplied more efficiently by importing oil at a price of P_w.

Studies have been conducted to estimate the welfare effect of limiting oil imports. To determine the price differential $\hat{P} - P_w$, one can use the resale price for import quota vouchers because the resale price should reflect the differential between the marginal cost of producing domestically produced oil and the price of importing another barrel of oil. Using this method, $\hat{P} - P_w$ was estimated to be \$1.174 per barrel for 1969.[17] To give an idea of the size of the differential, the average world price was around \$2.10 per barrel, so that import quotas raised the domestic price by over 50 percent. With this estimated price differential, one can derive a measure of the welfare loss from the MOIP if one has information on the domestic supply and demand curves. Based on estimated demand curves, Douglas Bohi and Milton Russell assume a long-run domestic demand elasticity of -0.5 and a long-run domestic supply elasticity of 1.0.[18] Their estimate of the cost to consumers in 1960 was \$3.2 billion, from which it steadily rose to \$6.6 billion for 1970.[19]

Crude Oil Price Controls

Regulatory Practices

There are two important aspects to the government regulation of the oil industry beginning in 1971.[20] First, a multitier pricing system was used that established different prices for oil according to the vintage of the well and other characteristics. The main reason for pursuing such a regulatory structure was to enhance incentives for domestic exploration by allowing higher prices for newly discovered oil. The second important aspect of regulatory practice was the entitlements program. This program determined how price-controlled oil was distributed among refiners.

Multitier Pricing

In setting price controls, EPAA delineated two types of oil, which were referred to as "old" oil and "new" oil. Old oil was all oil produced from an existing well at a production rate not in excess of the rate for May 1972. The price of a barrel of old oil was set at the price for May 15, 1973, plus $0.35. New oil included oil from new fields, oil produced in excess of 1972 levels from existing fields, and oil from properties that averaged less than 10 barrels per day. New oil was free of price controls. Furthermore, for each barrel of new oil produced, one barrel of old oil was released from price controls.

The pricing system became a bit more complicated under EPCA in that a three-tier system was instituted. The lower tier applied to oil produced below some base production control level (BPCL), whereas the upper tier applied to oil produced above the BPCL. However, all oil produced from wells developed after 1975 was classified as upper tier. BPCL was initially set at a property's average monthly production and sale of old crude oil during 1975. The initial price of lower tier oil was set at $5.25 per barrel in contrast to $11.28 per barrel for upper tier oil. Finally, the third tier included imported oil, stripper-well oil, and some other special cases. Third-tier oil was not subject to price controls. In addition to these three levels, the composite price of oil could not exceed $7.66 per barrel. The composite price was allowed to grow at the rate of inflation plus 3 percent with the growth rate not to exceed 10 percent.

Entitlements Program

At the inception of EPAA, the differential between the price of old and new oil was relatively small. This quickly changed when OPEC quadrupled the world price of oil between August 1973 and June 1974. Because the price of new oil was uncontrolled, a substantial difference between old and new oil prices emerged, which bestowed large windfall profits on refiners fortunate enough to be able to buy old oil. Because of the clear advantage given to some refiners, an entitlements program was instituted in November 1974 to allocate price-controlled oil.

To refine one barrel of price-controlled oil, a refiner needed to possess one entitlement. A refiner received entitlements equal to the number of barrels of price-controlled oil it would run if the percentage of price-controlled oil in its total crude oil input was the same as the national average. For example, the national average was 40 percent in December 1974 so that a refiner who processed 1,000,000 barrels of crude oil in that month would receive 400,000 ($= .40 \times 1,000,000$) entitlements. If it wanted to refine 500,000 of price-controlled oil, it would need an additional 100,000 entitlements, which it could acquire by buying them from other firms because entitlements were transferable.

Windfall Profits Tax

Like EPCA, the Windfall Profits Tax was a three-tier system but, unlike EPCA, it did not control prices. Rather, it levied an excise tax on domestic oil sales. Tier one included oil produced from fields that were producing prior to 1979. The difference between the price of tier one oil and some base price was taxed at a 70 percent rate. Tier two comprised stripper-well oil and oil produced from National Petroleum Reserves, and the differential between its price and a base price was taxed at a 60 percent rate. Finally, tier three was made up of new oil (that is, produced from wells developed after 1978) and oil released from tiers one and two. The tax rate on the differential between its price and a base price was 50 percent.

Effects of Price Regulation

In the absence of oil price regulation and with the assumption of price-taking behavior, the marginal revenue curve faced by domestic crude oil producers would be approximately equal to the world price. By distorting marginal revenue, regulation resulted in insufficient production by domestic suppliers. On the demand side, the imposition of price ceilings along with the entitlements program resulted in the price faced by domestic oil refiners being below the world price. Refiners processed too much crude oil relative to the social optimum. In this section, the welfare implications of these supply and demand distortions are analyzed.

Distortive Effect on Domestic Supply

Due to the multitier system of price controls, the marginal revenue curve faced by domestic suppliers was a discontinuous function of output. Depicted in Figure 18.7 is the marginal revenue curve faced by domestic suppliers under EPAA. Q_s denotes the maximum production rate whereby a supplier is classified as a stripper. Recall that a stripper is not subject to price controls. Thus, if output does not exceed Q_s, a supplier's marginal revenue from another barrel is just the world price P_w. For production greater than Q_s but less than the base production control level ($BPCL$), a supplier received the controlled price for old oil, denoted

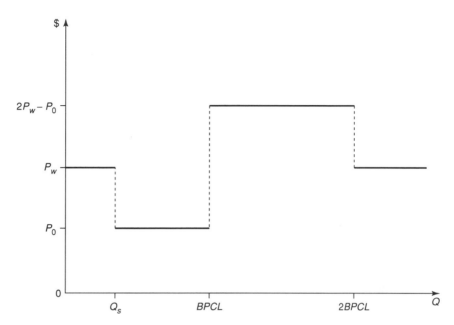

Figure 18.7
Producer Marginal Revenue under EPAA

Source: Joseph P. Kalt, *The Economics and politics of oil Price Regulation* (Cambridge, Mass.: MIT Press, 1981).

P_o. Oil produced in excess of *BPCL* is considered new oil and its price is uncontrolled. However, recall that for each unit of new oil produced, a supplier gets to release one unit of old oil from price controls. Thus, by increasing production of new oil by one unit, a supplier earns P_w from selling it on the market and also increases revenue by $P_w - P_o$ from being able to sell one unit of old oil at the world price rather than at the controlled price. Hence, marginal revenue for production in excess of *BPCL* equals $2P_w - P_o$. Of course, if production exceeded $2BPCL$ then there is no old oil left to release, so that marginal revenue falls back down to P_w.

In light of the complex nature of the marginal revenue curve under EPAA, it is difficult to draw any general conclusions about the effect of regulation on domestic supply decisions. If a firm's marginal cost was sufficiently steep so that the relevant production range was from Q_s to *BPCL*, then the relevant marginal revenue is P_o. In that situation, regulation reduced supply because the production of another barrel would only fetch the low regulated price of P_o. If instead the marginal cost function is less steep, so that the relevant production range is above *BPCL*, then marginal revenue is actually higher under regulation because another barrel would be worth more than P_w as it would allow

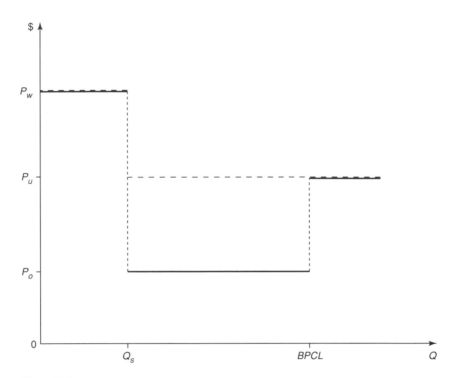

Figure 18.8
Producer Marginal Revenue under EPCA

Source: Joseph P. Kalt, *The Economics and Politics of Oil Price Regulation* (Cambridge, Mass.: MIT Press, 1981).

one barrel of controlled oil to be sold at the world price. One would then expect a firm's supply to be greater under regulation.

For the ensuing regulatory program of EPCA, the distortive effect on domestic supply is much more clear-cut. A firm's marginal revenue curve took the form depicted in Figure 18.8. Once again, production below Q_s is not subject to price controls so that marginal revenue is P_w. If the property was producing prior to 1975, then production between Q_s and *BPCL* received the old oil price of P_o while production in excess of *BPCL* earned the upper tier price of P_u. If the property was instead new, in that it did not begin producing until after 1975, it received the upper tier price of P_u for all production above Q_s. Because regulation under EPCA kept marginal revenue below the world price for all production in excess of Q_s, regulation would be expected to reduce domestic supply.

Distortive Effect on Domestic Demand

In the absence of the entitlements program, oil price regulation did not distort domestic demand. Because price-controlled domestic crude oil was in excess demand, a refiner who considered processing one more barrel of crude oil would have to buy on the uncontrolled market at the world price. Thus, the marginal cost faced by refiners was that based on the world price for crude oil. Because this is the same as in the absence of price controls, the marginal cost of refiners was not distorted by price controls. Hence, their demand for crude oil would be unaffected. The only effect of price controls would be to transfer profits from domestic oil producers to those refiners who were fortunate enough to get the price-controlled oil.

Of course, this system lasted for only a few months under Phase IV price controls. With the passage of EPAA, an entitlements program was introduced for allocating price-controlled oil. Recall that the number of entitlements a refiner received was equal to its total crude oil input multiplied by the national percentage of price-controlled oil of total oil. Let this percentage be denoted z and suppose a refiner considers buying one more unit of imported oil. The price it must pay to the foreign oil producer is P_w. However, by having increased its crude oil input by one unit, the refiner gets a fraction z of an entitlement. It can now buy z less of a unit of imported oil and z more of a unit of price-controlled oil. If $\overline{P}_d$ is the price of the latter then the refiner saves $z(P_w - \overline{P}_d)$ on this exchange. It follows that the net cost of one more unit of imported oil is $P_w - z(P_w - \overline{P}_d) = (1 - z)P_w + z\overline{P}_d$. Therefore, under the entitlements program, the marginal cost of one more unit of imported oil to a refiner is less than the world price P_w. Effectively, oil price regulation subsidized imported oil! We would predict domestic demand to be distorted upward as a result.

Measuring the Welfare Loss

Depicted in Figure 18.9 are the domestic supply curve for crude oil, $S_d(P)$, the domestic demand curve for crude oil, $D_d(P)$, and the world supply curve for crude oil, $S_w(P)$. For simplicity, we have assumed that the supply of imports is perfectly elastic at the world price. The effect of allowing $S_w(P)$ to be upward-sloping is considered later.

In the absence of oil price controls, the equilibrium price would be P_w, and refiners would demand Q^* units. At a price of P_w, domestic oil producers would optimally supply Q_d units so that imports would be $Q^* - Q_d$. Now suppose a price ceiling of $\overline{P}_d$ is imposed on domestic oil and an entitlements program is implemented so that the marginal price faced by domestic refiners is $(1 - z)P_w + z\overline{P}_d$, which we will denote P_s. Due to the lower price faced by refiners, their demand would increase from Q^* to Q^{**}. Because domestic suppliers receive the lower price of

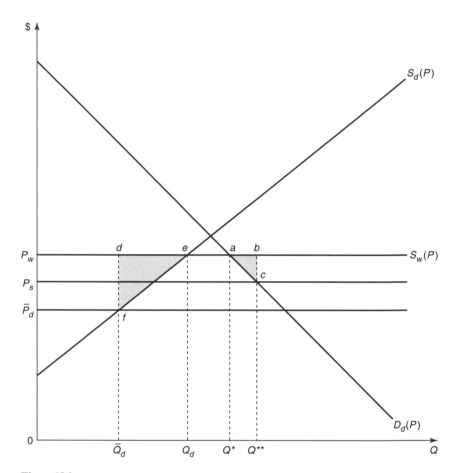

Figure 18.9
Equilibrium under Crude Oil Price Controls

$\overline{P}_d$, they are only willing to supply $\overline{Q}_d$ units. As a result, imports must increase from $Q^* - Q_d$ to $Q^{**} - \overline{Q}_d$.

We can now assess the welfare effects of regulation. Regulation induced domestic refiners to process too much oil by the amount $Q^{**} - Q^*$. For those additional units, the social cost, as measured by the world price P_w, exceeds the social benefit by the triangle *abc*. In addition, the reduced domestic supply means that more resources are used to supply $Q_d - \overline{Q}_d$. Thus, there is an additional welfare loss of triangle *def*. The total welfare loss from regulation is then measured by the sum of the two shaded triangles in Figure 18.9.

The size of these triangles have been estimated for 1975–1980 and is shown in Table 18.4. In 1975, triangle *abc* was estimated as $1,037 million (in 1980 dollars), whereas triangle *def* was estimated at $963

Table 18.4
Welfare Losses from Oil Price Controls, 1975–1980 (millions of 1980 dollars)

Year	Demand-Side Deadweight Loss	Supply-Side Deadweight Loss	Additional Expenditure on Imports
1975	$1,037	$ 963	$11,550
1976	852	1,046	15,052
1977	654	1,213	16,496
1978	300	816	11,319
1979	627	331	17,644
1980	1,038	530	34,475

Source: Joseph P. Kalt, *The Economics and Politics of Oil Price Regulation* (Cambridge: MIT Press, 1981).

million. The total deadweight loss from distorted supply and demand decisions was $2 billion. From 1975 to 1980, the average annual welfare loss due to demand and supply distortions was about $2.5 billion so that the total welfare loss from EPCA was on the order of $15 billion. The welfare loss from regulation fluctuated over time because of the changing price of world oil. Also note that expenditure on imports increased considerably as a result of oil price regulation.

There are several caveats that need to be mentioned with respect to these estimates. First, these triangles measure the welfare loss from regulation under the assumption that the marginal social cost of crude oil is properly measured by the world price. Thus, when regulation induces domestic consumption to increase from Q^* to Q^{**}, the value of that additional consumption is less than the cost of the resources used as measured by P_w. Because P_w represents the marginal social cost to the U.S. economy of another barrel of (imported) oil, triangles *abc* and *def* measure the welfare loss to the U.S. economy from demand and supply distortions. However, it does not measure the welfare loss to the world economy unless the world market is competitive. The world market was, in fact, not competitive, for OPEC was a price-setter acting in a monopolistic manner. As a result, the price of oil in the world market was set too high relative to other energy sources. Because this implies too little oil was being consumed, regulation that increased the consumption of oil need not have been welfare-reducing from the perspective of the world economy. The bottom line is that the estimated welfare losses are for the U.S. economy and not the world economy.

A second important caveat is that this analysis assumed that U.S. demand does not influence the world price. This assumption was implicit in specifying that the world price was fixed at P_w. On the contrary, the United States is a big player in the world energy market and its demand generally does influence the world price. To capture this effect, let us now specify a rising world supply curve so that changes in U.S. oil consumption affect the world price for oil.

Having made this modification in our model, there are two new effects introduced. Because greater U.S. consumption raises the world price, this higher price will tend to reduce the increase in domestic consumption as a result of regulation. If P_w is the world price in the absence of regulation, the world price with U.S. regulation will be above P_w because of the upward distortion in domestic demand resulting from the effective subsidization of oil imports. However, U.S. consumption will not rise as much with a rising world supply curve because of the resulting higher world price. Thus, the welfare loss from demand distortions are lower if increased U.S. consumption raises the world price. Under the specification of a rising world supply curve, the welfare losses from demand distortions have been reestimated. For a range of reasonable values for the elasticity of the world supply curve, the welfare loss was lower by 13 to 61 percent. For example, if the world supply curve is unit elastic, then the average annual welfare loss from demand distortions over 1975–1980 was $413 million in contrast to $751 million when we assume a perfectly elastic world supply curve.[21]

A second additional effect from regulation that arises with a rising world supply curve is that there is an increase in the transfer of wealth from the U.S. economy to foreign oil producers. This wealth transfer is due to the higher world price. Depending on the elasticity of the world supply curve, the average wealth transfer over 1975–1980 was between $1.625 billion and $8.115 billion per year.[22] These are substantial welfare losses to the U.S. economy.

Small Refiner Bias and Productive Inefficiency

In addition to the welfare losses from too much domestic demand and too little domestic supply, regulation also caused productive inefficiency by promoting the use of inefficiently small refiners. This bias was created by the entitlements program which allocated additional entitlements to small refiners. The additional number of entitlements was decreasing with the production of a refiner and were eliminated at 175,000 barrels per day. In 1977, the small refiner bias applied to 126 of 148 domestic refining firms. However, these 126 small refiners made up only 18 percent of U.S. refining capacity.[23]

This small refiner bias resulted in productive inefficiency because the minimum efficient size for a refiner was around 200,000 barrels per day.[24] That is, average cost was decreasing until around 200,000 barrels, at which point it became relatively flat. Thus, by providing additional entitlements to small refiners, regulation provided an incentive for inefficiently small refiners to operate. The small refiner bias was found to be increasing over the period of regulation. Refiners with less than 175,000 barrels per day made up 14.4 percent of total refined product sales in 1972 and this had increased to 17.8 percent by 1975.[25] Regulation not only resulted in inadequate domestic supply but also changed the composition of the domestic suppliers toward smaller, less efficient refiners. By doing so, industry average cost was raised and social welfare was reduced.

Reduced Incentives for Exploration

It has been argued by many economists specializing in the oil industry that regulation reduced the incentive to explore for new oil reserves. However, since marginal revenue from new oil production was higher than the world price under EPAA, one would think that regulation would have increased the expected profits from exploration and thus actually increased the incentive to explore. On the other hand, marginal revenue was constrained below the world price under EPCA so that the effect on expected profits from exploration would be just the opposite.

A concern of firms is that if they discover new oil reserves, future regulation may reclassify it as old oil and thus restrict its price below the world price. This effect would tend to reduce the incentive to explore under either regulatory program. Furthermore, uncertainty about future regulation can increase the variability of returns from exploration. There is already considerable uncertainty associated with exploration, even in the absence of regulation. A firm is uncertain whether it will discover new oil reserves and, if it does, it is uncertain as to the revenues that will be generated. Revenue uncertainty is due to uncertainty both over the size of the reservoir and what the world price will be. A regulatory structure adds uncertainty over what the regulated price will be. Because increased variability is thought to reduce the incentive to explore, price regulation can reduce exploration efforts by the domestic oil-producing industry.

Administrative and Compliance Costs

With any regulation, whether or not there is a rationale for it, there is always a welfare loss associated with the resources used to implement it. In light of the complexity of oil price controls and the entitlements program, the administrative and compliance costs were quite substantial. By the late 1970s, the industry was incurring an annual cost around $500 million (in 1977 dollars) for reporting and administrative duties while the cost to the FEA was around $40–50 million per year.[26] Adding these costs to those associated with supply and demand distortions, the annual welfare loss in 1979 due to regulation was around $3.2 billion (in 1979 dollars).[27]

On this note, it is interesting to mention that when the Windfall Profits Tax was repealed in 1988, it was creating a welfare loss in spite of the fact it was no longer collecting revenues. (Prior to that time, however, it did collect revenues totaling $77 billion over 1980–1988)[28]. The industry estimated that it incurred on the order of $100 million annually in reporting and complying with the law.[29] Even when a regulation is not binding, there can be welfare losses associated with it.

Price Regulation of the Natural Gas Industry

Like crude oil, natural gas is a hydrocarbon and is produced by drilling into an underground reservoir. In fact, gas is often found along with oil. Although oil has had a more significant historical role in the U.S. energy market, the first natural gas well in the United States was drilled in 1825, which predates the first oil well by more than thirty years. The standard unit of measurement for natural gas is 1,000 cubic feet, typically denoted Mcf.[30]

Technological Structure

The production of natural gas is almost identical to that of crude oil. Furthermore, about 20 percent of natural gas in the United States comes from wells also producing oil.[31] After extraction comes the transmission of natural gas from the wellhead to local distributors. The difficulty in its transmission is that natural gas is bulky. One million BTU of natural gas occupies about one Mcf at room temperature and atmospheric pressure whereas the same amount of energy is stored in only 7.5 gallons of gasoline.[32] Given its bulkiness, generally the only economical way in which to transport natural gas is by pipeline.[33] However, early gas pipelines suffered from serious problems with leakage. This caused pipelines not to be of great length, which meant that consumers had to be relatively close to producers. Consequently, the natural gas industry was slower to develop nationally than the crude oil industry. A sign of the future national scope of the industry took place in 1931 when a pipeline was built between Chicago and the natural gas fields of Texas. Nevertheless, it was not until after World War II that pipeline construction grew rapidly. Only then did the natural gas industry become truly national in scope.

After production and transmission, the last segment to the natural gas industry is local distribution. A local distribution network connects individual residential and commercial users with the pipeline and thus has many of the properties of a local electric utility.

Economic Structure of Transportation

Because a unique and essential aspect to the natural gas industry is its transportation system, let us briefly discuss its properties. First, both pipelines and local distribution systems are characterized by economies of scale since there is a large fixed cost component and a relatively low marginal cost. Given these investments are largely nonrecoverable, they require a long-term commitment from consumers. Hence, pipelines need a local distribution network to agree to buy gas from it for an extended length of time, and the local distribution network needs a similar commitment from commerical and residential consumers. Although a local distribution network is a monopoly and a pipeline may also be the only supplier for that network, it is important to recognize that competitive forces are still at work inasmuch as natural gas must compete with other energy sources. Manufacturing plants can choose between gas, oil, and coal to run their plants. Though switching in the short run is often difficult, in the long run residential demand for natural gas depends on the price of other energy sources such as electricity and oil.

Regulatory History

During the early part of the Great Depression, the natural gas industry was chaotic. Markets in the eastern United States suffered from rising prices and significant shortages, whereas there was enormous excess supply in the Southwest. Increasing pipeline construction would have greatly allievated this dilemma, but the Great Depression brought most pipeline construction to a halt. Amid this chaos, there were many abuses by local public utility holding companies. Many were acting essentially like unregulated monopolists and charging excessively high prices.

The Natural Gas Act of 1938

By the mid-1930s state public-service commissions and representatives of northern cities were lobbying the U.S. Congress to regulate the natural gas industry. In response, Congress passed the Natural Gas Act of 1938. This act gave the Federal Power Commission (FPC) control over the interstate transportation and sale for resale of natural gas in interstate commerce. However, the 1938 Act stipulated that it did not apply to the production or gathering of natural gas. The FPC was specifically given control over entry in the transmission segment of the natural gas industry. FPC approval was required to build an interstate pipeline that delivered gas to a market already served by another gas line. That type of entry control is reminiscent of airline and trucking regulation.

Phillips Petroleum Co. v. State of Wisconsin

After the 1938 Act, the FPC focused on reducing the risk associated with pipelines. This was largely accomplished by limiting access of pipelines to end-use markets. Before entering a market, the FPC required a pipeline to demonstrate it had large reserves under contract. While giving it the right to control entry, the FPC interpreted the 1938 Act as not giving it the right to control gas prices.

In a landmark case in 1954, the Supreme Court ruled in *Phillips Petroleum Co. v. State of Wisconsin* that the 1938 Act did indeed grant the FPC the task of regulating wellhead rates for natural gas. From that point onward, the FPC was very active in regulating gas prices. As will be discussed in detail in the section on regulatory practices, a key feature of price regulation was the establishment of different rates for "old" and "new" gas. This was done along similar lines to the regulation of crude oil prices.

Natural Gas Policy Act of 1978

By the late 1960s, shortages were beginning to emerge in natural gas markets in the Midwest and Northeast. Then, to further exacerbate the situation, the oil price shocks of 1973–1974 hit. By the mid-1970s there was considerable disequilibrium in the natural gas market as government-set prices were creating significant shortages.

The response of the government was the Natural Gas Policy Act of 1978. This act called for the gradual decontrol of prices for new gas, defined as gas produced by wells discovered since 1977. The objective was to have new gas prices at market-clearing levels by 1985. On the other hand, the 1978 Act continued to control old gas prices (that is, gas from wells discovered before 1977). Prices could only grow at the rate of inflation and, in addition, price control was extended to the intrastate market for the first time. Finally, government jurisdiction over the natural gas market moved from the FPC to the Federal Energy Regulatory Commission (FERC).

Because of the 1978 Act, deregulation has indeed taken place. Prices for gas produced from deep wells were fully deregulated in November 1979 and, according to plan, new gas prices were decontrolled in January 1985. Old gas prices were also effectively deregulated in 1986 when the FERC issued Order 451. It collapsed fifteen vintages of old natural gas into one and set the ceiling price above the market-clearing price. In July 1989, President George Bush signed the Natural Gas Wellhead

Market	Date	Production: Drilling, Prorationing, etc.	Production: Wellhead Pricing	Transportation	Sale for Resale	Final Sales
INTRASTATE	1978	STATE	STATE	STATE	STATE	STATE
			Federal Price Ceilings (FERC), NGPA			
	1985		Federal Price Ceilings, Many Categories Decontrolled (FERC), NGPA			
INTERSTATE	1938	STATE	NOT REGULATED	NOT REGULATED *Public Utility Commission of Rhode Island v. Attleboro Steam and Electric Co.*, 1927	NOT REGULATED *Missouri v. Kansas Natural Gas Co.*, 1924	STATE (for rates) *Pennsylvania Gas Co. v. Public Service Commission of New York*, 1920
	1954	Except for Federal Lands and Federal Offshore. Subject to Department of Interior	*Phillips Petroleum Co. v. Wisconsin*, 1954 Federal Rate Regulation (FERC), NGA	Federal Rate Regulation (FERC), NGA	Federal Rate Regulation (FERC), NGA	
	1978		Federal Price Ceilings (FERC), NGPA			
	1985		Federal Price Ceilings, Many Categories Decontrolled (FERC), NGPA			FEDERAL (FERC) (for certification)

Figure 18.10
Regulatory Jurisdiction of the Natural Gas Industry

Source: U.S. Department of Energy, Energy Information Administration, 1989. Figure from Paul L. Joskow and Roger G. Noll, "Economic Regulation and Its Reform During the 1980s," NBER Working Paper, October 1990.

Decontrol Act of 1989, which fully deregulated gas prices. An overview of the regulatory structure from 1938–1985 is provided in Figure 18.10.

Regulatory Practices

Rate-of-Return Regulation

The basic model used by the FPC in setting natural gas prices was rate-of-return regulation (see Chapter 12). Prices were set with the objective of allowing natural gas producers to recover the cost of supplying gas and earn a fair rate-of-return. In the early 1970s, the allowed rate-of-return was initially 12 percent and was then increased to 15 percent in 1974.[34] For example, the FPC set a rate of \$1.42/Mcf in 1976. This rate was calculated by allowing for each Mcf. \$0.37 for exploration and production costs, \$0.03 for operating costs, \$0.22 for royalties, \$0.38 for taxes, and \$0.42 for a return on investment.[35]

Initially, the FPC determined rates on a case-by-case basis and, before 1954, it averaged 700 gas-rate filings per year. However, after the Supreme Court ruling in 1955, the number of filings increased to around 11,000.[36] The result was a massive backlog of cases. By 1960 there were still 3,278 producer rate increase filings awaiting decisions.[37]

Given the burdensome nature of this approach to rate-making, the FPC changed tactics in 1960 by dividing the United States into twenty-three geographic areas and requiring price to be uniform within each area. The initial price set was based on prices in 1956–1958. The first area rate case was the Permian Basin Area Case. It took the FPC five years to decide it and after all that it was taken to court. Three years later in 1968, it was approved by the Supreme Court. Because of these delays, rates were basically frozen from 1960 to 1973.

Fourteen years after area rate-making was accepted, the FPC had still not completed even half of the twenty-three area cases. In its ongoing pursuit of a more manageable system, nationwide ratemaking was accepted in June 1974. A rate of $0.42/Mcf was specified for all interstate sales. This rate applied only to wells completed after January 1, 1973.

Multitier Pricing System

One of the key properties of natural gas price regulation was the specification of different rates for different vintages of gas. New gas was defined as gas discovered or first committed to the interstate market after some specified date, whereas old gas was discovered before that date. In the Permian Basin Area Case, new gas was priced at $0.165/Mcf and old gas was priced at $0.145/Mcf. The objective of the FPC was to keep new gas rates high to encourage exploration and old gas rates low to mitigate the transfer of rents from consumers to producers. It was believed to be unnecessary to keep old gas prices at the market-clearing level. This is a point we will return to shortly.

From November 1976 until the 1978 Act, a five-tier system was in place with prices ranging from $0.295 for gas produced from wells dating before January 1, 1973, to $1.42 for gas produced from wells dating after January 1, 1975. The number of tiers was increased in response to growing shortages in the interstate market. Finally, the system reached its acme in complexity with the 1978 Act, when twenty-eight different categories of gas were established for pricing purposes. New gas was defined as that from wells commencing production after January 1, 1977. Its rate was set at around $2.50/Mcf. Old gas prices were set close to pre-1978 rates. In addition, different rates were set for the interstate and intrastate markets.

Effects of Price Regulation

The important feature of gas price regulation was that both old and new gas prices were set below market-clearing levels. Because natural-gas producers were not required to meet demand, the result of price regulation was substantial excess demand in the interstate market. A multitier system of pricing improved incentives for exploration relative to setting a single price for all gas, but it also increased drilling and exploration costs.

Divergence between Interstate and Intrastate Rates

The best way to show that interstate gas rates were set too low is to compare them with intrastate rates. Because the intrastate gas markets were unregulated, it is reasonable to suppose that a competitive equilibrium was achieved there. Even though interstate gas rates were regulated by the FPC while intrastate rates were uncontrolled, before 1970 the difference between interstate and intrastate rates was relatively small. However, from 1969 to 1975, a considerable rift occurred due to

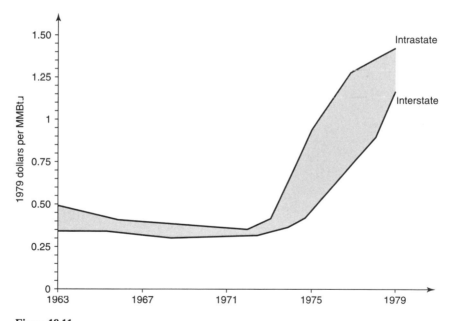

Figure 18.11
Comparison of Interstate and Intrastate Wellhead Prices

Source: Energy Information Administration, U.S. Department of Energy, *Intrastate and Interstate Supply Markets under the Natural Gas Policy Act* (Washington, D.C.: USGPO), October 1981. Figure from Arlon R. Tussing and Connie C. Barlow, *The Natural Gas Industry: Evolution, Structure, and Economics* (Cambridge, Mass.: Ballinger Publishing Company, 1984). Reprinted by permission of Arlon R. Tussing & Associates, Inc.

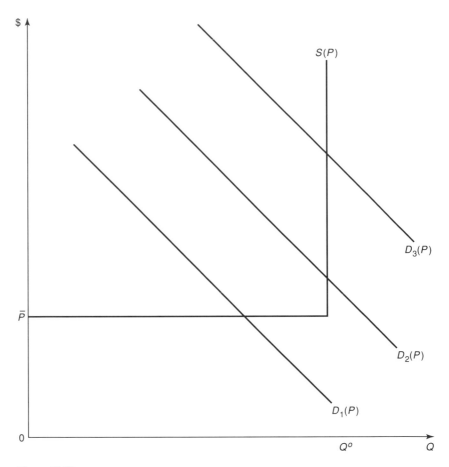

Figure 18.12
The Effects of FPC Policy with a Vertical Supply Curve

growing interstate demand and the oil price shock. During that time interstate prices for new contracts rose 158 percent from $0.198/Mcf to
$0.51/Mcf while intrastate prices for new contracts rose a whopping 650
percent from $0.18/Mcf to $1.35/Mcf.[38] Figure 18.11 shows the growing
differential between regulated interstate rates and unregulated intrastate
rates.

Diversion of Interstate Supply to the Intrastate Market

One interpretation of FPC policy is that it was based on the assumption
that the industry supply curve for natural gas was essentially vertical after some output rate, as depicted in Figure 18.12. If indeed the supply
curve had this property, given growing demand for natural gas due to
rising energy demand and the increase in the price of a substitute (that

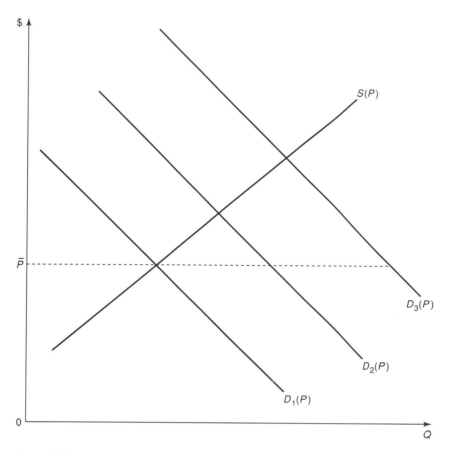

Figure 18.13
The Effects of FPC Policy with a Rising Supply Curve

is, crude oil), one would anticipate gas prices to increase but the supply response to be minimal once production of Q^o is reached. In light of this model, one can understand FPC policy. By keeping gas prices at $\overline{P}$ even when demand has shifted to $D_3(P)$, there is no welfare loss because supply is still Q^o while the transfer of wealth from consumers to producers is prevented.

Unfortunately, history has shown that the interstate supply curve for gas was indeed responsive to the price. A more accurate representation is that shown in Figure 18.13. In that case, with a price ceiling of $\overline{P}$, as demand grows from $D_1(P)$ to $D_2(P)$ to $D_3(P)$ an increasing shortage emerges because supply does not respond. With price ceilings in interstate markets, gas producers optimally diverted supply to intrastate markets where they could receive a higher price. This diversion was felt by interstate pipelines as they were forced to meet less than their contractual amounts to "interruptible" customers. Figure 18.14 shows the growing

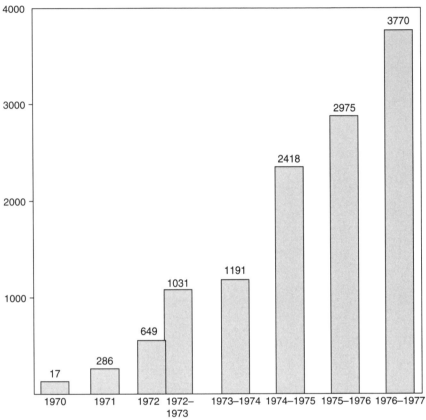

Figure 18.14
Firm Curtailments by Interstate Pipelines, 1970–1977 (Intercompany Sales Eliminated)

Source: 1970–1972 data from FPC, *Natural Gas Survey,* Volume 1, Washington, D.C.: USGPO, 1975; 1972–1977 data from FPC, 1976 *Annual Report.* Figure from Richard H. K. Vietor, *Energy Policy in America Since 1945* (Cambridge: Cambridge University Press, 1984). Reprinted by permission of Cambridge University Press.

number of curtailments by interstate pipelines. (A curtailment is an un-filled order.) By 1977, curtailments had reached a level of 3.7 trillion cu-bic feet. Gas reserves dedicated to the interstate market also dropped drastically, as shown in Figure 18.15. Although 67 percent of reserves were committed to the interstate market from 1964 to 1969, less than 8 percent were so committed from 1970 to 1973.[39]

Allocative Inefficiency

By setting price ceilings below market-clearing levels while allowing producers to freely choose how much to supply, regulation resulted in

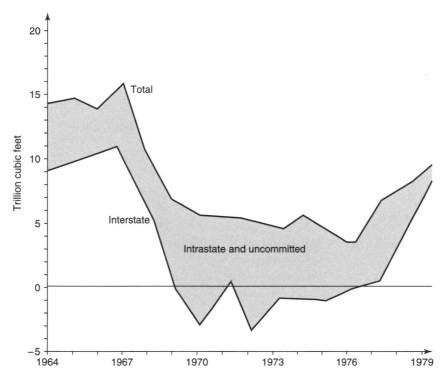

Figure 18.15
Comparison of Annual Reserve Additions for Intrastate and Interstate Markets
Source: Energy Information Administration, U.S. Department of energy, *Intrastate and Interstate Supply Markets under the Natural Gas Policy Act*, Washington, D.C.: USGPO, October 1981. Figure from Arlon R. Tussing and Connie C. Barlow, *The Natural Gas Industry: Evolution, Structure, and Economics* (Cambridge, Mass.: Gallinger Publishing Company, 1984). Reprinted by permission of Arlon R. Tussing & Associates, Inc.

inadequate amounts of natural gas being supplied to the interstate market. Consumers were forced to turn to more expensive and less efficient energy sources like oil and electricity. Potentially large welfare losses were incurred by the substitution of electricity for natural gas in providing heating to the residential market. In 1984, the price per million BTU faced by the residential market for electricity was $23.59 compared to just $6.26 for natural gas.[40]

A second source of welfare loss is associated with inefficient rationing. As shown in the section on the theory of price ceilings, when there is excess demand for a good, additional welfare losses occur when the good does not end up in the hands of the consumers who values it the most. One can make a strong case that this took place in the interstate gas market. Utilities and industries located in gas-producing states were able to receive ample supply of gas while residential consumers in the Northeast had to use expensive alternative energy sources like oil and electricity for heating. Because utilities and industries could have converted to coal, they had lower cost alternatives than were faced by the Northeast residential market. Thus, efficiency would have been increased by reallocating gas to residential consumers in the Northeast.

Excessive Drilling Costs and Productive Inefficiency

As it often does, regulation creates unusual incentives that can lead to productive inefficiencies. Consider a natural gas producer whose well was producing prior to some date so that all gas extracted from it was classified as old gas. If the gas could be reclassified as new gas, the producer's revenue would rise from the higher price ceiling applied to new gas. In some cases, a gas producer could accomplish this reclassification by drilling a new well on an already discovered gas reservoir. As a result, regulation resulted in the drilling of wells that were superfluous from a production standpoint but were profitable from a revenue standpoint. The resources used to build these additional wells must be added as an additional source of welfare loss. An offsetting effect is that the higher price from getting old gas reclassified as new gas would be expected to bring forth additional supply to the interstate market.

Reduced Incentives for Explorations

As in the case of oil price controls, it is generally believed that gas price controls reduced the incentive to explore for new reserves. Because the price one could expect from finding new reserves was lower under regulation, the expected profits from exploration were reduced so that less exploration would optimally take place. The evidence is consistent with this argument. Proved gas reserves rose quite steadily from 1948 to 1967 when they reached an all-time high of 297 trillion cubic feet. However, under gas price controls, these reserves steadily declined and were 31 percent lower in 1980 than in 1970.[41] This was particularly striking because the price of oil was way up. A higher price of a substitute for natural gas would tend to induce additional exploration.

Regulation specified higher price ceilings for gas from deep wells. There were, however, increased incentives to explore for high cost gas. With the early elimination of price controls for gas from deep wells, there was in fact a deep-gas boom during 1978 1982. Because drilling costs increase roughly in proportion to the square of well depth, considerably more resources were used to drill deep wells. Generally the incentive to explore was curtailed by regulation, but it was actually increased for higher cost gas.

Table 18.5
Take-or-Pay Provisions by Contract Vintage

Contract Vintage	Take-or-Pay Requirement[a]
Pre-1973	59.6%
1973 to April 20, 1977	85.9
April 21, 1977, to November 8, 1978[b]	82.3
November 9, 1978, to 1979	82.5
1980	78.3

[a] Weighted-average percentage minimum-purchase requirement (take-or-pay) based on percentage of deliverability or capacity.
[b] The Natural Gas Policy Act was enacted on November 9, 1978.
Source: U.S. Energy Information Administration, "An Analysis of the Natural Gas Policy Act and Several Alternatives," Part I (December 1981), II (June 1982), III (September 1982), IV (May 1983), Washington, D.C. Table from Ronald R. Braeutigam and R. Glenn Hubbard, "Natural Gas: The Regulatory Transition," in Leonard W. Weiss and Michael W. Klass (eds.), *Regulatory Reform: What Actually Happened* (Boston: Little, Brown, 1986). Reprinted by permission of HarperCollins Publishers.

Nonprice Competition and Take-or-Pay Contracts

For a pipeline to be profitable, it is essential that it have access to natural gas producers. For this reason, pipelines often enter into long-term contractual relationships with producers. Due to the shortages generated by regulation, there was a heightened incentive to sign such long-term agreements. Pipelines competed with one another to get gas producers to sign agreements that would contractually guarantee supply to the pipelines. Because the price they could offer producers was limited by regulation, pipelines turned to nonprice methods to compete. In particular, they competed through the take-or-pay provision of contracts.

A take-or-pay provision guarantees that a pipeline will purchase a minimum quantity each year at a specified price. It is equivalent to a fixed payment per year. As shown in Table 18.5, the minimum purchase requirement as a percentage of deliverability or capacity was distinctly higher after the 1973 oil price shock then before it. This reflects the fact that the difference between the regulated price and the market-clearing price was much greater after 1973. With a higher differential, competition drove pipelines to offer more attractive terms, like a higher take-or-pay provision, in order to get gas supplies.

The increased take-or-pay requirement has since created considerable problems for pipelines. Because oil prices did not rise as originally expected, natural gas prices have not risen as originally expected. As a result, pipelines that entered long-term agreements with a large take-or-pay requirement find themselves faced with financial obligations often in excess of their assets. This represents one of the major postderegulation problems with which the FERC has had to deal.

Path to Deregulation

In setting up a plan for the gradual decontrol of natural gas prices, the 1978 Act presumed that the price of oil would remain around a price $15 per barrel in 1978 dollars. Unfortunately, the price of oil shot up to $30 per barrel in 1979–1980 and resulted in severe disequilibrium in the natural gas market.

The effects of continued regulation from 1977 to 1985, as opposed to fully decontrolling prices in 1977, have been estimated.[42] These estimates reveal that continued price regulation reduced the revenues of gas producers by $106.3 billion over 1977–1985 but also reduced consumer expenditure by $98.7 billion. Rather interestingly, the impact on different consumer groups was quite varied. Continued regulation over 1977–1985 reduced gas expenditure for utilities by $41.3 billion, for commerical users by $3.0 billion, and for industrial users by $69.9 billion. In contrast, expenditure by residential users was actually higher by $8.6 billion as a result of gradual rather than full decontrol in 1977.

Summary

Both the regulation of domestic crude oil prices and the regulation of interstate natural-gas prices were characterized by price ceilings established at levels below what was required in order to clear the market. As a result, shortages emerged. However, due to differences in these two markets, the response to these shortages were quite different. In the case of the crude-oil market, consumers responded by increasing foreign imports. In the case of the interstate natural-gas market, consumers were forced to switch to less efficient energy sources like electricity and oil. The gas shortage was further exacerbated by intrastate prices' being unregulated. This provided increased incentives for gas producers to divert supply away from the interstate market and to the intrastate market.

Moving to other sources of regulatory-induced welfare losses, we found that price regulation caused productive inefficiencies in both the oil and gas markets. Oil price regulation created a bias for small refiners so that there were increased incentives to operate refineries with capacities below minimum efficient scale. The small-refiner bias raised industry average cost and wasted valuable resources. Both oil and gas price regulation increased drilling and exploration costs by providing higher price ceilings to oil and gas produced from more costly wells. Producers were then provided with incentives to explore for reserves that entailed more rather than less resources for production. Finally, energy regulation reduced the incentive for oil and gas producers to explore for new reserves, which resulted in even greater shortages in the future.

Although we have discussed the regulation of oil and gas separately, one would expect there to be important connections between the two markets since oil and gas are substitutes. In particular, the oil price shocks of the 1970s played a central role in the magnitude of the regulatory distortions in the natural gas market. When the price of oil increased, demand for gas naturally increased. Of course, the regulatory-imposed price ceiling prevented gas prices from rising, so that supply did not increase so to meet the greater demand. As a result, welfare losses from gas regulation were much greater because of the movement in world oil prices in the 1970s.

Questions and Problems

1. Is there an economic rationale for a state government to control the rate at which crude oil is extracted?

2. Describe how the optimal extraction rate of crude oil is affected when:

   a) information is revealed which raises the expected price of crude oil in the future;

   b) the interest rate rises.

3. When crude oil price controls were in place, what would have been the welfare implications of a ban on oil imports? (Use Figure 18.9.)

4. Assume the market supply curve is $S(P) = 30P$ and the market demand curve is $D(P) = 500 - 20P$.

   a) Derive the competitive equilibrium price.

   b) Suppose that the government institutes a price ceiling of 5. Derive the welfare loss from price controls.

   c) How much are producers willing to pay in order to get their legislators to remove the price ceiling?

5. How does the elasticity of the industry supply curve affect the welfare implications of price ceilings?

6. Let us consider the effects of the Emergency Petroleum Allocation Act (EPAA) on the domestic supply of crude oil. Assume the world price is 15, the price of old oil is set at 10, a domestic supplier is classified as a stripper if and only if its production does not exceed 10, and the base production control level is 20. Derive the effect of EPAA on the supply decision of a domestic supplier of crude oil when its marginal-cost curve is represented by:

   a) $MC(Q) = 5 + 2Q$

   b) $MC(Q) = 5 + .75Q$

   c) $MC(Q) = .02Q^2$

7. Assume that the domestic supply curve for crude oil is $S(P) = 5P$ and the domestic demand curve for crude oil is $D(P) = 500 - 20P$. Further assume that domestic oil refiners face a perfectly elastic supply of oil imports at a price of 16.

a) Derive the domestic price, the quantity processed by domestic oil refiners, and the amount of imports at the competitive equilibrium. Now suppose that domestic crude oil suppliers face a price ceiling of 8. Further suppose that for each two units of crude oil purchased, a domestic oil refiner gets one entitlement to domestic crude oil.

b) Derive the marginal price of crude oil faced by domestic oil refiners.

c) Derive the effect of regulation on the amount of crude oil processed by domestic oil refiners and the amount of imports.

d) Derive the welfare effect of regulation on U.S. consumers and producers.

8. Who gained and who lost by prorationing? By crude oil price controls? By natural gas price controls?

9. Why is the market for crude oil more international than the market for natural gas?

10. How did the combination of oil and gas price controls affect the incentives for exploration? (You should take into account the fact that a certain percentage of natural gas comes from wells also producing crude oil.)

11. The regulated price of natural gas for wells dating before January 1, 1973, was set lower than the regulated price for wells dating after January 1, 1973. Why did regulation create this price differential? Does it make a difference that natural gas is homogeneous?

12. In response to the doubling of the price of crude oil in 1979–1980, should the government have speeded up or slowed down the gradual decontrol of natural gas prices?

Notes

1. For specific data, see S. Schurr and B. Netschert, *Energy and the American Economy, 1850–1975* (Baltimore: Johns Hopkins University Press, 1960).

2. Ibid.

3. For an introduction to the technological aspects of petroleum, see chapter 2 in Stephen L. McDonald, *Petroleum Conservation in the United States: An Economic Analysis* (Baltimore: Johns Hopkins University Press, 1971).

4. Data is from the U.S. Bureau of Mines and Joel Darmstadter, Perry D. Teitelbaum, and Jaruslav G. Polach, *Energy in the World Economy* (Baltimore: Johns Hopkins University Press, 1971).

5. William Spangar Pierce, *Economics of the Energy Industries* (Belmont, Cal.: Wadsworth Publishing Company, 1986), p. 130.

6. All preceding price data is from Walter S. Measday and Stephen Martin, "The Petroleum Industry," in Walter Adams (ed.), *The Structure of American Industry*, 7th ed. (New York: Macmillan, 1986).

7. Erich W. Zimmermann, *Conservation in the Production of Petroleum* (New Haven: Yale University Press, 1957), p. 142.; and Gary D. Libecap and Steven N. Wiggins, "Contractual Responses to the Common Pool: Prorationing of Crude Oil Production," *American Economic Review* 74 (March 1984): 87–98.

8. The source for this description is McDonald, 1971, pp. 158–61. General background references for prorationing include Zimmermann, 1957; Melvin G. De Chazeau and Alfred E. Kahn, *Integration and Competition in the Petroleum Industry* (New Haven: Yale University Press, 1959); Wallace F. Lovejoy and Paul T. Homan, *Economic Aspects of Oil Conservation Regulation* (Baltimore: Johns Hopkins University Press, 1967); McDonald, 1971; and Libecap and Wiggins, 1984.

9. The ensuing analysis is from McDonald, 1971, chapter 5.

10. Federal Oil Conservation Board, *Complete Record of Public Hearings*, Washington, D.C.: USGPO, 1926, p. 30; *Report III*, Washington, D.C.: USGPO, 1929, p. 10.

11. Libecap and Wiggins, 1984.

12. Zimmermann, 1957, p. 286.

13. U.S. House of Representatives, Cole Committee, "Hearing on House Resolution 290 and HR 7372 to Promote the Conservation of Petroleum; to Provide for Cooperation with the States in Preventing Waste of Petroleum; to Create an Office of Petroleum Conservation," 76th Congress, Washington, D.C., 1939, p. 503.

14. J. H. Marshall and N. L. Meyers, "Legal Planning of Petroleum Production: Two Years of Proration," *Yale Law Journal* 42 (March 1933): 702–46.

15. Morris Adelman, "Efficiency of Resource Use in Crude Petroleum," *Southern Economic Journal* 31 (October 1964): 101–22.

16. This analysis is based on James C. Burrows and Thomas A. Domencich, *An Analysis of the United States Oil Import Quota* (Lexington, Mass.: Heath, 1970).

17. Douglas R. Bohi and Milton Russell, *Limiting Oil Imports* (Baltimore: The Johns Hopkins University Press, 1978).

18. Ibid.

19. For comparable estimates, see Burrows and Domencich, 1970.

20. General background references for crude oil price controls include Joseph P. Kalt, *The Economics and Politics of Oil Price Regulation* (Cambridge, Mass.: The MIT Press, 1981); W. David Montgomery, "Decontrol of Crude Oil Prices," in Leonard W. Weiss and Michael W. Klass (eds.), *Case Studies in Regulation: Revolution and Reform* (Boston: Little, Brown, 1981); Richard H. K. Vietor, *Energy Policy in America Since 1945* (Cambridge: Cambridge University Press, 1984); and R. Glenn Hubbard and Robert J. Weiner, "Petroleum Regulation and Public Policy," in Leonard W. Weiss and Michael W. Klass (eds.), *Regulatory Reform: What Actually Happened* (Boston: Little, Brown, 1986).

21. Hubbard and Weiner, 1986.

22. Ibid.

23. Joseph P. Kalt, *The Economics and Politics of Oil Price Regulation* (Cambridge Mass.: MIT Press, 1981).

24. Paul W. MacAvoy (ed.), *Federal Energy Administration Regulation* (Washington, D.C.: American Enterprise Institute, 1977).

25. Ibid.

26. Ibid.

27. Kenneth J. Arrow and Joseph P. Kalt, "Decontrolling Oil Prices," *Regulation*, September/October 1979: 13–17.

28. "Windfall Profits Tax Repealed with Trade Bill Signing," *Oil and Gas Journal*, August 29, 1988, p. 17.

29. Ibid.

30. General background references include Robert B. Helms, *Natural Gas Regulation* (Washington, D.C.: American Enterprise Institute, 1974); M. Elizabeth Sanders, *The Regulation of Natural Gas* (Philadelphia: Temple University Press, 1981); and Ronald R. Braeutigam and R. Glenn Hubbard, "Natural Gas: The Regulatory Transition," in Leonard W. Weiss and Michael W. Klass (eds.), *Regulatory Reform: What Actually Happened* (Boston: Little, Brown, 1986).

31. Pierce, 1986.

32. Ibid.

33. Actually, another method of transporting natural gas is to liquify it to 1/600th of its normal size and then ship it.

34. Vietor, 1984.

35. Ibid.

36. Helms, 1974.

37. *National Gas Survey, Volume 1* United States Federal Power Commission, 1975, p. 85.

38. United States House of Representatives, Report No. 94–732 (cited in Hubbard and Weiner).

39. Ibid.

40. Pierce, 1986.

41. Hubbard and Weiner, 1986.

42. Sickles, Robin C. and Mary L. Streitwieser, "The Structure of Technology, Substitution, and Productivity in the Interstate Natural Gas Transmission Industry under the Natural Gas Policy Act of 1978," Rice University, mimeo, March 1989.

III HEALTH, SAFETY, AND ENVIRONMENTAL REGULATION

19 Introduction: The Emergence of Health, Safety, and Environmental Regulation

As the review of regulatory costs in Chapter 2 indicated, environmental and other social regulations have become an increasingly prominent part of the regulatory mix. Indeed, the combined costs of these regulations in 1991 was double that associated with economic regulations, because of both the growth in the newer social regulations and the rise of deregulation for the economic regulations.

If this book had been written before 1970, it is likely that there would have been no discussion at all of health, safety, and environmental regulation. Since the early part of this century, there had been, of course, several efforts in the health, safety, and environmental regulation areas, but these were for the most part limited to the safety of food and drugs. Consumer advocates such as Ralph Nader became prominent influences on the national agenda in the mid-1960s, and the rising public concerns influenced national policy.

The decade of the 1970s marked the emergence of almost every major risk or environmental regulation agency. The U.S. Environmental Protection Agency, the National Highway Traffic Safety Administration, the Consumer Product Safety Commission, the Occupational Safety and Health Administration, and the Nuclear Regulatory Commission all began operation in that decade. Although in some cases these agencies absorbed functions that had been undertaken at a more modest level by other agencies, the advent of these regulatory agencies marked more than a consolidation of functions, inasmuch as each of the agencies also had their own legislative mandates that gave them substantial control over the direction of regulatory policies in these areas.

The early years of operation of these regulatory agencies were fairly controversial. Expectations were high, and for the most part these expectations regarding potential gains that would be achieved were not fulfilled. Congressmen and engineers often predicted dramatic safety gains achievable at little cost, but these predictions often ignored the role played by individual choice. Firms could ignore regulations, and indeed had an incentive to ignore them when compliance was expensive. Consumers might have chosen not to take certain precautions, such as wearing seatbelts. In addition, there was substantial resistance to the increased expansion of regulatory control over decisions that were formerly left to business. Many ill-designed regulations became the object of ridicule and vehement business opposition. Over time these regulatory efforts have become a more generally accepted component of the federal regulatory efforts. In addition, there has been an effort on the part of regulatory agencies to strike a better balance between the benefits achieved by these policies and the costs they impose.

Unlike the economic regulation areas, however, there has been no major push toward deregulation. Indeed, the recent emergence of concerns such as global climate change has increased the extent of this form of regulation. There is little doubt that actual market failures exist in the context of social regulation. In many cases, such as air pollution, no markets exist at all for the commodity being produced, and there is no market-based compensation of the victims of pollution. Markets could never suffice in instances such as this, so that our objective in the social regulation area will always be sounder regulation rather than no regulation whatsoever.

Consider, for example, the current regulatory agendas of the different agencies. At the U.S. Environmental Protection Agency, the emphasis is on dealing with the major regulatory problems that will have long-run ecological consequences. These include the "greenhouse effect," acid rain, and the depletion of the ozone layer in the atmosphere. EPA is placing increased emphasis on environmental problems that will define the well-being of the world at the beginning of the next century and beyond. None of these problems can be adequately addressed by free markets alone. At the Occupational Safety and Health Administration, the task is to devise more effective enforcement mechanisms, to update and make more performance-oriented the technological standards for workplace design, and to address in a more comprehensive manner the health hazards imposed by workplace conditions. Finally, in the product safety area, regulation of automobiles and other products is continuing as before, but there is also a new element as the increased role of product liability has highlighted the importance of coordinating the various social institutions at work in promoting health and safety. The main question in this area is one over which no one institution has responsibility—how the responsibilities should be divided among federal regulatory agencies, the market, and the courts.

Risk in Perspective

Before addressing the specific aspects of the efforts of the different regulatory agencies, it is helpful to put the scale of the problems they are addressing in perspective. Table 19.1 lists the various causes of death in the United States population.[1] The principal focus of the efforts of regulatory agencies is on accidents. All accidental deaths make up under 5 percent of the total death rate, so that even a fully effective safety regulation effort will necessarily play a small part in reducing overall mortality rates. In the accident category, roughly half of all accidental

Table 19.1
Causes of Death in the United States, 1991

Cause	Death Rate per 100,000 Population
All causes	860.3
Heart disease	285.9
Cancer	204.1
Stroke	56.9
Chronic obstructive pulmonary disease	35.9
Accidents	35.1
Motor vehicle	17.3
Falls	5.0
Poison (solid, liquid)	2.3
Drowning	1.8
Fires, burns	1.6
Pneumonia	30.9
Diabetes mellitus	19.4
Suicide	12.2
HIV infection	11.7
Homicide	10.5
Chronic liver disease, cirrhosis	10.1
Nephritis and nephrosis	8.5
Septicemia	7.8
Atherosclerosis	6.9
Certain conditions originating in perinatal period	6.7

Source: National Safety Council, *Accident Facts,* 1994 ed. (Itasca, Ill.: National Safety Council, 1994), pp. 6–7. Reprinted by permission of the National Safety Council.

deaths are due to motor vehicle accidents, which are a major component not only of nonworking accidents but also of work accidents as well. The second leading component is falls, which are concentrated almost entirely among the population over the age of seventy-five. These risks for the most part occur outside of the purview of government regulation. Similarly, drownings also tend to be age-specific, as a leading age group for drowning rates are children aged zero to four. Boating and swimming accidents are monitored by various parties, such as lifeguards. Moreover, there are government regulations of swimming pool slides, for example, that will influence drowning risks. However, for the most part these risks also fall out of the domain of regulatory policies. The categories of fires, burns, and poisoning are the subject of extensive government regulation, including safety-cap and flammability requirements of various kinds. Most, but not all, accidents are potentially under the influence of government regulation. Even a fully effective regulatory effort could not be expected to eliminate accidents, however, because individual behavior often plays a critical role. Studies assigning responsibility for job accidents, for example, generally attribute most of these accidents, at least in part, to worker behavior.

In contrast, many of the leading causes of death are more in the domain of individual behavior rather than regulatory action.[2] The main determinants of heart disease are individual diet and exercise. Similarly, many cancer experts believe that cancer risks are largely due to diet, smoking, genetics, and other person-specific factors. Environmental exposures generally rank low among the total determinants of cancer. Strokes likewise are not generally the result of risk exposures subject to government regulation, although air pollution is a prominent exception that will affect the propensity to have a stroke. Many of the causes of death that are less prominent than accidents, ranging from pulmonary disease to homicides, are also matters over which there is little regulatory control.

The Infeasibility of a No-Risk Society

These patterns do not suggest that regulation is unimportant, even though a fully successful regulatory program will not drastically alter death risks. What they do indicate is that our expectations regarding the overall effects of regulation should be tempered by an appreciation of their likely impact, even under a best case scenario. Moreover, it should also be recognized that many of the most prominent sources of death risks are in matters of individual choice, such as diet. In view of this, it seems inappropriate to adopt an extremist approach to government regulation in which we pursue a no-risk strategy while at the same time permitting risks of greater consequence to be incurred through individual action. Moreover, we need to place greater emphasis on policies such as hazard warnings and nutrition information that will foster better risk-averting decisions.

An interesting perspective on the variety of risks that we face is provided by the data in Table 19.2. Information provided in that table lists a variety of activities that will increase one's annual death risk by one chance in 1 million. This group includes some of the most highly regulated risks, as the risk of accident of living within five miles of a nuclear reactor for fifty years and the risk of smoking 1.4 cigarettes are tantamount to the risks one would face by riding ten miles on a bicycle, eating forty tablespoons of peanut butter, drinking Miami drinking water for one year, or eating a hundred charcoal-broiled steaks.

The risks that we have chosen to regulate are not altogether different from those that we incur daily as part of our normal existence. This does

Table 19.2
Risks That Increase the Annual Death Risk by One in 1 Million

Activity	Cause of Death
Smoking 1.4 cigarettes	Cancer, heart disease
Drinking 0.5 liter of wine	Cirrhosis of the liver
Spending 1 hour in a coal mine	Black lung disease
Spending 3 hours in a coal mine	Accident
Living 2 days in New York or Boston	Air pollution
Traveling 6 minutes by canoe	Accident
Traveling 10 miles by bicycle	Accident
Traveling 150 miles by car	Accident
Flying 1000 miles by jet	Accident
Flying 6000 miles by jet	Cancer caused by cosmic radiation
Living 2 months in Denver	Cancer caused by cosmic radiation
Living 2 months in average stone or brick building	Cancer caused by natural radio-activity
One chest X-ray taken in a good hospital	Cancer caused by radiation
Living 2 months with a cigarette smoker	Cancer, heart disease
Eating 40 tablespoons of peanut butter	Liver cancer caused by aflatoxin B
Drinking Miami drinking water for 1 year	Cancer caused by chloroform
Drinking 30 12-oz. cans of diet soda	Cancer caused by saccharin
Living 5 years at site boundary of a nuclear power plant in the open	Cancer caused by radiation
Drinking 1000 24-oz. soft drinks from banned plastic bottles	Cancer from acrylonitrile monomer
Living 20 years near PVC plant	Cancer caused by vinyl chloride (1976 standard)
Living 150 years within 20 miles of a nuclear power plant	Cancer caused by radiation
Eating 100 charcoal-broiled steaks	Cancer from benzopyrene
Risk of accident by living within 5 miles of a nuclear reactor for 50 years	Cancer caused by radiation

Source: Richard Wilson, "Analyzing the Daily Risks of Life," *Technology Review* 81, No. 4 (1979): 40–46. Reprinted with permission from *Technology Review*, copyright 1979.

not mean that the government should abandon regulation. But it does suggest that we will not have a risk-free environment no matter what regulations we pursue. Moreover, given the many risk-taking choices we make daily within the domain in which we institute regulations, it would not be appropriate to require that they produce a risk-free environment.

The basic issue is one of balance. Society should pursue regulations that are in our best interests, taking into account both the beneficial aspects of the regulation as well as the costs that they impose. These regulations may be stringent, or they may require that we have no regulation at all. The mere presence of a risk within the domain of a regulatory agency is not in and of itself a reason to institute a regulation. The key ingredient is that there must be some market failure to warrant government intervention. Moreover, there should be some ability of a regulatory policy to influence the risk outcome of interest.

Wealth and Risk

Our demand for greater regulation in our lives has developed in part from the increased affluence of society.[3] As our society has become richer, we have begun to place a greater value on individual health status and on efforts that can improve our physical well-being. These developments are not new. Sanitation levels and the cleanliness of food preparation, for example, were much greater in the early part of the twentieth century than they were several hundred years ago.

The influence of increased societal income is evident in the accident trends sketched in Figure 19.1. These accident statistics give the accident rate per 100,000 population, and as can be seen there is a general declining trend that has taken place. Overall accident rates are down, as are accidents at home, at work, and in other public places, other than those involving motor-vehicles. The main exception to the pattern of striking decline is that of motor vehicle accidents. Although the motor-

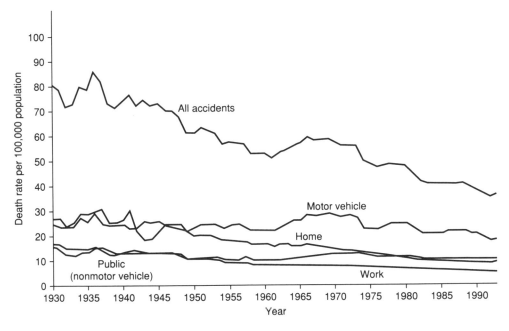

Figure 19.1
Trends in Accidental Death Rates in the United States, 1930–1993
Source: National Safety Council, *Accident Facts*, 1994 Edition (Itasca, Ill.: National Safety Council, 1994), pp. 24, 26–27.

vehicle death rate is lower now than it was sixty years ago, the change has not been great. This comparative stability is not a reflection of a failure to improve the quality and design of cars. Indeed, dramatic improvements have taken place with respect to automobile safety. Rather, the accident statistics are on a population basis, which does not take into account the level of driving intensity. If one were to examine figures based on the risk per mile driven, then the safety gains that have been achieved would be more apparent.

The existence of a downward accident trend provides a key element in terms of the historical perspective one should adopt in interpreting accident statistics. Regulatory agencies routinely announce this year's accident rates, which, if all has gone well, are lower than they were the previous year. The agency officials then tout these statistics as evidence of the efficacy of the agency's activities. Although this annual ritual may be effective political salesmanship, it ignores the fact that in all likelihood there would have continued to be a decline in the accident rate, as there has been throughout the century. The main evidence of the effectiveness of an agency should be a shift in the accident trend to a risk level below what it otherwise would have been.

The pattern of decline in accident rates also highlights the importance of technological progress. As a society we have benefited from a variety of technological improvements in our environment, and these have been a tremendous boost to our well-being. New technologies are often highly controversial and lead to demands that the risks be stringently regulated, but one should also recognize that new technologies have brought about many substantial benefits over the long run.[4]

Irrationality and Biases in Risk Perception

Whereas the negative relationship between risk levels and increased societal wealth reflects a rational economic response to risk, situations involving risk and uncertainty are also well known for the irrational decisions that they may generate. In particular, the risk statistics examined indicate for the most part that we are dealing with a low probability of events. Large risks, such as the risk of being killed in a car crash, are roughly one in 5,000 per year. Many other risks that we face are much smaller in magnitude; for example, the data in Table 19.2 indicated that we had to drink a thousand 24-ounce soft drinks from banned plastic bottles in order to incur a cancer risk of one in 1 million. Small probabilities such as this are very difficult to think about. Most people have little experience in dealing with risks such as one in a million or one in 100,000 on a sufficiently regular basis that would enable them to obtain enough experience in dealing with such events so as to

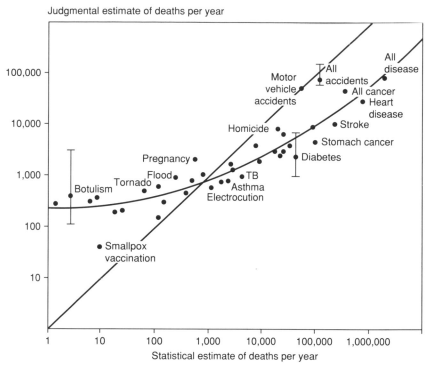

Figure 19.2
Perceived versus Actual Mortality Risks

Source: B. Fischhoff et al., *Acceptable Risk* (Cambridge: Cambridge University Press, 1981), p. 29. Reprinted with the permission of Cambridge University Press.

make sensible decisions. In some cases, the risk may not be understood at all, as the individual may be ignorant of the risk and consequently unable to make any decision with respect to it. For risks that are called to individuals' attention, there are also difficulties that arise because of biases in risk perception.

Figure 19.2 illustrates the relationship between perceived risks (on the vertical axis) and actual risks (on the horizontal axis) of death. Individuals tend to overestimate the risks associated with lower-probability events such as botulism, tornadoes, and floods. In contrast, there is a tendency to underestimate the risks associated with higher-risk events, such as the risks of cancer, heart disease, and stroke. This pattern of overreaction and underreaction suggests that market decisions will seldom be optimal. However, additional regulation will not be required in all cases. If risk perceptions are already excessive, then the market-provided risk will be too great, as the safety provided will be responding to exaggerated risk perceptions.

The overestimation of low-probability events also has substantial implications for government policy. To the extent that there is an alarmist reaction to small risks that are called to our attention, and if these pressures in turn are exerted on the policymakers responsible for risk regulation, society may end up devoting too many resources to small risks that are not of great consequence.

An interesting policy question is how the government should respond, if at all, to public misperceptions. Suppose, for example, that the public greatly overestimates the risks associated with hazardous waste sites. Should the government respond to these fears because, presumably, in a democratic society the government action should reflect the interest of the citizenry? Alternatively, one might view the government as taking a more responsible role in that it should attempt to educate the public concerning the overly alarmist reactions that it has. Moreover, ideally the government should be a steadying force in such context. If the general public underestimates the risk, one presumably would not expect the government to be idle and to let citizens incur risks unknowingly. An important function of the government is to acquire more scientific information than is feasible for an individual to obtain, to communicate this information effectively to the public, and to issue regulations that are needed to control the real risks that are present.

A related result that has emerged in the risk-perception literature is that highly publicized events often are associated with substantial risk perceptions, even though the risks involved may not be great. This finding is not a sign of individual irrationality. Typically the events themselves rather than frequency statistics are publicized. We learn that a number of people have recently been killed by a tornado, but we are not given a sense of the frequency of these events other than the fact that coverage of tornado victims in the newspaper occurs much more often than coverage of asthma victims. Because of the sensitivity of risk perceptions to the amount of publicity as well as the level of the risk, the pressures that will be exerted on risk regulation agencies will not necessarily be in line with the direction that fosters society's best interest. We will take as society's objective the promotion of societal welfare based on the true risk levels, not the risk levels as they may be perceived by society more generally.

Policy Evaluation

As a discussion of the various social regulation agencies will indicate, the stated objectives of these agencies are often quite narrow. The Clean

Air Act, for example, forbids EPA to consider cost considerations when setting air pollution standards, and the Supreme Court has explicitly prohibited the Occupational Safety and Health Administration from basing its regulations on benefit-cost analysis. Nevertheless, some balancing is required; otherwise the cost associated with the regulations could easily shut down the entire economy. Moreover, as a practical matter, cost considerations and the need for balancing enter in a variety of ways. Agencies may phase in a particularly onerous regulation. Alternatively, the agency may choose not to adopt regulations that threaten the viability of an industry or employment in a local area.

Regulatory Standards

By far the most stringent standards that promote a balancing of societal interests are those that have been imposed through regulatory oversight mechanisms of the Executive Branch.[5] The Ford administration instituted a requirement that the cost and inflationary impact of regulations be assessed. Under the Carter administration these requirements were extended to require that agencies demonstrate the cost effectiveness of their regulatory proposals. The Reagan administration went even further, requiring that agencies demonstrate that the benefits of the regulation exceed the costs imposed except when doing so would violate the legislative mandate of the agency. Moreover, even when there is such a legislative mandate, the agency must still calculate benefits and costs and submit these results to the Office of Management and Budget (OMB) for its review. The Bush and Clinton administrations have continued these policies.

The nature of the policy evaluation tools being discussed is not unique to the risk and environmental area. Procedures for assessing the benefits and costs of government policies have been in operation in the government for decades. Both the Army Corps of Engineers and the U.S. Department of Interior have been using benefit-cost analysis to govern their design and evaluation of water resources projects for several decades.

Rationale of the Benefit-Cost Approach

If one abstracts from controversies relating to how one calculates what the benefits and costs policies are, the rationale for the benefit-cost approach seems quite compelling. At a very minimum, society should not pursue policics that do not advance our interests. If the benefits of a policy are not in excess of the costs, then clearly it should not be pursued, because such efforts do more harm than good. Ideally we want to maximize the net gain that policies produce. This net gain is the dis-

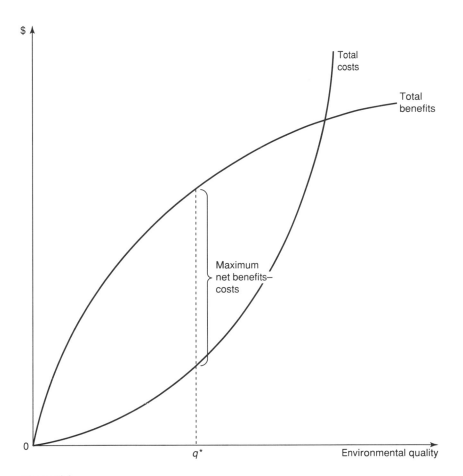

Figure 19.3
Benefit-Cost Analysis of Environmental Quality Control

crepancy between benefits and costs, so our objective should be to maximize the benefit-minus-cost difference.

Figure 19.3 illustrates how this would be done with respect to environmental quality. As environmental quality improves, the cost of providing environmental quality rises, and it does so at an increasing rate because improvements in an environmental quality become increasingly costly to achieve. As the most promising policy alternatives are exploited, one must then dip into the less effective means for enhancing the environmental quality, which contributes to the rise in costs.

The other curve in the diagram is the total benefits arising from improved environmental quality. The initial gains are the greatest, as they may affect our lives and well-being in a fundamental manner. The additional health and welfare effects of environmental quality improvements

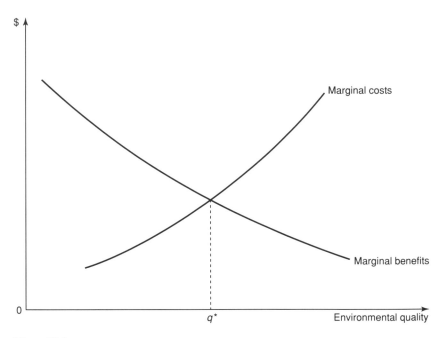

Figure 19.4
Marginal Analysis of Environmental Policies

eventually diminishes. Our task of finding the best level of environmental quality to promote through regulation reduces to achieving the largest spread between the total benefit and total cost curves. This maximum is achieved at the environmental quality level q^*. At that point, the gap between the cost and benefit curves is the greatest, with this gap giving the maximum value of the net benefits less costs that are achievable to environmental quality regulation.

The slope of the total cost and total benefit curves is equal at environmental quality q^*.[6] An alternative way to assess the optimal policy is to examine the marginal cost and marginal benefit curves, which are illustrated in Figure 19.4. Marginal costs are rising because of the decreasing productivity of additional environmental-enhancing efforts as we pursue additional improvements in environmental quality. Similarly, the marginal benefits shown in this curve are declining because they experience the greatest incremental benefits from such improvements when the environmental quality is very bad. The optimal policy level is at environmental quality level q^*, at which we equate marginal benefits and marginal costs. Thus the requirement for optimal quality choice can be characterized by the following familiar equation:

Marginal Benefits = Marginal Costs   (19.1)

Table 19.3
Cost-per-Life Values for Arsenic Regulation

Stringency	Standard Level (mg/m^3)	Average Cost per Life ($ millions)	Marginal Cost per Life ($ millions)
Loose	0.10	1.25	1.25
Medium	0.05	2.92	11.5
Tight	0.004	5.63	68.1

Source: W. Kip Viscusi, *Risk by Choice: Regulating Health and Safety in the Workplace* (Cambridge: Harvard University Press, 1983), p. 124. Copyright © 1983 by the President and Fellows of Harvard College.

Marginal Analysis

The importance of marginal analysis can be illustrated by examining some statistics on the efficacy of differing levels of stringency of arsenic regulation in the workplace. Table 19.3 provides pertinent statistics for three different levels of stringency of a standard—loose, medium, or tight. As the second column of the table indicates, lower levels of exposure to arsenic are associated with tighter standards. With increased tightness comes added costs. The third column in Table 19.3 gives one measure of the cost where it has been put into cost-effectiveness terms, in particular the cost-per-unit benefit achieved. In this case the measure is in terms of the cost per statistical life saved by the policy. This average cost-per-life-saved figure ranges from $1.25 million to $5.63 million, reflecting a substantial but by no means enormous variation in the efficacy of the policy.

In contrast, estimates of the marginal cost per life saved as appears in the final column of Table 19.3 indicate that successive tightening of the standard becomes very expensive in terms of the lives that are saved per dollar expended. In the case of tight levels of the standard, the marginal cost imposed per life saved is $68.1 million, which as we will see for the results in Chapter 20 is out of line with what a reasonable benefit value for life is. In this case, the substantial acceleration in the marginal cost-per-life values was not as apparent when the agency focused on average cost-per-life figures.

In some cases, the fallacy of focusing on averages rather than marginal changes is even more dramatic. In a policy decision involving one of the authors, the Occupational Safety and Health Administration (OSHA) was considering differing levels of stringency for a standard that would control ethylene oxide exposures, which occur primarily among hospital workers who are involved in the cleaning of surgical equipment. OSHA's regulatory analysis included calculations of the average cost per case of cancer prevented, but the officials responsible for the calculation had not noted that the last incremental tightening of the standard produced no reduction in cancer cases whatsoever. The marginal cost per case of cancer prevented in this case was actually infinite for the tightest level of the standard being considered. In contrast, the average cost per case of cancer remained fairly stable, thus disguising the inefficiency being created.

The Role of Heterogeneity

Examination of the benefits and costs of regulatory actions is important not only with respect to the stringency of any particular regulation, but also with respect to distinctions across different situations in terms of the stringency of the regulations. For example, pollution standards are generally set at a more stringent level for new enterprises than for existing enterprises, in part because the cost of compliance when introducing a new technology is believed to be less than the cost of adding pollution control devices to existing technology. There is the potential problem, however, of "new source bias." Although we want regulatory standards for new pollution sources to be more stringent so that the marginal costs are equalized across different kinds of facilities, we could err too much in this direction, as we will discuss in subsequent chapters.[7] Very often, in addition, one might want to make a distinction across industries in terms of the level of the standard because differences in industry technology imply different marginal cost curves. The optimal environmental quality level q^* that was shown in Figure 19.4 will not always be uniform. Even if the marginal benefit curve were the same in all situations, to the extent that regulated firms have differing marginal cost curves, the optimal environmental quality level will differ. As is apparent from the figure, higher marginal cost curves will shift the optimal level of environmental quality to the left, implying a less stringent regulatory regime.

The statistics presented in Table 19.4 illustrate how in practice one might approach such differentiation of a regulation. The health impact of concern here is the effect of noise pollution in the workplace on workers' hearing. In particular, the cases being examined are those involving a 25-decibel hearing threshold loss after twenty years of exposure to the noise. The statistics for the seventeen different industries represented indicate an order-of-magnitude variation in the cost per worker protected by differing levels of the standard. Suppose that one had to pick between setting the standard level at 80 decibels and at 90 decibels. In addition, for concreteness, let us assume that we are able to

Table 19.4
Industry Cost Variations for the OSHA Noise Standard

Industry	Cost per Worker Protected (thousands of dollars)	
	90 Decibels	80 Decibels
Electrical equipment and supplies	19	39
Rubber and plastics products	38	68
Stone, clay, and glass products	53	96
Paper and allied products	62	78
Food and kindred products	75	179
Chemicals and allied products	80	132
Transportation equipment	87	111
Tobacco manufactures	104	200
Printing and publishing	108	215
Electric, gas, and sanitary services	137	189
Furniture and fixtures	150	151
Fabricated metal products	192	188
Petroleum and coal products	215	257
Primary metal industries	218	372
Textile mill products	227	395
Lumber and wood products	228	303
Machinery, except electrical	233	245
Weighted average	119	169

Source: W. Kip Viscusi, *Risk by Choice*. Copyright © 1983 by the President and Fellows of Harvard College.

determine that a case of hearing loss has a benefit value of $200,000. A 90-decibel standard is justified in this case for all industries listed above petroleum and coal products in Table 19.4. Moreover, a more stringent 80-decibel standard is warranted for all industries listed above printing and publishing in the table. Thus the tighter 80-decibel standard can be justified in situations where the cost of protecting workers tends to be less. (In this instance there are also other policy options, such as protective equipment, so that hearing loss can be prevented for all workers.)

In general, policymakers should attempt to exploit cost variations such as this and take them into account when designing regulatory policies. Differentiated standards that recognize these cost differences will produce greater net benefits to society than those that do not. Uniform standards miss opportunities to promote safety and environmental quality in situations where it is cheap to do so, and impose substantial burdens in situations where the cost of providing environmental quality and safety is higher. Society should take advantage of differences in the ability to produce environmental quality and safety, just as we take advantage of other productive capabilities with respect to other goods and services that an economy provides.

Discounting Deferred Effects

If all the effects of regulatory policies were immediate, one could simply sum up these influences, treating effects today the same as one would treat an impact many years from now. Even if one ignores the role of inflation, it is important to take the temporal distribution of benefits and costs into account. If one could earn a riskless real rate of interest of r on one's money, then the value of a dollar today is $(1 + r)$ ten years from now. Thus, resources have an opportunity cost, and one must take this opportunity cost into account when assessing the value of benefit and cost streams over time. This issue is not unique to the social regulation area, but it plays a particularly important role with respect to these regulations because of the long time lags that tend to be involved, particularly when evaluating regulations focusing on cancer and the future of the planet.

Although a substantial literature exists on how one should approach the discount rate issue and estimate the appropriate rate of discount, these approaches can be simplified into two schools of thought.[8] One approach relies on the opportunity cost of capital. In this instance, market-based measures provide the guide as to the appropriate discount rate. A simple but not too unreasonable approximation to this measure is simply the real rate of return on federal bonds. The alternative is the social rate of time preference approach under which society's preference for allocating social resources across time may be quite different from the time rate expressed in private markets. How the social rate differs from the private rate and the extent of the difference from private rates of return has remained a subject of considerable debate.

From a practical standpoint, such controversies are not of major consequence in actual regulatory decisions. The U.S. Office of Management and Budget requires that all policy benefits and costs be assessed using a rate of interest of 10 percent, although regulatory agencies are free to calculate the present value of benefits and costs using other rates as well. Most choose to use some other rate as well because 10 percent is an extremely high real (that is, inflation-adjusted) rate of return.

Present Value

The procedure by which one converts a stream of benefits and costs into a present value is simply to divide any differed impacts in year i by $(1 + r)$. Viewed somewhat differently, if one could earn a rate of interest r on \$1 invested today, the value of this dollar i years from now would

Table 19.5
Discounting Example

	Year 0	Year 1	Total
No Discounting			
Benefits	1.00	2.15	3.15
Costs	−3.00	−0.00	−3.00
Benefits–Costs	−2.00	2.15	+0.15
Discounting at 5%			
Benefits	1.00	2.05	3.05
Costs	−3.00	−0.00	−3.00
Benefits–Costs	−2.00	+2.05	0.05
Discounting at 10%			
Benefits	1.00	1.95	2.95
Costs	3.00	0.00	3.00
Benefits–Costs	−2.00	1.95	−0.05

be $(1 + r)$. Thus the present value calculation simply puts the future payoff into terms that are comparable to payoffs today. More specifically, if one has project benefits B and C in year i, then the formula is given by

$$\text{Present Value} = \sum_{i=0}^{n} \frac{B_i - C_i}{(1 + r)^i} \tag{19.2}$$

To see the implications of the present value calculation, consider a simplified discounting example in Table 19.5. Three different sets of results are provided. First, the benefits and costs in which there is no discounting comprise the first part of the table. As can be seen, the benefits exceed the costs by 0.15, and the policy is worth pursuing. If one adopts a discount rate of 5 percent, then the deferred benefits one year from now have a lower present value. Nevertheless, the policy still remains justified on benefit-cost grounds, although the strength of the justification has been weakened. The final example shows the discount rate raised to 10 percent. This higher rate lowers even further the value of next year's benefits. In this instance costs exceed benefits, and the policy is no longer justified. Since costs are generally imposed early in the life of a regulation, and benefits often accrue later, as a rough rule-of-thumb raising the discount rate tends to reduce the overall attractiveness of policies. The exact relationship hinges on the number of sign reversals in the net benefit less cost stream over time. For one sign reversal—net costs in the early periods followed by net benefits—raising the discount rates reduces the attractiveness of a policy. The role of discounting is particularly instrumental in affecting the attractiveness of policies with long-term impacts, such as environmental regulations that address long-run ecological consequences or cancer regulations for which the benefits will not be yielded for two or three decades. Not surprisingly, a major battleground over discounting was asbestos regulation, inasmuch as the deferred nature of the risk made discounting a major policy issue in a debate involving EPA, OMB, and members of Congress. EPA advocated a discount rate of zero so that the benefits of the regulation would appear to be large.

Although the practice of reducing the value of deferred benefits may seem to be unduly harsh, it will be muted at least to some extent by increases in the unit benefit value over time. As society continues to become richer, the value we place upon environmental quality and risk reduction will also rise. As a result, there will be some reduction in benefits because of discounting, but there also will be some increase in the value benefits over time because of society's increased affluence, which generally raises the value that people attach to their health or environmental quality.

In general, on balance one will still discount in a manner that reduces the present value of future impacts. If one were in a situation in which one did not discount at all, which is a position that has been frequently advocated by the U.S. Environmental Protection Agency and by some Congressmen, then any action with permanent adverse effects could never be undertaken. A $1 annual loss that was permanent would swamp in value any finite benefit amount that was for one time only. No policies that would affect a unique natural resource or that would lead to the extinction of a species could ever be pursued. The cost of such efforts would be infinite. Trivial losses that extended forever could never be imposed, irrespective of how great the current benefits are. When confronted with the full implications of not discounting at all, it is likely that there would be few advocates of this practice. We certainly do not follow this practice in our daily lives. Otherwise, we would save all of our resources, earn interest, and spend the money in our last years of life.

Uncertainty and Conservatism

Most situations of risk regulation involve these elements but are not well understood. Typical regulation of carcinogens, for example, is based on laboratory tests involving animals. To make the leap from animals to humans, one must adjust for differences in the size of the dosage of a particular chemical, differences in body weight and size, differences in surface area, as well as possible differences in human as opposed to animal responses. Moreover, the results with different animal species may imply differing levels of riskiness that must then be assessed in such a manner that we can draw meaningful inferences for humans. Even in situations where we can reach a consensus on these issues, there is often a debate as to how one should model the risk relationships. For example, should one use a linear dose-response relationship or a nonlinear model? The fact that uncertainty exists does not imply that the risks are unimportant or should be ignored, but it does create an additional element that must be addressed in the course of risk regulation.

Even in the case of relatively common risks about which much is known, the range of uncertainty may be substantial. The range of uncertainty is indicated in the final column of Table 19.6. Risks posed by drinking water regulated by EPA, for example, could be ten times greater or ten times less than the mean estimate of the risk. Similarly, the risks posed by air pollution could be twenty times less than the mean estimate. In general, the regulatory approach is to use the upper end of the 95 percent confidence level around a particular risk. In the case of the statistics in Table 19.6, the risk levels as calculated by government agencies such as the EPA tend to reflect the annual risk level plus the uncertainty factor implied by the final column.

Table 19.6
Risks and Their Uncertainty

Action	Annual Risk	Uncertainty
Motor vehicle accident (total)	2.4×10^{-4}	10%
Motor vehicle accident (pedestrian only)	4.2×10^{-5}	10%
Home accidents	1.1×10^{-4}	5%
Electrocution	5.3×10^{-6}	5%
Air pollution, eastern U.S.	2.0×10^{-4}	Factor of 20 downward only
Cigarette smoking, one pack per day	3.6×10^{-3}	Factor of 3
Sea-level background radiation (except radon)	2.0×10^{-5}	Factor of 3
All cancers	2.8×10^{-3}	10%
Four tablespoons peanut butter per day	8.0×10^{-6}	Factor of 3
Drinking water with EPA limit of chloroform	6.0×10^{-7}	Factor of 10
Drinking water with EPA limit of trichloroethylene	2.0×10^{-9}	Factor of 10
Alcohol, light drinker	2.0×10^{-5}	Factor of 10
Police killed in line of duty (total)	2.2×10^{-4}	20%
Police killed in line of duty (by felons)	1.3×10^{-4}	10%
Frequent flying professor	5.0×10^{-5}	50%
Mountaineering (mountaineers)	6.0×10^{-4}	50%

Source: Richard Wilson and E. A. C. Crouch, "Risk Assessment and Comparisons: An Introduction," *Science*, 236 (1987): 268. Reprinted by permission of the American Association for the Advancement of Science.

By erring on the side of conservatism, in effect government agencies distort the true risk levels by differing amounts. We may be in a situation where a lower risk is the subject of more stringent regulation, not because it imposes a greater expected health loss, but because less is known about it. Indeed, the biases implied by Table 19.6 may be rather low compared with the actual biases that may be created by the conservatism approach when dealing with hazards that are far less well understood than the familiar risks covered in that table. These uncertainty factors ignore other biases that are present, such as the fact that government agencies generally rely on test results for the most sensitive animal species rather than a weighted average across all species.

Typically government policies are based on a series of conservatism assumptions rather than simply one. Consider the case of the EPA Superfund program, which is responsible for the cleanup of hazardous waste sites.[9] The EPA analysis of the risks of these sites includes a wide variety of the conservatism assumptions, a few of which are the following. First, who lives near the site and will be exposed to the risk? In addition to examining current populations, the EPA assumes there is a risk if there is some potential chance that a future population could be exposed to the risk even if such a chance is unlikely. Supreme Court Justice Stephen Breyer, for example, noted that at one Superfund site involving a case in which he ruled that a modest cleanup effort could make the dirt at the site clean enough so that children could eat the dirt for 70 days per year.[10] However, EPA spent an additional 9.3 million dollars to clean up the site so that children would be able to eat the dirt without risk for up to 245 days per year. What was noteworthy about the site is that no children lived near the site, which was a swamp. Similar unrealistic assumptions may affect the risk estimates at other sites, such as the North Carolina Superfund site at which it is assumed that a factory will be built in the future and that during their lunch break workers will swim in a nearby creek, exposing them to the contaminated water.

Most of the scientific components of the assessment are also highly conservative estimates. The concentration of chemicals at the site, the amount of the chemicals that individuals will be exposed to through ingestion and other mechanisms, the frequency of exposure, the duration of exposure, and the effect of the exposure on individual health are set at either the upper end of the 95th percent confidence limit or at the maximum level. The net result of the conservatism biases is to generate a risk assessment that may bear little relationship to the actual risk posed, making it difficult for policy makers to determine which sites pose risks and which do not.

The Role of Risk Ambiguity

If one were dealing with a single trial situation in which one rarely incurred risk, the precision of the risk judgment would not enter. Uncertainty should not be a concern in the case of one-period decisions.

This principle can be traced back to the well-known Ellsberg Paradox.[11] Suppose that you face two different urns, each of which contains red balls and white balls. Urn 1 contains fifty red balls and fifty white balls. Urn 2 contains an unknown mixture of red and white balls. Each urn contains a hundred balls, and you cannot see the contents of either urn. Suppose that you will win a prize if you can correctly guess the color of the ball that will be drawn. Which urn would you pick from and what color would you name?

The correct answer is that you should be indifferent between the two situations. Drawing from urn 1 offers you a known 50-percent chance of winning the prize. Because you did not know the composition of urn 2, you face an equivalent 50/50 chance of winning, by drawing from that urn, irrespective of the color of the ball you pick.

Most people confronted with the choice between the two urns believe that urn 1 is preferable because it offers a "hard" probability of success. However, the chances of success can be converted to an equally "hard" probability in the case of urn 2. Suppose you were to flip a fair coin before naming the color of the ball, and you had picked red if the outcome was heads and white if the outcome was tails. In that situation, you also face the same kind of precise probability of a 50/50 chance of success as you do with urn 1.

Although you should be indifferent between the two urns in the case of a single trial, this would not be the case if there were multiple trials. Suppose that you will be engaged in ten draws from the urn, where you have to replace the balls after each trial. From urn 1 you know you have a 50/50 chance of success on each trial, where this is a precisely understood probability. In contrast, from urn 2 the probability begins initially as a 50-percent chance of naming the correct ball, but with successive trials this probability will increase. For example, if the first three balls that you draw are red, then you will have acquired some information about the composition of that urn. In particular, the odds that there is a disproportionate number of red balls in that urn will have gone up, so that on successive trials your expected chance of receiving a prize after naming a red ball will be greater than 50/50. Even though this probability will remain a "soft" probability, it will still be in your interest to draw from the uncertain urn.

The same type of principle embodied in this example is true more generally. For one-shot decisions, the precision of the risk is not a matter of consequence. But in sequential decisions in which learning is possible and in which you can revise your decisions over time, it is preferable to have a situation of uncertainty rather than to have a precisely understood risk. In situations of uncertainty we can alter a course of action if the risk turns out to be different than we had anticipated originally.

In regulatory contexts, what this result implies is that the stringency of our regulation may depend in large part on uncertainty, but we will not necessarily respond in a conservative manner to this uncertainty. If you must take action now to avoid an environmental catastrophe, then uncertainty is irrelevant. The mean risk should be your guide. However, if we can learn about how serious the problem is and take effective action in the future, then it will generally be preferable to make less of a regulatory commitment than one would if this were a one-shot decision.

The conservatism approach to regulatory analysis runs the danger of confusing risk analysis with risk management. Ideally, the scientific analysis underlying regulatory policies should not be distorted by biases and conservatism factors. Policymakers should be aware of the true risks posed by different kinds of exposures so that we can make comparative judgments across different regulatory alternatives. Otherwise, we run the danger of distorting our policy mix and focusing attention on hazards that offer few expected payoffs but are not well understood.

The Role of Political Factors

Although benefit-cost analysis provides a convenient normative reference point for the determination of social regulation policies, in practice other political forces may be more instrumental. In particular, the same kinds of economic interests that influence the setting of economic regulations in a manner that does not maximize social efficiency also are at work in determining the structure of risk and environmental regulations. The Stigler/Peltzman/Becker models have applicability to social regulation as well.

Economic Models of Environmental Policies

One class of regulatory policies that has received very intense scrutiny by economists such as Robert Crandall, Peter Pashigian, Joseph Kalt, and Mark Zupan, is the determination of environmental policies. In each case they have documented that a driving force behind the congressional voting over key environmental provisions that govern regu-

Table 19.7
Determinant of Patterns of Congressional Voting on Environmental Issues

	Factors Influencing log $\left(\dfrac{\text{VOTE}}{1 - \text{VOTE}} \right)$	
Hypothesis Sign	Explanatory Variable	Estimated Effect
?	Air pollution	No significant effect
?	Water quality	No significant effect
?	Party	Significant negative
?	Natural lands	Significant negative
+	Income	Significant positive (1 out of 9)
−	Income growth	Significant negative
+	Frostbelt	Significant positive (3 out of 9)

latory policy has been dictated by the economic stakes involved. A chief source of these differences is regional. Representatives of districts from the declining areas of the Northeast have in particular used regulatory policies to limit the degree to which the emerging economic regions of the United States could compete with them.

Consider, for example, the results presented in the analysis of congressional voting by Crandall, which are summarized in Table 19.7.[12] Pashigian derived results that are more detailed and similar in character.[13] What Crandall found is that the current levels of air pollution and water pollution have little effect on the way in which a congressional delegation voted. The ones that were of greater consequence were more closely related to the economic interests involved.

The delegations with a larger share of Republicans in their districts were more likely to vote against environmental and energy policies, where the variable of interest in the analysis was the percentage of the delegation voting "right" on environmental and energy issues. This result is consistent with the greater orientation of the Republican party toward business interests, which are more closely linked to the economic impacts of such regulation. Congressmen representing districts with a large percentage of the national parks also are likely to vote no, perhaps because further expansion in these parks will take more land out of the economic base. The income level is positively linked with votes for environmental and energy issues, reflecting the fact that environmental quality is a normal economic good for which one's preferences will increase with one's income status.

The two key variables are the final ones in Table 19.7. States with substantial income growth are more likely to vote against environmental controls, because these controls will restrict the expansion of industry in these states. In contrast, the states in the Frostbelt of the North Central, New England, and Middle Atlantic states are more likely to vote for strict environmental controls, because these controls will hit hardest on the newly emerging sources in other regions of the country. In particular, because the main structure of EPA policy imposes more stringent requirements on new sources of pollution rather than existing sources, more stringent environmental regulation generally implies that there will be a differential incidence of costs on newly emerging industries and regions with substantial economic expansion. As a consequence there are important distributional issues at stake when voting on the stringency of such environmental policies.

The result was that the air pollution regulations that were promulgated imposed a variety of requirements with substantial redistributional impacts. For example, the legislation required that firms install scrubbers to decrease their sulfur dioxide pollution. An alternative means of achieving the same objective would have been for firms and power plants to rely more on the western low-sulfur coal. However, this option would have hurt the coal-producing regions of the Midwest and Northeast, and, as a result, the representatives from these regions opposed giving firms the more performance-oriented standard. By requiring that firms meet a technology-based standard that did not permit the substitution of types of coal to meet the pollution target, they could protect the economic interest of the eastern coal producers.

Although there have been a number of other analyses indicating a variety of social regulations as being subject to the influence of such political factors, there remains a question in the literature as to the extent to which economic self-interest is the main determinant of regulatory policy. In an effort to explore these determinants more fully, Kalt and Zupan have developed a model in which they analyze two different sets of influences—economic self-interest as reflected in the standard capture theory models of regulation and ideology, which are more closely associated with the more normative approaches to regulation.[14] The focus of their analysis was on the voting for coal strip-mining regulations. The requirement to restore strip-mine land to the premining state imposed substantial costs. The annual costs associated with this policy were believed to be $1.4 billion, where surface miners would bear roughly two-thirds of the cost and consumers would bear roughly one-third. The environmental gains were believed to be $1.3 billion per year. Overall, this policy would lead to a transfer from surface mine producers and coal consumers to underground producers and environmental consumers.

Table 19.8
Factors Affecting Voting Patterns for Stripmining Regulation

	Determinants of the Percentage of Anti-Stripmining Vote	
Explanatory Variables	Capture Model	Capture and Ideology
Proenvironmental vote	NA	Significant positive
Regulation-induced mine cost	Significant negative	Significant negative
Surface reserves	Significant negative	Significant negative
Underground coal reserves	Significant positive	Significant positive
SPLIT rights for strippable land	Negative	Positive
Environmental group membership in state	Significant positive	Positive
Unreclaimed value of land (stripped not restored)	Significant positive	Significant positive
Coal consumption in state	Negative	Significant negative
Surface coal mine groups	Negative	Positive
Underground coal mine groups	Positive	Positive
Environmental groups	Significant positive	Negative
Consumer groups in state	Significant negative	Negative

Voting Patterns

Under the capture theory, factors such as altruism, public interest objectives, and civic duty are believed to be insignificant determinants of voting patterns. In contrast, the ideological models of voting use the social objectives of the political actors as the objective function that is being maximized in the voting process. A potential role for ideological voting enters, because the market for controlling legislators meets infrequently. We vote for Representatives every two years and Senators every six years. Moreover, the voters have very weak incentives to become informed, and it is often possible for representatives to shirk their responsibility to represent the voters' interests in such a situation.

Table 19.8 summarizes the series of factors considered in the Kalt and Zupan analysis. These results suggest that both the capture and ideology models illuminate aspects of the determinants of the anti-stripmining vote. In particular, Congressmen are more likely to vote in favor of stripmining the higher the level of coal reserves in their state, the greater the environmental group membership in their state, the greater the unreclaimed value of the land that is stripped and not restored, and the greater the concentration of environmental groups in the state. They are more likely to vote against anti-stripmining regulations if there is a high regulation-induced mine cost for the state, a high amount of surface-coal reserves, or a high concentration of consumer groups in the state. Because it is the surface-coal industry that will lose from the regulation and the underground coal industry that will benefit, these influences follow the pattern one would expect.

The final column of estimates adds a capture theory variable, which is the proenvironmental voting record of the Congressmen. This variable has a positive effect on voting in favor of anti-stripmining legislation, and the magnitude of this effect is substantial. Kalt and Zupan interpret this result as indicating that ideology has an independent influence above and beyond capture. Indeed, the addition of this variable increases the percentage of the variation explained by the equation by 29 percent.

Interpretation of this measure as reflecting simply capture concerns also raises some difficulties, however. In particular, it may be that the proenvironmental voting record serves to reflect the influence of omitted aspects of the capture model. In particular, the fact that a Congressman has voted in favor of environmental measures in the past may be a consequence of the influence of a variety of economic self-interest variables pertaining to the stakes that his voters have in such legislation. This variable may consequently serve as a proxy for a host of concerns that were not explicitly included in the equation. The proenvironmental voting record consequently may not reflect concerns restricted to ideology, but may reflect the past influence of capture variables that will also be at work with respect to the anti-stripmining vote.

Interpretation of these models is also difficult because of the role of logrolling. If Congressmen exchange votes, agreeing to vote for measures they do not support in return for support of legislation in which they have a substantial interest, then the congressional voting patterns may be a misleading index of the impact of the political forces at work.

To the extent that there is a controversy in the economics literature over these issues, it is not with respect to whether capture models are of consequence, but the extent to which these influences are at work. The extreme versions of these models claim that the capture theory accounts for all of the pattern of voting and regulation. Even if such economic self-interests are only major contributors to the outcomes and not the sole contributors, they should nevertheless be taken into account as an important factor driving the determination of regulatory policy.

Summary and Overview of Part 3

Determining the optimal environmental policy typically involves only a straightforward application of benefit-cost analysis. Perhaps the main role for economists is in defining what these benefits are, particularly since environmental benefits typically are not explicitly traded on the market.

As a practical matter, environmental policies tend to be governed by a host of political factors that bear little relationship to the normative guidelines that might be prescribed by economists. Economic analysis nevertheless has a role to play with respect to these forces as well, as it illuminates how the different payoffs to the political actors have motivated the environmental policies that have emerged over the past two decades.

In subsequent chapters we will explore a representative mix of issues arising in the environment and safety area. This examination is not intended to be exhaustive, but we will address many of the problems that arise in this whole class of regulatory policies.

Chapter 20 begins with a discussion of the task of setting a price on the regulatory impacts. For the most part, social-regulation efforts deal with situations in which there are no existing markets available to set a price. We can draw marginal-benefit curves and total-benefit curves as convenient abstractions, but ultimately we would need to know how much benefit society does place on environmental quality or reduced birth defects before we can make any policy judgments that are more than hypothetical. Over the past two decades, economists have devoted considerable attention to devising methodologies by which we can establish these prices. Indeed, the principal focus has perhaps been on the area that one might have thought would be least amenable to economic analysis, which is the economic value of reducing risk to human life. The implications of Chapter 20 are pertinent to all subsequent discussions, inasmuch as they provide the best reference point that can be used for assessing the appropriate stringency of the regulatory policy.

Chapter 21 focuses on the specific cases of environmental regulation. The regulatory strategy there has been largely to set standards and to issue permits that allow firms to engage in a particular amount of pollution. The major difficulty is that compliance with these standards may be quite costly, and there is a need to set a balance between the economic costs to the firm and the benefits that will be achieved for society. Environmental protection efforts are utilizing increasingly imaginative means to strike such a balance, and we explore such approaches in this chapter.

In Chapter 22 we turn to a series of product safety regulations. These regulations also deal with risks that are, at least in part, the result of market transactions. The diverse forms of product regulation include auto safety regulation, food and drug regulations, general product safety regulations by the Consumer Product Safety Commission, and the impact of the liability system on product safety. This diversity has created a need for coordination among these institutions. Moreover, in the product-safety area in particular, the role of "moral hazard" has played a central role in economic analyses. Mandating seatbelts may have seemed like an attractive regulatory policy, but if nobody uses the seatbelts we will not experience any gain in safety. Other more complex behavioral responses are also possible, and we will examine these as well. Perhaps the main message of the product safety analysis is that the outcomes of regulatory policy are not dictated by regulatory technology, but instead involve a complex interaction of technological and behavioral responses.

Job safety regulations—the focus of Chapter 23—also involve markets that are in existence. In particular, workers incur job risks as part of the employment relationship, and in many cases these risks are understood by the worker who is facing the risk. Moreover, in return for bearing the risk, the worker will receive additional wages as well as workers'-compensation benefits after an injury. The presence of a market makes regulation of job safety somewhat different in character from environmental regulations.

Moreover, the main regulatory issues in the job safety area seem to be quite different as well. Because of the presence of a market before the advent of regulation, the initial wave of job safety regulation met with considerable resistance. In addition, perhaps the weakest link in the regulatory effort in the job safety area is the lax enforcement effort. In this area in particular, implementation aspects of regulatory policy loom particularly large.

Questions and Problems

1. Contrast the kinds of market failure that lead to regulation of automobile safety, as opposed to regulation of automobile emissions. In which case does a market exist that, if it were operating perfectly, would promote an efficient outcome? What kinds of impediments might lead to market failure?

2. Officials of the Environmental Protection Agency frequently argue that we should not discount the benefits of environmental regulation. Their argument is that it is acceptable to discount financial impacts, but it is not acceptable to discount health effects and environmental outcomes that occur in the future. What counterarguments can you muster?

3. What are the alternative mechanisms by which the government has intervened in the health, safety, and environmental area? How does the choice of mechanisms across agencies such as OSHA, EPA, and the FDA vary

with the regulatory context? Do you see any rationale, for example, for the difference in regulatory approach?

4.   Challenge question. Increasing the rate of discount typically makes one more present-oriented, but this is not always the case. Construct a sequence of benefit and cost payoffs for two different projects. It is easy to construct a sequence of payoffs for which project 1 is preferred at low discount rates, and project 2 is preferred at high discount rates. In this case, one would say that project 1 is more future-oriented. Can you construct a sequence of benefit and cost payoffs for three different projects so that project 1 is preferred at low discount rates, project 2 is preferred at intermediate discount rates, and project 3 is preferred at high discount rates? What is the minimum number of periods that you need to generate such a reversal in preference? What is the minimum number of sign reversals in the difference in the net benefit-cost payoffs to the three projects that is needed to achieve such a reversal?

5.   If future generations were able to contract with us, they would presumably bargain for a higher level of environmental quality than we would choose to leave them without such compensation. To what extent should society recognize these future interests? Should our views be affected at all by the fact that future generations will be more affluent and will probably have a higher standard of living? How will this difference in wealth affect their willingness to pay for environmental quality, as opposed to that of current generations? What will be the equity effects in terms of income distribution across generations?

6.   Should society react differently to voluntary and involuntary risks? Which risk would you regulate more stringently?

Recommended Reading

Health, safety, and environmental regulation has often been a prominent concern of the Council of Economic Advisors, who have frequently provided comprehensive and excellent perspectives on these issues. The best recent broadly based treatment of the class of issues to be considered in this part of the book appeared in Chapter 6 of the *Economic Report of the President, January 1987* (Washington, D.C.: U.S. Government Printing Office, 1987). A treatment of environmental risks in particular appears in Chapter 6 of the *Economic Report of the President, February 1990* (Washington, D.C.: U.S. Government Printing Office, 1990). The issue of long-term environmental risks has been increasingly prominent. The best overview of this class of issues appears in the National Academy of Sciences, *Policy Implications of Greenhouse Warming* (Washington, D.C.: National Academy Press, 1991).

Notes

1. For a detailed perspective on the various causes of accidental death, see the National Safety Council, *Accident Facts*, 1990 ed. (Chicago: National Safety Council, 1990).

2. A longstanding issue in health economics has been the role of individual consumption decisions, such as exercise and smoking, in influencing health status.

For a discussion of these factors, see Victor R. Fuchs, *The Health Economy* (Cambridge, Mass.: Harvard University Press, 1986).

3. For further discussion of the relationship between wealth and risk, see W. Kip Viscusi, "Wealth Effects and Earnings Premiums for Job Hazards," *Review of Economics and Statistics* 60, 3 (1978) 408–16, and W. Kip Viscusi, *Risk By Choice: Regulating Health and Safety in the Workplace* (Cambridge, Mass.: Harvard University Press, 1983).

4. For a discussion of the beneficial role of new technologies and their effect on longevity, see Aaron Wildavsky, *Searching for Safety* (New Brunswick, N.J.: Transaction Books, 1988).

5. The U.S. Office of Management and Budget periodically issues reports that describe in detail the character of its oversight efforts. The most recent of these documents is the U.S. Office of Management and Budget, *Regulatory Program of the United States Government, April 1, 1990–March 31, 1991* (Washington, D.C.: U.S. Government Printing Office, 1990).

6. The slope of the total costs curve is known as the marginal cost, as it represents the incremental increase in costs that arise from a unit increase in environmental quality. Similarly, the slope of the total benefit curve is known as the marginal benefit curve, as it represents the increment in benefits that would be produced by a one-unit increase in environmental quality.

7. For an excellent introduction to discounting issues and the calculation of present value within policy contexts, see Edith Stokey and Richard J. Zeckhauser, *A Primer for Policy Analysis* (New York: W.W. Norton, 1978).

8. See Stokey and Zeckhauser, 1978.

9. See W. Kip Viscusi and Jay Hamilton, "Superfund and Real Risks," *The American Enterprise* 5, 2 (March/April 1994): 36–45.

10. See Stephen Breyer, *Breaking the Vicious Circle: Toward Effective Risk Regulation* (Cambridge, Mass.: Harvard University Press, 1993).

11. The original Ellsberg Paradox is discussed in the article by Daniel Ellsberg, "Risk, Ambiguity, and the Savage Axioms," *Quarterly Journal of Economics* 75 (1961): 643–69.

12. This discussion is based on Robert Crandall, *Controlling Industrial Pollution: The Economics and Politics of Clean Air* (Washington, D.C.: Brookings Institution, 1983).

13. The important analysis by Pashigian appears in B. Peter Pashigian, "Environmental Regulation: Whose Self-Interests Are Being Protected?," *Economic Inquiry* 23 (1984).

14. See Joseph Kalt and Mark Zupan, "Capture and Ideology in the Economic Theory of Politics," *American Economic Review* 74 (1984): 279–300.

Establishing the appropriate degree of social regulation requires that we set a price for what the regulation produces. In the case of environmental regulation, we need to know what the value to society of additional pollution reduction will be before we can set the stringency of the standard. In the case of health and safety regulations, we need to know what is the value of preventing additional risks to life and health.

Although one can sidestep these issues in part by relying on cost-effectiveness analysis in which we calculate the cost per unit of social benefit achieved, such as the cost per expected life saved, the most that can be done with cost-effectiveness analysis is to weed out the truly bad projects. Ultimately, some judgment must be made with respect to the amount of resources society is willing to commit to a particular area of social regulation. In practice, this tradeoff may be implicit, as government officials may make subjective judgment with respect to whether a policy is too onerous. Implicit overall judgments come close to setting an implicit value on life, health, or pollution, but often these judgments may result in serious imbalances across policy areas.

One reason for these imbalances is that taking tradeoffs into consideration in an ad hoc manner may be a highly imperfect process. OSHA, for example, attempts to avoid regulatory actions that will lead to the shutdown of a particular firm. EPA likewise has similar concerns, as it has made an effort to phase in pollution requirements for the steel industry. When EPA policies would have serious repercussions for local employment, it has sought the advice of the residents in the affected area. Often the compromise that is reached is that the requirements will be phased in over a long period of time, which will reduce the costs of transition and which can better be accommodated given the normal process of replacing capital equipment over time. This practice of phasing in requirements has also been followed for automobile regulation, where pollution-control requirements and major safety innovations, such as airbag requirements, have been imposed with fairly long lead times so that the industry can adjust to the standards.

The focus of this chapter will be on how society can establish a more formal, systematic, and uniform basis for establishing tradeoffs between the resources expended and the benefits achieved through social regulation efforts. For most economic commodities, this would be a straightforward process. The U.S. Bureau of Labor Statistics gathers price information on hundreds of commodities, so that finding out the price of a market-traded good is a fairly trivial undertaking. In contrast, social-regulation efforts for the most part deal with commodities that are not traded explicitly in markets. Indeed, from a policy standpoint, it is in large part because of the lack of explicit trade that we have instituted government regulation in these areas. Victims of pollution do not sell the right to pollute to the firms that impose these pollution costs. Future generations that will suffer the ill effects of genetic damage likewise do not contract with current generations, the operators of genetic engineering experiments, or the firms that expose pregnant women to high levels of radiation. Nevertheless, to the extent that it is possible, we would like to establish a market reference point for how much of a resource commitment we should make to preventing these outcomes so that we can get a better sense of the degree to which various forms of social regulation should be pursued. We will use valuation of the risks to life as the case study for considering how the government can value the benefits associated with regulations affecting health and the environment.

Two approaches have been used. The first is to estimate the implicit prices for these social risk commodities that may be traded implicitly in markets. Most important is that workers receive additional premiums for the risks they face on the job, and the wage tradeoffs they receive can be used to establish an appropriate tradeoff rate. A second general approach is to ask people through an interview context how much they value a particular health outcome. This methodology may have greater problems with respect to reliability, but has the advantage in that one can obtain tradeoff information regarding a wide range of policy outcomes.

Policy Evaluation Principles

Suppose that this evening you will be crossing the street, and that you have one chance in 10,000 of being struck by a bus and killed instantaneously. We will offer you the opportunity to buy out of this risk for a cash payment now. For purposes of this calculation, you can assume that your credit is good and that, if necessary, you can draw on either your parents' or your future resources. To put the risk in perspective, a probability of death of one chance in 10,000 is comparable to the average fatality risk faced each year by a blue collar worker in American industries. How much would you be willing to pay for eliminating this risk?

This kind of thought process is exactly what the government should go through when thinking about how far to push various social-regulation efforts. In particular, the main matter of concern is society's total willingness to pay for eliminating small probabilities of death or adverse health effects.[1] Thus we are not interested in the dollar value of your future earnings that will be lost, although this of course will be relevant to how you think about the calculation. In addition, we are not interested in how much you are willing to pay to avoid certain death. The level of the probability of risk involved with certain death dwarfs that associated with small risk events by such an extent that the qualitative aspects of the risk event are quite different. It is noteworthy, for example, that society views suicide with disfavor, but the taking of small risks, such as the decision to drive a compact car rather than a larger car that offers greater safety, is generally viewed as being acceptable.

Let us now take your response to the willingness-to-pay question above and convert it into a value of life. What we mean by the value of life terminology is the value that you would be willing to pay to prevent a statistical death. This amount is straightforward to calculate. To calculate this magnitude, one simply divides your willingness-to-pay response by the level of the risk that you are reducing, or:

$$\text{Value of Life} = \frac{\text{Willingness to Pay}}{\text{Size of Risk Reduction}} \qquad (20.1)$$

This gives the amount you would be willing to pay per unit of mortality risk. For the specific values given in the example we considered, the value-of-life number can be calculated as

$$\text{Value of Life} = \frac{\text{Willingness to Pay}}{1/10,000} \qquad (20.2)$$

or

$$\text{Value of Life} = 10,000 \times \text{Willingness to Pay} \qquad (20.3)$$

An alternative way of thinking about the value of life is the following. Consider a group of 10,000 people, one of whom will die in the next year. As a result, there will be one expected death. If each person would be willing to contribute the same amount to achieve the risk reduction, then the value of preventing one expected death would be 10,000 multiplied by the willingness-to-pay amount per person. This calculation is identical to that in equation (20.3) above.

Your value of life implicit in the response you gave is consequently 10,000 times the amount of your response. Table 20.1 gives different value-of-life estimates depending on the level of your answer. If there is no finite amount of money that you would be willing to pay to prevent this risk, and if you were willing to devote all of your present and future resources to eliminate it (presumably retaining enough for minimal subsistence), then it would be safe to say that you place an infinite value on your life, or at least a value that is very, very large. Any finite response below this amount implies that you would be willing to accept a finite value of life or make a risk-dollar tradeoff when confronted with a

Table 20.1
Relation of Survey Responses to Value of Life

Amount Will Pay (Dollars) to Eliminate 1/10,000 Risk	Value of Life (Dollars)
Infinite	Infinity
Above 1,000	At least 10,000,000
500–1,000	5,000,000–10,000,000
200–500	2,000,000–5,000,000
50–200	500,000–2,000,000
0	0

life-extending decision. When viewed in this manner, making a risk-dollar tradeoff does not appear to be particularly controversial. Indeed, one might appear to be somewhat irrational if one were willing to expend all of one's future resources to prevent small risks of death, particularly given the fact that we make such tradeoffs daily, as some of the risk statistics in Chapter 19 indicated.

For the finite value of life responses, a willingness-to-pay of $1,000 to prevent a risk of death of one chance in 10,000 implies a value of life of $10 million. A response of $500 to prevent the small risk implies a value of life of $5 million. Similarly, at the extreme end, a zero response implies a value-of-life estimate of zero. Table 20.1 summarizes the relationship between various willingness-to-pay amounts and the value of life.

When presented with this survey task, most students tend to give fairly low responses, at the lower end of the range of the table. When we examine the implicit values of life of workers based on the wages they receive for the risks they face in their jobs, we will show that their values of life are much greater than those often given by students responding to the 1/10,000 death risk question. The best estimates of the value of life for a worker in a typical blue-collar job are in the $3 million to $6 million range.

Two explanations come to mind for these low responses. First, dealing with low-probability events such as this is a very difficult undertaking. Second, there is a tendency to think in terms of one's immediate resources rather than one's lifetime resources when answering this question. The current budget of a typical college student is substantially below that of an average blue collar worker, but the student's ultimate lifetime earnings will be greater.

Willingness-to-Pay versus Other Approaches

The procedure used to value life, health, and environmental outcomes more generally is exactly the same as is used in other contexts in which we are assessing the benefits of a government program. In particular, the benefit value is simply society's willingness to pay for the impact of the program.[2] This outcome may be in the form of a lottery, as in the case where the probability of an adverse event is reduced through a beneficial risk-regulation effort. Although reliance on the willingness-to-pay approach may seem to gain us little in terms of enabling us to assess benefit values in practice, it does offer a considerable advantage in terms of preventing one from adopting a benefit assessment procedure that is not economically sound.

The economic pitfalls that may be encountered are apparent from considering some of the alternative approaches that have been suggested. For the most part, these approaches rely on various human capital measures related to one's lifetime earnings.[3] However, the kind of approach that is useful in assessing the value of training or education may be wholly inappropriate for assessing the implications of life-extending efforts. The first human capital measure one can consider is the present value of one's lifetime earnings. This might be taken as a good gross measure of one's value to the GNP, and it is an easy number to calculate. The fallacy of using this measure is apparent in part from the fact that the elderly and people who choose to work outside of the labor force would fare particularly badly under such a procedure. In addition, although one's income level is clearly going to influence one's willingness to pay for risk reduction, it need not constrain it in a one-to-one manner. Thus, when dealing with a small risk of death, such as one chance in 10,000, one is not necessarily restricted to being willing to spend only 1/10,000 of one's income to purchase a risk reduction. One could easily spend 5/10,000 or more for small incremental reductions in risk. Difficulties arising from budgetary constraints are encountered only when we are dealing with dramatic risk increments. Moreover, if one were faced with a substantial risk of death, one might choose to undertake unusual efforts such as working overtime or moonlighting on a second job if one's survival depended on it.

A variant on the present value-of-earnings approach is to take the present value of lifetime earnings net of the consumption of the deceased. This is a common measure used in court cases for compensating survivors, inasmuch as it is a reflection of the net economic loss to the survivors after the death of a family member. This type of calculation abstracts from the consumption expenditures of the individual who is deceased, and it is certainly the individual whose health is most affected who should figure prominently in any calculation of the benefits of pursuing any particular social regulation.

A final approach that has appeared in the literature is to look at the taxes that people might pay. Focusing on tax rates captures the net financial contribution one makes to society, but it has the drawback of neglecting the income contribution to oneself or one's family.

Notwithstanding the inappropriateness of the various earnings approaches, this technique has not only appeared in the literature but has been widely used by government agencies. Much of the appeal of the method is that it lends itself to calculation.

A major policy event that led to a shift in the approach taken was the OSHA hazard-communication regulation that was the subject of intense debate in the early 1980s.[4] OSHA prepared its regulatory analysis, assessing the value of the risk reduction achieved by valuing these impacts according to the lost earnings of the individuals whose death or nonfatal cases of cancer could be prevented. OSHA justified this approach on the basis that it was much too sensitive an issue to value life, so that it would follow the alternative approach of simply assessing the costs of death.

Because of OSHA's overoptimistic risk assessment assumptions, the Office of Management and Budget rejected the regulatory proposal. OSHA appealed this decision to then-Vice President George Bush, who had delegated authority over regulatory matters. OSHA was ultimately permitted to issue the regulations after there was a reassessment of the benefits using the sound economic approach—willingness-to-pay measures for the value of life—which led to the result that benefits exceeded costs. Because willingness-to-pay amounts generally exceed the present value of lost earnings by roughly an order of magnitude, using an appropriate economic methodology greatly enhances the attractiveness of social regulation efforts and makes these regulations appear more attractive than they would otherwise be. Indeed, the substantial size of the benefit estimates that can be achieved using the willingness-to-pay measure, rather than its economic soundness, may be the principal contributor to the increasingly widespread adoption of this approach throughout the federal government.

There also appears to be less reluctance to address the life-saving issues directly. One or two decades ago, raising the issue of the value of life appeared to be intrinsically immoral. However, once it was understood that what is at issue is the amount of resources one is willing to commit to small reductions of risk, rather than to prevent a certain death, then the approach becomes less controversial. Moreover, because the measure is simply the total willingness of society to pay for the risk reductions, it does not use economic pricing in any crass or illegitimate way, as would be the case with the various human capital measures noted above. Society has also become aware of the wide range of risks that we face, including those imposed by our diets and a variety of personal activities. The idea that it is not feasible to achieve an absolutely risk-free existence and that some tradeoffs must ultimately be made is becoming more widely understood.

Variations in the Value of Life

One dividend of going through the exercise summarized in Table 20.1 is that individuals will give different answers to these willingness-to-pay questions. There is no right answer in terms of the value of life. Thus we are not undertaking an elusive search for a natural constant such as e or π. Rather, the effort is simply one to establish an individual's risk-dollar tradeoff. Individuals can differ in terms of this tradeoff just as they could with respect to other kinds of tradeoffs they might make concerning various kinds of consumption commodities that they might purchase. It makes no more sense to claim that individuals should have the same value of life than it does to insist that everyone like eating raw oysters.

A major source of differences in preferences is likely to be individuals' lifetime wealth. People who are more affluent are likely to require a higher price to bear any particular risk. This relationship is exhibited in the substantial positive income elasticity in the demand for medical insurance, as well as in a positive relationship between individual income and the wage compensation needed to accept a hazardous job. The amount workers are willing to pay to avoid a given injury risk increases proportionally with worker income, which is consistent with this pattern of influences.[5]

Overall, there is likely to be substantial heterogeneity in individual preferences, and this heterogeneity will be exhibited in the choices that people make. Empirical evidence suggests that smokers are more willing to bear a variety of risks other than smoking in return for less compensation than would be required for a nonsmoker.[6] Individuals who wear seatbelts are particularly reluctant to incur job risk, which one would also expect. If one examined a distribution of job-related risks, such as that provided in Table 20.2, one would expect that the individuals who are in the relatively safe occupations listed at the top of the table would generally be more averse to risk than those in the riskiest pursuits. In contrast, people who tend to gravitate to the high-risk jobs, who choose to sky-dive, or who smoke cigarettes are more likely to place a lower value on incurring such risks than do those who avoid such pursuits.

Although substantial differences such as those exist, from a policy standpoint it is not quite clear the extent to which we would use such distinctions. Should we provide individuals with less stringent government

Table 20.2
Average Annual Traumatic Occupational Fatalities Listed by Industry, United States, 1980–1985

Industry	Fatality Rate (per 100,000 workers)
Mining	31.9
Transportation, communications	25.4
Construction	24.1
Agriculture, forestry, fishing	20.7
Manufacturing	4.4
Services	3.7
Retail trade	2.7
Finance, insurance, real estate	1.2
Wholesale trade	1.0

Source: National Traumatic Occupation Fatalities, 1980–85, National Institute for Occupation and Health, Division of Safety Research.

regulations to protect them if they have revealed by other activities that they are willing to bear a variety of risks to their well-being? Viewed somewhat differently, should we override the decisions of people who find a particular wage-risk tradeoff in the labor market attractive or who find the nuisance of wearing a seatbelt to outweigh the perceived benefits to themselves? Although one should generally respect individual values in a democratic society, we may wish to distinguish situations in which individuals are believed to be irrational or where it is not feasible to educate people inexpensively with respect to the rational course of action. One danger of regulation of this type, however, is that we may impose the preferences of policymakers on the individuals whose well-being is supposed to be protected, which may not necessarily be welfare-enhancing for those affected by the regulation.

The one area in which the differences in the value of life should clearly be utilized is in assessing future impacts of regulatory programs. Because further benefits are deferred, discounting these benefits to bring them to present value reduces the current value of regulatory policies with long-run effects such as pollution control to reduce the depletion of the ozone layer around the atmosphere. If, however, we recognize that future generations are likely to be wealthier, then much of the role of discounting will be muted. Consider, for example, the situation in which the income elasticity of the value of the benefits is 1.0. Let the benefit n years hence be B, the growth rate in income between now and the time when the benefits are realized be g, and the interest rate be r. The equation below gives the present value of the benefits, which simply equal the dollar benefit value B multiplied by a growth factor, which is the spread between the growth rate in income minus the interest rate:

$$\text{Present Value of Benefit} = \frac{B(1+g)^n}{(1+r)^n} \approx B(1+g-r)^n \qquad (20.4)$$

Thus the growth in income will mute to a large extent the influence of discounting when weighing the consequences of policies in the future.

One might raise the question whether one should discount at all or simply treat all policy outcomes in different years equally, irrespective of the time in which they transpire. This procedure has been advocated by the U.S. Environmental Protection Agency because doing so will greatly enhance the attractiveness of its efforts, many of which have deferred effects. The fallacy of ignoring discounting altogether is apparent when one considers that in the absence of discounting one would never take an action in which there will be a permanent adverse effect of any kind. The costs of such efforts will always be infinite, and such policies would never be pursued.

The Labor Market Model

Most of the empirical estimates of the value of life have been based on labor market data. The general procedure is to estimate the wage-risk tradeoff that workers implicitly make as part of their jobs and to use implications of this tradeoff as an estimate of the value of life.

As the starting point for the analysis, consider Figure 20.1. Sketched in this diagram are two curves, EU_1 and EU_2, which are constant expected utility loci for the worker. This combination of wages and risk on each curve gives the worker the same expected utility. The required wage rate is an increasing function of the risk, which is true for a wide range of individual preferences. All that is required is that one would rather be healthy than not. It is not necessary that one be risk-averse in the sense of unwilling to accept actuarially unfair financial bets. Two expected utility loci offering constant expected utility are EU_1 and EU_2. Higher wage rates and lower risk levels are preferred, so that the direction of preference is toward the northwest.

Workers do not have all wage-risk combinations to choose from, but instead are limited to those that are offered by firms. Figure 20.2 illustrates how the available set of job opportunities is constructed. Each particular firm has a constant expected profits locus. Thus, one firm will have a locus MM, where this isoprofit curve gives the locus of wage-risk

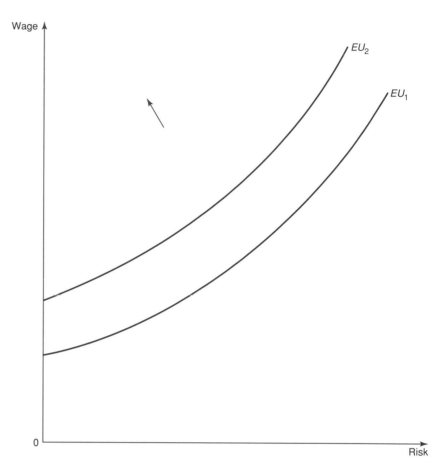

Figure 20.1
Worker's Constant Expected Utility Locus for Wages and Risk

combinations that give the firm the same level of profits. For example, if a firm lowers the risk level by investing in additional health and safety equipment, to maintain the same level of profits the wage rate must go down. As a result, the wage that the firm can offer and maintain the same level of profits will be an increasing function of risk. The curvature of the MM isoprofit curve is dictated by the fact that additional safety reductions become increasingly difficult to achieve, so that as one moves to the left along the risk axis, the additional cost expenditures on the part of the firm become increasingly great. Consequently, the magnitude of the wage increase required for any particular risk reduction becomes greater. Curve NN is another example of an isoprofit curve for a different firm in the industry.

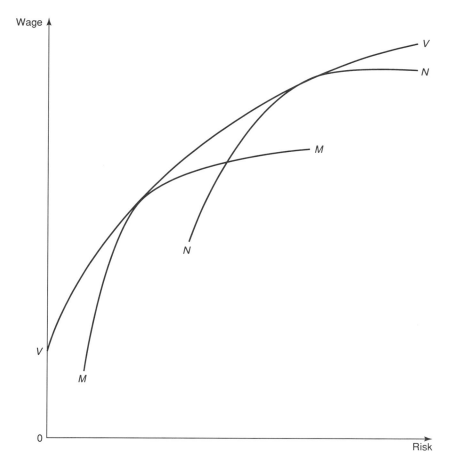

Figure 20.2
Derivation of Market Offer Curve

The outer envelope of the isoprofit curves for the entire industry provides the offer curve available to workers. Thus a worker's task is to select the point along the offer curve VV that gives the worker the highest level of expected utility. Points below this curve will be dominated by points along it, since a point below VV will be less desirable than a job that offers the same risk at a higher wage rate.

The nature of market equilibrium is illustrated in Figure 20.3.[7] Worker 1 achieves his constant expected utility at the point of tangency with the market opportunity locus VV, where his tangency point is at X. In contrast, worker 2 selects a higher risk-wage combination at point Y. Because of the aforementioned heterogeneity in individual tastes, the individuals will generally sort themselves along the part of the wage offer curve that best suits their preferences.

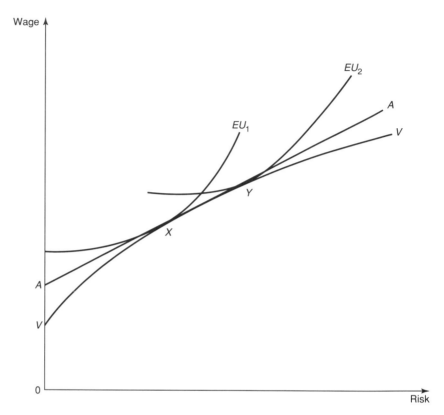

Figure 20.3
Equilibrium in the Market for Risky Jobs

The task of empirical analysis in this area is to analyze the nature of the observed market equilibrium points reflected in data sets on worker behavior. Thus, if we observe points X and Y, the estimation of a linear relationship between wages and risk would yield the curve AA shown in Figure 20.3. The slope of AA gives the estimated wage-risk tradeoff. In effect, what this curve does is indicate the terms of trade that workers, on average, are willing to accept between risk and wages. These terms of trade in turn can be used to extrapolate the implicit value that workers attach to a statistical death.

The details of the methodology vary depending on the particular data set used for the estimation. In general, the statistical approach involves the use of a large set of data on individual employment behavior. Table 20.3 summarizes the principal aspects of thirteen studies that have appeared in the literature.[8] These studies have been ordered according to the level of the risk being examined, with the studies focusing on the highest risk groups being at the top of the table. Although these studies

Table 20.3
Summary of Selected Value-of-Life Studies

Author/Year	Sample	Risk Variable	Mean Risk	Implicit Value of Life ($ millions)[a]
Smith (1976)	Current Population Survey (CPS)	Bureau of Labor Statistics (BLS)	0.0001	4.0
Thaler and Rosen (1976)	Survey of Economic Opportunity	Society of Actuaries	0.001	0.7
Viscusi (1979)	Survey of Working Conditions	BLS	0.0001	3.6
Brown (1980)	National Longitudinal Survey of Young Men	Society of Actuaries	0.002	1.3
Olson (1981)	CPS	BLS	0.0001	4.5
Viscusi (1981)	Panel Study of Income Dynamics (PSID)	BLS	0.0001	5.7
Arnould and Nichols (1983)	U.S. Census	Society of Actuaries	0.001	0.8
Dillingham (1985)	Quality of Employment Survey (QES)	Constructed by author	0.00014	2.2–4.6
Dillingham (1985)	QES	U.S. Department of Labor	0.00008	5.9
Gerking, DeHann, and Schulze (1988)	Mail survey conducted by authors	Perceived risk of death, based on Society of Actuaries	0.0007	3.0
Moore and Viscusi (1988)	QES	Discounted Expected Life Years Lost; based on BLS Death Rate	0.00006	6.4
Moore and Viscusi (1990)	PSID	BLS	0.00005	2.2
Moore and Viscusi (1990)	PSID	National Traumatic Occupational Fatality Survey	0.00008	6.4

[a] Expressed in 1988:3 prices using the GNP deflator, as reported in the *Economic Report of the President*, 1989.

are based on labor-market behavior, these estimates are now widely used throughout the federal government to value regulatory policy effects ranging from aviation safety to environmental health effects.

Empirical Estimates of the Value of Life

The general form of the estimation depends in part on the nature of the wage and risk information that is available, such as whether the data pertain to annual earnings or hourly wage rates.[9] One form of estimating the equation is the following:

$$\text{Annual Earnings} = \alpha + \beta_1 \text{ Annual Death Risk}$$

$$+ \sum_{i=1}^{n} \gamma_i \text{ Personal Characteristic}_i$$

$$+ \sum_{i=1}^{m} \psi_i \text{ Job Characteristic}_i + \varepsilon \qquad (20.5)$$

The dependent variable in this analysis is the annual worker earnings, which is not as accurate a measure as the worker's hourly wage rate, but for expositional purposes it facilitates our task of indicating how one constructs the value-of-life estimates in the equation. The explanatory variables include the annual death risk facing the worker. In general, this information is matched to the workers in the sample based on their responses regarding their industry or occupation.

The coefficient β_i in equation (20.5) indicates how annual earnings will be affected by an increase in the annual death risk. If the annual death risk were 1.0, then β_i would give the change in annual earnings required to face one expected death. Thus, for the equation as it has been set up here, β_1 is the value-of-life estimate. In particular, it represents the tradeoff that workers exhibit between earnings and the risk of death.

As the information in the third column in Table 20.3 indicates, several data sets have been used, including Society of Actuaries data on occupational risks and information on industry risk levels provided by the U.S. Bureau of Labor Statistics and the National Institute of Occupational Safety and Health, which has a detailed census of job deaths known as the National Traumatic Occupational Fatality data. Of the industry-based risk measures, the National Traumatic Occupational Fatality data is believed to be the most reliable.

The other variables included in equation (20.5) are designed to control for the other aspects of the worker and his job that will influence earnings. In general, the people who earn the highest incomes in our society also have fairly low-risk jobs. This observation, which can be traced back to the time of John Stuart Mill, reflects the positive income elasticity of the demand for health. By including a detailed set of other variables, including coverage of factors such as worker education and union status, one can successfully disentangle the premium for job risks as opposed to compensation for other attributes of the worker and his job.

The results of these estimations are summarized in the final column of Table 20.3. The value-of-life estimates range from under $1 million to more than $6 million. This heterogeneity is not solely a consequence of the imprecision of the statistical measures, but instead is due to the fact that these studies are measuring different things. The value-of-life estimates for samples of different riskiness are expected to be different because the mix of workers and their preferences across samples may be quite different. In addition, the degree to which different risk variables measure the true risk associated with the job may differ substantially across risk measures. Examination of the same sample of workers using two industry-based risk measures, the Bureau of Labor Statistics data, and the National Traumatic Occupational Fatality data, indicates that this measurement error alone can lead to a doubling of the estimates.

Even with the current state of econometric techniques and the substantial literature devoted to this issue, economists cannot yet pinpoint the value of life that is appropriate in every particular instance. However, we have a good idea of the general range in which such values fall, and from the standpoint of making policy judgments with respect to the ballpark in which our policies should lie, this guidance should be sufficient.

Value of Life for Regulatory Policies

It is useful to examine the government policies that have actually been pursued in the social-regulation area to see the extent to which they conform with an appropriate value of life. Table 20.4 summarizes a variety of key aspects of major regulations issued between 1967 and 1986.[10] These regulations covered such diverse issues as cabin fire protection for airplanes, grain dust regulations for grain handling facilities, and environmental controls for arsenic/copper smelters.

The main information of interest appears in the final column of the table, which is the cost per life saved by each of the programs. Some of these efforts, such as steering column protection for automobiles and other entries at the top of the table, are bargains. Their cost per life saved is well below $1 million. For concreteness, suppose that we took as the appropriate value of life a figure of $5 million. Then all regulations at the top part of the table including benzene/fugitive emissions regulations by EPA would pass a benefit-cost test. Similarly, all regulations at the bottom part of the table, including radionuclides/uranium mines, as well as all regulations with a higher cost per life saved could not be justified on benefit-cost grounds.

What is most instructive from this table is that in general it is not necessary to pinpoint the exact value of life that is appropriate for any government policy. For the most part, rough judgments regarding the efficacy of a regulation can tell us a great deal. We know, for example, if

Table 20.4
The Cost of Various Risk-Reducing Regulations per Life Saved

Regulation	Year and Status	Agency	Initial annual Risk[a]	Annual Lives Saved	Cost per Life Saved (millions of 1984 $)
Pass benefit-cost test:					
Unvented space heaters	1980 F[b]	CPSC	2.7 in 10^5	63.000	$ .10
Oil and gas well service	1983 P	OSHA-S	1.1 in 10^3	50.000	.10
Cabin fire protection	1985 F	FAA	6.5 in 10^8	15.000	.20
Passive restraints/belts	1984 F	NHTSA	9.1 in 10^5	1,850.000	.30
Underground construction	1989 F	OSHA-S	1.6 in 10^3	8.100	.30
Alcohol and drug control	1985 F	FRA	1.8 in 10^6	4.200	.50
Servicing wheel rims	1984 F	OSHA-S	1.4 in 10^5	2.300	.50
Seat cushion flammability	1984 F	FAA	1.6 in 10^7	37.000	.60
Floor emergency lighting	1984 F	FAA	2.2 in 10^8	5.000	.70
Crane suspended personnel platform	1988 F	OSHA-S	1.8 in 10^3	5.000	1.20
Concrete and masonry construction	1988 F	OSHA-S	1.4 in 10^5	6.500	1.40
Hazard communication	1983 F	OSHA-S	4.0 in 10^5	200.000	1.80
Benzene/fugitive emissions	1984 F	EPA	2.1 in 10^5	0.310	2.80
Fail benefit-cost test:					
Grain Dust	1987 F	OSHA-S	2.1 in 10^4	4.000	5.30
Radionuclides/uranium mines	1984 F	EPA	1.4 in 10^4	1.100	6.90
Benzene	1987 F	OSHA-H	8.8 in 10^4	3.800	17.10
Arsenic/glass plant	1986 F	EPA	8.0 in 10^4	0.110	19.20
Ethylene oxide	1984 F	OSHA-H	4.4 in 10^4	2.800	25.60
Arsenic/copper smelter	1986 F	EPA	9.0 in 10^4	0.060	26.50
Uranium mill tailings, inactive	1983 F	EPA	4.3 in 10^4	2.100	27.60
Uranium mill tailings, active	1983 F	EPA	4.3 in 10^4	2.100	53.00
Asbestos	1986 F	OSHA-H	6.7 in 10^5	74.700	89.30
Asbestos	1989 F	EPA	2.9 in 10^5	10.000	104.20
Arsenic/glass manufacturing	1986 R	EPA	3.8 in 10^5	0.250	142.00
Benzene/storage	1984 R	EPA	6.0 in 10^7	0.043	202.00
Radionuclides/DOE facilities	1984 R	EPA	4.3 in 10^6	0.001	210.00
Radionuclides/elem. phosphorous	1984 R	EPA	1.4 in 10^5	0.046	270.00
Benzene/ethylbenzenol styrene	1984 R	EPA	2.0 in 10^6	0.006	483.00
Arsenic/low-arsenic copper	1986 R	EPA	2.6 in 10^4	0.090	764.00
Benzene/maleic anhydride	1984 R	EPA	1.1 in 10^6	0.029	820.00
Land disposal	1988 F	EPA	2.3 in 10^8	2.520	3,500.00
EDB	1989 R	OSHA-H	2.5 in 10^4	0.002	15,600.00
Formaldehyde	1987 F	OSHA-H	6.8 in 10^7	0.010	72,000.00

[a] Annual deaths per exposed population. An exposed population of 10^3 is 1,000, 10^4 is 10,000, etc.
[b] F, P, or R = Final, proposed, or rejected rule.

Source: John F. Morrall III (1986), p. 30. These statistics were updated by John F. Morrall III via unpublished communication with the author, July 10, 1990.

OSHA arsenic regulations save lives at a cost of $92.5 million per life, that such efforts are out of line with what the beneficiaries of such an effort believe the value of such a regulation to be. Moreover, there are likely to be a wide range of other regulatory alternatives by OSHA or other agencies that are likely to be more cost-effective ways of saving lives.

Although the range in the value-of-life estimates for the policies summarized in Table 20.4 may seem to be substantial, in practice many government policies are proposed but not issued because the value of life is even higher than many of the outliers in this table. For example, in 1984 EPA proposed regulations for benzene/maleic anhydride that would cost $820 million per life saved. This regulation was rejected by the Office of Management and Budget as being too expensive. One of the all-time leaders in terms of the cost per life saved is a proposed OSHA regulation of formaldehyde exposures, which would have required an expenditure of $72 billion per expected life saved. Calculating the costs, benefits, and appropriate reference values for the value of life often highlights gross policy distortions such as this.

Survey Approaches to Valuing Policy Effects

There are many circumstances in which we do not have readily available market data that can be used to estimate either implicit or explicit prices. How much, for example, is it worth to prevent genetic damage or to reduce the risk of the greenhouse effect?

In the absence of existing data on these issues, an approach that has been used in the benefit-valuation literature for several decades has been to run a survey in which individuals are polled with respect to these values. This approach is now the dominant methodology for assessing environmental benefits because of the paucity of good data on explicit or implicit environmental transactions.

The actual procedures that have evolved for doing so in effect attempt to replicate the hedonic market estimate approach used to analyze wage-risk tradeoffs and similar factors using survey data. For example, such studies would not ask people how much they valued a job injury, but would instead ask how much wage compensation they would require to face extra risk. Similarly, assessment of an environmental amenity would focus on purchasing a reduction in certain risks in the environment rather than certain outcomes. The term *contingent valuation* has been used to describe such studies because they represent values that are contingent on a hypothetical market existing.[11] Thus they represent a hybrid between the initial survey approaches used in the literature and the market-based valuation econometric studies that began in the 1970s.

The objective is to elicit benefit values by constructing survey questions concerning hypothetical situations. There are a variety of ways in which one could pose the valuation question. In each case one must first give individuals information regarding the risk or other outcome to be valued. The first approach would be to ask individuals how much that particular benefit would be worth to them. This is a one-step procedure. The second approach would be an iterative one in which the individual first answered the open-ended question, and then was asked whether he or she would be willing to pay a small amount more than the initial response. A third variant on this technique is that instead of asking open-ended questions, individuals could be given a series of bids, and they would then have to determine how high or low they would go. These bids could be given in either ascending or descending order. In the ascending case, an individual might first be asked whether he or she would be willing to pay $1 for improved air quality, and if the answer is yes, the respondent would be asked if he or she would be willing to pay $2 for improved air quality, and so on, until the individual is not willing to increase the bid. A fourth approach is to utilize paired comparisons in which an individual is given an alternative product or other binary choices to make. Using interactive computer programs, one can then give an individual a succession of options to pick from to locate the point of indifference.

All of these variations in terms of the methodology are largely ones of process rather than economic content. The underlying issue is how we can best frame the survey questions to elicit the true underlying economic values that individuals have. In the case of market outcomes we know from revealed preference that these values will be expressed in individual decisions, but in the case of surveys the values that we elicit may be sensitive to the manner in which we attempt to determine individual preferences.

More generally, considerable care must be exercised in the design of such survey studies so that they will give us reliable results. Often such studies rely on "convenience samples" such as groups of students, but our ultimate objective is to ascertain the willingness-to-pay of actual beneficiaries of the project, not the willingness-to-pay of students in the class whose responses may be biased in part by substantial demand effects (they may give the answers that they expect their professor wants to see). Perhaps the major guidelines in assessing these studies is to determine the extent to which they replicate market processes in a meaningful manner.

When interview studies first became used in the literature, economists feared that there would be a major problem in individuals' misrepresenting their true values for strategic reasons. Advocates of pollution control efforts, for example, might give responses that indicate enormous willingness-to-pay amounts, knowing that they will not be taxed on the basis of their response and hoping that a high response will tilt the policy in their favor.

In practice, the strategic issue has not been a major problem with the survey studies. A more fundamental difficulty is that some individuals often may not give thoughtful or meaningful responses to the question, inasmuch as it does not involve a decision that they actually make. Moreover, because many of the decisions involve risks, some of which are at very low probabilities, the results will not reflect their underlying values but instead will be contaminated by whatever irrationalities influence one's decisions involving low-probability events.

Valuation of Air Quality

The nature of the performance of the survey approach varies from study to study, but some suggestions as to its likely precision are given by a recent study of air pollution valuation.[12] Two approaches were used to value air quality. In the first, a hedonic rent-gradient equation for the Los Angeles area was estimated, analyzing the relationship of home sale prices to a variety of factors likely to influence house price (such as house age, area, school quality, public safety, and distance to the beach). In addition, this equation included measures of pollution in the Los Angeles area, including either total suspended particulates or NO_2 concentration levels. The authors found substantial housing price effects of pollution; controlling for other aspects of the housing market, higher pollution levels lowered the price of the house.

A survey approach was also used to assess the amount the individuals would be willing to pay in terms of a higher utility bill to achieve cleaner air. The expressed willingness to pay for different levels of air quality was roughly one-third of the market-based estimates. These results suggest that at least in this case overstatement of valuations in surveys may not be a problem, although this conclusion may not be true more generally. In addition, there may not be an exact correspondence between survey valuation estimates and market estimates. Comparisons that have been done for worker-wage equations have yielded more comparable results to those obtained with market data, but in the job risk case one is dealing with a risk that is currently traded in a market and which individuals may have already thought about in this context, increasing the accuracy of the survey responses.

Exploratory Nature of the Survey Approach

Overall, survey approaches to establishing the benefits of social regulation represent an important complement to analyses using market data. This methodology should still be regarded as exploratory, however. Moreover, there will never be any general conclusions regarding the accuracy of such studies, because accuracy will vary from study to study depending on the extent to which a realistic market context was created and the degree to which the individuals running the survey motivated the survey participants to give thoughtful and honest answers.

Sensitivity Analysis and Cost Effectiveness

In the usual situation it will not be feasible to place dollar values on all outcomes of interest. In such circumstances one could undertake cost-effectiveness analysis to analyze the cost per unit outcome achieved, and indices such as this may often be instructive.

In addition, if there are multiple outcomes that one would wish to value but cannot, one can perform a sensitivity analysis assigning different relative weights to them to convert all of them into a common cost-effectiveness index. Table 20.5 summarizes calculations of this type for the OSHA hazard communication regulation. The three health outcomes involved are lost workday job injuries, disabling illnesses, and cases of cancer. Suppose that, based on past studies on the relative valuation of cancer, we know that lost-workday job injuries have 1/20 of the value of a case of cancer. In addition, suppose that the main uncertainty is with respect to the value of disabling illnesses, where our task is to assess how severe this outcome is compared with injuries and cancer. The

Table 20.5
Cost-Effectiveness Measures for Hazard Communication Standard

	Lost Workday Equivalents	
	Weight—1,1,20[a] Cost Effectiveness	Weights—1,5,20[a] Cost Effectiveness
Net discounted costs less monetized benefits	2.632×10^9	2.632×10^9
Total lost workday equivalents (discounted)	9.5×10^4	24.7×10^4
Net discounted cost/lost workday equivalent	$27,900	$10,700

[a] These are the relative weights placed on lost workday cases (always 1), disabling illnesses (1 or 5), and cancers (always 20) in constructing a measure of lost workday equivalents.

calculations in this table explore two different sets of weights, one in which lost-workday injuries and disabling illnesses are given the same weight, and a second in which disabling illnesses are viewed as being five times more severe than lost workday cases.

The first row of Table 20.5 gives the net discounted costs less benefits of other kinds from the project, which total $2.6 billion. The second row gives the discounted (at 5 percent) number of lost workday injury equivalents prevented, where these lost workday equivalents have been calculated using the two sets of weights indicated above. Finally, the third row of the table gives the net discounted cost per lost workday equivalent prevented. These estimates are in the range of $10,000–$30,000, which is in line with the general estimates of implicit values of nonfatal injuries that have been obtained in labor market studies.

The approach used here is to establish one class of outcomes as the unit of metric and to put the other outcomes in terms of them when calculating a cost-effectiveness index that can capture all of the diverse impacts of a particular effort. In this case the metric is that of lost workday equivalents, but in other situations the metric may be death equivalents prevented or number of birth defects prevented.

Risk-Risk Analysis

In the absence of a benefit-cost for risk or environmental regulations, agencies will not be constrained regarding the stringency of these efforts. Because of the restrictive legislative mandates that these agencies have that often require that they reduce risk irrespective of cost, the result is that many regulations that are promulgated generate considerable costs, sometimes as high as $100 million per statistical life saved or more. Other than wasting societal resources, is there any harm from such profligacy?

Two classes of costs can be identified, where these come under the general heading risk-risk analysis. First, there is a direct risk-risk trade-off arising from regulatory efforts. An automobile recall, for example, may require that consumers drive their cars back to the dealer for the repair. Because all motor vehicle traffic is hazardous, requiring that people undertake extra driving will expose them to additional risk which may be more hazardous than the defect being repaired, if it is minor.[13] In addition, risk regulations stimulate economic activity, such as manufacturing efforts to produce pollution-control equipment or construction efforts to carry away the waste at a Superfund site. All economic activity is dangerous, leading to worker injuries and illnesses. In many instances, roughly 4 percent of every dollar of production in industry is associated with the health and safety costs of that production. Regulations that stimulate substantial economic efforts to meet the regulatory objectives will necessarily create risks in the process of stimulating economic activity. Even if for some reason the regulatory agency chooses to ignore the dollar costs, a comprehensive tally of the risk consequences of the effort may suggest that it is counterproductive.

The newest form of risk-risk analysis that has emerged has drawn on the negative relationship between individual income and mortality. Regulatory expenditures represent a real opportunity cost to society as they take away resources from other uses, such as health care, that might enhance individual well-being. As a result, there is a mortality cost associated with these regulatory efforts. The U.S. Office of Management & Budget raised this issue with OSHA, suggesting that some of the more expensive OSHA regulations may in fact do more harm than good through these mortality effects.

Although the theoretical relationships are not controversial, the exact value of the regulatory expenditure that will lead to a statistical death remains a matter of debate. One approach has been to examine studies that directly link changes in individual income with mortality, where many of these estimates suggest that a statistical life may be lost for an income decrease on the order of $10 million to $15 million.[14] Another approach is to establish a formal theoretical link between the value of life from the standpoint of saving statistical lives and the amount of money spent by the government that will lead to the loss of a statistical life through its effect in making society poorer.[15] This approach leads to a value of $50 million in government expenditures, which will lead to the loss of a statistical life.

This literature is still in its early stages. However, the general principle suggests that regulatory agencies should be cognizant of the harm that is done when they fail to take costs into account. Economists concerned with cost is not a professional bias, but ultimately has a link to individual welfare. These links in turn involve our health and are just as real as the concerns that motivate the government regulations.

Establishing Prices for Health, Safety, and Environmental Regulation

Perhaps the most difficult policy issues arising in the social-regulation area will always stem from the setting of appropriate prices for the outcomes achieved. Because social-regulation efforts deal in large part with outcomes that are not the result of explicit market transactions, there will always be a need to establish the value of these efforts.

As a society we cannot allocate unlimited resources to any particular area of concern, however important it may seem. Because additional gains to health, safety, and the environment come at a diminishing rate for additional expenditures of money, we would quickly exhaust our resources long before we ran out of opportunities for spending.

As the discussion in this chapter indicated, the general economic approach to formulating a benefit assessment is not particularly controversial, but the empirical methodologies for establishing such values are still in their development stage. The greatest difficulties are encountered in situations where there are not even implicit markets that one could use as reference points for establishing appropriate risk-dollar tradeoffs.

As the discussion in subsequent chapters will indicate, in many instances the absence of a specific empirical estimate for the benefit value is not the most pressing policy problem. Rather, there is a more fundamental difficulty in that the importance of making tradeoffs at all has not even been recognized. In these cases, substantial gains could be made by noting that we are not in an unconstrained situation and that there must be some balancing among the competing objectives.

Questions and Problems

1. This chapter's discussion of the value of life has focused on estimates from the labor market. Economists have also estimated risk-dollar tradeoffs based on price data for risky products. Smoke detector purchases, differences in riskiness of cars, and seatbelt use decisions are among the contexts that have been considered. Can you think of any other market situations in which, if you had perfect data, it would be possible to infer an implicit risk-dollar tradeoff?

2. Environmental damage resulting from oil spills, such as that inflicted by the *Exxon Valdez*, is subject to quite specific environmental penalties. In particular, the companies responsible for the damage are required to pay an amount sufficient to compensate society for the environmental loss that has occurred. In economic terms, this compensation must be sufficient to put society at the same level of utility we would have had if it had not been for the accident. Can you think of methodological approaches for determining the appropriate compensation amount for oil spills such as the *Exxon Valdez*, which led to the death of thousands of fish and birds as well as oil residues on thousands of miles of Alaskan beaches?

3. Would you use the same value of life to assess the regulatory benefits in situations in which risks are incurred voluntarily, as opposed to situations in which they are incurred involuntarily? For example, would you treat smoking-risk regulation policies and nuclear hazard-risk regulation policies the same from the standpoint of benefit assessment?

4. Suppose we were faced with two policy alternatives. Under one alternative we will be saving identified lives, in particular Kip, John, and Joe. Under a

second policy option, we know that we will be saving three lives at random from the population, but we do not know whose lives they will be. Should we attach the same benefit value to each of these instances?

5. A variant on question 4 pertains to the girl trapped in a well. It has often been observed that society is often willing to spend almost unlimited resources to save identified lives. On the other hand, we seem to be willing to spend little on saving statistical lives. Does this inconsistency mean that we are spending too much to save the identified lives, too little on the statistical lives, or is it that we cannot tell?

6. Suppose there are two policy options. Policy 1 affects a population of 10,000, of whom 100 will die, so that the risk of death per person is 1/100. The second policy will likewise save 100 individuals, but from a population of 1 million, so that the individual risk is 1/10,000. From the standpoint of regulatory policy, should we exhibit any preference for one policy over the other?

7. One mechanism for obtaining contingent valuation bids is to ask the respondent how much he is willing to pay for some outcome and then to ask if the respondent would be willing to pay, for example, 10 percent more. This process continues until the respondent is no longer willing to increase his bid. Some researchers have argued that this approach will lead to a bias in terms of eliciting the true response. What direction do you believe the bias is, and why do you believe such a bias would occur?

Notes

1. This general approach to valuation of risks to life can be traced back to the work of Thomas Schelling, "The Life You Save May Be Your Own," in S. Chase (ed.), *Problems in Public Expenditure Analysis* (Washington, D.C.: Brookings Institution, 1968), pp. 127–62.

2. This principle is the same as in all benefit contexts. See Edith Stokey and Richard J. Zeckhauser, *A Primer for Policy Analysis* (New York: W. W. Norton, 1978).

3. Variations in the human capital approach are articulated in E. J. Mishan, "Evaluation of Life and Limb: A Theoretical Approach," *Journal of Political Economy* 79 (1971): 706–38.

4. The debate over the hazard communication regulation and over the value of life itself was the object of the cover story in *The Washington Post Magazine*, June 9, 1985, pp. 10–13, 36–41.

5. The role of these income effects is explored in W. Kip Viscusi and William N. Evans, "Utility Functions That Depend on Health Status: Estimates and Economic Implications," *American Economic Review* 80, No. 3 (1990): 353–74.

6. This relationship is documented in Joni Hersch and W. Kip Viscusi, "Cigarette Smoking, Seatbelt Use, and Differences in Wage-Risk Tradeoffs," *Journal of Human Resources* 25, No. 2 (1990): 202–27. The role of smoking behavior is also explored in Victor R. Fuchs, *The Health Economy* (Cambridge, Mass.: Harvard University Press, 1986).

7. For further elaboration on these market processes and the econometric basis for estimation of the value of life, see Sherwin Rosen, "The Theory of Equalizing Differences," in O. Ashenfelter and Richard Layard (eds.), *Handbook of Labor*

Economics (Amsterdam: North Holland, 1986), pp. 641–92. Also see, among others, Richard Thaler and Sherwin Rosen, "The Value of Saving a Life: Evidence from the Labor Market," in Nestor E. Terleckyj (ed.), *Household Production and Consumption* (Cambridge: National Bureau of Economic Research, 1976); Robert S. Smith, "Compensating Differentials and Public Policy: A Review," *Industrial and Labor Relations Review* 32 (1979): 339–52; and W. Kip Viscusi, *Employment Hazards: An Investigation of Market Performance* (Cambridge, Mass.: Harvard University Press, 1979).

8. A more comprehensive review of the literature is provided in W. Kip Viscusi, *Fatal Tradeoffs* (New York: Oxford University Press, 1992).

9. For elaboration on the methodology underlying this estimation procedure, see in particular Rosen, 1986.

10. For a fuller description of these issues see John F. Morrall, "A Review of the Record," *Regulation*, 1986: 30.

11. For a survey of this literature, see R. Cummings, D. Brookshire, and W. Schulze, *Valuing Environmental Goods: An Assessment of the Contingent Valuation Method* (Totowa, N.J.: Rowman and Allankeld, 1986).

12. D. Brookshire, M. Thayer, W. Schulze, and R. d'Arge, "Valuing Public Goods: A Comparison of Survey and Hedonic Approaches," *American Economic Review* 72 (1982): 165–77.

13. For a general discussion of risk-risk analysis issues such as these, see Lester Lave, *The Strategy of Social Regulation: Decision Frameworks for Policy* (Washington, D.C.: Brookings Institution, 1981).

14. See, for example, Randall Lutter and John F. Morrall III, "Health-Health Analysis: A New Way to Evaluate Health and Safety Regulation," *Journal of Risk and Uncertainty* 8, 1 (1993): 43–66.

15. This approach is developed in W. Kip Viscusi, "Mortality Effects of Regulatory Costs and Policy Evaluation Criteria," *Rand Journal of Economics* 25, 1 (1994): 94–109.

Environmental Regulation

The range of activities in the area of environmental regulation is perhaps the most diverse of any regulatory agency.[1] The U.S. Environmental Protection Agency has programs to regulate emissions of air pollution from stationary sources such as power plants, as well as from mobile sources such as motor vehicles. In addition, it has regulations pertaining to the discharge of water pollution and other waste products into the environment. These pollutants include not only conventional pollutants such as the waste by-product of pulp and paper mills, but also toxic pollutants.

In situations in which its regulations of discharges and emissions are not sufficient, EPA also undertakes efforts to restore the environment to its original condition through waste treatment plants and the removal and disposal of hazardous wastes. Insecticides and chemicals are also within the general jurisdiction of the agency's efforts. Moreover, the time dimension of concerns is also quite sweeping, as the environmental problems being addressed range from imminent health hazards to long-term effects on the climate of the earth that may not be apparent until well into the next century.

In this chapter we will not attempt to provide a comprehensive catalogue of environmental regulations, although we will draw on a number of examples in this area. The focus instead will be on the general economic frameworks that are available for analyzing environmental problems. The structure of these problems generally tends to be characterized by similar economic mechanisms for different classes of pollutants. In each case there is a generation of externalities affecting parties who have not contracted to bear the environmental damage. A similar economic framework is consequently applicable to a broad variety of environmental problems.

We will begin with an analysis of the basic economic theory dealing with externalities and then turn to variations in this theory to analyze the choice among policy alternatives. The issues we will address include policy concerns of the 1990s. Should EPA pursue various kinds of marketable permit schemes or rely on technology-based standards?[2] In addition, there is increasing concern with long-term environmental risks associated with climate change. How should we conceptualize the economic approach to regulating these and other risks that pose new classes of environmental problems? Finally, we will review the character of the enforcement of environmental regulation as well as the ultimate impact of environmental policy on environmental quality.

The Coase Theorem for Externalities

The fundamental theorem in the area of externalities was developed by Ronald Coase.[3] The generic problem that he considered was that of a cattle rancher. Suppose that Farm A raises cattle, but that these cattle stray onto the fields in Farm B, damaging Farm B's crops. The straying cattle consequently inflict an externality on Farm B.

What Coase indicated is that assessing these issues is often quite complex. Among the issues that must be considered from an economic standpoint are the following. Should the cattle be allowed to stray from Farm A to Farm B? Should Farm A be required to put up a fence, and if so, who should pay for it? What are the implications from an economic standpoint if Farm A is assigned the property rights and Farm B can compensate Farm A for putting up a fence? Alternatively, if we were to assign the property rights to the victim in this situation, Farm B, what would be the economic implications of assigning the property rights to Farm A?[4]

The perhaps surprising result developed by Coase is that from an economic efficiency standpoint the outcome will be the same irrespective of the assignment of property rights. If we assign the right to let cattle stray to Farm A, then Farm B will bribe Farm A to construct a fence if the damage caused to Farm B's crops exceeds the cost of the fence. Thus, whenever it is efficient to construct a fence, Farm B will compensate Farm A and contract voluntarily to purchase the externality so as to eliminate it.

Alternatively, if we were to assign the property rights to Farm B, Farm A could construct the fence to prevent the damage. If the cost of such a fence exceeded the damage being inflicted, Farm A could contract with Farm B to compensate Farm B for the damage imposed by the straying cattle. In each case, we will obtain the same result in terms of whether or not the fence is constructed irrespective of whether we give Farm A or Farm B the property rights.

From an equity standpoint, the results are, however, quite different. If we assign the property rights to Farm A, then Farm B must compensate Farm A to construct the fence, or alternatively Farm B must suffer the damage. In contrast, if we were to assign the property rights to Farm B, the cost of the fence construction or the cost of compensation for the damage would be imposed on Farm A. The outcome in terms of whether the crops will be trampled or the fence will be constructed will be the same regardless of the property right assignment. However, the well-being of each of the parties and the cash transfers that take place will be quite different under the two regimes.

Economists generally have little of a conclusive nature to say about which situation is more equitable. Coase observed that we should not be too hasty in making a judgment of which property right assignment was most fair. From an equity standpoint one should take into account the

Table 21.1
The Coase Theorem Bargaining Game

Feasible Bargaining Requirement:

$$\text{Maximum Offer} \geq \text{Minimum Acceptance}$$

Bargaining Rent:

$$\text{Bargaining Rent} = \text{Maximum Offer} - \text{Minimum Acceptance}$$

Settlement with Equal Bargaining Power:

$$\text{Settlement Outcome} = \frac{\text{Maximum Offer} + \text{Minimum Acceptance}}{2}$$
$$= \text{Minimum Acceptance} + 0.5 \text{ Bargaining Rent}$$

---

reciprocal nature of the problem. In this situation, Farm A inflicts harm on Farm B. However, to avoid the harm to Farm B means that we must harm Farm A. The objective from an efficiency standpoint is to avoid the more serious harm.

The Coase Theorem as a Bargaining Game

What Coase did not explore in detail was the nature of the bargaining process that would lead to the efficient outcome that he discussed. To address these issues, it is useful to cast the Coase Theorem problem within the context of a simple bargaining game. For concreteness, let us suppose that the property rights are being assigned to the pollution victims, so that it is the firm that must pay for the damage or control costs.

Table 21.1 summarizes the generic components of this and other bargaining games. The company in this situation has a maximum offer amount that it is willing to give the pollution victims for the damage being inflicted. The factors driving the maximum offer value are the expenditures that the firm would have to make to eliminate the externality of the cost that would be imposed on the firm by the legal rules addressing involuntary externalities. The maximum amount that the firm will be willing to pay will be the minimum of either the control costs or the penalty that will be imposed on the firm if it inflicts the externality.

From the standpoint of the individuals bearing the accident costs, the minimum amount they are willing to accept in return for suffering the impacts of the pollution will be that amount of compensation that restores their level of utility to what it would have been in the absence of pollution. We will refer to this amount as the minimum acceptance value.

There is a potentially feasible bargaining range if the maximum offer the firms are willing to make exceeds the minimum acceptance amount, which is the first inequality listed at the top of Table 21.1. If this condition is not satisfied, no bargain will take place, inasmuch as there is no feasible bargaining range. In such a situation in which the minimum acceptance amount by the pollution victims exceeds the maximum amount firms are willing to offer, there will be no contractual solution. Firms will select the minimum cost alternative of either installing the control device or paying the legally required damages amount. The absence of a feasible bargaining range does not imply that the Coase Theorem is not true or that the market has broken down. Rather, it simply indicates that there is no room for constructive bargaining between the two parties. In such situations, the resolution of the bargaining game will be dictated by the initial assignment of property rights.

An essential component of the bargaining game is the bargaining rent. This rent represents the net potential gains that will be shared by the two parties as a result of being able to strike a bargain. As indicated in Table 21.1, the bargaining rent is defined as the difference between the maximum offer amount and the minimum acceptance value.

This definition is quite general and pertains to other bargaining situations as well. For example, suppose that you were willing to pay $18,000 for a new Honda Accord, but the cost to the dealer of this car is $15,000. There is a $3,000 spread between your maximum offer and the minimum acceptance amount by the dealer, which represents the bargaining rent available. The objective of each of you is to capture as much of the rent as possible. You would like to push the dealer as close to the minimum acceptance amount as possible, and the dealer would like to push you to your reservation price. Much of the bargaining process is spent trying to ascertain the minimum offer and maximum acceptance amounts, because these values are not generally disclosed. Moreover, in the process of trying to learn these values, one may reveal considerable information regarding one's bargaining skill and knowledge of the other party's reservation price. A bid for the car that is substantially below the cost to the dealer, for example, does not indicate that one is a shrewd and tough bargainer, but rather usually suggests that one does not have a well-developed sense of the appropriate price for the car. In a situation in which the parties are equally matched with equal bargaining power, they will split the economic rent.

This symmetric bargaining weight situation provides a convenient reference point for analyzing the bargaining outcome. As indicated in Table 21.1, if there is such symmetry the settlement outcome will simply be an average of the maximum offer and the minimum acceptance amount, which is equivalent to the minimum acceptance amount plus one-half of the economic rent at stake.

Table 21.2
Property Right Assignment and the Bargaining Outcome

Basic Aspects of the Pollution Problem

Primary Treatment of Effluent $100	Water Purification < Costs $300	Environmental < Damage $500

Bargaining with Victim Assigned Property Rights

Bargaining equation:	Maximum Offer by Company = $100 < Minimum Acceptance by Citizens = $300
Outcome:	Company installs controls. No cash transfer.

Bargaining with Polluter Assigned Property Rights

Bargaining equation:	Maximum Offer by Citizens = $300 > Minimum Acceptance by Company = $100
Outcome:	Citizens pay company $100 to install controls and also pay company $100 share of rent if equal bargaining power.

A Pollution Example

To illustrate these concepts, let us consider the pollution problem summarized in Table 21.2. The upstream pulp and paper mill emits discharges that impose $500 of environmental damage. The citizens can eliminate this damage by constructing a water purification plant for a cost of $300. Finally, suppose that the company could eliminate this pollution through primary treatment at the plant for a cost of $100.

To see the impact that differences in the property right assignment make, consider first the situation in which the citizen victims of pollution are assigned the property rights. In this context, it is the company that must bribe the citizens for the right to pollute. The maximum amount the polluting firm is willing to pay for this pollution privilege is $100—the cost of installing a treatment facility. The citizens, however, have a reservation price of $300—the lesser of the costs of the water pollution treatment and the environmental damage. Because the maximum offer amount is below the minimum acceptance value, there is no profitable bargain that can be made by the two parties. The result will be that the company will install the pollution treatment system, and there will be no cash transfer between the parties.

The second situation considered is one in which the polluter has been assigned the property rights. In this situation, the maximum offer by the citizens to the firm will be $300. This amount exceeds the $100 cost of installing water-pollution treatment for the company, which is the company's minimum acceptance amount. As a result, there is a profitable bargain that can be arranged between the two parties, with a total bargaining rent of $200. The outcome will be that the citizens will pay the company $100 to install the pollution-control device. Moreover, if the bargaining power of the two parties is equal, the citizens will also pay the firm an additional $100 as the company's share of the bargaining rent.

Utilization of this bargaining-game framework to analyze the Coasian pollution problems provides a more realistic perspective on what will actually transpire than did the original Coase paper, which assumed that the purchase price for the transfers will equal the minimum acceptance amount by the party holding the property rights. In each case, the pollution-control outcome is the same, as the company will install the water treatment device. However, in the case where citizens do not have the property rights, not only will they have to pay for the water treatment, but they will also have to make an additional $100 transfer to the company that they would not have had to make if they had been given the property rights.

The difference in the equity of the two situations is substantial. The citizens must spend $200 if they do not have the property rights—$100 for the treatment cost and $100 to induce the company to install it. If the citizens have the property rights, the cost is $100 to the company for treatment. In each case, the water treatment is the same.

Long-Run Efficiency Concerns

What should also be emphasized is that this short-run equity issue also is a long-run efficiency issue. Ideally, we want the incentives for entry of new firms into the industry to be governed by the full resource costs associated with their activities. If firms are in effect being subsidized for their pollution by citizens paying for their pollution control equipment, then there will be too much entry and too much economic activity in the polluting industries of the economy. We will return to this point within the context of the debate over standards versus taxes. This long-run efficiency point is often ignored by policymakers and by economists who focus on the short-run pollution outcome rather than the long-run incentives that the property right assignment may create.

Transactions Costs and Other Problems

One factor pertaining to the bargaining process that Coase noted is that there may be substantial transactions costs involved in carrying out these bargains. Although we can generate an efficient outcome through a contractual solution without the need for any regulation, achieving this outcome may be quite costly. If there is a large number of citizens whose actions must be coordinated, then the cost may be substantial.

These coordination costs are likely to be particularly large in situations in which there are free riders. Some individuals may not wish to contribute to the pollution-control effort in hopes of obtaining the benefits of controls without contributing to them.

It has often been remarked that there is also a potential for strategic behavior. Some parties may behave irrationally in the bargaining process. However, by modeling the contractual components of the externality market in Table 21.2 using an explicit model of the bargaining structure, we capture these aspects within the context of a rational game-theory model. It may, of course, be true that people are irrational, but this is true of any economic context and is not a phenomenon unique to externality bargaining contexts. For example, people may misperceive the probability of a particular bargaining response or may not assess the reservation price of the other party correctly.

Perhaps the greatest caveat pertains to the degree to which we can distinguish discrete and well-defined assignments of the property rights. Even in situations in which there is a property right assignment, there are often limitations on the use of these property rights. Moreover, when the courts must enforce these rights, there is often imperfect information. The courts, for example, do not know the actual damages the citizens may incur. Moreover, they may not know with perfect certainty the pollution control and treatment costs. There are also costs to acquiring this information, and within the context of most judicial settings there is substantial error in the information being provided to the court.

The net result is that in actual practice we do not generally turn the market loose and let people contract out of the externalities that are imposed. The victims in the eastern United States who suffer the consequences of the acid rain generated by power plants in the Midwest cannot easily contract with these electric power plants. Even more difficult would be attempting to contract with the automobile users in the Midwest to alter their behavior. The bargaining costs and free rider problems would be insurmountable. Indeed, in many cases we cannot even identify the party with whom we might strike a bargain. Unlabeled drums of toxic waste in a landfill do not provide a convenient starting point for externality contracts.

Despite the many limitations of the voluntary contractual approach to externalities, the Coase Theorem does serve an important purpose from the standpoint of regulatory economics.[5] In particular, by assessing the outcome that would prevail with an efficient market given different assignments of the property rights, one can better ascertain the character of the impact of a particular regulatory program. To the extent that the purpose of government regulation is to eliminate market failures and to ensure efficiency, the implications of the Coase Theorem provide us with frames of reference that can be applied in assessing the character of the different situations that will prevail under alternative regulatory regimes. These concerns will be particularly prominent with respect to market-oriented regulatory alternatives that involve the explicit pricing of pollution.

Smoking Externalities

An interesting application of the Coase Theorem is to cigarette smoking. Environmental tobacco smoke has become an increasingly prominent public concern and a classic externality issue. Many nonsmokers find cigarette smoke unpleasant, and government agencies such as EPA and OSHA have concluded that there may be some adverse health effects as well, though the extent of these effects remains controversial.

What is important from the standpoint of the Coase Theorem problem is that nonsmokers would be willing to pay a positive amount of money to avoid being exposed to environmental tobacco smoke. Similarly, smokers would be willing to pay to be able to smoke in public places where they generate environmental tobacco smoke. As in the case of the Coase Theorem problem, the externalities are in many respects symmetric. Smoking will make the smoker better off and the nonsmoker worse off, whereas restricting smoking will make the smoker worse off and the nonsmoker better off. This is the classic Coase situation.

Applying the Coase logic, one might expect the nonsmokers in restaurants to walk over to the smokers' tables and attempt to strike a bargain to get them to stop smoking. Doing so, however, is unpleasant and consequently costly. However, there are other economic mechanisms that can reflect these concerns. If the restaurant does not have a suitable policy with respect to smoking, customers can eat elsewhere. In effect, the market operation in this context will be through the price system. The smoking policy of the restaurant is a local public good in much the same way as is the music, the lighting, and the overall restaurant environment. In situations in which customers are free to patronize different restaurants, the major remaining concern presumably would be with those who have found that they have made a mistake after arriving at the restaurant for the first time and finding it difficult to go elsewhere. Workplaces have responded similarly to the concerns of workers, inasmuch as some of them have banned smoking and others have instituted smoking areas.

The government has also become active in this area, as hundreds of local governments have enacted various kinds of smoking restrictions. National restrictions on public smoking and workplace smoking are also under consideration. If the Coase Theorem bargains were truly effective, additional regulations would not be needed. It is useful to explore in thinking about regulation which contexts the market will be expected to work and which it will not work. Moreover, if it is believed that the market will not work, should one then inquire what are the efficiency effects on both parties? What are the losses to the parties from the current situation and what will be the losses with regulation? This is the essential message of the Coase Theorem that is pertinent to all such externality contexts. In the case of cigarette smoking, the policy debate has been dominated primarily by equity concerns—the losses inflicted on the nonsmoking majority of the population—whereas the efficiency consequences have figured less prominently.

A final set of externalities associated with smoking pertain to insurance. If smoking is risky, as is the scientific consensus, then presumably the adverse health consequences will have widespread consequences for insurance costs. Health costs will clearly be higher. However, because smokers will die sooner under this scenario, their early departure will save society pension and Social Security costs. A comprehensive tally of these effects appears in Table 21.3. As is indicated by the summary of the insurance externalities in Table 21.3, the cost per pack generated by smokers are particularly high for health insurance. However, there are offsetting savings arising from the higher mortality rates of smoking, chiefly the lower pension and Social Security costs. Because smokers die sooner, they are also less likely to get long-term diseases

Table 21.3
External Insurance Costs per Pack of Cigarettes with Tar Adjustments

	20 Year Moving Average 1993 Cost Estimate
	Discount Rate 3%
Costs	
Medical Care <65	0.302
Medical Care ≥65	0.153
Total medical care	0.455
Sick leave	0.011
Group life insurance	0.114
Nursing home care	−0.197
Retirement pension	−1.000
Fires	0.016
Taxes on earnings	0.326
Total net costs	−0.274

Source: Viscusi, W. Kip, "Cigarette Taxation and the Social Consequences of Smoking," in James Poterba, ed., *Tax Policy and the Economy*, National Bureau of Economic Research, Vol. 9 (1995).

such as Alzheimer's, thus diminishing some of their medical expenses later in life. On balance smokers save money for society in terms of the net externality cost. This result does not mean that smoking is not consequential for the individuals whose lives are at risk or for the particular insurance programs whose costs are effected. However, this result does suggest that many externalities often involve competing effects with fairly complex ramifications.

Special Features of Environmental Contexts

In environmental contexts it should also be noted that the character of the markets that would emerge if we set up a market for pollution may be quite unusual. The usability of water tends to follow a step function such as the one indicated in Figure 21.1. Initially, the water quality is quite high, and we will label the water pristine. After a certain level of pollution the water is no longer pristine, but you can still drink it. After another increase in pollution the usability of the water for drinking declines, but you can swim in the water with appropriate vaccinations. As the pollution level increases further, water is suitable for fishing but no longer for the other uses. Finally, with a very high level of pollution, even the fishing option disappears. At this high pollution level, there is no additional marginal cost being imposed on the citizenry from addi-

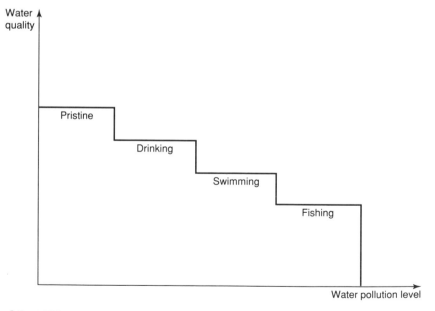

Figure 21.1
Changes in Water Usage as a Function of Pollution

tional pollution if we assume for concreteness that all of the beneficial uses of the water have disappeared. The citizens could then sell an infinite number of pollution rights without suffering any additional damage beyond what they have already suffered. Moreover, within any particular step of the declining water quality curve in Figure 21.1 there is no loss to the citizenry, so that the marginal costs to them of selling additional pollution rights will be zero.

This character of environmental contexts—known formally as an example of "nonconvexities"—suggests that instead of always dispersing the risks, it may be profitable to concentrate the risks in a particular location. For example, are we better off siting nuclear wastes throughout the United States, or should they be concentrated in one area? If they are concentrated, society can adapt by prohibiting residential housing and commercial operations near the facility so that a large environmental risk can be present without posing substantial costs on society. In contrast, dispersing nuclear waste siting on a uniform basis throughout the United States may appear more equitable, but it will impose larger risks to society at large because it is more difficult to isolate such a large number of individual risks.

The main difficulty with concentrating the risk in this manner involves the appropriate compensation of those who are unlucky enough to have been selected to be put at risk. The option of concentrating the risk is particularly attractive in theory, but in practice it implies that one group in particular will bear a substantial part of the costs. The NIMBY—not in my backyard—phenomenon looms particularly large in such contexts. It is these kinds of equity issues and the potential role for compensation of various kinds that are highlighted by application of the Coase Theorem and the implications that can be developed from it.

Selecting the Optimal Policy: Standards versus Fines

Lawyers and economists generally have different answers to the question of how one should structure regulatory policy. In situations in which there is an externality that we would like to prevent, the answer given by lawyers is to set a standard prescribing the behavior that is acceptable. The usual approach by economists is somewhat different, as they attempt to replicate what would have occurred in an efficient market by establishing a pricing mechanism for pollution.

As we will see, each of these approaches can potentially lead to the efficient degree of pollution control, depending on how the standards and fees are set. In analyzing these pollution-control options, we will assume that society approaches the control decision with the objective of providing for an efficient degree of pollution control. In tightening the pollution-control standard, we should consequently not do so past the point where the marginal benefits accruing to society from this tightening no longer exceed the marginal costs.

In actual practice, the standard setting guidelines administered by the Environmental Protection Agency are much more stringent. In the case of the Clean Air Act, for example, EPA is required by law to set ambient air quality standards irrespective of cost considerations. Moreover, not only is EPA required to ignore costs, ensuring safety is not sufficient. The agency's legislation requires it to provide a "margin of safety" below the zero risk level. The result is that standards are generally set at excessively stringent levels from the standpoint of equating marginal benefits and marginal costs, but there are informal efforts to achieve balancing based on affordability.

Figure 21.2 illustrates the character of the compliance costs with the degree of pollution control. By making allowances with respect to the availability and affordability of technologies, EPA and other risk regulation agencies attempt to limit the stringency of their regulations to a

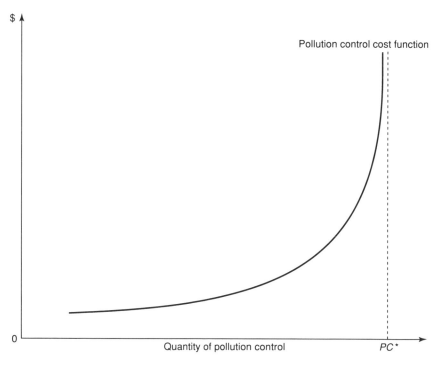

Figure 21.2
Technology-Based Standard Setting

point such as PC^*, where the cost function begins to rise quite steeply. Such informal considerations of affordability may lead to an equalization of marginal benefits and marginal costs in some instances, and at the very minimum will limit the most extreme excesses of regulatory cost impacts.

Setting the Pollution Tax

The shortcomings in the market that give rise to the rationale for government regulation stem from not only the character of the cost function but also the relationship of these costs to the benefits of controlling environmental externalities that will not otherwise be handled in an unregulated market context. Figure 21.3 indicates the character of the market equilibrium in a situation in which the externality is not priced, but was rather inflicted involuntarily on the citizenry. The focus of this curve is on the marginal benefits and marginal costs of the production of gasoline, where the externality consists of air pollution. The market is governed by the relationship of the demand for gasoline, given by the marginal-benefit curve MB. In setting the quantity level that will be

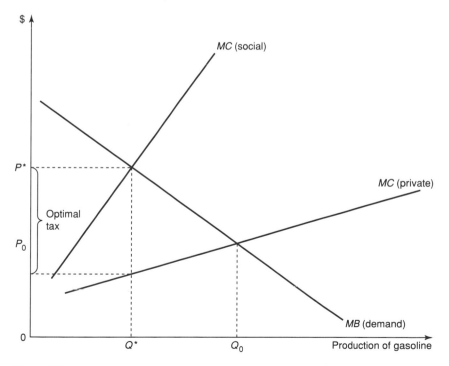

Figure 21.3
Market Equilibrium versus Social Optimum

produced, the market will be guided by the marginal cost curve reflecting the private marginal cost of gasoline, leading to a production of gasoline given by Q_0, whereas the socially optimal level of gasoline production is Q^*. The prevailing market price for gasoline is given by P_0. To achieve efficient pricing of gasoline what is needed is an optimal tax that raises the price of gasoline to the amount P^*. Alternatively, this can be achieved by constraining the quantity of gasoline produced to Q^*, where market forces will drive the price of gasoline up to the point P^*.

Focusing on either prices or quantities can each achieve the desired result. In the case of the quantity restrictions, the revenues accruing from the higher price of gasoline will go to the companies producing gasoline, whereas under a tax scheme the taxes will go to the government.

The choice between taxes and quantity constraints is not simply a question of administrative feasibility. There are also important dollar stakes involved in terms of the transfers among the various market participants. Because market outcomes will produce too much of the externality, some form of government intervention is potentially warranted. If we adopt the usual approach in which we wish to establish the appropriate pollution-control standard, the objective is to equalize the marginal benefits and marginal costs of pollution reduction.

The Role of Heterogeneity

Figure 21.4 illustrates the marginal-cost curve for pollution reduction to two firms. Firm 1 has a higher control cost for pollution, as is reflected in its higher marginal-cost curve MC_1. Firm 2 has a lower pollution-reduction marginal-cost curve given by MC_2. In situations in which the cost curves differ and where we can make distinctions among firms, the optimal solution is to have a differential standard in different contexts. Thus we should set a tighter standard in the situation in which the marginal cost curve is lower and we can achieve pollution control level PC_2, as compared with the looser standard of PC_1 for the higher-cost firm.

Distinctions such as this arise often among industries. It may be easier for some industries to comply with pollution requirements given the character of their technologies. If it is easier for chemical plants to reduce their water pollutant discharges than it is for dye manufacturers, then we should set the standard more stringently in that case to recognize the difference in the marginal costs of compliance.

Perhaps more controversial are the distinctions that regulatory agencies make among firms within a given industry depending on the character of their technology. For new facilities that can incorporate the new pollution equipment as part of the plant design, the marginal-cost curve for compliance is generally less than it will be for an existing facility that

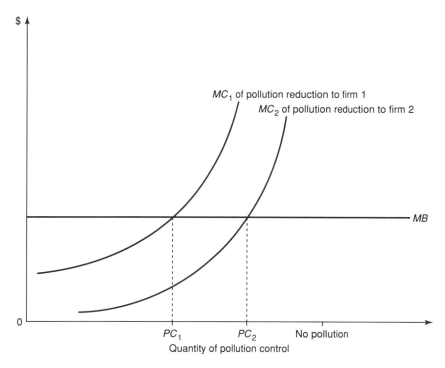

Figure 21.4
Differences in Control Technologies and Efficiency of Pollution Outcome

must retrofit the pollution-control equipment onto its existing technology. It is consequently optimal from an economic standpoint to impose stricter standards on new sources than on existing sources because of the differences in the marginal cost curves.

This economic principle has given rise to what many observers have identified as a "new source bias" in the policies of EPA and other government agencies.[6] A new source bias is efficient, but one must be careful in determining the extent to which one will have biased policies that set differential standards. For firms such as those in Figure 21.4 one can justify the differing degrees of stringency indicated by the difference in marginal costs. The danger is that we often move beyond such distinctions because of political pressures exerted by the representatives from existing and declining industrial regions that are attempting to diminish the competition from the growth areas of the economy, as B. Peter Pashigian has shown.[7] Economics provides a rationale for some new source bias, but it does not necessarily justify the extent of the new source bias that has been incorporated within the context of EPA policy.

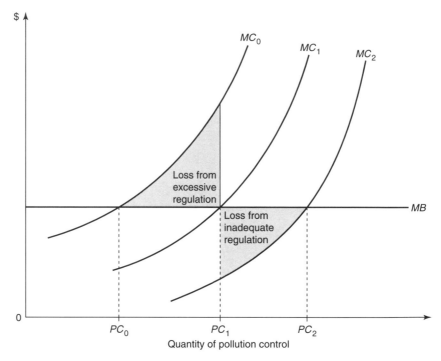

Figure 21.5
Standard Setting with Uncertain Compliance Costs

The Role of Uncertainty

Setting the optimal standard is most straightforward when compliance costs and benefits arising from policies are known. In the usual policy context, there is substantial uncertainty regarding these magnitudes. Figure 21.5 illustrates the familiar case in which the cost uncertainty is likely to be greater than the benefits uncertainty. For most policies with comparatively small impacts on the nation's environment, the marginal benefit curve will be flat. Firms' marginal cost curves for pollution control are not flat but rather tend to slope upward quite steeply. Moreover, there may be considerable uncertainty regarding the degree of compliance costs because the technologies needed to attain compliance may not yet have been developed. As is illustrated in Figure 21.5, the optimal degree of pollution control ranges from PC_0 in a situation in which the marginal-cost curve is given by MC_0 to the intermediate case of PC_1 for a marginal-cost curve of MC_1, to a very high level of pollution control at PC_2 for a marginal-cost curve MC_2. In situations in which the marginal cost curve can lie between MC_0 and MC_2 the standard consequently could have a very substantial range depending on how we assess compliance costs.

If we assess these costs incorrectly, then we run the risk of imposing costs that may not be justified. For example, if we set the policy on the basis of a marginal-cost curve of MC_1, where the true marginal-cost curve is governed by MC_0, then there will be a needless cost imposed by the regulation. The shaded triangle in Figure 21.5 that lies above line MB gives the value of the excess costs that are incurred because the regulation has been set too stringently. On the other hand, there could also be a competing error in terms of foregone benefits if the standard is set too leniently at PC_1 when the regulation should have been set at PC_0. If the true marginal-cost curve is MC_1 and it is believed to be MC_2, there will be a loss in benefits from inadequate regulation. This outcome is illustrated in Figure 21.5 by the triangle that lies below line MB, between PC_1 and PC_2.

Although setting standards intrinsically must address this problem of uncertain compliance costs, if we were to set a pollution fine equal to the level of the marginal-benefit curve in Figure 21.5, then firms could pick their quantity of pollution control on a decentralized basis after the pollution had been priced. This approach not only accommodates differences at a particular point in time in terms of technologies, but it also accommodates uncertainty regarding the present technology and uncertainty regarding future technological development. If the uncertainty with respect to cost is greater than with respect to benefits, as most regulatory economists believe, then a fee system is preferable to a standards system in such situations.

Pollution Taxes

The operation of a pollution tax approach to promoting optimal pollution control is illustrated in Figure 21.6. In particular, suppose that we set the price of pollution equal to the marginal benefits given by the horizontal curve in that diagram. This optimal fine will lead the firm to install the pollution-control equipment needed to achieve the level of pollution control given by PC^*. The amount of pollution reduced is indicated on the horizontal axis, as is the amount of pollution remaining. In addition, the shaded portion of Figure 21.6 indicates the total fine that firms must pay for their pollution. From the standpoint of short-run efficiency, achieving the pollution-control level PC^* through a standard or the fine system is equivalent. From the standpoint of the firms that must comply with this standard, however, the attractiveness of standards is much greater than that of fines. With a standard, the only costs

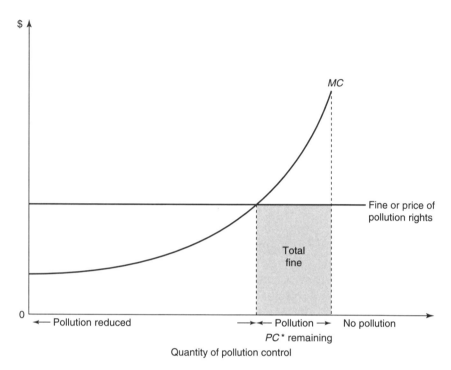

Figure 21.6
Setting the Optimal Pollution Penalty

incurred are the compliance costs, whereas under the fine system firms must pay both the compliance costs as well as the fine for all of the pollution that remains above the optimal control point.

This difference in outcomes raises two classes of issues. The first is whether the fine has any role to play other than simply being a transfer of resources from firms to the citizenry. In terms of the short-run efficiency, the fine does not alter the pollution control outcomes. However, from the standpoint of long-run efficiency, we want all economic actors to pay the full price of their actions.[8] If they do not do this, the incentive to enter polluting industries will be too great. In effect, society at large will be providing a subsidy to these polluting industries equal to the value of the remaining pollution. Imposition of fines consequently has a constructive role to play from a standpoint of providing correct incentives for entry into the industry and long-run efficiency, even though it will not alter the degree of pollution control by an existing firm.

A second observation with respect to the penalty proposals is that the imposition of costs on firms can be altered to make its impact more similar to that of a standard by making the fine asymmetric. In particu-

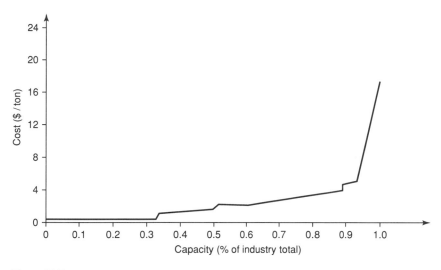

Figure 21.7
Distribution of Water pollution Control Expenditures in the Tissue Paper Industry
Source: W. Kip Viscusi and Richard Zeckhauser, "Optimal Standards with Incomplete Enforcement," *Public Policy* 26, No. 4 (1979): 443, Figure 2.

lar, if we impose a fine only for pollution levels below the standard PC^*, then the purpose of the fine is to bring firms into compliance with the standard. In situations in which firms choose to pay the fine rather than install the necessary control equipment, it may be an index that the original standard was not set appropriately given the firm's particular cost curves. Thus, fines may provide a mechanism to introduce flexibility into an otherwise rigid standard system that does not recognize the heterogeneity in compliance costs that does in fact exist.

Cost Heterogeneity for Water Pollution Control

Figure 21.7 illustrates the considerable variation in compliance costs with water pollution control standards for firms in the tissue paper industry. Although most firms in the industry can comply with the standards for under $6/ton of effluent, for some very high cost compliers the compliance costs could be four times as great. Rather than have to set standards that reflect the wide differences in compliance costs that may exist, offering the firms the option to pay a penalty if they fall short of the standard may be a way to promote efficient pollution control in situations in which there is uncertainty regarding compliance costs. Firms will not have an incentive to misrepresent their compliance costs in such an instance because they must pay the penalty if they cannot meet the standard.

Table 21.4
Summary of Emissions Trading Activity

Activity	Estimated Number of Internal Transactions	Estimated Number of External Transactions	Estimated Cost Savings (millions)	Environmental Quality Impact
Netting	5,000 to 12,000	None	$25 to $300 in permitting costs; $500 to $12,000 in emission control costs	Insignificant in individual cases; probably insignificant in aggregate
Offsets	1,800	200	Probably large, but not easily measured	Probably insignificant
Bubbles:				
Federally approved	40	2	$300	Insignificant
State approved	89	0	$135	Insignificant
Banking:	<100	<20	Small	Insignificant

Source: Robert W. Hahn and Gordon L. Hester, "Where Did All the Markets Go? An Analysis of EPA's Emissions Trading Program," *Yale Journal on Regulation* 6, No. 1 (1989): 138. © Copyright 1989 by the Yale Journal on Regulation, Box 401A Yale Station, New Haven, CT 06520. Reprinted from the Volume 6:1 by permission. All rights reserved.

Current Market Trading Policies

Although there has been substantial support for various kinds of fee systems in the economics literature for at least two decades, policy-makers have been slow to implement these concepts.[9] The four types of emissions trading options that are available are summarized in Table 21.4.[10] In each case firms must apply to EPA to be permitted to use these mechanisms, and the requirements on such systems are very stringent because there is a continuing suspicion among environmentalists of market outcomes that enable firms to buy their way out of meeting a pollution control standard.

Netting

The first of the mechanisms listed in Table 21.4 is that of netting. Under the netting system a firm can alter its current plant and equipment in a manner that increases the pollution emissions from one source at the plant, provided that it also decreases the emissions from other sources so that the net increase that occurs does not equal that of a major source. These trades cannot take place across firms, but are restricted to within firms. Such trades have occurred in several thousand instances. The estimated cost savings from having this flexibility range from $25 million to $300 million in terms of the permitting costs and from $500 million to $12 billion in terms of emission-control costs. For this as well as for the other market trading systems listed, the adverse environmental effect is believed to be minimal.

Offsets

The second most frequent market trading activity is that of offsets. Under an offset option, firms will be permitted to construct new facilities in a part of the country that exceeds EPA's maximum permissible level of pollutants. However, before the company can build a plant in such an area it must purchase pollution offsets from some existing facility in that area that provides for more than an equivalent reduction of the same pollutant. Moreover, the party selling these offsets must already be in compliance with EPA standards. Although there were 1800 offset purchases by the mid-1980s, for the most part these involved internal market trades rather than external transactions.

Bubbles

The third policy option was introduced with great fanfare in December 1989 by the Carter administration. Under the bubble concept a firm does not have to meet compliance requirements for every particular emissions source at a firm. Ordinarily, each smokestack would have to comply with a particular standard. Instead, the firm can envision the plant as if it has been surrounded by an artificial bubble. The compliance task then becomes that of restricting the total emissions that will emerge from this bubble to a particular level. This option enables the firm to have some flexibility in terms of what sources it will choose to control. If there are two smokestacks, for example, as in the case of Figure 21.8, the firm will choose to achieve the greatest pollution reduction from smokestack 1, as these costs will be lower than for pollution reduction in smokestack 2. There have been over a hundred such bubbles approved by EPA, with cost savings of $435 million.

Banking

The final option is that of banking. Under the banking policy, firms in compliance with their standards can store pollution rights over time, and then use these rights in the future as an offset against future pollution. The use of this policy option has been fairly infrequent.

The Future of Market Approaches

A major policy shift may occur in future years. President Bush, for example, declared a commitment to increase reliance on market trading options,[11] and some programs of this type were implemented. EPA has

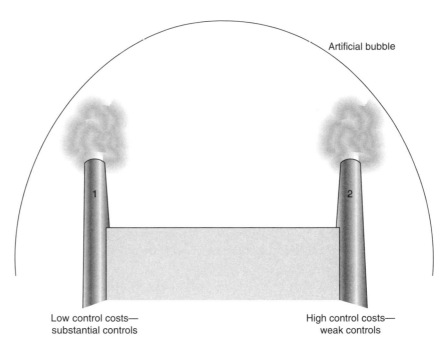

Figure 21.8
EPA Bubble Policy Standard for Total Emissions

not, however, replaced the thrust of its policy standards effort with a
tradable pollution permit system.

Nevertheless, permits have attractive economic features as firms with
the highest compliance costs can purchase them, thus fostering an efficient degree of control of pollution.

The first advantage of tradable pollution rights is that they enable
EPA to equalize the opportunity costs of pollution control. Second, they
encourage innovations to decrease pollution, whereas a rigid standard
only encourages a firm to meet the standard, not to go any further. Pollution rights systems also create less uncertainty for firms that must
make fixed capital investments. Changing technology-based standards
over time poses a risk that a firm's capital investments will become
obsolete.

The disadvantage of pollution rights is that we must set the number of
such rights. Establishing the quantity of such rights is not too dissimilar
from setting an aggregate pollution level. It requires a similar kind of
information, and it probably relies on more imperfect forms of information than would establishing a penalty scheme. However, a fee system for all pollution generated imposes such substantial costs that there
is currently political opposition to this approach.

Other criticisms of pollution-rights systems pertain to whether the market participants are really trading a uniform good. The impact of pollution depends on the character of the pollutants, the stack height, and similar idiosyncratic factors. These pollutants also may interact with other pollutants in the area so that their consequences may differ. There also may be decreased ability to enforce marketable permit systems, as compared with a situation where EPA mandates a particular technology for which officials can readily verify compliance. This concern may be of less consequence because many EPA standards, such as its water discharge requirements, are in terms of discharge amounts that must be monitored and reported on a monthly basis to EPA.

The final concern that has been raised relates to market power. Will some large players such as public utilities buy up all of the pollution rights? Thus far, such concerns have not been of practical consequences.

By far the greatest resistance to the marketable permit scheme is the general suspicion of markets among non-economists. Their counter-argument often takes the following form: "Should the government also sell rights to murder?" A more appropriate question to use is which policy approach will be most effective in reducing pollution at less cost? Although EPA has attempted to increase their salability by labeling such systems as ones in which firms sell pollution reduction credits rather than purchase pollution rights, these efforts continue to remain limited and fairly experimental in nature.

Global Warming and Irreversible Environmental Effects

Whereas the environmental policies of the 1970s focused primarily on conventional air and water pollutants, and efforts of the 1980s turned to toxic chemicals and hazardous waste, attention in the 1990s has shifted to the long-term character of the earth's climate.

Chief among these concerns is that of global warming. The accumulation of carbon dioxide and other trace gases in the earth's atmosphere in effect has created a greenhouse around the earth. This change in the earth's atmosphere is expected to produce global warming on the order of three to five degrees Celsius early in the next century, although scientists continue to debate the magnitude and timing of the effect. Some global warming is inevitable irrespective of current efforts to impose environmental controls because of the irreversible nature of the generation of the greenhouse gases. We have already taken the actions that will harm our future environment. The extent of the future warming is uncertain because of both the substantial uncertainty regarding climatological models and the uncertainty regarding factors such as population growth and our pollution-control efforts in the coming decades.

Even more problematic is the effect that global warming will have on society. Although the temperature will rise by several degrees, for northern regions this will be a benefit and for southern regions it will generally be a disadvantage. The warming in the winter will be beneficial and will occur to a greater extent than the warming in the summer, which will have an adverse effect. Some have even questioned the desirability of a temperature change. Will global warming, for example, be tantamount to getting on a plane in Boston and arriving in Los Angeles? U.S. retirement patterns suggest that warmer weather may in fact be preferable. Change of any kind will necessarily lead to the imposition of some adjustment costs, and climatologists also predict that there will be an increase in damage from natural disasters such as hurricanes.

Assessing the Merits of Global-Warming Policies

Although a precise assessment of the optimal policy relating to global warming is not possible, one can frame the issues and obtain a sense of the types of concerns that are being addressed within the context of what will prove to be an ongoing policy debate.[12]

Figure 21.9 sketches the marginal-cost curves for addressing global warming by controlling the emission of greenhouse gases. This has been the approach taken by economists such as William D. Nordhaus.[13] The first of the three policy options is that of reducing chlorofluorocarbons, such as bans on the use of freon in refrigerators. The second policy option listed is the imposition of a global carbon tax, which will penalize usage of gasoline or coal to produce energy, thus recognizing the environmental externalities they impose. The third policy option listed is reforestation. Additional forests serve to reduce the global warming problem by converting carbon dioxide into oxygen.

Also shown in Figure 21.9 are two marginal benefit curves—one designated MB (low) and another designated MB (high). The purpose of illustrating the two curves is to indicate how the policy might change depending on our uncertainty regarding the ultimate societal implications that global warming will have.

What is clear from this figure is that even in the case of the low marginal benefit curve, some actions are clearly worthwhile. Elimination of chlorofluorocarbons and the imposition of some global carbon tax is clearly efficient even in the case in which the low-benefit scenario prevails. If benefits are at a higher level, then policies of reforestation and a steeper global carbon tax are also worthwhile.

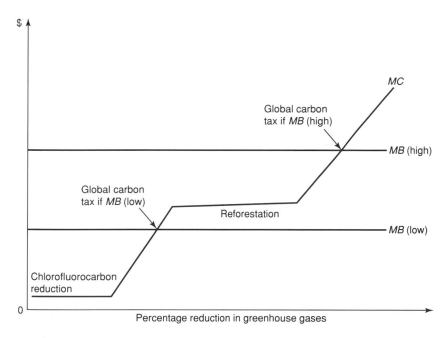

Figure 21.9
Establishing the Optimal Global Warming Policy

Whereas in most environmental contexts it is the marginal costs that are more uncertain than the marginal benefits, in this long-run environmental context, benefits also pose substantial uncertainty. This uncertainty is at a very fundamental level. There is even a debate over whether on balance global warming will be beneficial or adverse to our economy. However, even at the very low level of costs that are assumed in Figure 21.9, some policy options such as chlorofluorocarbon reduction are optimal.

How Should We React to Uncertainty?

Although further study to resolve these uncertainties is clearly a desirable policy alternative, if we were in a situation in which we had to take an action today, an economic issue arises as to whether the substantial uncertainties imply that we should err on the side of caution or err on the side of reckless abandon.

As we continue to study the climate change issue, there will also be calls for policy action. One approach that has gained widespread support is the "no regrets" option. We should clearly adopt policies, such as energy conservation, that would be desirable irrespective of what we

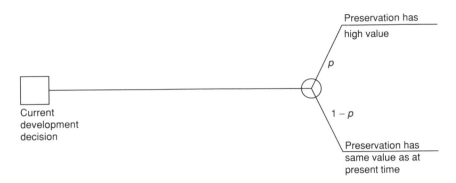

Figure 21.10
Irreversible Environmental Decisions

ultimately learn about the implications of climate change. Whether we should go beyond the "no regrets" policy is more controversial.

Some insight into resolving this problem is provided by examining the classic irreversible development decision situation.[14] Figure 21.10 illustrates the basic irreversible investment paradigm. A developer must choose the degree of current development, where the benefits and costs of this development at the present time are known. There is, however, uncertainty regarding the degree to which environmental preservation will be valued in the future. There is some probability p that the preservation will have a high value, and there is some probability $1 - p$ that the preservation will have the same value that it does at the present time. In such a situation of uncertainty, how should one choose the extent to which one will develop the scarce resource, such as conversion of a national forest into a shopping center and suburbs?

In general, the answer is that one should err on the side of underdevelopment in such situations. Moreover, the greater the probability that preservation will have a high value and the greater the increase that this value will be, the more one should alter one's current decision from what one would select based on a myopic assessment of the benefits and costs of the development policy.

This principle for underdevelopment does not generalize to every situation in which there are irreversible decisions to be made. For example, companies installing pollution-control equipment might rationally choose to overinvest in such equipment if they expect the standard to be tightened in the future. Much depends on the character of the problem and the nature of the uncertainty. However, for problems like global warming, where the main uncertainty is with respect to the potential increase in the benefits of controls above current levels based on the current benefits associated with pollution control, the general policy maxim is that conservatism is the best policy.

Moreover, it is noteworthy that this conservatism arises wholly apart from the presence of any risk aversion. Society does not choose to err on the side of caution because we are unwilling to engage in risks. Rather, the bias arises because the expected payoffs from development in the future may be much less than they are today, and we should take this possible change in values into account.

Multiperson Decisions and Group Externalities

Externality problems become particularly complex within the context of group decisions. In the situation of an individual firm and the citizenry, one has to worry only about the actions of one economic actor. However, in actual practice many of the most important externalities arise from the decentralized decisions of a variety of actors. In these contexts, some coordination mechanism is often desirable to promote behavior that will be collectively beneficial to society.

The Prisoner's Dilemma

The standard situation in bargaining theory where uncoordinated action gives rise to an inferior outcome is that of the Prisoner's Dilemma. Suppose that there are two partners in crime, each of whom has been captured by the police. The prisoners are held separately, preventing cooperation. The police offer to lighten each prisoner's sentence if he will incriminate the other. The prisoner must make a risky decision, based on what he believes the other is most likely to do. Following the standard scenario, the prisoners each choose their preferred strategy of talking to the police. Talking is a dominant strategy for each party, given any particular behavior on the part of the other prisoner. However, if both of the prisoners had agreed not to talk they would have been better off than they will be after they both incriminate one another. The outcome is consequently Pareto inferior (that is, each gets a lower valued payoff) when compared to a situation where both of them had remained silent.

The N-Person Prisoner's Dilemma

A variety of social situations also arise in which there are incentives for individual behavior that do not lead to optimal group outcomes. Figure 21.11 illustrates a multiperson Prisoner's Dilemma, using a methodology developed by Thomas C. Schelling, where the particular context

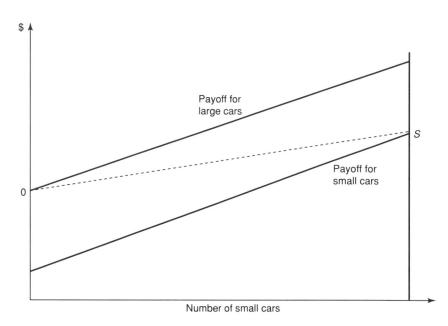

Figure 21.11
The Multiperson Prisoner's Dilemma

being considered is that of the purchase of a large or small car.[15] We will suppose for concreteness that consumers prefer large cars to small cars. Thus, for any given number of small cars on the market along the horizontal axis, the consumer's payoff received for using a large car exceeds that for a small car. The result is that because everybody has a dominant strategy to purchase a large car, we end up at the equilibrium 0. This equilibrium is not a social optimum, however. In particular, if we could constrain everyone to purchase a small car, we could reach the outcome at point S, which has a higher value than 0. The reason some constraint is needed is that this is not a stable equilibrium. Any individual driver has an incentive to break away and purchase a large car, leading to an unraveling until we reach the stable equilibrium at 0. Thus, some government regulation is required.

Applications of the Prisoner's Dilemma

Group externalities such as this arise in a variety of contexts. In international whaling, exercising some restraint in terms of the number of whales that are caught in any year will maximize the value of the whaling population. Thus, even if one were simply concerned with the commercial value of the whales, some limitation on whaling is optimal. However, from the standpoint of the individual fisherman it is always optimal to catch as many whales as you can. If all of the whaling vessels follow their dominant strategy, as most of them have, the result is that the whaling population will be overfished and that we will have a dwindling number of whales. In this instance, the optimal strategy is to provide for some restraint but not a complete abolition of whaling activities. Achieving this moderation in the degree of whaling has proven to be a long-term international regulatory problem.

The international whaling example has proven to be more than a hypothetical case. In 1994, the United States government proposed that the Georges' Bank fishing area off New England be closed so that the species could revive. This fishing ground, which had formerly been one of the richest in the Atlantic Ocean, was the source of fish such as cod and haddock. This fishing area also served as the principal source of livelihood for fishing villages in New England, such as Gloucester. Restraints on fishing proved to be ineffective, which led the Federal government in 1994 to propose the more drastic step of closing these fishing grounds altogether so that the fishing stocks could revive. Unfortunately, the difficulty in monitoring and enforcing appropriate fishing restrictions has proven to be so great that the government was led to a much more costly and disruptive regulatory policy option that has led to the abandonment of a fishing fleet and the shut down of a major industry throughout much of the New England area.

Similar classes of issues arise within the context of vaccinations. If a critical mass in society has received an inoculation, it is not optimal to get vaccinated because the risk of contracting the disease will generally be much less than the expected health loss due to an adverse reaction to the vaccine. We clearly need some coordinating mechanism to ensure that a sufficient portion of the population has received the vaccination, but given the fact that society has established such a vaccination requirement, each of us has an incentive to be exempted from the vaccination.

Similarly, home owners who are doing battle against Japanese beetles will be able to diminish their efforts if all of their neighbors use insecticides. However, it is essential to establish a sufficiently broad insecticide use to control the beetle population. The initial insecticide user may obtain little benefit unless a sufficient number of his neighbors also use the insecticides. At low and high levels of community-wide insecticide use, the individual incentive to use insecticides will be lacking. There is no voluntary incentive for an unassisted market process to begin generating the decentralized decisions needed to reach the social optimum.

The general result that pertains in situations in which there are group externalities is that some form of coordination is often worthwhile. This coordination often takes the form of explicit regulations. Hockey players are required to wear helmets, traffic rules require that we drive on the right side of the road, and daylight savings requirements establish uniform changes in the time schedule for everyone. Individually, the payoff of shifting to daylight savings is quite low if no one else in society shifts, but if we can all coordinate our actions we will all be better off.

The Enforcement and Performance of Environmental Regulation

Enforcement Options

The promulgation of regulations does not ensure that firms will comply with them. As a result, EPA and other regulatory agencies couple the issuance of regulations with vigorous enforcement efforts. In the case of major sources of air and water pollution, EPA attempts to inspect the emissions source at least once per year. Moreover, in the case of water pollution discharges, EPA requires by law that the firms submit a record of the nature of the discharge to EPA and that each firm reports its compliance status with the pollution permit that it has been given.

The enforcement task with respect to conventional pollutants is generally viewed as being the simplest. Next in terms of the degree of difficulty is enforcement with respect to toxic chemicals. These chemicals are often more difficult to monitor than are conventional pollutants because of specific chemical testing that must be undertaken.

The nature of the source of the pollution also affects the feasibility of effective enforcement. Hazards that arise on a decentralized basis, such as toxic wastes, radon in consumers' homes, and asbestos in buildings, often impose substantial enforcement problems because of the large number of pollution sources involved and, in the case of toxic chemical dumping, the difficulty of monitoring the party responsible.

Enforcement of environmental regulations pertaining to chemicals and pesticides varies in effectiveness depending on the nature of the regulation. The process of screening chemicals and regulating the chemicals that are being sold and used commercially is quite effective because of the ability to monitor mass-produced consumer goods. EPA also can readily monitor the hazard warnings attached to these products. Much more difficult to monitor is the manner in which the products are used. The disposal of chemical containers and the dilution of insecticides are among the decentralized activities that pose almost insurmountable problems. The best that EPA can achieve in these instances is to provide risk information to foster the appropriate safety-enhancing action on the part of the product users.

In these various inspection contexts, EPA has several enforcement tools that it can use. Not all of these involve fines, but they do impose costs of various kinds on the affected firms. EPA can inspect a firm. It can request that the firm provide data to it. It can send the firm letters, or it can meet with the firm's managers to discuss pollution-control problems. Most of the EPA contacts with firms are of this character.

In terms of sanctions, there are two classes of financial penalties that can be levied. The first consists of administrative penalties that are usually modest in size and limited in terms of the circumstances in which they can be levied. The main sanction that EPA has is not the penalties that it can assess, but rather the penalties that can be assessed through prosecution of the polluter by the U.S. Department of Justice. In severe, flagrant, or persistent cases of violations of EPA standards, the EPA frequently refers the case to the U.S. Department of Justice for civil or criminal prosecution. The costs associated with the prospective litigation as well as the possibility that substantial fines may be imposed often provide a compelling enforcement sanction.

Enforcement Trends

The level of such enforcement activities and the change in character of EPA's enforcement efforts is reflected in the summary of the EPA administrative actions in Table 21.5. Beginning in the 1980s, the agency became much more concerned with toxic substances and hazardous wastes. The Resource Conservation and Recovery Act of 1976 focused on the identification of hazardous wastes and the transportation of hazardous substances. The Superfund program established in 1980 focuses on hazardous waste site cleanup and hazardous waste disposal. Finally, the Toxic Substances Control Act requires premanufacture evaluation of all new chemicals and provides EPA with the authority to regulate existing chemicals. All three new areas of responsibility have exhibited substantial growth throughout the 1980s.

Table 21.6 provides a similar summary of the number of EPA civil referrals for prosecution by the U.S. Department of Justice. The number of these referrals is considerably less than the number of administrative actions. However, the general growth in these referrals follows a similar pattern. By 1988, the number of referrals to the U.S. Department of Justice for hazardous waste violations exceeded that for either air pollution or water pollution violations, which is a strong index of the changing focus of EPA enforcement activities and more generally a shift in the emphasis of EPA regulation.

Another notable pattern in these tables is the drastic decline in enforcement actions during the early 1980s. The initial head of EPA in the Reagan administration, Anne Gorsuch, sought to decrease the burden of

Table 21.5
EPA Administrative Actions Initiated (by Act), Fiscal Years 1972 through 1988

	Clean Air Act (1970)	Clean Water and Safe Drinking Water Acts (1972/1974)	Resource Conservation and Recovery (1976)	Superfund (CERCLA) (1980)	FIFRA[a] (1947)	Toxic Substances Control Act (1976)	Totals
1972	0	0	0	0	860	0	860
1973	0	0	0	0	1,274	0	1,274
1974	0	0	0	0	1,387	0	1,387
1975	0	738	0	0	1,641	0	2,352
1976	210	915	0	0	2,488	0	3,613
1977	297	1,128	0	0	1,219	0	2,644
1978	129	730	0	0	762	1	1,622
1979	404	506	0	0	253	22	1,185
1980	86	569	0	0	176	70	901
1981	112	562	159	0	154	120	1,107
1982	21	329	237	0	176	101	864
1983	41	781	436	0	296	294	1,848
1984	141	1,644	554	137	272	376	3,124
1985	122	1,031	327	160	236	733	2,609
1986	143	990	235	139	338	781	2,626
1987	191	1,214	243	135	360	1,051	3,194
1988	224	1,345	309	224	376	607	3,085

[a] FIFRA = Federal Insecticide, Fungicide, and Rodenticide Act.

Source: Based on Clifford Russell, "Monitoring and Enforcement," in Pual Portmey, ed., *Public Policies for Environmental Protection* (Washington, D.C.: Resources for the Future, 1990), Table 7.7, using data from *Mealey's Litigation Reports: Superfund* 1, No. 18 (December 28, 1988): C-5.

these regulations on business by scaling back the enforcement effort. This deregulation approach did little to alter the structure of EPA regulations or their stringency, which is the main area in which economists would advocate reform. Instead, the focus was simply on decreasing the cost burdens arising from effective enforcement. Because of the general consensus and support for effective environmental regulation of the various externalities addressed by EPA, this deregulation effort does not follow any of the prescriptions that would have been advanced by economists. In 1983, Anne Gorsuch was replaced as head of EPA by William Ruckelshaus, who quickly restored the enforcement efforts of the agency and was responsible for shifting the direction of the agency toward the new classes of hazards.

Environmental Outcomes and Enterprise Decisions

The statistics in Table 21.7 indicate that from the standpoint of firms' investments there has been considerable emphasis on pollution control

Table 21.6
EPA Civil Referrals to the Department of Justice

Fiscal Year	Air	Water	Hazardous Waste	Toxics, Pesticides	Total
1972	0	1	0	0	1
1973	4	0	0	0	4
1974	3	0	0	0	3
1975	5	20	0	0	25
1976	15	67	0	0	82
1977	50	93	0	0	143
1978	123	137	2	0	262
1979	149	81	9	3	242
1980	100	56	53	1	210
1981	66	37	14	1	118
1982	36	45	29	2	112
1983	69	56	33	7	165
1984	82	95	60	14	251
1985	116	93	48	19	276
1986	115	119	84	24	342
1987	122	92	77	13	304
1988	86	123	143	20	372

Source: Based on Russell, 1990, Table 7.6, using data from *Mealey's Litigation Reports: Superfund* 1, No. 18 (December 28, 1988): C-1.

efforts. First, the level of investment in pollution control has not been a one-shot expenditure that firms have made. Rather, there has been a continuing effort to make these investments. Moreover, the level of these investments has risen over time, even if we adjust for inflation. From 1972 to 1987 the investments in air pollution control almost doubled in real terms, to a value of $32 billion (1987 dollars). The rise in water pollution control expenditures was less striking, but nevertheless it was substantial, as firms' investments in water pollution control efforts increased by almost 50 percent in real terms from 1972 to 1987, reaching a value of $33 billion in 1987. Although evidence of substantial industry investments does not necessarily imply that these investments will enhance environmental quality, there are signs that environmental policies are having an impact on enterprise decisions. Moreover, these figures indicate the substantial stakes that are involved.

The objective of regulatory policy is not simply to promulgate and enforce regulations, but also to improve environmental outcomes. Assessing the impact of regulations is complicated by the fact that we observe trends in environmental quality, but we do not know what these trends would have been in the absence of regulation. Nevertheless,

Table 21.7
Pollution Reduction Efforts, by Year

| Year | Pollution Abatement and Control Expenditures (in millions of dollars) | | | |
| | Air Pollution | | Water Pollution | |
	Current Dollars	1982 Dollars	Current Dollars	1982 Dollars
1972	6,248	16,221	8,738	20,299
1973	8,094	19,593	10,095	22,037
1974	9,849	19,901	11,562	22,226
1975	12,225	22,192	13,445	23,607
1976	13,504	23,185	15,372	25,269
1977	15,151	24,407	16,667	25,518
1978	16,895	25,553	19,570	27,517
1979	19,932	26,254	21,489	27,355
1980	23,261	26,336	22,083	25,541
1981	26,450	27,272	21,579	22,795
1982	26,323	26,323	21,952	21,952
1983	28,419	28,070	23,214	22,297
1984	31,432	30,318	25,962	23,967
1985	33,302	31,480	28,443	25,457
1986	33,325	32,462	30,641	27,161
1987	32,273	30,136	32,987	28,700

Sources: Kit D. Farber and Gary L. Rutledge, "Pollution Abatement and Control Expenditures, 1984–1987," *Survey of Current Business*, U.S. Department of Commerce, Bureau of Economic Analysis (Washington, D.C.: Government Printing Office), June 1989, pp. 24–25. Kit D. Farber and Gary L. Rutledge, "Pollution Abatement and Control Expenditures," *Survey of Current Business*, U.S. Department of Commerce, Bureau of Economic Analysis (Washington, D.C.: U.S. Government Printing Office), July 1986, pp. 100–103.

even examination of pollution trends proves to be instructive in many instances.

Table 21.8 summarizes the pollution trends from 1960 to 1988 for five principal categories of air-pollution emissions. For the first four categories there continued to be steady progress of a fairly modest nature in terms of improved environmental quality. The categories for which the recent progress has been much less than in EPA's first decade of the 1970s are particulates (usually arising from fuel combustion, industrial processes, and motor vehicles), sulfur oxide emissions (chiefly arising from stationary fuel combustion and industrial processes), nitrogen oxide emissions (arising primarily from highway motor vehicles and cold-fired electric utility boilers), and carbon monoxide emissions (primarily arising from highway motor vehicles).

Table 21.8
National Pollution Emissions Trends

Year	Particulates	Pollutant (Teragrams/Year)			
		Sulfur Oxides	Nitrogen Oxides	Carbon Monoxide	Lead
(Gigagrams)					
1960	21.6	19.7	13.0	89.7	NA
1970	18.5	28.3	18.5	101.4	203.8
1975	10.6	25.8	19.5	84.1	147.0
1980	8.5	23.4	20.9	79.6	70.6
1981	8.0	22.6	20.9	77.4	56.4
1982	7.1	21.4	20.0	72.4	54.4
1983	7.1	20.7	19.3	74.5	46.4
1984	7.4	21.5	19.8	71.8	40.1
1985	7.1	21.1	19.8	67.0	21.1
1986	6.8	20.9	19.0	63.1	8.6
1987	7.0	20.6	19.3	64.1	8.0
1988	6.9	20.7	19.8	61.2	7.6
Percentage Annual Growth Rate					
1960–1970	−1.5	+3.7	+3.6	+1.2	—
1970–1980	−7.5	−1.9	+1.2	−2.4	−10.1
1980–1988	−2.6	−1.5	−0.5	−3.2	−20.0

Source: U.S. Environmental Protection Agency, *National Air Pollutant Emission Estimate, 1940–1988*, Office of Air Quality, Research Triangle Park, N.C., EPA-450/4-90-001 (March 1990), p. 2.

The category of greatest interest is that of lead pollution given in the final column of Table 21.8. The 1980s marked a period of dramatic gains in terms of the level of lead pollution, which can cause a variety of adverse health effects, including brain damage in children. The primary sources of lead emissions are motor vehicles and industrial processes. In 1985 EPA's regulations reduced the permissible lead content in gasoline from 1.0 grams/gallon to 0.5 grams/gallon. This regulation was tightened further in 1986, reducing the permissible level of lead to 0.1 grams/gallon. The dramatic effect of these policy shifts is apparent in Table 21.8. In 1985 and 1986 lead pollution emissions declined by half from the previous year, so that the emissions level in 1984 was almost five times as great as the lead emissions in 1986. It is also noteworthy that the estimated benefits for this regulatory success exceeded the estimated costs. This regulation was one of the few EPA regulations that passed a test of economic desirability, and the result was a dramatic improvement in lead pollution levels achieved at reasonable cost.

Although a precise test of EPA's impact on these various pollution measures has not yet been undertaken, it is clear that some progress has been made. Because one would have expected an increase in pollution levels with an expanding economy and a growing population, the fact that there was any decrease in the pollution, much less the dramatic declines that have occurred since 1970, is evidence of some payoff to society from the costs that have been incurred.

Summary

Environmental problems represent a classic situation in which there is an externality being imposed involuntarily. What is most noteworthy about this situation is that the optimal level of pollution is not zero. The fact that there is an externality that is being imposed without a voluntary contract does not mean that the activity should be prohibited. Whether we are talking about secondhand smoke or toxic waste disposal, the efficient level of pollution is generally not zero. However, the efficient level of pollution is also generally not going to be what arises within a market context, because the party generating the pollution has inadequate incentives to reflect the social cost imposed in their decisions.

Our review of the Coase Theorem indicated that the main focal point should be the efficient pollution level, which is the level that would arise under a voluntary contractual situation if parties could contract costlessly. Examining pollution problems within the context of the bargaining problems used to illuminate the Coase Theorem also sheds light on the distributional impacts involved. Assignment of property rights not only has distributional implication but also affects the long-run efficiency aspects of the system.

Similar concerns arise with respect to the choice of standards versus fines. Each of these approaches can provide for the same degree of short-run efficiency that can be achieved through a Coasian contractual outcome. However, standards differ from fines in terms of the total costs that will be borne by firms and in terms of their long-run efficiency. Moreover, there are a number of other features that distinguish the relative attractiveness of these options. Further exploration of the potential role of market trading options is long overdue, but in some contexts standards may be preferable so that it will not always be the case that a particular class of policy options will be dominant.

The same kinds of methodologies that we apply to analyzing conventional pollutants, such as air pollution, can also be applied to analyzing global warming as well as more complex externalities, such as the group decisions that lead to overfishing. Examination of these various contexts as well as the policies that have been developed to address them suggest that considerable insight can be obtained by assessing how efficient markets would deal with externalities, if such markets existed.

Questions and Problems

1.   Consider the following basic problem regarding a driver and a pedestrian in an accident situation. The driver makes a decision regarding his degree of care, but the pedestrian has no such decision to make. Payoffs to each party are given below.

Driving Speed	Total Benefit to Driver	Expected Cost to Pedestrian
Rapidly	170	160
Moderately	100	40
Slowly	90	10

Suppose that instead of an anonymous driver-pedestrian relationship we had a two-person society—one driver and one pedestrian.

a. If the driver could undertake voluntary bargains that would be enforceable, what driving speed would result?

b. If both parties have equal bargaining power, what is the predicted settlement amount (that is, amount of transfer from pedestrian to driver)?

2.   Suppose that a pulp and paper mill discharges water pollutants that impede the value of the stream for swimming. It would cost the mill $5000 to install pollution abatement equipment to eliminate pollution, and doing so would result in an additional $10,000 in swimming benefits to the residents downstream.

a. If the residents are assigned the property rights, and if each party has equal bargaining power, what will be the predicted outcome and the dollar transfer between the two parties?

b. If the firm is assigned the property right to pollute, what will be the predicted outcome and the income transfer between the two parties?

3.   The U.S. Department of Transportation has just rerouted the interstate highway through your yard so that you now have to sell your house. The government proposes that we compensate you an amount equal to the market value of your home. Is this fair? Is it efficient? Answer the same questions supposing that, instead of the government wishing to purchase your house, I have decided that I want to live in your house. Would it be possible for me to evict you and to pay the market value? Would your answer change if we could accurately determine your reservation price for selling the house so that we would ensure that you would experience no utility loss from such an eviction? How do you believe the functioning of society would change if such a compensation mechanism were instituted?

4.   The discussion in the chapter regarding the desirability of taxes and regulatory standards focused primarily on the short-run issues. However, these different policies also have important dynamic implications, particularly regarding the incentives for innovation. Under which type of governmental approach will there be greater incentives to innovate in a beneficial way from the standpoint of decreased environmental and health risks?

5.   Suppose that the government must undertake an irreversible policy decision regarding the extent of air pollution regulation. The government is making this decision in a situation of uncertainty, however. In particular, there is some probability p that the benefits will remain the same as they are this year for all future years, but there is some probability $1 - p$ that benefits will be less in all future years. If we take into consideration the multiperiod aspects, should we err on the side of overregulation or underregulation, as compared with what we would do within a single period choice?

6.   Figure 21.11 illustrates a multiperson Prisoner's Dilemma for a situation in which the payoff curves for the two kinds of cars do not intersect. However, there may be externality situations in which the payoffs do intersect, inasmuch as the desirability of different activities may change in a differential manner for the two different decisions. If these payoff curves intersected, with the bottom payoff curve intersecting the top from below, what would be the nature of the market equilibrium that would prevail? Would this equilibrium be efficient?

7.   Environmentalists argue that because the actions we take today will have an irreversible effect on climate change, we should take action now and err on the side of excessive restrictions. On the other hand, some economists have argued that because of the opportunity to acquire additional information, we should postpone a decision until we learn more about the merits of taking a regulatory action. Which strategy do you find more compelling and why?

Notes

1. For an excellent overview of environmental policy, see the Council on Environmental Quality, *Environmental Quality*, 21st Annual Report (Washington, D.C.: U.S. Government Printing Office, 1991). Chapters 1 and 2 provide overviews of environmental policy and the benefits and costs of these efforts.

2. For a detailed description of these policy options, see Robert W. Hahn and Gordon L. Hester, "Where Did All the Markets Go? An Analysis of EPA's Emissions Trading Program," *Yale Journal on Regulation* 6, No. 1 (1989): 109–54.

3. See Ronald H. Coase, "The Problem of Social Cost," *Journal of Law and Economics*, 1960: 1–44. The Coase Theorem has given rise to a large body of work in the field of law and economics. See, in particular, Richard A. Posner, *Economic Analysis of Law*, 3d ed. (Boston: Little, Brown, 1986).

4. One observant student noted that the manure left by the stray cows on Farm B may be a positive externality. For concreteness, we will assume the net externality is negative.

5. The role of the Coase Theorem in regulatory contexts is also elucidated in A.

Mitchell Polinsky, *An Introduction to Law and Economics*, 2d ed. (Boston: Little, Brown, 1989).

6. For more detailed exploration of new source bias, see Robert W. Crandall, *Controlling Industrial Pollution: The Economics and Politics of Clean Air* (Washington, D.C.: Brookings Institution, 1983).

7. See B. Peter Pashigian, "Environmental Regulation: Whose Self-Interests Are Being Protected?" *Economic Inquiry* 23 (1984).

8. A calculation of the optimal pollution tax to recognize these long-run incentive issues is a nontrivial economic problem. For an analysis of it, see Dennis Carlton and Glenn Loury, "The Limitations of Pigouvian Taxes as a Long-Run Remedy for Externalities," *Quarterly Journal of Economics*, 1980: 559–66.

9. It should be emphasized, however, that economists within these administrations have long advocated this approach. Most recently, see the Council of Economic Advisors, *Economic Report of the President* (Washington, D.C.: U.S. Government Printing Office, 1990), chapter 6.

10. For further discussion of these trading options see Crandall, 1983, or Hahn and Hester, 1989.

11. For the discussion of the position of the Bush administration, see the *1990 Economic Report of the President*, chapter 6.

12. This discussion of the greenhouse effect, particularly the graphical exposition, is based most directly on the article by William D. Nordhaus, "Global Warming: Slowing the Greenhouse Express," in Henry Aaron (ed.), *Setting National Priorities* (Washington, D.C.: Brookings Institution, 1990), pp. 185–211.

13. See Nordhaus, 1990.

14. An early exposition of the irreversible environmental choice problem appears in Kenneth J. Arrow and Anthony C. Fisher, "Preservation, Uncertainty, and Irreversibility," *Quarterly Journal of Economics* 88 (1974): 312–19.

15. The diagrammatic exposition that follows is based on the innovative work of Thomas C. Schelling, *Micromotives and Macrobehavior* (New York: W. W. Norton, 1978).

Although product safety concerns are not entirely new, they did not become a prominent part of the regulatory agenda until after the establishment of the social risk regulation agencies in the early 1970s. A pivotal event that led to the increase in public attention to product safety issues was the publication of Ralph Nader's *Unsafe At Any Speed*.[1] Nader charged that the automobile industry devoted insufficient resources to product safety, as was evidenced, for example, in the turnover risks posed by the Chevrolet Corvair. This compact, rear-engine car was marketed by Chevrolet in the early 1960s as a moderately priced compact that had some of the driving feel of a sports car. Its main disadvantage was that the car was highly unstable during cornering maneuvers, leading to a rash of deaths to Corvair owners. Among the victims was Ernie Kovacs, who at the time was the host of a popular television comedy show.

Emergence of Product Safety Regulations

The product safety era of the early 1960s was quite different from what it is today. There were no requirements that automobiles include safety belts, and in general they did not. Debates over passive restraint systems and air bags had yet to surface, as the primary concern was whether there ought to be any safety belt requirements at all.

Auto safety was not the only area where new regulations were emerging. In the mid-1960s Congress instituted requirements pertaining to the hazard warnings that had to be included on cigarette packages. The initial requirements for protective packaging were also instituted in that period so as to make aspirin products and prescription drugs child-resistant.

Even the subsequent establishment of the social-regulation agencies in the 1970s and the emergence of these new regulations did not lead to the same degree of sensitivity to safety concerns as is present in the 1990s.[2] In the 1970s, for example, the Ford Motor Company marketed a subcompact that it called the Ford Pinto. This car was the brainchild of Lee Iacocca, who wished to develop a budget-priced car that would compete with cheap imports. The design of the Pinto was a hurried affair, with catastrophic results. The main safety defect of the car was the placement of the gas tank too near the rear of the car. As a result, the car was highly vulnerable to rear-end collisions. Ford was conscious of the potential risks and the extra $11 per car that would have had to be spent in order to eliminate the hazard, but it chose to stick with the cheaper design. Ford estimated the costs likely to be imposed on the company by the comparatively inactive product liability regime at that time and concluded that these were less than the costs of making the design change. The result was a series of fatal accidents involving the Ford Pinto, which exploded upon rear impact, causing severe burn injuries and deaths. The substantial damages that were ultimately awarded by the courts became part of the increased product-liability price tag being imposed on the nation's businesses.

Current Safety Decisions

Firms currently contemplating product safety decisions no longer look solely toward the market. Rather, their efforts are governed by a complex set of regulations and judicial precedents. In some cases, these regulations are quite specific. The U.S. Department of Transportation regulations for municipal buses are almost tantamount to a comprehensive bus design. The focus of this chapter will be on how such product safety regulations affect the various market participants. We will also address how society should approach product safety regulation to achieve an appropriate balance between the competing objectives.

Figure 22.1 summarizes the main mechanisms at work in influencing product safety. Let us begin with the decisions by the producer. The producer's environment is governed by three sets of influences: the market through consumer behavior, government regulation, and tort liability. If the market were fully efficient, then there would be no need for social regulation or product liability litigation. In a perfect market, safer

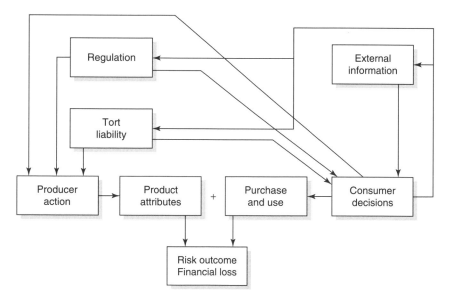

Figure 22.1
The Accident Generating Process

products will command a higher price. If consumers are unaware of the risks, however, market outcome will not be ideal. As was indicated in the discussion on the rationale for social regulation, assessing the degree and character of imperfect information is an area in which one should exercise caution. Even if consumers are not fully knowledgeable of all the implications of the product, that does not always mean that the market supplies too little safety. Indeed, the opposite result may pertain if consumers systematically overestimate the risk, as many consumers do for low-probability events called to their attention. Consequently, one must assess the particular context and nature of the risk involved before one can necessarily conclude that market incentives for safety will be adequate.

Consumer Complaints

One form of information that is frequently used as an index of informational failure is the presence of consumer complaints.[3] If consumers file complaints concerning the performance of a product, can we necessarily assume that there is a market failure warranting some form of regulation? To the extent that consumers are filing complaints for products that fail to meet with their reasonable expectations, there is clearly likely to be some informational value to examining the prevalence of complaints. However, in general it is difficult to distinguish the extent to which consumer complaints reflect a market failure or simply consumers who are unlucky. For example, suppose that consumers know that there is a 75-percent chance that new Hyundai cars will run well, but there is a 25-percent chance that these cars turn out to be lemons. Because of the car's low price, the consumers are willing to take this gamble. However, after the fact the 25 percent of the consumers who get stuck with a lemon are no longer facing an uncertain prospect. Rather, they must confront the certainty of definitely owning a bad car. Conditional upon knowing that they have purchased a lemon, this 25 percent of the consumers may voice regret with their purchase, but on an ex ante basis before they knew the outcome of the product quality lottery, they may have been making a sound decision from an expected utility standpoint.

One aspect of information provision in which there is more likely to be a clear-cut market failure is with respect to information that is of a public-good nature. Firms, for example, will have little incentive to investigate the safety properties of antilock brakes since disclosure of this information will benefit all manufacturers of cars with antilock brakes, not simply the firm undertaking the research.

Factors Affecting Producer and Consumer Actions

Based on the impacts of the market, regulation, and tort liability, the producer will choose the products it will make and their characteristics, leading to the product attribute outcome indicated in Figure 22.1. Consumers are also making decisions. Based on the information they have received from the media, from their experiences, firms, and government regulation, they will make a purchase decision. Moreover, they will also make a product use decision that may be influenced by the incentives created by regulation and tort liability. Government regulations, for example, mandate the use of safety belts in many states and prohibit the use of alcohol for minors. Similarly, tort liability creates incentives for consumer behavior because people who drive while intoxicated, operate an all-terrain vehicle negligently, and otherwise do not exercise appropriate care can be found guilty of contributory negligence, thus reducing or possibly eliminating their prospective court award after an accident.

Product Performance and Consumer Actions

The combined impact of product attributes and the consumer actions result in the risk outcome and financial loss component of Figure 22.1. The main issue that has been stressed by economists and generally ignored by the product-safety professionals is that product safety is not simply an engineering issue. Individual behavior is relevant both to market decisions as well as to safety-enhancing actions that individuals may take.

The performance of these products affects the experience base of information that consumers have in making subsequent purchases, which in turn will alter the market environment of the firm.

From the standpoint of regulatory policy, there are two aspects of these relationships that are particularly noteworthy. First, government regulation is not the only economic influence affecting safety incentives. The market and tort liability also are of consequence. Regulation generally affects firms either through design standards that influence the technology or by addressing observed product defects, as in the case of safety recall actions. In contrast, tort liability operates ex post facto. The courts do not address products that are potentially risky, but for which there have been no adverse outcomes. The focus instead is on observed defects. People must be injured to collect for bodily-injury losses. Consequently, the timing of the institutions in terms of how they can potentially influence product safety is different. Regulations have a greater opportunity to operate in a more anticipatory manner.

The second key feature of Figure 22.1 is that safety is the outcome of the joint influence of producers' safety decisions and user actions. The task of regulatory policy is to ascertain how best to influence both of these determinants of safety outcomes rather than restricting our focus on technological solutions to safety.

Changing Emphasis of Product Regulation

There has been a shifting emphasis of the determinants of the product-safety environment. The regulatory period of the 1970s concentrated on technological solutions to safety, such as mandated changes in automobile design. The decade of the 1980s marked a shift toward regulating consumer behavior, both through a wave of right-to-know policies as well as through requirements such as more stringent drunken driving rules and mandatory safety belt use requirements. In addition, there has been a change in the role of tort liability, as there had been an escalation in the role of tort liability through the 1970s, culminating with the explosion in liability insurance premiums in the mid-1980s.

Product-safety issues had previously been an afterthought. These matters were in the domain of corporate public-affairs offices, which dealt with product safety as part of their general public-relations efforts. By the 1990s product safety had become a central corporate concern. Safety and environmental regulations affecting the automobile industry were blamed by some critics as the source of that industry's collapse. Tort liability awards for workers in the asbestos industry led to the bankruptcy of a major American firm and the elimination of the asbestos industry. Other entire industries have also disappeared because of product safety concerns. The rising liability costs for private planes, which now average over $100,000 per plane, have led aircraft companies such as Beech, Cessna, and Piper all but to eliminate their production of private airplanes. The manufacturing of diving boards for motel swimming pools is also a vanishing industry. The focus of the remainder of this chapter is on developing the economic tools needed to approach such regulatory issues in a sensible manner.

Premanufacturing Screening: The Case of Pharmaceuticals

Regulations that hit products at a particularly early stage are those that pertain to the premanufacturing screening of products. Firms selling medical devices cannot market these products without prior government approval. Pharmaceuticals, insecticides, and chemical products are all subject to extensive testing and labeling requirements before they can be marketed. Food products are also subject to premarket testing, although these inspection procedures are generally viewed as more lax than the other premanufacturing screening regulations noted above. Notwithstanding food safety regulation, for example, imported produce drenched in pesticides and meat with major doses of hormones and antibiotics are staples in the typical American diet.

The most extensively analyzed premanufacturing screening effort is that of pharmaceutical regulation by the Food and Drug Administration. Before a firm is permitted to market a pharmaceutical product, it must establish the safety and efficacy of that good. Although the regulatory requirements have evolved throughout the century, a pivotal event was the 1962 Kefauver-Harris amendments to the Food, Drug, and Cosmetic Act. The major stimulus for this regulatory regime was the effect of the drug Thalidomide on pregnant women, many of whom had babies with serious deformities caused by the drug.

Although restrictions on drugs with severe side effects that create an overall net health risk to society are clearly desirable, establishing an appropriate balance in the premanufacturing screening decision is a complicated task.

The principal benefits of more stringent screening pertain to the decreased risk of approving a drug that might have adverse effects. This more stringent screening process also imposes costs. The first class of costs consists of the testing costs and the foregone opportunity to market a potentially profitable drug. There is an additional cost to society that may be deprived of potentially beneficial drugs with life-extending properties because they are tied up in the testing process. These costs have been of substantial concern to those with terminal diseases such as AIDS, for which a potentially effective drug that is possibly risky appears to be a good gamble. The regulator's task is to attempt to balance these competing concerns.

Weighing the Significance of Side Effects

Particularly in the case of pharmaceuticals, simplistic alternative policy objectives of eliminating all risks associated with pharmaceutical products are clearly inappropriate. Perhaps the main distinguishing feature of prescription drugs is that they pose potential hazards and, as a result, their use must be closely monitored by a physician. The Food and Drug Administration requires the information pertaining to the drug to be summarized in a label containing hazard warnings. These warnings are reprinted in an annual volume, the *Physicians' Desk Reference*, distributed to all doctors throughout the United States. Inspection of almost any entry in the *Physicians' Desk Reference* will indicate the

Table 22.1
The Competing Risks of FDA Decision Making on New Drug Applications

		STATE OF THE WORLD	
		New drug is safe and effective	New drug is not safe and effective
FDA POLICY DECISION	Accept	Correct policy decision	Type II error
	Reject	Type I error	Correct policy decision

Source: Henry G. Grabowski and John M. Vernon, *The Regulation of Pharmaceuticals: Balancing the Benefits and Risks* (Washington, D.C.: American Enterprise Institute, 1983). Reprinted with the permission of The American Enterprise Institute for Public Policy Research, Washington, D.C.

presence of potentially severe adverse effects or complications that may result from prescription drugs. These health impacts range from renal failure to anaphylactic shock. The presence of such potential hazards with prescription drugs does not imply that FDA regulation has been remiss, only that there are inherent risky attributes of the product and that ultimately society must strike a balance between the benefits these drugs provide and the potential hazards they pose.

Recognition of the need for balance does not completely resolve all of the policy issues at stake. The FDA must also decide on the stringency of the testing criteria.

Drug Approval Strategies

Table 22.1 summarizes the nature of the tradeoff.[4] Suppose that the FDA is analyzing a new drug that is both safe and effective, but the properties are not yet known to it. Ideally it would like to approve such beneficial drugs, but there is the potential that it may reject a beneficial drug because of misleading test results. In addition, firms seeking approval for beneficial drugs may be discouraged by the costs associated with the lengthy approval process and may abandon a drug. Situations in which the FDA review process leads to the rejection of potentially beneficial drugs are designated Type I errors.

If the FDA were to adopt a more lenient drug approval strategy, then it would incur the competing danger of approving dangerous drugs that should not be marketed. Errors of this type are designated Type II errors. Ideally, the FDA wants to approve all beneficial drugs and reject drugs that are not safe and effective. Achieving both of these objectives simultaneously is generally unfeasible, in large part because information about the drugs obtained through premarket testing is never fully informative. Moreover, because this information is costly to acquire, there are limits to the burdens the FDA can impose. As a result, there is always a need to strike a balance between the Type I and Type II errors.

Although a few critics have charged that the FDA has been too lax, the consensus in the economics literature is that the FDA has placed too great an emphasis on Type II errors. The FDA primarily seeks to avoid approving drugs with potentially adverse consequences, and it places insufficient weight on the Type I error of failing to approve beneficial new drugs. A political factor generating the motivation for this emphasis is the fact that the victims of Type II errors are more readily identifiable than the victims of Type I errors. In the case of Type II errors, specific people will suffer adverse consequences that can be linked to the drug. In contrast, Type I errors generally have a more diffuse probabilistic effect. One percent more of the 3000 patients suffering from a variant of heart disease may die if a new drug does not appear on the market, leading to a total of 30 expected deaths. However, the particular people who will die because the drug is not available may not be identifiable ex ante. Rather, there is simply a treatment-group population who will suffer a probabilistic loss in terms of their expected health if the drug is not available.

The identifiability of the parties suffering the adverse consequences becomes quite different when the lobbying group for the new drugs does not consist of a diffuse set of patients who are potentially at risk because of the absence of the drug's availability, but rather consists of a well-defined group with a clear-cut stake in the accelerated approval of such drugs. One such constituency that emerged in the late 1980s was that of AIDS patients who sought more rapid approval of AIDS-related drugs. The results of these efforts was an accelerated drug approval schedule for such drugs. We will consider the impact of this reform effort.

The FDA not only must set the criteria for whether it accepts or rejects a drug, but it also must determine the degree of premarket testing that it will require. Because full information is prohibitive and the cost of information acquisition may be substantial, the extent of premarket testing must necessarily be bounded. Figure 22.2 summarizes the shape of the health and nonhealth costs of premarket testing. As the downward sloping curve in the diagram indicates, the expected health costs from unsafe or ineffective drugs decline as the extent of premarket testing increases because the FDA is better able to avoid approving drugs that will turn out to have adverse consequences. However, minimization of health costs is not our sole objective, since testing also imposes costs. The cost of the research and development and the lost market oppor-

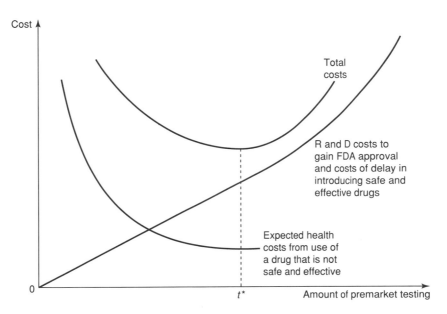

Figure 22.2
Cost Tradeoffs in Premarket Testing
Source: Henry G. Grabowski and John M. Vernon, *The Regulation of Pharmaceuticals: Balancing the Benefits and Risks* (Washington, D.C.: American Enterprise Institute, 1983). Reprinted with the permission of The American Enterprise Institute for Public Policy Research, Washington, D.C.

tunities stemming from delay in the drug's approval is indicated by the upward sloping curve in the diagram. The sum of the cost to the firms and the health costs lead to the total cost function at the top of the diagram. For total cost levels associated with the amount of premarket testing indicated by t^*, costs are minimized, establishing this amount of testing as the optimal amount.

Accelerated Drug Approval Process

Although economists have long urged that drug approval time be accelerated, the FDA has done little to change its overall policy. However, in 1987 the FDA instituted an accelerated drug-approval process for drugs that address life-threatening diseases such as AIDS. Table 22.2 summarizes the patterns of drug approvals and the time for approval for different classes of drugs. Consider first the rate of approval of drugs that represent legitimate innovations, in particular new chemical entities (NCE). The number of such approvals ranges from eleven to twenty-six per year for the 1980–1989 period. The average approval time for such drugs is on the order of approximately three years.

Table 22.2
New Drug Approvals and Time to Approval

Year	Number of NCE[a] Approvals		Avg. Lag Time (Months) from Submission to Approval	
	All Drugs	1AA/1A Drugs	All Drugs	1AA/1A Drugs
1980	11	2	35.18	26.38
1981	23	2	31.03	14.25
1982	22	4	26.02	9.81
1983	12	4	28.67	21.44
1984	21	2	43.44	27.75
1985	26	3	32.08	32.67
1986	18	1	34.19	17.50
1987	18	2	32.76	12.00
1988	16	4	36.39	41.00
1989	21	5	35.61	22.05

[a] NCE = new chemical entities.

Source: All figures based on calculations by the authors using chronology of new chemical entities developed by the University of Rochester Center for Study of Drug Development, July 10, 1990 (computer printout).

Now let us consider a subgroup of these drugs designated as 1AA/1A. These drugs consist of those that are targeted for fighting diseases such as AIDS as well as drugs that the FDA believes will have a substantial impact. Following the institution of the accelerated drug approval policy in 1987, there was an apparent increase in the rate of such drug approvals. The lag time for approval in 1988 was quite high even for these drugs, but this substantial lag time may reflect the fact that many of these drugs had been in the FDA drug-approval pipeline for years prior to the new policy. Beginning in 1989, there was a substantial speedup in the approval time for the 1AA and 1A drugs. One of the main factors leading to this apparent shift in FDA policy is the fact that accelerating the approval time of drugs that address life-threatening diseases not only has a well-defined constituency, but also there is less potential adverse health risk because of the high risk of mortality. Although there is a widespread consensus that this shift in policy was attractive, most FDA decisions are not as clear-cut. Even if officials are willing to commit to a particular tradeoff, there is a major difficulty in ascertaining what these tradeoffs are. In terms of Figure 22.2, the cost to the firms can be estimated reasonably reliably, but there is often substantial uncertainty regarding the expected health costs to the population. In situations in which we do not know the health-curve costs, FDA officials may be held responsible for their judgments regarding the entire shape of this curve if they adopt an aggressive drug approval policy. The incentives for bureaucratic risk aversion are clear.

The Behavioral Response to Product Safety Regulation

The usual approach to product safety regulation has been to alter the technology of the product in a safety-enhancing manner. If the behavior of the users of the product remains unchanged after the mandated safety device is instituted, then we will reap the benefits of the engineering controls. In the case of automobile safety, for example, engineering experts generated a variety of predictions of substantial gains in safety that would result from the wave of initial safety regulations. These experts predicted a 0.5 percent reduction in occupant death rates from dual braking systems, a 0–2.5 percent reduction in occupant death rates from improved windshields, a 4–6.5 percent reduction in occupant death rates from an energy-absorbing steering column, a 7–16 percent reduction in occupant death rates from lap seatbelts, and a 0.25–1 percent reduction in occupant death rates from shoulder belts. The benefits derived from these improvements all hinge on a key assumption, which is that the behavior of the driver will remain unchanged.

In an influential economic analysis, Sam Peltzman hypothesized that driver behavior would not remain unaffected.[5] In the case of safety belts, for example, the safety improvement from the new technology would reduce the potential hazards to the driver of driving fast. As a result, the relative benefits of taking the safety precaution of driving slowly would decline once an individual had buckled up. Faster speeds would become more desirable.

Figure 22.3 illustrates Peltzman's reasoning diagrammatically. Suppose that initially the driver is at point A, where the line $0A$ gives the relationship between driving intensity and the driver's risk of death before regulation. With the use of safety belts, the risk curve drops to $0BC$. After the introduction of the safety devices, if the driver leaves his degree of precautions unchanged he will be at a death risk at point B. However, because the marginal benefits to the driver of taking the precaution have been reduced, he will increase his driving intensity to a point such as C, thus muting some of the effect of the safety belts.

The factors driving the movement from point B to point C are based on elementary economic principles. Figure 22.4 indicates the marginal benefits and marginal costs to the driver of driving slowly. For simplicity, suppose that the marginal cost of driving slowly has a constant value per unit time, leading to the flat marginal-cost curve. Originally

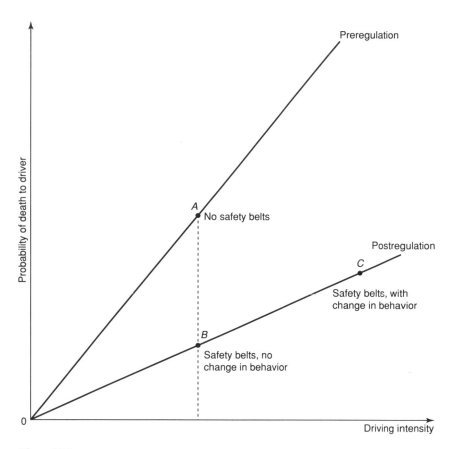

Figure 22.3
Relationship of Driving Intensity to the Regulatory Regime

the driver faced a marginal benefit curve of MB_0 for driving slowly. However, after the introduction of the safety device—in this case auto safety belts—the marginal benefit of driving slowly has been reduced, assuming that the belt is worn. As a result, the optimal slowness of the driving speed has been reduced, which is to say that the driver now finds it desirable to drive faster once he is using devices that will decrease his risk of injury or property damage from an accident.

Consumer's Potential for Muting Safety Device Benefits

The overall economic story is consequently that once individuals buckle up, they will have an incentive to drive faster, thus muting and possibly offsetting the beneficial effects of the safety device. This line of argument has long aroused considerable controversy because of the surprising nature of the results as well as the extent of the empirical effect that has been claimed for it.

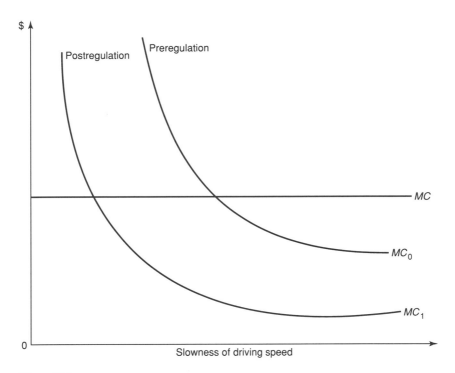

Figure 22.4
Choice of Driving Speed

The underlying theory is quite sound and is based on the same kinds of marginal benefit and marginal cost reasoning that is fundamental to all of economics. If one recast the safety belt issue in a somewhat different context, then most individuals would accept the economic mechanisms at work. Suppose that instead of making the car safer by introducing safety belts, we will make driving riskier by making the streets icy. Few would question that it is optimal for people to drive with greater care and slower speeds when the roads are icy and slick than when they are dry. Once the ice melts and the streets return to their dry conditions, one would expect people to drive faster. In essence, what safety belts do is take us from a risky regime such as that of icy streets to a safer regime such as dry streets, and the benefits from exercising driver care will decline.

How much of a decline will occur has long been a matter of dispute. In Peltzman's original paper he did not claim on theoretical grounds that the effect of safety belts would necessarily be counterproductive, although it could be. However, in his empirical analysis of both time-series and cross-sectional data pertaining to motor vehicle death rates he was unable to find any statistically significant effect of the introduction of safety belts. He concluded that the behavioral-response effect offset the technological gains.

This issue has become an ongoing controversy in the automobile-safety literature. Given data through the 1980s, the general consensus appears to be the following.[6] First, automobile-safety regulations have reduced the risks to drivers and motor vehicle occupants. However, there is also evidence that drivers wearing safety belts do drive faster, inasmuch as there has been an increase in the fatalities of motorcyclists and pedestrians with increased safety belt utilization. Thus the overall mechanism described here has strong support.

There is less general agreement on the extent of the offset from the deaths of motorcyclists and pedestrians. Although there remains some adherence to the view that these effects completely offset the beneficial impacts of automobile safety regulation, the mainstream view is that on balance safety regulation has a risk-reducing effect, although there is a muting of the impact of safety regulations by the decrease in the care exercised by drivers.

This role of individual responses to regulations is not restricted to safety belt issues. In particular, other product safety regulations that rely on changes in the technology similarly will interact with individual usage of the product to govern the ultimate product safety that will be experienced by the consumer.

The "Lulling Effect"

A case that is particularly intriguing is that of safety caps. The government has imposed child-resistant safety cap requirements for two decades for products such as aspirin, prescription drugs, and selected other hazardous products, such as antifreeze. Safety caps not only reduce the benefits to parents of putting medicines in a location for which access by children is difficult, but also may give parents a false sense of security. In a phenomenon that Viscusi terms the "lulling effect," there may be a misperception on the part of consumers of the efficacy of the safety device, leading to an additional decline in safety precautions.[7] Consumer product safety commissioners and the public at large routinely refer to these caps as being childproof, whereas in fact they are not.

Figure 22.5 indicates the impact of these various influences. Suppose that before the advent of safety caps the expected loss suffered by the consumer from any given level of safety effort is given by the curve EL_0. Suppose that the consumer originally was at point A, which reflects the optimal amount of expected loss that the consumer is willing to incur, given the costs associated with undertaking safety efforts. After the ad-

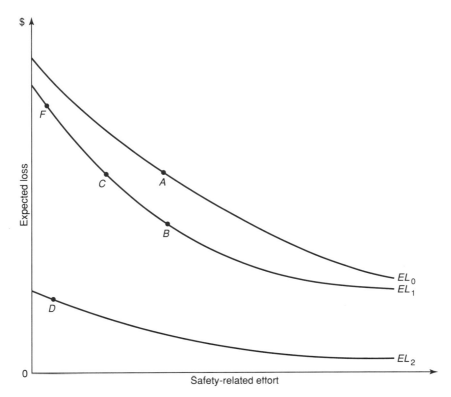

Figure 22.5
Safety Mechanisms and the Choice of Precautions
Source: W. Kip Viscusi, "The Lulling Effect: The Impact of Child-Resistant Packaging on Aspirin and Analgesic Ingestions," in *AEA Papers and Proceedings* 74, No. 2, p. 325.

vent of the safety caps, the expected loss associated with any degree of safety precautions declines to EL_1. If the consumer does not change his precautions, the postregulation safety effort will be at point B. For the usual economic preferences, one will necessarily decrease the level of safety-related effort so that the individual will be to the left of point B. If this decrease in safety precautions is sufficient, there will be no effect of the safety device on the safety outcome, and we will be at point C. For the safety device to be counterproductive, leading to an outcome such as point F, one must impose very severe restrictions on the shape of individual preferences. Such a counterproductive effect of regulations is conceivable, but it requires that very special and unusual assumptions be met.

Effect of Consumer's Perception of Safety Device Efficacy

However, matters are quite different if consumers do not accurately perceive the efficacy of the safety device. If they believe the safety mechanism reduces the perceived risk from the curve EL_1 to EL_2, then we may end up at a counterproductive outcome such as point D much more easily. Consumers believe they are at point D, whereas they are actually at point F. The danger of safety mechanisms is not simply that of a falloff in the optimal level of consumer behavior but also an inducement of misperceptions regarding the risk, leading to a further dropoff in safety precautions.

In the safety-cap case, there is detailed evidence regarding the character of consumer precautions before and after the caps went into effect.[8] Poisonings from safety-cap bottles are the main source of poisonings from aspirin and analgesic products. In most of these instances, the bottles have been left open by consumers. The rash of open bottle poisonings is not surprising, inasmuch as there have been widespread complaints regarding the difficulty of grappling with the caps. In an effort to deal with these caps, many consumers have responded by simply leaving the caps off altogether.

The poisoning context also provides some intriguing evidence regarding possible spillover effects for other products. If consumers undertake a common safety precaution for their medicines, then the introduction of safety caps may lead to a decrease in safety precautions overall. In the case of products with safety caps, the net effect of the decrease in precautions may be simply to have no observable effect on safety, which has in fact been the case for aspirin. For products not covered by safety caps, the decrease in the overall level of precaution taking will increase the risk from these products. Such an increase in risk has in fact been observed, as there has been an observed adverse spillover effect on other products. After the introduction of safety caps for aspirin, the poisoning rates for analgesic products such as Tylenol escalated from 1.1 per 1000 in 1971 to 1.5 per 1000 in 1980. Taking into account the rise in the sales of Tylenol and related products accounts for only half of this increase. The overall implication of this analysis is that there have been 3500 additional poisonings annually of children under five that resulted from the decreased safety precautions after the advent of safety caps.

The presence of such behavioral responses does not imply that all government regulations are bad or that these particular regulations are necessarily ill-conceived. What the responses do suggest, however, is that one cannot view safety as simply being a matter of engineering controls. Individual behavior plays a key element. These responses are not restricted to safety caps and seatbelts. Empirical evidence suggests that the newly introduced safety mechanism for butane cigarette lighters also reduces parental care. Regulations that attempt to influence safety behavior through hazard warning programs, safety training efforts, and other efforts should be regarded as a central component of any product safety regulatory strategy.

The Costs of Product Safety Regulation: The Automobile Industry Case

A principal target of product safety regulation has been automobiles. There have been dozens of regulations affecting the safety of autos as well as their environmental impact from emissions. Much of the impact of these regulations occurred in the 1970s—the decade in which the major wave of auto regulations emerged.

Let us begin with the various regulations affecting auto safety. These include occupant protection requirements, steering column protection, seatbelt assemblies, side door strength, bumper requirements, fuel system integrity standards, and a variety of other specific safety standards. Table 22.3 summarizes the costs over time of these various safety regulations. Costs are presented for two sets of assumptions: (1) assuming that there is no industry learning over time that would decrease these costs below their original estimates, and (2) assuming a learning curve that provides for a 5 percent annual reduction in the costs of compliance. The final column of Table 22.3 summarizes the level of the fuel penalty that will be assessed for the added weight that will be imposed on the car because of these safety devices. The standard that requires a bumper to withstand low-speed crashes is a chief contributor to this greater weight. The total costs are on the order of over $1000/car if we abstract from the reduction in the cost due to the learning curve.

These costs are in addition to the costs imposed by emissions standards. Table 22.4 summarizes these costs associated with compliance with environmental regulations pertaining to automobiles. As in the case of safety standards, the overall price tag by the 1980s had reached over $1000/car.

What we see then is a situation in which both safety and environmental regulations were imposing substantial and increased costs on the automobile industry in the 1970s. This decade was also a period of dramatic change because of the inroads being made by foreign imports of small cars as a result of the dramatically higher gasoline prices in the late 1970s. U.S. sales of Toyota, Honda, and Nissan (then known as Datsun) soared in the 1970s. Some critics charged that government regulation was undermining the previously superior position of the U.S. automobile industry by imposing a required shift in the technology for automobiles, thus making much of the U.S. production system and U.S. design of automobiles obsolete. With the sunk costs in the earlier

Table 22.3
The Total Costs of Safety Regulation, Model Years 1966–1984 Current Dollars per Automobile

Year	Equipment Costs		Fuel Penalty
	Without Learning Curve	With 5 Percent Annual Learning Curve	
1966	40	40	0
1967	75	73	0
1968	124	119	9
1969	156	144	14
1970	174	154	15
1971	184	155	16
1972	209	172	16
1973	293	245	73
1974	447	381	125
1975	452	361	116
1976	491	377	98
1977	530	390	94
1978	571	400	92
1979	641	431	116
1980	741	481	152
1981	822	512	159
1982	872	517	146
1983	900	508	123
1984	924	491	118

Source: Robert W. Crandall, Howard K. Gruenspecht, Theodore E. Keeler, and Lester B. Lave, *Regulating the Automobile* (Washington, D.C.: Brookings Institution, 1986), p. 37, Table 3-4. Reprinted by permission of The Brookings Institution.

Table 22.4
Estimated Cost per Car of Meeting the Automotive Emissions Standards, Pre-1968–1981

Model Year	Current Costs (1981 dollars)
Pre-1968	—
1968–1969	30
1970–1971	50
1972	370
1973–1974	950
1975–1976	640
1977–1979	700
1980	1,000
1981	1,400

Source: Lawrence J. White, *The Regulation of Air Pollution Emissions from Motor Vehicles* (Washington, D.C.: American Enterprise Institute, 1982), p. 61. Reprinted with the permission of The American Enterprise Institute for Public Policy Research, Washington, D.C.

designs no longer being useful, U.S. producers sacrificed much of their previous advantage over foreign competitors, thus making it easier for foreign firms to compete in American markets.

Even for political observers who did not blame government regulation as playing a central role in the demise of the automobile industry, the relationship between the health of the industry and government regulation was an important concern. The Carter administration, for example, undertook a substantial financial bailout of the Chrysler corporation in an effort to avoid its bankruptcy. In addition, it initiated some modest efforts designed to target regulatory relief at that industry.

On taking office, the Reagan administration instituted a sweeping program of regulatory relief for the automobile industry. Table 22.5 summarizes the components of this effort. The diversity of the regulations included in the auto reform package is quite impressive. Government regulations pertain to almost every aspect of the design of automobiles, ranging from speedometer standards to emissions requirements. Moreover, the price tags associated with many of these regulations are on the order of hundreds of millions of dollars. What is perhaps most impressive is the broad range of the twenty-nine regulations listed in Table 22.5 and the fact that a single industry could account for so much regulatory activity.

The automobile industry will remain a principal target of product safety regulation. The purpose of these efforts is not to drive a leading American industry out of business but rather to address the main source of product safety problems. Motor vehicles account for over half of all accidental deaths in the United States, and it is inevitable that continued regulation of automobiles and other motorized vehicles will remain a prominent policy concern.

Trends in Motor Vehicle and Home Accident Deaths

The purpose of regulation of home and automobile safety is to produce improvements in the accident rate. Focusing on these two classes of injuries can yield substantial dividends. In 1987, motor vehicles accounted for 52 percent of all accidental deaths, and home accidents other than motor vehicle accounted for an additional 22 percent. The contribution of these accident groups to disabling injuries is also quite substantial, although the emphasis is reversed. Motor vehicles account for 20 percent of all disabling injuries, whereas home accidents that do not involve motor vehicles account for 35 percent of all disabling injuries. The

Table 22.5
The Reagan Administration's Auto Reform Package

| Issue | Action (date of completion) | 5-Year Savings (millions) | |
		Industry	Public
	Rules Acted on		
Gas-tank vapors	Declined to order new controls on cars (April 1981).	$103	$1,300
Emissions tests	Streamlined certification of industry tests on vehicles (Oct. 1981, Nov. 1982).	5	—
	Raised allowable "failure rate" for test of light trucks and heavy-duty engines from 10 to 40 percent (Jan. 1983).	19	129
	Reduced spot checks of emissions of vehicles on assembly lines by 42 percent; delayed assembly-line tests of heavy-duty trucks until 1986 (Jan. 1983).	1	1
High-altitude autos	Ended assembly-line tests at high altitude, relying instead on industry data (April 1981).	0.2	—
	Allowed industry to self-certify vehicles as meeting high-altitude emission standards (April 1981).	1	1
Pollution waivers	Consolidated industry applications for temporary exemptions from tougher emissions standards for nitrogen oxide and carbon monoxide (Sept. 1981).	—	—
Paint shops	Delayed until 1983 tougher hydrocarbon pollution standards for auto paint shops (Oct. 1981).	300	—
Test vehicles	Cut paperwork required to exempt prototype vehicles from environmental standards (July 1982).	—	—
Driver vision	Scrapped existing 1981 rule and second proposed rule setting standards for driver's field of view (June 1982).	160	—
Fuel economy	Decided not to set stiffer fuel economy standards to replace those expiring in 1985 (April 1981).	—	—
Speedometers	Revoked rule setting standards for speedometers and tamper-resistant odometers (Feb. 1982).	—	20
Tire rims	Scrapped proposal to set safety standards for explosive multipiece tire rims (Feb. 1982).	300	75
Brake tests	Eased from 30 to 20 percent the steepness of grades on which post-1984 truck and bus brakes must hold (Dec. 1981).	—	1.8
Tire pressure	Scrapped proposal to equip vehicles with low-tire pressure indicators (Aug. 1981).	—	130
Battery safety	Scrapped proposal to set standards to prevent auto battery explosions (Aug. 1981).	—	—
Tire safety	Revoked requirement that consumers be told of reserve load capacity of tires; eased tire makers' reporting requirements (June 1982).	—	—
Antitheft protection	Eased antitheft and locking steering wheel standards for open-body vehicles (June 1981).	—	—
Fuel economy	Streamlined semiannual reports of auto makers on their progress in meeting fuel economy goals (Aug. 1982).	—	0.1
Tire ratings	Suspended rule requiring industry to rate tires according to tread wear, traction, and heat resistance (Feb. 1983).	—	10

Table 22.5 (cont.)

Issue	Action (date of completion)	5-Year Savings (millions)	
		Industry	Public
Vehicle IDs	Downgraded from standard to administrative rule the requirement that all vehicles have ID numbers as an aid to police (May 1983).	—	—
Seatbelt comfort	Scrapped proposal to set standards for seatbelt comfort and convenience (June 1983).	—	—
	Rules with Uncertain Futures		
High-altitude emissions	Failed to revise Clean Air Act order ending weaker high-altitude emissions standards in 1984; eased through regulatory changes.	38	1,300
Emissions reductions	Failed to revise Clean Air Act order to cut large trucks' hydrocarbon and carbon monoxide emissions by 90 percent by 1984; standard was delayed until 1985.	105	536
	Failed to ease Clean Air Act order reducing nitrogen oxide emissions from light trucks and heavy-duty engines by 75 percent by 1984. Regulatory changes under study.	150	563
Particulate pollution	Delayed a proposal to scrap specific particulate standards for some diesels in favor of an average standard for all diesels. Stiffer standards delayed from 1985 to 1987.	40	523
Methane standards	Shelved because of "serious" costs; questions a plan to drop methane as a regulated hydrocarbon.	—	—
Passive restraints	Delayed and then revoked requirement that post-1982 autos be equipped with passive restraints; revocation overturned by Supreme Court in June 1983.	428	981
Bumper damage	Cut from 5 to 2.5 mph the speed at which bumpers must resist damage; change is on appeal.	—	308

Source: Michael Wines, "Reagan Plan to Relieve Auto Industry of Regulatory Burden Gets Mixed Grades," *National Journal*, July 23, 1983, pp. 1534–35. Reprinted by permission of the *National Journal*.

remainder of the accidents that are not due to either motor vehicle or home accidents stem from accidents that occur at work or in public places, such as falls in public places, deaths from firearms, and crashes involving planes and trains.

The administrators of the regulatory agencies responsible for auto safety and home accidents generally refer to the improvements in the trends for these accidents as evidence of the efficacy of the agency. Annual press releases announcing decreases in accident trends portray these declines as evidence of the agency's success. As will be noted in Chapter 23, this approach has also been used by OSHA administrators in defending the accomplishments of their agency.

Accident Rate Influences

Such a test does little to show that regulation has had a demonstrable effect on safety. Most important is that because of the greater affluence of society, consumers have demanded greater safety from their products throughout this century. This wealth effect alone should lead to safety improvements.

These safety improvements are in evidence throughout the century provided that one defines the risk measure properly. This definitional issue arises most particularly with respect to motor vehicles. Two types of variations are most important. The first pertains to the intensity of usage of motor vehicles. People drive cars more often today than they did fifty years ago, so that we cannot simply compare death rates across the population, but must take into account the intensity of the product's use. One mechanism for doing so is to look at the automobile accident rate on a mileage basis rather than a population basis. Doing so yields a quite different picture of the trend in automobile safety. Automobile death rates have declined from 21.65 per 100 million vehicle miles in 1923 to 2.55 per 100 million motor vehicle miles in 1987, whereas the accident rate on a population basis has been quite stable, rising from 16.5 deaths per 100,000 population in 1923 to 20.0 deaths per 100,000 population in 1987.

Temporary shifts in the age structure of the population also may influence the accident rate. The rise in the proportion of teenage drivers in particular eras, for example, has also contributed to temporary swings in the motor vehicle accident rate. Changes in the character of highways and the driving speed on these highways also affect motor vehicle accident rates even though the safety of the car itself may not have changed.

In general, one should take all of these various factors into account when analyzing safety trends. The econometric analyses that have done so yield conclusions that are not starkly different from what one would have obtained by analyzing the statistics in Table 22.6.

The Decline of Accident Rates

Since the 1930s, motor vehicle-accident death rates per 100 million miles driven have remained in roughly the 3–4 percent range except during the 1960s, when the rate of decline was somewhat less. It is noteworthy that for the past sixty years motor vehicle accident rates on a mileage basis have been on the decline. The decline preceded the advent of government regulation two decades ago. In addition, one should be very careful in interpreting the rather modest dropoff in motor vehicle accident rates in the 1960s. That decade also marked a surge in the total

Table 22.6
Principal Death Risk Trends: Annual Rate of Increase in Death Rates

	Work (Per 100,000 Population)	Home (Per 100,000 Population)	Motor Vehicle (Per 100,000,000 Vehicle-Miles)
1930–1940	−1.8	−0.2	−3.3
1940–1950	−2.3	−2.2	−4.0
1950–1960	−2.8	−2.1	−3.5
1960–1970	−1.2	−1.7	−0.8
1970–1980	−1.6	−2.7	−3.3
1980–1990	−3.7	−1.5	−2.2

Source: Calculations by the authors using death rate data from the National Safety Council, *Accident Facts* (Chicago: National Safety Council, 1994), p. 27. Reprinted by permission of the National Safety Council.

motor-vehicle death risk arising from the changing age structure in the population and the growth of the interstate highway system.

The decline in home accident rates has been steady since the 1940s, with annual rates of decrease in home accident death rates on the order of 2 to 3 percent. Once again, the advent of a decline in the accident rate preceded the establishment of the Consumer Product Safety Commission. Statistical studies of the Consumer Product Safety Commission have failed to indicate any statistically significant impact of these efforts on product safety.[9] These studies do not imply that no regulations of that agency have ever been effective, only that their impact has been sufficiently small that their influence is not evident in examination of national accident statistics.

The econometric studies of motor vehicle accidents have yielded somewhat more optimistic results. Almost all of these studies have indicated that there has been an acceleration in the rate of decline in motor vehicle-accident death rates in the 1970s and 1980s, and controlling for other factors indicates that much of this decline is due to the impact of safety regulations. Much more controversial has been the assessment of the overall impact of motor vehicle safety regulation taking into account the spillover effects on the deaths of pedestrians and motorcyclists, which offset at least partially the favorable effect of safety regulations on motor vehicle accident rates.

From an economic standpoint, there is no reason why government regulations should not be effective, provided that the offset from the decrease in consumer precautions is not too great. The efficacy of these regulations in terms of promoting safety is not so limited that there should not be some beneficial effect observed. The main surprise from the earliest studies of these regulations, indicating the absence of a demonstrable effect, stems primarily from the imbalance between the initial projected impacts of these agencies and their observed impacts. This disparity suggests that other economic behavior such as users' precautions should also be taken into account.

The more important question from the standpoint of long-run regulatory policy is ascertaining whether on balance these regulations are in society's best interests. By the early 1980s, the price tag for safety in emissions regulations had reached over $2000 per car, but there were observable benefits as well. Econometric estimates indicated that the automobile death risk would be as much as 40 percent greater in the absence of such safety regulations. By some calculations, these regulations also produced benefits in excess of their costs, in large part because the safety regulations did not impose stringent deadlines for the adoption of specific technologies, but rather proceeded on an incremental basis in which there was a gradual development of the cluster of safety standards that reflected an evolving knowledge of the changing safety technologies.[10]

The Rise of Product Liability

Direct government regulation of product safety is not the only influence on firms' safety decisions. Increasingly product liability awards by the courts have played an important role in establishing safety incentives.[11] The rise in product liability costs is reflected in the trends in Table 22.7. In the 1960s the total insurance premiums that were paid for general liability insurance such as product liability coverage were only $746 million. In the last thirty years, however, there has been a dramatic expansion in the role of product liability. These changes have included shifts in the criteria used to assign liability to corporations. The earlier

Table 22.7
Trends in General Liability Insurance Premiums

Year	Premiums ($ millions)
1960	746
1970	1,658
1980	6,612
1985	11,544
1988	19,077
1990	18,123
1992	17,006

Source: A.M. Best and Co., *Best Aggregate and Averages*, various years and Insurance Information Institute, *The Fact Book 1994: Property/Casualty Insurance Facts* (1994).

negligence doctrine has been replaced by a strict liability doctrine that requires companies to bear the costs of product injuries in a greater share of situations. In addition, there has been a tremendous expansion in hazard-warnings cases and in the concept of what constitutes a product-design defect.

The net effect of these changes has been to increase product liability premiums to $1.7 billion in 1970, rising even further to $6.6 billion in 1980. The greatest expansion occurred in the mid-1980s, as liability premiums jumped to $11.5 billion in 1985, reaching $19.1 billion in 1988. Since that time, costs have been fairly stable. Even these impressive costs do not capture the full liability cost to firms. Corporations also must pay for the cost of extensive legal staffs. Moreover, there may be costs of liability judgments that are not covered by insurance, such as punitive damage awards and awards in excess of the policy limits. Many industries such as the pharmaceutical industry are unable to receive any liability insurance coverage at reasonable rates from conventional insurers and as a result have established separate insurance mechanisms outside of the standard industry channels. These insurance costs are in addition to the amounts in Table 22.7.

The impact of this product liability revolution on businesses has been substantial. Pharmaceutical companies have responded by withdrawing vaccines that have been hard hit by liability costs. A National Academy of Sciences panel blamed the lagging research and development of contraceptive devices by United States firms on the rise in liability costs.[12] The domestic aircraft industry manufacturing planes for private use has all but disappeared. Between 15 and 25 percent of the purchase price of ladders goes to pay for liability costs, and 17 cents of every fare dollar on the Philadelphia mass transit system goes to pay for liability insurance expenses.

One of the seminal legal events that led to this product liability revolution was the emergence of the strict liability doctrine that replaced the earlier negligence criteria. Under a negligence test, a firm is required to provide the efficient level of product safety. Consider the statistics in Table 22.8, which gives the benefits and costs of different levels of product safety. The objective is to set the level of product safety so as to minimize total social costs. This optimal point is achieved at the medium degree of safety, which offers a net social payoff of $50,000. Higher and lower levels of safety each provide fewer social rewards.

The Negligence Standard

Under a negligence regime, a firm is liable if it does not meet the medium degree-of-safety standard. Thus, all firms providing a low level of

Table 22.8
Summary of Social Costs for Product Safety

Degree of Safety	Consumer Accident Costs ($)	Safety Costs to Company ($)	Total Social Costs ($)
High	0	140,000	140,000
Medium	50,000	50,000	100,000
Low	150,000	25,000	175,000

safety become liable for the $50,000 in accident costs that could have been prevented if they had provided the efficient degree of safety at the medium level of safety. Firms facing this penalty consequently must choose between providing a low level of safety, which will cost them $25,000 from a manufacturing standpoint and $150,000 from a legal-liability standpoint, or choosing a higher level of safety such as the medium level of safety that will impose $50,000 of manufacturing costs but no liability costs. A negligence standard such as this will create incentives for firms to choose the medium level of safety, which in this case is the socially efficient level. Once they have done so, firms are free of any possible liability burden because they have met the efficient standard of care.

The Strict Liability Standard

In contrast, under a strict liability standard, a firm is liable for all of the accident costs incurred by the consumer irrespective of whether the firm has met the appropriate level of safety. (Actually, this is a variant of strict liability known as absolute liability, but consideration of this extreme case facilitates the exposition.) In the case of the high degree of safety, the cost to the company is the same as the social cost, which is $140,000. At the medium level of product safety, the social cost that must be borne by the company under strict liability is $100,000, and at the low level of product safety, the social cost that must now be internalized by the company is $175,000. The company will choose the level of product safety that minimizes these social costs—the medium level of product safety.

Strict liability achieves this outcome almost by definition. Since strict liability requires that the company bear all of the product-related costs associated with accidents, in effect what this doctrine does is force the company to internalize all accident costs. The social objective function and the company's profit function consequently become one and the same.

Tracing Accident Costs and Causes

A danger enters with respect to our inability to distinguish which are the accident costs traceable to the product. In addition, problems of moral hazard also arise. The result may be that entire product markets may disappear. If all ski manufacturers were required to pay for the hospital bills of those injured while using skis, the price of skis would become exorbitant. Similarly, the prices of automobiles would escalate if companies had to pay for all of the accident costs resulting from automobiles, irrespective of the parties at fault and the behavior of the drivers.

If we abstract from such complications, from the standpoint of achieving an economically efficient outcome, both the negligence rule and the strict liability rule are equivalent. Each leads to the medium level of safety. The difference is that under strict liability companies pay a share of the accident costs in a much broader set of instances. As a consequence, the legal system's movement toward a strict liability doctrine shifted the balance of power in the courts toward the consumers, who are consequently able to collect from companies in a larger share of cases than they were before.

Events Study Evidence on Liability Costs

The costs of product liability cases are not limited simply to the liability award. An adverse liability judgment may affect expectations regarding future awards of this type, particularly with respect to a design defect that influences an entire product line. There also may be broader reputational effects for the firm.

In an effort to identify influences such as these, economists have relied increasingly on event studies in which trends in stock market prices are analyzed to assess the change in the value of the firm attributable to particular events. Studies of this type have been undertaken to assess the costs associated with product recalls, the issuance of government regulatory standards, and airplane crashes. The example here will focus on the effect of liability costs on stock market prices.

Table 22.9 summarizes the estimates of the changes in the value of the affected firms resulting from various stages in the Agent Orange litigation. The Agent Orange litigation was one of the largest mass toxic tort cases in the country, as thousands of Vietnam veterans sued both the Federal government and major chemical companies like Dow Chemical for illnesses such as cancer allegedly contracted through exposure to large doses of the potent chemical herbicide Agent Orange. Table 22.9 summarizes various court decisions and publicity events (i.e., *Wall Street Journal* articles) in the Agent Orange litigation. From a

Table 22.9
The Effect of Agent Orange Suits on the Value of Individual Firms

Firms	Change in Value ($ millions)	
	Same Day	Ten-Day Period
A. Yannacone files class action suit, January 8, 1979		
Diamond Shamrock	35.03	−32.04
Dow Chemical	−60.74	−50.69
Hercules Inc.	−6.24	−30.82
Monsanto Co.	−20.68	9.76
North American Phillips Corp.	−1.09	1.57
Uniroyal Inc.	−1.93	3.80
Total change	−55.65	−98.42
B. Judge Pratt rules federal common law applies, November 20, 1979		
Diamond Shamrock	9.51	40.02
Dow Chemical	43.78	−178.83
Hercules Inc.	−2.12	17.45
Monsanto Co.	−14.52	−118.63
North American Phillips Corp.	−9.09	−18.71
Uniroyal Inc.	0.86	−8.74
Total change	28.42	−267.44
C. Agent Orange suit for $310 million reported in Wall Street Journal, May 30, 1980		
Diamond Shamrock	−32.49	−80.33
Dow Chemical	38.44	−220.68
Hercules Inc.	−0.94	27.28
Monsanto Co.	−9.33	193.41
North American Phillips Corp.	−5.12	30.57
Uniroyal Inc.	0.07	12.12
Total change	−9.78	−37.63
D. Agent Orange suit reported in Wall Street Journal, July 10, 1980		
Diamond Shamrock	−18.11	−136.42
Dow Chemical	−80.98	−97.23
Hercules Inc.	−13.47	−64.49
Monsanto Co.	33.49	−5.39
North American Phillips Corp.	−5.62	−15.81
Uniroyal Inc.	0.56	21.07
Total change	−151.11	−298.27
E. Judge Weinstein announces decision, May 7, 1985		
Diamond Shamrock	−11.63	20.86
Dow Chemical	83.35	300.69
Hercules Inc.	23.75	128.76
Monsanto Co.	66.27	204.26
North American Phillips Corp.	−16.567	28.61
Uniroyal Inc.	N.A.	N.A.
Total change	145.17	683.18

Source: W. Kip Viscusi and Joni Hersch, "The Market Response to Product Safety Litigation," *Journal of Regulatory Economics* 2, No. 3 (1990): 213–30.

theoretical standpoint, shareholders should react to information that affects the value of the firm in an efficient manner so that bad news will decrease the value of the firm and good news will increase its value. All of the early court decisions listed in Table 22.9 were adverse in that they indicated that the litigation would proceed and that there would be damages. However, the estimates of damages that were expected in this case were considerable. As a result, the final compromise settlement that was reached at urging of a judge who did not believe that there was a provable causal link between Agent Orange and the illnesses was in effect viewed as good news by the market, leading to a substantial increase in the value of the affected firms. Both adverse and favorable information were consequently reflected in stock market behavior in this particular instance.

Undertaking stock market analyses such as this is fairly straightforward, particularly in an era in which stock market price information by firm is readily available on computer. A major conceptual issue in this research is to define the event period, or what is often referred to as event window. If the market is likely to have foreknowledge of a particular event or to have anticipated an event, such as a presidential election result, then this knowledge will have a stock market impact before the event has actually taken place. Similarly, if it takes the market a period of time to assess the implications of an event, than one would want to include an extended period of time after the event has occurred to track the extent of the influence. The results in the Agent Orange case were estimated for both one day and five day event windows both before and after the event, yielding fairly similar results in each case. The appropriate approach in other contexts may of course vary depending on the different character of the way in which the information may be transmitted to shareholders.

Escalation of Damages

There has also been a rapid escalation in the role of damages. The penalties levied by regulatory agencies are often quite modest—on the order of $1000 or less and only a few million dollars even in the most severe cases. In contrast, million-dollar awards in product-liability cases are routine. Newspapers throughout the country gave prominent coverage to the woman who spilled a cup of hot McDonald's coffee on her lap and suffered burns for which she received a several million dollar award (later reduced by a higher court).

In addition to the phenomenon of runaway juries, there also may be a reasonable basis for some large liability awards. For a consumer who loses twenty-five years of his or her work life at a rate of pay of $40,000 per year, the lifetime earnings loss is $1 million. Because the size of the award roughly doubles when one also takes into account the pain and suffering associated with the accident as well as the loss to the family associated with such injuries, one can see how severe injury awards on the order of $1 million or more can become routine rather than exceptional.

This escalation has led to a variety of product liability reform efforts designed to limit the role of product liability damages. A chief target for these efforts has been the awards for pain and suffering because of the absence of well-defined legal criteria for determining such damages. Some lawyers, such as Melvin Belli, suggest that jurors should ascertain the value of pain and suffering for a small time interval such as a second and then scale it up by the length of time the pain and suffering was endured. In the case of very lengthy injuries this procedure could produce astronomical pain-and-suffering awards. A useful exercise is to consider whether from the standpoint of good economics one should simply multiply the value of pain and suffering for small time intervals by the amount of time the pain and suffering is experienced to generate the total welfare loss.

The lobbying over the economic stakes involved in product liability reflects the patterns of political influences one would expect for rent-seeking behavior. Table 22.10 provides a summary in the left column of the groups in favor of a pain-and-suffering damages cap, and a listing of the groups opposed to such a cap in the right column. This pattern reflects the economic stakes involved. Parties who bear the cost of such pain and suffering awards, ranging from business representatives at the

Table 22.10
Proposal to Impose Limits on Damages Awards for Pain and Suffering

For	Against
Alliance of American Insurers	Association of Trial Lawyers of America
American Consulting Engineers Council	Brown Lung Association
American Medical Association	Consumer Federation of America
National Association of Home Builders	Consumers Union
National Association of Manufacturers	Environmental Action
National Association of Realtors	National Council of Senior Citizens
National Association of Towns and Townships	Public Citizen
National Federation of Independent Business	United Auto Workers
National School Boards Association	United Steelworkers Union
U.S. Chamber of Commerce	Women's Legal Defense Fund

Source: Wall Street Journal, April 9, 1986, p. A64. Reprinted by permission of The Wall Street Journal © 1986 Dow Jones & Company, Inc. All rights reserved worldwide.

U.S. Chamber of Commerce to groups representing the construction industry, favor pain-and-suffering caps. In contrast, labor and consumer groups generally oppose such caps because they limit the awards that the victims of accidents can potentially receive. The debate over the pain and suffering cap proposals and the institution of these caps by various states has been almost devoid of compelling economic reasoning. In the case of each party's arguments, it has been the economic self-interest and the stakes involved that have driven the debate rather than any underlying rationale concerning the appropriateness of particular pain and suffering concepts.

Risk Information and Hazard Warnings

One of the rationales for market failure is that consumers do not have perfect information regarding the safety of the products they purchase. In some cases, consumers may be able to monitor the overall riskiness of products as a group, but not the riskiness of products manufactured by particular companies. Consumers know that chainsaws are hazardous, but they may have less ability to discriminate between the differing degrees of riskiness of Echo chainsaws and Stihl chainsaws.

In situations in which consumers know the average product risk, but not the risk posed by the individual product, there will be a phenomenon akin to the classic lemons problem.[13] Table 22.11 presents an example for the automobile-safety case. Suppose that there are three classes of cars ranging in safety from low to high. If consumers had perfect information regarding the properties of the cars, they would be willing to pay up to $30,000 for the safe car and as little as $20,000 for the average safety car. Because they cannot distinguish the differing degrees of safety, they will make their judgments based on the average safety across this entire group of cars, which produces an average value to consumers of $23,500. The losers from this group-based value approach are the producers of the high-safety cars, and the winners are the pro-

Table 22.11
Markets with Imperfect Information: Lemons Markets for Risky Cars (in Dollars)

Fraction of Cars	Safety	Consumer Value with Perfect Information	Group-Based Value	Gain or Loss
0.2	High	30,000	23,500	+6,500
0.3	Medium	25,000	23,500	+1,500
0.5	Low	20,000	23,500	−3,500

ducers of the low-safety cars. This kind of redistribution from the high-quality to the low-quality market participants is a standard property of lemons markets. This property holds whether we are dealing with the properties of used cars or the salaries given to graduates of a college in a situation where the individual's performance cannot be distinguished from the group average. The presence of such group-based pricing provides a disincentive for firms at the high end of the market because their safety efforts will not be rewarded. Rather, they will be sharing the benefits of safety with all of the other firms on the market.

Self-Certification of Safe Products

Firms can potentially avoid this pooling problem by identifying themselves as being producers of safer products. The gains and losses that would result from full disclosure of this type appear in the final column of Table 22.11. The incentives for such revelation are greatest at the highest end of the quality spectrum and decline as one moves toward the lower end of the spectrum. Firms that produce the low-quality cars in this example would be willing to pay to have information on the differing riskiness of the cars suppressed.

The practical issue from the standpoint of the companies producing the high-quality cars is how to convey credibly to consumers the lower riskiness of their cars. This is the classic economic signaling issue. Firms cannot simply claim that they produce high-quality products because such claims will have no credibility. All firms could make their claims without cost. The classic signaling problem is how to establish an economic mechanism so that the firm can credibly convey to consumers the safety of its products. Such mechanisms include the provisions of warranties and guarantees, since the costs of offering these product attributes are higher if one is marketing a risky product. Purely informational efforts such as ratings provided by government agencies and by consumer groups also may be of value in enabling consumers to make quality judgments.

Government Determination of Safety

Increasingly, the government has become active in trying to meet the informational needs of consumers. Beginning in 1965, Congress mandated hazard-warning labels on cigarettes. This system evolved over time, and in 1984 cigarettes began to include a system of rotating warnings alerting consumers to a diverse array of potential hazards from cigarettes.

Congress also instituted similar warnings for products containing saccharin. This artificial sweetener is potentially carcinogenic, but the scientific evidence and the extent of the risk have long been a matter of dispute. Moreover, the benefits of the product from the standpoint of reducing obesity and its associated risks have greatly complicated the debate over the appropriate regulation of this product.

Similarly, in 1989 Congress mandated the warnings on all alcoholic beverages. The first warning alerts consumers to the risk of birth defects from consumption of alcohol by pregnant women. The second warning notes the presence of health problems linked to alcohol and the effect of alcohol on one's ability to drive and operate machinery.

These measures do not exhaust all initiatives of this type. Many states have also joined in with these efforts. Chief among these state initiatives is California Proposition 65, which has mandated the labeling of all significant carcinogens in food products. Many companies have avoided the stigma of labeling by reformulating their products, such as Liquid Paper, which formerly contained carcinogens. Although the implementation of this regulation remains a matter of debate, the proliferation of right-to-know measures of various kinds is a major regulatory event of the 1980s.

Alternatives to Direct Command and Control Regulation

The rationale for employing an informational regulation rather than a direct command and control regulation is twofold. First, in many situations we do not wish to ban an activity altogether. The regulatory agency may not have sufficient information to proceed with a ban, but would nevertheless like to alert consumers to a potential hazard in the interim so that they can at least exercise caution until the information for taking more stringent action becomes firmer.

Second, regulation through information may sometimes be the most appropriate and most effective response even when the agency is in doubt as to the appropriate course of action. If individuals differ in their tastes and their willingness to bear risks, then information provides consumers with the ability to make these market judgments and to choose the level of risk that is most efficient given their own preferences.

In addition, many decisions must necessarily be made on a decentralized basis. The care consumers take when using household chemicals cannot be monitored by direct regulatory agency, so that the most effective way to promote safety is to give consumers the motivation to undertake the appropriate level of precautions.

More generally, the task of promoting product safety is not simply one of designing an appropriate technology for the product. As we saw in the case of safety belts and aspirin caps, consumer behavior often plays a central role in determining the safety level that will result from a

Table 22.12
Effects of Drain Opener Labels on Precaution-Taking (Percentages)

Precaution	No Warning ($n = 59$)	Drano ($n = 59$)	Incremental Effect
Wear rubber gloves	63	82	19
Store in childproof location	54	68	14

Source: W. Kip Viscusi and Wesley A. Magat, *Learning About Risk: Consumer and Worker Responses to Hazard Information* (Cambridge, Mass.: Harvard University Press, 1987).

particular product design. The government has at its disposal two mechanisms to influence safety—producer and consumer actions. In general, we will be able to achieve greater gains for safety if we take advantage of both these mechanisms rather than simply rely on a technology-based approach.

The potential impact of such regulations is reflected in the statistics in Table 22.12. This table provides information on the efficacy of the Drano label. Table 22.12 reports on the response of consumers to drain opener products for which the warning information had been purged, as opposed to their response to a label patterned after the current Drano label. The addition of risk information increases the frequency with which consumers wear rubber gloves or store the product in a childproof location.

Not all of the consumers would choose to wear rubber gloves even though the label urges that they take these precautions, because this precaution is onerous. Consumers might rationally choose to forgo this precaution if they believe that the benefits to them of taking it did not outweigh the costs associated with the nuisance value of wearing rubber gloves. The warning label also has an effect on storage in a childproof location, as 14 percent more of the respondents will store the product in a childproof location after receiving the label. Moreover, for the subsample of the population with children under age five—the high-risk-of-poisoning group—almost all respondents who received the hazard warning would take the appropriate childproofing precaution.

Finally, it is noteworthy that even when the hazard-warning information is purged, over half of all consumers would undertake the precaution. It is important to recognize that consumers are not working in a vacuum. Even for a drain opener purged of warnings, over half of all consumers know enough about the potential hazards to take the precaution. Moreover, the studies of hazard warnings indicate that these warnings are effective only to the extent that they provide new knowledge to consumers. Programs of education that are intended to browbeat consumers into changing their behavior or that are intended to remind consumers about desirable courses of action generally are not successful. The programs that have been shown to be effective are those that provide new information to consumers in a convincing manner rather than those that fail to recognize that consumers are rational decision makers who are sometimes in need of important risk information.

An attraction of informational regulations from the standpoint of economists is that such regulations do not interfere with market operations to the same extent as technological standards. Nor do they impose substantial costs on firms. Rather, by providing information to consumers, the market can work more effectively in generating the incentives for efficient levels of safety.

The Future of Product Safety Policy

The regulator choice process in the product safety area is even more diverse than Figure 22.1 suggested. As a society, we have a broad set of choices involving the appropriate role of government regulation and tort liability. However, within these classes of institutional mechanisms there are also important decisions with respect to the particular mechanism for intervention.

Consider first the case of regulation. The alternative mechanisms by which we can intervene through government regulation are quite diverse. The government can specify in advance the technological standards that must be met by a product. A second possibility is to have some premarket approval mechanism whereby the company submits the product to the government for review and approval before the product can be marketed. A third possibility is to have government regulations that operate after the fact, as in the case of the product-recall strategies for defective automobiles and consumer products.

One mechanism that has not been used as a regulatory arena is an injury tax approach, whereby the government imposes financial penalties on risky products rather than specify their technical characteristics. One reason why this final strategy has not met with widespread adoption is that in the product case it is particularly difficult to ascertain the contributory role of the product to a particular accident. The Consumer Product Safety Commission, for example, keeps a tally of all accidents involving use of particular consumer products, such as ladders. However, what we do not know is whether the ladder itself buckled under the consumer or whether it was simply the case that the consumer fell from the ladder. We know that the use of ladders is potentially risky, but ideally we want to establish a tax approach that will penalize unsafe ladders and not simply raise the price of all ladders irrespective of their safety. The latter approach is similar to the impact of a strict liability standard for ladders. In addition to raising the possibility of potentially substantial costs, this option also may create substantial moral hazard problems as well.

Since the mid-1980s the main policy debate has not focused on regulatory reform but rather on product liability reform. The reason for this emphasis is that the stakes imposed by product liability have escalated considerably and frequently dwarf the stakes involved with direct government regulation. Pharmaceutical companies are routinely faced with liability costs that may be in excess of the value of the sales of a product, particularly for small-market products such as vaccines, and the result is that such penalties have had a chilling effect on product innovation.

The fact that there has been some product innovation effect is not necessarily bad. Ideally, we do want tort liability to discourage the introduction of unduly risky new products. However, at the same time we do not want to deter beneficial innovations because firms are excessively cautious due to the prospect of potentially enormous liability burdens. A fundamental task that must be addressed in the coming years will be to restructure the tort-liability system to strike a balance between the competing objectives of promoting safety and at the same time fostering the legitimate interests of the businesses affected by the regulation.

A final issue on the policy agenda is the overall coordination of regulatory and liability efforts. These are two different institutional mechanisms that affect similar classes of economic concerns. In some cases, the companies are hit twice by these institutions. On the other hand, they may adopt particular technological devices to come into compliance with formal government regulations. However, the presence of such compliance does not provide any guarantees against additional liability costs being imposed on the firm.

In addition to this potentially duplicative impact, there is also the issue of the appropriate division of labor between these social institutions. Which classes of hazards are best suited to being addressed by government regulations, and which are better suited to the ex post facto approach of tort liability that addresses specific accident cases identified in the courts? Differences in the temporal structure and character of the accidents no doubt will be important considerations in making these institutional allocations, but another issue may also be the difference in expertise. Many observers are beginning to question the ability of jurors to make the society-wide product safety decisions that are often part of the judgments that must be made to determine whether a particular product design is defective. Resolving such issues, which only recently have begun to be raised, will remain a central component of the future regulatory agenda.

Questions and Problems

1. Ideally, we would like to determine whether there is a product market failure before we intervene. Suppose that we do not have information on consumer risk perceptions, but we do observe the price reductions consumers are willing to accept in return for greater objective levels of safety with their product. For example, economists have estimated the implicit values of life associated with purchases of different automobiles. How would you use these implicit value-of-life estimates to determine whether there is a market failure?

2. The Food and Drug Administration uses a premanufacturing screening program for determining the marketability of new pharmaceutical products, whereas the U.S. Consumer Product Safety Commission relies on recall actions for products found to be defective, such as electric coffeemakers that short out. Can you think of any rationale other than historical accident for the difference in regulatory approaches between the two agencies?

3. The AIDS lobbyists have forced the FDA to accelerate the approval of AIDS-related drugs. In some cases, this means that drugs that have not undergone the full FDA testing process to determine safety and efficacy will be used on patients. Is there a legitimate rationale for the expedited approval of AIDS-related drugs, or is this result simply due to the political power wielded by the AIDS lobbyists? Which other classes of drugs do you believe merit accelerated approval? More generally, if the FDA were to set up two different approval schedules, one being a thorough approval process and the second being a rapid approval process, what factors would you use in distinguishing whether a particular drug merited the thorough or the rapid approval approach?

4. Although Coase theorem types of influences can potentially lead to market provision of nonsmoking areas and similar restrictions, current smoking policies do not reflect market influences alone. Municipalities throughout the country enacted various smoking ordinances, and the federal government is considering measures as well. What do you believe has been the impetus for such policies? Are there any efficiency-oriented reasons why it might be desirable for the government to set uniform standards in this area? More specifically, is there any likely source of market failure? In addition, are there any equity concerns that may be motivating these measures? Which parties will gain from an equity standpoint, and which will lose? Is there any reason to believe that the political outcomes will be efficient, and how would we judge efficiency?

5. Much of the debate over the efficacy of seatbelt requirements and the influence of the counterproductive effect of decreased driver precautions noted by Peltzman stems from the crudeness of the empirical information that is available. If we can look only at accident rate totals by year or by state, then much key information will be lost. If you had unlimited resources and could commission your state police to develop an empirical

database for you, what factors would you ask them to assess so that you could test the Peltzman effect conclusively?

6. After the advent of an increased role of tort liability, some products have disappeared. Let us take the case of diving boards at motels. What factors would you want to examine to determine whether this change in product availability is efficient?

7. It has often been noted that Melvin Belli's procedure for determining pain-and-suffering damages is biased. Recall that his technique is to ask jurors to assess the pain-and-suffering value for a small unit of time, and then to extrapolate the value to the total time period over which the victim experienced the pain. Defense lawyers argue that the approach overstates the value of pain and suffering. What is the structure of the utility function for pain that must hold for the Belli approach to lead to an overstatement? Under what circumstances will it lead to an understatement?

Notes

1. See Ralph Nader, *Unsafe At Any Speed* (New York: Grossman, 1965).

2. For a review of the development of health, safety, and environmental regulations, see Paul MacAvoy, *The Regulated Industries and the Economies* (New York: W. W. Norton, 1979).

3. For an excellent economic analysis of the role of consumer complaints, see Sharon Oster, "The Determinants of Consumer Complaints," *Review of Economics and Statistics* 62 (1990): 603–9.

4. The role of pharmaceutical regulatory policy with respect to such tradeoffs is a principal theme of the book by Henry Grabowski and John Vernon, *The Regulation of Pharmaceuticals: Balancing the Benefits and Risks* (Washington, D.C.: American Enterprise Institute, 1983).

5. The original presentation of the Peltzman results appears in Sam Peltzman, "The Effects of Automobile Safety Regulation," *Journal of Political Economy* 83 (1975): 677–725. The role of driver precautions has been the focus of a number of other studies as well. See, among others, Glenn Blomquist, *The Regulation of Motor Vehicle and Traffic Safety* (Boston: Kluwer Academic Publishers, 1988); Robert Crandall, Howard Gruenspecht, Theodore Keeler, and Lester Lave, *Regulating the Automobile* (Washington, D.C.: Brookings Institution, 1986); Glenn Blomquist, "Motorist Use of Safety Equipment: Expected Benefits or Risk Incompetence?" *Journal of Risk and Uncertainty* 4, No. 2 (1991): 135–52; and William N. Evans and John Graham, "Risk Reduction or Risk Compensation? The Case of Mandatory Safety-Belt Use Laws," *Journal of Risk and Uncertainty* 4, No. 1 (1991): 61–74.

6. These overall themes are articulated in Crandall, Gruenspecht, Keeler, and Lave, 1986.

7. Viscusi's work on the lulling effect and consumer precautions more generally is synthesized in W. Kip Viscusi, *Fatal Tradeoffs* (New York: Oxford University Press, 1992).

8. See Viscusi, 1992, for empirical documentation of the effects discussed below.

9. In addition to Viscusi, 1992, see Peter Linneman, "The Effects of Consumer Safety Standards: The 1973 Mattress Flammability Standard," *Journal of Law and Economics*, 1980: 461–79. For a more general discussion of these issues, also

see Nina Cornell, Roger Noll, and Barry Weingast, "Safety Regulation," in H. Owen and C. Schultze (eds.), *Setting National Priorities* (Washington, D.C.: Brookings Institution, 1976).

10. See Crandall, Gruenspecht, Keeler, and Lave, 1986.

11. The discussion below is based most directly on W. Kip Viscusi, *Reforming Products Liability* (Cambridge, Mass.: Harvard University Press, 1991). Other treatments of these issues include Robert E. Litan and Clifford Winston, *Liability: Perspectives and Policy* (Washington, D.C.: Brookings Institution, 1988); Steven Shavell, *Economic Analysis of Accident Law* (Cambridge: Harvard University Press, 1987); and William M. Landes and Richard A. Posner, *The Economic Structure of Tort Law* (Cambridge, Mass.: Harvard University Press, 1987).

12. National Academy of Sciences, *Developing New Contraceptives: Obstacles and Opportunities* (Washington, D.C.: National Academy Press, 1990).

13. The discussion below is based most directly on W. Kip Viscusi, "A Note on 'Lemons' Markets with Quality Certification," *Bell Journal of Economics* 9 (1978): 277–79. The interested reader also should examine two of the seminal works on this topic: George A. Akerlof, "The Market for 'Lemons': Qualitative Uncertainty and the Market Mechanism," *Quarterly Journal of Economics* 84 (1970): 488–500; and A. Michael Spence, "Competitive and Optimal Responses to Signals: An Analysis of Efficiency and Distribution," *Journal of Economic Theory* 7 (1974): 296–332.

Workplace health and safety levels are governed largely by three sets of influences: the market, direct regulation of risk levels by the Occupational Safety and Health Administration (OSHA), and the safety incentives created through workers' compensation. In each case safety is promoted by creating financial payoffs for firms to invest in workplace characteristics that will improve worker safety. These incentives arise because improved safety leads to reduced wage premiums for risk, lower regulatory penalties for noncompliance, and reduced workers' compensation premiums.

The labor market incentives provide the backdrop for the analysis of job safety. As the discussion in Chapter 20 indicated, these wage incentives are often quite substantial. The principal direct regulatory mechanism consists of OSHA's health and safety standards. The Occupational Safety and Health Administration has long been a target of criticism. Critics have not questioned the agency's fundamental objective. Promoting worker health and safety is a laudable and widely shared objective. Rather, OSHA is generally regarded as not fulfilling its mission of promoting this objective. Some observers claim that the agency imposes needless costs and restrictions on American business, whereas others claim that the agency's efforts are not vigorous enough.

This branch of the U.S. Department of Labor began operation in 1971 after the Occupational Safety and Health Act of 1970 created it so as "to assure so far as possible every working man and woman in the nation safe and healthful working conditions."[1] Because ensuring a no-risk society is clearly an unattainable goal, the initial OSHA mandate established the unfeasible as the agency's mission. Nevertheless, a regulatory agency focusing on worker safety issues could serve a constructive function.

The early operations of OSHA did not, however, even begin to fulfill the agency's initial promise. OSHA was the object of widespread ridicule for standards that prescribed acceptable toilet seat shapes, the placement of exit signs, the width of handrails, and the proper dimensions of OSHA-approved ladders. Many of the more frivolous standards were never among the most prominent concerns in the agency's enforcement effort. Nevertheless, they did epitomize the degree to which the federal government was attempting to influence the design and operation of the workplace—matters that previously had been left to managerial discretion.

In recent years the stories of OSHA's misguided regulatory efforts have been less prominent. One no longer reads amusing anecdotes like that concerning the OSHA inspector who penalized a firm for allowing its employees to work on a bridge without the required orange life vests even though the riverbed was dry. The tone has shifted. Strident criticism in the 1970s gave way to comparative inattention in the 1980s. This inattention did not necessarily imply that the agency had been given a clean bill of health. There has been no widely publicized reform of the agency. Moreover, unlike transportation, natural gas, oil, and airlines, there have been no legislative changes or major administrative reforms. The decrease in coverage of controversial OSHA policies occurred because a continuation of past policies, however ill-conceived, was simply no longer newsworthy. Moreover, firms had complied in many instances, so that the decisions regarding the standards were behind them.

In the 1990s the tone of public debate concerning OSHA has shifted. After decreasing its enforcement effort in the early 1980s, OSHA became increasingly criticized for not doing enough. Instead of media coverage of apparently frivolous regulations, attention shifted to the continuing death toll in the American workplace. The status of job-safety regulation began to be epitomized by the meatpacking worker who had become disabled because of lax regulatory enforcement and the thousands of asbestos workers who will die from job-related cancers. The late 1980s and early 1990s marked a substantial increase in activity in the job safety regulation area. Job health and safety remains an area where society is still striving to devise workable and effective regulatory mechanisms.

This chapter focuses on a general assessment of the effort to promote worker health: why we have such policies, how the initial effort failed, whether there has been any improvement in this effort, and how these policies can be reformed. Although only about two decades old, OSHA has been the subject of a variety of proposed reform efforts.[2] That OSHA has already become a chief target of proposed regulatory reforms suggests the kinds of fundamental changes needed in the agency's initial orientation.

The previous two presidential administrations promised an overhaul of OSHA policies. The Carter administration sought to provide this risk regulation effort with greater legitimacy by eliminating some of the more frivolous standards and by enforcing the sounder portions of OSHA regulations more vigorously. Under the Reagan administration the attention shifted to decreasing OSHA's confrontational character so as to foster a cooperative business-government approach to promoting workplace safety. The Clinton administration initiated a long-overdue increase in the scale of regulatory penalties coupled with a substantial expansion in the scale of regulation. In 1994, for example, OSHA proposed indoor air-quality standards that would affect matters such as workplace smoking and, by OSHA's estimates, would cost $8 billion per year.

Although these efforts rectified many of the more extreme deficiencies of OSHA's initial strategy, calls for reform continue. Regulation of workplace conditions is a legitimate role for the government, but as with other regulatory policies, there is a continuing need to maintain a balance between competing objectives. In this case the principal tradeoff is between the costs imposed by the regulation and the health and safety benefits they provide. There is also a need to enforce the regulations that are promulgated in a manner that will foster effective incentives for compliance.

The Potential for Inefficiencies

There also may be more fundamental shortcomings whereby the government policy is failing to achieve as much safety improvement as is possible for the costs imposed. In more technical terms, the difficulty may be that we are not on the frontier of efficient policies (that is, those policies that provide the greatest safety for any given cost), as opposed to simply making the wrong tradeoff along such a frontier.

Consider the set of feasible risk-cost combinations in Figure 23.1. All points on the frontier ABC or to the right of it are potentially achievable. Ideally, the policy debate should be where along the policy frontier ABC our policy choice should be. Some finite rate of tradeoff is required inasmuch as complete safety is prohibitively costly in the case that is drawn. Unfortunately, a danger with ill-conceived policies is not that we are setting the tradeoff rate incorrectly, but rather that we are wasting resources. If OSHA policies are now at point D, we could have greater safety at the same cost as point C or the same safety at less cost at point B.

Often the debate over ill-conceived regulations is miscast as one of values—where along the frontier should we be—whereas the more fundamental problem is that a better policy could be designed regardless of one's disposition toward regulation. Many of the most widely publicized standards initially promulgated by OSHA fall in the category of policies dominated by less costly and more effective alternatives. As in the case of other regulatory reforms, proper application of fundamental economic principles will illuminate the nature of the policy changes required.

How Markets Can Promote Safety

Before instituting a government regulation, it is instructive to assess how the market functions. Basically, one should inquire whether there is any

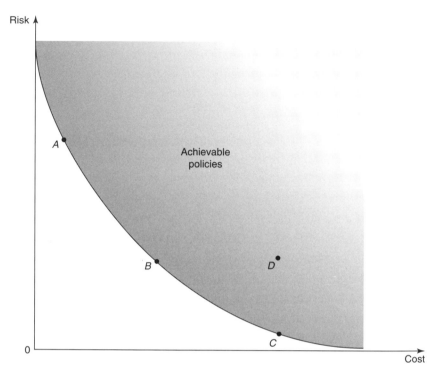

Figure 23.1
The Policy Frontier for Job Safety

inadequacy in the way in which market forces operate. Although individual life and health are clearly valuable attributes, there are many other market outcomes that are valued by consumers and workers but are not regulated by government. Because markets that operate well will allocate resources efficiently, there should be some perceived inadequacy in the way these forces function before one interferes with their operation.

To ensure that market outcomes will be efficient, a number of stringent conditions must be met. For example, the outcome of any employment decision must affect the worker and employer only, not society at large, because these broader concerns will not be reflected in the job choice. A particularly pertinent requirement is that the job choice must be the outcome of a fully rational decision. Individuals must be cognizant of the risks they face and be able to make sound decisions under uncertainty. As discussed below, these assumptions are especially likely to be violated for many important classes of risks.

Even if there is a consensus that market outcomes are not optimal, it is essential to ascertain the extent of the market failure. It is important to understand if the operation of the market is fundamentally flawed or whether there is a narrower market failure, such as an informational shortcoming that can be remedied through an information transfer effort rather than direct control of workplace conditions.

Finally, the market mechanisms will be pertinent insofar as they establish the context in which the government regulation operates. Regulations do not dictate health and safety outcomes, inasmuch as it is impossible for regulators to monitor and influence the health and safety attributes of all firms. Instead, these policies simply create incentives for firms and workers to take particular actions, such as installing new ventilation equipment. Whether regulations have any impact will hinge on the strength of the incentives created by the policy and the safety incentives the market generates for firms.

Compensating Wage Differential Theory

The fundamental economic approach to worker safety was sketched by Adam Smith over two centuries ago.[3] Smith observed that workers will demand a compensating wage differential for jobs that are perceived as being risky or otherwise unpleasant. This theory was the basis for the labor market estimates of the value of life discussed in Chapter 20. The two critical assumptions are that workers must be aware of the risk (which may not always be the case) and that they would rather be healthy than not (which is not a controversial assumption). Attitudes toward health will, however, differ. Hersch and Viscusi, for example, have shown that smokers and those who do not wear seatbelts are much more willing to work on hazardous jobs for less pay per unit risk than their safety-loving contemporaries, such as nonsmoking, seatbelt users.[4] These differentials in turn will establish an incentive for firms to promote safety, since doing so will lower their wage bill. In particular, these wage costs are augmented by reduced turnover costs and workers' compensation premium levels, both of which also provide incentives for safety improvements by the firm. In effect, it is primarily the risk-dollar tradeoffs of the workers themselves that will determine the safety decision by the firm.

Figure 23.2 illustrates how these forces will influence the level of safety provided. Suppose that the health outcome involved is reduction of job-related accidents and that improvements in safety have diminishing incremental value to workers, just as additional units of other types of "economic goods" have diminishing importance. The marginal value of the safety curve in Figure 23.2 consequently is a downward-sloping

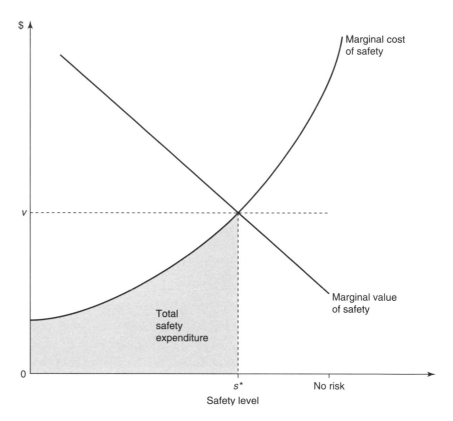

Figure 23.2
Determination of Market Levels of Safety

curve, for the initial increments in safety have the greatest value. Work-ers' marginal value of safety is transmitted to firms through the wage rate the firm must pay to attract and retain workers. The firm can pro-vide greater levels of safety, but doing so entails additional marginal (or incremental) costs that increase as the level of safety becomes increas-ingly great. Some initial safety improvements can be achieved inex-pensively through, for example, modification of existing machines or work practices. The addition of exhaust fans is one such measure for airborne risks. More extensive improvements could require an overhaul of the firm's technology, which would be more expensive. This marginal-cost curve consequently is increasing rather than staying flat because safety equipment differs in its relative efficacy, and the firm will choose to install the most effective equipment per unit cost first.

The price of safety set by worker preferences will determine where along this marginal cost curve the firm will stop. The optimal level of safety from the standpoint of the market will be s^*. The shaded area under the marginal-cost curve will be the total safety-related expenditure by the firm. This level is short of the no-risk level of safety. At the level of safety provided, workers would have been willing to pay v per expected accident to avoid such accidents. Additional safety beyond this point is not provided, because the cost to the firm for each extra accident avoided exceeds workers' valuation of the improvement.

The level of health and safety selected will not be a no-risk level, because promoting safety is costly. Almost all our daily activities pose some risk because of the costs involved in reducing the hazards. Consumers, for example, routinely sacrifice greater crashworthiness whenever they select more compact automobiles in an effort to obtain greater fuel efficiency, for the typical small car is less crashworthy than the average full-sized car. Moreover, the order of magnitude of risks we regulate are not too dissimilar from those that we encounter in other activities. As the data in Chapter 19 indicated, the accident risk posed by one day of work in a coal mine (a relatively hazardous pursuit) is comparable in size to the risks of smoking 3.7 cigarettes, riding 27 miles by bicycle, eating 108 tablespoons of peanut butter, or traveling 405 miles by car.[5] Individuals trade off these and other risks against other valued attributes, such as the recreational value of cycling.

Risk Information

The first link in the compensating differential analysis is that workers must be aware of the risks they face. For example, if there is no perception of the risks, workers will demand no additional compensation to work on a hazardous job. The available evidence suggests that there is some general awareness of many of the risks workers face. Given data from the University of Michigan Survey of Working Conditions, there is a strong correlation between the risk level in the industry and whether workers perceive their jobs as being dangerous in some respect.[6] This evidence is by no means conclusive, however, inasmuch as the risk assessment question ascertained only whether workers were aware of the presence of some risk, not the degree of risk posed by the job.

A more refined test can be provided using data based on a survey of workers at four chemical plants.[7] In that study workers were asked to assess the risks of jobs using a continuous scale that could be compared with published accident measures. Overall, workers believed that their jobs were almost twice as hazardous as the published accident statistics for the chemical industry suggest, which is expected in view of the degree to which health hazards, such as cancer, are not reflected in the accident data. Particularly noteworthy was that after the health hazards were excluded from consideration, the risk assessments equaled the accident rate for the chemical industry.[8]

These studies should be regarded as evidence of some reasonable perception of job risks by workers. They do not, however, imply that workers are perfectly informed. It is unlikely that workers have completely accurate perceptions of the risks posed by their jobs. These risks are not fully known even by occupational health and safety experts.

The degree to which there will be errors in the risk assessment will not, however, be uniform across all classes of risk. As a rough generalization, one would expect safety risks (external hazards such as inadequate machine guards) to be better understood than health risks (internal risks such as excessive exposure to radiation). Safety hazards tend to be more readily visible and familiar risks, such as the chance of a worker in a sawmill losing a finger. In contrast, health hazards usually are less well understood. These risks often involve low-probability events about which nothing is known whatsoever. Such risks may affect the individual decades after the exposure, so that learning by observation and experience is infeasible. These difficulties are enhanced in some instances by the absence of any clear-cut signals that a health risk is present. The odor and color of gases emitted in the workplace, for example, are not a reliable index of their potential carcinogenicity.

In situations where workers are aware of the hazard, the riskier jobs should be expected to command a wage premium. The value-of-life estimates in Chapter 20 indicated that these compensation levels are quite substantial, on the order of $5 million for each workplace fatality. This compensation in turn provides a financial reward to firms that promote safety, inasmuch as reducing the expected number of deaths will lower their wage bill. Overall, roughly $70 billion in wage premiums for risk is paid by the United States private sector each year, above and beyond the amount that is paid in workers' compensation.[9]

These figures represent what workers' risk-dollar tradeoffs are, given their current information about the risk, not what they would be if they had full information about the risk. In addition, the calculations assume rational decision making, whereas in practice workers may overreact to risks or they may neglect to take them into consideration. Although market behavior may not be ideal, the substantial magnitude of compensation per unit risk does suggest that there is substantial awareness of risks and their implications.

The value-of-life results are bolstered by analogous findings for nonfatal job injuries. These studies suggest that there is substantial compen-

Table 23.1
Risk Premiums as a Percentage of Total Earnings in Manufacturing Industries[a]

Risk premiums of 3% to 5%	Chemicals and allied products
	Petroleum refining and related industries
	Electrical machinery, equipment, and supplies
	Transportation equipment
	Instruments and related products
	Printing, publishing, and allied services
	Tobacco manufacturers
	Apparel and related products
	Nonelectrical machinery
Risk premiums of 6% to 9%	Textiles
	Paper and allied products
	Primary metals
	Rubber and plastics
	Fabricated metal products
	Leather and leather products
	Stone, clay, and glass products
Risk premiums of 12% to 15%	Food and allied products
	Furniture and fixtures
	Lumber and wood products

[a] These premiums are derived from earnings equations that are estimates of the relationship between injury rates and workers' earnings.
Source: W. Kip Viscusi, "Market Incentives for Safety," *Harvard Business Review* 63, No. 4 (1985): 137. Copyright © 1985 by the President and Fellows of Harvard College; all rights reserved.

sation for job risks, when viewed both in terms of the total wage bill (6 percent of manufacturing workers' wages) and the rate of compensation per unit risk.

The level of compensation may vary by industry. Unions, with a strong interest in health and safety issues, are particularly interested in securing workers' hazard pay. Some unions, such as that for petroleum and chemical workers, often have specialized expertise in the health and safety area and have the ability to bargain with greater expertise than workers could individually. Table 23.1 summarizes the overall breakdown in risk premiums by industry. These premium levels range from 3 to 5 percent of total earnings for industries such as apparel, to as high as 12 to 15 percent for the lumber industry.

On-the-Job Experience and Worker Quit Rates

The presence of possibly inadequate worker knowledge concerning the risks remains a potential impediment to the full operation of the compensating differential mechanism. The result will not be that market mechanisms will work less effectively, although some decreased efficacy will undoubtedly occur. Rather there will also be new market forces that may be influential.[10]

Consider a situation in which a worker starts a job without full knowledge of the potential risks. After being assigned to the position he or she will be able to observe the nature of the job operations, the surrounding physical conditions, and the actions of coworkers. Similarly, during a period of work on the job the worker learns about some particular difficulties in carrying out the job tasks, and even more directly, he or she observes whether coworkers are (or have been) injured. The worker can then use these experiences to evaluate the risk potential of the job.

If the worker's risk perceptions become sufficiently unfavorable, given the wage paid, he or she can quit and move to another firm. Overall, job risks account for one-third of all manufacturing quit rates. Similarly, the periods of time that workers spend at hazardous firms before leaving are shorter than for safe firms. As a consequence, there will always tend to be more inexperienced workers in high-risk jobs, because the high turnover rates from these positions lead to frequent replacements.

The standard observation that younger and more inexperienced workers are more likely to be involved in accidents is not entirely attributable to greater riskiness of this demographic group. Rather, the causality may be in the opposite direction, inasmuch as new hires are more likely to be placed in the high-risk, high-turnover jobs. The firm will also have a strong incentive to avoid placing its most experienced workers in these positions, because it will lose the training investment if the worker is injured or quits.

All of the labor market responses by workers are simply variations of the compensating differential theme. If the job appears to be risky initially, the worker will require extra compensation to begin work on it. Similarly, once he or she acquires information about the risks that are present, the worker will reassess the job's attractiveness and remain with it only if the compensating differential is sufficient.

Inadequacies in the Market

If market operations were fully efficient, there would be no need for government regulation of health and safety. The decentralized operation of the market would be sufficient to ensure appropriate levels of the risk. Two broad classes of shortcomings limit the efficacy of market outcomes: (1) informational inadequacies and problems with individual decisions under uncertainty and (2) externalities.

Informational Problems and Irrationalities

For the compensating differential model to be fully applicable, workers must be cognizant of the risks they face and be able to make sound decisions based on this knowledge. The available evidence suggests that in many contexts workers have risk perceptions that appear plausible, but these studies in no way imply that workers are fully informed. There is a general consensus that many health risks in particular are not well understood, and indeed workers may be completely ignorant of some of the risks they face.

With on-the-job experience, workers undoubtedly will revise their perceptions of many risks. Once again, safety hazards are more likely to be treated in a reliable manner because they tend to be readily visible and to occur with much greater frequency than many health risks, which are often low-probability events. Thus the worker has fewer observable incidents of adverse health outcomes to use in forming his risk assessment. The long time lags involved in many health risks further impede efforts to learn about the implications of these risks through experience. A worker may get cancer two decades after job exposure to a carcinogen, but tracing the cause to the job usually is not feasible. As a rough generalization, there is probably reasonable but not perfectly accurate perception of many safety risks and much less reliable assessment of the pertinent health risks.

Even with accurate perceptions of the risk, however, one cannot be confident that the decisions ultimately made by the workers will be ideal. Decisions under uncertainty are known to pose considerably more difficulties than decisions made in cases where the outcomes of alternative actions are known in advance.[11] These difficulties are likely to be particularly great in situations involving very low-probability events that have severe outcomes after a substantial lag. The low probabilities and substantial lags make these decisions difficult to conceptualize. How averse, for example, is a worker to taking a 1/20,000 risk of cancer twenty-five years from now? Because of the high stakes—possibly including the worker's life—the cost of mistaken choices will be high. Once again, it is likely that health hazards pose relatively greater demands on individual rationality than safety risks.

The final class of shortcomings in individual behavior relates to the degree workers can choose from a variety of alternative risk-wage combinations. For the relatively mobile, modern United States economy there seems to be substantial range of job options for almost all workers. Certainly, the classic textbook discussions of the one-company town no longer seem relevant and, even if true, would not have as great an impact in an era of interstate highways and substantial worker mobility. This mobility may be restricted during cyclical downturns when job opportunities are less plentiful, but because accidents move procyclically, the net influence of adverse economic conditions is not clear-cut.

Perhaps the most important constraint on individual mobility is related to the character of the employment relationship. Once on the job, individuals acquire skills specific to the particular firm as well as seniority rights and pension benefits that are typically not fully transferable. If workers had full knowledge of the risk before accepting the position, these impediments to mobility would not be consequential. The basic difficulty, however, is that workers may not have been fully cognizant of the implications of the position and will subsequently become trapped in an unattractive job situation. Available evidence for chemical workers suggests that the extent of serious job mismatches of this type is not high.

Externalities

An additional class of market inadequacies arises even if individual decisions are fully rational and ideal in all respects. Parties outside of the market transaction for the job may have a stake in the risky job insofar as there is a broader altruistic concern with individual health. This type of health-related altruism is probably of greater consequence than redistributional concerns in this context. Life and health are clearly quite special, as society has undertaken a variety of health-enhancing efforts, such as Medicare, to promote individual well-being.

The overall importance of these altruistic interests has not yet been ascertained, however. The evidence summarized in Chapter 20 was exploratory in nature. In contrast, individuals' values of life and health are considerable, and it is not obvious that the external interests of society would boost these values substantially. Whether society's broader altruistic concerns are of great consequence in this area is an open empirical issue that merits further attention.

Moreover, there is the ethical issue of whether there is a legitimate altruistic concern or simply an attempt by more affluent citizens to impose their own risk-dollar tradeoffs on others. High-income, white-collar workers may view most blue-collar jobs as unattractive, but this does not mean that social welfare will be enhanced by preventing anyone from working on this class of jobs. Until these questions can be resolved, the primary impetus for regulation of occupational hazards probably should be the shortcomings of worker decisions.

OSHA's Regulatory Approach

The general approach OSHA has taken to regulating job safety is dictated at least in part by the Occupational Safety and Health Act of

1970. This legislation authorizes OSHA to set standards and to do so in a manner that will ensure worker health and safety. OSHA's enabling legislation did not, however, specify what these standards should be, what general character they should take, or how stringent they should be.

In addition, the legislation did not specify the nature of the enforcement of the standards. For example, OSHA could couple standards with a penalty for firms out of compliance, where the penalty is set at a level that could give firms some discretion as to whether compliance is desirable. For example, the penalty could be related to the health impacts on workers, and the firm could comply with the standard only if the health benefits exceeded the costs to firms. (The frequency of OSHA inspections could also influence the penalty.) In actuality, OSHA imposes an ever-escalating series of penalties on firms out of compliance; thus the standards can be viewed as rigid guidelines. Because of this binding character, the level and nature of the standards is of major consequence to firms regulated by OSHA.

Setting OSHA Standard Levels

One could characterize OSHA's general approach as that of adopting technology-based standards whose stringency is limited only by their affordability. Cost considerations enter only insofar as OSHA is concerned with shutting down affected firms. To see how OSHA's strategy differs from a standard benefit-cost approach, consider Figure 23.3. For simplicity, suppose that the marginal safety-benefit curve is flat, so that there is a constant unit benefit value. The marginal cost of providing safety is rising, as it becomes increasingly more expensive to promote safety.

The strategy of OSHA is to look for the kink in the marginal cost curve—at what point does added safety become prohibitively expensive? For Figure 23.3 that point is at s_2, whereas the efficient level of safety is at s_1. The strategy advocated by most economists is that the agency should pursue a more balanced approach that recognizes the necessity of taking into account both the costs and risk-reduction benefits in a comprehensive manner. What matters is the relationship between marginal benefits and marginal costs, not whether costs happen to jump at a particular point. Costs should always be a matter of concern, not simply when a firm may go out of business as a result of OSHA policies. Such a shift in emphasis need not always lead to more lenient regulations. Some very hazardous firms probably should go out of business if provision for efficient levels of safety and health will not permit them to earn a profit.

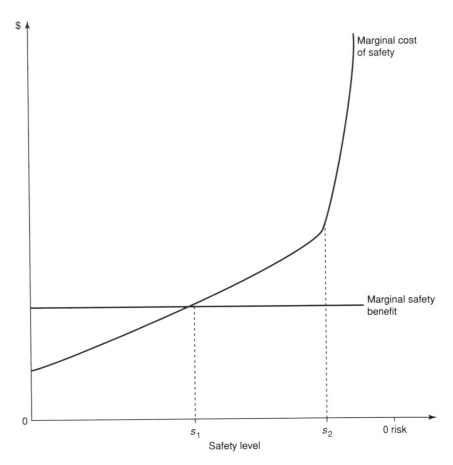

Figure 23.3
OSHA Standard Setting versus Efficient Standard Setting

Much of the policy-oriented debate over the safety standards has concerned their stringency. Those advocating a more balanced approach note that the Occupational Safety and Health Act does not require a risk-free workplace, only one that promotes safety "as far as possible."[12] This and other qualifiers in the act suggest that OSHA might have some leeway in being able to take costs into consideration. This view was bolstered somewhat by the U.S. Supreme Court's decision in the 1980 benzene case, in which it overturned the standard because OSHA had not shown that the reduction in risks would be "significant."[13] This significant risk criterion imposes a threshold benefit level, but it does not impose a requirement that OSHA balance benefits and costs.

Indeed, such benefit-cost tests were explicitly ruled out in the 1981 U.S. Supreme Court decision regarding the OSHA cotton-dust standard.[14] The court upheld the OSHA cotton-dust standard and inter-preted the feasibility provisions of the Occupational Safety and Health Act as meaning "capable of being done." It is the technical possibility of compliance rather than benefit-cost tradeoffs that should guide OSHA decisions.

In fact, however, in this instance OSHA had based its cotton-dust standards on cost-effectiveness concerns, not simply affordability. Spe-cifically, the standard is varied across different stages of processing because of difference in the severity of the risk in these areas and differ-ences in the cost of reducing the risk. Further reductions in the risk were clearly "capable of being done," and in fact many firms have already achieved cotton-dust levels well below those specified in the standard.[15]

Clearly, technological feasibility cannot be divorced from cost consid-erations, since almost any risk can be reduced at sufficiently large costs. Drivers, for example, would face a lower risk of injury in an auto acci-dent if everyone drove full-sized cars at speeds under 35 miles per hour. Such measures have not been undertaken, because the safety benefits do not justify the increased travel time and loss in fuel efficiency. Likewise, OSHA varied the cotton dust standard because the severity of cotton-dust exposures differs according to the stage of processing (because different types of fibers and dust are airborne at different stages) and because compliance costs differ.

Indeed, under the Reagan administration, OSHA began to routincly calculate the costs and benefits of its proposed regulations. The agency does not, however, explicitly compare these magnitudes when discussing the reasons for its policy recommendations. Inevitably, some compar-isons of this type are made by OSHA, the Office of Management and Budget, and other players in the regulatory process. There would be greater likelihood of balanced policies if the Supreme Court reversed its narrow and unrealistic interpretation of OSHA's mandate or if Congress amended OSHA's legislation. In the absence of such a change, primary emphasis will continue to be placed on the level of risk reduction rather than the associated costs. Regulations sometimes may impose costs that appear to be well out of line with any reasonable values, such as almost $70 million per expected life saved by the OSHA arsenic standards.

The Nature of OSHA Standards

The structure of OSHA's regulatory approach also has been overly restrictive, as the agency has adopted a narrow technology-based ap-proach to safety regulation. Ideally, OSHA should permit firms to achieve any given level of safety in the least expensive manner possible, consis-tent with having well-defined regulations that are enforceable. Instead,

OSHA has typically adopted uniform standards that attempt to prescribe the design of the workplace.

This orientation derives in part from the pattern set in OSHA's initial standard-setting activity. Shortly after beginning operations, OSHA issued over 4000 general industry standards for health and safety, the preponderance of which were safety-related. These standards, which continue to constitute most of OSHA's safety policies, were derived from the national consensus standards of the American National Standards Institute, the National Fire Protection Association, and some existing federal standards for maritime safety. In this process, OSHA converted a set of discretionary guidelines into a mandatory prescription for workplace design.

The upshot of this effort was to establish OSHA as a leading object of ridicule for its portable toilets for cowboys and other seemingly trivial standards. Perhaps more significant than these well-publicized OSHA horror stories was the specification character of the regulations. The OSHA handrail regulation specifies their required height (30 to 34 inches), spacing of posts (not to exceed 8 feet), thickness (at least 2 inches for hardwood and $1\frac{1}{2}$ inches for metal pipe), and clearance with respect to the wall or any other object (at least 3 inches).[16] Likewise, in its requirements for band guards for abrasive wheels, OSHA specifies the required thickness, the minimum diameter of rivets, and the maximum distance between the centers of rivets.[17]

In each case the specification standard approach may have imposed greater costs than equally effective alternatives. To provide guidelines for how such flexibility could be achieved, President Ford's Task Force on OSHA, headed by economist Paul MacAvoy, designed a model standard for machinery and machine guarding that indicated, for example, several ways to guard a punchpress.[18] This flexibility also may enhance the safety that could be achieved through a performance-oriented approach. A performance-oriented approach would stress the need for firms to achieve a particular health and safety level through whatever means they chose rather than be required to install a particular type of technology. The present OSHA specification standards are so narrowly defined that they pertain to only 15 percent of all machines.[19] This model standard has not yet been adopted, but it provides an operational example of how OSHA could achieve greater flexibility in its regulatory approach without jeopardizing worker safety.

It is also noteworthy that the primary orientation of the standards remains in the safety area. Externally visible aspects of the workplace, such as handrail width, are given comprehensive and meticulous treatment. In contrast, only a small fraction of the carcinogens in the workplace have been addressed by OSHA standards. There are some health standards, such as those for radiation exposure, but for the most part the standards have been dominated by safety concerns.

In view of the earlier discussion of market inadequacies, this emphasis seems misplaced. Health risks rather than safety risks are handled least effectively by the market. The greatest potential gains from OSHA regulation are likely to come from addressing the dimly understood health risks that pose the most severe difficulties for worker decision making.

Moreover, the structure of the health standards is also more likely to be conducive to more effective promotion of worker health. The health standards typically limit worker exposure rather than specifying particular technologies. For example, the cotton dust standard specifies permissible exposure limits to airborne concentrations of respirable cotton dust in different stages of processing, and it indicates the circumstances under which protective equipment must be worn. Respirators are needed during cleaning operations because of unusually high levels of cotton dust in that period. The standard does not specify how the lower levels of cotton dust are to be achieved, whether through use of exhaust fans, new machines for drawing and carding the cotton, or some other approach.

The Reform of OSHA Standards

Proposals for reforming OSHA standards have focused on three dimensions. The first recommendation is that there should be a shift in emphasis from safety to health. Second, there should be greater opportunities for firms to find less expensive techniques for promoting safety. Standards should consequently be more performance oriented when that is feasible. Finally, the level of the standards should be set in a more balanced fashion that attempts to recognize the health benefits to workers and the costs to firms.

Regulatory Reform Initiatives

Compared with its initial activity, OSHA's standard setting has been relatively modest in the past decade. During the Carter administration, much new regulation was stymied by the uncertainties caused by the court challenges of OSHA's legislative mandate in the cotton dust and benzene cases. The Reagan administration's emphasis was on slowing the pace of new regulation rather than changing its character, so that OSHA was less active than in its earlier years. Nevertheless, OSHA has not been completely dormant in the standards area.

Changes in OSHA Standards

The chief legacy of the Carter administration in the area of regulatory reform was its overhaul of the safety standards. The primary emphasis was not on a general restructuring of the standards approach but on eliminating those portions of the standards that were most extraneous and ill-conceived. This emphasis was quite appropriate, in view of the importance of establishing the agency's credibility. The Assistant Secretary of Labor for Occupational Safety and Health, Eula Bingham, eliminated or modified 928 OSHA regulations in all in October 1978. In many cases these changes were only editorial and had no major substantive impact. Nevertheless, the net effect of the elimination of the "nit-picking" features of OSHA regulation was to reduce some of the harsher criticisms of the agency's regulatory approach. Because of the magnitude of OSHA's initial credibility problem, the importance of even cosmetic changes in the standards should not be underestimated.

Chemical Labeling

The most important structural change in regulatory policy was OSHA's chemical labeling regulation, which was proposed at the end of the Carter administration and finalized by President Reagan.[20] By providing workers with information, this regulation represented an effort to use market forces to promote safety. The chief forms of information provision required were labels on the chemicals and a program for training workers in the handling of chemicals. This regulation addresses the primary source of market failure directly and, as a consequence, preserves the constructive aspects of the health-related decisions by firms and workers. In addition, the focus of the regulation is strongly oriented toward health hazards rather than safety risks.

Indeed, much of the impetus for this regulation came from the inability of direct regulatory controls to address the entire range of chemical hazards. Setting standards for all of the thousands of carcinogens in the workplace was viewed as unfeasible.

In addition to addressing long-term health impacts and acute health effects (for example, skin rashes from chemical exposures), the regulation also affects accidents from fires and explosions. These safety hazards also are likely to merit greater attention than more visible workplace characteristics, since the safety-related properties of chemicals will not be well understood in the absence of some information about risk.

The Economic Role of Hazard Warnings

The attractiveness of hazard warnings from an economic perspective is that they work in conjunction with market forces by eliminating the in-

Table 23.2
Workers' Response to Chemical Labeling

	Chemical Label			
	Sodium Bicarbonate	Chloroacetophenone	TNT	Asbestos
Change in fraction who consider job above average in risk	−35%	+45%	+63%	+58%
Annual wage increase demanded	$0	$1,900	$3,000	$5,200
Change in fraction very likely or somewhat likely to quit	−23%	+13%	+52%	+63%

Source: W. Kip Viscusi and Charles O'Connor, "Adaptive Responses to Chemical Labeling: Are Workers Bayesian Decision Makers?," *American Economic Review* 74, No. 5 (December 1984): 949. Reprinted by permission.

formational market failure directly. Moreover, in many instances it may be that altered worker actions are a more efficient means of promoting safety than technological changes in workplace conditions.

The manner in which hazard warnings exert their influence is reflected in the data in Table 23.2, which is based on reactions of workers in four major chemical plants to different hazard warnings. Each worker was shown a hazard warning for a particular chemical and was told that the chemical would replace the chemical with which the worker currently worked. In each case, the worker was shown a single warning, where the four different chemical labels used were for: sodium bicarbonate (household baking soda), chloroacetophenone (an industrial chemical that is an eye irritant), TNT (a well-known explosive), and asbestos (a leading occupational carcinogen). Workers were then asked a series of questions regarding their attitudes toward the job after it had been transformed in this manner.

The first row of statistics in Table 23.2 gives the change in the fraction of workers in the sample who viewed their jobs as being above average in risk after being given the hazard warning information. In the case of sodium bicarbonate, the fraction of the workers who viewed their job as above average in riskiness dropped by 35 percent, so that overall for the sample the workers all viewed their jobs as relatively safe. In contrast, for the remaining three chemicals there is a substantial increase in the fraction who believe that their jobs are risky, and this is particularly true in the case of the most severe hazards posed—asbestos and TNT. If the market operates efficiently, these risk perceptions in turn should lead to additional wage compensation for the jobs. Workers who were shown the sodium bicarbonate label did not require any additional wage compensation to work on the job, whereas workers shown the other three chemicals required amounts ranging from $1900 to $5200 per year in order to remain on the job. The final market mechanism discussed above is that if workers are not compensated sufficiently, they will quit. For this sample, if there were no change in the wage rate after the introduction of the hazard warning, quit rates would decline by 23 percent for sodium bicarbonate and would rise by up to 63 percent for workers who are exposed to asbestos. In terms of creating incentives for safety, hazard warnings serve to augment market forces by informing workers of the risks that they face. In addition, other studies of individual precautions indicate that hazard warnings are also likely to lead to increased precautions as individuals become better informed of the risks they face as well as the precautions needed to reduce these risks.

Effective Hazard Warnings

It should be emphasized that for these hazard warnings to be effective they must provide new information. Thus the source of the market failure is an information gap. Education efforts that are primarily efforts of persuasion and that attempt to browbeat individuals into changing their behavior have met with far less success.

Innovations in OSHA Regulation

The chief new safety standard under the Reagan administration is also noteworthy because it also marked a change in the character of OSHA regulation. That regulation consisted of a set of extensive rules intended to decrease the risks associated with grain handling.[21] These hazards are often well publicized, for explosions in grain-handling facilities may lead to the deaths of dozens of workers. Perhaps in part because of this publicity and the safety incentives created by the market and workers' compensation, there were no deaths from explosions in 1983.[22]

The 1984 OSHA regulation was intended to reduce this risk further by decreasing the dust levels in grain elevators, which in turn will reduce the risk of explosions. What is noteworthy about this standard is that firms are given several alternative options to decrease the dust: (1) to clean up the dust whenever it exceeds $\frac{1}{8}$ inch, (2) to clean up the dust at least once per shift, or (3) to use pneumatic dust-control equipment. This flexibility represented a major innovation in the design of OSHA safety standards. The regulation provides an opportunity for firms to select the most cost-effective option and will lead to lower compliance costs than would a uniform specification standard. OSHA's effort to use the advantage of a performance-oriented approach represents a significant, constructive contribution to OSHA policy development. Such efforts are likely to put us on the frontier of efficient regulatory policies.

Overall, there has not been a dramatic change in the structure of OSHA safety standards since OSHA's initial standard-setting efforts. Some of the extraneous and more frivolous standards have been pruned, other standards have been updated to take technological changes into account, and a few new standards have been added.

Further reform in standards that have already been promulgated is expected to be minimal, inasmuch as there is not a strong constituency for such changes. To the extent that more firms comply with the revisions of the OSHA standards, any impetus for relaxations or modifications of existing regulations will be diminished.

Some progress may be made regarding future standards in the form of greater recognition of the costs of the regulations and the introduction of innovative approaches to regulation. Two OSHA efforts of the 1980s—the chemical labeling standard and the grain-handling standard—represent significant advances in OSHA's regulatory approach. On balance, however, the level of activity in the standards area has not been great over the past decade, as OSHA has retained most of its original approach.

OSHA's Enforcement Strategy

To design and enforce its standards, OSHA now has over two thousand employees, ranking second behind the EPA among social-regulation agencies. This staff, in conjunction with the inspectors from states that choose to enforce OSHA regulations with state inspectors, come to the workplace, ascertain whether there are any violations, and penalize violators. The inspectors may return for a follow-up inspection, continuing to assess penalties until compliance is ensured.

Firms will choose to comply with OSHA standards if OSHA establishes effective financial incentives for doing so. The firm must consequently find it more attractive financially to make the safety improvements than to risk an adverse OSHA inspection. The penalties that result include fines levied by OSHA as well as possible adverse effects on the firm's reputation, which may in turn affect worker turnover or wages. To assess whether these safety incentives are strong, consider each link in the OSHA enforcement process.

Before OSHA can affect a firm's policies, it either must inspect the firm or create an effective threat of possible enforcement. OSHA undertakes four types of inspections: (1) inspections of imminent dangers, (2) inspections of fatalities and catastrophes, (3) investigations of worker complaints and referrals, and (4) programmed inspections.[23] This priority ranking has remained virtually unchanged since OSHA's inception. Somewhat surprisingly, complaint inspections produce few violations per inspection, which suggests that disgruntled workers may be using the OSHA inspection threat as a means of harassing the employer.[24] This pattern is unfortunate, since the role of workers and unions in promoting safety could potentially have been instrumental.

There have been five different eras of OSHA enforcement. The Nixon and Ford administrations established the general inspection approach, and there was little change in emphasis except for a gradual expansion in the enforcement effort. Under the Carter administration there was an attempt to eliminate some of the less productive aspects of the enforcement policy. The number of inspections and less important violations declined, and penalties for violations increased. The first term of the Reagan administration marked the start of what was termed a less confrontational approach. In effect, the inspection effort was scaled back. The Reagan administration also introduced more conscious inspection targeting. The biggest change was that the level of penalties assessed for OSHA violations plummeted. In the second Reagan term and in the Bush administration, the enforcement effort was not bolstered, with penalties at an all-time low. In the Clinton administration, the enforcement staff has remained sparse, but penalties have increased by several orders of magnitude. Fatalities now receive penalties that in some cases are on the order of several million dollars. This figure is comparable to the value of life and consequently will create strong deterrence effects.

Inspection Policies

The total number of inspections rose steadily through fiscal year 1976, after which it dropped by one-third as a result of the Carter administration's attempt to reduce the less productive inspections. The present level of inspections of below 70,000 annually may seem substantial, but it covers very few workplaces. At this rate of inspection an enterprise would be inspected less than once every two centuries.

Because many firms are small businesses with few employees, a more accurate index of coverage is the inspection rate per worker. At present, almost three million employees are covered annually by OSHA inspections. This figure represents the number of workers at sites covered by inspections, not the number of workers whose particular job conditions were analyzed. Yet even this generous estimate of OSHA coverage does not suggest a large-scale inspection effort, inasmuch as a worker at a site covered by an OSHA inspection will see an inspector only once every thirty-four years. In contrast, EPA inspects all major water polluters roughly once per year. Moreover, there has been a substantial drop in the rate of coverage of employees.

The drop in employee coverage may also reflect a failure of OSHA to target large firms sufficiently. During its early operations, OSHA was the object of criticism for focusing on small firms where few workers could be protected as a result of OSHA inspections.[25] This misallocation of resources diminished somewhat, as OSHA began to cite an equal number of violations per hour of inspection time in small firms as in large firms. Because more workers are affected per violation in large firms than small firms, some observers believe that this shift toward larger firms was still not sufficient. Under the Reagan administration the low level of employees covered by inspections led to suggestions that OSHA boost the coverage of large firms.

Two aspects of inspections that reflect desirable changes in emphasis pertain to the emphasis on health rather than safety and the emphasis on serious violations. Health violations merit relatively more attention, for there are greater inadequacies in the way these risks are treated. Safety risks are often well known to workers and generate compensating wage differentials, higher quit rates, and larger workers' compensation premiums—all of which establish incentives for firms to promote safety. In contrast, health hazards are less well understood and, because of difficulties in monitoring causality, are not covered as effectively by workers' compensation.

The role of health inspections doubled under the Carter administration, in part because the decline in overall inspections in fiscal year 1977 primarily represented a drop in safety inspections. The pattern through fiscal year 1981 was one of a gradual rise in the absolute number of health inspections. This increase was reversed under Reagan not so much because of a conscious decision to abandon the health area but because of the shift toward construction inspections, which are primarily safety-related.

Ideally, inspections also should identify serious violations rather than less consequential threats to worker safety. This emphasis on serious violations escalated considerably under the Carter administration, as almost one-third of all inspections began to generate serious violations. The frequency of serious violations under the Reagan administration was roughly the same as under the Carter administration.

Trivial Violations

On entering the workplace the OSHA inspector attempts to identify violations of OSHA standards for which he or she will assess penalties.

In determining whether a firm is in compliance an OSHA inspector cannot consider costs of meeting the standard, only technical feasibility.

In fiscal year 1977, when OSHA eliminated less important inspections and citations for trivial violations, there was a dramatic drop in the number of OSHA violations. Thereafter there has been a gradual and steady decline in the number of violations, with an additional small downward shift under Reagan. At present, each inspection results in just under two violations of OSHA standards. An important change has been the emphasis upon violations for serious threats to worker health.

OSHA Penalties

The ultimate determinant of the financial impact of an OSHA inspection is the amount of the penalties that are assessed for noncompliance. Notwithstanding the widespread notoriety of the enforcement effort, these penalty levels have always been inconsequential. Annual penalties have always been below $26 million and have often been below $10 million—roughly the same financial incentive created by the wage response to two additional deaths per year.

One change in the penalty structure occurred in the reforms of fiscal year 1977 when, at the insistence of Congress, OSHA eliminated penalties for firms with fewer than ten nonserious violations. The overall level of penalties, however, increased under the Carter administration to more than double its earlier level.

Under President Reagan, OSHA adopted a less confrontational approach in which penalties were well below their earlier levels. A particularly noteworthy change was that firms could obtain reductions in the assessed penalties by up to 30 percent if they made a serious effort to comply with the standards.

The resulting financial incentives for safety are not great. Penalties have long averaged about $50 per violation, though the Clinton administration has attempted to increase this level. In contrast, higher worker wages generated by job risks are $70 billion, and workers' compensation premiums are well in excess of $20 billion. OSHA enforcement efforts represent at best a modest addition to policies intended to promote workplace safety. These penalties are also dwarfed by the anticipated costs of compliance.

The level of the OSHA enforcement has declined by most measures of intensity, and this has been accomplished by a fundamental change in its character. Because of the reduction in penalties for firms that remedy OSHA violations, there is little threat from a random OSHA inspection. A firm need do little to promote safety, but simply await the OSHA inspector. The firm will avoid correcting safety problems that the inspector may not identify, and it will face few penalties if it makes the suggested changes. The elimination of the expected losses from inspections suggests that OSHA will have little impact on the great majority of firms that are not inspected, for inspections now have little deterrence value. Because the expected penalties have always been quite low, this loss may not be substantial, however.

Enforcement Targeting

In addition to changes in the level of OSHA enforcement, there have also been shifts in the focus of the enforcement effort. Perhaps the most controversial recent change in OSHA enforcement policies was the introduction of records-check inspections in October 1981. In these programmed safety inspections the OSHA inspector first examined the firm's lost workday accident rate for the past two years (three years for very small firms). If this rate was below the most recently available national manufacturing lost workday rate, the firm was not formally inspected. For example, a firm inspected in 1985 would have available its 1983 and 1984 lost-workday accident rates for comparison with the 1983 manufacturing rate, because there is a two-year lag in publishing the Bureau of Labor Statistics data.

Ideally, OSHA should target riskier firms. Inspecting these outliers provides greater opportunities for safety gains. Once the risk information has been acquired, it is clearly desirable to use the data to target OSHA inspections. Improved inspection targeting may have led to as much as a 50-percent increase in the citation rate per inspection. The OSHA procedure is not as sophisticated as it could be, however. From an economic standpoint, one would like to identify the risky outliers based on what is achievable within a particular context, which will depend on the costs of compliance for that industry. OSHA's procedure of targeting firms based on whether their record is better than the national manufacturing average does not incorporate this heterogeneity in the costs of promoting safety. A sawmill with an accident rate above the national manufacturing average may have a very safe technology for that industry, whereas a garment manufacturer with an injury rate just below the manufacturing average may be a high-risk outlier for that industry.

The changing character of the OSHA enforcement effort is exemplified as well by the change in the mix of violations cited by OSHA inspectors. Although the OSHA standards have not changed dramatically over the past decade, the role of different violation categories has undergone many significant modifications. In OSHA's initial years violations for walking and working surfaces (for example, misplaced exit signs) constituted about one-fifth of all violations. Many of these violations were for less important risks, some of which were readily visible to workers as well. The roughly 50 percent drop in this category suggests that OSHA's resources have been redirected from a less profitable area.

The two categories that displayed the greatest relative increases are health-related. The role of health and environmental control (for example, noise, ventilation, and radiation) has risen to 8 percent, and violations for toxic and hazardous substances (for example, asbestos and coke oven emissions) now include a similar amount. OSHA enforcement policies remain primarily safety-related, but health hazards no longer constitute a trivial portion of the enforcement effort.

The Impact of OSHA Enforcement on Worker Safety

Firms will choose to make the necessary investments in health and safety if the OSHA enforcement policy in conjunction with market incentives for safety makes it in the firm's financial self-interest to do so. More specifically, a firm will comply with an OSHA regulation if

$$
\begin{array}{cccc}
& & \text{Expected no.} & \text{Average} \\
\text{Expected cost} < \text{Probability} \times & \text{of violations} & \times & \text{penalty per} \\
\text{of compliance} & \text{inspection} & \text{per inspection} & \text{violation}
\end{array}
$$

As discussed, the three links in establishing these incentives—inspections, violations, and penalties—are all relatively weak. A firm has less than one chance in 200 of being inspected in any given year. If inspected, it expects to be found guilty of less than two violations of the standards, and for each violation the average penalty is under \$60. Overall, the financial cost per worker is just over fifty cents. A useful comparison is that market forces through compensating differentials in combination with workers' compensation premiums imposed costs in excess of \$800 per worker for the same time period. Quite simply, OSHA's enforcement effort is too modest to create truly effective financial incentives for safety.

The manner in which the safety incentives created by OSHA influence the decisions of firms can be seen by examining the payoffs from safety investments for a firm on a compliance-no compliance margin, which is illustrated in Figure 23.4. The curve ABC gives the payoffs to the firm from different levels of safety investment in the absence of OSHA policy. If there were no government regulation, the firm would choose the optimal level of safety, which is that at s_0, because that point yields the highest payoff on the curve ABC. Suppose now that OSHA standards

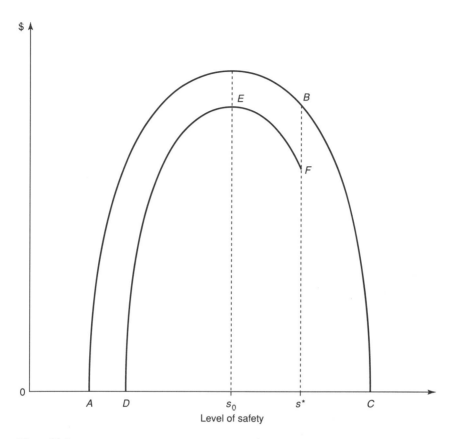

Figure 23.4
Payoffs to Safety Investments for a Marginal Firm

require a minimal safety level given by s^*, which is above the level at s_0 shown on the diagram. For safety levels below s^*, the firm will face an expected penalty level that will shift its curve downward, so that over what formerly was the payoff curve range AB, the firm's payoff levels now are given by DEF. If the firm invests enough in safety to achieve a safety level equal to or in excess of s^*, its payoff function will be given by BC as before. The real issue from the standpoint of compliance is whether the OSHA enforcement effort is sufficiently stringent so that the expected cost of noncompliance shifts the firm's payoffs downward sufficiently to make compliance worthwhile. In this example, the highest payoff the firm can get from complying with the standard will be at point B, whereas the highest payoff that the firm can get from noncompliance will be at point E. For the case shown, the expected costs of noncompliance are sufficient to induce the firm to choose to invest in greater safety.

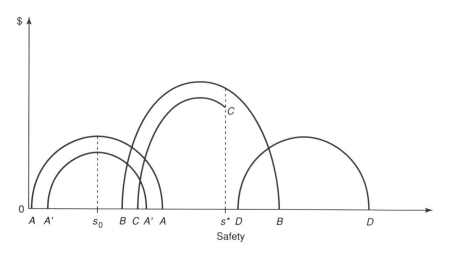

Figure 23.5
Payoffs for Safety Investment to Heterogeneous Group of Firms

OSHA Regulations in Different Situations

This need not always be the case. In particular, as the three situations in Figure 23.5 indicate, there are three broad classes of situations that can arise. In the first case, a firm initially has a payoff curve AA, which is shifted downward to $A'A'$ once OSHA penalties are introduced for safety levels below s^*. That firm will continue to choose safety level s_a, because in this diagram the firm's safety level is so far below that needed to achieve compliance that it would not be feasible or desirable for the firm to comply with the standard. In the intermediate case, the firm's initial payoff curve is given by BB, which shifts downward to CC. For that firm, the standard will be sufficient to induce compliance, because the downward shift in payoffs introduced by the additional expected penalties has given the firm enough of a financial incentive to make additional investments in safety up to the standard worthwhile. The final situation, given by the payoff curve DD, represents a situation of a firm that already is in compliance with the standard, so that OSHA regulation will be irrelevant to its conduct.

What Figure 23.5 illustrates is that in general there will be three classes of firms. For two of these classes, firms that are already in compliance with the standard and firms that are substantially below the safety level required, one would expect little effect from the regulation. Effective enforcement in terms of raising the expected penalties for noncompliance is essential, inasmuch as that will drive the extent to which there is a substantial population of firms who will choose to comply with the regulation. Moreover, the level of stringency of the regulation is also of consequence, because if a regulation is very tight many firms will choose not to comply at all, so that a very tight regulation that is ignored may actually produce less of a beneficial safety effect than a more modest regulation for which compliance is feasible.[26] In terms of its regulatory strategy, OSHA in effect may have adopted a strategy that was doomed to fail—stringent regulations coupled with weak enforcement.

OSHA and Other Factors Affecting Injuries

Because of these limitations and the weakness of the OSHA enforcement effort, it is not surprising that OSHA has no dramatic effect on workplace safety. Not all workplace injuries are due to factors under OSHA's influence. Many accidents stem from aspects of the work process other than the specific technological characteristics regulated by OSHA. That most workplace risks have not been readily amenable to the influence of OSHA regulations is in stark contrast to the optimistic projections of the framers of OSHA's legislative mandate, who anticipated a 50 percent drop in workplace risks.[27]

The chief contributing factor relates to worker actions. Although the estimates of the role of the worker in causing accidents vary, in part because of the difficulty in assigning accidents caused jointly by worker actions and technological deficiencies, it is clear that worker actions play a substantial role. OSHA found that over half of all fatal accidents on oil/gas well drilling rigs were caused by poor operating procedures, and worker actions also have been found to be a major contributor to 63 percent of the National Safety Council's accident measure, 45 percent of Wisconsin workers' compensation cases, and the majority of accidents among deep-sea divers in the North Sea.

Recent studies reinforce the view that at best OSHA regulations could have a significant but not dramatic effect on workplace safety. One recent statistical analysis estimated that if there were full compliance with OSHA standards, workplace accidents would drop by just under 10 percent.[28] A recent detailed analysis of workplace accidents in California presented somewhat more optimistic conclusions. At most, 50 percent of all fatal accidents were contributed to by violations of OSHA standards that potentially could have been detected by an OSHA inspector visiting the day before the accident.[29]

Because even a fully effective set of OSHA regulations would not revolutionize workplace safety, it is appropriate to take a more cautious view of the prospective effects of OSHA regulation than did the original framers of the Occupational Safety and Health Act. The critical economic issue is whether OSHA regulation has had any beneficial effect on safety. Agency officials at OSHA as well as other safety-related agencies frequently point to improvements in accident-rate trends as evidence of the efficacy of their agency. There are two difficulties with this approach. First, there may be year-to-year changes in risk levels for reasons wholly unrelated to changes in safety standards or their enforcement, such as cyclical fluctuations. More important is that there has been a long-run trend toward safety improvements throughout this century as a result of the increased wealth of American society and the increased demand for safety that we have placed on our social institutions. Thus, even in the absence of any government regulation, one would have expected a safety improvement as a result of society's increased affluence.

The extent to which there has been such a safety trend is evidenced in the death rate statistics sketched in Figure 23.6. The death risk for American workers dropped from 15.8/100,000 workers in 1928 to 6.8/ 100,000 workers in 1970, more than a 50 percent decline, and these improvements were achieved before the existence of OSHA. In the post-OSHA era these improvements have continued, as the risk level in 1987 was 4.6 deaths per 100,000 workers. The appropriate test of the agency's

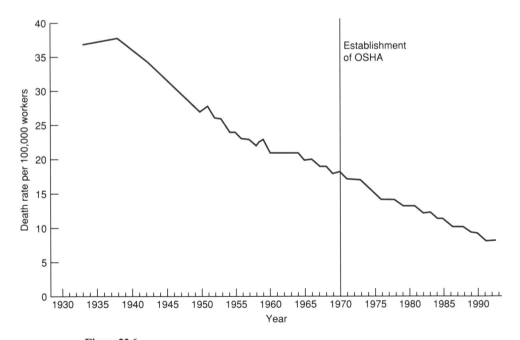

Figure 23.6
Death Rate Trends for Job-Related Accidents

Source: National Safety Council (1994). *Accident Facts, 1994 Edition* (Itasca, Ill.: National Safety Council), pp. 34, 37.

effectiveness is whether OSHA has shifted this trend in any demonstrable fashion, controlling for determinants of accident rates other than
occupational safety and health regulation.

The methodology for approaching this issue is illustrated in Figure
23.7, which presents a stylized view of the statistical tests. The curve *AB*
represents the injury trend before the establishment of OSHA, and the
curve *BC* represents the predicted trend in injuries after OSHA, had
there been no safety regulations in place. Similarly, the curve *BC* represents the actual trend that injuries have had. If there is no statistically
significant difference between the actual and predicted injury trend, then
the agency has not had the intended effect. It is the vertical spread between *BC* and *BD* that represents the incremental effect of the agency on
the injury rate, not the extent to which the injury level at point *D* lies
below point *B* at the establishment of the agency, because much or all of
the injury decline may have occurred in the absence of the agency.

Determining OSHA's Impact on Safety

Two approaches can be used to ascertain the efficacy of the agency.
Under the first, one estimates the equation to characterize the injury-

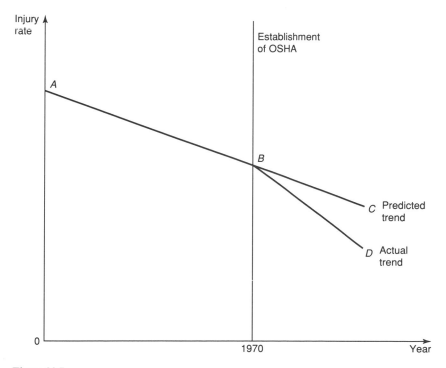

Figure 23.7
Statistical Tests for the Effect of OSHA

rate performance during a pre-OSHA era, which is the injury-rate trend given by AB. One such model that could be used to estimate this relationship would be

$$\text{RISK}_t = \alpha + \beta_1 \text{ RISK}_{t-1} + \beta_2 \text{ Cyclical Effects}_t$$

$$+ \beta_3 \text{ Industry Characteristics}_t$$

$$+ \beta_4 \text{ Worker Characteristics}_t + \varepsilon \qquad (23.1)$$

The dependent variable in the analysis is the risk level in some year t, which will be determined by the series of variables on the right side of the equation. The risk level in the previous year is influential, inasmuch as it is a proxy for the character of the technology of the industry, and typically this lagged risk level has a positive effect. Cyclical effects are also pertinent because accident rates generally move procyclically as additional shifts of workers are added, new hires are added to the work-force, and the pace of work is increased. Industry characteristics are also consequential because the mix of industries in the economy and factors such as the presence of unionization may be influential. Principal worker characteristics include the experience mix of the work force. Once an equation such as (23.1) has been estimated, one can use the fitted value of this equation to project out the accident-rate trend BC in Figure 23.7 and this predicted trend can be compared with the actual observed risk levels along BD to determine whether the agency has, in effect, shifted the injury rate downward.

The main prerequisite to using this postregulation simulation approach is that one must have a substantial period of preregulation data to do so. Although this is the case for overall accidental death statistics presented in Figure 23.6, all data series gathered by the U.S. Bureau of Labor Statistics on an industry-specific basis changed after the advent of OSHA, so that no preregulation and postregulation comparison is possible. In this situation, one can adopt an alternative approach in which one estimates an equation using only data from the postregulatory period. Equation (23.2) summarizes such a model:

$$\text{RISK}_t = \alpha + \beta_1 \text{ RISK}_{t-1} + \beta_2 \text{ Cyclical Effects}_t$$

$$+ \beta_3 \text{ Industry Characteristics}_t$$

$$+ \beta_4 \text{ Worker Characteristics}_t + \beta_5 \sum_{i=0}^{n} \text{OSHA}_{t-1} + \varepsilon \qquad (23.2)$$

This equation is the same as the preregulation simulation equation (23.1) except for two differences. First, it will be estimated using the postregulation data rather than the preregulation data. Second, it includes variables that capture measures of the effect of the regulation, where the principal variables that have been used in the literature pertain to the rate of OSHA inspections for the expected penalty level. The equation indicated that a distributed lag on the OSHA variable has been included to recognize the fact that it may take some time for an OSHA inspection to have an effect. Health and safety investments that require capital investments on the part of the firm take some delay before they can be made, so that it would be unrealistic to assume that OSHA regulations will always have a contemporaneous effect. In practice, most studies have indicated that to the extent that OSHA has an effect it is with a one-year lag.

Mixed Opinions Regarding OSHA's Impact

The general consensus of the econometric studies is that there is no evidence of a substantial impact of OSHA. Viscusi analyzed the 1972–1975 period and failed to find any significant OSHA impact.[30] Smith found a drop in the lost workday rate at firms inspected in 1973, but not for firms inspected in 1974.[31] A replication of Smith's analysis by McCaffrey for the 1976–1978 period failed to yield any significant effects on manufacturing firms.[32] Similarly, Bartel and Thomas's analysis of the 1974–1978 experience did not reveal any significant OSHA impacts.[33] Mendeloff's analysis of the California workers' compensation records from 1947 to 1974 likewise produced mixed results, as some risk levels rose and others declined.[34] The strongest published evidence of OSHA's efficacy is by Cooke and Gautschi, who found a significant drop in lost workdays because of accidents in Maine manufacturing firms from 1970 to 1976.[35] A more recent study by Viscusi of the 1973–1983 period suggested that there may have been a modest decline in the rate of accidents as a result of OSHA enforcement, although this effect was not great.[36] The greatest effect appears to be in the most severe category of injuries, for OSHA regulations have reduced the total number of lost workdays due to injuries by 5–6 percent. The OSHA policy variable that seemed most instrumental was the rate of OSHA inspections rather than the penalty level. The degree of OSHA's presence in the workplace and the threat of penalties for continued noncompliance appear to be the fundamental determinants of OSHA's impact.

Ruser and Smith similarly found that the recent OSHA efforts had a beneficial effect. They estimate that the records-check inspections of the early 1980s decreased injuries by 5–14 percent.[37] Evidence reported by Scholz and Gray for 1979–1985 also indicated significant OSHA effects.[38]

The possibility of a favorable impact of OSHA on workplace conditions is also borne out in more refined studies of workplace standards. One case study is that of the OSHA cotton-dust standard, which was the subject of a Supreme Court decision. That standard was directed at controlling cotton-dust exposures in the workplace, because these exposures lead to potentially disabling lung diseases. The promulgation of such a regulation was viewed by the business world as a dramatic event, as there were severe stock-market repercussions of the various regulatory events that were involved in the issuance of the regulation. Overall, an event study analysis indicates that the market value of the cotton firm fell by 23 percent in response to the cotton-dust standard.[39] If it was expected that firms would be able to completely ignore the regulation, then no market effect would have been observed. A major reason for the expected compliance with the regulation was that the controversy surrounding it as well as the vigorous action by the union involved in this particular instance ensured that the cotton dust standard would be a prominent target of OSHA enforcement.

Although compliance with the cotton-dust standard was not required until 1984, by the end of 1982 the majority of the exposed workers were in work situations in compliance with OSHA standards. Firms' investments in cotton-dust controls from 1978 to 1982 will lead to an annual reduction of about six thousand cases of byssinosis (a lung disease) annually. The standard remains controversial, however, because it is a costly means for promoting worker health. For example, the cost per case year of total disability prevented has been estimated at $1.2 million.

In addition, there remain a number of advocates of the greater use of more performance-oriented alternatives to control cotton. One possible policy alternative is to require the use of lightweight dust masks for low-to-moderate cotton-dust levels, which would produce the same benefits as engineering controls at negligible cost. Because byssinosis is a progressive disease that moves through a series of grades and is reversible in its early stages, disposable masks could be coupled with a worker rotation policy. Only for severe cotton-dust levels would respirators or engineering controls be required. To date, protective equipment alternatives have not been treated as a viable policy option because of union opposition to such efforts.

The available empirical results for the overall OSHA impact and in the cotton dust case suggest that OSHA enforcement efforts may be beginning to enhance workplace safety. An improvement over the early OSHA experience should be expected, as the standards have been refined and there is more systematic targeting of the inspection effort.

Agenda for Policy Reform Efforts

Even with a reform of its policies, OSHA will not be the dominant force influencing worker safety. The role of the market in determining safety will continue to be instrumental. OSHA can augment the existing forces for safety, but even full compliance with all current OSHA regulations or those likely to be promulgated will not markedly reduce workplace risks. The no-risk society that some might envision as OSHA's ultimate goal is simply unattainable.

Nevertheless, constructive reform of OSHA could enable this agency better to foster the interests of workers and at the same time diminish the associated burden on society. A number of specific reforms have been advocated in the literature. Rather than review each of these proposals, the following focuses on changes for which there is likely to be a broad consensus about the nature of OSHA's inadequacy or the proposed remedy.

The first area of proposed reform concerns the area of emphasis. In over two decades of regulation, OSHA policies have exhibited a slight shift toward health but have remained largely safety oriented. The emphasis of both the structure of new regulations and OSHA enforcement has continued to be predominantly in the safety area. This emphasis is misplaced, for market forces are better equipped to address safety risks through compensating differentials and related mechanisms. In addition, the incentives created by workers' compensation premiums already augment to some extent the market incentives for safety. Health hazards are handled less adequately by both the market and workers' compensation. Moreover, the coupling of substantial uncertainties with low probability events involving potentially catastrophic outcomes makes health risks a promising target for governmental regulation.

A second class of reforms is to ensure that we are "on the frontier" of efficient policies; that is, that we are achieving as much health and safety improvement as possible for the costs imposed. Much of the adverse reaction to OSHA's initial wave of regulations of toilet-seat shapes and the like stemmed largely from the belief that the regulatory mechanisms had not been well chosen. Much more beneficial improvements in safety and health could have been achieved if OSHA had focused its efforts on issues of more consequence.

Some of the most extraneous features of OSHA policy have been pruned, but there is continued need in all regulatory contexts to find ways to promote safety at less cost. The use of performance standards rather than narrowly defined specification standards could, for example, enable firms to select the cheapest means of achieving the health and safety objective. Such flexibility would reduce compliance costs and increase the incentive of firms to develop innovative technologies to foster health and safety. Moreover, if structured appropriately, as in the grain-dust standard, a performance standard need not greatly increase firms' uncertainty whether they are in compliance.

The final reform target is to strike a more explicit balance between the health improvements and the costs imposed on society. Labor-market estimates of the value of life are now being used to provide guidance in terms of the appropriate tradeoff. Such exercises remain controversial, but the need for making some kinds of tradeoffs is apparent. It is unlikely that economic research will soon be able to pinpoint the compensatory value of a case of cancer, decreased lung-function capacity, or a partial work disability. Nevertheless, if policymakers viewed regulatory alternatives in light of the cost per health benefit achieved, they would at least confront explicitly the nature of the tradeoffs and ideally would pursue only those policies that they judged to be in society's best interest.

Although reforming OSHA's regulatory strategy remains a major item on any agenda of important regulatory reforms, it would be an oversimplification to say that OSHA has not improved its efforts over the past decade. The agency has introduced several promising new regulations, has eliminated some of the worst initial regulations, and has better targeted enforcement efforts than they once did.

The future of OSHA policies no doubt will continue to exhibit the need for reflecting the three classes of reform elements suggested above, for they are at the heart of any regulatory strategy for workplace health and safety. As a result, complete regulatory reform will never be achieved with the same finality as economic regulation, where, for example, deregulation has transformed the airline industry into what some observers consider to be a more competitive situation. The need in the health and safety area is for better regulation, not deregulation, and opportunities for improvement will always remain.

Questions and Problems

1. What are the rationales for occupational safety and health regulation? Does the existence of compensating differentials for risk imply that there is no rationale for regulation? What if we also knew that workers have perfect information regarding the risks they faced and markets worked competitively? Could you think of any other possible rationale for intervention?

2. OSHA inspectors could guarantee compliance by imposing infinite penalty amounts on firms that did not comply with their regulations. If arbi-

trarily large penalties were permitted by OSHA's legislation, would it be desirable to adopt such penalties? What are the factors that you would want to consider in establishing the penalty level?

3. Suppose that a technological innovation has made it easier for firms to provide a safe work environment. How would you illustrate this effect using the diagram in Figure 23.2? Can we tell whether safety expenditures will rise or fall after such a shift?

4. OSHA and other regulatory agencies have typically followed a specification standard approach rather than a performance-oriented approach. What are the considerations that make a technology orientation attractive to government officials even though they have not found great favor among economists?

5. When setting the optimal penalty level for noncompliance for the regulation, should the regulatory agency vary the penalty with firm size? Should the profitability of the company be a concern?

6. Suppose that there are different types of firms in the industry, old firms and new firms. Suppose that old firms have existing technologies for which it is more costly to adopt risk reducing innovations, whereas new firms can incorporate these innovations in their new plant investments. Illustrate using a variant of Figure 23.2 how the optimal safety level will differ in these two different situations. Should there be heterogeneity in the standards set by regulatory agencies?

7. Economists frequently advocate the use of personal protective equipment, such as gas masks and ear muffs, as less costly solutions for promoting worker safety. These cost considerations typically focus only on the purchase cost of the equipment. What other cost components are associated with personal protective equipment that might make engineering controls a more attractive alternative?

8. New information becomes available pertaining to potential safety innovations on a very regular basis. There are always new potential engineering controls that could be adopted by OSHA. Yet the agency tends to vary its standards very little over time. Can you think of any economic rationales for having a relatively stable regulatory regime even in the presence of technological changes that might enhance safety?

Notes

1. Section 26 of the Occupational Safety and Health Act of 1970, 29 U.S.C. 651 (1976).

2. For an early critique of OSHA, see Albert Nichols and Richard Zeckhauser, "OSHA After a Decade: A Time for Reason," in Leonard W. Weiss and Michael W. Klass (eds.), *Case Studies in Regulation: Revolution and Reform* (Boston: Little, Brown, 1981), pp. 202–34. Other earlier critiques of OSHA's efforts include Walter Oi, "On Evaluating the Effectiveness of the OSHA Inspection Program," unpublished manuscript, University of Rochester, 1975; Robert S. Smith, *The Occupational Safety and Health Act: Its Goals and Achievements* (Washington, D.C.: American Enterprise Institute, 1976); John Mendeloff, *Regulating Safety: An Economic and Political Analysis of Occupational Safety and Health Policy*

(Cambridge: MIT Press, 1979); Lawrence Bacow, *Bargaining for Job Safety and Health* (Cambridge: MIT Press, 1980); and W. Kip Viscusi, *Risk by Choice: Regulating Health and Safety in the Workplace* (Cambridge: Harvard University Press, 1983). See W. Kip Viscusi, *Fatal Tradeoffs* (New York: Oxford University Press, 1992) for a review of the evidence on OSHA's impact.

3. Adam Smith, *The Wealth of Nations* (New York: Modern Library, 1937).

4. See Joni Hersch and W. Kip Viscusi, "Cigarette Smoking, Seatbelt Use, and Differences in Wage-Risk Trade-Offs," *Journal of Human Resources* 25, No. 2 (1990): 202–227.

5. These calculations were made by the authors using data from Richard Wilson, "Analyzing the Daily Risks of Life," *Technology Review* 81, No. 4 (1979): 40–46.

6. W. Kip Viscusi, *Employment Hazards: An Investigation of Market Performance* (Cambridge, Mass.: Harvard University Press, 1979).

7. W. Kip Viscusi and Charles O'Connor, "Adaptive Responses to Chemical Labeling: Are Workers Bayesian Decision Makers?" *American Economic Review* 74, No. 5 (1984): 942–56.

8. The health risks were in effect excluded by informing one subsample of the workers that the chemicals with which they worked would be replaced by sodium bicarbonate (household baking soda).

9. See Viscusi, 1983.

10. This discussion is based on W. Kip Viscusi, *Employment Hazards: An Investigation of Market Performance* (Cambridge: Harvard University Press, 1979), and W. Kip Viscusi, *Risk by Choice* (Cambridge, Mass.: Harvard University Press, 1983).

11. For a diverse set of essays on the empirical aspects of decisions under uncertainty, see Daniel Kahneman, Paul Slovic, and Amos Tversky (eds.), *Judgment and Uncertainty: Heuristics and Biases* (Cambridge: Cambridge University Press, 1982).

12. Section 3b, part 7 of 29 U.S.C. 651 (1976).

13. Industrial Union Department, AFL-CIO v. American Petroleum Institute, 448 U.S. 607 (1980).

14. American Textile Manufacturers Institute v. Donovan, 452 U.S. 490 (1981).

15. Centaur Associates, *Technical and Economic Analysis of Regulating Occupational Exposure to Cotton Dust*, Report to the Occupational Safety and Health Administration, 1983, pp. 1–4.

16. 29 CFR Part 1910.23.

17. 29 CFR Part 1910.215.

18. Paul MacAvoy (ed.), *OSHA Safety Regulation: Report of the Presidential Task Force* (Washington, D.C.: American Enterprise Institute, 1977).

19. Ibid., preface.

20. Federal Register 48, 228 (November 28, 1983): 43280.

21. Federal Register 29, 4 (January 6, 1984): 996–1008.

22. Office of Management and Budget, Executive Office of the President, *OSHA's Proposed Standards for Grain Handling Facilities, April 1984*, p. 17. Because of the random nature of major explosions, however, one should not conclude that the risk has been eliminated.

23. OSHA, Field Operations Manual II-3 (January 27, 1984).

24. U.S. Department of Labor, Assistant Secretary for Policy Evaluation and Research, *Compliance with Standards, Abatement of Violations, and Effectiveness of OSHA Safety Inspections*, Technical Analysis Paper No. 62, 1980.

25. Walter Oi, "On Evaluating the Effectiveness of the OSHA Inspection Program," working paper, University of Rochester, 1975.

26. W. Kip Viscusi and Richard J. Zeckhauser, "Optimal Standards with Incomplete Enforcement," *Public Policy* 26 (1979): 437–56.

27. See Nichols and Zeckhauser, 1981, p. 202.

28. Ann Bartel and Lacy Thomas, "Direct and Indirect Effects of Regulation," *Journal of Law and Economics*, 1985.

29. John Mendeloff, "The Role of OSHA Violations in Serious Workplace Accidents," *Journal of Occupational Medicine*, 1984.

30. W. Kip Viscusi, "The Impact of Occupational Safety and Health Regulation," *Bell Journal of Economics* 10, No. 1 (1979): 117–40.

31. Robert S. Smith, "The Impact of OSHA Inspections on Manufacturing Injury Rates," *Journal of Human Resources* 14 (1979): 145–70.

32. David McCaffrey, "An Assessment of OSHA's Recent Effects on Injury Rates," *Journal of Human Resources* 18, No. 1 (1983): 131–46.

33. Ann Bartel and Lacy Thomas, 1985.

34. John Mendeloff, *Regulating Safety: An Economic and Political Analysis of Occupational Safety and Health Policy* (Cambridge, Mass.: MIT Press, 1979).

35. William Cooke and Frederick Gautschi, "OSHA, Plant Safety Programs, and Injury Reduction," *Industrial Relations* 20, No. 3 (1981): 245–57.

36. W. Kip Viscusi, "The Impact of Occupational Safety and Health Regulation, 1973–1983," *Rand Journal of Economics* 29 (1986): 29–60.

37. John Ruser and Robert S. Smith, "The Effect of OSHA Records Check Inspections on Reported Occupational Injuries in Manufacturing Establishments," *Journal of Risk and Uncertainty* 1, No. 4 (1988): 415–35.

38. John T. Scholz and Wayne B. Gray, "OSHA Enforcement and Workplace Injuries: A Behavioral Approach to Risk Assessment," *Journal of Risk and Uncertainty* 3, No. 3 (1990): 283–305.

39. John S. Hughes, Wesley A. Magat, and William E. Ricks, "The Economic Consequences of the OSHA Cotton Dust Standards: An Analysis of Stock Price Behavior," *Journal of Law and Economics* 29 (1986): 29–60.

In Chapter 4 we discussed the importance of technical progress (or dynamic efficiency) in comparison to static efficiency. It was observed that an economy may have to tolerate market power that stimulates or results from technical change if a rapidly rising standard of living is desired. In this chapter, we focus on the economics of patents and their role in one of the most technologically progressive U.S. industries: pharmaceuticals. It is generally believed that patents are more important in pharmaceuticals and chemicals than in any other industries. Pharmaceuticals is also an industry in which there is current controversy about this very tradeoff—some argue that its profits and prices are excessive, and others warn that policies to curb prices will likely harm the innovativeness of one of America's most progressive industries.[1]

There are two main sections in this chapter. In the first section, the economics of patents in providing incentives for innovation will be discussed. Both positive and normative lines of analysis will be pursued. It should not be surprising that a definitive set of results does not exist. For example, there are some market factors that make for too little investment in inventive activities, and others that make for too much—from a welfare point of view. Nevertheless, economic analysis can be quite instructive for policy purposes in certain cases.

The second half of this chapter is a case study of the U.S. pharmaceutical industry with a particular emphasis on the role of patents. A principal topic is an examination of a 1984 law that increased the life of patents in the pharmaceutical industry while simultaneously easing entry conditions faced by imitators.

Economics of Invention and Patents

In an important article in 1962, Nobel laureate Kenneth Arrow explored the problems created for the market by inventive activity. Arrow observed that the product of inventive activity is new knowledge, or information. For example, after spending $200 million on research, a pharmaceutical firm might come up with the chemical structure of an important new drug. In principle, the information is extremely valuable and may be worth more than $200 million in terms of future revenues. However, the point here is that the product of the research and development (R&D) is simply knowledge of the chemical structure. This knowledge, or information, can often be described completely in a short document of five to ten pages!

As Arrow has explained,

Information is a commodity with peculiar attributes, particularly embarassing for the achievement of optimal allocation. In the first place, any information obtained, say a new method of production, should, from the welfare point of view, be available free of charge (apart from the cost of transmitting information). This insures optimal utilization of the information but of course provides no incentive for investment in research.... In a free enterprise economy, inventive activity is supported by using the invention to create property rights; precisely to the extent that it is successful, there is an underutilization of the information.[2]

One difficulty is the problem that the inventor has in appropriating the economic value of the invention. Because what is possessed is information, the problem is how to sell the information. Suppose the inventor discovers an important drug, Panacea. The inventor could keep the chemical structure secret and try selling the drug as a cure for certain diseases. But a rival could easily buy a few pills, hire a chemist to figure out the structure, and begin selling exact copies at a lower price. In such a case, the inventor would not appropriate all of the economic benefits of the invention; rivals would share in the rewards although having invested very little. From a social point of view, this situation would result in too little investment in inventive activity.

Of course, if the inventor could obtain a legal right to exclusive use of Panacea—a patent—then the problem is partially resolved. The patent gives the inventor property rights to the invention for a fixed period of time. But, as Arrow has described, patents cannot solve all problems of appropriability:

Suppose, as a result of elaborate tests, some metal is discovered to have a desirable property, say resistance to high heat. Then of course every use of the metal for which this property is relevant would also use this information, and the user would be made to pay for it. But, even more, if another inventor is stimulated to examine chemically related metals for heat resistance, he is using the information already discovered and should pay for it in some measure; and any beneficiary of his discoveries should also pay.[3]

If the inventor cannot expect to appropriate all of the economic value of the invention, there will be underinvestment in inventive activity. The real quandary though is raised when we consider the optimal *use* of the information. Now the argument is that the price of the information should be zero, implying that the inventor would appropriate none of the economic value of the invention!

The argument that the price of the information should be zero follows from the fact that its marginal cost is zero. Once the information exists, any number of people can "consume" it without any cost to anyone else. Anyone who would derive any benefit whatsoever from the information should be permitted to use it freely; if not, the information would not be used efficiently.

Clearly, firms would not invest in inventions without expectations of rewards. Arrow suggested one way out of the dilemma: "In an ideal socialistic economy, the reward for invention would be completely separated from any charge to the users of the information."[4] That is, "prizes" could be given by the government to successful inventors, with the understanding that the inventions would be freely available to all. In response to this suggestion, Harold Demsetz observed that there would be serious problems in implementing a system of prizes. "How would such a system produce information on the desired direction of investment and on the quantities of resources that should be committed to invention?"[5] Similar problems would exist if the government implemented a system of subsidizing or contracting with firms to undertake research deemed worthy by the government.

Patents, then, can be regarded as one way of achieving a balance between appropriability and use. In brief, a long patent life (by giving the inventor a monopoly of long duration) favors appropriability at the expense of use. That is, optimal use is not achieved during the patent life because of pricing above marginal cost. On the other hand, a short patent life favors use at the expense of appropriability—with the result being levels of investment that are too low. Hence, a "second best" patent life lies somewhere in between. Later in this section we will consider a model of the optimal patent life in detail.

Background on Patents

A patent is an exclusive right to one's invention. In the United States, the right lasts for twenty years. Basically, either products or processes can be patented; an idea itself cannot be patented unless it is applied. To obtain a patent, the inventor must make an application to the U.S Patent and Trademark Office. The Patent Office must be satisfied that the invention is *new, useful, and non-obvious*. The twenty-year life begins when the patent application is made. In most other countries the patent life is twenty years also.

The idea of patents is quite old; the first patent law was adopted by the Republic of Venice in 1474, and the first U.S. patent statute was enacted in 1790. The usual rationale for the patent includes the belief that the inventor is entitled to his or her discovery, that the patent is a device for promoting invention, and that the patent system encourages inventors to disclose their inventions to others. The granting of a patent in itself does not ensure the inventor exclusive rights. Rather, the inventor must bring suit against anyone who infringes the patent, and the courts then make the final determination of the validity of the patent.

Although patents are technically issued only to individuals, many large corporations engaged in R&D require their employees to assign the right to any invention that they make to the company. Less than a quarter of the patents issued today are assigned to individual inventors.

The holder of a patent may either make sole use of the discovery or license others to use the invention at a mutually agreed-on royalty rate. For example, General Electric once licensed Westinghouse to produce electric lamps at a royalty rate of 2 percent of Westinghouse's sales revenues. The rate jumped up to 30 percent once a certain level of revenues was reached.

Incentives to Invent: Monopoly versus Competition

In this section[6] we consider the following limited question. Assume that an industry can be organized either competitively or as a monopoly. In either case, assume that a single inventor is considering investing in R&D in order to achieve a cost reducing[7] invention of a particular size. The inventor is not concerned about competition from other inventors, and complete protection from imitation is assumed. In the competitive case, the inventor has an infinitely lived patent; and, in the monopoly case, the inventor *is* the monopolist and entry is completely barred.

Minor Invention Case

Figure 24.1 shows both the competitive industry and the monopoly for the case of a minor[8] invention. That is, the original equilibria for both cases is based on a constant cost of production C_0 and the demand DD'. Hence, the competitive industry equilibrium before the invention is at price P_0 and quantity Q_0, where demand and the constant cost supply curve intersect. The original monopoly equilibrium is determined by the intersection of marginal revenue, DJ, and marginal cost (constant at C_0), or at the quantity M_0, yielding price P_m.

First, we focus on the incentive to the inventor in the competitive industry. What royalty rate (expressed in dollars per unit output) would maximize the inventor's total royalty if the invention lowers cost from C_0 to C_1? Analytically, we can proceed in either of two equivalent ways. The derived demand for the patent could be determined,[9] or the inventor could be assumed to monopolize the industry (because the inventor alone has access to the lower cost process). Because the second method is analytically a bit simpler, we will use it.

The monopolist-inventor in the competitive industry would face a kinked demand curve, P_0AD'. The price could not be set above C_0 or the existing firms would find it profitable to compete. Thus the maximum price for output levels up to Q_0 would be P_0 (or just a bit below),

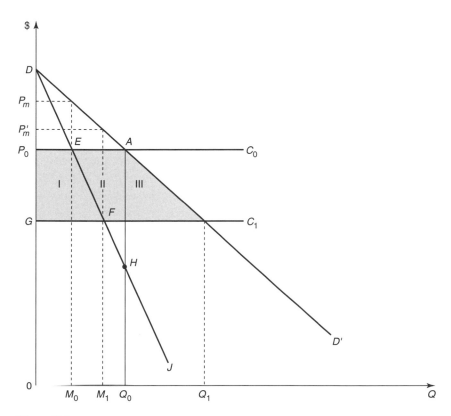

Figure 24.1
Incentives to Invent in Monopoly and Competition: Minor Invention Case

and above that output level the market demand curve would be the relevant demand. The marginal revenue curve would be P_0AHJ, with the usual vertical discontinuity at the kink. Hence, the monopolist-inventor would choose price P_0 and output Q_0, because marginal revenue intersects marginal cost (C_1) at this output.

We pause for a moment to distinguish exactly what the difference is between a minor invention and a major invention. Notice in Figure 24.1 that the marginal cost C_1 lies within the "gap" AH of the marginal revenue curve. This insures that the quantity Q_0 remains unchanged after the invention. However, if the marginal cost C_1 should be so low as to intersect the HJ segment of the marginal revenue curve, then the monopolist-inventor's quantity would be larger than Q_0, leading to a price decrease as a result of the invention. Large cost reductions of this sort that induce price reductions are termed major inventions. For minor inventions, market price is unaffected. (A major invention can also be defined as one that makes the inventor's monopoly price below the original marginal cost.)

Given the inventor-monopolist's equilibrium as explained above, the inventor's profit in the competitive industry case is therefore the rectangle equal to the cost saving per unit $(C_0 - C_1)$ multiplied by the output level Q_0. Or, the incentive in the competitive case is the sum of the two shaded areas I and II in Figure 24.1.

We now consider the case in which the industry is organized initially as a monopoly. Originally, the monopoly would charge a price of P_m as noted earlier. At this price the monopoly profit is the triangular area DEP_0. It equals the area under marginal revenue (or total revenue) less the area under marginal cost (or total cost).[10] The monopolist's incentive to invest in a cost reducing invention is simply its increment to profit due to the lower cost process. It is easy to show that this is the trapezoid P_0EFG in Figure 24.1, or area I. The reason is that profit with the lower cost process increases from DEP_0 to DFG, and the difference is P_0EFG.

The key conclusion is that the incentive to invent in the competitive industry case is the sum of areas I and II, while in the monopoly case it is only area I. Hence, for the minor invention case, the incentive is greater if the industry is organized competitively.

Before examining the same question in the case of a major invention, it is useful to consider the "first-best" social benefit of the cost reducing invention in Figure 24.1. If the lower cost process were made available to firms at the efficient price of zero, the competitive equilibrium would change to a price equal to C_1 and a quantity of Q_1. The social benefit would then be equal to the sum of areas I, II, and III, the increase in consumer surplus due to the price decrease. The ranking is therefore that the social benefit (I + II + III) exceeds the incentive in competition (I + II) which, in turn, exceeds the incentive in monopoly (I).

Major Invention Case

Figure 24.2 shows the case of a major cost reducing invention. As we explained earlier, the major invention leads to a price decrease after the invention—unlike the minor invention case.

Before invention, the two equilibria are exactly as in the minor invention case. Competition has price P_0 and quantity Q_0 while monopoly has price P_m and quantity M_0. After invention, both the inventor-monopolist in the competitive industry and the monopolist choose price P'_m and quantity M_1. The inventor-monopolist in the competitive industry therefore obtains a profit incentive equal to the large shaded rectangle, P'_mSVW.

To find the profit increase for the monopolist, and therefore its incentive, simply subtract the pre-invention profit, which equals the small

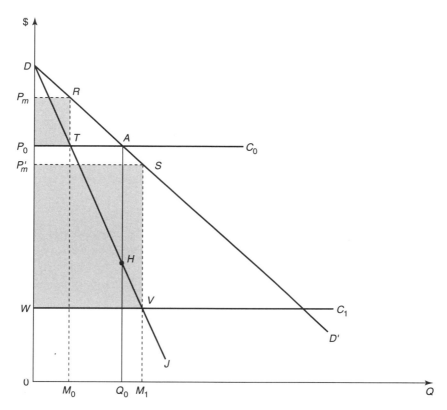

Figure 24.2
Incentives to Invent in Monopoly and Competition: Major Invention

shaded rectangle P_mRTP_0, from the large shaded rectangle. The comparison of incentives is therefore clear. It is again the case that the incentive is greater in the competitive industry than in the monopoly—the monopolist has a pre-incentive profit that must be subtracted from the large rectangle, whereas the inventor in the competitive industry does not need to subtract anything.

Tirole has described this lesser incentive in monopoly as the *replacement effect*. "The monopolist gains less from innovating than does a competitive firm because the monopolist "replaces himself" when he innovates whereas the competitive firm becomes a monopoly."[11]

Welfare Analysis of Patents

Earlier we noted that patent life could be too long or too short from a social viewpoint. Longer life increases the inventor's appropriability at the cost of a longer period of monopoly pricing. A shorter life reduces appropriabilty but brings about efficient pricing sooner. The implication is that an optimal patent life lies somewhere in between the extremes. In this section, we describe an optimal patent life model developed by Nordhaus.[12] This section also considers some complications regarding the Nordhaus model—competitive patent races and new product inventions when close substitutes exist.

Optimal Patent Life Model

Nordhaus assumed the case of a single inventor in a competitive industry who makes a minor cost reducing invention. Hence, the model builds directly on the development of that case earlier in this chapter.

The Inventor's Equilibrium

In the analysis relating to Figure 24.1, the magnitude of the cost savings per unit $(C_0 - C_1)$ was taken as given. Here, we shall examine what determines the magnitude of the cost savings, or what can be termed the *size of the invention*. The magnitude of the cost savings will be referred to as B.

Although one of the major characteristics of inventive activities is the uncertainty of the outcome, the model rules out uncertainty. Hence, it is assumed that the inventor has a total cost of R&D function, TC, that gives TC as a function of the cost savings, B.[13] In Nordhaus' book, he justified this assumption by observing that "if there is no relationship between pecuniary rewards and inventive inputs on the one side and inventive output on the other, the optimal life is zero."[14]

Hence, assume that the inventor's total cost of R&D, TC, is a quadratic function of B. This means that there are diminishing returns to R&D as the size of the invention increases. It is:

$$TC = \alpha B^2 \tag{24.1}$$

where

TC = total cost of R&D

B = cost savings $(C_0 - C_1)$

α = a positive constant

The problem is now easily formulated. The inventor must choose the amount of cost savings, B, that will maximize the difference between the present value of the stream of royalties, PV, and the R&D cost, TC. Recall that the royalty (or profit), as determined earlier for the minor invention case, is the rectangle equal to Areas I + II in Figure 24.1. The rectangle is also simply BQ_0. An important parameter is T, the patent life, because the stream of royalties will cease after year T. It is easy to show that the present value of the stream of royalties from the present to year T is:[15]

$$PV = BQ_0(1 - e^{-rT})/r \qquad (24.2)$$

where

PV = present value of royalties

B = cost savings

r = inventor's interest rate

T = patent life

Figure 24.3 shows both PV and TC as functions of B. Notice that PV is just a straight line from the origin with its slope dependent on the value of the patent life, T. Two patent lives are assumed in the figure: $T = 10$ years and $T = 20$ years. The inventor will choose the value of B

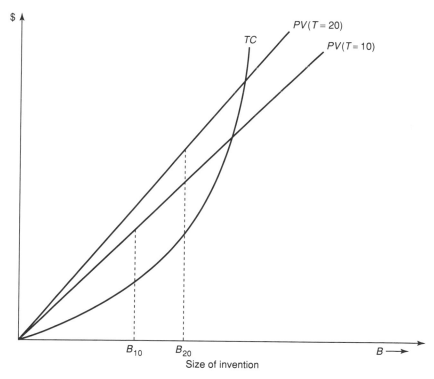

Figure 24.3
The Inventor's Choice of Size of Invention Varies with Patent Life, T

corresponding to the largest vertical distance between PV and TC, or where the slopes of the two functions are equal. Hence, if $T = 10$ years, the inventor will choose to have a cost saving invention of magnitude B_{10}; if a longer life of $T = 20$ years is in effect, the inventor will choose the larger invention B_{20}. The result is clear—the longer the patent life, the larger the cost saving invention.[16]

Determination of Optimal Patent Life

Because the size of the invention, B, is positively related to T, the patent life, why shouldn't T be set at an infinitely large number? The reason it should *not* be is the need to balance off a larger invention against the inefficiency of monopoly pricing. As discussed earlier, the price of new knowledge should be set at zero if it is to be used efficiently—but, of course, this would provide no incentive to the inventor.

In order to understand the tradeoff as T varies, consider Figure 24.4. Figure 24.4(a) shows the benefits of the invention to be the rectangle, Area I, *for the period of the patent life.* Area I represents the total cost savings in real resources, which is captured in the form of a royalty by the inventor. *After the patent expires,* price falls to P_1 and output increases to Q_1, as shown in Figure 24.4(b). The benefits are now shown as two areas: Area I is the same as in Figure 24.4(a), though it is now part of an enlarged consumers' surplus, and Area II is the gain of the former deadweight loss triangle due to the removal of monopoly.

Now as T increases, the size of the invention increases and C_1 shifts downward in both panels of Figure 24.4. This increases Area I benefits

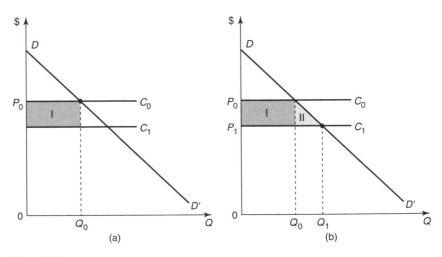

Figure 24.4
(a) Benefits during Patent Life. (b) Benefits after Patent Expires.

but Area II is put off further into the future, thereby reducing the *present value* of the stream of Area II benefits.

The actual derivation of the optimal patent life requires one to choose the value of T that maximizes the present value of Areas I and II, less the total R&D cost, TC. Because the mathematical analysis becomes rather complex, we shall merely indicate the result as the intersection of a marginal benefit curve with a marginal cost curve, as shown in Figure 24.5. The optimal patent life is therefore T^*.

The marginal-benefit curve is a function of the patent life, and it declines as the life increases. The marginal benefit from an additional year of patent life is the gain in social welfare generated by the ensuing larger size of invention. For convenience of exposition, it is net of the additional R&D cost. The decline is primarily because of diminishing returns to R&D investment.

The marginal cost in Figure 24.5 is really a marginal *opportunity* cost. It is the loss of Area II in Figure 24.4 for an additional year of patent life. For example, as the patent life increases from T' to $T' + 1$, consumers forgo the deadweight loss triangle that they would have attained in $T' + 1$. It also declines with patent life, but not as steeply as the marginal benefit curve. Marginal cost declines because the lost triangle is discounted more heavily as the life increases.

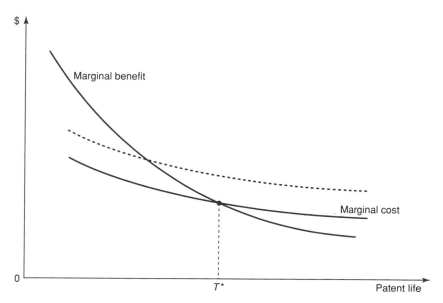

Figure 24.5
Determination of the Optimal Patent Life, T^*

One simple result that the model predicts is that the optimal patent life should vary with the industry's demand elasticity. For example, higher elasticities of demand imply that Area II in Figure 24.4 will be larger. This, in turn, suggests that the primary effect will be to shift the marginal cost curve in Figure 24.5 upward (as is indicated by the dashed curve). The result is an optimal patent life that is smaller.[17]

Complications

Of course, there are a number of strong assumptions underlying the optimal patent life model above. We will consider the relaxation of two important ones here. The first is the restriction of the analysis to a single inventor unconcerned about rival inventors. Recent work has developed the concept of competition among inventors for the patent—so-called patent races. The second assumption is that the invention is cost reducing. We will examine the welfare economics of a new product invention that has a close substitute that already exists.[18]

Patent Races[19]

Unlike the model above of a single inventor, there are now numerous potential inventor/firms all seeking a particular invention. The winner gets the patent and the others get nothing. For simplicity, it is assumed that there is a social benefit of amount B that also equals the private benefit to the inventor—problems of monopoly pricing are therefore not considered here.

It is useful to conceive of a "discovery function" that gives the probability of the invention being made and the patent awarded. Assume that all inventors are equal in size—each must commit an R&D investment of amount R up front if they decide to join in the race. Hence, we indicate the discovery function as $P(n)$, where P is the probability of discovery and n is the number of inventor/firms. As the number of firms increases, P rises but at a decreasing rate, approaching $P = 1$.

There are two problems to be solved. First, what is the optimum number of firms from society's viewpoint? Second, what is the number of firms that will engage in the race in a competitive (or free-entry) equilibrium? Looking ahead, it will be shown that there are too many firms in a competitive equilibrium as compared to the social optimum. That is, the model as structured here leads to *overinvestment* in R&D. We shall explain the rationale for overinvestment as simply a variation of the well-known *common pool* problem in economics. Next, we consider whether the model's assumptions are likely to describe the real world.

The social welfare problem is to find the number of firms, n, that maximizes the *expected value* of social benefit less social cost. In a statistical sense, the expected value of benefit is the "average" benefit if the race were repeated over and over—it is just the probability of discovery multiplied by the benefit amount, or $P(n)B$. The social objective function is then $P(n)B - nR$, where nR is social cost, or just the number of firms times the cost per firm.

Solving this maximization problem by differentiating the social objective function with respect to n gives the marginal condition that marginal social benefit, MSB, should equal marginal cost, MC. Or,

$$P'(n)B = MSB = MC = R \qquad (24.3)$$

In words, $P'(n)B$ is the marginal increase in probability of discovery brought about by adding another firm, times B. It is the expected increase in social benefit due to one more firm joining the race—and, at the social optimum, it should equal the cost of that firm, R.

The socially optimum number of firms, n^*, is shown in Figure 24.6 as determined by the intersection of the MSB curve and MC. The fact that MSB declines as n increases is inherent in the assumption about the shape of the discovery function made earlier. The probability of discovery is assumed to increase with n but the increases ($P'(n)$) become smaller and smaller.

Next, consider the competitive equilibrium. A firm must decide whether to enter the race by comparing its expected profit, EP, with its

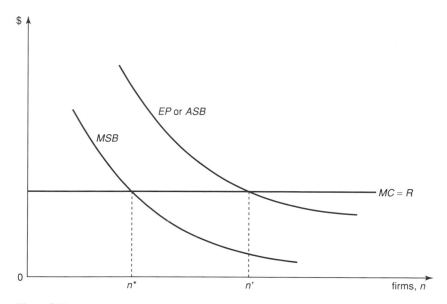

Figure 24.6
Marginal Social Benefit and Expected Profit in Patent Race versus Marginal Cost

cost R. As long as EP is greater than R, firms will continue to join the patent race. Hence, the number of firms is determined by the condition of zero profit at the margin, or by $EP = R$. The expected profit can also be written as $P(n)B/n$. That is, each firm would believe that it is equally as likely to win the expected prize of $P(n)B$ as any other firm—so its probability is just $1/n$. Hence, its expected profit is $1/n$ times $P(n)B$. Or,

$$P(n)B/n = EP = MC = R \tag{24.4}$$

The EP equal to R condition is shown in Figure 24.6. It is also possible to interpret EP as the average social product, ASP. That is, ASP is the expected social product divided by n. This makes it easy to understand why it lies above MSB in the figure—the two curves stand in the usual relationship of average and marginal curves. As the average social product declines, the marginal must lie below it. The competitive equilibrium leads to n' firms which exceeds the optimum number, n^*.

Just as competitive fishing in a lake can result in overfishing, or competitive drilling of oil from a single pool can lead to too much drilling, our assumptions here lead to too much R&D. The explanation for this result is that there is one "production function" that links the firms in these cases—here it is the discovery function. Each firm affects the others directly through this function but ignores the effect that it has on others in its private decision. This is known as an *externality*.

One prescription for solving the externality problem is to "internalize" it by placing a single decision maker in charge. In the oil industry, there are cases where the owners of land above an oil pool combine to place the oil drilling decision under a single management, known as unitization.[20] The implication here is that the patent race should be placed under the command of a single decisionmaker.

It is likely that placing R&D decisions under a single decision maker—private or public—would lead to harmful effects that are not captured by this model. That is, the value of independent inventors trying new approaches that may not coincide with the majority view is often important. A single management committee coordinating multiple R&D projects could easily overlook promising approaches.

Another concern about the patent race described here is the assumption that there is one and only one product. In fact, it is often not the case that there is only one winner. In pharmaceuticals, for example, many firms might be seeking a cure for high blood pressure or cancer, and the outcome is a variety of different drugs with different properties—sometimes a drug for a disease not even being considered may be discovered.

Furthermore, patent monopolies are often temporary and can be displaced quite early in their product lives by newer, better products. Hence, it is probably reasonable to say that before R&D overinvestment becomes a widely accepted policy concern, patent race models will need to be refined to incorporate more realistic assumptions.[21]

A New Product Invention when Substitutes Exist

The optimal patent life model assumed a cost reducing invention. Here we consider a new product invention that is a close substitute for an existing product. What is the social benefit of a new product N that is a close substitute for an existing product E? As we shall see, the introduction of substitute products leads to significant changes in the way social benefits are measured. It is also true that it becomes possible for private incentives to invent to become either too large or too small from a social welfare perspective.

In Figure 24.7(b) the demand and cost of the new product N is shown. Demand is dd with a constant average cost of c'. The demand dd takes as given the price P_0 of a substitute product E (in panel a of Figure 24.7). The introduction of N at price p' leads to consumers purchasing quantity q'.

After N is introduced, the demand for E, which was originally DD, shifts leftward to $D'D'$. The constant average cost of N is assumed to be C_0. This is shown in Figure 24.7(a). For simplicity, we shall assume that

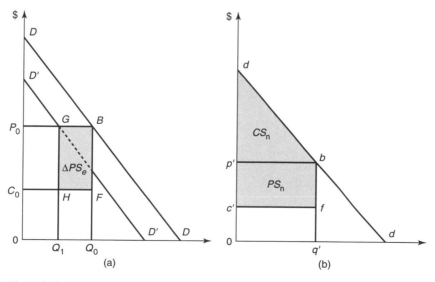

Figure 24.7
(a) Existing Product E. (b) New Product N.

the supplier of E keeps the price of E fixed even after the introduction of N.[22] As shown, the quantity of E purchased decreases from Q_0 to Q_1, leading to profits that fall from $P_0 BFC_0$ to $P_0 GHC_0$, or by the amount $GBFH$, or ΔPS_e.

Now, consider the question of how to measure the social benefit of the introduction of product N. Clearly, the total economic surplus of N (dbp' of consumer surplus, or CS_n, and $p'bfc'$ of producer surplus, or PS_n) is a major component of the social benefit of N. However, unlike the case we considered earlier in the optimal patent life section, we must make an adjustment for the effect of N on the substitute product E.

The adjustment is that the loss in profit on E, ΔPS_e in Figure 24.7, must be subtracted. This is the "business stealing" effect. The idea is that the firm introducing the new product does not internalize the loss of profit suffered by its rivals. By itself, the effect suggests a tendency for too much innovation.

The social benefit, SB, of the new product N is:

$$SB = CS_n + PS_n - \Delta PS_e \tag{24.5}$$

An often troublesome theoretical point for some is why the shift leftward of demand for product E does not necessitate a subtraction of consumer surplus for product E of, say, area $DBGD'$. The answer is that the demand for product N assumes the availability of product E at price P_0, and it therefore gives the *increment* to consumers' willingness-to-pay due to the introduction of N. This is exactly what is desired.[23]

The social benefit, given by equation 24.5, leads to another possibility for private investment in R&D being socially too large or too small. Assuming that the two products are supplied by different firms, then the private incentive to N's inventor is simply PS_n. Comparing PS_n with SB, it is clear that the private incentive can be either larger than the social benefit (if $\Delta PS_e > CS_n$) or smaller than the social benefit (if $\Delta PS_e < CS_n$). Interestingly, the portion of the social benefit not appropriated by the inventor (CS_n) acts to offset the business-stealing effect (ΔPS_e) in bringing the social and private benefits closer in value.

It is obviously difficult to know how these magnitudes might compare in particular real world cases. It would be useful to at least know whether too much or too little inventive activity might be stimulated by this factor. Based on admittedly rough estimates, Scherer and Ross argue that the ready-to-eat cereal industry of the 1960s and the soft drink industry of the 1980s probably had excessive new product innovation.[24] The basic idea is that CS_n was probably low because consumers did not perceive great differences among products, while ΔPS_e was probably large because of the high profit margins in those industries.

Pharmaceuticals and the Role of Patents

We turn now from the theoretical analysis of patents to consider the actual role of patents in the pharmaceutical industry. In particular, the 1984 Drug Price Competition and Patent Term Restoration Act will be examined. Although there was no pretense by policymakers that they were adjusting the patent life in pharmaceuticals to the socially optimal life, it nevertheless represents a rare case in which the legal patent life in an industry was actually changed. We will discuss the reasons for and economic effects of that change.

First, we provide a brief overview of the structure of the U.S. pharmaceutical industry as background.[25] The following section will describe the 1984 Act and its economic effects.

Industry Structure

The pharmaceutical industry is sometimes referred to as the ethical drug industry. It can be thought of as the industry that discovers, manufactures, and sells drugs that require a doctor's prescription. It is a leading high-tech industry and is consistently at the top of American industries in terms of R&D spending per dollar of sales. The industry has contributed greatly to improved health by virtually eliminating certain diseases (e.g., diphtheria, smallpox, and polio) and by reducing deaths from others (e.g., tuberculosis and heart disease). Expenditures on pharmaceuticals account for about 6 percent of total health care expenditures in the United States.

It is a relatively young industry—its beginning as a research-oriented industry dates back to the mid-1930s, when the first important group of antiinfective drugs were introduced. After World War II, pharmaceutical research broadened to cover many different therapeutic areas. Drugs were introduced to deal with cardiovascular, respiratory, neurological, and other disease categories.[26]

Government Regulation

The development of the industry into a research-based industry competing in terms of new drug innovation was accompanied by the development of extensive government regulations of new drugs.[27] Government regulation of this industry dates back to the Pure Food and Drug Act of 1906. This regulation was directed primarily at the adulteration and mislabeling of food and drugs sold in interstate commerce. In 1938, following a drug disaster that killed over a hundred children, the Food, Drug and Cosmetic Act of 1938 was passed by Congress. This law

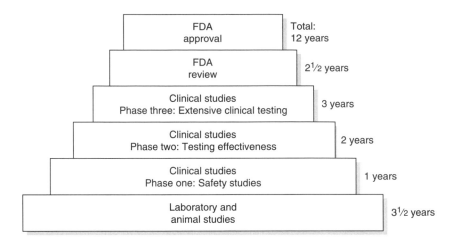

Figure 24.8
Steps in R&D Process from Discovery to Product Launch

required new drugs to be approved as safe by the Food and Drug Administration (FDA) before they could be introduced into interstate commerce. And, in 1962, Congress passed the important Kefauver-Harris Amendments to the Food, Drug and Cosmetic Act.

As described in Chapter 22, the 1962 amendments required that a drug's efficacy as well as safety be demonstrated on the basis of well-controlled scientific tests prior to marketing approval by the FDA. Chapter 22 also explains the market failure rationale for product quality regulation in pharmaceuticals as a case of imperfect information.

The 1962 Amendments added considerably to the length and cost of the R&D process. Figure 24.8 is an illustration of the average length of the process. It begins with a highly uncertain period of discovery involving laboratory and animal studies. This is shown in the figure as lasting about 3.5 years. After a new chemical compound is discovered that has the potential for being an effective drug product, the first of three phases of clinical testing is initiated (FDA approval is required before testing in humans is permitted). On average, the clinical testing adds six more years to the process.[28]

Following the clinical tests and assuming the drug is still regarded as a promising new therapy, a New Drug Application (NDA) is submitted to the FDA. These applications cover, on average, clinical trials of over 3000 patients and contain 90,000 pages. After another 2.5 years the FDA gives its decision, which, if positive, permits the firm to begin selling the drug. Of every four drugs that begin clinical trials, one will be eventually approved by the FDA.

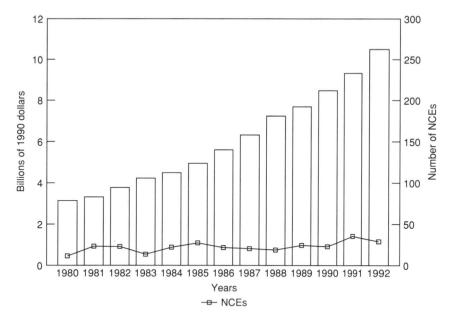

Figure 24.9
R&D Expenditures and NCEs

The industry typically introduces between twenty and thirty new chemical entities[29] (NCEs) each year. Figure 24.9 shows the trend in total industry R&D expenditures and the number of NCEs introduced between 1980 and 1992. It indicates that total R&D expenditures have been growing rapidly in real terms since the 1980s. The figure suggests the the average R&D costs per NCE are also rising.[30]

Demand

The concentration of buyers in the retail market is low if one thinks of patients taking their prescriptions to their local pharmacy. Of course, the key decisionmaker is the doctor who writes the prescription, and who has typically been the main target of pharmaceutical marketing.[31] It is often noted that the doctor is more concerned with the quality of the drug than its price—and, in fact, may not even know the price.[32] This characteristic of the demand side makes for relatively inelastic demand. This inelasticity is reinforced by the facts that often drugs are seen as vital for one's health and many consumers' drug purchases are covered by insurance.

It should be noted, however, that the above characterization of demand is rapidly changing as "managed care" organizations and other large group buying institutions are becoming increasingly important.

For example, health maintenance organizations (HMOs) are "firms" of health care providers that are quite cost conscious because they sell care to patients for a fixed price per year. They often bargain with drug manufacturers over prices and receive large quantity discounts. Their leverage is based on a "formulary," or list of approved drugs for the HMO doctors. The HMO pharmacy committee's decision to include or exclude a drug is therefore very important to the manufacturer. Government agencies such as Medicaid also employ various tactics to obtain lower prices.

In addition, firms known as "prescription benefits managers" (or PBMs) have become quite important. These firms are hired by large employers, insurance companies, HMOs, and other health care providers to lower drug costs. Because they represent many customers, they can negotiate big discounts with manufacturers. In 1993 and 1994 the three largest benefits management firms were bought by manufacturers. Eli Lilly bought the largest manager, PCS Health Systems, which covers prescriptions for 50 million people, in July 1994. It remains to be seen whether these acquisitions will lead to antitrust actions. In brief, the demand for drugs has become much more price sensitive in recent years.

Seller Concentration

Although the pharmaceutical industry is multinational in character, we focus here on the U.S. market.[33] The first point is that there are a large number of research intensive firms. Considering pharmaceutical sales by manufacturers to drug stores and hospitals in the United States as a single market (about $60 billion in aggregate), the top four sellers in 1993 with their respective market shares (percentages) were:

Merck	6.21
Bristol Meyers-Squibb	5.86
Glaxo	5.46
American Home Products	5.27
Total	22.80

Hence, the four-firm concentration ratio is relatively low at 22.8. However, if one considers the more meaningful markets to be "therapeutic categories" rather than pharmaceuticals in aggregate, then the concentration ratios are higher. One study found that the average therapeutic market concentration ratio was 70.[34] The rationale for the more narrowly defined markets is that on the demand side, categories like antibiotics and cardiovasculars, for example, are poor substitutes.

In addition to the research intensive firms listed above, there are many "generic" manufacturers. Biocraft, Mylan, and Zenith are examples of generic firms that do little research; rather, they specialize in copying brand-name products after the brand product's patent expires. For example, when the popular brand-name tranquilizer Valium went off patent in the mid-1980s, some fifteen to twenty generic suppliers began selling the generic version of Valium—known as diazepam—at large discounts. In 1993 the average generic price of diazepam was only 2 percent of Valium's price. Even so, Valium with its much higher price still had a market share of 25 percent of total diazepam pills sold.

Barriers to Entry

Three sources of entry barriers can be identified: patents, brand loyalty, and scale advantages in R&D (which includes winning FDA approval).

Patents

As noted earlier, patents are generally regarded to be more important to foster innovation in the pharmaceutical industry than in most other industries. The reason is that once a new chemical structure is marketed, the cost of imitation is usually quite low.

An important ruling by the Patent Office in 1948 concerning the antibiotic streptomycin opened the door to the patenting of new drugs. That is, new drugs would not be patentable if they were simply natural substances. In the case of streptomycin, the Patent Office ruled that the natural materials found by Waksman, streptomycin's discoverer, were not in suitable form for medical use. By making chemical modifications to streptomycin so that it could be purified, however, the Patent Office rule that a "new composition of matter" had been created.

A patent barrier can be overcome by the development of chemically distinct substitutes for the original product. One strategy for inventing around an existing firm's patent is termed "molecular modification." This refers to the development of a similar compound so as to retain a rival product's main therapeutic effects, but at the same time to have a chemically distinct structure so that it can be patented. This is a controversial practice and some see it as wasteful; on the other hand, it has sometimes led to superior products not having the harmful side effects of the original product.

The antiulcer drug Zantac is an example of such molecular modification. In 1977 SmithKline introduced its newly discovered anti-ulcer drug, Tagamet, on the U.S. market. It was a drug that was "designed" to fit a receptor site in the body to "turn off" the release of histamine in the stomach. Histamine, in turn, could no longer stimulate the secretion of gastric acid in the stomach. This proved to be far superior to the use of antacids or surgery in the treatment of ulcers. By 1980, Tagamet became the largest selling drug in the world and, according to a *Fortune* article, "ranks as one of the most stunningly successful products in the history of American business."[35]

In the mid-1970s Glaxo began a search for a similar molecule that would also fit the histamine receptor site. It was granted a patent for its molecule, Zantac, in 1978, and by 1987 Zantac had overtaken Tagamet and had become itself the best-selling drug in the world. Its advantage over Tagamet was claimed to be fewer side effects. Zantac's daily dosage also was only twice daily compared to Tagamet's four times daily— fewer dosages per day are generally preferred by doctors because it increases patient compliance.

By 1992, Zantac's sales amounted to $3.2 billion worldwide—over $1 billion more than the next-best selling drug. As might be expected, other companies have also come up with similar antiulcer drugs, but they have not been as commercially successful as Zantac. In 1994, however, the patent on Tagamet expired and it can be expected that vigorous price cutting by generic suppliers will significantly impact the sales of Zantac.

Glaxo owns two patents on Zantac. One expires in 1995 and the second in 2002. Glaxo has been involved in a number of patent infringement cases that it has brought in order to defend its belief that the 2002 patent is the valid one. The 1995 patent covers the basic molecular structure of Zantac and one crystalline form of the drug. The 2002 patent covers a second crystalline form, and is the form actually in use. Hence, the actual determination of the 2002 patent's validity will be determined by the courts. Such patent infringement cases are common in the pharmaceutical industry.[36]

Brand Loyalty

Brand loyalty was illustrated above by the case of Valium and the fact that it maintained 25 percent of the total sales of diazapam despite generic prices being only 2 percent of the price of Valium. The point, of course, is that generic versions of the tranquilizer are necessarily bioequivalent[37] to Valium. This is required by the FDA for generics to be marketed. Hence, quality differences are quite small and must be due largely to consumers' perceptions that the brand name is superior. Of course, consumers often have poor information about the availability, price, and quality of generic substitutes.

In a 1992 study,[38] eighteen major drug products whose patents expired in the 1984–88 period were analyzed with regard to the pattern of

Table 24.1
Generic Penetration on Patent Expiration: 18 Drugs

	At Date of Entry	One Year after Entry	Two Years after Entry
Average brand name price index	1.0	1.07	1.11
Average generic price index	1.0	.78	.65
Average ratio of generic price to brand name price	.61	.46	.37
Average generic market share in units	.09	.35	.49

Note: Each value is an unweighted average of the values for the eighteen drug categories.
Source: H. G. Grabowski and J. M. Vernon, "Brand Loyalty, Entry, and Price Competition in Pharmaceuticals after the 1984 Drug Act," *Journal of Law and Economics*, October 1992.

generic penetration. The key results are reported in Table 24.1. As can be seen, the average generic product was introduced at a price equal to 61 percent of the brand name product's price, and after two years it fell to 37 percent. Despite these low relative prices, the total market share in units that generics won after two years was only 49 percent. In other words, half of the units sold were made by the brand-name products, even though their generic rivals had prices of only one third the brand price. Furthermore, as the table shows, the brand name prices on average rose in the face of entry! The table indicates an increase of 11 percent.[39]

One interpretation of the results in Table 24.1 is that the market is segmented into two groups—a price-sensitive group and a group that has strong loyalties to the branded products. If a brand-name product can keep half the market at the unchanged price as opposed to keeping the whole market by lowering price to one-third the original level, simple calculations indicate that the unchanged-price strategy is more profitable.[40]

It should be noted that managed care organizations and other cost-containment market forces are becoming increasingly important. Hence, brand loyalty should become less and less important over time. In terms of the segmented market story above, the price sensitive group is likely to become larger and larger.[41] This is true not only of pressures to substitute lower-cost generics but also of pressures to substitute lower-cost brand name drugs for higher cost ones.

R&D Scale Economies

The final type of entry barrier is that of economies of scale in R&D and the need to obtain FDA approval for newly discovered drugs. Several factors can be mentioned here. First, a firm must maintain a portfolio of R&D projects because only one in four that enter clinical testing are ever marketed. Furthermore, it turns out that only three out of ten drugs that are marketed cover their total costs—including their share of failures.[42] This means that a firm must maintain a large enough R&D budget to insure that it will have at least the minimal number of successes necessary to maintain financial viability.[43]

The R&D process presents several opportunities for traditional economies of scale. For example, the discovery process is characterized by significant fixed costs. Multidisciplinary teams of biologists, chemists, and other scientists are engaged in research to develop concepts and hypotheses concerning new compounds. The clinical development process also requires significant regulatory and legal expertise, which is also characterized by fixed costs and specialization. In principle, larger firms can spread these fixed costs over more R&D projects.

The R&D cost per NCE marketed is also quite high in absolute dollars, and has been increasing in real terms quite rapidly. This point is clear from Figure 24.9. A 1993 study by the U.S. Office of Technology Assessment concluded that the average aftertax R&D cash outlay for each new drug that reached the market in the 1980s was about $65 million in 1990 dollars. It went on to say, "The R&D process took 12 years on average. The full aftertax cost of these outlays, compounded to their value on the day of market approval, was roughly $194 million."[44]

In an 1991 article[45] in *The Wall Street Journal* about a number of recent mergers in the industry, several executives observed that the mergers were occurring for R&D needs. According to the head of SmithKline Beecham—which resulted from the 1989 merger of the U.S. firm, SmithKline, and the British firm, Beecham—"few drug companies on their own can afford truly innovative research these days. More consolidation is inevitable." The chief executive of Glaxo noted that "to be a big player a company must spend somewhere north of $500 million a year [on R&D] and grow it by more than 10% or 15% a year. Those who can't spend that will be left behind; they'll be good candidates for a merger."

There have also been a number of statistical studies of R&D productivity in pharmaceuticals.[46] The general findings seem to be that there are economies of scale or advantages to larger firms that at least partly result from the increased regulatory stringency of the FDA after 1962.

This completes our brief overview of the structure of the pharmaceutical industry. It is an industry in which patents are essential to provide incentives for R&D investment and a major form of competition is through the introduction of new drug products. On the other hand, recent developments are leading to an increasing role for price com-

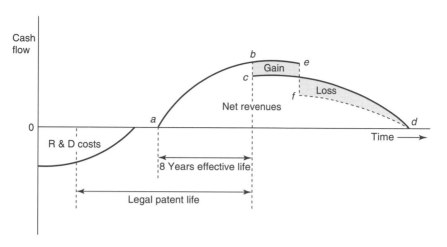

Figure 24.10
Effect of 1984 Act on Expected Revenues of Average Drug

petition. We turn now to the analysis of an important 1984 law that simultaneously increased patent lives and lowered barriers to generic competition.

The 1984 Drug Price Competition and Patent Restoration Act[47]

In 1984 President Reagan signed into law the Drug Price Competition and Patent Restoration Act. The law facilitated the entry of generic competitors after patent expiration, thereby leading to price competition. It also restored part of the patent life lost during the premarket regulatory process for new pharmaceuticals.

Provisions of the Act

Figure 24.10 can be used to make these two main provisions clear. The figure is a representation of the cash flows of the average new drug innovation. First, there is a twelve-year period of R&D costs and FDA review time from the origin to point *a*. Point *a* represents the beginning of marketing, with the pre-1984 profile of net revenues being shown by the path *abcd*. The post-1984 profile is *abefd*.

Considering the pre-1984 period, the legal patent life begins during the R&D period and extends, on average, for eight years into the marketing period. Hence, as shown in Figure 24.10, there was an "effective patent life" of eight years. The point, of course, is that part of the legal patent life is consumed in premarket R&D and regulatory activities, leaving only eight years for exclusive marketing.

The act provides for an extension in effective patent life equal to the sum of the FDA review time plus one-half the clinical testing time, subject to certain constraints. For example, there is a maximum extension of five years and no extension beyond fourteen years of effective patent life. In Figure 24.10, the amount of patent restoration is represented by the distance *be*.

Figure 24.10 also indicates the second provision of the act as the relatively large drop in net revenues upon patent expiration in the post-1984 case, the distance *ef*, as compared with the smaller drop in the pre-1984 case, or *bc*. The loss is relatively small in pre-1984 because of the significant barriers to entry that confronted generic competitors. (The size of the losses is the product of two factors: the probability of generic entry and the losses of revenues to generics given that entry occurs. It should be recalled that the cash profile is for the *average* drug—and in the pre-1984 case generic entry simply did not occur in many cases.)

The entry barriers in the pre-1984 period were due to the fact that generic firms frequently could not rely on the safety and efficacy evidence submitted by the brand name firms (the innovators). Unless the relevant data were publically available in the scientific literature, an imitator had to duplicate many of the innovator's tests to gain FDA approval. Under the 1984 law, a generic firm need only submit an "Abbreviated New Drug Application" (ANDA). This requires only that bioequivalency be demonstrated, a relatively low cost test.

Reasons for and Welfare Effects of the Act

With regard to the brand-name drug's revenues, one effect—patent restoration—leads to a gain, whereas the second effect—easier generic entry—leads to a loss. The gain and loss areas are shown in Figure 24.10. Of course, the loss to the brand name firm are gains to generic firms. Hence, as might be expected, the act was passed after a long period of compromises among various interest groups. (In addition to the pharmaceutical firms and their associations, groups representing consumers favored the lower prices and sided with the generic firms.) Obviously, the optimal patent-life model discussed earlier in which the policymaker was assumed to choose the life that maximizes total surplus was not applied!

Senator Hatch, one of the two sponsors of the act, described the bill to the Senate as "carefully balanced ... in ways that only lawyers could have devised." More generally, he said:

This is a groundbreaking compromise in the public interest. It reconciles the opposing, competitive interests of two segments of the pharmaceutical industry which have often stymied each other's attempts to improve the law. The re-search-based drug industry obtains an extension of patents for new drug discoveries to compensate them for the time spent off-market in FDA review. The generic drug industry gets to bring generic copies of off-patent drugs to market as soon as the patent expires, without the needless reduplication of studies and tests already in FDA's files.

The public receives the best of both worlds—cheaper drugs today and better drugs tomorrow.[48]

From the perspective of economic welfare, the act is the source of large potential positive gains of two types. First, it eliminated costly scientific testing which served no valid purpose. Second, the act lowered prices to consumers with some elimination of deadweight losses and large transfers from producers to consumers.

At the same time, the act had the potential of lowering the expected returns from drug innovation—it depends on the relative magnitudes of the gains and losses in Figure 24.10. One might interpret Senator Hatch's remarks quoted above "of better drugs tomorrow" as his belief that the act would *increase* incentives to invest in R&D. Of course, as we discussed in the earlier part of this chapter, it is possible from society's viewpoint to have too much appropriability as well as too little. However, if it was the intention of Congress to at least maintain the incentive to introduce new drugs, one can attempt to examine this question empirically.

The Net Effect on R&D Incentives

In this section we present an attempt to examine the effect of the 1984 Act on R&D incentives that was published shortly after the act was enacted. Hence, it should be regarded as suggestive of the relative effects and not in any sense based on current research findings.

The results are shown in Table 24.2. Figure 24.10 indicates the trade-offs involved graphically. The baseline case with the act *not* in effect has the net revenues life cycle *abcd*. The present value of the net revenues is based on a study of the average new drug discovered and introduced in the United States in the 1970s. The baseline net present value (NPV) is set at 100 so that the effect of the 1984 act can be compared with a world without the act in effect.

The two key parameters (the magnitudes of *be* and *ef* in Figure 24.10) are quite uncertain. Hence, Table 24.2 gives a sensitivity analysis for three values of patent life restored (1, 3, and 5 years) and three values of net revenue losses to generics (30, 40, and 50 percent). For the intermediate case (3 years and 40 percent), the NPV is shown in Table 24.10 as only 93 percent of what the NPV would have been without the Act in

Table 24.2
Index of NPV for Average Drug under Alternative Assumptions (NPV without Act in effect = 100)

Patent Extension (years)	Net Revenue Loss to Generics		
	30%	40%	50%
5	110	104	98
3	102	93	84
1	91	79	67

Notes: Patent extension is distance *be* in Figure 24.10. New loss to generics is distance *ef* in Figure 24.10.
Source: H. G. Grabowski and J. M. Vernon, "Longer Patents for Lower Imitation Barriers: The 1984 Drug Act," *AEA Papers and Proceedings*, May 1986.

effect. In short, for this choice of parameters, the net effect of the Act is estimated to have a moderate negative impact on R&D investment incentives.

It should be noted that the analysis deals with an "average" drug. Firms that are optimistically seeking "blockbusters"—such as Tagamet and Zantac—are unlikely to be deterred by the act's possibly negative effect on the NPV. At the same time, firms that rely heavily on internal funds to finance R&D are likely to experience significant financial pressures when the patents on major products expire.

Recent evidence—such as that presented in Table 24.1—suggests that losses to generics may be closer to 50 percent or more.[49] The patent life restored for 142 patent extensions (as of May 1992) has most often been for a period of two years.[50] This would suggest that the 1984 act has, on balance, reduced incentives for R&D.

Other Policies that Affect R&D Incentives

Of course, patent policy is only one of various ways that the government affects the incentives to invest in R&D. Here we shall discuss several briefly. These include favorable tax treatment, market exclusivity for so-called "orphan" drugs, and various types of price controls.

Tax Subsidies and Orphan Drugs

The tax code favors R&D relative to investment in plants and equipment because R&D can be "expensed" rather than depreciated and written off over time. That is, a drug company can deduct its R&D expenses from income in the year incurred, thereby recovering the expenses much quicker than it can recover its investment in plant and equipment. Also, in 1981 Congress passed a law that permitted a tax credit for increases[51] in R&D. The tax credit was reduced to 20 percent in 1986.

The 1983 Orphan Drug Act, which was passed to encourage firms to develop new treatments for diseases that affect small numbers of people, provides for a tax credit equal to 50 percent of R&D expenses for clinical trials. The trials must be for drugs that have been given orphan drug status—primarily drugs that treat diseases or conditions affecting less than 200,000 people in the United States. The idea, of course, is that drugs for such small markets would not be profitable for firms in the absence of subsidies.

The first firm to receive FDA approval for an orphan drug also may market it exclusively for a seven-year period beginning on the date of approval. Any patent protection covering the drug runs contemporaneously with the market exclusivity. Through September 1992, the FDA had granted orphan status to 494 drugs.[52] There has been much controversy about certain orphan drugs that are perceived by critics as being too profitable—sometimes because of very high prices. Legislation to limit excessive profits has been proposed, but has not yet been successful.[53]

Price Controls and Profits

Price controls for pharmaceuticals has become a widely discussed issue in recent years. Although most foreign countries have some type of price control system for drugs, the United States generally does not.[54] However, the possibility of including expanded coverage for prescription drugs under health care reform proposals, and the perceived need for accompanying cost controls, has made price controls an issue. In addition, critics of the industry have long been convinced that the industry is too profitable and charges prices that are too high.

To illustrate the two points of view in this debate, we quote some of the arguments from a 1992 debate on the Senate floor. The legislation being discussed was a proposal by Senator Pryor to penalize drug companies that increase their prices faster than the rate of inflation.

Senator Pryor:
From 1982 ... to 1992, 10 years, while the general inflation rate was just 46 percent in that decade, prescription drug prices increased 142 percent.... *Fortune* magazine, July 29, 1991, said the manufacture of pharmaceuticals is America's most profitable business....

I would only say that today those profits are being made at the expense of the most vulnerable members of our society.... In the United States, we spend $270 for every man, woman, and child a year for prescription drugs and most of this is not covered by insurance, it is not covered by Medicare, it is coming out of the pockets of our citizens who are least able to pay....

In 1990 ... the average rate of profit for the Fortune 500 companies was 4.6 percent....What about the pharmaceutical companies?... Let us see how they are getting along—15.5 percent, that was their average profit in the year 1990.... Now how do they make these enormous profits?... By outright price gouging of our American citizens who can least afford the medications—the elderly, the poor, and other vulnerable parts of the American population.[55]

Of course, Senator Pryor's arguments are more detailed than indicated by his statements. However, his major point is that he thinks that the industry has too much monopoly power. It is interesting that his solution is to use price controls to directly attack what he perceives to be the problem. Given that much of the market power presumably stems from patents, one might think that shortening the patent life would be considered.

Senator Bradley:
So, Mr. President, what I believe is a major concern about Senator Pryor's amendment is its effect on investment, research, and innovation in this country. Senator Pryor has singled out one sector in the health care economy that is the most heavily research oriented and funds a significant amount of all research on health care....
And although it is not easy to predict the reactions in the marketplace to Government intervention, this one is simple: Price controls, as envisioned in this amendment, will significantly reduce incentives for investment.... Reduction in research will lead to fewer innovations, fewer cures, and fewer hopes for many Americans who are counting on medical breakthroughs to lengthen their lives.
Certainly, lower prices will help consumers to be able to afford prescription drugs. But the question is, what are they going to be able to buy?[56]

As is perhaps natural in a debate, the senators tend to focus on the extremes—one on the monopoly pricing of existing drugs and the other on the benefits of invention, or future drugs. However, there is a background issue that deserves further analysis, and that is the question of the level of profits in this industry.[57] It is a complex issue and we cannot devote the necessary space to it here. Hence, we will simply make a few key points here, and refer the reader to several relevant articles.[58]
Perhaps the most important point is that profit rates taken from the annual financial reports of firms can be very misleading. The profit rates referred to by Senator Pryor from *Fortune* are of this type. We briefly commented on some of these problems in Chapter 9. With regard to pharmaceutical accounting profit rates, the most serious problem is that accountants expense R&D rather than capitalize and depreciate it as they do other plant and equipment. R&D is the major form of investment for pharmaceutical firms and it clearly has economic effects that last for years—just as plant and equipment do. However, accountants

do not attempt to depreciate it over time—probably because of the difficulty of determining its "useful life."

A simple example may be helpful:

Accounting profit rate $= (R - VC - r\&d - d_kK)/K$

Economic profit rate $= (R - VC - d_{rd}RD - d_kK)/(RD + K)$

where

R = revenues

VC = variable costs

$r\&d$ = current expenditures on R&D

d_k, d_{rd} = depreciation rates of K, RD capital

K = plant and equipment capital stock

RD = R&D capital stock

As stated above, the accounting profit rate expenses R&D. The current expenditures on R&D appear in the numerator. Economic profit rates depreciate the R&D capital stock just as physical capital is depreciated. Assume for simplicity that the firm is in a "steady state" in which its R&D expenditures each year exactly equal the amount needed to offset the depreciation of the R&D capital stock. For this particular case, notice that the two profit rates have equal numerators, but the economic profit rate has a larger denominator. That is, the economic profit rate has both RD and K in its denominator, not just K. Clearly, for this particular case, the accounting profit rate overstates the economic profit rate.

Although the particular case above—a steady state—is not necessarily applicable to pharmaceuticals, it does indicate the possibility of accounting profit rates being too high. In fact, based on a review of six sophisticated studies of pharmaceutical industry profits, the Office of Technology Assessment concluded that "correcting pharmaceutical industry profit rates for investment in intangible capital reduces rates of return by roughly 20 to 25 percent."[59]

The reference to "intangible" capital stock above indicates that the argument about R&D also applies to advertising—which is also expensed rather than capitalized. In 1993, the largest drug firm, Merck, invested about $1.2 billion in R&D, $1 billion in physical capital, and about one quarter of a billion dollars in advertising.[60] Hence, the problem of intangible capital is particularly important to pharmaceuticals because of unusually high levels of both R&D and advertising.

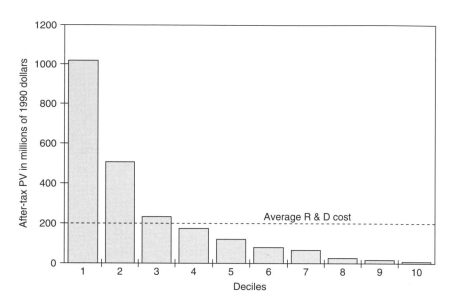

Figure 24.11

An alternative to *firm* profitability is the profitability of new product introductions from an industry-wide perspective. In a study[61] of the sixty-seven new drug introductions in the United States in the 1980–84 period, the average rate of return on pharmaceutical R&D was estimated to be 11.1 percent. This return was compared to the industry's cost of capital of about 10.5 percent (based on a study by S.C. Myers and L. Shyam-Sunder[62]). This finding of the average return being above the cost of capital, but by a relatively small amount, is broadly consistent with a similar study by the Office of Technology Assessment.[63]

It is instructive to note that underlying the *average* return is a highly skewed *distribution* of returns. Figure 24.11 illustrates this point. Using a 10.5 percent cost of capital, and grouping the sixty-seven drugs into deciles by sales revenues, the figure compares the average net present value of net revenues to the average capitalized value of R&D cost—all on an aftertax basis. The top decile has an estimated present value of cash flows after launch that is more than five times average R&D costs. In addition, only the top three deciles have present values that exceed average R&D costs.

This extreme skewness of returns to R&D has an important implication for the type of price controls described in the President Clinton's proposed Health Security Act of 1993. The proposal was to create an Advisory Council on Breakthrough Drugs that would focus on the "reasonableness" of the prices of such drugs. Because breakthrough drugs are likely to correspond to the top decile or "blockbusters," restricting their prices to a breakeven level would significantly reduce the attractiveness of investing in R&D.[64] If one regards R&D investment as somewhat like a lottery—with low probabilities of achieving huge returns—top decile regulation changes completely the nature of the game. Winning the lottery now provides only a reasonable or breakeven return, with other outcomes worse!

Opinions certainly differ, but according to one expert,

> If profits were held to "reasonable" levels on blockbuster drugs, aggregate profits would almost surely be insufficient to sustain a high rate of technological progress.... Should a tradeoff be required between modestly excessive prices and profits versus retarded technical progress, it would be better to err on the side of excessive profits.[65]

Summary

The chapter has two main parts. The first part dealt with the economics of inventions and patents in general and from a theoretical perspective. We compared the incentives to invest in inventive activity for an inventor in a competitive industry with the incentive that a monopolist would have. Under the relatively special assumptions made, it was found that the incentive was greater for the inventor in a competitive industry.

The welfare economics of patents was next considered, and a simple model of the optimal patent life was presented. The model highlighted the tradeoff between greater incentives to invest by giving a patent monopoly, and the cost of that monopoly in terms of inefficient pricing. Two complications were then discussed: so-called patent races and the special problem of measuring social benefits when the invention takes the form of a new product which is a close substitute of an existing product.

The second part of the chapter turned to the role of patents in the pharmaceutical industry. First, some background material on the structure of the industry was presented: the nature of government regulation, and the traditional discussion of demand, concentration and barriers to entry. The 1984 Drug Price Competition and Patent Restoration Act was described and analyzed as to the net effect that it has had on the incentives to invest in R&D. Finally, other policies that affect R&D incentives were discussed with particular attention given to the possibility of the imposition of price controls because of perceived excess profitability of the pharmaceutical industry.

Questions and Problems

1. If patents were no longer available under the law, would technical progress cease? Explain.

2. Assume that the market demand for shoes is $Q = 100 - P$ and that the constant average cost of production is \$60. Consider two alternatives. In Case C the industry is initially organized competitively and in Case M the industry is organized as a monopoly. In each case an invention leads to a lower, constant average cost of production of \$50. The R&D cost of the invention is not relevant for this problem, inasmuch as the issue is the magnitude of the incentive to invent in the two cases. Finally, there is no rivalry to make the invention: in Case C the inventor may be assumed to have a patent of infinite life and in Case M the inventor is the existing monopolist and entry is barred.

    a. Find the initial price and quantity equilibria in the two cases.

    b. What is the return that the inventor in Case C could expect from its lower cost production process? Assume that the inventor monopolizes the shoe industry.

    c. What is the return to the monopolist in Case M that results from inventing the lower cost process?

    d. Interpret your results regarding the incentive to invent under monopoly and competition.

    e. In Case C, if society could require that the new process is used efficiently—by making it freely available to all—what would be the increase in total economic surplus? How does this magnitude compare to the returns found in (b) and (c)?

3. Refer to problem 2 above and answer the same questions where the only change is that the invention lowers average cost to \$10 (rather than to \$50). This is a so-called major invention as compared to the minor invention of problem 2. Does this affect the comparative incentives under monopoly and competition?

4. In this problem rivalry to make the invention is introduced. Assume that the demand for shoes is $Q = 100 - P$ and the constant average cost of production is \$60. The incumbent monopolist, M, faces competition from a single potential entrant, E, in being first to invent and patent a new, lower cost process for producing shoes. Let the new, lower cost process be one with a constant average cost of \$50. If E wins the race for the patent, a Cournot equilibrium will result with M having an average cost of \$60 and E having an average cost of \$50. If M wins the race it will remain a monopolist, but with an average cost of \$50.

    a. What is M's incentive to win the race?

    b. What is E's incentive to win the race?

    c. Explain the intuition underlying this result. It can be argued that this so-called efficiency effect leads to the "persistence of monopoly." Why?

5. A breakfast cereal product, Cheers, has demand $Q = 5 - P/2$ and constant average cost of \$1. Under existing conditions, the supplier of Cheers charges \$5.50. Now, a new product, Kips, is introduced by a rival supplier. After equilibrium is reached, Cheers' price is unchanged at \$5.50 and Kips'

price is also $5.50. Cheers' demand has shifted leftward and can be described as $Q = 4.25 - P/2$. Kips' demand can be described as $q = 4.25 - p/2$ and its constant average cost is $1.

a. What is the social benefit resulting from the introduction of Kips? (Ignore R&D cost for now.)

b. What is the private benefit of Kips introduction?

c. If the R&D cost of introducing Kips is $6, what is the *net* social benefit? That is, subtract $6 from your answer to part (a). Compare this with the *net* private benefit.

d. Discuss the findings above from the perspective of welfare economics. In this instance, Kips would be introduced even though it is not socially beneficial. Is this finding true in general? Explain.

6.   This problem illustrates the possibility that excessive resources can be expended in search of a new product, say, Panacea. For an excellent treatment—on which this problem is based—see Chapter 17 of D. W. Carlton and J. M. Perloff, *Modern Industrial Organization*, 2nd ed. (New York: HarperCollins, 1994).

Assume that there are an unlimited number of firms that can each undertake one research project at a constant marginal cost of $1. The probability P of discovery of Panacea by one of the n firms searching for it is an increasing function of the number of research projects (firms). In particular,

$$P = 1 - e^{-0.5085n}$$

If Panacea is discovered, it will be priced competitively and the present value of total surplus is $25. Research all takes place this year; if Panacea is not discovered this year, no research can take place in the future.

a. From society's viewpoint, find the optimal number of research projects (firms). Hint: Define the expected social benefit as the probability of discovery multiplied by $25. Using calculus, find the marginal social benefit as the derivative of expected social benefit with respect to n and equate the result to the marginal cost of $1.

b. Assume now that a competitive R&D industry exists and that n is determined by the zero profit condition. That is, firms will join the search for Panacea as long as the expected payoff to a firm is greater than its $1 cost. If the government promises the firm that discovers Panacea the entire social benefit of $25, how many firms will enter? Hint: The solution to the equation in which expected social benefit divided by n equals 1 is $n = 25$.

c. Explain the intuition underlying this so-called common pool problem.

Notes

1. See, for example, "President Assails Shocking Prices of Drug Industry," *New York Times*, February 13, 1993, p. 1. Arguments for both positions are also given by various senators in a floor debate in the *Congressional Record*, March 11, 1992, beginning at p. S3183. For a historical perspective on the public policy debate regarding pharmaceuticals, see W. S. Comanor, "The Political Economy of the Pharmaceutical Industry," *Journal of Economic Literature*, September 1986.

2. K. J. Arrow, "Economic Welfare and the Allocation of Resources for Invention," in NBER, *The Rate and Direction of Inventive Activity* (Princeton, N.J.: Princeton University Press, 1962).

3. Ibid.

4. Ibid.

5. Harold Demsetz, "Information and Efficiency: Another Viewpoint," *Journal of Law and Economic*, April 1969.

6. This section is based on the analysis of K. J. Arrow, "Economic Welfare and the Allocation of Resources for Invention."

7. There are two types of inventions: cost-reducing processes and new products. Here we focus on inventions that lower costs. Although a bit strained, the same analysis can be used for new products. Imagine that the demand exists but is everywhere below the current cost of production, so quantity purchased is zero. Now a cost reducing invention lowers cost such that positive quantities are purchased—and we have a new product!

8. A minor invention reduces cost by a relatively small amount. The exact difference between a minor and a major invention will become clear later in this section.

9. The inventor would then equate the marginal cost of the patent (zero) with the marginal revenue, thereby determining the optimal royalty rate to charge users of the lower cost process.

10. For a more detailed explanation of this geometrical method for measuring profit, see the section in Chapter 8 on successive monopolies.

11. Jean Tirole, *The Theory of Industrial Organization*, (Cambridge, Mass.: MIT Press, 1988), p. 392. Tirole also describes an *efficiency* effect. By assuming that there is rivalry to make the invention in the monopoly case, it can be argued that the incumbent monopolist has a *greater* incentive to invent than a rival inventor who is a potential entrant into the industry. That is, if the rival inventor is successful and develops the low cost process C_1 first, a Cournot duopoly would result between the incumbent with cost C_0 and the inventor. Hence, the incumbent monopolist's incentive is the difference between winning the race and obtaining monopoly profit with C_1 and its duopoly profit with C_0. This is larger than the entrant's duopoly profit. For a specific example, see problem 4 at the end of this chapter. Also, see R. Gilbert and D. Newbery, "Pre-emptive Patenting and the Persistence of Monopoly," *American Economic Review*, June 1982.

12. W. D. Nordhaus, *Invention, Growth, and Welfare* (Cambridge, Mass.: MIT Press, 1969).

13. The use of this cost function is based on exercise 10.4 in J. Tirole, *The Theory of Industrial Organization* (Cambridge, Mass.: MIT Press, 1988).

14. Nordhaus, p. 74.

15. Evaluate the integral $\int BQ_0 e^{-rt}\,dt$ between $t = 0$ and $t - T$. The integral simply adds up the flows of royalties over the period, properly discounted.

16. In the case here of a single inventor, this result is straightforward. However, other models have been developed in which there is competition among firms to lower costs. In these models, information "spillovers" among the firms increase the efficiency of the industry's cost reducing efforts. Larger spillovers, of course, mean that appropriability is lower. Hence, in these models cost may *decrease* with higher appropriability (lower spillovers). See, for example, A. M. Spence, "Cost Reduction, Competition, and Industrial Performance," *Econometrica*, January 1984.

17. For further comparative static results and citations to recent literature on the Nordhaus model, see F. M. Scherer and D. Ross, *Industrial Market Structure and Economic Performance*, 3rd ed. (Boston: Houghton Mifflin, 1990), p. 625.

18. Of course, this issue has been examined to some extent earlier in the book in Chapter 6 under the heading "Preemption and Brand Proliferation."

19. The discussion here draws heavily on the excellent, detailed model of patent races in D. W. Carlton and J. M. Perloff, *Modern Industrial Organization*, 2nd ed. (New York: HarperCollins, 1994), Chapter 17.

20. A more detailed discussion is given in Chapter 18, "Solutions to the Common Pool Problem."

21. In a study of pharmaceutical R&D that attempted to test statistically for the existence of patent races, it was concluded that there was no support for that hypothesis. R. Henderson and I. Cockburn, "Racing to Invest? The Dynamics of Competition in Ethical Drug Discovery," *Journal of Economics and Management Strategy*, Fall 1994.

22. If the price of E is reduced after entry, a further demand shift for N occurs and the computation of social benefit becomes a bit more complex. An excellent exposition of this case can be found in a comment by R. W. Hansen in R. B. Helms (ed.), *Drugs and Health* (Washington, D.C.: American Enterprise Institute, 1981), p. 295.

23. Another way to explain the point is that total consumer surplus for products N and E is DBP_0 plus dbp'. It is *not* the sum of the two *marginal* consumer surplus areas $D'GP_0$ and dbp'. Each marginal surplus assumes the availability of the other product at its equilibrium price; hence, the consumers' value of E without N available is not captured by the latter sum.

Thus, the change in consumer surplus is simply total consumer surplus after N is introduced, $DBP_0 + dbp'$, minus the total before N is introduced, or DBP_0. This is simply dbp', or CS_n.

24. Scherer and Ross, p. 606.

25. Recent case studies of the pharmaceutical industry are contained in L. L. Duetsch, *Industry Studies* (Englewood Cliffs, N.J.: Prentice Hall, 1993), and W. Adams and J. Brock (eds.), *The Structure of American Industry* (Englewood Cliffs, N.J.: Prentice Hall, 1995).

26. On the historical development of the industry, see P. Temin, "Technology, Regulation, and Market Structure in the Modern Pharmaceutical Industry," *The Bell Journal of Economics*, Autumn 1979.

27. For a more extensive discussion of the history of regulation of the industry, see H. G. Grabowski and J. M. Vernon, *The Regulation of Pharmaceuticals: Balancing the Benefits and Risks* (Washington, D.C.: American Enterprise Institute, 1983), Chapter 1.

28. J. A. DiMasi, et al., "Cost of Innovation in the Pharmaceutical Industry," *Journal of Health Economics*, July 1991.

29. An NCE is a new therapeutic molecular compound that has never before been used in humans.

30. Because of the lengthy gestation period for an NCE, and the fact that the period is increasing, the average cost per NCE is not simply the yearly expenditure divided by the number of NCEs in that year. Nevertheless, the cost per NCE has been found in the DiMasi et al. study to have increased dramatically. The reasons include higher clinical trial costs, the adoption of expensive new technologies, and that "firms are focusing development more on treatments

for chronic and degenerative diseases, which typically require longer and more expensive testing." See J. A. DiMasi, et al., "Cost of Innovation in the Pharmaceutical Industry," p. 133.

31. It is possible for pharmacists to substitute a generic drug for a brand name prescribed by a doctor if the doctor does not specify that the brand name is required. Of the new 1989 prescriptions written for drugs that were multisource, only 19 percent were written generically. Of the remaining brand-written multisource prescriptions, 29 percent were dispensed generically.

Because it is generally more profitable for pharmacists to dispense a generic than a brand name drug, it is interesting to consider why generic substitution is so low. One reason is that doctors frequently prohibit substitution. For example, in states where doctors can prohibit substitution by simply signing their name on the appropriate line, substitution was prohibited 41 percent of the time. In states where doctors must write "Dispense as Written," or something equivalent, substitution was prohibited only 11 percent of the time. J. K. Hellerstein, "The Demand for Post-Patent Prescription Pharmaceuticals," unpublished working paper, Harvard University, January 1994.

32. Because over a thousand new drugs have been introduced into therapeutic practice in the past forty years or so, it is very difficult for doctors to be fully informed on such large numbers of drugs.

33. The U.S. market is about one-third of the world market. Also, in 1990 nine of the largest twenty pharmaceutical firms in the world were based in the United States. International Trade Commission, *Global Competitiveness of U.S. Advanced-Technology Manufacturing Industries: Pharmaceuticals*, September 1991.

34. M. Statman, *Competition in the Pharmaceutical Industry: The Declining Profitability of Drug Innovation*. (Washington, D.C.: American Enterprise Institute, 1983), Table 20.

35. *Fortune*, June 30, 1980, p. 63.

36. They are especially common in the emerging biotechnology sector of the industry. This is the sector in which recombinant DNA techniques, for example, are used to produce certain human proteins. TPA, a protein useful for people who have had heart attacks, is produced by inserting human genes in the ovary cells of Chinese hamsters. Genentech and Burroughs-Wellcome had a dispute over whether Genentech's patent covered TPA with one less amino acid than natural TPA. Another case involved EPO, used for treating anemia. Here, Genetics Institute had a patent on a method for purifying EPO from natural sources and Amgen had a patent on a process for using recombinant DNA to make EPO. The court upheld the patent of Amgen.

37. To be bioequivalent, the rates at which the active ingredient of two drugs are absorbed by the body must not differ significantly.

38. H. G. Grabowski and J. M. Vernon, "Brand Loyalty, Entry, and Price Competition in Pharmaceuticals after the 1984 Drug Act," *Journal of Law and Economics*, October 1992.

39. It should be noted that an 11 percent increase over two years during the period in question is probably less than the average pharmaceutical price increase for all products. The main point is that the brand name products did not cut their prices. A similar study, but one using a different sample of drugs, found broadly equivalent results. R. Caves, M. Whinston, and M. Hurwitz, "Patent Expiration, Entry, and Competition in the U.S. Pharmaceutical Industry," *Brookings Papers on Economic Activity: Microeconomics*, 1991.

40. Using an estimate of marginal cost of 25 percent of price and assuming that the market is perfectly inelastic with respect to price, profits will fall by 89 percent with price-cutting and by only 50 percent with the price unchanged.

For a theoretical analysis, see R. G. Frank and D. S. Salkever, "Pricing, Patent Loss and the Market for Pharmaceuticals," *Southern Economic Journal,* October 1992.

41. In 1980, generic drugs accounted for 23.3 percent (in units) of all pharmaceuticals sold in the United States. By 1991, the share had grown to about 40 percent. A. Masson and R. Steiner, *Generic Substitution and Prescription Drug Prices: Economic Effects of State Drug Product Selection Laws* (Federal Trade Commission, 1985), p. 113; and S. Morrison, "Prescription Drug Prices: The Effect of Generics, Formularies and Other Market Changes," Congressional Research Service, August 17, 1993, p. 1.

42. H. G. Grabowski and J. M. Vernon, "A New Look at the Returns and Risks to Pharmaceutical R&D," *Management Science,* July 1990. See also Figure 24.11 in this chapter.

43. An interesting theoretical analysis of this problem of the gambler's ruin is T. R. Stauffer, "Discovery Risk, Profitability Performance and Survival Risk in a Pharmaceutical Firm," in J. D. Cooper (ed.), *Regulation, Economics, and Pharmaceutical Innovation* (Washington, D.C.: American University, 1976). A computer simulation model is developed in H. G. Grabowski and J. M. Vernon, "Pioneers, Imitators, and Generics: A Simulation Model of Schumpeterian Competition," *Quarterly Journal of Economics,* August 1987.

44. U.S. Office of Technology Assessment, *Pharmaceutical R&D: Costs, Risks and Rewards.* Report, February 1993, p. 1.

45. The Wall Street Journal, June 25, 1991.

46. The more recent studies include S. N. Wiggins, "Product Quality Regulation and New Drug Introductions: Some New Evidence from the 1970s," *Review of Economics and Statistics,* 1981; E. J. Jensen, "Research Expenditures and the Discovery of New Drugs," *Journal of Industrial Economics,* September 1987; and L. G. Thomas, "Regulation and Firm Size: FDA Impacts on Innovation," *Rand Journal of Economics,* Winter 1990; and J. DiMasi, H. Grabowski, and J. Vernon, "R&D Costs, Innovative Output, and Firm Size in the Pharmaceutical Industry," *International Journal of the Economics of Business,* 1995.

47. This section is based on H. G. Grabowski and J. M. Vernon, "Longer Patents for Lower Imitation Barriers: The 1984 Drug Act," *American Economic Review,* May 1986.

48. *Congressional Record—Senate,* August 10, 1984, p. 23764.

49. A security analyst's report (Kidder, Peabody of April 4, 1994) found that in 1993 the average generic share in units twelve months after the first generic entry was 53 percent.

50. OTA, *Pharmaceutical R&D: Costs, Risks and Rewards,* p. 292.

51. The increases equal the difference between R&D expenses in the current year and the average amount spent during the previous three years.

52. OTA, p. 226.

53. OTA, p. 232.

54. An exception is the Omnibus Budget Reconciliation Act of 1990, which requires drug manufacturers to give Medicaid programs rebates for drugs based on the lowest prices available to any purchaser.

A description of price control systems in Europe is contained in U.S. General Accounting Office, *Prescription Drugs: Spending Controls in Four European Countries*. Report, May 1994.

55. *Congressional Record*, March 11, 1992, p. S3183.

56. *Congressional Record*, March 11, 1992, p. S3192.

57. In addition to the level of profits, there is a different point about the rate of increase in pharmaceutical prices being excessive. We have reason to believe that the government pharmaceutical price index is flawed and overstates the true price increase. For an analysis of this issue, see E. R. Berndt, et al, "Auditing the Producer Price Index: Micro Evidence from Prescription Pharmaceutical Preparations," *Journal of Business and Economic Statistics*, 1993.

58. For an excellent overview discussion, see F. M. Scherer, "Pricing, Profits, and Technological Progress in the Pharmaceutical Industry," *Journal of Economic Perspectives*, Summer 1993. See also Chapter 4 of OTA, *Pharmaceutical R&D: Costs, Risks and Rewards*, 1993, and H. G. Grabowski and J. M. Vernon, "Returns to R&D on New Drug Introductions in the 1980s," *Journal of Health Economics*, November 1994.

59. OTA, p. 96. The most recently published study that they reviewed was H. G. Grabowski and D. C. Mueller, "Industrial Research and Development, Intangible Capital Stocks, and Firm Profit Rates," *The Bell Journal of Economics*, Autumn 1978. In a study presented after the OTA report was published, Clarkson found that the pharmaceutical industry's rate of return on equity fell from 21 percent to 13 percent after correction for intangibles. This compares to an average of 11 percent for a fourteen-industry sample. K. Clarkson, "Intangible Capital and Profitability Measures: Effects of Research and Promotion on Rates of Return," in R. Helms (ed.), *Competitive Strategies in the Pharmaceutical Industry* (Washington, D.C.: American Enterprise Institute, 1994).

60. Most of the marketing expenses of pharmaceuticals have traditionally been promotional visits to doctors, known as detailing. Advertising expenses constitute only about one quarter of total marketing expenses, with detailing accounting for most of the rest.

61. H. G. Grabowski and J. M. Vernon, *Journal of Health Economics*, November 1994.

62. The study was prepared for the OTA report and is partially described in that report.

63. OTA, 1993.

64. The Congressional Budget Office notes, however, that if breakthrough drugs are to correspond to the FDA's past rating of "significant therapeutic advances," there may not be a close correspondence to commercial importance. U.S. Congressional Budget Office, *How Health Care Reform Affects Pharmaceutical Research and Development*, June 1994, p. 35.

65. F. M. Scherer, *Journal of Economic Perspectives*, p. 113.

Author Index

The letter n following a page number indicates that the name will be found in a note. The letter f following a page number indicates a figure; the letter t indicates a table.

Subject Index

The letter *f* following a page number indicates a figure, the letter *t* indicates a table.